Latinization of AMERICA

How Hispanics are Changing the Nation's Sights and Sounds

Eliot Tiegel

PHOENIX BOOKS

Latinization of AMERICA

How Hispanics are Changing the Nation's Sights and Sounds

Eliot Tiegel

ISBN: 1-59777-514-2
Library of Congress Cataloging-In-Publication Data Available

Book Design by: Sonia Fiore

Printed in the United States of America

Phoenix Books
9465 Wilshire Boulevard, Suite 315
Beverly Hills, CA 90212

10 9 8 7 6 5 4 3 2 1

Table of Contents

Dedication page

For my wife Bonnie Gail, whose dynamic personality, loving and caring attitude, combined with the neatest birthday present imaginable, makes this book adventure a memorable time in my life.

Acknowledgements

RECONOCIMIENTO

Undertaking this first-of-its-kind contemporary overview of the growth of the domestic Latin entertainment industry and its natural impact on English-language show business is among the most fascinating and challenging experiences of my journalistic career. I am beholden to scores of people for their assistance in putting this living history together.

My publisher, Michael Viner, tops the list of the people who help bring this project to fruition by seeing the value and importance of this subject where other publishers see none; my editor Rochelle O'Gorman with her keen interest in the topic and her incisive editing suggestions keeps this transitional flowing story on track; to Julie McCarron, editor, who adroitly sees that late chapter additions are properly positioned while shepherding the manuscript through the various production phases prior to publication; to editor Henrietta Tiefenthaler whose final editing ensures smooth transitions, and to art director Sonia Fiore for her awesome cover design, photo layouts, chapter graphics, and assistance with inserting late news developments where appropriate. In helping get this book beyond the idea stage, attorney Leon Gladstone's legal assistance and expertise are crucial in solidifying all the contract details. Authors Peter Levinson and Stan Cornyn take the time to give me invaluable information on how to plan out and effectively pursue the research and writing aspects of my first book.

This work is dedicated to the memory of my two sons, Scott Edward, who tragically passed away too early at age 39, and Blake

Harris, 38, who died six months later. They both would regularly ask me how the book was coming along. Scott, the guitarist in the family, whose music and lyrics remain memories in my mind, had a good nature and helping hand, and once told me I gave him these qualities. Blake, a poet lost in his dreams, wanted the world to be a better place like his brother Scott, but never saw this wish happen for him. My daughter Alexis and my other son Ken infuse me with their gifts of curiosity and enthusiasm for this project when Scott and Blake are no longer voices I hear. My cousin Steve Peck and his wife Pat, who constantly travel on business together, always cheer me up with their regular check-ins to see how the writing is going from wherever they happen to be in this vast nation. My mother-in-law, Frankie Kauffman, who's originally from Montreal, Canada, speaks no Spanish; but her healthy curiosity about the book's progress helps prod me forward. As do the regular "How's the book coming?" queries from her daughter, Elizabeth.

A number of other family members actually wind up assisting me with this book. My wife Bonnie, an Emmy-winning television producer, uses her industry expertise to assist me in tracking down sources and actually arranges my interview with George Lopez. When I need Latinos who will talk about their entertainment experiences, my nephew Steven Tiegel and cousins Howie Peck and Marilyn Zolondek provide me with names in New York, Chapel Hill, and Phoenix, respectively. Marilyn's husband Joel, a respected sports photographer, provides me with the action pictures that enhance the photo section. My brother Joseph and his wife Barbara provide a warm haven on Long Island prior to my research trip into New York City. My daughter-in-law Diana Kaplan writes all the Spanish translations for each chapter when I come up with the idea to add a multilingual tinge to the book. My brother-in-law, Mike Mink, a Los Angeles County Superior Court Judge and a golf maven, proffers his golf expertise.

During the six years I work on the book, I conduct 100-plus interviews, and I owe these people my gratitude for seeing value in this project and allowing me to come into their lives. I cannot say this cooperation is the rule with all companies I ask for interview time. A number of record companies choose not to respond to my request, including BMG U.S. Latin, Sony Discos, EMI Latin, Fonovisa, Univision, Balboa, and Crescent Moon, part of the equally uncooperative Estefan Enterprises empire in Miami. I also have no luck with requests for time with Carlos Santana, Gloria Estefan, Christina Aguilera, Alejandro Fernandez, Rubén Blades, Ricky Martin, and Marc Anthony. I'm also told don't try for Jennifer Lopez because she's too busy with other projects. The president of Spanish Broadcasting System, the second largest music radio network, is also unavailable, while his counterpart at the number one Hispanic Broadcasting Corporation is cooperative. People with whom I've conducted interviews for stories in several publications are melded into the book's narrative. There are no anonymous sources, except in two instances when I include a question about payola in radio during my interviews and I'm told, "Don't quote me."

Since the book deals with sundry branches of entertainment, I've broken down my thank-you appreciations by category. In music, I am most indebted to critically ill flutist Herbie Mann, who speaks with me by phone from his home in Santa Fe, New Mexico, during a medical crisis regarding an unorthodox treatment for his malignant prostate cancer. I am also grateful to his loving wife Janeal for her cooperation and courage in speaking about Herbie's illness and the final months of his life following his passing. I also find much of value in interviewing musicians Poncho Sanchez, Eddie Palmieri, Larry Harlow, Arturo Sandoval, Paquito D'Rivera, Quincy Jones, Bobby Rodriguez, Susie Hansen, and Rolando Sanchez, as well as executives Bruce Lundvall, Ralph Kaffel, Chris Strachwitz, George Zamora, John Echeverría, Jesus Lopez, Freddie Martinez, Jr., Bruno Del Granado, John Burk, John Iervolino, concert promoter Tom Moffatt, and talent agent Michael Vega.

In radio, the following add their perspective and perceptions: McHenry "Mac" Tichenor, Jr., Carey Davis, Bill Tanner, Jerry Ryan,

Howard and Jim Kalmenson, José Cancela, Walter F. Ulloa, Claudia Puig, Don Graham, Brad Chambers, Jon Denny, José Molina, Sean Heitkemper, Cephas Bowles, David Lapovsky, Nancy Ortiz, and Ray Cruz. Special kudos go to Steve Pailet, the able assistant to Jim Kalmenson.

In television, I gain invaluable perspective from: George Lopez, Cristina Saralegui, Andres Cantor, Carlos Ponce, Jim McNamara, Betty Ellen Berlamino, Steve Paulus, Maritza Puello, Joanne Tombrakos, Jeff Wald, Ken Ehrlich, Linda Bell Blue, Augustine Martinez, Luis Patiño, Jodie Mena, Luis J. Echarte, David Faitelson, John Perez, Jorge Ramos, Sylvia Rosabal-Ley, David Downs, Joe Peyronnin, Jorge Hidalgo, David Sternberg, Lino Garcia, Tom Maney, Ian Stoilkovic, Emilio Nicolás, Jr., Guillermo Nicolás, Constantino Voulgaris, Eileen Montalvo, Karen Plount, Lindsay Polumbus, Jose Antonio Espinal, Brian Forti, and Kevin Layne.

Special thanks are in order for Kevin Gershan, Bruce Thompson, and Annie Tang for all the computer-related questions they answer and problems they solve, generally in the early morning when I hit a technical snag, and for George Nicholis for his efforts in rounding up many of the photos that put a human face to the people I write about.

Andy Garcia is the lone film actor/director/musician I chat with, Miami's Michael Hardy is the lone concert venue executive who explores his world with me, and Ron DeBlasio is the single personal manager providing clarifying chronological information for one of his clients' show business ascendancy. Two of Andy Garcia's office associates, Kathy Fisher and Evan Payne, are most helpful—Kathy in coordinating my interview and Evan in gathering and sending me photos.

In the realm of non-entertainment figures, or "civilians" as they're known in many industries, including show biz, I learn their entertainment life patterns from: Christine Reyes, Luis Pillich, Jimmy Vasquez, Maria De Los Angeles, Frank Delgado, Diana Kaplan, James Mendez, Clemencia Tafur, Mayitza Frederick, Elva Chavez, Jose Villa, Susana Ho, Juan Carlos Kennedy, and Alan J. Fernandez.

Advertising agency executives who have a keen perspective into Spanish media who open this door to me include: Jean Pool, Maria Cueva, Jose Aybar, and Luis Miguel Messianu.

Reporters who allow me to interview them include: Leila Cobo, Cary Darling, and Kevin Baxter. Cobo, located in Miami, along with Ramiro Burr in San Antonio and Augustin Gurza in Los Angeles, are perhaps the most sought-after journalists working for major English-language newspapers.

Public relations mavens who are helpful in gathering information and arranging interviews are of inestimable assistance to me and include: Jack Loftus, Jo Foster, Rosemary Scott, Gerardo Oyola, Daniel McCosh, Matthew Gould, Thom Mocarsky, Ed Pachetti, Ted Farone, Terri Hinte, Jennifer Serna, Luis Silva, Cristina Romano, Eric Schuster, Saskia Sorrosa, Elias Makos, Ginny Gutierrez, Manfred Westphal, Marleah Leslie, Stu Glauberman, Stan Rosenfield, and Bill Farley.

Steve Tenenbaum, one of my oldest friends from our youth in the New York borough of the Bronx, who like me is a transplanted New Yorker, besides being one of the top business managers in show business, has suggested on more than one occasion: "You should write a book." Here it is.

Photo Credits

CREDITOS DE LAS FOTOS

FILM—Ken Regan: Antonio Banderas; Rob McEwan: Benicio Del Toro; Phil Caruso: John Leguizamo; Ron Batzdorff: Jennifer Lopez.

MUSIC—Omar Cruz: Ruben Blades; Ivan Otis: Jane Bunnett; Izzy Sanabria: Celia Cruz with Johnny Pacheco; Don Hunstein: Paquito D'Rivera; Cathy Callahan: Herbie Mann; Eliot Tiegel: Miami record executives Bruno Del Granado, John Echeverria, Jesus A. Lopez; Kwaku Alston: Carlos Santana; Nick Cardillichio: David Sanchez; Juliana Thomas: Chucho Valdes.

RADIO/TV—Stewart Shining: Eva Longoria; Gittings Portraiture: Mac Tichenor; Eliot Tiegel: Jim McNamara.

SPORTS—Los Angeles Dodgers: Fernando Valenzuela; Fox Sports En Espanol: Manny Ramirez; Joel Zolondek: baseball: Roberto Alomar, Felipe and Moises Alou, Orlando Cabrera, Cezar Izturis, Russ Ortiz, Albert Pujols, Sammy Sosa, Alex Rodriguez; basketball: Manu Ginobili; boxing: Oscar De La Hoya; golf: Sergio Garcia and tennis: Marcello Rios.

Foreword

ADELANTE

Invasion! The Latinization of America and Its Impact on Show Business

!INVASION!
EL LATINIZATION DE AMERICA
Y EL IMPACTO EN EL ESPECTACULO

This is a first-of-its-kind book.

I know that's a strong statement, but this is the first time anyone has attempted to write a book about the growth of the domestic Latin entertainment industry and its component parts, each fueled by the explosive growth of the Hispanic population. Under one cover are the escapades, successes and failures in the fields of music, records, radio, television, film, theater, dance, and professional sports. Each year more companies are formed or merged, more entertainment is created and designed to appeal to Latinos from Mexico, Central and South America, and Cuba. The popularity of talented musicians, in particular, creates a cultural crossover phenomenon, resulting in Spanish-surnamed artists gaining exposure in mainstream media and developing fans in both the Spanish- and English-language communities.

In looking for a way to make this contemporary history—which is also my personal odyssey—alive and of the moment, rather than recasting past developments, I felt a new way to make reading history an interesting, even intimate, experience was necessary. In seeking a method for turning a history lesson into a moment of reality, I kept thinking about the CBS Television series *You Are There*, hosted by Walter Cronkite. During its 1953 to 1957 black and white lifetime, it provided the viewer a front-row seat to historical events. This live show, with Cronkite at the anchor desk and actual CBS correspondents filing reports from their vantage points, was created on a large soundstage in New York City. Still, it was riveting television because you actually saw famous names in history portrayed by actors. Whether it was an "army" of Roman soldiers trekking through the scenery, or Joan of Arc facing her tormentors, you were there. I thought I would follow CBS's example of presenting history through a modern prism, which brings the past to the present, by writing this book in a present tense style, intended to bring a sense of immediacy and currency to this historical saga.

I've been an advocate of writing in the present tense to liven up a story, using it in my articles for national business and consumer publications and during my own 17-year tenure with *Billboard* magazine. It's a style utilized accordingly in *Time*, *Newsweek*, and *The New Yorker*, along with other national and local periodicals. And it works.

An excellent and timely example of covering history in a contemporary fashion occurs on May 1, 2006 (May Day), when an estimated one million people across the nation take to the streets to peacefully protest stricter immigration laws being considered by Congress. Spanish- and English-language media focus on the marches, informally called "A Day Without Immigrants" in such cities as Los Angeles, Sacramento, Oakland, Santa Ana, San Ysidro, Chicago, New York, Houston, Dallas, San Antonio, Miami, Orlando, Phoenix, Denver, New Orleans, Las Vegas, Detroit, and Atlanta. Thousands of companies are forced to close by the absence of protesting workers. When I take a walk through my Brentwood, California, neighborhood to assess the economic impact, I find a number of major restaurants closed while Baja Fresh, a Mexican eatery, is open and staffed by Hispanics.

Watching the coverage on TV, you see a preponderance of American flags, in sharp contrast to an initial March 25 demonstration across the country in which Mexican flags proliferate. During the May Day marches, signs, mostly in Spanish, are also omnipresent, with some English or a combination of languages, such as "Legalizacion: We Are

Not Criminals." While opponents to catering to undocumented immigrants stress they are here illegally, the overall emphasis is on the huge turnout of people, including students who skip school and who are making their presence known to the world. Jose Ramos, Univision's Miami-based key news anchor, reports from New York, and during an interview with CNN, he stresses the demonstrations "made visible to millions of Americans what was invisible." He admits illegals break the law, "but they are here. We eat the food they harvest, live in homes they built, and they take care of our children. Americans hire them and the President says they fill jobs Americans don't want to do." Cristina Saralegui, star of her own hit Univision show, dedicates the day's segment to the immigration hot topic under the banner, "*Latino Phobia.*"

May Day 2007 has a totally different feel in Los Angeles as violence erupts at the conclusion of two downtown Immigration rights rally/marches, which combined attract around 35,000 people, far fewer than the estimated 650,000 who peacefully parade last year. Caught in the mele between demonstrators and the Los Angeles Police Department in the late afternoon are news crews from Telemundo's KVEA (Channel 52), Univision's KMEX (Channel 34), Fox TV's KTTV (Channel 11) with one of its veteran Hispanic reporters, CBS' KCAL (Channel 9), and public radio's KPPC-FM. The media stationed at MacArthur Park covering this second march, capture participants who have moved into the park and been told by officers to disperse around 6:45 p.m., start throwing rocks and plastic bottles at police who respond by firing volleys of foam bullets into the crowd.

Five minutes later as I'm watching a live shot, a police car is blasted with bottles and a line of police in riot gear, with batons at the ready, confront the protesters; a number of citizens and police are injured, as are seven journalists. I switch from station to station to observe and gasp at the unfurled anger and physical force unleashed by both sides as seen from overhead news helicopter cameras. It's like being a silent witness to some horrible clash of cultures. The next morning, KVEA's reporter Maria Garcia tells KNX-AM, the CBS all-news station, while I'm listening, that "Mario my cameraman was hit twice in the knees and head and fell to the ground. I thought he was dead." She also feels the imbroglio "can backfire with people thinking we don't deserve immigration reform." KNX also reports that KTTV's veteran reporter "Christina Gonzalez (who I write about in Chapter 3) and her crew are roughed up." I'm looking at surreal, live, raw, unedited video of police chasing people, hitting them, and in the middle of this crush of people—her white blouse a stark contrast to the dark blue uniforms of the marauding police—stands Christina, holding her wireless mike and yelling at the intruders. In footage captured by her station, she is pushed out of the way as she bends over to protect her camerawoman, who is on the ground after being hit by a baton. As she struggles to right herself, she is pushed by her shoulders. "You cannot do that and you know it," she yells at the officer, the *Los Angeles Times* reports in its second day coverage. She suffers a minor shoulder injury while her camera operator has a fractured wrist. A few hours later, attired in a multi-colored spring dress, Garcia tells KCAL's noon news she tried to alert her crew about the impending police rush, but four members of her crew are injured. She says three rubber bullets hit the KVEA van and she is amazed this is happening in America. There is video shot of police storming the KVEA setup, with people running away, falling down, being jostled by police, and a cameraman hitting the ground with his equipment still in his hands.

During the police rush, Telemundo's news anchor Pedro Sevcec is preparing to go live with his 6:30 p.m. broadcast. I see him ducking rubber bullets and rushing away from his open air set, a look of fear on his face. A Miami-based reporter continues the newscast. Sevcec tells the *Times* he sees the confrontation prior to going on the air. Then the cops come into his area and he sees people falling to the ground, police hitting reporters and cameramen with their batons. He tells the *Times* a policeman points a weapon at his face and he's struck three times by a baton on his neck and back. "Police ran over us. Lights were flying and monitors were on the floor," he tells the paper. These are the pictures I watch transfixed to the TV screen. Sevcec's comments clarify what I was watching. A KCAL reporter says he and his cameraman are confronted and impacted by the LAPD. The next morning, the chief of police, William J. Bratton promises an investigation will be undertaken anent the use of such force against the public and the media, and the city's mayor Antonio Villaraigosa, in El Salvador on a business trip, promises a full investigation into the situation as well.

You'll find numerous mini-stories throughout the book, which I trust will pop out at you through the descriptive powers of a present-tense writing style. My goal is to have the reader at my side as I encounter events memorable enough to be part of this history.

A good example of accompanying me as an eyewitness occurs during my trip to Havana in 1979. I was one of a handful of American journalists invited to cover the historical musical event called "Havana Jam," designed to defrost the chill between Fidel Castro and the U.S. government. What is supposed to be three days of the best music from Cuba and CBS Records also turns into a plethora of heart-rending experiences for me.

An empty row at the back of the Karl Marx theater is roped off each night for Fidel, so the obvious question we reporters ask is, "When will he be here?" to which an official curtly replies, "He's coming," but never says when. One young Cuban boy who lands a front-row seat next to me on the night Billy Joel is the headliner tells me he's a Billy Joel fan and knows all the words to his hit records; he hears them on powerful Miami radio stations 90 miles away. He then hits me with an alarming thought: he wants me to help him defect. "Take me with you, take me with you," he pleads several times during the concert, despite my telling him that's an impossible wish. He persists, adding that he'll meet me at the airport tomorrow when we return to New York City. I have no idea how this will play out and confess to another journalist I'm a bit worried he'll try to sneak out of the country with the CBS contingent. When we do depart from our bus on a warm and sunny afternoon, there he is on the street outside the José Marti Airport among a large crowd of young people, and he somehow makes his way into the stifling terminal where we're unloading our luggage, but he never leaves his native soil, and a potentially explosive political imbroglio is avoided.

Here are some additional first person experiences:

When I chat with actor/director/musician Andy Garcia in 2004 about growing up in Cuba before his family migrated to Miami and he moved to Los Angeles, his ranting about people imprisoned for their opposition to the Castro government is a fresh reminder of the inhuman treatment meted out to those who dissent from the official party line.

During my research trip to Miami in 2002, I encounter stories from many of the Cuban-born executives who escaped with their families. Each story seems more horrific than the previous one, detailing prison stays and, in one instance, of a relative being lined up against a wall and shot in front of his family. When I ask one record executive how it was growing up in Miami as a child without his father (who's in a Cuban jail) he tells me it wasn't that bad; other children have fathers similarly rotting away in Cuban jails.

One of the most unusual experiences lending itself to a "right now" description occurs during my 2002 research trip to New York City where I visit the offices of NY1 News, the 24-hour local cable news channel, which is setting up a Spanish-language news version. The offices are in the historic downtown Chelsea Market and my walk past 28 retail businesses and a waterfall while searching for the elevator to take me to the NY1 offices is an experience far afield from visiting any entertainment company I've ever had.

When comic/TV show star George Lopez is called to testify at the Michael Jackson child molestation trial in Santa Maria, California, in 2005, the reader is right alongside me in the courtroom that morning, listening to George and his wife recall their dealings with the family of one of the principal young boys allegedly fondled by the pop star. Everything that happens that morning—from the arrival of the attorneys for both sides, to the judge, to the Jackson family's slow walk to their front-row seats, to Lopez's comedic quips during his testimony—makes for colorful narrative through words that carry the weight of immediacy.

In writing this story of the growth of an industry, while recognizing the years in which events take place, the key consideration is that the information is presented in such a way that you are an observer with me as history comes alive, careers are made, lives affected, stars are born or cast aside, and cultural barriers are broken as milestones unfurl. You read about them as they're happening right now—not 20 years ago.

—ELIOT TIEGEL

Chapter 1
CAPITULO 1

An Evolving Odyssey
UNA ODISA EN EVOLUCION

During my 45 years as an entertainment journalist, I have been touched and affected by Latin entertainment. With the development of the motion picture industry and the growth of the record and radio industries, English-speaking Latin entertainers have become well-known personalities, melding into the reservoir of show business. During the past decade, as Latin TV networks spread their tentacles, major Hispanic TV personalities begin to be sporadically profiled in the Anglo media, but the spotlight always shines more brightly on English-speaking show business celebrities. In 1999, mainstream America rediscovers Latin entertainers when ex-Menudo member Ricky Martin makes a sensational appearance at the Grammy Awards. The general media then turns inward to discover a number of other dynamic Latino artists, and the hyperbole begins.

Throughout our nation's musical history, two major foreign influences induce a cross-fertilizing effect on our popular musical styles: Latin and African music. Their melodies and rhythms stretch through motion pictures to New York's songwriting industry, euphemistically called Tin Pan Alley, to Broadway musicals, television series scores and into jazz, rhythm 'n' blues, and rock 'n' roll. They also influence new forms of Latin music reflecting the diversity of our Latin heritage from coast-to-coast. From the tango craze of the 1920s to the rumba-craving 1930s to the mambo mania of the 1950s to the merengue and string-laden pachanga patterns of the 1960s to the Mexican-flavored and Tejano Tex-Mex diversities of past decades, America's heritage is strongly linked to its acceptance of Latin music, with or without an accent.

I first hear Latin music growing up in New York City in the 1950s. The music is either Latin jazz hosted by English-speaking disc jockeys or Afro-Caribbean-style tunes interlaced among Spanish-language programming. "Symphony Sid" Torin, Mort Fega, Art "Poncho" Ramos, and Dick "Ricardo" Sugar are the music's advocates, playing to both Anglo and Latino music lovers. Stations like WEVD, WBNX, and WADO, all on the AM dial, are the principal places to go to feast on the mosaic of Latin music and rhythms at a time when rock 'n' roll is taking over the music business, and New York radio stations—like others around the country—cater to the teen audience with the exuberance of new rock sounds that inexorably alter the landscape of popular music.

Within the popular music idiom there are a number of Hispanic artists achieving mainstream pop success, performing primarily in English, but who in later years return musically to their roots and occasionally sing in Spanish. These artists, whose music I hear and enjoy on the pop hit parade, include Ritchie Valens, Trini Lopez, Eydie Gorme with the Trio Los Ponchos, Vikki Carr, Jose Feliciano, and Gloria Estefan. With the exception of Valens, who dies in a plane crash with Buddy Holly in 1959, and Estefan, during my career I wind up interviewing the rest, including three hit-making groups that infuse pop music with south of the border panache: Herb Alpert and the Tijuana Brass; their Latin counterpart, the Baja Marimba Band; and the smaller Eddie Cano ensemble. Latin music snares me because it's very exciting and so different sounding from what's being played on the radio. The beats and the rhythms, and the driving solos are so propulsive that I know this New York-bred music is very special.

So special that during the '50s, the Palladium Ballroom on 53rd Street and Broadway in Manhattan become the home for the mambo, booking all the top New York City mambo and Latin jazz bands. The often-competitive on-stage battles between ensembles, called "cutting sessions," draw lots of sweat, but no blood. The musicians play so fiercely that the temperature in the large ballroom rises and mixes with the absolutely fantastic displays by New York City's top teams of mambo dancers. Each couple tries to outdo the others with their precision routines, and all captured in black and white by *Life* Magazine in a feature on those fiery nights when the Big Apple's "mamboniks" come out to dig the sounds of the top line bands of Machito, Tito Puente, Tito Rodriguez, Joe Cuba, Jose Curbelo, La Playa Sextet, Miguilito Valdez, Noro Morales, Pacheco, Charlie Palmieri, Eddie Palmieri, Alfredito, Randy Carlos, Vicentico Valdez, and the Orquesta Broadway. Oddly, Pérez Prado, RCA Record's self-proclaimed "King of the Mambo," whose hit records help flame the mambo craze in the '50s, does not play the Palladium according to New York musician Larry Harlow, who works the venue.

The Palladium is also the place where you go to learn to do the mambo under the guidance of instructor "Killer Joe" Piro and then watch the pros dominate the dance floor. Occasionally I'll walk by the venue and see the people, all dressed up going into the building. On Mondays the Anglo crowd shows up in force, Friday and Saturday draw the city's Hispanics, with Puerto Ricans dominating on Saturdays, and on Sundays it's African-American aficionados.

The first Latin jazz band I review is Cal Tjader at the Village Gate in Greenwich Village in Manhattan in the early '60s for *Playback*, a New York monthly music magazine. DJ "Symphony Sid," he of the deep-toned announcer's voice, also runs a series of "Salsa Meets Jazz" shows at "The Gate," as the club is known in 1966. In 1962, I join Columbia Records in Los Angeles, where the major jazz-recording artists of all stripes play the top club of the decade, the Manne Hole in Hollywood. This colorful venue is owned by the omnipresent jazz drummer Shelly Manne, a mainstay of the modern jazz scene, who leads his own group and plays on other artist's studio dates and movie-scoring sessions.

In 1963, I'm in San Juan, Puerto Rico, for the first time to attend a Columbia convention and in addition hear a new, laidback, shy folk singer named Bob Dylan perform. I also get a chance to hear some hot Puerto Rican bands perform in-person. Both experiences are mind-openers. Later that year, I join *Billboard*, the entertainment newsweekly, as West Coast bureau chief, and regularly attend the Manne Hole to review a gamut of jazz bands.

During the remainder of my 17 years at the magazine, in a variety of editorships including record review editor, special issues editor, and culminating with six years as managing editor, I review albums by top pop and jazz artists, including those with a penchant for fusing jazz with Latin elements. So my enthusiasm for Latin jazz follows me from coast to coast, and that's pretty cool. In 1967, I spend a week in Mexico City researching a special section I write and edit on Mexico's music/records/radio/TV/audiotape industries.

It features the first bilingual headlines in the magazine's history. This first time in the Mexican capitol affords me the opportunity to hear first-hand top Mexican artists in their recording studios and nightclubs. The sounds of mariachi bands, marimba groups, and singers who all seem very dramatic, are totally different from anything I've heard in New York. There, the emphasis on music from Cuba, the Dominican Republic, and Puerto Rico produces Caribbean and Afro-Cuban dynamics fused into something very American.

In the late '70s, I sense a bubbling of the Hispanic creative cauldron and mention this to editor/publisher Lee Zhito. It's the same feeling I have a few years earlier about the power of soul music, which results in the hiring of the magazine's first African-American reporter and increased coverage of black music. Lee agrees with my recommendation that we hire the magazine's first Hispanic reporter, so Augustin Gurza joins the staff to cover the Latin scene. By the 21st century, he's reporting on Hispanic entertainment for the *Los Angeles Times* entertainment department.

One of my career highlights occurs in March 1979, when I'm selected to represent *Billboard*, along with a handful of American journalists, to spend a weekend in Havana covering the first-ever attempt to create a cultural bridge over the political and economic barriers erected by Cuba's revolutionary leader, Fidel Castro, following his 1959 coup. The event, created by CBS Records with State and Treasury Department authorization, and the Cuban government's participation, is called "Havana Jam." It features the host nation's best artists performing on the stage of the Karl Marx Theater, along with a handpicked array of CBS' top pop and Latin musicians.

This prescient event, from March 2 through 4, helps open the door years later to the subsequent release in the U.S. of records by Cuban artists, as well as allowing some of them to also perform in various venues around the country, including Miami, where the Cuban exile community's didactic pressure on the city keeps Castro's musical emissaries away from their new home. "Havana Jam" also opens the gates for American artists to enter Cuba to record, perform, and even win Grammys for their efforts. "Havana Jam" earns me my first and only trip to Cuba, and the Cuban artists on display are all unfamiliar names to me; subsequently several will defect and become well-known and popular in this country.

This cultural Cuban connection, which seems to fade from most people's memories once the initial hoopla ends, is so important in helping the growth of contemporary and traditional Cuban entertainment in this country during the existing U.S. embargo against Cuba that it warrants a chapter of its own.

In addition to writing about music, I begin writing about radio and television for several broadcasting business publications, collecting articles on these industries as reference sources. Within the clippings are the inklings of a change under the surface of mainstream show business, the palpable but steady emergence of Hispanic companies that are achieving success to the point they are becoming real competitors in the Anglo entertainment world. Since I live in Los Angeles, these early clippings often, but not always, focus on L.A.'s Latin music, radio and TV stations spreading their growth tentacles.

I quickly realize my clip file has historical value in developing a book on the Latinization of America and its impact on show business. This historical odyssey will cover the growth of domestic Latin show business from the '90s on, and avoid recapping the well-documented early achievements of Latin entertainers. The major domestic creative powers are in Miami (the headquarters for Latin show business), Los Angeles, New York, Puerto Rico, and isolated cities in Texas and New Mexico.

Thus the first chapters generally concentrate on what is the nation's No. 1 Hispanic market, with subsequent chapters taking a broader look at how this Hispanic invasion is taking hold across America and how it propels little-known domestic Latin music and broadcasting entities into an ancillary force focusing on keeping pace with the ever-expanding community of transcultural Latinos.

This, then, is a story about people and the drama of their struggles for success. It is abutted by cold statistics that unrelentingly reflect the changes occurring every year. It is a history of the modern growth of an exciting creative force with an accent, one that mainstream America inexorably becomes aware of. It is also the transformation of America into an interethnic nation in which a new generation of parents and the children of Hispanic–Caucasian marriages forgo past prejudices against interracial bonding.

This is also my personal odyssey into reporting on Latin show business. It's a subject for which I receive my initial experience in fact recapping journalism by working with noted journalist/critic, the late Leonard Feather, in putting together the music section for the *World Book Encyclopedia*'s Annual Year Book Supplement from 1971-'82. When it's applicable, I include opinions, personal and mood setting experiences, awkward moments, and problems encountered along the journey that help humanize and personalize this trek through history.

The first story I write about Spanish-language broadcasting occurs in July 1988 for the biweekly broadcasting business magazine *Television/Radio Age* where I am its West Coast correspondent. It's a seven-page special report dealing with the growing Hispanic market in the Western United States and its headlines portend America's present and future: "TV, Radio Stations Multiply As Job Seekers Trek Across the Border/Hispanic Culture Thrives Like Mesquite in Western U.S."

Two months later, I chronicle the first project ever to reach out to the region's Hispanic community by offering a Spanish simulcast of its 10 p.m. newscast, by KTLA-TV, Los Angeles' oldest TV station and one of the first English-language stations in the nation. The station utilizes the second audio program (SAP) channel of TV sets to reach its target audience. The banner headline for that two-page feature: "KTLA Says It In Spanish." KTLA, which is still offering Latinos the Spanish news service, along with several off-network situation comedies dubbed in Spanish, is joined in February of 2003 by another Tribune Broadcasting station, WPIX in New York. It offers its 10 p.m. news in Spanish via the SAP channel as an adjunct to airing a number of situation comedy reruns with a Spanish dialog voice track provided by the movie companies.

The mercurial rise of the once isolated Latino subculture takes on a broader profile as "Spanglish," the blending of Spanish and English words in the same sentence, spreads beyond the major U.S. Latin cities to gain a broader foothold in the new millennium. This is the result of both commercials and Latino TV series on English-language television cementing the two languages into a homogenized form. The term will wind up as the catchy name for a major motion picture in 2004 that introduces Spain's beautiful 28-year-old actress Paz Vega to American audiences.

California is home to two-thirds of all Mexican-American interracial marriages, five times the number for the nation's similar mixed heritage, or *mestizos*, representation. From my *Billboard* years I'm aware there are successful Hispanic record companies and radio stations catering to the dominant Mexican population in parts of the country. One special issue we publish in the early '70s focuses on Freddie Records, a small Corpus Christi, Texas label formed in 1969 specializing in regional Mexican music. Today it remains a successful stalwart for this traditional brand of Hispanic music.

In 1992, I notice something major starting to happen in Los Angeles radio—an indicator of what's bubbling in other large U.S. Hispanic-populated cities. Spanish Broadcasting System's KLAX-FM changes its music format to appeal to the region's overwhelming Mexican population and also become the market's No. 1 station through the fall of 1994.

By 1995 and '96, I'm writing about how Hispanic radio and TV in L.A., the nation's No. 1 Hispanic market, are making their imprints on the region for *Electronic Media*, a leading broadcasting newsweekly. KMEX, the Univision TV network's flagship station, has the most watched early evening newscast in '95, beating out all the English-language network affiliates.

In 1995, I'm also jolted to see Spanish-language radio stations regularly appearing at the top of the market's Arbitron ratings. Instead of a Top 40 station being most popular, KLVE-FM, which plays romantic music, is No. 1 and KLAX-FM, which now features up-tempo dance music is No. 3, with KPWR-FM, the top hip-hop station sandwiched between them. Spanish stations regularly show up in the top 30 positions in the Arbitron surveys.

In July of 1996, as Univision's L.A. station KMEX retains its early evening lead and starts to make inroads into late night news, I cover the ratings news battles that continue to favor a Hispanic station, recapping how for 13 straight survey periods, encompassing the so-called sweeps months of November, February, May, and July, KMEX is the 6 p.m. news leader. Then for nine straight sweeps reports, its 11 p.m. newscast also becomes the city's No. 1 watched newscast. Hispanics coast-to-coast are loyal fans of Univision's evening novelas, which are dramatic mini-series or soap operas.

By 1999, the Anglo and Latin entertainment industries, cognizant of the presence of Hispanics outside the traditional West Coast border state repositories and the enclaves of Latinos in Miami and New York City, begin expanding their presence in the record, radio, and TV and concert fields. Major secular concert venues are booking Latin acts before sellout crowds of their fans who heretofore attend their shows in smaller, less glamorous locales near Hispanic neighborhoods.

By 2000, having already covered Hispanic media, I start reporting on its changing patterns for *Advertising Age*'s multicultural media section. And in 2003, I start writing again about Hispanic TV for the revamped *Electronic Media*, renamed *TelevisionWeek*.

The Hispanic population, while estimated by the 2000 U.S. Census at 37 million, still cannot accurately calculate all the illegals that cross our borders. Among the top 15 Hispanic states by population, according to the Census, are some surprise locales: California, Texas, New York, Florida, Illinois, Arizona, New Jersey, New Mexico, Colorado, Washington, Georgia, Massachusetts, Pennsylvania, Nevada, and North Carolina. There are also growing niche communities in Hawaii, Alaska, Wyoming, South Carolina, Tennessee, Alabama, Mississippi, Kentucky, Oregon, Indiana, Minnesota, Rhode Island, and Oklahoma.

After all the population shifts, a picture emerges as to where the top 10 Hispanic TV cities are located, according to Nielsen Media Research: Los Angeles, New York, Miami/Fort Lauderdale, Houston, Chicago, Dallas/Fort Worth, San Antonio, San Francisco/Oakland/San Jose, Phoenix, and the Texas cities of Brownsville/McAllen/Harlingen. The top 10 Arbitron radio markets bear some similarities with their television counterparts: Los Angeles, New York, Miami, Chicago, Houston, San Francisco, Dallas, San Antonio, McAllen, and Phoenix.

On the city level, between 1980 through 2000, 18 localities see significant growth by Hispanics, according to the Pew Hispanic Center of the Brookings Institution: Raleigh, Atlanta, Greensboro, Charlotte, Orlando, Las Vegas, Nashville, Fort Lauderdale, Sarasota, Portland (Oregon), Greenville, West Palm Beach, Washington, Indianapolis, Minneapolis/St. Paul, Fort Worth, Providence, and Tulsa. Hispanics are also found in cold regions like Buffalo and Rochester (New York), Chicago, Baltimore, Allentown, (Pennsylvania), and Grand Rapids (Michigan). They've also settled in

Wichita, Toledo, Tulsa, Torrington (Wyoming), Fort Smith (Arkansas), Dalton (Georgia), Liberal (Kansas), Rupert (Idaho), Dodge City (Kansas), Grand Island (Nebraska), Marshalltown (Iowa), and the Tennessee towns of Smyrna and Pulaski. And the list keeps growing.

The U.S. Immigration and Naturalization Services estimate the nation's undocumented aliens at seven million in February of 2001, with 2.2 million living in California. The majority are Hispanics from Mexico, El Salvador, Guatemala, Colombia, Honduras, Ecuador, the Dominican Republic, and Brazil. By 2003, the illegal estimate is eight million; by 2004 the government broadens the figure to 11 million, but it's still a guess. Through the years this count encompasses not only Hispanics but Haitians, Asians, and Europeans, all of whom traverse entry points into this nation with impunity.

With Latin jazz moving in multiple directions, guided by the appearance of American artists in Cuba and Cuban-born musicians living and working in the U.S., I cover this immense development in a 2001 feature for *Down Beat*, my first Latin-themed story for the leading jazz monthly.

In the fall of 2002, I visit Miami for the first time in 25 years to talk to leaders in the Latin entertainment industry and discover a city dramatically altered. It has become not only the Latin entertainment capitol of the world, but also a city overwhelmed by its Hispanic citizens and dominated by the Cuban exile community.

Here are some of the things I learn during my odyssey:

No public or private agency has an accurate count of the Hispanic population in this country. Conflicting figures are provided by different research companies on a yearly basis.

America's Hispanic girth is being swollen by a number of disparate figures: a high birth rate among Latinos living here and the rolling tides of immigration, legal and illegal. The lure of freedom and the ability to enhance one's career and earn previously unattainable amounts of money act as a magnet in attracting people with a purpose to come to these shores.

A handful of radio stations claim to be the nation's first Hispanic outlet: KWKW-AM Los Angeles in 1941 and KCOR-AM in San Antonio in 1945. KWKW starts parttime Spanish broadcasting of news about World War II, becomes a fulltime Spanish broadcaster in 1957 under second owner William Beaton, and in 1962 is bought by Lotus Communications Corp.

KCOR's founder is Raúl Cortez, a native of Veracruz, Mexico, who comes to San Antonio in the 1940s as a music promoter for such artists as Pérez Prado, becomes a citizen, and in 1945 branches into radio with the launching of KCOR. In 1953, he starts KCOR-FM, his second Mexican music station. That same year, his company launches KCOR-TV, probably the nation's first Spanish TV station, which broadcasts from 4 p.m. to 10 p.m.

Additionally, in 1949 the Tichenor family forms Harbenito Radio in Harlingen, Texas, and launches its first station, KGBT-AM, which features regional Mexican music. In 1960, KALI-AM becomes L.A.'s second Spanish station. In 1965, WADO-AM, New York, offers some Spanish and goes fulltime 10 years later. And in 1975, Liberman Broadcasting's KLVE-FM Los Angeles asserts itself as the nation's first Spanish FM.

Some Hispanic families reside for centuries in the Southwest, which is part of Mexico until the U.S. declares war on Mexico and claims California for its own. Eight months later, the treaty of 1848 cedes the land to the U.S. The modern mass invasion of America by immigrants from Mexico occurs between the 1970s and the '80s, when political strife in Central America, especially El Salvador, Nicaragua, and Guatemala also forces hundreds of thousands of refugees north of the border, dramatically ascending the Hispanic presence in California. A study by Pepperdine University's Institute for Public Policy reveals that by 1990 a new Latino middle class emerges in Southern California, with four times as many Hispanic families in the more secure middle class than are living in poverty.

In 1993, California's Finance Department forecasts that by 2040 Latinos will account for 49.7 percent of the population, overtaking whites who will represent 32.4 percent of the Golden State's populace. In fact, by 1996 Latinos represent 29.8 percent of California's population. And, according to the U.S. Commerce Department, California is the No. 1 state in the nation in the number of Latino-owned businesses, followed by Texas, Florida, New York, and New Jersey. California has 250,000 firms, representing 32 percent of all the country's Hispanic companies, followed by Texas with 155,909, and Florida with 118,208.

In 1996, before the Latin invasion moves into the Midwest and South, the nation's top 25 Hispanic-populated cities are Los Angeles, New York, Miami, San Francisco, Chicago, Houston, San Antonio, McAllen/Brownsville, Dallas/Ft. Worth, El Paso, San Diego, Albuquerque, Fresno, Phoenix, Sacramento, Denver, Philadelphia, Corpus Christi, Washington, D.C., Boston, Tucson, Austin, Tampa, Salinas, and Orlando, according to Strategy Research Corp. of Miami's domestic Hispanic market report. A futuristic peek by the Municipal Research Institute of New York in 1996 at the projected dramatic shift in New York City's population in 2000 reveals that of the region's 7,489,000 residents, Hispanics will hit 2,175,000 behind 2,604,000 whites, but ahead of 1,948,000 blacks and 762,000 Asians. The New York City Department of City Planning projects that 35 percent of the city population will be white in 2000.

By 2005, the top 21 Hispanic markets differ in several numerical instances. Here's how they rank as determined by research/analysis firm BIAfn MediaAccess: Los Angeles, New York, San Juan, Miami-Fort Lauderdale, Chicago, Houston, Dallas-Fort Worth, San Francisco-Oakland-San Jose, San Antonio, Phoenix (10), Harlingen-McAllen-Brownsville, San Diego, Sacramento-Stockton-Modesto, Fresno-Visalia, El Paso, Denver, Albuquerque-Santa Fe, Washington, Philadelphia, Atlanta, and Orlando-Daytona Beach.

Hispanic radio grows from 67 stations in 1980 to 564 by 1997 and 699 in 2003. Latin radio and TV stations become the umbilical chord that keeps migrants connected to news of their homelands. Spanish formats proliferate so steadily that by the summer of 1995 and

1996 they are the fifth fastest growing branch of radio behind news/talk, black music (euphemistically called urban to hide its racial slant), adult contemporary, and country, according to ad agency Caballero Spanish Media. In 1995 there are 14 Spanish stations in L.A., including the market leader, thus crowning the city the nation's No. 1 Latin radio market. In 1996, the number increases by one and in 1997 there are 18 Spanish stations. By 2002, L.A. boasts 20 Hispanic-themed outlets among the market's 82 out of 87 stations covered by the Arbitron ratings service. In the ensuing years, low-rated Spanish stations are sold off so that by 2005, the number is down to 17—still the most for any city in the country.

Regional Mexican remains the most listened to format through the decades, encompassing such genres as ranchera (Mexican country style songs about love and life); norteño (bands using accordion); bajo sexto (12-string Mexican bass); grupo (bands playing romantic Mexican music); cumbia (songs based on the Colombian dance rhythm of the same name); vallenato (accordion fueled style from Colombia's Atlantic coast); mariachi (bands featuring trumpet, violin, and guitar playing sentimental Mexican music); conjunto (Texas-based material using accordion and bajo sexto rhythm); banda (horn-driven bands using tuba polka style with electric keyboards and bass); and Tejano (hybrid Texas music combining ranchera, cumbia, and country-string elements).

The Hispanic population expansion, while enriching America's multicultural heritage, fuses the growth of the American Latin entertainment industry still owned by some pioneering independent companies, with Anglo conglomerates in a buying frenzy to instill the kind of consolidation that now controls English-language show business. Every major Anglo record company (CBS, BMG, Warner Bros., EMI, and the Universal Music Group) has its own Spanish stand-alone label. Clear Channel, the conglomerate that dominates American radio with its ownership of 1,270 stations, also operates concert venues and a concert promotion firm. By 2005, the media giant has drawn so much ire for its monopolistic power that it announces it'll split its radio and live-entertainment divisions into two separate companies.

Where there are Spanish population bursts, Spanish-language radio and TV stations usually spring up, altering the broadcasting landscape in rural and urban areas where people migrate to fill available blue-collar jobs in construction, harvesting crops, and laboring in poultry plants. On a higher plane, as more Hispanics seek political office, Spanish media benefit from the influx of political advertising.

There are a number of unique characteristic similarities found in the domestic Latin entertainment industry. While American TV networks use homegrown programming, Hispanic networks like Univision and the upstart Azteca America initially rely on shows primarily developed in Mexico. Telemundo shares facilities and domestic news and special event programming with its parent company, NBC, in addition to creating original Spanish offerings done in Miami, Colombia, and Brazil.

In a major refocus toward Mexican-Americans, which Univision caters to, Telemundo begins aiming original programs in 2003 at this dominant audience. In addition, a growing list of Hispanic-American actors and actresses are making their presence felt on English-language broadcast TV and cable TV channels. A number of new cable networks provide a wide-array of Spanish-language programming aimed at different age groups, thus mirroring the pattern found within the domestic cable community where there are niche channels for a wide variety of interests. Where once there was the Grammy Awards, now there is a companion televised Latin Grammy celebration.

American and Hispanic radio stations equally operate with a plethora of formats. The big difference in Spanish radio is the major role geography plays in programming. Yet these regional tastes are subject to change as population growths prod stations to adjust their formats to accommodate new migrants in their communities. While regional Mexican music and its subcategories are heavily played in the

West and the Southwest, two new L.A. stations begin programming differently for new arrivals. One station focuses on Central and South American émigrés, while the other targets Central Americans and Mexicans. On the East Coast, tropical Caribbean music dominates, with little regional Mexican music played. In Miami, Cuban music is generally eschewed within the tropical mix because of the political clout of the exile community. Spanish talk is heard throughout the country. It seems to have a neutral political stigma except in Miami, where anti-Castroism reigns.

Commercials on radio and TV are read in a machine-gun, rapid-fire pattern. The impression I get is that Latinos live in a fast-paced environment, if the pace of pitching products is any indication. This pacing mirrors the up-tempo style utilized in Mexico, which is reaffirmed when in 2005 I'm in Punta Mita, Mexico, 45 minutes from Puerto Vallarta, and listening to radio stations all pitching products with lightning speed.

On TV, female singers dress seductively and novela actresses act like sex sirens, strengthening the message to young women that sensual is the way to dress and behave if you want to get your man.

Latin jazz, the homegrown art form, is caught in a perpetual pincer. It is eschewed on Spanish-language radio as well as on any of the popular English-language formats. It's thus relegated to the handful of true jazz stations still catering to this niche audience.

American radio has been tainted with payola and the same payoff tactics by record companies has allegedly made its way into the relationship between some Spanish radio and record companies. This despicably illegal practice is discussed in Chapters 5, 13, and 14. This quiet spectrum of payola is a hot topic that's hard to confirm by the Federal Communications Commission, which probes payola charges on a sporadic basis.

What's fascinating about the Hispanic record industry is the evolving musical styles within the Byzantine maze of formats used by major and independent labels to "Americanize" their music. The intention in developing disks that blend Spanish lyrics with some

English lyrics to create "Spanglish," plus the blending of spicy/upbeat Latin tempos with rock rhythms, rhythm and blues, hip-hop, and even reggae, is to broaden the music's appeal to keep bilingual teens and young adults in step with Spanish-language records rather than favoring popular English-language artists. Latin music has its own brand of pop, often featuring lush arrangements and a less raucous rock beat to envelop the themes of love and romance. And in a move that might be called blasphemous, some young regional Mexican groups are adding elements of hip-hop and Latin pop to the most traditional of Latin genres. They are even dressing differently from their older, hit-making brethren by eschewing cowboy hats, boots, and performing clean shaven.

Latinos start rapping in Spanish, which along with rock en Español falls under the confusing genre called urban Latin, while a new, fresh breeze from Puerto Rico called reggaeton, which mixes the reggae dancehall beats from Jamaica with true stories from the barrio, inexorably explodes on the Mainland and becomes the hot sound of 2004 and 2005. This dance music even worms its way onto the playlists of some Anglo rap stations around the nation, including L.A.'s influential No. 1, KPWR-FM.

This targeted terrain fuels the adventurous spirit of artisans exploring idiosyncratic creations, including the fresh sound out of Chicago, of all places, where local area bands develop the breakout sound of 2004 called música Duranguense, based on the dance music of Durango, Mexico. A number of Chicago bands with their own takes on the regional Mexican style will attract a national following and result in appearances on the national Latin Album chart published by *Billboard.*

Despite all these attempts at modernization, the mainstream media generally over-emphasizes the handful of artists with Hispanic surnames that have found some crossover success with Anglo audiences and then seem to fade from popularity, to the detriment of all the pure ethnic Latin performers who remain the backbone of the Hispanic record industry. Spanish and English show business remain two separate worlds except when Latinos successfully crossover into the general market. If a Latin artist doesn't make the cross-market trek, he or she remains invisible to the English-speaking world while being loved by their compatriots.

Well into the 21st century, despite the dichotomy between cultures, these two worlds of entertainment attempt musical and nationality marriages, and to a degree the record industry is the most successful in its efforts to create new styles of music—like rap en Español and reggaeton—which appeal to both bilingual listeners and Spanish speakers. However, as the record industry grows to meet the burgeoning Latin population, it encounters similar problems tarnishing the English-language industry, notably tightly controlled radio formats, the quietly nefarious use of payola to gain airplay, piracy in Latin America that cuts into U.S. sales, and the downloading of music off the Internet. The major Spanish TV networks already romancing Spanish - and English-speaking homegrown viewers with U.S.-produced and - themed novelas, are joined by several new cable channels launched in the new millennium featuring English-language programs for English-dominant speakers. While the majority of Hispanic artists never crack the national radar, a growing number start appearing on the general market album chart in 2004-'05. However, most Spanish-speaking artists in the U.S. have no illusion that they will be discovered by mainstream America and enjoy the crossover success of the past two decades by Julio Iglesias, Gloria Estefan, Carlos Santana, Ricky Martin, Marc Anthony, Shakira, Jon Secada, Elvis Crespo, Enrique Iglesias, Christina Aguilera, Paulina Rubio, and Mariah Carey in 2005.

Marc Anthony, born in New York City's East Harlem of Puerto Rican ancestry, disavows the crossover term in 1999, saying it only applies to Latinos who land on the pop charts rather than Latinos singing in Spanish on the mainstream charts. The key to the big bucks is singing in English, although a hit album in Spanish can also reap financial rewards, but for a smaller audience.

There's one film industry here and, a handful of growing Hispanic actors and actresses are gaining prestigious roles in important films, especially the constantly in play and in wedlock multimedia artist Jennifer Lopez. A small number of Hispanic-focused homegrown film companies have sensed the timing is right and are gearing up to produce movies expressly for the U.S. Latino audience. By 2004, the full impact of the offshore Spanish-language film industry on the U.S. is in full glory, as a host of established, familiar names like Antonio Banderas, Salma Hayek, Penélope Cruz, Jennifer Lopez, and directors Robert Rodriguez and Pedro Almadóvar, to new names in America like Javier Bardem, Gael Garcia Bernal, Diego Luna, and Paz Vega participate in critically acclaimed projects, with several reaping Golden Globe or Oscar buzz.

While Latinos are regularly seen in English-language films, in a growing number of highly acclaimed Spanish-language imports, and in important roles on general market TV network series, they remain a minority, albeit with a growing presence, in the worlds of theater and dance.

In professional sports, while soccer is the favorite among Latinos here and worldwide, baseball employs the most Hispanic players, with football having a surprising number of solidly built Hispanic participants. Latino boxers help attract large fan bases for this brutal punch-a-thon. Basketball teams become aggressive in signing Latinos from outside the U.S. in the 1990s, with 16 on NBA teams in 2005. Even though there are no breakout Latin superstars, the sport is favored by bilingual Hispanics. The fanaticism among Hispanics for their favored sports prompts the emergence of several Spanish-language cable sports networks as adjuncts to Spanish-language coverage of kingpin baseball on broadcast TV networks using the SAP (secondary audio channel) and on Spanish-language radio.

All are media activities these spurred by the geographical expansion of 38.8 million Hispanics with their concurrent $452 billion buying capability in 2003. Census projections place Hispanics at 42.7 million in June 2006 and at 43.7 million in July 2010. Georgia's Selig Center for Economic Growth Studies projects the population rising to 63 million with $926.1 billion in disposable income by 2007 and reaching $2.3 trillion by 2020. With nearly two-thirds of all Latinos residing in the U.S. coming from Mexico, the Hispanic population comprises 12.5 percent of the nation's population and 32.4 percent of Californians in 2003, according to the National Hispanic Medical Association. And with Hispanics having the highest birthrates in the nation there's another generation of fans and consumers in the wings to be cultivated. These Herculean figures are propelling companies to seek their share of the escalating bounty in what sociologist Nathan Glazer has called "the permanently unfinished nation."

One of the most remarkable and tangible effects of the Hispanic population on show business is the proliferation of Latin artists appearing on the nation's general market best-selling album list in 2004. The appearance of Latin acts in different genres of music on the *Billboard* Top 200 album survey, and selectively on the Hot 100 singles chart, supports the truism that Hispanics, with their buying power, are transforming the sounds of music America now accepts.

There can be no more proof of capitalism's embrace of the Hispanic culture than the actions of four powerhouse, blue-chip companies. GE-owned NBC acquires the troubled Telemundo network in 2001 and integrates it within its corporate world. In 2004, the giant Viacom conglomerate and ABC Radio hook up with the Spanish Broadcasting System's radio network to both provide programming and dual advertising opportunities for national marketers. Clear Channel, the nation's largest radio network with 1,270 stations, starts in 2004 to convert upward of 29 of its low-rated stations to Spanish formats in a move to possibly compete against Univision Radio, now the nation's leading Spanish-language network. Univision acquires this status as a result of parent Univision Communications' acquisition of the former Hispanic Broadcasting Corporation, melding it into its entertainment empire which includes the Univision TV Networks and a number of acquired independent record companies grouped together in the Univision Music Group.

Faced with declining audiences for broadcast TV programs, ABC becomes the first English-language network in September of 2005 to reach out to Latinos by offering a combination of Spanish dubbed dialog and subtitles for its fall primetime entertainment programming. This is a very big deal for mainstream TV in the new America. ABC's move is the latest in a series of awakening moments for the broadcast and advertising industries, all buoyed by new, enticing statistics pointing to golden opportunities within the Hispanic community. These upbeat statistics, cited by the *Los Angeles Times*, include Nielsen Media Research's newly estimated 11.2 million Hispanic households that watch TV, of which an estimated 34 percent are under 18, according to research firm HispanTelligence. What also portends heady times for English-language broadcasters is that resident Latino births are now overtaking the entry into this country of new immigrants whose loyalty is to their Spanish language. U.S.-born Hispanics grow up as acculturated consumers who easily split their TV and radio loyalties between their dual cultural backgrounds, often leaning toward Spanish media during evenings at home with their families. The keys are having a total understanding of how to reach Latinos through their heritage, language, culture, and lifestyle within these 50 retro-acculturated states.

This awareness obviously produces a major cultural impact on the radio industry in 2005 as English-language stations add Spanish-language records to their playlists with greater frequency, spurred on by the explosive popularity of reggaeton, the mixture of rap with reggae and Caribbean influences emerging from Puerto Rico to become the hottest form of Hispanic music with bilingual Latinos.

While Hispanics are currently the fastest growing "minority" in the nation, get ready for the takeover...in 2050. That's when Census Bureau projections indicate Hispanics will become the majority of Americans, based on their rapid domestic birth rate and migration. This Latin takeover is heightened by a U.S. Census report in June of 2005 depicting one of every seven Americans as Hispanic, representing 41.3 million of the nation's 294 million people. Of the

41.3 million, 14 million are under 18. A 2005 study by the Pew Hispanic Center appearing in *Advertising Age* also affirms the Latinization of America, in which 88 percent of the U.S.-born Hispanics are under 18. It's the first time they outpace the foreign-born immigrant population. And by 2020, 34 percent of all Hispanics will be foreign-born first generation, 36 percent will be U.S.-born second generation and 30 percent will be third-generation children of U.S.-born Latin parents. These are very heady figures for biculturalism.

The Pew Center also cites data from the Census Bureau and the Bureau of Labor Statistic's 2004 current population study, which graphs a continual dramatic shift in undocumented immigrants during the last 15 years that eschew the traditional six destinations states of California, Texas, Florida, Illinois, and New Jersey to create "settlement areas" in nine states. These new homes are in Arizona, Utah, Colorado, Nevada, North Carolina, Tennessee, Georgia, Maryland, and Massachusetts. The government now claims illegals arriving in the U.S. at an average rate of 500,000 a year since 1990. The majority are still arriving from Mexico, which produces 57 percent of the undocumented residents, with 24 percent arriving from other Latin American nations. For states with no previous experience in dealing with Hispanic arrivals (many of them non-English-speaking illegals), there are major problems in providing schooling, healthcare, and housing for these families and workers who tend to find jobs in agriculture, food processing plants, construction, and as unskilled labor. These are all serious, tension-creating problems between townsfolk and the new arrivals, especially if crime rates rise.

The changing nature of U.S.-residing Hispanics also reveals that 72 percent of first-generation immigrants speak Spanish as their primary language, while English and Spanish are spoken by 47 percent of second-generation bilingual residents and English is the dominant language among 78 percent of third-generation Latinos. Aware of this generational difference, MTV Español plans developing a bilingual format under the slogan "Two Worlds" in 2004. Already exploring this bilingual world is cable's year-old

English-language Si TV, whose slogan captures its dichotomy with the tag "Speak English. Live Latin."

It's hard to separate political polemics from the Latino life experience, which is often at the core of Latin media coverage, whether it's the growing number of Hispanics gaining prominence on state and federal levels or the constant invasion across America's open borders by illegal migrants. The subject of arrest by Border Patrol officers and the deaths of people trying to navigate across desert areas is a volatile topic year after year. As a result of 300 illegals' deaths in Arizona in 2004, the Bush administration beefs up its Arizona–Mexico security force in 2005, deploying an additional 500 Border Patrol agents to scrutinize the 370-mile Arizona frontier as a key component of its year-old Arizona Border Control Initiative. The additional personnel increase the total number of Border Patrol agents looking for illegals in this part of the country to 3,000.

Some skeptics claim the government's additional personnel is in response to a new citizen protection movement called the Minuteman Project, which begins a month-long operation on April 4, 2005 and involves roving patrols of around 750 civilians from across the U.S., some armed with guns, seeking to spot illegals crossing the border and calling the Border Patrol to arrest them. The volunteers plan to patrol 23 miles of desert in Southeast Arizona, the most trafficked area in the country, where around 500,000 arrests were recorded last year of illegals sneaking into the U.S., principally from Mexico. These public monitors attract more than 200 media from around the world as the story becomes more politicized. The Minuteman movement doesn't sit well with immigration-rights groups, generally supported by Hispanic politicians who curry the votes of the Latin communities and by Mexico's President Vicente Fox, who wants the U.S. government to protect illegals streaming across the Arizona desert. Mexico also adds more federal troops and police to thwart its border breakers. President Bush calls the volunteers vigilantes and they in turn label him the co-president of Mexico who fails to secure the nation's porous borders.

Just about the time the Minutemen leave Arizona, the federal government announces a new surge of illegals from Honduras, Guatemala, El Salvador, and Nicaragua prodded by political and economic problems, to seek relief in the U.S. Their route is through Mexico. The U.S. faces another immigration problem that adds to a topic being covered in-depth by Hispanic media: the number of illegal immigrants caught who are fighting to stay in the U.S. for any number of reasons. Inspired by the Minuteman project, a new organization, Friends of the Border Patrol, announces it's forming Border Watch to patrol areas around San Diego. The volunteers will include pilots and medics who will assist other volunteers made ill by the warm weather. Volunteer groups also appear in a number of other states from California to Maine to watch the U.S. Canadian border as well as porous crossing points on the U.S. Mexican border.

Reacting to rising public displeasure, the Border Patrol launches a historic and innovative $1.5 million Spanish-language ad campaign on Mexican radio and TV during the summer, using Mexican actors and *corrido*-singing musicians under the banner "No Mas Cruces En La Frontera" ("No More Crosses on the Border"). The commercial's key message, according to the *Los Angeles Times*, is "There are many reasons for crossing the border. None are worth your life."

Three weeks later, and in a sharp rebuke to the Bush administration's condemnation of the patrols as vigilantes, Customs and Border Protection Commissioner Robert C. Bonner, during a visit to the Port of Los Angeles, tells the *Times* the peaceful conduct of the citizen patrol groups "eases his initial concern about possible vigilantism."

When Antonio Villaraigosa, the 52-year-old Los Angeles city councilman and former state assembly member and assembly speaker stunningly defeats one-term Los Angeles mayor James K. Hahn, 55, in May of 2005 in a low turnout, runoff election, this local upset becomes a national story for the Anglo and Spanish media. The new mayor, who's last name is Villa and is raised in the East L.A. Mexican barrio, adds his wife's surname to create the longer moniker. He becomes the 47-percent Hispanic city's first Latin mayor since José Cristóbal Aguilar serves two terms and departs the office in 1872. The victory is redemptive for Villaraigosa who loses in 2001 to Hahn, a former city attorney for 16 years and son of the late Kenneth Hahn who had been elected to the L.A. County Board of Supervisors 10 times. Villaraigosa's sweep into office is a combination of white, black, and Asian support coupled with a record boost from 84 percent of the city's 25 percent of registered voting Latins.

He's also the first challenger to remove a sitting mayor in Los Angeles in 32 years. The new mayor joins a growing list of 22 Hispanic mayors in cities with 100,000-plus populations, including such major Hispanic metropolises as San Antonio, Miami, San Jose, and the improbable locale of Wichita, Kansas.

The new surge of Latin political power, already reflected in the number of Latinos in elected office in Texas, is explosively clear in the city and county of Los Angeles, where in addition to the mayor, the city attorney, president of the city council, chairman of the Metropolitan Transportation Authority, county sheriff, and chairwoman on the county Board of Supervisors are all Hispanics. Seven years ago, none of these posts are occupied by Hispanics; today, Alex Padilla is the first Hispanic president of the L.A. City Council since 1868 and city attorney Rocky (Rockard J). Delgadillo is the first Hispanic to hold that post prior to 1851, according to the *Los Angeles Times*. All of these high-profile positions lend themselves to regular media coverage. Gloria Molina is arguably California's best-known pioneering Latina politician, becoming the first Latina in the state Legislature in 1982, the first Latina on L.A. City Council in 1987 and the first elected Latina to the County Board of Supervisors in 1991.

There are now more than 6,000 Hispanic elected officials in this country, showing how far Hispanics have come in the so-called ethnic integration of mainstream American politics. The highest-ranking Hispanic in the second Bush administration is Alberto R. Gonzalez, the 49-year-old Attorney General replacement for John

Ashcroft. Born in San Antonio and rising to become the Texas Secretary of State and a three-year member of the state Supreme Court, he follows his friend President Bush to Washington as his legal council.

Within the federal government are the Senate's first two Hispanics, Democrat Ken Salazar of Colorado and Republican Mel Martinez from Florida. Hispanics in the House of Representatives include Democrat Robert Menendez of New Jersey, Republicans Heana (Ileana) Ros-Lehtinen of Florida, and Henry Bonilla of Texas. On the state level, Bill Richardson is the Governor of New Mexico while Brian Sandoval is Nevada's Attorney General.

The pervasiveness of Hispanics in positions of power and influence in the new America of the 21st century is markedly displayed in *Time*'s cover story of August 22 titled, *The 25 Most Influential Hispanics in America*. Eight Latino show business figures are included in the list along with Attorney General Alberto Gonzalez, Los Angeles Mayor Antonio Villaraigosa, and the nation's first Hispanic Senator from Miami, Mel Martinez. The notable Latinos include Mexican American comic George Lopez, star of his eponymous hit ABC series; actress/entrepreneur Jennifer Lopez of Puerto Rican ancestry; Robert Rodriguez, the Mexican American film director who casts Hispanics in major mainstream films; Gustavo Santaolalla, the Argentinean owner of Surco Records, which helps develop rock en Español; Arturo "Arte" Moreno, the fourth-generation Mexican American billionaire owner of the Anaheim Angels and the first Latino to own a major league baseball team (he's also named one of the nation's richest people and the lone Hispanic with a net value of $1 billion, tying him for 26th place among 27 sports team owners by *Fortune*); Cristina Saralegui, the Cuban-born host of her own influential Univision talk show who crosses over into English-language TV shows and owns a number of related business ventures; Jorge Ramos, the Mexican-born male lead news anchor on Univision since 1986, whose network clout enables him to interview every American president since George H.W. Bush; and Mexican actress Salma Hayek, who starts appearing in American films in 1995, including the starring role in her own production of *Frida*, which wins two of its six Oscar nominations in 2002. Along with Moreno, *Fortune* also ranks Andrew Jerrold (Jerry) Perenchio, principal owner of Univision Communications with $2.6 billion, in 14th place among 38 film and broadcast moguls.

In the "It Seems They're Everywhere Department," you see capitalism's open market concept at work over the years as the Hispanic population increases in recent years. AOL zeros in on Spanish speakers who don't own a personal computer with the specially priced $300 package of its Optimized PC, 17-inch monitor and a one-year subscription to AOL's on-line service. Staples, the leading office products retailer, uses its first-ever Spanish-language, 30-second TV commercial to pitch back-to-school merchandise in Los Angeles on Univision, TeleFutura, Telemundo, and Azteca America. New York's Ambassador Yellow Pages directory, which already has a bilingual edition in the borough of the Bronx, introduces its first Spanish-language directory for the borough of Manhattan in 2005. Doritos hooks up with Universal Music & Video Distribution to place photos of its Latin music artists on 180-million bags of its nine flavors. AT&T joins Verizon Wireless, U.S. Cellular, and Alltel in offering Latin songs obtained from a company called Latin Garage to cell phone subscribers as incoming ring tones. AGmobile and Versaly Entertainment sign with Univision and Telemundo, respectively, to provide their content for cell phones. Versaly is the company working with Sprint, Nextel, AT&T, Cingular, and T-Mobile.

McDonald sponsors its first all-male Hispanic rock band tour, "Lo McXimo De La Música," which plays Miami, Houston, and Los Angeles. Proceeds from the package, which includes Motolov, El Gran Silencio, Rabanes, and Maldita Vecindad, plus local acts, goes to the Ronald McDonald House Charities and the Hispanic American Commitment to Education Resources Scholarship Program. The fast food chain also shifts from pure Spanish in its TV ads to Spanglish for its Big Macs, an acculturation move to appeal to young people living in the English and Hispanic cultures; it earlier targets young

Hispanics with TV spots running in the West and Southwest on popular teen networks like the WB, UPN, Fox, and NBC. PepsiCo also uses Spanglish to sell Mountain Dew on TV.

Dunkin' Donuts, CVS Pharmacies, and Mitsubishi begin using original Spanish-language commercials on TV. Dunkin' Donuts' first Spanish commercial airs in cities where it has large numbers of stores: New York, Miami, Chicago, and Philadelphia. The chain previously uses a Spanish translation for its general market spots. Mitsubishi, which also uses Spanish language converted Anglo commercials, shifts its TV marketing to original Spanish spots. CVS' first Spanish commercial airs in Texas and Florida, where its stores also introduce bilingual signage. Toy manufacturer Fisher-Price allocates $1 million for Spanish radio/TV ads in Los Angeles, Houston, and Chicago to introduce its products to parents during the 2004 Christmas buying season. It also sponsors street fairs in which parents can bring their children to play with its line of toys. Nissan boosts its advertising budget for Latinos to $50 million from 2003's $20 million in an effort to reach the next level of awareness.

Hennessy Cognac signs Saúl Hernández of the Mexican rock band Jaguares as its first Latin figurehead in a new ad campaign touting independent-oriented performers. Verizon Wireless sponsors Alejandro Sanz's U.S. tour, which includes advertising on radio, TV, the Internet, and in print publications, linking him to the tour and his new Warner Music Latina album, *No Es Lo Mismo*. The campaign also promotes the downloading of his songs as the ring tones for cell phones. Heineken sponsors a five-city tour for Nortec Collective music groups that blend electronics with Northern Mexican music aimed at 21- to 24-year-old males. Absolut Vodka creates its first marketing campaign aimed at Latinos, *Absolut Ritmos*, which includes a touring music presentation starting in Miami and then expanding to New York and other Hispanic markets.

Two other liquor companies, Jack Daniel's and Chivas Regal, also sponsor music tours. Jack Daniel's sponsors concerts in Miami, New York, and Los Angeles, all featuring acts in the 21-to-34-years of age group that the company is targeting. The concerts are promoted under the "Studio No. 7" banner featuring local alternative unknown acts as well as national figures. In Miami alone, a special CD featuring local rock en Español bands is released as another means of connecting with potential new liquor drinkers. Chivas Regal ties with La Ley, Chile's successful pop trio, for its second U.S. tour, which also promotes *Libertad*, its 2004 album. The group's 2000 release *Uno* wins a Grammy for best Latin rock/alternative album.

Kellogg's also sponsors a six-city tour of six totally different Latin acts. GE increases its Hispanic advertising budget. Hallmark Cards offers 2,500 greeting cards in Spanish. Blockbuster adds nearly 1,000 videos dubbed in Spanish. Kraft Foods aligns with Universal Music Special Markets to create a customized CD to celebrate Hispanic Heritage Month.

On the fashion front, Kmart sells a clothing line named after pop star Thalia; Sears plans to feature dressy women's clothes with the brand of Lucy Pereda, a Spanish TV lifestyle personality; and the Jennifer Lopez's JLO brand of clothes is featured in the teen departments of major stores. Lincoln uses Oscar-nominated actress Salma Hayek to sell Navigator models. Daisy Fuentes, who breaks into TV in 1986 as weather girl/news reporter on Univision's New York station WXTV and then becomes the show host on *MTV Internacional*, MTV's *House of Style*, and the *Miss USA Pageant*, is recruited by Regatta USA, designer and manufacturer of private label apparel items. She will front a line for the Kohl's department store's 542 outlets in 36 states. The Cuban American actress' Daisy Fuentes Collection includes clothing, shoes, and jewelry. Using a different approach, Shakey's Pizza chain in Southern California targets Latinos in its media commercials with regular actors, not celebrities.

The Belo Corp., owner of the *Dallas Morning News*, launches *Al Dia*, a Spanish-language daily paper, while Knight Ridder's Fort Worth *Star-Telegram* changes the name of its nine-year-old *La Estrella* to *Diario La Estrella* as it increases publication from two to five days a week. New York City has two dailies, *Diario La Prensa* and *Hoy*. By

2003, when the *Dallas Morning News* launches *Al Dia*, there are 500 Spanish newspapers in the nation, up from 232 in 1970. By 2005, there are 700-plus Spanish-language papers in the nation. They're found in the major Hispanic centers of Miami, Los Angeles, Houston, Dallas, Fort Worth, and Laredo, as well as in Arlington, Virginia, Lexington, Kentucky, and Wichita, Kansas, and points in between. One year later, L.A.-based *La Opinion*, which concentrates on Mexican and Central American readers and New York's *El Diario/La Prensa*, which focuses on Puerto Rican and Caribbean readers, are merged into a new company, Impremedia, as the first step in building a national print media company. One week after this announcement, the Tribune Company, which publishes *Hoy* in Chicago and New York, launches the paper in Los Angeles in March of 2004. It covers Mexico, Puerto Rico, the Caribbean, and South and Central America. The Hearst Corporation launches bilingual weeklies in two cities where it operates English-language dailies. In San Antonio, its *Express-News* launches *Conexión*, while its *Houston Chronicle* introduces *La Vibra*.

San Antonio-based Meximerica Media launches the Spanish-language daily paper *Rumbo De Houston* as the latest in its chain of *Rumbo* papers in its home city, plus Austin, and in the Rio Grande Valley. The *Houston Chronicle* counters the invasion into its city by buying *La Voz (The Voice)*, founded in 1979 by two Cuban refugees. The weekly is distributed on Wednesdays to *Chronicle* subscribers. The purchase in December follows the *Chronicle*'s launch in April of *La Vibra*, a weekly Spanish-language entertainment magazine with distribution to bilingual and Spanish speakers in Hispanic neighborhoods. With the addition of these publications, the number of Spanish newspapers in the U.S. continues to exceed the 666 tallied in 2003 by the Latino Print Network of Carlsbad, California.

Also during 2004, the *New York Post* debuts *Tempo*, a monthly English-language Latin section that boasts of "capturing the rhythm of Latin New York." Rival tabloid *New York Daily News* introduces a free weekly Spanish-language paper, *Hora Hispana*, to 200,000 Hispanic families in the boroughs of Manhattan, the Bronx, Brooklyn, and Queens. In addition to general news and entertainment features, two of *The News'* columnists will cover immigration and other developing issues facing the various Latino communities. Puerto Rico's largest daily, *El Nuevo Dia*, available in Orlando since 2003, expands into Tampa in 2005.

People En Español leads the parade of companies debuting Latin issues. Parent company Time Inc. is testing three Spanish-language themed *Sports Illustrated* issues in 2005 with professional baseball, football, basketball, and World Cup 2006 previews. Editorial Televisa, the Mexican media giant and the largest publisher of Spanish-language magazines in the world, publishes 20 titles in this country including *Cristina*, *Vanidades*, *TV Y Novelas*, and *Cosmopolitan En Español.* In 2004, it acquires 51 percent of English-language *Hispanic* and *Hispanic Trends* magazines from the Hispanic Publishing Group. In 2005, it debuts *Prevention En Español.*

Focusing on Hispanic college students, LatCom Communications unveils the quarterly *Icaramba U* in time for fall 2004 semester. In 2005, Meredith launches *Siempre Mujer*, a service magazine for Latinas. On a regional level, Emmis Publishing, the latest owner of the monthly *Los Angeles* magazine, debuts the English-language bimonthly *Tu Ciudad Los Angeles (Your City)* for well-heeled Latinos.

AARP's three-year-old *Segunda Juventud* bilingual magazine for 50-plus Hispanics switches from a quarterly to a bimonthly with its February/March 2005 issue. Sports channel ESPN, in partnership with Mexico's media giant, Grupo Televisa, launches *ESPN Deportes*, a monthly Spanish-language magazine in May. The slick magazine will provide U.S. Hispanics with coverage of global soccer, Major League Baseball, the National Football League, Mexican and Caribbean League baseball, boxing, and auto racing. Aiming at a younger audience, Emmis Publishing launches *Tu Ciudad (Your City)* as a free, English-language bimonthly magazine in Los Angeles focusing on an upscale Latin readership. The debut issue appears in May covering June/July of '05.

Best Buy and Circuit City, two major mass merchandisers, begin advertising consumer electronics products in Spanish. It's a first for both chains. Best Buy is targeting older Hispanics less likely to purchase high-tech equipment. Kmart distributes a Spanish ad circular in 160 stores and in 10 Spanish newspapers. Wal-Mart Stores has its own monthly circular in Spanish found in states bordering Mexico. Both discounters, plus the Big Lots chain, all carry food, health, and beauty aid products for Hispanics. Ikea, Circuit City, Home Depot, Target, and JCPenney all add bilingual staff, signage, and merchandise appealing to Latinos in select stores. Also debuting TV commercials in Spanish are Ikea and Circuit City.

Washington Mutual Bank has bilingual talking ATMs in eight states. Hispanic cooks account for a quarter of the jobs at U.S. restaurants. Cartoonist Lalo Alcaraz's "La Cucaracha," the first Latino-themed comic strip to focus on social and political topics, is sold to 60 newspapers in the U.S. by the Universal Press Syndicate.

Microsoft, AOL, and Yahoo, with their Spanish portals, join shopping giants Sears, Roebuck & Co., Home Depot, Target, Sharper Image, and a growing list of other companies romancing Hispanics online. Book publisher Knopf becomes the first American publishing house to issue a Spanish book (Gabriel Garcia Marquez's *Viva Para Contarla)* without an accompanying English translation. Barnes & Noble adds thousands of Spanish-language titles to its inventory. Simon & Schuster begins a Spanish-language children's line while Scholastic Inc. releases a Spanish translation for Madonna's children's book, *The English Roses*. Fast-food chains from Latin America open franchises around the country. Pepsi employs Latin sex kitten Shakira in its TV ads. Frito-Lay launches an assortment of spicy snacks in cities with large Hispanic populations.

Home Depot, which already sponsors Telemundo's home improvement show, *Una Estrella En Casa*, signs a product placement deal with the network's *Mi Primer Hogar*, a reality/documentary show debuting in April of '05. It will provide all the appliances, home improvement products, and services for the show's design experts and participants.

Chicago-based JossClaude Products introduces the Formula Latina Hair Care line specifically designed for Hispanic women, with Miami the first city to receive the line with 12 different hair treatments. It's joined in the competition for skin tone products for Hispanic women with different pigmentations by Zalia Cosmetics, whose line of 110 items gains the big boost of being carried initially in Victoria's Secret Beauty Shops in Miami, New York, Los Angeles, and Dallas. Prior to landing the test with Victoria's Secret, the cosmetics line is only available at three Zalia BeautiLounges in New York and New Jersey. Procter & Gamble plans adding two shampoo and conditioner products to its Extra Liso line of Hispanic hair-care items in February of 2006.

In one of the most unusual and far-reaching commercial connections, the Nickelodeon Channel hooks up with four blue chip advertisers in February of 2005 in sponsoring a national mall tour, "La Casa De Dora," aimed at the parents of preschoolers centered around the seven-year-old bilingual animated children's series, *Dora The Explorer*. Housed outside and within a 1,000 plus square foot modular house, designed like Dora's TV home, are products by Daimler Chrysler (a Dodge Grand Caravan minivan), Procter & Gamble (Bounty paper towels), Burger King (burgers), and General Mills (Kix cereal). The tour package, which includes the stage show "Dora The Explorer Live," will travel to 10 malls in heavily populated Hispanic cities, explains the *Wall Street Journal*. Cost of the project: an estimated $40 million to interact with Hispanic parents and their tagalong children.

Interstate Bakeries Corporation, known for its top-selling Twinkies snack, enters the Spanish market with a line of cakes under the moniker Las Delicias De Hostess in San Diego, Phoenix, and Dallas in September of '05.

Despite Latinos being the nation's largest ethnic group, 54 percent of people surveyed by the Pew Hispanic Center and the Kaiser Family Center say they identify themselves by their country of origin rather than as Hispanic or Latino. The term "Hispanic" is created by the U.S. Census Bureau in the 1970s. "Latino" is another domestic creation supposedly designed to focus on marketing and political endeavors. Yet in the U.S., "Hispanic" and "Latino" dominate the way Spanish-speaking artists are identified. "Chicano," a third identification for Americans of Mexican lineage in California, seems to be fading in popularity. Go figure.

One thing's for sure, the growth of the U.S.-Hispanic entertainment industry is a living, evolving entity. Despite the branch of show business they're in, these entertainers seeking success and glory in the U.S.A. all speak Spanish, the one element that unifies them despite their cultural differences. So fast and vast is the Latinization of America occurring that in 2002 Tajamika Paxton, a film producer working on a joint venture movie aimed at the Latin market with Fox 2000, a division of 20th Century Fox, prophesizes that in 30 years Hispanics will be the nation's mainstream audience.

This melting pot of peoples, first, second, and third generation, bilinguals or strictly Spanish speaking, and the companies catering to their artistic and cultural needs (and relishing the feel of those green American dollars) are the components I set out to explore on my odyssey into the wildly competitive, highly political, eagerly sought-after, multi-tiered world of the American Latin entertainment industry. As for now, the Latin industry is a brilliant rainbow of visuals and sounds. Effusive jazz bandleader Eddie Palmieri predicts in 1996 that "Latin music will overwhelm the 21st century." Whether or not his prophecy comes true, the new century has all the benchmarks for historically securing a dominant position for the Latin branch of show business...with one caveat. Companies will fall short in achieving this recognition if they short-circuit their industry's growth by devouring each other to eliminate competition while striving to be both players in the crossover, megabuck Anglo market, and remaining powerhouses in their separate but distinct cultural oasis.

Articles

"BIAFN's Rankings Of The Top 21 Hispanic Markets." Multichannel News, Oct. 17, 2005

"Forbes 400 Richest People In America." Oct. 10, 2005

"P&G Heads Into Hispanic Hair Battle." Advertising Age, Oct. 3, 2005

"A Growing Passion For The Latino Market." New York Times, Aug. 31, 2005

"The 25 Most Influential Hispanics In America." Time, Aug. 22, 2005

"No Plans For Citizen Border Patrols Seen." Los Angeles Times, July 21, 2005

"Immigration Official Praises Citizen Patrols." Los Angeles Times, July 21, 2005

"Border Patrol Tries New Tune To Deter Crossers." Los Angeles Times, July 4, 2005

"Latinos, Flexing Political Muscle, Come Of Age In L.A." Los Angeles Times, June 27, 2005

"Under The Sun." U.S. News & World Report, June 20, 2005

"Illegal Population Flows To Southeast." Los Angeles Times, June 15, 2005

"In The U.S., 1 In 7 Residents Is Latino." Los Angeles Times, June 9, 2005

"Charming The Angels." Time, May 30, 2005

"A Latin Power Surge." Newsweek, May 30, 2005

"Not-News Week." LA Weekly, May 26, 2005

"Villaraigosa's Support Goes Beyond Latinos." Los Angeles Times, May 19, 2005

"Big Numbers That Finally Add Up." Los Angeles Times, May 19, 2005

"Giving Upscale Latinos In L.A. A Fresh Voice." Los Angeles Times, May 11, 2005

"Volunteers To Patrol Border Near San Diego." Los Angeles Times, May 5, 2005

"Multicultural? No Mainstream." Advertising Age, May 2, 2005

"Immigrant Pleas Crushing Federal Appellate Courts." Los Angeles Times, May 2, 2005

"A Surge South Of Mexico." Los Angeles Times, May 1, 2005

"Border Watchers Capture Their Prey-The Media." Los Angeles Times, April 5, 2005

"Minutemen Prepare To Lay Down The Law." Los Angeles Times, April 2, 2005

"Daisy Blooms." Hispanic Magazine, April, 2005

"U.S. To Bolster Arizona Border Security." Los Angeles Times, March 30, 2005

"Telemundo & Home Depot Product Placement Agreement." HispanicAd.com, March 29

ESPN To Launch Magazine In Spanish." Los Angeles Times, March 17,

2005

"Colorado Activists Push Immigration Initiative." Los Angeles Times, March 13, 2005

"New 'Dora' Plug: Mi Casa Es Su Casa." Wall Street Journal, Feb. 17, 2005.

"Papers Chase Markets To Add Reach." Advertising Age, Jan. 31, 2005

The New Generation." Advertising Age, Jan. 31, 2005

"Mexico's Border-Crossing Tips Anger Some In U.S." Los Angeles Times, Jan. 4, 2004

"Ikea, Circuit City Stores Go Bilingual." Advertising Age, Jan. 3, 2005

"Chronicle Buys La Voz Spanish Newspaper." Houston Chronicle, Dec. 3, 2004

"Hispanic Income Rising, Expected To Grow." Miami Herald, Nov. 12, 2004

"New Acts Try Ol' No. 7." Latin Notas Billboard, Oct. 30, 2004

"Nissan Taps Vidal For $50M Hispanic Account." Advertising Age, Oct. 25, 2004

"AARP's Juventud Ups Frequency." MediaWeek, Oct. 18, 2004

"Chile's La Ley The Latin Rock Band's Popularity Grows." Hispanic Magazine, October 2004

"Who Left The Door Open?" Time, Sept. 20, 2004

"NY Daily News Launches Hora Hispana Newspaper." HispanicAd.com, Sept. 15, 2004

"Dunkin' Donuts Creates Spanish-Language Spot." Advertising Age, Sept. 6, 2004

"Zalia Cosmetics Shows True Face." Miami Herald, Aug. 17, 2004

"Staples Unveils First Hispanic Television Commercial." HispaniaNews.com, Aug. 15, 2004

"Ambassador Yellow Pages Launches Spanish Language Directory In Manhattan." HispaniaAd.com, Aug. 12, 2004

"AOL To Market Low-Cost PC To Latinos." Los Angeles Times, Aug. 12, 2004

"Versaly Puts The World In Wireless Hands." Billboard, Aug. 7, 2004

"Best Buy Targets Hispanic Patriarchs." Advertising Age, Aug. 2, 2004

"New Spanish Daily Paper Debuts." San Antonio Express-News, July 26, 2004

"Verizon Crunches Data On Sanz Tie-In." Advertising Age, June 7, 2004

"Doritos Has A Taste For UMVD Acts." Billboard, May 22, 2004

"Print Sees Hope In Hispanics." Advertising Age, May 3, 2004

"Another Spanish-Language Paper For L.A." Jan. 20, 2004

"Spanish-Language Newspapers La Opinion, El Diario To Merge." Los Angeles Times, Jan 16, 2004

"The House That Used To Be In Mexico." Los Angeles Times, Jan. 11, 2004

"AT&T Wireless Offers Latin Mobile Content." Billboard, Jan. 10, 2004

"Calculating The Latino Influence." Los Angeles Times. Jan. 8, 2004

"A Hybrid Tongue Or Slanguage?" Los Angeles Times, Dec. 27, 2003

"Verizon Courts Latins With Sanz." Billboard, Dec. 27, 2003

"Reading All About It En Espanol." Hispanic magazine, December 2003

"Formula Latina To Hit Miami Stores In Spring." Miami Herald, Nov. 24, 2003

"Latin Acts Attract More Companies." Billboard, Oct. 11, 2003.

"AOL Launches Spanish-Language Service." Los Angeles Times, Oct. 1, 2003

"Barnes & Noble Gets Better Read On Spanish Market." Los Angeles Times, Sept. 15, 2003

"Open Markets." Hispanic Magazine, September 2003

"Mestizo Culture Already Has Erased Many Of The Differences That Split Californians." Los Angeles Times, Aug. 31, 2003

"McTour For Latin Rock." Aug. 9, 2003

"Texas Dailies Battle For Hispanic Readers." Wall Street Journal, Aug. 4, 2003

"Heineken Loves Leche." Billboard, June 14, 2003

"With Immigrant Boom, South Makes Translation." Los Angeles Times, May 27, 2003

"Retailers See Potential In Growing Latino Population." Los Angeles Times, May 19, 2003

"Online Sellers Woo Spanish Speakers." Los Angeles Times, May 19, 2003

"Surging Interest Ignites Regional Mexican Scene." Billboard, May 10, 2003

"CFA Becomes Clear Channel/Televisa." Billboard May 10, 2003

"McD's Lets Music Speak To Latino Teens." AdWeek, May 7, 2003

"Telemundo: Latino Buying Power To Soar." Multichannel News, May 5, 2003

"Cereal Support." Billboard, May 4, 2003

"Watch Out, He Bites." Los Angeles Times, Los Angeles Times May 2, 2003

"Buying Power Of Hispanics Is Set To Soar." Wall Street Journal, April

18, 2003

"Hispanic Boom's Here To Stay." Multichannel News, March 17, 2003

"For Millions Of Latinos Race Is A Flexible Concept." Los Angeles Times, March 11

"Top 15 States By Population." Billboard, March 1, 2003

"Hispanic Magazines Sizzling When It Comes To Ad Revenue." Miami Herald, Feb. 22, 2003

"Latinos Face Significant Barriers To Health." Los Angeles Times, Feb. 28, 2003

"Latino Majority Arrives Among State's Babies." Los Angeles Times, Feb. 6, 2003

"Number Of Illegal Migrants Growing." Los Angeles Times, Feb. 1, 2003

"Belo Preps New Spanish Daily For Growing Segment." MediaWeek, Jan. 27, 2003

"Absolut Launches Absolut Ritmos." Hispanic PR Business Wire." Jan. 27, 2003

"Office Depot Launches New Spanish Language Web Site." Hispanic PR Business Wire, Jan. 16, 2003

"Noel Laureate's Memoir Is A Success In Any Language." Los Angeles Times, Jan. 14, 2003"

"America Adds Salsa To Its Burgers And Fries." Wall Street Journal, Jan. 2, 2003

"Latino Survey Shows Optimism About Assimilation." Los Angeles Times, Dec. 18, 2002

"Hispanics Speak Out," Miami Herald, Dec. 18, 2002

"As Latinos Fan Out Across America, Businesses Follow." Wall Street Journal, Nov. 26, 2002

"Latin Magnet Markets." Multichannel News Hispanic Market Report, Oct. 28, 2002

"Latinos Take Root In Midwest." Los Angeles Times, Oct. 25, 2002

"From Prep To Chef: Latinos Sway In U.S. Restaurants." Wall Street Journal, Oct. 7, 2002

"¿Cuanto? Talking ATMs Going Bilingual In S. Fla." Miami Herald, Sept. 12, 2002

"New Kmart Magazine Targets Hispanics." NY Times, Sept. 9, 2002

"Pepsi Looks To Pop Stars To Reach Minorities And Mainstream." NY Times, Aug. 27, 2002

"A Film Of Their Own" Miami Herald, Aug. 20, 2002

"Great Third Wave On The No. 7." Financial Times, Sept. 8, 1999

"Crank It Up." Los Angeles Times, Aug. 8, 1999

"Crossing Over? Hello-o They're Already Here." Los Angeles Times, June 6, 1999_

"Latin Jazz Fermentations. Down Beat, August 1997

"New Middle Class On The Rise, Study Shows." Los Angeles Times, Oct. 10, 1996

"Reverse Assimilation." LA Weekly, Aug. 9, 1996

"Number Of Latino Firms Up 76% In 5 Years; California Has The Most." Los Angeles Times, July 11, 1996

"The Browning of Black L.A." Los Angeles Magazine, May 1996

"Latinos, Asians To Lead Rise In U.S. Population." Los Angeles Times, March 14, 1996

Chapter 2
CAPITULO 2

Early Indicators 1977–1979 "Havana Jam:" The Cuban Connection
LOS INDICADORES PRIMARIOS 1977–1979
"HAVANA JAM:" LA CONEXION CUBANA

In 1977, a Caribbean jazz cruise makes an unexpected layover in Havana, and when the American jazz stars walk down the gangplank, scores of Cubans are at the dock to greet them, including some members of Cuba's top fusion-jazz band, Irakere. Stan Getz, Dizzy Gillespie, and Earl Hines all jam with the local musicians that evening at the Havana Hilton, including trumpeter Arturo Sandoval, who will wind up playing with his new mentor, Dizzy Gillespie, and later defect to the U.S. along with several other Irakere members. Word of the spontaneous jam, including enthusiastic comments from saxophonist Getz, who is signed to Columbia Records, reaches Bruce Lundvall, president of the CBS Records division. Knowing of Cuba's rich musical heritage and curious to learn about the new music emerging within the Castro government, Lundvall asks Jerry Masucci, president of Fania Records, the New York Latin label which Columbia Records distributes, to do some investigating. Masucci is able to establish contact with Cuban officials, which opens the door in 1978 for Lundvall and a number of CBS associates to make an initial exploratory trip to Havana. All together, Lundvall makes three trips to the communist nation. Masucci and several other CBS bigwigs also have their turns talking to Cuban officials about the state of music and a possible festival.

Lundvall's exposure to the exciting, burgeoning music scene in Cuba, which remains unrecognized in the U.S. despite both nations' long-history of musical fusions, is the basis for what will emerge as a historic music festival between the two nations in 1979.

"We went to Havana in April 1978 piqued by the enthusiastic comments of a few musicians we respected, to explore the quality and intensity of the current Cuban musical scene," Lundvall says at the time. "The fact that pre-revolutionary Cuba had contributed more than any Latin country to our popular music culture, made the prospects of discovery even more intriguing. As guests of the Ministry of Culture, we were able to feast our senses on a broad spectrum of Cuban musical life, including a thriving contemporary musical scene strongly supported by the revolutionary government. Throughout our subsequent trips, the overriding impression and inspiration is the musical spirit of the people. Music is everywhere: on car radios, transistors on the beach, in hotels, bars, restaurants, and in the streets. Despite the very different lifestyle that has emerged in the last 20 years of Castro's government, the musical spirit survives. It was that impression on our first trip that instigated the idea for 'Havana Jam.'"

Lundvall is so impressed by Irakere he signs, and records them. He then arranges for the government-sponsored ensemble to perform unannounced at the 1978 Newport Jazz Festival, New York, where rave reviews result in their being invited to perform at the Montreux Jazz Festival in Switzerland. The next year they return to the U.S. to perform 16 concert dates with Stephen Stills.

The Newport Jazz Festival in New York is an outgrowth of producer George Wein's historic and troubled Newport, Rhode Island, festival which starts in 1954, ends in 1971, and opens in the Big Apple the next year. The '78 version goes all out for Latin music and discovers Irakere's blistering artistry. "The year 1978 found Latin jazz making a definite impact on the festival in 'A Schlitz Salute to Jazz Latino'," Wein writes with collaborator Nat Chinen in his biography, *Myself Among Others.* The lineup features Machito's Afro-Cuban Jazz orchestra, the Tito Puente band, Mongo Santamaria, and Irakere.

"Columbia Records brought them to America to play at the festival. Because we feared political demonstrations by any-Castro émigrés, we decided not to publicize their appearance, but rather to add them onto an existing concert. Their long set surprised everybody; the band danced, sang, and even paraded through the aisles of the audience like a New Orleans street band. And their musicianship was at a high level," says Wein.

In 1978, I'm attending an international music conference in Venice with my wife Bonnie, sponsored by *Billboard* magazine where I am the managing editor. During a reception at the world famous Hotel Cipriani on Giudecca Island, I overhear Bruce Lundvall mention to one of the other attendees that he's working on a music festival between CBS Records and Cuba. My curiosity is so peaked by what sounds like something impossible during the Cold War era when Cuba's President Fidel Castro and the U.S. government are distant neighbors, even though the two countries are 90 nautical miles (and millions of miles politically) apart. So I casually inch up to Bruce, with whom I've done numerous interviews during both our careers. He is so enthused about the idea that he gives me the early outline for the event, but says I can't write anything about it since there are details to be cleared with various U.S. government agencies. He says it will take some time before everything is politically correct and the event can be announced.

So I say something to the effect that I'll hold off breaking the story if I can get it exclusively and be part of the press contingent that will go to Havana to cover the three-day festival. Bruce, ever the politician/savvy record company executive, says we have a deal and for me to keep in touch with him on a regular basis, and when all the logistical paperwork and clearances are done, I can write my story. So for a lot of Thursdays, which is the magazine's main deadline day, I call Bruce and ask if the time is right, and one Thursday he says everything has been cleared. And that's how *Billboard* breaks the story January 1, 1979, about this historic cultural bridge-making effort named "Havana Jam." I wind up in cold New York City embarking on March 1 with

180 passengers, including artists from CBS' pop, jazz, and Latin rosters, CBS Records employees, and a select group of American journalists on a TWA 707 charter flight to hot and steamy Havana.

In that exclusive announcement story, Lundvall emphasizes, "This will be musical event for both Cuba and the U.S. It has nothing to do with politics; it is a cultural exchange between two countries that have much in common in their music."

However, getting to Havana, and returning, is not a simple matter. In January, an anti-Castro group calling itself Omega 7 has initiated a series of bombings around New York City, including Lincoln Center, to protest an appearance by Orquestra Aragón. In response, CBS initiates a security/secrecy policy. We are told to arrive at the New York Sheraton hotel by 9 a.m. where we're informed the flight from John F. Kennedy Airport will last three-and-a-half hours. What's puzzling is we're not told when we'll depart nor when we'll return to New York the following Monday. Before we even get to Castroland, the mood among some of the musicians is somber, even scary, and very un-show businesslike, as companies usually like to boast about their endeavors with great flair and publicity. There's no media coverage for our departure: CBS doesn't want to entice Omega 7 into action. It feels like we're all going on a secret mission. In a few days the original 5 p.m. departure time from Cuba will be tossed to the wind by a series of mysterious mishaps at the airport.

On the flight to Havana, percussionist Willie Bobo tells me he and Getz are the only two American musicians who have played in Cuba before, and he's also recorded two albums with Mongo Santamaria for Fantasy before Castro took control. "It's a wish of mine to go back to Cuba" and he believes the people are "eager to hear what we're going to play." He and Getz are both members of the CBS All Stars. Several members of the Fania All Stars are of Cuban descent and looking forward to seeing their families. Two of them will, in fact, have their first family reunions in 20 years. "Havana Jam" becomes more than just about music, even though it marks the first time since Castro's revolution overthrew dictator Fulgencio Batista

20 years earlier that American artists perform there; it's about Cuba and its people.

When we finally land at the airport there are lots of people on a viewing platform above the one and only terminal. It's blistering hot and even hotter inside the non-air-conditioned building. A radio reporter from the Canadian Broadcasting System interviews Kris Kristofferson inside the tepid building. We are all bused to the beachfront Hotel Marazul, a 20-minute ride from Havana. Next door to the hotel, which is supposedly off-limits to the populace (a ban which aggressive Cubans somehow overcome), is a Russian beach retreat with cabins for top government bigwigs and their wives. Inside our hotel rooms, which are not air-conditioned, is an object which catches my attention. It's an imposing brown ashtray built like a tank and manufactured in China. A hole where the turret usually sits is where you toss your Cuban cigar ashes. It becomes a prized souvenir and today rests in a prominent place on a shelf in my office.

Havana in 1979 is a city frozen in time; there are Russian cargo ships unloading much needed necessities of life. Political posters with pictures of Fidel and his brother Raul are omnipresent. Old American cars with bald tires roam the streets. In the center of the city sits the imposing Museum of the Revolution, formerly known as the presidential palace.

On arrival night, we all attend the show at the famous outdoor Tropicana nightclub, Havana's version of Las Vegas glitz, where time and music seem stuck in the '50s and '60s. Since the "Havana Jam" concerts are all at night in the 4,800-seat Karl Marx Theater, there's ample time to sightsee and mingle with the populace. The only request we are given by government officials is not to photograph soldiers with guns, and there are plenty all over the capital city, as are anti-American posters. Children in school uniforms are not afraid to come up to me and Bob Altshuler, Columbia's PR vice president (who invites me to tour the city in his government provided car) and ask us for gum and writing pencils. Cuban women, who sneak into the Hotel Marazul where we're staying, are willing to swap sex for shoes. There are some transactions, which the musicians boast about the next morning at breakfast. The show venue, formerly the Chaplin Theater, was renamed the Karl Marx in 1975 at the first Congress of the Cuban Communist Party. On its stage three months ago Fidel Castro makes a scathing speech before a Parliamentary meeting castigating the U.S. government's trade embargo, initiated after Castro's revolution. Three months later, the stage is set for music at "Música Cuba-USA" as the Cubans call it, and the "Bay of Gigs" as some of the American players will tag it.

Several weeks before the main entourage enplanes, CBS Records sends a DC-6 and a C-46 to Havana carrying 40 tons of sound and lighting equipment from the CBS Recording Studios, Showco, and the Record Plant, which includes a stereo sound recording console and 40 microphones. Much of the equipment will be left for Egram, the state-owned record label. The total cost for this endeavor is an estimated $300,000. CBS records two concert albums, *Havana Jam* and *Havana Jam 2* (for which I write the liner notes), while CBS TV sends gruff-voiced features reporter Hughes Rudd and a crew to tape the festival for a slot on its popular *Sunday Morning* program hosted by its first host, Charles Kuralt. Rudd, I discover during one of the media breakfasts, isn't too savvy about the music business, so I offer him some tidbits on the CBS musicians. He winds up doing a two-part story on the music and political ramifications of the event that airs on successive Sundays.

Tickets for the concerts go to connected officials, people who make their job quotas, or those who do well in school. There are some $10 tickets available for tourists. I wind up sitting in the front row next to several young men who are enamored of American pop artists more than the jazz players. One of them, who says he's a Billy Joel fan, admits he wants to defect and wants to know when we're going back to the U.S. I tell him it would be very hard for him to get on the plane and I don't even tell him the departure time. On the night Billy Joel headlines, he's sitting next to me again and asking me to help him defect. "Take me with you, take me with you," he extols, between singing the lyrics along with Joel. "I can't," I answer strongly, but sadly. Lots of young people in the audience sing along with the pop stars. I ask him where he's learned the lyrics and he says he hears all the pop records on Miami stations WGBS and WQAM. In a few days he shows up outside the airport still intent on getting to America, but he never leaves the ground. Plainclothes Cuban security guards will check every person boarding the TWA plane, making any defection impossible.

In the theater there's an empty row and one roped off seat for Fidel every night, who we are told by government officials "is coming." When? They don't say. "I had expected to meet Castro," Lundvall recalls, "but apparently there was some spat with the Carter administration that week so he refused to come. That I don't meet him is disappointing. Late in the afternoon before the final concert, I'm told we're going to have a very important meeting. I thought we're finally going to meet Fidel. A small group of us, including Hughes Rudd and his camera crew from CBS News, are brought to a secluded beach area where there's a fenced-off house with guards with machine guns. We go upstairs to the second floor where a bunch of Cuban officials are watching a baseball game. We're served mojitos, the Cuban rum and lime juice drink, and a government limo drives up, which is a Ford Falcon. I said, "My God, it's got to be Fidel." It isn't. It's Armando Hart, the minister of culture. He is pleased with the way the festival is going and we end up doing an interview for Cuban television, during which he tells me, "You see, if Americans come down here and bring guns, we will respond with guns. But if you bring music, we will respond with music. I said, "No, we didn't bring any guns, just music."

Government officials who do show up for the concerts are vice president Carlos Raphael Rodriguez, former president Osvaldo Dorticós, and Armando Hart.

The Americans bring plenty of pop, jazz, and Latin music. The Cubans arrange the three nights to feature a potpourri of their musical best, from traditional violin-flavored dance bands like

Orquestra Aragón to the contemporary jazz of Irakere to Nuevo Trova or "new song" political folk singers Sara Gonzáles and Pablo Milanés (called Cuba's Bob Dylan) backed by the Grupo Managuaré. There's also revolutionary vocalist Elena Burke, modern band Orquestra De Santiago De Cuba, and 25 Afro-Cuban percussionists in the group Percusión Cubana. There are samples of cha-cha, mambo, and the traditional son style, as well as music stressing the country's endemic African and Spanish heritage. Of the bands, Irakere impresses me the most. Its fusion of jazz ensemble and solo work, the pulsating drive of native Yoruba and Carabali rhythms, and the addition of European classical influences create a three-pronged energy explosion. Since I'm writing for an American audience, I concentrate on the performances of the Americans while underplaying the Cubans, as I am less familiar with those bands.

Since the Cubans are starved for live American music, they warmly receive the visitors except for the Fania All Stars, who close the opening night concert with their hot brand of New York salsa. The Cubans seem unappreciative of their music and leave the theater in large numbers. Maybe it's the late hour and the midnight curfew on public transportation, but they sure don't appreciate the band's Nuyorican style of playing performed by mostly musicians of Puerto Rican ancestry. Despite the tepid audience response, the 24-piece band plays a specially written composition, *Tres Lindas Cubana*, which I write has as much "fire, excitement, and flair" as anything else performed during the three concerts. Its members include Johnny Pacheco, Rubén Blades, Pete Rodriquez, Hector Lavoe, Pupi Legarreta, and Larry Harlow.

The selection of the CBS artists, after the Cubans reject Santana, is designed to showcase the broad scope of American music, rather than focus mainly on Latin and jazz. So the roster encompasses Weather Report, Billy Joel, Kris Kristofferson, Rita Coolidge, Stephen Stills, and the CBS All Stars including Dexter Gordon, Stan Getz, Jimmy Heath, Tony Williams, Arthur Blythe, Woody Shaw, Hubert Laws, Bobby Hutcherson, Willie Bobo, Cedar Walton, and Percy Heath.

Weather Report opens the festival with its blend of synthesized, electronic keyboard driven jazz, sparked by Joe Zawinul. Bassist Jaco Pastorius' use of controlled feedback, digitally delayed notes, and distortion is obviously a new sound for many Cubans.

Vocalists Stephen Stills and Bonnie Bramlett work well together in a powerful showing of their vocal strengths. Stills offers a tune written expressly for "Havana Jam," *Cuba Al Fin*, which promotes a sense of brotherhood: "We are brothers, not enemies, there should be an end to tension and the only thing that makes sense is friendship." Kris Kristofferson and wife Rita Coolidge individually run though their familiar material, including "Help Me Make It Through the Night," a shouted request from the audience, again reinforcing that American music via Miami radio is beaming into this island nation. Like Stills, Kristofferson makes a political statement in his song "Fallen Angels," stressing a better tomorrow: "There's got to be a better way...the future is ours you see...we've got a chance to change today." The high-energy amplified trio of guitarist John McLaughlin, bassist Jaco Pastorius, and drummer Tony Williams also find favor with the audience.

Billy Joel, who flies in on his own private jet and does not give his permission to have his performance recorded or videotaped, mesmerizes the audience with his string of pop power hits, his playing of acoustic and electric pianos, and his leaping around the stage. All this energy is returned by the shouting, singing crowd in a city in a country in which American artists are off-limits. "Bee-lee Yo-el" they shout. After his exciting performance, which draws the crowd to the edge of the stage, he tells me: "It was a total surprise. I figured since my Spanish is not too good, I'd just play my music. I didn't know I was going to get that kind of reaction." He also adds a political comment: "We've been isolated from the Cubans so long I felt it would be a good thing to have music, which is a universal language, bring us together."

After the concert ends, Joel supposedly flies out of town to Miami and misses the debacle at the airport. When the CBS contingent arrives at Jose Marti airport, we discover that a luggage conveyor belt is not working. So after unloading our bags and sitting interminably in the insufferably hot terminal, we're told to move them to another area. Musicians, rock stars, jazz stars, Latin stars all groan and curse, and begin moving their bags. And we sit and wait for a second time. Finally, some Cuban handlers come to assist the CBS coordinators designated to help the musicians and the bags are moved. Then we get in a single line, all 180 of us, and wait to go through passport clearance. We wait and wait and watch in frustration and with a growing anger as Russians walk right past us and are cleared to board their Soviet passenger planes. One famous rocker gets drunk and begins cursing the passing Russians before being hustled away to avoid any politically embarrassing incident from happening.

After another interminably long wait, the line starts to move and once we've been cleared by unsmiling people in their control booths, I surmise the wait is over and we'll board our plane. No such luck. We wind up in an empty terminal and I can see the TWA plane, its red and white emblem, sitting on the tarmac maybe 200 yards away. My hotel roommate, Frank Meyer, *Weekly Variety*'s music editor, and I sit down on the floor, our backs against the wall and begin writing our stories in longhand on our pads. When we first sit down its late afternoon and the sun warms the area, oblivious of the other soon-to-be passengers. Soon it turns dark and we're still there and that TWA plane looks like a symbol of freedom that remains out of our reach. Did all of these delays just happen or was there some ulterior motive? Is the transportation ministry showing us "Yanquis" who's in control? Some of the musicians feel the delays are intentional, with the government controlling our exit movements as a final action against the hated capitalists. It may have been around 8:30 p.m. when we finally are passed through the door and walk briskly to the plane. Stern-faced Cuban security guards check our boarding passes and compare our passport photos to our tired faces.

I thought we'd get on board and take off. It doesn't happen that way. A CBS official calls the roll and one of the musicians doesn't answer when his name is called the first and second time. We start to squirm in our chairs. Could someone have stayed behind? Finally on the third or fourth call, the musician, who is fast asleep, awakens and calls out his name and everyone feels relieved. And I'm thinking, "didn't the people sitting next to him know who he was?" With everyone accounted for, the engines start, we taxi to the end of the runway and speed into the night sky. As the plane makes a sweeping turn over Cuba, the pilot comes on the intercom and utters the most welcome and memorable comment of the trip: "Say goodbye to Cuba and welcome to freedom. We're going home." The cabin erupts in cheers and then falls silent as the assemblage takes a nap or reflects on what we've all been through. Instead of arriving at JFK at 8 p.m., it's midnight, and by the time I clear customs it's 12:30 and close to 1:30 a.m. when I get to my hotel in Manhattan, where my wife Bonnie is fast asleep. While I'm in Cuba, she vacations in San Juan and is back at the hotel in time for my 8 p.m. airport arrival.

After the initial flurry of stories in such publications as *The New York Times*, *Washington Post*, *Miami Herald*, *Time*, *Newsweek*, *People*, *Rolling Stone*, *Variety*, and *Ebony*, among others, "Havana Jam" disappears from the music radar screen. It's a happening of the time, of the moment. I write five stories about "Havana Jam" for *Billboard*, starting with two articles March 17 and ending with the final article July 14. The color and black and white photos I shoot capture the musical intensity and camaraderie. A feature I do for *High Fidelity* runs in June. I don't think about "Havana Jam" and its impact on music until years later when Cuban artists begin to appear in the states and their records emphasize the rich musical heritage and the ever-lasting gift bestowed on America.

"Havana Jam" Postscript:

In 2001, *Jazziz* magazine publishes a second issue devoted to Cuba. I contribute an article on the historical importance of "Havana Jam." I ask Bruce Lundvall, now president of Blue Note Records since 1984, what he feels is "Havana Jam's" historical impact. He replies, "What we did was peak the interest in America in Cuban music. I don't know if 'Havana Jam' was the linchpin that opened the door for Cuban music to come to the U.S., but it had a big influence in the sense that Cuban music is now coming into the states. It's more the dance music and Buena Vista Social Club stuff featuring the older musicians. No one here had any idea about Cuban music for the longest time." During 2001, Lundvall has lunch in New York with Cuban piano virtuoso Gonzalo Rubalcaba. "He was not part of 'Havana Jam' but was a young pianist and he was in the audience. He said to me, 'You have no idea what you did.' I said, 'What do you mean?' He said the impact was enormous within Cuba for years." Lundvall, who becomes president of Columbia Records in 1976, replacing the fired Clive Davis, says he strove to make his mark by having Columbia "viewed as a company that does adventurous things. I though 'Havana Jam' was something adventurous. From a business standpoint it was hard to justify, but I was encouraged to do it nonetheless."

I also query Irakere's two most notable defectors, Paquito D'Rivera and Arturo Sandoval, to reflect back on "Havana Jam" and how their lives have changed since moving to America.

In 1980, Paquito D'Rivera defects in Madrid while on tour with the band and establishes himself as a major saxophone soloist in the U.S. One of Irakere's founding members from 1970-'80, he settles in Weehawken, New Jersey, and in 2001 he tells me "there was too much pressure and abuse of power in Cuba." Leaving is "liberation" despite leaving his wife and five-year-old son, which the Cuban government keeps hostage for nine years. "I had to pay a lot of money and wait a long time for them to be let go." He calls "Havana Jam": "a wonderful event for us because of the limited amount of foreign artists we had a chance to see in Cuba."

Arturo Sandoval, a member of Irakere from 1973 through 1981, winds up driving Dizzy Gillespie around Havana and jamming with him, Stan Getz, and other musicians in the jazz cruise who come ashore in 1977. In 2001, he tells me that as a result of defecting in Rome in 1990 while on tour with Gillespie and his United Nation

Orchestra, and eventually settling in Miami, his life "has changed drastically. It's a priceless feeling to know you can express yourself, say what you want and do what you want to do. I left Cuba to find freedom, because life without freedom is no life." Since establishing himself in the U.S. without any constraints as a featured soloist, he says his trumpet playing has changed because "I hear different kinds of music and so I have more influences."

In 2003, I ask Lundvall if the legacy of "Havana Jam" is still potent. "I think the repercussions have been perhaps quiet but they're very real and very much felt. Chucho Valdés, Paquito D'Rivera, and Arturo Sandoval, all members of Irakere, are now major stars in this country. Chucho is revered as the Art Tatum of Cuban jazz piano. Gonzalo Rubalcaba, who is signed to our Japanese company, got permission from the State and Treasury Departments in 1996 to live in Miami, work here, and travel outside the country even though he continues to be a Cuban citizen, which is highly unusual." Would Lundvall ever do another "Havana Jam"? "While I'd love to do it, there's no need because there's the Havana International Jazz Plaza Festival every year in Havana now and American musicians go there and play with Cuban artists."

Rubalcaba, whose albums are released in the '80s on Messidor, a German label, breaks into the American market in a roundabout fashion with his 1990 album, *Discover*. The album is recorded in Switzerland, released by British EMI's Japanese label Somethin'Else and then licensed to Blue Note, another EMI record company. In a story the Tower Records publication, *Pulse* magazine, does about Cuban music, Rubalcaba, now settled in the Miami suburb of Coral Gables, defends his Cuban citizenship and U.S. residency thusly: "Citizenship has nothing to do with residency." Previously living in the Dominican Republic for six years, he stresses he has "no political, economic, or other ties with Cuba," and that's legally why he's been given a U.S. residency permit. In 1993, he makes his U.S. debut at Avery Fisher Hall in Manhattan. In 1996, attempting to perform in anti-Castro Miami, a group of hardcore exile protestors prevents him from doing so. It's a bitter experience, perhaps indicating his past is not that simple to eradicate at this stage of his life in Southern Florida. Nowhere else in America will he confront Cubans seeking to prevent him from performing in public.

Despite the U.S. government's 42-year trade embargo, a number of significant developments occur since "Havana Jam" creates a cultural bridge between the two nations. Here are some of the things which I believe couldn't have happened had there not been "Música Cuba-USA":

In 1988, Congress passes an amendment to this troublesome embargo that permits Cuban musicians to come to the states and perform if they are part of a cultural exchange, such as participating in an educational workshop. Among the bands enjoying this entry into the U.S. in later years are popular dance music groups Los Van Van and NG La Banda.

In 1996, The Buena Vista Social Club's eponymous recording on World Circuit/Nonesuch, the brainchild of guitarist and producer Ry Cooder, is released and introduces Americans to a host of vintage and timeworn Cuban legendary musicians and their evergreen style of music. It wins a Grammy the next year. And the year following that, film director Wim Wenders and a camera crew accompany Cooder to Havana where he records 70-year-old singer Ibrahim Ferrer's solo album. His theatrical film documentary, which he calls a "muiscumentary" captures Ferrer in the studio reunited with his former music pals called "Super Abuelos," or "Super Granddads" who help define a century of music. The two projects help spur interest in Cuban music.

Answering this interest during the past seven years, American record companies, large and small, known or untested, distribute albums by Cuban artists recorded in their native country and licensed from companies in Japan, Canada, and Europe. U.S. labels are also recording Cuban artists living in the U.S. or visiting. One such project features Cuban band ¡Cubanismo! traveling to New Orleans to marry its music with local stylists John Boutté and the Vocamo All Stars for the Hannibal release, *Cubanismo in New Orleans.*

Los Hombres Calientes, a New Orleans-based sextet, blends the music of Cuba, the Caribbean, and America on its popular Basin Street CDs. Its two leaders are trumpeter/composer Irvin Mayfield and percussionist/vocalist Bill Summers. They record in Cuba, Brazil, the Dominican Republic, and Jamaica on their Grammy-nominated *New Congo Square* release. The band also works major venues and is a critically acclaimed hit during the 2003 25th anniversary Playboy Jazz Festival at the Hollywood Bowl.

Cuban artists D'Rivera, Sandoval, Valdés, and Irakere all earn Grammy nominations over the years, with D'Rivera and Sandoval winning three and four trophies, respectively. Pianist Valdés, Irakere's founder and leader, tells *Pulse* magazine in 1997 that "culture and politics are two different things and culture is not confined by laws." Valdez, who cannot see his expatriate famed musician father, Bebo Valdés, for close to 20 years because of the revolution, is unable to come to the U.S. until 1995 to perform as a solo artist. And for the first time Sandoval uses music maven Quincy Jones as the co-executive producer for his 2003 release *Trumpet Evolution* on Crescent Moon, along with Emilio Estefan, who co-owns the record company with his wife Gloria. Sandoval's life is also featured on HBO in the made-for-TV movie *For Love or Country*, with Atlantic releasing the soundtrack. The film subsequently wins two Golden Globe nominees for best-made-for-TV-movie and a best actor nod for Andy Garcia, who portrays Sandoval.

Starting in 1997, American trumpeter Roy Hargrove, violinist Susie Hansen, and Canadian flutist Jane Bunnett are among the artists recording CDs in Cuba for Verve, Jazz Caliente, and Blue Note, respectively.

Music Bridges Cuba '99, the fifth in a series of international goodwill concerts taking place in Havana, pairs 48 American artists, including Dave Koz, with 45 Cubans. President Castro hosts a reception; in 1979 he is noticeably absent from "Havana Jam."

In recent years at the Havana international Jazz festival, the U.S. contingent includes Herbie Hancock, Nicholas Payton, Dave

Valentine, Kenny Barron, and Ronnie Mathews. BET on Jazz, the cable channel, tapes the event for later broadcast.

Once diplomatic relations are established with Cuba and there is a change in government—whenever that is—the floodgates of Cuban creativity will truly be open, nudged in this direction by the oft-forgotten but historically significant 1979 musical happening called "Havana Jam."

Articles

"Resounding Still." Jazziz, April 2001

"CBS Firms Fest In Havana With Cubans." Billboard, Jan. 27, 1979

"Music Of U.S. And Cuba Mixes At Havana Jam." New York Times, March 5, 1979

"Billy Joel Brings Cuban Crowd To Its Feet." New York Times, March 6, 1979

"U.S. Cuban Fest: A Bang With No Bombs." Weekly Variety, March 7, 1979

"U.S. Musicians Feel They're Doing More Than Just Blowing." Billboard March, 17, 1979

"U.S. Acts Record CBS LPs In Cuba." Billboard, March 17, 1979

"Havana Jam Due Out In June." Billboard, May 2, 1979

"U.S. Artists Eager To Please Cubans At Historic Havana Jam." Billboard, March 31, 1979

"CBS Pays For Cuban Tapes Ok'd By U.S." Billboard, July 14, 1979

"It Happened In Havana." High Fidelity, June 1979

Chapter 3
CAPITULO 3

Muscle Stretching: 1990-1996
ESTIRAMIENTO DE MUSCULOS: 1990-1996

• In the decades following the Second World War, Los Angeles emerges as a cultural and fashion trendsetter for the nation. It also becomes the gateway for the growth of Hispanic broadcasting as Latinos flock to the City of Angels in the '70s and '80s and create an eager audience for Spanish-language radio/TV and Mexican-dominated music.

• Gloria Estefan's successful crossover career is tragically halted on March 20, 1990 when her tour bus is rammed from behind on Interstate 380 by a tractor-trailer. She suffers major back injuries that require surgery and put a halt to the final leg of her tour.

• In 1990, Christina Gonzalez becomes the first TV journalist from a Spanish-language station, KMEX, to reportedly cross over into English-language news when she joins the Fox station KTTV in Los Angeles to become a general assignment reporter.

• In 1992, Los Angeles and its neighboring counties of Orange, Ventura, Riverside, and San Bernardino begin to hear the growing strains of the Latinization of radio, a harbinger of how the growth of the Hispanic population will impact broadcasting around the country.

• What starts out as a simple purchase in 1992, Jerry Perenchio teams with Televisa and Venevision International to acquire five TV stations and the SIN Network for $550 million and turn them into Univision.

• In 1995, Selena, a rising Tejano music star, is murdered.

• Cable television begins to acquire a Spanish accent.

• The San Diego Padres become the first major league team to actively romance fans from outside the country in 1995. They bus in followers from Tijuana, Mexico (population 2 million), for $11, which includes a ticket plus the roundtrip bus ride. Mexican food items are available at special stands. Between '95 and '97, Hispanic attendance at Padres games increases from seven to 25 percent. The Arizona Diamondbacks and the Florida Marlins launch their Hispanic marketing in '97.

A harbinger of change within the radio industry occurs in Los Angeles in 1992 and will be felt in the years to come. The historical event centers around Spanish Broadcasting System's KLAX-FM L.A., whose banda music, a form of regional Mexican patterned after German tuba polka sounds, but infused with electronic instruments, catapults it to the top of the fall Arbitron ratings. It's the first time a Spanish-language station is the region's most popular, attracting an audience of Hispanics that alters and shocks the Arbitron listener sampling. A new power is emerging to challenge English-speaking stations as KLAX retains the No. 1 position until the fall of 1995 when another Spanish formatted station, KLVE-FM, becomes the frontrunner.

This key radio breakthrough on the West Coast centering around KLAX-FM, while it surprises, even shocks English-language stations, actually makes numerical sense. Mexicans, including Chicanos born in the U.S., account for 80 percent of the growing Hispanic community. For nine straight rating periods the Spanish Broadcasting System station ranks No. 1, through the fall of 1994. That's when its zany morning drive-time team of Juan Carlos Hidalgo and Jesús "El Peladillo" García beats out KLSX-FM's Howard Stern for the most listened to slot in the fall ratings period, with Stern dropping to fifth place, his lowest ranking since entering the market in 1991. The second most popular Spanish station is Heftel Broadcasting's romantic ballads KLVE-FM in 11th place. Years later, the company will merge and become Hispanic Broadcasting Corp. and then be acquired in 2003 by Univision for its TV–radio–records empire.

As KLVE recaptures the No 1 spot it loses to hip-hop/R&Bish KPWR-FM in the summer survey, 15 Latin stations rank among the fall survey's top 23 positions. The strong showing among Hispanic stations has general managers at 13 Anglo stations procrastinating over the rise of all these Latino outlets, and point to the Arbitron ratings service company as the culprit. There's no brotherly love among Hispanic and Anglo broadcasters, as English station general managers claim Arbitron's decision last October to shift to bilingual telephone interviewers has altered the results toward the Spanish-language stations. While that's just swell with the Latinos, especially KLVE, which sees its ratings leap nearly 44 percent over the previous quarter, Anglos are doing a slow burn. As a result, they ask the company to rethink its usage of bilingual surveyors and to limit the influence of language preference in the survey.

In the past, if the English-speaking interviewer reaches a Spanish speaker, the conversation ends and the interviewer moves to another household. KLVE's general manager, Richard Heftel, supports the bilingual questionnaires, saying they "allow Arbitron to accurately portray the habits of listeners and it would be a mistake to eliminate the bilingual phone surveyors." Roy Laughlin, president and general manager of KIIS AM/FM, home of morning personality Rick Dees, whose contemporary hits format has been slipping in popularity and is now tied for fifth place with two other Anglo stations, KROQ-FM and KOST-FM, believes Arbitron needs to distinguish the difference between English-speaking Hispanics and those who exclusively speak Spanish. He naturally believes the Spanish-dominant response is being given too much weight in the survey.

In the winter of '95 KLVE is still No.1 and KLAX falls to third place. KLVE's morning personalities Pepe Barreto and Lupita Pena become the most listened to a.m. drive-time personalities, overcoming KLAX's morning duo of Hidalgo and García, who drop to eighth place. Rick Dees, KIIS-FM's previous top English-language morning personality before Howard Stern invades the market along with the influx of mass-appeal Spanish stations, ties for second place with CBS' all-news station KNX-AM. Stern moves up to fourth place. By choosing two pairs of Latino funnymen over the better-known raunchy Stern and the often wacky Dees, Hispanic radio listeners are affirming a new class of popular radio personality, familiar to Latino families but unfamiliar to Anglos who stay tuned to their favorite stations.

Shoot forward to the spring '95 survey and while KLVE is now second behind Emmis Broadcasting's hip-hop power KPWR-FM, its morning personalities Barreto and Pena continue to top the 6–10 a.m. slot. KPWR, which claims its music has appealed to English-speaking Latinos since 1986, says Hispanics also account for 60 percent of its listeners, according to Emmis' president and station manager Doyle Rose. And KLAX? It slips to number nine. So there's a lot of movement within L.A. radio, as Latino stations smash egos, create new egos, and begin to make their presence felt. The ratings game for Latino stations, like their Anglo brethren, begins to resemble a ping-pong match.

In fact, by 1995 Spanish-language radio and television stations have broken out of their niche and are changing the sound and look of local broadcasting around the nation. The Latinization of Los Angeles transforms the City of Angels into the nation's No. 1 Hispanic market, with an estimated 5.6 million legal and uncounted illegal aliens as the foundation for the 14 Spanish-language radio stations (among the region's 87) and two-and-a-half TV stations offering Hispanic programming. By the late '90s, there will be 22 Latino radio stations in L.A., a record number for any U.S. city.

So dramatic is the impact of the burgeoning Latin community on broadcasting that nine Hispanic radio stations are listed among the top 40 positions within the Arbitron rating service's summer quarterly report behind the overall market leader KPWR-FM. KLVE is second and KLAX is eighth. As for Howard Stern, he bounces back to the top a.m. slot after a year of not holding the gold ring in L.A. Of the stations in the upper tier of the rankings, two are previously pop and hard rock legends, switched to Spanish by their new optimistic owners: KKHJ-AM (number 15) was previously the pioneering Top 40 "KHJ Boss Radio" in the high-flying '60s and KBUE-FM (tied for 26th) was formerly '90s heavy metal KNAC-FM, whose new format of regional Mexican music is similar to that featured on KKHJ and KWKW-AM (in 28th place).

The importance of Hispanic stations charting along with the Anglo stations reflects the diversity of formats aimed at listeners from Mexico, Guatemala, Costa Rica, El Salvador, Nicaragua, Honduras, Cuba, and Puerto Rico. They show the growth of Latin radio from the market's first two: KWKW and KALI-AM, lone voices in the '60s.

The growth of Latin radio in L.A. enables an enlarged number of Latin acts, including the East L.A.-bred Los Lobos, to gain promotional tie-ins for their concerts with these stations, which is a big deal. And there are deals galore to be made. The 6,000-seat Universal Amphitheatre adds a heavy dose of Latin entertainment to its annual concert business, now averaging 25 percent Latino attractions. The year's lineup includes comic Paul Rodriguez, Juan Gabriel, Rocio Durcal, Vilma Santos, Ariel Rivera, Lucero, Carlos Vives, Vincent and Alejandro Fernández, Ballet Folklorico De Mexico, and a singer named Ricky Martin.

If anyone in L.A. has seen the explosion of Hispanic culture and immigration, it's Luis Torres, a veteran general assignment radio reporter for KNX, the CBS all-news station in Los Angeles. If there's a major story anywhere, Luis is usually on the scene, reporting both the happy and the gritty details. He is one of the first Latinos to work in Anglo radio, starting as editorial director in 1972 with KLOS-FM, the ABC-owned hard rock station. His major complaint is that "English-language station coverage of Latin issues isn't all what it should be. They react to particular crisis, big demonstrations, and who did what to whom. But there's a need for comprehensive investigation of root issues." It's a concern which still bears fruit within the Hispanic community.

In 2003, Torres has another complaint that he reveals in a story he writes for the *Los Angeles Times.* This time he's concerned about the all too frequent police policy of using broad generalities like "Hispanic" when looking for an alleged crime subject. He has two concerns: "the importance of sensitivity and thoughtfulness in using race and ethnicity to describe crime suspects...and the meaninglessness of the term 'Hispanic' in physical descriptions of crime suspects. 'Hispanic' should be retired as a term of physical description, unless accompanied by precise details on such characteristics as weight, height, hair color, and distinguishing marks. Otherwise, it's like saying 'Police are looking for a skinny New Yorker or a fat Minnesotan.'"

In November 1996, plans for the first national long-form programming radio network are unfurled. Radio Unica, as the Miami-based company is called, will debut in April of next year. Joaquin Blaya, former president of both Univision and Telemundo TV networks, heads a new venture that will target 25-to-54-year-olds with news, talk, and sports programming available on a projected network of 70 AM affiliates, plus company-owned stations in major cities like Miami and Los Angeles. Programs via satellite will include a mix of U.S.-produced shows along with top-rated shows from Mexico. Barrett Alley, former president of the troubled and soon to be closed Cadena Radio Centro network, is named executive vice president of the new venture. By 2002, Radio Unica will become a powerful and respected national radio network, operating out of modern facilities in Miami and featuring a number of top Hispanic TV personalities hosting their own talk shows. By 2003, it's financial fortunes are failing.

In L.A., two radio stations make significant programming changes and a third is sold. Heftel's KTNQ-AM drops its regional Mexican music in favor of a talk/news/sports format, abandoning the dominant Mexican music format which continues through the years to be the most popular among the nation's Latino stations. The second change occurs at low-power general market KGRB-AM, which has featured big band music for 32 years and is now simulcasting the Latin music of KMQA-FM. Conservators for 84-year-old owner Robert Burdette, who suffered a stroke a year ago and is unable to manage the station, abruptly fire the staff and engineer the switch to Latin music. Liberman Broadcasting of Houston increases its strength in the market by buying KYFK-FM, licensed to the suburb of San Fernando from Chagal Communications, for $10.8 million. The acquisition adds to its market portfolio of regional Mexican stations KKHJ-AM, KBUE-FM and KWIZ-AM/FM Santa Ana.

Meanwhile, reports of the sale by Gene Autry's Golden West Broadcasters of faltering KSCA-FM—currently playing adult alternative rock by the likes of Dave Matthews, Alanis Morissette, Joni Mitchell, and Elvis Costello, to Heftel Broadcasting—will add further strength to Latin radio's growing influence. The station will, in effect, be purchased by Heftel and eventually air regional Mexican music as the Hispanic Broadcasting Corp.

In what on the surface appears to be a simple, smart transaction in Spanish-language television in 1992, Andrew Jerrold Perenchio (later called A. Jerry Perenchio) teams with two programming giants, Mexico's Televisa and Venezuela's Venevision International, to purchase five stations and the SIN network for $550 million and change the company's name to Univision. These stations are added to New York's independent Spanish station WNJU (Channel 47), which Perenchio buys in the late '80s to form the new Univision network. His hard-line position against company officials giving unauthorized interviews to the press results in one unnamed executive being fined $25,000 in 1995 for crossing this line. In 1996, the company goes public, and according to a *BusinessWeek* feature in 2004, he takes no salary but owns 11.5 percent of the company. In terms of employee relations, Univision is a hardnosed operator in terms of unionism and payrolls. In 2002, it holds fast against a 32-day hunger strike by Spanish-speaking staffers at its Fresno station demanding to be paid the same amount as English-speaking counterparts before it raises their pay. It's also adamant in dealing with the American Federation of Radio and Television Artists, which represents editorial workers at its New York and Los Angeles stations. In 2004, of its 4,300 employees, only around 10 percent belong to the union.

Prior to his entry into TV, Perenchio was the owner of Chartwell Artists, a talent agency in Los Angeles whose clients include singers Andy Williams, Jose Feliciano, and later Julio Iglesias, as well as promoting major boxing and tennis matches like Muhammad Ali-Joe Frazier in 1971 and a wacky tennis match in '73 between Billie Jean King and Bobby Riggs, called the "Battle of the Sexes."

Univision has a rather unusual history. It dates back to 1961 when the owners of Mexico's Grupo Televisa buy a San Antonio station (KCOR-TV) and then establish Spanish International Communications Corp. and the Spanish International Network. In 1986, an administrative law judge rules the Mexican network has more control of its U.S. stations than is allowed by federal law and orders Televisa to sell both properties.

Hallmark Cards buys the companies and renames them Univision. In 1992, Perenchio and his overseas investors purchase the network and begin adding imported shows to those produced stateside. I recall doing interviews with Perenchio, the talent agency maven, when I was *Billboard*'s West Coast bureau chief in the 1960s and he's known as Jerry. I run up against his no public interviews policy myself when I attempt to arrange an interview with him in 2004, which is detailed in Chapter 19.

Univision's first station, KMEX, which begins broadcasting in September 29, 1962, as Los Angeles' first Hispanic TV station, commences outdrawing all the English-language stations news at 6 p.m. with its Spanish-language newscast in 1995. It is another indicator that Anglo stations have a new competitor to do battle with besides themselves. *Noticias 34*, as the 6–6:30 p.m. newscast is called, rates tops with persons 18 to 49 and 25 to 54. The station's

11 p.m. report also outperforms its English-speaking competition in the 18 to 34 demographic, but ranks third behind KNBC and KABC in the 18 to 49 age group.

KMEX's strength within the Hispanic community is emphasized when, working with a viewer tip, it tracks down and videotapes the highly sought-after Rosa Lopez, an elusive O.J. Simpson murder trial witness, beating out all news organizations to gain a sweet exclusive. "Our reporter Rosa Marie Villapando tracked down Rosa Lopez," boasts Augustine Martinez, general manager of the flagship station for the network in a story I write for *Electronic Media*. "We caught her two times but she was reluctant to do an interview. The taped footage we did get was picked up by other stations." She is subsequently called as a trial witness and allowed to return to her native Mexico.

KMEX also flexes its muscle for the first time when it challenges the all-mighty Nielsen Media Research company, and what it believes are disparities in the methodology used in its general market survey: the Nielsen Station Index (NSI) and the three-year-old Nielsen Hispanic Station Index (NHSI). I cover this imbroglio for *Electronic Media*, its importance being that the data showing audience strength is the basis on which local advertising is sold. KMEX's key beef is that the NHSI, which measures Spanish-language stations exclusively, indicates higher viewership for the city's two Latino stations than does the NSI measure which covers all the TV stations.

The NHSI study is launched in L.A. and is slated to be in use in 15 other cities by the end of the year. KMEX's director of research and marketing, Maureen A. Schultz, says, "Nielsen has been producing two different sets of numbers which are out of statistical tolerance. We're looking at 28 to 86 percent differences. So we went to Nielsen and said, 'Explain why the numbers are different.' General market station ratings are being overstated by the wrong methodology."

While NSI uses meters and diaries, NHSI employs a device called a people-meter, samples 200 Hispanic households and uses a bilingual field force to make in-person visits six times a year. (Field force is the industry term for workers around the country, not in the home office.) NHSI reports are issued monthly. Nielsen Hispanic households are queried as to each member's primary language. Along with other personal data, the households are then classified in five language groups: Spanish only, mostly Spanish, Spanish/English, mostly English, and English only.

One of the drawbacks for Hispanic stations in the NSI methodology is the use of the English-speaking person calling on the phone to make the initial contact. If the person answering the phone doesn't speak English, there's a problem right away, notes Ms. Schultz. That household doesn't get polled.

In response to the complaint, Nielsen dispatches Ceril T. Shagrin, its senior vice president for market development, to L.A. to meet Schultz at a press conference at the Regent Beverly Wilshire Hotel. Shagrin acknowledges the NHSI measuring techniques are superior to those of the NSI in gauging Hispanic viewership. She notes the company is looking at the NSI sample and will address the issues of concern. KMEX combines data from the two surveys to support its claim that February's primetime rating averages for the two major Spanish stations, KMEX and KVEA, increase by up to 95 percent, while the Anglo stations lose between 1.3 and 11 percent.

Following this assertion, Robert Taragan, Nielsen executive vice president, quickly dispatches a letter calling the NSI service "the benchmark for measurement of the Los Angeles television market" and that the two surveys were never designed to be combined. The higher ratings for the Latino stations do not sit well with the Anglo stations. While citing the different methodologies, Taragan notes that at a future time the company, in consultation with its customers, "may wish to consider some crossover involving the two samples."

Skip to 2003 and Nielsen hopes to add a "weighted" Spanish language element to its national People Meter sample by September. And by 2005, it plans to have its national general market survey incorporate Hispanic household findings to produce a unified source for the planning and buying of all national TV media, Anglo and

Spanish. This data combining is what KMEX does in 1995 and which Nielsen says is ill-advised.

Among the nation's TV stations hopefully benefiting from the exclusively focused Nielsen research data is KVEA, Telemundo's L.A. outlet since 1985. After unsuccessfully competing against KMEX with novelas (soap operas) produced outside the U.S., it drops 10 hours of soaps in '95 in favor of developing four original programs: sports, games, a comedy, and a talk series; the latter two hosted by KTNQ-AM morning personality Humberto Luna. KVEA also offers local entertainment and community affairs shows, prompting station general manager Roland Hernandez to stress that the shows focus on issues "relevant to this market and the Southwest. We need to bring this regional flavor using local talent to the network."

KVEA goes up against KMEX with local news at 6 and 11 p.m. and maintains a two-person bureau in Tijuana, Mexico, which produces stories focusing on border issues. One interesting side effect of the emergence of Spanish-language TV in this country is the opportunities they provide for pros and neophytes alike. KMEX's Augustine Martinez says its reporters stay rather than leave for general market stations because "they have a commitment to serve the community. The best kept secret is that people are leaving general market stations to come to Spanish-language television because of its great potential."

An opposite view is proffered by KVEA's former general manager, Michael Martinez: "The station trains people, usually college students, who then seek general market jobs. It's a hassle in some respects," he admits, "but it's important because we bring people into the business."

Christina Gonzalez is one Latina who sees greater growth working in Anglo TV, despite working as an anchor on KMEX's 6 and 11 p.m. newscasts. She's had a taste of general market broadcasting with stints at KTVW-TV Phoenix and at radio stations KVVA Phoenix and WNWS Miami. In 1994, I happen to see her perform a heroic action live on TV while covering a fire for KTTV. That sparks an idea for a story and I interview her for an *Emmy* magazine feature about reporters who cross the line between being an impartial observer at a news event and helping someone they see is in danger. Here's the scenario: on a warm sunny afternoon in May, L.A. news helicopters are capturing the drama of an apartment house fire. On the street firefighters and one civilian woman are attempting to revive several unconscious people that have pulled from the burning building.

Christina, whom I had never heard of before this incident, recalls that when she arrived on the scene in a predominantly Spanish neighborhood, a fireman is telling a gathering crowd to move away in English, but to no avail. She tells them in Spanish to move back. And when she asks a fireman if there's anything else she can do, "he says, 'CPR'" not knowing that this helpful woman was a premed student with hospital emergency room experience. So after telling her cameraman what she plans to do and to keep on shooting, but not to put her in any live shot, she joins three rescue personnel and begins applying heart massage to an unconscious little girl while a fireman tries to clear her air passage. As firefighters bring out other victims, the fireman working with Christina tells her to stay with the child while he goes to assist other people.

Christina is now working on clearing her airway. "You have to pull the black phlegm out of her mouth and in essence she's throwing up in my mouth and I'm thinking, 'don't get sick.' It's not pleasant." The girl is shortly taken by ambulance to a hospital without a heartbeat and is among several people who die in the inferno. Unbeknownst to Christina, other TV stations are broadcasting her life-saving efforts live.

When she is beeped by the station and told to get out of the area, she goes back to being a reporter and after composing herself, Gonzalez and her field crew edit the videotape of the fire and she does her live stand-up. The next day she meets with news director Jose Rios—another barrier breaker—who tells her he saw her on several live shots by the other TV stations and he was concerned when he saw her performing CPR. So he tells the assignment desk to call and ask if she is experienced in doing the rescue procedure. Although she is deluged with requests for interviews from her own news department and from other stations, she refuses to talk about her actions.

"I didn't want to talk about it," she tells me. "I'm the storyteller, not the story." Although she does not make a point of it, Christina has intervened two other times to assist someone in trouble during her first 10 years in TV news. Rios says the station has no hard rule covering this kind of situation.

This kind of participatory journalism is found at a few other Anglo TV stations around the country, but is not a general practice, especially at L.A.'s third Hispanic TV station, KWHY, a Spanish programmer in the afternoon-evening hours for four-and-a-half years. When its owners, Harriscope of Los Angeles, purchase the station in 1982, it is running business news from 6 a.m. to 3 p.m. and ethnic programming in the evening. It continues its split personality as first the Business Channel and then as Canal 22, where it blends its own three locally produced Spanish shows with films and novelas from Televisa.

But it lacks any general news coverage, only brief newsbreaks. "We decided there was room for a third Spanish signal because of the size of the Hispanic market," explains owner Burt Harris. Initially the station acquires programming from Mexico's Univisa, but in a complicated deal involving a change of ownership for Univision, KWHY loses its Univisa contact because the programmer goes to Univision and cannot provide shows to two different Spanish channels. So the station signs with another Mexican source, Televisa, for programs and movies, and begins augmenting these with its own locally produced shows.

Guiding this effort is newly hired director of Spanish programming Sara Garibay, former producer of Univision's popular Saturday night three-hour *Sabado Gigante* hosted by "Don Francisco." The in-house produced shows encompass entertainment, talk, medical advice, and public service, which Marty Dugan, KWHY's general manager stresses allows the station "to focus solely on the wants and needs of the viewer in Los Angeles. The other two channels, which offer network programming, are concerned with what's going on in other places.

The station's most popular evening show is *Facilismo*, a weeknight, hour-long variety show with live bands, dancing, contests, and a small studio audience. "This was our first attempt to allow the home audience to participate using the phone to win game prizes," says Dugan. "We were receiving 100,000 calls a week and one night the calls blew our switchboard."

Years later, KWHY becomes a fulltime Spanish-lingo station when it's acquired by Telemundo and begins running newscasts that are enhanced when Telemundo in turn is purchased by NBC in April 2002 for $2.7 billion. In June 2003, the Federal Communications Commission loosens media ownership rules, allowing NBC to retain the station, among the three it can now own in L.A. Under previous rules it would have had to sell KWHY to keep within a two-station limit per market.

In an effort to connect with the Hispanic populace, a number of L.A. Anglo stations offer Spanish simulcast interpretations for their news programs via the second audio program channel of their stereo signal, notably KTLA, KCBS, KCAL, and KTTV.

In a major show of discontent, on April 24, 1995, the National Hispanic Media Coalition begins a series of planned protests at ABC-owned TV stations in Los Angeles, New York, Chicago, Houston, and Fresno, charging what they say is ABC's failure to act on its promise to have more Latinos on the network. The picketing begins at ABC's KABC-TV in L.A. It is the result of a meeting held in January between a group of Latino groups who react to a promise made by Robert Iger, president of Capitol Cities/ABC, in 1993, to the National Hispanic Media Coalition to have a Latino-flavored show on the fall 1994 schedule, and to also offer upstanding portrays of Hispanics in its primetime shows. The coalition also asks viewers to bypass ABC on May 5, National Hispanic Unity Day.

The Coalition charges that since its meeting with Iger two years ago, there is no Latino-themed series on ABC and there are only three series on the network with Latinos in key roles: Jimmy Smits on

NYPD Blue, Theresa Saldana on *The Commish*, and Wilson Cruz on *My So-Called Life*.

Preceding the ABC protests is a study by the Washington-based Center for Media and Public Affairs revealing that Latinos represent one percent of all speaking parts in primetime TV series during the 1992–'93 season, down from three percent in 1995.

What's the story behind the National Hispanic Coalition? While it was formed in 1986 to improve the employment and wages for Hispanic-Americans in radio, TV, and films, it expands its lobbying-political activism into protesting the lack of cooperation with broadcasters who promise to improve the visibility of Hispanics, like ABC. It also chases sponsors away from offending personalities who impugn the reputation of Hispanic artists. Its actions draw media coverage, including the *Los Angeles Times* and my own for *Electronic Media*.

Thirty Hispanic groups, along with 125 organizations nationwide, make up this pressure group, totaling 200,000, according to Esther Renteria, the Coalition's chair emeritus. "Bob Iger promised that ABC would include us in background roles of judges, cops, and doctors that were neither ethnic or gender-specific and there'd be a Hispanic-themed show on the air by the fall of 1994," Renteria recalls. "His reneging on his promise made him the target for the picketing." By 2002, there are still a minuscule number of Latino TV series on broadcast and cable TV.

And when Howard Stern utters a series of insensitive comments April 3, 1995 on his nationally syndicated radio show following the fatal shooting of Tejano star Selena on March 31 in Corpus Christi, the Coalition, along with the League of United Latin American Citizens, and the American GI Forum (a Latino veterans organization), all call for stations to pull the program and for listeners and sponsors to boycott the show. Also coming under the coalition's ire are talk show hosts Joe Crummey and Bill Handel, of KMPC-AM and KFI-AM, respectively, "for deriding Mexican-Americans, their culture, and their music."

All this hot and steamy action is chronicled by the *L.A. Times* in a series of articles. Stern's derogative comments as quoted in the paper include such jabs as Selena's fans "live in refrigerator boxes, like to make love to a goat and like to dance with velvet paintings and eat beans." Stern says the comments were all in jest and his on-air apology given in Spanish is called "insulting" by Alex Nogales, the Coalition's chairperson, who replaces Renteria and calls Stern "absolutely gross." Nogales says Stern's remarks indicate a "lack of respect for the 25 million Americans of Hispanic descent as well as the dead." He also chides Stern for insulting Hispanics in English and then apologizing only in Spanish.

The station strikes back forcefully in an editorial by general manager Bob Moore in which he dismisses the groups' "bullying" tactics and prods fans to voice their objection to people who seek to "silence voices they disagree with."

Setting aside personal vindictiveness to focus on English-language stations employing Hispanics, Renteria stresses to me the organization's efforts open the doors for Latinos at local Anglo stations. And while there are Hispanic-named on-camera anchors and reporters, and people working behind the scenes in Anglo radio and TV, there is an obvious lack of Latinos in top managerial positions. With one exception: Jose Rios, news director at KTTV, is the market's lone Hispanic in this decision-making position, joining the station in that capacity in May 1992 from a news position at the cross-town CBS station.

By 2002, Rios has company: Nancy Bauer-Gonzales, news director at Viacom's KCBS and KCAL duopoly. The Coalition's Alex Nogales claims one reason for the lack of Hispanics in top management jobs at English-language stations: "Out and out racism and discrimination. The majority of general managers come from another market where they don't have large numbers of Latinos to help them run their station. So when they come here, they bring in people like themselves. The danger is everyone's thinking the same way and they have no sense of reality (about Hispanics) with which to work in their new environment. The coverage of the Latin community on English-speaking television is abysmal. It becomes a crime blotter."

The California Chicano News Media Association, which is 22 years old, has 400 members spread over nine statewide chapters and stays away from political action causes. It focuses instead on getting jobs and using an 800 number to "help us hook up employers with our members," says Albert Reyes, its executive director. It doesn't apply any political pressure, explains Reyes, "because we feel it would be a conflict of interest to put our members in a position of reporting on a company they work for that they might have to rake over the coals."

While Reyes says there has been progress in landing jobs for Hispanics in the last 20 years, "we'd like to see an improvement in management representation. We need to confront the glamour aspect of being in front of the camera. It takes a different frame of mind to get into management, and we need to start making Latinos aware that this is also the way to go." While Hispanics holding top positions at Anglo TV stations do not raise any eyebrows, coverage of the Latin community remains strongly tilted toward crime, simply because there's lots of gang-related violence and murder, and illegal immigration concerns, of which there are multitudes within the border states.

The American Federation of Television and Radio Artists senses there is a scarcity of union members at Telemundo's KVEA and attempts an organizing effort at the station. To its chagrin, the station's on-air broadcasters vote not to become unionized. Although the vote is a tie, seven to seven, the union must have a majority in order to win, so the defeat is a major one for the union that represents on-air talent at Telemundo's station in New York, WNJU and at Univision's KMEX in L.A., and WKTV in New York. In a first round vote at KVEA, the union leads seven to six, with two disputed ballots not yet counted. The National Labor Relations Board, which supervises the election, rules one of these two ballots has to be counted, causing the tie and defeat for the union in August.

Despite being spotlighted for its labor matters, KVEA's newly launched primetime program schedule produces a happier mood; it more than doubles its ratings from July to August, sparked by several telenovelas, including its first pickup from TV Azteca, the Mexican network. Yet these achievements are not enough to overtake KMEX, which remains the dominant Hispanic station in the May Nielsen ratings. Buoyed by its continued success, KMEX wins the 1996 Edward R. Murrow Award for overall excellence in TV news from the Radio/Television News Directors, Association. This is the first time a non-English-language station wins the competition.

This fact is not overlooked by the station's news director, Luis Patiño, who cheerfully states: "The very fact that America's best and L.A.'s No. 1 rated newscast is in Spanish, honors the hard work of every member of our news team and support of our station's owners and management." Going one boastful step further to herald its *Noticias 34* news ranking No. 1 through nine ratings books, from May 1994 to May 1996, the station promotes its achievement in a full page in *Daily Variety* with the clever closing statement: "KMEX-TV's *Noticias 34* continues to grow as the most-watched early local news in Los Angeles among adults 18 to 49. A story that's tops in any language."

Hispanics are comfortable having KMEX tell their stories exclusively in their native tongue. Patiño notes: "We had an exclusive interview with Alicia Soltero, an undocumented immigrant who was beaten by Riverside police. I know her lawyers felt comfortable with us because we would give her the proper time to tell her story." Patiño also attributes the station's gains to bilingual viewers. "They watch for two reasons. The broadcast quality is just as good or better and we talk about issues that are important to them and their families. And we also feature news from Mexico."

The station's viewer base is principally 75 percent Mexican here legally and illegally. General manager Augustine Martinez, in addressing this sticky issue, tells me that "from a consumer base standpoint, whether you're legal or illegal and you're buying products, it really isn't an issue. When you go to the television and watch the programs and advertisements, it doesn't have much of a bearing."

Anglo stations like KTLA are attempting to attract bilingual Hispanics. "We are attempting to include more stories of importance to Hispanic viewers," remarks the station's news director Craig Hume. These include adding the value of the peso versus the dollar to its *Wall Street Report* financial segment on its 10 p.m. news, "because," says Hume, "people are sending money back to their relatives."

Television in 1996 is expanding its romance with Latinos into cable as several companies announce Spanish-language news services. Joining NBC, which starts Canal De Noticias in 1993, are CBS and CNN. CBS buys TeleNoticias for an estimated $20 million from the Telemundo Group and will begin producing a half-hour newscast for Telemundo, as well as launching its 24-hour news channel, CBS TeleNoticias, for cable systems in Southern California, Arizona, South Texas, Miami, and hopefully New York City. TeleNoticias, owned by three investors, including Telemundo, debuts in 1994 and is available in 22 countries. Since Telemundo buys out its partners, Westinghouse, CBS' parent, only deals with the Florida company in making the acquisition.

CNN's Noticiero CNN Internacional, which already beams newscasts into South America, plans to expand into Latin America in March of 1997 and then bring it to domestic Latinos. NBC's early cable entry initially targets Hispanics in 21 countries outside the U.S. and is starting to expand into domestic markets. Within years the NBC and CBS entities will be history.

What's making history are the growing number of Hispanic names, as well as other ethnic sounding monikers appearing on America's English-language TV news programs. This seems to be the year it's cool to be Hispanic and broadcast to the mainstream audience, which is still dominant in America, but fading around the edges. A major exposé in the *Los Angeles Times* chronicles the quiet ethnic pseudonym craze, as journalists with Anglo last names, established and newcomers, draw upon the federal affirmative action rules aimed at benefiting minorities to enhance their careers. Since 1969, the Federal Communications Commission has structured rules based on regional demographics. Each station is required to fill out a form describing its minority and female hiring activities. The hiring formula is based on adding a proportion of each minority that is equal to at least half of that minority's workforce presence unless it falls below 5 percent or less of the region's workforce.

In 1996, Jim Avila joins NBC News as a national correspondent working out of the Chicago bureau after working for the NBC-owned station in L.A., KNBC. Twenty years earlier he changes his on-air name from Jim Simon to Avila because his father is a former broadcast executive and the union they both belong to eschews having members with the same name. Avila says his heritage in Mexican-American and Avila is his mother's maiden name. Today, Avila is a highly visible member of the NBC News team and possibly the best-known name changer. In 1999, he'll win the National Association of Hispanic Journalists TV News Feature Award, and in January of 2004 the now 48-year-old leaves NBC for ABC as a correspondent for its newsmagazines, remaining in the Windy City where he earlier reports for ABC's WLS-TV and CBS' WBBM-TV.

By stressing their ethnic roots, Anglo-named TV journalists are reversing the often familiar process of immigrants altering their last names to become more Americanized. While there are no figures to support any claim for a nation wide name change practice, the *Times* cites "Los Angeles, Chicago, and other markets where there are at least a dozen confirmed examples."

Among the TV reporters cited by the paper as changing their last names to Latino are Denise Valdez at KSAT San Antonio and Cathy Warren, who becomes Cathy Warren-Garcia (by adding her mother's maiden name) at KTVL in Medford, Ore., when she's assigned to cover Hispanic community stories. She subsequently drops Warren to be known as Garcia on-air, and uses that identity when she shifts to KDBC in El Paso. The story also focuses on several individuals who adopt Asian last names.

The name changing has its boosters and detractors. Henry Mendoza, a member of the Chicano News Media Association, calls the practice of reporters utilizing name changing and station officials who condone it as "unscrupulous intent on both sides." Broadcast talent scout Bill Slatter admits "there are benefits to be labeled Hispanic" because "Hispanic reporters and anchors are a scarce commodity."

In the year 1996 KMEX celebrates its 34th birthday. It is L.A.'s first UHF station and the flagship of the Univision network, with company-owned outlets in New York, Miami, San Francisco, Chicago, Dallas-Fort Worth, Albuquerque, Phoenix, Houston, and Fresno. Another nine stations are affiliates. The station celebrates a number of national firsts: first Latino station to have a morning talk show, first to introduce a weekend newscast, first to acquire telenovelas from Mexico's Televisa, first Hispanic station to have its own helicopter and three live remote microwave news vans, first Spanish station to compete news-wise against the Anglo stations and to pull ratings away from them for its early evening news.

Despite all these editorial successes, the station says it's still a hard sell with advertisers, who seem to have blind spots about spending dollars on Hispanic television. According to Bob Bradley, the station's director of new business development, industries that are on board include automotive, telecommunications, wire transfer, package goods, fast food chains, department stores, gas and oil companies, electronics retailers, auto parts stores, grocery chains, drugstores, and furniture stories. Industries that eschew Hispanic TV include financial, cosmetics, and healthcare firms. In 2003, some national marketers remain unhip to the potency of the exploding Hispanic market.

KVEA, which begins operation in 1985 as the second UHF station in the market, calls its competing 6 and 11 p.m. news *Noticias 52*, one of three shows being produced in its major new production facility. A second show, *Los Angeles En Acción* (Los Angeles in Action), wins a local Emmy as the best weekly half-hour public affairs show, making KVEA the first Spanish-language station in L.A. to win an Emmy. The third program emanating from the new production center is *Marcador Final*, a sports show airing Sundays from 8 to 8:30 p.m.

The two biggest news events in Latin entertainment, as well as in the music industry, occur in 1990 when Gloria Estefan suffers major back injuries when her tour bus is rear-ended by a tractor-trailer truck en route from New York City to upstate Syracuse, and in 1995, with the shocking murder of a rising Tejano star named Selena.

Riding with her husband Emilio and young son Nayib, as well as members of her entourage, the Estefan's $345,000 customized Silver Eagle Coach is pushed by the tractor-trailer that runs into the rear of the bus and into another tractor-trailer that jackknifed across the icy, snowy western lanes of Interstate 380 in an earlier accident. Gloria is knocked off the couch she is sitting on and slammed to the floor, resulting in severe back injuries. Emilio suffers a broken rib. Passersby call 911 and she is taken to the Community Medical Center in nearby Scranton, Pennsylvania, 45 minutes away. The next day she is flown to New York City to the Orthopedic Institute for Joint Diseases and undergoes a complex three-hour surgery which leaves her with a 14-inch long scar and 400 stitches. The accident is covered by the world's media, recognition of her superstar status. Two weeks later, she returns to her Miami home to recuperate and makes her first public appearance in January of 1991 as a presenter on the *American Music Awards* televised on ABC. She then embarks on a tour to coincide with the release of her new album, *Into the Light.* The Estefans file a multimillion dollar lawsuit against several defendants and are eventually awarded $8.3 million out of the total amount of $8,950,632, with monies also going to her son, her assistant, who also suffers back injuries, the tour bus company, and its driver.

As for Selena, I confess, like most non-Hispanics, I had never paid much attention to regional Mexican music even thought it blared out of radio stations around the country with alacrity. That branch of the domestic Latin music industry is more of a background presence in my professional life since I've dealt primarily with other forms of music, including Latin jazz, while at *Billboard.* When 23-year-old Selena from Corpus Christi, Texas, is shot and killed in a motel on March 31 by Yolanda Saldivar, her personal assistant and founder of her fan club, it is all fuzzy news to me. Yet the maelstrom created by the mainstream media, which falls all over itself covering the death and the emerging star's life, kick-starts the nation's awareness of Tejano music and the role Selena Quintanilla Perez played in altering its sound and moving her career to the point where she was destined to become a Latin crossover phenomenon.

Tejano is Spanish for Texan, and Selena helps turn the Tex-Mex musical style, with its hot dance rhythms and a cauldron of multi-influences including accordion-driven polkas and sax-influenced ensemble sounds, into modern music with tastes of salsa, rhythm and blues, synthesizers, electronic sounds, and pop ballads, all propelled by a very danceable cumbia beat. Cumbia is a Colombian-based rhythm which Tex-Mex musicians alter by emphasizing the accordion over brass instruments, and dancers trot counterclockwise to the snappy rhythm.

Little known is the fact that at age 12, Selena, her 11-year-old sister Susette, and her older brother AB, 14, form the band Selena Y Los Dinos and record their debut album, *Mis Primeras Grabaciones* (*My First Record*) for their hometown label, Freddie Records. Her father Abraham and the owner/founder of the record company, Freddie Martinez, Sr., are friends and acquaintances. When Abraham calls and asks his friend if he'd be interested in recording the children, the answer is "yes," recalls Freddie Martinez, Jr., the label's vice president of operations and a son of the owner. That LP, released in 1984, he tells me in 2003, is still in the company's catalog, with Martinez, Jr. calling it "a collector's item for hardcore Selena fans." In 1989, the band signs with EMI Latin, which after her death begins reissuing and repackaging her albums for these hardcore fans. Within the shadow of her death, eight albums, eight books, five videos, and the film *Selena* starring Jennifer Lopez all help to keep her image alive. Lopez, incidentally, is reportedly paid $1 million in 1997 to portray the murdered singer, also supposedly making her the highest-paid Latina actress ever. Selena's last CD, *Dreaming of You,* released four months after her death, includes three English tunes intended to help break her into the mainstream market.

"I don't think most Anglos had heard of her at the time of her death," admits Martinez, Jr. "She was a young and up-and-coming beautiful performer in the prime of her life who was getting ready to crossover into the English market. She was at the top of her game in the Tejano industry, and nothing of this magnitude had ever happened to an artist in this part of the business. After the tragedy people who hadn't heard of her before wanted to discover her music, see what she was all about, and that's when non-Latinos became interested in her. The media attention was so surreal; people couldn't help but pay attention. And for the tragedy to be showcased on such an international scope created a bigger-than-life image. At the time of her death she was the number one or two female artist in Tejano and on the cusp of crossing over into bigger things."

If timing is everything, 1996 sees the early seeds for the rock en Español movement, nurtured by such bands as La Ley, Jaguares, Maldita Vecindad, Fobia, La Lupita, Aterciopelados, Puya, Sol D'Menta, Soraya, and Los Rabanes, among others. Ironically these groups from Mexico, Colombia, Puerto Rico, and Panama express a yearning to break out of traditional music molds and get with the "in crowd."

Three major concert venues in Southern California, the Greek Theater, Universal Amphitheatre, and Blockbuster Pavilion open their doors to rock en Español groups for the first time. And the first radio station in the nation to reportedly play rock en Español is KRTO-FM in L.A. *Radio Ritmo*, as it's called, targets Spanish-speaking 18- to 34-year-olds who eschew the predominant radio music formats of regional Mexican, salsa, or romantic ballads. KRTO calls its format alternative music, which includes playing merengue and disco half the time. Owned by El Dorado Communications, which operates a second L.A. station, KRRA-AM (ranchera music) and eight stations in Texas, the company says it's hoping to lure listeners away from such English-language stations as KPWR, KROQ, and KKBT as well as Spanish stations. Within years, KRRA, KRTO, and its format will have faded away and been absorbed by other owners.

The year after her death, Selena is being credited with inspiring a growing number of female vocalists to seek their fortunes in the regional Mexican music community, a field traditionally dominated by men. Record labels, big and small, are all looking for their Tejano diva as regional Mexican music continues its popularity surge within the domestic Latin record industry, a segment comprised various niche styles: banda, cumbia, conjunto, grupo, mariachi, Norteño, ranchera, son, Texachi, and tropical/cumbia.

Selena's father, Abraham Quintanilla, who helped launch her career, signs a 13-year-old singer Jennifer Peña to his Q Productions label, which is distributed by EMI. She even performs at a Selena tribute concert at the Houston Astrodome. Selena remains EMI's top seller. The label also has a number of female Tejano singers it's now pushing, since radio and concert promoters are more open to working with females, a situation some observers claim wasn't the case in the 1980s.

It also obtains male artists through licensing deals with Alacrán and Disa, which had formerly been distributed by Fonovisa. Alacrán's first hit acts for EMI Latin include Graciela Beltrán and Los Tucanes De Tijuana, while Disa provides EMI with additional growth artists, or as the industry coldly calls it, "product." Especially important in EMI's efforts to increase its standing in regional Mexican music is the special release by Mexican superstar Juan Gabriel, along with three top female Mexican warblers, the late Lola Beltrán, Lucha Villa, and Amalia Mendoza, titled *Juan Gabriel Y Los Tres Señoras.*

Sensing profits, major labels (which start to chase male Tejano artists in 1990) are now going after increased female representation in the regional Mexican genre, the original roots music one hears on the early Hispanic stations and which transmogrifies into a powerful musical force. It's all very simple: play music that is popular with Mexican immigrants in the West and Southwest, who account for around 65 percent of the nation's Latinos, thus making it the most played format on Hispanic radio. It's a situation that remains in effect in the 21st Century.

Sony Discos adds the one-name artist Lares, whose initial album offers Vince Gill, a top country music personality, performing on a number of the tunes in an effort to enter the untapped country music crossover market. It also enters the regional Mexican battle by licensing albums from Mexico-based Maya, which can now release its albums simultaneously on both sides of the border. La Mafia heads the list of its commercially viable bands. With a name like that, what program director will resist playing its music?

Fonovisa (owned by Mexican TV network Televisa) is the power in the genre, retaining among its females, Laura Canales, who makes her breakthrough in the '80s. Its male superstars include Marco Antonio Solís and Los Tigres Del Norte. Its all-around success in lining up licensing deals with Mexican firms is the reason for its front-running position and a key factor in being acquired by Univision 20 years later as the foundation for a new music group the TV network creates.

PolyGram Latino is building domestic awareness for the Monterrey, Mexico, band, Grupo Límite, featuring lead singer Alicia Villarreal, whose initial release, *Por Un Amor*, sells a reported 600,000 copies in both Mexico and the U.S. Pedro Fernández is one of the label's enduring male acts.

Arista Latin, which starts selling regional Mexican three years ago, debuts 16-year-old mariachi-flavored Nydia Rojas, who comes from Hacienda Heights, California. She performs with the group Mariachi Reyna De Los Angeles for four years and wins first place in an international talent contest on the Univision hit series *Sabado Gigante*.

Of course, there are also a number of small labels—the bellwether undersurface of the industry each year—that also offer male and female artists, including Freddie of Corpus Christi, Balboa of Los Angeles, Exitos Latinos and Barbed Wire in Dallas, AFG Sigma in San Antonio, and Voltage Discos in Houston, among others. Miami's MP Records, a specialist in developing salsa and merengue acts, forms MP Mexico through which it sells Mexico-based bands domestically.

In its third decade in business, Freddie's top seller is Ramón Ayala, Sr., the so-called "Norteño King," among its roster of 22 acts.

WEA Latina looks to build up its roster by obtaining albums from Mexican independent label MCM, which the company's Mexican label purchases this year. Still to be resolved is for MCM to get out of its U.S. distribution deal with Fonovisa.

In 1996, Los Lobos, the Latin fusion band from East L.A., releases a two CD compilation on Warner Bros., *Just Another Band from East L.A.: A Collection*, which is a rich cornucopia of 20 years of blending the roots sounds of the Mexican-American barrio with tastes of Americana: pure blues, rhythm'n'blues, and rock. The CD is not a greatest hits package. Rather, it is an exploration of he band's roots, explains drummer Louie Pérez, one of its founding members. And when film producers want the raw energy of Latin crossover music for *La Bamba* and *The Mambo Kings*, they call upon this aggregation. The band continues to work shows and does an occasional TV appearance, but it appears to have reached the pinnacle of its commercial viability, while retaining its connection to its loyal fans, a fate which befalls many in show business.

The year 1996 is also the year the Los Angeles Latino Film Festival debuts, founded by Marlene Dermer, actor/producer James Edward Olmos, and film/music producer George Hernández. It starts out with 42 films shown over a five-day period. By 2002, the sixth year of its existence, the festival showcases more than 100 films and includes workshops and lectures, and is attended by 25,000 film buffs over its 10-day run at the historic Egyptian Theatre in Hollywood.

The National Council Of La Raza, a major Latino artists' interest group, unveils its first Bravo Award winners in 1995 and '96. By 1998, they will have a new name: the ALMAs (Amerian Latino Media Arts). But for now, under the original moniker, here are the early winners:

1995: Ricardo Montalban wins the lifetime achievement award named after him; *Selena* is named the outstanding album; *Sesame Street* is the top TV program; and Jacob Vargas the emerging artist of the year.

1996: Edward James Olmos captures two awards, as outstanding actor in a film (*Caught*) and for his performance in the TV film *Larry McMurtry's Dead Man's Walk.* Liz Torres wins for her performance in the TV comedy series *The John Larroquette Show;* Jimmy Smits for his performance in the TV series *NYPD*; Theresa Saldana wins for her performance in TV series *The Commish*; Michael DeLorenzo and Lauren Vélez for their performances in the TV series *New York Undercover;* and Los Lobos for its music for films and TV.

Articles

"The Heavyweight On Latin Airwaves." BusinessWeek, Aug. 9, 2004

"One Crime, A Million 'Hispanic' Suspects." Los Angeles Times, Sept. 26, 2003

"Gloria Estefan: The Pop Superstar From Tragedy To Triumph." Signet Books, September 1997.

"Feeding Latin Rock And La Banda Elástica." Los Angeles Times, Dec. 19, 1996

"Translating No-Nonsense News Into High Ratings." Los Angeles Times, Dec. 2, 1996

"Hispanics The Target Of Radio Unica." Hispanics Broadcasting & Cable, Nov. 25, 1996

"Major League Baseball Teams Tap Into Latin American Talent." Christian Science Monitor, Nov. 17, 1997

"Liberman Buys KYKF: Begins KBUE Simulcast." Radio & Records, Nov. 8, 1996

"Rock En Español Is Slow To Get Rolling In America." Hollywood Reporter, Oct. 10, 1996

"Spanish-Lingo KLVE Still Leads Radio Race." Daily Variety, Oct. 10, 1996

"Numero Uno, Salute To KMEX Channel 34 On It's 34th Anniversary." Hollywood Reporter, Sept. 30, 1996

"Regional Music Of Mexico." Billboard spotlight, Aug. 17, 1996

"AFTRA Organizing Effort Fails At Telemundo's KVEA." Hollywood Reporter, Aug. 19, 1996

"Playing The Name Game." Los Angeles Times, Aug. 18, 1996

"KVEA Debuts Boost Ratings." Hollywood Reporter, Aug. 16, 1996

"Radio Ritmo Has Rock?But Not Salsa." Los Angeles Times, Aug. 16, 1996

"KLVE-FM Continues Run In Top Local Ratings Spot." Los Angeles Times, July 13, 1996

"KMEX Ratings Mirror Ethnic Growth In L.A." Electronic Media, July

1, 1996

"CBS Parent Buys TeleNoticas; Spanish News Service Planned." Hollywood Reporter, June 28, 1996

"CBS Enters Spanish-Language News." USA Today, June 28, 1996

"KLVE-FM No.1 In Arbitron Survey." Electronic Media, Jan. 15, 1996

"KGRB Radio Is Dis-Banded." Hollywood Reporter, Jan. 2, 1996

"L.A. Spanish Stations Thrive." Electronic Media, Dec. 18, 1995

"Summer Wind Barely Moves Radio Ratings." Los Angeles Times, Oct. 11, 1995

"Hip-Hop Powers Its Way To Top." Daily Variety, July 19, 1995

"Universal '95 Tickets Go On Sale Sunday," Los Angeles Times, April 30, 1995

"Latinos Protest At ABC Stations." Los Angeles Times, April 27, 1995

"KLVE-FM Romances To The Top." Los Angeles Times, April 21, 1995

"L.A.'s KMEX Seeks New Ratings System." Electronic Media, April 17, 1995

"Latinos To Stern: Apology Is Not Accepted." Los Angeles Times, April 11, 1995

"Latinos: We're Underrated In L.A." Hollywood Reporter, April 6, 1995

"Taking Tejano Beyond Texas." USA Today, April 6, 1995

"Stern Gets A Bit Of A Ratings Shock." Los Angeles Times, Jan. 7, 1995

"The Rescuers." Emmy, April 1994

Chapter 4
CAPITULO 4

A New Presence: 1997
UNA NUEVA PRESCENCIA: 1997

• A select group of Hispanic actresses makes its presence felt in the mainstream market.

• A new form of music, rock en Español, displays its presence as well.

• The nation's first 24-hour Spanish-language radio news and information network debuts to offer an alternative to the Hispanic music radio networks which are expanding and ingratiating themselves to audiences in major cities; formats splinter into programming designed to cater to newly arrived immigrants and second- and third-generation U.S.-born bilinguals.

• Sony Pictures Entertainment and Liberty Media Corp. purchase the financially ailing Telemundo TV network for $537 million plus $200 million in debt.

Two years after the murder of rising Tejano star Selena Quintanilla Perez, her life story hits the big screen with Jennifer Lopez in the leading role and Jackie Guerra as her co-star. The murder also elicits books and prods *People* magazine to publish an issue on the Latino community.

The timing also seems appropriate for Elizabeth Peña to receive several honors for her role in John Sayles' *Lone Star*, including nominations for an Oscar and Independent Spirit Award plus an accolade from the National Council of La Raza, all for her portrayal of Pilar, a Mexican-American mother who's also a schoolteacher—a multidimensional role far a field from the stereotypical roles of sexy temptress or maid. Gilbert Avila, executive administrator of affirmative action at the Screen Actors Guild, the actors' union, tells the *Los Angles Times* he believes the film industry is entering an era where there will again be Latino stars who can generate the kind of box-office success that ensures their career growth. He cites Cameron Diaz and Lopez as the kind of young, skillful performers "who are breaking out in non-Latino-themed films," and are qualified to be either co-stars or stars in major budgeted feature films.

And why not? The 1990 Census finds the Hispanic population has jumped 56 percent to 23.3 million, excluding illegals. According to Census projections, in the 21st century Latins will replace African-Americans as the nation's largest minority. By 2050, America will be 52.8 percent white, 24.5 percent Latin, 13.6 percent black, and 8.2 percent Asian. The present U.S. population in 1997 is 73.6 percent white, 12 percent black, 10.2 percent Latin, and 3.3 percent Asian. This estimate proves correct as the Census Bureau in June 2003 declares Latinos the nation's largest minority at 38.8 million as of July 2002. The INS in 1996 estimates the number of undocumented aliens, the majority Latinos, at more than 5 million, and growing by 275,000 a year. California alone has an estimated 2 million and rising as the porous border between Mexico and U.S. invites illegal entry.

This massive population represents "a country within a country," says Ramon Pineda, president of Caballero Spanish Media, a 27-year-old New York firm which secures advertising for 100 Spanish radio stations, for a story I do for *Gavin GM*, a monthly radio periodical. "In 1970 there were 50 or more Spanish stations. Today, there are 500. Format fragmentation is good," she believes "because you can narrow and pinpoint your audience."

The buying power of Hispanics this year is projected to reach $348 billion, up from $325 billion in 1996, according to the University of Georgia's Selig Center for Economic Growth good news to the growing Latin entertainment industry which sees more greenbacks on the horizon.

Five years after Spanish radio takes over the top popularity slots on Los Angeles radio, KLVE-FM retains its No. 1 position two years running as the most listened to station among the 18 Spanish radio stations out of 87 in the market, the most in the nation. Besides owning KLVE, Heftel Broadcasting Corp. also owns KSCA-FM, its newest $112 million station purchased from Gene Autry. It's hasta la vista to alternative rock and buenos dias to Mexican regional music, much to the angst of alternative rock fans who mourn listening to a mix of Alanis Morissette, Joni Mitchell, Sting, Elvis Costello, and the Wallflowers.

Two short-lived L.A. Spanish stations target non-Mexican listeners. KWNK-AM Simi Valley, broadcasting English sports/talk provided by the new national network, Radio Unica, is switched in April by Lotus Communications to KVCA-AM (*Radio Centro America*) which programs for the one million estimated arrivals from war-torn El Salvador, Guatemala, and Honduras with a combination of cumbia, punta, salsa, merengue, and other forms of tropical music. In 2000, Lotus changes the station to all Farsi KCRN, catering to the huge Iraqi exile community. KRTO-FM (*Radio Ritmo*), which has been romancing the emerging rock en Español crowd, is sold by owner El Dorado Communications to Cox Radio for $19 million and becomes KPRO-FM, a classic rhythm 'n' blues station, one of the few instances where a Spanish lingo station is sold and goes English. One new station which aims at the youth audience is KSSE-FM, which makes a dent in the market by focusing on artists like Shakira, Chayanne, and the Barrio Boyzz. This concentration on Latin pop hits earns the station the fifth most listened to Spanish station rating, despite a weak signal. Outside New York and Miami, L.A.'s KTNQ-AM is the only other station programming talk around the clock. With funny morning host Humberto Luna, the station is the sixth most listened to AM station and the top-rated AM broadcaster in Spanish. Weekdays from 5 to 9 p.m. Guatemalan-born Rolando González takes the mike for the station's popular sport talk stanza, *Hablando De Deportes.* It's the city's longest-running Spanish sports chat show, and González has been its host since the beginning 10 years ago. His current co-host is Mexican-born Hipólito Gamboa.

In November, Liberman Broadcasting's KKHJ-AM switches to all talk from regional Mexican music, gaining the accolade of becoming the nation's only Spanish-language all news station. The station, formerly KHJ (Boss Radio) during the '60s and '70s, offers long news blocks and shorter news-talk programs. The format is designed to halt declining ratings, credited to a large extent by the departure of morning drive-time host Reñan Almendarez Coello. After a 14-month break, he reappears on KSCA as its morning drive host. Like the other morning show hosts, Coello—known affectionately as *El Cucuy De La Manana*—blends scripted skits with improvised comedy in a fast-paced style. What sets him apart is his syndication by HBC across the country to such cities as New York, Washington, Las Vegas, San Francisco, and Chicago.

KWKW-AM follows in August as the second Spanish talk station in the West, its lead newsman Antonio Gonzaléz, formerly the host of two issue-oriented programs on KTNQ. Despite the format switch, the station remains the popular flagship for the Los Angeles Dodgers, which it has broadcast for 25 of the 40 years the team has been in L.A. after its move from Brooklyn in 1958. KWKW's two baseball broadcasters are René Cárdenas, who starts in 1958 and Jaíme Jarrín, who begins the next year. With the changing composition of the city's Hispanic population an ever-present reality, the station unfurls a new green and red banner in front of its broadcast booth in Dodger stadium.

Instead of the station's familiar slogan *LA Mexicana*, the new banner offers the station's dial setting, 1330. Cárdenas, who's from Nicaragua, says the original banner made a lot of people mad, since not everyone now is from Mexico. Jim Kalmenson, the station's general manager, who formerly held the same post when KVCA was on the air, says the Latin community needs a radio station that provides them with information while adjusting to their new home.

In one of the first consolidations within Spanish radio, Heftel of L.A. and Tichenor Media System of Harlingen, Texas, merge as Hispanic Broadcasting Corp. on February 14, 1997. Mac Tichenor, Jr., president of the merged firm, says the two companies joined forces to increase their reach into the top 10 Latin markets. "We had six and Heftel had five, with one overlap in Chicago when we merged," says Tichenor. Several months later it has 36 stations in Dallas, New York, Los Angeles, Miami, San Francisco, Chicago, San Antonio, Houston, El Paso, McAllen-Brownsville, and Las Vegas, with others on the horizon.

Among its rival networks, 14-year-old Spanish Broadcasting System has seven stations in New York, Los Angeles, Miami, and Chicago. The company is selling off some AMs to focus on FM, with its cleaner music signal. During the spring of 2002, Spanish Broadcasting System and rival Hispanic Broadcasting Corp. negotiate a merger. Several months later on June 12, HBC announces it will be acquired by Univision Communications. Right after this announcement, Alarcón, Jr. and SBS vociferously oppose the acquisition of HBC by TV-music giant Univision, filing an antitrust lawsuit in Miami against HBC and radio station goliath Clear Channel Communications, which is a minority partner in HBC. HBC and Clear Channel file their own counter suit, heating up the legal battlefield.

WSKQ (La Mega) has the distinction of being New York's first Spanglish station. "It's a combination of Spanish and English," says Carey Davis, vice president/general manager of SBS' two New York FMs, WSKQ and WPAT (Suave), adding: "There are second- and third-generation Hispanics who speak both languages, so the station reflects this by broadcasting bilingually. The station's morning show, *Vaciulon De La Manana* with Luis Jiménez and Junior

Hernández, ranks second in the morning behind the better-known irascible Howard Stern. Still, for the market's 3.2 million Hispanics, the Latino duo is doing mighty fine against Stern."

New York's third Spanish station, WADO-AM, goes through several formats, starting out in 1936 as an English broadcaster bartering time periods to advertisers, opening some hours for Spanish in '65, and goes all out 10 years later with salsa and merengue music until January of 1996, when it switches to news/talk.

In Chicago, while music is the all-important entertainment element at Heftel's WOJO-FM, offering regional Mexican for its large Mexicano population and at its WLXX-AM, which has a tropical music format, WIND-AM, its third outlet, counters with an all-news operation. WIND's six fulltime news crew are augmented by Notimex, a Mexico City news service, and freelancers. Notes Jim Pagliai, general manager for all three stations: "For a Spanish station we have a large news operation. We have to super serve our audience with news, information, and gossip about Mexico plus soccer scores and sports reports. We also broadcast play-by-play of the Bulls and White Sox. Mexican Hispanics, immigrants, and U.S.-born represent 25 to 30 percent of Chicago's growing Hispanic community." WOJO is first among the city's six Spanish stations and 12th in the general market rakings in listeners 12-plus and fifth among 18- to 34 year-olds.

In San Antonio, Heftel has three stations: KCOR-AM, KXTN-FM, and KROM-FM. "When we all cover a major event, we can impact the Hispanic community," says Dan Wilson, general manager of the triplets. Fifty-year-old KCOR (*La Primera*) plays traditional regional Mexican; KXTN (Tejano *107.5*) caters to Tejano fans, while KROM (*Stereo Latina*) plays more mass appeal pop stars. "The different formats work because we don't see a lot of audience sharing," says Wilson, except when all three broadcast a fundraiser for residents of Jarrel, Texas, torn apart by tornado Jarrel, or they cover the 17th annual Hispanic State Fair each July featuring a full day of music in one of the city's major parks. Within the top 10 Arbitron slots, two of the three rank: KXTN is third and KROM is seventh.

In the San Diego-Tijuana market, XLTN-FM plays Spanish pop hits while XHKY-FM appeals to cross-border listeners with regional Mexican mariachis, rancheros, and groupos. XHKY ranks No. 8 among Arbitron stations. "With the two stations we have the Hispanic population covered in San Diego," says Randy Phillips, sales director for both California radio stations. The company's third station, XKTZ-FM, is an English-language contemporary hits outlet which boasts a large listenership among Hispanics since "35–40 percent of Hispanic listeners are English speaking." Both FMs have been on the air 15 years, each attracting a different 18 to 49 demographic: XLTN appeals to females while XHKY is favored by males, according to Phillips.

The San Francisco region is unique within itself. The city's major Spanish outlet is a simulcast combination of KSOL/KZOL-FM, purchased by Tichenor Media in 1996 for $40 million. KSOL is a former rhythm 'n' blues power whose DJs include Sly Stone, before he becomes a music superstar during the late '60s psychedelic hippie era with his Sly and the Family Stone aggregation. The combination called *Estereo Sol* in less than one year gains a major presence among the region's 10 Spanish stations, including those in San Jose and Sacramento.

Another chain, Z-Spanish Radio, avoids paying the top dollar fees paid by Tichenor by buying three low-power stations for $8 million to cover the area with KZSF-FM in San Francisco, KZWC-FM in Concord, and KZSJ in San Jose. In San Jose, EXCL Communications, which operates KLOK-FM for five years, merges with the Latin Communications Group to own 17 Spanish radio stations around the country. In the Bay Area, Latinos are a hot commodity to be romanced.

With this sense that the timing is right, Radio Unica announces its rollout in January, rather than in April, of the nation's first Spanish 24-hour news and chat network. While conceding there are dangers, Radio Unica's chairman Joaquin Blaya believes "this is an idea whose time has come," he informs the *Los Angeles Times*. Due to delays in building the network's Hialeah, Florida, headquarters, the launch is postponed several times last year. When the network debuts January 5, 1997, it has 32 affiliates in such cities as Miami, San Antonio, San Francisco, Houston, and Los Angeles where its affiliate is KVCA-FM in the suburb of Simi Valley. In the hot, muggy days of October 2002, I visit Radio Unica to interview its president and tour its impressive array of studios and production facilities for this book.

Despite skeptical claims that the diversity of the Hispanic community nationwide presents problems in programming for so different an audience, Blaya dismisses these comments by pointing to his experience at both Univision and Telemundo where he developed award-winning programming for their national audiences. Investors like New York's Warburg Pincus Ventures LP and Mexico's Cadena Radio Centro help fund the new venture with millions of dollars, obviously believing it's a sound investment.

Although it happens in November, the most epochal TV news is the acquisition of Telemundo by Sony Pictures Entertainment and Liberty Media Corporation, a division of Tele-Communications that owns cable systems, for $537 million plus $200 million in debt. The deal marks Sony's entry into U.S. broadcasting. Due to Federal Communications Commission network ownership regulations regarding foreign investments, more than 50 percent of Telemundo will be owned by Bastion Capitol, the nation's largest Latin-owned private equity fund, headed by Daniel Villanueva, owner of the Los Angeles Galaxy soccer team, and Apollo Management, whose founder Leon Black is Telemundo's chairman since 1994. Both firms currently own 35 percent of the network.

Sony will own 25 percent and Liberty will own five percent of the voting stock, and 20 percent of the nonvoting stock. The new owners plan to overhaul the network's programming with Sony, the managing partner, producing Spanish-lingo entertainment, some of which will be based on its popular TV series. Jeff Sagansky, Sony Pictures Entertainment president, projects the company will utilize the Latin creative community for original programming expanding

Telemundo's competitive capabilities. Another Sony official, Jon Feltheimer, executive vice president of Sony and president of the Columbia TriStar Television Group, adds to *Daily Variety*'s coverage that Sony "already produces programming in eight languages and the Telemundo brand will become the centerpiece of our worldwide Spanish-language programming strategy." Other companies vying for Telemundo: Clear Channel Communications in association with TV Azteca of Mexico and News Corp., bidding with financial interests Abry Partners and Thomas Lee.

Prior to its sale in mid-summer, Telemundo announces a major primetime programming realignment designed to make it more competitive with Univision. Nationally, Telemundo stations will shift their local nightly newscasts up an hour to 10 p.m. boasting they have the earliest nightly news in most cities. *CBS TeleNoticias*, which provides the network with a national broadcast, follows at 10:30. Telemundo also moves films into the 8–10 p.m. block instead of soap operas. In Los Angeles, the network's KVEA overhauls both its 6 p.m. news half-hour and its primetime broadcast by replacing anchors, adding a consumer advocate, features for the so-called Gen X populace, and an exclusively tagged report on Central America for Southern California's growing Central American community. Viewers will be able to interact with newscast stories by dialing a special phone number to communicate their feelings about the coverage or seek additional information.

Liberty Media Corporation, the programming arm of cable giant Tele-Communications Inc., announces in December it will launch a digital tier package, as it's called in cable TV, encompassing 12 Spanish-language networks next spring, including Telemundo. Among the other networks offered are Discovery Channel's Spanish version, CNN En Español, music channel The Box's Latin music service, Home Shopping Network's Spanish cousin, Fox Sports America, and Locomotion, an animation service. Being developed are two general show business channels, one featuring action and the other comedy, both developed with partner Sony.

Univision Communications Inc. is where Henry Cisneros, former Housing Secretary in the Clinton administration and San Antonio mayor from 1981 through 1989, winds up as president and chief operating officer. After one term with the federal government, he heads to Los Angeles in February to oversee Univision, the leading Spanish TV network. The job offer comes from Univision owner A. Jerrold Perenchio, who remains chairman, chief executive officer, while giving up his presidency title to Cisneros. In 1997, Univision owns 18 stations, has 39 network affiliates, is carried on hundreds of cable systems and reaches around 92 percent of domestic Latin households. It's viewed by around 80 percent of U.S. Latinos. Cisneros tells the *Los Angeles Times* he'll be "assisting the company in finding its way into the mainstream of American life."

Univision's New York station, WXTV, is making its own headway into this mainstream consciousness. During the May sweeps period, its morning show *Dispierta America* ties with WCBS' *This Morning* for fourth place among 18- to 49 year-olds. What's the big deal? Fox Broadcasting's WNYW's morning stanza, *Good Day New York*, has been the favorite among this same age group for years, but it's knocked out of this leadership position by WNBC's airing of the network's *Today* show plus WXTV's strong showing, indicating that perhaps Hispanics have discovered something more to their interests and are saying good-bye to *Good Day.*

WXTV's viewers are also tuning into the station's 6 p.m. local news, hosted by Liliana Marín and Rafael Pineda, positioning the station third among the 18 to 49 bracket behind ABC and NBC's stations and ahead of the troubled WCBS. During the July ratings survey, WXTV's morning show's ratings rise from a May level of 0.5 rating, 4 share to a 0.9/3 combination, a major increase over what the station averages in the same time period with non-news shows one year ago. And in August, the station's 6 p.m. newscast continues to outdraw 18- to 54 year-olds ahead of similar aged followers for WCBS' newscast.

Univision's sole cable network, Galavision, introduces its first program for English-speaking Latinos, *Café Olé*, hosted by Giselle

Fernandez, whose mainstream TV gig is co-hosting *Access Hollywood.* What is she doing on Spanish TV? With a heritage of being half-Mexican, half-Jewish, she fits the role of the bilingual, bicultural host. The half-hour talk show airs Sundays at 7 p.m. until Si TV, its producer and Galavision end their relationship in August of '98, when the show goes into syndication in 52 markets. Fernandez ultimately leaves the show, stays with *Access* until joining the *KTLA Morning News* in Los Angeles in October 2001 as the replacement for original co-anchor Barbara Beck, who debuts with the show July 21, 1991, and stays with it until departing in 1997. Fernandez departs the program in August 5, 2003.

Café Olé's creators, Si TV executive producers Jeff Valdez and Bruce Barshop, believe there's a wide gap for programming which caters to Latins who speak English.

Valdez says he tells Henry Cisneros that young Latins prefer watching Anglo sitcoms rather than Univision. According to the *Los Angeles Times*, Cisneros is not prepared to air a bilingual show, but Galavision's president, Javier Saralegui, savors the idea, based on the channel's good response to airing reruns of *Que Pasa USA?*, a bilingual sitcom from public television. Barshop makes the point that the program is geared for second- and third-generation U.S.-born Latinos who grow up watching football and American TV shows. Crossover media actors scheduled to appear during this first season for *Café Olé* include Hector Elizondo of *Chicago Hope*, Michael DeLorenzo of *New York Undercover*, Erik Estrada of *CHiPs* fame, and Laura Harring of *Sunset Beach.*

Also heating up the TV wars are CNN, which launches CNN En Español on the same day, March 17, that CBS (owned by Westinghouse) begins its news channel CBS TeleNoticias. The CNN spin-off is aimed at Latin America, where CBS TeleNoticias already has a presence. Both networks will utilize their parents' worldwide bureaus. Exiting the scene is NBC's short-lived Canal De Noticias which fails to meet advertising expectations, especially in light of NBC and Microsoft's joint venture 24-hour news channel, MSNBC.

For the second time in two years, the National Hispanic Media Coalition again goes after the Walt Disney Co. for not increasing the number of Latinos hired at its ABC radio and TV stations. The organization calls for a national boycott of the Disney Co.'s holdings including the Anaheim Angels baseball team, the Mighty Ducks hockey franchise, the two theme parks in California and Florida and the Disney retail store chain. Alex Nogales, national chair of the organization, tells *Daily Variety* that "after three-and-a-half years of talks with the company, less than one percent of those in creative and policy-making positions at Disney/ABC are Hispanic."

Despite statistics that the Hispanic population now accounts for 10 percent of the nation's population, and "despite this sea of brown faces, we're nowhere to be found in the entertainment industry," contends Nogales. Disney does not respond to these concerns, but a spokesperson cites the company's "long policy of nondiscrimination and good working relationships with numerous Hispanic groups, including La Raza and Imagen."

Taking its cue from MTV, KSUV-TV in Bakersfield, California, begins airing Spanish-language videos around the clock to entice 12- to 34 year old Hispanics. Calling itself *MasMusica TeVe* (More Music TV), the format debuts September 16 and its owner Tri Caballero LLC, says it plans to build and operate stations in a number of other California cities with strong Hispanic communities which will rebroadcast KSUV's signal. The target demographic is similar to what music radio successfully romances. While MTV Latino already airs Spanish-language videos offering a variety of musical styles, *MasMusica TeVe* will focus on local tastes and favorites, mainly Mexican pop and Tejano artists, for viewers in Texas and California.

On the music front, the major new happening is rock en Español in Los Angeles, San Antonio, Miami, New York, Chicago, and San Francisco, but without the support of Spanish music radio stations, which look askance at this hybrid style, sometimes called rocanrol and aimed at the hearts of young Latinos. The music is also called alternative rock and Spanish rockers coming from both

Mainland U.S. and overseas sources are just now starting to gain the attention of record labels, big and small. The movement often blends indigenous Latin music styles with rock rhythms, electric instruments, punk, and ska ingredients. Recognizing the importance of rock en Español, the English-language Grammys add a statue for Hispanic rock music. It's a major addition for the mainstream Grammys, especially since the music is aimed at a young audience.

Among the early bands fusing these elements with Spanish or Spanglish lyrics are Los Fabulosos Cadillacs from Argentina; Jaguares, Maldita Vecindad, and Café Tacuba from Mexico; Aterciopelados from Colombia; King Changó from New York; Los Olvidados from Southern California's San Gabriel Valley; plus L.A.-area bands Yeska, Calavera, Pastilla, Maria Fatal, Chencha Berrinches, Voz De Mano, Chiles, and Viacrucis among others.

Of all these groups, Aterciopelados has been performing since 1995 and is the headliner on "Rockinvasión '97," the most adventurous tour for rock en Españolers in the U.S., with stops in Los Angeles, San Diego, El Paso, Houston, Chicago, New York, and Miami. Also on the bill are Los Fabulosos Cadillacs, Maldita Vecindad, and La Unión. It's also the first tour with a major U.S. sponsor, PepsiCo, which seeks to reach young Hispanic consumers. The tour is the outgrowth of the success of a concert titled "Wateke '96" which features Shakira and Aterciopelados and is held at the Universal Amphitheatre, a major L.A. area venue which welcomes this music and the customers it attracts.

Jaime Vasquez, Southern California marketing manager for PepsiCo, says American companies miss the mark by not realizing "that Latino teens are now living in two worlds," he tells the *Los Angeles Times*. And having been nurtured on English rock while being raised in Hispanic families, "many are interested in a mature rock formula that borrows the rhythms and the melodies that are credible and relevant to the Latino community and incorporates them into the rock format."

Southern California venues, from the Hollywood Bowl to the Amphitheatre in Universal City to the outdoor Greek Theatre in L.A.'s

Griffith Park to the Arrowhead Pond in Anaheim, seem particularly eager to book Latin acts, a major change for these mainstream theaters. Previously, Latin acts played lesser-known venues. The exception is Julio Iglesias, the romantic heartthrob, who has been playing to Anglos and Hispanics at the Amphitheatre since 1983, when his career breaks open in the states.

Booked for two evenings in 1983 at the Amphitheater, the demand for tickets is so great that the engagement stretches to five nights. Iglesias is among a wide-ranging array of talent besides the rock en Español festival playing the venue, including ranchera king Vicente Fernández, followed by his son Alejandro plus Lucero, Ana Gabriel, Los Del Rio, Julio Sabala, Linda Ronstadt with the Mariachi Los Camperos De Nati Cano, and Juan Gabriel.

The main attraction at the Arrowhead Pond is Julio Iglesias' son Enrique, who is gaining a strong fan base totally apart from his father's. He sells out his two performances, an indication in the years to come he will emerge a major star and overshadow his father.

On the Greek Theatre's bill are: La Mafia, Emmanuel, Viva Mariachi '97 (Jose Hernandez, Maria Conchita Alonso, and Mariachi Reyna), Santana, Los Lobos, the L.A. International Latin Jazz Festival featuring Jerry Gonzales, and the Fort Apache Band, the Caribbean Jazz Project featuring Paquito D'Rivera, Andy Narell, and Dave Samuels, and a tribute to Antonio Carlos Jobim featuring Lee Ritenour, Dave Grusin, Eric Marienthal, and El DeBarge. The venue books its first Hispanic performer in 1984, José Luis Rodríguez, a Venezuelan recording and soap opera star.

The Spanish uprising is also being felt on the East Coast where New York's Madison Square Garden has no problem selling out Latin performances by headline status acts. Miami, naturally, as well as Orlando, Chicago, San Antonio, Houston, and Dallas are also favorite stopping off points for top name Latin performers. Concert venues often watch the sales of Latin CDs and ticket sales at other venues as a guideline for which acts are hot and ready for top-line venues.

In sports, a remarkable, even historic marketing effort by the San Diego baseball Padres is in full bloom at this border town with Tijuana, Mexico.

Looking to tap into Tijuana's two million population, including hardcore baseball lovers, the team takes a series of steps starting in 1995 that results in greater cooperation in getting through the ever-clogged San Ysidro border checkpoint. This allows buses from the border town of Tecate to shuttle fans to Padres games from six Mexican border cities on Sundays and during the week, where they are greeted by mariachis, Spanish-speaking attendants, and booths selling Mexican food favorites. The buses are provided by Tecate, one of Mexico's most popular beers, which is (naturally) sold at the games.

The Hispanic community, on both sides of the border, is today the fastest-growing segment of the Padres audience, with attendance increasing 350 percent between 1995 and 1996, according to Enrique Morones, the team's director of multicultural marketing. In 1996, the team says 20,000 fans make the border crossing bus ride to see a Sunday game, arriving from Tecate, Tijuana, Mexicali, Ensenada, Rosarito, and San Luis Rio Colorado in Sonora.

Why does all this Hispanic romancing actions occur in San Diego? *The Los Angeles Times* credits Larry Lucchino, the team's top executive, who looks at Tijuana in 1994 and sees an untapped market, in addition to recognizing the historic popularity of baseball in northern Mexico going back decades. Two Mexican circuits, the Mexican League and the Pacific League, both feed players into the majors. When Tijauna's team in the Pacific League folds in 1992, a void develops which the Padres seek to fill with this "come on over" enticement scheme.

In order to expedite fans through the oftentimes-agonizing drive through San Ysidro, reportedly the world's busiest border crossing, the team invites Immigration and Naturalization Service Commissioner Doris Meissner to a meeting with local business officials in September 1995. Out of the meeting emerges a plan to keep border crossing waits to less than 20 minutes. Then the team develops its bussing program and stadium welcoming efforts.

Seeking an additional connection to the Tijuana community, the team opens a Padres store in a mall in the city, replete with local musicians and folk dancers. The families of Tijuana players on opposing teams visiting Padres Stadium are given free tickets to the games. As more Mexicans spend their days at the ballpark, TV Azteca, one of the major Mexican networks with a station in Tijuana, begins broadcasting the Sunday games in January of 1997. Tijuana radio station XEXX-AM acquires the radio rights to the Padres games and resells them to eight Mexican stations.

In 1996, the Padres and New York Mets play what is called the first American big-league series held outside the U.S. and Canada. The three-day event is held in Monterrey, home to Mexico's Baseball Hall of Fame. Padres lefthander Fernando Valenzuela, who is from Mexico, is on the mound for the first game. After 10 years with the Los Angeles Dodgers, who release him in 1991 following injuries and a declining winning record, he winds up playing for Anaheim, Baltimore, Philadelphia, San Diego in 1995, and St. Louis before ending his career in 1997.

With the Dodgers starting in 1981, he creates "Fernandomania" by throwing five shutouts in his first eight games to become the first player to win both the Rookie of the Year and the prestigious Cy Young awards in the same year, and lead the team to the World Series title. When Fernando and his transported "Fernandomania" fan frenzy arrives in San Diego, upwards of 20 Mexican radio stations sign up to carry the games and follow the exploits of their hometown favorite.

Articles

"Fernandez Exits KTLA 'Morning.'" Daily Variety, Aug. 6, 2003

"L.A. County Leads U.S. In Numbers Of Latinos, Asians." Los Angeles Times, Sept. 19, 1998

"Ready For Drive-Time Players." Los Angeles Times, Dec. 14, 1997

"An Experiment In Unity." Los Angeles Times, Dec. 12, 1997

"TCI Preps Package Of Spanish-Lingo Nets." Daily Variety, Dec. 11, 1997

"Sony-Led Venture Wins Bidding For Telemundo." Daily Variety, Nov. 25, 1997

"Telemundo Agrees To Be Acquired By Sony, Liberty." Los Angeles Times, Nov. 25, 1997

"All-News Is News." Los Angeles Times, Nov. 20, 1997

"A Spanish-Language TV Network Tries Bilingualism." Los Angeles Times, Nov. 8, 1997

"Station goes 24-Hour With Latin Music." Electronic Media, Oct. 20, 1997

"Talking Sports En Español." Los Angeles Times, Oct. 16, 1997

"En Español Por Favor." Gavin GM, October 1997

"L.A.'s Spanish Media Face New Latino Reality." Los Angeles Times, Aug. 21, 1997

"Catch A Flame: The U.S. Generates Its Own Rock En Español Movement." Pulse! August 1997

"Conversation, Not Corridos." Los Angeles Times, Aug. 21, 1997

"Vying For New York Stories, For Beguiling Announcer And, Yes, For People's Trust." New York Times Television Guide, Aug. 17, 1997

"Ch. 41's Good News." New York Post, Aug. 8, 1997

"Spanish Signal Grows Louder." San Francisco Examiner, July 22, 1997

"Race In America." Los Angeles Times, July 20, 1997

"Telemundo, KVEA-TV Will Revamp Nighttime Schedule." Los Angeles Times, July 19, 1997

"'Today' Gets Bilingual Assist In N.Y. Sweeps." Weekly Variety, June 23, 1997

"Latino Buying Power Surging, Study Finds." Los Angeles Times, June 19, 1997

"Feeling The Heat With Los Van Van." Los Angeles Times, June 16, 1997

"Latino Artists Pack 'Em In." Los Angeles Times, June 12, 1997

"The Talk Of L.A. En Español." Los Angeles Times, June 5, 1997

"Pitch To Fans In Mexico Pays Off For Padres." Los Angeles Times, May 27, 1997

"The Second Wave." Los Angeles Times, May 15, 1997

"The Rising Language Of Latino Media: English." Los Angeles Times, May 4, 1997

"A Good-Humored Change." Los Angeles Times, May 1, 1997

"Hispanic Group Aims Ire At Disney." Daily Variety, April 30, 1997

"Changes In Law Lead To 27% Hike In Legal Immigration." Los Angeles Times, April 23, 1997

"Central American Outlet." Los Angeles Times, April 8, 1997

"Rock En Español In Demand." Los Angeles Times, April 3, 1997

"Salsa Hot Spot." Los Angeles Times, March 27, 1997

"A Positive Immigrant Portrait." Los Angeles Times, March 27, 1997

"Greek Theatre 1997 Schedule." Los Angeles Times, March 23, 1997

"Universal Amphitheatre 25th Anniversary Schedule." Los Angeles Times, March 20, 1997

"CNN, CBS Seek To Expand Hispanic Audience." Broadcasting & Cable, March 19, 1997

"More Stations Say Adios To English." Los Angeles Times, March 17, 1997

"In The Game At Last." Los Angeles Times, March 16, 1997

"¡Basta Con Los Adultos Contemporaneos!" Los Angeles Times, Feb. 3, 1997

"Univision Names Departing Housing Secretary Cisneros As President." Los Angeles Times, Jan 24, 1997

"Spanish Stronghold." Los Angeles Times, Jan. 7, 1997

Chapter 5
CAPITULO 5

Calm Before the Storm: 1998
LA CALMA ANTES DE LA TORMENTA: 1998

• While America's Anglo majority focuses inward on their lives, the nation's Hispanics are stretching their collective influences to become a 30.4 million strong minority, representing a $273 billion consumer spending treasure.

• Miami's strength grows as the nation's Latin entertainment capital for music and television.

• A number of new artists such as Ricky Martin, Marc Anthony, Luis Miguel, Juan Gabriel, and Enrique Iglesias strongly make their presence known.

• The Justice Department investigates charges of payola between the Fonovisa label and a number of Hispanic radio stations.

• Heftel Broadcasting becomes the nation's largest Spanish-language radio company.

• Telemundo and Univision switch their emphasis from acquiring programming from overseas sources to producing shows in the U.S.

• The ALMA (American Latino Media Arts) Awards are unveiled by the National Council of La Raza.

• The National Academy of Recording Arts & Sciences announces the formation of a separate Latin Recording Academy with plans for its own Latin Grammys by 2001.

• The Los Angeles area Latino market continues to lead the nation, with 6.3 million Hispanics, excluding undocumented aliens, spread throughout Orange, Ventura, San Bernardino, Kern, and Inyo Counties.

• The state of California, which sees its Latin population rise mercurially from 1970 to 1990 by 253 percent, from 2.1 million to 7.6 million, also sees the number of Latino-owned businesses grow by 787 percent between 1972 and 1992, according to a study by the Latin Business Association and the UCLA Center for the Study of Latino Health.

Los Angeles County is home to 4.4 million Hispanics and scores and scores of people who have snuck into the country from Mexico and neighboring Latin nations. Compare the L.A. figure to New York's 3.6 million Latinos and Miami's 1.4 million Hispanics, and you see why the battles among Hispanic entertainment companies for the hearts and dollars of Angelinos are becoming so hot and contentious. Los Angeles, which always plays second to New York, is now the biggest Hispanic market in the nation and the place where trends begin and then spread across the country, much in the manner trends within the general market have emerged here and morphed into acceptable tendencies in other parts of the country.

An entrepreneurial mood encompasses two regions in Southern California where the Hispanic population is settling: to the south of Los Angeles County in Riverside and San Bernardino Counties, where business growth is graphed at 124 and 125 percent, respectively. These locally owned companies become the advertising backbone for local Spanish radio and TV stations. Another happy indicator for Spanish entertainment companies is revealed by a federal government study into the nation's youth. There are 10.5 million Hispanic children under 18, the most of any minority group, a new source of consumers to be romanced, and an early indicator that Hispanics are on the road to becoming the nation's largest minority block—a feat they accomplish in 2003.

Despite its larger population, Los Angeles Hispanics have less money to spend that Hispanics in 25 other cities, reports Strategy Research, a major Latin marketing/research company whose study is sponsored by the U.S. Hispanic Chamber of Commerce, Spanish Broadcasting System, and the L.A. newspaper *La Opinion*, among others. Miami's Hispanics have the most annual buying power, \$10,777 compared to L.A.'s \$9,013 average. There's a simple reason for this, Strategy Research's David Thomas tells the *Los Angeles Times*. While Los Angeles has a more fractionalized Latino community, Miami is less structured, with the dominant exile Cuban community comprised of the upper class levels of society that fled the Castro revolution, bringing with them their style of living and whatever assets they could assemble. In other words, more money.

Money, of course, is at the core of Miami's growth as the center for the growing domestic Latin entertainment industry. While Miamians are well aware of the city's evolution into a Latin-populated city from its original destination as a vacation magnet for winter-logged East Coasters, Canadian "snowbirds," and the home-base for such domestic hit TV series as *The Jackie Gleason* show and *Miami Vice*, the south Florida community is fast becoming the home for Latin American music and television stars. Begun quietly five years or so ago, Miami is the gateway for membership in the domestic Latin show business community, with record companies and cable networks the first entities to drop anchor, including BMG, WEA, PolyGram, and the powerhouse independent label Fonovisa; the two main TV networks, Univision and Telemundo, and a number of cable networks, including MTV. Each broadcasts their Latin spin-off channels into the Caribbean and Latin America. There's also a great influx into tony South Miami Beach, which boasts its own entertainment row in refurbished buildings housing the Latin divisions of such music conglomerates as EMI, Sony, Universal, plus homegrown Estefan Enterprises and its Crescent Moon Records, owned by singer Gloria and her producer husband Emilio.

This burst of Latin action results in the growth of the production and support systems needed to feed the creative community, encompassing agents, managers, producers, press agents, music publishers, and recording studio operators. Miami's glistening star is even called the "Hollywood of Latin America" by Jeff Peel, director of the Miami-Dade (County) office of film entertainment, in the *Los Angeles Times*. The Latin entertainment industry is becoming a major cash cow for Dade County, worth $1.4 billion in 1996 alone, almost twice the amount for the previous year, according to the newspaper.

Of the Miami-based companies, one, Telemundo, placed under bankruptcy protection in 1995 and purchased in August by Sony and Liberty Media for $539 million, has plans to become a dual coast operation, since Sony's motion picture and television program division are located in the Los Angeles area suburb of Culver City. The projection is for Los Angeles to become a show producing center for Hispanic TV. It's a wide-eyed projection with more promise than realism.

Sensing the exciting pulse of Miami, a major music trade show, the 33-year-old MIDEM, which gathers the world's music mavens to Cannes, France, each January, invades Miami with its MIDEM Latin America and Caribbean music conference in the city's convention center, bestowing respectability to the city's role as the gateway to Latin America, bolstered by Dade County's population being two-thirds Hispanic.

The growth of the nation's Hispanic population results in Latin record sales in 1998 rising 16 percent to $571 million, according to the Recording Industry Association of America, an optimistic indication that Latin records can exceed its current 4.1 percent apportion of the $13.7 billion domestic record sales. It's the fourth consecutive year of growth for the Latin music industry, despite the industry plague of piracy which takes its toll of legitimate record sales. Latin music videos are also on the rise, with a 62 percent spike in sales to $2.1 million from $1.3 million the previous year. Hilary Rosen, President/CEO of the RIAA, calls the growth rate for the Latin music industry "phenomenal."

So there's a lot of excitement during MIDEM's second appearance in Miami, as the trade show attracts artists and record labels from overseas and the U.S., engenders a hateful demonstration by members of the Cuban exile community and a bomb threat against the inclusion of Cuban musicians outside the convention center. It is the backdrop for an announcement by NARAS, the National Academy of Recording Arts & Sciences, the presenter of its annual televised Grammy Awards, to create a separate Latin Academy in Miami that will develop its own Latin Grammy telecast in 2001. The new show will feature a full slate of award categories to augment the small number of Latin accolades included in the English-language Grammy presentation.

Politics cannot be avoided. When Dade County fearfully cancels an opening night party at the last moment at a county-owned facility because of the inclusion at MIDEM of the Cuban musicians, Miami Beach provides the musical/political release by producing its own sunset beach party for attendees. During the protest by around 400 people sign label the cultural exchange "offensive."

Musically, the convention attracts some of Latin America's top acts who perform at various venues throughout the city. Immigration delays prevent two Cuban bands, Irakere and Charanga Rubalcaba, from teaming up with Compay Segundo, the 90-year-old singer with the Buena Vista Social Club. Once the clearances are given, the reunion takes place on stage. Afterward, according to a story in the *Los Angeles Times*, participant Chucho Valdés is quoted as saying it's "wonderful to be playing in Miami."

Among the talent performing around the city are Miami's Volumen Cero, Panama's Rubén Blades, Venezuela's Los Amigos Invisibles, Colombia's Los Aterciopelados, Brazil's Só Pra Contrariar, Cuba's Irakere, Chucho Valdés, Carlos Varela, and defector Paquito D'Rivera.

The sounds of Latin music continue to produce a fusion of styles, often far-reaching in their content, as they marry the electronic instruments of rock en Español with the softer sounds of the bolero, bossa nova, the flowing tempos of disco, even reflections of '70s rhythm and blues, English and a host of other dialects besides Spanish. The intended audience? The U.S. youth market, Spanish and English. This blending of cultural and musical influences is reflected in the attitudes of emerging artists who are stretching beyond the traditional Latin music confines. Acts like Spain's male vocalist Manú Chao, Venezuela's Los Amigos Invisible, and the ever-present Colombian band, Aterciopelados, are among the critic's favorite border breakers. Universal Records is so impressed by two rock en Español producers, Gustavo Santaolalla and Anibal Kerpel, that it signs their Surco label for distribution. The pair is the best-known within the Latin music industry for producing three albums by Mexican group Café Tacuba. Another of their bands, Mexican quartet Molotov makes its Los Angeles debut at the prestigious House of Blues on the Sunset Strip in L.A.

Argentinean-born Santaolalla is compared to producing legends George Martin and Phil Spector by Zach Horowitz, the president of the Universal Music Group. Among the groups being produced by the duo are Puerto Rican band Puya, which combines mambo, salsa, and heavy metal elements; Uruguayan band Peyote Asesino, and Argentinean groups Arbol and Beresuit Vergarabat. Two of these bands, Molotov and Tacuba, are in contention for best rock en Español Grammy, but lose out to Argentina's Los Fabulosos Cadillacs. By 2003, the Argentinean band ceases to exist and Vicentico, its former single-named lead singer, is working solo.

Santaolalla will subsequently work with superstar Juanes and move into movie music with partner Kerpel. In 2003, they will write the scores for two films, *The Motorcycle Diaries* and *21 Grams*.

In addition to Universal signing Puya, other mainstream companies join the signing fray. Capitol signs Mexico's Plastilina Mosh; Warner Bros. Records owned Luaka Bop label and releases Venezuela's Los Amigos Invisibles, while its Warner Music Latin America distributes Café Tacuba. Nearly half the tunes on Mosh's debut CD are in full or part English. And some of the production is by two Anglo producers, Rob Schnapf and Tom Rothrock, who have produced records by the best-selling Anglo act Beck as well as for artists on their own Bog Load Records. Universal is also going with half an English album for Puya. Hollywood Records, the Disney Company's rock label, expands into Latin with the signing of Nydia Rojas. Shanachie releases *Voices of Latin Women* as part of its *Holding Up Half the Sky* series. Scouring a 30-year period, the disc features La Lupe, Celia Cruz, Albita Rodriguez, Fefita La Grande, La India, Lola Beltrán, María Teresa Vera, Patricia Teheran, and the group Paracumbe.

One band, Los Amigos Invisibles, is even touring with two English-speaking bands as their opening act during the summer. It opens for Soul Coughing in the East and for Cornershop, an English band, in the West. The band follows the example of Fabulosos Cadillacs, which plays to large non-Spanish-speaking audiences during its junket through Cleveland and Minneapolis. Both bilingual-seeking bands are managed by Tomás Cookman, who thinks in terms of breakthroughs by having his bands play their brands of rock en Español before language diverse audiences.

Equally competing for their portion of the Latin pop market are a number of male singers, who combine fire with romance in their presentations, as they seek acceptance from both the Anglo and Spanish worlds. This is the year Ricky Martin, Luis Miguel, Juan Gabriel, Marc Anthony, Enrique Iglesias, Cristian, and Alejandro Fernández, are all starting to leave their footprints in the cement pathway to stardom.

For Martin, a member of Puerto Rico's hit teenybopper group Menudo from 1984 to 1989, this is the year he garners international headlines for performing his *La Copa De La Vida* hit during the closing ceremonies of the World Cup soccer championship in Paris. An estimated global audience of two billion people watches—and remembers—his performance. The single becomes No. 1 in Europe and the album, *Vuelve*, becomes a best seller in copious foreign nations. After he leaves the group, which peaks in popularity, he moves to New York where he begins acting, including a recurring role in the soap opera *General Hospital* from 1994 to 1995 and a key role for three months in the Broadway production of *Les Miserables* the next year, before eventually moving to his new home in Miami.

For Enrique Iglesias and Alejandro Fernández, sons of famed singers, Julio and Vicente, respectively, the challenge is to develop their own independent stardom away from their dads' success and fan base. For Marc Anthony, the timing seems right for the Nuyorican singer to record his first album in English, apart from his salsa image and reputation. Cristian, the son of soap opera actress Verónica Castro, is also recording in English. Luis Miguel, with his strong popularity in Latin and South America, keeps singing in Spanish despite the strong push by other singers to gain crossover appeal.

In an attempt to build audience for salsa music, which is starting to lose some of its luster, record labels try adding tinges of rap and overreaching studio arrangements. Despite this attempt to broaden the music's ingredients, artists keeping the genre authentic include jazzman Eddie Palmieri, who returns to his roots after 10 years, Celia Cruz (with a bolero compilation), Tony Vega, and Joe Arroyo. One fledgling salsa label, Ahi-Namá, draws attention for its Arte Mixto band, one of several it imports from Cuba.

On a sad note, Eddie Serrano, a member of one of the 1960s seminal Latin rhythm 'n' blues crossover pop groups, Cannibal and the Headhunters, dies in August from injuries suffered in a motorcycle accident in Los Angeles. The band scores national attention for its *Land of 1000 Dances* hit single in 1965, which results in the quartet from East Los Angeles' Ramona Gardens housing project opening for the Beatles' U.S. tour that year. After the original group disbands in late '68, it is reformed by one of the original members, Francisco "Little Cannibal" Garcia who leads it in the '70s and '80s. Serrano will take over the name in the '90s and lead the group, with none of the original performers, until his accident.

The television landscape is undergoing its own transformation. For the first time in its 29-year history, ABC Sports

Monday Night Football will provide a Spanish-language version of the contest on the secondary audio programming (SAP) channel of stereo TVs. The broadcast team gaining this distinction is play-by-play announcer Alvaro Martin and action analyst Roberto Abramowitz. ABC Sports executive vice president and general manager Brian McAndrews stresses the network is seeking a broader audience by using the SAP technology.

Troubled Telemundo unveils a dramatic turnaround programming schedule for the fall which involves sitcoms, game shows, and action dramas based on past Sony-owned TV series, but now in Spanish with Spanish actors and actresses. The company's new president Peter Tortorici (formerly president of CBS Entertainment from 1994 to 1995) stresses all its sitcoms and dramas, will, for the first time, be produced domestically. One of Telemundo's original primetime shows breaking new ground for Hispanic TV is *Solo En America*, a sitcom focusing on a divorced 34-year-old mother raising her two teenage daughters alone in New York City. The network's first original primetime drama is *Reyes Y Rey*, patterned after *Miami Vice*, but focuses on two cops, one Mexican, the other Mexican-American, working along the two nations' border.

The overhaul involves 75 percent of the network's programming and the retirement of 30-year-old movies which will be replaced by more current and library titles dubbed in Spanish like *La Bamba*, *Desperado*, and *Stand and Deliver*. Everything is designed for younger eyes and for bilingual U.S. Hispanics. The most controversial aspect of the Sony plan involves Columbia TriStar Television, the parent company's TV programming arm, which will create dubbed shows based on past year successes like *Starsky & Hutch*, *Charlie's Angels*, *One Day at a Time*, *Who's the Boss?*, *The Dating Game*, *The Newlywed Game*, and *Candid Camera*.

Sony also plans securing morning children's programming from Nickelodeon and documentaries from Discovery Communications for evenings. Telemundo currently reaches 85 percent of Hispanic households and hopes its new programming concept will attract more cable systems and additional viewers, principally young and bilingual.

While this all sounds spectacular for Telemundo, a number of Hispanic critics take aim at the new Telemundo and its programming concept. Of Telemundo's four-person executive team, only one is Hispanic: Nely Galán, Cuban-born president of programming. The other execs are Tortorici, the former CBS programmer, Rachael Wells, executive vice president for marketing, and Alan Sokol, the chief operating officer, who shifts over from Sony corporate development. This doesn't sit well with Alex Nogales, head of the National Hispanic Media Coalition, one of the most active Latino advocacy organizations. Nogales is concerned whether having three white executives at the helm of the network and only one Latina is the right balance and whether that lone Hispanic will have enough clout and insight to get her new programs on the air. There's also concern that redoing past American shows truly reflect the domestic Hispanic culture. And while Tortorici helps create several hit CBS shows, there's concern he'll have trouble with Spanish-language TV.

And while Telemundo plans to replace its imported shows with its remakes of U.S. programs, Galán admits it will take time to include English dialog with the Spanish. In a dig to imported shows from Latin America, she tells *New Times Los Angeles*, a weekly entertainment/political weekly, that the network's shows "will be about being Latino here and not about living vicariously through Latin America." And while she admits the concerns that other top executives are not bilingual are correct, she points to "300 people on staff who are also Latino."

Univision, which debuts in 1961, has two Miami-based superstars, *Cristina* talk show host Cristina Saralegui and the Mario Kreutzberger alter-ego "Don Francisco" hosted *Sabado Gigante* Saturday night variety show in which the audience sings along with the commercials. This year, the network reaches 92 percent of domestic Latin households and in its Miami hometown, WITV, is the market's top station from sign-on to sign-off, beating out

Telemundo and the Anglo network affiliates in the February and May rating periods. WITV also has the city's top early and late night local news.

Univision's primetime programming, stressing novelas, results in its stations in Los Angeles, Dallas, Houston, San Francisco, Fresno, and Phoenix also winding up No. 1 with 18- to 34 year-olds to beat out the ABC, CBS, NBC, and Fox affiliates. The network's three-hour morning show, *Despiert América*, launched a year earlier, is similar to the news/chat/entertainment shows like NBC's *Today* and ABC's *Good Morning America.* The show replaces a 10-year-old Mexican comedy series and doubles its morning ratings in New York, Miami, and Los Angeles.

While Univision's main program suppliers remain Mexico's Televisa and Venevision of Venezuela, the network launches its first effort to produce a greater percentage of its shows domestically, with two locally taped programs slated during a weekday mid-afternoon low spot preceding *Cristina*. The newcomers are game show *El Bla-Blazo* and celebrity magazine show *El Gordo Y La Flaca*. In an effort to bolster Friday and Sunday evenings, the network drops a low-rated music/variety series, *Al Ritmo De Fiesta*, and replaces it with a talent show and variety/game show from Televisa from 7–9 p.m.

In New York City, Univision's company-owned, 30-year-old station WXTV emerges as a power to be reckoned with. For the first time in broadcast history, for one day in May it rates higher than an English-language TV station from the moment it signs on to the time it ends the entire broadcast day, bolstered by a special Latin music special in addition to its regular programming. Ratings represent the percentage of a market's TV homes—in New York's case that's 6.75 million TV homes—while a share represents the percentage of sets in use.

The station also breaks through the Nielsen Company's May sweeps report, beating out all English-language stations in the 18- to 34-year-old category during the 6 p.m. and 6:30 p.m. newscasts. It also achieves a first-ever tie with WABC, the ABC-owned station, for first place among 18- to 49-year-olds at 6 p.m., with a 3.0 rating and a 14 share. But it dominates with males 25 to 54 between 6–7 p.m. During competition for the 6:30 p.m. network news audience, WXTV lands in second place with *Noticiero Univision* behind ABC's *World News Tonight*, with *NBC Nightly News* falling to third place and the *CBS Evening News* in fourth position.

In June, Univision's coverage of World Cup Soccer matches from June 10 through July 12 draws devotees to all the Univision stations, including WXTV. Ratings for soccer (as opposed to regular shows) rise sharply, up 90 percent for the early mornings and 75 percent from 11 a.m. to 1:30 p.m. Nationally, Univision chalks up a 9.7 rating for its broadcasting of 13 contests and puts ESPN's coverage on a lower scoring level, much to the chagrin of its ABC/Disney parents. For the total of 47 games Univision carries against either ESPN or ESPN2, it attracts a huge number of Hispanic households for contests pitting Mexico against Belgium and South Korea, Argentina versus England, Paraguay versus France, and anyone defending champion Brazil plays. This coverage achieves a 10.0 average rating. Ecstatic over the network's performance, Henry Cisneros, Univision's president, tells the *New York Times*: "It's amazing to get good ratings and beat ESPN." WXTV is the city's only local station to carry every World Cup match.

Soccer fans across the country can also tune in six-month-old Radio Unica's 17 hours of games, post-game analysis, and discussion show. While the Hialeah, Florida, network employs announcers in a studio reacting to the TV picture, it sends them overseas to report live from France. Univision's play-by-play announcer, Andres Cantor, enlivens his TV reporting with his famous long "gooooaaaalll" call. Unica's Jorge Ramos tends to be hyperactive all the time, with shorter goal calls, but there are more of them, accompanied by music from the scoring nation.

Riding a crest of viewership popularity, WXTV adds two local weekend newscasts on its birthday, August 4. Similar to its weekday news, *Noticias 41* also airs at 6 and 11 p.m. in the timeslots formerly held by the network's national weekend newscasts. Joining the station to work the half-hour weekend programs are co-anchors Adhemar Montagne (who'd been with the station in 1991 but left to join KMEX Los Angeles) and Arly Alfaro (who comes from Univision's Miami station WLTV). Sportscaster Salvador Cruz is doing double duty at local Spanish radio talk station WADO. Sol Sostre, the meteorologist, arrives from WIPR in San Juan. In 2003, Montagne jumps ship to join NY1 Noticias, New York City's first Spanish-language news channel as one of three anchor/producers.

In Los Angeles, Univision's KMEX adds a weather and entertainment reporter to its evening local news and news director Jairo Marin increases the number of stories during the half-hour newscasts by around one-third by cutting lengths or adding them to roundup reports. When two hurricanes, George and Mitch, belt the Caribbean and Latin America, weather is the station's major story, with meteorologist Francisco Javier Quiroz providing insight into this natural disaster.

This is the year that Spanish Broadcasting System's New York tropical music radio station, WSKQ-FM, becomes the most listened to Spanish station among the handful in the nation's number two Hispanic market behind Los Angeles. Its presence attracts fans of salsa and merengue music from the Puerto Rican and Dominican Republic communities to this pioneering Manhattan station, aided and abetted by modern techniques in programming, promotion, and marketing. This is the year that major advertisers take note of the clout of major market Hispanic stations playing to their ever-growing Latin populations. Even in secondary cities with growing Latino representation like Tucson, Arizona and Monterey, California, Spanish-language radio is building strong followings. One of several reasons for audience growth around the country is that when there is social unrest in a Latin nation, the U.S. is the target for immigration. This produces unexpected increases in population resulting in larger audiences for Latino media, but not necessarily an equal increase in advertising dollars as sundry marketers are still not savvy to the potential of Hispanic radio and television.

This is the year that Heftel Broadcasting, which buys two stations in L.A. from Liberman Broadcasting in 1986, KLVE-FM and KTNQ-AM, grows to 39 stations and becomes the nation's largest Spanish radio company. Along the way, the company makes history by placing Latinos in top management positions around the country, contrary to what has happened in the past in Spanish radio. When an Anglo company buys a Spanish station in the '80s, management usually shifts over white males with little or no expertise in Spanish to run the new acquisition. Heftel changes all that. In New York, David Martinez, born in Chicago but with Puerto Rican ancestry, runs WADO-AM and WNWK-FM; Pio Ferro, a Cuban American, and Maria Nava, a Mexican, are the program directors for KLVE and its latest purchase, KSCA, respectively, in L.A.; Jose Valle, a Cuban, runs KLSQ-AM in Las Vegas; and Claudia Puig, a Cuban, manages four Miami stations, WAMR-FM, WAQI-AM, WRTO-FM, and WQBA-FM. In 2002, I interview Puig during my research trip to Miami anent the complexity of overseeing four different formatted stations.

This is also the year that payola casts a dark shadow over Latin radio. Fonovisa, the record label owned by Mexican media conglomerate Grupo Televisa, is at the center of an emerging payola scandal. Payola is the illegal payment to radio stations to play music unless the broadcaster announces the sponsorship. Grupo Televisa admits its record division broke the federal law by making promotional payments and says it is cooperating with a federal investigation. The scheme reportedly involves kickbacks up to $10,000 a month being given to radio station program directors throughout the Southwest in exchange for playing certain Fonovision tunes, according to a *Los Angeles Times* story.

These songs air on Spanish stations for 30 straight weeks in 1997 and allow Fonovisa, the nation's largest Latin music label, to dominate the Hot Latin Tracks chart in *Billboard*. Among Fonovisa's artists who obtain No. 1 positions on the industry chart are Enrique Iglesias and Marco Antonio Solis. During the first five months of '97, Fonovisa discs control the top three chart positions, while also holding six of the top 10 positions on the survey, which is based on an electronic airplay sample of 97 radio stations. In October, Fonovisa's domination ends. It's also coincidentally the same month the label allegedly stops paying out cash to radio station programmers. Fonovisa specializes in such regional Mexican music styles as mariachi, banda, ranchera, and norteño.

In June, around two dozen stations reportedly receive subpoenas from the Justice Department to turn over payroll records going back to 1994 as well as other documents that could show illegal payment to program directors and other station officials, the *Los Angeles Times* reports. Eighteen independent record distributors are also supposedly subpoenaed for any documents relevant to the investigation, which begins in December when Fonovisa attorneys contact the Justice Department to reveal possible wrongdoing within its radio promotion operation. Radio station and record company employees are under scrutiny for payola, a misdemeanor, and tax evasion, a felony.

Los Angeles stations being studied include the market's three top stations, Heftel's KSCA-FM and KLVE-FM and Spanish Broadcasting System's KLAX-FM as well as EXCL Communication's KSSE-FM. Naturally, station managers are tight-lipped about discussing under-the-table payment and none want to be quoted by name. One station official who goes on the record in a second *Times* story is XPRS-AM's Teddy Fregoso, who admits payola is commonplace in Spanish radio. He cites one unnamed "program director who accepts payments to buy a Mercedes for his girlfriend," while "drugs were offered to deejays to play certain records." XPRS uses a legal "pay for play" policy in which cash is paid the station for playing certain records so long as an announcement is made on the air explaining the deal. Fregoso calls it a "legal alternative to payola."

The probe is the first major federal investigation in 12 years. It brings back strong memories of when I broke a major payola scandal in Los Angeles in 1964 in *Billboard* involving a number of top rock and rhythm 'n' blues stations and a very long list of very popular

DJs, plus program directors, record librarians, and station managers. The probe and legal action last nearly four years, draws a team of FCC investigators, an FCC law judge who holds closed door hearings which last five days and subsequently causes one major broadcasting company, Crowell-Collier, to get out of Top 40 radio and sell KFWB-AM, which subsequently becomes all-news.

Covering that story is one of my most difficult journalistic journeys. In the early days of the exposure, I receive death threats for myself and my children. Suddenly, being an entertainment journalist is not fun. I am probably the most hated reporter in L.A. I am ridiculed by top DJs who are named defendants in a civil lawsuit by an independent record promoter, Al Huskey, who charges he cannot get his records on the radio because several labels are paying off DJs in a number of ways. Huskey seeks $250,000 damages.

In the long run the FCC does nothing. Some of the DJs leave radio to go into TV to host game shows. Several stations change formats. The original lawsuit is dismissed for "lack of diligent prosecution" in 1967. The dismissal does not affect the FCC investigation, which holds hearings for another year.

And when this new scandal breaks I fully understand the defensive position the stations take. This same defensive attitude emerges in 2002 when the *Miami Herald* breaks a payola story and the Spanish radio industry goes into denial mode. I will encounter this defensiveness the next year when I talk to an executive from the Spanish Broadcasting System, whose New York market leading station, WSKQ, is mentioned in the story as being a haven for payola cash. The corporation denies the allegation and the New York executive refers to that official statement.

KLVE and KSCA, two of the L.A. stations under government scrutiny, nonetheless capture the first two places in Arbitron's fall '97 ratings. For KLVE it's the ninth quarter in a row the adult contemporary station has been No. 1. For KSCA, which switches from alternative rock last February to regional Mexican music, it's a slight jump in the ratings. For talk station KKHJ-AM, which is not listed among the market's top 25 stations, Alfredo Nájera's sex-laden program, *Alfredo Contigo*, reflects a growing trend within the last two years for Spanish stations to carbon copy Howard Stern's raunchy style. Nájera first appears on Heftel Broadcasting's KTNQ-AM in 1995 and leaves that station one year later for KKHJ when he refused to tone down the sexy banter. KSCA has its own off-the-wall morning personality, Renan Almendárez Coello, known as *El Cucuy* (The Bogeyman) who is also known to get sexy on the air with double entendres. While KSCA general manager Richard Heftel denies that Armendárez's material is obscene, the omnipresent National Hispanic Media Coalition says otherwise. Its national chair, Alex Nogales, calls what the two personalities do "filth radio" or "radio porqueria" in the Los Angeles alternative weekly *New Times*. The format allows listeners to call in and discuss their sexual encounters in specific terms, with the show host responding with equally graphic sexual exhortations. Sexual pressure aside, Coello's six-hour morning show, begun in 1997 on KSCA, is now being syndicated to Heftel stations KSOL-FM San Francisco, KZOL-FM San Jose, and KLSQ-AM Las Vegas.

The Coalition petitions the FCC to deny KKHJ's owner Liberman Broadcasting a renewal of its license, alleging the station airs obscene material "at all hours of the day and night," thus violating the FCC's rules against indecent programming. Nogales also claims Coello crosses the line of decency. After the Coalition's complaints, Najero's show is revamped to broadcast news and current events. He claims his previous format encompassed relationships directed at adults, according to *New Times*.

In one of those topsy-turvy conditions within the L.A. radio industry, KSCA overtakes sister Heftel station KLVE for the top slot in the Arbitron ratings for the first three months of the year. Reflecting the region's growing Latin population, English-language KCMG-FM, with its strong female Latin audience, rises from 25th to 14th place as it switches from dance music to R&B oldies.

In another instance of station hopping, Humberto Luna, KTNQ's zany morning man for more than 20 years and supposedly

Spanish radio's first $1 million personality, switches to rival KLAX. He apparently dislikes KTNQ's shift from regional Mexican to talk a few years ago and resents being passed over for the morning slot on sister station KSCA, which goes to Almendárez. At KLAX, Luna plays regional Mexican music interspersed with skits, jokes, and prank calls—all the elements of his KTNQ show.

In December, Radio Unica announces it is purchasing two stations in New York (WBAI and WJDM), KAHZ in Dallas, and KIDR in Phoenix from Children's Broadcasting Corp. for $29.3 million. They will be added to the network's owned and operated stations in Miami, Los Angeles, Houston, San Francisco, San Antonio, and Chicago. This newest transaction reinforces Radio Unica's position as the nation's top Latin radio network, broadcasting 24 hours of news, sports, and talk.

The National Council of La Raza unveils its newly named ALAMAs (American Latino Media Arts Awards). The major category winners include: *Selena*, the film, which wins four accolades: outstanding film, outstanding actor Edward James Olmos, outstanding actress Jennifer Lopez, and director Gregory Nava; Cameron Diaz for her role in the film *My Best Friend's Wedding;* Hector Elizondo for his role in the made-for-TV-film *Borrowed Hearts*; Evelina Fernandez for her role in the made-for TV film *Hollywood Confidential;* Elizabeth Pena for her role in the TV movie *Contagious;* Benjamin Bratt for his role in the TV series *Law and Order;* and Rita Moreno for her role in the TV series *Oz*.

Articles

"There's No Holding It Back Now." Los Angeles Times, Jan. 3, 1999

"Luna Takes A Morning Berth At KLAX." Los Angeles Times, Dec. 12, 1998

"Latino Businesses Surge In Southland." Los Angeles Times, Nov. 11, 1998

"Telemundo: Time For Plan B." Broadcasting & Cable, Nov. 8, 1998

"Radio Unica To Acquire 4 Stations." Los Angeles Times, Oct. 28, 1998

"Numero Uno." Los Angeles Times, Oct. 22, 1998

"Monday Night Spanish." Los Angeles Times, Oct. 22

"Vanilla TV." New Times Los Angeles, Oct. 22, 1998

"Two Top Spanish Stations Tie For No. 1 In Ratings." Los Angeles Times, Oct. 14, 1998

"It Doesn't Add Up." Los Angeles Times, Sept. 17, 1998

"Latin Music Wave Rolls Over Miami." Los Angeles Times Aug. 28, 1998

"Eddie Serrano: Revived 'Cannibal' Rock Band." Los Angeles Times, Aug. 27, 1998

"Latin America Looks To Miami, Not Hollywood, For Music, Film." Los Angeles Times, Aug. 26, 1998

"Ch. 41 Adding Its Own Weekend Newscasts." New York Post, Aug. 4, 1998

"Spanish-Language Radio Gains Market Share." Los Angeles Times, July 16, 1998

"Latino Children Outnumber Blacks In U.S." Los Angeles Times, July 15, 1998

"The Accent Is On The Future." Los Angeles Times, July 5, 1998

"Gooooaaaalll! Univision's Audience Takes Off." New York Times, July 3, 1998

"Local Stations Feel Inquiry's Impact." Los Angeles Times, July 2, 1998

"Latin Label's Cash Sharply Boosted Play." Los Angeles Times, June 24, 1998

"Spanish Station Delivers Strong Demos." Broadcasting & Cable, June 22, 1998

"Telemundo Changes Format To U.S.—Style Dramas, Sitcoms." Los Angeles Times, June 20, 1998

"World Cup: Alive And Kickin'." New York Post, June 18, 1998

"WNBC News Wins Late." Daily Variety, June 17, 1998

"Payola Probe Focuses On Latin Music Airplay." Los Angeles Times, June 4, 1998

"Radio En Español Makes Strides In U.S." Billboard, May 30, 1998

"Small Nielsen Coup For Hispanic Ch. 41." New York Daily News, May 18, 1998

"A Shake-Up At Top Of L.A. Radio." Los Angeles Times, April 22, 1998

"Really Southern Rock." Los Angeles Times, April 19, 1998

"Sales Of Latin Music Expand 16% In 1998 Despite Piracy." Daily Variety, March 12, 1998

"The Next Generation?" Los Angeles Times, Feb. 26, 1998

"Radio Porno." New Times Los Angeles, Jan. 22, 1998

"Spanish-Language Stations Capture No. 1 And 2 Spots." Los Angeles Times, Jan. 9, 1998

Chapter 6
CAPITULO 6

Crossover Explosion: 1999
CRUZANDO LA BARRERA DEL IDIOMA: 1999

• This is the year of the crossover explosion by a phalanx of Latin entertainers, names generally unknown to mainstream America, but who suddenly emerge into the spotlight of national media exposure and exploitation by Anglo record companies eager to feed the nation's insatiable hunger for new role models, especially since they have Hispanic last names.

• It's also the first time a Hispanic record official is charged with the federal crime of payola, admits his guilt in paying radio programmers for airplay for his Fonovisa artists and is fined $50,000.

• Jennifer Lopez, with a modicum of notoriety for her TV dancing and film work, parlays her performance in the *Selena* tribute movie into a recording career, which establishes her credentials in this field big time.

• The National Academy of Recording arts And Sciences, which presents the Grammy Awards, reveals plans for its separate Latin Grammy competition.

• Mainstream TV networks begin adding Spanish-language translations or English programming specifically for Hispanics.

• The Baltimore Orioles travel to Cuba to play its national baseball team in an exhibition, marking the first time a major league team is welcome in the island nation in 40 years. And for the second time in history, Major League Baseball opens its season outside the U.S. with the San Diego Padres playing the Colorado Rockies in Monterrey, Mexico. In 1998, the historic season's opener occurs in Tokyo and pits the New York Mets against the Chicago Cubs.

• While America has always swayed to the rhythms and styles of the amorphous Latin music industry, this year is different because there is a growing Hispanic population, now pegged at 31 million, excluding illegals, which provides the foundation upon which artists can build their fan base. In bringing their fractious musical styles into the equally fractious popular music world, these artists are turning Americans on to the nation's rich Hispanic heritage once again.

Artists led by Ricky Martin's headline-grabbing performance at the nationally televised Grammy Awards, on February 24, present a new face to Latin music's crossover invasion. In addition to possessing heat on stage, they all possess the three "S's": sizzling, sensual styles. These newly discovered performers by mainstream America include Marc Anthony, Jennifer Lopez, Shakira, Elvis Crespo, Jon Secada, Carlos Ponce, Enrique Iglesias, Christina Aguilera, India, Millie, Chayanne, Luis Miguel, and Rubén Blades. The politically active Blades, one of Panama's leading musical exports, calls crossover "a racist term for people who cannot accept the mixture" of styles and cultural ingredients that excite Latin music.

These artists seek the path to fame and largess already traversed by the likes of such pioneering crossover artists as: Xavier Cugat the rumba bandleader in 1934; Tito Guízar, one of the first Latino singers to star in films starting in 1938 through the '40s, hosts his own CBS radio network show, *Tito Guízar and His Guitar*, and makes Mexican folk music popular in the U.S., notably with his version of *Cielito Lindo*; Andy Russell, the vocalist who popularizes *Besame Mucho* in the mid-40s; Cuban bandleader/conga player Desi Arnaz and his *Babalu* Afro-Cuban chant, first popularized in films in the '40s and then rekindled in the '50s during his co-starring role with wife Lucille Ball Arnaz in the TV hit series *I Love Lucy*: Pérez Prado and his string of mambo hits, starting with *Mambo No. 5* on RCA in 1949; Pete Seeger and then the Sandpipers with their versions of the Cuban tune *Guantanamera* in the 1960s; Eydie Gorme with her 1963 hit single, *Blame It on the Bossa Nova*.

Also: Tito Puente with his blending of Afro-Cuban rhythms with jazz improvisations in 1949 and his *Oye Como Va* composed breakout hit in 1963; Ritchie (Valenzuela) Valens with his marriage of Mexican music and rock rhythms in his 1959 hit *La Bamba*; Herb Alpert and the ersatz Tijuana Brass and Julius Wechter and the Baja Marimba Band in the '60s; Vikki Carr with her 1960's smash Liberty single and album *It Must Be Him*; Joe Bataan with his Latin soul hits *Gypsy Woman* and *Subway Joe* and Joe Cuba's equally Latin and R&B-ish *Bang Bang* in the mid-'60s; Jose Feliciano and his 1968 breakout vocal single smash *Light My Fire* from his hit RCA album *California Dreamin'*; Carlos Santana with his blazing electronic guitar riffs over Latin tempos and rock rhythms in 1969 and his hit version of *Oye Como Va* in the 1970s.

And: Los Lobos, the East Los Angeles band formed in 1973 by fusing its Spanish-language Chicano heritage with rock and rhythm 'n' blues, and then performing the title tune in the 1987 film *La Bamba*; Julio Iglesias with his smooth romantic love ballads aimed at American women in 1984; Gloria Estefan with her marriage of salsa tempos, heavy Latin rhythm instrumentation which provide the undercoating for her hit English and Spanish language recordings starting in 1985 with *Conga*; and Linda Ronstadt, a female rock superstar of the '70s, who tributes her Mexican heritage by doing an album with Nelson Riddle, *Canciones De Mi Padre*, in 1987, followed by another album of Mexican music in the '90s.

Ricky Martin's blending of sexual hip swagger, his handsome demeanor, and a spectacular performance of his hit single, *Livin' La Vida Loca*, all help ignite his Grammy performance. But how does he get to be on the program in the first place? It doesn't happen by any quirk or accident. I find out the answers by speaking with Ken Ehrlich, the veteran TV music specials producer, who annually produces the Grammy telecast and has done other Latin-oriented TV shows, including a two-hour pre-Super Bowl show from Miami featuring Gloria Estefan, Linda Ronstadt, and Carlos Santana as well as the Desi and ALMA Awards, formally known as the American Latino Media Arts Awards.

"America didn't know who Ricky was," Ehrlich says from the Encino, California, offices of his Ken Ehrlich Productions, despite his acting as the long-haired Miguel in the ABC soap, *General Hospital*, from 1994 to 1996 and as Marius in the '96 Broadway musical, *Les Miserables*. "There is some disagreement about how his booking happened. I recall Michael Greene (the president of the National Academy of Recording Arts and Sciences) being the first person to mention Ricky to me. I had been following his career by watching his Sony album sales on the Billboard international charts and seeing how popular he was overseas. Sony was hyping him to me about the time his first English album was coming out. It was a real priority for the label and Sony executives Tommy Mottola (chairman/chief executive of the Sony Music Entertainment), Don Ienner (chairman/president of Columbia Records), and (PR chieftain) Larry Jenkins made sure I was aware of him. America certainly wasn't. Tommy wanted me to talk to Ricky and meet his manager. Tommy was really the visionary because the old war horses were not selling a lot of CDs and Sony was looking for a new niche to get into, even though it was still the biggest label group. He had a vision that Latin could break big for an Anglo audience.

"So I took a trip to Miami and met with Ricky and Angelo Medina, his manager. They played some songs for me from a Spanish-language album and some footage from the video of his performance of *La Copa De La Vida* at the World Soccer Cup the previous year before 100,000 people. He held the stage and was electric. The Grammys were not known for taking chances; it was a reasonably safe show, and I felt safe booking Ricky. Ricky was a home run, there was charisma and a great arrangement for his song. As I recall the press didn't pick up on the fact he was performing on the show. After the show, they all wrote about how spectacular his performance was as well as calling the staging with rope dancers and stilt walkers a 'spectacle.'

"Because of the fact he was under-promoted, nobody expected to see what happened. It was a shock to the audience. During his performance we showed Sting screaming and yelling at him. After the performance, we did interviews with various artists and their response vindicated his performance. In three-and-a-half minutes he went from a not well-known international star in the U.S. to an overnight sensation, even though he'd been working 15 years with Menudo. There's no question his moment was the highlight of the Grammys. Ricky's was a defining moment and I really feel he helped create the pathway for Marc Anthony and Jennifer Lopez. The next morning I got phone calls from the record company executives wondering why they weren't in this market.

"Following the Grammys we did a special with Ricky for CBS. We also did a Thanksgiving weekend special with Ricky, Shania Twain, and Celine Dion. Ricky performed from Liberty State Park in New Jersey with the World Trade Center twin towers and the New York City skyline as the backdrop. He just nailed the crowd."

In 2004, Ehrlich celebrates his 25th year with the CBS broadcast as well as working the first two telecasts of the new Latin Grammy spin-off and co-producing and co-writing the 2003 event for CBS from Miami—a city who's vitriolic Cuban exile community forced the first Latin Grammys the previous year to leave Miami due to pressure against including Cuban musicians on the telecast. Ehrlich will tell me he'll be "walking a fine line" (the next time), and while he doesn't want to offend anyone, the show principals say "they will recognize all achievements in music."

In the years to come, after the media hype has moved on to the next flavor of the month topic, the doors of acceptance will close somewhat, leaving many of these artists out of the national spotlight and competing for their palpable images and egos with the onslaught of other artists seeking a beachhead in the all-inclusive mainstream music business. After 1999, other Hispanic entertainers will seek breakout status in music, films, and television with a modicum of success, but they lack the exaltation of the faddish frenzy seen this year, when crossover Latino artists are prominently featured in national publications from *Newsweek* to *Time* to the *Wall Street Journal* to *Billboard* and beyond into major city newspapers.

It's not just the English-language Latin pop crossover community that is invading America—other genres are percolating and hoping for cross-culturalization. Latin rockers combing rap, heavy electric guitar patterns, and often times politically cutting lyrics are a growing factor to be reckoned with, led by such bands as Puerto Rico's Puya, Mexico's Molotov, and Argentina's Beresuit Vergarabat. There's also a spawning rock-rap en Español genre fueled by such groups as Mexico's El Gran Silencio and Control Machete, and Argentina's Valderramas and Illya Kuryaki. American labels are additionally looking at a fusion between R&B and Latin, opening a new avenue for cross-promoting artists on radio. The audience they are going after are not fans of Ricky Martin, per se.

In one of the first Latin/R&B fusions, the Interscope label, releases *Your Eyes*, the debut single by Elsie Muniz, in both English and Spanish, and markets her as the "Queen of Latin R&B." While there's always been a close affinity between Latin and black music, the current motivation is for English- and Spanish-speaking stars to create commercial, contemporary Latin/R&B connections. Motown star Smokey Robinson, for example, has a Latin/R&B cut, *Tu Me Besas Muy Rico*, on his *Intimate* album. The single's title is certainly enticing enough: *You Kiss Me So Good.*

Two younger top acts, Sean "Puffy" Combs and Cypress Hill, enter the fray: Combs with a Spanish remix of the single *P.E. 2000* and Cypress Hill with 13 redone tunes in Spanish for its album, *Los Grandes Exitos en Español.* And LaFace Records signs Joy Enriquez, its first Latin/R&B vocalist, whose debut single is *Shake Up the Party.*

Salsa music, a mainstay along the East Coast, is undergoing a whole lot of shakin' as this tropical warm wind shows ineluctable downward signs of cooling and mellowing. In Puerto Rico, the creative pulse for salsa, something seems to be missing. Musicians are undergoing a self-examination as how to best retain the island's musical heritage and strengthen the use within groups of local rhythms like plenas and bombas. Victor Manuelle is Puerto Rico's superstar salsa sonero style singer and an obvious top seller for Sony Tropical, a wing of Sony Discos, who easily sells out Puerto Rico's largest indoor venue, the Roberto Clemente Coliseum. Since debuting in 1994, he's had 18 singles on *Billboard*'s best-selling tropical chart, of which eight hit No. 1, and 13 on the Latin pop chart. Along the way he's recorded duets with label mates Melina León and Elvis Crespo. Three of his albums also hit the top Latin album chart while achieving sales of 400,000 copies apiece.

Heading in an opposite direction from salsa stars aiming for the crossover market is New York Anglo singer George Lamond, whose music in Spanish is geared toward a dance market that likes its salsa laced with spicy soul. Lamond's debut Prestigio/Sony single, *Que Te Vas*, is a national tropical hit on the mainland and in Puerto Rico. Lamond boasts about being part of the "Puerto Rican Brat Pack," comprised of former pop disco artists like himself and Frankie Negron (who appears in *The Capeman* on Broadway), India (salsa's top female artist since 1992), Safire, and Huey Dunbar, lead singer for salsa/hip-hop band Dark Latin Groove (DLG). Lamond, whose real name is George Garcia, is asked to drop the Spanish surname by two independent record producers before releasing his debut English-language dance single *Bad of the Heart* in 1988. The album sells 200,000 copies and remains his top seller even after signing with Columbia and releasing three albums. Marc Anthony, salsa's top male singer since 1993, is now focused on a crossover career.

So what's the best way to gain crossover credibility, find recondite Spanish acts that can sing in English, or English acts that can meld their styles with a Latin gusto? Apparently both ways.

One of Latin music's leading producers, Rudy Pérez, an industry favorite in Miami, feels the Anglo market has awakened to the potential of Latinos recording English hits. There is one rub:

artists recording for major labels who want only to perform in English have to maintain their Spanish alter egos. Christina Aguilera, for example, cuts two versions of her RCA single, *Genie in a Bottle* and *Genio Atrapado.*

Running parallel with these movements remains the often coruscating yet underreported and unappreciated Spanish-language industry, which nonetheless helps expand the current Latin music explosion. This year, an impressive number score gold RIAA certifications for their albums, indicating 500,000 copies sold, including Los Angeles Azules, Los Tigres Del Norte, Elvis Crespo, Alejandro Fernández, Bronco, Marco Antonio Solís, and Conjunto Primavera. One act, Charlie Zaa, achieves platinum status for one million copies. What's significant about the transcultural Spanish-language industry is its devotion to recording music for the parents of the kids buying the flash of the younger bilingual crossover performers. Included in this older age bracket are adults who purchase the *Buena Vista Social Club* album performed by an assembled array of older Cuban musicians who revitalize a collection of pre-Castro revolution songs, for which nearly 500,000 copies are sold in the U.S.

It is a collage of Anglos and bilingual Hispanics who help break Ricky Martin into the mainstream market. These bilingual Hispanics—sometimes known as the Latin Gen Ñ version of the Gen X generation—are among the 45 percent of domestic Hispanics residing in Los Angeles, New York, Miami, San Francisco, San Jose, and Chicago. The largest Latino populations are in California, Arizona, New Mexico, New York, New Jersey, Florida, Illinois, and Colorado.

New York City is especially important in light of the changing nature of its Hispanic community. Within the city's collage of Latino communities, Mexicans are now its third largest Hispanic group, trailing Puerto Ricans and Dominicans. It's a strange phenomenon for New York, which until the early '80s has very little Mexican representation. The migration can be traced as far back as 1943, when several residents of the inland state of Puebla visit New York City and discover an open job market caused by World War II. Word spreads back and scores of Puebla residents move north to New York. Over the years, residents from neighboring states of Oaxaca and Guerrero, part of the Mixteca region, also head for work in New York.

With Mexico's financial downfall in the '80s and the peso's devaluation in 1994, the flow of residents from Mixteca continues to New York, one of the nation's remaining hallmark cities that hasn't experienced a major influx of Mexican immigrants.

In 1990, around 55,698 undocumented Mexicans are estimated to have arrived unheeded and begin the Mexicanization of New York City, which unlike California, is not sensitized to the escalation of undocumented Mexicans slipping into the country. By 1998, the number of illegals in New York City escalates to around 306,283, according to City University of New York sociologist John Mollenkopf. They reside in all five boroughs of the city, creating a powerful listening and viewing block for the two Spanish TV networks and New York's Latin radio stations. They also position New York sixth among cities with large Mexican populations, behind Los Angeles, Chicago, Houston, San Francisco, and Dallas/Fort Worth, according to the U.S. Census.

In the '90s, the city's Mexican population triples, according to Robert Smith, a Barnard College sociologist. For the 2000 Census, Smith will estimate the city's Mexican population, documented and undocumented, as approaching 300,000. Nevertheless, within 15 years, Mexicans are predicted to become the city's dominant Hispanic populace, ahead of Puerto Rico and the Dominican Republic. They are also taking root in the previously untapped South.

In one example of growth, in Dalton, Georgia, the "carpet capital of the world" located in the northern part of the Peach State, newly arrived Latinos, primarily from Mexico, account for one-third of the city's 22,000 population. WDAL, the city's first and only Spanish radio station, plays regional Mexican music and competes with three Hispanic newspapers for local Hispanic business advertising. Overall, Latinos comprise just three percent of the state's population. It will grow in the years to come.

The U.S. Census now predicts that by 2005, Latinos will overtake blacks as the leading minority and by 2050 they will represent around one-quarter of the nation's population. With one-third of the population under 18, there's a booming new audience ready for romancing and star-gazing.

With memories of Ricky Martin's catchy, exulted phrase, *olé, olé, olé* from his hit single, *Livin' La Vida Loca* still resounding after the Grammys on a broad spectrum of radio formats on English and Spanish radio, his self-titled first all-English album released in May tops the five million sales mark, to become the best-selling album by a Latin artist. Martin's 1997 album release, *Vuelve*, his fifth as a solo performer after leaving Menudo, falls far short of the record-setting *Ricky Martin* title, but does gain a sales boost because of the Grammy notoriety.

The expansive romance with Latin music also impacts seven Spanish-speaking artists, the largest number up to this point, who wind up with awards from the RIAA, the Recording Industry Association of America. These performers include Alejandro Fernandez, Elvis Crespo, and Jennifer Lopez, all platinum recipients for sales of one million copies, and these gold plaque winners: Conjuncto Primavera, Los Tigres Del Norte, Marco Antonio Solís, and Los Bukis. Overall, sales of Latin discs for the first half of the year are up 11 percent, while English-language record sales are flat for the same period, notes the RIAA. Latin records, which must be 51 percent Spanish-language in order to be called Latin music, represent 4.9 percent of total U.S. sales, up from 4.5 percent during the same half-year in '98. Propelling the sales of Latin records are two obvious names, Ricky Martin and Jennifer Lopez, and a sadly macabre Selena, whose EMI Latin compilation, *All My Hits—Todos Mis Exitos*, accounts for eight percent of the sales increase. Selena has been dead four years, but her catalog continues to sizzle and sell.

The growing popularity, and familiarity for Latin artists in this country, can be compared to building a house brick by brick. Colombia's Shakira, one of the newly emerging sex sirens, credits Emilio Estefan, Jr. and wife Gloria for their trailblazing efforts in opening paths to the broader crossover market for herself and other aspiring artists. EMI Latin's president José Behar, takes the process one step further in his reflections in *Billboard*: "Gloria helped pave the way for Selena who helped pave the way for Ricky." Executive Estefan believes the crossover currents flow more freely today because the public is open to new sounds.

Jennifer Lopez is an anonymous member of the Fox TV comedy series *In Living Color*'s Fly Girl dance group. While she's also featured in two films, *U Turn* and *Out of Sight*, her big break comes when she is cast by director Gregory Nava to portray Selena in the 1997 film. Although Lopez will sing during the actual filmed scenes, Selena's voice is heard during all the musical sequences. But the experience prompts Lopez to break into music with the debut in October of her bilingual Sony album, *On the 6*, whose rhythms reflect her Puerto Rican ancestry and Bronx, New York, upbringing. She calls it "Latin soul." The number 6 is the train she rides for 40 minutes from her neighborhood into Manhattan. A single, *If You Had My Love*, sells more than one million copies and adds to her notoriety. Her popularity and beauty will lead her to the open pockets of movie moguls who help her ascend to super superstardom within a few years.

Finding the next crossover star is the chief concern for a record number of 337 American record companies (out of 818 registered in Miami) for the third annual Latin music conference sponsored by the Paris-based MIDEM organization. Originally called the MIDEM Latin America & Caribbean Music Market, the organizers change the name this year to MIDEM Americas to reflect the growth of Latin music in the U.S. and the concomitant impact of domestic rock and rap in Latin America. MIDEM is important this year for a number of other reasons.

The National Academy of Recording Arts & Sciences (NARAS), which presents the Grammy Awards, uses the event to formally announce the creation of a separate Latin Grammy Awards ceremony, nine months after the formation of the Latin Academy of Recording Arts & Science (LARAS), which will handle the spin-off award. One month after the Latin Grammy announcement, NARAS is jolted by the resignation of Sergio Rozenblat, LARAS' first president. No official reason is given for his resignation, although the departure is reported to be a mutual decision with Michael Greene, president/CEO of the parent NARAS.

Among MIDEM's varied panel discussions, the Internet sparks serious concern as a source for downloading and distributing Latin records without paying for them. Rock en Español is provided a major boost in a showcase sponsored by MTV Latin America, which features Los Angeles' hard to define Mexican-Asian rock band Ozomatli, Mexico's Control Machete, Puerto Rico's El Manjar De Los Dioses, and Argentina's Beresuit.

The event sponsors 18 concerts throughout Miami Beach, with a stress on the impact of black music in the Americas. This is especially paradoxical since black Latinos, who are concentrated in the Caribbean (including Cuba), Colombia, and Brazil, are non-existent on the rosters of the major domestic Latin labels, but are finding homes on small, independent labels. The lack of regional Mexican artists in the talent showcases involving 300 performers is underscored even though this is the leading sales genre within the spectrum of Latin music styles. The four-day event is expected to pump $20 million into Miami's economy, long a bastion of resistance to both Cuban artists and regional Mexican music.

The event's artistic director, Dominique Leguern, who programs all the concerts, indicates the lack of Mexican artists is due to her belief that they are not popular, an astonishing revelation by an official who should know better. Christophe Blum, MIDEM America's director, is a bit savvier when he acknowledges that the increased attendance by U.S. labels is due to the crossover successes of the highly publicized American bilingual artists Ricky Martin, Marc

Anthony, and Jennifer Lopez. Cuban-born Jon Secada, who grew up in Miami and records in Spanish and English, admonishes the audience at the "Crossing Borders" panel that domestic Latin labels should not automatically expect U.S. born Latins to want to record in Spanish.

On the other hand, Universal Music Group's reported record $40 million signing of Enrique Iglesias to its Interscope label indicates to panel member KC Porter, a songwriter/producer, that the crossover pop market welcomes Latin artists. Iglesias, who formerly sings for Fonovisa, will record in English for Interscope and in Spanish for Universal Latin.

The fusion of Afro-Caribbean music with R&B and rap by black Latinos opens a new avenue for expression, with New York's three-year-old H.O.L.A. Records, among the independents seeking its mainstream market breakthrough artist from among its roster. Among these labels, Reign combines Spanglish with R&B and reggae, Proyecto Uno blends merengue with rap, and among its artist, D'Mingo is a salsa vocalist, Veronica, a Puerto Rican R&B singer, and the Voices of Theory, a Philadelphia group which has the distinction of opening for Mariah Carey.

While Cutting Records from New York promotes Fulanito, which pairs rap with merengue played on the accordion from the Dominican Republic, Putumayo Records from San Francisco pushes the Congolese Cuban music of the band Makina Loca, led by Ricardo Lemvo. Lemvo, who was born in Kinsasha, Zaire, and lives in L.A., tells the *Los Angeles Times* of his pleasure that "young Latinos are finally embracing their African heritage." In subsequent years I will chat with a New York black Puerto Rican about the difficulties he and other black Latins encounter in their lives.

Unlike last year's MIDEM, at which around 400 Cuban exiles protest the appearances by several Cuban artists, this year a small handful of exiles show up one night to protest an appearance by singer Elio Revé, Jr. Upward of 300 Cuban Americans attend the singer's concert. NARAS, on the other hand, is being confronted by the anti-Castro movement, which is bolstered by a Dade County ordinance disallowing the city of Miami from contracting with any group which does business with Cuba. Michael Greene, NARAS' president/CEO, stresses that NARAS and its Grammy Awards are nonpolitical, and while he understands the feelings of the anti-Castro community, he requests the exiles not to "punish musicians" for the misdeeds of President Fidel Castro.

Spokesperson Ninoska Perez of the exile organization, the Cuban American National Foundation, which supports the rule, tells the *Los Angeles Times* that the First Amendment gives the organization the right to protest concerts by Cuban artists. "These types of cultural exchanges are not really cultural exchanges," she opines, "because the Cuban government gets to pick who goes in and out of Cuba." Pressure from the anti-Castro hardliners, supported by Miami officials, and Miami's vitriolic Spanish-language news/talk radio stations, forces Cuba's top dance band, Los Van Van, to cancel its Miami debut in October. This kind of political pressure and clout will force the neophyte Latin Grammys to abandon Miami in favor of Los Angeles.

Following concerns by Latin record labels that their sales are being undercounted by SoundScan, a company which receives sales figures from major chain retailers, including Latin leader Ritmo Latino, the RIAA conducts its first-ever study into the buying patterns of domestic Hispanics. It discovers the record companies are correct; SoundScan does not obtain sales figures from small community mom and pop record stores or outlets without electronic cash registers. Among the label presidents complaining is George Zamora, head of WEA Latina in Miami. He claims SoundScan is shy half of his pop sales, 70 percent of his tropical sales and 85 percent of his regional Mexican music tallies. More embarrassing are the figures for its superstar rock en Español group, Maná. The label claims 900,000 copies of its last album; SoundScan reports 300,000 sales.

The musical tastes of young and older U.S. Hispanics reveal 14- to 29-year-olds have an open-minded attitude about all types of music, while 30- to 54-year-olds are loyal to radio and feel music is a vital element in their lives. While these older people enjoy listening to music in Spanish and English, 65 percent of the 900 phone interviews in New York City, Los Angeles, Miami, Houston, Phoenix, Chicago, and San Francisco, conducted by the Market Segment Group of Miami, favor Spanish music on the radio, while 20 percent favor English-language easy listening, and 20 percent favor rap.

Sony, whose English and Spanish label rosters include Martin, Anthony, Lopez, Fernandez, and Crespo, among the recent RIAA winners, is also home to Shakira, Julio Iglesias, and Gloria Estefan. Tommy Mottola, head of Sony Music Entertainment, who helps market Gloria Estefan and Julio Iglesias to the fledgling crossover market during the past decade, acknowledges in *Billboard* that "Ricky's Grammy performance set the world on fire." In the '90s, Mottola will help boost the career of Mariah Carey, who he will marry and later divorce. In 2003, after leaving Sony, he'll marry another Latin songbird, Thalía, who records for EMI Latin.

For New Yorker Anthony, who gains fan acceptance in the Hispanic world for his tropical/salsa albums over a five-year span on Sony Discos, he debuts this year on Columbia with an English-language CD. It's a priority project for Columbia, which believes the eponymous LP, with its salsa ingredients, will retain his Latino fans while snaring enough English and Spanish buyers to reach crossover nirvana. The first single from this 1999 Grammy best tropical performance winner is *I Need to Know*, which will become his new, familiar calling card with English and Spanish versions.

His latest appearance in the Martin Scorsese film, *Bringing Out the Dead*, provides Columbia with an additional promotional element. He's also acted in three other movies: *Hackers*, *Big Night*, and *The Substitute*. A co-leading role with Rubén Blades in Paul Simon's Broadway debut crime musical, *The Capeman*, fails at the box office and does nothing to further Anthony's career as a stage actor.

One act that keeps on romping year after year for 20 years is Los Lobos, one of the pacesetting bands from L.A.'s East Los Angeles Mexican neighborhood, which keeps inventing itself as time passes, all to the delight of fans who appreciate its rambunctious forays into TexMex, blues, and rock. Whether playing at New York's Bowery Ballroom or at L.A.'s Greek Theatre, or at venues in between, the sextet, built around four graduates of Garfield High School, begins life in 1973 as Los Lobos Del Este De Los Angeles, trims it name when it starts recording in 1983, and remains true to its core Mexican roots. In addition to singing and playing regular guitar, David Hidalgo plays a button accordion while Cesar Rosas attacks the 12-string bajo sexto guitar and Victor Bisetti provides propulsion on timbales and drums. The band split from Warner Bros. Records 1998 after 13 years and this year joins Hollywood Records, which releases its newest album, *This Time*.

A second band, equally hard to define is Ozomatli, which also causes heads to turn because its music mirrors its 10 members of Mexican, Cuban African, European, and Japanese descent. Its debut album is released by Almo Sounds in 1998, a label owned by Herb Alpert and Jerry Moss, the co-founders of phenomenally successful '60s and '70s A&M Records. It showcases a mixture of Latin, rap, electric, and eclectic rhythms. While it's been called the future of Latin pop, Latin radio eschews the band's multi-cultural music because it doesn't easily fit into any formal format category. So it resorts to touring and doing interviews on college radio stations and Spanish-language TV to get its message out and about. In 2003, it will find a home on Concord Records, the jazz label which has its own Concord Picante Latin label, and will cause consternation among jazz critics at the 25th annual Playboy Jazz Festival at the Hollywood Bowl because it is not a true jazz band.

Latin mania is also responsible for several major national tours with improbable pairings, probably unimaginable 15 years ago. Try Maná and Carlos Santana on the same bill, for starters. Maná, the supreme rock en Español band from Guadalajara, with a reported six million albums sold in Latin America and Spain and one million in the U.S. since is start in 1986, will visit 18 cities with Santana. The sojourn brings together two bands with totally different followings despite both being from Mexico, Anglo Santana buffs who aren't into Mexican rock, and rock en Español fans who aren't old enough to appreciate Santana's fusion of rock dynamics, jazz improvisations, and Latin rhythms.

The tour is the result of Maná's lead singer, Fernando Olvera, warbling two songs on Santana's new album, *Supernatural*, which will become a benchmark success for the guitarist/spiritualist in this decade and revitalize his career. The two musicians decide a tour is just dandy for both their band's careers. Maná's exploits in Latin America are hardly known in this country. Its 1992 album, *¿Dónde Jugarán Los Niños?* racks up sales of three million copies globally to become the most sold Spanish-language rock album up until now. Three years later, the band crashes into the U.S. market by becoming the first rock en Español ensemble to sell more than 500,000 copies of a WEA Latino album.

The second 12-city tour unites Latin rock and rap bands for the first time and is the idea of the producers of the Anglo punk rock "Warped Tour." This event is called the "Watcha Tour" and features Café Tacuba, Molotov, Control Machete, Todos Tus Muertos, lllya Kuryaki, and the Chris Perez Band. The tour provides the first national exposure for Perez, husband and guitarist for Selena, the slain Tejano vocalist. The "Watcha Tour" is an idea fermented between co-producer Kevin Lyman, Molotov's manager, Jorge Mondragón, and tour co-creator CAA agent Darryl Eaton after Molotov is invited to join this summer's "Warped Tour."

One key venue for Latin musicians to play in downtown Los Angeles, which had lain dormant for years, is about to be resuscitated. The 2,332-seat Million Dollar Theater on Broadway, which opens in 1918 as a movie house and begins presenting Mexican artists in the '50s, has been refurbished and reopens as an outpost for Latino stage shows seven years after it stops presenting Hispanic talent and becomes a locale for evangelical revivals with a primarily Hispanic following.

Continuing to act as a magnet for Latin immigrants, Los Angeles explores ways to appeal to its diverse ethnic community. The 10th annual Cinco De Mayo Festival, sponsored for the 10th year by Bud Light in the suburb of South El Monte, draws a huge crowd to the diversity of music, including local Tejano band Cindy Y Los Cholos; Los Tiranos Del Norte, a norteño band from Mexico; Graciela Beltrán and her banda band from Mexico; Los Tri-O, three vocalists from Colombia; Juan Luis Guerra, Dominican singer/songwriter; Puerto Rican vocalist Maya; Rocio Durcal, Spain's top ballad singer; and Shakira, Colombia's sexy full-energy singer and the heads-up favorite with the audience at the public Whittier Narrows Recreation Area.

Among the popular styles not represented at the event is East Coast salsa, which finds a home at a hardcore number of venues, led by the year-old Conga room, which allows local salseros to dance to the music of a coterie of local salsa bands, a number of whom move here from New York in the '90s. Salsa bands, generally 10-member strong, work an informal club circuit involving local area venues.

Saluting Latino Heritage Month, the city of Los Angeles creates Festival Los Angeles featuring a variety of music, dance, drama, art, and sport events highlighting the cultures of Mexico, Central and South America, and the Caribbean. The event runs from August 17 through October 18 and features a lot of top name musicians ranging from Tito Puente to Lalo Schifrin, Chucho Valdes, and Eddie Palmieri. Legendary Mexican actor, Tito Guízar, who has been acting in TV novelas on Mexico's Televisa network, is the grand marshal for the September 12 Mexican Independence Day parade, which Univision's KMEX televises live.

L.A.'s smoldering Latin scene is also the home for a major Latin artist management firm, Hauser Entertainment, with national clout. Ralph Hauser's company provides the MCA Universal Amphitheatre with around 25 percent of its Latin talent, is in partnership with MCA Concerts to co-produce all concerts at other MCA venues, and is the exclusive Latin booker for concerts at the Las Vegas Mandalay Bay Hotel. Hauser's talent roster includes Juan Gabriel, Vicente and Alejandro Fernández, Ana Gabriel, Antonio and Pepe Aguilar, and Rocio Durcal. The Universal Amphitheatre, incidentally, hosts the first Ritmo Latino Music Awards in October, with predictable winners in 15 categories. Telemundo airs the awards voted by the public in November. Ricky Martin wins three awards as male pop artist, best album, and best video. Double winners are Shakira as best female artist and artist of the year and Juan Gabriel as best regional Mexican artist and lifetime achievement winner. The event is also the city's first Latin music awards ceremony.

Latinos who want to join the surge by young people towards previewing music and downloading songs from the Internet now have an online outlet all their own. Ritmoteca.com, a Miami firm, claims to be the first Latino online retailer to offer this global online service for receiving music on computers and MP3 players. Its music will come from such labels as Sony Discos/Sonolux, RMM/Universal Latino, Hacienda, Cutting Records, and Discos Fuentes. It costs $1.99 to download a single tune and $9.99 for an album.

Despite early inroads with online Hispanic websites, radio remains the key promotional tool, and for the first know time Latin radio is being contaminated by illegal payoffs to garner airplay. After its initial investigation into promotional ties to radio last year, federal prosecutors charge the head of promotions for Fonovisa Records, Jesus Gilberto Moreno, with a single count of payola, according to the *Los Angeles Times*. He is charged with doling out $2,000 to an unnamed radio programmer to favor Fonovisa artists. Moreno pleads guilty, and is fined $50,000 and placed on two years' probation. Fonovisa's president, Guillermo Santiso, pleads guilty to a felony payola associated tax charge. He is accused of writing checks totaling $450,000 to a phony company which launders the money so it can be paid to radio programmers. Moreno's attorneys tell the judge in Los Angeles Federal District Court their client's actions reflect accepted practice in Mexico where pay for play is legal. While this public white-washing is a first for the Hispanic record and radio industries, other than Moreno being the first top record official in the U.S. to be successfully brought to justice, there are no fallout effects, no craze in the making.

The nation's Latinization craze is, however, causing consternation among many of the nation's English-language pop music stations that are wary of playing too many Latin records that sound alike. L.A.'s chief Top 40 station, KIIS-FM, chooses not to give Marc Anthony's English version of *I Need to Know* heavy airplay rotation, even though the disc is being aired heavily around the country. The same limited airplay applies to *Groove with Me Tonight*, a new disc by MDO, the restructured former Menudo group. Michael Steele, KIIS' music director, tells the *Los Angeles Times* his decision to limit the Anthony record is based in part on the song having "a similar sound to records by Ricky Martin and Enrique Iglesias. They've all got the same pacing, kind of a salsa beat." Roy Laughlin, the station's president/general manager, expresses surprise at Steele's appraisal of the two artist's songs, asserting instead that having too many Latino-sounding records is not the station's music policy.

In New York, super popular hit station WHTZ-FM's music director/air personality, Paul "Cubby" Bryant, provides crossover Latin artists strong on-air support. The key, he explains in the *Times* article, is not to play them one after the other, while supporting Steele's belief that the Anthony, Martin, and Iglesias discs are similar sounding.

Around the same time KIIS is undergoing self-analysis, another L.A. station, the low-rated, three-year-old alternative rock station KLYY-FM, begins airing a one-hour rock en Español show, *The Red Zone*, Sundays in September. One month later, after strong listener response, the station increases the show to two-and-a-half hours, starting at 5 p.m. In December, the station's owner, Big City Radio, drops alternative rock and becomes a fulltime Spanish contemporary hits/rock en Español/ballads outpost under the banner *Viva 107*. A second station also switches formats...again. After 14 months as the region's lone Spanish-language news station, KKHJ returns to music, as *La Ranchera*, stressing Mexican tunes, old and new.

There's also action on the Spanish sports front. After 17 years, the KWKW Dodgers broadcast team has changed. In for the retiring René Cárdenas is Pepe Yñiguez as the partner for veteran announcer Jaíme Jarrín, who has been broadcasting the Dodger games since 1959. Yñiguez had been the pre- and post-game show host since 1993 and has covered the World Series, American League playoffs and the All-Star Game for cable network Fox Sports America. One year after the California Angels reinstate complete coverage in an attempt to attract Hispanic fans in Orange County after a six-year absence, its broadcasts on XPRS-AM are producing the desired effect. Raising attendance in Anaheim, where the team plays, are Ivan Lara calling the game and José Tolentino providing color analysis. While Lara has seven years experience with the minor league Tucson Toros, Tolentino, who played 14 years as a professional, is a novice in the broadcast booth.

As the nation's Latin population grows, so grows the Radio Unica network, which snares exclusive Spanish-language broadcast rights to the 2000 and 2004 Summer Olympics from programming giant Westwood One. The 19-month-old Miami-based company is home to Spanish coverage of all the major soccer contests and the NBA playoffs. Its 24-hour programming is carried on upward of 60 affiliates. On a smaller level, Heftel Broadcasting, which owns 40 Spanish-lingo stations, launches its own version of a network called the "Heftel Circuit." It provides 12 hours of regional programming each day to 12 of its stations in nine of the top 15 Hispanic markets. Based on its credo that radio is a local medium in which indigenous cultures impact on audience acceptance, Heftel syndicates its Reñan Almendárez Coello wacky morning show from its L.A. KSCA to stations in the Southwest, while a Miami talk show airs on East Coast stations.

The crossover phenomenon captures the financial attention of the English-language broadcast networks. ABC, Fox, and CBS see benefits in providing bilingual programs. ABC, which debuts Spanish simulcasts for *Monday Night Football* last fall, broadcasts the 1997 theatrical release *Selena* starring Jennifer Lopez with a Spanish version on the second audio program channel (SAP) available on newer TV sets. Following the film, ABC airs the world premiere of *Best I Can*, a music video tribute to the slain singer by her husband, Chris Perez, and his band. The film, written and directed by Gregory Nava, starts the network's season of Saturday night movies. Nava is tapped by CBS to develop a family drama series focused on several generations of a Mexican American family in…where else…Los Angeles. While Nava covers a similarly themed idea in his 1995 film, *Mi Familia*, this is his first foray into episodic television. A documentary he does for Showtime titled the *American Tapestry*, about immigrants seeking the good life in America, airs in November.

CBS' Los Angeles-owned station, KCBS, signs an agreement with production company Si TV to use its library of English/Latino flavored programs for an hour-long, late-night series and another at 1 a.m. Sunday mornings for 30 minutes, starting in July for seven weeks. In an unusual arrangement, the two companies will split all advertising revenue, rather than KCBS paying Si TV a license fee.

Si TV, owned by Jeff Valdez, a former executive producer at TriStar TV, is formed 20 months ago to provide TV shows for English-speaking Hispanics. Its initial deal is with Univision's Galavision cable network which runs two of its bilingual shows, *Cafe Olé* and *Funny Is Funny*, for one year before the shows are switched to broadcast syndication. Si TV, which hopes to start a cable network for bilinguals next year, is also involved in developing half-hour programming for the Disney Channel and Nickelodeon. Its debut plans, however, are put off until the fall of 2003.

Fox, which already airs a Spanish SAP track for one of its most popular series, *Cops*, expands its Spanish coverage into football in the fall, following its first-ever Spanish coverage for Major League Baseball. The network reports both baseball and *Cops* gain a five percent ratings boost because of increased Latin viewers. Joining *Cops* in the SAP arena is the network's second popular series, *America's Most Wanted* criminal catching saga.

NBC is taking the Latino plunge by broadcasting the *Latin DanceSport Championships* in primetime following its foray last spring into ballroom dancing with a telecast of the International Dance Sport Championship. That one-hour program draws 6.6 million viewers, besting NBC's regular performance for that same Saturday primetime period. The Latin dance broadcast offers a faster paced, more physical form of competition than most other forms of ballroom dancing. Translation: more exciting images.

Univision is also seeking exciting pictures for the small screen. It's newly announced Univision Productions plans to produce between 10 to 12 made-for-TV films in the comedy, drama, and adventure fields. The challenge for the front-running Hispanic network is to generate programming for both a vortex of new immigrant viewers from Central and South America and the Caribbean while at the same time retaining its core audience of primarily immigrant and U.S.-born Mexicans. According to the Nielsen ratings company, 60 percent of Latino households watch English-language TV. And while the English-language networks encounter declining audiences because of other programming options, notably cable, Univision reports an audience growth of 25 percent since the previous season, to a record four million daily viewers.

This audience increase affects standing of the network's New York-owned station, WXTV, for the second time since 1997, when it makes major inroads in the general market ratings. This year, for the first time, the station outperforms an English-language station, Chris-Craft United's WWOR, on a Tuesday in September, albeit by a slim margin. The station's growing strength is also evident in other parts of the day. WXTV relies on its network-fed array of dramatic telenovela mini-series, and one of these daytime programs, *El País De Las Mujeres*, exceeds the viewership for both CBS' *As the World Turns* and NBC's *Sunset Beach* during the May sweeps period. The station's 6 p.m. local newscast also records a higher rating than the local news on CBS' WCBS.

Univision may be feeling optimistically confident because of the ill fortunes of rival Telemundo, whose new owners Sony and Liberty Media scrap its traditional imported telenovela programming last year in favor of domestically produced novelas and Spanish-language copies of past Sony TV drama series, like *Charlie's Angels*, retitled *Angeles*. This is designed to attract a younger audience by focusing on the domestic Hispanic lifestyle. However, due to the failure of this lineup, the network's audience dramatically falls by a third since the new owners take over in 1997 to less than eight percent of Hispanic households. So out go the weekly primetime cop dramas, *Angeles*, and *Reyes Y Rey* and back are the popular telenovelas from TV Azteca, Mexico's powerful second network.

(Univision garners its novelas from Mexico's Televisa, the leading producer of Spanish-language TV programming.) Also disappearing are the dubbed versions of Sony-owned movies which run weeknights.

While Telemundo adds two new Miami-situated talk series, more newscasts, a reality show and a family sitcom, *Los Beltrán*, whose pilot show includes dialog in Spanish and English, Sony's Columbia TriStar TV wing is in discussions with veteran TV executive, Jim McNamara about replacing the current Telemundo president Peter Tortorici. One month later, McNamara is in as Telemundo's president/CEO. Tortorici winds up with a production deal with the Columbia TriStar TV Group.

McNamara says the network is committed to developing new programs for the ever-expanding 18- to 34-year-old Hispanic audience. He comes to his new assignment after operating his own consulting firm, JMM Management. From 1996 to 1998 he's president of Universal Television Enterprises and before that is with New World Entertainment for nine years, rising from senior VP of New World International to CEO of the parent firm. Raised in the Panama Canal Zone, he speaks fluent Spanish. McNamara moves the Los Angeles operation back to the Hialeah headquarters and downsizes its L.A. office. In October of 2002 I get to converse with him in-person in English and listen to him talk in Spanish on the phone when I visit the network's sprawling Hialeah complex to do an interview for this book. That experience appears in Chapter 13.

With Telemundo focusing on creating original series domestically, the American Federation of Television & Radio Artists signs a three-year contract with Sony to represent all actors and actresses performing in U.S. videotaped shows handled by Llamame Loco Productions, Sony's Spanish-language production company. The first show to be produced under the AFTRA pact which covers wages, residual payment, health, and retirement plans is the Spanish version of *One Day at a Time*, called *Solo en America*.

Three months after McNamara takes the helm, one of Telemundo's veteran executives, Nely Galán, president of entertainment, exits to start her own Galán Entertainment company, with a two-year exclusive contract in hand to develop comedy, drama, and reality series for the network. She gets to executive produce three shows she brings to Telemundo, *Los Beltrán*, *Solo en America*, and *Padre Alberto*. She chooses not to relocate to Florida from L.A. In 2003, Galán will executive produce one of Telemundo's new fall series out of its new Miami production center, the reality/game show, *La Cenicienta*.

Cognizant of the power of the new Latin music pantheon, Telemundo sets its sights on adding music to its schedule. During May it produces and airs the *Billboard International Latin Music Awards*, which becomes one of its highest-rated shows. During the summer it airs a week of music specials, including the *Festival Presidente De La Música Latina*, culled from a three-day bash in the Dominican Republic featuring Chayanne, Shakira, and Enrique Iglesias. The week also includes an acoustic performance by rock band Maná, dubbed versions of the films *Salsa*, featuring former Menudo member Robi Rosa, and *La Bamba*, with Lou Diamond Phillips playing Ritchie Valens. There is also a closing concert by Ricky Martin before 40,000 fans in his native Puerto Rico.

On the cable dial, Galavision, Univision's bilingual network, sees its prime time ratings jump up 60 percent among 18- to 49-year-olds.

Among its slate of new shows is the Sunday evening entry *En Persona*, patterned after A&E's popular *Biography*. It will accompany *Dímelo*, a half-hour celebrity gossip show that premiers in January. In February, Galavision bows what it calls its most expensive bilingual offering, *Kiki Desde Hollywood*, an hour-long variety show hosted by comedienne/actress Kiki Melendez.

One of the nation's leading cable systems operators, Liberty Media Group, creates Canales ñ, a digital package of Spanish-language channels which reaches one million Hispanic households, one-eighth of all Latino homes in the nation. The special package includes Discovery en Español, CNN en Español, Toon Disney Español, Fox Sports World Español, CBS TeleNoticias, Cine Latino, video channels Box Exitos and Box Tejano, and eight channels of Spanish music. Still in its infancy, Spanish programming on cable is being introduced on a city-by-city basis. Charter Communications, which has a system in Long Beach, California, has 5,000 subscribers to its analog *Cable Latino* package which provides the Cartoon Network, CNN en Español, CBS TeleNoticias, Gems, HTV, and Cine Latino. HBO en Español is also available on a request basis.

Two Los Angeles Anglo broadcasting stations, KTTV and KTLA, set marks for their Hispanic staffs. While L.A.'s stations generally have Hispanics on-camera, KTTV's on-air staff is nearly one-third Latin, supposedly the largest number in the city. The station's 10 p.m. hour-long newscast is the time period's No. 1 news show, outreaching the former 10 p.m. news leader, KTLA, since May of 1996. During the last four November sweeps periods, KTTV's primetime programming, preceding its news, attracts more Latino households than any station, including Spanish KVEA and KWHY, but not that of Univision's KMEX.

KTTV's staff is led by news director Jose Rios, who expands the scope of stories to report on major events in Mexico. Among his Hispanic staffers are sports anchor Rick Garcia, plus reporters Christina Gonzalez, who joins the station in 1991 from Univision, David Garcia, Bernard Gonzales, and Tony Valdez. KTTV, along with

KCAL and KCOP, join KTLA in offering Spanish translations of their news. KTLA, the city's first TV station, hires its first Hispanic sports reporter Claudia Trejos from KWHY, the independent Spanish station. She joins weekday sports anchor Tony Hernandez to give the station the lone all Latino sports team on Anglo TV and the city's only regular female sports anchor. KTLA is her first English language gig after two years at KWHY where she also covered sports. In a few years she fades off the KTLA screen.

Although Latin music and broadcasting capture the majority of the nation's attention, Latinos are also flexing their skills in sports and films. Sammy Sosa, the National League Dominican-born slugger, and Jose Canseco, a Cuban-American in the American League, top the list of homerun hitters. Oscar De La Hoya, the WBC welterweight champion (with a 31 to 0 record), decides to move his career into a field which guarantees no physical punches: the record business. He signs with EMI Latin as a singer and heads of his own label. Latin labels are romancing him after his singing performance on *Cristina*, Univision's popular daytime talk show. Singing is not the boxer's greatest asset, however, and he continues to be a major presence in the ring. But that too will change in a few years when he loses three matches, including his super welterweight title twice to Shane Mosley, the last time in 2003 in a controversial decision in Las Vegas.

The Baltimore Orioles become the first American major league baseball team in 40 years to visit Cuba in March for the first of two exhibitions against the Cuban national team. The Orioles win 3 to 2 in the 11th inning. Two months later, the Cubans receive a sendoff by President Castro and arrive in Baltimore for the second game. A charter flight brings the team, plus a delegation of 300 to Baltimore, eager to equalize the series. It is also the first time a Cuban team faces a major league team in this country. Perhaps for that reason the Cubans bushwhack their hosts 12 to 6 at Camden Yards. The Cuban government is concerned about someone defecting. It doesn't happen.

In a highly charged political imbroglio, two Cuban baseball players signed by the Los Angeles Dodgers, first baseman Juan Carlos Diaz and outfielder Josue Perez, assert their signings are illegal and request they be given free agent status. The two charge that the Dodgers held secret tryouts, arranged their escapes from Cuba to the Dominican Republic, and told them to lie. Both players are signed while they are in the Dominican Republic. Diaz receives a $65,000 singing bonus in 1996 and goes to the Dodgers' double-A team in San Antonio, while Perez receives a $40,000 bonus in 1998 and joins the team's Class-A Vero Beach franchise, according to the *Los Angeles Times.* The two players allege that the Dodger's regional scouting supervisor, Pablo Peguero contacted them in Cuba and arranged their departures. Peguero counters he hasn't been in Cuba for 10 years. Major League Baseball is investigating the whole mess as the number of foreign-born players escalates, led primarily by Hispanics.

Baseball commissioner Bud Selig's office fines the Dodgers $200,000 and declares the two players in the club's farm system free agents because they are scouted illegally in Cuba and signed in the Dominican Republic without the required tryout camp open to other players. Several months later, following a six-week investigation of the underage signing by the Dodgers of Adrian Beltre, Selig again fines the club for violating major league rules and declines the player's request for free agency.

During the course of the investigation, the Dodgers admit they purposely falsify Beltre's birth date and sign the player as a 15-year-old in '94 when he's one year under the league's age limit. The team is ordered to pay Beltre the difference between his initial bonus and the amount he would have received a year later. The team is also prohibited for one year from scouting and signing any first-year players who reside in the Dominican Republic and are ordered to close its Dominican training facility. Beltre's request for free agency is denied because he fails to raise this issue of free agency in a timely fashion and is apparently complicit in the signing violation.

While baseball's annual amateur draft for players from the U.S., Canada, and Puerto Rico is held in June, and candidates have to be a high school senior or college junior; non-drafted foreign players need only be 16 years old. A growing number of defecting Cuban players cause agents to establish residencies for them in either the Dominican Republic or Costa Rica to which team scouts are invited to view the players in tryouts. Four Cubans go straight to major league teams: the highly touted fastball pitcher Orlando "El Duque" Hernández to the New York Yankees; his half-brother Liván Hernández to the Florida Marlins; Rolando Arrojo to the Tampa Bay Devil Rays; and Rey Ordonez to the New York Mets. Baseball is a very chaotic business. Yankees pitching phenomenon "El Duque" starts off fast but undergoes a slow burnout and by 2002 is traded to the Montreal Expos, where by 2003 he is no longer with the team. In 2004, he's back with the Yankees, but only for a brief period due to health reasons. He then plays for Arizona and in 2006 is traded to the New York Mets. At age 40, he wins four straight games for the National League East leaders.

In the film world, equally chaotic at times, actors Benjamin Bratt and Salma Hayek are gaining breakout respectability in an industry in which the Screen Actors Guild (SAG) dimly reports in its first nationwide survey of Hispanic membership that roles for Latinos in films and on television represent less than one-third of their 10.7 percent of the nation's population. This places the burgeoning Latin community at the top of the list of underrepresented ethnicities.

According to SAG, which in 1992 begins surveying employment by ethnicity, age, and gender, Latino actors are cast in only 2.8 percent of film/TV roles in 1992, in 3.2 percent in '93, 3.5 percent in '94, 3.7 percent in '95, 3.9 percent in '96, 4 percent in '97, and 3.0 for leading roles and 3.8 for supporting roles in '98. For Hispanics struggling to get into mainstream show business, especially in the visual arts, the lack of an open door is frustrating and unfathomable, considering all the spiking population statistics.

In fact, the lack of Latino-themed films underscores the annual ALMA Awards, which hand out a plethora of accolades but nothing for Latin movies, a situation which Lisa Navarrette, spokeswoman for the National Council of La Raza, which presents the awards, calls "unconscionable." The awards are meant to recognize English-language films and TV programs and the performers who portray positive Latino role models. Repeating TV winners are Benjamin Bratt for *Law & Order*, Nestor Carbonell for *Suddenly Susan*, Jimmy Smits for *NYPD Blues*, Rita Moreno for *Oz*, and Mark Consuelos for *All My Children*. First-time winners: Bruno Campos for *Jesse*, Maria Conchita Alonso for *My Husband's Secret*, Edward James Olmos for *The Taking of Pelham One, Two, Three*, and Socorro Santiago for *All My Children*.

In the movie category, Jennifer Lopez is lauded for her role in *Out of Sight*. Director Gregory Nava (who has worked on such Latin-themed film as *Selena*, *El Norte*, and *Mi Familia*) is honored for his work on *Why Do Fools Fall in Love*, Antonio Banderas for *The Mask of Zorro*, Kirk Acevedo for *The Thin Red Line*, Andy Garcia for *Desperate Measures*, and Elizabeth Peña for *Rush Hour*.

To provide more clout for Hispanic-themed movies, a number of Latin organizations form the Premiere Weekend Club which pledges to motivate one million Latinos to attend any movie portraying Latinos in a positive manner. Jimmy Smits, the Emmy winner and co-founder of the National Hispanic Foundation for the Arts, tells the *Hollywood Reporter:* "We need Latinos to vote with their pocketbooks in support of Latino-themed projects." Vincent Miller, a club vice president and director of the film *Gabriela*, explains the enticement "is the opposite of an economic boycott. We will financially reward Hollywood for making more positive Latino films." Films cited with positive Latino themes and actors include *Stand and Deliver*, *Selena*, and *Like Water for Chocolate*.

Film producer Moctesuma Esparza, whose credits include *Selena* and *The Milagro Beanfield War*, announces plans to start a national, urban chain of movie theaters for Latin films. He'll start with six theaters in California. He tells the *Los Angeles Times* that between 1940 and 1960 there were 600 outlets for Spanish movies in the country, plus another 300 which screened Latino films part-time. They are all history by the end of the 1980s. Now, paradoxically, there's an immense audience, but no movie theaters.

Still, there is hope at the creative end of the business. While there are no Latin-themed movies produced this year, a number of production deals by Hollywood players portend some change in this situation. Miramax will release *Frida*, a movie about Mexican artist Frida Kahlo starring Salma Hayek which begins filming next year. In 2003, she wins a best actress Oscar nomination for her role in the film, which also garners five other nominations. Latin Universe will distribute the Mexican romantic comedy *Santitos* in domestic theaters in December. The company plans to pick up distribution for several other Mexican titles. New Latin Pictures will release *Luminarias*, a Mexican-American English-language film, in Los Angeles theaters next February.

Additionally, New Line Cinema signs Gregory Nava and partner Susana Zepeda's El Norte Productions to work on several Latin-themed movies. Artisan Entertainment plans releasing Nava's 1983 drama *el Norte* next April to the Latin market and speaks enthusiastically about producing and distributing a number of Hispanic movies. And Jimmy Smits signs up to star in *Price of Glory*, about a boxing family in East L.A., which New Line will release sometime next year.

Also, actor John Leguizamo and his Lower East Side Films will produce the story of Juan García Esquival, the Mexican composer known for a string of hit LPs in the 1960s, with Fox Searchlight handling domestic distribution. Also on Lower East Side's agenda is the story of the controversial New York-based Puerto Rican poet Miguel Piñero. Benjamin Bratt will portray the controversial, emotionally troubled lead character in the 2001 release, *Piñero.* His powerful performance will win him a 2002 ALMA Award to add to his two TV achievements for *Law and Order* in 1998 and '99.

Showing a growing interest in Latin films, more than 23,000 people pack the 10-day Latino International Film Festival in L.A. in

October, up from 15,000 people who attend last year. Among the most popular films screened are *Luminarias* and *Santitos*. The American Film Institute increases the number of Latin films during its annual film festival from one last year to seven this year, with titles coming from Mexico, Spain, Argentina, Brazil, and Cuba. The movies attract 3,500 interested film buffs.

The nation's changing multicultural landscape prompts *TV Guide* to introduce 16-page inserts in Spanish at newsstands in the top 15 Hispanic markets, beginning in October. But there are still mucho problemas getting a Latin-slanted show on the small screen. Two incidents illustrate this conundrum. Producer/director Gregory Nava pitches a primetime drama series to Warner Bros. Television focusing on an East L.A. Latino family, which is rejected. One month later, Warner Bros. TV signs a pact to develop Latino comedy and drama series for broadcast and cable with Silverlight Television, run by two non-Spanish-speaking Anglos. Co-owner Stephen Drimmer says his mandate is "to be a conduit for all Latino talent," and if the company does get a show on the air, it will be staffed with Latinos, he tells the *Los Angeles Times*, adding he has represented Hispanic talent for close to nine years.

The Silverlight WB alliance is announced five months after the broadcast networks announce their fall show lineup of 26 programs, none of which casts an actor of color in a lead role. Hispanic reaction to the fall lineup eschewing Hispanics, the bypassing of Nava's story suggestion, and the WB deal with Silverlight, all cause consternation within the Latin TV corps.

With professional baseball continuing to employ more Hispanic players, the Hispanic Heritage Baseball Museum is established in San Francisco under the aegis of Gabriel Avila, Jr. It is the first museum of its kind in the world and displays artifacts from past and present Major League Baseball players. Hispanics comprise 11 percent of baseball's fans, according to an ESPN/Chilton survey. Some 86 percent report they watch baseball on TV, up from 12.2 percent in 1996; 25.5 percent claim they listen to games on the radio, while 11.6 percent say they listen to Spanish-language baseball broadcasts, according to Strategy Research Corp. of Miami. In the major Hispanic cities of Los Angeles, New York, and Phoenix, baseball feels the impact of the transnational population. The New York Mets see a six percent increase to 17 percent in its Hispanic attendance during the past five years. The Mets broadcast 100-plus games on WADO-AM. In Los Angeles, KWKW-AM, the Dodger's flagship station, sees a 20 percent increase in its advertising revenue every year for the past five years, the majority from top national accounts. Pennzoil, a major oil company, in addition to sponsoring the Dodgers, also sponsors broadcasts of the Houston Astros and San Diego Padres. In Phoenix, the Arizona Diamondbacks broadcast 14 games in Spanish on KDHX-FM in an obvious move to endear itself with the city's expanding Latin audience. The city's Hispanic population is projected to increase by 44 percent in the next 10 years.

Articles

"The Loud And Quiet Explosions." Los Angeles Times, Dec. 26, 1999

"Streetology." LA Weekly, Dec. 17, 1999

"Y107 Will Switch To Spanish Hits Format Monday." Los Angeles Times, Dec. 10, 1999

"Ritmoteca.com Devoted To Latin Music Fans." Billboard, Dec. 18, 1999

"New Faces Spice Up A Record Year." Billboard, Dec. 11, 1999

"Latin Music: Bigger Than Reported." Los Angeles Times, Dec. 10, 1999

"Latin Music Mixes It Up With R&B." Billboard, Dec. 2, 1999

"Latin Grammys Need A Venue: Miami Waits." Los Angeles Times, Oct. 30, 1999

"The Real Crossover." Los Angeles Times, Oct. 28, 1999

"Galan Hoists Banner, Ankles Telemundo." Daily Variety, Oct. 26, 1999

"Ritmo Latino Winners." Los Angeles Times, Oct. 22, 1999

"Latin Music Is No Passing Fancy." Billboard, Sept. 18, 1999

"Anthony's Columbia Debut A Departure For Latin Star." Billboard, Sept. 18, 1999

"Univision Crows In N.Y." Daily Variety, Sept. 16, 1999

"In New York, Spanish TV Stations Tops Ratings Of An English

Station." New York Times, Sept. 16, 1999

"CBS, Nava Set Latino Dramedy." Daily Variety, Sept. 14, 1999

"Festival Los Angeles." Los Angeles Times, Sept. 13, 1999

"Exiles Force Top Cuban Band To Cancel Concert In Miami." Los Angeles Times, Sept. 12, 1999

"Latin Sound Faces A Defining Problem." Los Angeles Times, Sept. 11, 1999

"Following A Legend." Los Angeles Times, Sept. 8, 1999

"Emerging Salsero." Los Angeles Times, Sept. 2, 1999

"'Selena's' Two-Track Mind." Daily Variety, Sept. 1, 1999

"Música Equals Dinero As Latin Sales Up 11%." Daily Variety, Aug. 26, 1999

"Border-Hopping Music With A Mestizo Beat." New York Times, Aug. 25, 1999

"Ole! Fans Taking Control Of First Ritmo Latino Awards." Hollywood Reporter, Aug. 17, 1999

"Martin Sets Latino Record." Billboard, Aug. 14, 1999

"Networks See Benefits Of Becoming Bilingual." Los Angeles Times, Aug. 9, 1999

"Martin's Rise Elevates Other Latino Crooners." Daily Variety, Aug. 2, 1999

"Liberty Gears Up For Hispanic Tier Push." Multichannel News, July 26, 1999

"Ozo Rising." Los Angeles Times, July 25, 1999

"Telemundo Hears The Sound Of Music." Los Angeles Times, July 19, 1999

"Rozenblat Steps Down From LARAS." Billboard, July 17, 1999

"Mexican Consulate Honors Pioneer." Los Angeles Times, July 13, 1999

"Univision: TV Success That Will Last?" Los Angeles Times, July 13, 1999

"McNamara's New Band Is Telemundo." Daily Variety, July 8, 1999

"The Other Chili Peppers." Entertainment Weekly, July 7, 1999

"Too Much Of A Good Thing." Los Angeles Times, July 1, 1999

"Columbia TriStar May Be Considering Leadership Changes At Telemundo." Los Angeles Times, June 30, 1999

"Welcome To The Club." New York Daily News, June 29, 1999

"KTLA Sports Team Boasts New Look, Accent." Los Angeles Times, June 28, 1999

"A Country Now Ready To Listen." New York Times, June 27, 1999

"In Ever-Expanding Musical Universe, Crossover Rules." Los Angeles

Times, June 26, 1999

"New Latin Grammys Introduced." Los Angeles Times, June 25, 1999

"KCBS Will Test Seven Weeks of Late-Night Latino Shows." Los Angeles Times, June 23, 1999

"De La Hoya In Music Ring." Daily Variety, June 23, 1999

"Embracing A Heritage." Los Angeles Times, June 23, 1999

"Mexican Music Recognized Yet Unheard At Industry Events." Los Angeles Times, June 22, 1999

"The Burden Of Success." Los Angeles Times, June 19, 1999

"Latin Music Is Becoming The New Language Of Pop." Hollywood Reporter, June 18, 1999

"AFTRA Reps Spanish-Lingo Thesps." Daily Variety, June 17, 1999

"Latin Warped Tour To Cross U.S." Hollywood Reporter, June 17, 1999

"Televised Dance Competitions Cutting Into Ratings Circle." Los Angeles Times, June 12, 1999

"Iglesias, U In Tune." Daily Variety, June 10, 1999

"Lovin' La Vida Loca." Newsweek, May 31, 1999

"Spicing The Mix." Time, May 31, 1999

"Unica Wins Olympics Radio Rights." Los Angeles Times, May 25, 1999

"Latin Music Pops." Time, May 24, 1999

"U.S. Latin Sales Soar In 1st QTR." Billboard, May 22, 1999

"U.S. Latin Music Sales Continue To Surge." Billboard, May 22, 1999

"Album's Debut At No.1 Signals Boom In Latino Music." Los Angeles Times, May 20, 1999

"Univision Vision." Daily Variety, May 20, 1999

"Martin's 'La Vida Loca' A Latin Crossover Thriller." Daily Variety, May 19, 1999

"Ailing Telemundo Seeks Cure By Adopting Proven Format." Los Angeles Times, May 18, 1999

"Stronger Hispanic Identity Sought." Advertising Age, May 10, 1999

"Pop Music's Latin Locomotion." USA Today, May 7, 1999

"Attorney Says Dodgers Erred." Los Angeles Times, May 5, 1999

"Special Series Transcends Politics, Policies." USA Today, May 4, 1999

"Cinco De Mayo Festival." Los Angeles Times, May 4, 1999

"Cuban Team Makes Late Arrival, But Set For Exhibition." Los Angeles Times, May 3, 1999

"Rap Movement Gaining Strength In Spanish Rock." Los Angeles Times, May 2, 1999

"Orioles Throw A Curve Ball In Cuba Baseball Diplomacy." Financial Times, April 30, 1999

"¿Estás Preparado Para El Rock En Español?" Wall Street Journal, April 29, 1999

"U.S. Warms To Latin Sounds." Billboard, April 24, 1999

"Hauser Leads Field In Act Management." Billboard, April 17, 1999

"United By Diversity." Los Angeles Times, April 15, 1999

"Univision Means Success In Any Language." Los Angeles Times, April 13, 1999

"Million Dollar Theater Set To Reopen." Los Angeles Times, April 8, 1999

"Eastside Chronicles." L.A. Weekly, March 12, 1999

"New Si TV Wants To Be In Tune With Young Latino Viewers." Los Angeles Times, March 10, 1999

"Galavision Speaks The Language of Success." Los Angeles Times, Feb. 20, 1999

"Latino Presence Boosts KTTV News." Los Angeles Times, Feb. 19, 1999

Chapter 7
CAPITULO 7

Explosive Fallout: 2000
CAIDAS EXPLOSIVAS: 2000

• As the 21st Century unfurls, the nation reels with the expansive expansion of new Hispanic immigrants from Mexico, Central, and South America who are setting their roots in small towns in rural America, affecting every facet of life and straining the capabilities of local schools, police departments, medical facilities, and local businesses trying to deal with their new, Spanish-speaking neighbors.

• Carlos Santana's time to glow is in the first year of the new millennium. There's no getting around the fact that the 52-year-old rock and blues guitar stylist's winning eight of 10 Grammy nominations catapults his career into orbit after two decades of fallow sales.

• This is the year the new Latin Grammy spin-off debuts in Los Angeles, not Miami, one year ahead of schedule, with CBS becoming the first Anglo network in TV history to air a bilingual program. Nonetheless, the Grammys are mired in behind-the-scenes controversy.

• Democrats and Republicans reach out to Latin music stars to spark up their nominating conventions to demonstrate their affection for the Hispanic community, hoping to garner their votes.

• The film industry takes aim at the Hispanic market, signing talent whose artistic heft will attract ticket-buyers.

• Of all the players in baseball, Alex Rodriguez snares the highest paying salary ever: $252 million to play 10 years for the Texas

Rangers. Two days later, Manny Ramirez signs an eight-year, $160 million deal with the Boston Red Sox.

• Azteca America, the spinoff by Mexican-owned network TV Aztca, is set to debut in the U.S. in 2001.

While the influx of new Hispanics creates community relations problems, these new residents bode well for Spanish radio and TV, which open affiliates in many of these communities. Of the 13.1 million Hispanic immigrants, close to half move to the U.S. between 1989 and 1997, reports the U.S. Census Bureau. Of these immigrants, 65.2 percent are from Mexico, 14.3 percent from Central and South America, 9.6 percent from Puerto Rico, 4.3 percent from Cuba, and 6.6 percent from other Latin nations. This influx turns the U.S. into the fifth largest Spanish-speaking nation behind Mexico, Spain, Argentina, and Colombia, trumpets the *Jim Lehrer News Hour* on PBS. California continues to lead the nation as the chosen home for 25 percent of immigrants, the majority Hispanics, with 20 percent of this figure residing in the three Southern California neighboring counties of Los Angeles, Orange, and Riverside. Of California's population of 33 million, 25 percent are Latinos.

An estimated six million undocumented immigrants currently reside in the U.S., according to the Immigration and Naturalization Service. And with intermarriage between races on the rise, and cultural barriers and prejudices of past centuries slowing fading, America, to some degree, is becoming more accepting of the differences in peoples. In fact, the nation's second language is now Spanish, a result of the blurring of linguistic borders between the U.S. and its Latin neighbors.

A coterie of second- and third-generation U.S. Hispanics choose to make their recording debuts singing English with a Latin rhythmic twist, a combination they hope catapults them into the mainstream market while riding the record industry's leitmotif by tapping into all segments of the Latin feeding frenzy.

Major Latin record companies create multiple versions of the same song in different musical styles to garner radio airplay on different format genres.

Just as last year's Grammys provided Ricky Martin with the national exposure platform to impact mainstream America, so too does this year's 42nd annual Grammys rekindle interest in Carlos Santana, with one major caveat. His Arista album, *Supernatural*, wins eight awards and includes performances by a host of major name rock artists, which undoubtedly helps propel the album's sales up by 166 percent after the CBS telecast, according to SoundScan, the company which electronically measures album sales in major retail outlets. The album sells 583,000 copies during the seven days after Santana's performance and trophy walkathon during the program. It's a record for a Grammy-exposed album, which also sells 520,000 copies overseas, a 200 percent increase outside the U.S., which boosts the album's total global sales to 13 million plus copies.

Clive Davis, Arista's president, who originally signs the San Francisco musician to Columbia Records in 1969 before departing that company in an unfavorable light to form Arista, brings Santana along with him. In a *USA Today* story, Davis says of the post-Grammy sales: "In my entire career, I've never seen anything like this." Known for his hands-on involvement in selecting material for his artists, Davis directs that half the album match up new names who will lure in their own fans. So with half the album featuring his bluesy, high-decibel electric guitar over sybaritic Latin rhythms, the other half features Lauryn Hill, Dave Matthews, Wyclef Jean of the Fugees, Rob Thomas of Matchbox Twenty, as well as evergreen blues guitarist Eric Clapton. Prior to the Grammys, the album sells four million copies. Among Santana's eight statuettes are record of the year, album of the year, song of the year, top rock album (which includes his guest collaborators), pop and rock collaborations with vocals, and pop and rock instrumental performances.

As a result of the Hispanic cultural explosion, the Grammys add two new Latin categories: salsa and merengue, to its Latin pop, rock alternative, traditional tropical, Tejano, Mexican American, and Latin jazz offerings, bringing the total for Latin music categories to eight from the low of three in 1985. It also includes six Hispanic performers on the February 24 telecast: Santana, Marc Anthony, Chucho Valdes, Ibrahim Ferrer, Poncho Sanchez, and Ricky Martin. These additions are a result of the formation in 1997 of the Latin Academy of Recording Arts and Sciences (LARAS) by the parent National Academy of Recording Arts and Sciences. Having helped raise the profile of Hispanics on the Anglo Grammy show, LARAS sets September 15 and Los Angeles as the date and locale for its premiere Latin Grammy Awards presentation, which CBS will air for two hours in primetime.

If Santana has a domineering male role as the new year unfolds, 19-year-old Christina Aguilera is music's distaff darling, followed by established salsa star India. Christina gains her position by being named best new artist at the Grammys, overpowering Britney Spears, Macy Gray, Kid Rock, and Susan Tedeschi.

What's fascinating and important about these regular Grammys are the wide swatch of artists who are nominees and/or winners: besides Aguilera's being named best new artist (not best new Latin artist), Ricky Martin is nominated for song of the year with *Livin' La Vida Loca* and best pop album for his eponymous title; Gloria Estefan is nominated for best pop vocal collaboration with *NSYNC for *Music of My Heart* and best dance record for *Don't Let This Moment End.* In the best male pop vocal category, three of the five candidates are Latinos: Marc Anthony for *I Need to Know;* Lou Bega for *Mambo No. 5 (A Little Bit of...),* and Ricky Martin's ever-familiar *Livin' La Vida Loca.*

Latin category winners show individualism at work: Rubén Blades wins the best Latin pop award for *Tiempos;* Chris Perez Band (Selena's brother) wins the rock/alternative prize for *Resurrection;* Tito Puente and *Mambo Birdland* take the traditional tropical award; Los Van Van with its *Llego Van Van: Van Van Is Here* captures the salsa title; Elvis Crespo and *Pintame* nails the best merengue category; Plácido Domingo and *100 Años De Mariachi* earn the Mexican-American prize; Los Palominos with *Por Eso Te Amo* wins the Tejano title; and Poncho Sanchez claims the Latin jazz category with *Latin Soul.*

Aguilera arrives at the Grammy podium with a rich show business background. At the age of 12 she's a singing/dancing member of the Disney Channel's revamped *New Mickey Mouse Club.* Her Disney connection channels her to sing the ballad, *Reflection*, for *Mulan*, the studio's animated feature, which in turn lands her an RCA recording contract, resulting in a eponymous debut album last year. Following a series of small media showcases in New York, Los Angeles, Las Vegas, Minneapolis, and Toronto, she receives offers to appear with the Backstreet Boys and *NSYNC and instead joins the all-female Lilith Fair tour. RCA hires an Internet marketing firm in New York to create a cyberspace buzz for its new artist, which helps build a fan base.

After performing in English and winning the Grammy for these efforts, she decides to take on the Latin market as she begins to show interest in her Latin culture on her father's side. He's from Ecuador; her mother is Irish-American and they divorced when she is seven. First, she re-records her hit single, *Genie in a Bottle*, in Spanish as the prelude to cutting a Latin version of her debut RCA album, even though she speaks little Spanish. Veteran Spanish hit making producer Rudy Pérez is hired to work on the album which will feature Spanish versions of her hits, including *Genie*, plus some new Latin tunes. A language coach is helping with her Spanish skills. Pérez prophesizes to *Time* that Christina's penchant for rhythm 'n'blues while she was growing up will enable her to add these music ingredients and take "Latin music to new places."

India, who is nominated in the best salsa category for *Sola*, her fourth solo album for New York label RMM, plans to jump into the big leagues this year by signing with Sony after recording a final album for RMM, which will also lose Marc Anthony, Celia Cruz, and José Alberto before ultimately going out of business. Legally named Linda Caballero, the 27-year-old India, whose lyrics are compared to Alanis Morissette's, emerges from a horrific life in the Bronx section of New York City, where according to published reports she hid under her bed at age seven while her father beat her mother. Those scars turn her into a feminist who uses music to champion against male chauvinism and a determination to control her own path in life. After her parents split, India begins singing professionally as a teen to help her mother pay bills.

After meeting DJ Little Louie Vega, the two connect with Jellybean (John) Benitez's record label where she cuts several disco tunes before coming to the attention of David Maldonado, then managing Rubén Blades. She's 17. Maldonado also signs Marc Anthony and debuts his own label, Soho Records, with the two and RMM as its distributor. On her first album in 1992, India works with pianist, salsa exponent Eddie Palmieri. On her second album in '94, she duets with Anthony. In '96 she teams with timbale star Tito Puente and the Count Basie Band on a disc which is dismally received within the salsa community. RMM makes up for this flop by releasing remixes of India's top salsa cuts, while she is featured on two other RMM releases. In a field devoid of feminine salsa singers, India and veteran Celia Cruz are its two female shining stars.

Although he misses out on a Grammy, Marc Anthony's charisma earns him his first HBO showcase in February, *Marc Anthony: The Concert from Madison Square Garden* where the 31-year-old native New Yorker performs for his hometown fans. Anthony likes to stress he's no overnight sensation despite last year's crossover hoopla. He's been performing for the last 19 years in music, on Broadway as the lead in Paul Simon's failed 1998 murder musical, *The Capeman*, and Martin Scorsese's 1990 film, *Bringing Out the Dead.* Having sung on commercials and as a backup singer for pop acts including Menudo, he makes his recording debut in 1991 with his English-language disco album, *When the Night Is Over*. Two years later he starts working with his Puerto Rican heritage's salsa music and records three strong selling albums. He's 25 years old and has gained the respect within the mainstream music industry. "He's a bright, shining star," is the way Carlos Santana describes him to *TV Guide*. Two months later Anthony is on a national concert tour. His star status will later earn him a coveted slot within the tribute to the late Celia Cruz during the opening segment of the fourth annual Latin Grammys broadcast on CBS from Miami September 3, 2003.

Aside from the Grammys, Gloria Estefan, Selena, and a group of Latin Christian artists are adding remarkable diversity to Latin music. Estefan releases her third Spanish-language album, *Alma Caribeña* (*Caribbean Soul*) on Sony label Epic, which features a potpourri of sounds and influences from her native Cuba, Puerto Rico, Panama, and the Dominican Republic. Her first Spanish foray for Sony is in 1993 with the one million plus selling *Mi Tierra*, followed in 1995 by *Abriendo Puertas*, which sells 400,000 copies, according to SoundScan. Summarizing the three LPs, Estefan tells *Billboard:* "Latin music culture is so rich and diverse, there's no way to capture it all on one record." In fact, it takes Gloria and husband/producer Emilio four years to plot this latest record, time she says allows her to be totally comfortable with the lyrics of all the tunes. Appearing on the album with her are Celia Cruz and Jose Feliciano, who is also enjoying a resurgence in popularity after many years out of the pop spotlight.

Having star power lands Gloria Estefan major promotional television exposure as part of the latest album's marketing efforts. Prior to its release, she stars in her first network special, *Gloria Estefan, Caribbean Soul: The Atlantis Concert*, which airs on CBS May 12. During the taping at the new Bahamas Atlantis hotel, she's joined by such audience attractors as *NSYNC, Marc Anthony, Celia Cruz, and Jose Feliciano. On May 24, during the week of the LP's release, you can find her on *Cristina* on Univision, the *Late Show with David Letterman* on CBS, the syndicated *Rosie O'Donnell Show*, performing on the *Today* show on NBC during its summer concert series, and taping PBS' *Sessions at West 54th* for a later airing. A single from the album, *No Me Dejes De Querer*, has double exposure on Latin radio and in a remixed version plays at dance clubs.

Latin radio is also the target for Latin Christian music, whose artists are aching to get into the now available crossover Anglo market. The most successful new artist in the Latin Christian field is Jaci Velasquez, a two-time winner of the Gospel Music Association's Dove Award as female vocalist of the year. For the first time, the Dove Awards are aired in Spanish on the Internet in the U.S. and on a satellite-delivered broadcast to Latin America.

One year following a 1997 appearance at the Dove Awards, Velasquez is signed to Sony Discos, even though she doesn't speak fluent Spanish, but with tutoring is able to release two Spanish singles, *Llegar A Ti and Sólo Tú*, both from her Myrrh/Sony Discos *Llegar A Ti* album, which will subsequently sell 115,000 copies in both the Christian and Latino markets. She looks upon this recording as helping her reach her "ministry which is the Latin industry," she tells *Billboard.* Both singles, incidentally, do well with radio airplay and consumer sales for the 20-year-old Texas vocalist.

In one of those not uncommon label-switching moves when an artist gets hot, Velasquez shifts from the parent Word Entertainment's Myrrh label to the more renowned Word imprint. Word's Latin roster already encompasses Miguel Guerra, Ricardo Rodriguez, Dani Driggs, and Salvador, a five-man group from Austin. Driggs performs at the "2000 Years with Jesus" festival in Maracahna, Mexico, before 115,000 believers. Salvador is booked to perform at one of the nine concerts presented at Exploit, an annual Latin/Christian music conference taking place this year in Miami. The event starts out as a bookseller's convention but adds record label exhibitors that now account for about 35 percent of the booths, or "music ministries," as conference director Marie Tamayo calls them. Words Latin general manager Luis Fernandez, a 22-year business veteran, calls all the interest "a new era for Spanish Christian music."

What's not generally reported in the mass media is the convergence of the Latin and Christian genres, which sees secular labels like Sony and Fonovisa creating Spanish gospel labels, English-speaking gospel acts recording in Spanish, and Latino artists recording their religious messages for the larger contemporary Christian music market. In addition to Velasquez, who lands an opening act slot on Ricky Martin's Nashville tour stop in July, there are other gospel artists that also record in Spanish, including Steve Green, Margaret Becker, and Dove recipient Crystal Lewis, who starts testifying in Spanish in 1992 and has six LPs to her credit. Artists going in the opposite direction toward the Christian market are found on such labels as the EMI Christian Music Group's EMI CMG and One Voice, a four-year-old Spanish Christian label operating out of Miami, as does gospel market leader Word. One Voice has a reciprocal distribution deal with the Provident Music Group, an Anglo firm, to place its product in the Latin market, while Provident moves One Voice releases into the Anglo Christian retail arena. One Voice's vice president, Gloria Garcés-Alvarado, notes in *Billboard* that the distribution deal is "the first time a Spanish label has crossed over into the contemporary Christian music market" and she hopes it's a door-opener for other Latino religious labels.

Open to exploitation by the Spanish invasion are the more than 400 Christian bookstores in the country, the foundation for gospel album sales. Provident Music Group anticipates selling both its English and Spanish versions on One Voice in this highly influential branch of retailing. Despite all the optimism anent breaking Spanish acts in the Anglo Christian market, there are voices of dissent. One belongs to Bill Hearn, president/CEO of the British EMI-owned EMI CMG operation. He doesn't believe Anglo artists singing in Spanish are gaining support from Latinos. "Indigenous artists that make an effort to tour, work churches and do concerts do okay, but (with) Anglo artists doing translation records, we just have not seen very good sales," he tells *Billboard*. Jaci Velasquez he calls an exception "because of her mainstream airplay and Sony Discos making her a priority."

In a bizarre display of forlorn love, fans of murdered 23-year-old Tejano singer Selena Quintanilla Perez are scooping up her albums five years after her death and the release of seven posthumous albums, the Jennifer Lopez-starring *Selena* feature film and a score of books. Putting her life in perspective is the $2-million budgeted stage musical, *Selena Forever*, which opens in San Antonio, and is scheduled to play Corpus Christi, Houston, Dallas, Chicago, Los Angeles, and San Diego. A planned 30-city tour, with an eye on eventually landing on Broadway, never materializes. With a cast of 35, the San Antonio performance is attended by Selena's parents and sister as well as Tejano stars Bobby Pulido and Jennifer Peña and the president of EMI Latin, her label which is reissuing all her recordings.

The stage play is called the first professional musical about a Latina music star, written by Latinos and featuring a 95 percent Hispanic cast. It's the brainchild of its producer, Tom Quinn, who dreams up the production after seeing the movie. The director is William Alejandro Virchis, normally director of the theater department at Southwestern College in San Diego and co-founder of San Antonio's Old Globe Theatre's Teatro Meta project. Quinn also hires Fernando Rivas, a Cuban-born composer/arranger/producer to write the score which encompasses 27 new songs and nine new arrangements for Selena tunes. Script and lyrics are written by Edward Gallardo, winner of a Joseph Papp national Latino play competition in New York, who says he focuses on cultural issues not covered in the movie. Auditions in San Antonio, Corpus Christi and Dallas are sparked by casting announcements made on *Cristina*, Univision's highly rated daytime talk show.

One year after the crossover detonation and awakening by the nation to the existence of handsome and beautiful Latino artists swinging and singing in English, the fallout also touches other crossover hopefuls and tinges the traditional Mexican music branch of Hispanic show business.

This is the year Colombian artists seek a beachhead along with other youthful rock en Español enthusiasts from Mexico, Venezuela, Argentina, Spain, Chile, and Cuba. One Colombian vocalist, Shakira, prepares to enter the U.S. with an English-language album. Others, like Juanes and Bloque, seek to follow the path patterned by Aterciopelados, which made an impact in 1998 with its Grammy-nominated album, *Caribe Atómico.* Other aspiring bands trying to follow suit are Molotov, Café Tacuba (which uses a drum machine instead of a real-live musician), Fabulosos Cadillacs, El Gran Silencio, and Los Amigos.

In the field of less raucous Latin pop, artists set for a push across the border include Mexico's José José, Chile's La Lay, Spain's Alejandro Sanz, Venezuela's King Changó and Guaco, and Cuba's Rolo Martinez. Other Cuban artists getting around the U.S. economic embargo are Rubén González, the Buena Vista Social Club's 80-year-old pianist, with his second solo album, plus Barbarito Torres, Pío Leyva, and Arte Mixto.

Traditional Mexican music, with diverse sub-genres that generally lack crossover appeal to Anglos, is poised to snatch some of the spinoff affect of last year's media attention for the sexy young Hispanics singing in English. The problem is Mexican-flavored music remains within its cultural confines, a world unfamiliar to non-Latinos. Nonetheless, mariachi, conjunto, norteño, and Tejano, for example, attract loyal fans, primarily in the Southwest.

Of all these musical styles, mariachi remains the most family-oriented form of Mexican music, germinating in the home country hundreds of years ago and reportedly crystallizing into an easily identified form in the 19th century in the state of Jalisco. Once dominated by all-male bands, there are now all-female mariachi bands playing their brass, wind, and violin instruments (along with emotional vocals) with the same devotion and intensity as their male brethren. There are also bands that have expanded their instrumentation and repertoire to include English-language songs. One ensemble, the 12-member San Antonio band, Campanas De América, which forms in 1979, is noted for its inclusion over the years of trombone, flugelhorn, and lots of percussion.

There are also mariachi conferences, festivals, and concerts attracting large followings, including, among others, the 21-year-old San Antonio International Mariachi Festival, now known as the Ford and Lincoln Mercury Mariachi Vargas Concert and Extravaganza, the 18-year-old Tucson International Mariachi Conference, the 10-year-old Mariachi USA Festival at the Hollywood Bowl, and the equally as old San Jose International Mariachi Festival and Conference.

If mariachi is the musical export from Mexico since the 1920s, conjunto is the rural folk music of the Southwest, performed by three- or four-man groups that play accordion and the bajo sexto bass guitar. Norteño bands, which employ accordions and the bajo sexto, are a close cousin to conjunto groups. Tejano, the uptown sound of the energy-laden big city, with bands fusing electric guitars and keyboards with the culturally rich sound of the region, appears to be the brand of regional music most able to cross cultural borders, much the way Selena was poised to do. Two major Tejano events are San Antonio's 19th annual Tejano Conjunto Festival and its six-day long Tejano Conjunto Festival, which draws fans from California, Minnesota, Montana, and Canada.

How does the accordion wind up being used by so many regional bands? Historians point to its being brought to Northern Mexico and South Texas by German immigrants in the late 1800s.

Of all the forms of Mexican music, conjunto impacts "people's everyday life by being played at weddings, dances, and funerals," emphasizes Cynthia L. Vidaurri, the Smithsonian Institution's coordinator of its Latin Cultural Resource Network to *Hispanic* Magazine.

One artist who seeks his own identity apart from the crossover phenomenon is Panama's political polemist Rubén Blades, a failed candidate for the presidency of Panama in 1994 but the winner of several Grammys in the U.S. and the welcome collaborator with Lou Reed, Elvis Costello, and Willie Colón. His latest album on Sony Discos, *Tiempos*, blends elements of jazz and classical music with fairly known rhythms from Latin and South America. This album eschews the strong and powerful political statements he's made in the past calling for social change in Latin America and against the U.S.' anti-embargo policies against Cuba.

Working with the Costa Rican band, Editus, the underlying rhythm is the chacarera, found more commonly in Chile and Argentina than in the salsa centers of Havana and New York. Combining indigenous musical ingredients on this recording will serve as the linchpin for a similar project in 2003, the equally adventurous *Mundo* on Sony Discos, which includes Gallic bagpipes and some English-sung tunes. While it wins Latin Grammy nominations for album of the year and contemporary tropical album, Blades walks away empty handed in this popularity contest.

Latin show business is becoming big business, so it's rather appropriate that a talent agent is honored during *Billboard*'s seventh annual Latin Music Awards at the Jackie Gleason Theatre of Performing Arts in Miami Beach. Jorge Pinos, vice president of the international department at the world-famous Williams Morris Agency, is given the El Premio special award for helping bring Latin music to non-Hispanic markets. Of course, having such stalwart clients like Enrique Iglesias, Shakira, and Thalía, certainly helps. He is one of the first talent agents to book Hispanic acts in the U.S. and overseas.

One artist known in the Caribbean and the U.S. is Cuban-born bandleader Machito, whose 1943 recording of the Mario Bauzá composition, *Tanga*, is credited with helping build Latin jazz in America. Seven of his classic albums are being reissued by Sonido Records. They cover the period from 1956-'71 when Machito is one of New York's top band attractions playing alongside such contemporaries as Tito Rodriquez, Tito Puente, and Eddie Palmieri at the fabled Palladium. Born Frank Grillo in Havana in 1912, Machito dies in 1984. In this new 21st century, the nation's swelling Latino population, which has been exposed to jazz before migrating to the U.S., is driving in part the popularity of such artists as Danílo Perez, David Sánchez, Ray Vega, William Cepeda, and Arturo O'Farrill.

Artists already fusing the excitement of Africa and Cuba are also aware of creative movements developing in other nations.

Venezuela, which is spawning its share of alternative rock groups, has another treasure for domestic audiences. For the first time in the U.S. the music of Guaco, the country's highly touted 18-piece band, is heard on reissues by two labels. Universal Music Latino releases a 12-track hits compilation under the title *Exitos*. Latin World Records offers the band rerecording current works and old favorites.

The band's blending of salsa with rock and electronic elements, while it alienates some Venezuelans, is accepted by Carlos Santana and Rubén Blades, who hire them to play on their stadium shows, thus ensuring sellouts.

Looking for sellout concert dates in the U.S. is the second annual "Watcha Tour" this year concentrating not on Latin pop acts, but on hard-edged rock en Español bands like Café Tacuba, Molotov, Aterciopelados, Los Enanitos Verdes, A.N.I.M.A.L., Maldita Vecindad, and Ozomatli. Two of these groups have gained some crossover exposure, Café Tacuba opening for Beck and Ozomatli for Santana.

The 18-city tour, up from last year's 11 stops, is sponsored by Coors Light. "Watcha," is a Spanglish term which means "check it out." This sojourn is the end result of last year's "Warped Tour" featuring Anglo bands. When "Warped" ends in Miami, Kevin Lyman, its producer, decides to explore the Latin market and employs much of the "Warped" road crew to keep the new Latino venture moving. Although "Watcha's" initial effort loses money, there's enough interest to bring this year's project into uncharted waters, aiming at a primarily Hispanic audience, which shows up in force last year. This summer tour showcases five bands on weeknights, eight on weekends, with local concert promoters bringing in local favorites to bring the total of working bands to 20, compared to the 140 employed during the "Warped" tour.

Working to also build up Latin touring business is the upstart New York agency Martinez, Morgalo & Associates, whose goal is to create a network of new cities beyond the traditional "cuchifrito" circuit of cities with major Hispanic populations. "Cuchifrito" relates to the "bread and butter" stop-off points which Latin acts traditionally play. The new agency specializes in tropical salsa by such artists as Rubén Blades, Luis Enrique, Son By Four, and Luis Damón. Its partners are Arturo Martinez and Robert Morgalo, in association with Blades, who seek to change the current pattern of booking scattered dates in the Northeast, then in the South, the Midwest, and finally the West.

The first artist set by the agency to blaze the new touring circuit is Damón, sent first to Kansas City to bridge dates between Minneapolis and Chicago. Partner Morgalo hooks up with a Kansas City radio station that plays salsa and merengue and a local promoter who wants in on the project and books the Grand Emporium on a Sunday night. Everything clicks and the show is a success. The singer's self-titled album on Sonolux/Sony is available in local stores for the first time as part of the promotion. Damón ultimately plays 32 shows during April. In October, he hits the trail again for a month and a half. Besides the Grand Emporium, venues like the Club Viva in St. Louis and the Quest in Minneapolis are now booking Hispanic groups for the first time. The agency also has tours for Blades on college campuses, and Luis Enrique, and Son by Four in the fall to more commercial venues.

Rock en Español is on the minds of the participants at the Latin Alternative Music Conference in New York in August where bands from the U.S., Mexico, Colombia, Argentina, Chile, and Venezuela perform around the city. Among the 700 registrants attending seminars, there is no definitive term used to describe alternative Latin music, although it generally has a most difficult time being played on formatted Spanish radio stations, which prefer regional Mexican, tropical salsa, and Latin middle ground pop styles. Among the musicians performing are these disparate acts: Juliet Venegas, who grows up in Tijuana, learns English by watching American television beamed across the Mexico border and writes her lyrics in Spanish; Austin, Texas' bilingual band Vallejo, which fuses Caribbean rhythms with rap, heavy metal, and Southern rock; Chile's La Ley which explores rock patterns, and Tijuana's Nortec, proponents of electronic sounds. Of prime importance to this movement is acceptance by the growing domestic bilingual Hispanic community.

Puerto Rico, New York's musical cousin and historical bastion for tropical music, is undergoing a musical evolution of sorts, with reggae and rap joining the stalwart genres of merengue and salsa, the latter led by new quartet Son by Four. And these creative ripples are being felt on the Mainland. Islanders still cite the success in the English-language market by Menudo, Ricky Martin, Marc Anthony, and Jennifer Lopez, all of Puerto Rican descent. Now new merengue stars Gisselle, Luis Fonsi, Melina León, and Jéssica, join the ranks of established merengue proponents Elvis Crespo and Olga Tañon.

While the Commonwealth's 100 radio stations usually guarantee airplay for all genres of music, a consolidation of formats due to the arrival of major chains like Spanish Broadcasting System is causing concern among record labels. As Fernando Ramos, BMG Puerto Rico's general manager relates to *Billboard*, "Now it's harder to break an artist in radio because the formats are very similar to those in the U.S."

A number of Commonwealth artists are gaining Mainland exposure as their record companies create multiple style versions of their records to appeal to diverse listeners. Gaining from this exploitative technique are Son by Four, Gisselle, Olga Tañon, Millie, Jerry Rivera, Frankie Negron, and Elvis Crespo. Rogelio Macín, general manager of BMG Latin, asserts in the *Los Angeles Times* that this multiple-style concept is the real "crossover" involving selling musical genres rather than language. The domestic Latin market, he stresses, is comprised of "immigrants from all over the world," and because their tastes are different, record companies must provide these consumers with music "the way they like to hear it."

Gisselle's BMG single, *Jurame*, sounds like a pop ballad rather than a traditional merengue record and is sold in markets where the singer is not associated with merengue music. Salsa specialists Son by Four's single, *A Puro Dolor*, becomes the No. 1 Latin single in the country after being issued as a combination salsa/R&B mixture in Puerto Rico, Miami, and New York. In the Midwest, South, and Southwest, the version gaining airplay is a sweet pop ballad. The R&B version, with some English lyrics, even makes the general market pop singles chart in *Billboard* at No. 13. The group's album contains the salsa and pop versions of the hit. Salsa singers Jerry Rivera and Frankie Negron, and merengue vocalist Olga Tañon, all find accepting ears for their regional Mexican and romantic pop remixes. Alejandro Fernández's multi-designed single, *Quiereme*, plays primarily as a pop ballad, while in New York and Miami, the version has the requisite Afro-Caribbean rhythms for those cities. Elvis Crespo sees his merengue image burnished by an early crossover into the disco dance market in 1998 and '99 with the refashioned single, *Suavemente*, which remains on the *Billboard* dance chart for a record-making 99 weeks. A more expansive, detailed look at Puerto Rico's rich entertainment history through 2005 is provided in Chapter 15.

Arturo "Chico" O'Farrill, born into a Cuban-Irish-German family in Havana in 1921 and becomes one of Cuban's most promising musicians after moving to New York City in 1948 to make his mark in Latin jazz, passes away on June 27, 200l, at age 79 from pneumonia. At the time of his death he's working on the score for a Broadway musical patterned after the film, *The Mambo Kings*. Feeding into New York City's creative cauldron, O'Farrill becomes one of the most sought after player/arranger/composers and a key proponent of Afro-Cuban jazz. His works are used by Count Basie, Benny Goodman, Stan Kenton, Wynton Marsalis, David Bowie, and Ringo Starr. Among his compositions, *The Afro-Cuban Jazz Suite* finds favor with Charlie Parker and Machito; *Afro-Cuban Jazz Moods* is a workhorse for Machito and Dizzy Gillespie and *Manteca Suite* is lionized by Gillespie.

Among his two dozen albums, his best-known titles on Milestone are *The Afro-Cuban Jazz Suite*, *Gone City*, and his last, *Carambola*. O'Farrill is featured in the new film documentary *Calle 54*, the subject for a soon to be completed documentary by Cuban American filmmaker Jorge Ulla.

During the past six years, O'Farrill leads his own ensemble, the Afro-Cuban Jazz Orchestra, on Sunday nights at Birdland. His son, pianist Arturo, Jr., produces three of his father's albums and will carry on the family tradition of big band leadership next year when he and Wynton Marsalis create the Afro-Latin Jazz Orchestra for Lincoln Center's new jazz program, and Arturo becomes the orchestra's leader. In 2005, almost to the date of the fourth anniversary of his father's death, New York City names the intersection of West 88th Street and West End Avenue after him.

While there is often much similarity in television programming, on September 24 a historic event takes place: CBS' telecast of the first annual Latin Grammy Awards from the new downtown Los Angeles Staples Center marks the first time in television history an English-language network airs a bilingual program with all the performances in Spanish or Portuguese. The show is also broadcast to 120 overseas countries.

Originally scheduled for 2001, the show is moved up one year, explains Michael Greene, president/CEO of the parent National Academy of Recording Arts & Sciences, because the timing is appropriate for NARAS' new sister organization, the nearly three-year-old Latin Academy of Recording Arts & Sciences, to publicly emerge amidst the growing popularity for Latin music. The Latin Grammys are also in the City of Angeles because of a 1996 Miami-Dade County ordinance prohibiting the dispensation of monies for the presentation of Cuban artists or the works. Groups must sign an affidavit that they have no connections to Cuba in order to use county-owned venues or receive county cultural grants. These stipulations are the result of disfavor among the Cuban exile community when Miami considers hosting the Latin Grammys, which will include Cuban nominees and possibly even winners. In May, a federal judge issues a temporary injunction to allow groups to apply for grants without signing any affidavits.

Controversy follows the Latin Grammys to Los Angeles. There, Gilberto Moreno, general manager of Fonovisa, the largest independent Latin label in the country, says his company will not support the new awards because they ignore Mexican regional artists in favor of artists associated with Sony's labels and Emilio Estefan, and eschews having any Mexican regional artists performing on the telecast. Moreno is especially piqued at what he perceives as a cozy relationship between Estefan and the Latin Recording Academy, both of whom reside in Miami. Estefan's response to the criticism is to cite disappointment in the lack of unity and the need to unite and put aside differences. Fonovisa, it turns out, has five artists nominated in the Mexican regional category, La Banda El Recodo, Conjunto Primavera, Ana Bárbara, Los Temerarios, and Los Tigres Del Norte. By the end of the night, Banda El Recodo, Los Temerarios, and Los Tigres are all winners.

Greene says he chose CBS as the best network to present Latino music to a mainstream audience, one which associates the Eye Network with its long coverage of the English-language Grammys held in February. The 40 category Latin telecast starts off attracting nine million viewers and ends with a 7.47 million average and a 3.2 rating/9 share among 18- to 49-year-olds, according to the Nielsen company. By contrast, the Anglo Grammys in February attract an average of 24.7 million viewers and a 12.6/31 for the same 18 to 49 demographic.

The disappointing ratings results are palpable. I'm curious as to why the show draws so few viewers, and during a research trip to Miami a few years later, I query record company executives for their opinions. They generally agree CBS doesn't promote the show properly in the Hispanic media, Latinos are accustomed to tuning in with regularity to the Hispanic networks and they aren't motivated to change their viewing habits by switching to an English-language network even when there's mucho Spanish spoken.

Audience composition aside, among the show's major and multiple Latin Grammy winners are: Luis Miguel, Mexico's pop singer with three trophies including album of the year and top pop album for *Amarte Es Un Placer* and top male vocal with *Tu Mirada;* Carlos Santana who wins three times for record of the year and rock duo vocal for *Corazón Espinado*—both with Mexican rock band Maná—and for top pop instrumental with *El Faro;* Shakira who wins pop female vocal award for *Ojos Así*, which includes *elements from* her

Lebanese upbringing and top rock female vocal with *Octavo Dia;* producer/songwriter Emilio Estefan, Jr., nominated for six awards for working with various artists in several capacities, garners two awards—producer of the year and director of his wife Gloria's best music video *No Me Dejes De Querer;* rock vocalist Fito Páez wins two honors, rock male vocal and top rock song, both for *Al Lado del Carmino;* tropical performers Juan Luis Guerra Y 440 for merengue performance with *Ni Es Lo Mismo Ni Es Igual* and tropical song *El Niágara En Bicicleta.*

Single winners include: best new artist Ibrahim Ferrer, the 72-year-old Cuban singer with the Buena Vista Social Club who wins for his debut solo album; pop duo or group vocal: Maná with *Se Me Olvidó Otra Vez*; rock album: Café Tacuba's *Revés/Yosoy*; tropical salsa performance: Celia Cruz with *Celia Cruz and Friends: A Night of Salsa;* traditional performance: posthumous award to Tito Puente for *Mambo Birdland;* ranchera performance: Alejandro Fernández with *Mi Verdad*, beating out his legendary father Vicente; banda performance: La Banda El Recodo with *Lo Mejor De Mi Vida;* groupo performance: Los Temerarios with *En La Madrugada Se Fue*; tejano performance: Los Palominos with *Por Eso Te Amo;* norteño performance: Los Tigres Del Norte with *Herencia De Familia;* regional top song: Alejandro Fernández with *Mi Verdad;* jazz: tie between *Spain* by Michel Camilo and Tomatito and *Tropical Nights* by Paquito D'Rivera; Brazilian pop album: *Crooner* with Milton Nascimento; Brazilian rock album: *Acústico MTV* by Os Paralamas do Sucesso; Brazilian samba album: *Zeca Pagodinho Ao Vivo* by Zeca Pagodinho; and Brazilian song: *Acelerou* by Djavan.

Among the show's performance highlights are an opening tribute to the late Tito Puente featuring Gloria Estefan, Ricky Martin, Celia Cruz, and *NSYNC performing in Spanish with Puerto Rican-bred salsa vocal group Son by Four.

Since this is an election year, both major parties reach into Latin music for name acts to appear at their conventions, both during primetime convention hours and at separate concerts for delegates, another first. The Republicans hire Vicente Fernández, the legendary ranchera superstar to sing *Cielito Lindo* during the closing moments of their conclave in Philadelphia, a significant move considering his age and appeal to older Hispanics. They also play Ricky Martin's *Livin' La Vida Loca* tune innumerous times during the convention. The Democrats, obviously seeking younger voters, book Los Lobos, a favorite among younger Latinos, for the opening day of their convention in Los Angeles. It's all about numbers: the U.S. Census' proclaims 32 million Latinos were counted in the survey, which is 12 percent of the population, excluding all those illegals who've snuck into the country. The Republicans look to Emilio Estefan to put together a concert extolling the party's new interest in their presence. He comes through with powerful singers Celia Cruz, Jon Secada, and Carlos Ponce. Cruz Bustamente, California's little known Lieutenant Governor, develops a "Latin Talent Showcase" at the Universal Amphitheatre featuring another group of heavy hitters: Enrique Iglesias, Los Lobos and Tex-Mex band Little Joe Y La Familia.

Everyone is romancing the eight percent of Latinos registered to vote...with music. Steve Loza, a UCLA professor of ethnomusicology, explains the reasoning behind all this Latin talent to the *Los Angeles Times:* "What the Democrats and Republicans have figured out is that music is the heart and soul of Hispanics. They need the vote in all the key states, Texas, California, and Illinois, where we've got big numbers."

Following the Republican convention, criticism arises over some of the music usage. Robi Rosa, composer of the hit Ricky Martin tune, issues a statement protesting the repeated playing of the song. And fans of Vicente Fernández are also critical of his appearance. Performing in his normal rodeo cowboy charro outfit, topped by his giant sombrero, he is viewed by fans as a working-class booster, and they cannot understand why he is performing for a party which in 1992, '96, and '98 showed a lack of openness toward Hispanics. In 1998, for example, California Republicans, seen as unfriendly toward Mexicans, lose big time, while Republicans in Texas, seen as being friendlier to Mexicans, win their races. Fernandez quickly goes on Spanish-language TV to defend his appearance and stress it is not a political statement of any sort.

As the year closes out, record companies are focusing on the nation's English-speaking Hispanic population, a populace which Sylvia Rhone, Elektra Records chairman, tells *Billboard* is an invisible link within the mainstream market. Elektra has two domesticated Latin acts targeted toward the Anglo market first: Angie Martinez and Lugo, a one-name teen singer, both of whom will debut with hip-hop singles.

In addition to Elektra, other companies sensing the surging Hispanic population's potential for supporting artists who are Latin and sing in English, include Virgin, MCA, Arista and Crescent Moon. Unknown names like Crystal Sierra (Virgin), Joy Enriquez (Arista), Christina Sarazola Valemi (MCA), and Vallejo and Daniel Reno (Crescent Moon), all have one thing in common. Their musical direction reflects their companies' desire for mass appeal, rather than Latin market, penetration. But that, too, holds the potential for additional marketing and dollars.

Joy Enriquez, a Mexican-American from Whittier, California, who is Arista's entry into the mainstream market with an album produced by hit-maker Kenneth "Babyface" Edmonds, is the voice paired with EMI Latin's Carlos Ponce on the tune *Bella Notte* in English and Spanish for the Walt Disney animated feature, *Lady and the Tramp II, Scamp's Adventure.* Babyface is the former producing partner with Arista's current president/CEO Antonio "L.A." Reid in the team of LaFace, which produces hits with Whitney Houston and Sheena Easton. When Edmonds strikes out on his own, he produces hits for Mariah Carey, Toni Braxton, and TLC. Crystal Sierra, who records for EMI-owned Virgin, ties Colombian rhythm elements with her hip-hop vocal on her initial single, *Morena*, which features rappers Cuban Links and Styles Skillz. A second single, *Playa No More*, is also designed for pop and R&B radio plays.

The fusion of musical styles is also affecting the sound and look of television commercials. Major advertisers from Miller Light to the Macy's department store chain to McDonald's, to clothing and cosmetics firms, are all using Latin actors, actresses, and musicians to reach into the English-language TV. The sensuous sounds of salsa, mambo, cha-cha, merengue, samba, bossa nova, and other variants of Afro-Caribbean music are all heard propelling the on-screen action. The parallel action by ad agencies is a result of the media coverage of the Latinization of America and the acceptance of the nation's Hispanic culture.

Mainstream is what English-language TV stations are concerned Latino TV is becoming. Nielsen Media Research, which produces the industry's ratings figures on which the industry's fates and fortunes rise or fall, is in the cross-hairs of Univision, the leading Latin network, which claims Nielsen undercounts its viewers, while Anglo executives have their backs up against any technology changes that will reflect greater Hispanic viewership and diminish their ability to charge higher ad rates. Nielsen first begins calculating Hispanic ratings in 1992 and eight years later it admits that while it may measure the correct number of Hispanic households in its survey, it may not have the right amount of people in those homes whose principal language is Spanish.

In New York, the nation's largest TV market where there are 6.8 million TV households, Nielsen estimates Hispanics account for more than one million of those TV viewing homes and Spanish is the main language in 500,000 of those residences. During a field survey by Nielsen to estimate the size of the New York area's Spanish-speaking population, the company projects that 43 Latino homes should be represented in its 500 households that have its TV-viewing meters, rather than the 21 now in the survey. English-language TV stations aren't buying this, according to a *New York Times* article of the dispute. In May, discrepancies surface in Nielsen's two surveys, one for the general market, which includes Hispanic TV, and a second Latin TV exclusive report, for the New York market.

In the general market survey, Univision's WXTV averages 144,375 households weekdays from 6-7 p.m. for a 2.1 rating. In the

Hispanic Ratings index, which comes into play in 1995, WXTV has 236,168 homes tuned in for a 3.4 rating. WXTV is on a roll, beginning with the February sweeps in which its 6:30 p.m. newscast beats the ABC, CBS, and NBC nightly newscasts with 18- to 49-year-olds. In the general ratings, the Univision network news on WXTV finishes behind ABC and NBC, but not CBS. To appease Latin TV, Nielsen says it will add a minimum of five meters in Spanish-dominant New York homes, which translates into an additional 60,000 Latino households.

Progress is marked by slowly taken steps: in 2003 Nielsen announces it will not include new Hispanic measurements into its national People Meter System until 2006. The national People Meter sample of around 5,000 households will be expanded to nearly 10,000 households, of which 1,000 will be Hispanic, "and should be sufficient to provide a solid audience estimate for Hispanic programmers," claims Susan Whiting, Nielsen's president/CEO.

Univision and Telemundo, the two prime Latin TV program distributors, are attempting new programming strategies for their new seasons. Univision will launch its first million dollar version of ABC's *Who Wants to Be a Millionaire*, simply titled *A Million*, hosted by Mexican film and novela star Daniela Romo, and its first-ever produced sitcom, *Estamos Unidos* (*All Together*), starring Mexican actor Carlos Bonavides and Alicia Machado, the 1996 Miss Universe and current telenovela actress. The show's theme about a Mexican family adjusting to life in the U.S. is one Mexican immigrants can relate to. Univision president Ray Rodriguez says the network has been developing the sitcom for nearly two years and has 26 scripts ready to be produced from its Miami headquarters.

Rodriguez's hyperbole for the millionaire game show is first-rate. He tells *Electronic Media* it's "the most expensive property in the history of Spanish-language television," intentionally not mentioning the cost. While Televisa of Mexico continues to supply around 35 percent of Univision's programming, the network plans to accelerate its output of internal productions from 52 to 55 percent this year. Included are several four to six-hour miniseries, the first of which deals with the career of Mexican rock star Gloria Trevi and her husband, who are awaiting a trial date in Mexico for allegedly debauching minors.

In a highly political action, Univision airs a 10-part series featuring home videos smuggled out of the country of Fidel Castro on its New York, Miami, and Puerto Rico stations. *The Secret Life of Castro* videos were supposedly shot by Castro's adult children and somehow get to Castro's son Antonio's disgruntled former girlfriend who leaves Cuba with them.

Univision is also launching an hour-long newsmagazine titled *Ver Para Creer*, a children's novela, *Serafin*, and the new Televisa drama/novela, *Ramona*. It's expanding its sports weekly roundup to two hours, will offer live boxing Sunday afternoons, and has secured rights to several soccer tournaments, including elimination matches prior to the 2002 World Cup. Univision will also air the sports roundup show on its Galavision cable outlet.

Univision's Los Angeles-based Univision Productions film division is gearing up to handle 10–12 telepictures for its 4 p.m. Sunday movie slot. Formed last year, the division churns out 10 films in its fledgling period.

Telemundo has its own array of new shows for the fall, all designed to make audiences forget its disastrous 1998 attempt to refashion parent Sony's old Columbia TriStar TV series with a Spanish accent. Those Latinized sitcoms were a ratings disaster. The new shows include a first attempt at a morning news/information program, *Esta Manana*, weekdays from 7–9 a.m. co-hosted by José Díaz-Balart and Gloria Calzada. Diaz-Balart returns to Spanish TV after anchoring CBS News' *This Morning* from 1996–'99. Calzada is a former anchor on the network. There's also the U.S. introduction of the Spanish game show, *Numeros Rojos*, Saturdays at 8 p.m., following World Wrestling Federation matches at 7, and the debut of a Brazilian telenovela, *Tierra Nuestra*, dubbed from Portuguese to Spanish, during the 7–11 p.m. drama saga block. Network president, Jim

McNamara, calls it a centerpiece of the evening lineup. Another import from South America, this time from Colombia, is the dream come true novela, *Yo Soy Betty, La Fea* (*I Am Betty, the Ugly*). And on Sunday at 8:30 p.m., *Viva Vegas*, follows the exploits of two brothers from Venezuela who move to Las Vegas.

Underscoring both network's programming directions is a study by Strategy Research Corp. stating that teenagers who are bilingual and bicultural watch Spanish TV with the parents in the evenings. The research firm indicates that of the estimated 33.8 million domestic Hispanics, 11.6 million are 17 or younger and they watch general market TV with their friends, but when at home, view Spanish-language programs with their families at night. Univision claims 86 percent of its primetime viewers are Spanish-speaking teens, according to Nielsen audience composition breakouts. Two weekend shows specifically aimed at this audience are the magazine show *Control* and *Caliente*, a dance program.

Voting age Hispanics are the target for the first time for Spanish-language ads during the presidential primaries. A 30-second spot for Republican candidate George W. Bush runs on the Hispanic networks prior to the Arizona Republican primary. It's reportedly the first usage of a Spanish-language ad during the primaries and a barometer that the nation's Latino voters are a prime target to be coveted in order to gain the White House. In the spot, Bush, wearing his cowboy-ranch outfit of jeans and a work shirt intones: "Es un nuevo dia," this is a new day. Actually, the new day begins in 1998, according to Henry Cisneros, Univision's CEO, who tells the *Los Angeles Times* the network garners $8 million in political advertising that year. This year, he's predicting the figure will double. Telemundo's sales executive vice president, Stephen J. Levin, anticipates a political advertising bonanza for Spanish-language TV of "three to four hundred percent."

So it is indeed a new day for Latin broadcast and cable networks, as a number of niche channels seeks to siphon audiences from the broadcasting companies and entice new viewers with differing interests. Nickelodeon, Showtime, and HBO are among the powers adding Hispanic shows to their lineups. Other new channels involved include ESPN, the History Channel, and Home Shopping Network. Cable's penetration in the nation is now at 58 percent, up from 49 percent in 1995, according to Nielsen.

Showtime's initial entry is *Resurrection Blvd*, a drama about a South Los Angeles Latino family with an all-Latino cast and crew. Showtime estimates that of its 20 million subscribers, between 11 and 12 percent are Hispanic. Nickelodeon, recognizing the paucity of programs for Hispanic children on TV, creates three series, *The Brothers Garcia*, *Dora the Explorer*, and *Taina*. Each focuses on a different age bracket. HBO is moving into Latin territory on a number of levels. Its made-for-TV film, *For Love or Country: The Arturo Sandoval Story*, is the true saga of the Cuban trumpeter who defects to the U.S. with help from his idol, Dizzy Gillespie. HBO is also adding its HBO Latino service to its digital package of other features, including Spanish-language films and a Spanish translation for its *World Championship Boxing* series. It will also offer dubbed versions of the hit series *The Sopranos*, *Sex and the City*, and *Oz*. The channel also plans to film original material that it will insert as interstitials between films and series. HBO Latino becomes the seventh version of its brand. It plans searching for new films by sponsoring the 16th annual Chicago Latino Film Festival.

ESPN and Major League Baseball are offering Spanish-language simulcasts of select games from July 10 through the division playoffs on the ESPN2 channel. This first-time effort is designed to attract more Hispanic baseball fans who subscribe to cable and satellite-distributed services in the nation's top 10 markets, encompassing some 2.9 million Hispanic households. DirecTV, the largest satellite provider, is offering the games on its DirecTV Para Todos service. The History Channel, while not offering a new Spanish service, is nonetheless pitching Latinos by airing a Spanish-language commercial by Giselle Fernandez, co-host of its *This Week in History* series. The 30-second spot will run for five weeks during the summer on Univision, Galavision, and Telemundo in cities with heavy

Latino populations, including Dallas, Houston, and Los Angeles. Home Shopping Network launches Home Shopping en Español aimed at Hispanic home shoppers, who account for 85 percent of its sales, according to the network. It will include added features covering information and entertainment. The new service with the difficult to pronounce name, HSeE, is an update to a daily, three-hour version it has been running on Galavision for the past two years. Within two years HSeE is closed down.

About to open are two new Hispanic broadcast networks, individually and collectively no threat to Univision or Telemundo. The newcomers are Fort Worth-based Hispanic Television Network (HTVN), and Mexico City-based Azteca America, a new entity from Mexican programming power TV Azteca. Publicly held HTVN, which merges with the financially ailing American Independent Network, a producer of Spanish programming in 1999, is purchasing clusters of low-power TV stations that are blended into one signal to provide full coverage to that city. Its first purchase offer of $35 million for KLDT in the Dallas/Fort Worth area is its first effort to buy or affiliate with full-power stations in the top 20 Hispanic markets. CEO Marco Camacho says the network will go after Univision by programming all Mexican films, dramas, game shows, and sitcoms. To accomplish this, it signs with Mexico's MVS to develop and distribute its original shows. HTVN will be able to utilize MVS' production facilities and on-air talent. By the end of the year, HTVN will own or have affiliations with 25 stations, including outlets in Phoenix, Los Angeles, and San Antonio.

TV Azteca is pairing with Pappas Telecasting of Visalia, California, in the formation of Azteca America. Pappas will own 80 percent of the network and Azteca, which is handling the original programming, will own the remaining 20 percent and receive $1.5 million a month under a 20-year licensing agreement. Some of the 14 Pappas TV affiliates will start airing Azteca America in the second quarter of next year. These initial stations only can reach between 35 and 45 percent of domestic Hispanic households, excluding key markets like New York, Chicago, and San Diego. The company's goal is to spend upward of $435 million to buy additional stations to reach 65 percent of targeted homes by the end of next year. In December, it receives the Federal Communications Commission's approval to build its own full-power station in Los Angeles, KIDN, Channel 54. By 2003, Azteca America will have 24 affiliates around the country.

In what could be a major breakthrough for network TV, a Gregory Nava directed series about a Latino household called *American Family* is pitched to all three major networks. Nava chooses CBS, which green lights a pilot starring Edward James Olmos, Esai Morales, Raquel Welch, and Sonia Braga. It plays well with the critics when it airs, but is not on CBS' fall schedule. A CBS official explains it has a sufficient number of dramas that fit better into its line-up. However, Nava is given the opportunity to place it elsewhere and it winds up on PBS as one of its most popular and renewable primetime series.

Although ABC has no specific Latin-themed series, Latinos appear on its shows: Rubén Blades on *Gideon's Crossing*; Ian Gomez in *Norm*; Lana Parrilla in *Spin City*, and John Ortiz in *Leary*. While some of these shows will be canceled in the next few years, Esai Morales will join *NYPD* and George Lopez will star in his own self-titled hit comedy series. Besides Smits, other Hispanic actors who bask in the glow of national network celebrity include Hector Elizondo on *Chicago Hope*, Jaime Gomez on *Nash Bridges*, and Randy Vasquez on *JAG*, all on CBS.

What these isolated instances underscore is the small percentage of Latinos who work in television. Statistics from the Screen Actors Guild, for example, indicate Latino membership in its union at 4.4 percent—that's 4,973 of its 113,009 members. Of the Writers Guild of America's 10,173 members, 1.21 percent are Hispanic; only two percent of the Directors Guild of America's 11,825 dues payers are Latinos.

If TV is slow to employ Hispanics, there are award shows and film festivals to glorify Latin achievements in the arts. The fifth annual American Latin Media Arts Awards, the ALMAs, presented by the National Council of La Raza, honors Antonio Banderas as outstanding actor for *The 13th Warrior*; Cameron Diaz for the film *Any Given Sunday*; A Martinez for the daytime soap *General Hospital*; a tie for outstanding TV correspondent in a special between John Quiñones (*The Latin Beat*) and Geraldo Rivera (*Back to Bedlam*); Wilson Cruz as emerging actor in the TV series *Party of Five*; Laura Ceron for the TV series *ER;* Christina Aguilera, new entertainer of the year; Ricky Martin male entertainer of the year; and Jennifer Lopez as female entertainer of the year. Cristina Saralegui, Univision talk show host, is presented the community services award and actor Ian Gomez with a special achievement award.

This year marks the 30th anniversary of Nosotros' presentation of its Golden Eagle Awards, which were founded by Ricardo Montalban, who emerges as a contract actor in 1945 with MGM and has a commanding presence in films and TV up to the 1980s. The outstanding achievement this year goes to trumpeter Arturo Sandoval with the Hall of Fame award; actor Carlos Rivas with the Lifetime Achievement award; *Los Beltrán* as the top Spanish-language sitcom; *Resurrection Blvd.* as the top English-language series; and Martin Sheen with the *Ricardo Montalban* award.

Although the general public may not be aware of them, Latin film festivals surface around the country. The granddaddy is the 17-year-old Miami International Film Festival, followed by the 16-year-old Chicago Latino Film Festival, the four-year-old Los Angeles Latino International Film Festival, and the first-year New York International Latino Film Festival. Each provides exposure to films from all over the Americas, Spain and Portugal, including titles with major name stars like Penélope Cruz, John Leguizamo, and Rosie Perez.

Also making inroads around the country, especially in rural communities amidst the Rocky Mountains, Great Plains, and Southeast, are syndicated Spanish radio programs airing on former English-language stations that have been converted to meet the needs of newly arrived immigrants. In Laurel, Kansas, for example, KYUU-AM provides a familiar voice to new arrivals working in the beef processing plants. In many parts of the country, Spanish-language TV is only available on cable, so having a free radio station to listen to fits perfectly within the budgets of the new arrivals. KYUU and KMMJ-AM, Grand Island, Nebraska, are buying their programming from Z-Spanish, a Sacramento, California, company originally formed to provide programming for stations in the state's central valley area. Its satellite-fed, 24-hour regional Mexican music service is heard on 68 stations, usually in small markets, so as not to compete with Hispanic Broadcasting Corp., which targets major cities.

The company's co-founder John Bustos notes that when the company goes to satellite distribution, its signal reaches the entire nation. "We discovered what growing populations there are in places like Arkansas and Nebraska," he says in the *Los Angeles Times.* These rural Spanish-language stations blend local remotes with the syndicated programming, switching from farm reports to the beats of ranchera, corrido, and norteño. With converted stations cropping up in new parts of the U.S., Spanish-language radio is now available in 44 states, with at least 560 of the nation's 12,800 stations now broadcasting in Spanish. Twenty years ago there were only 67 Spanish-language radio stations in the nation, according to the Arbitron ratings service.

In Los Angeles, the nation's No. 1 market with 19 Spanish-language radio stations, a number of format alterations are changing the sound of Hispanic radio. KLYY-FM, a floundering alternative rock station, becomes *Viva 107* as it switches to upbeat Latin pop and romantic ballads. KLVE-FM, the second rated station, adds upbeat pop and dance cuts to its ballad-dominated format. KACE-FM and KRTO-FM, two rhythm 'n'blues specialists, both purchased by Hispanic Broadcasting Corp. from Cox Communications for $75 million, are converted to a new format called Hispanic oldies or *Recuerdo*. KRTO-FM becomes KRCV, and continues to simulcast KACE-FM's signal.

The new format goes against the grain at Hispanic FMs, which target 18- to 34-year-olds. The new oldies simulcast is designed to appeal to people 35 and older who may not be listening to younger skewing programming. One station, KWKW-AM, with its news/talk and broadcast of the Los Angeles Dodgers, attracts the oldest and wealthiest Hispanics, states Arbitron. KLAX-FM, which is the first Hispanic station to hold the No. 1 slot from 1992–'94, adds more Mexican styles, including oldies and standards, to a basic regional format that appeals to 18- to 49-year-olds, but has slipped in the ratings to 12th place. The Spanish Broadcasting System station's low rankings are countered by the company's KSCA-FM, which also plays regional Mexican, remaining the market's most popular station through two survey quarters from September through March. KSCA's popular morning personality since 1997, Reñan Almendarez Coello, by being syndicated to eight cities, has the largest audience of any Spanish radio show in the country. He's also looking to broaden his appeal by recording an album of poetry for the Fonovisa label after recording a comedy album for BMG Latin.

The motion picture industry, led by small- to medium-sized companies like Miramax, New Line Cinema, Screen Gems, and Artisan Entertainment, are leading the march into the Latin arena. Jimmy Smits, with television credits on *L.A. Law* and *NYPD*, moves to the big screen to headline New Line Cinema's boxing feature, *Price of Glory*. Major and minor studios are cognizant of the Latin community's cultural diversity and how it affects box office totals. When New Line released *Mi Familia* (*My Family*) five years ago, it plays well in the Mexican-heavy West and Southwest, but poorly in Cuban-dominated Miami.

Nevertheless, studios are aware that some English-language films aimed at Latinos can do well ticket-wise. According to the Directors Guild of America, the top grossing Latin-themed films are *A Walk in the Clouds* (1995), which earns $50 million, followed by *Selena* (1997) and *Bound by Honor* (1993) tied with $35 million each, *Desperado* (1995) with $25 million, *Born in East L.A.* (1987) $17 million, and both *Mambo Kings* (1992) and *Stand and Deliver* (1987), each earning $14 million.

Articles

"Baseball Stars Discover Owners Now Have The Upper Hand." Los Angeles Times, Dec. 23, 2002

"Azteca American Gets FCC Approval To Build Spanish TV Station In L.A." Los Angeles Times, Dec. 21, 2000

"Latin Jazz Musician Arturo 'Chico' O'Farrill Dead." CNN.com, June 29, 2001

"Hispanic Net Deals For Original Programming." MediaWeek, Dec. 11, 2000

"Latin Crossover's New Twist." Billboard, Dec. 9, 2000

"Casa, Sweet Casa." Hollywood Reporter, Oct. 12, 2000

"El Cucuy Recites Poetry." Billboard, Oct. 7, 2000

"State Leads As Home To Immigrants." Los Angeles Times, Oct. 5, 2000

"Cable Sets Pace Via Assimilated Hispanic Fare." Advertising Age, Sept. 18, 2000

"Teens Under Watchful Eye." Advertising Age, Sept. 18, 2000

"Showing Off To The Mainstream." Los Angeles Times, Sept. 14, 2000

"Azteca, Pappas Plan Spanish Net." Electronic Media, Sept. 11, 2000

"Hispanic TV Takes Off In The U.S." Wall Street Journal, Sept. 7, 2000

"Telemundo Sees New Day With Live 'Esta Manana.'" Daily Variety, Sept. 5, 2000

"Latin Grammys Bow With Bland Ratings." Daily Variety, Sept. 5, 2000

"Minorities Become Major, Census Officials Say." Los Angeles Times, Aug. 30, 2000

"Controversy Over Latin Grammy Nominees." Los Angeles Times, Aug. 30, 2000

"Latin Rock Seeks A Global Moment." New York Times, Aug. 17, 2000

"Conventions Strike Up The Band (With A Latin Beat)." New York Times, Aug. 15, 2000

"History Channel Sets Its Sights On Latino Viewers." Electronic Media, July 31, 2000

"Latinos In Entertainment." Daily Variety, July 28, 2000

"Innovative Route For Latino Tours.." Billboard, July 22, 2000

"Hispanic Net To Fix Itself First." Broadcasting, July 17, 2000

"TV Advertising Drives Fight Over Spanish Audience." New York Times, July 17, 2000

"The Spotlight's On La Música." Los Angeles Times, July 8, 2000
"ESPN Covers Hispanic Bases." Hollywood Reporter, June 30, 2000
"Salsa To Tejano To Banda, Latin Crossover Hits." Los Angeles Times, June 24, 2000
"Heartland Tuning In To Spanish." Los Angeles Times, June 23, 2000
"Watcha Tour Aims To Rock Latin World." Billboard, June 10, 2000
"Small Towns Shaped By Influx Of Hispanics." USA Today, May 23, 2000
"Hispanic Rivals Gear Up." May 22, 2000
"Judge Blocks Cuban Arts Law." Daily Variety, May 22, 2000
"Stateside Spots Swing To Latin Groove." Billboard, May 20, 2000
"Univision's Got Game." Daily Variety, May 18, 2000
"Telemundo Has A New Game Plan." Los Angeles Times, May 16, 2000
"HSN Readies Spanish-Language Version." Multichannel News, May 8, 2000
"Latin Music: Next Stage Of Success Story." Billboard, May 6, 2000
"Halfway There." Hollywood Reporter, April 14, 2000
"Commanding Respect." Los Angeles Times, April 9, 2000
"New Vista For Hollywood." USA Today, March 31, 2000
"New Line Preps Latino Pix." Daily Variety March 31, 2000
"Selena Forever." Los Angeles Times, March 25, 2000
"Cable Catering To Latinos." Electronic Media, March 13, 2000
"HBOs Latino To Dub English, Dabble In Spanish." Daily Variety, March 7, 2000
"Christina Aguilera: Building 21st Century Star." Time, March 6, 2000
"Santana's 'Supernatural' Sales Jump 166%." USA Today, March 2, 2000
"It's All About The Audience." Los Angeles Times, March 2, 2000
"A New Form Of Oldies." MediaWeek, Feb. 28, 2000
"Santana's The Top Banana." Daily Variety, Feb. 24, 2000"
"Latin Music Moves Sales, Souls And Feet." Los Angeles Daily News, Feb. 23, 2000
"To Sing Of her Own People." Billboard, Feb. 19, 2000
"Finalists Tapped For Latin Awards." Billboard, Feb. 19, 2000
"AFO-CIO Calls For Amnesty For Illegal Workers." Los Angeles Times, Feb. 17, 2000
"Smooth As Santana." Newsweek, Feb. 14, 2000
"Everything You Need To Know About Marc Anthony." TV Guide, Feb. 12, 2000

"Bush Hopes Spanish Ads Will Garner Votes." Los Angeles Times, Feb. 7, 2000

"Machito Albums Get To The Root Of Latin Jazz." Los Angeles Times, Feb. 6, 2000

"LARAS Makes Its Mark On NARAS." Billboard, Feb. 5, 2000

"Latin Academy Debuts Own Grammy Awards." Billboard, Jan. 29, 2000

"Keep 'Em Laughing." Los Angeles Times, Jan. 27, 2000

"Can KLAX Return To Numero Uno?" MediaWeek, Jan. 17, 2000

"Viva 107 Ready For Its Closeup." Los Angeles Times, Jan. 6, 2000

"¿Oye Como Va, Carlos?" Los Angeles Times, Jan 5, 2000

"Young Rockers Are Expected To Fill The Void." Los Angeles Times, Jan 2, 2000

"Our New Look: The Color Of Race." Newsweek, Jan. 1, 2000

"El Nuevo Milenio." Jazziz, January, 2000"

"The Hot New Sound Of Tradition." Hispanic Magazine, January/February, 2000

"Razor Blades." Hispanic Magazine, January/February, 2000

"Playing The Name Game." Los Angeles Times, Aug. 18, 1996

"KVEA Debuts Boost Ratings." Hollywoode Reporter, Aug. 16, 1996

"Radio Ritmo Has Rock-But Not Salsa." Los Angeles Times, Aug. 16, 1996

"KLVE-FM Continues Run In Top Local Ratings Spot. Los Angeles Times, July 13, 1996

"KMEX Ratings Mirror Ethnic Growth In L.A." Electronic Media, July 1, 1996

"CBS Parent Buys TeleNoticas: Spanish News Service Planned. Hollywood Reporter, June 28, 1996

"CBS Enters Spanish-Language News." USA Today, June 28, 1996

KLVE-FM No. 1 In Arbitron Survey." Electronic Media, Jan. 15, 1996

"KGRB Radio Is Dis-Banded." Hollywood Reporter, Jan 2, 1996

"L.A. Spanish Stations Thrive." Electronic Media, Dec. 18, 1995

"Summer Wind Barely Moves Radio Ratings." Los Angeles Times, Oct. 11, 1995

"Hip-Hop Powers Its Way To Top." Daily Variety, July 19, 1995

"Universal '95 Tickets Go On Sale Sunday, Los Angeles Times, April 30, 1995

"Latinos Protest At ABC Stations." Los Angeles Times, April 27, 1995

"KLVE-FM Romances To The Top." Los Angeles Times, April 21,1995

"L.A.'s KMEX Seeks New Ratings System." Electronic Media, April 17, 1995

"Latinos To Stern: Apology Is Not Accepted." Los Angeles Times, April 11, 1995

"Stern Gets A Bit Of A Ratings Shock." Los Angeles Times, Jan. 7, 1995

"The Rescuers." Emmy, April 1994

Chapter 8
CAPITULO 8

Viva Mexico: 2001
VIVA MÉXICO: 2001

• Despite attempts to crack rocanrol and increase the number of artists making inroads with crossover English-language recordings, America's Latins continue to favor regional Mexican music. And why not? Sixty percent of the nation's Hispanic population of 35 million continues to be made up of descendants from our neighboring nation.

• Regional Mexican music is being programmed by a greater number of radio stations both those established and newly arrived to the format either as newly licensed stations or format switchers.

• Attempts fail for the second year to present the Latin Grammys in Florida's Latin entertainment capital of Miami due to perceived problems by the Cuban exile community. The event is transferred to Los Angeles and scheduled for September 11 at the Great Western Forum in nearby Inglewood.

• Telemundo and Univision are both the objects of major corporations eager to buy their way into Spanish-language TV. Despite reported inquires from AOL Time Warner, Viacom, and the Walt Disney Company, General Electric's NBC offers the right figure, $1.98 billion in cash and stock worth a total of $2.7 billion for Telemundo, the No. 2 network behind Univision. These same media behemoths shift their interests towards the market leader, who chooses to control its own destinies for now.

• Mexico's TV Azteca launches its planned new Azteca America network with its first station in Los Angeles. Programming naturally emanates from its Mexico City studios and is slanted toward Mexicanos living in L.A.

• Although from Colombia, not Mexico, Shakira looms as the sensuous new Latina crossover darling with Sony's clout behind her first all-English CD.

Mexican residents and new immigrants, legal and illegal, are producing some new and interesting changes to the nation's population composition, according to the updated Census numbers. Mexicans account for 58.5 percent of the 35 million Latins, with an estimated 4.5 million illegals scatted across the U.S. as well. Half of the nation's Latinos continue to be found in California and Texas, with East Los Angeles housing the most Latinos, 96.8 percent. Of all the cities in America, California's Santa Ana has the highest concentration of Spanish speakers at 74 percent. The nation's top 10 largest Hispanic-populated cities include New York (2.16 million), Los Angeles (1.72), Chicago (753,644), Houston (730,865), San Antonio (671,394), Phoenix (449,972), Dallas (422,587), San Diego (310,752), Philadelphia (128,928), and Detroit (47,167).

On a statewide basis, Hispanics more than double and help Oklahoma's population grow 9.7 percent to 3.5 million, enabling Oklahoma City's population to grow 23.8 percent to reach 506,132. Kansas' population, urban and rural rises to 2.6 million, bolstered by the 94,582 Hispanics representing 7 percent of the population, up from 3.6 percent in 1990. Nevada sees its Hispanic population skyrocket from 124,419 or 10.4 percent in 1990 to 17.8 percent, bringing the figure up to a current 355,452 people. Texas adds an unbelievable 2,018,310 Latinos, for a 30 percent population boost. In Connecticut, Hartford elects Eddie Perez its first Latino mayor, the first of any capitol city in New England. Hartford's population is 39 percent Hispanic, primarily Puerto Ricans who come to Hartford in the mid-1940s to work in the tobacco fields and factories.

The strength of the regional Mexican music genre is seen by the number of record companies seeking to strengthen their regional artist roster and go after market leader Fonovisa as a reflex reaction to figures from the Recording Industry Association of America revealing that regional Mexican/Tejano music accounts for 51 percent of the $608 million worth of all Latin albums shipped to retailers last year. Fonovisa, the Los Angeles independent label, has nearly 60 regional Mexican artists under its imprint, led by heavy hitters Marco Antonio Solis, Los Temerarios, Los Tigres Del Norte, La Banda El Recodo, Los Angeles De Charly, and Conjunto Primavera. Of these bands, Los Tigres has been together since 1968, initially helping launch Fama Records on the West Coast as its first artists. By 2003, the band will have 55 albums to its credit as well as being considered the top norteño band in this brand of regional Mexican music.

The music's appeal also propels the concert appearances by 61-year-old mariachi master Vicente Fernández and his 30-year-old son Alejandro, who's only been recording 10 years on his own. The duo, backed by a 36-piece band at the Universal Amphitheatre in the San Fernando Valley section of Los Angeles, performs for four hours. While Vicente charms his legions of older fans with his élan, Alejandro, the youngest of three sons, uses his sybaritic appeal to charm his female boosters. Mariachi music and Vicente reign with the combustible concept of father and son working together.

Overall sales for Latin records decline, notably for lack of breakout new superstars in the tropical category, which seems to lack a new rhythmic dynamic, but Mexican music grows by more than 20 percent over previous years. Universal Music Latino, Sony Discos, and WEA Mex, a spin-off by WEA Latina, are all aggressively developing rosters for regional Mexican station airplay. A gradually increasing number of stations are playing alternative music, which encompasses hard-driving, rock-flavored pop music. It's a mélange of styles fit for 18- to 34-year-olds. Despite a select number of radio stations like Puerto Rico's WCOM (*Cosmos 94*), Miami's WRTO (*Salsa 98*), New York's WCAA (*Latino Mix*), Los Angeles' KLYY (*Viva*

107), and KSSE (*Super Estrella*), the musical style continues to have a tough time gaining a national foothold. This paucity undercuts personal appearances by the international top guns of the movement, Maná, Café Tacuba, Molotov, Fabulosos Cadillacs, Beresuit, and Jaguares, and the efforts by majors BMG and EMI Latin, and independents Balboa and Disa. It also affects new companies like the Univision Music Group (which buys 50 percent of Disa), EMI's New Alternativa imprint and Madonna's Maverick Música. Rock en Español seems to be the Latin version of the school of hard knocks, or rocks.

Still, there are efforts to mix genres and come up with alternative styles that cross social class taboos and create a latticework of styles, notably established bands attaching R&B and electronic rock to their bedrock styles while hipper bands dig back into their roots for elements that will broaden their appeal and break onto the playlists of restrictive formatted stations. In Mexico, for example, social status directs people's musical preference. Pop music is favored by the upper class while the middle and lower class prefer regional Mexican, Adolfo Valenzuela, a producer/arranger who collaborates with his brother Omar on a banda album for Thalía, comments to *Billboard.*

One New York band, Fulanito, which records for Cutting Records, fuses hip-hop with merengue and reggae, adds the sound of an accordion and comes up with Puerto Rico's emerging reggaeton style. The label calls the quartet's third album, *Americanizao*, a blending of hip-hop with reggae. A new New York label, Flia, focuses on rap in English and Spanish. It's a spinout from J&N Records and Flia Entertainment and its roster is from New York, Puerto Rico, and the Dominican Republic. Juan Hidalgo, president of J&N, which specializes in tropical music, says rap is becoming a popular form in Puerto Rico. Flia's head and Hidalgo's partner is Magic Juan, himself one of the new label's Dominican artists. A number of Flia's artists record a single, *Nuestro Destino* with proceeds assisting victims of the September 11 World Trade Center Twin Towers terrorist attacks.

For Fonovisa, the pop market is its next crusade. Having savored some pop success with a separate Mexico-based label,

Fonovisa, owned by Mexican media conglomerate Televisa, starts its Melody pop label in Miami, and builds a roster of 20 artists. The original Discos Y Cintas Melody in Mexico is credited with starting such acts as Thalía, Enrique Iglesias, Lucero, Cristian Castro, Lucero, and Timbiriche. In addition to starting its new domestic label, Fonovisa also handles distribution for a number of independents in the regional Mexican, tropical, and rap/reggae fields.

With memories of the 1999 crossover implosion, the Latin industry is pinning its hopes on the vocal power and sensuality of Shakira Mebarak Ripoll, the half-Lebanese, half-Colombian dynamo whose first Epic release in English is *Laundry Service*, a love paean to what she calls her "two great passions of love and music" written since her romance with Antonio De La Rúa, the son of Argentina's president. Shakira, as she is best known, has the support of Sony Music's chairman Tommy Mottola and her manager, the out of retirement veteran Freddy DeMann, who last works with Madonna and is an owner in her Maverick label before having a fallout of sorts in 1999 and heading for quieter environs. With this album she becomes the decade's first true crossover Hispanic artist to sing in English since Julio Iglesias romanticized *To All the Girls I've Loved Before* in 1984. Three of her Sony Spanish-language albums, starting with *Pies Descalzos* in 1995, help establish her as the best-selling female pop artist of the moment.

Mottola calls Shakira "a volcano waiting to explode into the Anglo market" in the same *Los Angeles Times* article that Freddie DeMann admits that accidentally catching her on TV in 1999 while switching channels causes him to come out of retirement. "She just mesmerized me," he says of her appearance on a special with Melissa Etheridge one year prior to rocking the first Latin Grammys with her dynamically sensuous performance. Her half-Lebanese, half-Colombian background generates enticing music with electric guitars intertwined with Middle Eastern rhythms and Andean melodies. Using her established Latin American fan base from the past 10 years, she preps for her eventual break into the English market by teaching herself to write in English and uses a rhyming dictionary, along with the creative guidance from writer-producer Glen Ballard, to compose eight of the tunes in the album. Her former manager Emilio Estefan Jr., who produces her 1998 album *Ladrones,* is listed as executive producer on the new Epic release. As Emilio is quite busy she claims she needs someone who can devote 100 percent to her career. DeMann eventually negotiates a worldwide deal for Shakira to be a Pepsi spokesperson, in which her sultry image will flash across TV screens and appear in print ads.

For Marc Anthony's return to salsa via his first Spanish-language studio session since hitting the big time last year, there's both creative elation and professional concern caused by a dispute with three of the *Libre* album's writers over song credits. What should be a free and open ride for the album, which is being distributed to Latin markets by Sony Discos and to the general market by Columbia Records, becomes instead an imbroglio between Anthony and the three composers. They are angered when Anthony claims songwriting credits for arranging and writing the added choral refrain, using a series of improvised vocal inserts. In what becomes a he says–they say word battle, Anthony claims he informs the writers he will be adding parts to their written compositions, similar to the way salsa singers traditionally contribute, and they agree. The writers claim they are unaware of the co-authorship arrangement and learn about it when contacted by Anthony's attorney.

While this may seem like a legal misunderstanding, there are serious underpinnings to Anthony's crossing over from the salsa tradition in which singers never demand writing credits for their vocal improvisations. Through his breakthrough success last year he's learned there's a big difference in the pop market, where writing one line in a song gets you a writing credit and part of the seven-and-a-half cent royalty per song, while in the salsa field, one line gets you *nada*. As a result of the impasse, Anthony drops four tunes from the projected 13-song album. One singer who comes to Anthony's support is Rubén Blades, who tells the *Los Angeles Times* (which amplifies on *Billboard*'s original story), "I think Marc has an argument. There's no doubt in my mind that when you add *soneos*, you are contributing to a song. The question is, to what degree?"

The Latin Grammys seem to be wrapped up in a question of their own: How do they present the annual event without any political pressure from Miami's Cuban exile community? After announcing the second annual awards presentation will take place in Miami September 11 at the AmericanAirlines Arena, the event is switched three weeks before the telecast to Los Angles and the Great Western Forum in Inglewood when NARAS officials decide staunch anti-Castro Cubans represent a major security problem for artists and audience guests. It's a repeat of what happened last year when the inaugural show, also set for Miami, is switched to Los Angeles because of a Miami ordinance prohibiting Cuban musicians from appearing at the arena. This time, Michael Greene, the NARAS president/CEO, reveals a number of uncomfortable situations that can endanger the show and its guests. He says more than 100 Cuban Americans will be allowed to demonstrate within a new two-block protest area, part of which is a half-block from the arena's main entrance, and that places the expected 7,000 attendees in close proximity to these protestors. He also claims protestors have purchased tickets for the event and are planning to disrupt the live CBS broadcast. In another slap for Miami, its prohibitive ordinance is eventually ruled unconstitutional.

Back home in Los Angeles, Greene, who also oversees the new Latin Recording Academy, makes his anger known in the *Los Angeles Times* by admitting: "I do feel betrayed, in that everybody knew what we were trying to do. We weren't there to cram a Cuban national performance in the face of the people of Miami. We were there trying to celebrate a coming of age of tolerance." The decision does not sit well with the Cubans and Miami officials. Cuban exile Emilio Estefan, a flag-waver for Miami, indicates he won't be making the flight to L.A. Although no Cuban artists are scheduled to perform, by shifting the locale to Los Angeles, pianist Chucho Valdés indicates he plans attending the ceremonies. Lined up to perform are Latin artists well known within the Latin community, but are blank checks with mainstream America.

Despite last year's disappointing ratings with only 7.5 million viewers, CBS states it won the evening with male and female viewers in the 18- to 49-year-old bracket, even though it failed to win the night with total household viewers. CBS senior vice president for specials, Jack Sussman, notes in the *Los Angeles Times* this year that the network considers the Latin Grammys an "investment and a franchise that could live for many years on the network." Then America is attacked on September 11, President George W. Bush declares war on terrorists, and the Grammys, like so many other show business events, are on hold. The Latin Grammys go from a high profile, televised event to a low-key news conference in October at the Conga Room nightclub in Los Angeles. Winners in 22 of 38 categories are announced by two investors in the club, actor Jimmy Smits and comic Paul Rodriguez. In an unusual step, winners are told in advance so others need not make an unnecessary trip to Los Angeles. The only performance is by Juanes, winner of the best new artist, best rock solo vocal, and best rock song.

Despite the hoopla in Miami against Cuban artists, only one Grammy goes to Cubans for best folk album. The evening's supreme winner is Spain's Alejandro Sanz with four trophies for the album, *El Alma Al Aire*, followed by Juanes with three. Here's how the top awards are handed out:

Record of the year, album of the year, song of the year, and male pop vocal album: *El Alma Al Aire*, Alejandro Sanz; new artist: Juanes; female pop vocal album: *Mi Reflejo*, Christina Aguilera, RCA/BMG Latin; pop duo or group vocal album: *Duetos*, Armando Manzanero, Warner Music Mexico; pop instrumental album: *This Side of Paradise*, Nestor Torres, Shanachie; rap-hip-hop album: *Un Pasa A La Eternidad*, Sindicato ArgentinoDel Hip Hop, Interdisc; rock solo vocal album: *Fijate Bien*, Juanes, Surco/Universal; rock vocal album by duo or group: *Gozo Poderoso*, Aterciopelados, BMG Entertainment, Mexico; rock song: *Fijate Bien*, Juanes, Surco/Universal; salsa album:

Obra Maestra, Tito Puente, Eddie Palmieri, RMM; merengue album: *De Vuelta Al Barrio*, Chichi Peralta, Caiman; tropical song: *Juarme*, Gisselle; songwriter Kike Santander, BMG U.S. Latin; ranchera album: *Yo No Fui*, Pedro Fernandez, Mercury; banda album: *Contigo Por Siempre*, Banda El Recodo, Fonovisa; grupo album: *Por Encimade Todo*, Grupo Límite, Universal Music Mexico; Tejano album: *Quien Iba A Pensar*, Jimmy Gonzalez Y El Grupo Mazz, Freddie; norteno album: *Quemame Los Ojos Amigos Del Almo*, Ramon Ayala Y Sus Bravos Del Norte, Freddie/Harmony; regional Mexican song: *Borracho Te Recuerdo*, Vicente Fernández, songwriter José Vaca Flores; Latin jazz album: *Live at the Blue Note*, Paquito D'Rivera, Half Note; contemporary pop album: *Memorias, Cronicas E Declaracoes*, Marisa Monte, EMI Brazil; and rock album: *3001*, Rita Lee, Mercury.

One of the new artists in the competition is Vicente Amigo, Spain's renowned flamenco guitarist, who wins the best flamenco album Grammy for *Cuidad De Las Ideas*, released overseas on BMG. It was also nominated in the album of the year category. Next year, it will be released in the U.S. on Windham Hill, one of the BMG labels and mark the guitarist's first-ever album release in this country. The Grammy winning title is his fourth album dating back to 1991. Although he's not a household name, jazz guitarist Pat Metheny calls Amigo the greatest player of the Spanish guitar. A number of other American musicians with whom he's worked, who call him their playing amigo, include Stanley Jordan, Al DiMeola, and John McLaughlin.

In a compilation of who's hot and who's not, *Billboard*'s yearly recap blends familiar names and newly emerging personalities. In the overall album and regional Mexican album sales categories, Vicente Fernández is tops, Paulina Rubio heads the pop album sales category, Sony Discos is the top Latin album and tropical/salsa label, Son by Four is the top salsa/tropical album sales artist, and Fonovisa is the top regional Mexican label.

Like all of entertainment, music artists struggle to maintain their popularity against inroads by new performers and evolving styles. So it's quite amazing in the yearly report to see Vicente Fernández beating out such upstarts as Paulina Rubio, who finishes second behind him, and Christina Aguilera who's in fifth place, and Ricky Martin in 10th position, a major slide downward in his sales potency since his 1999 year of adoration. In fact, his sales will keep declining in the next couple of years, a victim of the record industry's push to create the next flavor of the month and a fickle public's abandonment of its artist loyalties, based in a large part on how a performer's music ratchets up their emotional connections and sensibilities.

Following NBC's $2.7 billion acquisition of Telemundo in October from principal owners Sony Corp. and Liberty Media Corp, Bob Wright, a GE vice president and NBC's chairman, calls Hispanic TV "the most dynamic television market in the U.S." Jim McNamara, Telemundo's CEO is equally effusive, stating: "This is the most significant day in the history of Spanish-language television." NBC's money acquires Telemundo's 19 owned and operated stations, 40 affiliates and two cable networks, mun2 and Telemundo Internacional. Under the deal terms, NBC lays out half in cash and half in GE stock and also assumes an estimated $700 million in debt. Since Sony and Liberty Media buy the troubled network for $537 million in 1997, life is good. One month earlier Telemundo launches mun2, a cable network zeroing in on 18- to 34-year-olds, with at least half of its programming music flavored.

At a time when the broadcast networks are losing audiences, Hispanic TV keeps growing as its audience keeps enlarging. While California and Texas are home to half of all Hispanic Americans, the last census reports major population increases in Georgia, North Carolina, Virginia, Nevada, Utah, Oregon, and Washington, while immigrant arrivals from Central and South America and the Caribbean rise by 97 percent.

Telemundo provides NBC with entry into an estimated 10 million Hispanic TV homes, providing advertising and programming opportunities never available before, but certainly imagined. Two of its stations are in Los Angeles, KVEA and KWHY, the latter an independent purchased in February for $239 million from owner

Harriscope, which shifts its bilingual daytime English-language business reports and evening Spanish programming to all Spanish in 1999. Last year, the station made history by airing the nation's first Spanish-language high definition TV broadcast, one of its few hallmarks. With the acquisition, Telemundo becomes the first Spanish broadcaster to operate a duopoly in the same city as a result of the FCC's opening up the rules to allow multiple station ownership in the same market. Univision also takes advantage of this rule loosening by purchasing, for $1.1 billion, the 13 stations owned by the USA Network that will become the core for a planned second network.

Prior to the NBC purchase, Telemundo makes several important moves to increase growth. It begins adding newscasts in the morning and evening at KVEA and covering major events outside the U.S. When a 6.6 magnitude earthquake unnerves El Salvador, the station treats it as a local story for its expatriate Salvadoran viewers, possibly the largest community in the U.S. Telemundo also recasts its female cable network called Gems, which it acquires in May 2000 as mun2 or "mundos" as its known within the Spanish community. It relaunches the channel on October 10 as a home for 18- to 34-year-olds including bilinguals, with a programming mix of 60–70 percent original entertainment fare. And it signs with Argos Communicacion of Mexico City, known for its unorthodox telenovelas. Under a three-year contract, the company will provide more than 1,200 hours of programming. It's novelas in Mexico deal with subjects normally eschewed by the genre, such as the changing roles of men and women in Mexican society, political corruption, and drug distribution. The company previously produced several novelas exclusively for Mexico's TV Azteca network. Telemundo also acquires programs from Brazil's TV Globo.

One of Telemundo president McNamara's winning actions, according to *Electronic Media*, is shifting the new *Laura En America*, with host Laura Bozzo from 2–3 p.m. to 4–5 p.m. to compete against Univision's popular *Cristina* with Cristina Saralegui. In a major upset during the all-important November sweeps rating period, Laura beats

Cristina in three of the top five markets, Los Angeles, Chicago, and San Francisco, according to the Nielsen Station Index report. Nationally among the 18–49 demographic, the show achieves a 3.0 rating 42 share, an 88 percent increase in the 3–4 p.m. time period, according to the Nielsen Hispanic Television Index report. However, Cristina retains her national lead with a 4.1/58, which is down 11 percent from the same period last year.

One company apparently taking note of KVEA's push for Central American viewers is Venture Technology, which operates foreign-language low-power stations. It starts a 24-hour Spanish station, KSFV, aimed at the estimated 1.5 million Central Americans residing in the L.A. region.

While Telemundo and its NBC parent are formulating plans for joint operations to come in the future, Univision makes its first foray into the Puerto Rican TV market by spending around $50 million for Raycom Media independent stations, WLII in San Juan and WSUR in Ponce. It then announces it is canceling several of its programs due to the nation's slowing economy, or as it calls it, "a challenging economic environment," according to the *Bloomberg News* service. Among the shows axed are game show *A Million*, variety show *Gran Blablazo*, and sports show *Compacto Deportivo* in development at Galavision. Network president Ray Rodriguez tells financial analysts that the shows will be replaced with programming from existing outside show creators. The company says it will take a first-quarter charge of between $8 million and $12 million for the cost-savings efforts. It also boasts about its new TeleFutura network, slated to debut next January. The name, which means television of the future, is selected from hundreds of entries by company employees. The new network's programming will include films, news, novelas, as well as talk, variety, and sports shows. TeleFutura is designed to attract viewers away from the Anglo networks. Its core will be the 13 full-power stations acquired from the Barry Diller-operated USA Networks, with programming coming from sources in Venezuela and Colombia.

These same sources, RCTV in Venezuela and RCN in Colombia, sign contracts with Univision to create 1,100 hours of exclusive programming each year. Some industry observers believe the alliance with these two companies is designed to counter Univision's heavy reliance on Mexican telenovelas from Televisa, whose contract runs through 2017. In a story in the *Los Angeles Times* detailing these new relationships, a 10-year deal with RCTV calls for 800 hours per year of first-run novelas, game shows, comedies, and variety programs. A five-year pact with RCN Television specifies 300 hours of exclusive telenovelas each year. On its own, TeleFutura produces a weekday chat show, *Marta Susana*, from Miami, which offers advice on medical, family problems, and legal matters.

While Univision attempts to lessen its reliance on programs from Mexico, it does nothing to alter another company policy, known within the TV industry as a company with a closed-mouth public edict, meaning its executives eschew talking to the media except at specific occasions. Owner/chairman and chief executive A. Jerrold Perenchio, has in place a policy prohibiting company executives from generally speaking to the media without his permission. In a story about Univision, the *Los Angeles Times* reports that one errant official who broke the credo "was fined $25,000 for being quoted in a publication, according to a personal familiar with the incident who asked not to be identified." When I attempt to set up interviews with Univision officials I'm informed by PR executives about the no-speak policy and am told that Perenchio doesn't want his executives to become more important than the company. In 2003, I crack the anti-media barricade for a series of articles I do for *TelevisionWeek* in which I'm given access to Univision network and local news officials.

Matters between Grupo Televisa, the world's largest Spanish-language media company, and Univision are a bit sticky since talks between the two companies about restructuring Univision's rights to continue receiving Televisa's soap operas are at a standstill. Televisa, according to the *Wall Street Journal*, is using the planned new TeleFutura network as a basis to renegotiate its original revenue sharing pact on advertising that runs in its programs on Univision. The current ad deal provides Univision with about 40 percent of its revenue. Televisa receives nine percent of the ad revenue. Televisa is reportedly asking for 15 percent of the ad revenue from its shows airing on both networks and will throw in expanded rights to its programming, including in Puerto Rico, where Telemundo has those rights. Univision is not happy with these terms. Six months later, in December, Univision and Grupo Televisa resolve their differences on a much broader scale. Univision also signs a deal with Venevision of Venezuela for its programming.

Under the complex terms of the Televisa deal, Univision secures its programming for TeleFutura and Galavision, expanding the pact which formerly only covers shows on Univision. Televisa increases its holdings in Univision to 15 percent, paying Univision $375 million for its increased equity position and will receive an additional three percent fee for its shows seen on Univision and Galavision, and a 12 percent fee for its shows running on TeleFutura next year.

Univision is also asserting its rectitude by moving its muscle into the record business and purchasing Televisa's Los Angeles-based regional Mexican label, Fonovisa, for $240 million in stock. Univision will merge Fonovisa with Disa Records in which it has a 50 percent stake acquired in April. These two labels form the basis of the Univision Music Group that will become a power in Latin records.

The arrival of Azteca America, the nation's third Spanish-language network spawn by Mexico's TV Azteca conglomerate, begins broadcasting in late August from one station, KAZA in Los Angeles. It's a scaled down version of a grandiose plan to start with 10 stations this summer. The new outlet obtains its programs from its Mexico City parent and the nation's No. 2 broadcaster behind Televisa. Pappas Telecasting of Visalia, California, which owns stations in small markets, owns 80 percent of the network, with the remaining 20 percent held by TV Azteca. Bad economic times in the U.S. halts the company from starting with its intended 10 stations, so it loses out on the 13 USA Network stations it hoped to buy, which are acquired instead by Univision for its forthcoming TeleFutura network.

Meanwhile, Univision continues to shake things up in the New York market. With the help of its *Mujeres Enganadas (Deceived Women)* novela, its local outlet, WXTV, racks up its highest primetime rating since September 9, 1999, and positions the station in fifth place in the market rankings. This is not unusual since Census data indicates that Hispanics represent 18.6 percent of the region's TV viewers, up from 15.1 percent in 1990. The growth boom also boosts the 11 p.m. newscasts of both Univision and Telemundo's WNJU during the May sweeps. Univision is up 55 percent to finish seventh, while WNJU is up 58 percent to place it eighth during that time period. With a mayoral election this year, WXTV presents the first-ever Spanish-language TV mayoral debate between candidates Mike Bloomberg and Mark Green. Questions will be asked in Spanish and the English answers will be translated for viewers. The station is also offering an English translation for all New York broadcast outlets.

Credit the following to New York's loyal Hispanic audience: For the first time in the history of New York TV ratings for station's total sign-on to sign-off performance, WXTV beats out WNYW, the local Fox Television Network station. In November, the station sets two records, first achieving the highest weekday average rating in the history of New York Spanish-language TV: a 2.9 rating, fueled in part by its coverage of the crash of American Airlines flight 587 enroute to Santo Domingo, killing everyone on board and people on the ground in the Rockaway section of Long Island. And second, by racking up the highest rating in the history of Spanish TV in New York, a 2.3 rating and 5 share to pass one of the city's six major Anglo stations in total viewership, Fox-owned WWOR, for sixth place.

Companies with specialty cable niche networks continue to join the growing ranks of the cable en Español community. Or at least indicate they're intentions. Fox Sports World Español starts offering live, Spanish translations of Major League Baseball's playoffs and the World Series. Time Warner Cable and the Fox network target New

York, Orlando, El Paso, and Milwaukee for a special fall classic package. Why Milwaukee? The city's Hispanic population grows 82 percent in the last 10 years to nearly 72,000, reports the U.S. Census. Scripps Networks, which operates the popular Home & Garden and Food Networks, indicates it is looking to develop Spanish lingo versions of these two channels. DirecTV Para Todos, a spin-off by the leading satellite provider DirecTV, is pitching its service exclusively to Hispanics, of which less than two percent subscribe to the parent English service. ESPN starts a four-hour sports block called *ESPN Deportes*, which by 2003 ESPN hopes will morph into a fulltime network. It debuts instead in January of 2004.

Home Shopping Network provides Latinos with their own home buying capability on HSeE, Home Shopping Español. Discovery En Español provides a mix of dubbed shows from parent Discovery Channel and from its international cousin, Discovery Latin America. Adelphia Communications in Los Angeles becomes one of the first cable system operators to create a Latin package of 15 channels as a means of attracting Spanish-speaking customers.

Hispanic radio seems to have unbridled growth. Entering this year, according to the radio business periodical, the *M Street Journal*, there are 571 Spanish programmed stations in the nation, up from 527 in mid-1999. In 1990, there are 376 up from a low of 67 in 1980. The regional Mexican format, once sacrosanct, is now blending formats, with stations specializing in Tejano (or Texas sounds), fusing banda, norteño, and groupo to broaden its audience reach.

In Houston alone, where most of the city's immigrants hail from Mexico, especially the Monterrey region where norteño rules, there are seven regional Mexican stations. The genre also rules on El Dorado Communications' two FM stations, KLTN and KQQK. You need look no farther than Los Angeles, the nation's top Hispanic radio market with 19 stations, to hear the impact of regional Mexican music. For the first time in the city's history, according to Arbitron statistics, Spanish stations finish one-two-three in the September 24 to December 16 survey, with regional power KSCA-FM in clear control of first place by attracting 6.9 percent of the listening audience. In second is KLVE-FM, which plays adult contemporary artists, followed by KLAX, another regional Mexican proponent tied with hip-hoping KPWR-FM, which claims a large Latino listenership. In the previous quarter, KSCA and KLVE tied for first with KLAX in 11th place.

In addition to L.A. and Houston, other cities with top-rated regional Mexican stations include San Antonio, Dallas/Fort Worth, Chicago, San Francisco, and San Diego. No surprises here for these cities with large Mexican populations. Nearly 8.8 million Mexican immigrants arrive in this country during the 1990s, creating a built-in audience for regional Mexican music from coast to coast. Besides Hispanic Broadcasting Corp. (HBC) and the Spanish Broadcasting System (SBS), several other chains keep the regional Mexican sounds flowing and diversified. Liberman Broadcasting, begun in 1988, operates 10 regional Mexican stations, all of which play local favorites. Entravision Radio, a chain with 52 stations that can choose from any of its three syndicated formats, finds its regional Mexican format, called *Radio Tricolor*, is the most utilized. The other two formats are the rock flavored *Super Estrella* and the romantic ballad *Radio Romantica.* La Máquina, a company which begins operation in 1994 in Northern California, owns 11 stations and provides regional Mexican programming to 12 others, reaching listeners in California, Oregon, Washington, and Minnesota.

The crossover fallout from 1999 is also affecting Latin radio and pop music as a growing array of U.S.—raised Latino artists record in English, opening an opportunity, however heretic, for Spanish stations to include English-language records by these artists. It's a bilingual bonus. HBC, for example, programs for bilingual audiences with stations in Houston and San Antonio that play a compendium of Spanish and English tunes, a crossing of the cultural bridge attempting to romance two audiences. SBS, in a dramatic move to strike gold in the L.A. market, purchases religious station KFSG-FM for $250 million and converts it to KXOL *El Sol* (*The Sun*) with a regional Mexican format based on grupera music aimed at 25- to 54-year-olds, especially women. This is a brand of Mexican music the company asserts HBC's market leader KLVE doesn't emphasize. SBS' first regional Mexican station, KLAX, is having a hard time maintaining audiences with its corridos story songs about violence, gangsters, and drug trafficking, so the station is rebranded *La Raza* (*The Race*) from its previous moniker *La Lay* (*The Law*) and emphasizes banda and norteño bands. HBC, already the top Hispanic radio broadcaster, with 52 stations, announces it's going on a buying spree in the top 15–20 Latin markets where many of its stations already operate. It plans to build additional station "clusters" as they're called, as an extra tool in competing against SBS, which operates 13 stations, including groupings in major cities.

What is surprising and of concern to record companies—once they get past the good news that regional Mexican continues to significantly outsell tropical and Latin pop—is the incursion by regional Mexican radio of Top 40 radio strategies, like tight playlists that make it difficult for unknown acts to easily get airtime and the use of research to pinpoint audience preferences and dislikes.

A major break occurs in the film industry, which is still under employing Hispanics, when Universal Pictures and the Arenas Group, a 12-year-old talent/management/advertising/public relations firm, form Arenas Entertainment to produce, finance, distribute, and market films for the domestic Latin market. Universal thus becomes the first major studio to create a specific film entity targeting this branch of the population. Arenas has worked with a number of other Hispanic projects, including the first Latino Film Festival in Los Angeles, the Ballet Folkloric De Mexico, and the Spanish Film Institute.

Behind the camera, Latinos are making strides as well. Emanuel Nuñez, a Cuban-American, is an agent with the Creative Artists Agency whose clients include Gloria Estefan, Antonio Banderas, Robert De Niro, Al Pacino, and Neve Campbell. Nuñez, along with several other success stories, is profiled in the *Los Angeles Times*: film producer David Valdes (*The Green Mile* and the *Columbo*

TV series); vice president of programming at Showtime, Poncho Mansfield (overseeing *Resurrection Blvd.*); New Line Cinema producer Julio Caro (*The Cell*); screenwriter Cynthia Cidre (*The Mambo Kings*); executive story editor Alfonso H. Moreno (*The Practice* TV series); vice president of talent development and casting for Big Ticket Television, Donna Eckholdt; co-executive producer of CBS' *Yes, Dear*, Joey Gutierrez; and screenwriter Ernie Contreras. Nuñez, who naturally speaks Spanish when required, is optimistic about doors opening in mainstream show business: "There is no one standing there blocking the gate. There is a gate, but there is no guard." Other Latinos still trying to find their place in the industry will question his assertions.

This year's ALMA Awards continue tributing those successful artists and projects with high visibility: *Traffic* as both outstanding film and for its Latino cast; Lauren Velex as outstanding actress in the TV series *OZ*; Elizabeth Peña as outstanding actress in a new TV series *Resurrection Blvd.;* Martin Sheen as outstanding actor in the TV series *The West Wing*; Rubén Blades as outstanding actor in the new TV series *Gideon's Crossing*; Joe Menendez, director of the TV comedy series *The Brothers Garcia;* and Felix Alcala, director of the TV drama series *Third Watch.*

One branch of show business often overlooked, but acting on the growing Latin population, is the circus. The 31st edition of Ringling Bros. and Barnum & Bailey's Circus is now a bilingual affair for its entire run at the downtown Los Angeles Sports Arena. For the second straight year the show has two ringmasters for its Los Angeles appearances, regular ringmaster Johnathan Lee Iverson and Roberto Miguel, a Mexican singer and soap opera star who handles the Spanish introductions. The L.A. run at the Sports Arena is the only one in the country in which the program is done in two languages, an effort to attract the predominantly Hispanic community residing near the venue. While in the L.A. area the circus also plays the Great Western Forum in Inglewood and the Pond in Anaheim, but these performances are conducted in English. Around 70 percent of the Sports Arena show is in Spanish, with act introductions beginning in Spanish, continuing in English, and ending in Spanish. Iverson, in his third season with the circus, admits to the *Los Angeles Times* he was unsure about the bilingual concept. "But when I did it, it was exciting." Four years ago, the circus presents two Sports Arena shows in two languages. Last year for the first time, the number increases for the entire week. On a sporadic basis the circus presents bilingual performances in Miami, New York, Chicago, Houston, and Phoenix.

While the appeal of the circus as a family outing for immigrants is the reason Barnum & Bailey seek to entice this community, another presentation is designed specifically for this audience, with one major alteration: all the performers in the new $5 million *¡Circo Fantástico!* are Latinos. The two-hour show is playing large Hispanic communities in Southern California, including Pomona, El Monte, and Huntington Park. The acts are from all over Latin America and the music ranges from mariachi to Latin pop to salsa. There are no clowns or animal acts. Doriana Sánchez, the show's writer, director, and choreographer, calls the production "A celebration of Hispanic culture through music, dance and traditional circus acts" in a *Los Angles Times* article. Before called by the show's producers to write the script within two weeks, she choreographs concerts for such talents as Cher, Peter Gabriel, and Jane's Addiction.

Another activity highly popular with Hispanics around the world is futbol, which the seven-year-old Major League Soccer (MLS) focuses on with teams in 12 regions, including New York/New Jersey, Washington, D.C., Los Angeles, Miami, San Jose, Chicago, Dallas, Kansas City, Colorado, and New England. Lots of Hispanic players keep U.S. Latinos interested in the league. During its six years, DC United wins the league title three times, followed by one-timers San Jose, Kansas City, and Chicago. L.A. gets shut out three times in the championship. Seeking national TV exposure, MLS signs a new five-year pact with ABC, ESPN, and ESPN2 that stretches through 2006 and includes next year's World Cup presented by Japan and South Korea, and the 2006 Cup in Germany. Univision holds the Spanish TV rights for both World Cups. International matches, especially with Mexico, regularly fill the Rose Bowl in Pasadena and Los Angeles Coliseum, and non-U.S. soccer telecasts on Spanish TV are regular ratings toppers. Univision's initial broadcast in July of the Copa America, the hemispheric championship in professional soccer with Mexico pitted against Brazil, helps its New York station, WXTV, score a 4.0 rating and a 6 share between 8:30 and 11 p.m., a 74 percent increase over the station's primetime average in May.

In a highly familiar move, Hispanic immigrants regularly seek out local soccer teams in their new homes. In Phoenix, for example, the 20-year-old Liga Latinoamericana De Futbol soccer league for Hispanics has 125 adult and 40 youth teams, up from eight teams in 1981. Jesse Cadena, a member of the league's board of directors, tells the *Arizona Republic* he "believes soccer brings the community closer together than anything." Four Arizona players are on Major League Soccer teams, including Pablo Mastroeni of Phoenix, who plays for the Miami Fusion. He says Hispanic players have changed the league's style of play from a kick and run strategy to more of a dynamic attack. "Growing up in Arizona, the Mexican community has definitely rubbed off on me in terms of my style of play."

With a strong footing among U.S. soccer fans, primarily Hispanic immigrants, the MSL has preliminary plans for the construction of soccer stadiums in Harrison, New Jersey, for the New York/New Jersey MetroStars and in Washington for the D.C. United. Denver billionaire Phil Anschutz and his Anschutz Entertainment Group (AEG), which operates five of the 12 MLS teams, the L.A. Galaxy, Chicago Fire, Colorado Rapids, Washington D.C. United, and his newest acquisition the MetroStars, plans building a new soccer-tennis stadium in Carson, California, next year.

Responding to critical concerns that the Anschutz group controls the league because of its five-team monopoly, which can cause conflicts of interest, league commissioner Don Garber effusively supports AEG's position in the *Los Angeles Times:* "I believe we are in a far better position with fewer investors who are fully committed to the long-term success of the sport than with a greater number who don't have that same commitment."

There are also problems at the Los Angeles Coliseum, home for the Galaxy, which files a lawsuit in federal court against Major League Soccer and the United States Soccer Federation, alleging "anticompetitive practices" by the two organizations. The Coliseum wants to stage soccer matches with foreign clubs and national teams without interference from the USSF, the governing body for amateur soccer in this country. The Coliseum alleges it is limited in its ability to stage matches because of fees imposed by the USSF and by blackout periods to cover its own events as well as MLS games.

Articles

"The Year In Latin Music 2001." Billboard, Dec. 29, 2001

"Univision Strikes Pact With Televisa." Los Angeles Times, Dec. 22, 2001

"A Delicate Dance Over Credits." Los Angeles Times, Dec. 19, 2001

"Fútbol A Way Of Life For Valley Latinos." Arizona Republic, Dec. 15, 2001

"Telemundo Gains New Ground." Electronic Media, Dec. 11, 2001

"Latins Back To Roots Music." Billboard, Dec. 1, 2001

"Tuning Into Hispanic Music." Billboard, Dec. 8, 2001

"Univision 41 Ratings Tops In Sweep In NYC." HispanicAd.com, Dec. 4, 2001

"Fonovisa Eyes Expansion With New Pop Imprint, Melody." Billboard. Dec. 1, 2001

"Universal Pictures And Arenas Group Form Latino Film Label, Arenas Entertainment." PRNewswire, Nov. 26, 2001

"San Jose Breaks Down Galaxy." Los Angeles Times, Nov. 22, 2001

"Anschutz Expands Empire." Los Angeles Times, Nov. 22, 2001

"Channel 41 Sets Spanish-Language Ratings Record." New York Post, Nov. 20, 2001

"Santa Ana No. 1 In Spanish." Los Angeles Times, Nov. 20, 2001

"Hartford's Latinos Revel In Securing Mayor's Post." New York Times, Nov. 18, 2001

"Fulanito Turns American On Cutting Records." Billboard, Nov. 17, 2001

"Latin Notas: Welcome To The Family." Billboard, Nov. 17, 2001

"Marc Anthony's Amazing Salsa On Sony's 'Libre'." Billboard, Nov. 17, 2001

"Coliseum Commission Puts Up A Red Card." Los Angeles Times, Nov. 13, 2001

"Fernandez And Son A Dynamic Duo." Los Angeles Times, Nov. 12, 2001

"Fox Hits Homer With Latino Series Promo." Multichannel News, Nov. 12, 2001

"Epic's Shakira Serves A Bilingual Album." Billboard, Nov. 10, 2001

"Across The English Divide." Los Angeles Times, Nov. 4, 2001

"NBC Deal Promises Telemundo New Leverage." Billboard, Nov. 3, 2001

"Sanz Wins Big At Latin Grammys." Los Angeles Times, Oct. 31, 2001

"Channel 41 Airing Mayoral Debate En Español." New York Post, Oct. 30, 2001

"Galaxy Tries It Again." Los Angeles Times, Oct. 21, 2001

"NBC Touting Volume, Synergy With Telemundo." Electronic Media, Oct. 15, 2001

"Telemundo To Enter TV Production Deal With Mexican Firm." Los Angeles Times, Oct. 18, 2001

"NBC To Acquire Telemundo Network for $1.98 Billion." Los Angeles Times, Oct. 12, 2001

"Changing Face Of Latin Radio." Billboard, Oct. 6, 2001

"Spanish-Language TV Weathers Stormy Economic Conditions So Far." Broadcasting & Cable, Oct. 1, 2001

"Telemundo Polishes Gem." Daily Variety, Sept. 26, 2001

"Scripps Has Eye On Hispanic Cable Nets." Multichannel News, Sept. 24, 2001

"Media Giants Are Glued to Latino TV." BusinessWeek, Sept. 24, 2001

Fox TV Loses To Channel 41 In NYC." HispanicAd.com, Sept. 10, 2001

"4 Stations To Hispanic B'casting." Hollywood Reporter, Sept. 6, 2001

"Latin Grammys 'Betrayed' By Miami." Los Angeles Times, Aug. 31, 2001

"Azteca America On Air To Tap L.A.'s Latino Market." Los Angeles Times, Aug. 1, 2001

"Univision Sees What's Next In TeleFutura, Its New Net." Hollywood Reporter, July 31, 2001

"Out Of The Shadows." Time, July 30, 2001

"Greatest Bilingual Show On Earth." Los Angeles Times, July 25, 2001

"Univision 41 Scores With Copa America." HispanicAd.com, July 23, 2001

"Latin Grammys Do Cuban Slide To Los Angeles." Daily Variety, July 8, 2001

"Univision Adds Muscle To Its Original Lineup." Los Angeles Times, June 19, 2001

"Spanish TV's Soapiest Soap Is Off-Screen." Wall Street Journal, June 7, 2001

"SBS Launches El Sol Station In L.A." Billboard, May 26, 2001

"WNYW Pulls News Surprise." Daily Variety, May 25, 2001

"Univision Unveils New Lineup, Network." Los Angeles Times, May 17, 2001

"Fox Sports' Spanish Net To Televise World Series." Multichannel News, May 7, 2001

"Mexicans Change Face Of U.S. Demographics." Los Angeles Times, May 10, 2001

"Station Seeks Unusual Niche In Spanish-Language Market." Los Angeles Times, May 1, 2001

"Mexican/Tejano Rules Latin Genre." Billboard, April 21, 2001

"Ops Mine Hispanic Gold Rush." Multichannel News, April 9, 2001

"Miami To Host Second Year Of Latin Grammys." Daily Variety, April 4, 20001

"Nevada Jumps 66.3% In 10 Years, Census Shows." Los Angles Times, March 14, 2001

"Hispanics Spur Population Growth." USA Today, March 14, 2001

"Deep In The Heart Of Texas, The Population Destination Is Suburbia." Los Angeles Times, March 13, 2001

"Hispanics Boost City Growth." USA Today, March 13, 2001

"Adelphia Tailors Pitch To L.A.'s Hispanics." Multichannel News, March 12, 2001

"Radio Rises To The Bilingual Challenge Quickly." Billboard, Feb. 17, 2001

"News They Can Use." Los Angeles Daily News, Feb. 20, 2001

"Univision To Cancel Programs To Save Money." Los Angeles Times, Feb. 13, 2001

"KWHY's The Answer." Daily Variety, Feb. 13, 2001

"Telemundo To Buy L.A.'s KWHY For $329 Million." Los Angeles Times, Feb. 13, 2001

"Spanish-Language Radio Tops The Arbitrons." Los Angeles Times, Jan. 13, 2001

"Novela Pushes Univision Outlet To New High." New Jersey Herald News, Jan. 12, 2001

"An Accent On Progress." Los Angeles Times, Jan. 6, 2001

"A Neglected Giant." New Times Los Angeles, Jan. 2, 2001

Chapter 9
CAPITULO 9

Which Way to Go? 2002
QUE CAMINO? 2002

• Latin music, which obtains the most media coverage of any branch of Latin entertainment, continues to haltingly pursue the growth of alternative music or "alterlatino," its new two/words/glued/together identity.

• Puerto Rico's El Gran Combo celebrates its 40th anniversary.

• Salsa faces fading fans and declining radio exposure.

• Hispanic Broadcasting Corporation's marriage to Spanish Broadcasting System is aborted in favor of a new suitor, Univision, which prompts legal action by a miffed SBS.

• FCC clears NBC's historic purchase of Telemundo for the higher price of $2.7 billion.

• Latin theater's roots entrenched in a growing number of cities.

• Film industry in high gear with Latin-flavored titles, some controversial, in both English and Spanish.

• The Immigration and Naturalization Service discovers 24 Latin-born baseball players lie about their age in order to appear younger and attract major league team interest.

• Hispanics play unheralded roles on the gridiron for National Football League teams.

• Major League Soccer restructures itself into a two-conference league.

The continuous Hispanic population expansion is now setting roots in America's suburbs, notably Las Vegas, Little Rock, Raleigh, Atlanta, Greensboro, Orlando, Nashville, Fort Lauderdale, Sarasota, Portland, Oregon, and Elgin, Illinois. Utah's Latin population increases by 138 percent in the last decade to 200,000, where it will represent 20 percent of the state's populace and 40 percent of Salt Lake City's by 2010. In the greater Los Angeles area, Central-Americans have a larger presence than is reported in the 2000 Census, according to the Pew Hispanic Center, which sets the figure at 645,000, rather than the Census count of 437,000. The Census also claims there are 8.7 million immigrants who have entered the country surreptitiously, of which 3.9 million are from Mexico. Nonetheless, *Hispanic* magazine's annual survey lists the top 10 locales for Latinos to reside as being (in descending order) San Diego, Austin, Miami, San Antonio, El Paso/Las Cruces, Albuquerque, Tucson, Los Angeles, New York, and the Raleigh/Durham/Chapel Hill area.

The key question no one knows the answer to in music is: Will "alterlatino" be an evanescent trend? Enrique Fernandez, the new president of the fledgling Latin Recording Academy of Arts and Sciences, which presents the Latin Grammys, asserts in the *Miami Herald* that, "'alterlatino' is the very near future, almost the present of Latin music."

Attendees to the third annual Latin Alternative Music Conference in New York hear plenty of alternative music pros and cons, buffeted by comments that Latinos all over the hemisphere incorporate American rock 'n' roll into their endemic music on display in the U.S. by the likes of true believers Juanes, Maná, Volumen Cero, Bacilos, Molotov, Aterciopelados, Manú Chao, Los Rabanes, La Lay, Locos Por Juana, and even Miami's favorite son, Jorge Moreno. Tomás Cookman, the conference's co-founder, cites Latin music's stretching out beyond its traditional orders. He tells the *Miami Herald*, it's a "thriving bazaar."

The acceptance of a rock-based music mixed with lots of other influences and cresting with Spanish-language lyrics is competing with this year's crop of new crossover hopefuls singing in English, succeeding, and inspiring other erstwhile Latino artists, to join the campaign to reach the nation's important bilingual audience.

This bazaar of sounds and fashions is butting up against the reality of the Latin record industry, which is beset by record piracy in much of Latin America and a concern among some musicians that Latin music's uniqueness is being watered down by the industry's rush to copycat hit pop acts.

Two independent Anglo record labels with major connections to Latin music are Fantasy and Concord. Fantasy is the catalog home for two major Latin artists, Cal Tjader and Mongo Santamaria. Ralph Kaffel, the label's president says from his office in Berkeley: "We've seen a spike in their catalog sales." There are 21 Tjader titles in the company's catalog, with a number being reissued. Reissue sales fall in the 10,000 to 17,000 range, figures that record industry veteran Kaffel calls "quite good." The younger Latin population is more focused on current salsa stars, Kaffel notes, adding with a tinge of sadness in his voice, "A lot of them don't know who Mongo or Cal are."

However, the Latin community sure does know who Poncho Sanchez is. "The Hispanic populace's financial clout is producing a major influence on the sale of Poncho's new releases," states John Burk, Concord's vice president/general manager, who oversees the Concord Picante Latin line. Concord and Concord Picante are owned by Norman Lear's Act III Communications Company of Beverly Hills, which acquires Concord after its founder, Carl Jefferson, sells it to Alliance Entertainment, which then goes bankrupt. Within three months of selling the company, Jefferson is diagnosed with terminal liver cancer. Before he dies in March 1995, Burk says, "He asked me and Glen Barros (another company executive) to take over. We went through a two-year sale bidding process until Lear buys the label and moves it to Beverly Hills."

Burk notes that Picante, established for Cal Tjader in 1980, has a higher sales performance "than other musical genres we record." Since sales leader Sanchez's music is hard driving, danceable Latin jazz, it gets no Latin radio exposure. "So," continues Burk, "we've been experimenting with buying television advertising time, using direct response ads in target markets on the West Coast where he has a fan base. This is a viable alternative to radio exposure" (or the lack of it).

Picante's new alliance with Eddie Palmieri has the label attempting new promotional methods for the respected New York musician. "We had him perform live on Univision's *Sabado Gigante* variety show and it was a big thing because it was the first time they let a band perform live. Usually it's lip synching," explains Burk.

Another major project being developed is *Jam Miami* for a 2003 release on DVD. Notes Burk: "I've always wanted to have a big star Latin jazz record since I have a passion for this music. There are people on the roster I want to get together, so we lined up Poncho and Chick Corea (another Concord pactee) along with Pete Escovedo, Arturo Sandoval, Dave Valentin, Oscar D'Leon, Steve Turre, Ray Vega, Claudio Roditi, Avishai Cohen, Hilton Ruiz, Dave Samuels, Nestor Torres, Ed Calle, and Horacio Hernández and interchanged them in different settings in front of a big band and percussion section. One of the goals of the jam is to take lesser-known players and couple them with Tito Puente. He is supposed to be on the show but he has heart problems two months before the session and passes away. I talked to him about the repertoire and arrangements. I wanted him to do a medley from his Palladium days. So we do a tribute to Tito instead. The loss of Tito is a real blow because he was a great ambassador for the music. We've lost a lot of those icons and that's not good for the music."

Two acts with Concord Picante Records that attract a different audience are Tânia Marie, from Brazil, and the Caribbean Project, whose recent release is *The Gathering*. Led by Dave Samuels and Dave Valentin, the sextet appeals to Afro-Cuban devotees. "Generally," says Burke, "someone who enjoys Brazilian music doesn't necessarily have the same affinity for Afro-Cuban and vice versa. *Gathering* is a little different because the guitar is replaced by a piano and Paquito D'Rivera plays alto sax on some cuts."

Does recording a Latin album come with its own unique problems in the studio? "It takes a little longer to do a Latin jazz session because of the miking. While a Latin pop album will be layered with prerecorded sections, that's not done in Latin jazz and jazz sessions. In some ways it makes it more difficult because you need a certain amount of isolation between all the percussion elements. You need to get the clarity of the conga, timbales, cowbells, and chekere, which is a large gourd and a very loud instrument. You need to mike the instruments so they sound like they would in a live performance."

One company building its own powerful sound identity is Univision Communications, parent to the leading Spanish-language TV network. It becomes a force in the record industry by buying West Coast-based Fonovisa in December of 2002 for $230 million and incorporating it into its expanding and recently formed Univision Music Group, which includes a 50 percent ownership in Disa, a Mexican-based label. With the acquisition, the group's sales will account for 22 percent of all Latin records in the U.S. Two casualties of the Fonovisa purchase are the departure of its president, Guillermo Santiso, and the closing of its subsidiary, Melody Latina, whose artists will be shifted to the Fonovisa roster in the Woodland Hills suburb of Los Angeles, which makes it in close proximity to the regional Mexican music's hegemonic hold over the Latin record industry.

In one of its major growth moves, Univision signs a joint venture record label deal with hot producer/songwriter Rudy Pérez. The label, with the original title of Rudy Pérez Enterprises, will focus on Miami acts. Its first act is Area 305, a quartet of Miami singers/instrumentalists who have worked on record dates for Perez. Perez will continue to produce other artists through his Bullseye Productions. The producer's credits include working with Julio Iglesias, Christina Aguilera, Michael Bolton, Luis Miguel, Marc Anthony, and Univision vocalist Jennifer Peña, whose hit, *El Dolor Du Tu Presenica* (*The Pain of Your Presence*), he writes and produces.

Another top Miami producer working with Univision acts is Kike Santander. He and Perez co-produce Peña's album *Libre* (*Free*) while Perez writes Univision act Pilar Montenegro's hit single, *Quitame Ese Hombre* (*Take That Man Away*), which comes out in different versions: a pop ballad for East Coasters and their Caribbean roots, and a norteño sound for Mexican fans in Chicago and the Southwest. Peña says he adds new melodies and lyrics to the traditional sound of regional Mexican music's accordions and drum patterns to create a new regional sound. Peña is credited with being a pioneer in creating multi-versions of a song for different audiences. José Behar, Univision Music Group's president, who leaves EMI Latin for this new assignment, labels Los Angeles the right place to be. A Cuban-American who grows up in Miami, he tells the *Miami Herald* that being in L.A. allows the company greater access to "trends and marketing needs and the different flavors that 65 to 70 percent of the market needs and wants. When you're in Miami, you're insulated from that 65 to 70 percent of the market."

For Sony Discos, while very hip to the importance of regional Mexican music, led by ranchero scion Vicente Fernández, its roster is an eclectic potpourri of stylists, including Rubén Blades, the Panamanian political overseer and musical boundary pusher; Sin Bandera, vocal duo from Mexico and Argentina that blends R&B and jazz into its pop style; Puerto Rican 25-year veteran contemporary vocalist Gilberto Santa Rosa; Spanish ballad singer Jordi; and Guatemalan provocative lyricist singer Ricardo Arjona Fernández. Tommy Mottola, while chairman and CEO of Sony Music Entertainment, calls Fernández, "Mexico's greatest living singer" in a *Billboard* spotlight to the legendary ranchero vocalist. Among his album releases this year is an acoustic work featuring guest vocalists, including Juanes and Alejandro Sanz, who accompany him on several of his greatest hits. The LP will be the centerpiece of a special on Televisa, the Mexican TV network. A second album, *35 Anniversario Lo Mejor De Lara*, pays tribute to the late Mexican composer Augustin Lara. Sony's regional music is augmented by distribution deals with genre specialists Titán Records, Cintas Acuario, and with Luna Records purchased from departing executive Abel De Luna, hired three years ago to strengthen Sony's regional Mexican music department. Sony will now distribute Costarola Music, the label De Luna now heads.

Of all the contemporary artists on the Sony roster, Rubén Blades latest album, *Mundos*, is the most adventurous since it goes beyond the multifarious Latin community by mixing in Irish bagpipes, violins with Afro-Cuban congas, jazz guitarist Pat Metheny, and the Irish-American favorite *Danny Boy*, which is sung in both English and Spanish.

In a first effort, two Sony Discos artists, record the theme song for Telemundo's first music reality series, *Protagonistas De La Música (Music Stars)*. Notes the labels chairman Oscar Llord in *Billboard:* "The opportunity to team up with Telemundo on an extensive, national talent search is enormous and unprecedented for Sony."

Although it seems a natural thing to do, Miami Beach-based Warner Music Latina is one of a few labels to sign local talent. Its roster includes two such bands, Bacilos and Volumen Cero. It's also home to Maná, a Guadalajara-based pop rock quartet that becomes the industry's most successful Latin rock ensemble.

While Bacilos members produce their first self-titled rock album in 1999, the band lands on Warner Music when a label employee attends a release party and brings the trio to WB's attention. Its second album, *Caraluna*, is produced by two veterans, Luis Fernando Ochoa and Sergio George. The trio, singer/guitarist Jorge Villamizer from Colombia, vocalist/bassist André Lopes from Brazil, and vocalist/drummer José Javier Freire from Puerto Rico, meet while attending the University of Miami. Volumen Cero is a proponent of alternative rock. The bilingual quartet, Luis Tamblay, Martín Chan, Cristian Escuti, and Fernando Sánchez, grow up in Miami and in their family's native Chile, Colombia, and Peru. Each is influenced by '80s bands The Cure, New Order, current favorites Radiohead, and early Latin rock bands. Their debut CD, *Luces* (*Lights*) features all-Spanish language tunes but no Latin tempos. Rock rhythms dominate. The band's history is full of ironies. It begins as an Anglo rock band, Orgasmic Bliss in the early '90s, but shifts to all-Spanish in '97 under its new name, enters and wins a local talent contest and then finishes second in the national competition sponsored by Telemundo. After signing with a small label it winds up on Warner Bros.

This seems to be the supreme year for 15-year-old Maná, which blends social concerns with its mixture of musical textures and is often derided by music critics for its sweet memorable lyrics, lack of cutting edge emotions, and its reliance on light rock and tropical rhythms. Its major breakthrough, which tends to shut up its detractors, occurs when it performs with Carlos Santana on the track *Corazón Espinado* from his 1999 Grammy-winning LP, *Supernatural.* The band also accompanies Santana on 28 concert dates and records a hit *MTV Unplugged* CD on its own. Collectively the band wins four Grammys and sells more than 16 million albums globally. Its new album, *Revolución De Amor*, is both its seventh studio album and its first of this nature in five years. Guests on the album include Santana and Rubén Blades. Warner Latino calls the album the most important LP it will release toward the end of the year. The band, in its early formative years in 1984 is called Sombrero Verde (Green Hat). It changes it name to the one word Maná three years later.

The four members, Fehr Olvera, Juan Calleros, Sergio Vallin, and Alex González, have a major tour sponsor, Coors Light, which also places them in Spanish and English TV commercials, which means much exposure before a potential crossover audience.

Crossover is not necessarily on the minds of Universal Music Latino's two marquee attractions, Enrique Iglesias and Juanes. For Iglesias, the oldest son of 1984 crossover Latin idol Julio Iglesias, this is the first time in five years he's recorded an album in Spanish, *Quizas* (*Perhaps*). This is the Spanish debut for his new label and it bumps right up against last year's release of the English-language album *Escape* on Universal-owned Interscope, which also released his initial 1999 Anglo CD, *Enrique.* So he's promoting both the Spanish and

English albums during a U.S. tour. Initially recording three albums for Fonovisa, starting with his 1995 debut, Iglesias signs a multi-album deal worth an estimated $40 million with Interscope/Universal International Music, with his Spanish-language albums to come out on Universal Music Latino, the company's domestic Latin imprint.

Juanes, whose given name is Juanes Esteban Aristizabal, and is last year's best new artist in the Latin Grammy competition, makes his debut as a headlining tour attraction, performing works from a new album, *Un Dia Norma* (*A Normal Day*). On the sad ballad, *Fotografia* (*Photograph*), he duets with female pop vocal Grammy winner Nelly Furtado. The two were supposed to perform on last year's Latin Grammys, which were reduced to a small ceremony because the September 11 Twin Towers attacks cancelled the telecast. The album reflects the agony of being born in Medellín, Colombia, where drug trafficking rages and is a contrast to the love songs he espouses. This album, the follow-up to last year's debuting, harder-edged, *Fifate Bien* (*Pay Close Attention*), is more pop-oriented and includes smidges of vallenato, a form of Colombian folk music, rock, salsa, and cumbia. Jesús López, Universal Music Latino's chairman, tells the *Miami Herald* the new album is "the reality of his life."

The company also signs Puerto Rican alternative music band Circo, acquires its Latin Grammy nominated album *No Todo Lo Que Es Pop Es Bueno* on Head Music, and signals its intention to support rap en Español by signing a distribution deal with VI Music, a Puerto Rican label specializing in *reggaeton*, the hybrid form of reggae and rap. It also releases albums by two established rappers, Spain's Maria Rodriguez Garrido, known as "La Mala" and Cuba's Orishas, a trio now based in Paris. With U.S. Latino radio stations unenthusiastic about adding this form of music, its exposure is highly problematical. On a more realistic level, the company strengthens its regional Mexican department with the hiring of Gilberto Moreno, and also picks up distribution of his 20-artist MusiMex label, which specializes in two tropical genres of regional Mexican. It also signs regional Mexican vocalist Carmen Jara. Universal also lands an exclusive licensing deal with Barcelona, Spain's Vale Music, which releases music from the weekly TV series *Operación Triunfo*. Launched in 1997, Vale is also a specialist in dance music.

BMG U.S. Latin sprinkles its roster with artists from Mexico, Puerto Rico, and Cuba. El Gran Combo, celebrating 40 years as Puerto Rico's leading salsa band, is tributed on its first live recording, *40 Anniversario*, recorded at the Coliseo Rubén Rodríguez in Bayamón, Puerto Rico, in April. The 13-piece ensemble's 20th anniversary produces a tribute LP, *De Ayer, Hoy, Manaña Y Siempre*, on the Combo label. Combo, an independent label in New Jersey, forces the halting of BMG's album when it alleges the label did not secure a licensing agreement to include several songs on the new CD. One Puerto Rican artist changing musical directions is Gisselle, who shies away from the fading merengue style to encompass a Latin pop sound in her BMG title, *En Alma, Cuerpo Y Corazón* (*In Soul Body and Heart*). Born in New York where she speaks both English and Spanish, the CD mirrors her bilingual upbringing by including two songs in English.

Following the trend among labels to release soundtracks from Spanish TV series, BMG issues three CDs from the TeleFutura novela, *Cómplices Al Rescate* (*Accomplices to the Rescue*). One release features cast members while the other two feature 13-year-old actress Belinda Peregrin in her roles as twin sisters with different singing styles. Reaction to the soap in Puerto Rico, where it runs on an Univision station, has been strong among youngsters four to 12, prompting initial sales of 60,000 copies, according to the label. Peregrin's appeal is so strong in Puerto Rico she headlines two concerts at Roberto Clemente Stadium.

Tropical singer Jerry Rivera, in a quest to gain strength in the rock en Español field, works with three different producers: his Puerto Rican A&R man, Ramón Sánchez, Estéfano (who's clients include Thalía and Paulina Rubio), and Italy's Emanuele Ruffinengo (who's produced the newest sensation Alejandro Sanz on his CD, *Vuela Muy Alto*). Rivera thinks he may be the first Puerto Rican artist to work with Ruffinengo, who comes highly recommended. One artist, Mexico's ballad singer Cristian Castro, makes sure he keeps BMG's managing director Adrian Posse happy by including a tune with lyrics written by Posse in his compilation CD, *Grandes Hits*. Another Mexican artist, Patricia Manterola, returns to recordings after four years in TV and film, including an appearance in Telemundo's 1998 recasting of *Charlie's Angels*. Originally a member, with Pilar Montenegro, of the music group Garibaldi from 1989 to 1994, she reemerges on BMG with *Que El Ritmo No Pare*, an album in which she helps select the musicians and songs.

Of all BMG's artists, Manolín González arguably has the most bizarre background. A medical doctor in Cuba, he drops that career in order to become a salsa singer. After three years of pressure from the Cuban government to cease his conciliatory songs anent reuniting with Cuban exiles in the U.S., and being banned from traveling abroad, and having his music disappear from state-owned radio and TV, he defects to Miami in May 2001. There he reunites with his band, which had earlier defected, and resumes his career as a musician. Manolin, known as "El Médico De La Salsa" ("The Doctor of Salsa"), records his first U.S. album for local label Cioca Music, which leads to a four-album deal with BMG Latin.

When Los Fabulosos Cadillacs, Argentina's popular rock en Español band goes on hiatus due to the departure of bassist and composer Flavio Oscar Cianciarulo from Buenos Aires to Monterrey, Mexico, BMG signs the band's singer/songwriter Gabriel Fernández Capello. His first solo album, *Vicentico*, is much softer and melodic in tone than the band's previous brash explosiveness.

Romanticism is the mood at Miami's Crescent Moon, the label owned by the Estefans, Gloria and Emilio, where Jon Secada duets with Gloria on the song, *Por Amor*, from his *Amanecer* (*Awakening*) album, his first Spanish LP in seven years. Another single, the ballad *Si No Fuera Por Ti*, is turned into a hit by utilizing a number of different rhythms—the vallenao (Peruvian waltz), bachata, merengue, and bolero. Born in Cuba, Secada utilizes his bilingual skills in 1992 when he records his debut EMI album, *Just Another Day*, in English and in Spanish as *Otro Dia Mas Sin Verte*. It wins a Latin pop Grammy and is followed by another Latin Grammy winner, *Amor*, in 1996.

Panamanian rock band Los Rabanes, with Crescent Moon for two years, ventures into new turf with *Money Pa' Que* (*Money for What?*), a fusion of punkish rock with Caribbean flavors from Jamaica. Things are not as smooth for Vallejo, the bilingual rock band from Austin, Texas, and Crescent Moon's first band to be performing rock in 2000. After releasing the all-English *Into the New*, the band independently releases its second album, the all-English *Stereo*. Lead singer A.J. Vallejo alleges to the *San Antonio Express-News* that there were problems in producing the debut CD because of the non-English speaking producers assigned by Estefan to work with the band. Nonetheless the band hopes to release its first Spanish-language LP on Estefan's label next year.

Estefan is individually honored by the U.S. Congress for his contributions to Latin communities in this country. Secretary of State Colin Powell makes the presentation during a ceremony celebrating Hispanic Heritage Month. The day after the honor, Estefan produces a music special at the White House hosted by Carlos Ponce and featuring Jaci Velasquez, Gian Marco, and Jennifer Peña.

Reacting to the nation's changing Hispanic population and its alternating musical styles, EMI Latin USA creates a unit to work with its alternative rock bands, which include two Argentinean acts, La Mosca Tsé Tsé, an emerging band, and Charly Garcia, a pioneer in the musical style who signs a three-album deal with the label after previously recording for Sony. His initial U.S. album release is *Influencias* (*Influences*). He'll be put on a select city domestic tour including Miami, Los Angeles, and two cities where he's already performed to packed audiences, Boston and New York.

EMI Latin also adds Colombia vocalist Andrés Cabas to its roster. He specializes in fusing little-known African rhythms with strident guitar riffs, which Jorge Pinos, EMI Latin USA's president, feels is more self-contained than fusing musical styles from multi-national sources. As part of its Selena reissue program, the label releases a new Selena single, *Con Todo Amor* (*With All Love*). The disc is actually a medley of three of the late singer's ballad hits: *Amor Prohibido* (*Forbidden Love*), *Como La Flor* (*Like a Flower*), and *Si Una Vez (If Once)*.

Meanwhile, Mexico's Paulina Rubio seeks to become her nation's new crossover sensation with her first English debut album, *Border Girl*, which includes hip-hop and rock elements. Following this is the release by the label's top seller, sexy vocalist Ariadna Thalía Sodi Miranda, best known simply as Thalía, of her new eponymous CD, which includes three songs in English. Rubio's is planning an all-English album by the end of the year. Last year, her *Paulina* album is the nation's top-selling Latin album, so with a solid global Spanish-language fan base, her challenge, like those crossover sensations before her, is not to alienate these loyalists by singing in English. *Border Girl* winds up spending 10 weeks on *Billboard*'s top 200 chart, an important achievement for a first-time effort by the 31-year-old artist, who also becomes the first Mexican singer to border hop from Spanish to English.

Thalía hires Emilio Estefan to produce and co-write eight songs on her new EMI album. She's looking for the same creative forces Estefan utilizes to produce a 2000 hit for Rubio. The new record features high-profile guest artists on three tunes, the Kumbia Kings, Los Rabanes, and Marc Anthony. The vocalist gains notoriety by marrying Tommy Mottola, chief executive of Sony Music Entertainment, after he divorces Mariah Carey, and has a single from the album, *Tu Y Yo*, released for various Spanish and English radio formats. It's the same cross-format concept that helps promote a tune by another female vocalist, Pilar Montenegro. Thalía's name is dragged across the headlines one week after she performs on the Latin Grammys in Los Angeles when two of her older sisters, Laura Zapata and Ernestina Sodi, are kidnapped in Mexico City, the latest victims of criminal extortion plots plaguing that nation. The women are eventually freed after a ransom is paid.

While these women generally lack a unique vocal style and are not known for interpreting lyrics, they are known for their energetic sensuality on stage, which accounts for a lot during their in-person appearances.

Perhaps the most wacky, fun Latin hit records are Las Ketchup's debut single, *Asereje*, from the album, *Hijas Del Tomate (Tomate's Daughters)*, named after their father, flamenco guitarist El Tomate (Juan Muñoz). The tune by the three sisters, Pilar, Lola, and Lucía Muñoz, and the dance craze it spawns in Spain, which then spreads to other parts of Europe, is given added sales momentum by the trio's fall promotional tour in the U.S. Like the dance craze built around another one-tune sensation of six years ago, the *Macarena*, Las Ketchup runs out of sauce.

There's a lot of soul-searching and changing going on in the record business. Like Rubio and Thalía, who add new elements to their music, pop acts like Juanes, Sin Bandera, and Area 305 are also expanding their styles by infusing new ingredients. Tropical music sales for salsa and merengue are declining. Listeners are abandoning salsa in Puerto Rico and on the Mainland, forcing a number of radio stations to change formats. Salsa buffs apparently feel the music from the past two decades is old hat. The result is artist trimming at such salsa supporters as Sony Discos and Universal Music Latino. Artists are adding disco, rap, and reggaeton, which mixes reggae with rap to the tropical beat. Carlos Ponce, a Miami-raised novela actor on Univision, whose earlier EMI albums focus on pop ballads, adds rock and rumba colorations into a new self-titled album he calls "Caribbean Rock."

One locale rejecting the salsa slide is Dallas/Fort Worth, where the popular norteño and Tejano styles are seeing strong competition from an array of artists ranging from drop-ins Celia Cruz, Marc Anthony, and Oscar D'Leon to local favorites, Havana Boys and a spin-off, Havana NRG! "Dallas is even stronger than Houston, which used to be the big salsa city," boasts Willie Martinez, Havana NRG!'s manager, and percussionist in the *Dallas Morning News*.

"What has helped here are the salsa dance classes in the clubs," adds band member Ivan Martinez. "We see a lot of Mexicans dancing salsa at the shows. People do want more than just Tejano and norteño here."

Three Latino superstars are also on the move, and not all necessarily down a positive path.

Carlos Santana explodes with *Shaman*, his first-ever album to debut at No. 1 on Billboard's Top 200 album chart. It's his follow-up to the eight Grammy award-winning 1999 spectacular, *Supernatural*, which sells 25 million copies worldwide. Santana calls the new album "a multi-dimensional" collection of songs, aided by vocalist Michelle Branch's efforts on the single *The Game of Love*. The new LP (whose title means healer) is the 37th for the 55-year-old spiritually motivated musician since debuting sensationally at Woodstock in 1969.

Jennifer Lopez's private life begins to overshadow her musical career. Her new release, titled quixotically, *This Is Me*, may have a subliminal message that there are many facets to her personal life than just shifting from marriage one to marriage two to a romantic fling in-between to finally landing in a relationship with actor Ben Affleck, underscored in her song, *Dear Ben*. Her latest film is *Maid in Manhattan* with Ralph Fiennes, with whom she does not get involved romantically off the big screen. That isn't the case with Affleck, with whom she stars in *Jersey Girl* and with whom she's living with in Philadelphia during the filming. With the lovebirds every move reported by the frenzied tabloid press, Lopez's talent agency, International Creative Management, drops her. The agency's vice chairman, Ed Limato, e-mails ICM staffers: "We have decided that we no longer wish to represent Jennifer Lopez, and we have so informed her manager (Benny Medina)." *Daily Variety* gets a copy of the e-mail and prints it in a story about the separation. *Jersey Girl* is scheduled for release in 2004. It'll be preceded by *Gigli*, another film the current hot celebrity duo does, which comes out in 2003 to devastating reviews. In

January of 2004, Jennifer and Ben call its splitsville after previously canceling their planned $2 million wedding in Santa Barbara, California, which dominates the tabloid press.

Marc Anthony's second all-English album, *Mended*, does well but not spectacularly. Panned by critics, it fails to produce a breakout single hit. His last LP, *Libre*, returns him to his Latin roots, so while he's a success as a bicultural pop act, he still finds himself distancing himself from the term "crossover." "Everyone seems to think crossover is the ultimate thing," he remarks to the Phoenix-based *Arizona Republic*. "I'm not crossing over to anything." His personal life is also starting to draw headlines. Two years after marrying former Miss Universe, Dayanara Torres, the couple announces they are separating. Five months after their separation, they renew their vows in Puerto Rico.

El Gran Combo, Puerto Rico's seminal salsa big band, celebrates its 40th anniversary, apparently above the sales slippage fray affecting other artists. The band, which tours globally, is known affectionately as *La Bandera De La Salsa* or *The Salsa Flag*. The 13-man ensemble founded by pianist, arranger, director Rafael Ithier, is known for its evolving style, playing the soul-flavored boogaloo, merengue, tango, and bolero, as well several island rhythms and featuring a string of sonero, or improvising vocalists, that carry the message of yearning and passion to new decades of listeners. Its latest double album on BMG U.S. Latin, *Aniversario 40 En Vivo*, celebrates its historic birthday, is recorded live at a concert in Bayamón, Puerto Rico. The ensemble features a mixture of repertoire from the CD with its old chestnuts during its appearance at the 27th annual Salsa Festival in Manhattan's Madison Square Garden. The band's stature in Latin music pays off with a *Billboard* Lifetime Achievement Award. Puerto Rico's musical importance is explored, along with its other entertainment assets in Chapter 15.

The bolero, the timeless romantic music born in Cuba, accepted within the Caribbean and Mexico, and performed by any number of today's vocalists and instrumentalists, ranging from vocalists Luis Miguel and Adela Dalto to Gonzalo Rubalcaba and David Sánchez, is given an academic tribute at the Smithsonian Institute's International Latin Music Conference and Festival in Washington, D.C.

There's a dramatic decline in the number of artists emphasizing the controversial narco-corrido tributes to drug runners, murder, and corruption in Mexico and the U.S. Los Tigres Del Norte, pioneers in this brand of story-telling from the Mexican state of Sinola, backs away from this subgenre of corrdio stories, which previously lauds a mixture of folk heroes ranging from gunfighters battling over the love of a woman to smugglers and bootleggers fighting U.S. law officials. Now the genre is filled with newcomers whose profane, sexually laden lyrics include thoughts that can induce fights among rowdy fans. Radio stations in the Baja California state of Mexico, which includes Tijuana, sign an agreement not to play narco-corridos, and to emphasize songs that promote good thoughts. The genre is a popular mainstay on Tijuana radio, which can be heard in San Diego. Author Elijah Wald's excellent book, *Narcocorrido, a Journey into the Music of Drugs, Guns, and Guerrillas*, calls the musical genre "analogous to gangster rap."

Classical music, too, is adding a Latin tinge to its concert repertoire.

In the Los Angeles area, a number of classical organizations are aiming programs at L.A. County's 44.6 and Orange County's 30.9 percent Latino populations. The Los Angeles Philharmonic, the Long Beach Symphony, UCLA, the Orange County Performing Arts Center, and the Eclectic Orange Festival are all upbeat on reaching this new audience. The Los Angeles Philharmonic devotes two weeks to what it calls "Latin Influence on U.S. Culture." This program features a world premiere by Mexican composer Gabriela Ortiz, John Adams' *El Nino, a* choral version of the birth of Christ, and chamber music from Latin America.

The Orange County Performing Arts Center in Costa Mesa, under the banner The Eclectic Orange Festival, adds a strong Latin music presence to its 2002 to 2003 season, including the American debut of the Orquestra De São Paulo, Brazil, and the appearance by the National Symphony of Mexico, the West Coast debut of the 14-member jazz ensemble Banda Mantiqueira, and the West Coast premiere of Argentine composer Osvaldo Golijov's *La Pasión Según San Marcos* (*The Passion According to St. Mark*), previously performed in New York, Boston, Tanglewood, Chicago, Caracas, and Stuttgart, Germany. It's a major work with a Latin Jesus, a mixture of a big band brass section with classical cellos and violins, vocals by a Brazilian soloist, the Venezuelan chorus Schola Cantorum De Caracas, and classical soprano Dawn Upshaw, Brazilian and Cuban percussion, and Afro-Cuban dancers, all conducted by Maria Guinand, music director of Schola Cantorum.

The Eclectic Orange Festival also features the Cuarteto Latinoamericano and the famous San Francisco-based Kronos Quartet, which appears earlier at UCLA's Royce Hall performing similar selections from its all-Latin *Nuevo* CD. On the LP, the group plays Silvestre Revueltas' *Sensemayá* with Mexico City's percussion group Tambuco, as well as playing along with a tape of Mexican alternative rock band Café Tacuba.

The Long Beach Symphony announces it will feature the works of Latin composers in four its six concerts.

When the Orquestra Sinfónica Nacional De México, the official title of the 74-year-old Mexican National Symphony, brings its program of varied moods to Chicago's Symphony Center, a Hispanic community group, the United Neighborhood Organization, distributes 1,500 tickets to area families. The orchestra's on-the-road repertoire includes such non-traditional, exploratory pieces as Villa-Lobos' (*Bachianas Brasileiras*), Piazzolla's (*Tangazo*), Arturo Marquez's (*Danzon No. 2*), and Revueltas' (*Night of Jaranas*).

Two artists from Latin nations not often mentioned, Argentina and Chile, are seeking their places among Latinization luminaries. Argentinean tenor saxophonist Gato Barbieri, who cracks the American market 30 years ago with his theme music for the controversial film, *Last Tango in Paris*, and then records his groundbreaking fusion of Latin American idioms with his jazzy avant-garde style for Flying Dutchman Records, Impulse, and A&M in the '70s, is back. His newest work, *The Shadow of the Cat* on Peak, reunites him with A&M Records former co-owner/trumpeter Herb Alpert, with whom he recorded in 1976. Now 70, Barbieri plays three tunes with Alpert, who hasn't reached that age yet.

One artist struggling for her own breakthrough is jazz vocalist Claudia Acuña from Santiago, Chile, one of the few Chilean artists to be signed by an American record company. Verve, which takes a chance on her in 2000 with her debut album, *Wind from the South*, gives her a second shot with the CD, *Rhythm of the Heart*, and a national nightclub tour. Canada's piano nobility, Oscar Peterson, is also on the scene as Verve reissues in digital sound his 1967 Limelight release, *Soul Español.*

Two of the seminal alternative bands, Los Lobos and Ozomatli, are going in different directions. Ozomatli's current Interscope CD, *Embrace the Chaos*, is a polyglot mixture of dynamic sounds from its Chicano, Cuban, African American, Japanese, and Filipino members. Politics weaves a strong influence amidst its lyrics when the band appears in an anti-Iraq war protest concert, Not in Our Name—Art Speaks Against the War, the latest in its efforts to raise its collective voice against police brutality and for immigrant rights.

For Los Lobos, the 29-year-old East Los Angeles quintet, writing the music for the WB TV Network series, *Greetings from Tucson*, and appearing in one of the episodes as a band looking for a place to practice on Christmas Eve, marks its presence in dual roles on the small screen. The band's current Mammoth/Hollywood album, *Good Morning Aztlan*, continues its eclectic escapades, fusing cumbia rhythms with reggae beats, rockabilly guitar riffs with lyrics of a social and political nature. "This record covers everything we're about," explains member Louie Pérez. The album is also recorded for the first time in guitarist member Cesar Rosas' home rather than in a commercial recording studio.

The growing interest in Latin music, especially by major mainstream venues wanting to book the big names and by companies seeking to align themselves as tour sponsors, results in a major expansion of Hispanic artists appearing in your town, wherever that is, be it in Oregon, Michigan, or in the South. Among the performers fortunate enough to have sponsors are Vicente and son Alejandro Fernández (Jack Daniel's), Maná (Coors), Carlos Vives (Sears Hispanic Concert Series), Juanes (Bud Light), and Shakira, the sponsorship queen with her consorts Pepsi and Reebok. Other appealing names on tour include Enrique Iglesias, Marc Anthony, Juan Gabriel, and Luis Miguel.

On a lower level of name power, also touring are such groups as Los Hombres Calientes, MDO (the 1997 successor to Menudo), Calle 54, featuring 14 musicians from the Miramax film of the same name and playing music from the film's soundtrack on Blue Note, and Peruvian singer Susana Baca, with appearances in New York, Chicago, Los Angeles, Seattle, Edmonton, and Calgary, Canada. She is often called "Peru's musical ambassador to the world" and "the voice of black Peru" because of her African descent. African slaves are first brought to Peru by Spaniards in the 16th century. She's been recording for pop star David Byrne's Luaka Bop label since 1995, and her newest disc, *Espiritu Vivo*, is scheduled to be recorded in New York on September 11, but is recorded a few days later in Manhattan.

Latin music is also showing up at some new locales: Dodger Stadium in Los Angeles where the first Veranazo 2002 Festival features six-hours of music by the likes of Enrique Iglesias, Thalía, José Manuel Figueroa, and La Banda El Recodo, among others, and at the L.A. County Fair in Pomona, where the spotlight is on the music of El Salvador, Guatemala, Honduras, Nicaragua, Costa Rica, and Panama, marking the first time the Central American community in L.A. gathers together in one locale to honor its culture. Santa Ana, California, with one of the largest Hispanic populations in the nation, treats mothers to its first-ever Festival De Mariachis at the city-owned Santa Ana Stadium.

In New York, the first all-Colombian concert at Madison Square Garden features nine Colombian acts, including Latin Grammy winner Juanes. The Brooklyn Academy of Music in the city's borough of Brooklyn hosts Brazil's touring dance troupe, the 27-year-old Grupo Corpo, during its month-long North American tour.

San Antonio, a major repository of regional Mexican music, is the site for several first-time events, including the Puro Conjunto Festival at Rosedale Park, featuring 12 bands; the appearance of the Los Angeles-based Hollywood Bowl's Mariachi USA Festival at the new 23,000-seat Verizon Wireless Amphitheater (where fewer than 2,000 people attend), and the Que Locos Live Comedy Tour at the Majestic Theater, featuring four Latino comics. The annual Hispanic State Fair at Rosedale Park is loaded with regional Mexican, Tejano, and pop acts. In Houston, the 12th annual Houston International Jazz Festival attracts a broad range of Latino artists to the Verizon Wireless Theater: Celia Cruz, Arturo Sandoval, Poncho Sanchez, and Houston's own salsa star vocalist Norma Zenteno.

Michael Vega, a talent agent with the New York office of the powerhouse William Morris Agency, whose clients include Enrique Iglesias, opines that the Latin business shows more growth than any other aspect of the touring industry. In one year, Vega will transfer to Miami to open the Agency's first office there and I'll wind up chatting with him about the business of putting Latin artists on the road.

The bachata music of the Dominican Republic is branching out beyond its New York City stronghold to engulf radio listeners in New York, Miami, and Houston. Bachata is an evolution of the Cuban bolero, developed in the Dominican during the 1960s. The catchy sound is heard on New York's WSKQ-FM, the city's top tropical formatted station, at Dominican nightclubs in uptown Manhattan and during a Latin music festival in Madison Square Garden. The music's lyrics may be romantic, melancholy, even bitter, prompting WXDJ-FM Miami DJ Ruddy Hernández to tell the *New York Times* it's "music to slit your wrists to." Yet by playing bachata during his hour program, Hernández's rating shoots skyward during the fall 2001 Arbitron survey period, besting every show on the station, and earning him a second hour of airtime. While some Latinos say bachata is crude, it is gaining acceptance alongside salsa, merengue, and even regional Mexican. When Houston's KOVE-FM plays *Hoja En Blancho* (*Blank Page*) by the top bachata act, Monchy and Alexandra, 468 times in six months, the exposure ensnares the city's Mexican and Central-Americans who go club dancing.

The influx of Latinos to Las Vegas in recent years is adding a richness to the local salsa scene, with one new 10-piece band, the Generación Habanera, performing the Cuban rhythm called timba at the Venetian Hotel and Casino. The year-old band's leaders are Leonardo "Leo" Chansuolme, a Cuban native and Mike Eckroth, from Bismarck, North Dakota, whose musical studies at the University of Arizona lead to his joining a Brazilian music band and visiting Cuba under the auspices of the State Department.

Three major historical albums provide glimpses into the roots of Latin music in this country. A Columbia four-disc retrospective recalls the artistry of Machito, Xavier Cugat, the Fania All Stars, and such Latin jazz artists as Mongo Santamaria, Herbie Mann, Ray Barretto, Paquito D'Rivera, Gato Barbieri, Arturo Sandoval, and Cachao. Arhoolie Records releases a 21-track compilation titled *Pachuco Boogie*, the 1948 tune written by bandleader Don Tosti that symbolizes the music of Los Angeles from 1948 to 1954, when zoot-suited Mexican-American youngsters chose to bypass traditional Mexican music for their own neighborhood music reflecting life in the barrios of L.A. Also on a historical note, Smithsonian Folkways Recordings issues *Latin Jazz* as a companion to the Smithsonian Institution's *Latin Jazz: La Combinación Perfecta* bilingual touring exhibition beginning a four-year, 12-city tour across America and then the Caribbean. The story relates the evolution of the music; the CD features classic tunes by Tito Puente, Mongo Santamaria, Dizzy Gillespie, Charlie Parker, David Sánchez, and Chucho Valdés.

History may also be made at the third annual Latin Grammys, set for September 18 at Hollywood's Kodak Theater and broadcast for the second time on CBS. Historic in the sense this could be the year in which nothing affects the event. As has already been detailed, in 2001 the show is pulled from Miami by Michael Greene, the National Academy of Recordings Arts and Sciences (NARAS) president and chief executive, who also oversees the new Latin Recording Academy (LARAS), because he feels planned protests by anti-Castro exiles in Miami will endanger guests and artists if they are from Cuba. So you have NARAS, which creates LARAS, maintaining influence over its award show's actions. Reset in Los Angeles for September 11 at the Staples Center, the telecast is cancelled after the Twin Towers attack in favor of a scaled-down presentation at a news conference in the Congo Room restaurant/nightclub. The Latin Recording Academy, governing body of the Latin awards, adds two new categories, best contemporary tropical album and best Christian album, bringing the total to 41.

Shortly after announcing the Kodak date, Greene resigns in April after 14 years, clouded by questions over his compensation (with a $2 million annual salary, plus country club membership, and a luxury car, reportedly making him the highest paid non-profit executive in the nation) and personal behavior, focusing on accusations by female employees of sexual harassment. He denies all the allegations, and his severance is reported to total $8 million. He's replaced by Neil Portnow, a 30-year record industry figure, who's worked with a number of companies including the Zomba Group, EMI America, Arista, 20th Century Fox, and RCA. His replacement as executive director of the Latin Academy, Enrique Fernandez, oversees the organization's 4,000 members, almost half of whom are in Mexico, Brazil, and Spain. After a short period, from May to November, Fernandez resigns to join the *Miami Herald* as features editor.

On the evening of the awards presentation, September 18, 22 Cuban artists and producers are not present, including several nominees, the result of a tightening of security measures on foreign visitors from seven nations the U.S. lists as terrorist countries, causing delays in the granting of visas. The State Department says it now takes 12 weeks for a security clearance, but that doesn't ensure a visa. The exclusion of Cuban artists is protested by a small group of demonstrators outside the Kodak Theatre.

As for the CBS broadcast itself, Spain's Alejandro Sanz is the big winner for the second year in a row. He wins three trophies this year; last year he won four Grammys in a scaled down, non-televised ceremony. Sanz is honored with record and song of the year for *Y Solo Se Me Ocurre Amarte*, and for album of the year, *MTV Unplugged*, all on Warner Latina. Sanz's victories come at the expense of two other multiple nominees, Celia Cruz and Carlos Vives. Vives, Colombia's hot new vocalist, with six nominations, wins two for best contemporary tropical album, *Déjame Entrar* (EMI Latin), and tropical song of the same name. And in a bittersweet moment, Vicente Fernández tops his son Alejandro for the best ranchera album.

Although the show features performances by Sanz, Cruz, crossover successes Shakira, and Marc Anthony, as well as Carlos Santana, Carlos Vives, Juanes (who teams with Nelly Furtado on *A Dios Le Pido*), Vicente Fernández, and son Alejandro, the presentation of awards in absentia to Cuban artists, and father and son Bebo and Chucho Valdés, the broadcast is seen by an average 4.2 million viewers. This is a significant 45 percent drop from the 7.5 million viewers who tuned into the inaugural broadcast two years ago. During the same period, ABC, Fox, and NBC each draw an average 9.5 million viewers to their counter-programming.

During a post-mortem interview with *Billboard*, Manolo Díaz, president of the board of the Latin Academy of Recording Arts and Sciences, blames the lack of strong ratings on poor marketing by CBS. "No one knew the Latin Grammys took place September 18," he asserts. He suggests the marketing has to be directed towards both the English-speaking audience and bilingual Hispanics.

The broadcast is a bilingual marriage with Spanish-language commercials by Southwest Airlines, Yoplait, Heineken, Dr. Pepper, and Red Fusion. Spanish-language commercials with accompanying English subtitles, a first for a CBS telecast, are by Covington Clothes, Sears, and Neutrogena. The majority of the spots are in English. The hosts, Gloria Estefan and Jimmy Smits, speak English, although Smits does make a reference that "this isn't your grandma's CBS." The show's announcer, Carlos Amezcua, a co-anchor on the *KTLA Morning News* in Los Angeles, works entirely in English. Cossette Productions, the same company producing the general market Latin Grammy telecasts for CBS, handles the sight and sound for this endeavor, which is broadcast in Spanish on the SAP channel. Technically, CBS has nothing to be embarrassed about, except it's not attracting major viewership.

Here are the key winners:

Record and song of the year: *Y Solo Se Me Ocurre Amarte*, Alejandro Sanz; album of the year: *MTV Unplugged*, Alejandro Sanz; best new artist: Jorge Moreno; best female pop vocal album: Rosario with *Muchas Flores;* best male pop vocal album: Miguel Bosé with *Sereno;* best group pop vocal album: Sin Bandera with *Sin Bandera;* best pop instrumental album: Chucho Valdés with *Canciones Inéditas;* best rock group album: La Lay with *MTV Unplugged;* best tropical salsa album: Alejandra Guzman with *Soy;* best tropical merengue album: Olga Tañon with *Yo Por Ti;* best tropical traditional album: Bebo Valdés Trio with Israel López "Cachao" and Carlos "Patato" Valdés with *El Arte Del Sabor;* ranchera album: Vicente Fernández with *Más Con El Número Uno;* banda album: Banda Cuisillos with *Puras Rancheras Con Cuisillos;* grupo album: Joan Sebastían with *Lo Dijo El Corazon;* Tejano album: Jimmy Gonzalez Y El Grupo Mazz with *Siempre Humilde;* norteño album: Ramon Ayala Y Sus Bravos Del Norte with *El Numero Cien;* jazz: Gonzalo Rubalcaba Trio with *Supernova;* Brazilian pop album: Lenine with *Flange Canibal;* Brazilian rock album: Cássia Eller with *Acústico MTV;* Brazilian samba album: Zeca Pagodinho with *Deixa A Vida Me Levar;* Brazilian song: *Saudade De Amar* by Dori Caymmi and Paulo César Pinheiro.

In one of the most bizarre legal decisions, the .38-caliber revolver that kills Tejano star Selena in 1995 is ordered smashed with a sledgehammer, shredded and the parts thrown into Corpus Christi Bay by state District judge Jose Longoria. "It's time to finally bring closure to such tragedy," he tells a wire service. Believed to be lost, the gun used by Yolanda Saldivar to kill Selena is found in the home of the court reporter at the trial. Supporters and detractors respond to the judge's ruling.

Despite all the industry's creative twists and turns, Latin record sales decrease sharply. It's the same bad news for the overall record industry with album sales down 10.7 percent over last year, which was also a drooping year. The Latin malaise, according to the Recording Industry Association of America, is reflected in the 26 percent drop in overall CD shipments to retailers to less than 19 million units during the first half of the year, a loss of an estimated $80 million, compared to the same period last year. For the same time frame, the dollar value of Latin records shipped to the Latin market exclusively is down 24 percent at mid-year to $249.5 million from $329.3 million for the same half-year in 2001.

While Sony remains the No. 1 overall Latin label, the two-year-old Univision Music Group comes from nowhere to land in the runner-up position on the Latin label album chart. According to *Billboard's* year-end compilation, Universal Latino continues to reign as the top-distributing label.

Latin theater is starting to flourish around the nation.

The first International Latino Theatre Festival at the Japan American Theatre in downtown Los Angeles presents plays by 11 theater companies from nine nations, and symposiums involving 70 playwrights, actors, and directors. Productions are in either Spanish or Portuguese. The organization bemoans the fact that L.A. has been slow in having its own Latino theater summit, since New York, Miami, and cities in Texas all have similar gatherings. A spokesperson also says the theater festival is a result of the interest and heavy attendance at the recent sixth annual Los Angeles Latino International Film Festival.

Miami's 17-year-old International Hispanic Theatre Festival, which this year offers a barrage of productions from 13 nations during its 17-day run in five South Florida cities, heads to Los Angeles and

Albuquerque for the first time. The Los Angeles branch of the festival takes place at the outdoor Ford Amphitheater down the street from the Hollywood Bowl. Mario Ernesto, the event's Miami-located director, is 15 when he comes to the U.S. from his native Cuba and eventually winds up in Miami. The festival's appearance is part of the Ford Theater's Latino Audience Initiative and is supported by a $450,000 grant from the James Irvine Foundation. The two troupes launching the Hispanic Theater Festival are from the Pia Fraus Teatro of São Paulo, Brazil, and the Compañia Marta Carrasco of Barcelona, Spain. The Brazilian company performs in Portuguese with English overhead supertitles, while the Spanish company performs in its native tongue with English supertitles. Ernesto is aware that the majority of Hispanics in L.A. are Mexican-American, but believes some people will go beyond listening to mariachi music.

Hispanic dancers are cracking the world of ballet as well. Two Cubans are with the American Ballet Theater in New York. Neither Carlos Acosta nor José Manuel Carreño are defectors, only great dancers. Twenty-nine-year-old Acosta comes to the American Ballet Theater after performing with the Houston Ballet from 1994 to 1998 and England's vaunted Royal Ballet, where he's a guest artist. Acosta is also the top black Cuban star in international ballet and a guest artist when he returns to dance with the National Ballet in Havana.

The blockbuster event among Spanish-language TV networks is the Federal Communication Commission's clearance of NBC's 2001 acquisition of Telemundo, originally announced as $1.98 billion and stock to the amended price of $2.7 billion. The financially ailing operation is jointly owned principally by Sony Pictures Entertainment and Liberty Media. NBC also assumes a debt load of around $700 million. NBC plans consolidating back-office functions and sharing of news and other programming with Telemundo's 11-owned stations. By year's end, it will acquire four additional stations.

Univision makes three acquisitions that turn it into a goliath in Spanish-language media. Its major efforts are the launch in January of a second network, TeleFutura, which debuts on 42 stations, including 13 it acquires for $1.1 billion from entrepreneur Barry Diller's USA Networks. There is also the purchase of the Fonovisa record label, the leading independent purveyor of regional Mexican music, and Univision's acquisition of the top Hispanic radio group, Hispanic Broadcasting Corp. for $3.5 billion.

Television in general is faced with the paradigm of perpetual immigration, spurring Spanish-language programming, while those people born in the U.S. portend an audience which will be bilingual and bicultural in nature and seek programming that reinforces their presence in the two-language world. This creates new opportunities for broadcast and cable, which begins producing more of its shows domestically. The Hispanic market is also especially sought after since research indicates Latinos watch more TV than any other group. According to a study by ad agency Initiative Media, as reported in the *New York Daily News*, Hispanics watch 58.6 hours of TV, an increase of 4.4 hours over non-Hispanics. Close to 50 percent of the viewing is for Spanish-language programming, but Latinos are also selectively viewing programs on the six broadcast networks, including *WWF Smackdown!* on the UPN, *Friends* on NBC, *The Simpsons* and *Malcolm in the Middle* on Fox, *Monday Night Football* on ABC, and *The George Lopez Show* on ABC.

English-language television, in either an offensive or defensive move, starts going after the Hispanic community with impunity. All across the nation, stations and networks are airing programs aimed at pulling bilingual Latinos away from Univision and Telemundo.

This move on the part of these broadcasters is designed to also counter the mercurial rise of Spanish-language TV as the fastest-growing advertising medium this year, according to CMR, a New York firm that tracks advertising expenditures. Additionally, program providers are also offering Spanish-language dubbed versions of their hit series heard by using the secondary audio program, or SAP, button on their sets. Cable TV continues its growth direction, with a plethora of new Latino networks debuting.

The array of Hispanic-themed shows centers on either drama or comedy, and includes *Resurrection Blvd.* on Showtime, *Brothers Garcia and Lorena* on Nickelodeon, the *George Lopez Show* on ABC, *Good Morning Miami*, *The Kingpins*, and *American Dreams* on NBC, *Greetings from Tucson* on the WB, and *American Family* on PBS. There are also Latin actors working in high profile mainstream TV series, including Alfred Molina in *Bram and Alice* on CBS, Freddy Rodriguez on HBO's *Six Feet Under*, A Martinez on ABC's *General Hospital* and Lifetime's *For the People*, Giancarlo Esposito on *Girls Club*, Gina Torres on *Firefly*, and Ricardo Antonio Chavia and Michael Cera on *The Grubbs* on Fox.

These actors follow in the footsteps of such predecessors as Hector Elizondo on CBS' *Chicago Hope*, Jimmy Smits on ABC's *NYPD Blue*, Cheech Marin and Jaime Gomez on CBS' *Nash Bridges*, and Randy Vasquez on CBS' *JAG*.

The roster of actors and actresses presently working is a blending of established names as well as relative unknowns, but there's a political caveat that displeases proponents of more Hispanic faces on the small screen: only around five percent of roles on TV feature Hispanics, whereas Latinos account for close to 13 percent of the nation's population. One actor, Esai Morales, has the distinction of appearing in three series, *NYPD Blue*, *Resurrection Blvd.*, and *American Family*. One actor, perhaps the best known of the Latinos holding down a lead role on a major series, but who is not generally known by his Hispanic name is Ramon Estevez, or Martin Sheen, of *The West Wing* on NBC. Sheen reveals the story behind his name change when he's the guest on Bravo's signature show, *Inside the Actors Studio*. He tells host James Lipton that when he senses his Hispanic name is a hindrance during acting job interviews, he changes it to that of New York Catholic Bishop Fulton J. Sheen, whose weekly TV show makes him a secular personality in the early 1950s. "I thought of him as a magnificent actor," he says. Sheen does not explain why of his two actor sons, Carlos is known as Charlie Sheen, while Emilio uses his original birth names, as does his sister Reneé.

Local Anglo stations are also romancing Latinos. In Charlotte, North Carolina, Fox affiliate WCCB finds that offering its local news with a Spanish translation on the SAP channel fills a void in the market with a growing Hispanic population and no Spanish-language newspaper. It also allows local advertisers an outlet to reach new customers.

Two Texas cities are miles apart as far as providing Spanish translations for their English-language newscasts. In El Paso, KVIA, an ABC affiliate, offers a Spanish interpretation on the SAP channel of its 6 p.m. news, which news director Eric Huseby tells the *San Antonio Express-News*, "people like." In the story, Margarita Lozano, the station's interpreter, admits her job is difficult because anchors don't always adhere to her script. Univision's KINT, which airs Spanish-language newscasts at 5 and 10 p.m., discounts the SAP offerings. Zoltan Csanyi-Salcedo, its news director, points to market studies that 70 percent of the city's Spanish-speakers are bilingual, and that residents can view four stations that program in Spanish, including several beamed in from Mexico. The San Antonio market, which has Spanish TV network coverage, eschews Spanish simulcasts. KENS news director, Thomas Doerr, explains the avoidance thusly to the *Express-News*: "Most people, if they're bilingual, would watch in English, or in Spanish on Telemundo or Univision. We found that broadcasting in our second audio channel was not very effective."

In Houston, for the first time, a 30-minute bilingual infomercial advising parents to warn their children about alcohol usage airs on KXLN, the Univision-owned station in Spanish and on KHOU, a CBS affiliate. The Spanish version, *Familias Hablan Sobre El Alcohol*, airs at 9 a.m. Saturday, while *Making the Right Choice about Drinking* follows at 11:30 a.m. Notes John L. Nau, III, President/CEO of Silver Eagle Distributors about the bilingual offering: "This message has not gone out in the past anywhere in Spanish. As far as a TV show dealing with this subject, this is the first of its kind nationwide." Nau, whose company pays for the airtime and contributes to its production costs, makes this claim to the *Houston Chronicle.*

In Las Vegas and Reno, which see growth in their Hispanic communities, TV stations add bilingual reporters to communicate with Latinos. KTNV, Las Vegas, adds Veronica Sanchez to its news staff. She is one of the first hires made by new news director Denise Clodjeaux at the ABC affiliate. Clodjeaux stresses that having a bilingual reporter opens the door for covering the city's emerging Hispanic population. This is the same logic behind Reno's KRNV hiring of Melissa Santos, who speaks English and Spanish. Jon Killoran, news director at the NBC affiliate, is quoted in an *Electronic Media* story anent bilingual reporters that if "you are going to attract those viewers, you need to reach out to them."

Los Angeles, already a bastion for Spanish-language TV, has a new addition, *LATV Live*, a year-old, two-hour block from 8–10 p.m., Monday through Thursday on KJLA, which features a potpourri of Latin music videos and bilingual VJ hosts, all geared to young viewers who eschew traditional forms of Hispanic radio and TV in favor of alternative music styles. The 13-year-old station barters its time to religious shows, infomercials, and shopping programs, with Latin night its growing favorite among young Latinos who comprise the studio audience at its West Los Angeles studio. The show is the only locally produced Latin music video program and features live performances by top names in music.

If names truly make news, then Anglo TV is name-dropping. Lynda Lopez, she of the famous last name, joins WNBC in New York as an entertainment reporter after toiling on local TV station WPIX's *Morning News*, at VH1 as co-host of *The Daily One* show, and at two Long Island radio stations, WBAB-FM and WLIP-FM. She now files entertainment reports for the network's 13-owned stations, its cable channels, and its Telemundo Spanish-language network. At 29, she's the youngest of the three Lopez sisters, megastar Jennifer, 31, and music teacher Leslie, 34. By 2003, she will have left NBC to co-host the morning-drive show on WNEW-FM and after a housecleaning at the station she joins WCBS-TV as a pop culture reporter. It's her third local TV station job in two years. In 2004, she is being pitched for her own daytime syndicated TV talk show by Universal Television. Jennifer's Nuyorican Productions will produce the ensemble show and she may herself occasionally appear. Neither happens.

ABC TV adapts a major concept of Spanish telenovelas for its daytime low-rated soap opera, *Port Charles*, by shortening its story arcs and climaxing a story within 13 weeks. The result: an increase in female viewers, and the motivation by the ABC Daytime Department to also integrate shorter story plots into another of its daytime soaps, *One Life to Live*. In its seventh season, *Port Charles*, sees a 10 percent rise among women 18 to 49 and a 13 percent rise in women 25 to 54, all because of the shortening of story arcs.

Felicia Minei Behr, ABC Daytime's senior vice president of programming, tells *Electronic Media* that the show's writing staff spends several weeks visiting with Latin American telenovela production companies to learn how they create the shorter segments flowing through their novelas.

Good Morning America hires Alex Cambert away from Telemundo as a Los Angeles correspondent. NBC hires Cheech Marin for its planned series, *The Ortegas*, about a multigenerational upper middle class Mexican family in Los Angeles. Marin, who previously works on *Nash Bridges* and *Resurrection Blvd.*, is the top name in a cast that also includes Al Madrigal, Terri Hoyos, and Renee Victor.

CBS-owned station in L.A., KCBS, lures news anchor Laura Diaz away from ABC's KABC, after nearly 20 years there, to beef up its low-rated 5 p.m. and 11 p.m. newscasts and also attract Hispanic viewers. KCBS plasters the city with billboards in English and Spanish, one of the few instances in which a bilingual ad campaign is launched by an Anglo TV station, as well as ads on Spanish radio and in the local Spanish newspaper. Ratings results do not immediately show a spike in audience viewership. By 2005, Diaz's presence still hasn't elevated KCBS from third place among network affiliates in the local news battles until the May sweeps when the 11 p.m. weeknight news, co-anchored by Diaz and Paul Magers, moves into second place behind longtime leader KNBC. And ahead of KABC.

KCBS' beefed-up news coverage and the new anchor team are among the key reasons the station draws 3.6 million viewers, including a boost in the target audience of 25- to 54-year-olds. It's the first time in 20 years that KCBS is rated No. 2 for its late local newscast. Diaz is also playing to her strength and reaching out to Hispanic viewers with an occasional public service show, *La Vida*, airing Sundays at 6:30 p.m. It displaces *Studio 2*, the station's regular community service half-hour she co-hosted with Magers. *La Vida*'s initial show on May 1 focuses on Cinco De Mayo, actors Jimmy Smits and Adam Rodriguez, and musicians Sergio and Francisco Gómez. As a result of a strong showing in the May 2006 sweeps, the 11 p.m. newscast, anchored by Diaz and Magers and augmented by the merged newsroom staffs of KCBS and KCAL, the city's second CBS-owned station acquired in 2002, is elevated to No. 1 after a 30-plus-year drought.

As for the heavyweight names appearing in series *The George Lopez Show* on ABC in primetime—after starting off slowly, gains steam and is given a full season commitment. Lopez also carries creator, producer, and writer credits. Los Angelinos are familiar with him as he's been doing a morning drive-time show for two years on KCMG-FM, an English-language station. The Lopez show, which is based on his personal life, features sparse use of Spanish words since it's aiming for a basically English-speaking audience. Still, there is ethnic humor. The obvious challenge of attracting Anglos and an ethnic audience to a show built around minority figures pays off when ABC renews the show for the next season. Lopez, a third-generation Mexican-American, is discovered during a comedy club appearance by Sandra Bullock, who is looking to get into TV with a Latin-themed program. His stand-up routines do show up in the program, which also stars Constance Marie as his wife and Belita Moreno as his beloved 83-year-old grandmother. Lopez is among the celebrities I interview in Chapter 11.

Greetings from Tucson, on the WB in primetime, is a story focusing on a Hispanic family in which a promotion allows Julio Oscar

Mechoso to move his Irish-American wife Rebecca Creskoff and their family to the suburbs. Other cast members include Pablo Santos, Aimee Garcia, Jacob Vargas, Bobby Chavez, Lupe Ontiveros, and Sara Paxton. Santos dies tragically in a private plane crash September 15, 2006 in Toluca, Mexico.

HBO's hit mortuary series, *Six Feet Under*, includes one Hispanic actor among the ensemble players: Freddy Rodriguez, who plays Federico Diaz, the mortuary's main embalmer, and his performance earns him a respected Emmy nomination.

Two Miami-based series, *CSI: Miami* and NBC's *Good Morning Miami*, each have tiny regular Latino cast members, despite the city's being 60 percent Hispanic.

CSI: Miami's lone Hispanic is Adam Rodriguez, while its star headliners include David Caruso, who is joined by another *NYPD Blue* alumni, Kim Delaney, who is hired when her own *Philly* series is canceled by ABC after she leaves *NYPD*. Problems emerge with both Caruso and Delaney, who subsequently leave the show. The Caruso role is originally written for a Latino, but somewhere along the creative process the characters ethnicity was altered.

NBC's *Good Morning Miami*'s solo Hispanic is Tessie Santiago, a Cuban-American from Miami, whose scatterbrained co-anchor on the TV show is criticized for her stereotypical vapidity and Cuban-accented one liners. Santiago tells *Entertainment Weekly* the accent "adds to her character" the way Megan Mullally's high-pitched voice defines her character on *Will & Grace*. The cast for the network's *American Dreams* includes Sarah Ramos and Arlen Escarpeta.

NBC is also taking a major risk with the David Mills' created *Kingpin*, which revolves around the life of a wealthy family of Mexican drug dealers that sells marijuana, cocaine, and heroin. The six-episode limited run, announced this year, will debut next January, but is already drawing flack for a story content that includes violence and drug usage, and, of course, brutal assassinations. There are also Latino law enforcement officials who battle the bad guys and gals. Among its stars are Yancey Arias and Bobby Cannavale.

Jeff Zucker, president of NBC Entertainment, in commenting on the variety of roles in the network's new series against the backdrop of stereotypes that have confronted Hispanic actors and actresses, like playing maids or poor people or recent immigrants, tells the *New York Times*, "As diversity increases, the span of roles increases. It's an evolution."

Resurrection Blvd's cast on Showtime includes Michael DeLorenzo, Nicholas Gonzalez, Ruth Livier, Mauricio Mendoza, Marisol Nichols, Elizabeth Peña, Tony Plana, and Esai Morales. It's a story about three generations of an East Los Angeles family whose lives are centered on boxing.

Of all the programs, PBS' story about an East Los Angeles family, called *American Family*, has the largest ensemble of well-known names, including Edward James Olmos, Sonia Braga, Esai Morales, and Raquel Welch as well as Kate Del Castillo, Austin Marques, and Constance Marie. Welch, incidentally, is playing a Latina for the first time on television. During her nearly 40-year career, she plays a Latina in only two films, a Mexican in *Bandolero* and in *100 Rifles*, a Mexican Yaqui Indian. The creator/executive producer/director is the respected film figure Gregory Nava, who brings the entire cast to Mexico to film the season's final two episodes during which they have separate missions to accomplish in the land of their heritage.

The story behind the appearance of this first Hispanic-oriented weekly dramatic series on U.S broadcast television is a remarkable tale of ingenuity and determination. Nava brings the project to CBS, which finances a pilot but cannot find a place for it on its 2001 schedule. So the director of *El Norte*, *My Family/Mi Familia* and *Selena* offers it to the other networks, but they also pass. Pat Mitchell, president and chief executive of PBS, reads about the series being passed by CBS. She contacts the president of CBS Television, Les Moonves, who tells her, according to *The New York Times*, that if she can find the funding to finance the series, CBS will donate its investment in the pilot show. So Mitchell obtains the funding from various sources for 13 episodes, and signs Johnson & Johnson as the sole corporate underwriter.

Nava slashes his fee, shoots the series on high-definition videotape rather than on the more expensive 35 m.m. film and cuts salaries for all actors, producers, directors, and writers. Using a common cliché, the project becomes a labor of love. That love is exhibited in a reflective thought given by 60-year-old Welch in another *New York Times* feature: "I do feel very fortunate now at this point in my career, where I'm definitely middle-aged and I'm not getting the kind of young leading lady parts anymore, that I have discovered and have been gifted with this role where I can feed myself personally as a human being."

One project showing corporate synergy is the animated kids series, *Mucha Lucha*, which runs on the WB Saturday mornings and has its soundtrack released on Warner Latina. In what could be a first, the English-language series and its Spanish-language compilation album are both targeted to bilingual Hispanics. The theme by Los Chicos Del Barrio, a popular Mexican group, as well as tunes performed by Volumen Cero, Bacilos, Tito Nieves, Pesado and Frankie Negron, add diversity to the album.

One TV critic, Ann Hodges of the *Houston Chronicle*, says, "The music is better than the show." The cartoon show features three students at the Foremost Renowned International School of the Future, who turn to wrestling to settle disagreements. Every character wears a mask, an idea show creators Lili Chin and Eddie Mort credit to lucha libre, Mexican wrestling, where combatants wear masks and costumes.

Despite these programming efforts, several multi-ethnic lobby groups continue to find fault with the number of Hispanic shows on television, two years after they've launched their pressure campaign to foster greater cultural diversity in primetime programming. The National Latino Media Council, along with the Asian Pacific-American Media Coalition and American Indians in Film and Television, give low grades to the broadcast networks for their diversity efforts: CBS earns a D minus (down from last year's D plus); NBC receives a D plus (down from a C); ABC goes from last year's D minus to a C minus, and Fox rises to a C from a C minus. The networks counter by claiming these groups fail to acknowledge legitimate cultural progress, according to a story in the *Los Angeles Times*. They all assert they are making progress in casting minorities.

As if this furor isn't enough, the National Association of Hispanic Journalists issues a devastating report claiming that out of 16,000 stories aired on the four major broadcast networks last year, only 99 are about Latinos. The report does, however, find something to boast about: Of these 99 stories, 68 percent include interviews with Hispanics, up from the 84 stories airing last year in which 24 percent feature Latinos speaking.

One artist making his own primetime progress is Marc Anthony, who stars in his first network TV special, *Marc Anthony: I've Got You*, taped at the Mohegan Sun Arena in Connecticut and broadcast on CBS. The all-English show is produced by Ken Ehrlich, the veteran music TV specialist, and is Anthony's first major appearance before an audience in this country in close to two years. He calls the Spanish Harlem section of New York where he grows up "a melting pot of music" and is rewarded during the concert by a sea of waving Puerto Rican flags in the audience. The concert, part of his North American summer tour, is aptly named after his new Sony single, which elicits lots of screams from the teenage girls in the crowd. This is Marc Anthony, crossover sensation of the moment, parlaying a program of English tunes, including the Eagles' *Hotel California*, for a national audience, which may have heard of him, but not seen him personal and close-up as he is in this taped performance.

His repertoire of ballads and up tempo tunes during this very slick production includes *I Need You*, *Faithfully*, *Half a Man*, *Tragedy*, and "the one song I never get tired of singing," *I Need to Know*, which he dramatizes on a runway into the audience.

Financially troubled three-year-old Hispanic Television Network files for Chapter 11 bankruptcy protection. The Fort

Worth-based network, seen on broadcast and cable, is available in 130 cities, but has always been undercapitalized and affected by the nation's economic decline. Sensing a more upbeat future, a New York Latino show seen on local cable, *Urban Latino*, becomes one of the first Hispanic cultural/entertainment magazine shows to go into national broadcast TV syndication by signing up 25 stations, including the key markets of New York and Miami and adding segments from Los Angeles, Miami, and Texas to appeal to its broader audience.

MTV Latin America, which broadcasts from Miami to viewers outside the U.S. and Puerto Rico, sets its first *MTV Video Music Awards Latin America* show to be seen domestically, as well as overseas, for the first time. MTV2 airs the show simultaneously from the Jackie Gleason Theater in Miami. An edited version also airs on MTV five days later, in October. Colombia's Shakira wins five honors, including artist and video of the year. Chile's La Lay is the only other act to win multiple awards for best rock artist and best rock group. The public votes for winners online.

The telecasts include the Rolling Stones' taped greeting in Spanish and Carlos Santana and Michelle Branch performing *The Game of Love* in English, with Santana later introducing Maná in Spanish. The heavily edited version on MTV includes performances in English by Avril Lavigne and Paulina Rubio, Spanish "thank yous" by the winners, a combination of commercials in Spanish and English, English promos for MTV's Saturday night show lineup, and putdown jokes by artists in Spanish.

And where are all these multi-cultural audiences being focused on by large companies? The top 20 Hispanic TV markets, according to Nielsen Media Research, are: New York, Los Angeles, Chicago, Philadelphia, San Francisco/Oakland/San Jose, Boston, Dallas/Fort Worth, Washington, D.C., Atlanta, Detroit, Houston, Seattle/Tacoma, Tampa/St. Petersburg, Minneapolis/St. Paul, Cleveland/Akron, Phoenix, Miami/Ft. Lauderdale, Denver, Sacramento/Stockton, and Orlando/Daytona Beach.

The importance of Hispanics also reaches Beverly Hills, and I'm not taking about domestic help employed by the city's super-rich residents. With a financial grant plus programming examples from Univision, the Museum of Television and Radio, located in this wealthy city in its trendy shopping area, will begin offering visitors 100 hours of the network's programming, plus radio and TV shows from the U.S., Spain, and Latin America.

In what starts out as a smart idea offered by the New York-headquartered National Academy of Television Arts and Sciences (NATAS) to its L.A. counterpart, the Academy of Television Arts and Sciences, for the creation of a Latin Emmy Awards turns into a shooting match between the two organizations. Split apart 25 years ago when the West Coast group questions its sister academy's voting procedures, the New York group is given jurisdiction for news, documentaries, sports, and daytime programs while L.A. retains the primetime Emmys.

Now the New York group claims its West Coast counterpart is moving too slowly and announces it will move on its own to launch the new awards show. Tentative plans by NATAS are to recognize programs in a full array of categories, with Univision and Telemundo alternately airing the show starting in 2003. The New York group says it will seek arbitration to allow it to organize the new event. NATAS president, Peter Price, says Latin programs need their own national exposure platform since they are usually not included in the regular Emmy awards. The last time a Spanish-language program wins a national Emmy is in 1998 when Univision's national newscast, *Noticiero Univision*, garners two news Emmys. However, as 2003 concludes, there are still no Latin Emmys in sight; the issue will be resolved in January of 2004 as the rival academies drop their legal maneuverings and begin discussing ways to honor Hispanic television. The West Coast chapter will handle the International Academy of Television Arts and Sciences, which can issue Emmys for programs on Univision, Telemundo, and Azteca America that emanate from overseas sources, while the East Coast chapter can issue Emmys for shows produced in the U.S. by the Hispanic networks.

Meanwhile, when the 25th annual *Kennedy Center Honors* air on CBS in 2002, one Latina, 60-year-old Chita Rivera, is among this year's five honorees including Elizabeth Taylor, James Earl Jones, Paul Simon, and James Levine. Among Rivera's achievements recalled are appearances on Broadway in *Bye Bye Birdie*, *Sweet Chariot*, *Life Was Sweet*, and *Chicago*, and in the film, *Kiss of the Spider Woman*.

As for the two key Hispanic networks, Univision looks to secure affiliates for its TeleFutura network by signing up English-language stations in Texas, notably in El Paso and Harlingen/Brownsville/McAllen. Along with rival Telemundo, both networks alter their programming schedules to include more of their own produced telenovelas, even expanding story themes into new areas, like Telemundo's four-hour religious mini-series based on the miracles credited to the Virgin of Guadalupe, Mexico's patron saint.

Univision's pact to carry World Cup Soccer pays off. The game between the U.S. and Mexico becomes the highest-rated sports event in Spanish-language TV among 18- to 49-year-olds, delivering an average of 4.2 million men and women viewers, the network claims. ESPN also carries the competition, but Hispanics prefer the Univision broadcasts. Univision also holds the rights to the 2006 tournament as part of its two-tournament, $150 million contract. During the first nine matches broadcast from South Korea and Japan and airing in the U.S. in the early morning hours, Univision reaps 54 percent more viewers than ESPN and ESPN2, according to Nielsen Media Research. In Los Angeles alone, Univision's coverage of the U.S.'s 2-0 victory over Mexico draws more than three-and-a-half times the viewers than does the ESPN coverage, resulting in an 11.5 rating, 32 share. Translated into English, that means KMEX's coverage is seen in 648,000 of the market's 1.573 million Hispanic households. The match is the most watched late night program that day in the history of cable TV among men 18 to 34.

Aiming to appeal to U.S. Latino families, Univision launches the first animated series in Spanish, *Baldo*, based on the popular two-year-old newspaper strip and co-created by Hector D. Cantú and

Carlos Castellanos, the show's executive producers working with an all Latino writing and directing team. The series is being produced by L.A.-based Paloma Productions, which also produces the novela, *Te Amare En Silencio* (*I Will Love You in Silence*), a story involving a deaf female lead character.

Univision's cable channel, Galavision, reduces its U.S.-produced primetime programs in favor of entertainment and news provided by Mexico's Grupo Televisa and Venezuela's Venevision. The company claims the need to shift programming aimed at bilingual teen and adults in their 20s results from halting ratings.

If there's one sure bet in New York television, it's the continued winning ways of Univision's WXTV, whose 6 p.m. newscast, *Noticias 41*, outdraws the ABC, CBS, and NBC affiliate newscasts among 18- to 49-year-olds during the February sweeps and outdraws CBS in the same age category during the July sweeps ratings period. The broadcast is also named best newscast by the New Jersey Associated Press State Broadcasters Association. The show's anchor, Rafael Pineda, who helms the broadcast for 28 years, is inducted into the Silver Circuit of the New York chapter of the National Academy of Television Arts & Sciences. Cuban-born, he arrives in the U.S. after the Castro revolution in 1959, and as the first Latino inducted into the Silver Circuit, he proudly tells the *New York Daily News*, "This is by far the highlight of my career."

TeleFutura is aimed at 18- to 34-year-olds, many bilingual, with a schedule loaded with films, talk, soccer, boxing, and music shows, plus dubbed English-language movies in primetime. Novelas are aired in the daytime rather than at night. It carries Puerto Rico's main awards show for its artists, *Premios Tu Música*, on the Mainland, while the local Univision station airs it at home. The biggest challenges for TeleFutura are luring bilingual teens who are accultured towards Anglo TV, and not pulling audience away from the parent Univision network, which could split its ratings with its two networks and provide Telemundo with a stronger presence. Ray Rodriguez, CEO of Univision Networks, asserts TeleFutura will be a different entity from Univision, and be more experimental in its programming.

Two months after its debut on January 14 with its counter-programming schedule, which does not appeal to around one-third of its core audience, the network makes two significant changes. It adds an entertainment variety show and a novela, *El Inútil* (*The Useless*) to its primetime lineup. The novela airs at 10 p.m. after Univision has already run its soap operas, but Telemundo is still airing this genre.

Once Univision broadcasts live its 64 World Cup soccer games, they are repeated on TeleFutura in the morning and in primetime on its Galavision cable network. Univision will also debut its first domestic-slanted telenovela, *La Gata Salvaje* (*Untamed Heart*), shot entirely in the U.S. Its novelas are called "accent-neutral" and are not targeted at any one Hispanic culture, an unidentified Univision official tells the *Miami Herald*, unidentified because of the company's press policy initiated by A. Jerrold "Jerry" Perenchio, the company's chief executive. The paper quotes from Perenchio's, "Rules of the Road," which includes 20 don'ts: "stay clear of the press, no interviews, no panels, no speeches, no comments, stay out of the spotlight; it fades your suit." What amazes me about this policy is that Univision is a publicly held company, whose news departments seek quotes from public officials, yet its own executives are told to avoid cooperating with the media.

Several growth moves by Univision cause concern within the Latin entertainment industry. Its purchase of Fonovisa Records last December combined with its intriguing planned purchase of Dallas-based Hispanic Broadcasting Corp. (HBC) in a $3.5 billion stock deal, leaves interested parties worried about the possible conflict of interest in Univision's owning a major record company, major radio network, and three TV networks: Univision, which owns 22 stations, TeleFutura, which owns 28 stations, and Galavision on the cable dial. If federal regulators approve the merger with HBC, Univision will be in the power seat to attract an estimated two-thirds of all Spanish-language advertising, which is on a steady rise, fueled by Latino consumers whose purchases hit an estimated $580 billion mark.

McHenry "Mac" Tichenor, President/CEO of HBC, which owns and operates 55 stations in 14 markets, tries to allay any fears by noting the acquisition of Fonovisa will not affect the radio network's decisions regarding which records get played. HBC was created in 1996 with the merger of two radio station groups, Tichenor Media System and Heftel Broadcasting Corp. of Las Vegas. The move into radio will create a chasm of dissent among politicians in Washington who take sides as to the wisdom of the purchase in light of possible domination of Spanish broadcasting by the soon to be conglomerate once it's authorized by the Federal Communications Commission, a process that will stretch until 2003, when the green light is given for the merger.

Telemundo, now part of the NBC empire, will co-present the 2004 Olympics, the Golden Globe Awards, and a number of feature films. NBC will move its L.A. Spanish stations, KVEA and KWHY (if it's allowed to keep the latter station as part of its triopoly) to its Burbank lot along with its station, KNBC. KVEA, on its own, makes history during the May sweeps period by tying KMEX, its dominant rival for first place among 18- to 34-year-olds, with its 11 p.m. newscast. The ratings boost is a result of its reconfigured news concept called *Mejorando Su Vida* (*Making Your Life Better*) in addition to boosting its community service outreach programs.

NBC begins cross-promoting its Telemundo talent. Maria Celeste Arrarás, an Emmy-winning anchor, is hired away from Univision after 10 years to be the anchor of a new newsmagazine, *Al Rojo Vivo*, and is also given the opportunity to do features for NBC's *Dateline*. She also makes a guest appearance on NBC daytime drama, *Passions*. In other synergistic efforts, Telemundo reporter Angie Sandoval covers an attempted coup in Caracas, Venezuela for MSNBC, and WTVJ/NBC Miami reporter Patricia Andreu helps host a telethon on Telemundo's WSCV. Telemundo's efforts to upgrade, redirect, and promote the local newscasts for its stations in New York, Los Angeles, Chicago, Miami, and Dallas begin to show results by mid-year. Its New York station, WNJU shows a 24 percent year-to-year rise in audience for its 11 p.m. news. Of its two Miami outlets, WTVJ finishes first at 11 p.m., followed in second place by

WSCV, another first-time accomplishment. In Los Angeles, KVEA grows its ratings among 18- to 49-year-olds by 53 percent. In Dallas, KXTX launches its own news operation, which garners major percentage rises at 5 p.m. and 10 p.m. over the previous year. In Chicago, WSNS shows a 14 percent increase at 5 p.m. and a 45 percent increase at 10 p.m.

Telemundo's programming begins to show new directions. It launches the first reality series in Spanish, *Protagonistas De Novela* (Novela Stars) in primetime. The show pits actors competing for a chance to win a part in a novela. It will be followed by another reality effort, *Protagonistas De La Música* (*Music Stars*) in which seven male and seven female musicians are sequestered in a Miami TV studio as they compete to win a recording contract. Telemundo also debuts Spanish-language TV's first primetime animated series, the romantic comedy, *Simplemente Rita* (*Simply Rita*). It obtains rights to nine segments of the popular PBS series, *American Family*, which will air with a dubbed Spanish-language voice track. Seeking a serious image for its programming, the network debuts its first public affairs show, *Enfoque*, hosted monthly from Washington by José Diaz-Balart. Seeking to attract young viewers, the network airs *Jennifer Lopez En Concierto* with Spanish lyrics and Spanish commentary one night after an English-language version runs on NBC, and *Chayanne En Concierto*, *Grandes Exitos*, featuring the hot male Latin romantic vocalist.

The network also beefs up its sports muscle. It signs a three-year deal to broadcast 15 regular season NBA games as well as 10 WNBA (Women's National Basketball Association) games starting in the fall. With parent NBC's 12-year connection with the NBA and the WNBA ending this year, the Telemundo broadcasts will fill weekend programming slots formerly occupied by NBC. Hired to host the NBA pre-game show is Andres Cantor, the soccer play-by-play announcer best known for his looong gooooallll calls. Other talent working the NBA are Jessi Losada, Edgar Lopez, Claudia Trejos, and John Sutcliffe. It also acquires U.S. Soccer in a five-year deal, covering 10 games per season plus two women's national team games through the 2006 World Cup in Germany. Telemundo has carried some U.S. matches, including last year's World Cup qualifier between the U.S. and Mexico, but not the championship.

Telemundo is in the sights of the American Federation of Television and Radio Artists, the union that represents NBC reporters and anchors. AFTRA seeks to organize 36 on-air employees at L.A. stations KVEA and KWHY, claiming they are paid less than their NBC counterparts at NBC-owned KNBC. The union alleges that when it attempts to organize KVEA in 1995 to 1996, Telemundo fires six employees interested in joining the union. The only Spanish-language TV employees in L.A. represented by AFTRA are at Univision's KMEX.

Curious as to what the situation is in January of 2004, I call AFTRA and Leslie Simon, its director of legislative and public affairs and Spanish-language media, provides the update. "The stations remain non-union," she says. "We are continuing to attempt to organize the stations and we continue to find a large amount of fear among the unit members because of our previous organizing attempt at KVEA, which resulted in six union supporters being fired." Several attempts to reach Manuel Abud, general manager of KVEA and KWHY are unsuccessful. He doesn't return my phone calls.

There seems to be a feeding frenzy among cable networks that don't want to be outdone by their broadcast competing cousins. So you have:

ESPN, which currently carries a Spanish-language service for five hours on Sunday nights called *ESPN Deportes*, announces it will go into a fulltime, 24-hour mode next year as a stand-alone channel. It actually debuts in January of 2004. The original program traces its origin back to 2000 when the service began airing Major League baseball games on Sunday evenings and then goes full bore as a weekly Sunday block the next year. When it goes fulltime, *ESPN Deportes* will go head-to-head against Univision and Telemundo and Azteca America, and Fox Sports World Español, which all have significant sports rights agreements.

TBS superstation, part of the Turner Broadcasting System's cable outlets, also offers Spanish-speaking announcers on its SAP channel for its regular season coverage of the Atlanta Braves.

The Inspiration Networks, whose three-year-old La Familia Network airs on low-power TV stations in Texas, expands its Latin service to a national audience via cable systems. Its family-friendly programming includes music, variety, talk, cooking, films, and shows for teens and younger children, besides religious-flavored offerings.

Time Warner Cable launches a new Spanish-language news service in Tampa Bay, Florida, called Bay News 9 En Español. It's a spin-off from its four-year-old English-language Bay News 9, which covers the city's 327,000 Hispanics in the Tampa Bay area. Time Warner recognizes that having a specific Latino news channel is the proper way to connect with this growing populace, home to the fourth largest Cuban community in the nation. The spin-off will be the model Time Warner Cable uses in 2003 to debut an all-news Spanish channel in the New York City market, an operation I will visit in the cold, dark days of March 2003 when I'm doing interviews in the Big Apple for this book that appear in Chapter 14.

Turner Classic Movies, still another AOL Time Warner company, pays tribute to all the Hispanics working in the motion picture industry, in front of the camera and behind it, during Latino Heritage Month by airing 25 films Mondays throughout September under the unifying banner *Hispanics in Hollywood.* Artists represented include: Rita Moreno, Ricardo Montalban, Maria Conchita Alonso, Rubén Blades, Katy Jurado, Edward James Olmos, Lupe Ontiveros, Raquel Welsh, Henry Silva, Jimmy Smits, Cheech Marin, Rita Hayworth, Lupe Velez, Anthony Quinn, Cesar Romero, Dolores Del Rio, José Ferrer, and Lalo Schifrin.

A second channel, Cinemax, also honors Hispanics in film with its *The Bronze Screen: 100 Years of the Latino Image In Hollywood Cinema*. Artists interviewed include Rita Moreno, John Leguizamo, Esai Morales; and directors Alfonso Arau, Gregory Nava, and Leon Ichaso. The range of films covered reflects the diversity of celluloid down through the decades: *West Side Story*, *The Gunfighter*, *Touch of Evil*, *Flying Down to Rio*, *Stand and Deliver*, *La Bamba*, *Selena*, and *El Norte*.

The major transformative story in radio is the potential high-power merger between HBC (Hispanic Broadcasting Corp.) and SBS (Spanish Broadcasting System). The merger, SBS chairman/CEO Raul Alarcón, Jr., intonates to HBC's McHenry Tichenor, Jr. "would have strategic merit" in a letter that the *Wall Street Journal* reveals Tichenor receives from his chief rival. Tichenor, the story continues, suggests Alarcón, Jr. discuss the merger with HBC's board of directors.

Thirteen days later in June, HBC pulls a switch and announces it will be purchased by Univision Communications, parent to the leading Spanish-language TV network for $2.97 billion in stock. HBC issues a statement that it chooses to merge with Univision for a number of reasons, including the appeal of the radio–TV pairing, which it cannot obtain from radio-only SBS. SBS and HBC have long been at odds over a number of testy issues, including luring away each other's employees. Immediately following this explosive news, SBS files an antitrust suit in U.S. District Court in Miami against HBC and its largest shareholder, Clear Channel Communications, the leading owner of mainstream radio stations. That suit alleges that Clear Channel and HBC seek to depress SBS' share price after SBS rejects a bid in 1996 by Clear Channel to buy the Miami area network.

One month later, SBS files a second U.S. District Court suit in Miami against Clear Channel, seeking $500 million in damages, and according to a Bloomberg News dispatch, again alleges that "Clear Channel and HBC tried to undermine Spanish Broadcasting's 1999 initial public offering, convince industry analysts to drop coverage of Spanish Broadcasting, and persuade institutional investors to sell their stock in the company." The two firms "allegedly took these steps to facilitate their ultimate objective of acquiring SBS and eliminating it as a competitive threat." Matters get testy when Clear Channel files its own suit in Miami to dismiss the SBS suit, claiming SBS has failed to state any reason for which "relief can be granted."

The proposed merger will turn political and acrimonious until the government clears the merger in 2003.

In the meantime, HBC's Tichenor attacks the Arbitron Company, charging its methodology does not "ensure that its survey sample reflects the population being measured." Tichenor especially notes that during the summer ratings results for Los Angeles and other unnamed cities, alleged flaws in the methodology "have radically affected the ratings in the country's largest media market and largest Hispanic city." Steve Morris, Arbitron's President/CEO, answers the charge by explaining the number of people listening to Spanish-language radio in Los Angeles remains flat and that ratings' declines during the summer are the result of changes in listening to any number of English-language radio formats, including urban (black).

Aside from its concerns over Arbitron ratings, HBC, which already owns 55 stations, purchases five Albuquerque Anglo FMs from the Simmons Media Group for $22.5 million and converts two to Spanish-language music formats. The other three retain their classic rock, smooth jazz, and Top 40 formats.

There are a handful of fulltime, all-jazz radio stations in the nation that include Latin jazz in their programming, notably WBGO-FM in Newark, which covers the New York area, KKJZ-FM, in Long Beach, California, which covers Los Angeles, and some of Southern California, and KUVO-FM in Denver. They are outnumbered by the 40 smooth jazz stations across the country, down from a high of 83 in 2002 and which also include Latin jazz. "Latin music is the icing on the cake," says record industry veteran Don Graham, president of Progressive Marketing, a Los Angeles promotion firm that works with both formats as well as adult standard formatted stations. Graham tracks the number of stations in each format, so he knows that "Latin jazz shows up on specialty shows on the two public-supported jazz stations." Smooth jazz stations play "Latin-influenced music like *Look of Love* by Diana Krall and bossa novas by Dave Koz, Kenny Rankin, and Peter White. Natalie Cole's first Verve album features Latin percussion on several tunes." Graham sees Latin-flavored music continuing to gain jazz radio play "because of the Latin population growth and because it's great refreshing music." Latin jazz is also played sporadically on college radio and other public radio stations like WPFW-FM, Washington, D.C., where Nancy Alonso starts hosting the Monday night *Latin Flavor* show in 1999, which specializes in classic salsa and Latin jazz.

At WBGO, the East Coast jazz voice, which has been on the air since 1979, Latin jazz is a part of the overall straight-ahead jazz programming for the past six years, notes Cephas Bowles, the station's general manager. The expanding Hispanic population in the New York metropolitan area has not affected the station in any way, he informs me. Why not? "We feel it's part of the jazz experience so the population growth doesn't affect the amount of Latin we play. Our DJs program their own shows and Latin jazz is interspersed around the clock. We also have a Saturday night show that's been on 10 years, *The Latin Jazz Cruise*, from 9 to midnight, whose current host is Awilda Rivera. She plays salsa, Brazilian, Cuban, Caribbean, and American artists. When we started playing Latin, we found some liked it, some didn't, but it's rare when you get someone who says, 'I hate what you're playing.' We also don't experience any pressure from the Cuban community to our playing Cuban artists like Chucho Valdés and Paquito D'Rivera (who lives in New Jersey)."

Bowles also believes he knows why new Hispanic arrivals to the region aren't adding to his audience numbers. "They're not getting exposed to the music in their native countries. Many are trying to assimilate into the American culture and do American things. Mainly, it's a lack of exposure in their home country and here in the States where there aren't a lot of stations that program Latin jazz." As one of National Public Radio's 274 affiliates, WBGO's Bowles is tapped by the organization's board of directors in 2004 to oversee its investment committee, which is beyond happy as a result of a $235-million gift by Joan Kroc, wife of the founder of McDonalds. At the meeting, NPR speaks of using digital technology in the years to come, which will allow stations to simulcast different programs in their cities, including Spanish programming.

KKJZ, which changes its name several years ago from KLON after a station in Alameda, California, KJAZ drops its all-jazz format and similarly sounding call letters become available, increases its Latin music significantly, especially during the daytime hours. The station, licensed to California State University at Long Beach, and operating from its campus, has been programming jazz since 1987. It identifies itself as "Kjazz." "Our DJs select their own music and know people want upbeat, snappy music to help them get through their work day. Latin jazz is an upbeat, catchy form of music," explains Sean Heitkemper, the station manager. "We're aware of the fact that 60 percent of the metro Los Angeles area is Hispanic and we've found that the Latino population enjoys straight-ahead jazz more than Latin jazz. I don't know why this is the case, but it's directed us to stick with a correct mix of straight-ahead jazz and some Latin jazz."

KKJZ is one of my favorite music stations, and it's always an energizing, uplifting experience to hear the fiery, upbeat, or smoothly flowing Latin music throughout the day, especially in the early morning when I do a lot of writing. The station's Latin showcase is its Friday night *Jazz on the Latin Side*, with host José Rizo, from 7 to 11 p.m. It's been on 13 years, allowing its host to develop concerts and records as an ancillary benefit of the airplay. A more recent show following Rizo is *Caribbean Jazz* from 11 to 1 a.m. hosted by Eric Kohler. The station also connects with Hispanic listeners by sponsoring its twice-annual Latin Jazz Caravan, in which listeners are virtually transported to multiple clubs where Latin jazz artists explore the boundaries of the music. The promotion celebrates its seventh effort this year. As a non-commercial station, KKJZ, like WBGO, runs membership drives, and Heitkemper says station surveys indicate Hispanic membership has increased. "It's been a gradual change."

KKJZ undergoes a startling change, when after years of being satellited and paid for by Playboy Enterprises to listeners all over North America, dating back to its time as KBCA in the '70s, the service is terminated when Playboy needs the satellite channels for its own English and Spanish adult channels. KKJZ now offers its programming to a worldwide audience on its Website.

Perhaps the most unusual Latin radio program in the country is 28-year-old *Alma Del Barrio*, a bilingual show airing Saturday and Sunday on KXLU-FM Los Angeles from 6 a.m. to 6 p.m. The public-supported station is owned by Loyola Marymount University in the suburb of Westchester and transforms itself into the home for Brazilian, Afro-Cuban, salsa, and merengue music, which tempts Latinos from many parts of the globe with their favorite forms of music, but nothing radical. For a station in a region where the majority of Hispanics are from Mexico, it's significant that regional Mexican music, a mainstay of commercial radio, is hardly heard in favor of what the program classifies as non-commercial music, meaning records that aren't aimed at the commercial Hispanic marketplace. Each morning begins with Brazilian music and expands from there. As many as 14 volunteer hosts participate speaking English and then repeating everything in Spanish, or reversing the languages. Artists often drop by to promote their new recordings, and these interviews are also conducted in two languages. The two-language approach makes for a lot of banter between music. It's one of my favorite shows because there are always musical surprises exploding out of the song selection of instrumentals and vocals.

The show is the creative idea of two freshmen, Raoul Villa and Enrique "Kiki" Soto, who seek to add Latin music to the station's all-classical format in 1973. The university grants the duo an hour to prerecord their music on Sunday nights—provided they and other volunteers act as engineers for some of the classical programs. Within a year, the show on the 5,000-watt station is so popular among Hispanic and Anglo listeners that it expands to four hours. From four hours the show increases to 12 commercial-free hours on Saturdays and Sundays, using student volunteers and outside personnel to host the various programs. The show's name is patterned after the tune, *Barrio Suite*, by the popular band Tierra. The two hosts decide "suite" would sound too much like the word "sweet," so they keep barrio and plant "Alma Del" in front of it to create the title, "Soul of the Barrio." While Miami radio stations refuse to air Cuban records during the 1980s for fear of repercussions by the frenetic Cuban exile community, *Alma* offers Cuban artists exposure. And when Nina Lenart, who's been playing Cuban artists in 1980 on KCRW-FM's *Latin Dimensions* show, joins *Alma* the next year when that program goes off the air, she and newcomer Emilio Vandenedes, a Cuban émigré, herald the arrival of new Cuban bands like Los Van Van. They receive angry calls from listeners asking why they are backing the Castro regime. Lenart recalls this discomforting period for the *LA Weekly*: "Back in the '80s, Emilio and I were playing more Cuban artists because he was getting all the latest imports before anyone else. We were asked a few times by irate callers why we were supporting Castro, and we'd reason back: How was exposing Cuba's musicians and major classical composers on the radio supporting Castro?" These calls have no effect on the show's inclusion of Cuban artists.

When the show celebrates its 30th anniversary in 2004, its birthday party aboard the Queen Mary in Long Beach, California, attracts former staffers as well as the current on-air hosts. The station's live, seven-hour broadcast on March 21 features the music of several local area bands.

If you're in Miami and want to hear Latin jazz, including some Cuban acts, you tune to WDNA-FM, which calls itself the "jazz and rhythm station." The city has nine Hispanic stations, none of which program Latin jazz, favoring other forms of music and talk. I'd heard about WDNA, so when I'm in Miami in late September of 2002, I monitor the station and also chat with general manager Maggie Pelleya. "The station has always had a crazy quilt of music styles since its inception in 1980," she says, adding that jazz programming begins in 1991. Jazz is aired Monday through Friday from 7 a.m. to 7 p.m., with the *Latin Jazz Quarter* airing from noon to 3 p.m. weekdays and from 8 to 11 p.m. on weekends. WDNA also offers *Fusion Latina* on Mondays from 7 to 10 p.m., hosted for six years by Viviám López, which encompasses Latin jazz and Latin dance motivating music from

Puerto Rico, the Dominican Republic, and Africa. "There's more Latin jazz getting airplay because the exploding Hispanic population is affecting our schedule," notes Pelleya. There are also shows featuring Brazilian, reggae, folk, polka, French, Jewish, Indian, Pakistani, and Haitian music, resulting in the crazy quilt patterns. "We're a bilingual station," says Pelleya, who's been with the station since 1981, first as a volunteer and for the last eight-and-a-half years as general manager. "It depends on the host. Some are more comfortable in Spanish or Portuguese." With the exception of morning drive-time host Frank Consola, all the other 50 on-air hosts are volunteers.

Los Angeles, with 20 fulltime Spanish stations, the most of any Mainland U.S. city outside of Puerto Rico, is called "a bellwether" for what will happen in other major Hispanic cities by Betina Lewin, an executive with Caballero Spanish Media, a New York firm representing radio stations in their advertising sales. "With Los Angeles having more Spanish format niches catering to ethnic populations than any other part of the country, all the other Latino markets are catching up to what's happening there," she tells me for a story I write for *Advertising Age.*

Population alterations around the country are impacting the growth of Hispanic radio. Of Dallas' 66 stations, 16 are for Hispanics. In Phoenix, there are 13 Spanish outlets out of a total of 55 stations. In Houston, which ranks seventh among the nation's radio markets up from 10th place, KLTN-FM becomes the city's first Spanish-language station to hit No. 1. The HBC outlet finds favor with its northern Mexican music format, which captures 6.7 percent of listeners 12 and older and with its morning show personality Raúl Brindis, with a dominating 9.9 share of the audience.

When the quarterly Arbitron ratings are released covering September 20 through December 12, the terrorism attacks of September 11 affect people's listening around the nation as they turn to all-news radio, but then they return to music stations. In L.A., KSCA-FM's morning personality, Reñan Almendarez Coello, remains the top drive-time listened to voice, with 7.5 percent of the audience while his station is the city's fourth most listened to. Coello and KSCA remain in their positions in the Arbitron winter survey, while during the spring survey, the station jumps to second place as Coello retains his front-running position. New York City, which has a new Hispanic station, former country outlet WYNY-FM, remains loyal to SBS' tropical power WSKQ-FM, the highest ranked Spanish station in the city and fifth in the spring ratings.

The most listened to format across the country remains regional Mexican, followed by contemporary and tropical. The most listeners to Hispanic radio are in the West, followed by the South Central part of the country and then along the Atlantic Coast, according to Arbitron statistics published in a *Billboard* story. The fastest growing areas for Hispanic listeners are in the mountain states of Colorado, Montana, Utah, and adjoining Nevada. An indicator of the bicultural power of Hispanic teenagers is the statistic that they represent nearly 35 percent of Latinos who favor Top 40 English-language programming.

The film industry is in high gear with new releases and future projects tailored for the mainstream Hispanic audience and the more esoteric art house circuit. A growing coterie of familiar names and faces, those talents whose names can sell tickets, seem to be hired for one project after another.

Following the success of Lionsgate's release of *Amores Perros*, directed by Mexico's Alejandro González Iñárritu, which grosses $5.4 million, the film company distributes *Intacto* from director Juan-Carlos Fresnadillo, which wins accolades at the Cannes Film Festival. Tom Ortenberg, Lionsgate's president, credits the new array of Latin actors, along with the growing Hispanic population, for the consumer interest in Hispanic films. IFC Films scores with domestic Hispanics with the release of the sex-laden *Y Tu Mama Tambien*, another Mexican import whose cast includes Diego Luna, Gael García Bernal, and Maribel Verdú, while Sony Classics goes with *Hable Con Ella*, by director Pedro Almadóvar, and Palm Pictures adds the erotic drama

Sex and Lucia to the mix. This film runs into trouble in Seattle, where two newspapers, the *Times* and the *Post Intelligencer* ban ads for the film because of its content. Miramax doesn't see that fate befalling its Salma Hayek-starring *Frida*, based on the tumultuous life of Frida Kahlo, the Mexican artist and her marriage to equally egotistical muralist Diego Rivera, played by Alfred Molina. Miramax also distributes the Robert Rodriguez saga *Once Upon a Time in Mexico*.

For Hayek, bringing the story of *Frida* from the time she is 16 to her death at age 47 to the screen is a seven-year journey. The former star in the Mexican novela *Teresa* says she became fascinated with the painter as a teenager in Veracruz, Mexico. Even as her U.S. film career begins to take shape after moving to Los Angeles in 1991, she maintains her interest in oing the film until she meets Broadway director Julie Taymor, recipient of two Tony Awards in 1998 for *The Lion King*, which leads to their agreement to do the film, with Hayek as producer and star. Miramax Films will handle distribution. The original score by Elliot Goldenthal is seamlessly melded with traditional Mexican songs that were favorites of the volatile married couple. Despite its powerful story, the film is ripped by Mexican critics who complain a film about a famous Mexican artist should have been made in Spanish, not English, and that the film trivializes the couple's lives. Hayek and Taymor defend their film, relays a story in the *Hollywood Reporter*. While they say the film is "an American production, backed by American money, the film's theme is universal."

Film companies are aware that Latinos spend around $500 million annually on movie tickets, based on a Screen Actors Guild report, and that figure includes English-language titles like *Blood Work*, whose cast includes actor/director Clint Eastwood, Paul Rodriguez, Wanda De Jesús, Jeff Daniels, Anjelica Houston, Tina Lifford, and Dylan Walsh in the Malpaso/Warner Bros. release; *Real Women Have Curves* from HBO/Newmarket Films; *Blue Crush*, the Universal Hawaii surfing film starring Michelle Rodriguez; *Scorpion King* from Universal (which uses its partner Latino marketing experts, the Arenas Group); and *Spy Kids 2*, the Antonio Banderas-starring/

Robert Rodriguez-directed Dimension Films project whose cast includes Carla Gugino, Alex Vega, Danny Trejo, Cheech Marin, Daryl Sabara, Steve Buscemi, and Mike Judge. It's the sequel to director Rodriguez's *Spy Kids*, which introduces moviegoers to a Latin family led by Banderas as family head Gregorio Cortez.

Banderas, Jennifer Lopez, and John Leguizamo all have multiple projects to keep them busy. Banderas is signed to play the title role in *Pancho Villa As Himself* for HBO Films and co-star with Emma Thompson in *Imagining Argentina*, focusing on the government's war against political dissidents from Arenas Entertainment, the Hispanic label formed in partnership with Universal Pictures. Also in the cast are Maria Canals and Rubén Blades.

For Banderas, this is an extremely busy year, as he appears in four films, *Spy Kids 2*, *Femme Fatale*, *Ballistic: Ecks Vs. Sever*, and *Frida* in the role of Mexican painter David Alfaro Siqueiros. He makes his English-language film debut in 1992 with *The Mambo Kings*, followed by 20 other films, some forgettable—including the 1996 comedy *Too Much*, where he meets future wife Melanie Griffith—to some memorable, including director Pedro Almadóvar's, *Law of Desire*, *Matador*, and *Labyrinth of Passion*. Regarding the opening for Hispanic actors and directors to make mainstream films, Banderas is optimistically philosophical in discussing his career with *Hispanic* magazine. "I don't think Spanish-speaking actors in Hollywood are just a fashion trend like they were before. We are there to stay."

Real Women Have Curves turns out to be a charming sleeper. The film, based on a play written by Josefina Lopez that recasts her life growing up in the Boyle Heights section of Los Angeles, wins the 2002 Sundance Film Festival's Dramatic Audience Award. Making their dramatic film debuts are Colombian director Patricia Cardoso and America Ferrera in the title role of Ana Garcia, a heavyset high school graduate who irons dresses at her older sister's garment factory. The cast includes Ingrid Oliu as the sister, Lupe Ontiveros as the oppressive mother who also works in the factory and berates her daughter about her weight, George Lopez as a schoolteacher who supports Ana's dreams of being more than a factory worker, and Jorge Cervera, Jr. as the sympathetic father.

Arenas, with its Universal clout, also acquires distribution for the independently financed gangster/morality saga, *Empire*, starring John Leguizamo, along with Sonia Braga, Carlos Leon, Isabella Rossellini, Denise Richards, and Peter Sarsgaard, with music by Rubén Blades. Leguizamo also stars in Newmarket Films *Spun* and in the boxing/drug film *Infamous* for HBO, with a cast including Blades, Sonia Braga, Rafael Báez, Vincent Laresca, and Nestor Serrano. Obviously a hot commodity, Leguizamo is signed by Universal Films to star and co-write the script for an untitled romantic comedy.

Jennifer Lopez links with Columbia Pictures to star in *Shrink!*, the Internet comedy strip her Nuyorican Productions will handle. The project is the first film acquired by the studio for Lopez's company as part of a three-year first-look feature film development deal. She is also signed to produce and co-star for Screen Gems, another Sony-owned company, the story of the late salsa singer Hector Lavoe, who dies in 1993 at age 43. Lopez will play the musician's widow, Nilda Roman Perez.

Diego Luna, who stars in *Y Tu Mama Tambien*, signs for the male lead in *Havana Nights: Dirty Dancing 2* for Miramax/Artisan Entertainment. The female lead goes to Romola Garai. The story is inspired by 1987's hit *Dirty Dancing*, but with a storyline involving life in revolutionary Cuba. One year later, Artisan will be purchased by Canada's Lionsgate for $160 million and assume $60 million in debt. Cuban-born Andy Garcia, who flees to the U.S. with his family when he's five, is signed to star and make his directorial debut in *The Lost City*, an independently financed $20 million drama about life in Havana prior to the Fidel Castro revolution. Other cast members: Benicio Del Toro, Robert Duvall, Dustin Hoffman, Javier Bardem, Benjamin Bratt, and Tomas Milian. Garcia will play a Havana nightclub owner, one of three brothers dealing with the transition from the oppressive dictator Fulgencio Batista to the Castro installed Marxist government. In another Cuban-flavored story, Del Toro will star in a biography of the assassinated revolutionary Ernesto "Che" Guevara for an as yet unnamed company. Garcia's comments to me about his new film and record projects appear in Chapter 11.

In a first for a major studio, 20th Century Fox's Fox 2000 art house imprint will film *Papi Chulo* (*My Sexy Man*), which it calls the first romantic comedy aimed at the Hispanic market. Signed to the leading role in the English-language film is Eduardo Verástegui, whose limited credits involve working with the Mexican band Cairo and appearing in several Univision novelas, including *Tres Mujeres* (*Three Women*) and a Jennifer Lopez music video. He's also learning to speak English. The romantic comedy centers on a lothario who is dating three women. Other unknowns in the film: Sofía Vergara, a Colombian Univision novela actress who has a role in the Disney release, *Big Trouble*; Puerto Rican actress Roselyn Sanchez (who appears in *Rush Hour II*), and Jaci Velasquez, a Mexican American Christian pop vocalist. The director is another neophyte, Linda Mendoza. While Fox previously released the comedy *Woman on Top* in 2000 with Penélope Cruz, Mendoza boasts to the *Miami Herald* that her film is different because "we were able to cast four Latinos in a lead, three of whom have accents. I don't think that's ever happened before."

Benjamin Bratt hopes his decision to star in the thriller *Abandon* is the right move following his emotional, dramatic performance in *Piñero*, the story of Michael Piñero, the Puerto Rican playwright-junkie living in New York City released by GreenStreet Films. The actor, the son of a Peruvian-Indian mother and German-English father, meets his future wife, Puerto Rican actress/model Talisa Soto, on the set of *Piñero*. The romance/marriage enabled him to overcome his highly publicized four-year romance with Julia Roberts. For nine years Bratt is one of the stars of the highly successful TV drama, *Law and Order* as the partner to detective Jerry Orbach. After leaving the show in 1999, he appears in a string of unsuccessful films and then comes across the script for *Piñero*.

Abandon is his first starring film role in which he plays a familiar part, that of a detective.

The most controversial film of the year, *El Crimen Del Padre Amaro* (*The Crime Of Father Amaro*), is a Mexican production that is both scorned at home by members of the Catholic church and favored by film buffs, who make it that nation's highest-grossing film of all time. Directed by Carlos Carrera and modernized from the original 19th century Portuguese novel about actual scandals in Mexico, it is a story of free sex, debauchery, and murder in a small Mexican village. Gael García Bernal plays the innocent father, Amaro, who discovers all sorts of wrongdoing by the church in his new home and becomes a victim of his own carnal desires when he deflowers a 16-year-old girl who flirts with him, played by Ana Claudia Talancón. Released on IDP/Goldwyn, a branch of Samuel Goldwyn Films, the movie is the target of protests from American Catholics. Director Carrera says the film is fiction but adapted from widely reported incidents in Mexico that include pedophilia and molestation, which help make the film timely for American viewers who are aware of sexual abuse charges emerging in the American Catholic church. Samuel Goldwyn, Jr., chairman of IDP/Goldwyn, acknowledges the film is controversial in Mexico, but doesn't expect the controversy to also play out in the U.S., he admits to *Daily Variety*. There is certainly negative reaction by staunch Catholics, but nothing overpowering to halt its showing.

Several of these intense projects are included among the awards presented for outstanding performances by a number of organizations.

At the American Latino Media Arts Awards (ALMAs), triple awards are presented to *Piñero* for outstanding motion picture and screenplay, accepted by writer/director Leon Ichaso and leading actor Benjamin Bratt. Marc Anthony also wins three accolades for outstanding male performer, Spanish album of the year, and outstanding performance in a music/variety/comedy TV special. Robert Rodriguez wins outstanding director for *Spy Kids*. Andy Garcia wins outstanding supporting actor for *Ocean's Eleven*. There's a tie for supporting actress between Elizabeth Peña (*Tortilla Soup*) and Elpidia Carrillo for *Bread and Roses*. *Resurrection Blvd.* wins for top TV series while Esai Morales is named outstanding actor for his role in *NYPD Blue* and Rita Moreno is named outstanding actress for her part in HBO's *Oz*.

Other winners: Ozomatli as breakout music group of the year and outstanding Latin group, while Jennifer Lopez wins the people's choice award for outstanding video. Antonio Banderas receives the Anthony Quinn award for achievement in films; Freddie Fender wins the Ritchie Valens pioneer award, Ricky Martin gains the National Council of La Raza's initial Vanguard award, and John Leguizamo wins entertainer of the year.

The 17th annual Imagen Awards name Esai Morales, Penélope Cruz, and Andy Garcia among its top recipients. Morales is named entertainer of the year, Cruz leading female entertainer, and Garcia receives the creative achievement award. Univision TV personality Cristina Saralegui wins the Lifetime achievement award.

Among the 32nd annual Nosotros Golden Eagle Awards: Antonio Banderas wins the Ricardo Montalban award; José José the life achievement award; Join Secada excellence in music award, and Laura Harring best actress.

Legendary Mexican actress Katy Jurado dies at age 78. She makes her American film debut in 1951 in *The Bullfighter and the Lady* and wins an Academy Award nomination in 1954 for her supporting role in *Broken Lance*. In 1984, shc plays Paul Rodriguez's mother in the ABC sitcom *Pablo*, and continues to act until 1998.

There are no detracting voices raised in sports to the records achieved by Hispanic baseball players. Francisco Rodriguez, a 20-year-old right-hander from Venezuela, makes history when he helps his Anaheim Angles defeat the San Francisco Giants 4 to 1 during a World Series game, to become the youngest pitcher to ever win a championship series game. The Angels go on to beat San Francisco 4 to 1 in the seventh game to win their first-ever Series title. Rodriguez is one of seven Hispanic players among 31 on the Angels' roster. The others are brothers Bengie and Jose Molina, Benji Gil, Alex Ochoa, Orlando Palmeiro, and Ramon Ortiz.

Oakland Athletics shortstop Miguel Tejada is named the American League's Most Valuable Player. The Dominican's accomplishments include hitting in 24 straight games, the league's highest this year, whacking 34 homeruns and batting in 131 runs. His salary is $3.5 million and he is the third Dominican to reap the MVP, following Toronto's George Bell in 1987 and Chicago Cubs' slugger Sammy Sosa in 1998. In second place: Texas Ranger shortstop Alex Rodriguez, the highest paid player in the leagues with his 10-year, $252 million pact signed in 2000. Both Tejada and Rodriguez receive bonuses for their MVP positioning: Tejada with $100,000 and Rodriguez with $200,000. During the season, Rodriguez hits five home runs in two games to tie the league record with three other players, including Manny Ramirez of Cleveland in 1998. Other Hispanics in the American League's top 10 MVP positions: New York Yankee second baseman and fellow Dominican Alfonso Soriano in third, Chicago White Sox right fielder Magglio Ordonez, eighth, Boston Red Sox left fielder Manny Ramirez ninth, and New York Yankees center fielder Bernie Williams 10th. In the National League, while San Francisco's home run champ Barry Bonds wins his second consecutive MVP, three players with Latin names are in the top 10 positions: St. Louis' Albert Pujols in second, Montreal's Vladimir Guerrero in fourth, and Chicago's Sosa in ninth place.

One day after the American League MVPs are awarded, Latinos are among the winners for American League Gold Gloves awards presented since 1957 by glove manufacturer Rawlings. Angels catcher Bengie Molina bests 10-year winner Ivan Rodriguez of the Texas Rangers, Texas shortstop Alex Rodriguez ends Cleveland's Omar Vizquel's nine-year streak, and Oakland third baseman Eric Chavez wins his second straight accolade. Rodriguez lands a $100,000 bonus for winning his Gold Glove award one day after picking up a $200,000 bonus for finishing second in the MVP poll.

Boston's right-handed pitcher Pedro Martinez finishes second behind the Oakland A's left-handed pitcher Barry Zito in the American League's Cy Young Award standings. Martinez has a 20 to 4 record to Zito's 23 to 5 record.

Of the 849 players in the major leagues, 222 are born abroad, with the Dominican Republic topping the list with 65, followed by Puerto Rico and Venezuela each with 38.

One veteran who retires is Cuban-born, Miami-raised Jose Canseco, who plays 20 seasons. The 37-year-old former superstar ends his career with a Triple A Chicago White Sox team in Charlotte, North Carolina. He hits 462 home runs, has a .266 career batting average, finishes with 1,407 runs batted in, 200 stolen bases, and plays in 1,887 games with Oakland, Texas, Boston, Toronto, Tampa Bay, the New York Yankees, and Chicago White Sox. He's among an elite group of nine players who hit 400 homers and steal 200 bases. During seven of his last 10 seasons he is on the disabled list with back problems. In 2005, three years later, his explosive revelation in a book he writes anent taking steroids along with other major name home run sluggers will spark a Congressional investigation which turns baseball and the sports world's quiet acceptance of illegal enhancing drugs into a major public issue, all of which is explored in Chapter 20.

After being fired in 2001 following 10 years as coach of the Montreal Expos, Felipe Alou, 67, becomes the oldest manger in baseball when he takes over the San Francisco Giants from Dusty Baker. The Dominican native, who begins his 17-year playing career with the Expos, also plays for the Giants from 1958 to 1963. He will be superseded as the oldest manager next year by the World Series winning Florida Marlin's 72-year-old Jack McKeon.

Age is also on the mind of the Immigration and Naturalization Service, which begins cracking down on immigration documentation following last year's September 11 terrorist attacks. At least 24 Latin-born major league players are outed for under reporting their ages in attempts to appear younger and gain major league contracts. In a major expose in the *Los Angeles Times*, a State Department spokesman indicates most of the fraudulent papers are from the Dominican Republic. Among the reported Dominicans hedging on their accurate ages are California Angels right-handers Joel Peralta, 26 not 22, and Hatuey Mendoza, 23 not 22. Angel pitcher Ramon Ortiz turns out to be 29 not 26 as is San Diego Padres shortstop Deivi Cruz. Chicago pitcher Juan Cruz is 23 not 21. The deception goes back to 1999 when the Los Angeles Dodgers sign Adrian Beltre, whom they believe to be 16, the minimum age a player may be signed. He's actually 15. Players are now required to show their official birth certificates to clubs in order to be signed.

Cuban players, notably defectors, generate equally dramatic and sympathetic headlines on their own. One little forgotten fact, recalls *The New Yorker*, is that the Cincinnati Reds in 1911 drafted two Cuban players, the first of an avalanche of more than 100 players signed to play in the majors during a 50-year period. That all stops in 1961 when Cuban dictator Fidel Castro cut the tie with American teams by signing National Decree 83A, which outlaws professional sports in Cuba in favor of amateur teams, whose top players will be paid a government stipend. So it's major news whenever a Cuban defects. José Ariel Contreras, the top pitcher with Cuba's national team for seven years, becomes the latest defector, choosing Mexico City as the place of departure and setting up residence in Nicaragua so he can be pursued as a free agent, rather than going through baseball's June draft as a U.S. resident. The right-hander, with a 93 m.p.h. fastball, pitches eight innings of shutout ball against the Baltimore Orioles exhibition game in Havana three years ago, though the Orioles win 3 to 2 in 11 innings. With the Boston Red Sox and New York Yankees pursuing him, it's the Yankee dollars that talk the loudest and he is signed to New York with a $32 million four-year contract. It's the largest sum ever paid to a Cuban defector, surpassing the $14.5 million paid pitcher Danys Baez by the Cleveland Indians three years ago.

Already playing hardball for the Yankees is right-hander Orlando "El Duque" Hernández, who receives $3.2 million upon his defection three years ago. Since he does not speak English, Hernández is provided an interpreter for five years. But the team decides this year he'll need to learn English on his own. Hernández, whose career takes off phenomenally, is in a downward spiral. The team's decision sets off a firestorm among other Cuban defecting players, especially since several Asian players in the majors use interpreters. Michael Tejera, a Cuban defector who pitches for the Florida Marlins, calls the Yankees decision "unfair" in the *Miami Herald.* Tejera points out that when he comes to the U.S. as a 16-year-old, he is able to learn English, while Hernández, who is much older, has no exposure to English in Cuba, so it's much harder for him. In the story, Marlin's pitcher Alex Fernández calls the Yankees' decision "unheard of." Liván Hernández, Orlando's half-brother, who defects with him and signs with the Marlins, is initially given an interpreter by the team, which also provides language assistance to Luis Castillo. Other players who have used or currently use interpreters include: Fernando Valenzuela, the Dodger's star pitcher from Mexico, who is assigned an interpreter in the 1980s; Bartolo Colón, who has one at both Cleveland and Montreal; and Vladimir Guerrero, who uses one for a year while with Montreal.

The Marlins wind up being home to two other Cuban defecting pitchers, Hansel Izquierdo and Vladimir Nuñez. All three pitch in one game, a 1 to 0 shutout over the San Diego Padres, with Izquierdo the winning hurler in his first major league start. Nuñez, who defects in 1995, signs with the Arizona Diamondbacks and then joins Florida. Izquierdo and Tejera both defect when they're 16-year-old pitchers for the Cuban junior national team and grow up in Miami. Both are drafted by the Marlins in '95; Izquierdo is released and joins the White Sox in 1997, then the Cleveland Indians and then rejoins the Marlins in 2000.

Cubans have been defecting since René Arocha left the Cuban national team at the Miami International Airport in 1991. Of the estimated 60 Cuban baseball players who defect since then, the *Miami Herald* says 14 make the major leagues. In 1995, Larry Rodriguez defects with Nuñez from the Cuban national baseball team training in

Venezuela and receives a $1.3 million bonus for signing with the Arizona Diamondbacks, who assign him to their minor league franchises. While working three seasons, he injures his arm in 1998, which ends his pro career.

It's the lure, though not always the realization, of big bucks that attracts Cuban athletes, especially baseball players with families. In 1999, Rigoberto Betancourt, a former hotshot pitcher in Cuba for nearly 20 years and the pitching coach for the Cuban national team, defects during the team's exhibition game in Baltimore against the Orioles, leaving behind his wife and two grown children, reports the *Miami Herald.* His hopes of landing a coaching job are dashed when he moves to Miami and is reunited with his 29-year-old son, a doctor in Cuba, who somehow arrives in South Florida. Betancourt, a cashier in a convenience store who coaches little leaguers, is anticipating the arrival this year of his wife and second child, both of whom secure visas to come to the U.S.

Baseball teams, eager to build their Hispanic fan bases, attempt new promotional schemes. The hapless Montreal Expos announce they will make Puerto Rico's Hiram Bithorn Stadium their home away from home for 22 games next season, including three with the World Series champs, the Anaheim Angels. The Expos, whose roster includes Caribbean players Jose Vidro and Vladimir Guerrero, will also meet the New York Mets, Atlanta Braves, Cincinnati Reds, and the Chicago Cubs in the Commonwealth. The team is being operated by the office of the Commissioner of Baseball, which buys the franchise from Jeffrey Loria, who purchases the soon-to-be 2003 World Series champion Florida Marlins.

The renamed Anaheim Angels initiate their most adventurous marketing plan to attract more Latinos to Edison Stadium from Orange County and adjacent San Bernardino and Riverside Counties, all of which show increased Latin populations. The nearby city of Santa Ana has the largest Latin population—71 percent—of any large city in the nation. Multi-cultural ads promoting the team and its six Latino players appear at bus stops, on rock en Español radio stations, and on Hispanic TV. Radio station XPRS-AM, which broadcasts Angels games for five years, tells the *Los Angeles Times* that more people are listening to Angels baseball than listening to soccer matches and the number of sponsors for the broadcasts is overflowing. Latinos now account for between 15 and 20 percent of game attendance.

In voting for the National League's championship series most valuable player, the winner this year is the revitalized Benito Santiago of San Francisco, the venerable slugger who starts his career in 1987 with the San Diego Padres and wins the Rookie of the Year award. The Ponce, Puerto Rico, native winds up playing for the Cincinnati Reds, Philadelphia Phillies, Toronto Blue Jays, Chicago Cubs, and Florida Marlins before being called to San Francisco by Dusty Baker. Other Hispanic National League playoff series MVPs include Atlanta's Eddie Perez in 1999, Florida's Liván Hernández in 1997, and Atlanta's Javy Lopez in 1996.

During this year's World Series, which the Anaheim Angels clinch in the seventh game against the San Francisco Giants, 4 to 1 at Edison Field, Hispanic players on both teams perform to the pleasure of the home team fans. In game three when Angel's pitcher Ramon Ortiz from the Dominican Republic competes against the Giants Liván Hernández from Cuba, the match-up is a big news event in the Hispanic press, here and overseas. The Angels series line-up besides Ortiz includes catcher Bengie Molina, who gains the distinction of becoming the first catcher with two doubles in a World Series game since October 25, 1995, when Atlanta's Javy Lopez notches the same results in game four against Cleveland; relief pitcher Francisco Rodriguez, who at 20 years of age becomes the youngest pitcher to win a World Series game, and second baseman Benji Gil.

The Giants series lineup includes, besides Hernández, shortstop Rich Aurilia, catcher Benito Santiago, and pitcher Russ Ortiz. In a breakdown of the champion Angels 31-man roster, seven are Latinos: Alex Ochoa, brothers and catchers Bengie and Jose Molina (the first siblings to catch for the same team since 1887 when Amos and Lave Cross perform for the Louisville Colonels), Benji Gil, Orlando Palmeiro, Ramon Ortiz, and Francisco Rodriguez.

In the voting for the World Series most valuable player, Latinos are blacked out. Since 1955, five Latinos have been named MVP: New York's Mariano Rivera in 1999; Florida's Liván Hernández in 1997; Cincinnati's Jose Rijo in 1990; Dodger's Pedro Guerrero who ties with teammates Ron Cey and Steve Yeager in 1981; and Pittsburgh's Roberto Clemente in 1971.

Amidst all of the hullabaloo anent the Angels, Carlos Peralta, a Mexican billionaire, announces his interest in buying the team from the Walt Disney Co., which has been trying to unload it for three years. Peralta owns one of Mexico City's top baseball teams, the Tigers De Angelopolis. While the team's new owner next year will have a Hispanic name, it's Arturo Moreno, fourth-generation Mexican American and Phoenix advertising mogul, not Carlos Peralta. Moreno will pay $183.5 million for the franchise and the distinction of being the first Latino owner of a major league team.

There is a Latino part owner of a major league team: Linda Alvarado, owner of Denver-based Alvarado Construction, a partner in the Colorado Rockies. She is asked in 1990 to become part of the group to attract a Major League team to the area. The team opens its inaugural season in 1993.

This is Telemundo's inaugural season to televise 15 National Basketball Association games. Basketball, known as baloncesto in Latin America, is taking aim at the Hispanic community in the U.S. Four teams sport Latin players: the Denver Nuggets with Arturo "Nene" Hilario from Brazil, Dallas Mavericks Eduardo Nájera, Mexico's first import to the NBA, Minnesota Timberwolves Felipe López from the Dominican Republic, and Golden State Warriors Oscar Torres from Venezuela. Since Telemundo reaches Hispanic American youth familiar with basketball, national advertisers like Reebok are signing up and even securing endorsements, the first of which locks up the Warriors' Torres.

In Dallas, Mavericks home and away games are broadcast on KESS-AM, a Hispanic Broadcasting Corp. affiliate whose sponsors include Budweiser and Dr. Pepper. And when the team is home,

Grupo Bimbo, Mexico's top baked-goods company has uniformed reps giving out free samples to arriving fans; kids under 12 receive a free Nájera jersey with the Bimbo logo. Nájera, in his second season, according to the *Wall Street Journal*, supplements his $420,000 salary with $1 million in endorsements from Anheuser-Busch, Nike, and Telcel, Mexico's major cell phone service.

The National Football League is doing the best of all the other pro leagues besides baseball in integrating Hispanics on the playing field. For many second and third generation Hispanics, football is more popular than fútbol, the name for soccer in Latin America. While there is an NFL ban against Spanish-language football telecasts, the *Miami Herald* reports the league looks to open the door for Super Bowl coverage for Hispanic TV in cities with large Latino populations.

Among teams with Hispanic players, according to *Hispanic* Magazine, are: the San Francisco 49ers with quarterback Jeff Garcia of Gilroy, California, and El Salvador's place-kicking Jose Cortez, whose previous teams included the San Diego Chargers and New York Giants; Tampa Bay's kicking brothers Martin and Bill Gramatica from Argentina; Jacksonville's defensive tackle Stalin Colinet from the Dominican Republic; Cleveland Browns' Miami-raised lineman Joaquin Gonzalez; and San Diego Chargers' linebacker Zeke Moreno, raised in the San Diego suburb of Chula Vista, among others. Mexico contributes the most players to the NFL. Perhaps the most notable is Anthony Muñoz, all-pro with the Cincinnati Bengals for 13 seasons, starting in 1980. His extraordinary record includes being elected to 11 straight Pro Bowls, being named all pro from 1981 to 1991, playing in two Super Bowls, named offensive lineman of the year in 1981, '87, and '88, and the NFL Players Association Lineman of the Year in '81, '85, '88, and '89. All these stellar achievements earn him a place in the Pro Football Hall of Fame in 1998.

According to San Diego's *La Prensa*, in 1998 there are 16 Hispanics in the league: Louie Aguiar with Kansas City; Tony Gonzalez, Kansas City; Leo Araguz and Danny Villa, Oakland; Tony

Ramirez, Detroit; Marco Rivera, Green Bay; Stalin Colinet, Minnesota; Norbeto Davidds-Garrido, Carolina; Juan Roque, Detroit; Jorge Diaz, Tampa Bay; David Diaz-Infante, Denver; Daniel Gonzalez, Dallas; Pete Gonzalez, Pittsburgh; Moses Moreno, Chicago; Juan Castillo, Philadelphia offensive line coach, and Pete Rodriguez, Seattle special teams assistant head coach.

Hispanic coaches? There are several. Two are with the Philadelphia Eagles: Ron Rivera the linebacker coach who plays linebacker with the Chicago Bears team that wins the 1985 Super Bowl, and Juan Castillo, offensive line coach.

Nine teams offer their games on Spanish radio: Arizona, Dallas, Denver, Houston, Miami, New Orleans, New York (Jets), San Diego, and Tampa Bay. The 49ers air a Spanish weekly highlight show on Telemundo affiliates in San Francisco, Sacramento, and Fresno. *ESPN Deportes*, ESPN's weekly Spanish service, airs NFL games. Last year, when ABC's *Monday Night Football* opens in Mexico City with the Cowboys and Raiders, Mexico President Vicente Fox welcomes the audience at the start of the telecast.

During its seventh year Major League Soccer goes into retractive mode and closes down its troubled Miami Fusion and Tampa Bay Mutiny franchises, returning to a 10-team league. MLS commissioner Don Garber says the move will cut losses by 30 percent. The restructuring also includes a two-conference format with the Eastern Conference teams the Chicago Fire, Columbus Crew, D.C. United, New York/New Jersey MetroStars, and New England Revolution (who play in Gillette Stadium, specifically built for soccer). The Western Conference's members include the Colorado Rapids (playing on soccer specific Invesco Field at Mile High), Dallas Burn, Kansas City Wizards, Los Angeles Galaxy, and San Jose Earthquakes. Unlike other pro sports where there are different team owners, MLS is dominated by one owner, Colorado billionaire Phil Anschutz, who controls the Los Angeles, Chicago, Colorado, Washington, and New York/New Jersey teams through his Anschutz Entertainment Group. The league has additionally given Anschutz the right to become half-owner of the defending champion San Jose Earthquakes. Dallas-based Hunt Sports Group, led by Lamar Hunt, operates three teams, Dallas Burn, Columbus Crew, and Kansas City Wizards. Hunt and several other investors form the league in 1996, two years after the World Cup is played in this country to enthusiastic fan support. League commissioner Garber, in the *Los Angeles Times*, disavows any problem with Anschutz having too much power. He says there have always been multiple owners. “We have a wide variety of checks and balances in place and will continue to enforce them.”

The MLS also operates in another unique fashion. Under its single entity concept, owners invest in the league and then operate teams. Player contracts are owned by the league and all teams share revenues.

As the league concludes its seventh season with Los Angeles winning its first MLS championship by beating New England 1-0 in overtime, commissioner Garber is predicting the league will expand to 20 cities, with candidates including Philadelphia, Seattle, Tulsa, Atlanta, Cleveland, Houston, Minneapolis/Saint Paul, and Oklahoma City.

While still a young league, MLS championship matchups include: 2001—San Jose 2, Los Angeles 1; 2000—Kansas City 1, Chicago 0; 1999—D.C. United 2, Los Angeles 0; 1998—Chicago 2, D.C. 0; 1997—D.C. 2, Colorado 1; and 1996—D.C. 1, Los Angeles 0. This year, MLS players lead the U.S. team to the World Cup quarterfinals, where they lose to Germany 1 to 0 in the second round in Arlington, Virginia. In the first round from Korea and Japan, the team beats Portugal and upsets Mexico 2 to 0 en route to this historic level of World Cup competition. The shutout victory over Mexico in the quarterfinals is the first time since 1950, when the U.S. shut out England, 1 to 0, that a U.S. team has accomplished this same achievement. Univision, which pays $150 million for U.S. Spanish-language rights for the 64 matches this year and for the 2006 games, finds viewership this year extremely supportive of its financial outlay for the soccer coverage, averaging 4.2 million male/female viewers per game.

Ironically, the World Cup is also drawing close to as many Anglo viewers to ESPN as are watching Univision. ESPN, which has close ties with MLS, pays $50 million for the English-language rights to the Cup competition, which it has broadcast since 1982, though not in 1990.

What's interesting about the MLS is that throughout its history, the players are a mixture of top talent from all over, including the U.S. Knowing that soccer is the sport of choice of Hispanics, I expect to see lots of Latinos on the teams, but that's not the case, according to the MLS' own player rosters. For example, this year six are the most Latinos playing for the D.C. United, MetroStars and Dallas Burn, followed by five at Los Angeles and New England. Other teams have two to four players. When the league debuts in 1996, here's the breakdown of Hispanic players: New York/New Jersey eight; Dallas and Los Angeles seven; Tampa Bay and San Jose five; D.C. four; New England three; and Kansas City one.

The Galaxy's Guatemalan striker, Carlos Ruiz, who boots in the winning left-footed goal in the 113th minute of this year's championship against the New England Revolution at its stadium, scores 24 goals this season and becomes the first player in the league to score more than half his team's goals all season. He also wins the league's Most Valuable Player award. It's the Galaxy's first title after losing in the finals three times since 1996. A record crowd of 61,316 is on hand at Gillette Stadium in Foxboro, Massachusetts, to witness the match. Of the champion's 30-player roster, Latinos come from El Salvador, Venezuela, Guatemala, Pasadena, and Riverside. Overall attendance for the league is up for the second straight year, a six percent increase over last year and a 15 percent jump for the last two seasons. Attendance averages 15,822 a game, with the top three teams Colorado, Los Angeles, and New York/New Jersey.

Major League Soccer is the second attempt at a pro league hoping America's soccer kids of the '70s and '80s are ready to see professional competition following the 17-year run of the North American Soccer League, which closes down in March of 1985. This pioneering league was the fusion of the United Soccer Association and the rival National Professional Soccer League, both of which begin in 1967 and merge the following year into the 17-team NASL. After its first season, 12 teams fold. In 1975 the league makes headlines when the New York Cosmos sign Brazilian retired superstar Pelé to a three-year, $4.5 million contract. Also joining Pelé (Edson Arantes Do Nascimento) on the Cosmos is another super name, Germany's Franz Beckenbauer. With attendance rising, the league expands to 24 teams in 1978, but a dramatic financial downturn, due to rising costs, forces the closing of 17 franchises, followed by a final adios in March 1985.

In one of the most contentious fights in pro boxing, superwelterweight champion Oscar De La Hoya shuts down fellow Mexican American Fernando Vargas, who blatantly calls himself the "real Mexican" of the two in the pre-battle war of words. De La Hoya racks his opponent with 16 unanswered punches in the 11th round of the fight at the Mandalay Bay Events Center in Las Vegas, with the referee stopping the fight at 1:48 as the 154-pound De La Hoya retains his World Boxing Council title. During the heated word fight build-up, Vargas (22-1) charges that Mexicans favor him over his opponent. "I'm proud of being a Mexican," boasts Vargas, born in the agricultural city of Oxnard, California, in the *Los Angeles Times*. "I fight like a warrior, like Mexicans do." Vargas boasts of representing the immigrants while De La Hoya (34-2), with his 1992 Olympic boxing gold medal, singing career, and celebrity pals fits the description of his "Golden Boy" moniker. De La Hoya, born in East Los Angeles, says nothing of his participation in the Olympics on the boxing team, but does jab at Vargas with the pointed comment that his characterization of a Mexican reminds him of a gang member. "What he says is insulting to a lot of hard-working people," De La Hoya says.

For De La Hoya, who hasn't fought in 15 months after losing to his last two opponents, Felix Trinidad and Shane Mosley, the victory is vindication against all the bad blood comments. To make matters worse for Vargas, after his TKO loss, he takes a urine test that reveals the presence of an illegal anabolic steroid. He becomes the first boxer to test positive for steroids in Nevada. Three months later, in November, the Nevada State Athletic Commission votes 4 to 1 to suspend Vargas for nine months and fines him $100,000. Vargas pleads no knowledge of the steroid and alleges someone in his staff gives it to him without his permission. He claims steroids are slipped in with vitamins and supplements he was taking.

Articles

"KCBS Makes News With A Late Comeback." Los Angeles Times, June 19, 2006

"KCBS Makes Headlines In L.A." Hollywood Reporter, May 31, 2005

"KCBS Rises To An Unfamiliar Place." Daily Variety, May 27, 2005

"Anchorwoman Lives 'La Vida.'" Los Angeles Times, April 29, 2005

"TV Acads Miss, Make Up." Daily Variety, Jan. 23, 2004

"Latinos Tune In To Watch As George Lopez Pursues American Dream On ABC." Walls Street Journal, Dec. 31, 2002

"Hispanics Driving TV Growth." New York Times, Dec. 30, 2002

"2002's Pop Artists Unable To Duplicate Crossover Success." San Antonio Express-News, Dec. 29, 2002

"The Year In Latin." Billboard, Dec. 28, 2002

"Marc Anthony & Miss Universe Tie Knot Again." Star, Dec. 24, 2002

"Are We At The Crest Of Another Creative New Wave In Latin Music?" Miami Herald, Dec. 22, 2002

"Sony Strengthens Regional Mexican With Titan." Billboard, Dec. 21, 2002

"Establishment Of Latin Emmys Is Headed To Arbitration." Los Angeles Times, Dec. 20, 2002

"Diversity Coalition Is Now Under Fire." Los Angeles Times, Dec. 17, 2002

"A Hispanic Drama, Rejected Once, Finds A Home." New York Times, Dec. 16, 2002

"Few TV News Stories Focus On Hispanics." USA Today, Dec. 16, 2002

"Miami Folk-Rock Group Aims To Keep Tropical Roots." San Antonio Express-News, Dec. 15, 2002

"Regional Mex Tops Top 40, West Is Best." Billboard, Dec. 14, 2002

"'Greetings From Tucson' Takes A Holiday Detour With Los Lobos." Los Angeles Times, Dec. 13, 2002

"Vallejo's New Disc Isn't From Miami." San Antonio Express-News, Dec. 1, 2002

"'Latin Jazz: La Combinación Perfecta." Jazziz, December 2002

"The Bolero's Timeless Appeal." Hispanic Magazine December 2002

"La Timba Llegó A Las Vegas." Latin Beat, December 2002

"Secada Sings Duet With Gloria Estefan." Hispanic Magazine, December, 2002

"Andy Garcia's Directorial Debut." Hispanic Magazine, December 2002

"Real Women Have Curves." Latin Beat, December 2002

"KCBS Still Waiting." Daily Variety, Nov. 27, 2002

"A Comedian Mines A Rich Vein Of Gloom With All-Latino Sitcom." New York Times, Nov. 27, 2002

"Arriba, Arriba, Arriba." Broadcasting & Cable, Nov. 25, 2002

"Regulators Face A Bilingual Conundrum." Los Angeles Times, Nov. 24, 2002

"Fernandez Handy With Lara Songs." Los Angeles Times, Nov. 23, 2002

"Latin Notas: Child's Play." Billboard, Nov. 23, 2002

"Expos To Call Puerto Rico Home." Los Angeles Times, Nov. 21, 2002

"Vargas Suspended 9 Months." Los Angeles Times, Nov. 21, 2002

"Museum to Add Shows In Spanish." Los Angeles Times, Nov. 20, 2002

"Talks Underway On Latin Emmys." Los Angeles Times, Nov. 18, 2002

"TV Academies Mull Latin Emmys." Electronic Media, Nov. 18, 2002

"No Blessing For 'Amaro' At L.A. Bow." Daily Variety, Nov. 18, 2002

"Switching Over." Billboard, Nov. 16, 2002

"Sony's Arjona Delivers 'Saintly Sin.'" Billboard, Nov. 16, 2002

"Latin Notas: UMVD Pacts With VI." Billboard, Nov. 16, 2002

"UPN Plans Latina Laffer." Daily Variety, Nov. 14, 2002

"Giants Believe Alou Is Answer." Los Angeles Times, Nov. 14, 2002

"Tejada Wins Short Battle For MVP." Los Angeles Times, Nov. 13, 2002

"NL MVP Voting." Los Angeles Times, Nov. 12, 2002

"Sports Court The Ethnic Market." Miami Herald, Nov. 11, 2002

"Marin Plays Pop On NBC's 'Ortegas.'" Hollywood Reporter, Nov. 11, 2002

"Mexican Critics Cool To 'Frida.' Hollywood Reporter, Nov. 11, 2002

"Equal Time?" TV Guide, Nov. 9, 2002

"Diaz On Future Of LARAS, Latin Grammys." Billboard, Nov. 9, 2002

"Tropical Music Falters Despite Latin Boom." Billboard, Nov. 9, 2002

"Soul Searching." Latin Notas, Billboard, Nov. 9, 2002

"Fusion Duo Sees A World Sin Bandera." Houston Chronicle, Nov. 8, 2002

"Setting Frida Kahlo's World To Music." Wall Street Journal, Nov. 7, 2002

"Orquestra Sinfónica Indulges Many Moods." Chicago Sun-Times, Nov. 6, 2002

"Manolin Goes Pop." Miami Herald, Nov. 5, 2002

"Top Ensemble Fires Up Cuban." Daily Variety, Nov. 5, 2002

"Is This Classical Music's Next New Thing?" Wall Street Journal, Nov. 5, 2002

"HBC's Mac Tichenor Jr. Slams Arbitron On L.A. Results." Radio And Records, Nov. 4, 2002

"New Faces Of The NFL." Hispanic Magazine, November 2002

"Universal Loves Romance Pitch From Leguizamo." Hollywood Reporter, Oct. 30, 2002

"Heating Up On-Screen." Multichannel News, Oct. 28, 2002

"Rhythms of Brazil, With Diverse Flavors." Los Angeles Times, Oct. 28, 2002

"Artisan Buoys Library Card At Lions Gate." Daily Variety, Oct. 28, 2002

"Grammy Boss Tries To Settle Harassment Case." Jam Music, Canoe.com, Oct. 26, 2002

"Shakira Sweeps MTV Awards For Latin America." Los Angeles Times, Oct. 25, 2002

"TV Academy Honor For Ch. 41's Pineda." New York Daily News, Oct. 25, 2002

"Social Conscience Still Striking Maná's Chords." Miami Herald, Oct. 25, 2002

"Red Hot 'Mama.'" Entertainment Weekly, Oct. 25, 2002

"Catholic Groups Target Film About Clerical Misdeeds." Los Angeles Times, Oct. 23, 2002

"Baseball Sees A World Of Possibilities." Los Angeles Times, Oct. 23, 2002

"As Angels Diversify, So Does Fan Base." Los Angeles Times, Oct. 22, 2002

"Can Laura Diaz Rescue KCBS?" Los Angeles Times, Oct. 22, 2002

"His Rise Has Been As Fast As His Fastball." Los Angeles Times, Oct. 22, 2002

"Uproar Over A Movie Priest Going His Own Way." New York Times, Oct. 21, 2002

"A Composition For The Ages?" Los Angeles Times, Oct. 21, 2002
"Cantor Scores NBA Spot." Hollywood Reporter, Oct. 21, 2002
"Ruiz's Overtime Goal Defeats New England, 1-0, As L.A. Ends String of Near Misses To Win First MLS Title." Los Angeles Times, Oct. 21, 2002
"A Brazilian Company That Zigs Where Others Zag." New York Times, Oct. 20, 2002
"¡Pop!" Billboard, Oct. 19, 2002
"ABC Commits To Full Season For Lopez Sitcom." Los Angeles Times, Oct. 19, 2002
"Latin acts Expand Presence At Arenas." Billboard, Oct. 19, 2002
"Latin Notas: Jordi's Unsuspecting Public." Billboard, Oct. 19, 2002
"Latin Notas: Estefan Honored." Billboard, Oct. 19, 2002
"Mother Vs. Daughter: A Love Story." L.A. Weekly, Oct. 18, 2002
"City Of Brotherly Gloves." Los Angeles Times, Oct. 17, 2002
"Spirit Of Santana." USA Today, Oct. 16, 2002
"Luna To Star In 'Havana' Dance Pic." Daily Variety, Oct. 14, 2002
"Juanes Wins A Show Of Hands." Los Angeles Times, Oct. 14, 2002
"Lopez Joins WCBS As Reporter." Hollywood Reporter, Oct. 13, 2003
"Casting Doubts." Entertainment Weekly, Oct. 11, 2002
"MLS Adding Two Teams Within Year." Los Angeles Times, Oct. 10, 2002
"The Bronze Screen: 100 Years Of Latino Image In Hollywood Cinema." Daily Variety, Oct. 9, 2002
"Lopez, ICM Part Ways But Who Dumped Whom?" Daily Variety, Oct. 9, 2002
"A Little Respecto." New Times Los Angeles, Oct. 3, 2002
"Cuban Ace Has Possibly Defected." Miami Herald, Oct. 2, 2002
"Ruben Blades: Speaking A New Pop Language," Pulse Magazine, October, 2002
"Expect More Sensual Telenovelas On Spanish-Language TV." Hispanic Magazine, October 2002
"The Cat's Nine Lives." Hispanic Magazine, October, 2002
"A-Rod Breaking Home-Run Records." Hispanic Magazine, October 2002
"A Hands-On Dream Builder." Hispanic Magazine, October 2002
"More Hispanics On Prime Time." Hispanic Magazine, October, 2002
"Salma Living Free Like Frida." Hispanic Magazine, October 2002
"ESPN Plans 23-Hour 'Deportes.'" Multichannel News, Sept. 30, 2002
"Sanz Reigns Again At Latin Grammys." Billboard, Sept. 28, 2002
"Mexican Billionaire Interested In Team." Los Angeles Times, Sept. 28,

2002
"Vargas Drug Test Reveals Steroids." Los Angeles Times, Sept. 28, 2002
"Singer's Sisters Apparently Abducted." Los Angeles Times, Sept. 25, 2002
"MLS Attendance Again Rises." Los Angeles Times, Sept. 24, 2002
"WCCB Offers News And Ads In Spanish." MediaWeek, Sept. 23, 2002
"Telemundo Plans 'Idol' Type Show For Latin Audience In The U.S." Billboard, Sept. 21, 2002
"Latin Grammys Needs Wider Appeal To Survive." Miami Herald, Sept. 20, 2002
"Latin Grammys Make Downbeat Showing." Los Angeles Times, Sept. 20, 2002
"Enrique Iglesias Promotes Two CDs With A Miami Tour Stop." Miami Herald, Sept. 20, 2002
"One Mas Time For Sr. Sanz." Hollywood Reporter, Sept. 19, 2002
"The New Spanish Conquest." Los Angeles Times, Sept. 19, 2002
"22 Cubans Can't Attend Latin Grammys." Miami Herald, Sept. 18, 2002
"Kronos Goes Beyond Kitsch To Capture Musical Mexico." Los Angeles Times, Sept. 16, 2002
"Latin Artists Expand Their Reach By Thinking Global." Chicago Tribune, Sept. 16, 2002
"The Road To Latin Music Leads To L.A." Miami Herald, Sept. 15, 2002
"De La Hoya Beats Vargas." Los Angeles Times, Sept. 15, 2002
"Ketchup Girls Relish Chart Success." Billboard, Sept. 14, 2002
"Fall Preview." TV Guide, Sept. 14, 2002
"Tour Targets Latina Teens." San Antonio Express-News, Sept. 13, 2002
"New Kid On Latin Block Is Old School." Miami Herald, Sept. 11, 2002
"Heartthrob." Los Angeles Times, Sept. 11, 2002
"A Band's 40th Birthday Party As Salsa Festival." New York Times, Sept. 10, 2002
"Salute To Area's Ethnic Diversity." Los Angeles Times, Sept. 10, 2002
"Culture Clash." Los Angeles Times, Sept. 10, 2002
"More Steamy Novelas, Reality Shows On Spanish TV." Miami Herald, Sept. 9, 2002
"It's Not Just A Translation Of Rap." Los Angeles Times, Sept. 8, 2002
"Ruben Blades Tours World Styles On Sony Discos' 'Mundos.'"

Billboard, Sept. 7, 2002

"New Moon." Latin Notas, Billboard, Sept. 7, 2002

"For Hispanic Radio, A Feud Boils Over In A Market On Fire." Wall Street Journal, Sept. 6, 2002

"Golden But Not An Oldie, A Salsa Band Turns 40." New York Times, Sept. 5, 2002

"Secada Finally Heard From." New York Daily News, Sept. 4, 2002

"Metro's 'Urban Latino' Takes Syndication Flight." Multichannel News, Sept. 2, 2002

"Series Pays Tribute To A Pioneering Cast Of Latino Actors." Los Angeles Times, Sept. 2, 2002

"The Tempo Of Politics." Hispanic Magazine, September 2002

"El Gran Combo De Puerto Rico." Latin Beat, September 2002

"U.S. Latin Market Joins Downward Trend." Billboard, Aug. 31, 2002

"Label Loyalty." Billboard, Aug. 31, 2002

"Santa Rosa Mixes It Up On Sony Discos' 'Vice Versa.'" Billboard, Aug. 31, 2002

"Universal Star Iglesias Returns To Latin Roots." Aug. 31, 2002

"Local Salsa Bands Carry Torch For Cuban Music." Dallas Morning News, Aug. 29, 2002

"Latin Music Sees 26% Drop In '02." Hollywood Reporter, Aug. 29, 2002

"A Bronx Cheer For Owners." National Review Online, Aug. 29, 2002

"'American Family' Visits Mexico." Los Angeles Times, Aug. 28, 2002

"Radio's Future? Listen To L.A." Advertising Age, Aug. 27, 2002

"Telemundo To Air NBA En Español." Multichannel News, Aug. 26, 2002

"January 1, 2003 Nielsen Media Research Estimates." Electronic Media, Aug. 26, 2002

"Patricia Manterola Wants To Break Mold." San Antonio Express-News, Aug. 25, 2002

"Will Controversy Over Sins Of 'Padre' Translate?" Los Angeles Times, Aug. 24, 2002

"Volumen Cero Zeroes In On Alt Rock Without A Lot Of Gimmicks." San Antonio Express-News, Aug. 22, 2002

"Hispanics Lead Nation In Amount Of Television Watched." New York Daily News, Aug. 20, 2002

"A Film Of Their Own," Miami Herald, Aug. 20, 2002

"Bilingual Reporters Have The Inside Track." Electronic Media, Aug. 19, 2002"

"Santana Sees 'Supernatural' Sequel As A Healer." Newhouse News Service, Aug. 19, 2002

"Latin Music Wave Goes South Of Border." Daily Variety, Aug. 19, 2002

"Two Papers Abstain From 'Sex' Ads." Daily Variety, Aug. 15, 2002

"American Bowls Highlight Third Preseason Week." La Prensa San Diego, Aug. 14, 2002

"Burn Soccer Takes A Foothold." Dallas News, Aug. 13, 2002 "Rivers Shows More Pop, More Confidence On His New CD." San Antonio Express-News, Aug. 11, 2002

"WB Hopes Everyone Gets 'Lucha.'" Billboard, Aug. 10, 2002

"Latin Luminaries Know Trials And Triumphs." Dallas Morning News, Aug. 10, 2002

"Austin Tops S.A. In List Of Best Hispanic Cities." San Antonio Express-News, Aug. 10, 2002

"Look Out For New WB Series 'Mucha Lucha!'" Houston Chronicle, Aug. 9, 2002

"Union Seeks Telemundo Contract." Los Angeles Times, Aug. 9, 2002

"Classic Clint: 'Blood' Sweat And Golden Years." Los Angeles Times, Aug. 9, 2002

"That's Amore." Arizona Republic, Aug. 8, 2002

"Sending Out A Message In Two Languages." Houston Chronicle, Aug. 7, 2002

"He Woos Fans In Two Languages." Los Angeles Times, Aug. 7, 2002

"Mission Accomplished, Yet Again." Los Angeles Times, Aug. 7, 2002

"Letter From Cuba Rough Diamonds." The New Yorker, Aug. 5, 2002

"WXTV's Spanish-Lingo News Cleans Up In July Sweeps." New York Daily News, Aug. 4, 2002

"Veranazo Fest Debut A Hit At Dodger Stadium." Los Angeles Times, Aug. 3, 2002

"Reel Word," Entertainment Weekly, Aug. 2, 2002

"Spanish Broadcaster Sues Clear Channel." Aug. 1, 2002

The Bratt Pact." Vanity Fair, August 2002

"Emphasis On 'International' Gives Festival Salsa Flavor." Houston Chronicle, July 31, 2002

"Latinos Finding New Homes In Suburbs, Study Shows." Los Angeles Times, July 31, 2002

"'GMA' Nabs Cambert For L.A." Daily Variety, July 30, 2002

"Arenas Spices Up Myriad Pic." Daily Variety, July 29, 2002

"Distribs Usher In New Spanish Wave." Daily Variety, July 29, 2002

"Arbitron Results." Billboard, July 27, 2002

"Latin Market Seeks Lift From Warner's Mana." Billboard, July 27, 2002

"From Colombia, Music Of Both Terror And Joy." New York Times, July 27, 2002

"Hispanic Television Files For Bankruptcy." Los Angeles Times, July 26, 2002

"Arbitron Ranks Spanish-Language KLTV-FM Numero Uno." Houston Chronicle, July 25, 2002

"Family Connects With Its Roots." Los Angeles Times, July 24, 2002

"Numero Uno And Growing." Houston Chronicle, July 22, 2002

"Triumph Of A Common Touch." Los Angeles Times, July 20, 2002

"KPWR-FM Experiences Ups, Downs." Los Angeles Times, July 19, 2002

"Lo And Behold, The Sister." New York Daily News, July 18, 2002

"Coalition Faults Networks Over Lack Of Diversity." Los Angeles Times, July 18, 2002

"Crest Of The Crossover." Miami Herald, July 14, 2002

"Los Lobos Wake Up to New Episode Via Mammoth/Hollywood's 'Good Morning.'" Billboard, July 13, 2002

"Rudy Perez Launches Joint Venture With UMG." Billboard, July 13, 2002

"Cultural Disconnect Masks The Diversity Of Latin Music." Miami Herald, July 11, 2002

"A World Of Colorful Concoctions From Ozomatli." Los Angeles Times, July 9, 2002

"Kath Jurado, 78: Mexican Film Star Had U.S. Roles In The '50s." Los Angeles Times, July 6, 2002

"Just About Every Genre Fills Hispanic State Fair." San Antonio Express-News, July 5, 2002

"Players Go To Bat For El Duque." Miami Herald, July 3, 2002

"2 Families Worth Knowing." Los Angeles Times, July 1, 2002

"Latino Actor Humbled By Success." Hispanic Magazine, July

"Mariachi USA Fest Makes Amphitheater Ring." San Antonio Express-News, June 30, 2002

"De Luna Departing Sonya Discos To Helm Indie Label Costarola." Billboard, June 29, 2002

"The Iconic Charly Garcia Returns On EMI." Billboard, June 29, 2002

"For Tosti, The Zoot Suit Still Fits." Los Angeles Times, June 27, 2002

"Screen Gems Chipping In On Salsa Pic." Daily Variety, June 25, 2002

"News Bueno For Hot KVEA." Daily Variety, June 24, 2002

Univision Acquisition Of HBC Creates Media Giant." Billboard, June 22, 2002

"World Cup Ratings Wake Up Network Projections." New York Times, June 21, 2002

"Banderas Will Ride As 'Villa.'" Daily Variety, June 21, 2002

"Univision, Perez Spin Deal." Hollywood Reporter, June 20, 2002

"In L.A. Univision Outdraws ESPN On U.S. Soccer Upset." Los Angeles Times, June 19, 2002

"Soccer Starts Scoring With U.S. Viewers." Los Angeles Times, June 18, 2002

"Hot! Hot! Hot!" Multichannel News, June 17, 2002

"A Latin Dance Music Sings The Blues." New York Times, June 16, 2002

"Spanish Simulcasts Not Catching On." San Antonio Express-News, June 15, 2002

"Sony's 'El Rey' Goes Acoustic." Billboard, June 15, 2002

"Spanish Broadcasting Suit Alleges Antitrust Actions." Los Angeles Times, June 13, 2002

"Univision Making Radio Waves." Hollywood Reporter, June 13, 2002

"Giving New York A Glimpse Of Ballet Magic From Havana." New York Times, June 13, 2002

"Univision Acquiring Dallas Network." Dallas Morning News, June 12, 2002

"Univision's Cup Runneth Over ESPN." Hollywood Reporter, June 11, 2002

"Raquel Welch Is Reinvented As A Latina." New York Times, June 11, 2002

"Los Lobos' Universal Note." Los Angeles Times, June 10, 2002

"Carlos Ponce Takes Different Tack On His Album." Houston Chronicle, June 8, 2002

"Gun Used To Kill Singer Selena To Be Destroyed On Judge's Order." Associated Press, June 8, 2002

"Every Day's Dicey For Juanes." Miami Herald, June 8, 2002

"Fox Tries Latin Beat." Daily Variety, June 5, 2002

"Columbia, Perez Psyched About 'Shrink!' Feature," Hollywood Reporter, June 4, 2002

"NBC Will Take Advertisers To The Edge." Electronic Media, June 3, 2002

"For Cuban Athletes Who Defect, Success In Sports Is Elusive." Miami

Herald, June 2, 2002

"Los Hombres Calientes Featuring Bill Summers & Irvin Mayfield." Down Beat, June 2002

"Hispanic Theater Opens Tonight; 8 Countries Will Be Represented." Miami Herald, May 31, 2002

"Pavos Reales To Cap Puro Conjunto Fest." San Antonio Express-News, May 31, 2002

"Hispanic Networks Hone An Edge In Race For TV Ad Dollars." New York Times, May 30, 2002

"Telemundo Attacks Rivals With 'Hyperlocal' News." Electronic Media, May 27, 2002

"Latin Singer-Actress Shucks Her Clingy 'Has Been' Label." Miami Herald, May 27, 20032

"CD Review: Juanes Moves Past The Hype In Sunny Style." Dallas Morning News, May 26, 2002

"Rabanes: Dancehall Is Up Our Street." Miami Herald, May 26, 2002

"Popular Latino Stand-Up Tour Returns To S.A." San Antonio Express-News, May 24, 2002

"Hispanic Nets Offer Up Strategies." Multichannel News, May 20, 2002

"'Piñero,' Anthony Lead ALMAs." Hollywood Reporter, May 20, 2002

"Thalía's 'Crossover Success' Target Is Entire World." San Antonio Express-News, May 19, 2002

"Latin Grammys Struggle With Loss Of Momentum." Los Angeles Times, May 17, 2002

"Acuña Deftly Fuses Latin Roots With Imagination." Los Angeles Times, May 17, 2002

"Trying To Get Behind The Role Of The Maid." New York Times, May 16, 2002

"Univision Unveils Edgier Lineup." Miami Herald, May 16, 2002

"Telemundo Enhances Lineup With NBC's Help." Miami Herald, May 15, 2002

"Jose Canseco Announces Retirement." Miami Herald, May 14, 2002

"With Added Muscle, Ratings Bump, World Cup Coverage, Hispanic Outlook Brighter." Advertising Age, May 13, 2002

"Two Is A Party For Owners." Los Angeles Times, May 11, 2002

El Gram Combo." Billboard, May 11, 2002

"Importing Latino Theater." Los Angeles Times, May 10, 2002

"Moms Get Treated To Mariachi Festival For Their Special Day." Los Angeles Times, May 10, 2002

"Cubans Izquierdo, Tejera And Nuñez Help Shut Out Padres." Miami Herald, May 10, 2002

"A Latino Censes Recount." Los Angeles Times, May 9, 2002

"Commissioner: Serving Hispanic Fans." NFL. Com, May 2, 2002

"PBS Extends 'Family' With Back Nine Order." Daily Variety, May 1, 2002

"Arrarás Turns Up Heat At Telemundo." Electronic Media, April 29, 2002

"Grammy Prez Quits." Stereophile, April 29, 2002

"Univision Becomes A Major Player." Billboard, April 27, 2002

"A Return To Normal After 9/11." Los Angeles Times, April 26, 2002

"Kodak Site For Latin Grammys." Daily Variety, April 26, 2002

"'Scorpion,' 'Spider' Draw Latino Auds." Daily Variety, April 25, 2002

"Unchanged Tunes." Los Angeles Times, April 23, 2002

"February Reign." New York Post, April 21, 2002

"Telemundo Under Microscope." Hollywood Reporter, April 15, 2002

"Latin Music's Growing Pains." Billboard, April 13, 2002

"FCC Gives Peacock A Go On Telemundo Acquisition." Daily Variety, April 11, 2002

"Will This One Click?" Los Angeles Times, March 26, 2002

"Tampa Bay Launches News En Español." Multichannel News, March 25, 2002

"Galaxy's Stars Have That Familiar Look." Los Angeles Times, March 23, 2002

"MLS Insists Less Is More This Season." Los Angeles Times, March 21, 2002

"Univision's New Network Revises It's Programming." Los Angeles Times, March 21, 2002

"Telemundo Leaps Into Reality TV With 'Protagonistas De Novela.'" Miami Herald, March 11, 2002

"Like Players, This Story Is An Old One." Los Angeles Times, March 11, 2002

"U.S. Gets Promising TV Deal." Los Angeles Times, Feb. 28, 2002

"Young Maverick Sits On Sidelines But Stars In Ads." Wall Street Journal, Feb. 27, 2002

"ABC Soap Takes A Page From Telenovela Playbook." Electronic Media, Feb. 11, 2002

"Univision Network Enters 3 New Markets." Los Angeles Times, Jan. 16, 2002

"Philharmonic Society Emphasizes Latin Works." Los Angeles Times,

Jan. 15, 2002

"Univision Aims 3rd Network At Bilinguals." Los Angeles Times, Jan. 14, 2002

"Hispanic TV Network Faces Daunting Odds." Electronic Media, Jan 14, 2002

"Univision Leaps Into TeleFutura," Hollywood Reporter, Jan. 14, 2002

"Universal Music Latin America Licenses Vale." Billboard Jan. 13, 2002

"Sept. 11 Effect Figures Into Radio Ratings." Los Angeles Times, Jan. 11, 2002

"Musimex Label Joins Uni Family." Billboard, Jan. 11, 2002

"Viva Los Outlaws!" New Times Los Angeles, Jan. 10, 2002

"White And Hispanics Fall Out Over Quest For Suburban Dream." Wall Street Journal, Jan. 10, 2002

"MLS Eliminates Florida Teams." Los Angeles Times, Jan. 9, 2002

"PBS's Latino Drama Gets 2nd Window." Electronic Media, Jan 7, 2002

"Nets Gird For Spanish War." Daily Variety, Jan. 2, 2002

Chapter 10
CAPITULO 10

Public Passion
PASION PUBLICA

While there's no doubt the growth of the domestic Latin entertainment industry is the No. 1 story in show business and translates into money and power for those successful artists and companies, how is the public reacting to all the hullabaloo and hype? To find out I query a cross-section of Hispanics on how the exploding Latin population and the expansion of Spanish-language entertainment is impacting their lives. Each story has its own distinctiveness, like the multifarious Latin mixture of the nation itself.

Christine Reyes is a 36-year-old research associate at a management consulting firm in New York City whose mother is from the Dominican Republic and whose father is from Puerto Rico. Growing up she says she spoke Spanish to her mom and English to her dad. "My Spanish was bad," she admits, "until my teen years when I was required to take a language in high school, so I took Spanish. As a bilingual I had a broad upbringing. My dad listened to classical music on eight-track cassettes. Initially, I didn't appreciate Hispanic music and the merengue from the Dominican Republic. Now I appreciate it because I understand it's the roots and origins of Dominican music."

A single parent raising her four-year-old son Christopher, "he speaks Spanish better than I did because he's been watched by my mom and cousin while I'm at work. So he's being raised in a Hispanic household." As a teen, while her mother watches Spanish-language

TV, she doesn't. She does listen to New York's top Spanish radio station, WSKQ-FM, as well as general market stations WBLS-FM for its rhythm and blues, WRKS-FM for its pop, and CD 101.9 for its jazz. While a teenager, her musical tastes run from The Mamas & The Papas to Simon & Garfunkel to the Tokens. When she turned 23, she joins the ranks of New Yorkers digging salsa music and now she's progressed to rock en Español specialists Maná.

She also prefers to watch English-language news rather than the Spanish stations because "the Spanish newscasters talk too fast. While I understand the content, it's harder to understand what they're saying. I prefer English because I don't have to listen so hard as I have to do with the Spanish networks." When she sees the film *Y Tu Mama Tambien*, she's glad "there's English subtitles because the Spanish is so quick."

Luis Pillich is a 25-year-old New York investment banker with a fascinating background. Born in Puerto Rico to two black Hispanics, when he's nine his dad joins the Army and he becomes a traveling "Army brat," spending 12 years in Germany. "In our household, we speak Spanish; with my friends it's English. Although I'm definitely bilingual, I think in Spanish," he says. His background has multicultural roots. "On my father's side my great grandmother is from St. Lucia and my great grandfather is Croatian. They meet in St. Lucia and settle in Puerto Rico. My mom's side has an African heritage." Luis is among the 939,000 Hispanics who describe themselves as black Latinos, according to the 2000 U.S. Census as analyzed by sociologist John R. Logan in his report, "How Race Counts for Hispanic Americans." His project also lists 17.6 million Hispanics who call themselves white while 16.7 million Latinos refer to themselves as either of another race or a combination of races.

When Luis returns to New York, he lives with his grandfather, who's been in New York 50 years and is a big Latin jazz fan. At the University of Hartford his undergraduate thesis was on "Puerto Rico and Race Relations." His graduate studies are accomplished at Oxford in England. "While I was doing my research, it dawns on me my ties to Puerto Rico aren't that deep and solid, even though I speak Spanish, so I start listening to Latin jazz and became interested on a surface level." Now he listens to Latin jazz on records and hip-hop and R&B on WQHT-FM. "I tend to listen to old records; they're my only musical connection to my heritage," he explains.

Luis estimates 20 percent of his TV viewing is on Telemundo and Univision where he watches soccer and international news. When he was living in Germany, his parents have satellite TV and he watches Telemundo and TV from Spain.

Luis is bothered by the term "Latin crossover." "I didn't feel Ricky Martin, Marc Anthony, and Shakira are bringing me strong Latin influences. They're crossing over to play American music. I didn't feel the Latinization I read about is evident in their music, a lot of which is catchy pop tunes and there's nothing wrong with that."

He becomes more intense as we touch on other aspects of the Latin entertainment explosion. "While we're seeing more Hispanic faces in films, it's a double-edged sword for me. I'm happy for that, but in some ways they don't especially represent me and my parents who are black. I don't see a lot of myself in those characters. If you look at Spanish TV in Puerto Rico, servants in soap operas tend to be black; musicians or Sambo-like characters tend to be black as well. That is the basis for my undergraduate thesis on racial politics in Puerto Rico."

Luis admits there's pressure to adapt to American culture. "Especially among people who don't go to college, it's very strong. People shouldn't think in dualities. They should think the concept of America is we come from a lot of different places. Being American doesn't necessarily mean we're losing our own culture and heritage. I was guilty as a kid of not wanting to listen to Spanish music with my parents. I wanted to assimilate as an American and listen to American music. Music is a very important key to having this connection. I didn't want to be identified as a kid who listens to Spanish music. When I was in elementary school I listened to LL Cool J and other rap groups. Today, I wouldn't be offended if someone spoke to me in Spanish."

Across the country in Los Angeles, Jose Jaime Vasquez is another person struggling with his own identity. Jimmy, as he prefers to be called, is a 33-year-old hospital pharmacy technician who's married to Laura (Duckman) and they have two children, Sam, four, and Abigail, 20 months. Jimmy, he explains, "stuck with me since I was five years old." Now, he candidly admits, "My generation is feeling the pressure to be more Hispanic. It's not something I want to do. I don't feel connected. Since I'm first-generation American, I have a little pressure to be more American than Hispanic. I've met other people in my age group who have similar feelings. Here in America we speak English; we're not Hispanic, we're not Mexican, we're really caught between two worlds. I'm being affected because of the greater awareness of Hispanics in the U.S. Sometimes I feel if I spoke clearer Spanish I wouldn't get smears from some Hispanics."

Jimmy's mother Eloisa came to Los Angeles in 1969 from Jalisco, Mexico, pregnant, unmarried, and facing her nation's great pressures against an unwed mother. "She wanted me to be born in the U.S. not Mexico," he tells me. He is born in Glendale within Los Angeles County. When he was growing up he doesn't listen exclusively to Spanish radio or Spanish-language music. "I do now because there's more emphasis on the Spanish-language, and it's more accepted to speak Spanish anywhere. Before, it wasn't like that." Now he listens to KCRW-FM, the National Public Radio station, KISS-FM, the contemporary hits outlet, KKJZ-FM, the all-jazz outpost, and some classical music. He doesn't listen to Spanish radio or watch Spanish television. Since he works from 2:30 to 11 p.m. he doesn't get to watch much TV, but when he does, it's all English. Wife Laura and her family are non-Hispanics, so this marriage crosses cultural and religious boundaries. His mother, who speaks very little English, primarily watches Spanish TV, and she and Jimmy converse in Spanish. As a teenager, he enjoys reggae and some Spanish music "because my mother listened, but it wasn't a big influence on me.

"Fifteen years ago," he continues, "if a Hispanic owned his own home and a large car the perception was he was doing something illegal. Today, I own my home, drive a large car, and don't get too many smears and odd looks from the Caucasian population. I feel fairly normal."

Although he hasn't been impacted by the exploding Hispanic population in Los Angeles, he tells me about a very sensitive and disturbing situation he encounters when his Latino characteristics automatically elicit the same response from Spanish clerks at McDonalds. "They always ask me for my order in Spanish. This irritates me. This is America and this is an American business, and you go there with the expectation of speaking English." So how does he order his Big Macs and fries? "In English."

Although some of his friends attend concerts by Latin artists, Jimmy doesn't. He also has no sense of connection with artists in other branches of Latin entertainment.

Maria De Los Angeles Lopez holds dual citizenship in the U.S. and Mexico, where she is born in the city of San Diego in the state of Jalisco and lives on a farm with her parents and six brothers and five sisters. She and her husband Ramon are both 49. They met in Mexico and have been married 32 years. No pun intended, Los Angeles is their home. They have a son Francisco, 29, who has two children and a daughter Maribel, 26, who has four children. She is usually called Angela, she explains, "because my formal first name is so long." She came to the U.S. 29 years ago "for a better future. Life is hard in Mexico." She gains her citizenship in 1990, learning English from the people for whom she works and by going to night school.

While she speaks Spanish to Ramon and her children, she speaks English to her grandchildren. She admits it's a little hard to switch to English because sometimes she doesn't understand some of the things the grandkids say.

When she is by herself, she listens to several Spanish radio stations for their specialty formats, KWKW-AM and KTNQ-AM for their talk shows and KLVE-FM for its romantic music. She especially enjoys KWKW in the morning when Dr. Ernesto Prado "helps people" and Antonio Gonzaléz "gives people tips on solving problems." While

Pepe Barreto is the humorous personality who attracts her to KLVE, Amalia Gonzalez keeps her attention on KTNQ with helpful advice. She generally listens to Spanish radio six hours a day. When she's in the car with her son, they listen to English-language radio.

At home, she watches more English TV than Spanish, and this pattern surprises me. Why is this the case? "Ramon likes the English movies," she explains, and the two watch them together. "Ramon usually watches English TV until 3 a.m. He speaks better English and he understands everything," she admits, noting, "There are some words I don't understand." Angela is also a faithful viewer of Spanish networks Telemundo, Univision, and its TeleFutura second network "which shows English movies with Spanish translations." She watches news, telenovelas, and films on Hispanic TV. "Telenovelas always have sad endings," she laments.

Her dual citizenship causes a bit of a conflict during the World Cup playoffs in 2002 when the U.S. defeats Mexico 2-0. "I love both Mexico and the United States," she says, adding: "to tell the truth I wanted Mexico to win, but I'm happy here. I love the U.S.A. I came here when I was 17. Ramon came to Los Angeles five years before me and learns to speak English here. Then he returns to Mexico. We are best friends in Mexico and we live in the U.S. four years before we get married. I have all my children in Los Angeles." Ramon is part of a growing Hispanic fan base that follows the Los Angeles Dodgers and Lakers.

Frank Francisco Delgado is 44 and from war-torn El Salvador. He arrives in Los Angeles in 1981 with his brother Luis, 35. He came to the U.S. to get away from the political war erupting in his home nation. "The situation in my country is so bad because of the right-wing guerillas. I was working for the government in the Department of Health, and I have to go to rural areas and try to educate the people on health matters. If you work for the government you never know when the guerillas will attack you. They kill three of my associates. It was getting dangerous. You couldn't be neutral, either with the government or the guerillas." To come to the U.S., he explains, "You have to go through Guatemala and Mexico. It takes five days on the bus to get here."

Frank speaks a little English when he arrives in Los Angeles. He attends night school to improve his vocabulary. "When I first come here I listen to Hispanic radio and TV, but by watching the news in English it helps you learn the language." Today, he's bilingual and listens to Spanish music station KLVE-FM and English-language country station KZLA-FM. Since he does maintenance work for a management company with 13 buildings, his days are long and he arrives home after 9:30 p.m. "So there's little time to watch television." When he does, he watches the news on Anglo stations KTTV and KCAL and movies on KTLA and KCOP. He finds there is news for Salvadorans on several of the Spanish channels, but he doesn't hear too much music from El Salvador. He lives in La Puente with his wife Yolanda and their two sons, Daniel, eight, and Kevin, a year-and-a-half. "I speak English to my kids, but I also try to talk Spanish because I don't want them to lose their Spanish heritage."

Frank's father Jose comes to the U.S. in 1976, followed by his mother Maria Ofelia in 1982 and his brother Salvador, 38, and his sister Vilma, 32, in 1984. He has family in El Salvador, which he visits. "My family started a road assistance, car body shop," he says, which sounds like a good, solid, safe business. But then he adds a frightening footnote: "They're getting anonymous phone calls demanding $40,000 or they'll kidnap my sister Esperana (who is 43), or her two daughters. They've had to hire bodyguards, but it's been quiet. It's the style of life there, I guess."

There are also bad things happening within the Hispanic community in L.A. linked to the region's expanding Latino population that impact Frank on an emotional level. "You see a lot of people on the streets doing bad things," he relates. "Then you see that on television and that affects all Spanish people. We came here to do something good, not bad."

Diana Kaplan, formerly Diana Rodriquez, typifies the contemporary cross-cultural phenomenon confronting and encompassing America. She and her husband are the second couple I interview whose Hispanic-Caucasian backgrounds create a colorful pastiche of melding attitudes and tastes. Born in Los Angeles to parents who migrate from Mexico-Olivia from Sonora and Donaldo from Durango—Diana, along with brother Donaldo and sister Dayami, speaks Spanish until she is in kindergarten and she starts learning English and watching English-language cartoons on TV while in the first grade. During her formative years, she listens to Spanish radio and TV, "whatever my parents listen to, like KALI (AM), KWKW (AM), and KLVE (FM)," she recalls. In the third grade she pays attention to Menudo and in the fifth grade her favorites aree Madonna and Michael Jackson. In her teen years she listens to Anglo radio stations KISS and KROQ, two very popular stations.

Her life dramatically changes when she meets Ken Kaplan while working for the same downtown Los Angeles produce company; romance blossoms into marriage in January of 1996. It's the first time either have dated someone with a different cultural and religious background. When they're dating, Diana recalls she "feels uncomfortable singing along to the radio in Spanish, but Ken gets used to listening to Spanish music."

Work takes Ken, 36, and his 28-year-old bride on an interminable journey, first to Seattle, then to Maui, Hawaii (where first daughter Samantha is born), back to L.A. and finally to San Diego, where Ken becomes a real estate agent. Two more daughters, Lauren and Sophia, are born in San Diego, where the family establishes its synergistic Latin and Anglo lifestyle.

In her new home, Di listens to Anglo FM stations KFMB for pop and KIFM for smooth jazz and Spanish FM outlets XLTN (*Radio Latina*), KLQV (*K-Love*), and KLNV *(La Nueva)*. Comments Diana about the difference between Los Angeles and San Diego: "When we first moved to San Diego, I was searching for Spanish radio stations and thought that being so close to the Mexican border there'd be more stations than there were in L.A. But that's not the case."

While her parents, who also moved to San Diego, watch Univision and Telemundo and a Tijuana station, Diana prefers general market TV. When (in 2002) the girls, Samantha, six, Lauren, four and Sophie, one, are home, she tends to listen to Spanish radio with them, explaining: "I want my girls to enjoy that type of music. It's good for them to start learning Spanish. I want them to know my culture. This is who I am. I don't want to lose my identity and I want them to know where I come from. It's so easy to lose my identity when I live with somebody who is of a different culture. I want to pass the beauty of the language along to my girls. I'm bilingual as are most of my friends and relatives, and I want my girls to have equal skills. There are so many opportunities being bilingual."

Diana employs Spanish with the girls as an attention-grabber. "When I'm angry I tend to yell in Spanish. They'll stop, turn around and pay attention to me because they don't understand what I'm saying. Lauren will say, 'Mom, stop that and talk right.'"

Diana's parents speak Spanish to their siblings and to the Kaplan girls; they speak English to Ken, whose formal name is Kenneth Douglas and is often called Kenny by his parents. Ken's musical tastes, which encompass James Taylor, John Mayer, the Dave Matthews Band, Sting, Sade, and the Dixie Chicks, are embraced by Diana and the two attend concerts by several of these acts Diana has never seen before. But she can't get away from her Latin roots. "I love to listen to music I can dance to," she explains, "especially salsa, merengue, and cumbia." She also attends a limited number of concerts by top Latin stars like the father and son duo of Vicente and Alejandro Fernández, and Juan Gabriel.

"My parents grow up listening to Vicente Fernández," says Diana. "He's my father's all-time favorite. I used to get annoyed when my dad turned up the radio to hear him better. Now I do the same thing. There's so much Mexican history in the music. I had seen them both with my parents in San Diego. The last time I see them, it's in Los Angeles at the Universal Amphitheater with my friends and sister. I was surprised to see around 90 percent of the audience in their mid- to late 20s, early 30s. Alejandro tends to sing more ballads while his father sings more ranchero/country music. I wound up with a hoarse voice because I was yelling at Alejandro. He's so good looking. And he can sing."

(I should mention that while Diana is my daughter-in-law, who's married to my son Ken, her inclusion in this chapter is designed to show how her acculturated status keeps her shifting between English and Spanish show business entities.)

James Mendez is an 18-year-old bilingual Hispanic born in San Antonio as are his mother Virginia and his father Juan. What makes his story interesting is that he comes from a show business family. His father is the general sales manager for Hispanic Broadcasting Corp. stations KROM-FM and KCOR-AM/FM, now operating as Univision Radio, part of the Univision Communications empire.

"Although my dad works for HBC it doesn't affect my musical tastes," says James, who straddles two cultures. "Naturally he plays Spanish radio so I grow up listening to it, but now I like hip-hop and rhythm and blues, Tejano and some salsa. Tejano is big in San Antonio. I like its cool rhythm. It's similar to hip-hop." He fills his Tejano needs by tuning to KXTN-FM (another Univision-owned station), KCOR-FM for its contemporary romantic Latin music, and KBBT-FM for hip-hop. At home, he listens to more Spanish radio; in the car, it's the English-language stations. "My dad tends to tune in Spanish radio and television at home. My mother prefers more English." He attends R&B and hip-hop concerts at the Freeman Coliseum or Alamodome, two of the city's main concert venues.

He mostly watches Anglo TV, but "if something on Spanish TV catches my eye, like shows from Televisa that target youth, I'll watch them. I'll also watch some programs on Galavision."

He speaks Spanish when he's around people who only speak it or when he's around his dad. "If I want something really bad, I have to ask my dad in Spanish, or I won't get it. He's really big on us learning our culture." At his high school, it's mainly English that's spoken, but he'll switch to Spanish if a student has trouble with his English. Most of his friends speak two languages. "It's a big advantage because you can talk to more people and see how some are different. It's very cool. Being bilingual also opens the door for job opportunities." James works several late afternoon hours at KMOR/KCOR putting music commercials, or "I.D.s" in order for airing. He also works at KBBT on Sundays handling control room panel functions.

Clemencia Tafur is a 56-year-old Bogotá, Colombia, native living in Phoenix for 22 years who strongly asserts, "I don't like Spanish television because the telenovelas are boring. There's more interesting things to do than watch people's terrible life. I have friends from Colombia who like the telenovelas and ask me why I don't watch them."

Clemencia is a teacher's aide in a kindergarten class in a Phoenix public school. Her husband Mario is a psychiatrist. They've taken a circuitous route to get to Phoenix, initially going to St. Louis where Mario does his internship, then to Topeka, Kansas, where he works at the Menninger Clinic for four years and then practices psychiatry there for six years. They have three sons. Mario Jr., 31, is an attorney in Los Angeles for Amnesty International; Joseph, 28, is in his fourth year of medical school in San Diego, and Camilo, 27, is a teacher in Albuquerque. "Camilo," Clemencia says with a chuckle, "is more a gringo because he's more American in his ways." Clemencia says she self-taught herself English here in the States. "I never took any classes."

Clemencia favors classical music, which she initially listens to in Colombia and then in her new country on the radio and on CDs. "I don't listen to Spanish radio because I don't like the music. I only watch Spanish TV for the news." While she says she heard about the Latin Grammys being broadcast on CBS, she didn't watch the show "because I don't watch too much TV. I read and go to bed early."

The exploding Hispanic population impacts the Phoenix public school system and, of course, Clemencia, who is in her seventh year as a teacher's aid. "In our school, more than 300 of 800 children in grades kindergarten through the sixth grade are Hispanic. A lot are newcomers. They stay here, disappear, and then come back. We don't know where they go. My advantage to being bilingual is I can help the children who speak Spanish with their English. The state used to have bilingual education; now it's only English."

At school, she'll speak Spanish to four co-workers, one from Peru and Paraguay and two who are Mexican-Americans.

Mayitza Frederick's burning desire as a teenager in CD. Obregon, Mexico, in the state of Sonora, is to learn English and find a better life in the U.S. So 18 years ago, when she was 15, she moves by herself to Phoenix, "a jump across the border from Mexico. Being a second language learner and a Mexican, I didn't feel welcome," she admits. While taking English lessons in school, she reveals, "she wants to only have Anglo friends and assimilate fast." Her perseverance pays off when she becomes a first grade teacher in Phoenix, a city in which she has relatives.

"This country has given me so much. I crumbled inside on September 11. I feel this is my country now," she proudly informs me. "I obviously love Mexico and my family who's still there, so when I really miss them, I switch to *Amor*, the Spanish radio station which plays the regional Mexican music I grow up with. It takes me back to when I'm with my four brothers and four sisters. I feel like I'm close to my family when I'm listening to that music."

Mayitza, 33, and her husband Mark, 29, who works for a financial company, have a 14-month-old son, Michael. She watches *Elmo* with her son on Anglo TV, as well as the news and several sitcoms. "During the summer when school's out, I get into the Mexican soaps totally, and when my mom comes to visit, we watch Spanish TV together." Linguistically, there's a cultural divide. "I do speak English to my son, but not as much as I speak Spanish, and I speak English to Mark, who is Anglo. I want Michael to grow up bilingual. I feel my husband is the model for English conversation and I'm the model for Spanish conversation."

She's really become Americanized, listening to radio stations *Power 92* which plays pop music, and *The Zone*, which offers the Dave Matthews Band and other rock groups. When I ask her the call letters of the radio stations, she doesn't know them, only their slogans, a situation I encounter in chatting with other Hispanics. The first band Maritza sees when she comes to Phoenix in 1985 is U2. "I couldn't understand what Bono is saying, even though he comes across with such emotion. I loved the music, and since I come from a little town, I don't have many opportunities to see live shows. I did attend two shows in a baseball stadium to see Menudo when I was 12 and Timbiriche when I was 13."

There's a period during her early years in Phoenix, up until she's 20, when she'd be listening to Spanish radio in her car and "when I got to a red light, I'd switch to an English station." Why the switch? "Because I didn't want people around me to know I was listening to a Spanish station. Once I gained more esteem, I didn't care. Now I speak Spanish to my son in the Target store and I'm not embarrassed anymore because I see a lot of Hispanics everywhere I go in Phoenix." Eighty percent of her students are Hispanics, mostly from Mexico. "I started this year with 20 Hispanic students, the lowest number I've had in years. Last year I had 25 Hispanic students. I average two from Mexico who can't speak any English at all. I've lost several students. They move; they're a very mobile community."

Elva Chavez is a 44-year-old native of the state of Colima, Mexico, who's been in this country for 25 years, the last eight in the Chapel Hill area of North Carolina, where she does translations for companies whose clients include non-English speaking Hispanics. The day I call to speak with her, things are not going well. Yesterday, a 7.8 earthquake shook the state of Colima where her family lives. Twenty-nine people die and 200 are injured. Her family is spared any injury. She's also got such a bad cold that she can't talk, so her 12-year-old daughter Dennise listens to my questions, repeats them to her mother in Spanish and gives me her response in English. Elva and husband Miguel, also 44, initially move to Michigan where for 12 years they work on farms, then move to Okeechobee, Florida, where they both work in the orange groves for five years before moving to Graham, North Carolina. Elva and Miguel both have family living in the state. The two are now living apart, with Miguel back in Mexico. They have six children, three girls, and three boys. Dennise and her two sisters, Jasmine, 13 and Sulema, seven, live with their mom, while her brothers live in Florida, Ardian in Orlando, and Miguel and Alexandro in Saint Cloud. Of Elva's 12 brothers and sisters, four live in North Carolina and four in Florida.

Elva says she learned English by watching soap operas. She watches Univision and buys Mexican CDs rather than listening to Spanish radio. She grows up listening to the Beatles and other successful Anglo pop bands.

Elva speaks Spanish and English. "When mom makes a mistake in English, we correct her," says Dennise. While Elva listens to rock music, Dennise listens to R&B and rap stations. With her Spanish friends, Dennise speaks Spanglish, the combination of Spanish and English expressions. Otherwise, it's English for Anglo friends. Dennise enjoys the Spanish telenovelas as well as sitcoms on general market stations.

One of the locales in which I personally discover a growing Hispanic community is the state of Hawaii, a place I've visited regularly since 1968 on both business and vacation trips. What I find fascinating about Hawaii is the melding of races comprising its population: native Hawaiians whose ancestors are Polynesian, Samoan, Chinese, Japanese, Korean, Vietnamese, Caucasian, and African American. Intermarriage creates a unique cultural collage, a situation I first learned about in the pages of the old *Look* magazine while living in New York. Hawaii seemed an impossible dream far away from the wintry environs of New York. It's only when I move to California that I'm within striking distance of this exotic locale.

I have no knowledge of there being a quiet Hispanic presence in the state, starting with the arrival of the first Puerto Rican migrants to work in the sugar fields in 1900 and 1921. The first two groups number around 10,000 people, brought to the Islands by the Hawaiian Sugar Planters Association to fill the needs for field hands when laws mandate a reduction in the number of workers coming from Asia.

I never encounter any Hispanics on the streets of Honolulu or on the outer islands in all the years I spend time in Hawaii. And in writing about the Hawaiian entertainment industry, no one ever mentions anything about a Hispanic presence. That changes one typically warm and sunny day in May of 2001 as I'm walking along the beachfront in Waikiki and spot a group of men sitting under a tree chatting enthusiastically in Spanish and watching girls in their bikinis stride by-Ole! The sounds of their voices speaking a language I don't associate with the Aloha State catches me off guard and alerts me to something significant occurring within the state's polyglot composition.

One year later, when I start research for this book, a Honolulu friend, Stu Glauberman, steers me to an online Hawaii Hispanic newspaper, and then I uncover three Latin radio programs, a network of venues offering Latin dances, and a local label that records homegrown Latin artists all feeding a population swelling with new arrivals from Mexico. Jose Villa, editor and publisher of the eight-year-old *Hawaii Hispanic News*, cites the 2000 U.S. Census figure of 87,699 Hispanics in Hawaii out of the state's population of 1,211,537, excluding illegals. "We know there are also a large number of undocumented people from Mexico, El Salvador, and Guatemala," adds the host of the paper's weekly public affairs radio show on KWAI-AM.

The majority of Hispanics are on the island of Oahu, where the state capitol of Honolulu is situated, along with pockets on the islands of Hawaii, Maui, and Kauai. In the Census breakout by island, Oahu's total population is 876,156, of which 58,729 are Hispanics; out of the Big Island of Hawaii's 148,677 residents, 14,111 are Hispanics; of Maui's 128,241 residents, 10,056 are Hispanics; and of Kauai's 58,463 population, 4,803 are Hispanics. By genre, Puerto Ricans total statewide 30,005, followed by 19,820 Mexicans. Lumping all other Latinos, except Cubans, into one category produces a total of 37,163, while the standalone Cuban community totals 711 persons.

By 2003, the total resident population by island and county of the same name are all on the rise. The state's total population is now 1,257,608, of which Oahu claims 902,704, Hawaii 158,423,

Maui 135,734, and Kauai 60,747. For this interim report, there are no ethnic breakouts to indicate whether the Latino community is also increasing.

Hispanics may be found working in the hotel, construction, and agricultural industries. In fact, while vacationing on the Big Island of Hawaii in 2004, my wife Bonnie and I are served dinner at the Four Seasons Hualalai Resort by Juan Carlos Kennedy, who says he's from Cabo San Lucas, Mexico, and has been living and working at the hotel for five-and-a-half years. He indicates other Hispanics work at the hotel and he feels isolated from his Hispanic roots because he doesn't have easy access to any Spanish radio or TV on this island, and he's not into listening to Mexican music on CD.

Susana Ho, who works with the 10-year-old Hawaii Hispanic Chamber of Commerce, believes the Census figures for Hawaiian Hispanics aren't accurate. "It's more like 100,000 with the undocumented and the military," she says. "We're also seeing Argentinean arrivals besides Mexicans. Hispanics now comprise 7.2 percent of the total population." Ho's cross-cultural background is one-quarter Hispanic and three-quarters Chinese, emphasizing the state's quilt work-type of citizenry.

Hawaii's key local label, which adds Latin music to its repertoire of Hawaiian, reggae, and world music is Quiet Storm and its president is John Iervolino. Born in the Bronx, New York, where his family is in construction, he moves to Hawaii in 1983 where he gets into the same business and meets his future wife Debra, whose lineage reads like a mini-United Nations: "Puerto Rican, Portuguese, Hawaiian, Japanese, Spanish, English, French, and Indian." In 1999, the two attend a Puerto Rican Centennial celebratory event at a local mall where Grupo Lelolai is performing for several thousand people.

"I thought to myself, 'is anyone recording Hispanic music in Hawaii?' I found out nobody is, so I decide to get into the field, using money from my construction work," says Iervolino. The label's inaugural Latin release is *Salsa from Hawaii*, which features six acts, including the state's top Latin attraction, bandleader/percussionist/

vocalist Rolando Sanchez and Salsa Hawaii. The LP focuses on music from Puerto Rico, performed primarily by local Puerto Rican groups Latin Fire, Second Time Around, and El Leo, The Jarican Express, while military personnel from Puerto Rico comprise Orquestra SalsAloha and Grupo Lelolai. Nicaraguan-born Sanchez, who comes to the islands in the early '80s from his home in San Francisco and forms his band in 1988, is also prominently featured.

Sanchez and Iervolino co-produce the recording, which had its high-point professional moments. Of course, New York salsa bands don't shout "aloha" the way Sanchez does on his track *Salsa*, one of four by the band on the album. Latin Fire and Second Time Around incorporate elements of traditional jibaro or Puerto Rican folk music in their arrangements. Their Japanese co-workers named the percussive sound "katchi-katchi" for its scratchy guiro sound and for the legend of Kachi Kachi Yama, an otter who creates fire on Mount Fuji by striking sticks together. El Leo, The Jarican Express offers a rap ditty, *La Boringue Rap*, in English above a reggae beat, saluting Puerto Rico in lyrics that proclaim, "Puerto Ricans and Hawaiians in the house."

Based on favorable reaction to the initial Latin release, Iervolino says he's going to record a *Salsa from Hawaii* volume 2 featuring Son Caribe, a popular Waikiki band, organized by two former members of Rolando Sanchez's Salsa Hawaii ensemble, trumpeter Eddie Ortiz, and vocalist Cynthia Romero. "I was with the group for three years, Cynthia for four years. We formed Son Caribe two years ago and it has five permanent members," Ortiz tells me, noting the others are multi-instrumentalist/vocalists Arvin Lucio, Jerry Rivera and vocalist Frankie Ramirez. "I heard them play at Rumours on a Tuesday night," notes Iervolino. The second volume, the self-titled *Son Caribe Salsa from Hawaii II* appears in June of 2004. Wayne Harada, the *Honolulu Advertiser*'s entertainment editor, cites the mixing of vocals with seductive brass and the rhythms of Puerto Rico, Cuba, and Brazil is "like going to Latin America without boarding the plane."

When I listen to the album, several elements pop out: the varying styles of salsa, merengue, cha cha cha, and Puerto Rico's bachata. Several of the tunes sport English lyrics. The quintet's sound is tight and catchy, especially *La Negra Tiene Tumbao* with its Spanish rapping, vocal harmonies, and pulsating rhythm, and two other infectiously pulsating tracks, *Ella Fue* (*She Was the One*) and *No Speaki Spanish*. This combination of ingredients proves that being on an island in the Pacific 2,500 miles from the Mainland is not a deterrent to creating authentic Latin music.

Two months later, Iervolino releases the album, *Moemoelutionary Music*, a blending of Island rhythms with reggae, soul, and world beat influences featuring the Big Island septet Moemoea.

Nancy Ortiz, a Latin radio show host who operates Alma Latino Productions, which books Hispanic acts including Son Caribe, brings son Caribe to the Iervolino's attention. She gives John and Debra tickets to one of its performances, motivating the duo to think about recording the band. Notes Ortiz: "We play a variety of styles including salsa, merengue, cha cha, bachatas, mambo, and Latin pop. Sometimes when we play at corporate conventions we play contemporary and Top 40 music as well." Although its main venue is the Espirit nightclub in the Sheraton Waikiki Hotel, the quintet plays resort hotels and conventions throughout the state.

While the number of Hispanics continues to rise around the state, Iervolino faces hurdles in a tight economy. "The Hispanic community is a divided community and hard to work with because of cultural differences," says Iervolino, adding he can't find any good Mexican groups to record. "The problem with the Latin community is while it's rich culturally, it's poor economically."

Sanchez gears his music to the Puerto Rican community when he's doing shows in clubs and hotels. A large percentage is military personnel who stay two to three years and compliment second- and third-generation Hawaiian-Puerto Ricans. A working musician in San Francisco, he says after visiting his sister here in 1984, he decides a change of lifestyle and scenery is appropriate. So he moves, gains a foothold in the local music scene as the leader of a Latin band that records for several labels, plays local venues, and appears with touring acts ranging from Michael Franks to Tito Puente, Sheila E., and Sting, he points out.

"When I came here, I was one of the first non-Puerto Rican musicians to promote Latin music at the hotels in Waikiki. I took the music out of the barrio and into the city." In his photos he looks like Marc Anthony, and when I mention this to him, he replies jokingly: "He looks like me. I even started wearing dark glasses." What does salsa mean in Hawaii? "It's a combination of Afro-Cuban, merengue, cha cha, and salsa from Puerto Rico." Fourteen years ago he begins producing Latin music events, capped by the annual Latin American Music Festival of Hawaii, which takes place in September. Club and hotel budgets for Latin bands per night run in the $350—$500 range for the entire ensemble, Sanchez says. "It used to be $100 a man." In order to attract tourists and other non-Hispanics, his shows are bilingual. He is arguably the busiest Latin musician in the state, working shows on the outer islands as well as in Honolulu. With salsa the "flavor of the month," dance instructors teaching the right moves become a cottage industry.

Sanchez initially hosts a Latin music show *La Onda Latina*, on KTUH-FM, on Saturdays from noon to 3 p.m. The program runs three years and ends in 1999. Long before him, and still on the air, are two ladies, Nancy Ortiz and Audrey Rocha Reed, pioneers in Latin radio on non-Latin radio stations. Ortiz was born and raised in Hawaii of Hawaiian parents who arrive in the state during the 1900 to 1901 migration. She starts in radio in the 1970s, working 15 years at KISA-AM and 10 at KHPR-FM and for the last three years is heard on KWAI-AM, the latest home for her three-hour *Alma Latina* show. "I started doing five minutes on Puerto Rico every Saturday on KISA," she explains. "Then I co-hosted a six-hour show on Saturday mornings, first with Jimmy Carvalho, who has a heart attack and is replaced by Audrey Reed, who is now on Maui and doing her own show."

Ortiz plays salsa, merengue, tipica (a Puerto Rican folkloric style), and local Puerto Rican bands. While her Alma Latino Productions promotes concerts, it also secures Puerto Rican bands for Saturday night appearances at the club C'est La Vie, and lines up talent for the visiting Univision show *Caliente*, which tapes four segments in the state. Sanchez and Salsa Hawaii are among the groups booked, along with dancers and models.

Reed, born and raised on Maui, plays the music of Portugal on KISA in Honolulu from 1974 through '82 on her *Nancy's Corner* segment, teamed with Ortiz's *Alma Latina*. After 20 years in Honolulu she moves back to Maui and begins *Sounds of Portugal and the Latin World* on KMVI-AM, which runs for 12 years before the station is sold to KNUI-AM, the all-Hawaiian music station, several years later. For the past two-and-a-half years KNUI airs her show Sundays from 8:30 to 11 p.m. "There are so many ethnic groups here, the music appeals to a broad base," she says, noting: "Mexicans begin arriving on Maui five years ago. Now we're seeing a lot of Brazilians who speak Portuguese. There are clubs for Mexican and Guatemalans in Lahaina, Kihei, Wailuku, and Kahului," all key regions where tourists and locals mingle.

Univision, the leading Spanish-language TV network, entered the market in 1999, but is not widely available. While there are Asian-language local TV stations appealing to this segment of the population, there are no local Latin-themed outlets. The radio stations, which do offer time for Hispanic programs, are generally not the top-rated nor do they have strong signals. But word gets around so devotees know where to tune in. Frankie Villalobos hosts a music show Sundays on Honolulu's KNDI-AM from 3:30 to 5:30 p.m. Ray Cruz's *Sabor Tropical*, on KHPR-FM Saturdays from 5 to 8 p.m., is in its 10th year and has expanded from spinning salsa in the '60s and '70s to encompass Afro-Cuban Latin jazz. Of all the people who host Latin radio shows and hold fulltime jobs, Cruz has the most interesting: he's a flight attendant with United. He's been with the airline since 1979, first in Chicago, then in Denver, "and when I get tired of the snow, my girlfriend suggests we move to Hawaii and that's what we did in 1988."

Cruz explains that when he plays salsa music with Spanish lyrics, "it's limiting to non-Hispanics. When I play Afro-Cuban Latin jazz, I don't have any language problem and the music can be appreciated by everybody." He's played Rolando Sanchez's salsa album, which has Spanish lyrics as part of the music mix, during the first half of the program.

Cruz rates the professionalism of local Puerto Rican bands as "good, considering they don't have any role models here. The guys in the military from Puerto Rico take up the music as a hobby more or less, but they're not accomplished musicians. Rolando's band is the best because he's been here the longest and is a professional." On the jazz portion of his show he plays Tito Puente, Machito, Cal Tjader, Mongo Santamaria, Ray Barretto, Alejandro "Alex" Acuña, Poncho Sanchez, and Cuban bands Los Van Van and Irakere.

Honolulu's Latin music scene consists of various venues offering entertainment different nights of the week, live or with DJs playing discs. A major gathering is the annual Puerto Rican Salsathon. One fixture on the circuit is Augie Rey Fernandez, whose Cuban-Puerto Rican roots are reflected in his music at the various Waikiki clubs in which he appears. Salsa clubs include Planet Hollywood, Pipeline Cafe, Players Sports Bar, Rumours (Ala Moana Hotel), Wonder Lounge (W Hotel), Espirit Lanai (Sheraton Waikiki Hotel), Mambo Café, Zanzabar, Amerasia, Rainbow Lounge, Mai Tai Bar (Royal Hawaiian Hotel), Las Palmas Restaurant, and the Emporium Lounge. When Ray Cruz is not flying, or doing his radio show, he's one of the Latin DJs Saturday nights at the Café Sistina, playing records by Tito Puente, Johnny Pacheco, Celia Cruz, Grupo Niche, and La Sonora Carruseles. Joining the club list in May of 2005 is Bamboleo in the Spada bar and restaurant's outdoor courtyard, which livens up the deserted downtown financial district with hot-recorded salsa, mambo, and merengue rhythms Friday and Saturday from 9 p.m. to 2 a.m.

Salsa music attracts local devotees to the Dia De San Juan Puerto Rican Cultural and Salsa Festival and Salsathon. In 2004, the fourth annual bash in Honolulu at the McCoy Pavilion in Alan Moana Beach Park in June features local bands Son Caribe, Batacumbele, El Conjunto Tropical, and Wally Rita and his Latin Amigos, as well as several salsa DJs keeping the pace hot and sultry.

Alan J. Fernandez is not in show business, but he encounters musicians in his work. He lives on the island of Lanai and is the food and beverage manager at the Lodge At Koele, which features an artist-in-residence program and is the upscale sister hotel to the oceanfront Manele Bay Hotel. His background is typical of the state's multiple ethnicities. "My dad is half Chinese and Portuguese. My grandfather was born in Argentina, his father was born in Spain." Born in Honolulu 52 years ago, he toils in the hotel industry before moving to Lanai 13 years ago when the Lodge opens inland from the Manele Bay Hotel, both resorts owned by Castle & Cooke Resorts. He has nine brothers and four sisters from his parent's two marriages. As a result of both parents remarrying, he takes his paternal grandfather's last name. Alan himself has been married twice and has three children, his son Branson is nine and lives on Lanai while his two other offspring, Shane, 33, and Margaret, 30, both live on Oahu. He doesn't listen to any Spanish media, and since he works nights, he only listens to Spanish CDs, including Arturo Sandoval's *Trumpet Evolution.* "I discovered him when he came to the Lodge with his band to perform," says Fernandez. Other Latin acts appearing as part of the artist-in-residence program are Four Amigos, Antonio Carlos Jobim, Laurindo Almeida, and Cerro Negro, whose CD he also enjoys.

Growing up in Honolulu he listens to Spanish music on the radio. "I hear a lot of Puerto Rican music. My grandfather Joseph sang Spanish songs like *Cielito Lindo*, which Tito Guízar made famous." When he needed to hear Spanish close-up, his family on the Big Island and in Honolulu provide the cultural connection. As for his last name, "I'm asked about it a lot," he says. "I don't mind reminiscing; I love trivia."

Although he's not Hispanic, Honolulu-based veteran concert promoter Tom Moffatt is an integral link to bringing a plethora of Hispanic stars to the islands. So his views of Latin entertainment in the Aloha State carry weight. In addition to bringing in the biggest names in show business, from Elvis Presley to the Rolling Stones to Michael Jackson, Moffatt also presents Hispanic talent, new or established, which he senses will be accepted by local audiences. In the lexicon of show business, if there's a "buzz" pulsating around their persona on the Mainland, he'll gamble that buzz will work in Hawaii as well.

Since 1952, when he leaves frigid Detroit for the warmth of Hawaii and begins his dual career, first as a rock 'n' roll disc jockey on a number of stations and then as a concert promoter—eventually handling both jobs simultaneously—Moffatt is the Man most artists work with in Hawaii. "The first Hispanic act I introduce is Richie Valens in 1958. I also present Pérez Prado in the late '50s," he recalls as we chat in the bar of the Kahala Mandarin Oriental Hotel, the resort of choice for Mainland show business luminaries in the spotlight or in the executive offices.

His other attractions include Christina Aguilera, Linda Ronstadt, Gloria Estefan, Julio Iglesias, Menudo, Santana, and tenor José Carreras. "Julio is the first major Spanish act I book at the beginning of his career in the early '80s in the Blaisdell Concert Hall for one night. I'm very concerned because people in Hawaii didn't know him." But once powerful KGMB-AM morning radio personality Hal "Akuhead" Lewis starts playing his record, *Amor, Amor*, Moffatt says, "he becomes well-known and we sell out the first show and add a second. In 1984, I bring him back when the single *To All the Girls I've Loved before* becomes a hit and it's a lot easier to sell tickets for his shows at the Sheraton Waikiki Hotel's Hawaii Ballroom and the Blaisdell Arena for two nights."

Gloria Estefan is another story that proves that timing is everything. "I book her into the Blaisdell Arena in 1987 when she's with the Miami Sound Machine, which has the top billing. She isn't that well known yet. But I have faith in the group because it's getting some radio play. They're singing mostly in English with some

Spanish. It's a gamble that doesn't pay off. The show isn't a sellout and loses money. The second time in 1988 I bring her to Guam and then the Waikiki Shell. She's just broken out as Gloria Estefan and the Miami Sound Machine. I'm a little concerned since we're promoting the show as the Miami Sound Machine and all of a sudden it's Gloria Estefan and the Sound Machine, but it works.

"The third time I book her is after she recovers from her tragic car accident, which almost leaves her paralyzed in 1990. After seeing her perform in Puerto Rico, I decide to put her in Aloha Stadium, where I'd recently presented Michael Jackson. A concerned representative from CBS Records comes to see me and asks where I'm going to put her. I say 'Aloha Stadium,' and the record company rep says, 'I don't think so. That won't work.' I just have a feeling that since she's recovered from the accident and is on a concert tour it would work. The most people you can get in the stadium for a concert is 30,000 plus, depending on the size of the stage. We did over 25,000 for Gloria."

With Hawaii's Hispanic population on the rise, isn't there a place for Hispanic shows? "The problem is you've got to go with the local audience. I call the visitor audience 'gravy.'" One local group that is really Hawaii's first partial Hispanic breakout act is Cecilio (Rodriguez) and (Henry) Kapono. Their sweet harmonies in English and Hawaiian, which blend in like gentle ocean breezes with their guitar -dominated soft folk rock material, gains acceptance among locals.

It also appeals to Columbia Records, which has a sales office in Honolulu, and when its local reps start talking up this duo known as C&K, the company senses crossover potential across the wide Pacific Ocean, signs the act, and promotes its two albums and singles on the Mainland. While I'm in Honolulu in 1973 working on a Hawaii report for *Billboard*, people in the local record and radio industries are talking up Cecilio and Kapono as Hawaii's hot act. So when Moffatt books them for the first time into the outdoor Waikiki Shell, which is a sellout and indicates how popular they are, I'm in the audience anticipating their performance under threatening skies.

Rain seems imminent. Fortunately I'm with a Columbia Records promotion man who conveniently brings along an umbrella. A little while after the concert begins, it starts pouring. I'm sitting under the umbrella, other people are opening theirs, the duo is singing as if nothing's happening, and nobody moves. Granted it is Hawaii and a warm night, but it's coming down really hard, yet the audience remains fixed on their local favorites.

Over a four-year span, Moffatt stages seven dates with C&K, including two sellouts at the Blaisdell Center in addition to the Waikiki Shell. When C&K appear on the Mainland, they gain a major promotional break by touring with the Beach Boys. In ensuing years the duo goes its separate ways but reunites for special occasions. One such event occurs in September 2002 on the Big Island, where Bonnie and I are vacationing. I notice they're appearing along with a long list of other popular Hawaiian music acts as part of the Hilton Waikoloa Village's first-ever month-long celebration of Hawaiian music, culture, and food. They are the only act with a Hispanic heritage on the bill. Rodriguez strikes out on his own again in 2004 with the release on HanaOla of *Sweet Surprise*, which includes the Latin-flavored *Liliana* and *Ensenada* among the 14 tracks.

According to the Census, about 25 percent of Hawaii's residents consider English their second language. The state ranks fifth in the nation in terms of non-English speakers behind California, New Mexico, Texas, and New York. Spanish comes in fifth here among languages after Pacific Island, Tagalog, Japanese, and Chinese. More Spanish is spoken than Korean, which is very telling about how the state's population is changing.

Articles

"Salsa Under The Stars Lures Dancers Downtown." Honolulu Advertiser, Aug. 5, 2005

"'Sweet Surprise,' Teen Tunes, Spooky Tales Offer Enjoyment." Honolulu Advertiser, Oct. 31, 2004

"Hot Stuff At The Salsa-Thon." Honolulu Advertiser." June 25, 2004

"Salsa, Hula Songs Set Mood For Dancing." Honolulu Advertiser, June

27, 2004

"Weekend Scene." Honolulu Star-Bulletin, June 28, 2004

"Report Shows How Racial Identities Affect Latinos." Los Angeles Times, July 11, 2003

"Kohala Coast Cultural Festival Is Planned." West Hawaii Today, Aug. 18, 2002

"After Hours, Café Sistina A Stage For Salsa Dancers." Honolulu Advertiser, June 7, 2002

"Spice Of Life". Hana Hou Hawaiian Airlines Magazine, April/May, 2002

"Hispanic TV Shoot Coming." Honolulu Advertiser, Jan. 16, 2002

"Hot Salsa: It's Music And Dance With Heat." Honolulu Advertiser, Jan. 11, 2002

Chapter 11
CAPITULO 11

Artistic Expressions
EXPRESIONES ARTISTICAS

Artists implant their distinct creative imprimatur on their work. How are these avatars of the public's ever-changing tastes dealing with the Hispanic cultural explosion within the 50 states? Are they seeking new avenues of expression? Are they being impacted by the expanding universe for their art? Getting inside their exulted world is my challenge. Here are the responses from a representative array of performers, including some remarkable stories of courage and determination in the face of life-threatening illnesses.

George Lopez seems to be everywhere...on ABC with his eponymous weekly hit comedy series, on CBS hosting the Latin Grammy Awards three years in a row, strolling the stage alone during his Showtime comedy specials, bringing laughter to cross-cultural audiences during a national concert tour, recording hit comedy albums, making high rollers forget their losses during a stint at the Las Vegas Hilton, popping up on the big screen in a series of films, hosting a breakthrough morning radio show in Los Angeles, even testifying as a defense witness at the Michael Jackson trial in Santa Maria, California. George Lopez at age 44 is currently the hottest comic in show business who happens to be Hispanic, with the skills to keep both English and Spanish speakers tuned to his brand of cultural comedy which smartly avoids any walls of separation and exclusion.

I first meet George at an Emmy Party in 2004 and get to chat with him on the phone during a break from taping his weekly TV series several months later in 2005. His professional life is built around the strong belief about not putting restrictions on oneself.

His credits being "the right guy at the right time, living the right type of life and running parallel with the explosion of Latinos in this country" undeniably helps boost his career. "Other guys have tried with less success," he says. "You can't correct all the ills you feel America has done to Latinos. The only way to change things is to not to become a preacher but to stay funny. My priority was to be funny in the clubs and not to change that when I got on TV. I just wanted to stay funny. When I was a kid I was funny even though I was very shy, but I always had something funny to say around guys I was comfortable with. I wanted to be a comedian as a career because of seeing Freddie Prinze when I was 11 years old. I became a professional comedian in 1979 when I was 18 and started to work at the Comedy Store in Los Angeles." George is a native of Los Angeles who grows up in the Mission Hills community within the sprawling San Fernando Valley, with its cauldron mixture of Latinos, Anglos, and other cultures.

He admits that while he dreams of being a success in show business, he doesn't believe it can happen. "For Mexican American and African American kids it's a dream, when for white kids it's a goal. The day I turn 40 I'm on the radio on KCMG-FM, Mega 92.3 in Los Angeles and I look in the mirror, and this is before the TV show, and it really dawns on me I've achieved my goal which I used to call a dream. And I thought I'm short-sighting myself for calling it a dream and not a goal." Then adding additional philosophical spin to our conversation, the 43-year-old megastar says: "If there's anything to put in the book, it's that we set limitations on ourselves which we should stop doing, like I've done. The minute I let those things go and realized there is nobody really responsible for my success or failure but myself, my career starts to take off."

He doesn't believe being Hispanic at a time of media consciousness about the importance of the growing Hispanic community plays a role in the early stages of his 25-year show business career. "The first thing is you have to be good, and being Mexican is great. But if I wasn't funny and Mexican I wouldn't be here. It's all about being prepared. If you have two actors and one's Mexican and he's not prepared, he's going to lose the part to a white dude who is prepared, and that's got nothing to do with being Mexican."

When I ask if he encounters any problems being Hispanic at the start of his stand-up career, he replies: "I was doing material that nobody really wanted to hear. Now here's the funny part. Since nobody wanted to hear what I was talking about, they didn't get it. They weren't listening; they were only seeing. And yet when I got to the level where American saw what I was doing on television, they got it."

George's comedy schtick brings him to the attention of Clear Channel Communications, the nation's leading radio company, which hires him on November 27, 2000, to do the morning drivetime show on its oldies rock station, KCMG-FM (later called KHHT), the first Hispanic to ever host a morning program on an English-language station in L.A., the nation's leading Spanish radio market. Ten months later in September of 2001, a consultant switches the station to a modern soul format hosted by a series of short-lived DJs including Sinbad the comic. "I actually got fired for showing up every day and moving the station from No. 22 to No. 9, and they thought it had gone as far as it could," George tells me, obviously still smarting from the decision: "I don't understand. If you're doing a good job, why do they kick you out?"

His comedy routines translate easily onto recordings, *Right Now Right Now* in 2001 and *Team Leader* in 2003, which contains a parential advisory about explicit content and wins a 2004 regular Grammy best comedy nomination. The recording from the Ice House in Pasadena, California, dissects the worlds and words of the Chicano and Mexican cultures in Southern California, with more expansive use of Spanish words that will be used in the TV series and curse words, which are never allowed on the broadcast network. References to his powerful grandmother figure do transfer to the TV show as a key storyline inspiration. What's the difference in doing a comedy album which relies exclusively on spoken material and doing a concert where movements and facial expressions can enhance the words? The difference, he explains, "is with the album I don't use words that don't need to be there, so it's like listening to old-time serials on the radio. The words I use can make you feel like you're at the concert. I'm not a visual comedian like someone who uses props, I'm a real wordsmith-type dude." He says he uses Spanglish, the mixture of Spanish and English words in the same sentence, on the records and in his act; it's something he's heard growing up and it works in his style of storytelling.

Listening to the album I realize is like being given a pass into George's world, albeit one in which he finds humor, like his routines on listening to unintelligible English by an order taker at Jack In the Box, or the way Latinos rely on disposable cameras for major events, or how dogs owned by Hispanics live a different kind of life, or how homespun are Hispanic weddings taking place in someone's back yard.

George owes his being signed to his ABC series to being seen by actress Sandra Bullock at the Improv comedy club in Brea California, in August of 2000. At that time, she and her partner Jonathan Komack Martin are looking to develop a TV show with a Hispanic theme, and are searching for a lead actor. According to George's manager Ron DeBlasio, Jonathan's father is the producer of *Chico and the Man*, the hit 1970s TV series starring Freddie Prinze, whom DeBlasio represents at that time, and the comic George says inspires him to go into comedy.

Recalls DeBlasio: "In August of 2001 we started our development meetings with Sandra and Peter Roth of Warner Bros. and in September with Stu Bloomberg, the head of programming at ABC after both companies see George at the Ice House that summer. Sandra has several ideas for the show including a Latin version of the hit CBS series *Beverly Hillbillies*. George tells her stories about his life and they decide to use this material and his grandmother as the model for the mother in the show. George's talent agency, CAA (Creative Artists Agency) tells us the networks won't buy the show because it's too Latino and they're looking for other kinds of comedy." Nevertheless, "Warner Bros. says they love him and an ABC rep says, 'I want this.' So we don't have to shop the show around to the other networks.

"Around this time, Clear Channel decides to shake up things at the radio station and go more in the direction of hip-hop and older R&B classics and feel they need another face to host the show rather than George. They want him to do a weekend Top 40 show. As we're walking out of the building in Burbank, they're removing his photo from the lobby and George says to me, 'What do you think of this?' I said, 'our deal is for morning radio. This is trouble. We're sitting out our contract.' The Clear Channel dismissal is a great blessing because it allows us to start working on the Warner Bros. show. In September, ABC tells Warner Bros. it wants six episodes of the show for January of 2002. There's not a lot of time to develop six episodes so Warner Bros. says it'll do four. In TV land, that's pretty fast." George, Bruce Helford and Robert Borden create the show, with Sandra Bullock and Helford two of its exec producers. In addition to being co-creator and star, George also holds writer and producer positions on the show.

With George playing himself, the first assembly line worker promoted to plant manager, his ensemble cast includes Emiliano Diez, Luis Armand Garcia, Stacey Haglund, Constance Marie, Belita Moreno, Valente Rodriguez, and Trevor Wright, *The George Lopez Show* debuts March 27, 2002, at 8:30 p.m. on Wednesdays and attracts 9 million viewers during its premier season. In its second season starting October 2, 2002, as simply *George Lopez*, running on Fridays at 8 p.m., it averages 10.37 million viewers, and in it's third season starting Septtember 26, 2003, on Tuesdays at 8:30 p.m., it's viewership drops to 7.49 million people. In its fourth season commencing September 28, 2004, and running until May 17, 2005, it remains ensconced on Tuesdays at 8:30, but not with the same high ratings found in earlier seasons-due primarily to its being affected like all the shows up against *American Idol*, the No. 1 show in the nation. During the week of May 9–15, the period when Lopez is the subject of an insightful interview May 12 on ABC's *Primetime Live*, the exposure could be a factor in the show's ratings bouncing up from a low of 80th place with a 4.94 rating to 72nd place with a 5.47 rating. And during the final week of the season, the show rebounds to 40th place with a 6.41 rating. When the season's final standings are tallied, the show winds up in 88th place, according to Nielsen Media Research. The good news is the show is renewed for a fifth season, moving to Wednesday at 8 p.m. where it's followed by *Freddie*, the new Freddie Prinze Jr. comedy, marking the first time two Latino shows air back-to-back and explore the star's Mexican and Puerto Rican heritages. On a historic note, the Lopez show will air its 100th episode during the new season, the first time a Hispanic-themed family show reaches this key level.

Of his TV experience, George says he's never encountered any problems from ABC in his triple role. "Not once have they given me a note about being too Mexican or not Mexican enough. They have not even tried to dissuade me from the way I want to run the show. They have not ever said people aren't going to get it. I've peppered the show with about three percent Spanish words that you only hear from a real Chicano, and ABC has always been supportive of what I do from day one."

Having seen the show, I ask George something I suspect drives the program's acceptance with non-Hispanics as well as with bilingual Hispanics: Is he patterning the show to gain general market acceptance the way Bill Cosby steered his last NBC series rather than aiming expressly at a black audience? "Absolutely," he parries, noting that 65 percent of his audience are Anglos, with the summer reruns building an even larger audience of Caucasians. "In the history of TV," George points out, "there are three shows driven by a person of Latin descent. The first is *I Love Lucy*, in which Desi Arnaz (a Cuban) creates the way we shoot sitcoms today (three cameras in front of a studio audience with no laugh track). Twenty-five years later, there's *Chico and the Man*, starring Freddie Prinze who is Puerto Rican-Hungarian-German, and then there's us, the only show that's ever been led by Mexican Americans." Actually, the first national TV series with a Mexican American cast stars Mexican American comic Paul Rodriguez in the 1984 short-lived ABC primetime series *A.K.A. Pablo* created and written by Norman Lear, which the Smithsonian Institute acknowledges is the first TV show about a Mexican American family airing on mainstream television.

During the Christmas holidays, Lopez stars in the ABC TV movie *Naughty or Nice*, in which he plays a repugnant sports radio show host. Lopez makes the TV show a family affair since his wife Ann is the exec producer. George tells me he and Ann, a Cuban from Ft. Lauderdale, and their almost nine-year-old daughter Mayan, watch his TV series together every week. He savors the idea of family viewing because "it's not going to be on forever, so I want to remember what it was like to watch with my family when the show's in its hey-day."

Lopez's cross-cultural success makes him an excellent host for the Latin Grammys on CBS in 2003 and 2004, where he needs to communicate primarily in both English and then Spanish. He's slated to again host the show in 2005. During his first telecast from Miami, he uses a Spanish expression when discussing Arnold Schwarzenegger who has his eyes on the California governorship which gets bleeped but has the AmericanAirlines Arena audience in an uproar. This incident is covered in Chapter 13, devoted to Miami. The next year he comes out on stage at the Shrine Auditorum in Los Angeles riding a white stallion and wearing a traditional sparkling Mexican charro outfit with a huge sombrero. After dismounting, he chides new California governor Arnold Schwarzenegger's opposition to granting driver's licenses to illegals, noting: "That's the way we gotta get around in Los Angeles since Governor Schwarzenegger took away our driver's licenses." A crude Spanish remark about President Bush is deleted from the program. But most of the time, he's funny and disarming, not irritating.

Lopez's film career is on an ascendancy curve. Having appeared first in *Bread And Roses* for Lionsgate followed by the HBO Film *Real Women Have Curves* in 2002, he plays a teacher in his newest family film, *The Adventures of Shark Boy and Lava Girl in 3-D*, written and directed by Robert Rodriguez for Dimension Films/Columbia Pictures, which unfurls June 10, 2005, and will be followed by *The Richest Man*, a comedy with some dark overtones, for Universal Pictures. He believes the reason Latin actors and actresses are being seen more in this country in films is due to "a groundswell of knowing we can do the job. It's still like putting a toe in the water. You're never going to see parity (with Anglo actors). But look at Eve Mendes in the romantic comedy *Hutch* with Will Smith and Jennifer Lopez, Salma Hayek, and Carmen Diaz, they're all working but because they're beautiful, they don't get counted as Latinas, but there are a lot of them working."

Following his recent concert swing patterned after his *Why Are You Crying* Showtime special which conveniently includes the title of his first book, *Why Are You Crying? My Long Hard Look at Life, Love and Laughter*, he says he's comfortable "settling into talking about the past and dysfunction and family and life. It's not even about the future as much as it's resolving issues of the past and that's where I'm most fertile comedically."

It's his past which causes Lopez to take the witness stand March 28, 2005, to testify about his dealings with a cancer stricken Hispanic youngster and his family at the Michael Jackson child molestation trial in Santa Maria, California. The defense calls him to show the mother is money-hungry and tapping Lopez for finances, so they hope that'll rub off on the son and discredit his testimony. But Lopez will testify all his dealings are with David the father, not Janet the mother.

My wife Bonnie, a senior supervising producer with both *Entertainment Tonight* and its new companion show, *The Insider*, which are covering the trial, and I drive to the Santa Maria courthouse from Los Angeles to observe Lopez and also hear Judge Rodney Melville decide whether to admit previous allegations of sexual misconduct by the accused.

When we arrive in Santa Maria, 163 miles from Los Angeles, the sight we see in front of the courthouse is all too familiar because of the massive television interest. TV mobile units with their circular satellite dishes reflect the national coverage: NBC, CNN, and New England Satellite Systems, are among the bigwigs, plus smaller microwave trucks from the local area, Los Angeles and San Francisco, all ready to go into action later in the day and a mobile unit from KNX, the CBS all-news radio station in Los Angeles, which broadcasts updates throughout the day. A large group of people are lining up to gain the 50 public access tickets to the courtroom based on a lottery outside. They're waiting outside of the white fencing which separates them from the line of fixed television camera positions which stand empty at this hour. The trial attracts a large international horde of print and TV reporters, including NBC and CBS News reporters, with whom we wind up sitting next to in the media section of the courtroom.

The courtroom is packed with spectators, all wearing their yellow passes, many carrying note books. Jackson's lead attorney Thomas Mesereau, Jr. and one of his assistants, Susan Yu, are the first to arrive at 8:05, followed by lead prosecutor and Santa Barbara County District Attorney Tom Sneddon at 8:12, Brian Oxman, the Jackson attorney who's removed on a stretcher last week and taken to a local hospital with a touch of pneumonia, at 8:25 and Judge Melville at 8:40. A female bailiff explains the rules: "no eating, sleeping, smoking or talking, no standing in the aisles, and no individual outbursts of support for either sides. There'll be three breaks: 9:45 for 10 minutes; 11:30 for 15 minutes; and 1:15 through 1:25." There's no lunch break.

Following arguments by the prosecution and defense, Judge Melville rules in favor of District Attorney Sneddon's motion to introduce into evidence testimony of previous alleged sexual offenses and groping of others by Jackson, which the D.A. says shows a pattern of abuse common with pedophiles. Defense attorney Mesereau's arguments that to go back to the 1990s when these alleged incidents take place is "too remote" and will stretch the length of the trial, since each of these instances will be "full-blown trials" within the trial, are rejected by the judge. It's a major victory for the prosecution, which has media pundits calling it the decisive moment in the trial. The judge's ruling is based on a 1995 California law, Section 1108, specifically written to allow into evidence previous charges of sexual misconduct, including those for which no charges were filed.

Following this strongly argued session which begins at 8:40 and concludes at 10:25, without the presence of the jury and Jackson, Judge Melville announces a lengthy break until 11:30 a.m., which affords me an opportunity to observe the pro and con Jackson fans stationed on the other side of the white fences. The crowd is small by comparison to the first week when Jackson busses fans from Los Angeles to bolster his support and provide fodder for the TV cameras. One man, who's a regular Michael booster, shouts at the media, "stop the lies, shut up," followed by "fight Michael fight" despite there being no Michael to flash his familiar V for victory sign. Red or green signs wave in the cold breeze. One proclaims "we support the victim" with a large X drawn through the word "victim" followed by the word "survivors." Another sign proclaims: "we've had enough, Michael's innocent," while an opposition sign heralds: "the glove fits let's convict," a play on words which refers to Jackson's often wearing of gloves and the famous phrase reverberating around the world by O.J. Simpson's lead attorney Johnny L. Cochran, Jr. during his 1994 murder case: "If it doesn't fit, you must acquit," referring to a pair of gloves Simpson fails to squeeze into during the trial. Cochran, 68, who dies of an operable brain tumor at his home in Los Angeles two days after we visit the courtroom, is Jackson's attorney for the 1993 multi-million dollar settlement in the initial molestation allegation. This victim may now appear among the witnesses called to testify because of Judge Melville's ruling this morning.

At 11:20, Michael's mother and father walk slowly down the aisle to their seats in the second row, mom in seat two, father on the aisle. Mom is dressed in a purple suit, her husband in a black suit with white stripes, a black shirt and tie. Suddenly and silently Michael arrives accompanied by one bodyguard and Mesereau. While all the attorneys are dressed in conservative business suits, Michael's court attire consists of a black jacket with a gold crest and red stripe on the right arm, black pants, white shirt, and red and white striped tie. He's back to wearing his customized showy outfits. It's sad to watch this thin 46-year-old former king of music walk by and realize he's in the fight of his bizarre life.

George and Ann his wife of 12 years arrive at 11:30 and are seated in the front row where a female court artist begins sketching him. He's dressed appropriately for his legal appearance. When court is reconvened shortly thereafter, Lopez is called first followed by his wife. Lopez discusses how he meets Gavin Arvizo, the cancer victim and his family in the fall of 1999 when Gavin, his brother and sister all attend the comedy camp operated by the Laugh Factory, a popular comedy club in Hollywood. He notes he meets Janet the mother and the children who travel by bus to the club. "Anybody who rides the bus from East L.A. to Hollywood is a hero to me," he says. Lopez says he works with the youngsters several weekends. Lopez also notes he visits the family at the grandparent's home in El Monte. Mentioning both locations prompts defense attorney Mesereau during his cross examination to ask Lopez whether El Monte is in East L.A. (a prominent Hispanic community), which gives Lopez a chance for some levity in his response. "El Monte is not East L.A. Any Chicano knows better than that. That's Chicano 101."

Lopez also testifies that when Janet tells him Gavin is seriously ill and in the hospital, he visits the cancer-stricken child several times by himself.

In March of 2000, Lopez says Gavin's father David "made it known he was strapped for cash, so I'd give him whatever I had, $20 or $40. Then he asked me to do a fundraiser for Gavin, and it became apparent I was about how Gavin was feeling and David was more interested in the money than his son. I was going to do the fundraiser myself at the Ice House in Pasadena (another popular comedy club). But because of my work with the radio station I fell behind. I received a lot of calls from David asking how much I thought we could raise and I told him I didn't know. He'd even call me while I was on the air, and I told my wife it wasn't a good idea to do the fundraiser." On May 5, 2000, while doing his radio show live from 5 to 10 a.m. from the Acapulco restaurant in El Monte, Lopez says David "approached me aggressively and asked me about the fundraiser. I told him it wasn't going to happen and we had words." It's when Ann testifies that the startling reason for calling off the fundraiser is revealed.

Lopez testifies on one occasion he takes Gavin, who's released from the Kaiser Permanente hospital and in remission from his cancer, his brother and sister and father to the Sherman Oaks Galleria in the San Fernando Valley on a shopping trip and is aware that the father doesn't intervene when the kids ask for several gifts, which he pays for.

On the one occasion that Gavin visits Lopez's home, the entertainer tells the court about "the room we have which is very popular with Mexicans. No one is allowed in, even me. I saw a wallet on the fireplace mantle and it's not mine. It's Gavin's, with his school ID and a $50 bill. When I saw the wallet on the mantle, I thought that was odd because nothing is supposed to be in that room and it was also odd to have $50 in the wallet. So we call Gavin and tell him he left his wallet and we'll send it to him. Sometime later, David tells Jamie Masada (the owner of the Laugh Factory who befriends the family before they meet Lopez and is the one responsible for having Gavin meet Jackson, his idol) that I had taken $300 out of Gavin's wallet. On May 5, I told David he was an extortionist. And I don't use big words like that," which elicits new laughter. "I had no more conversations with David after that day. I later found out Jamie paid him the money. I asked him, 'How could you do that?' and he said he wanted to make amends."

When Ann takes the stand, her testimony both fills in spots and reinforces her husband's sworn statements. She tells the D.A. she met Gavin in the hospital two months after the comedy camp. "I never met his mother, although we had phone conversations. She told me he was gravely ill with a large tumor in his stomach cavity. I was told the mother didn't go to the hospital because she was distressed and couldn't handle it. David would hint they were having financial problems. He said he had taken a leave of absence from his job and was worried about his insurance running out. I also thought it was strange for the kid to have a crisp $50 bill in his wallet with his school ID."

During the time when the fundraiser is being discussed, Ann testifies David "asked continually how much could be raised. I started feeling uneasy and decided I want to test him to be sure his intentions are honorable. So I told him to send us his bills so we can start paying them. He said, 'Aren't I going to get the cash?' He got real agitated. I said the radio station was going to be involved and they needed documentation. He called me a fucking bitch and motherfucking whore and that's when I hung up the phone. I was shaking. I called my husband at the radio station and George was really angry. He decided the fundraiser was off."

Following their testimony, George stops to answer questions for the pool camera whose words and pictures are provided free to all media. Asked the simple question how he felt being in court, George finds another opportunity for some biting levity: "Hispanics are genetically comfortable in court," he answers. "I'm not making a case for the prosecutor or defense. I'm here to tell my story. I knew I had pertinent information about the wallet." He says it's "not uncommon for celebrities to help impoverished families." Asked how he got to the courthouse, he replies with a smile: "Private jet and white limousine." The stretch limo is indeed parked impressively in front of the courthouse, the only prestigious vehicle on the property. And it allows George, Ann, and two of the comic's associates, manager Ron DeBlasio and publicist Marleah Leslie, who have flown up with them, to be whisked away to the Santa Maria airport for the return flight to Los Angeles.

The next evening during E! Entertainment Television re-enactment of the Jackson trial, an actor portrays Lopez and reads his comments from the court transcript. Seeing Lopez in-person on the witness stand and then watching an actor recreate his words, but not his aura, separates the drama of the real courtroom testimony from the tensionless television experience.

Four weeks after he becomes the first show business celebrity to testify at the Jackson trial on March 28, Lopez undergoes a renal kidney transplant at Cedars Sinai Medical Center in Los Angeles April 19. Ann, his Cuban American wife, is the organ donor after both undergo a series of compatibility tests, Ron DeBlasio, George's manager tells me two weeks later. Remarkably, the tests show Ann is a complete match, a condition not always true between husbands and wives. The operation lasts five-and-a-half hours. How are they both doing? "They're doing very well," DeBlasio responds, noting that as the donor whose surgery is more complicated than George's, Ann is recuperating a bit slower. At the time of his court appearance "George had been feeling badly for many months" due to a genetic condition which causes his kidneys to deteriorate. "He never felt 100 percent good," continues DeBlasio, with whom I have dealings when I'm with *Billboard* and he represents musicians. "He always says, 'I'm okay' which to me means 'I'm not good or great.' This morning (April 28), he told me, "I can now say I feel great.'"

Lopez postpones his transplant until he's taped all 24 episodes of his ABC series on March 31. The final episode of the season airs May 17. Several weeks before the final episode airs, an ad appears in the *Los Angeles Times* heralding his first concert since the surgery, June 12 at the newly named Gibson Amphitheatre, formerly the Universal Amphitheatre. The ad's tag line reads "George Lopez ¿Sabe Que?...I'm Alright!" This concert, I'm told by his manager's office, is a special date in which he says hello to his fans and will be followed during the second half of the year with select weekend dates numbering between 15 and 20. Among the cities he'll play are Indianapolis, Washington, Seattle, Chicago, San Jose, Anaheim, Fresno, Oakland, and Phoenix, with other locales to be added.

It is only after Lopez appears on ABC's *Primetime Live* on May 12 that he reveals how long he's suffered with his kidney disease, a life-threatening aspect of his life which includes a troubled upbringing as a child by his grandmother and some major problems in his marriage with Ann. In his interview with George Quinones he traces a line from his childhood when he first encounters problems to his adult life when his two kidneys are deteriorating. "In Hollywood, if you're not well, you're labeled damage goods," Lopez says, so he keeps his secret from everyone. "I worked but I didn't feel good." He even uses his medical secret as a theme for an episode on his ABC series in which his TV father needs a kidney transplant. "I was going to give him one of my kidneys," George says of the story plot, "but he died before I could do it." It's not a happy thought for Lopez who faces the harsh reality there's a five-year waiting list for a new kidney. His wife Ann alters that statistic when she volunteers to give him one of her kidneys. "When she matched," says an amazed Lopez, "it ended all the stress in my life. All I had to do was get to April 19 at Cedars."

Ever the comic, Lopez mixes humor with caution by checking into the hospital under the assumed name of "Tom Ace." His story about gaining consciousness once the transplant is completed has a humorous twist. "I'm coming out (of the anesthesia) and they're yelling 'Ace…Mr. Ace…Tom…breathe…open your eyes…Tom.' And I'm thinking who the hell...oh that's me. So as I wake up I'm like, oh yes, Tom Ace. Alrighty then. I'm fine, I got a new kidney."

Three weeks after the surgery, he's shown playing golf with his buddies Andy Garcia and Cheech Marin. When questioned, Andy admits he doesn't know George is sick. "I called him up to see if he wants to play golf and he tells me he's 'lying in bed in the hospital. Ann just gave me a filter.' I said, You got a Cuban filter? You'll be okay."

The segment ends with George and Ann sitting together. George: "I'm feeling better than I ever have in my life. It hasn't even been a month and I feel alive. I feel as good as I did bad." When Quinones notes that Ann gives George the thankful gift of life, she replies: "He doesn't need to thank me; I love him." To which George responds: "I'm a lucky man."

Several weeks later during the media campaign, Lopez admits to the *Los Angeles Times* his frustration over the lack of credit and importance the show receives. "This is the first sitcom with a Latino family, and this is the first time in history that's been done," he says, adding: "This is groundbreaking and yet everyone has just kind of ignored it.... They don't want to acknowledge we're important."

Lopez himself is certainly important enough to be named host for the 2005 Primetime Creative Emmy Arts Awards, airing September 11 from the Shrine auditorium in Los Angeles on E! Entertainment Television at 7 p.m.

Following the conclusion if its fifth season in May of '07, in which Lopez airs against Fox's powerhouse *American Idol*, ABC cancels the series, prompting an angry Lopez to denounce ABC's decision based on financial reasons. ABC says it will lose money if it renews the show; Lopez believes the cancellation has more to do in part because the show is produced by Warner Bros. Television rather than by ABC itself. Still, the show will go into money-producing syndication and the star has a deal with Warner Bros. to produce TV movies among his other projects.

Cristina Saralegui is Hispanic television's female superstar. She's been Univision's talk show stalwart since 1989 when her daily *The Cristina Show* premieres and after 12 years of probing heavy topics like teenage sex, homosexuality and AIDS, she chooses to relax from the grind of daily TV by switching to a Monday evening at 10 slot and focusing on a mix of zany lighthearted topics to more serious subjects. Having arrived with her family from her native Cuba in 1960 and settling in the Miami area where she learns English, she starts her career in Spanish-language print media, which leads her into television. Cristina, as she is known, becomes a bilingual TV personality, appearing on a growing number of general market TV series including an English-language 13-week syndicated version of her talk show which Columbia TriStar TV places on the CBS-owned stations in 1992; appearing in NBC's daytime soap *Passions* and doing a cameo appearance on *Taina* on Nickelodeon in 2001; being interviewed on *20/20* by Barbara Walters in 2002, and also appearing on *Hollywood Squares* in September and November, which prompts a return appearance in February of 2003, the year she makes her primetime acting debut on ABC's hit *The George Lopez Show*. With husband/manager Marcos Avila and Whoopi Goldberg, they plan developing a film based on the life of the late Celia Cruz, the Queen of Salsa. Cristina also signs with Touchstone TV to star and co-executive produce with Marcos a half-hour sitcom centered around her life.

Cristina and Avila, a former member of the Miami Sound Machine, build a media empire, Cristina Saralegui Enterprises, which encompasses Blue Dolphin Studios—a state of the art TV production facility—*Cristina Opina*, a daily radio show which shifts from Radio Unica, a domestic network to ABC Radio International, *Cristina La Revista*, a monthly magazine and a bilingual Website.

When I contact her about doing an interview for this book, I'm told she's tied up in projects, but will gladly answer e-mailed questions. Sure enough, she comes through with answers about her life and career which form the basis for her coverage in this chapter. When I contact her male superstar counterpart at Univision, Mario Kreutzberger, the "Don Francisco" host of the network's popular Saturday night variety extravaganza *Sábado Gigante* since 1986, following its launch in his native Chile in 1962, his office replies he can not do a book interview for three years since he has his own book coming out. Nevertheless, he is making history. The *Guinness Book of Records* in 2002 lists his show as the longest-running program in TV history after 40 years. Cristina's own biography, *Cristina! My Life As a Blonde*, is published is in 1998, so she has no conflicting problems.

Twice in her career, in 1992 and in 2001, in addition to doing her own Spanish-language show, she also appears on an English-language program, which makes her one of a rare breed of Hispanic TV show hosts: a multi-cultural TV personality. Her Columbia

TriStar 13-week test run of her *Cristina* show in English on the CBS-owned stations in 1992 is her first major exposure before Anglo viewers. "At the time of the test, I was already the No. 1 talk show on Spanish television," she notes, adding that problems arose with the English version "over the production budget. So much so that I decided I could not produce a quality show with the budget CBS was offering me at the time. I knew I could not do English and Spanish daily at the same time and I did not want to take the gamble of losing everything. Of course, I got killed by the media when I pulled out after the 13 weeks. They said I was a ratings failure, which was nonsense. During the summer run, we had a 2.9 rating with a combined 10 share for the 13 weeks in 26 markets, which is not bad. But I remember opening the *Miami Herald* and seeing my photo on the people's column under the heading 'Another one bites the dust.' But there's a saying I just love: 'What doesn't kill you will eventually make you stronger.'"

The second dual assignment occurs during the week in the summer of 2001 when she appears in nine episodes of the NBC soap, *Passions*, another grind in multi-language television. "I didn't feel I was working in two cultures, because I was playing a Latina," she explains.

The reason she shifts from daily to week television in January of 2002 is simple, she explains. "Daily television is a heck of a grind, especially in Spanish-language, since we do not go on hiatus like people in English-language TV do, so after a dozen years I was honestly burned out." Since the ratings for the weekly show are higher in her time period than they were before she got there, Cristina believes her daily show viewers have followed her to primetime. "But I've also gotten a lot of complaints from people who would like me to go back to the daily format, which I don't think I'll ever do." The weekly format allows her to do "a lot more comedy since our primetime program is mostly geared towards having fun. I think laughing is very therapeutic, especially after what American has gone through after September 11.

"What doesn't evolve dies. It's just human nature. I have invented and re-invented my show many times over the last 13 years."

She shifts to tackling more serious topics in 2003. Why has she changed the tone of her weekly program? On November 24 the subject is the unsolved killings of 263, possibly more women in the Juarez city area of Mexico since 1993. By January 2004, the Mexican government's figure escalates to 370 missing women.

So I e-mail her again one year later and she responds with her explanation. "When the show goes to primetime after 12 years as a daily show, I have to be aware of the male dominance on the TV set after 9 p.m., so we're primarily catering to this audience segment.

"Some issues simply have to be addressed and such is the case of the women of Juarez." Cristina has four of the victim's mothers in her Miami studio who are part of a support group, while others remain in Juarez where they testify to their pain via satellite. The show is full of anger from the mothers. One day after the broadcast, the slayings are a topic of major discussion in Mexico following a report by a National Human Rights Commission to the Mexican Senate in Mexico City. The 1,600-page document charges neglect by officials since the victims are poor and also criticizes what it calls falsified evidence, torture, and questionable investigative techniques during investigations.

"I have always mixed what people want to see with what I consider they need to see," Cristina continues. "That's how my work with HIV and AIDS awareness begins in 1996. Our program has tackled many important issues and this has kept my work interesting and worthwhile. If not, it would be a very banal exercise." Some of the topics she discusses on the daily program are the kinds of issues you'd expect to appear on the nightly news broadcasts: kids and sex, cancer, teenage pregnancy, gay marriage, homophobia, domestic violence, illegal immigrants, pedophiles, priests and sex, alcoholism, mail-order brides, adoption, gun control, abortion, and Alzheimer's.

On the occasion of her 15th anniversary as a show host, she presents her national audience with a two-hour special which reflects on the show's history and includes invited celebrities. It airs May 24, 2004.

One topic I'm interested in having her respond to concerns the pressure the Cuban exile community exerts on Latin radio and television and music, vigorously protesting the appearance by Cuban musicians at the Latin Grammys, or any Hispanic who thinks its time for the U.S. to disengage its 40-year trade embargo against Castro and tries to make that point on the five local Spanish talk stations which are strongly anti-Castro. She responds with a correct political answer which will not create rancor among the aging exiles: "I think that since we have the privilege of living in a free society, all people have the right to protest if they dislike something," she says. "The Cuban issue is a very painful one for me and my people. Miami is considered the capital of all Cubans in exile and is a place we feel at home in. We may not be perfect, but I feel we've contributed tremendously to the development of the city."

What contributions, I ask her in the second e-mail. "In the early '60s after Fidel Castro's revolution, about 600,000 people leave Cuba, primarily all types of professionals and their families to start anew in South Florida. They bring their knowledge and desire to succeed and this unique influx of hard-working people changes the landscape of Miami."

One move which tremendously aids her growing empire is the construction of her own studio complex which houses all elements of her company beginning in May 2001. Blue Dolphin Studios "is basically an extension of my home," she enthuses. The lot consists of a 50,000 square foot state of the art TV production facility with three soundstages and editing rooms. The building is the home for *The Cristina Show* and is rented out to TV commercial production companies." Notes Cristina: "We found an existing building on two-and-a-half acres that we purchase for $3.1 million. It housed a marble business and we convert it into TV studios and offices. Originally it has about 30,000 square feet and we end up with the 50,000 square foot building and a total investment of $10 million." With the opening her own studio, Cristina becomes the fourth woman in show business besides Mary Pickford, Lucille Ball and Oprah Winfrey, to own her own studio. She's often referred to as the "Oprah of Hispanic television." How does she feel about this high honor and comparison? "When Anglos make comparisons and call me the Latin

Oprah, it's an honor to be compared hands down to the best talk show host of all time," she responds.

As for the studio acquisition, she labels it "a very savvy business move on the part of my husband and business partner, because it's basically paying for itself from the proceeds of the studio rentals alone." These include shooting TV commercials for the likes of AT&T, Master Card, Wendy's, Capital One, and Colgate-Palmolive, while providing private studio space for artists like Carlos Vives, Jennifer Lopez and Gloria Estefan.

Life for Cristina extends beyond her television show. In 1996, she forms Arriba La Vida to assist people with HIV and AIDS. "I was already a member of AmFar (the American Foundation for AIDS Research), which has done an incredible job trying to find a cure. But what happens to people who already have the disease and must live with the hardships of the virus? Arriba la Videa mainly helps finance hospices." In addition, she's a board member of the National Council Of La Raza, the Latino organization which "advances important causes to help our people." She's also co-chairing a committee to establish a permanent collection of Spanish-language TV shows for the archives at the Museum of Television and Radio in Beverly Hills. The project, she believes "will be another milestone for our industry."

Cristina and her family arrive in the U.S. with a heritage in Cuban media. She is the granddaughter of Don Francisco Saralegui, whose publishing company produces a number of magazines before being forced to immigrate to Miami in 1960. Cristina is 12 years old. She attends the University of Miami and begins her media career as an intern at the Spanish-language magazine, *Vanidades*, a stepping off point to becoming editor-in-chief of *Cosmopolitan En Español*, a post she holds from 1979 to '89 when she quits the print medium to become host and executive producer of her own talk show on Univision.

In her autobiography, she notes that her father and grandfather are both in publishing and life before Castro is "idyllic" for this wealthy family. Her father, Tony Menéndez, attends school with Fidel, and then when the revolution begins to show its communist leanings, he decides his wife and their two daughters and son should leave Cuba first. So they depart for Trinidad via airplane to stay with an aunt and uncle for a month. Meanwhile, Cristina's dad goes straight to Miami's suburb of Key Biscayne, and once he's found a house and schools, he flies to Trinidad and returns with his family. In her book Cristina says the "small house with only three bedrooms was not necessarily traumatic for my family, but it was strange after the level of comfort we had known in Cuba. She also recalls that as a teenager she encounters "something I had never known before: prejudice. In those early days there were not many Latinos in Miami," and going to school she faces innumerable questions about her departed homeland. "In the sixties, discrimination was universal in Miami," notably against blacks. "The pure truth is I learned about prejudice and hatred in the United States, in Miami."

During her 20-year stay at the magazine *Vanidades*, which her father founds and then sells, she handles a variety of editorial jobs. Since words have different meanings in different Latin American countries, she learns to use a "Pan-American vocabulary," a skill she believes helps her to "become a good communicator on television." That magazine experience leads to a position with *Cosmopolitan En Español* from 1973 to '76 which leads to a six-month job on a Latin supplement by the *Miami Herald* which proves too restrictive, so she returns to Vanidades where she also works on one of its other publications, *Intimidades* and then when the editor of the Spanish *Cosmopolitan* leaves, she's hired for that position which she holds for 10 years before making the leap into Spanish-language TV.

Wherever Andrés Cantor goes, his trademarked long "gooooooal" significantly identifies this Argentinean-born soccer play-by-play announcer. Since 1987, when he begins his 13-year association with Univision by broadcasting his first match between America of Mexico and Roma of Italy at the Los Angeles Coliseum, and through his current four-year affiliation with competing Telemundo, Cantor's goal calls add an additional sense of drama to the telecast.

People often recognize him on the street because of his distinct goal call. "They either start to yell 'goooal' or come up and say 'gooal.' It's weird because they seem to know me and I don't know them. But I cherish every moment. I'm thankful for the attention the viewing public gives me."

His long calls are also heard on matches he covers for Futbol De Primera, a company he co-founds in 1989 to provide soccer programming for radio. He also does a daily two-hour soccer show 363 days a year in addition to his TV commitments. Cantor says growing up in Buenos Aires, where he plays soccer, he listens to Argentinean radio soccer announcers extending their goal calls. That's the core reason for his own trademarked long call "It's a passionate way to call a game," he says, providing the action warrants the dramatic emphasis. The length depends on a number of factors. "It's not a gimmick," he said. "If it's a long play and I'm talking for two minutes, I may not have the breathe to give a long call. If it's a lopsided 5-0 route, there's no sense in yelling my guts out. It depends on the emotion of the play, the way the play develops, the beauty of the goal and the esthetics of the goal."

What does he mean by esthetics? "If there's a bicycle kick, with a high degree of difficulty, in which the player gets the ball in midair with his back behind the goal and makes an acrobatic kick without looking at the goal, that deserves a long call."

During the Sydney Summer Olympics in 2000 when he's calling his first English-language broadcast for NBC, "Bob Costas times one of my calls in the U.S. Women's semifinal round and it runs 26 or 28 seconds long. I'm never conscious of how long it is."

During the women's final game against Norway when the team ties the game on the last play of regulation time to go into overtime, "that's as dramatic as it gets," Cantor recalls, and warrants a long "goooooal." The team loses in sudden death overtime.

While NBC covers the 2004 Summer Olympics in Athens, Cantor and Jessi Losada provide Telemundo with its first-ever Spanish-language coverage of the games. When Telemundo carries mens' and womens' soccer, Cantor handles play-by-play while Alejandro Blanco handles the color commentary.

As a teenager, Cantor arrives in the U.S. in 1976 with his family when his father, a gastroenterologist, receives a fellowship to the University of California Davis campus in Northern California. In 1977, the family settles in Los Angeles, where after graduating from high school, he studies journalism at USC while working fulltime for *Editorial Atlantida*, an Argentinean publishing company, filing stories for its five magazines. While covering sports events in 1987 at which Univision is present, he's told the network is looking for a soccer play-by-play announcer. "So they give me an audition and I do color commentary to two taped matches, including America versus Roma. I thought it was a trial, but they hire me and air the games several weeks later in February." When Univision moves from Laguna Niguel, California, to Miami in 1992, Cantor and his wife Lilana are among those relocating. Their two children, Nicolas, 10 and daughter Andrea, 8, grew up in Miami.

During his tenure at Univision—where he averages 150 games broadcast—he covers the 1990, '94, and '98 World Cups and the European, Copa America and Mexican League qualifying rounds. How does the World Cup compare to the Super Bowl and World Series? Answers Cantor: "I say it is 64 Super Bowls in one month. You have the best 32 countries participating in 64 games in a knockout round to eliminate teams for the championship."

Since he calls 150 TV games a year, "there's no way to be everywhere at one time. So 80 to 90 percent of the time, I work off a video feed in the studio," he explains. "It's not the same experience as being there," he admits. "But after 16 years, I'm used to it." He also uses a video feed when covering a number of contests for radio.

Soccer has two seasons, January through June and August to December. "In between," notes Cantor, "there's always something going on during the off-season. This summer (of 2004), it's the European Cup in Portugal, South American teams in the Copa America in Peru and the Olympics in Athens." Which means lots of continued long calls from Cantor, either on location or in the studio, but all equally dramatic.

Stepping outside the world of soccer, Cantor unleashes his long call during *Billboard*'s Latin Music Awards 2004 ceremony from Miami telecast for the first time on Telemundo. Opening the envelope to announce the best Latin Jazz trophy, he explodes with a happy "Arturrrroooo" to signal the winner as trumpeter Arturo Sandoval and his *Trumpet Evolution* CD. Cantor expands his horizons and financial wealth in 2005 by partnering with XM Satellite Radio in the creation of its XM Deportivo 24-hour sports channel on which he hosts two weekday shows, the flagship soccer news and analysis program *Futbul De Primera* from 6 p.m. to 8 p.m. and *Las Voces Del Deporte*, an hour one-on-one interview show from 11 p.m. to midnight. Cantor is among a number of well-known Hispanic sports broadcasters signed to work on the new service.

Andy Garcia's portrayal of the defecting Cuban trumpeter in the acclaimed HBO feature *For Love or Country: The Arturo Sandoval Story*, airing in 2000, is one of three key events in the Cuban American's career linking him to his heritage. Born Andrés Arturo Garcia Menéndez, he's five years old when he and his family depart Cuba in 1961 en route to Miami a year-and-a-half after the revolution, as he aptly describes the family's flight by air to freedom. In addition to playing key roles in major motion pictures like the vindictively determined Las Vegas casino owner Terry Benedict, a victim of a $160 million robbery in *Ocean's Eleven*, who seeks the return of his lucre in the gleeful sequel, *Ocean's Twelve* in 2004, Garcia maintains strong emotional ties with his former homeland in his film and music projects as a hyphenated actor-producer-director-musician.

Besides playing Sandoval, Garcia acts, produces and directs for the first time his independent film *The Lost City* in 2004, which is set in Havana during the Castro revolution; produces and plays bongos and other percussion instruments on four albums showcasing Cuba's 86-year-old legendary bassist Israel "Cachao" Lopez, who along with his older brother Orestes creates the mambo in 1938. Garcia also produces a film documentary during the musician's visit to the U.S.

When we finally connect on the phone after several postponements, Garcia is effusive in discussing his film career since arriving in Los Angeles from Miami in 1978 and his film and record projects which are steeped in Cuban legend and legacy. I'm most anxious to discuss his growing up in Cuba and his present projects which assert his personal élan over keeping Cuba's troubled past and its present artistry alive in the minds of Americans.

When I ask him is there anything he's done career-wise which is most important from a historical Hispanic standpoint, he responds: "I think the most important things that I've done to contribute to my culture are my associations with Cachao."

Had it not been for Garcia being in San Francisco in 1989 prior to filming *The Godfather: Part III* for which he receives Academy Award and Golden Globe nominations for best supporting actor for his portrayal of Don Vincent "Vinnie" Mancini-Corleone in 1990, his life might never have become personally entwined with Cachao. Explains Garcia: "I knew of his music after I'd left Cuba and was an avid collector of Cuban music, specifically his albums. I was visiting Francis Ford Coppola prior to doing the movie and Tom Luddy, a friend of mine who works for Coppola tells me Cachao is appearing at the San Francisco Jazz Festival on the night they're showcasing Afro-Cuban music, headed by a local group the Machete Ensemble. After seeing him perform, I met him backstage." Garcia is so inspired, he asks Cachao if he'd consent to a tribute concert in his honor, which will be filmed as a documentary titled *Cachao...Como Su Ritmo No Hay Dos* (*Like His Rhythm There Is No Other*). The feature length film marks Garcia's directorial debut; he's also the film's co-producer. From that emotional connection between the actor and the musician an expansive musical bonding develops.

The documentary is followed by four recordings including a one-hour film on the making of the latest CD, *¡Ahora Si!*, "which is sort of a behind the scenes documentary," explains director Garcia. The recordings: 1994's *Master Sessions Vol. 1* wins a Grammy while the next year's *Master Sessions Vol. 2* only gains a Grammy nomination. Both CDs are distributed by Crescent Moon/Sony. *Cuba Linda*, released in 2000 and distributed by EMI, earns both a Latin Grammy nomination and a regular Grammy nomination in 2001. When *¡Ahora Si!* (*Now Yes*) is released in 2004, it's distributed by Univision. All these CDs are produced by Garcia's CineSon Productions, his Sherman Oaks, California, company formed in 1991.

"Cachao," Garcia stresses, "is a forgotten, extraordinary figure in our culture, and that's my basic motivation for doing the albums and the film. He brought so much solace to me over the years in his music that I wanted to give something back to him and enlighten people about artists like Cachao who have been at our doorstep and may have been overlooked."

The musicians on all Cachao's recordings done in the U.S. are a plethora of top-name instrumentalists aiding in the revival of the leader's career. While a number of players appear on multiple albums where the ensembles range in size from 11 to 17 to 20 musicians, several have greater name recognition, notably Paquito D'Rivera (clarinet and alto sax), Jimmy Bosch (trombone), Justo Almario (tenor sax), Nestor Torres and Danilo Lozano (flutes), Richie Flores (congas), Francisco Aguabella (Batá drum), Orestes Vilató (timbales), Luis Conte (congas), and Federico Brito (violin). Garcia adds a percussive touch on bongos, congas, cowbell, rain stick and, jawbone, in different combinations on the four albums. The bands spin their infectious magic through descaragas and mambos on volumes 1 and 2 and *¡Ahora Si!* while salsa and Cuban son rhythms earmark *Cuba Linda*.

¡Ahora Si!, nominated for a mainstream Grammy traditional tropical Latin album, wins the category during the CBS telecast Feb. 13, 2005. Producer Garcia is effusive in his comments anent the win, and his creative connections with "Cachao," telling the *Hollywood Reporter* backstage: "I'm proud to say the documentary and our first albums resurrected his life, and to have done this for him is one of the highlights of my life."

Cachao is also lending a helping hand on Garcia's new film, *The Lost City*. "He's collaborating on the music with me," Andy informs me. "I've already written some things and he's going to come in and augment and orchestrate the score. I'm also using some music by Paquito D'Rivera who did some work for me in the film *Just the Ticket* I produced in 1999. We'll have some symphonic, chamber orchestra and a heavy percussion section. I play all the Latin percussion instruments, piano and a little harmonica. We'll record in Capitol Records Studio A, where we did the *¡Ahora Si!* session" and where Frank Sinatra records all his hit albums before forming Reprise Records which he subsequently sells to Warner Bros.

What's the significance for you personally in the film's taking place in Havana during the Castro revolution having come from Cuba yourself? I ask. "Well, it's a subject matter that's very close to me obviously being a product of the exodus," he responds. "So therefore I've a great nostalgia for the Cuba of the '50s, and I always thought there'd be a great movie with a story to tell about it."

Written by Guillermo Cabrera Infante, the film's cast includes American and Cuban actors and actresses. In addition to Garcia as actor/producer/director, other top name English-speaking actors include Dustin Hoffman, Bill Murray, Richard Bradford, and Millie Perkins. Among the Cuban cast members are ballerina Lorena Feijoo (whom Garcia first meets while shooting the film *Twisted* in San Francisco one-and-a-half years ago). He wants her to play a flamenco dancer in that film but she says no to that particular role. Ever persistent, Garcia makes another pitch, this time to play a cabaret star patterned after Havana's fabled Tropicana nightclub, after he sees her dance the ballerina part in *Don Quixote* at the downtown Los Angeles Dorothy Chandler Pavillion in October of 2003. This role is more appealing and she dances two solos in *The Lost City*. Lorena and her sister Lorna's defection to the U.S. where they resume their separate ballet careers is detailed in Chapter 20. Among the other members of the large Cuban heritage cast are Tomás Milian, Tony Plana, Julio Oscar Mechosa, Elizabeth Peña, Enrique Murciano,

Nestor Carbonell, Ruben Rabasa, Juan Feranandez, Steven Bauer, and William Marquez.

Obviously not being able to film in Cuba, the production shoots the story of Havana during the Cuban revolution in the Dominican Republic in 35 days. "The story covers two years prior to Bautista's exit in 1959 and a year-and-a-half years afterwards," explains Garcia in giving the film its historic perspective. At the time we speak, Garcia is in the post-production stage of completing the movie. "We'll be finished by February (of 2005) and hope to have it out sometime next year." While Garcia has some distribution in Europe, he still needs to lock in the all-important U.S. distribution. So to draw attention, he debuts the film at the Telluride Film Festival in September, screens it for Florida Governor Jeb Bush and his wife Colombia during the state's Hispanic Heritage Month celebration in October and then screens it at the AFI Festival in Los Angeles in November. Returning to acting, he plays the director of the FBI in *Smokin' Aces*, an action comedy whose cast include Ben Affleck and singer Alicia Keys.

When Andy emerges himself in the life story of trumpet ace and Cuban defector Arturo Sandoval for HBO, playing both the lead role, executive producing the movie, and producing the Atlantic soundtrack album, I'm more than curious to see the film since I'd seen Sandoval perform with Irakere, the Cuban-funded jazz/fusion band in Havana in 1979, and interviewed him twice years later on the phone from his Miami home. Both these encounters are covered in Chapters 2 and 13 and here as well. After telling Andy how impressed I am with his performance, I inquire about the kind of research he does in order to play trumpet on camera. While the film is shot in Puerto Rico and Miami, Andy says he spends "a lot of time with Arturo in developing the script." He's aware of Sandoval's musical prowess and his flight for freedom at age 41 in 1990 in Rome while on tour with Dizzy Gillespie and his gaining U.S. citizenship in 1999. In addition to recording all his solos, writing the original score and arranging several of the tunes, Sandoval performs two of Gillespie's most famous compositions, *Night*

In Tunisia and *Manteca*, and several selections from Irakere's 1970 Grammy-winning album.

Did Arturo teach you how to play the trumpet? I ask. "He gives me some tips, but he isn't physically present giving me any training; a friend of his in Los Angeles does that since he's on tour and living in Miami. Once we get together when we're filming, he oversees what I'm doing and offers some tips. But my actual fingering and mouthing techniques are the work of the friend. When we start working together, I 'play' for him and when we actually start recording the music I videotape Arturo doing all the licks so I'm able to study his style and mimic the way he plays." Obviously Hollywood is impressed enough with Andy's acting in and producing the film and Sandoval's original score which wins an Emmy award for outstanding music composition for a movie as well as Emmy nominations for best made TV movie or miniseries and best cinematography. The film also reaps two ALMA Awards as best TV movie or miniseries and as outstanding Latin cast in a TV film or miniseries, and is nominated for a Golden Globe in the same dual category.

Helping Garcia recreate Sandoval's life in the film, directed by Joseph Sargent and written by Timothy J. Sexton, are the following thespians: Gloria Estefan, Mia Maestro, David Paymer, Charles Dutton, Tomas Milian, Freddy Rodriguez, Andy Mendez, Felix David Manrique, José Zúñiga, Fernanda, Andrade, William Marquez, Steve Bauer, Fionnula Flanagan, and Michael O'Hagen.

Of his celluloid story, Sandoval will state: "The chance of a movie being written about one's life is one in a million and I am humbly honored."

Garcia's own journey to freedom begins as a child living on the family farm in the community of Buenaventura outside the city of Bujucal and during the summer and on weekends in an apartment in Havana in the section called Club Nautico, he explains. "My father is a lawyer and a notary but he also has the family farm. Besides my mother and an older brother and older sister, we have an aunt and uncle with two children. My father's the only child and my mother has one brother, so our direct family is fairly small. In 1961, our entire family comes to the U.S. about a year-and-a-half after the revolution. We arrive on a commercial flight out of Havana to Miami just before they shut the flight down. You have to have visas to get out and they aren't easy to get. But we are able to find our way out and my father comes later."

When I mention that during my trip to Miami in 2002 I encounter tragic horror stories about life in Castro's Cuba right after the revolution from the Cuban American executives I interview (discussed in Chapter 13), Garcia adds his own scenarios. "There was tragedy all around," he begins, "starting with the disappearances right after the revolution itself. Unfortunately, Castro betrays the revolution, the 26th of July movement and the mandate 'De Directorio Revolucionario' to reinstate the constitution and have an election to reinstate democracy. By the time we luckily get out, he's declared himself a Marxist and abolished elections."

Garcia also talks about the prisoners who refuse to wear prison uniforms "because they don't consider themselves criminals but rather prisoners of conscience. They are called the plantados or the planted ones. There is a whole group of them who refuse to wear prison clothing. They are tortured constantly and live in cells that are called gabetals, which literally means drawers because the cell is as big as a drawer. There would sometimes be five men to a cell which is the width of a human body and they would take turns with one laying down on the floor and the others standing, and then that one would get up and someone else would lay down and try to get some rest. Within the first year, people are either getting shot or arrested, whether they are guilty or not."

Those are terrible thoughts to carry within one's psyche.

Andy's cinematic career, encompassing a diversity of roles earned through his acting ability, transcends his Hispanic ancestry. Since 1983, he appears in 41 films, produces eight and directs three. In 2004, he appears in five films, the aforementioned *The Lost City* and *Ocean's Twelve Plus Modigliani* (in which he plays the 36-year-old Italian expressionist painter/sculptor in the final days of his life), *The*

Lazarus Child and *Twisted*. His other diverse films include: *Just Like Mona*, *Confidence*, *Ocean's Eleven*, *Man from Elysian Fields*, *Lake Boat*, *Swing Vote*, *Just the Ticket*, *Desperate Measures*, and 1997's *Hoodlum* in which he plays gangster Lucky Luciano. Since 1985, he makes 17 TV appearances.

He plays dark, foreboding characters and cops. Are there certain types of roles you seem to land more often which may typecast you? "It's hard to say," he parries. "I've certainly played my share of cops, but that's a genre they make a lot of movies about. I don't gravitate to them because I like them. I gravitate towards them because of the inherent value of the material, who's directing and who else is in the cast."

When asked how the nation's exploding Hispanic population is affecting his career, he responds that "any culture will tend to innately support someone they identify with, and that can only be a positive thing. The Spanish culture in America is very diverse, held together with a common tread of sharing a common language. Even though there are sub-cultures with different tastes and customs, the prevailing view is that if you happen to be Hispanic, you do tend to get a support system from the community. It's only natural because people identify and want to come out and see what you're doing or at least pay attention to what you're doing."

Does he find new Latino actors are having a hard time cracking through in movies and television or are the doors of opportunity opening wider now than when he starts out? "There's much greater opportunity now than when I was starting out when there are four TV networks including PBS and five major film studios. Today, the studios have their sub-studios (which often deal with small budget, art house projects including foreign-language entries) and you have all the cable networks which also provide the young actor with audition opportunities."

Arturo Sandoval is one of the best-known and proficient trumpet players in music. His interests and skills range from classical to jazz. And since defecting in 1990 from the repressive regime of Fidel Castro with the assistance of his friend and mentor, the late

Dizzy Gillespie, he's called South Florida home—a home from which he regularly tours the U.S. and the world, able to travel so freely without any governmental oversight in stark contrast to his life with the Cuban-sponsored fusion band Irakere, which he helps co-found in 1973. Despite living a much better style of life in Cuba because of his association with Irakere than the average Cuban, Sandoval successfully frees himself of the shackles of a government-controlled society.

I've followed his career in the U.S. since arriving first in Hialeah with his wife and son, moving to Miami and becoming a sought-after player by American record companies, ranging from GRP to N-2-Coded to Columbia/Crescent Moon for whom he's a headliner in addition to working as a studio player for other companies. Along the way he befriends Emilio Estefan, the Miami Latin music mogul and Quincy Jones, the better-known music and TV mogul, former trumpeter, film music composer and Grammy-snatching record producer for superstars ranging from Count Basie to Sammy Davis, Jr. to Frank Sinatra to Michael Jackson.

The morning in November of 2003 I plan to write about him for this chapter, a large photo of Arturo accompanies an announcement of his appearing for two days at the Orange County Performing Arts Center appears on page three of the *Los Angeles Times* Calendar section. Arturo is truly living the American dream of making it in the open-market capitalistic society. Along with another member of Irakere, saxophonist Paquito D'Rivera, who defects in 1980 and lives in New Jersey, Sandoval represents a Cuban émigré who finds success in the crossover world of music, television and films.

During a trip to Miami in October of 2002, I chat with Arturo at home on the phone during a break in his writing regimen. He reiterates his happiness in being in the U.S., and his joy of working so uninhibited, a theme he first expresses to me the year before. In this country, he's free to map his own creative paths. "In Cuba, I studied classical music as a kid and then became a big fan of bebop when I heard Dizzy Gillespie and Charlie Parker. But jazz music was called the music of the imperialists."

Arturo says he performs at least three times a week with his seven-piece band. Not only doesn't he play Miami often "because there aren't a lot of jazz venues in South Florida," but the nation's transcultural Hispanic community is not his target audience. "Latinos," he says, "are not my forte because I don't play Latin music, I play Latin jazz and classical gigs."

Sandoval's dramatic life story in the 2002 HBO film, *For Love or Country: The Arturo Sandoval Story* starring Andy Garcia in the lead role, wins an Emmy for Arturo's original score and gains Garcia a best actor nomination. The pay TV film exposes Sandoval to Americans who may not be as yet tuned into his music or know of his life altering experiences. Sandoval continues to expand his creative opportunities by writing the scores for two film documentaries with a Cuban connection: *The Fuente Family: An American Dream* and *Fuente Fuente Opus X: Making of a Legend*. He composes 45 minutes of music for the two stories about Carlos senior and junior, third and fourth generation cigar makers from Cuba who now grow tobacco in the Dominican Republic.

Although he's recorded 10 albums for American companies, plus a score of others for overseas labels since arriving in the U.S., his most adventurous project is a tribute to 19 trumpet stylists in jazz and classical music, *Trumpet Evolution*, on Columbia/Crescent Moon in 2003. The CD traces the stylistic evolution of the trumpet and, of course, includes Gillespie whom he first meets in 1977 when a jazz cruise stops in Havana and Arturo drives the horn giant around and the two strike up a friendship which culminates with Dizzy helping Arturo defect in Rome while he's touring with the American legend's United Nation Orchestra. The two remain friends and performers together years later in the UNO, Gillespie's last ensemble before he succumbs to pancreatic cancer on January 7, 1993.

Although I hadn't pressed Arturo for details on his meeting with Dizzy in Havana in the past, I discover these facts while reading Donald L. Maggin's book, *Dizzy the Life and Times of John Birks Gillespie* on rainy morning in February of 2005. Arturo is 27 when the life-altering event occurs in Havana. As Maggin explains, when then president Jimmy Carter eases travel restrictions to Cuba, the jazz cruise ship heads to Havana instead of Montego Bay in Jamaica. Sandoval hears about the ship's arrival and heads for the dock, where he recalls his inability to speak English leaves him feeling restrained as the musicians head his way. Sandoval tells Maggin: "Percussionist Ray Mantilla, who is walking behind Dizzy says in Spanish, 'Can I help you?' I said, 'Oh yeah.' I wanna tell this guy that I love his music and I'm here for whatever he wants. I never told them I was a musician; I was embarrassed to say that. Or to tell them that I served three months in prison for being caught listening to Willis Conover's jazz program on Voice of America radio. I was happy when Dizzy asked if I had a car and could I take him right away to where people played those Afro-Cuban rhythms. It was a '51 Plymouth, falling apart, which I had just painted with tar and gasoline." Sandoval next says he takes Gillespie and Mantilla to several locales to hear local musicians perform African rhythms and chants. The next day, Gillespie jams with local musicians including Irakere, the band in which Sandoval, Chucho Valdes, its founder and pianist and saxophonist Paquito D'Rivera are members, and a valuable, life-saving connection is established for Sandoval with Gillespie.

The book explores in detail the complex and frightening aspects of Sandoval's defection once he makes the critical decision to run for freedom with his wife and son, utilizing the European tour with the UNO as the launch pad. According to Charles Friedman, an associate of Gillespie traveling with the band, Sandoval reveals his intentions to defect, which prompts Friedman to contact a member of President George H.W. Bush's National Security Council he's recently met, who in turn instructs Sandoval to contact the U.S. Immigration Service representative in Athens, Greece, when the band arrives there to perform. Which is what he does and is told the request is being worked on and Sandoval will be told when the paperwork clears. When the American Cultural Attache at the Athens embassy hears the musicians are in town, he invites Dizzy and Arturo to dinner. When a photo of Sandoval at the dinner runs in a local newspaper, the Cuban Secret Service takes more than a passing look at the photo and instructs Sandoval to cut his tour short and return to Cuba with his family. Ten days later, the troupe is in Varese, Italy, when Friedman is awakened at 2 a.m. by Sandoval accompanied by two band members. He tells Friedman the Cubans are threatening him. Friedman calls the White House and asks for David Miller, his NSC contact. After explaining the political situation, Miller contacts someone from the Immigration and Naturalization Service in Washington who calls Friedman with instructions to fly to Rome the following day while the band continues its tour. Once the plane lands in Rome, Friedman and Sandoval are instructed to stay on board and four armed Italian policeman come into the cabin and escort them to the tarmac where an American Embassy car drives them to the embassy. Sandoval's wife and son, who are in London, are picked up and taken to the American Embassy and put on a plane to New York. That same day, July 22, Sandoval is also ticketed to New York where he's reunited with his family.

One year after he tells me how happy and secure he feels in his adopted country, he's still enthusing about having an extremely happy existence and working in his chosen field. The trumpet tribute album, he says in the liner notes, pays homage "to a group of artists that have not only been a significant influence on my life and career, but also to many other musicians." He's had this project in mind for many years and "Emilio was the first one to say, 'let's do it.' This is a project which required me to understand and fully grasp the essence of 19 extremely diverse styles." These musicians include King Oliver, Louis Armstrong, Bix Beiderbecke, Rafael Mendez, Bunny Berrigan, Charles "Cootie" Williams, Roy Eldridge, Harry James, Dizzy Gillespie, Clark Terry, Timofei Dokshizer, Fats Navarro, Miles Davis, Maynard Ferguson, Chet Baker, Clifford Brown, Maurice Andre, Freddie Hubbard, and Wynton Marsalis. One year after its release, this most honorable CD wins the best Latin Jazz accolade during *Billboard*'s Latin Music Awards first live telecast on Telemundo.

The trumpeter/pianist is never far from his jazz roots. His *Live at the Blue Note* album, recorded in 2004 at the revered New York club, comes out in '05 on the Half Note label. The octet jamming session is a combined CD/DVD package featuring a strong bebop flavor, some zesty electric guitar runs and Sandoval playing piano on the ballad *A Lovely One*.

Arturo's trumpet tribute album brings Quincy Jones into his world. "Q" as he's known within show business, is hired to co-executive produce the recording with Cresent Moon owner Emilio Estefan. I've been writing about Quincy for a number of magazines since the late '60s when I first interview him about his score for the film, *The Slender Thread*, for *Billboard*. As his career blossoms and he moves into pop music while retaining his jazz roots, I've told him he knows how to "marry commerce with art." So it's really no surprise when he brings his producing expertise to this project with Arturo. "Arturo is one of the most multi-talented dudes I've ever heard in my life," he tells me from his Bel-Air, California, hilltop residence. "Cubans are serious musicians. I think he's one of the few people who have conceptually the ability and chops to go from Louis Armstrong to Rafael Mendez to Miles to Clifford Brown to Dizzy Gillespie. It's a long trip. He called me to help him work on the album. So did Emilio, who's like family with Gloria. I'm godfather to their son Nayib, so this is just a family affair. Arturo's album," he continues, "reflects the life I've led for 50 years. These are my roots going from King Oliver to Louis Armstrong straight through to Fats Navarro. He plays the solos note for note in the original versions we have transcribed, yet he puts his own nuances on each tune. For the most part, he's faithful to the original artists."

What are his responsibilities on the album? "I help pick the material, deal with the instrumentation, interpretations, and chronological way the songs should be done. Half of the job of producing a record is picking the songs. There weren't too many question marks. It's a joy really because you have so many tunes. The fun part is to try and get the songs you think are most representative of each artist."

Working on this album rekindles memories of Quincy's own years as a trumpet player. "It brought back memories of my being 12-years-old and listening to Louis Armstrong and Roy Eldridge, man. Clark Terry taught me how to put my horn in my mouth. I was 14. I played with Lionel Hampton when I was 18 and I also played trumpet in Dizzy's band."

Arturo, Tito Puente and Celia Cruz all appear at a special concert Quincy puts on for the Clinton Administration in Miami before 34 Latin American presidents. "Gloria has just had her new baby, Emily, so she couldn't perform, but I asked her if we could film her with the new arrival instead. I was hurt when we lost Celia (on July 16, 2003). I just loved her. She was a serious spirit who I enjoyed working with. In a way she reminded me of the lady I started out with, Dinah Washington. They were in totally different genres of music but Celica had Dinah's spirit."

Years later and in a time of crisis for the nation, Arturo joins a number of other artists in a show Quincy produces for the Economic Forum at the Waldorf Astoria in New York after the September 11 destruction of the World Trade Center Twin Towers, which launches the Bush Administration's war against terrorism in Afghanistan and Iraq.

While I have Q's attention, I ask him a number of wide-ranging questions about the status of the record industry. With the nation's Hispanic population now 37 million and growing, why haven't Latin jazz records sales spiked? "I don't know," he parries. "It depends on people's cultural background. There are jazz musicians all through Latin America , but Cuba has a very serious connection with the music and it's African and Spanish roots. If you go back to 1946–'47 Dizzy was playing such tunes as *Cubana Bebop* and *Manteca.*"

What isn't being done by jazz labels to reach and motivate this new domestic potential audience? "Jazz, salsa, hip-hop, all their sales are down. The record business faces a serious crisis," Quincy opines. This crisis starts out as a fun activity by computer savvy college students who swap songs which then escalates into a full-blown nightmare for the record industry which is caught unaware of this emerging new form of free direct distribution into a person's home, bypassing the traditional manner of buying records in a retail store. "Napster (the free Internet down-loading songs nightmare) put a big dent in the record business. It made everyone wake up and see that full access is important. When you have full access to everything that's recorded we're going to have more people get into jazz and Latin jazz so long as they pay for the music.

"Technology is outrunning humanity. Binary numbers don't care whether they transport images, text or sound. In a third of a second they go around the world and the genie's out of the bottle and you can't get it back in. The RIAA (Recording Industry Association of America, the trade group representing major U.S. manufacturers) is trying to enforce copyright laws by suing people and is making enemies out of consumers. You've got to remember there are 13- and 15-year-old kids who don't know anything about paying for records. It's like kids asking did Paul McCartney work with a group before Wings? The problem has to be solved to everyone's satisfaction otherwise there won't be any more music written and played in this country. I've heard more and more attitudes that intellectual property should belong to the public." Another problem he cites "is the consolidation of companies owning radio stations who control the playlists." With the Univision and Spanish Broadcasting System networks, the two giants of Hispanic radio, this same concern holds true for Latin radio.

What should Anglo record companies be doing to impact the Hispanic audience when they do release albums with a Latin jazz flavor? "How about advertising on Spanish radio and television?" Quincy responds. Apparently it's not on the must do lists of record label's marketing plans.

Carlos Ponce makes history by becoming *Entertainment Tonight*'s first correspondent of Hispanic heritage in 2003. The 30-year-old Puerto Rican born vocalist/bilingual actor arrives at the popular 22-year-old daily show business syndicated program through a latticework of achievements, starting out as an actor in Miami on telenovelas for Telemundo, hosting a newsmagazine on Univision, recording three hit albums and three successful singles for EMI Latin which is followed by acting roles on English-language TV series *Once and Again*, *7th Heaven* and *Karen Sisco* and returning to Telemundo to host a musical reality show.

Ponce, known within Latin entertainment as a charismatic, romantic heartthrob, is hired by *ET* to attract more Latina viewers to the program. Linda Bell Blue, the show's executive producer, also hires a second correspondent to strengthen its appeal with female viewers, Steven Cojocaru, the eccentric, highly energized fashion and pop culture maven. Of the two, Ponce faces the most challenges in luring new bilingual females to the daily half-hour program.

Ponce acknowledges he hopes to attract bilinguals. "I know the shows I've done in the Latin market have increased the number of bilinguals," he tells me. "My question is will the people who speak both languages, people like me who are 18 to 30 and watch Anglo television, be interested in watching *ET* because I'm there. I hope to interview Latin artists although I wasn't hired just to do that. It would be an interesting mission for me to create a little awareness by bringing in important figures in the Latin market that mainstream or middle America doesn't know about."

When I chat with Bell Blue about Carlos, she says she's known about him for some time. "He was on the Paramount lot in May and we invited him to come to *ET* and everyone here simply stopped breathing when he walked in. He has this amazing charm about him that makes him easy to be around. Then he went back to his home in Miama and we kept talking over the next few weeks and in late June I flew there to talk with him. This man is a very big star in Latin America. He's been in show business 15 years and has been successful with his singing and acting careers. It took a little bit of wooing on my part. I told him I wouldn't leave town until I had him ready to negotiate a contract." She won't say how long the pact is for, only to opine, "I think we're going to be together for quite a while. The people who watch *ET* are overwhelmingly female and I think there aren't many women who won't be attracted to him. Hiring *ET's* first Latin on-air personality is a big deal. We are breaking new ground. He has lived the life of a celebrity and that to the outside world that's a very glamorous thing. But, in reality, it involves a lot of travel and fatigue. Since he's lived that life, he brings this unique perspective to chatting and interviewing other celebrities."

Carlos says he wasn't seeking a position in television when he comes to L.A. in 2003. "After my recording contract with EMI expired in March, I went to L.A. and was making the rounds of the film studios when I met Linda," he recalls, adding candidly: *ET* is not what I went looking for, but I was completely seduced by her. She told me she wanted to break the show's newsy format and have more of a camaraderie with the artists by having someone like me who has been through the same path of touring or filming something."

He says he wants to ask questions of public interest the artist might not necessarily want to respond to and "get an answer, not a complete shutdown. As long as the format is casual and it's about having fun with the artist, it'll work." He does, however, admit that since the show's format and language are different from Latin TV, "I always have to find my words in English because it's my second language. I somehow think in Spanish and then I translate those thoughts into English. So I have to be a little more prepared and do a little more homework in English than I would in Spanish. But I don't want to lose the spontaneity. I have to make sure I know how to pronounce a word correctly before I use it in a question."

During his two-segment assignment which airs July 29, Carlos adds a personal physical touch to his first segment interviews, a technique not generally utilized by interviewers on Anglo TV. When he meets Kate Hudson and Naomi Watts, stars of the film *Le Divorce*, on the outdoor set in Los Angeles, he kisses both on the cheek. "What a way to start things off sitting between two beautiful women," he says beaming. "I love this job." Among the questions he asks Hudson are about her relationship with Russell Crowe, her pregnancy and where she conceived. He suggests she name the baby Carlos. "Carlos? That's a beautiful name," Kate replies, looking pensive before modifying that to "Carl" without making any commitment. He next asks Naomi about friends of hers who are also expecting. Then the subject switches to the real reason he's there—to discuss the movie—and filming in Paris, which Carlos calls "the fashion capitol of the world." It's a natural lead-in to asking Kate if she ever wanted to become a model, to which she replies, "no."

In the promotion for his second interview with Beyoncé about her music video, he tempts viewers with: "This is a song you won't hear anywhere else." In this interview taped in Miami, Carlos relates to Beyoncé singer-to-singer, fulfilling exec producer Blue's concept of using his show business experience as a common ground for interviewing other celebs. "I've spent most of my life in the recording studio and touring the world. So I know how tough it is to stay on top," he states. "And nobody is at the top now more than Beyoncé, and I've got the new music video and the song you won't find on her album," he boasts. "Her new hit comes straight off the soundtrack of her upcoming film, *The Fighting Temptations*." The tune is naturally called *Fighting Temptation*. Clips from the video appear under Carlos' gushing voiceover which concludes with, "I'll be sitting down to talk with her pretty soon about her new movie." Among the things he chats with her about is her new hairstyle.

After he interviews Will Smith in Vancouver on the set of the film, *I Robot*, he compares that interview with Kate and Naomi. "Will is a funny guy but not as good looking as Kate and Naomi and the questions are a little different. Kate and Naomi are also a lot of fun." Obviously interviewing is fun, but no kissing on the cheek with Will.

During another appearance on *ET*, Carlos the actor is on the set of *7th Heaven* where he has a recurring role. Maria Menounos, a fledgling *ET* correspondent, asks what it's like to be a sex symbol. His answer: "Sex symbol...wow...no way." Nonetheless, Ponce plays on his sexual appeal to women in his other interviews with young, sexy starlets.

Carlos' show business career is connected to his parents' decision to move to Miami when he is 14. "I was born and raised in

Santurce, Puerto Rico, but my parents are Cuban from the pre-Castro generation who leave before the revolution. They meet in Denver. My father is in the Army and stationed there during the Vietnam War.

"Miami altered my career plans. I never thought about acting; music was going to be my focus. I went to a conservatory in Miami and took musical theater and I did some acting in high school which introduced me to the acting world. How did I get into telenovelas? At one point I had $300 in the bank from valet parking jobs and I said, 'this is enough, I'm going to quit my job and go to casting calls and auditions.' I had been visiting the set of the Spanish soap opera, *Maria Elena*, which is near my house and almost every day I tried to get a job on the show. Finally the casting director got fed up with me and said, 'Listen, if you go home and not come back again,' and then he starts to laugh before continuing the thought, 'I promise I'll let you read for the next soap opera,' and he actually gave me a call to come back and audition for *Guadalupe* on Telemundo. I was booked for nine episodes and ended up working a full year." He also hosts the magazine show, *Control*, on Univision. His acting career takes off when he stars in the telenovea *Sentimientos Ajenos* in 1995 for Univision. It's because of his appearance on this series which includes singing *No Puedo Vivar* that he attracts attention from EMI Latin, also located in Miami. He records three albums, *Carlos Ponce*, *Todo Lo Que Soy*, and *Ponce*, all of which achieve double platinum status and produce three top-selling singles during his three years with the label, an association which kick starts his Spanish-language record career, but never moves beyond that to cross over into the general market. He also duets in English and Spanish with Joy Enriquez on the song *Bella Notte* for the soundtrack of the Walt Disney film, *Lady and the Tramp II, Scamp's Adventure*. During 2001, he shoots the novela, *Sin Pecado Concebido*, in Mexico, which airs in the U.S. In 2002, he's signed by Telemundo to host its first-ever domestically produced music contest reality series *Protagonistas De La Música*.

Following the September 11 Twin Towers terrorist attack, he collaborates on the song, *El Ultimo Adiós*, with a host of other Latin artists and proceeds from the record go to victims of the tragedy. In October, during Hispanic Heritage Month, he's invited to sing the tune at the White House for President Bush and other dignitaries.

Ponce's established position within the Latin entertainment industry and his exposure on *ET* undoubtedly results in two additional national exposure career events: being selected a presenter on the 2003, Latin Grammy Awards telecast on CBS and singing the *National Anthem* in game four of the National League playoffs between the Florida Marlins and the Chicago Cubs in Miami's Pro Player Stadium which Fox broadcasts and the Cubs win 8-3. The Marlins go on to beat the New York Yankees in the World Series in the sixth game, 2-0, which certainly provides the Miamian with another reason to smile.

In an effort to revive his recording career, he signs a management deal with Houston-based EarthTown Entertainment, a new firm established by the former president of Crescent Moon Records. The goal in 2004 is to find a record company for whom he can record in English and Spanish. EMI Latin, his former label, takes advantage of Ponce's national TV exposure, and releases a greatest hits compilation on CD and DVD in December of 2003. By 2005, he's hardly seen on *ET* anymore, although in July he co-hosts along with Lara Spencer, the fast-paced, slickly produced *ET* hour special for CBS *Celebrity Weddings Unveiled* taped at the new Wynn Hotel in Las Vegas and has a cameo role in the Rob Schneider comedy film, *Deuce Bigalow European Gigolo*, released the next month.

Eddie Palmieri is one of the longest sustaining stars in Latin entertainment, encompassing two fields of music: salsa and Latin jazz over a 50-year period. I've read about his exploits, his ornery personality, fights with record companies in New York City and Gloria Estefan over his musical compositions, and have always been impressed by his musical talents as a pianist and bandleader. When I sit down to speak with him in Los Angeles prior to an engagement at the Conga Room, he's just arrived from a tour to Italy, Switzerland, Germany, England and then onto Miami to appear on Univision TV's highly popular Saturday night extravaganza, *Sabado Gigante* with host

Don Francisco. His son and manager for the past nine years, Eddie Palmieri II, misses the flight to L.A. During our chat in Eddie's hotel room, the phone rings and it's his son who's made it to Los Angeles. The two chat about meeting later in the afternoon.

One of the most interesting prescient projections 63-year-old Palmieri makes in 1999 is that "Latin jazz will overwhelm the 21st Century." What is the status of Latin jazz today? I ask. "It's healthy; it's bringing in a lot of young players and a lot of Hispanics from all over the Americas," answers Eddie. "It will always be the maximum because it's the combination of the most difficult, complicated, rhythmic patterns and compositions. Latin jazz will overwhelm the 21st Century because musicians know they have to go towards the harmonic structure of jazz. Salsa is going nowhere. It will never reach the levels of the '50s with the mambo and cha cha because today's young players don't know the history of the music and there is no conscientious effort on their part to learn the music's history."

With the passing of Tito Puente in 2000, Palmieri becomes the patriarch of Latin music in this country. While his prediction is not totally happening, the pianist's 2001 debut album on Concord Picante, *La Perfecta II*, strongly links jazz improvisations within the Afro-Caribbean rhythmic dance framework of the pianist's original 1961–'68 octet, *Eddie Palmieri and His Conjunto La Perfecta.* That band's substitution of two trombones, orchestrated by Barry Rogers, and one flute rather than trumpets, alters the traditional sound of New York bands which play mambo, cha cha, charanga and salsa styles of energizing music. When Rogers dies and other members drift away, the soul of the ensemble starts to dissipate, a signal for Eddie to close things down.

Palmieri says the time is right in 2001 to resurrect the ensemble's "trombanga" sound of trombone/flute, since several key players are available to relaunch the band. Trombonist Doug Beavers, for example, transcribes five of the band's classic charts off the original album; trombonist extraordinaire Conrad Herwig cuts into his solo career to become a driving force within the ensemble, (augmented by two other trombonists on different selections); Eddy

Zervigon, the last of the wooden flute experts, fills in on that vital instrument, while jazz trumpeter Brian Lynch infuses his contemporary colorations. The album is also Palmieri's 34th and will be followed two years later by *Ritmo Caliente*, featuring the enlarged instrumentation of a string quartet for the first time, along with trumpets, trombones, flutes, tenor saxophone, flugelhorn and bass plus heavy Latin rhythm. It's music for listening and dancing, choose your preference.

Eddie's previous releases are on Alegre, Tico, Coco, Mango, Barbaro, Roulette, Elektra/Nonesuch, and RMM/Tropijazz. A number of them cause him such grief that he gains a reputation as a hard-headed individual, when in effect, he claims he's simply protecting his creative rights. The fights he has with record companies and the tragic death in 1988 of Charlie, his nine-year older brother, who's a major bandleader in the era of Machito, Tito Rodriguez, and Tito Puente, are indelible hallmarks on the dark side of his career.

Palmieri claims his compositions are stolen by unscrupulous record companies which no longer exist. "Record companies did a number not only on me but on other artists as well. You never saw any royalties and if you wanted to audit the books, there'd be several sets of books. When I signed my contract with Morris Levy at Roulette (a strong-arming, brash character), I noticed a sign behind his desk which said 'Oh Lord, bring me a bastard with talent.' My compositions were subtly and methodically taken by force. The companies that took my compositions were Tico Records (owned by Roulette) and Coco Records. When fame runs ahead of preparation, that's a mental situation you don't wish on anyone because all your thoughts are constantly negative. By being put on the defensive, I became a defensive rebel. My normal reaction was to become rebellious and untouchable. I was everything you could think of to be able to survive under the conditions I faced." With his life now seemingly on course, Palmieri seems a much mellower person. One key reason, he acknowledges, is "my son has cleared up all my past problems," including dealing with alleged mob controlled record companies.

His problem with Gloria Estefan centers on his allegations that in 1989 her song, *Oye Mi Canto*, contains material pilfered from his own 1981 composition, *Paginas De Mujer*, which he recorded for Barbaro Records. His $10 million lawsuit, filed in the spring of 1991 under federal copyright laws, winds through legal corridors four years; some of Palmieri's evidence is tossed out and a lower level court dismisses the suit when he refuses to go to trial. Based on that action, the U.S. Court of Appeal for the Second District, refuses to hear the case, bringing it to an end. Estefan claims she did not copy Palmieri's composition, but rather used notes commonly found in Cuban folk music. These notes appear on both artists' recordings.

During his evolutionary career, in addition to changing the instrumentation for Latin bands, he enthusiastically engages lengthy compositions beyond what is normal for Latin bands, is inspired by jazz pianists Bill Evans, McCoy Tyner, and Thelonious Monk to incorporate stronger improvisational elements to his playing, and melds jazz-based harmonies with his Afro-Caribbean rhythms. During the hiatus between versions one and two of *La Perfecta*, Palmieri writes heavily politically flavored compositions against the Vietnam War, delves into the boogaloo R&B field on the Roulette album *Harlem River Drive*, records with Cal Tjader, the Fania All Stars, the Tropijazz All Stars, does an album with Tito Puente, the timbalero's last before he dies during heart surgery on May 31, 2000, and gains favor at the Playboy Jazz Festival in Hollywood with his often avant-garde pianistics overshadowing the playing of *montunos*, the normally utilized repetitive, often monotonous simple note figures heard regularly in Latin dance music.

One of his many achievements is helping prod the National Academy of Recording Arts and Sciences in 1994 to add a Latin jazz Grammy to its roster. "I'm very proud of my contribution to having a Latin Jazz category," he says. He winds up winning five of them. As for the formation of the new, separate Latin Recording Academy which proffers its own Latin Grammys, Eddie calls its creation "totally ludicrous. We don't have two Oscars or Tonys," the latter a reference to the accolades for top Broadway plays.

Having come full circle with *La Perfecta II*, which extols dancing, inculcates three trombones, flute and trumpets on different cuts, and allows for *montunos*, I ask if his career is being boosted by the Hispanic population injection. The answer by the New York-born musician whose parents are from Puerto Rico surprises me. "No, because our genre of salsa music is suffering dearly. The music coming out of the orchestras is being called salsa monga, which means deadwood salsa. If you're a conscientious musician and you hear Latin music radio, particularly in New York, you'd want to drink something like Pepto-Bismol to settle your nerves. The compositions lack tension and resistance so there's no climax. It's dull and bland. It's being called salsa but it's not our music. There are no more dances and very few club venues for me to play in this country, and at those that are available, there's a financial ceiling that I cannot accept. It's insufficient for the price that the orchestra charges. So I have to do small jazz rooms or festivals or travel overseas. I've been to Europe 45 times since 1984. There are Hispanics in Sweden, Denmark and Germany. A man from Colombia owns the club Zapata in Stuttgart, Germany. His wife is German and he's having the time of his life and we packed the place for him."

In 2005, Palmieri's 50th year in show business is commemorated by the release on Concord Picante of *Listen Here!* featuring a cast of all star jazz caliber soloists Michael Brecker, Regina Carter, Christian McBride, Nicholas Payton, David Sanchez and John Scofield who join his recording ensemble of Brian Lynch, Conrad Herwig, Donald Harrison, John Benitez, Horacio "El Negro" Hernandez, and Giovanni Hidalgo. The 68-year-old pianist/composer/arranger's CD is among a number of releases also celebrating the label's 25th anniversary, including Dianne Schuur with Dave Samuels and the Caribbean Jazz Project, and conguero Poncho Sanchez with the R&B group, Tower of Power.

Listen Here! Is a different kind of Palmieri album. It's the first time he includes jazz works by other composers along with his own compositions, which requires him to alter his salsa piano playing technique. It's also the first time he eschews the full Latin rhythm section of timbales, congas and bongos, choosing instead a full drum kit, congas and bass. In dealing with jazz compositions, Palmieri adjusts his piano technique to differentiate from Latin music where "you play the full octave which locks your hand and the harmonic extensions are minimal. This isn't the way you finger for jazz. I had to do basic fundamental fingering exercises in order to play the different styles of jazz." In shifting away from his spicy salsa support, Palmieri notes to *Down Beat* the genre is now integrated with rap and reggaeton elements which appeal to kids and is far afield from the traditional salsa sound he calls "la salsa dura," or the hard salsa. In fact, he's even thinking about recording an album extolling this hard salsa sound of years gone by.

Conguera master Poncho Sanchez is a major selling musician whose career is being impacted by the growing U.S. Hispanic population. "It's helped me a great deal," he tells me one afternoon when he and his band are not on the road. The 50-year-old Los Angeles area bandleader, who straddles both the "salsa and jazz sides of the fence," as he puts it, "remembers when people could care less about Latin jazz. There were small groups in San Francisco, New York, Los Angeles, and Chicago that liked it. Now I'm trying to reach this new Hispanic population which may not be interested in Latin jazz with a music which has both the sophistication, quality, harmony and melodies of jazz but also has the flavor and feeling of the heartbeat of traditional Caribbean music."

Sanchez is aware that the influx of people from Cuba, Colombia, the Dominican Republic, El Salvador, Nicaragua, Honduras, and Guatemala, adding to the already established Puerto Rican enclaves on the East Coast and the steady stream of Mexican immigrants relocating all across America, opens new avenues of creative opportunity. "I'm thinking we should reach out to these people and try to add something they'd enjoy hearing in my music. I'm open to recording music from these countries because their music is getting more popular. Maybe I should stretch out a little bit and see if I can invite them into our circle. I've had newly arrived people from El Salvador, Nicaragua, and Venezuela tell me, 'I didn't know anything about Latin jazz until I heard your music and I love it.'"

Sanchez admits that in order to keep his music "real," he needs to tap into some of the new Latin rhythms, flavor and style on his records which the new arrivals are familiar with. He says he's already using rhythms from Colombia and the Dominican Republic in his songbook. This way, he reasons, "the music will keep growing. I'm a purist and I respect the music so much that I don't want to change it too far, but I have broadened my scope to include rhythm 'n' blues material on my last two albums, *Soul of the Conga* (2000) and *Latin Spirits* (2001)." In 2002, Concord releases the *Ultimate Latin Dance Party* two-disc compilation of the hottest tracks from 18 of Poncho's 20 albums dating back to 1983. Amidst this representation of the band's various styles is funky soul. Having interviewed Poncho for this book, I wind up writing the liner notes for the compilation, an upbeat best of collection.

Despite an interest in ensnaring new Latino arrivals with more indigenous sounds, Poncho's next album in 2003 is laden again with 1960's funky American R&B ingredients which blend well with the band's trademark salsa spice. It's the 21st he's done for Concord Picante and is titled *Out of Sight.* It features blues legends Ray Charles singing *Mary Ann* and Sam Moore (of the Sam and Dave duo) vocalizing with Poncho on *Hitch It to the Horse*. Other blues artists jamming with the ensemble include Billy Preston playing the Hammond B-3 organ on *One Mint Julip* and trombonist Fred Wesley and saxophonist Pee Wee Ellis from the old James Brown band playing on five tracks. Brown's importance is felt on his tune, *Out of Sight* (sung by Poncho), and the original tribute *JB's Strut.*

Sanchez's regular infusion of the East Coast-bred boogaloo combining Afro-Cuban rhythms underlining R&B tunes in English, is an extension of his early exposure to this music when his six older sisters begin listening to the genre before it becomes known as soul music. It's part of his musical education which he explains starts with regional Mexican music, which he'll eschew when his professional focus is on other forms of Latin music.

"I love Tex-Mex music and I respect the mariachi music of Mexico. When I was a kid growing up in L.A., I played in a Tejano band called Little Jimmy and the Vagabonds for five years. I played congas on the cumbias and cha chas and I'd sing all the English songs while Jimmy would sing all the Tex-Mex songs in Spanish. My parents are from Mexico, my mother from the north so she's into ranchera and conjunto music, while my father likes mariachi because he's from the center of Mexico. We'd hear Tex-Mex music all the time at home, but my six sisters got into rhythm 'n' blues and I liked that. But then they got into the mambo and cha cha, which was very rare for my neighborhood because it was 90 percent Chicano people from the barrio and everybody was listening to doo-wop music, or Ricky Nelson. In those days we called the mambo or cha cha *Musica Latina*. Nowadays people call it salsa. I learned about Latin jazz from my brothers and sisters. They got into the first wave of the mambo and cha cha cha that came from New York City to Los Angeles in the late '50s.

"There were Latin dances at the Hollywood Palladium with DJ Chico Sesna once a month and my sisters went to that show. There was also a Latin music show on an AM radio station for one hour a week that they'd also listen to. So I grew up hearing Machito, Tito Rodriguez, Tito Puente and Cachao (bassist Israel Lopez) before anyone knew who he was. As a little kid I'd see my sisters dance the mambo, cha cha, or pachanga, so that's also how I learned about this music. I'm the youngest of my 11 brothers and sisters and I turned out to be the only musician, but my sisters are great dancers, man."

For seven-a-half years in Poncho's early career he plays congas with the pioneering Cal Tjader Latin jazz band, starting on New Year's Eve of 1975. He vividly remembers being on the band's 1982 tour of the Philippines when Tjader dies of a heart attack in Manila. When I query him about that event, his recall is crystal clear with jarring sadness. "Cal had a heart attack a year before we went to the Philippines and was under a doctor's care for six months. The tour had been planned before he had his first attack. He wanted to go there because he was a Navy medic during World War II in the Philippines. He looked sick from the moment we left. He said the doctor had given him some medicine and he'd be fine. I was a kid at that time and didn't know what was going on. When we got to the Philippines, his wife took him to visit a statue of General MacArthur and then he went to the beach where he'd been a medic during a major battle. He said he was 17 years old at the time.

"He told me, 'I was shooting all my friends with morphine because their arms and legs were blown off.' His wife later told me about his crying like a baby on the beach during that battle and here he was 54 years old and right back on the beach. He'd done a complete circle. He had his second heart attack the next day. I remember when they were wheeling him out of the hotel, someone called a doctor to see him at the Manila Medical Center and it turned out to be Philippines president Ferdinand Marcos' private physician. Cal died the next day."

Having established a solid reputation, the Grammy-winning bandleader who's voted percussionist of the year in the 2003 *Down Beat* Readers Poll, says for the past five years he's on the road Thursday through Sunday playing in major cities with large jazz and Latin populations like New York, Miami, and Chicago and playing in small towns in-between. "Places," he is pleased to say, "you'd never think Latin music would be popular, like Billings, Montana, that has no business, my man, with Latin music. We sold out a concert at a beautiful concert hall and that's living proof that Latin music is on a roll. We'd gone there after playing the Sedona Jazz on the Rocks Festival in Sedona, Arizona, so we went from desert weather to freezing cold on the same weekend."

Sanchez's popularity during his 20-year career with salsa and jazz buffs produces an audience he explains is mixed between the two camps. "When I do salsa dance Latin clubs, the audience is 90 percent

Latino. Then when I play a jazz club or supper club the next night the jazz aficionados turn out. So we play on both sides of the fence. I feel real blessed because we can play all these different markets and I prefer that because each draws a different audience."

When our conversation turns to the growing Mexican population around the country, Poncho keys into his personal feelings. "The first time I went to New York many years ago, you didn't see any Mexicans, no burritos or tacos. People in New York didn't even know what that was. They'd call it Spanish food, but I'd say, 'No Mexican food.' Now when I go there I see Mexican people and Mexican restaurants." When I mention there is a huge Mexican population among Hispanics now living in Hawaii, Poncho laughs and says with a tinge of an accent: "Oh jes, look out, here we come."

In 2005, as part of Concord Picante's silver anniversary, Sanchez releases *Do It!*, a blending of tropical Latin, jazz and R&B styles featuring the entire nine-member Tower of Power on two tracks and South African trumpeter Hugh Masekela on two other tunes. These two guests continue the Chicano conguero's tradition of selecting soloists ranging from Freddie Hubbard, Eddie Harris, Tito Puente, Mongo Santamaria, and the late Ray Charles to jam with his band.

Herbie Mann is one of the first Caucasian musicians to sense the commercial beauty of marrying the flute with Afro-Cuban music. In 1958, he begins adding conga drums to his ensemble and over the years he employs some of the top players on the instrument: Candido, Ray Barretto, Ray Mantilla, Olatunji, Potato Valdes, and Willie Bobo. In 1961, he begins his romance with the music of Brazil, which he starts recording for Atlantic. He's also one of New York's first Latin music crossover pioneers, conscientiously pollinating genres of music to create pop music hits like *Comin' Home Baby*, *Memphis Underground*, *Push*, *Push*, and *Hijack*.

I've been a big fan of his and it's always fun chatting with him for any number of stories we do about his musical expeditions for *Billboard.* One time, my wife Bonnie and I are on vacation in Hawaii and staying in Honolulu at the Kahala Hilton in the late '70s when I spot Herbie poolside. Sidling over to chat with him, I wind up doing an interview about his tour of Japan and the status of Latin music in the Orient. During our chat about music and Japan, he's enthused about a new kind of king bee health liquid he found in Japan. "This stuff's great," he says and then goes up to his room to retrieve a few small bottles of the darkish-colored substance. I think it tastes awful when we try it later in our room.

During the summer of 2000, I learn about his three-year battle with inoperable prostate cancer, and despite undergoing radiation and chemotherapy treatment, he performs 13 concerts, some close to his Santa Fe, New Mexico, residence, where he's lived since 1989. He forms a nonprofit foundation, Herbie Mann's Prostate Cancer Awareness Music Foundation, which provides information about the disease during his concerts. Knowing he's ill and wanting to chat with him for the book, I call him at home and because he's traveling, working on a new album and planning a medical trip to Ireland, we end up chatting several weeks later on November 20, 2002. His voice sounds a bit weak from the treatment he's undergoing and he reveals he's trying to set up a trip in a few weeks to a clinic in Cork, Ireland, to undergo photodynamic luminescent therapy, which he says may be his last chance to save his life. During our conversation, he tells me about the eight concerts he's already booked for the new year, a positive indication he plans being able to continue performing in public.

What I envisioned being a simple discussion about Latin music, now touches on three areas: his music, the current status of instrumental Latin music, and his health.

With a backdrop of a growing Hispanic population, is this a good time to be playing instrumental Latin music? It's an easy question for Herbie, who responds: "The new generation of Latinos are listening to who's ever a hit at the moment, Jennifer Lopez, Enrique Iglesias and Ricky Martin. Here's the thing I've always found about Latin dance music. It doesn't sell because the records are not the star; it's the people on the dance floor. As for Latin jazz records, I don't know who's buying them."

Do the new arrivals from Mexico, Central and Latin America have any connection with Latin jazz? "I would venture to say if you spoke to the record companies, you'd find out these new immigrants have no connection to Latin jazz. Even if Roy Hargrove does a record with the Buena Vista Social Club, I'll bet you it's the same fringe jazz audience that buys the record. It's the same audience I always tried to go toward rather than the traditional Latin fan.

"When I first started playing jazz on the flute in 1951, there were no role models for flute in traditional jazz, so I was a freak. I grew up in New York (in the borough of Brooklyn) listening to Latin music and DJ Symphony Sid Torin, the Latin jazz guru, recommends that I add two Latin percussionists to my band because he was a mambo man. I followed his suggestion and all of a sudden the audience could relate to the flute because in Latin music the flute is a solo instrument along with the trumpet and piano. While I play the same repertoire, *I'll Remember April* and *Caravan* with two percussionists, I now have an identity people can relate to. I have the first pachanga crossover record in 1960 on Atlantic with the Ray Charles tune, *This Little Girl of Mine*, which also gets me the black audience. The pachanga/charanga is the Cuban dance which features three violins playing traditional Cuban music. I knew we'd have Latin people listening to this record, and the Ray Charles tune drew in this second audience. All of a sudden there was this crossover. Since I didn't have any traditions I had to adhere to, everything I did was against the books. I went from Latin to Brazilian. As much as I loved the music and the grooves, harmonically it began to get redundant playing Latin music. Playing salsa, it's all two chords, and with four drummers in my bands, I was almost a sideman. So when I heard Brazilian music and went there in 1961, I heard amazing rhythms with Antonio Carlos Jobim. It was my salvation."

Mann tells me that after specializing in both Latin and straight-ahead modern jazz, he's turned off to playing Latin jazz. "The bottom line is at 72, I have to play what I love personally and I don't find any challenges in that music anymore. What challenges me now is Eastern European music." He's done two albums of this music, the first, *Eastern European Roots*, is recorded in Budapest, Hungary, with his Sona Terra band and released in 1998 on Herbie Mann Music/Lightyear Records and distributed by Warner Bros. "I just came back from Hungary in November where I did another album with Hungarian musicians and my son Geoff on drums," he says. The title is *Carpathia*. "If this is to be my last album," he says prophetically, "what do I want it to be? I'm a second-generation American, an East European Jew that wants to be recognized by exploring this music. It's the most original music I've heard in 20 years." It will not be his final recorded farewell, supplanted by a pure jazz LP with some Latin influences which comes out in August of 2004.

During his vaunted career, this strong-minded saxophonist/flutist/record company owner records 90 plus albums under his own name for Bethlehem, Prestige, Verve, Epic, Milestone, Savoy, Atlantic, and his own Embryo and Kokopelli Music labels. In 1980, after 20 years with Atlantic—where he scores his pop crossover hits—he decides to return to playing Brazilian bossa novas, and the parties sever their relationship.

Regarding his health, he reveals personal aspects which have not been detailed before and which I feel are historically important for they show the stumbling blocks he encounters in the final years of his life. "Five years ago I discover I have prostate cancer which is already out of the prostrate, so I can't have an operation. I go through all the runarounds, the chemo and radiation and the cancer is not responding to any treatment.

"So I decide I don't want to do anymore traditional or alternative treatments since they're all short-term, temporary stuff. Now there's this treatment in Ireland I'm looking into. My doctor, Andrew Weil, recommends this place. I called the clinic today to confirm my appointment and they said they haven't received my full payment, so they have to cancel my appointment. Needless to say, we're in a little bit of a war with this clinic. I hope to resolve this situation."

Everything gets resolved, his wife Janeal explains to me months later. Dr. Weil intervenes with the Irish clinic which refunds the Manns' $20,000 deposit. One month later, however, the cancer has spread into his bones, Janeal says. Then another health problem crops up, worsening the situation.

While in the Cayman Islands for a prostate cancer meeting in February of 2003, Herbie falls and incurs bleeding in the brain. "That's the turning point in his health," Janeal says haltingly. They are planning to try a clinic in Germany which offers the same radical treatment as the clinic in Ireland. But the fall cancels that. It sends the Manns home where Herbie has surgery, "but he never recovers his health," Janeal laments. Despite his waning condition, Herbie is determined to perform at the New Orleans Jazz & Heritage Festival May 3. So he and Janeal leave Santa Fe, elevation 7,500 feet, for Phoenix where they remain two months and hope the lower altitude will help him feel better while he practices for the New Orleans gig. "That was a very special occasion," Janeal says with pride. "He came on stage hooked up to an oxygen tank and played his hour show with Larry Coryell and David 'Fathead' Newman and four other musicians. The tunes he played were mostly funk rather than the Eastern European material. I think everyone knew he was dying. It was his grand finale. And his last gig. He canceled the other two he had lined up."

I ask her if he speaks to the audience about his illness. "He didn't speak about his illness on stage. In fact, he didn't speak at all, an absolute first for Herbie, since his stories were a great accompaniment to his playing."

In early 2003, he records what becomes his final album, *Beyond Brooklyn*, a small group jazz album in Pittsburgh featuring alto saxophonist Phil Woods that includes bossa nova and tango rhythms. So, minimally, he's still in the Latin music genre. The last time these two stylists perform together is in 1957 on Mann's *Yardbird Suite* LP. The new album on the Manchester Craftsmen's Guild jazz label features two rhythm sections for the contrasting moods and tempos. The album is the result of the two musicians performing in 2002 at the non-profit arts organization's 15th anniversary of its jazz subscription series in its 350-seat music hall, which inspires Marty Ashby, MCG Jazz's producer, to suggest Mann and Woods cut an album.

Six months later, the duo starts recording its reunion album featuring new charts for several jazz standards plus original compositions. The LP's title is a reflection of where Mann is born and of the two playing together for the first time in 1951 in Tony's Bar on Flatbush Avenue, the New York borough of Brooklyn's main downtown street. It's at this location the two begin experimenting with modal harmonies. This final recording shows where the two master soloists end up musically after all these years.

Two months after his final concert and last public appearance and seven months after our interview, Herbert Jay Solomon of Brooklyn, New York, dies on July 1, 2003, in Santa Fe. He's 73 years old. I'm among the last journalists he talks to before his passing. I'm certainly one of the few writers who knows about his planned trips to Ireland and Germany because none of the obituaries I read mentions anything about his last efforts to obtain the radical treatment for his disease and the stumbling blocks he encounters trying to accomplish that goal.

One year later in late July, *Beyond Brooklyn* is released to the public. It is called a "fitting farewell to a master" by *Jazziz* magazine. The final tune of the 12 recorded, *Time after Time*, is recorded at Glen Campbell's home studio in Phoenix. Although the original intent in using the studio is to make minor alternations to several of the already recorded tracks, Mann decides he wants to record a new version of *Time after Time* for Janeal. It turns out to not only be the last song he ever records, but a farewell love statement to his wife.

A few days after I listen to the album, I call Janeal to ask her some questions about this recording and the album titled *Carpathia* which precedes it. Did *Carpathia*, which Herbie believes will be his final recording, ever come out? Janeal says she and son Goeff are working on a new remix and she hopes to have it released in 2005. When I tell her that after listening to Herbie's strong and lyrical playing on *Beyond Brooklyn*, I cannot detect any weakness in his breathing or phrasing; he really sounds strong. Janeal says he's breathing oxygen through a nose clip connected to the tank for this session similar to the way he is when he plays his final performance in May at the New Orleans Jazz & Heritage Festival. "During the session I sat next to him and gave him every ounce of energy I had," she tells me. "He is 100 percent dependent on oxygen at this time. While every song is labored, on the first take of *Time after Time*, he plays all the way through. And when they need a second take as a safety, he again plays all the way through without stopping. He looked at me and said, 'that's for you baby.'"

Larry Harlow is an anomaly. He's one of New York's busiest Latin music composers, pianists and recording artists. He's also a Caucasian Jew, whose legal name is Kahn and who goes by the moniker *El Judio Maravilloso*, which translates into marvelous Jew. Long steeped in salsa music, he's branched out into writing music for Spanish-language TV and radio commercials, has made his foray into Latin jazz and performs at Hispanic cultural children's programs around the country he helps create. It's a busy life for Harlow, 64, who grows up listening to Latin music, winds up playing piano with a neighborhood band, spends two years in Cuba studying music and learning Spanish and hastily departs when Fidel Castro comes to power. He returns to his native New York and becomes a chief maven among New York musicians specializing in salsa music for such labels as Fania where he's a member of the Fania All Stars, featuring the gold of New York Latino musicians. Only he's not Latin.

I get to meet Larry in person at his West Side apartment off Central Park during a wintry week trip to New York in March of 2003. Larry tells me that the expanding Hispanic population in the U.S. is helping revive his career in salsa music. "I am going through a renaissance," he says. "Hispanic kids who weren't born when I was in my heyday in the '60s and '70s, have discovered the re-releases of my records. And they like the traditional salsa much better than what's available now, the romantic salsa. The young kids don't know the poetry and melodic content of salsa. Since the big radio chains have no new traditional product to play, they've been playing the romantic salsa which has only the one theme of love. Whereas when salsa develops in the '70s we talk about politics and war and humanity and also love."

Salsa music, Harlow believes, is going through a cyclical change. "After I start my career in 1964, the first obstacle Afro-Cuban music comes up against is the boogaloo in 1967–'68. Seven years later it's the Latin Hussle. Seven years later it's the salsamonga and now that's gone. Salsa will always come back to the real Afro-Cuban dance form because of its purity. Hispanics seem to want to be more American and lean towards the rock scene and try to get away from their roots. I'm trying to keep them connected to their roots." Harlow gets his wish in 2006 when he is among the stalwarts on the defunct Fania label who are reintroduced to new fans of classic salsa by the company's new owners, Protel Records, which schedules the re-release of albums from the '60s and '70s. The Fania label, dormant following the death in 1997 of co-owner Jerry Masucci, was the home to Ray Barretto, Eddie Palmieri, Hector Lavoe, and the Fania All Stars.

Harlow calls himself a "survivor" because he says with a bit of braggadocio, "Being an American and having a little more business sense than most Hispanic musicians, I have other interests. I write music for Spanish-language radio and television commercials, I'm writing two books, I'm an antique music instrument dealer selling instruments from the 14th and 15th centuries, I've expanded into Latin jazz and I married a rich lady on top of all that."

Harlow is among an elite group of musicians advertising agencies hire to write commercials for Spanish media. "I do Tex-Mex music for the West Coast, salsa for the Northeast, charanga for the Southwest and Tejano for Texas and California. I usually have 48 hours to write and arrange the music for a 30- or 60-second commercial. The copyist has overnight to copy the score, we record it the next morning and then mix the sound and deliver the finished product all in one day." His music propels commercials for Sony,

Campbell's Soups, Miller Beer, Miller Light, Lowenbrau, and Magnum Malt Liquor.

Harlow says he's playing less but earning more because he's playing more concerts with his salsa band, "since there are very few dance clubs left to play around the country, especially in New York." One reason he shifts into Latin jazz for the very first time is partially due to economics and because he feels jazz is a new creative challenge for him and his new band the Latin Jazz Encounter, whose first release, *Live at* Birdland, is released on the new Latin Cool label. "I'm not a jazzer; I'm a dance music guy. I always wanted to be a jazz player but I never followed it up."

Harlow then offers an example of how math plays a role in his shifting musical gears. "If a festival director in Chicago wants to hire me and my salsa band, I tell him we get $10,00 plus 15 plane tickets, 15 hotel rooms plus per diems and the cost of schlepping all the instruments. So it's going to cost $20,00 to bring me in for one night. Whereas if I play Latin jazz, I go with a sextet and I do it for $2,000, six plane tickets and six hotel rooms. So it's opening new areas for me, 300-seat rooms. But jazz is music for the head, it's not for dancing, and Hispanics don't really understand jazz. They're used to hearing two or three chords and they can't follow the chord changes in jazz or the creative process of the soloists who are blowing and creating music over a structured chord line. They're looking for rhythmic music to dance to. Don't forget the majority of Latinos in the United States are Mexicans. The Mexican culture is not African-based. It's a European/Indian-based culture. I find their music boring."

What he finds energizing is participating in the children's learning experience called *Sonfrito* which is salsa music he writes to blend with stories written and narrated by David Gonzalez, who holds a Ph.D. in music. "It's a multi-media kind of presentation we started in 1997 for bilingual children which gives them pride in who they are, and give American kids a little insight into what the Hispanic cultures are like." The kids between five and 12 are bussed to venues Saturday mornings. "It's all free to the children. We get paid by sponsors in different cities like New York, Newark, Cleveland, Buffalo, Minneapolis, Los Angeles, and Fayetteville, Arkansas. Now there isn't a Hispanic within 500 miles of Fayettville, yet we brought the show there."

In 1996, Harlow and Ray Barretto form the sextet Latin Legends which morphs into Thunder Drums several years later and differs from the original instrumentally and conceptually. "It's more of a concert-style band," Harlow says. The new ensemble features six drummers, including one from each country visited, instead of three, one singer instead of three and two trombonists who double on violin. There's also five horns, bass and piano."

Inevitably our conversation gets around to his names. How does Larry Kahn become Larry Harlow? "My father, who's a saxophone player, is in a car crash when he's 19. His lung is punctured and he has two ribs removed so his lung can be collapsed by a doctor named Harlow. In appreciation, my father takes the name Harlow for his own and adds an 'e' on the end. After the loss of his lung, he can't play the sax anymore, so he becomes a bass player and subsequently the bandleader at the Latin Quarter in Manhattan for 25 years. I just assumed his last name. My social security card reads Larry Harlow Kahn."

What's the origin of his nickname? It's based on his appreciation for Arsenio Rodriguez, a blind black Cuban pioneering bandleader whose family is from the Congo, Harlow explains. "He is the spokesperson for black Cubans in the '40s and '50s. When he becomes a bandleader he adds piano, conga drum, three trumpets and written arrangements. And he starts the mambo diablo, or devil mambo. And that's what the people call his music, devil dancing. He is the father of the mambo and since he's blind, the people call him *El Ciego Maravilloso, the Blind Marvel.* He was one of my idols and one day during a show as I was about to play a piano solo on one of his songs, Adelberto Santiago, our singer says, 'Ahora viene (here comes) the *Maravilloso* (*the marvel*), the Jewish marvel, *El Judeo Maravilloso.*' During the early seventies the doors were just opening for salsa in

South America but the Hispanics could not pronounce the name Larry Harlow. They called me Carlo Harlow or Harry Marlow. But they could pronounce *Judeo Maravilloso*, so that kind of stuck with me and the next album I did, I gave it that name."

If Harlow, a free-spirit and extremely confident artist is a major musical force in the Big Apple, Bobby Rodriguez holds a similar power position in Los Angeles, where he's both a musician and educator. I initially meet Bobby in 2001 to discuss his multiple exploits for a story I'm doing for *Down Beat.* The assignment takes me to the campus of California State Los Angeles where he teaches a class in improvisation at the Los Angeles County High School for the Arts, located on the college's campus in the Eastern part of the city. Bobby heads the high school's instrumental jazz studies program. A few days later, my wife Bonnie and I attend the 23rd annual Playboy Jazz Festival at the Hollywood Bowl to catch trumpeter Rodriguez conduct the high school's 30-piece studio band which opens the festival. It sounds pretty professional on this warm afternoon in June, performing four tunes, three in a Latin vein.

After their performance, three of the musicians head off to work the rest of the evening as Bowl ushers. The sellout crowd of 17,965 hears an array of Latin music from violinist Regina Carter's blending of Latin and modern jazz; Ozomatli's off-kilter salsa/rap/rock gumbo and Los Van Van's charanga dance temptations. The high school band's Playboy appearance is its second at the gala in three years. Fittingly, the concert begins with Latin jazz and ends with the energy of Cuban-style dance music. Rodriguez spends the rest of the summer at the Bowl in the trumpet section of the Clayton-Hamilton Jazz Orchestra, the venue's current resident ensemble.

When I next chat with Bobby in May of 2003, he's in his third year of teaching Latin jazz at Pasadena City College and second year as a member of the UCLA jazz studies department headed by famed guitarist Kenny Burrell. He's also effusive about the increase in work he's getting with his salsa and jazz band as a result of more Latinos translating into more music, por favor. "The growing Hispanic population is providing me with opportunities to work in different venues besides clubs, such as shopping malls and parks which are funded for the most part by the Professional Musicians Local 47," he says. He's currently leading the 23-piece Bobby Rodriguez Salsa Orchestra, formerly known as the Hispanic Musicians Association's HMA Salsa Jazz Orchestra. Consisting of both top name professionals and some college neophytes, Rodriquez says of this orchestra: "This is where the light shines through the brightest."

As a professional, Rodriguez records three albums on his own LatinJazz Productions label: *LatinJazz Romance* (2001); *LatinJazz Explosion* (nominated for a Latin Grammy in 2002), and this year's *Trumpet Talk*. His forte on trumpet expands his horizons to perform with the likes of Quincy Jones, Ray Charles, Tina Turner, Chaka Kahn, the Emotions, Diana Krall, Gerald Wilson, Buddy Collette, Don Ellis, Louis Bellson as well as Poncho Sanchez, Lalo Schifrin, Tito Puente, Willie Bobo, and Arturo Sandoval.

Born in East Los Angeles, Rodriguez believes Latin jazz combines the best of two worlds. "The magic of the music pulls together the jazz and Latin audiences. People can dance to it. It's exciting music. In the 1940s we called Machito's instrumental music Latin music because of the rhythms. Tito Puente, Eddie Palmieri and Poncho Sanchez sold the music as Latin jazz."

Growing up in a major Latino community, Rodriguez recalls he hears mariachi, ranchera, pop music and a little Latin jazz on the radio. "When I was 10 and starting to play the trumpet, I never wanted to play mariachi music. When I was 14 and a student at Salesian High School in Boyle Heights, I joined a band of older kids, the Three Counts, who knew I could play trumpet and that's when jazz improvisation comes into my life."

Today, while wearing various musical hats, he feels music "is part of the whole essence of what life is. It makes some of us musical poets and allows us to communicate, which is essentially what music does."

If anything, Bobby is a communicator, a fact he underscores during his third Playboy Festival appearance in June of 2003 when he appears for the first time leading his Salsa Orchestra on a bill replete with Latin artists. This wide array of Latin music styles is the draw for Bonnie and I to attend the 25th edition of this most popular of music festivals in the City of Angels. Representing the wide horizon of Latin music are: Poncho Sanchez and his Latin jazz band, Los Hombres Calientes (an octet co-founded by percussionist Bill Summers and trumpeter Irvin Mayfield which explores the connections between New Orleans and Afro-Caribbean music), Ozomatli (the multi-cultural, racial dynamite stick which tries to be hip by adding hip-hop to the mix of jazz and Latin elements), and Daniela Mercury (a Brazilian vocalist stressing the samba and reggae rhythms).

Los Hombres Calientes offers a lesson in cultural blending, percussive grooves from Cuba, Haiti, Jamaica, New Orleans, African chants, flighty trumpet solos and the inspiration for the audience to rise up, dance and wave white hankies at the band. Ozmatli is also a crowd pleaser in its own way, its 10 members bombarding the Bowl with its array of percussion instruments, Mexican music, minimal jazz, English rap lyrics, rock guitars, saxophone, trumpet, electric piano. Everyone is in motion, first starting out in the middle of the Bowl and weaving its way to the stage and then jumping up and down and swaying sideways. It's high-energy music for people digesting their dinner deserts. It's also not everyone's cup of espresso.

Of these acts, Rodriguez stresses and re-stresses his East L.A. roots during his turn Sunday on stage at 4 p.m. "Well, East L.A. has made it to the Hollywood Bowl," is one of his proud proclamations. The band plays hot jazz over salsa, cha cha, and bossa nova rhythms. In introducing one of his signature compositions-a traditional 12-bar blues-titled *East L.A. Blues* (which appears on the *LatinJazz Explosion* and *Trumpet Talk* CDs), Bobby jokes that "everybody knows the blues started in East L.A." The lyrics are full of neighborhood references to being born "at the corner of Bonnie Beach and Hubbard Street, right next to Calvary Cemetery, where half my family's there, to Whittier Boulevard, Johnny's hotdog stand, East L.A. College, Rio Hondo College, and Cal State L.A. East L.A. is like no other place. If Bobby Rodriguez can make it, so can you, that's the message I bring."

Bobby also tributes his neighborhood on a second tune on the *Explosion* LP, *East L.A. Rasta*, which carries the homeboy message via a reggae beat.

I've noticed in recent years that Playboy keeps adding Latin acts to the line-up, so backstage I ask Bill Farley, Playboy Jazz Festival's vice president, marketing events, about this expansion of its artist roster. "Six years ago it became evident that Latin music and Latin jazz in particular are experiencing bursts of popularity," he says. "It became evident we needed more of this music and we've found it to be a tremendous crowd-pleaser each year. It'll never be the Playboy Latin Jazz Festival. We feel we have to include all forms of Latin music so patrons who come here to see their favorite Latin act will be exposed to other forms of jazz. We've had three or four Latin acts for several years, some marginal like Ozomatli."

After asking Bill to ascertain when Latin artists begin appearing, he comes through with the historical data. "We've included Latin jazz since the festival's inception in 1979 when both Flora Purim and Willie Bobo perform. Willie is a favorite and is back in 1981 and '83, when he teams up with Mongo Santamaria and his band for a Latin reunion. In 1984, Tito Puente makes his festival debut. In 1990, we added more than one Latin act for the first time with the return of Tito as a special guest with Poncho Sanchez's band, and the introduction of the Eliane Elias trio. In 1997, we had two Latin acts on each of the two days: on Saturday Gato Barbieri and Cuba's Los Van Van, and on Sunday Tito Puente and India and Roy Hargrove's Cristol group which features Chucho Valdes, David Sanchez, Changuito and John Bnitez, among the players. In 2000, we have Los Van Van, Rubén Blades, Celia Cruz, and Ozomatli."

Electric violinist Susie Hansen has been leading her own Latin band in Los Angeles since 1990, her instrument playing the melody lines, rather than the trumpet which plays that role in many salsa bands. Yet after listening to her two albums, *The Salsa Never Ends* and *Solo Flight* on her own Jazz Caliente label, you'd never know she has a background in classical, folk music and rock 'n'roll and a degree in electrical engineering from the prestigious Massachusetts Institute of Technology. As one of the few female violinists in Latin music, Hansen is a prime example of definitely being in the right place at the right time. Her chance meeting in January of 1997 in L.A. with Cuba's touring Los Van Van lands her a guest appearance at the band's engagement at the Grand Avenue Club. Another chance meeting with Orquesta Aragon in Cuba several months later also turns into a performing opportunity when that band visits L.A. the next year.

Performing a brand of music patterned around the traditional charanga style which utilizes violin and flute, plus Afro-Cuban rhythms, straight-ahead modern jazz harmonies and both English and Spanish lyrics, Hansen and her 10-member plus band including singers, plays around 200 concerts annually, she says. She also records and plays with other aggregations. She recalls one such engagement in 1991 at the Hollywood Palladium with Tito Puente "who has Marc Anthony and La India (Linda Caballero) singing backgrounds." She calls her own music "danceable Latin" and says her growing audience consists of first- and second-generation Hispanics from all the Americas, pro- and semi-pro salsa dancers and jazz buffs. "It's hard not to have multi-cultural friends; white middle class Americans are more open to my music because our culture is accepting all things Hispanic." Susie says her music is designed to motivate people to dance. "With some Latin bands you don't see people dancing. I think all Latin jazz is danceable. If you play a song with tempo changes or extended solos without a bass or beat, people sit down." The salsa album, she stresses during our conversation, is "mambo-based. It's between 160 and 220 beats per minute on the metronome."

How does she get to play with Los Van Van? Word of mouth. When she finds out through a friend from Cuba that Los Van Van's violinists are having trouble with the solid metal E string on the new Zeta violins they've purchased in Miami prior to coming to Los Angeles, she tells her friend to relay to the Cubans she knows how to fix the problem. They eagerly say come on by, so she brings her fiddle and fine sandpaper and shows them how to sand down the troubling portion of the violin's bridge. "I wound up jamming with them at their hotel and they got excited because I know their Cuban heritage music. So they invited me to play with their two violinists during the two nights they're appearing at the club.

"Then when I tell them I'm going to Cuba for two weeks in February to study at a Caribbean music and dance conference/festival, they meet me in the Havana hotel's lobby. I'm talking with people from all over Latin America when one of the violin players says to me, 'That's Fidel,' pointing out the Cuban leader who's accompanied by his entourage and is surrounded by people. When the violinists invite me to play with them on opening night of Carnival at El Palicio De La Salsa, I said I didn't know their planned repertoire, so they let me join the rhythm section with the violins playing repeat phrases or harmony. Then bandleader Juan Formell let's me play a solo. And that's a blessing. The place where you get to speak your heart is during an improvised solo."

During one of her classes, two violinists from the Orquesta Aragon are her teachers and this chance meeting results in another musical opportunity. One year later, when the band's performing at the Hollywood Palladium, she drops by after finishing her own gig. "Since I had my fiddle they invited me to play on their second set along with their three violins and then let me solo."

This is all heady stuff for Hansen, who at age five is given her first violin by her father, a violinist with the Chicago Symphony for 37 years. "My father is my teacher, who has me play by ear." This early training enables her as a student at the University of Illinois to join a rock band where she discovers she can easily improvise on the blues tunes the band plays. "So I was familiar with improvising in rock and from there it's easy to move to jazz. By the time I had gone through folk, rock, jazz, and started playing Latin jazz with Victor Parra's Mambo Express All Stars in the Chicago area, I was no longer pursing a career in classical music."

The Chicago native, degree in hand, decides instead to go into music and works for several Chicago bands ranging from rock to society music, starts her own ensemble in 1977 which plays society swing music, straight-ahead and Latin jazz and moves to Los Angeles in 1988, trusting the electric violin she's been playing since the late '70s will be her entrée into the West Coast music scene. It does. She meets conga player Angel Figuera from Chicago who introduces her to another congero, Cuban/San Franciscan Francisco Aguabella, who invites her to join his new Latin band. From that band she joins a new group Bobby Matos organizes and then starts her own ensemble which plays a style she devises which is "melodic, rhythmically oriented, and light and flowing. I'm definitely a melody from the heart player," says the woman whose virtuoso violin playing adds luster to her career.

And then there's....

Jennifer Lopez, arguably the most reported upon female Hispanic in show business. From simple beginnings, the second of three daughters of Puerto Rican-born parents being raised in New York City's borough of the Bronx, she emerges to become a triple dynamo in dance, television and films and an entrepreneur with her own $350 million clothing and perfume lines, a restaurant in Pasadena, California, and a well-paid TV spokesperson for Pepsi. It seems she's constantly being signed to develop some kind of project in TV or appear in one more movie. The complexity of her personal and professional lives with their roller coaster ups and downs reflects a woman seemingly impatient and eager for new challenges. Her three marriages spanning 1997 to 2004, along with a highly visible three-year romance from 1999 to 2002, seamlessly blur into another happening in her pursuit for fame, fortune and happiness and not necessarily in that order.

In discussing this beautiful, dynamic celebrity, I've chosen to graph her career by genres, starting with television, her launching pad for national recognition.

Having taken dance lessons as an 11-year-old, in 1990 she tries out to become a "fly girl" backup dancer on Fox TV's pioneering biracial comedy series *In Living Color*. She doesn't get the job, but is called back to replace a dancer who leaves the show. She is one of the unannounced bubbly dancers who add a sense of big city dance routines to the show. She then advances to the TV movie *Nurses on the line: The Crash of Flight 7* and the series *Second Chances*, both in 1993 and two more series in '94: *South Central* and *Hotel Malibu*. In 2003, Lopez and her partner in Nuyorican Productions Benny Medina are signed by NBC-owned Telemundo to a production deal, whose first project is a novela about a girl from a Latin neighborhood in the Bronx who seeks a career in show business and overcome the barriers to this success story. The story line is similar to Lopez's experiences in the Castle Hill section of the Bronx. That year she guests on the season-closing episode of NBC's hit *Will & Grace* series playing herself. In 2004, she returns to the season premiere of the show to continue the short story arc. Lopez's Nuyorican Productions and her new partner in this venture, Simon Fields (who replaces Medina, who's ousted in 2003), sign a development deal with the UPN Network. This time the project is a novela set in toney South Miami Beach, with Lopez one of the executive producers. The series bows on January 11, '06, to tepid reviews. Her company also signs a first-look production deal with Fox TV Studios and Regency TV, but that venture quietly fades away. In 2005, she and husband of nine months Marc Anthony perform their first public duet together on the Grammy Awards, singing in Spanish *Escapémonos* (*Let's Escape*). Jennifer hits a few off-key notes while Marc is very on target. Several weeks later, *People* magazine reveals her off performance is due to a sore throat and swollen glands. During fashion week in New York a few weeks later, MTV airs the special *Jennifer Lopez: Beyond the Runway* showcasing her new Sweetface fall clothing line. She also reactivates her record career with the Epic hit album *Rebirth*, which spawns the hit single *Get Right*.

Films: During her career from 1995 to 2005, she appears in 17 movies, many faded memories, others successful titles, and along the way becomes the highest paid Latina actress ever. Her big screen career starts in 1995 with the drama *My Family/Mi Familia* and the action film *Money Train* opposite Wesley Snipes and Woody

Harrelson; She appears in Francis Ford Coppola's comedy *Jack* in 1996; in 1997 she appears in four films: the thriller *Blood and Wine* opposite Jack Nicholson, *Anaconda*, a horror-adventure-thriller; the steamy *U Turn* opposite Sean Penn and Nick Nolte and *Selena*. For portraying the slain Tejano superstar, she's paid $1 million, the most ever received by a Latina. From this point on, her price escalates. One year later, she receives $2 million for her role as a U.S. Marshal chasing George Clooney and Ving Rhames, two escaped convicts in *Out of Sight*. She also does a voiceover in the animated feature *Antz* and in 2000 is paid $4 million to appear in the psychological drama *The Cell* opposite Vince Vaughn; by 2001 she's receiving $9 million apiece for playing in *Angel Eyes*, a romantic drama and *The Wedding Planner*, a romantic comedy. By 2002, when she's featured as Billy Campbell's battered wife in the revenge thriller *Enough*, her price is $12 million. She also signs to star opposite Robert Redford, Morgan Freeman and Camryn Manheim in the drama *An Unfinished Life*.

In 2003, she films *Gigli* and *Jersey Girl* with Ben Affleck and both turn out to be major flops at the box office; in 2004, she portrays a hotel maid in *Maid In Manhattan* with Ralph Fiennes playing a rich guest who becomes enamored with her; in 2004, she plays a dance instructor in the sad story of marital disconnect in *Shall We Dance* with Richard Gere and Susan Sarandon. She's also signed to star with Nicole Kidman in the period drama *American Darlings*. In 2005, she completes the adversarial comedy *Monster-in-Law* with Michael Vartan and Jane Fonda who's appearing in her first film in 15 years, and her first job since separating from TV mogul Ted Turner whom she marries in 1991. She is next signed to co-star with Antonio Banderas in *Bordertown*, the story of the wanton murders of 300 women in Juarez, Mexico. Gregory Nava, who directs her in *Selena*, is at the helm on this project.

Lopez's Nuyorican production company is signed in 2006 by newly formed Sony BMG Films to co produce *Reggaeton*, the story of a 21-year-old South Bronx rapper who flees to Puerto Rico to avoid trouble with New York thugs and becomes a reggaeton star in the commonwealth. Moving to television, she signs with MTV to to co-executive produce *Moves*, an eight-part reality series about neophyte dancers seeking to become professionals. She auditions and selects the six dancers for the show premiering in the fall of '06.

Records: Her outlet is sporadic and often tied to her film releases once she becomes a powerhouse box office attraction and cultural icon. Overall, her first four CDs click with fans, resulting in an estimated 35 million sales. In 1998, Thomas "Tommy" D. Mottola, chairman and CEO of Sony Music Entertainment, signs her to Sony Records which releases the album *On the 6* in 1999. The title refers to the train she takes from the Bronx to Manhattan. During this project she works with Sean "Puff Daddy" Combs on one tune from the CD and begins a romantic fling with the flamboyant producer, which ends in 2001. Mottola, mentor to once married Mariah Carey and other female stylists Gloria Estefan, Celine Dion, and Shakira, works with J.Lo's manager, Benny Medina, in planning her career moves.

In January of 2001, her new CD, *J.Lo*, becomes the nation's top album, along with her film, *The Wedding Planner*. In 2002, the hit CD *This Is Me…Then* spawns the single *Jenny from the Block*, which casts her as still being a home girl rather than someone having become extremely wealthy. During 2002, Sony also issues *J to the L O: The Remixes*, and in 2003 releases the EP *Reel Me* with a bonus DVD, while her single with LL Cool J, *All I have*, hits No. 1 on the *Billboard* Hot 100 singles chart.

In 2005, the single, *Get Right* from the forthcoming album, *Rebirth*, is released January 22, debuts on the Hot 100 in 53rd place and moves upward to No. 1 on March 26.

Rebirth, her fifth studio session, is released as both a single CD and DualDisc with a DVD component, blends elements of rap, R&B, Latin and pop music, and debuts on the general market best-selling list March 19 at No. 2. For the CD, Jennifer pens two songs, *Cherry Pie* and *(Can't Believe) This Is Me*. A number of writer/producers including husband Marc Anthony contribute other tunes. *(Can't*

Believe) This Is Me will also appear in the all-Spanish album she and Anthony are working on for a fall release. Because of her stormy marital and romantic encounters, dissected with alacrity by celebrity-driven publications, critics look for hidden meanings behind her music.

The new release, she reveals to *Billboard* is designed "to put the spotlight back on my career." *Rebirth* and *Get Right* both begin sliding down their respective charts after 18 weeks. By May 21, the single is off the Hot 100, while the album slides downward; By June 25, the album is in 151st place. A new rap-like style single featuring Fat Joe, *Hold You Down*, also makes its appearance on the new *Billboard* Pop 100 survey in April and after 16 weeks it's nestled in the 97th slot, its final resting place.

2006 is the year J.Lo stresses her Hispanic roots with her first all-Spanish album, *Cómo Ama Una Mujer*, featuring ballads written and produced by hitmaster Estéfano.

Personal relationships: They're as diverse and explosive which naturally attracts the celebrity media, which keeps her in the spotlight, providing millions of dollars worth of free publicity, some of it with a negative tinge. In 1999, her first marriage to model and waiter Ojani Noa ends after 13 months. In September 1999, she begins dating Sean "Puffy" Combs, a hotshot New York rap music mogul, whose late night escapades with Jennifer results in their being stopped by New York City police after they flee a shooting at a Manhattan nitery. Although she's not charged and the 32-year-old Combs is acquitted of charges of bribery and possessing a concealed weapon (a gun), the fracas places her in an awkward situation, which ends three years later when she breaks off their romance on Valentine's Day. The next man in her life is Cris Judd, 32, a dancer who appears in one of her music videos in 2000, with whom she sparks a romance resulting in their getting engaged in June of 2001 and marrying in September. In April of 2002 when she opens her Cuban restaurant, Madrés, in Pasadena, she hires ex-hubby Noa as manager. Nine months after they're married, the couple separate, with Jennifer subsequently filing divorce papers on July 25, 2002.

In December of 2001, Jennifer and her next beau to be, A-list actor Ben Affleck meet while they're filming *Gigli*. By mid-July of 2002, they're a romantic "item," another irritant in her marriage with Judd. Affleck showers Jennifer with expensive gifts during their courtship in 2003. When *Jersey Girl*, in which they costar, flops at the box office, their flamboyant spending on homes in Georgia, Miami and the Hollywood Hills, cars and jewelry keeps them in the public spotlight, especially when they announce plans to wed in September in Santa Barbara, California. Instead, their 18-month romance ends in January 2004. One general reason given for the breakup of two high-profile show business personalities: they each seek different goals in life and there seems to be no middle ground to keep them together.

Enter Marco Antonio Muniz, better known as Marc Anthony, with whom Jennifer has worked in 1998 in Anthony's music video, *No Me Conoces* (*You Don't Know Me*) and with whom she records their first duet, *No Me Ames* (*Don't Love Me*), in 1999 on her debut album, *On the 6*. She also dates him in 1998 but as history shows, moves on to other romances, starting with "P Diddy." In May 2000, Anthony marries Dayanara Torres, 29, the 1993 Miss Universe one year after meeting her in her native Puerto Rico. They have two sons, Cristian and Ryan (Anthony also has a daughter, Arianna, now 11 by a previous relationship with ex-girlfriend Debbie Rosado, a former New York City policewoman, with whom he shares custody) before separating in July of 2002. After five months apart, they renew their vows in December. Torres files to dissolve the marriage in January of 2004; Cristian is three and Ryan is five months old. After rebounding from her Affleck misfire (labeled "Bennifer" by the media) by dating Anthony, in June of 2004, Jennifer, 34, and Marc, 35, are married in the backyard of her Beverly Hills mansion, five days after his divorce with Torres is final and two months shy of her 35th birthday. During the filming of *Monster-in-Law*, Arianna joins her dad in visiting Lopez on the set.

Although the two share Puerto Rican heritage and a New York upbringing, Jennifer's career outshines Anthony's. By 2004, she has four platinum albums and 17 film credits. He has two platinum albums and 11 films on his resume. Of her 2005 coming out Grammy duet with her husband, she proclaims in *People:* "It's great singing with Marc, it is great singing with hugely talented people." The duo are also represented on the best-selling charts in '05: Jennifer with the single *Get Right* and the album *Rebirth* and Marc with two Spanish-language albums, *Amar Sin Mentiras* (*To Love Without Lies*) and *Valio La Pena*. The duo will work together on *El Cantante*, the film of the late Puerto Rican salsa star, sonero Hector Lavoe with him playing the lead role and her as the producer. Lavoe, born in Ponce, where he begins his singing career, moves to New York in 1963 where he's teamed with Willie Colon for a series of Fania albums. Along with the late Cuban bandleaders Mario Bauzá and Machito, Lavoe helps create the 1970's salsa splash in New York. In 1973, Lavoe and Colon split up, Lavoe forms his own band and subsequently enters a dark period of drug use and poverty and passes away purportedly of AIDS in 1993 in New York at age 47.

Interim romances aside, life gets nasty between Jennifer and her longtime personal manager Benny Medina. In August of 2002, as a sign of a strained relationship, their verbal management pact in effect since 1998 is formalized in a written contract. In June 2003, she fires him and files a complaint with the California Labor Commissioner, accusing him of obtaining jobs for her as an unlicensed talent agent, a legal no no in California. In a separate lawsuit, she alleges he misappropriates more than $100,000 and seeks to recover the money he makes during the five years he represents her plus 10 percent interest. Medina denies any wrongdoing.

Business ventures: Clothing lines J.Lo (2004) and the new high-end Sweetface (2005); fragrances: Glow and Still Jennifer Lopez (2002) and Miami Glow by J.Lo (2005). Restaurants: Madre's (2002).

Amid all this capitalistic success, J.Lo or "Jenny from the Block," as she's also been referred to because of her Bronx upbringing, is eagerly sought by a media all too cooperative in promoting her latest branded item. That's why in 2005 she's

Billboard's page one feature promoting her new *Rebirth* album and performs songs from the CD on NBC's *Today Show* from the plaza outside the show's Rockefeller Plaza studio. And why she appears in glossy magazine layouts, or does a revealing interview with the *Associated Press*—which guarantees widespread exposure—and allows her to explain the sensitive reasons her business activities are publicly exploited, like the new album and fashion line, while her private life is kept...private. In the story appearing in the *Houston Chronicle*, which notes she takes eight months before acknowledging her marriage to Marc Anthony, she details her reasons for her determined control of her life. "I don't want to talk about anything that is personal or private at all, because what's the use? You're open with people and then they try to make a soap opera out of your life. Then it's not about your work anymore, it's not about the movie you're promoting or the record you hope your fans will enjoy," she says. "It becomes about other silly stuff and it's damaging." She also notes: "I used to be the kind of person who would talk about a lot of things, but as I've matured I've realized that's not the best way to go. You have to set boundaries...and you have to protect what's sacred to you."

It's a safe assumption that performing smartly in public for her fans is a sacrosanct function of retaining her fan base and remaining a popular show business celebrity. So when she makes one of her first musical appearances on May 14, 2005, at contemporary hits radio station KIIS-FM's annual Wango Tango concert at the Angel Stadium in Anaheim before an audience of 12-year-old girls and older teens following good reviews for the release of *Monster-In Law*, her first film with formerly retired actress Jane Fonda, you'd assume she'd do everything right. Wrong.

Not only is she given mixed reviews for her singing and is suspected by some reviewers of lip-synching to a prerecorded track, she shows unquestionably bad taste by wearing a T-shirt with "Fuck It" clearly in full frontal view. What message is this profane prose sending to her teen fans? For someone selling her own upscale, classy clothing line, this raunchy, classless statement may reveal a facet of her emerging persona which has never been exposed before.

Articles

"George Lopez Lashes Out At ABC." Los Angeles Times, May 15, 2007

"MTV 'Moves' With Lopez Reality Series." Hollywood Reporter, May 22, 2006

"Lopez En Espanol." Latin Notas, Billboard, Feb. 4, 2006

"Born Again." Hispanic, February 2006

"Sony BMG Cues 'Reggaeton.'" Daily Variety, Jan. 23, 2006

"Garcia Dealt An 'Aces' Gig." Daily Variety, Oct. 14, 2005

"They're Linked In Spirit And Schedule." Los Angeles Times, Oct. 12, 2005

"State Of The Clave." Down Beat, September 2005

"Creative Emmy Stint For Lopez." Daily Variety Aug. 19, 2005

"Chicanos And The Man." LA Weekly, June 17, 2005

"Lopez Tackles U's 'World.'" Daily Variety, June 9, 2005

"A Stand-Up Wife Helps Lopez Stay On A Roll." Los Angeles Times, June 3, 2005

"Wife Donates Kidney To Lopez." Los Angeles Times, April 27, 2005

"Lopez Keeps Music In Spotlight, Private Life In Dark." Houston Chronicle, March 7, 2005

"Jennifer Lopez This Is Me…Now." People, March 7, 2005

"Her Hot New Designer Line." Star, Feb. 28, 2005

"New York's New Style Stars." Us, Feb. 28, 2005

"Jennifer Back On Track." Billboard, Feb. 19, 2005

"Miami Spice For UPN." Daily Variety, Dec. 8, 2004

"Right On Time." Jazziz, September 2004

"Jennifer Lopez Her Crazy Busy Fall." Star, Aug. 30, 2004

"Monster Comeback." Weekly Variety, Aug. 23, 2004

"A Star Turn On Screen For Feijoo." Los Angeles Times, Aug. 22, 2004

"J.Lo To Perform 'Will & Grace' Encore." USA Today, Aug. 18, 2004

"Nest In Peace." People, July 26, 2004

"Jennifer's Big Surprise," People, June 21, 2004

"Getting Serious." People, June 14, 2004

"Cristina Marks Anniversary, Plans More Ventures." Houston Chronicle, May 14, 2004

"Why Is Jennifer Hiding Marc Anthony?" Us, May 10, 2004

"J.Lo In First Look Deal With Fox TV, Regency." Daily Variety, March 10, 2004

"Reency Gets Into The Swing." Daily Variety, March 10, 2004

"J.Lo's Steamy New Affair." Star, Feb. 24, 2004

"Ssshhh! The New Lovebirds!" Star, Feb. 24, 2004

"Why J.Lo Gave Up On Ben." InTouch, Feb. 9, 2004

"Prosecutor To Probe Juarez's Serial Killings." Los Angeles Times, Jan. 31, 2004

"Commission Criticizes Probes Of Juarez Slayings." Los Angeles Times, Nov. 25, 2003

"Touching Cuba." Hispanic Magazine, October 2003

"Herbie Mann, 73: Jazz Flutist Explored Genres." Los Angeles Times, July 2, 2003

"What A Difference A Year Makes." People, Aug. 4, 2003

"Payback Time." People, July 21, 2003

"When Jenny Dumped Benny. New York Times, July 15, 2003

"J.Lo Inks Prod'n Pact With Telemundo." Daily Variety, May 5, 2003

J.Lo & Ben Surprise Surprise!" Us, August, 12, 2002

"J.Lo & Cris-The Split Explained." Us, June 24, 2002

"Mags: Divorce Looms For Lopez." USA Today, June 13, 2002

"It Seems J. Lo Has Had Enough Of Judd." USA Today, June 10, 2002

"Livin' La Vida Lopez." People, May 27, 2002

"In 'Enough,' No Victimhood for Lopez." Los Angeles Times, May 20, 2002

"Concord In 'Perfecta' Deal." Billboard, May 18, 2001

"Music For The Millennium." Los Angeles Times, April 28, 1996

"Hollywood: Are Two J-Fleck Movies Too Many?" Newsweek, April 14, 2003

"Double Play: NL, Lopez Cuff Blair Cop Spec." Hollywood Reporter, Feb. 3, 2003

"Keeping J. Lo In Spotlight Has Risks As Well As Rewards." New York Times, Dec. 9, 2002

"Wife Gives Abusive Husband Just Deserts?" Los Angeles Times, May 24, 2002

Redford's 'Life' With Lopez." Daily Variety, Feb. 12, 2002

"J.Lo-CEO." Us, June 10, 2002

Chapter 12
CAPITULO 12

Cuban Connection: 1979–2005
CONEXION CUBANA: 1979–2005

• Politics dominates efforts by U.S. firms to easily gain access to Cuban entertainers.

• New Cuban music stars and styles receive enthusiastic reception in the U.S. after a long absence due to continued U.S. trade embargo.

• Defecting Cuban musicians establish a new life in the U.S.A., but it's not all glory.

• The *Buena Vista Social Club* album breathes new life into an aging group of retired musicians performing music of the pre-revolutionary decades and spawns a cottage industry of spin-off albums and a film/TV documentary.

• Festivals, concerts, and clubs welcome elite visiting Cuban artists.

• American record companies compete to gain new Cuban artists.

• Steven Spielberg attends a film festival in Havana showcasing his eight movies and joins a growing list of people calling for the end of the 40-year U.S. trade embargo.

• Superstars Celia Cruz and Mongo Santamaria pass away.

Cuba and the United States have been musical romantics since the 1920s when the first Cuban jazz bands emerge in Havana. In the 1930s, the first American style Cuban big bands add another dimension to the romance. And in the '40s, Cuban musicians start melding their own roots ingredients to their American-inspired jazz ensembles. Out of this mixture emerge the mambo, cha cha, and Afro-Cuban jazz. Once New York's vibrant music community catches hold of the fiery blending of Cuba's Afro-Caribbean inventions, there's no stopping the infusion of these elements into the music which feeds the passions of New York City's Hispanic populace, principally from Puerto Rico. Musicians like Mario Bauzá and Francisco Grillo, better known as Machito, along with Luciano "Chano" Pozo and Arturo "Chico" O'Farrill, are the pioneering musicians credited with the growth of Afro-Cuban music which influences a host of American musicians to add a Latin spice to their repertoires. Of these pioneers, Pozo tragically dies when he's only 33 in 1948, a bullet through his heart resulting from a dispute over a marijuana sale in a Harlem café, ending his career and his life, tragically young.

With the messianic takeover by Fidel Castro in 1959, the free-flow of musical ideas from Cuba across the 90 miles of Atlantic Ocean to the U.S., abruptly ends and is enforced by a U.S. embargo against Castro which means no more business dealings between the two nations. No more business, no more creative ideas, no more new musical treats. But that void will be filled by rules which allow restricted visits to Cuba and the importing of records which are produced by a second party company and licensed to American firms.

We are left to our own inventions in the decades to come, until 1979 when the first attempt at a cultural bridge between the two countries is attempted. It's the "Havana Jam" music festival sponsored by Columbia Records and sanctioned by the U.S. and Cuba, which I fully detail in Chapter 2. The most significant thing to come out of that three-day weekend in February is the discovery of how advanced Cuban music has become, how it is fusing endemic parts of its history in modern ways to create new styles of music. In the years to come, these forms of Cuban music start trickling into this country, and by the early '90s, Americans are hearing on record and seeing in person, albeit on a very small scale, the makers and shakers of the new Cuban school of music. And it's at this point that I take up the story of how the Cuban Connection once again impacts America, only this time it becomes a vital contributor to the growth of the domestic Latin entertainment industry. In a sense, it's hidden fruit status makes it all the more appealing to people looking for something new to latch onto—besides the salsa styles of Puerto Rico and New York, the stimulating merengue rhythms from the Dominican Republic and the inbred music of Mexico, which dominates much of the Latin music scene—something with a Caribbean flavor all its own.

Cuban artists, those that defect or visit these shores, discover an accepting audience in cities across the nation—except in Miami. There will be isolated cases where political pressure is used to frighten Cuban musicians from playing in Miami, where musicians will join the list of defectors and where some Cuban players will have problems gaining their visas to perform in this country.

Several Cubans become known by their first names: Paquito and Arturo and Chucho, for example. In early 1993, two of them, Paquito D'Rivera and Arturo Sandoval, tour the nation leading their own bands. Both are former members of the influential Cuban fusion band Irakere which is one of the musical highlights of "Havana Jam." Nineteen years later, I don't recall their solo performances, only the creative power of the ensemble, so when I read Paquito and Arturo are on the same bill, that's a must-see event for me. During their concert at UCLA's 64-year-old Royce Hall, D'Rivera leads his aptly titled Havana New York Ensemble. In this band are a pianist and trumpeter from Argentina, a bassist from Peru and a drummer from Spain. Sandoval chooses to work with an all American quintet.

Ever aware of his Cuban roots, D'Rivera who defects in 1980, links his country's musical heritage to his opening remark: "Good evening ladies and gentlemen, welcome to the Tropicana," Havana's famous open air nightclub, now state-operated, which I visit in 1974 during the "Havana Jam" excursion. D'Rivera tells the audience he's on a mission to change this nation's "Carmen Miranda syndrome," a reference to the late 1930s to 1940s film star whose singing is often overshadowed by her signature high hats adorned with fruit. "There's such a lack of knowledge about Latin American music by Americans," he adds.

Sandoval, who defects in 1990, arrives for the show after an overnight flight from Osaka, Japan, admits "he's very tired. But I'm going to try my best." The comment draws applause. Sandoval's stratospheric and flighty trumpet catches on with American audiences. After recording his first band album in the U.S., *Hot House*, for K2K Encoded Music in '98, he embarks on a nine-city U.S. tour to gain visibility within the Latin community. One track from the album aimed at radio play is *Tito*, a salute to Tito Puente, who performs on the tune along with Cuban salsa artist Rey Ruiz.

Chucho, known formally as Jesus "Chucho" Valdés, Cuba's legendary pianist and leader of its Irakere fusion fireworks ensemble, is barely known in the U.S. because of the trade embargo against Cuba which makes it difficult for Cuban artists to easily appear in the U.S. That changes in 1997 when Valdés, director of the Havana Jazz Festival, invites American trumpeter Roy Hargrove and a host of other American musicians to perform at the festival. Unlike the first Havana Jazz Festival two years ago where a group of lesser-known American perform, this year's version features top names like Billy Taylor, David Sanchez, Steve Coleman, and Latin Flavor, among others. Valdés tells *The New York Times:* "I made a special effort this year to invite as many people as possible because the time is really right." Several of the musicians, including Hargrove and Sanchez jam with Cuban bands after the concerts, and a number of U.S. talent scouts and concert promoters are looking for bands to bring to the U.S., following the passage in 1994 of California's U.S. Democratic Representative Howard Berman's "Free Trade in Ideas Act" which includes the right to travel and the free exchange of ideas inside Cuba.

As for Roy Hargrove, he reciprocates by inviting Valdés to Rome to guest solo in the 10-piece band he calls Crisol which records an eponymous album for Verve. The band then returns to New York where it plays several dates, providing Chucho with major city exposure. Another New York musician trekking to Cuba to record is alto saxophonist Steve Coleman, who combines his Mystic Rhythm Society with Cuba's Afro Cuban De Mantanzas Society to create *The Sign and the Seal: Transmissions of the Metaphysics of a Culture* on RCA. The album melds roots music from West Africa with the chant sounds of Cuba's Yoruba culture.

Chucho and Irakere (which means forest in African) both gain entry into the domestic market in 1997 by signing with EMI Canada, for whom he records his first studio album, *Bele Bele En La Habana*, a melding of Cuban, Caribbean, and American musical forms, which is released the next year and earns Valdés a Grammy nomination. Following the album's release, Valdés launches his first U.S. tour with his quartet of bassist Alain Peréz Rodriguez, percussionist Roberto Vizcaino, and drummer Raul Piñeda Rogue. First stop: two weeks at New York's venerated Village Vanguard, which is also a hallmark for the pianist: it's his first-ever extended booking at a major venue. Other cities on the itinerary are Philadelphia, Washington, St. Paul, Minnesota, Palo Alto, California, and Los Angeles.

Irakere actually makes its premier appearance in the U.S. in 1979 on two CBS/Columbia Records albums recorded live during "Havana Jam." The new deal allows EMI's American labels Blue Note or Metro Blue, which specializes in world music, to release their recordings in the U.S. It's a major first for a major American label. Bruce Lundvall, CBS Records former president and creator of "Havana Jam" and now president of Angel, Blue Note, and Metro Blue, indicates 56-year-old Valdés' first live album will be his solo appearance at the Jazz at Lincoln Center concert series in January of '98. "We've also got a licensing deal through EMI Spain to release new albums from the Cuban label Caribe, which gives us a number of artists, including Manolin, who calls himself *El Medico De Salsa*."

Valdés, the mercurial pianist, records two additional albums, *Yemayá*, with Irakere and *Briyumba Palo Congo* (*Religion of the Congo*), with two percussionists and bass, in which his lightning bolt fast arpeggios and complex phrasing reflect the influences on him of American pianists McCoy Tyner and Bill Evans. Lundvall infers other as yet unsigned Cuban bands will be coming through the EMI pipeline.

Meanwhile, Valdés, whose musical heritage dates back to his famous father, Bebo Valdés, the pianist/composer and musical director of the Tropicana, becomes Blue Note's top Cuban artist. Live is the key to his winning his first Grammy for *Live at the Village Vanguard*, named the best Latin jazz album. He follows this up with *Chucho Valdés Solo: Live in New York*. A resident of Cancun, Mexico, he also records two albums which feature tunes by his father Bebo, *Encantando* for Town Crier and *La Timba* for J&N. He and Irakere also perform together on *Cubanismo Live!* on Bembe, along with pianist Hilario Duran and the Cuban All Stars' *Killer Tumbao* (with guest Canadian saxophonist/flutist Jane Bunnett) on the Canadian label Justin Time, which has its own Cuban connection for recordings it can import into the U.S., and are among the year's most adventurous albums.

In an amazing display of the power of old Cuban musicians and their music, 1997 is the pivotal year guitarist Ry Cooder's produced album, *Buena Vista Social Club*, is released in the U.S. on World Circuit/Nonesuch and unleashes a cottage industry of concerts and albums by its key senior citizen members, who suddenly see their limp careers re-energized as a result of the album, which in 1998 wins a Grammy as top tropical album, sells 500,000 copies in the U.S. to be certified gold, and is the subject of a similarly titled 1999 documentary by German filmmaker Wim Wenders. Buena Vista Social Club members totaling nearly 20 men and one woman, whose average age is 70, include bandleader Juan De Marcos, vocalists Compay Segundo, 91 (who also plays guitar) and Ibrahim Ferrer, 71, pianist Rubén González, 79, bassists Barbito Torres and Orlando Lopez Vergara, guitarist Eliades Ochoa, and female vocalist Omara Portuondo, represent the golden era in Cuban music, pre-Castro, when the son, danzón, mambo, cha cha, and bolero are the popular musical styles. Despite little Latin radio play in the U.S., somehow linked to fear of reprisals by right-wing Cuban exile groups, the album is one of the year's amazing success stories and nonetheless starts appearing on *Billboard*'s Latin best-selling chart in 1998 and eventually hits No. 1; by 1999 it crosses over to the mainstream top 200 album chart at No. 97 and then rises to number 80, propelled by the release in 1999 of the Wim Wenders documentary. By 2003, the album will sell 5.5 million copies globally, as the world rediscovers and obviously enjoys the vintage sounds of Cuba.

Ry Cooper, a guitarist who records 11 albums under his name from 1970 to 1987, becomes enthralled with Cuban music while living in New York in the 1960s. In 1977, he visits Cuba as part of a jazz cultural exchange boat tour with Dizzy Gillespie which docks in Havana. In collecting tapes of Cuban music he ends up with one by an unidentified musician playing the six-stringed tres guitar. Cooder finds Cuban music deeply emotional and is impressed by its intricate rhythms and melodies. In 1996, Nick Gold, owner of the British label World Circuit, invites him to join him in Havana where he's recording an album by the Afro Cuban All Stars and then plans to have Cooder help record Cuban and African musicians from Mali. When the Africans are unable to obtain visas, the duo refocuses on recording evergreen Cuban music. Gold reveals to the *Los Angeles Times* in 2001 that the idea for this album featuring older Cuban musicians comes from Juan De Marcos Gonzalez, head of the traditional Cuban band Sierra Maestra which records two CDs for the label. In hiring top tres player González to line up the musicians for the all-star album, and then conduct that ensemble as the Buena Vista Social Club, Cooder discovers that's González on the 20-year-old tape. The second band is given the name for a previously popular Havana hangout, whose address no one seems to recall in the east Havana hills. State-run Egram studios, in a terrible state of decay, is where the two sessions take place, and since Cooder has brought his son Joachim with him, Joachim sits in with band playing a Cuban drum.

In attempting to get to Cuba in 1966, Cooder fails to apply for a license from the U.S. Treasury Department's Office of Foreign Assets Control, claiming he believes cultural exchanges do not require a license. Nevertheless, he is fined $25,000 upon his return, a fact which does not surface until 2001—when Cooder attempts a second trip to Cuba for additional Buena Vista projects, which also involve political intrigue, which I'll get to.

Veteran German-born film director Wenders knows Cooder for 20 years. While the two are working on the soundtrack for Wenders film, *End of Violence* in 1997, he hears the *Buena Vista Social Club* album and Cooder enthusing about the great stories the musicians relay about their past and present lives. So he tells Cooder he'll accompany him on his next trip to Havana to film the principals. One year later, Wenders will film the Cooder-produced documentary which will be released in 1999. The film is shot in three weeks and shows the musicians as they record vocalist Ferrer's solo album. Each of the featured players are filmed in different parts of the city, which itself becomes a star of the movie, crumbling buildings amidst historic Spanish-themed edifices. Wenders both praises the city while noting its state of atrophy. "Havana is very imposing. It's so incredibly colorful. All the faded colors are so strong in that light. But it is very sad to see the city crumbling," he tells the *Los Angeles Times.* Cuba's economy is crumbling since the end of Soviet subsidies in 1990. Wenders also includes footage of the band's 1998 concert appearances first in Amsterdam and then at Carnegie Hall, where guitarist Cooder joins the band on stage. After filming more than 80 hours, Wenders edits it down to 90 minutes.

While watching a tape of the documentary at home, one particular poignant scene recalls my own experiences walking the streets of mid-Manhattan laden with stores selling tourist-attracting items. Band members Manuel Licea and Pio Leyva, walking amidst all the towering skyscrapers and gaping at the imposing buildings with awe, pass a souvenir store whose window offers enticing statues of celebrities. They stop to gaze at the figures and begin identifying those they recognize like Louis Armstrong and film stars Laurel and Hardy. There's one person whose name eludes them. Talking in a quiet manner, they try to figure out who they're looking at. "I can't remember, but he's one of the great leaders," is one of their searching comments. They're looking into the face of John F. Kennedy, the assassinated American president, who orders the failed Bay of Pigs invasion of Cuba in 1961 and thwarts Soviet premier (from 1958 to 1964) Nikita Khrushchev's attempts to arm Cuba with missiles capable of hitting the U.S.

The documentary film, distributed by Artisan Entertainment and playing on around 50 screens in major markets, is credited with boosting the sales of solo albums by Ferrer and Rubén Gonzàlez. Following the release of the original *Buena Vista* album in 1996, 77-year-old González records his first-ever LP as a bandleader, *Introducing Rubén González* in April of that year. Three years later, spin-off albums emerge. *Buena Vista Social Club Presents Irbrahim Ferrer* is the 72-year-old's solo debut as is Omar Portuondo's self-titled release. All these albums plus the Buena Vista spin-off band, the Afro Cuban All Star's LP, *Distinto Diferento*, are on Nonesuch which is licensed from the U.K.'s World Circuit. The dual label credit is the result of a U.S. embargo prohibiting American labels from making records in Cuba.

World Circuit/Nonesuch—having achieved success with its Buena Vista Social Club album—now reaches into Cuba's musical past for two albums among four recorded in 1979 by the Estrellas De Areito, a group of musicians focused on recording their native song format called son, which takes on the formal identity of salsa in the U.S. Among the band's personnel at the Egram studios sessions in Havana are several names now familiar to American audiences: Arturo Sandoval, Rubén González, and senior citizen vocalist Pio Leyva, who appear on the two albums, *Los Héróes* and *Cuban All Stars.*

World Circuit/Nonesuch is by no means finished with Buena Vista product. The band's concert appearances at Carnegie Hall and in Amsterdam last year, comprise the nucleus for the live album coming out later this year at the same time the Wim Wenders documentary premieres in this country, following its initial showing in Havana.

Two other members of the band record solo albums for different labels. Singer Eliades Ochoa records his album, *Eliades Ochoa Y El Cuarteto Patria Sublime Illusion*, for Higher Octave, while Cuban lute virtuoso Barbarito Torres headlines *Havana Cafe* for Havana Caliente. Nonesuch also packages tunes for a new album, *Los Heroes*, originally recorded in earlier jam sessions by the band Estrellas De Areito, whose members are part of the ensemble on the main Buena Vista album. To the surprise of most people, sales for *Buena Vista Social Club* are close to 2 million worldwide, and by 2000 exceed three million copies. PBS acquires TV rights to Wenders' similarly titled documentary, which further exposes the lives of the featured band members and their recollections of music in pre-revolutionary Cuba.

While the World Circuit/Nonesuch albums of vintage Cuban music are targeted towards Ry Cooder's world music following, the Higher Octave CD focuses on the Latin market. So there's a dichotomy between who's buying what, reveals the *Los Angeles Times*. Buena Vista Social Club patrons are second- and third-generation Latinos, not their parents, and 35- to 55-year-old Caucasians, whose interests are piqued by the general market media splurge coverage over the albums and the documentary.

Buena Vista musicians, in the guise of the Afro Cuban All Stars, make their first appearance on the West Coast in 1998 at the fifth annual Hollywood Salsa and Latin Jazz Festival at the Hollywood Bowl. Cooder joins them for one tune.

When the entire Buena Vista Social Club attempts to perform in Miami in February of '99, fears for their safety forces the band to cancel its concert. They cite an earlier incident in which thousands of Cuban exile protesters' anger over the appearance of Los Van Van results in insults and bottles being directed at concertgoers. As a result of this fracas, politicians in Miami-Dade and the city announce they are opposed to Los Van Van appearing in Miami again, citing public safety concerns. Protests by Cuban exiles primarily in Miami over the years against the appearance by musicians living under the Castro regime, underscores the irony of their living in a nation which espouses free speech, yet they refuse to grant this right to the visiting musicians, and those sympathetic people who wish to hear their music. Cuban anger aside, individual Buena Vista Social Club members Ferrer, González, Torres, Ochoa, and Segundo hit the touring circuit in '99 with their ensembles to cities where they are welcome.

By 2000, Ferrer's fortunes outshine all the other band members. Five years after he's discovered shining shoes, his solo LP is among the Grammy nominees in the traditional tropical Latin category. He and pianist González perform a song during the telecast's salute to Latin music along with two young studs, Ricky Martin and Marc Anthony. His elation over his newfound star status emerges during an interview with *USA Today*. "I would have liked this to happen when I was younger. But I'm happy it's happening now. I can see that it was destined. It's a magical thing." Sales from his solo record—which by 2001 total 1.4 million sold copies—enable him to upgrade his lifestyle, he explains, by buying and remodeling a house and providing assistance to his enlarged family which includes his wife, five children, two stepchildren, 13 grandchildren, and five great-grandchildren.

There are, of course, other developments occurring in Cuban music besides Buena Vista's vast tentacles. In what is certainly a first for Latin instrumental music, both Juan Formell and his Los Van Van band and Formell's 36-year-old son, Juan Carlos, are nominated for Latin Grammys in 2000. The Van Van gang is competing in the salsa category with *Llego Van Van* on Caliente Records, while the younger Formell, who significantly defects from his homeland in 1993 while performing in Mexico with Rumbavana to subsequently reside in New York, is vying in the traditional tropical category with his debut album, *Songs from a Little Blue House*, on Wicklow. Although father and son, who writes music and plays the bass, keep in touch by phone, they are at opposite polls of the political spectrum; the father is part of the establishment while Juan Carlos refers to himself as being part of the generation of Cubans who object to the government's oppressive policies. He tells the *Los Angeles Times* he calls his music "post-Castro because I sing for the heart and soul of a Cuba that has lost her voice, and I tell the truth."

While stories abound of Cubans defecting under different circumstances, Juan Carlos literally swims to freedom. Working its way north through Mexico from Chiapas, Juan Carlos is reported to have stripped off his clothes and swam across the Rio Grande from Nuevo Laredo, Mexico, holding his clothes over his head. Once in Laredo, Texas, he's arrested, and when he tells the police he's Cuban, he's told he can either go to Mexico or to a jail in the U.S. He chooses jail and a relative in New York posts his bond and he heads to the Big Apple and a life in music.

Cuban music with a French flair by two Paris-based groups, and one living in Miami, are being showcased on Higher Octave Records of Malibu, California. Among the bands are Sergent Garcia, a singer/guitarist/rapper whose musical base is a blending of the traditional son style with the newer timba; P18, a 13-piece band proponent which plays a combination of electronic and tropical music, and Orishas, ex-Cubans living in Miami who rap about problems in their former home. This wave of musicians living in Paris tends to focus on lyrics which dissect the underbelly of society in terms of immigration, justice, and poverty, all to a modern Cuban beat. Higher Octave's chief operating officer, Joe Rakauskas has stated that Paris nourishes musical experimentation, resulting in hybrid forms developing. Garcia's debut album, *Un Poquito Quema'o*, reflects his Spanish/French heritage. P18's debut album, *Urban Cuban*, reflects its ethnically mixed French and Latin backgrounds.

Cuban music with a New Orleans twist is what makes *Cubanismo in New Orleans Mardi Gras Mambo* so appealing to American ears. The 13-piece Cuban band, as well as a New Orleans contingent, John Boutte and the Vocamo All Stars, consisting of 22 musicians, explore commonalities in the musical connection between New Orleans and Havana. The bilingual album, with English spoken by the New Orleans players, offers gutsy bluesy tunes, brass band marching tempos, African-Cuban rumbas, and American jazz of Bourbon Street which seems natural when juxtaposed against the blazing Cuban rhythms of the Malecon, Cuba's famed seafront region. This album is an update of the close connection between New Orleans and Havana dating back to the 1920s and '30s. Jesús Alemañy, the band's trumpet-playing leader notes that while Cubanismo visits New Orleans during the past five years, the idea for the fusion of cultures CD belongs to local Hannibal Records, which is distributed by Rykodisc. The recording at two New Orleans studios produces one big, happy, spicy, enticing gumbo.

Blue Note cooks up its own menu of enticing historic recordings featuring Cuban musicians in a reissue series titled *The Roots of Afro-Cuban Jazz* which focuses on achievements in the '50s and '60s by both Latin and American musicians. Among the musicians showcased in the series are Machito and his orchestra (*Machito: Kenya*), percussionist Candido "Sabu" Martinez (*Sabu: Palo Congo*), and Carlos "Patato" Valdes. Anglo musicians paying tribute to Latin music include Julian Cannonball Adderley and his Bossa Rio Sextet, and Art Blakey.

Two small labels, FTC and Winter and Winter, also check in with Cuban compilation sets. FTC's Canciones *Cubanas Del Milenio* spotlights Beny Moré, Celia Cruz, Miguelito Valdés, Bole De Nieve, Machito, and Sexteto Habanero. Winter comes early via *Cuadernos De La Havana* with tracks by Frank Emilio Flynn, Cuarteto Tradicion Cubana, Dúo Enigma, and La Cantoria Coralillo.

In 2001, when Ry Cooder plans returning to Havana to record a second album with Ibrahim Ferrer and a separate album with guitarist Manuel Galbañ, he receives help from the outgoing Clinton administration which authorizes his trip and clears all legal hurdles. In January of 2000, Cooder applies for a license and is told he can travel to Cuba provided he receives no proceeds from the two albums, a stimulation he rejects, according to *Billboard*. In September, he donates $10,000 to Hillary Rodham Clinton's run for the New York state senate seat. In November, he reapplies for a license, and writes to Sandy Berger, President Clinton's national security adviser, explaining his problem with the Treasury Department's Office of Foreign Assets Control and the State Department, which must approve all travel requests. According to the *Baltimore Sun*, Berger calls Madeleine Albright, the Secretary of State, about the imbroglio, who agrees with Berger that Cooder should be granted permission to travel and do business in Cuba. The license is granted on the final day of the Clinton administration. Denials from Senator Clinton and former administration officials assert there is no connection between Cooder's contribution to candidate Clinton and the Treasury Department's granting of the travel license. On the day President Clinton prepares to leave office, Cooder is on a plane for Cuba.

Once in Havana, Cooder records Ferrer at the home studio of Jesus "Chucho" Valdes, who plays piano on all the tunes, including two new works of his own. For the album, *Buenos Hermanos,* Cooder adds Tex-Mex accordionist Flaco Jiminez and the Blind Boys of Alabama to build new harmonies around Ferrer's winsome voice. Cooder notes that while his Treasury Department license allows him to record with Cuban nationals, it expires within a year, so he needs to complete the second album with electric guitarist Manuel Galbán, 72, while he's on site. These 10-hour sessions at the Egram studios for the album, *Mambo Sinuendo*, are motivated by Galban's playing and arranging with the adventurous vocal group Los Zafiros from the 1960s through 1975. Cooder assembles a band to create music which goes in several directions and includes himself on electric guitar, American drummers Jim Keltner and Cooder's son Joachim, Cuban bassist Cachaito Lopez and congero Miguel Diaz, supported by three bata drummers, organ, electronic percussion, and two female voices harmonizing on the title tune. Galbán is the lead melody player on guitar, piano, or electric organ. His guitar tone has the twangy quality of '50s bluesmen. Back in Hollywood, Cooder rents time at the Capitol Records studio for editing, overdubbing Herb Alpert's trumpet on the title tune, and using an old microphone which he places in front of a bass speaker, he runs Cachaito Lopez's bass parts through the mike to create an old fashioned sound for the ensemble. The LP will be released in 2003 on Cooder's Perro Verde label, distributed by Nonesuch, and marking the first time in 10 years that Cooder plays electric guitar. The musician will tell *Time* in 2003 that his Cuban sojourns are at an end since he faces prison if he returns there. "It's totally impossible for me to go back until some comprehensive change occurs in the embargo. The sad thing is, these players are indispensable, and none of them are getting younger."

While the Buena Vista mystique remains viable in the U.S. during 2001, vocalist Ferrer and pianist González plus Chucho Valdés, headline the Hollywood Bowl's "A Night in Havana" program.

Two of Buena Vista's charter members, Compay Segundo, 95, and González, 84, both die of reported kidney failure in Havana. González passes first on December 8, 2002, followed by Segundo on July 13, 2003. Born Maximo Francisco Repilado Munoz, Segundo is in frail health for some time and dies two days after appearing at a tribute concert in his honor hosted by his sons at the Hotel Nacional in Havana. A statue of Compay is unveiled on December 30 in the lobby of the hotel where the guitarist performs in recent years. Segundo's son Salvador Repilado places a real cigar in the free hand of the statue, while the other hand rests on his guitar case.

Behind the scenes, World Circuit's Nick Gold and bandleader Juan De Marcos Gonzalez come to a creative parting of the ways, with the musician seeking to work with younger, more modern Cuban musicians, noting in the *Los Angeles Times*, this is the proper way to go "so the public won't have the erroneous impression that the only legitimate music in Cuba was made 40 years ago and that the only worthwhile musicians are 80 years old."

World Circuit, having mined gold with its Buena Vista album, also releases albums by two historic Cuban bands, Los Zafiros and Estrellas De Areito, for the first time in the U.S. Another first takes place in Los Angeles with the creation of the Latin Jazz Festival at the Greek Theater in October of '97. Among the artists performing on the event subtitled *Con Ritmo Y Sabor* (*With Rhythm and Flavor*) are Arturo Sandoval, the Caribbean Jazz Project (which features Paquito D'Rivera, Andy Narell, and Dave Samuels), bassist Israel "Cachao" Lopez, saxophonist Justo Almario, and Tres Maestros Congueros tributing fellow percussionist Mongo Santamaria. Actor/musician Andy Garcia is the master of ceremonies. I get to chat with Garcia about his Cuban upbringing and multifaceted career in Chapter 11.

If Cuban music inspires people to dance, there's plenty of hoofing going on around the country in 1998, inspired by recordings and personal appearances. Jane Bunnett is the Toronto, Canada-based soprano saxophonist/flutist, whose trips to Havana with trumpeter Larry Cramer for inspiration starting in 1982, results in a series of Cuban-inspired albums recorded with the island nation's top musicians at the government-owned Egram studios. After her initial foray to Cuba, she writes in the notes for her 2001 release *Alma De Santiago*: "I've always been drawn to music that has enriched my life, but I never realized how deep the connection with Cuban music would go." Starting with *Spirits of Havana* in 1991 on Denon and then joining Blue Note through EMI Canada, her prodigious output through 2000 includes *The Cuban Piano Masters*, *Alma De Santiago*, Cuban *Odyssey* and *Ritmo and Soul*. Bunnett, as a result of trips to Cuba, is called *Havana Jane* by the musicians she works with there.

Blue Note sister label Metro Blue is the newest home for Los Van Van, Cuba's 29-year-old primo dance band, who's dashing sound is described by leader Juan Formell as an advanced form of the son style of music through the addition of a strong trombone section and three frontline vocalists. Before it goes out of business, New York's RMM Records, best known for its salsa releases, makes a dramatic turn towards Cuban music with the release of a 16-album series of archival recordings called *Forbidden Cuba*. Among the forbidden fruit are artists Chucho Valdés, Frank Emilio Flynn, Los Van Van, NG La Banda, Grupo Afrocuba, and La Orquestra 440. Another compilation, *Sexto Y Sexto Habanero* on Tumbao, features four discs by the early Cuban band Sexteto Habanero which helps develop the son musical idiom, a form of early folk/blues by incorporating complex rhythms played on bongos, claves, and maracas to provide the kick for intimate lyrics and harmonic interplay between guitar and the tres, a small, guitar-like instrument prior to the addition of a trumpet to up the sextet to a septet.

One American label, Milwaukee-based NARADA, looks to Los Angeles' Cuban community and strikes gold with the album *Cuba L.A.* Danilo Lozano, the band's musical director/flutist, says the album adds credibility to the city's Cuban connection. A founding member of the Hollywood Bowl Orchestra, Lozano admits, "The West Coast has always lagged in terms of how the world has seen its Latin music contribution. It's always been New York, especially with salsa music and all the great Puerto Rican musicians. In fact, many pioneering Cuban artists who bring their music with them to the States settle in L.A., including my father Rolando Lozano (known in Cuba for his flute playing within the charanga movement), plus Cuco Martinez, Armando Peraza, Humberto Cane, Francisco Aguabella, and Lalo Ruiz."

Lozano says the LP allows the musicians "to play the music our fathers left for us, the music that was around the house when we were growing up. As Cubans we listen to our music with our feet. If it sounds good (after its been recorded) and it makes you dance, you have satisfied the artistic and aesthetic criteria for the session." This band of merry men includes, in addition to Lozano, Ilmar Gavilan (violin); Alberto Salas (piano); Raymundo Olivera and Harry Kim (trumpets); Carlos Puerto (bass, clave), and Mitch Sanchez, Orestes Vilato, and Luis Conte (percussion).

Building the domestic Latin market by building the Cuban presence is high on the agenda for the American companies attending the second Cubadisco trade fair in Havana in '98. Two major U.S. companies, EMI and Universal Music, and a New York independent label, Qbadisc, are among the 41 foreign firms at the five-day event at the Pabexpo Convention Center, featuring conferences, product presentations, and evening concerts at both the Karl Marx Theater and the Havana National Theater, which attract upwards of 5,000 music lovers. Ciro Benemelis, president of the trade show, explains in *Billboard*, "The main goal of Cubadisco is to promote Cuban music's presence in the world." Universal Music Latin America, which has a distribution deal with Magic Muse, a Spanish-owned record company with an office in Havana, lists two prime projects: La Charanga Habanera, a dance band which includes hip-hop elements, and a 12-album series, *La Isla De la Musica*, which features music endemic to different regions of Cuba.

The maze of companies involved in getting product into the U.S. is on display at this gathering, all utilizing a 1988 amendment to the U.S. trade embargo, which allows American firms to distribute Cuban products on an indirect basis. Caribe Productions, a five-year-old Panamanian firm headquartered in Havana, specializes in popular dance bands like Los Van Van, NG Banda, and vocalist Mandolin. Caribe is distributed by EMI Spain which passes the material onto EMI's Metro Blue in the States. Ire Productions, also from Panama, licenses its product to Ahi-Nama in the U.S. Qbadisc, is among the companies looking to reissue discs made by such Cuban labels as Egram, Artex, and Bis Music, which are peddling their merchandise to interested foreign companies.

Festival talent bookers around the U.S. and Canada show their interest and enthusiasm for Cuban music power, often introducing American audiences for the first time to a growing coterie of acts finding acceptance here. Paquito D'Rivera headlines at the Cuban American Cultural Institute's Festival '98 in Los Angeles in April with a band consisting of members from the Caribbean Jazz Project, with whom he performs last year. In September, he appears at the nation's longest-running festival, the 41st annual Monterey (California) Jazz Festival with his U.N. Orchestra. One month later, the Cuban American Institute presents its fourth annual Cuban Festival in the Plaza José Marti at Echo Park in L.A. featuring Israel "Cacao" Lopez plus a number of local groups including orchestra Makina Loco with vocalist Ricardo Lemvo. With an estimated 80,000 Cubans in L.A., the city ranks third behind Miami and New York/New Jersey, whose Cuban populations are larger. Eighty-year-old bassist Lopez, credited with helping establishing the mambo, is also saluted at the second annual Los Angeles Latin Jazz Festival in September, where he performs with his orchestra at the Universal Amphitheatre. He also appears at last year's first L.A. Latin Jazz Festival.

The prestigious JVC Jazz Festival in New York in June of '98 is rich with Cuban artists: Arturo Sandoval and his Hot House Big Band, Los Van Van, and Jesús Alemañy and Cubanismo, all perform in Carnegie Hall. Sandoval is also slated for JVC dates in Newport and Denver and the Montreal Jazz Festival in July as part of a Latin Crossings tour which also features Tito Puente and Steve Winwood. Cubanismo is also booked for the 10th annual Santa Barbara (California) Jazz Festival in September. Los Van Van is also performing in 13 other North American cities during June, featuring music from its BlueNote/Metro Blue album, *Esto Te Ponte La Cabeza Mala*, which Blue Note says translates to "This'll mess up your head." The tour is the dance band's third consecutive in North America in the past three years. Among the cities it'll play are Boulder, Colorado; California cities Santa Ana, San Diego, and Los Angeles; Oregon locales Portland and Jacksonville; Chicago, Toronto, New York City; Saratoga Springs, New York; Philadelphia, and Boston. Chucho Valdés, while touring the country with his quartet, plays Philadelphia's Mellon Jazz Festival and the Toronto Jazz Festival in June and the Montreal Jazz Festival in July. The San Francisco Jazz Festival, in its 16th year, beckons Valdés and two members of the Buena Vista Social Club, pianist Rubén González and singer Ibrahim Ferrer to its party in November. Two nights are themed to California's growing Hispanic population, with non-Cuban acts Marc Anthony, Poncho Sanchez and David Sanchez among the better-known attractions.

Those acts which stop in L.A. include an array of bands playing either traditional or fusion arrangements, notably Bellita, one of the few female jazz pianists and her band, Jazztumbata, which includes famed percussionist Pancho Quinto; two 14-piece ensembles,

Cubanismo led by trumpeter Jesús Alemañy and Otra Visión, led by flutist Orlando "Maraca" Valle and featuring 82-year-old singer Pio Leyva, and Vocal Sampling, a sextet without any backing instruments, which favors the new song movement of the '60s and '70s called nueva trova which focuses on social issues. Los Van Van is brought back for a second straight appearance in '98 at the Playboy Jazz Festival in L.A. following its initial warm reception last year. Many of the Cuban bands play the Conga Room, which as the home for hot Latin music, is referred to metaphorically as the House of Blues for Latinos.

One touring Cuban salsa band, Arte Mixto, cannot complete its U.S. tour this year. Vocalist Iris Sandra Cepeda, defects following the eight-member band's appearance at Whittier College (in Whittier, California) and prior to its gig at the Mayan Theatre in L.A. Jimmy Maslin, owner of the band's L.A. record label, Ahi-Nama, informs the *Los Angeles Times* Cepeda told him of her plans midway through the tour, forcing the label to cancel engagements in New Orleans, New York, and Puerto Rico and return to Cuba. Alexis Correa, the band's leader expresses his anger at Cepeda by stating: "Iris has betrayed all the love and trust that was placed on her, and ruined the countless hours spent rehearsing in order to make Arte Mixio the band it is today."

Across the Atlantic in Cuba, young contemporary musicians in 1999 are building the latest musical bridge into the future. It's called timba and its components are polyrhythmic sophistications coupled with advanced harmonics and elements of hot salsa and cool merengue to create a fusion dance music decades removed from the traditional mambo beat of the '50s. This mixing of Cuban and other Caribbean dance rhythms along with sophisticated jazz elements is being heard in America by record producers looking for the new sound from Cuba, according to *Billboard.* They are incorporating *timba* tinges into their music to create what Juan Formell, director of Los Van Van, calls "something new."

One problem with the new music, in addition to having no domestic radio play, according to New York producer Sergio George, is that by being so sophisticated rhythmically and harmonically, the music may be too advanced "for the market outside Cuba" where musicians selected by the government learn all elements of their craft in music conservatories. That's why the Cubans are adding the different Caribbean tempos to generate acceptance in other Latin markets including the U.S.A. Vocalist/musician Manolin, fresh from a club tour in the U.S., admits to *Billboard* Cubans need to be more "international. Our music can be very complex and our lyrics are too local. We have to start to recognize the market outside of Cuba."

One Cuban band trying to get into the U.S. in February of '99, Sierra Maestra, runs afoul of the State Department, which withholds visas for two of its nine members. State informs the promoters that the two are undergoing security checks by the FBI and CIA. The nine-piece ensemble remains stranded in Toronto, where its month-long tour begins. After petitions are filed by a San Francisco attorney, visas are finally granted to the percussionist and tres (small guitar) player and the band does fulfill its two-night engagement at the Conga Room in Los Angeles two weeks later. Despite its lack of traditional Cuban instruments like timbales, regular drums, piano, and a brass section, the band's utilization of voices, bongos, claves, maracas, guiros, cowbells, bass, and the tres guitar, provides the rhythmic flow for its traditional son dance formula.

This kind of paper blockage against the band shouldn't have happened since President Bill Clinton announces new steps one month earlier to ease the process for cultural exchanges between the U.S. and Cuba. These measures include speeding up the visa process for Cuban musicians with jobs in the States. The band's attorney, William Martinez, tells the *Los Angeles Times*, the Cuban arts organization called MINREX is the culprit since it takes too long to provide the U.S. with the band's paperwork. Once the State Department does receive the applications, visa are approved for seven of the members since they were cleared for entry in 1997 for the band's initial American tour. The other two are new to the ensemble, so the U.S. says it needs 21 days to conduct its security check. Bandleader Alejandro Galaraga admits being confused by the delay. "I don't understand why this has to be so difficult," he tells the *Times*. "We're artists, not terrorists."

The Clinton Administration also authorizes charter flights to Cuba from New York and Los Angeles later in the year (for a controlled group of travelers: journalists, government officials, U.S. residents with family living in Cuba, news organization technical personnel, athletes, and people invited to business meetings) which it believes will enhance "people-to-people" contact, providing they have permission from the Treasury Department's Office of Foreign Assets Control. The loosening of the rules against visiting Cuba by the U.S. draws mixed reactions from the Cuban exile community around the country.

American record labels continue their romance with Cuba. Atlantic, a giant in rock, blues, and jazz, signs a distribution pact with the Havana Caliente label, whose artists include Adalberto Alvarez Y Su Son, Pedro Luis Ferrer, and Buena Vista's Barbarito Torres, who's album, *Havana Café*, is the label's first release in the U.S. Lute player Torres also appears on a second album featuring Buena Vista members in the band calling itself the Afro Cuban All Stars.

Arhoolie, the 39-year-old specialist in esoterica from various forms of folk and world music, issues the compilation, *The Cuban Danzon: Before There Was Jazz*, which features Cuban dance bands circa 1906 to 1929. Label owner Chris Strachwitz, notes these early recordings remind him of early jazz bands since the instruments are similar, trumpet, trombone, and clarinet. But the addition of violins and, of course, Latin rhythms, provides the Cuban stamp of authenticity.

Rhino Records, which specializes in creating box sets from previously released recordings by other companies, turns its spotlight on Ramon Mongo Santamaria with a two-disc, 34-track anthology, *Skin on Skin: The Mongo Santamaria Anthology (1958–1995).* Rhino calls the Cuban-born, New York residing conguero "The Godfather of Latin Soul." The tunes are collated from Mongo's Atlantic, Riverside, and Columbia releases and include his signature songs *Afro Blue*, *Watermelon Man*, *Para Ti*, *Yambu*, *Canta Bajo* plus mainstream-directed *Sweet "Tater Pie*, *Cold Sweat*, *Bahia*, *Groovin*," and *Son of a Preacher Man.*

Canada's Justin Time continues adding to its Cuban catalog; its latest addition is pianist Hilario Durán's *Habana Nocturna* which features a string quartet, soprano saxophonist/flutist Jane Bunnett, her husband trumpeter Larry Cramer, drummer Horacio "El Negro" Hernandez, and bassist Roberto Occhipinti all jamming on charanga, danzon, and cha cha stylings.

Spain's Tumbao Cuban Classics label, releases *El Tambor De Cuba*, its Chano Pozo 3-CD memorial set in the U.S. The selections include the deceased percussionist's early Seeco discs, transferred for the first time to CD, plus his connecting forays fusing African rhythms, American jazz, and Cuban melodies. The first disc features Pozo tunes performed by other players; disc two contains Pozo playing congas on Cuban melodies, while disc three consists of Chano's New York jazz sessions, following his move from Cuba to New York City in 1947, where he begins working with trumpeter Dizzy Gillespie, only to be murdered the next year in a Harlem drug dispute.

One American label, Ahi-Namá, formed in 1995 to specialize in Cuban music, becomes a major supplier in 2001. The Studio City, California, company founded by Jimmy Maslon, following his tourist trip to Havana in '95, is devoted to contemporary, cutting-edge Cuban bands, which on paper sounds like a swell idea, with one key caveat: hardnosed Cuban exiles in the U.S. don't like any American company doing business with Cuba, and traditionalists prefer their salsa unfettered by new spices of any kind. There is no way for Maslon to know what hurdles he faces. Raised near Mankato, Minnesota, he moves to California as a teenager with his family and has no connection with either Spanish or Latin music until his trip to Havana coincides with the emergence of progressive bands in Cuba. "I was just blown away at the talent I saw there," he tells the *Los Angeles Times*, which profiles his Cuban connection.

After starting with Latin videos of Cuban acts, since the U.S. embargo locks out Cuban performers from performing here, Maslon forms his label, which loosely translates to the slang expression "Right On," He is able to sign Bamboleo, a Latin funk fusion quintet, singer

Isaac Delgado, flutist Orlando Valle, and Arte Mixto, a fusion folk/salsa band. Two years after his visit to Cuba, Maslon sets up a concert for Bamboleo at New York's Lincoln Center, one of the first Cuban contemporary groups to appear in this country. The label begins to make inroads in the domestic Latin record industry when Delgado's *La Formula* album and title tune are nominated in 2001 for a best Latin Grammy salsa album and for best tropical tune. Despite a general lack of Latin radio play for his contemporary, edgy groups, a station in Los Angeles, KLVE-FM, begins to air Delgado's song, *El Pregón Del Chocolate*. Latin dance club disc jockeys are also provided the tune and begin offering ancillary exposure. Close on the heels of this radio break, Maslon signs a production partnership with New York's top salsa producer, Sergio George, who acknowledges that Cuba's current crop of adventurous musicians influences his own music.

Despite attempts to upgrade the sound of Cuban music, several traditional acts tour the U.S.A. during the fall of '01. Orquesta Aragón, the 12-man band which traces its beginnings to 1939, gets an upgrade of its own which includes an electric bass and a silver flute replacing the original model. Los Fakires, Cuba's traditional top vocal quintet, which performs together for more than 30 years, makes its first American appearance during its three-week tour beginning in Miami in mid-November. And Raúl Malo, a Cuban American singer/songwriter, who successfully dabbles in country music with the group the Mavericks in the early '90s, stresses Latin rhythms, Cuban songs, and Cuban-American musicians during his December sojourn to promote his new Om Town/Higher Octave album, *Today*.

One Cuban artist who defects and now resides in Miami is timba/vocalist Manolin, whose open-minded songs anger Cuban cultural officials, prompting his entry into the exile community.

Frank Emilio Flynn, one of Cuba's most heralded pianist/composers, dies at age 80 in Havana. His versatility in propelling a number of musical styles, running from the 1930s through the development of Afro-Cuban jazz two decades later, will be remembered during select tributes in the U.S. which spill over into 2002.

Los Van Van and a number of other Cuban bands find freedom in the U.S. comes with a price in 2002. Van Van and its U.S. label, Havana Caliente, are at odds over its contract. The priceless dance band, despite its constant policy of updating its sound, claims its contract is unenforceable because the New York company produced its album in Havana, violating the U.S. embargo which only permits American companies to distribute finished albums created by another party, or release records by Cuban artists signed to companies in another nation. Technically, the band is signed to a company in Curacao named Harbour Bridge, according to a *Los Angeles Times* feature on the dispute. Marla Zenoz, Havana Caliente's owner, says the company follows the rules and she plans to release a live album of the band's 1999 Miami concert. Juan Formell, the band's leader, claims the label failed to exercise an option for a new album under the prescribed deadline. He also vows to halt the live album's release.

Two avowed anti-Castroites, and defectees, Arturo Sandoval and Paquito D'Rivera, wind up recording on the album, *Generoso Que Bueno Toca Usted* for the German label Termidor, which is recorded in Cuba, and features 84-year-old trombone legend Generoso Jimenez. While on the surface this may seem hypocritical, but the two former Irakere members keep their distance from Castro's Cuba by overdubbing their parts in the U.S.—a rare instance of Cuban exile musicians appearing on an album by a still residing artist in their former homeland. Sandoval records his trumpet parts in his Miami studio while D'Rivera adds his sax solos in New York. Juan Pablo Torres, himself a member of the Miami exile community, who produces the album, says all the exile players know the album is being recorded in Cuba with the bandleader who has not recorded in 30 years. While modern technology allows the musicians to tribute Jimenez without leaving the U.S., they are still open to criticism by the vocal anti-Castro element in this country for their participation in this project.

Politics continues to disturb relations with Cuban artists seeking to work. It seems to be a hit or miss proposition, with some musicians being accepted by the U.S. government for work entry while others are stymied. Among the acts allowed to appear are the 20-member Ballet Folklorico Cutumba; singer/songwriter Issac Delgardo, former lead singer with the timba band NG La Banda; flutist Orlando "Maraca" Valle and his dance band Otra Vision and the popular Cuban ensemble, Carlos Manuel Y Su Clan. While in Miami, two musicians and two sound technicians with the Clan band file for political asylum four days after they appear at the Club Cristal. Both Chucho Valdés and the Afro Cuban All Stars, are prohibited from entering the country following the September 11 Twin Towers suicide attacks. A federal law, the U.S. Enhanced Border Security And Visa Reform Act, signed by President George W. Bush after the terrorist attacks, requires a lengthy screening process to keep out residents of seven nations named in the act as "state sponsors of terrorism" notably Iran, Iraq, Syria, Libya, Cuba, North Korea, and Sudan.

The new law prevents Valdés and 21 other Cuban musicians from attending the Latin Grammy Awards in Los Angeles, and also partaking of a solo concert tour in this country. The Afro Cuban All Stars are forced to cancel their five-week domestic tour. Scott Southland, head of the Massachusetts-based International Music Network, which books foreign acts in the U.S., including Valdés and the All Stars, tells *Newsweek*, "The short-term impact is that this is costing me tens of thousands of dollars. But the true cost is the long-term negative impact on the cultural arts marketplace."

Two former Cuban residents, singer Albita and Bebo Valdés, father of Chucho Valdés, have recording projects which explore the island nation's musical heritage. Albita, who starts recording in Havana in 1988, relocates to Colombia two years later and moves to the U.S. in '93 with her band. She forms Silva Screen/Times Square records and releases its first album, *Hecho A Mano*, which explores her personal takes on life, reflecting the Cuban tradition of the singing troubadour. For 84-year-old Valdés, recording four albums for Calle 54 Records is the culmination of his desire to capture on disc his past accomplishments. The senior Valdés, during a stop in Miami to do a concert and also record one of the albums, tells the *Miami Herald* he wants "to do one thing before dying because I know I'm one of the ancient ones." That one thing is a suite which focuses on different Cuban rhythms. During his musical renaissance since leaving Cuba in 1963 to marry a Swedish woman and reside there, the former arranger/accompanist for top Cuban vocalists Benny Moré and Rolando Laserie, and orchestra leader of the famed Tropicana outdoor nightclub in Havana, comes out of retirement in 1994 to record the LP, *Bebo Rides Again.* The first of the four new albums is recorded in Madrid with flamenco singer Diego "El Cigala"; the others are the suite of Afro-Cuban rhythms with a big band, a smaller octet session and the Miami session which also involves a small group including Uruguayan violinist Federico Britos. Several of these musicians appear with Valdés during his concert appearance at the Gusman Center for the Performing Arts.

Major name American show business figures show up in Cuba to participate in a variety of events. Director Steven Spielberg and his wife actress Kate Capshaw accept an invitation by the Cuban Institute of Cinematographic Arts and Industry to attend a festival showing eight of his films, including *Minority Report, E.T. The ExtraTerrestrial, Jaws, Schindler's List, Saving Private Ryan, Empire of the Sun, Duel,* and *Raiders of the Lost Ark.* Visiting Cuba for the first time, the filmmaker criticizes the U.S. trade embargo. "I personally feel this embargo should be lifted. I do not see any reason for accepting old grudges being played out in the 21st century," he tells the *Reuters* news agency.

Following the film festival, Matt Lauer and the *Today Show* on NBC arrive to report on an international conference focusing on the 40th anniversary of the Cuban missile crisis, which is narrowly averted by the Kennedy Administration in its face-off against the Russians.

The TV crew is followed by an array of American-based musicians who attend the semi-annual 20th annual Havana International Jazz Festival. During the five days of the festival, American artists perform with Cuba's top players and appear on

Cuban television. This is the first festival since President George W. Bush takes office and musicians and their managers voice complaints about obtaining licenses and visas. The atmosphere is very different, one of the Americans tells the *Chicago Tribune*. "The last time I was here in 1998, it was totally different," says trombonist Steve Turre. "Last time you had Cuban and American musicians getting together at parties hosted by the American government. You don't see that this time."

Among the other visiting musicians are guitarist Larry Coryell and blues singer Taj Mahal, who both play with festival director Chucho Valdés; trumpeter Roy Hargrove, saxophonist David Sanchez, Panamanian pianist Danilo Peréz, pianist Kenny Barron, vibist Dave Samuels, flutist Dave Valentin, violinist Regina Carter, saxophonists Joe Lovano and David Murray, pianist Ronnie Mathews, trombonist Jimmy Bosch, vocalist Claudia Acuña, and the vibraphone quintet Ritmo Caliente.

One of the highlights is a piano gathering of Chucho, Gonzalo Rubalcaba, Ernán López-Nussa, and American Arturo O'Farrill, who dedicates his performance to his father and noted big band arranger Chico O'Farrill, who passes away on June 27, 2001, in a New York hospital at age 80. The senior O'Farrill, a native of Havana studies composition and then moves to New York in 1948 and begins writing music for such musicians as Machito, Benny Goodman, Stan Kenton, Dizzy Gillespie, Gato Barbieri, and Count Basie. In the '50s he records his own Afro-Cuban jazz compositions for the Clef and Norgam labels. From 1995 to 2000, he records three albums for Milestone and Orfeon tributes the pioneering musician with the CD, *In Memoriam*, in 2001.

For Cuban musicians, performing with the visiting stars affords them exposure before these influential visitors and the hope they may crack the American market the way pianist Frank Emilio did by attracting the attention of Blue Note, which in 1999 releases a second government produced album, *Ancestral Reflections*, in the U.S.

Through the years attempts are made on political levels to cool down the heat between Cuba and the U.S. and find some accommodating comfort zone to appease the virulently anti-Castro Cuban exile community, whose voting clout clouds the attitudes of Cuban elected officials in Miami and Washington.

Among the more recent politically inspired moves, President Bill Clinton in October of 2000 signs the Trade Sanctions Reform and Export Enhancement Act which allows Cuba to buy American food and medicine on a cash basis, resulting in Cuba purchasing 550,000 tons of U.S. goods by May of 2002, the month current President Bush says he won't lift the 42-year-old trade embargo unless Castro frees all political prisoners, allows other parties to: speak freely, form independent trade unions, and allow human rights organizations in to ensure that free elections will be created, and outside monitors to observe the 2003 elections.

Pressure to ease the embargo also comes from a 40-member Congressional bipartisan group, led by House Majority Leader Dick Armey. The House also votes to also lift travel restrictions, citing trade and travel with Cuba is the best way to show Cubans the good points of democracy. The Bush administration believes new travel restrictions allowing only Cubans who are U.S. citizens to visit their former homeland is the right way to go. According to U.S. estimates, around 160,000 Americans travel to Cuba in 2001 with or without the required travel permits, placing America fourth behind Canada, Germany and Italy in terms of foreign visitors to the Caribbean nation.

Political actions and events in 2003 draw Cuban artists and 76-year-old Fidel Castro's 44-year-old government into confrontational, headline-making situations. The Cuban government's arrest of a reported 78 dissidents, the retention of the American embargo launched by President Dwight Eisenhower in October of 1960, the U.S. crackdown on travel to the island nation and the defection of Cuban gymnasts, dancers, and musicians, all cast a shadow over the strained relations between the two nations.

The intertwining of these events prompts one Cuban official, Darsi Fernández, of the Spanish Authors and Publishers Society, to tell *Billboard*: "Cuba is living in an especially complicated political moment, one of significant isolation. When the political issues come forth, it's harder to get tours and promoters outside of Cuba. And inside, it's harder to get your travel papers in order." Cuban artists suffer more of an emotional than economic impact because of stringent U.S. travel visa regulations, the executive also believes.

Despite the U.S. House and Senate favoring opening travel to Cuba, both bodies back down when President George W. Bush says he'll veto any such plan, thus keeping a 42-year-old ban in place. The House vote is its fourth in a row to end travel restrictions. Cuba needs the American dollars U.S. turistas coming in on special visas and through other nations provide to prop up its economy following its loss of life-supporting subsidies in 1990 when the Soviet economy collapses.

Sadly, two of Cuba's most well-known American residents, Celia Cruz and Mongo Santamaria, die in 2003, Santamaria on February 1, Cruz on July 16. Santamaria, the Cuban congero who moves to New York before the revolution to work with a plethora of top musicians, including Tito Puente, Perez Prado, and Cal Tjader, dies in the Baptist Hospital in Miami at age 86 of a stroke which put him on life support systems. His long association with Columbia Records produces the crossover hit *Watermelon Man* in 1963 and inculcates conga drums as a staple on pop records. He is credited with recording the first album of traditional Afro-Cuban drumming in this country, *Chango*, later reissued as *Drums and Chants*.

Cruz, 77, loses a yearlong battle with brain cancer, culminating in surgery in December to remove a tumor, and passes away at her home in Fort Lee, New Jersey, on a Wednesday. Her death comes two days after she and husband Pedro Knight celebrate their 41st year of marriage. Her body is then flown from New Jersey to Miami where an estimated 100,000 mourners file past her coffin before a Cuban flag on Friday and Saturday; on Sunday "The Queen of Salsa's" remains are returned to the New York area for the funeral service the next day. A horse-drawn carriage draped in purple, Cruz's favorite color, carries her down Fifth Avenue to St. Patrick's Cathedral from the Frank E. Campbell funeral home on Madison Avenue and 81st street, where tens of thousands of fans say adios. Guests attending the service at the famous Catholic Church where Patti Labelle and Victor Manuelle both perform, include New York Governor George Pataki and Democratic senators Charles Schumer and Hillary Rodham Clinton.

She is buried in the Bronx section of New York City, her coffin containing a jar of Cuban soil and a copy of her last recorded Sony Discos CD, *Regalo Del Alma*, (*Gift from the Soul*), which she works on laboriously while still ill following her hospital stay. She carries her show business flair and image to her grave, appearing in her coffin in a platinum blonde wig, sequined gown, and sparkling jewelry, her nails painted white in contrast to her lips colored hot pink, according to *People* magazine.

Since she defects in 1960 and becomes a U.S. citizen, the Cuban government calls her a traitor and refuses her permission to return home for her mother's funeral two years later. Her passing receives scant attention in the Cuban media; the government newspaper *Granma* reports her death in a two-paragraph story on page six of the eight-page edition. Cuban entertainers in America pay tribute to her lovingly. Singer Jon Secada reflects on her career as a powerful member of the New York salsa community, working with Tito Puente, Willie Colon, and Johnny Pacheco and winning three Latin Grammys and two regular Grammies. "What a legacy she left," he tells *People*. Two other high profiles musicians are quoted in *Hispanic* Magazine: Saxophonist Paquito D'Rivera laments: "Cuba's soul has just died," while bandleader Johnny Pacheco notes she "is the kind of star that cannot be equaled."

New York's love for the powerfully voiced singer results in New York City Mayor Michael Bloomberg naming a portion of the city's second oldest public high school, 106-year-old DeWitt Clinton, the DeWitt Clinton High School/Lehman College Celia Cruz Bronx High School of Music. The new school's first 90 students take their academic classes at Clinton and their music studies at the nearby Lehman College, where the music school is located. I read about this development in the Clinton alumni bulletin which also reflects on this year being the 10th anniversary of girls being admitted to the former all-boys school. The bulletin explains that Mayor Bloomberg, who now has control of the city's schools, is reducing the size of the student population at schools with academic or crime problems. Clinton, which has none of these maladies, nonetheless is selected to be part of the awkwardly long named new school. During my four years at Clinton in the 1950s, there are hardly any Hispanics, if any at all, in the student body. By 2003, Latinos are omnipresent due to population shifts into the borough of the Bronx.

Three weeks after her death, Celia makes her posthumous debt on *Billboard*'s mainstream top 200 album listings with three albums, *Regalo Del Alma* (Sony Discos) at number 40; *Exitos Eternos* (Universal Latino) at number 95 and *Hits Mix* (Sony Discos) at number 106. Five weeks later, these same titles appear on the magazine's Top Latin Albums chart. *Regalo Del Alma* is first; *Exitos Eternos* is second, and *Hits Mix* is fourth. In November, three DVDs are added to the available product list by the late superstar, who would have celebrated her birthday October 21. They include *Cuba Mia*, a DVD/CD documentary on Cuban music released by Sony Norte which is shown on Florida PBS stations; *Celia Cruz: An Extraordinary Woman… Azucar!* on Havana Caliente, and *Celia Cruz…Azucar!* a tribute with a similar name which Telemundo airs and which Image Entertainment distributes. All proceeds from the sale of the DVD, notes Telemundo, will go to the Celia Cruz Foundation, which donates scholarship money to youngsters.

One of the most unusual Cuban troupes making its first tour of the U.S. in March of 2003 to five California cities is La Colmenita, whose 25 members include those with physical and mental handicaps. The 13-year-old troupe, whose name means "The Little Beehive," initially performs at pediatric hospitals in rural areas of the country, the group's assigned psychiatrist tells the *Los Angeles Times*. A group of California legislators on a trip to Cuba last year are so awed by the company, they recommend a U.S. tour. The trip, sponsored by Global Exchange of San Francisco, is replete with political underpinnings designed to foster people-to-people connections between the two nations. "We feel the policy of no engagement with Cuba needs to change," says Ana Perez, who oversees the organization's Cuba programs. "Having children come together was a really great statement for that goal." The group's bilingual musical performances are in San Diego, Los Angeles, Sacramento, Oakland, and San Francisco.

Following the defection 18 months ago by popular Cuban salsa vocalist Manolin, who settles in Miami, a second salsa star, Carlos Manuel Pruenda defects in May after performing a concert in Mexico City at the Hard Rock Cafe. The vocalist, along with his mother, sister, her boyfriend, one band member, and a sound technician, fly to the northern Mexican city of Monterrey and take a 180-mile cab ride to Matamoros where they walk across the bridge over the Rio Grande into Brownsville, Texas, are granted asylum and the head to Miami. A news crew accompanies them from Telemundo filming the singer's Mexican exploits in support of a new album, *Enamora'o*, released on the Miami label, Ciocan Music. This company, owned by Hugo Cancio, also provides Manolin with his first American record contract and his debut release, *El Puente*. The two defectors are the first name performers of their generation to flee Cuba for the U.S.

Manuel, the leader of the salsa band Carlos Manuel Y Su Clan since 1996, tells KGBT, a Harlingen, Texas, TV station his defection is based on the need for "greater freedom to play his music around the world." In other words, for money and professional growth, Manolin cites "personal and political" reasons for his defection.

Once Cuban pop musicians become part of the American Cuban community, they are often shocked to learn their past reputations hold no influence with traditional salsa fans who eschew their newer, more complex form of the music called timba, which includes elements of hip-hop mixed in with the hot salsa tempos. "People don't buy music to support politics," Joe Garcia, president of the Miami-based political lobby group the Cuban American National

Foundation, which virulently opposes the incumbent Cuban regime, stresses in a *Billboard* article. "Exile organizations cannot create the hits," emphasizes Garcia during a press conference for Carlos Manuel, who drops his last name for the shorter stage moniker.

In August, three members of the Cuban team competing in the World Gymnastic Championships in Anaheim, California, defect and seek asylum. Michel Brito Ferrer, 24, Charles León Tamayo, 22, are the first to leave the team's hotel, followed eight days later by Janerky De La Pena, 20, who is picked up by Ferrer's uncle Ramon, who lives in nearby Los Angeles. The three gymnasts tell a news conference their actions are all individual choices, there is no advance plan to defect, and they've received no assistance from anyone.

Five members of the touring Ballet Nacional De Cuba next defect during its national tour in October. Two members, Gema Diaz, 32 and Cervilio Amador, 20, slip away from the touring troupe in Daytona Beach and head for the exile community in Miami one day before they are to appear in *Don Quixote.* A week later, three others defect in New York: Adiarys Almeida, Violet Serrat, and Luis Valdés. Since November of last year, the *New York Times* reports a total of 20 dancers defect in the U.S., Spain, Mexico, and the Dominican Republic.

The dancers cite the lack of a good quality of life as the reason for their decision to defect. They claim their government salary of around $14 to $18 a month, plus a $10 monthly bonus is not sufficient and that they have to purchase items on tour which they can resell in Cuba, like American videos.

A fresh start is provided the four dancers in December. Although they need work permits or legal status, all four find work performing *The Nutcracker*. Both Diaz and Amador perform with the Arts Ballet Theater of Florida in Miami, while Alemeda appears with the South Florida Ballet Theater in nearby Hollywood. Valdés journeys to Philadelphia to dance with the Rock School for Dance Education.

While Cuban artists seek the security of life in America, saxophonist Jane Bunnett continues to venture to Cuba to mine its musical heritage. There's an educational ingredient to Bunnett's fifth album for Blue Note, *Cuban Odyssey*, which features musicians from Havana, Matanzas, Cienfuegos, and Camaguey. The Toronto soprano saxophonist, and her trumpet-playing husband Larry Cramer, have made more than 40 visits to the Caribbean island nation during the past 15 years, so they know where the strong local players are for her Spirits of Havana ensemble. Bunnett says making the album is truly an odyssey "because as we ventured outside Havana and landed in the various provinces of Cuba, it became clear how different the (music) styles really are."

Five additional albums capture the essence of the new Afro-Caribbean beat as well as the energy of pre-revolutionary Cuba. Rounder, a U.S. label which specializes in eclectic music, weighs into the Cuban romance with the CD *!Cubalive!* which presents nine bands performing live in various venues "where Cubans play for Cubans." Miami-located Cion introduces Clan 537, a Paris-based quintet, which seeks a new sound by incorporating strong lyrics about the dark side of life in Cuba within a hip-hop formula on its self-titled CD. Yerba Buena, a New York sextet including Cuban exile vocalist Zuiomara Laugart, which is gaining creative buzz for its sprinkling of various Caribbean influences blended with rap and Santeria religious exhortations, debuts with the album *President Alien* on the Fun Machine/Razor and Tie label. *Festival in Havana*, recorded in 1955 by Riverside Records and unavailable for 40 years, re-emerges as a reissue from parent Fantasy records of Berkeley, California. Bassist Andy Gonzalez, in his notes for the repackage, says it's "like opening a time capsule of Havana before the revolution." Finally, Cuban pianist and émigré Omar Sosa teams with Venezuelan percussionist Gustavo Ovalles in a live concert recorded in Yokohama, Japan, in 2002 which matches the pianist's adventurous note clusters with the heartbeat flow of Afro-Cuban rhythms on *Ayaguna* from Otá Records. Sosa, who migrates to San Francisco in the mid-'90s, receives a Latin Grammy nomination in 2002 for his previous *Sentir* album.

Cuba's artists and their music continue to frustrate the U.S. government in 2004, while encountering a welcome mat from that portion of the public that eschews any political linkage to their presence. The most dramatic and historic event occurs on November 15 when 43 members of the Cuban musical revue "Havana Night Club—The Show" appearing In Las Vegas at the Stardust's Wayne Newton Theatre, defect, joining six other cast members who defect while in Germany. The troupe is the hotel's musical attraction since opening August 21 and is the first major defection by such a large number of Cuban artists ever in this country.

Prior to the show's American debut, rumors of planned defections reach these shores because of the problems the performers face from a recalcitrant Cuban government over their going to the U.S. Despite their confrontation with the Castro government, which tells them they will not be allowed to resume their careers if they go to the U.S., behind the scenes pressure on the Cuban government by a number of individuals, greases the way for the singers, dancers, and musicians to leave and open at the Stardust Resort & Casino. After the 43 cast members apply for asylum at the Lloyd D. George Federal Building and fill out their 10-page applications, they are forwarded to the Los Angeles office of the Department of Homeland Security. Earlier, the six other defecting members in Germany are granted entry visas on the same day and fly to Las Vegas for the November 16 reopening of the revue. Two members of the 53-person show, citing family ties, state their intention to return to Cuba once the engagement closes next January 11. Others believe they will be free to return home when either Castro dies or the hot war of political differences between the U.S. and Cuba is resolved. Nicole Durr, the German-born group's founder/producer/director, attributes the defections to the unclear future the artists face if they return home. Seven months after they defect, all 49 members are granted asylum by the U.S. government.

The American premier of the Cuban music and dance troupe arrives in the nation's gambling capitol one year behind schedule following the U.S. Government's 2003 clamp down on visas for Cuban artists, resulting in a major lobbying effort this year involving a New

York law professor, a top film actor, a former State Department official, the U.S. Secretary of State, and the anti-Castro Cuban American National Foundation. When all the political back channel efforts are completed, "Havana Night Club—The Show," debuts in the Wayne Newton Theater August 21 (23 days later than it's planned opening) through late October and then returns for 12 weeks from November 15 through January 11, 2005. This show is the first to play Las Vegas since the 1960s when Fidel Castro rids his country of the American mob, which controls Havana's gambling casinos.

The show's plight and opening hardly draws any national attention and I only become aware of its presence as a result of a one paragraph reference in an August 26 *Los Angeles Times* story about Siegfried and Roy's refusal to provide a video to federal investigators of the near-fatal tiger attack on illusionist Roy Horn, 59, on October 3, 2003. The paragraph also mentions Roy attends the show in a wheelchair last August 24 and that he and his partner, Siegfried Fischbacker, 65, are the show's presenters and associate producers. Roy and Siegfried's presence that night is captured during the Maria Shriver NBC special, *Siegfried and Roy: The Miracle*, broadcast September 15, which naturally includes some very short footage of the actual on stage action. The interview is a major scoop for Shriver, who returns to NBC following her self-imposed hiatus following her husband, actor Arnold Schwarzenegger's recall victory to become California's governor last fall.

The Stardust venue is also the room in which the two illusionists make their Las Vegas debut in 1976. This reference to the show prompts me to contact the hotel and the show's outside PR company for information about the production. On September 4, a few days before the material arrives, the *Times* runs an investigative story anent the show's travails, which reveals this is more than just the U.S. debut for a touring Cuban ensemble.

"Havana Night Club—The Show" is the 1998 creation of Nicole "ND" Durr, which mines the cultural richness of Cuba through its African and Spanish heritage. Since then, it performs in

17 countries and in 2002 Durr invites friends Siegfried and Roy to Havana to ask them to be the show's American presenters, with its first appearance at the Universal Amphitheatre in L.A.'s San Fernando Valley in February 2003. When the troupe undergoes personnel changes, the L.A. date is cancelled. Before the Las Vegas date is firmed, Horn suffers his major mauling injury in October just as a new visa policy initiated by the Bush administration prohibits Cuban artists who've already appeared in this country as part of cultural exchanges initiated by the previous Clinton administration, from gaining new entry.

The 90-minute show, with some words in English for the American audience, but primarily in Spanish, features 32 dancers, eight singers, the 13-piece Cubaximo band, and 23 scene changes. One of the dance numbers choreographed by Maurice Hines showcases the island's chancleta wooden shoe tap dance. The music encompasses the traditional son and pilon dance tempos plus the "newer" rumba, mambo, cha cha cha, salsa, and Cuban flamenco blended with contemporary choreography, modern dance, and the traditionally sensuous movements of today's Cuban dance.

Durr, determined to get her show before American audiences after the Cuban government refuses to allow then to leave the country as a group, but instead permits them to apply for exit permits individually, also finds she has to overcome the U.S. State Department's refusal to allow the company to land on U.S. shores in February. Thus begins her lobbying efforts, reports the *Times*, contacting New York law professor Pamela Falk, who has had dealings with the Cuban government. The two contact Kevin Costner to write a letter to Castro, believing his visit to Cuba three years ago during which the actor screens his Cuban missile crisis film *13 Days* for the Cuban president, will carry some weight in getting the visas cleared. Falk then contacts the vehemently anti-Castro Miami-based Cuban American National Foundation, asking them not to oppose the entry of the Cuban ensemble, as it has other Cuban artists. Joe Garcia, the organization's president, agrees to not thwart this group's arrival, urges Cuban exiles in Las Vegas not to protest the show's stand at the Stardust and writes a supporting letter to Colin Powell, the U.S. Secretary of State. Also enlisted in the lobbying is Dennis K. Hayes, a former State Department official, who serves as coordinator for Cuban affairs during the Clinton presidency and later as a contact for the Miami exile organization.

This diplomatic pressure pays off as the U.S. has a change of mind and grants the show its requested visas. What causes the Castro regime to change its mind is not clear. During its run, it is the only Cuban revue playing on the Strip amidst its flashing neon lights and gambling casinos.

Cuban musicians help infuse Latin jazz with new energy with the release of CDs by former Cuban bandleader/drummer Horacio "El Negro" Hernandez and pianist Gonzalo Rubalcaba.

Hernandez's *Italua* on Pimienta, reflects the direction the drummer takes by building a quartet of Cuban émigrés living in Italy whom he meets while on a tour, notably Amik Guerra on trumpet and flugelhorn; Ivan Bridon Napoles on keyboards and Daniel Martinez Izquierdo on bass.

Rubalcaba's *Paseo* on Blue Note is his first new release in three years, reprising the quartet format he utilizes on two previous Blue Note CDs, *Rapsodia* (1992) and *Antiguo* in '98. Rubalcaba calls saxophonist Luis Felipe Lamoglia, electric bassist Jose Armando Gola and drummer Ignacio Berroa his "new Cuban quartet." The sound often has a more hard-edged avante-gardist feel to it as a contrast to the relaxed sound on several of his reworked originals heard on earlier albums. Gonzalo tours the nation from late September to early December with the New Cuban Quartet, which has a substitute drummer and bassist on two of the dates.

Arguably one of the most adventurous cultural barrier crossing releases year this is *Bridge to Havana* on Pyramid/Universal, featuring a plethora of American artists of diverse musical persuasions who visit Cuba in 1999 under U.S. Treasure Department and Cuban government sanction to work with local musicians. Making the cultural connection with Cuban musicians are Dave Koz, Gladys Knight, Bonnie Raitt (who sings in Spanish), Jimmy Buffet, Peter Frampton, Mick Fleetwood, Joan Osborne, Montell Jordan, Beth Nielsen Chapman, Paddy Moloney, and Andy Summers. The resulting album released this year blends Cuban lyrics and rhythms with jazz, R&B, son, salsa and rock 'n' roll.

Cuba is also the subject of four different historical recordings.

Cuba 21-Nueva Música Cubana on EMI showcases new artists who are fusing the island's Afro-Cuban musical connection with rap, R&B, acoustic pop, and electronic sounds.

Ritmo Afro-Cubano on Fantasy puts into perspective the way Cuban jazz in the U.S. evolves through the stylistic recordings of luminaries ranging from Joe Loco to Chico O'Farrill.

Benny Moré Y Su Banda Gigante on Tumbao Cuban Classics, is a compilation of the late singer/percussionist/bandleader's works between 1953 and 1960. Moré, who dies in 1963, is credited with creating a band in 1952 which records for RCA, trail blazes the fusion of Cuban's venerable son style with boleros and up tempo guarachas amidst blazing trumpet and trombone sections, all connected to the leader's emphasis on placing African-based drumming into the Afro-Cuban landscape.

El Gran Tesoro De La Musica Cubana (*The Great Treasure Trove of Cuban Music*) celebrates 60 years of music from Cuba's two national labels, Panart and EGREM. The music presented in the six-CD boxed set released in the fall, also commemorates EGREM's 40th anniversary. The CDs are assembled chronologically and provide six hours of evolutionary and revolutionary music, ranging from early works in 1969 by Los Van Van to 1985s revolutionary era poet and songwriter Silvio Rodriguez and copious other artists unfamiliar to U.S. listeners ranging from Frank Fernandez to José Antonio Méndez to Los Muñequitos De Mantanzas to Antonio Maria Romeu to Noel Nicola, among others.

In addition, Cuban guitarist/singer/songwriter Roberto Poveda now living in Miami, makes his solo debut after 25 years as a supporting musician with *Son Eléctrio* on ALG Entertainment. The album expands the trova traditional style of ballads and political commentary with more cautious lyrics, rather than uplifting ones, and the utilization of electric guitars, a blues feel and muted horns, all kept moving with Cuban flavored rhythms, and a very conscious effort to crack the American Latin market.

Cuban musicians trying to get into the U.S. continue to face visa problems. Cuban nominees for Grammy awards denied visas to attend the ceremonies in Los Angeles in February include vocalist Ibrahim Ferrer, lutist Barbarito Torres, and timbalero Amadito Valdes. The Cuban government claims the visa requests are denied by U.S. Immigration because the musicians are considered security threats. Visas are also denied Cubanismo, the 15-piece pop/jazz band, forcing the cancellation of its 34-city, 43-concert tour in May.

On the one-year anniversary of the death of Celiz Cruz July 16, two albums and a television special mark the occasion. The records are *Que Disfrute A La Reina* on Universal Music Latino which features previously unreleased tunes recorded in 1999, and *De Cuba Con Amor* on independent Miami Kubaney Records featuring the Cuban children's group, Los Niños Cantores De Cuba, tackling tunes made famous by the "Queen of Salsa." The TV show running on Telemundo is a repeat of its last year's tribute, *Celiz Cruz: Azucar!*, taped prior to her passing and the last event she's able to participate in, according to the network. When the fifth annual Latin Grammys take place in September, Cruz wins the best salsa album award. Several weeks after the awards are announced, Cruz, a Cuban defector, is in the headlines as her dark secret is revealed, her lengthy political battles with the U.S. government over being granted permanent residency.

The *Miami Herald* breaks an exclusive story about the late salsa queen's struggles with the U.S. government to gain permanent status in this country. Using the Freedom of Information Act, the paper obtains her FBI counterintelligence file which indicates she is taken off the government's blacklist of suspected communists in 1965 when she performs and raises money for anti-Castro causes while in exile from her native country, and is granted permission to stay in the U.S. The documents reveal her thwarted attempts to obtain visas to enter the U.S. since 1952. The action comes five years after she defects from Cuba. U.S. government officials call her a communist for her membership in the Popular Socialist Party and for her work for a communist radio station prior to the Castro revolution, according to documents quoted in the story. The late singer's battle with the government is a secret untold by the 77-year-old until this year.

The 10th annual Cuban American Music Festival at L.A.'s Echo Park's José Marti Plaza, alters its name this year to the Cuban Music Festival Honoring Celiz Cruz in tribute to the late Salsa Queen. Music from her albums is played between the sets by local groups Orquesta Guamá, Long John Oliva and Timbache, Yamila and Family, the LA Salsa Kids, and Charanga Cubana.

Two years after her death, she is the subject of a planned musical set for a 2007 premiere in Spain, followed by an engagement in New York City's off-Broadway. The Spanish-language play, *Assuca!*, will feature her career's top tunes as well as original material written by Oscar Gómez , the show's Cuban-born, Spain-based co-producer with Henry Cárdenas, the Chicago headquartered chieftain of his eponymous promotion/marketing firm. The title is a takeoff on the singer's famous shout of "Azucar! (Sugar!)" during her performances. Auditions to find the actress for the lead role will take place in Madrid, Miami, and New York, according to *Billboard*. Reggaeton star Daddy Yankee, an investor in the play, will also act as a musical consultant.

Israel "Cachao" López, the 86-year-old Cuban bassist credited with inventing the mambo rhythm in 1957, becomes Univision Records first living Cuban legend, expanding the label's roster from its regional Mexican and Latin pop strong points. The Miami resident's debut album, *!Ahora Si!*, recorded at Capitol Records in Hollywood and produced by perennial fan, friend and actor Andy Garcia, features his CineSon All Stars band of international players in a program featuring Cuba's rich musical heritage. In addition to the

CD, the release encompasses an hour DVD which includes coverage of the recording session, which features several impromptu tunes. Cachao's U.S. exposure lands him a gig with his orchestra at the 27th annual Playboy Jazz Festival at the Hollywood Bowl June 11, 2005.

Verve Records, one of the bastions of modern jazz in the '50s through 70s, includes three Cuban legends among its four re-releases of classic Latin jazz titles to hook into the Hispania craze: *Candido Featuring Saxophonist Al Cohn* (originally released in 1956 on ABC-Paramount); *Vacation at the Concord* by Machito and his Afro-Cubans (released in '58); *Manhattan Latin—The Sensuous Rhythms of Spanish Harlem* by Dave Pike (released in '64) and followed by *Patato Y Totico* featuring an all star band including Cachao and Arsenio Rodriguez.

Reedman Paquita D'Rivera celebrates 50 years as a musician, dating back to when he's six and playing a small soprano saxophone, with an all-star concert at New York's fabled Carnegie Hal on January 10, 2005. Appearing on the grand stage with the expatriate Cuban saxophonist/clarinetist are Cuban artists congero Cándido, pianist Bebo Valdés, grupo Las Hermanas Márquez, Dominican pianist Michel Camilo, Brazilian singer Rosa Passos, Brenda Feliciano, Paquito's opera singing wife, Yo-Yo Ma, the classical cellist and members of the Youth Orchestra of the Americas. One month later, the National Endowment for the Arts honors Paquito with its respected Jazz Masters award presented during the International Association for Jazz Education's annual conference held this year in Long Beach, California. He is the second foreign-born artist following British pianist Marian McPartland to receive the honor since its inception in 1982. It's also his second national honor, having been named in 2004 Clarinetist of the Year by the Jazz Journalists Association. In 2003, he wins Grammys in the jazz and classical categories for two different nominations, *Brazilian Dreams* (jazz) and *Historia Del Soldado*, featuring music by Igor Stravinsky. Besides Wynton Marsalis, he's only the second jazz performer to win dual category Grammys in the same year. He's also won four Latin Grammys.

Since making America his country and Weehawken, New Jersey, his home, he's written his life story, *My Sax Life*, whose English translation is released domestically in June following its initial debut in Spanish in Spain in 1998. Paquito's first novel, *!Oh, La Habana!* is also available in Spain, and he admits to *Hispanic* magazine that "99 percent of the characters are real." His next literary project—when he's not touring or recording—will detail life on the road and his connection to artists like Dizzy Gillespie and Yo-Yo Ma. "The book's title is appropriately *Portraits and Landscapes*," he tells the magazine.

Noel Nicola, who plays a key role in developing the trova style of protest ballad music, dies of cancer August 7, 2005, in Havana at age 58. Trova's roots are in the early troubadour songs extolling the Island's battles for independence from invading nations which are updated to lyrics dealing with Cuba's social issues, notes the *Los Angeles Times*. Born into a family of musicians, he makes his professional debut in 1968 with Silvio Rodriguez and Pablo Milanes, who also contribute to the emergence of the contemporary protest folk song movement

Articles

"Musical Fetes Cruz's Life." Latin Notas Billboard, Dec. 17, 2005

"Noel Nicola, 58; Cuban Composer, Co-Founder Of Modern Trova Music." Los Angeles Times, Aug. 14, 2005

"Cuban Cast Is Granted Asylum." Los Angeles Times, July 23, 2005

"Cuban Artists Stage Mass Defection." Los Angeles Times, Nov. 16, 2004

"Asylum Papers In, It's Back To Work For Cuban Dancers." New York Times, Nov. 16, 2004

"Bush's Cuban American Support May be Slipping." Los Angeles Times, Sept. 21, 2004

"Breakthrough On The Strip." Los Angeles Times, Sept. 4, 2004

"Cuba's Music Endures." Hispanic Magazine, September 2004

"Cuban American Music Festival." Latin Beat, August 2004

"U.S. Blocks Tour Of Cuban Band." Los Angeles Times, April 9, 2004

"Visa Trouble For Cuban Musicians." Los Angeles Times, Feb. 6, 2004

"Statue Of Compay Segundo Unveiled In Cuba." Houston Chronicle, Dec. 31, 2003

"Preparing For A Mass Exodus-Into Cuba." Time, Dec. 22, 2003

"Fleeing Cuba, Hoping To Soar On New Stage." New York Times, Dec. 5, 2003

"Conferees OK Keeping Ban On Travel To Cuba." Los Angeles Times, Nov. 13, 2003

"Trio Of DVD Releases Savors Cruz's Sweetness." Billboard, Nov. 8, 2003

"Ban On Travel To Cuba May Survive." Los Angeles Times, Oct. 25, 2003

"Cuban Dancers To Seek Asylum." Los Angeles Times, Oct. 22, 2003

"Defying Crackdown, Travel Executives Visit Cuba." Los Angeles Times, Oct. 20, 2003

"The Soul Of Cuba." Hispanic Magazine, September, 2003

"Third Cuban Athlete Defects." Los Angeles Times, Aug. 25, 2003

"School Named For 'Salsa Queen'." Los Angeles Times, Aug. 22, 2003

"Cubans Seek Asylum." New York Times, Aug. 20, 2003

"Celia Sets Cruz To Top." Billboard, Aug. 16, 2002

"Adios, Celia." People, Aug. 4, 2003

"Freedom's Downside." Los Angeles Times, Aug. 1, 2003

"Singer's Death Little Noticed In Cuba." HispaniaNet, July 23, 2003

"Fans In N.Y. Say Their Goodbyes To Queen Of Salsa." Newsday, July 22, 2003

"Salsa Fans Ache To Say Farewell To Their Queen, Celia Cruz." New York Times, July 21, 2003

"A Fitting farewell For Salsa's Queen." Los Angeles Times, July 20, 2003

"A Legend And Rarity In The Fractious Latin World." Los Angeles Times, July 18, 2003

"Celia Cruz, 77; Queen Of Salsa's Passing Marks The End Of A Musical Era." Los Angeles Times, July 17, 2003

"Defection Worth It, Cuban Star Says." San Antonio Express-News, July 6, 2003

"Cuban Defectors Face Hurdles To U.S. Success." Billboard, June 21, 2003

"Popular Cuban Musician Given Asylum." Los Angeles Times, June 12, 2003

"Grammy Winner Compay Segundo Dies At 95." USA Today, July 14, 2003

"New York Style, Cuban Substance." Los Angeles Times, May 25, 2003

"An Angel On His Shoulder." Newsweek, May 5, 2003

"Ry Cooder Offers Cuban Projects Beyond The Buena Vista Social Club." Down Beat, May 2003

"Castro Risks World's Ire, Envoy Says." Los Angeles Times, April 8, 2003

"Albuquerque Band In Havana." Down Beat, April 2003

"Afro-Cuban Pioneer Mongo Santamaria Dies." Down Beat, April 2003

"U.S. Bristles At Cuba's Arrest Of Dissidents." Los Angeles Times, March 20, 2003

"Cuban Children A Beehive Of Spirit." Los Angeles Times, March 8, 2003

"The Club's Last Session." Time, Feb.24, 2003

"A Union Of Older Hands In Havana." New York Times, Jan 26, 2003

"Omar Sosa Stands At The Head Of This Piano Class." Los Angeles Times, Jan. 19, 2003

"Bound By Embargo, Cooder's Cuban Era May be Capped With New Sets." Billboard, Jan. 18, 2003

"Many Question Embargo As Cubans Suffer." Los Angeles Times, Jan. 2, 2003

"Personal Journey." Down Beat, January 2003

"Jazz Triumphs At A Cuban Festival That's harder To Get To." Chicago Tribune, Dec. 16, 2002

"U.S. May Tighten Cuba Travel." Miami Herald, Dec. 15, 2002

"Ruben Gonzalez, 84, Pianist With Buena Vista Social Club." Los Angeles Times, Dec. 9, 2002

"Cubans Touring With Band Defect To the U.S. For Encore." Miami Herald, Nov. 20, 2002

"Timeless Romance: A Man And His Music." Miami Herald, Nov. 20, 2002

"Spielberg Havana Good Time." Daily Variety, Nov. 7, 2002

"Spielberg Criticizes Cuba Embargo." Los Angeles Times, Nov. 6, 2002

"Ry Cooder Can't Escape Cuba's Pull." Los Angeles Times, Oct. 27, 2002

"From Albita, A New Look, A New Sound." Houston Chronicle, Oct. 25, 2002

"Stopped At The Border." Newsweek, Oct. 14, 2002

"Quick Takes." Los Angeles Times, Oct. 1, 2002

"New Sept. 11 Law Keeps Cuban Musician From Getting To Concert." Houston Chronicle, Sept. 25, 2002

"Cuba Trade Show Whets Appetites Of U.S. Firms." Los Angeles Times, Sept. 24, 2002

"A Final Tribute To A Little-Known Cuban Music Great." Los Angeles Times, Sept. 1, 2002

"There Was Plenty Of It And It Was All Cuban." New York Times, Aug. 28, 2002

"U.S. Firms Set Course For Cuba." Dallas News, Aug. 25, 2002

"Armey Urges End To Cuba Sanctions." Los Angeles Times, Aug. 9, 2002

"House Votes To Lift Curbs On U.S. Travel To Cuba." Los Angeles Times, July 24, 2002

"Cuba's Delgado Returns With Pleasant Surprises." Los Angeles Times, June 17, 2002

"Bush Refuses To Life Cuba Embargo." Miami Herald, May 20, 2002

"A Cuban Blend As Diversified As Cuba Itself." New York Times, May 19, 2002

"Carter Visit May Boost Growing Cuba Trade." Los Angeles Times, May 17, 2002

"Cuban Trombone Master's Album Signals A Dawning Detente." Los Angeles Times, April 13, 2002

"Music: That Cuban Twang." Wall Street Journal, Jan. 23, 2002

"From A Fiery Conga Player, Jazz's Latin Tinge." New York Times, Jan. 20, 2002

"A Tempest Of Success." Los Angeles Times, Jan. 13, 2002

"A Beat That Demands Dancing In The Aisles," New York Times, Dec. 5, 2001.

"An Eye On Cuba While Blending In Country Music." New York Times, Dec. 3, 2001

"Bitten By A New Cuban Sound." Los Angeles Times, Aug. 12, 2001

"Afro-Cuban Pioneer's Brief Career Left Lingering Legacy." Los Angeles Times, July 27, 2001

"Cuba's Chucho Valdez Now Has The World's Ear." Los Angeles Times, March 28, 2001

"Fusion With Tradition." Los Angeles Times, Sept. 7, 2000

"Bunnett, Spirits Of Havana Link Genres." Los Angeles Times, May 15, 2000

"Stardom Is Sweet With Age." USA Today, Feb. 22, 2000

"An Apple Far From The Tree." Los Angeles Times, Feb. 22, 2000

"Cuban Sound Has Paris Sizzling." Los Angeles Times, Feb. 2, 200

"Bowing To Protester's Pressure." Los Angeles Times, Oct. 22, 1999

"Buena Vista Bring Back Old Cuban Sound." San Francisco Chronicle Sept. 9, 1999

"Buena Vista Touring Club." Los Angeles Times, Sept. 9, 1999

"Who's Buying Cuban Phenom?" Los Angeles Times, Aug. 14, 1999

"U.S. Authorizes Charter Flights To Cuba from L.A., N.Y." Los Angeles Times, Aug. 4, 1999

"Capturing A Cuban Sound Before It Could Die Out." New York Times, June 6, 1999

"Who Put The Honky Tonk In 'Honky Tonk' Women?" Esquire, June 1999

"Cuban Lute Player Shares Sound, Rhythm Of Life." Los Angeles Times, May 14, 1999

"Buena Vista Explorers Club." Los Angeles Times, May 1, 1999

"Caliente Stays Hot." Latin Notas, Billboard, April 3, 1999

"Cuba's Sierra Maestra Brings Salsa's Past To Life." Los Angeles Times, Feb. 27, 1999

"Cuban Music Goes Commercial." Billboard Feb. 20, 1999

"Two Cuban Musicians Awaiting U.S. Clearance." Los Angeles Times, Feb. 11, 1999

"Buena Vista Social Club's Success In World Music 'Real Enough'." Los Angeles Times, Feb. 5, 1999

"Sacred Steel And More Adorn Arhoolie's Eclectic '99 Slate." Billboard, Nov. 21, 1998

"Cuban Singer Defects." Los Angeles Times, Nov. 11, 1998

"S.F. Fest Matches The Music To The Venue." Los Angeles, Oct. 23, 1998

"Cuba's Arte Mixto Stirs Spicy Salsa." Los Angeles Times, Oct. 12, 1998

"Salsa & Latin Jazz Fest Has Rough Spots, Rewards." Los Angeles Times, Oct. 5, 1998

"Cachao Gives Latin Fest A Grand Evening." Los Angeles Times, Sept. 28, 1998

"Jazz On The Beach." Los Angeles Times, Sept. 18, 1998

"In Monterey Lineup, He Plays First Bass." Los Angeles Times, Sept. 11, 1998

"14-Piece Otra Vision Visits From Cuba." Los Angeles Times, Sept. 5, 1998

"U. S. Authorizes Charter Flights To Cuba From L.A., N.Y." Los Angeles Times, Aug. 4, 1998.

"Hidden Gems," Los Angeles Times, July 7, 1998

"Angel Calls Back Forgotten Music Of Old Havana." New York Times, July 1, 1998

"Vocal Sampling: Musical Magic Using No Instruments." Los Angeles Times, June 23, 1998

"Cubanismo Kicks Latin Music Into High Gear." Los Angeles Times. June 19, 1998

"JVC Jazz, Latino Style." Latin Notas, Billboard, May 30, 1998

"An Infusion Of New Fusion From Cuba." Los Angeles Times, May 18, 1998

"Where The Latin Beat Goes On." Los Angeles Times, May 17, 1998

"Int'l Biz Flocks To Cuba." Billboard, May 15, 1998

"K2K's Arturo Sandoval Taps Afro-Cuban Big-Band Spirit." Billboard, May 9, 1998

"Bruce Lundvall On Blue Note, Angels And The Cuban Experience." Gavin magazine, April 24, 1998

"D'Rivera Lights Up Cuban Cultural Fest." Los Angeles Times, April 13, 1998

"Keeping The Ear On Dance." Los Angeles Times, March 19, 1998

"A Virtuoso Who Riffs Over Borders And Embargoes." New York Times, Jan. 21, 1998

"International Dissonance Aside, Harmony In Cuba." Dec. 24, 1997

"Cuban Legend Comes To Blue Note Via Canada." Los Angeles Times, Nov. 21, 1997

"Bebop's Night In Havana." Los Angeles Times, Oct. 19, 1997

"Latin Jazz Fermentations." Down Beat, August 1997

MUSIC

DIVERSE FACES

Ricky Martin sets the modern crossover parade, recording in a fiery style in both English and Spanish.

Rap En Espanol hitmakers Akwid, born in Mexico and raised in Los Angeles. The brothers **Sergio** and **Francisco Gomez** blend rap with elements of regional Mexican music to create a West Coast urban regional sound.

Enrique Iglesias combines romantic lyrics with upbeat Latin pop elements to become a modern-day favorite with young Latinos, especially the ladies.

Luis Fonsi is a singer in transition, adding harder edged rock ingredients to his regular string-laden albums.

Paulina Rubio records in both Spanish and English to keep both sides of the cultural community appeased.

Sultry Shakira's release of a dual language album, her hit single with Alejandro Sanz and an album, which both crack the general market surveys, fuel her distinct presence.

MUSIC
POWER PLAYERS

CARLOS SANTANA's pioneering work in fusing Latin riffs with pop and rock music helps maintains his popularity. **RUBÉN BLADES** politically aware lyrics propel his varied recorded projects.

Miami-based record executives **JOHN ECHEVERRIA**, **BRUNO DEL GRANADO** (center) and **JESUS A. LOPEZ**.

MUSIC
Latin Jazz Instrumentalists

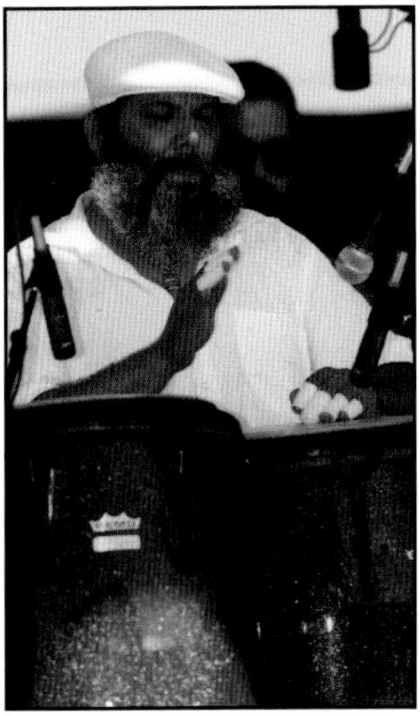

Conguero **Poncho Sanchez**, saxophonists **Paquito D'Rivera** and **David Sanchez** add their own fire to Latin jazz.

Pianists **Chucho Valdes** and **Gonzalo Rubalcaba** and soprano saxophonist **Jane Bunnett** have one thing in common: Cuba. The two pianists are from there; Canadian Bunnett records several albums there.

Latin music's lost icons touch all bases. **CELIA CRUZ**, shown performing with **JOHNNY PACHECO**, passes away July 16, 2003 of brain cancer in her home in Ft. Lee, New Jersey. She's 77. **TITO PUENTE**, the timbales playing bandleader (center) dies in New York University Hospital after an operation to repair a faulty heart valve May 31, 2000. He's 77. Flutist **HERBIE MANN** loses a long fight against cancer July 1, 2003 in Santa Fe, July 1, 2003. He's 73.

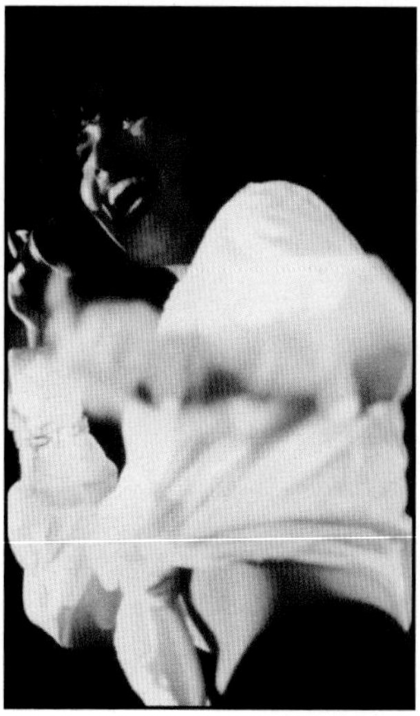

MONGO SANTAMARIA, one of the busiest conga players on English and Spanish discs, dies in Miami's Baptist Hospital Feb. 1, 2003 following a stroke. He's 86. **SELENA**, the rising Tejano star (center) is murdered in Corpus Christi March 31, 1995. She's 23. **ADAN SANCHEZ**, a rising Tejano star, dies March 27, 2004 in a car crash in Sinaloa, Mexico. He's 19.

RADIO/TV
BROADCAST LEADERS

KWKW-AM Los Angeles starts broadcasting war news in Spanish in 1941 and goes fulltime in 1957. Its current owners since 1962 are **JAMES KALMENSON** and his father **HOWARD** top row left. **RAUL CORTEZ**, founder of KCOR-AM San Antonio in 1945, is honored at a ceremony by Bob Hope, center, **MAC TICHENOR**, right, is the former CEO of Hispanic Broadcasting Corp. sold to Univision Communications in 2003.

JIM MCNAMARA, Telemundo's president, left, is in a happy mood in 2002 one year after NBC's acquisition; six years after he takes the top post, he resigns in 2005. **WALTER F. ULLOA** is chairman/CEO of Entravision Communications which owns radio and TV stations.

RADIO/TV
Powerful Personalities

Noticiero Univision, the network's popular newscast is coanchored by **Jorge Ramos** and **Maria Elena Salinas**.

Cristina Saralegui is Spanish TV's leading female show host who also crosses over to do mainstream TV appearances.

Telemundo's historic 2004 Olympics coverage in Spanish is coanchored by **Andres Cantor** and **Jessi Losada**. Cantor is also noted for his soccer play-by-play.

Radio veteran **Bill Tanner** oversees programming decisions for the Spanish Broadcasting System's radio network from Los Angeles.

Claudia Puig is the Miami-based vice president/general manager for four Hispanic Broadcasting Corp. stations. She's also the only female in the market overseeing that many stations

RADIO/TV
Mainstream Players

George Lopez, star of his self-titled hit ABC series, sits on his backyard set with Valente Rodriguez who plays his friend Ernesto.

Jimmy Smits campaigns on-location for his run for the presidency in NBC's *West Wing*.

TV/music personality **Carlos Ponce** sings the National Anthem before a Marlins home game in Miami where he resides.

Eva Longoria is the Latina sexy housewife seeking love outside her marriage on ABC's breakout hit *Desperate Housewives*.

FILM
Box office Draws

Andy Garcia, in his role as star/producer/director, views a shot during filming of his first independent production, *The Lost City*, in the Dominican Republic used to substitute for Havana, Garcia's home. The film tells the story of Havana during the Castro revolution.

Hector Elizondo, in addition to appearing in all of Garry Marshall's films, is a sought-after dramatic actor.

Salma Hayek, left, and **Penelope Cruz**, are two leading dramatic and romantic actresses with separate careers, who in 2005 appear together for the first time in the film *Bandidas*.

FILM
SET SHOTS

Actors need to get it right when the camera's rolling. Here are some examples: **JENNIFER LOPEZ** dances with Matthew McConaughey in the 2001 release *The Wedding Planner*.

JOHN LEGUIZAMO, playing a New York painter, is interrogated by detective Anthony LaPaglia in the 1992 release *Whispers In The Dark*.

BENICIO DEL TORO charms Alicia Silverstone in the 1997 release *Excess Baggage*.

ANTONIO BANDERAS ponders his thoughts in the 1993 release *Philadelphia Story*.

Predominant Players

Arizona Diamondbacks second baseman **Roberto Alomar** jumps over St. Louis Cards sliding Tony Womack after getting him out and throwing to first for a double play.

Chicago Cubs home run slugging **Sammy Sosa** during his halcyon years prior to being called to testify about alleged steroid use in 2005.

Alex Rodriguez, the richest player in baseball after being traded by Texas to the New York Yankees.

Orlando Cabrera, one of the Anaheim Angels top sluggers.

Cezar Izturis provides left handed power to the Los Angeles Dodgers.

SPORTS
SOLID PERFORMERS

The only father-son combo playing on the same team in major league baseball is San Francisco manager **FELIPE ALOU**, left, and son **MOISES**.

Phoenix solid hurler **RUSS ORTIZ** looks to be standing still in this photo taken on his home field.

St. Louis Cardinals **ALBERT PUJOLS** becomes the first major leaguer in 2005 to hit 30 homers in each of his first five seasons.

MANNY RAMIREZ of the World Series champions Boston Red Sox, attends the Fox Sports En Espanol awards in Miami with his wife Juliana where he's named the series most valuable player.

SPORTS
LEGENDS & HOPEFULS

FERNANDO VALENZUELA, the Los Angeles Dodgers ace pitcher from 1980-'90, becomes the first pitcher in 1981 to win both the Cy Young Award and the National League's rookie of the year accolade.

MANU GINOBILI, the NBA's leading Latin superstar, who helps San Antonio win the NBA championship in 2005, drives up for a shot against the Phoenix Suns' top two players, Amare Stoudemire, center, and Steve Nash.

OSCAR DE LA HOYA, boxing's "Golden Boy," (right) jabs Sugar Shane Mosely before losing his welterweight title in 2000 at Staples Center in Los Angeles.

SERGIO GARCIA, the current leading Hispanic golfer in action in 2000 at the Williams Challenge World, left, while **MARCELLO RIOS**, one of a number of competitive Latinos, shows his power at the Franklin Templeton Tennis Classic in Scottsdale in 2000.

Chapter 13
CAPITULO 13

Miami: Latin America's Intersection 2002–2005
MIAMI: INTERSECCION DE AMERICA LATINA 2002–2005

- Cuban community's anti-Castro rhetoric starts to cool.
- Telemundo talks, Univision balks.
- Record labels seek new niches, sign local acts.
- Performing Arts Center snafus delay 2004 opening to 2006.
- Calle Ocho celebrates 25 years of Little Havana festivals.
- Radio payola allegations emerge anew.
- Talent agency William Morris focuses on Latinos in new office.
- Cuban musicians continue being denied visas to local events.

Miami is the creative headquarters for this nation's Latin entertainment industry. It's the home base for the two primary Hispanish-language television networks, Univision and Telemundo; two of the major radio networks, Spanish Broadcasting Systems and Radio Unica; a variety of Latin TV network offsprings of their Anglo parents; TV and film production outfits; Latin record companies owned by the major mainstream labels; several independent record operations trying to counter the major labels; freelance record producers hawking their winning ways; recording studios in which to be creative; high-powered talent agents for securing big-money bookings and the Latin Academy of Recording Arts and Sciences, hoping to keep political pressure out of the Grammy Awards ceremony.

Since 1960, Miami is home to the Cuban diaspora as well as the magnet drawing Hispanics from all over the Latin world, which radically alters the city's population composition. It's a city with a "Floribbean" flavor, in which Caribbean and Latin influences jell together to create the ultimate Hispanish experience. It's also the fiery home for the strongest anti-Castro political lobby in the nation, the Cuban American National Foundation, which aggressively asserts its power and disdain towards anyone or anything it feels brings glory to the despised demigod, including Latin entertainment events which dare to present visiting Cuban artists whom it believes are political foils of the current government. Spanish talk radio is a hotbed of hatred, its commentators spewing venom against those who disagree with their anti-Castro views.

Despite these overpowering attitude, there's a strong undercurrent of change roiling the Cuban community. A poll in May of 2002 by the Cuba Study Group, four months before I arrive in South Miami Beach, indicates a softening of this anti-Castro attitude, as most Cuban exiles favor reconciliation rather than confrontation and a gradual and peaceful transition to democracy in their native land. During my stay, I'll hear about this softening attitude, especially among young Cuban Americans, indicating a major shift among some members of the Cuban community. I'll also encounter a sense of unease by several people I'll interview over speaking publicly about the pressure the exiles exert in Miami.

Nevertheless a book published in 2002, *Cuba Confidential: Love and Vengeance in Miami and Havana* by investigative journalist Ann Louise Bardach, explores in graphic detail the smoldering cauldron of hate and control the powers in the exile community wield. She writes that this vitriol is turned against her because of a 10,000 word series she writes for the *New York Times* in 1998 with Larry Rohter about Luis Posada Carriles, one of the leaders of a group of 20 men aligned with most of the extreme anti-Castro groups, and currently a resident of El Salvador. Not only does the Cuban American National Foundation attack the paper for publishing "offensive, slanderous, and defamatory" articles about Carriles, but Bardach writes her associate is accosted by angry people and later someone tries to drive her off a freeway. Spanish radio calls her both "the lover of Fidel Castro" and *una tortillera*, a Cuban abusive term for lesbian.

Spanish radio, she writes can only have one unified voice against Castro; to go against this can be "injurious to one's image and security." Character assassinations and denunciations of people who oppose the views of the exile community leadership are common. Hispanic Broadcasting Corporation's WAQI-AM, *Radio Mambi* and show host Armando Pérez-Roura, are the favorite antagonists. He also has his own show on Radio Marti, the U.S. government funded news station beaming its own slanted news into Cuba. Other biased radio stations, according to Bardach are HBC's WQBA, *La Cubanisma*; Fenix Broadcasting Corp.'s WWFE, *La Ponderosa;* and Spanish Broadcasting System's WCMQ. Local Spanish TV stations also echo the same strong anti-Castro stance. WWFE's Ramón Saúl Sánchez, I discover in the *Miami Herald*, is a key protagonist who trades diatribes with WAQI's Pérez-Roura.

Living in Los Angeles where news of the Cuban exile community is hardly reported on, the book recounts incidents which carry the mark of retribution against miscreants and unbelievers. Among occurrences cited: There are more than 100 politically motivated attacks by anti-Castro groups between 1972 and '76. In 1996, the dinner music club Centro Vasco is bombed when Cuban entertainer Rosita Fornes is invited to perform. The popular Havana club, reopened here in 1960 by owners Juan and Totty Saizarbitoria, are the subject of death threats following attacks by *Radio Mambí* hosts Pérez-Roura and Marta Flores. With their business ruined, the duo are forced to sell the venue. None of the prominent artists who've appeared in the room, Gloria and Emilio Estefan, Jon Secada, Arturo Sandoval and Julio Iglesias, speak out against the violence. Two other incidents in '96 are also mentioned: La Orquestra Aragon's planned appearance is cancelled by the promoters following threats against them, and people attending pianist Gonzalo Rubalcaba's concert are assaulted and jeered at by 200 protesters. One year later, WRTO receives bomb and death threats following the addition of Cuban artists to its playlist. Naturally, the music ceases.

Spanish talk radio plays a pivotal role in allowing listeners to vent their opinions in the Elian Gonzalez situation, according to the book. The youngster is one of three survivors among the 15 who set out November 22, 1999, from Cárdenas, Cuba, on a 17-foot aluminum hand-built boat with a 50 horsepower outboard motor. Elian's mother is among those who perish at sea; he is found tied to a large black inner tube 30 miles north of Ft. Lauderdale. He'll be six years old 10 days after he arrives in Florida on Thanksgiving day. Almost immediately Elian becomes the central figure in the battle between his father, Juan Miguel Gonzalez, and his relatives in Miami. Spanish radio runs a two-day fund raiser which produces more than $204,00 to cover legal and other expenses incurred by the family. The Cuban American National Forum leads the fight to keep Elian with his Miami family rather than returning him to his father in Cuba. Eventually the U.S. government decrees Elian should be with his father, who is reunited with his son in Washington and they both fly back to Havana a few days later.

Spanish radio, still smarting from losing the Elian battle, tells its listeners to invalidate the Democratic federal government's decision by voting Republican in the 2000 elections. Pérez-Roura is especially singled out in the book for extolling listeners to never vote Democratic.

Despite all this bombast, or perhaps because of it, some Cubans are saying enough is enough. In January, Oswaldo Payá, the leading dissident to his nation's communist government and head of the Varela Project, a referendum designed to produce a peaceful transition to democracy, visits Miami to gather support for the movement. He's called "Fidel's ambassador" on some of the Spanish talk stations, reports the *Los Angeles Times.* In addition to the Cuba Study Group's poll, which indicates a softening attitude toward reconciliation, a *Miami Herald* poll indicates a majority of Cuban Americans support the Varela Project. Carlos Saladrigas, who heads the Cuba Study Group, comprised of leading Cuban Americans, points to the Elian Gonzalez incident as a turning point in altering local minds.

Although I don't run into any political pressure of any sort during my visit, one radio official expresses concern about doing an interview for fear any comments expressed about Cuban exiles will create problems for the person within the company. We chat and nothing untowardly happens.

Miami is a city whose statistics tell the story of its transformation from a winter retreat haven for Easterners and Canadian "snow birds" to the bridge with Latin America, where Latinos become the majority of the population. Up until 1960, Anglos represent the majority of Miami's population. By 1990, they are down to 10 percent of the population. Among the Cuban exiles living in Miami are 10,000 plus ex-prisoners of the regime. In 1980, there are an estimated 586,479 Cuban Americans in South Florida of which 125,000 arrive via the Mariel Boatlift. Since the 1994 migration agreement between the U.S. and Cuba, around 250,000 Cubans, mostly young people and those who arrive on rafts, come to the U.S. In 1997, the number grows to 600,000 in the greater Miami area. The 2000 Census reports the number at 701,512, representing 65.7 percent of Miami-Dade County. In nearby Broward County, the Census reveals there are 271,652 Hispanics, of which Puerto Ricans represent 20 percent, Cubans 18.7 percent, Colombians 11 percent, Mexicans 7 percent, and Central Americans 6.7 percent. In Tampa, the Census turns up 35,000 Cuban-Americans.

Miami is still a hot, muggy exciting city by the ocean, where I discover first-hand during my visit the first week in October of 2002 to conduct interviews for this book that Spanish, or "Cubonics" is spoken just about everywhere. "Cubonics" is an alteration of

"Spanglish" heard in New York, in which Spanish idioms are Anglicized. At the end of four-and-a-half days, I'll have conducted 16 interviews, including several unplanned. A number of executives who are members of the Cuban exile community, candidly talk about how the Castro government dramatically impacts their lives, with stories the likes of which I have never heard before. These people bear the personal scars of what happened to them 90 miles across the Atlantic. How can someone in charge of a Spanish-language radio or TV network or station be fair and impartial and accept the idea of Cuban artists funded by the Castro regime appearing in their city? How can the general manager of a Latin radio station add Cuban music to the playlist when memories of past injustices which cause them to escape to America are still vivid in their minds? How indeed can they function fairly without their bias affecting their business judgments? It's a question I will come to ponder during my week in Miami.

One morning, while walking along Washington Avenue in South Miami Beach, where the record companies are ensconced, the sound of merengue music wafts through the air. It's a delightful welcome for me to Miami Beach, and to my initial surprise, the music's drifting out the open door of Sopranos Pizza. Caribbean music from a place which sells Italian pizza? The dichotomy causes me to stop, look and listen, and I suddenly realize on this first day of going to interviews, I may be in for a lot of unforeseen surprises.

The last time I'm in Miami Beach is in 1960 when a friend and I take leave time from Ft. Stewart, Georgia, the fairly obscure Army post an hour's drive north of Savannah where we're stationed, and head for a week of sun and fun at the popular tourist destination. During my two years at Ft. Stewart, with a permanent military contingency of 2,500, its principal reason for staying open is to provide a summer training ground for thousands of Southern National Guard and Reserve tank and artillery units. By the new millennium, the base is a major Army installation, sending troops to answer the call of the Bush administration's wars against Iraq and racking up their share of soldiers tragically killed or injured in combat.

Now in the fall of 2002, I'm situated in the trendy South Beach portion of the community's hotels and refurbished art deco buildings all ablaze with coats of colorful paint, a rainbow of subtle tints which engage the eye and house the Latin spin-offs of the major English-language record companies like Warner Music Latina, Universal Music Latino, Universal Music Latin America, Sony Discos, BMG U.S. Latin and EMI Latin America. The two prominent independent labels are Maverick Musica owned by Madonna and Crescent Moon, owned by Gloria and husband Emilio Estefan, which they will sell to Sony in a few years. Of these eight companies, four top executives grant me interviews: Warner Music, Universal's two operations and Madonna's Maverick Musica.

Despite extensive phone calls and e-mails over a three-month period, the others choose not to be part of the project, but not before I'm given a royal runaround involving lies, obfuscation and being deceived into believing I'll be able to meet Oscar Llord of Sony Discos when he comes to the company's Santa Monica, California, complex months later. After returning to Los Angeles, I attempt to arrange a phone interview with the elusive Llord and am told he'll be on the West Coast at his office and we can do an in-person interview there. Although several dates and times are mentioned, the meeting never takes place. Two other company PR officials ask me to provide them with specific subjects I'd like to discuss, so I e-mail Jorge Pino at EMI and Adrian Posse at BMG the topics I plan to discuss with them. I never hear back from them as well as from Mauricio Abaroa, president of Crescent Moon. In all of these incidents I'm communicating with both the executive's assistant or the company's public relations representative.

For whatever reason, Crescent Moon, Sony, BMG, and EMI see no value in being part of this project which chronicles the growth of their industry. In my 45 years as an entertainment journalist in which I've interviewed the presidents of powerful record companies and superstars ranging from Frank Sinatra to Barbra Streisand to Ray

Charles, The Supremes and Dave Brubeck, I've never encountered such a lack of cooperation and been lied to so much about doing an interview. Naturally, I'm disappointed and frustrated and not accustomed to being turned down by so many companies. In a move to counter a total lack of cooperation from Estefan Enterprises, the company owned by the Estefans, which informs me Emilio is too busy to do an interview and Gloria is on tour, I send Emilio, the acknowledged power figure in the Latin music industry, a personal letter requesting time and listing the names of superstars who've found time in their schedules to do sit-down interviews with me. I never hear back from him and even simple requests for background material on the company and bios of its principals from its PR people also go unanswered. Touring, I discover, is the excuse author Anthony M. Destefano is given for being unable to interview Gloria for his 1997 bilingual unauthorized autobiography, *Gloria Estefan The Pop Superstar from Tragedy to Triumph.*

Still trying to connect with the Estefans, I try another approach several months later by contacting the New York head of PR for Sony Music in New York, which distributes Crescent Moon, and leave several requests via e-mail and phone to ask his assistance in connecting with Emilio and Gloria, who records for Sony, as well as label mate Ricky Martin. I'm told he'll get back to me, but he never does. It's another surprising turndown by a company I never have any problem dealing with during my 17 years with *Billboard.*

Two years later, with three quarters of the book completed, I attempt to set up interviews with the Estefans, but again run up against a wall of indifference.

Of the two major Spanish TV networks, Telemundo is accessible; Univision has a policy of its executives not talking to the media. While Radio Unica, the first Spanish news and information network welcomes me, I get the cold shoulder from Raul Alarcón, Jr., Spanish Broadcasting System's owner/chairman, whose major music radio network competitor, Dallas-based Hispanic Broadcasting Company, is eager to cooperate.

Unknown to most Americans are the large number of Hispanic TV networks, owned by English-language TV parents, whose broadcasts originate from this epicenter, but are beamed to viewers outside the U.S. These Miami-area companies operating Latin American networks include such familiar brands as Discovery Networks, MTV, HBO, TNT, Universal Television, E! Entertainment Television, and MGM. MTV Latin America is perhaps the best known of these offsprings for carrying the first *MTV Music Video Awards* telecast in 2002.

This growing television industry with a global reach, now provides employment for technical as well as artistic personnel, buoyed by the presence of Latinos who are migrating here from Latin American countries with political and economic problems, including Colombia, Chile, Argentina, Nicaragua, and Venezuela. Venezuela, incidentally is the headquarters for the parent of local film/TV production company Venevision International, and is also home to Ole Communications, which partners with the HBO Latin American Group.

Miami's concert halls which increasingly cater to Hispanic musicians, will be augmented and overshadowed by the grand daddy of all venues, the new $344 million Performing Arts Center of Greater Miami, running behind schedule and now planned for a summer 2006 opening rather than its original February 2004 debut.

I arrive in town on a Sunday afternoon with my business interviews commencing the next morning. I'll be socializing with two people on the periphery of show business to gain some background and a sense of what modern Miami is like. While scanning the *Miami Herald*'s Website, I spot a byline by someone I know and have lost contact with. His name is Cary Darling and I offered him an internship at *Billboard* while he was a senior at Loyola Marymount College. He worked out so well that I provided him with his entry into journalism when he graduated and added him to the magazine's Los Angeles reportorial staff. While exchanging e-mails Cary tells me he's been in Miami two-and-a-half years and is the paper's entertainment features editor. He was last writing about pop music for the *Orange*

County Register in Santa Ana, California. So we make a dinner date for Sunday evening and he takes me to Collins Avenue where we select Solé an Italian restaurant for an al fresco dinner, not too far from the Jackie Gleason Theater, one of the main concert venues.

"People here prefer to be called Hispanic rather than Latinos," Cary informs me. "They think Latino has a lower class connotation. Hispanic has more of a European, Iberian feel to it. Nicaraguan, Argentinean, Colombian and Venezuelan immigrants comprise the newest arrivals during the last 20 years. It's the middle class which comes here because of economic or political problems in their countries. Many of these people settle in Coral Gables, which is the Beverly Hills of Miami."

Is there any alteration in the dominant Cuban community's ire against Castro and the ferocity with which it protests Cuban musicians playing here? "Protests are more sporadic," Cary says, adding: "The younger generation doesn't care as much. Slowly, the Cuban community is becoming more moderate. It's the older Cubans who come here in the '60s that are still anti-Castro."

On my second combination social/business evening with Ginny Gutierrez, a former New Yorker who's lived in Miami 22 years, she takes me to Little Havana and we dine at the fabled Versaille Restaurant, which she points out is a key hangout for leaders of the Cuban exile community. "The recent migration brings great cultural vitality to Miami," she says as we dine on traditional Cuban food and a strolling quartet of musicians stops at our table to offer a musical background to our conversation. "The community has become multi-cultural and music is a very important aspect of this growth," she says. "You can go to restaurants, hotels and nightclubs hear singers from all over the world."

Her tastes run from salsa to Brazilian to Cuban music, all of which have African roots, she stresses. She's a radio station button-pusher, splitting her time between American pop and Latin music. " I find American music makes me sentimental because I like the older pop music and Latin music makes me want to get up and move, tap my fingers, shake my shoulders and roll my hips." She watches the news on Univision, reads Spanish newspapers and glossy magazines "to keep my Spanish vocabulary current." Her initial exposure to Spanish is in language classes in high school and college.

Ginny, who works in public relations, meets her then Cuban-born husband in San Juan, Puerto Rico, where they live for several years before moving to Miami. He comes from a wealthy family. "When I met my father-in-law, he told me how horrific it was to have spent 20 years building his women's underwear business in Cuba, and within two years of Castro taking over, he walks into the building to discover the workers have taken over the business and he is told he is no longer the owner. The father, mother, two sons and a daughter are exiled to Venezuela, leaving behind other members of their family in Cuba."

With these two social/business background dinners completed, my first interview meeting is with Warner Bros. Latin label president George Zamora, whose office is a few blocks away from the hotel I'm staying at in South Beach on Collins Avenue. Warner Music Latina is on Washington Avenue in a white building with blue highlights. Neighboring buildings are a blaze with pastel colors. My interviews with record companies are all within walking distance of the Royal Palm Crowne Plaza Resort, one of the area's oldest art deco buildings, which itself sports a fresh makeover and ownership. Visiting the television and radio networks involves driving to the industrial section of Hialeah, on the other side of Miami International Airport.

Zamora, dressed in a colorful sports shirt, works out of a large office with delightful views of the city. He's been with the company since 1997, after 11 years of running Sony Discos. His family migrates from Cuba in 1960 when he's 11 years old. "As soon as Castro walked it, I walked out," he says, adding he and his brother are the first to come to the U.S. "We live with uncles and relatives here for a year before my parents arrive."

Zamora knows first-hand how the nation's soaring Hispanic population is impacting the Latin record industry. "We have grown tremendously since 1983–'84 when I started in the U.S. Latin market. At that time, there were only two major labels based in the U.S. dealing with Latin music, CBS and RCA." Warner's Latin label, Zamora explains, starts in 1987 "to market Luis Miguel. Now we have great success with Alejandro Sanz, who's the biggest artist ever to come out of Warner Music Spain." Both artists are winners in the new Latin Grammy competition during the formative period from 2000 to 2002. Four of the label's additional top sellers are rock groups Maná, Volumen Cero, Bacilos and La Ley. The label, Zamora explains, competes in all genres of Latin music, rock, Mexican, tropical and pop.

With the ability of Latin artists to cross into the mainstream market on a selective basis over the years, is that the company's ultimate goal? "Just because you can sing in Spanish does not mean you can sing in English. Everybody wants a crossover act, but just because you're a superstar in the Hispanic marketplace does not mean you are going to succeed in the U.S. market," Zamora responds. That said, he believes crossover "is a little easier today because we have a stronger sales base for Spanish music in the U.S. than it was 15 years ago."

What about regional Mexican music being played in Miami and rock en Español being aired around the country? "Mexican music," Zamora says, "does get played in (tropical music favored) Miami, "but it's usually a Mexican pop idol like Vicente Fernández, or a Marco Antonio Solís or Pepe Aguilar or someone with a mariachi sound singing a ballad that will get it played everywhere. But not the tuba banda bands, which seem to work best in Los Angeles. With rock en Español bands, it's been a struggle since they're copying rock'n'roll. Volumen Cero plays a pretty heavy type of rock."

Is the Latin industry losing second- and third-generation Hispanics who prefer English-language artists as they become more Americanized? "I think there's a certain amount of loss occurring," Zamora admits. "If we're talking about Puerto Ricans in New York and Cuban Americans born here, I'd say yes. The biggest Hispanic population, the Mexican population, stays a little more loyal to its heritage when it comes to music sales. But I think they also are buying music in both languages. A lot of Hispanic kids are going to

Tower or Musicland, Transworld or Wherehouse to buy the new Maná or Juanes or Enrique Iglesias or whatever happens to be hot at the time. I remember when I first began, I had to convince mainstream retailers to carry Latin product, and it was a very difficult thing to do. But as the Latin music business grew tremendously throughout the late '80s and '90s, retailers started looking for new areas for incremental sales, and began hiring specialized people who understood the language and the product. Today, probably all major retailers have Hispanic buyers and they have given us more space, especially in the main metropolitan Hispanic areas around the country."

While retailers enthusiastically see additional profits, Latin radio is not as gung-ho about all the genres of Latin music being churned out. Notes Zamora: "We always have problems with radio because of its conservative approach. Sometimes it's very difficult to convince them to open their doors to new artists and new music. Because of this problem, we haven't been able to develop a new artist in the last few years. It's not only us, everyone has the same problem. It's always a battle and it will continue to be a battle." So how do you get around radio's resistance? "We're doing a lot of street and dance club promotions. We use word of mouth and place posters on the street. It's costing us twice as much money in marketing as well as a tremendous amount of human effort. As for television, we do get exposure on certain shows on Univision and Telemundo, but unfortunately we don't have a Latin MTV or VH1. I think if we did, our growth would have been phenomenal the last three years. We do get play on MTV Latin America." But that doesn't impact domestic sales.

By April of 2004, sales obviously matter as the Warner Music Group drastically reduces the staffs for Warner Music Latina and Warner Music Latin America (which handles the other Latin markets). Zamora is among the staffers departing both firms. Inigo Zabala, president of Warner Music Latin America, now has oversight of Zamora's operation, who's top acts include Luis Miguel, Alejandro Sanz, La Ley, Alex Ubago, and Olga Tañon.

Zamora subsequently hooks up in July with hit making producer Sergio George to form SGZ Entertainment, a record production, management and publishing firm, whose records will be distributed by Sony Music. The label will record new acts and established names like former Warner artist Tito Nieves. With Zamora the company president, George is the vice president/A&R director who moves from New York to work here with him. He'll continue to function as an independent producer, a safe hedge against any possible label failure.

Domestic sales are a natural concern in 2002 for John Echeverría, president at Universal Music Latino, who's offices are in an imposing coral building on Lincoln Road in the closed to car traffic Lincoln Mall. From his windows, the executive in a white short sleeve shirt, can gaze across the mall and its plethora of outdoor restaurants and shops to the Sony building where Sony Discos is located, and in another direction palm trees and the Atlantic Ocean. It's a nice setting to work in.

"While the exploding Hispanic population has created a very important market in the U.S. probably the size of Spain, we are facing the problems that all mature markets are facing, like piracy and downloads, resulting in a first time industry decrease in sales of 26 percent for the first half of the year," he says. Also affecting sales, continues the executive, is Latin radio which "targets very old and conservative audiences while second- and third-generation Latino kids are listening to Anglo radio where they hear hip-hop and rock. So why should they listen to rock en Español when they have the real rock'n'roll?" Echeverría, born in England but raised in Madrid, Spain, where his three children are born, says his 16-, 11-, and nine-year-old kids all prefer listening to Anglo radio. The executive and his family are six-year Miami residents and he's been with Universal 14 months. Through a number of ownership deals, the label traces its formation to 1992 when it is PolyGram Latino which becomes Universal Latino four years later.

Universal's roster reflects the Latin American community with artists from Puerto Rico, Mexico, Colombia, and Spain. "Puerto Rico used to represent 50 percent of the U.S. Latin market, but it's suffered a severe decline," Echeverría says. "The young kids are listening to reggaeton, which is hip-hop and jazz rather than salsa."

The label's top attractions are Enrique Iglesias and Juanes. After recording two hit albums in English, Iglesias records his next album, *Quazas*, in Spanish. It's been five years since he last records in his native language. Why the return now? "Enrique is one of the very real bilingual kids I know. He doesn't speak Spanglish like most of the second-generation kids in L.A. or Miami or New York do. Sooner or later he's got to express himself in Spanish; it comes from his heart," Echeverría explains, underscoring the point that now is the hour for a discourse in Español. So optimistic is the label about the album which the executive calls its "most important release ever" that it ships 600,000 copies within the U.S. Latin market. Echeverría also emphasizes the company is treating this album like it would an "American release." Don't all your releases in the U.S. get treated like American releases? I ask. When Latin labels release a Spanish-language album domestically, he explains, "the expectations for success are all going to start at 200,000 units, while the expectation for an American (English-language) album is going to be over one million copies."

On Juanes new album, *Un Dia Normal*, he has a duet in Spanish with pop star Nelly Furtado. How unusual is this? Parries Echeverría: "It's very unusual. You don't very often have Anglo acts doing duets in Spanish."

One of Universal's acts, Jessie Morales, focuses on a modern form of the corrido, musical stories about the poor and oppressed masses, the narco-corrido tales extolling Mexican drug traffickers. Isn't this glorifying criminals? "Corridos are part of the Mexican tradition," responds Echeverría, "and many of the big regional and norteño Mexican acts like Los Tigres Del Norte perform this form of the corrido. I've got mixed feelings about it. It's not very nice to sing and do homage to traffickers. On the other hand, what are the musicians doing? They are reflecting what's going on around them, and that has always been the case. I would never censor an artist.

Would I try to convince them not to sing that someone dealing drugs is a hero? Definitely."

One subject I'm really interested in concerns the lack of a huge audience for the first Latin Grammy telecast on CBS. Despite a potential audience of 37 million Hispanics, the telecast only attracts 4.5 million viewers. What is the problem? Echeverría says "part of the problem is the Latin media which is focused on keeping older viewers tuned to Spanish-language TV. Are the 40-year-old Hispanic ladies who watch the novelas ready for the Grammys? I don't know. Probably part of the mistake is that the awards are on CBS, a typical American mainstream network. So what is the solution? "If the awards are on Univision, they would have a higher rating. CBS needed to have artists liked Santana and Shakira, whose names have an appeal to the American audience. But they forgot the big majority of Hispanics in this country are Mexicans who watch Spanish television."

Universal, like Warner Bros. and Sony, has both its domestic and international Latin labels in Miami. How does Echeverría's operation interrelate with Universal Music Latin America? The latter company deals with bringing music into the U.S. market and exporting domestic releases into the overseas Latin markets. Notes Echeverría: "The great thing about the Latin market in the U.S. is that's it's so open. The big advantage of Latin music is that it flows so freely across borders." With rare exception, Echeverría points out, "no one becomes a big pop act in the U.S. without being successful in Mexico. It's the same situation for all the U.S. Latin labels. When we have a big success here, that pattern follows into Latin America, and when there's a huge act in Latin America, it will also become big in the U.S."

So to get the overseas perspective, I stroll over to chat with Jesus Lopez, chairman of Universal Music Latin America/Iberian Peninsula. The company is situated on fabled Collins Avenue in a gray three-story building with pink highlights which was formerly a hotel. Walk past the adjacent towering Loews, St. Moritz, and Royal Palm Crowne Plaza hotels, representing modern Miami Beach, past the shuttered and fenced off Charles Hotel with its court-ordered auction signs, past the "Coming Soon 5 star condo hotel, the De Soleil," which will replace the current businesses, a scooter rental, Wok & Roll Chinese eatery, the Frooty market, a toy store, a roller blade store and two small hotels, the Henrosa and Carlton, and you arrive at 1425, the building with the silver lettering proclaiming you've arrived at Universal Music Latin America. The building is sandwiched between two aging hotels, the aforementioned Carlton and the President.

Across the street are several apartment houses and the newly opened Jerry's Famous Deli from Los Angeles, a 24-hour eatery, which hopes to replace the shuttered Wolfie's delicatessen, a Miami Beach landmark which closes along with several other businesses along Collins Avenue after the September 11 Twin Tower attacks in Manhattan diminishes the region's tourist trade. This is a section of South Beach apparently in transition from hotels and apartments to refashioned offices for Latin entertainment companies.

A Rock-Ola Jukebox in the Universal lobby plays the label's Spanish CDs. The receptionist greets me in English when I tell him I have a meeting with Jesus Lopez. Like all the companies I visit, English and Spanish are interchanged, one minute someone's speaking English, the next minute Spanish, or the other way around, whether it's to a co-worker or someone on the phone. Spanish is definitely the prime means of communication within this branch of Latin show business. Alejandro Maya, Lopez's assistant, has been tremendously helpful during our phone conversations and e-mails in setting up this appointment. So we share an enthusiastic in-person greeting in English.

I catch Lopez at both an opportune and inopportune time. Both apply since he tells me he's leaving shortly for the airport for a trip that will take him to Madrid, London and Rio De Janeiro all in the same week. Lopez is a traveling exec, out of the U.S. 80 percent of the time, meaning he's away from his wife so much "that she wants to kill me," he says jokingly. "This is not an easy life," continues Lopez dressed for this flight in a white polo shirt with white slacks, not yet looking at his watch in his third floor office.

Lopez is in charge of the whole of Latin America including Spain and Portugal. He oversees an operation begun in 1992 with offices in Mexico, Venezuela, Central America, Colombia, Brazil, Argentina, and Chile, with the U.S. joining the roster in 1996. "This is a very young operation," he says.

While Lopez also handles American, French, Italian and Japanese acts for sale in Spanish-speaking nations, in addition to importing U.S. domestic product, Echeverría's main focus is on artists who perform in Spanish for domestic Latino consumers. The top-selling acts from Echeverría which Lopez sells overseas include Enrique Iglesias ("a kid who grew up in Miami and is completely bilingual and bicultural and that's important"), Paulina Rubio and Juanes.

While the U.S. market is open to artists who shift from Spanish to English for the crossover market, Lopez feels Hispanics should keep singing in Spanish. "It's very important to keep one's cultural roots," he says, adding: "Music is one of the most important parts of our lives, and artists need to perform and preserve their native language."

Do your overseas companies fill the needs of the U.S. Latin community? "Yes," he answers, "because with the real boom in migration during the last 10 years from South America, Spain, Colombia, Argentina, Brazil, and Portugal, we're able to provide them with records by the artists they're familiar with. A person coming from Argentina is completely different from a person coming from Colombia or Spain. The only thing they have in common is the language; their cultures are all different."

Globe-traveling Lopez notes there are healthy pockets of Latin music fans in France, Germany, Sweden, and Norway. "A lot of refugees from South America live in Northern Europe. You can find thousands of Colombians dancing and listening to Colombian music in the center of Madrid. In Asia, the Japanese are very interested in flamenco music from Spain, regional Mexican music or tango from

Argentina. But the most constant forms of music in small quantities that you can find in every place around the world are tangos, flamencos and tropical music from Cuba or Colombia."

Seven months after our interview, Lopez cuts his personnel in all nations due to sales dips based on rampant piracy and counterfeiting. He also launches disco and regional Mexican divisions and licenses music from the catalogs of Univision and Vale Music.

One executive riding the growth crest is Maverick Musica's president Bruno Del Granado. His arrival in Miami takes a circuitous route. Leaving his native Majorca, Spain, to come to the U.S. in 1986 and work in marketing for CBS Records, he moves to Miami in 1993 to help launch MTV Latin America, becomes an independent Latin music and TV consultant four years later and in 2000 is hired by Madonna to oversee the growth of her new Latin label.

Del Granado strikes gold with three of the company's first four cross-cultural artist signings, Hialeah-raised Cuban American vocalist Jorge Moreno, 27; Chilean vocal star Nicole, 25; and Ibiza, Spain, DJ and instrumentalist José Padillo, 45. All three win Latin Grammy nominations-Moreno as best new artist; Nicole for her pop female album, *Viaje Infinito* and Padilla for his pop instrumental album, *Navigator* which features English-language vocals on such tracks as *The Look of Love* and *Adios Ayer* by guest artist Seal. The fourth act, Santos Inocentes, an Argentinean electronic rock band, is ineligible to compete because of the timing of the CD's release. Prior to releasing albums by these acts, the label's debut CD is a compilation, *Platinum Rhythm*, featuring tracks by Enrique Iglesias, Marc Anthony, and Spanish-language cuts by Madonna and *NSYNC.

So while the Warner Bros.-distributed label is three for three, only Moreno wins his Grammy category. He is born in a Miami suburb following his parents departure from Cuba prior to the revolution and who subsequently divorce when he's 13. His self-titled debut album showcasing his pleasant voice, includes some perky tracks, acoustic and electronic instruments and even some album scratching elements. His updated merengue version of *Babalu*, the tune made famous by Desi Arnaz, so impresses the producers of the CBS special, *I Love Lucy 50th Anniversary*, that he's invited to perform the song on the national telecast. Moreno is an anomaly in Miami, one of a few local homeboys to be signed by a Miami record label, which makes the city very proud. Moreno grows up listening to salsa artists on his father Tony's record labels, Top Hits, home to Oscar D'Leon, El Puma De Sinaloa, Frankie Ruiz, Tito Rojas and José Luis Rodríguez and the more current Musical Productions (MP) label, which features salsa and merengue artists Puerto Rican Power, Manny Manuel, La Banda Gorda and Limite 21. Jorge's older brother Mark, 30, is employed at MP. Another older brother, Tony, runs a record store in Hialeah.

Del Granado's offices are on Lincoln Road, in an older building, reflecting the Miami Beach of years past. From his window he can see CBS and Sony Disco across the street. MTV Latin America, his former employee along with MTV Networks and Nickelodeon Latin America are in the same building down the street. Other entertainment entities right off Lincoln Road include the Latin Recording Academy, the Jackie Gleason Theater and EMI Music. The casually attired executive in a blue checkered long-sleeved shirt sees I'm looking out one of his windows at the distant blue ocean, chimes in, "not a bad view." His focus on business is much closer than is the Atlantic. Moreno, he says has been knocking on doors in Miami the last five years. His music is a combination of old Cuban from the '40s and '50s which he hears at home with his parents sprinkled with alternative Radiohead-influenced music and straight-ahead pop and rock by the likes of the Beatles, Rolling Stones, The Cure and Depeche Mode, which he listens to with his friends. I signed him because he has that special sense of being an Anglo and a Latin artist. The kinds of artists I'm signing are certainly left of center."

During a trip to Los Angeles while a music consultant in 1999, Del Granado meets Madonna. "I was kind of a bridge at that time between the Anglo and Latin cultures, working with companies that wanted to get into the Latin market and companies in Spain and Latin

America that wanted to get into the U.S. market," he says. "One of my clients is in L.A. and while I'm there, I receive a call from Madonna's people, who say she's interested in what I'm doing. I initially thought this might not be the right thing for me to go to work with an artist. I was used to doing things my own way, being my own boss.

"It's while living in Miami that she discovers Latin music and is very much into Latin culture. That's what I found fascinating about her. She says she wants to start a Latin division that would mirror what her Maverick label in Los Angeles has accomplished in 1992 as an alternative music label. My personal interest is in becoming an alternative niche boutique label to what the major labels are. And she said 'that's what we want to do,'" an assertive vision which prompts Del Granado to join Madonna's world.

The executive senses a new musical sound—"the Miami sound of the new millennium"—emerging from the city where WPOW, the leading pop station blends Spanish-language records among its English-language playlist "because 60 to 70 percent of its audience is Hispanic." Gloria Estefan and her husband Emilio, he says "were the precursors in the '80s and '90s. But now Miami's gone from being a purely Cuban city of the '70s and '80s to being a multi-Latin melting pot. You have a homogeneous Argentine community of around 150,000 people, which is into the rock en Español scene. You have a tremendously powerful Colombian community of around 250,000. There's also huge Venezuelan and Nicaraguan communities. These are recent arrivals drawn here because of the troubled economies of their countries.

"So what's happening is these people are bringing their musical identities with them. When you go to a rock en Español concert at the Miami Arena, you'll see people waving flags from Colombia, Bolivia, Peru, and Ecuador. If you look at the group Volumen Cero on Warner Music Latina, its members are Colombian, Cuban and Peruvian. These are musicians who are either born or raised in the United States from South American origins and their music sounds like what's coming out of Miami now, a mixture of rock, pop, and ethnic sounds."

In addition to dealing with the record label, Del Granado is also executive producer of a Maverick Films two-hour production, *How to Be the Perfect Latino Star*, "which is about the Hispanic music scene in Los Angeles and discovering and breaking an artist. It's supposed to air on VH1 next year. "We're hoping it will attract a crossover, bilingual, bicultural audience." It's his first shot at exec producing a film. "One of the reasons why I'm involved," he explains, "is because I bring in the Latin perspective to make sure the film's being done properly." Several months later, Maverick forms a new division, Maverick Latino to acquire and distribute Spanish-language films with English subtitles for the home video market, and one year later it's ad in *Weekly Variety* promoting seven films unabashedly asserts "Blazing a new trail in the Latino market."

Being a Hispanic in America now comes with a timely pastiche. "When I first came to American 20 years ago," Del Granado opines, "being Hispanic was not really cool. You spoke Spanish with your own kind but you also made sure you assimilated. I leaned to speak English without an accent. Now it's cool to be Hispanic; it means we've become part of the fabric of the nation.

"I think America's future lies in the Spanish-speaking world, mainly Latin America. Everybody's been talking about the 21st Century being the century of the Pacific Rim nations. That's not happening. The future is intertwined between America, which is the third largest Spanish-speaking country in the world, and Latin America. These bonds are unbreakable. I think mainstream America will wake up and realize Latin music is as much a part of the American fabric as are rap and rhythm 'n'blues."

While Latin music certainly has its devotees, enough are downloading and pirating records that after four years of declining sales, Maverick's joint venture partner, Warner Bros., decides to close its label down in 2003. When I call Bruno to inquire what happened, he utters the now common Latin record industry mantra of sales being down which makes it hard to be in the record business. "Some of the artists go to Warner Bros. Latin and others go home," Bruno tells me on the phone. Then he tells me something significant which he hadn't mentioned when we meet in-person: "Our purpose is to be an A&R (artist and repertoire) farm team to find and develop talent for Warner Bros. Latin, which is to market the music and fund our operation."

He says his energies are now in film development, and the film he tells me about, *How to Be the Perfect Latino Star*, is retitled *30 Days Until I'm Famous* and it's scheduled for airing on VH1 in May of 2004. "It's about an aspiring Latina singer who meets two agents who work on making her a top Hispanic music star," he says. While operating his film consulting firm Entertainment Media Factory in 2005, he's also back in the record business, tagged to help launch a Spanish-language album for the Special Olympics organization. The record, *A Very Special Latin Christmas: Noche De Pez*, is also the title for a two-hour TV special for Telemundo, which is shot October 5 at the Staples Center in Los Angeles for airing in December. The actual CD and an accompanying DVD will be released in 2006. It's the first Spanish language CD in the *Very Special Christmas* series of recordings dating back to 1987. Del Granado lands the gig after being recommended to Tim Shriver, chairman of the Special Olympics (whose mother Eunice Kennedy Shriver founds it in 1968) by Venezuelan entrepreneur Carlos Cisneros, notes *Billboard*.

Getting to the record companies in Miami Beach is an easy task. I simply walk a few blocks from my hotel, or walk from one interview to the next. It's when I start driving to the radio and TV networks in Hialeah through interconnecting highways that things turn complicated...and troublesome. While the instructions I've gotten from the MapQuest Website to get to all my record company appointments are correct, there's a problem with the directions on how to get to Radio Unica, the 24-hour news, sports and information network. Even though I've allocated enough time to make the half-hour drive to Hialeah from Miami Beach to be there on time for the 2 p.m. meeting, I can't find the building on the street I'm directed to turn onto, and it looks like I'm going to be a little late. I'm driving around an industrial park of low-level buildings looking for the address and the satellite antennas I know will signify I've found the structure which houses a radio network.

So I find a gas station on another street and ask the clerks if they know where Radio Unica is located. All I get are puzzled looks from the clerks who don't speak too much English. Out of frustration, I head one block past the street I've been driving down and make a right and eventually spot the satellite antennas which indicate I've found the right building. José Cancela, the network's president, is himself a few minutes late in returning from a meeting, so we balance each other out. It is so hot and humid that my sunglasses fog up every time I take them out of the case and put them on. And after a few interviews, I stop wearing my sports jacket, which only adds to the oppressive heat.

After my earlier interviews I'm starting to feel that execs here prefer the casual look rather than conservative business suits…until I observe Cancela and the company's CEO, Joaquin Blaya, returning from their meeting and walking past me in the company's lobby. Despite the oppressive heat, they're both wearing dark suits and white long-sleeved shirts and ties. Fortunately for me, I've put on my blue sports jacket rather than leaving it in the car, so I don't look too underdressed compared to these sharply dressed broadcasters.

By the time I arrive at Radio Unica, I've heard remarkably touching personal stories from the executives I've interviewed about their migration to the U.S. I know from Jose Cancela's biography that he came to Miami from Cuba, but nothing I've heard so far prepares me for his story. There'll be additional horrific tales before this South Florida journey is complete.

His journey to Miami begins in 1961 when he's three-years-old and he arrives with "my two brothers, a sister and my mom on a freedom flight. My dad is a political prisoner and it's only after he serves his time in prison, that the government lets him out and I meet him in Miami when I'm 14." When I comment that it "must have been very hard on you as a kid, knowing your father is in prison," his answer unnerves me since I have no way of understanding what life must have been like for him growing up in a new country without his father. "There are so many of us going through this same experience in Miami that it doesn't seem awkward," he says. "Growing up in my neighborhood, 90 percent of my friends either had their dad still in Cuba or in a third country waiting to come to the United States. It became awkward later in life because it was the Castro regime's strategy to separate families."

Cancela spends 13 years at Univision in executive positions at its stations in Miami, Phoenix, and San Antonio, and six at Telemundo, where as president of its station group, he oversees management of its stations in Puerto Rico and here on the U.S. Mainland before joining Radio Unica in July 1998, six months after the network commences with its news, information, sports and entertainment programming. When we meet, Radio Unica has 15-owned stations and 35 affiliates.

The network's mettle is challenged, like all of America's media, by the calamity of the terrorist attack on the World Trade Center's Twin Towers. "We dedicated 72 straight hours to coverage to the events of the day provided by our station in Manhattan, WNMA-AM. It's the culmination of Joaquin Blaya's vision to have talk radio in Spanish available to the entire country. His vision really pays off as we have the vehicle that helps bring a lot of people across the country together. We even aired a non-denominational mass for the hundreds of Hispanics that are killed when the two buildings collapsed."

Among the station's on-air personalities are several who are on Spanish TV. That, too, Jose credits to network founder Blaya. "One of the biggest challenges in radio is that you may be well known in Los Angeles, but no one knows you in Miami. Spanish television creates personalities who are known cross-country, so we select the best ones we believe have a chance to make an impact on radio." Among TV's familiar faces working on the network, Cristina is probably the best known. Between January of 1999 and December of 2002, she does her daily two-and-a-half minute commentary, *Cristina Opina*, but her work load at Univision forces her to drop her radio show.

Another TV veteran is Guillermo Descalzi, with 30 years of news experience at Univision and Telemundo, who joins the network in June 2002 to host a weekday talk show, *Descalzi En Directo* (*Descalzi Live*) from 10 a.m. to noon Eastern time. Cuban-born Lucy Pereda, who becomes a TV personality in Puerto Rico and Miami, hosts a self-help show, *En Casa De Lucy*, from noon to 1 p.m. Eastern. Cuban-raised Dr. Isabel Gomez-Bassols, host of the popular *Doctora Isabel* advice show weekdays from 1 p.m. to 4 p.m. Eastern, heads in the opposite direction to guest in several episodes of the CBS daytime soap, *The Bold and the Beautiful.*

When Arbitron ranks radio stations, music purveyors usually are the market leaders, so how do Unica's news/talk/sports/entertainment shows do against its music and talk competition? "We definitely skew a lot younger than the traditional talk format station does in the general market," Cancela answers. "The Hispanic marketplace is a lot younger. We skew very much to 18- to 49-year-olds. Within that bracket, it's about 50-50 between 18-to-34 and 34-to-39. In the general market, talk radio usually attracts 25- to 54-year-olds. A second reason is that our programming, especially in entertainment, skews younger. Dr. Isabel, who's been on the network since its inception, hosts one of our most popular shows. We also corner the market in sports, meaning soccer. We broadcast every important soccer match starting with the World Cup in 1998. We do four hours of sport talk every night and then have three hours on Saturday and Sunday. We have one minute of network news at the top of the hour and at the half hour. On weekdays, our affiliates have an opportunity between 3 and 4 p.m. for their own local public service or news-oriented shows."

Cancela acknowledges that the expanding Hispanic population around the country provides the network with its own expansionism. "It's given us a platform to acquire affiliates in markets that are not yet ready to have their own fulltime radio and television stations. These are stations that could not afford to provide the kind of programming we offer them." Like a variety of evening music shows for different age groups. Or carrying a three to four minute address by Vicente Fox, Mexico's president, aimed exclusively at domestic Hispanics, which begins airing Saturday afternoons in June of 2002.

Is Cancela concerned about second-generation Hispanic youth becoming Americanized and choosing Anglo radio over his Spanish-language network? Responds Cancela: "I guess the answer is Hispanic USA is here to stay. Programming, whether it's on radio or television is culturally relevant. The Spanish language is a reality of the United States of America to the point where even politicians are finally using it."

How does the network help integrate new arrivals who only speak Spanish? Cancela says by being a source of information on topics and issues that relate to their well-being, like how to understand how interest rates may affect you and what's new with immigration laws. "We let people express their frustrations with life while entering the U.S. We provide an outlet for new arrivals who get to hear themselves through the people who call in to our programs with similar concerns. The reality is that while it may be tough when we first get here, there's light at the end of the tunnel."

Are Spanish-language radio and TV stations keeping people in their cultural ghettos by only broadcasting Spanish to them? Cancela promptly answers "no," citing as sponsors on all the major radio and TV networks, as well as on Unica's affiliated stations, "companies that offer English teaching lessons. In no way are Hispanic broadcasters saying that staying proficient in Spanish is a way of singling yourself out and being unpatriotic. On the contrary, all we do is provide programming that gives people the opportunity to have a choice. But as broadcasters, we all understand that the English-language is an important part of being successful in this country, and we promote that."

Cancela stresses the network welcomes political opinions. There's the situation in Miami in which political discourse on the city's six talk stations against Castro or people who may have a propensity to establish relations with his government result in very heated discussions. Cancela says he allows his show hosts to air their strong slant against Communist Cuba, even though a generation of young Miami-born Cuban Americans are softening their anti-Castro vitriol. "Talk radio is about being opinionated. There's a saying in the business, no opinions, no ratings. So all our hosts have an opinion about current events and they open up the phone lines to other opinions."

Do people who are changing their minds about Cuba and are saying 'enough already, let's co-exist,' and hope the U.S. drops its economic embargo, react to the opinions of some of your hosts who may be staunchly anti-Castro? "Oh yes, we get it all."

Cancela admits that passions burn feverishly with the generation of Cubans who flee the country after the revolution and there's less passion within their children born in the U.S. "For the first generation that leaves their homes and families and are uprooted by coming to this country, they're going to have tremendous passion, and the second generation's going to have less of it, as will the third generation. The reality in Miami is for the most part that while there is definitely a transition taking place, it's still a transition that has a tremendous and profound respect for its elders. There's also a tremendous sense that while change is in the air, no one's taken a leadership role in the U.S. promoting that change out of respect for all those thousands of people that have died."

When I ask Cancela why the network is headquartered in Miami rather than in New York or Los Angeles, he says Miami is the proper home since Univision and Telemundo are also located nearby in Hialeah. It sounds logical and won't take on a greater significance until the next day.

When I tour the network's studios and production facilities, everything looks slick and in order. Radio Unica's financial future, however takes on a sobering tone in February 2003 when it pays $9.3 million in interest on its 11.75 percent discount notes due in 2006. Had the company not made this payment, its entire $158 million principal amount of the notes and interest could have been due immediately and payable, setting the company up for possible default. To solve its financial nightmare, it will sell off its owned stations in February of 2004 to New York-based MultiCultural Radio Broadcasting Inc. for $150 million in cash and cease to exist. Multicultural will in turn broker the time on the 15 stations to outside producers.

The next day I have an appointment at 3 p.m. with Jim McNamara, president/CEO of Telemundo since 1999. Since Cancela says his company is not too far from Telemundo, I check my MapQuest driving instructions and notice they are totally different from the ones I've just used to get to Radio Unica. So I call Jim McNamara's office and ask his secretary if she can give me simple instructions to get there since the ones I have involve a different highway and lots of turns from one street to the next. I tell her how I got to Radio Unica and she gives me the same highway pathways. The only problem is she neglects to tell me to exit off one of the interconnecting highways and I drive past the exit I'm supposed to use to get onto the local streets heading towards the Telemundo complex.

When I suddenly realize I'm lost and heading towards the Florida Keys, I get off the highway, find a gas station and someone who directs me to head back the way I came and switch onto the highway the secretary neglected to tell me to use. Consequently, I'm around 20 minutes late when I arrive at Telemundo's broadcast complex spread over several streets. From the outside, the buildings appear to be aging former warehouses, a stark contrast to the colorful, cheery South Beach offices of the record companies.

When I apologize to McNamara's secretary from the lobby phone for being late and never say anything about her incorrect instructions, she tells me he's been on a phone call which is just ending. After waiting and watching the Telemundo and TeleFutura feeds on the lobby TV sets for a few minutes, I'm escorted to his office. Waiting for me is a public relations executive with whom I've had one phone conversation in Los Angeles. "You're 20 minutes late," she tells me a bit perturbed. When Jim gets off the phone, I apologize for my lateness but say nothing about being given the wrong driving instructions by his secretary. He's gracious and eager to chat. I have a long list of questions and he's very effusive in his answers.

With about five questions remaining to be answered, the PR lady says since I was 20 minutes late, we have to stop, and she reaches over to my tape recorder to hit the stop button. In my entire career, I have never had anyone attempt to touch my tape recorder and turn it off. Taken aback by her aggressive action and attitude, I tell her to keep her hands off my equipment and I continue my dialog with Jim. For a second time she says a bit more annoyed that we have to stop and again reaches to hit the stop button on the recorder and again I tell her not to do that. McNamama doesn't say a word.

When I mention that I have a few more questions, he tells the PR lady that it's okay to continue. "He came all the way out here to talk with me so let's continue," he says and I'm relieved by his assertiveness on my behalf. "Only one more question," she warns. When I go beyond that one question without any resistance from McNamara, she says she has to leave and departs in a bit of a huff. When I mention the tape recorder incident to friends in the media, they are flabbergasted about this very unprofessional action taken by this woman. "You have to include that since it's part of the story," one friend tells me. Since what happens is intimidating, rude and totally unprofessional, I decide to follow his advice and make it part of this narrative.

Now here's a real twist. While doing several articles for *TelevisionWeek*, a major newsweekly in 2003, I need her assistance in arranging several interviews with Telemundo officials. She's of great help and nothing's said by the two of us about the tape recorder incident. I obviously don't bring it up, and since this phone contact is months after my visit to Miami, she doesn't indicate she relates me to the person she was miffed at. We have a second contact in January of 2004. She calls me as a result of my placing a call to the general manager of Telemundo's two L.A. stations asking for an update on whether AFTRA, the union representing news personnel, has been successful in organizing the stations. She calls me to say the executive I called contacts her after receiving my request for information. "I understand you're doing a book about unions," she says, to which I respond: "No, it's for my book on the Latin entertainment industry, the one I was doing interviews for when I was in Jim McNamara's office." Several months later, when I call her to set up some interviews I'm doing for a story on soccer on Spanish TV for *TelevisionWeek.* I'm told she's no longer with the network and has returned to General Electric, NBC's parent company.

McNamara is the 47-year-old executive whom I regularly read about in the broadcast media with a dual cultural upbringing. He's born and raised in the Panama Canal Zone where he speaks both English and Spanish. His father is a financial executive working for the U.S. government there. After moving to the U.S. Mainland and graduating from Rollins College in 1976, he works at a number of jobs selling TV shows, enroute to Telemundo, notably as an agent with the International Management Group in Brazil handling sports events; the Learning Corp., an educational film company which is purchased by New World Entertainment which places him in charge of New World International's global distribution of American soap operas, and finally with Universal Television Enterprises, handling international and domestic TV syndication.

When I finally sit down with McNamara who's dapperly dressed in a white, gray stripped long sleeved shirt in his spacious office, my first topic is obviously how the network is being affected by its purchase last year by NBC for $2.7 billion. "The biggest area of support right now is moving our stations into NBC facilities here, in Chicago, Dallas, Los Angeles, San Jose, and San Francisco. We won't be moving into the NBC facilities at 30 Rockefeller Plaza in Manhattan because of space constraints, so we'll probably keep our newsroom where it is in Teterboro, New Jersey. On the network level, there's cooperation on the news and sports fronts, primarily with soccer, baseball and boxing. We're also going to have 15 men's NBA games and 10 women's games on weekend afternoons, especially with teams in Hispanic markets like Miami, Dallas, Los Angeles and New York. The Dallas team has a player from Mexico, who's a local favorite.

"One of our news personalities, Maria Celeste Arrarás, who hosts her own newsmagazine show, *Rojo Vivo*, appeared on *Dateline* covering the story on the separation of Guatemalan twin girls. She's one of several people who've left Univision to join us. She left at the end of April and we started her in May. Maria is like other successful people in television, whether its Katie Couric, Dan Rather, Diane Sawyer, or Cristina, they all have a strong creative drive."

McNamara sees Telemundo airing several entertainment events with NBC, including the Golden Globes and the Billboard Latin Music Awards, with other events to be added. "We've also attracted about 20 new advertisers as a sort of halo effect to being part of NBC."

The Hispanic population explosion, McNamara admits, "has helped us immensely and we've grown in a parallel manner to the growth of the markets. I can't imagine a single company that markets a product of any mass nature that isn't also focused on the Hispanic market, so that's a major benefit for us." Separate from its NBC sports connection, Telemundo has been airing the Mexican national soccer team's season for two years and U.S. national soccer team's World Cup competition, with Andres Cantor and Norberto Longo handling the action. Cantor, McNamara points out pridefully is "Mr. Goal" for his signature long shout of "goooaall."

In its battle with market leader Univision, and now obviously under the observation of its parent NBC, Telemundo is looking for a new programming image, best reflected in its slogan, *Si Es Diferente, Está En Telemundo* (if it's different, it's on Telemundo). The network is seeking to distance itself from Univision's strength: its telenovelas and programming from Mexico's powerhouse programmer Televisa. It's begun its own reality contest series, *Protagonistas De Novela*, followed by *Protagonista De La Musica* in which men and women compete over a series of elimination programs with the public voting for their favorite candidates.

Are reality shows (the hot favorite on mainstream TV) risky for Spanish TV? "I believe some people will think they're a risk. I think they're actually low-risk because they're different and innovative and they differentiate us from the competition." McNamara has another low-risk first to his credit. For the first time in Spanish television he says, a novela, *El Clone*, has an English-language closed caption feature available on the SAP channel. "It's a major breakthrough. The show is a unique product produced by TV Globo of Brazil. It's an Arab-Christian love story that also deals with human cloning. Bear in mind that after September 11 there's a huge interest in all things Muslim and at the same time there's a flurry last fall in the advances being made in human cloning. "So we said this is very contemporary, let's subtitle it because there are a lot of second- and third-generation Hispanics that understand Spanish, but since they tend to speak more English now, they've stopped watching Spanish-language television because of the subtitles, so let's use close captioning to provide access to the dialog. While we close caption by U.S. government regulation around 50 percent of all of our programs for the hearing impaired, we realize that by close captioning in English as well as in Spanish, we have a new marketing strategy.

"We'll be close captioning in English another novela for next January, *El Beso Del Vampiro* (*The Kiss of the Vampire*), which is light and campy and not a deep, dark horror novela."

McNamara wants to make a strong point that Telemundo—and its TeleFutura second network aimed at bilinguals—relate Univision's reliance on Mexico City-based Televisa for its novelas as representing "something that's slightly in the past. Televisa is very good and they are primarily making programming for their local market. What happens is when Mexicans travel north and arrive in the U.S., they start to undergo a transformation of becoming the next wave of immigrants and eventually they become part of the mainstream U.S. So if we try to imitate Televisa's programming, we're going to be staying behind the times, when what we're trying to do is program out in front of that evolutionary curve and be there when the new wave reaches us. That's strategically what we're trying to do."

One additional key change in Telemundo's programming which McNamara stresses is "we have shifted from 100 percent acquisitions to a much higher mix of internally produced programs." While this sounds super, a closer look has Telemundo still using overseas suppliers for novelas, only now involved as a co-producer. While a novela normally has a six to eight week arc, Telemundo is producing what McNamara calls "an actual U.S.-style miniseries, *La Virgin De Guadalupe*, which will air for four hours on two nights. We're shooting it in Mexico and for the first time ever, we received government permits to actually shoot in the historical Mexican ruins of the Aztec civilization."

The same production company that produces *Protagonistas De Novela*, has been hired by Fox Television to create a Spanish-language version of *Temptation Island*, the sensually laden series running on the Fox Network for Telemundo. The 13 episodes are being shot in Thailand with Spanish-speaking actors for airing next spring. "We cast the show in Miami, Chicago, Houston and Los Angeles," says McNamama, noting the series will retain the original show's sexual undertones, "but not as strong as the English-language version."

Will this show cause any problems with prudish viewers? Parries McNamara: "I don't think so. The whole premise of the show is the slightly preposterous proposition that before I enter into a committed relationship, I want to test that relationship, These people are not married but they're thinking about getting engaged. So they go to this island for the express purpose of being tempted. Let's face it, in some cases sparks are going to fly and relationships will be put to the test."

Audiences will also be tested with Telemundo's and Spanish TV's first animated primetime novela, *Implemente Rita*, slated for December or January. Notes McNamara: "We're taking a big risk with it because the audience has never seen a primetime animated novela before. We're targeting the show to 18- to 54-year-olds first and then the whole family."

When I ask why the company isn't shooting its novelas in Miami, McNamara responds: "We're in that process now. We'll shortly start production of a youth-oriented novela, *Los Teens*, designed to appeal to and reflect the young Hispanic experience in the States. We conducted research in Miami, Texas and California to find the issues Hispanic teens are dealing with, and we found they're similar to what the concerns of general market teens are, but with some slight differences."

As the company increases its output of in-house productions, McNamara envisions writers, producers and actors who live in Mexico, Colombia, or Venezuela "will move here. We will also develop our own home-grown talent."

Telemundo will have a first class array of U.S. grown actors and actresses currently starring in *The American Family* series which CBS passes on and which finds a home on PBS, when it starts airing the first 22 episodes in the first quarter of 2003. Is the story anent a Mexican-American family living in Los Angeles going to be of interest to Hispanics around the country from the Dominican Republic, Cuba, Argentina and Puerto Rico? "The short answer is yes," McNamara replies, "because it's good story-telling about a multi-generational immigrant family and their problems. Themes like the sanctity of the family unit touch every person's soul whether they're from Latin America or the U.S. It may not be as relevant to a Puerto Rico or a Cuban family in New York or Miami as it will to a Mexican family in Texas or California, but it will overcome the country of origin partly because it's so good."

While it will cooperate with NBC News on major stories of interest to Hispanics, Telemundo's own network news operation employs around 200 and feeds its 18-owned stations (10 full-power; eight low-power) and 44 affiliates three hours of news in the morning—the hour with Maria Celeste, an evening newscast at 6:30 and a newsmagazine show on Sunday evenings. On a local market level, McNamara says Telemundo's owned and operated stations will be building up their news clout to differentiate from what their Univision competition provides. By doing what? I ask. “By being more relevant, more local and better broadcasters,” McNamara responds. “It’s exactly what NBC, ABC and CBS do to duke it out in every market.”

Three years after our interview, McNamara steps down on April 6, 2005, and is replaced by Don Browne, the former head of NBC News’ Miami bureau and president/general manager of NBC’s Miami station WTVJ, who shifts over to become Telemundo’s chief operating officer in May of 2005. McNamara’s departure is based on several factors including disagreements over his contract renewal. Nothing is said publicly by NBC about the $2.7 billion it pays for Telemundo in 2001, its takeover the next year, and Telemundo’s subsequent inability to overcome Univision’s lead despite creating more U.S. flavored novelas in the past two years designed to attract new viewers. McNamara remains in Miami where he’ll pursue creative endeavors. In 2005, he teams up with Lionsgate Films in Hollywood, which will utilize his Panamax films to acquire and produce Latin American movies for bilingual U.S. Hispanics. Further details are covered in Chapters 19 and 20.

Claudia Puig has her own battles to fight. As the only female vice president/general manager of four radio stations in Miami, I’m most anxious to chat with this Hispanic Broadcasting Corp. executive. But she’s very hard to get to despite phone calls and e-mails dating back to July 14. She finally responds by e-mail Aug. 13 requesting more information about the book. The next day she e-mails me that she needs to clear the interview with her PR rep, Jorge Plasencia. I’ve also left messages on her answering machine which she claims she never receives. I send her three more e-mails suggesting interview times and never hear back. Then seven days before flying to Miami on September 29, I e-mail the PR rep and ask him to clear the interview. I never hear back from him. During August, she’s on a short vacation and then I’m on vacation a few weeks later, so we still haven’t arranged a meeting time. While I’m in Miami, I attempt to contact Claudia and the PR rep to no avail. Monday, the night after I arrive in Miami, I receive a call from my wife Bonnie to tell me that Jorge has called my home phone number, not the number I've left for the hotel I'm staying at, to say the interview is not going to happen. This is becoming one drawn-out runaround and the call to L.A. when I'm in Miami only acerbates the situation. So when I return to Los Angeles quite frustrated by this serpentine put off, I call HBC's headquarters in Dallas and am directed to Rosemary Scott, the director of research and marketing in the San Antonio office, who listens to my frustration. She does something magical and I wind up chatting with Claudia on the phone several weeks after I'm back in Los Angeles.

Although it takes some taking to finally hook-up with Claudia, my persistence pays off. Her story is a fascinating saga of survival and success, survival when she and her family are among the Cuban exiles who come to Miami in 1961, and success when she displays the determination and grit required to manage four radio stations in the basically male environment of Miami radio and compete against nine other Spanish-language stations. The HBO stations Claudia oversees are adult contemporary WAMR-FM; news/talk WAQI-AM; tropical WRTO-FM; and news/talk WQBA-AM.

So recognizing how unique her position is, my first question is how she juggles her time to oversee four stations, split between music and news/talk. "The most important aspect for a general manger in running a cluster effectively is to have clearly defined goals and objectives for the cluster and each individual station," she says. "I have eight department heads who cover everything from engineering to programming to sales that I channel my energies through." Sounds logical and simple enough.

Up until this point, I thought I've heard some terrifying and shocking stories. Then Claudia reveals her own unmatched horror. Her life in Cuba and what happens to her parents reflects the tenor of the times and undoubtedly affects her attitude as a radio broadcaster. Claudia is seven when she arrives here. Her story is mesmerizing and I listen quietly as it unfurls in spurts, one shock after another. What do you remember about living in Cuba and then arriving in Miami? I ask. "I remember being in the womb of a very big, loving, united family. My family suffers quite a toll from the Castro government. Two of my uncles serve prison time as political prisoners, one 15 years; the other eight years. I also have a cousin who is in prison. My father is executed by the Castro government.

"My father is an Olympic athlete, a businessman and a freedom-loving person. He goes to Florida and is in some kind of CIA training camp and then he infiltrates back to Cuba one month before the Bay of Pigs invasion, is captured and executed. I think the government knows he is out of the country but they don't know he's back until he's captured. When my father comes back, he and my mother are reunited and she joins him in the underground. They have a very good marriage and are very close. He is 37; she is 30. My mother is captured with my father and taken to prison. Several months later my mother is released. When my father goes on trial she is with him. My grandfather is his lawyer. My father's sentence is signed before the trial begins. He is executed by a firing squad at 2 a.m. on April 20, during the Bay of Pigs, and we leave Cuba that August."

How is her mother able to get out of prison? "My great grandfather was part of the government that wrote Cuba's 1940 constitution. So he still has some connections which he uses."

When first arriving with her mother and her four small children, she says she "feels a little uncomfortable and aware of accent. My first impression is that it is peaceful and safe here. My mother is able to get a master's degree in psychology and she becomes a teacher at Miami Dade Community College." Claudia migrates into Spanish radio after initially working for BellSouth Yellow Pages. After spending 1984–'97 with Spanish Broadcasting System (SBS) in various positions, she joins HBC overseeing its Miami station cluster.

Does Miami's powerful exile community exert pressure on Miami radio to keep Cuban music off the air the way it forces the Latin Grammys to move to Los Angeles two years ago? "The stations just choose to play the music they think the audience will appreciate," she answers, deflecting the politically oriented question. "Miami radio is unique because it reflects Miami being the gateway to the Americas. Now we have a growing population of Colombians, Venezuelans, and Nicaraguans. As a result of the upheaval in South America, we have Brazilians and Argentineans also coming here. They are the middle/upper class who are well educated and usually upscale, and it's political issues which drives them here. When you get out of the airport in Miami, you know you're visiting a Latin city and Hispanics here feel proud to be Hispanic and feel comfortable in their culture."

How do HBC's two music stations differ? WAMR, called *Amor* (fourth in the Arbitron ratings in September), plays what Claudia tags light adult contemporary music from the '80s, '90s and today by Gloria Estefan, Julio Iglesias, Marco Antonio Solís and Chayanne, intermixed with some salsa and a tinge of the top English-language hits. Its morning drive time show, *Desayuno Musical*, is co-hosted by the popular duo of Javier Romero and Osvaldo Vega. WRTO, called *Salsa 98* (tenth in the survey), is called a Top 40 dance station by Claudia, which includes salsa, merengue, pop, rock en Español and bachata, a form of Dominican dance music (airing Sunday afternoons for two hours), as well as selections by Marc Anthony, Gilberto Santa Rosa, Carlos Vives, Tito Nieves, and Las Ketchup. Its morning team of professional comedians Carlos Lanzas, Gilberto Reyes and Jorge Miguel González, who call themselves *Los Fonomemecos*, are competing in the morning zany race against their former station, WXDJ-FM SBS' (in nineteenth place) tropical music exponent. González, a member in 1980 of a Cuban comedy team called *Los Fonomemecos*, defects in 1991 to Miami where he starts the Miami group with Reyes and Lanzas. While performing in a local club, they are discovered by SBS' vice president of programming Jesús Salas, who hires them for WXDJ's morning slot, which they hold down for a brief period before jumping over to the competition. SBS operates two additional stations in Miami, Spanish adult contemporary WRMA-FM (seventh in the standings) and Spanish oldies WCMQ-FM (eighth in the rankings).

How are HBC's two talk stations, WAQI and WQBA, different from each other? WAQI (sixth in the rankings) and called

Radio Mambi La Grande "is basically a station that's focused on Cuban issues for the Cuban community and the majority of the staff is Cuban," she explains. WQBA (22nd in the rankings) "reflects Miami, with a personality mix of Venezuelans, Colombians, Dominicans and Cubans. We are the Spanish voice for the Florida Marlins and we cover the World Cup soccer competition." The station whose slogan is WQBA *Cuarenta Sepega*, also has Castro's estranged daughter, 45-year-old Alina Fernández Revuelta, who defects in 1993, as one of its show hosts weeknights from 11 p.m. to 1 a.m. Does she focus on her father's regime? "Not really," Claudia answers. "She talks about lifestyle and general issues since WQBA focuses on non-political issues." That's not what I hear from a veteran broadcast reporter on the *Miami Herald* who covers the Latin beat and whose comments I'll get to later in this chapter.

Is this her first radio job and had she not been Castro's daughter, would you have hired her? "It is her first radio job and I've hired other people with no radio experience. I didn't really have any intention of hiring her, but she is so persistent, tenacious and intelligent that I changed my mind. She's led an interesting life. She came here a few years ago with her teenage daughter after living in Spain. She's a gutsy lady. This is a tolerant society. You can see that by us having Fidel Castro's daughter on the air."

Are the city's bilingual young Hispanics tuning in more to the Anglo stations? Puig believes Spanish-language radio retains an ineffable grasp on this audience. "When my generation arrived here," she explains, "there was a little bit more pressure to assimilate. Now that our subculture has grown, when the younger kids hit the 25-year-old mark, a lot revert back to their roots and they enjoy finding out what's happening in their native countries. They may be comfortable speaking in English but they definitely still enjoy Latin roots and Latin music, which is a huge element in their lives."

Does Spanish radio and TV keep people in their cultural conclaves to the point where they're so comfortable they don't have to learn to speak English as part of their adjustment to living in America? "I don't think that makes sense," she answers, adding: "We encourage everyone to speak English and be part of America. I think most Hispanics are more patriotic sometimes than even the American people. I think all of them want to be able to function and work in English. At the same time, in Miami we actually have successful entrepreneurs who don't speak English because there's enough of a subculture that embraces them."

When I ask Claudia whether she has any complaints about how the Arbitron company measures the radio audience, she replies without missing a breath: "The usual. I don't think the diary method being used now (marking down stations and programs being listened to) is the right way to measure Hispanics. Hispanics listen to radio; that's a habit they bring to this country, but they're not in the habit of filling out diaries. That's a very American thing. Then there's the issue of the level of acculturation and the need to make sure Spanish-speaking households are included and they fill out their diaries." Which may not be as simple a task as it sounds within Hispanic households.

One company also facing the task of enticing Latinos to savor its products is Coral Gables-based Venevision International, the nearly 30-year-old U.S. subsidiary of Venevision, the 40-year-old Venezuelan TV network. The local company, headed by president Luis Villanueva since 1997, is expanding into national film distribution and producing plays for South Florida patrons. Both operations are part of the Cisneros Group of Companies, a privately held conglomerate which owns or holds an interest in 67 companies, including DirecTV Latin America and Univision Communications, whose Univision and TeleFutura networks air programs produced by the local Venevision branch. Villanueva, incidentally, has been with the company in various positions since 1982, but this is his first posting in the U.S.

Venevision's first talk shows are *Martha Sousana* for Univision and *En La Intimidad* for TeleFutura. "We also distribute these shows all over Latin America," explains Jose Antonio Espinal, Venevision International's marketing director. During 2001, the company produced five hours of local original programming a week. Now, in addition to its five hours locally, it's also handling two more hours in Peru. All these programs air in Venezuela as well as on the domestic Univision networks. The company has a deal with Nostromo América, a division of Nostromo Europe, which specializes in developing genre formatted TV series. "We'll produce shows for the U.S. and Venezuela next year," Espinal tells me during a phone interview. He's sitting in for Villanueva who's out of town while I'm in town. The best formats have contests and extreme situations, he notes. One show planned is *Quien Dijo Miedo* (*Who Said That*).

While TV production for the small screen appears to be the company's foundation, large screen theatrical releases loom larger on the horizon as a new revenue source, albeit one with greater risks of failure. In its first year of distributing movies, Venevision International releases five titles in multiplex theaters rather than the esoteric art house circuit. "We're generally releasing our films progressively in Miami, Chicago, Dallas, Houston, San Antonio, Austin and Los Angeles," says Espinal. "This is the first time we've exhibited Spanish films on commercial screens in the U.S. A theatrical window is the riskiest of all outlets," he continues, "because if the release doesn't do well, you really get hurt financially." Each print is "bicycled" from city-to-city and the length of the run varies by locale. The initial titles include three from Spain: *El Arte De Morir*, *Cha-Cha-Cha*, and *Nadie Concoe A Nadie*, plus *Pantaleón Y Las Visitadoras* (Peru), and *Bolivar Soy Yo* (Colombia). "While it was hard at the beginning building an audience here in Miami, progressively it became easier as word spread about the films," recalls Espinal. "In the case of *Pantaleon* and *Bolivar* we increased the distribution based on the number of Colombians living in Miami." It costs the company around $10,000 per screen while the cost to print each film copy is around $3,000.

Espinal admits initial box office revenue is "weak because we're building the market. There weren't any Spanish films in the multiplexes before, only in the art houses. But we will release some films in both forms of commercial cinema." One year later, the company releases the 1999 hit Mexican film, *Herod's Law*, on 15 screens in Los Angeles, the city with the largest Mexican population. It also gains a major partner for its film releases when 20th Century Fox Home Entertainment signs a deal to distribute Venevision International's films on DVD and VHS under the newly created Cinema Latino brand. Mike Dunn, the Fox division's president, tells the *Hollywood Reporter* the movies are "entertaining films with tremendous crossover appeal that just happen to be in Spanish." During February–March of 2004, Venevision, 20th Century Fox Home Entertainment and the Mexican Consulate, send out a dual language invitation to attend "Cinema Latino: A Celebration of Mexican Films" featuring five films on five evenings at the Consulate. The movies to be screened before entertainment industry bigwigs include: *La Ley De Heródes* (*Herod's Law*), *Por La Libre* (*Dust to Dust*), *Sin Dejar Huella* (*Without a Trace*), *Santitos* (*Little Saints*) and *Todo El Poder* (*Gimme Power*).

Several months before I arrive, Villanueva tells the *Miami Herald*: "Miami allows you to test among different Hispanics. You can find an Argentinean, a Bolivian, a Chilean, without ever leaving the country."

When I ask Espinal about the value derived from the company's research prior to releasing a film by unknown companies on a market by market national basis, he offers his own market savvy answer, echoing the theme first espoused by Villanueva: "We conduct focus groups and test the product and that tells us what works and what doesn't. It's half art and half science."

Mounting a stage production takes more than art and science. The company has produced seven Spanish-language plays locally since last year in Coral Gables, Miami's Little Havana and Fort Lauderdale. "We select productions that entertain; we're staying away from political, social or plays that are too dense," explains Espinal. "We look for sponsors to finance the plays. There are lots of Hispanic businesses in Miami that are willing to sponsor the arts."

Two of the plays I notice which earn good reactions from *Herald* critic Marta Barber are *Master Class*, Terrence McNally's Tony-winning endeavor about opera diva Maria Callas conducting master classes at New York's Julliard School of Music in 1971, following her stage retirement, and *La Lechuga*, about a family sharing the burden of taking care of their father who's been in a vegetative state nine years.

With Puerto Rican actress/singer Yolandita Monge in the lead role in *Master Class*, Barber extols: "Directed by César Sierra, with a handsome set by Raúl De La Nuez and stunning lighting by Ivan Inguanzo, this *Master Class* is up to the standard of any Broadway version. And if Monge's Callas doesn't quite soar, her performance flies high." In discussing *La Lechuga*, whose cast includes veteran actors and actresses Marilyn Romero, Gellmar Baralt, Gerardo Riverón, Diana Quijano, and Claudio Giúdice, Barber gushes: "As *La Lechuga*, which runs without intermission, approaches the end and its humor get more caustic, the audience is caught between laughter and tension. That's the sign of a good play."

In February of 2006, Venevision partners with Universal Music Group Latino in a new, unnamed record company. New acts will be enticed to sign by possible roles in Venevision novelas and having their songs in film soundtracks.

Among the dozen or so show-producing entities in Miami, one especially catches my attention, Forti Layne Entertainment, which specializes in producing music videos and TV specials for Hispanic media. Its owner/executive producers are two Anglos, Brian Forti from Boston and Kevin Layne from New York, whose migration to Miami causes them to cross paths in 1984 and begin selling advertising time on cable and then two years later they form their production company to create commercials and low-budget music videos. In 1991, they strike gold with Gloria Estefan following her near fatal bus accident. "Her husband Emilio wants us to document her life," recalls Brian during our phone conversation. "We do a series of shoots, including a session for her new album. The video, *Coming Out of the Dark*, is released on the Estefan's home video company and winds up as a special on Univision. Then Emilio hires us to cover her world tour and the video, *Gloria Estefan Going Home*, runs on the

Disney Channel in 1992." This project wins the company a CableAce Award as the best music video from the cable industry in 1993.

Following these two projects, the duo handles two additional projects for the Estefans, including its first all-digital technology shoot of *Live for Loving You*, which is inducted into VH1's Hall of Fame in late '93. The second project in 1994, *Mi Tierra My Homeland*, airs later in the year on Univision as an hour special and on VH1 as a half-hour in English. Sticking close to the Estefans, the duo works on two videos for Jon Secada, a new crossover name on their Crescent Moon label during '92–'93. *Just Another Day* airs on VH1 while its Spanish counterpart, *Otra Dia Mas*, wins best director and best new artist accolades at the *Billboard* Music Video Awards.

Kevin estimates 75 percent of the company's work is for Spanish media. Are there any other production firms owned by Anglos in Miami which specialize in Latin music? "I don't think so," he responds, adding cryptically: "I'm not sure that's a good thing." He does admit that "our Spanish (language) skills are growing," while underscoring that "having a bilingual staff from Puerto Rico, Colombia, Venezuela and Honduras" is a necessity and fills any of their language voids.

This year, the company is working on its second season of two weekly music series, *Cartelera Pepsi* (*Pepsi Chart*), an hour show and *Pepsi Music*, a half-hour, both airing on TeleFutura, Brian points out. *Pepsi Music* also airs in 12 Latin American countries. Both shows are drawn from artist appearances at the South Beach located Club Crobar before an audience. "We tape four to five hours of artists singing to prerecorded tracks of their records. The countdown show also includes interviews with the stars. The charts are compiled by "an independent company from local radio station playlists," explains Brian, who notes participating artists cover the gamut of Latin and English pop talent: Shakira, Enrique Iglesias, Britney Spears, Paulina Rubio, Juanes, Elvis Crespo, Nicole, and Red Hot Chili Peppers. Naturally Pepsi is the key sponsor with its name in the title, but there are others, including Ford and some hair product companies, who see validity in tapping into the Hispanic TV market.

The city's enormous Latin population is on the mind of Michael Hardy, president of the new $334 million Performing Arts Center of Greater Miami, a 570,000 square foot landmark, originally slated for a fall 2004 opening, purportedly the largest arts center to be built in the U.S. since the John F. Kennedy opens in 1972, and certainly the largest public–private enterprise in Miami–Dade County history. The center will consist of the 2,200-seat Carnival Symphony Hall, the 2,480-seat Ziff Ballet and Opera House, the 200-seat Studio Theater (for dance and music acts) and the 57,000 square foot Plaza for the Arts outdoor performance area (for festivals). It will be the third major center for South Florida's 4.8 million residents besides the Broward Center for the Performing Arts in Fort Lauderdale and the Raymond F. Kravis Center for the Performing Arts in Palm Beach.

Hardy, who arrives in Miami from Louisville, Kentucky, where he's been the president of the Kentucky Center for the Arts for four years, sees the Latin community's "60 percent of the population making a major impact on the center's arts presentations. My thinking is this will be the first Hispanic performing arts center in the U.S. where the staff will be international and bilingual. It's important if we're going to appeal to the entire community. I've hired a director of operations from Venezuela and hope to have a Hispanic program director booking talent. I'm doing this because the population is now more than just Cubans, which comprise 50 percent of the Hispanic population. But that's shrinking because of the arrival of people from Venezuela and Argentina and other Latin American countries. During the summer when Anglos go to the mountains, Latins in Brazil, Venezuela and even Mexico come here because it's their winter, and the city becomes more Hispanic or Portuguese. Except for New York, this is the most international center in the country."

Hardy tells me during our phone interview he's taking Spanish lessons twice a week for 90 minutes in his office." Although he's headed performing arts centers in New York, Texas and Illinois, this is the first time he's immersed himself in Latin culture and among his musical preferences are salsa and merengue.

He says he's "looking to break new ground with his Latin attractions. I'm looking into bringing in an orchestra from Buenos Aires and a ballet from Caracas to do productions like *Live from Lincoln Center*, which we would send back as a pay-per-view television event." While he says "there's no problem booking entertainment for Cubans, there is a problem in booking acts from Cuba itself." So he's forming a "Hispanic Council, an informal group of influential people, heads of law firms and businesses from which I'll seek advice. My approach is to have an open discussion to find a path to travel." He says he needs assistance to counter what he expects to be "compelling logic from the most vociferous of the exile community against booking Cuban artists. It's a volatile community, but with enough allies we can accomplish these kinds of bookings."

The only problem Hardy foresees is "the competition for dates and the rental costs of the halls. The venue's current resident companies—the Florida Philharmonic, Concert Association of Florida, Miami City Ballet and New World Orchestra, and Florida Grand Opera—have the first choice on dates now and three years out."

"Our programming philosophy," Hardy emphasizes, "is to include all kinds of performing arts, from jazz to hip-hop to Broadway musicals to dance to Latin pop to classical, including new commissioned works. My philosophy about the arts developed over the years is that when someone has a successful experience, it's both emotional and intellectual. I contend that the response to the arts is universal, and if we confine ourselves to just select groups, we're excluding huge portions of the population."

Last year, Hardy hires Justin Macdonnell from the Australian Opera, to handle the booking of Latin and South American national symphonies, comedy acts, children's shows, pop performers, jazz artists and solo musical attractions. It's a heady challenge for an untested multi-showroom venue.

Hardy faces another wrenching problem. His grandiose plans have been delayed until 2006. Last year, a series of somber articles in the *Miami Herald* details major problems with the project ranging from structural and acoustical problems to cost overruns to a budget deficit to the collapse of the Florida Philharmonic Orchestra. The grand opening projected for February 2006, is pushed back six months to the summer, washing away the original October 2004 date. The overall cost of the project is now an estimated $344 million, up from the estimated $334 million in 2003. In 2000, the construction cost alone, projected at $208 million, rises to $254 million by 2003. There's also an annual deficit of $2.7 million by 2003. Miami–Dade County, which issues bonds and a hotel bed tax to pay for the construction, has more than $20 million in contingency funds built into the original budget. But by March of 2004, Miami–Dade County officials tell the *Herald* that cost overruns could add another $100 million to the price tag. Construction delays push the budget $67 million over its original price by August of 2005.

With the demise of the Florida Philharmonic, the center will have four resident companies whose collective schedules will fill 125 nights annually of the 730 combined evenings available in the venue's two largest halls. They include the Concert Association of Florida, Florida Grand Opera, Miami City Ballet and the New World Symphony, all finalizing their programming for the premier October opening of the 2006–'07 season, 20 months later than planned. Culled from his experience managing arts centers, Hardy attempts to temper local frustrations and put some balance to the open dates created by the Philharmonic's tragic fate, reflecting the dire situation faced by a number of symphonies around the country facing a financial abyss or actually shutting down. He says on average, symphony halls are active 40 percent of the time, while ballet and opera venues offer performances on 60 percent of the available evenings.

In April of 2007, the renamed Carnival Center for the Performing Arts faces a $3 million shortfall due to ticket sales lagging 50 percent below projection following its October 2006 opening. The Center, according to the *Miami Herald*, is looking to close for 30 days during the upcoming summer as a cost saver, and also seeks financial assistance from the county.

A number of journalists here specialize in measuring the news and hype quotients of the Latin entertainment industry, including Colombian born Leila Cobo. She's a former *Herald* writer for two-and-a-half years, who, for the past two years as *Billboard*'s Miami Bureau chief, provides a window on key local happenings for a national audience. Miami's role as a recording center has been enhanced, she says, by a growing number of well-known producers setting up shop here. "We're starting to see more bands created here and signed as opposed to someone from another country signed by a local record company," she adds. "This has not been a place where local talent was actively developed." While talent may be nurturing here, Cobo says one of the city's shortcomings is its lack of a good club circuit for them to perform in.

"When a label hears an artist they think will work in English, like Shakira or Enrique Iglesias, they release them on their English-language label which knows how to sell to the American market. A number of American labels have their own versions of what they think sounds Latin. DreamWorks, for example, has a group, Soluna, which are four girls from Los Angeles who are Latin descendents. They don't speak Spanish and they sing mostly in English coupled with Latin rhythm tracks. That is truly abandoning their roots, yet they're marketed as a Latin group."

One day while reading the *Herald*, I recognize a familiar byline and call Kevin Baxter at his office. He's the same person who covers Latin radio and TV for the *Los Angeles Times* for 11 years before joining the Herald to cover Latin broadcasting in 1999. Why, I want to know, are there six Hispanic news/talk radio stations? "Because politics drives the Hispanic community. If you're running for political office you have to be on those stations." Kevin says it's the same script all the time: "what Fidel says today or who's going to replace him." Does Castro's daughter Alina draw an audience to her evening show on HBC's WQBA? "Yes. She talks about how bad Cuba is, how people still have no freedom and even about her father dying. She holds sway with the older Cubans, the upper classes who arrived here in 1960. The young people are not as passionate about Cuba as the 'professional Cubans' who think about it 24 hours a day and when Castro will die. She knocks her father. If she didn't she wouldn't be on the air," comments which strongly contrast with those given to me by Claudia Puig, the vice president/ general manager of WQBA and HBC's three other stations.

Baxter affirms what's been written about the pressure the Cuban exile community exerts on the talk stations and within the entertainment industry. "The Latin Grammys were forced out of here because of the threat of protests. There's the perception they're still powerful. We cover radio because of the political reasons, not the programming." In essence, controversy stimulates the writer, not which tunes are being played.

In discussing music, Baxter says it's difficult for new talent, rock en Español and regional Mexican music to gain airplay on the local stations. "Even the English stations rarely break new artists."

Baxter stresses that Miami radio especially avoids playing regional Mexican music. And "any attempt to write about it in the paper draws letters asking why we're covering it. People want to know why Latin music awards or Univision or Telemundo give time to Mexican music, despite it's being the top-selling category of Latin music in this country."

When he mentions Univision, that leads me to ask how the paper deals with the network's policy of restricting its top behind the camera executives from openly talking with the media, except in specific instances when it's to their advantage. News personnel, on-camera and department heads seem to be the exception. "We're selective in the stories we do about Univision," he says. "Jerry Perenchio (the owner) wants to focus on talent and not have executives in the media spotlight. Henry Cisneros (Univision's fifth president/CEO) left after he was unable to get more of his executives in the media."

I've heard payola continues to be present within the Latin radio and record industries. So I ask Kevin and several others about it. Kevin calls it "unofficial payola to program directors. I've heard from enough radio industry and music people that money speaks and that a song that's not especially good receives heavy rotation." Then I run into the three words journalists hate: "don't quote me." When I ask the head of a local record company to comment, his first comment is "don't quote me." He admits "it's a known fact that it happens, even with big artists and big releases." When I mention the subject to a well-connected local writer, the scribe acknowledges "the subject is well-known" and suddenly becomes worried and says "don't quote me. I'd lose my job if I spoke about it without any proof." Does the writer have any proof to speak of? No because the topic has never been aggressively pursued, it's inferred by this individual.

Now these conversations take place in October. On December 8, the *Herald* runs a front page story by Jordan Levin in which a former SBS official, Ruben Estrada, is quoted as saying "You don't pay, you don't play." He also states that when he works at WSKQ-FM in New York from 1992 to 2000, payola affects the programming there. "No question" about that he says. The lengthy, well-written article carries denials from the radio network as well as no comments from several record companies. Strengthening her article, Jordan appears to be listening while Edgar Alvarez, a former record promoter now in the talent agency business, calls several disc jockeys in Orlando and Puerto Rico from his South Miami offices to ask what the price will be to get a song on their air. The prices range from $500 to $1,100, $3,000 to $10,000. It's explosive material and the kind of nitty gritty data which is generally impossible to obtain. It's something I know about, having spent months investigating the subject and finally breaking a major payola scandal in Los Angeles in 1964 in *Billboard*, which is covered in Chapter 5.

The writer also quotes William Otero, a New York DJ, and other unnamed persons who claim record companies "have come to accept payola as a necessary part of doing business" due to several factors. Including financial pressure for labels to show a profit, declining spots on playlists and the fierce battle for airplay. Jordan also quotes SBS attorney Jason Shrinsky who says "payola does not affect his company. We have very strict policies on that. Disc jockeys sign affidavits on a regular basis affirming they don't do that."

After the story has been out a while, I e-mail the writer to ask if she's had any reaction to her story from the industry and if she has, is she planning any follow-ups. I tell her I'm doing this book and have gone through the uncomfortable aftermath of breaking my story and becoming a most hated journalist in Los Angeles. She never replies. Her story will, however, set up an acrimonious moment between me and an SBS executive in New York when I spend a week there doing interviews and I ask him to comment on the story. His reaction, along with other salient thoughts about Latin music and radio, as well as other interviews I conduct, appear in Chapter 14.

This cosmopolitan city, as it's referred to in 2002, is a hotbed of Latin rock activity by second-generation Hispanics, fueled by labels reaching out for the first time to sign local contemporary-thinking musicians. The goal is to develop music which incorporates endemic American rock and hip-hop influences with reggae, ska, cumbia and ranchera as a contrast to the mainstay tropical rhythms of salsa and merengue. An Argentine rock festival in April draws thousands in the rain to the Bayfront Amphitheater in Miami to hear Argentine bands like Los Piojos presented by promoter Enrique Kogan. Argentine music, especially the bailanta, a working class dance music blending cumbia with merengue, is especially popular among Argentines. While the 2000 Census counts 19,000 Argentines in Miami-Dade, and 10,000 split equally in Broward and Palm Beach counties, according to the *Herald*, the Argentine Consulate has a higher estimate: 100,000 in South Florida, the paper reports.

In November, Kogan's working at the Bayfront again with his *Rock En Miami Festival* featuring homegrown acts Volumen Cero and Javier Garcia, Mexico's El Tri, Panama's Los Rabanes, and Peru's Pedro Suarez-Vertiz and La Mosca Tsé Tsé.

Local acts are the hot new flavor of the month and are being romanced by Miami labels. In addition to Jon Secada signed to Crescent Moon and Jorge Moreno signed to Maverick Musica,

Volumen Cero, Los Hidalgo and Bacilos join Warner Music Latina, Seliné is nabbed by BMG and Area 305 is signed by RPE/Univision. Two independent labels, Delanuca, which specializes in importing established rock en Español acts from Latin America, and J&N, which specializes in tropical music from the Caribbean, North and South America, are important contributors to the local music scene.

The local recording scene is also attracting such experienced producer/songwriters as Kike Santander, Rudy Pérez, Bebu Silvetti, AT Molina, Alejandro Jaén, Juan Vicente Zambrano, Fabio Estéfano Salgado, and Lester Mendez, among others. Salgado and fellow Colombian Santander, formerly work for the pioneering czar of Latin music production, Emilio Estefan Enterprises. Two years ago, Santander sues Estefan, claiming he is not receiving both the compensation and credit he feels he deserves. Estefan denies the charges, counter sues and the dispute is settled out of court. Santander goes on to win this year's top Latin Grammy producer accolade, while Estefan and his staff of 42 songwriters and 16 producers remain sought after and active. One of Emilio's projects is co-producing with Sebastian Krys Panamanian trio Rabanes latest album, *Money Pa' Que*, which fuses rock with Caribbean rhythms salsa, reggae and Jamaican ska into a danceable mixture.

Recording studios are also capitalizing on the expanding talent scene. New York's famous Hit Factory acquires and renovates Criteria Studios to become Hit Factory/Criteria, joining such other facilities like Crescent Moon (part of the Estefan operation), South Beach Studios, the Warehouse and Bogart Recording Studios.

The region is also cementing a performance circuit for Latin acts which encompasses BillboardLive, Señor Frogs, the Jackie Gleason Theater, Lincoln Theater, and Macarena in Miami Beach; Bongos, Hard Rock Café, Hoy Como Ayer, Café Nostalgia, Tobacco Road, and the Bayfront Park Amphitheater in Miami; Churchill's in Little Haiti; Coconut Grove Playhouse in Coconut Grove and such major venues as the AmericanAirlines Arena, Miami Arena, and James L. Knight Center in Miami and the Office Depot Center in the Fort Lauderdale locale.

The Miami Beach city commission envisions a new concert hall for the New World Symphony designed by world-renowned architect Frank Gehry called Soundscape, beginning construction in 2007 and hopefully completed within two to three years. The *Herald* reports the cost at $40 million, with the city leasing the land now used for parking lots an a garage for $1 a year in rent.

Some of the night spots specialize in niche music. Restaurant 190 in downtown Miami features rumba Saturdays by Adalberto Delgado and La Fé for an audience comprised of Cubans, Cuban-Americans, Haitians and other rumba fanatics. Club La Covacha in West Dade, has evolved from offering Cuban and tropical sounds to a pastiche of Mexican rock and endemic music from Colombia, the Dominican Republic and Argentina for a crowd which includes natives from these nations plus Hondurans and Venezuelans, the result of immigrants from these countries fleeing to Miami for political and economic relief.

BillboardLive and the Jackie Gleason Theater play featured roles during the magazine's Latin Music Conference in May. While the 13th annual three-day conference takes place at the venerable Eden Roc Hotel in Miami Beach, BillboardLive hosts the welcoming party while the Gleason Theater—from which the late comic Jackie Gleason did his CBS TV series—is the site for the awards show which includes such top-tier names as Marc Anthony, Carlos Vives and Celine Dion, who sings in Spanish on her new album, and which airs on a tape delayed basis May 12 on Telemundo and on Hispanic Broadcasting System's 40 radio stations.

Bachata, the forlorn dance rhythm from the Dominican Republic, is being heralded by two tropical formatted radio stations, WXDL and rival WRTO. Juan Luis Guerra, a bachata /merengue vocalist of some duration since the release in 1991 of his album, *Bachata Rosa*, makes his first local headlining appearance in nine years at the Miami Arena as the premier event of SBS Entertainment, the new concert promotion firm owned by radio network Spanish Broadcasting Systems.

Having lost the Latin Grammy Awards last year to Los Angeles because of pressure from the Cuban community, the city is hoping its being selected as the site for the inaugural MTV Video Music Awards Latinoamérica will bring new luster and prestige to the metropolis. The two-hour show on October 24 from the Jackie Gleason Theater, will feature local and international acts, and will be beamed live out of the country on MTV Latin and run in the U.S. on MTV2. It will air on the main MTV channel in the U.S. eight nights later. Hosts will be Argentine TV star Mario Pergolini and Mexican actor Diego Luna. Artists appearing on the inaugural telecast include Carlos Santana, Colombia's Juanes and Sofia Vergara, Mexico's Paulina Rubio, Molotov, Ely Guerra, and Kinky.

Miami's insular Cuban community maintains connections with its homeland. In honor of the 100th anniversary of the Cuban Republic on May 20, Florida International University hosts a concert featuring pianist Sergio A. González and violinist Andrés Trujillo, just one of many arts celebrations taking place throughout South Florida. Miami's Little Havana section goes all out with its own summer cultural event, *Cultural Viernes*, along main thoroughfares Calle Ocho and Southwest Eighth Street, where three Cuban presidents are buried in Woodlawn Cemetery. During Hispanic Heritage Month in October, *Viva Broward*, a popular Fort Lauderdale weekend festival for the past 13 years, features music and vittles from 21 nations in the Caribbean and South America. This year's event is expected to attract 35,000 plus visitors.

The eighth annual International Ballet Festival of Miami, originally cast to showcase Latin dance from all over the Latin world, this year features an expanded roster of styles and participating nations besides the U.S. and Latin America performing over six days at the Broward Center for the Performing Arts, the Jackie Gleason Theater and the Manuel Artime Theater. Among founder Pedro Pablo Peña's contemporary ballet troupes is Mexico's Compañia Nacional De Danza, originally scheduled to appear last year on the weekend following September 11, but cancelled instead.

In January of 2003, two major events occur, one upbeat, the other sad.

The 104-year-old William Morris Agency announces it will open a Miami outpost in April to gain a strong foothold in the Latin market.

One month later, world-renowned percussionist Ramon "Mongo" Santamaria, 80, dies in a hospital following a recent stroke, and being on a life support system. The Cuban-born musician spends the last years in retirement in the Miami suburb of Kendall. Throughout his career, he infuses the excitement of Afro-Cuban drumming to his work with Pérez Prado, Dizzy Gillespie, Tito Puente, and Cal Tjader, as well as to his Fantasy, Riverside, Fania, Milestone, Columbia, and Pablo recordings starting in 1958 and running through 1998. His one major crossover hit in 1963, Herbie Hancock's *Watermelon Man*, remains one of the elite Latin jazz singles to reach the top 10 on *Billboard*'s pop singles chart.

In September, I call Michael Vega, Williams Morris' New York vice president who is dispatched to open the office and provide the talent agency with its first presence in Miami in 30 years. Vega, whose background includes 10 years as a theatrical booking agent before joining William Morris, cites 1989 as his entry into the Latin market, working with legendary bandleader Mario Bauzá and in 1996 producing the first American tour for the Cuban National Folkloric Dance Ensemble.

Along with an office staff of seven, including three agents, the company's Latin artist roster totals 30 names, ranging from Thalía to Juanes, Luis Miguel, Arturo Sandoval, Jaci Velasquez and José Carreras. "It's very important that we're making this formal commitment to the Latin market," Vega opines.

Dealing with Latin artists involves traveling. "This week I'm going to the White House with Bacilos and Alexandre Pires who will perform at the annual Hispanic Heritage Month ceremonies," Vega tells me. Is the agency pushing artists to try the crossover route? "It's a case-by-case situation," he says. "While some artists would love to reach out to as broad an audience as possible in another language, others are content to sing only in Spanish. Luis Miguel only sings in Spanish. Jaci Velasquez has a dual career, with Christian albums in English on Word and Latin pop for Sony Discos. Jon Secada records in both English and Spanish. Huey Dunbar, the lead singer with DLG, which mixes R&B with salsa in the '90s, now has a solo career where he sings in both English and Spanish for Sony."

Vega calls Spanish radio "one of the biggest problem areas because it's "segregated into three basic regimens: regional Mexican, pop and tropical and it's hard to break anything different from these formats. You can hear more rock en Español on college stations than you can on Spanish stations. One local station, *Zeta 94.9*, where 60 percent of its listeners are bilingual, plays alternative music on weekends." The main Spanish TV broadcast networks "are very important because a lot of Latino households still don't have cable."

What about the Cuban community's the so-called power grasp on the city? "I think the Cuban community has a great deal of power. But I don't think it has a great deal of reach into the actual workings of the music business." He senses a different attitude among some Cubans towards Cuban artists performing in the U.S. "It's not so much a mellowing attitude towards Castro," he explains, "it's more a feeling that an occasional Cuban artist is no big thing. Prior to 1955, Miami was a sleepy Southern town. Now it's become the capitol of Latin American trade. It's becoming less Cuban every day. You hear dialects in Spanish from all over Latin America. Miami's become more of a cosmopolitan city."

In January of 2003, nearly two years after the Latin Grammys abruptly pull the show following pressure by the powerful exile community to place protesters across the street from the AmericanAirlines Arena, and shift it to Los Angeles, the city makes a renewed bid for the fourth annual event, which is granted and will take place again in the same arena.

Cuban musicians are still having visa problems entering the U.S. this year. None of the Cuban artists nominated for the September 3 Latin Grammys to be hosted by comic George Lopez are granted visas by the Bush Administration, which also fails to clear visas for three Cuban musicians living in Madrid to perform here in concert one month later. In August, nominees vocalist Ibrahim Ferrer of the Buena Vista Social Club, pianist Chucho Valdés, and Los Van Van are informed they are denied access to appear in Miami for the Grammy CBS telecast. Pathetically, this is the second instance that Valdés is denied entry. The four-time regular Grammy winner is unable to make the 2001 L.A. Latin Grammys because of similar visa problems based on bickering between the U.S. and Cuban officials.

The current U.S. denial follows action in April by Miami city commissioners who pass a 4-0 resolution asking the Latin Recording Academy which opens its national headquarters here in March, under new president Gabriel Abaroa, "to refuse to recognize or invite any Cuban artists" as a counter action to the Cuban government's crack down on dissidents, including the killing of three men.

One month later, the city commissioners vote to withhold city funds if Cuban artists are invited to the telecast, but will provide police and fire protection. Miami mayor Manny Diaz tells the *Herald* he believes the proposal "is a good decision because it showed that we can send a strong message to the Cuban government while preserving constitutional rights."

Two well-known exiles, who want the Grammys in Miami, entrepreneur Emilio Estefan and singer Willy Chirino, proclaim in August they will boycott the ceremony if any Cuban musicians actually perform on the telecast. One member of the Latin Recording Academy's board, Manolo Diaz, reflects the exile's banishment philosophy when he tells the *Herald:* "If the Cuban community doesn't like Cuban artists performing here, they have the right to protest. That does not mean the show cannot be done here."

Once the Latin Grammys are set, tempers start to heat up again. A contingent of anti-embargoists obtains a permit to hold a demonstration blocks from where the anti-Castroites in the National Council of Political Prisoners will protest the inclusion of any Cuban artists in the awards presentation.

"We are demanding that the United States government permit cultural liberty in this community, so we can see Cuban artists from Cuba participating in cultural events in this city," is the statement Andrés Gómez, national coordinator of the Antonio Macéo Brigade provides the *Herald*.

Francisco Garcia Martinez, spokesman for the National Council of Political Prisoners goes in a different direction with his statement to the *Herald*: "We are protesting the presence of Cuban agents, not Cuban artists, because there are a lot of good Cuban artists that Castro does not permit to leave the island. Those who are coming, come with the Cuban regime's blessing and to spread Castro's propaganda."

Once the Latin awards are returned here, the community sets up a series of "hallelujah, we're glad you're here" events in addition to dozens of parties and dinners all tied to the happiness of the Latin Grammys finally coming to downtown Miami. A series of free street parties with local talent begins in August as part of a four-month festival prelude to the actual event. These street parties are in Hialeah, Homestead, West Dade and Fort Lauderdale. Local officials anticipate 12,000 people arriving in South Florida to attend the telecast and participate in the various galas at several upscale hotels, a boost to the local economy, which slows down after the tourism season ends after Labor Day. How much revenue will the awards show generate? While party-laden Miami Beach, the city of Miami, the Greater Miami Convention and Visitors Bureau and the Greater Miami and the Beaches Hotel Association cannot guestimate how much money will be spent, the Latin Grammys estimate the event is worth $35 million to the community, reports the *Herald*, adding it's "a number that's hard to verify."

The fourth Latin Grammys hosted by George Lopez, the multi-hyphenated co-creator-writer-producer-star of ABC's hit *George Lopez Show*, airs in a setting designed to look like a concert within the AmericanAirlines Arena, with audience members often standing up during performances and waving their arms to the rhythm of the music. Presenters and commercials are heard both in Spanish and

English. In fact, 26 national companies run 60 commercials for 42 products, with only 14 in Spanish, according to the Media Economics Council, reports *Billboard.*

The two-hour program begins with a tribute to Celia Cruz, who passes away July 16, featuring the Fania All Stars and several of today's hot salsa stars.

Unfortunately, Lopez chooses to aim low with jokes denigrating Latinos, which fortunately draws little laughter from the audience. In his introducing to Juanes performing with the rap act, Black Eyed Peas, Lopez foolishly says: "Juanes is performing with a group named after beans. How do you like that? That's when you know Latins have really made it when there's a group named after beans." Or: "There are 39 million Hispanics living in a two-bedroom apartment in Hialeah. I'd like to see more Latinos on reality shows. On 'Big Brother' you have 12 people living in a house. We Latinos call that half-full." He fares better in another attempt to breach the Anglo and Spanish audience, noting: "Arnold Schwarzenegger just called. He's trying to recall me as host. Arnold Schwarzenegger will never be governor of California because Latinos will never vote for someone who speaks worse English than we do. *Hasta la vista*" followed by a word which CBS bleeps. It draws the biggest laughs of the evening. Lopez's reference to recall relates to Schwarzenegger's intention to recall the present Governor Gray Davis, and, of course, in the recall election he does just that and becomes the latest celebrity without any political experience to become California's governor two months later.

Entertainers performing between the awards include Bacilos, Thalía, Ricky Martin, Alexandre Pires dueting with *American Idol* winner Kelly Clarkson, Juanes and the Peas, David Bisbal, La Banda El Recodo, Kumbia Kings, Molotov, and Tribalistas.

The broadcast's Nielsen rating of a 3.4 is an improvement over last year's 2.9 figure. This year, some 3.69 million homes tune in, compared to last year's 3.1 million homes. The event is not without its share of controversy and conflict, centered naturally around Cuba. An estimated crowd of between 100 and 200 persons for and against the presence of Cuban musicians at the Grammys voice their strongly held opinions on opposite sides of the arena where they can not come into close contact. Signs read "Music, yes, censorship, no" or "Down with Castro." Host Lopez interjects himself into the politically charged dispute by appearing in one segment wearing a black shirt with the slogan "Cuba B.C." in white lettering. "B.C." apparently means before Castro.

Brazilian artist Gilberto Gil, honored as the Latin Grammy Academy's person of the year, also expresses concern about the American embargo against Cuba, which obviously affects the ability of Cuban artists to easily appear in the U.S., including on the Latin Grammy show. As quoted in the *Los Angeles Times*, Gil calls the 40-plus year embargo "the residue of a horrible historic situation, the apartheid to which they have submitted Cuba in recent times. It's time to put an end to it, so Cuba can be incorporated into the Latin community (and) the American community."

Nonetheless, three Cuban musicians, exile Paquito D'Rivera, Orishas and Ibrahim Ferrer of the Buena Vista Social Club, all garner Latin gramophones.

Colombia's Juanes is the evening's big winner nailing all five of his nominations: record and song of the year for *Es Por Ti*; rock solo vocal album and album of the year for *Un Dia Norma* and rock song for *Mala Gente*.

Other key winners include: David Bisbal, best new artist, who beats Mexican singer Natalia Lafourcade, who's shut out in three other categories as well; Bacilos, the Miami based folk–pop trio, for its best pop album, *Caraluna* and best tropical song, *Mi Primer Million;* Puerto Rico's Olga Tañon for her female pop vocal album, *Sobrevivir;* Enrique Iglesias for his male pop vocal album, *Quizás*; Maná for its rock album, *Revolución De Amor;* Bajofondo Tango for its eponymous pop instrumental album; Orishas for its rap album, *Emigrante;* El Gran Combo for its salsa album, *40 Anniversary En Vivo*; Milly Quezada for her merengue album, *Pienso Asi*; Rubén Blades for his contemporary tropical album, *Mundo*; Ibrahim Ferrer for his traditional tropical album, *Buenos Hermanos*; Vicente Fernández for his ranchero album,

35 Aniversario Lo Mejor De Lara; Joan Sebastían for his banda album, *Afortunado;* Atrapado for its grupero album, *¿Qué Sentirás?*; Jimmy Gonzalez Y El Grupo Mazz for its tejano album, *Si Me Faltas Tú*; Los Terribles Del Norte for its norteño album, *La Tercera Es La Vencida...Eso!*; Paquito D'Rivera for his Latin jazz album, *Brazilian Dreams* and his top classical album, *Historia Del Soldado*.

Aside from Ibrahim Ferrer, Chucho Valdés and Los Van Van not being permitted into the country for the awards, three Madrid-based Cuban musicians denied visas to perform at a concert here, Pepe Del Valle, Luis Barberia, both singer/songwriters and drummer Kike Ferrer, belong to the ensemble Habana Abierta which espouses change and freedom at home. Five members of the band are nonetheless granted visas, and along with three local replacement musicians, perform before enthusiastic crowds on two weekend nights at the Coconut Grove Playhouse. In checking on why the visas are denied, the *Herald* reports being told by a State Department official who deals with Cuban matters, that the delays result from obtaining all the required post September 11 inter-agency clearances.

Several Cuban cultural acts with close ties to the Cuban government, like the Cuban National Ballet and Los Van Van, apparently have no problem working here. One theory is the Cuban government clears these act's paperwork expeditiously, while groups critical of the Castro regime find their requests to leave Cuba slower in being granted.

On another cultural level, albeit homegrown, the 25-year-old Calle Ocho Festival spread over 10 days in March, is both internationally known and arguably the largest annual Hispanic street party in the U.S. Its theme is celebrating "25 years of history and success," and among the 30 artists performing for the more than 1.5 million people who attend, are Oscar D'Leon, Elvis Crespo, Oro Solido, Willy Chirino, Tito Nieves, La India, Victor Manuelle, El Gran Combo De Puerto Rico, Orquesta Salsa Gorda, Gilberto Santa Rosa, and Juan Pablo Torres. One year later, the festival's lineup of performers includes such diverse names like New York's Yerba

Buena, Puerto Rico's El Gram Combo, Victor Manuelle and Tego Calderón, Colombia's Bacilos and Cabas, Venezuela's Oscar D'Leon and Spain's Rosario.

While people dance in the streets along Calle Ocho, Cubans across America rejoice in the selection of Nilo Cruz, the first-ever Hispanic playwright to win the Pulitzer Prize for drama for *Anna in the Tropics*. Cruz's play focuses on Cuban Americans working in a cigar factory in Tampa in 1929. The 42-year-old author, who comes to the U.S. in 1970 with his parents when he's 10 on a Freedom Flight from Havana, receives a commission from the New Theater in Coral Gables, plus a grant from the National Endowment for the Arts/Theater Communications Group to write the play. He subsequently has several other plays in production while teaching playwriting at Yale. With *Anna* playing on Broadway with an all-Latino cast starring Jimmy Smits, the play is nominated for a Tony Award in 2004, but the award goes to *I Am My Own Wife*.

In a major boost for the record industry, superstar Gloria Estefan releases her first English-language studio album in five years, *Unwrapped*, which includes 14 tunes, including duets with Stevie Wonder and Chrissie Hynde and eight tunes in Spanish. Sony Norte, the new name for Sony Discos, handles the Latin market while Epic covers the English-language market. With the recent demise of Celia Cruz, Estefan is called the "queen of Latin music with international appeal" by Sony international official Frank Welzer in a *Billboard* spotlight to the artist. The new release is her 20th since 1977 and her 12th since her breakthrough 1985 *Primitive Love* album and its hit *Conga* single.

The latest member of the musical Valdés family, vocalist Mayra Caridad Valdés debuts in the U.S. The sister of star pianist Chucho Valdés, marks her solo appearance in the U.S. with her six-piece band on the album *La Diosa Del Mar* for Jazzheads records. The vocalist previously performs with Irakere, Cuba's national fusion band which her brother co-founds in the '70s. Her father, pianist extraordinaire Bebo Valdés, nicknames her "the Ella Fitzgerald of Cuba" because of her vocal virtuosity.

Radio network Spanish Broadcasting System, which is already in concert promotion with its own operation, is now a partner in the record industry with songwriter/producer Robert Livi. Their label, Megamusic, will be distributed by Universal Music and Video Distribution to the domestic Latin market. Its first signings are from Argentina: Emanuel Ortega and Meno Fernández. Livi has a lock on all his artists, signing them for management, bookings and the very lucrative music publishing rights.

Two local festivals, all with major sponsors, reflect the marriage between commerce and the Latin community. Soulfrito, the Pontiac Urban Latin Music Festival, features Latin hip-hop and mainstream hip-hop acts at the Bayfront Park Amphitheater. Its sponsors include General Motors, GMAC Financial Services and Jack Daniel's. The Bud Light II Rock En Miami Festival also at the Bayfront Amphitheater, features rock en Español groups. Its title sponsor is naturally Bud Light, with Toyota, Coca-Cola and McDonalds also involved.

Among Miami's 11 TV stations in 2003, its three Spanish outlets, WLTV (Univision), WAMI (TeleFutura), and WSCV (Telemundo), are well represented in the ratings standings. During the key November sweeps period, WLTV has the top-rated 11 p.m. newscast Monday through Sunday, with a 6.7 number, beating out the NBC affiliate WTVJ (6.2) and CBS affiliate WFOR (6.0) who follow in second and third places, respectively. WSCV is in fourth place with a 5.8. During primetime, WLTV is No. 1, while WSCV is fifth and WAMI is in 10th place. From sign-on to sign-off, WLTV is first, WSCV sixth and WAMI ninth.

Miami is now the locale for four televised Latin music awards, the most emanating from any U.S. city—the Latin Grammys (airing on CBS), *Billboard*'s Latin Music Awards (airing on Telemundo and simulcast on Univision Radio), the MTV Latin America accolades, and Premios Los Nuestro a la Música Latina (airing on Univision). In 2005, the Latin Grammys shift to Univision for the first time, with the broadcast emanating from Los Angeles.

Two artists stand out at the 14th annual *Billboard* Latin Music Awards announced May 8 and telecast on Telemundo three days later. Mexican vocalist Pilar Montenegro and Puerto Rican romantic singer Chayanne each win three honors. Montenegro wins her trophies for the tune *Quitame Ese Hombre* as top female Latin pop and regional Mexican airplay track and new artist regional Mexican airplay track of the year. Two of Chayanne's trophies, top Latin track and top male Latin Pop Airplay track, are for *Y Tú Te Vas*. His third accolade, Latin greatest hits album of the year, is for the retrospective *Grandes Exitos*. Seven acts in the regional Mexican, tropical and pop categories earning two awards include Los Temerarios, Lupillo Rivera, Monchy and Alexandra, Brenda K. Starr, Maná, Sin Bandera and Las Ketchup.

In its second year, the MTV Video Music Awards Latin America are also a celebration of parent MTV Latin America's 10th anniversary. The presentation October 23 on MTV Latin America and MTV2 domestically is followed on MTV November 1. The inaugural telecast last year reaches 410 million homes around the Latin world and four million in the U.S. according to MTV. Performers include Shakira, Maná, Paulina Rubio and Avril Lavigne. This year's show from the Jackie Gleason Theater has a strong Latin rock flavor, with four acts all garnering five nominations: Café Tacuba, Molotov, La Ley and Natalia Lafourcade, and three others earning four nominations: Juanes, Maná and Gustavo Cerati. Host this year as he was last year is actor Diego Luna, whose performance in the film *Y Tu Mamá Tambien* earns him accolades. Performing this year: Alejandro Sanz, Control Machete, La Ley, Natalia Lafourcade, Mars Volta, Café Tacuba, Dido, Sum 41, and Iggy Pop, to add a tinge of aging punk.

Mexican artists stand out at the awards. Rock band Molotov wins four trophies and new vocalist Natalia Lafourcade earns three. Molotov dominates in the categories of top group, alternative artist, Mexican artist and video of the year. Known for its socially conscious lyrics, the band's accolades are sparked by its Universal album, *Dance and Dense Danso*. Lafourcade's trophies are for best solo, pop artist, new Mexican artist. Juanes, Colombia's top selling vocalist, wins two awards as top rock star and artist of the year. Singles winner include Avril Lavigne, international pop artist; Coldplay, international rock artist; Evanescence, new international artist; Beresuit Vergarabat, top Argentinean artist; Vicentico, new Argentinean artist, and Peruvian band Libido, top central region artist.

Heading MTV Latin America is Antoinette Zel, a Cuban American former general counsel for eight years with parent MTV Networks. She believes that MTV Latin America's music videos which reach across Latin America parallels the growth and impact which MTV enjoys during its 20 plus years in the U.S.

If Viacom's MTV is a power in Latin America, how far behind is Time Warner's HBO Latin America Group? Close enough to jump into digital TV with a 10-channel digital package including HBO Latin America and the new HBO Family channel, which Time Warner hopes will stimulate the growth of digital cable TV.

Based on radio programmers' selections, ill salsa queen Celia Cruz wins four awards at the 2003 15th annual Premio Lo Nuestro Awards, broadcast live by Univision from the James L. Knight Center. Recuperating at home following brain surgery, Cruz's album, *La Negra Tiene Tumbao* (*The Black Chick Has Swing*), is the basis for her winning tropical song of the year, best album, female artist and salsa performance. Other multiple winners: Juanes and new Mexican vocalist Pilar Montenegro. Juanes' four accolades are for pop male artist, rock performance, pop song of the year and video of the year. Among her three wins, Montenegro shares the pop song of the year with Juanes. Marc Anthony, named male tropical artist of the year, dedicates his honor to Cruz. Two Mexican acts produce major surprise wins. Sin Bandera gains the pop album of the year with its similarly titled debut disc to best the likes of Enrique Iglesias, Thalía and Alejandro Sanz. And accordionist Celso Piña Y Su Ronda Bogotá overtakes Carlos Vives, and Monchy & Alexandra for the best traditional tropical performance.

During Premio Lo Nuestro's live February 2004 telecast from the Miami Arena, featuring a headline-attracting array of artists, Marc

Anthony is the top awards earner with three trophies in the categories of best salsa performance, best male tropical artist and best tropical song. Key winners in the pop area include Ricardo Arjona and his *Santo Pecado* for top album of the year; Juanes as best male artist; Shakira as best female artist; Sin Bandera as best group/duo; David Bisbal as best new artist, and Maná's *Mariposa Traicionera* as song of the year. Double winners include Olga Tañon, Juanes, Marco Antonio Solís, El General, Kumbia Kings, and La Onda. For Tañon, the recognition is especially significant since her two trophies are for best merengue performance in her field and as the best tropical album performer with *A Puero Fuego*.

Ricky Martin is presented his lifetime achievement award by Jose Feliciano. In addition to Martin, who opens the show singing *Jaleo* from his new Spanish-language CD, other performances are by Marco Antonio Solís (who wins two awards in the regional Mexican category for best male artist and best album); Joan Sebastían (best banda performance winner), Intocable (best norteño performance winner); Ricardo Arjona (best pop album); plus Thalía, India, Akwid, Montez De Durango, and La Oreja De Van Gogh.

Lo Nuestro, according to Nielsen research, outshines such powerhouse general market attractions as the Super Bowl and Oscars among Hispanic households in February. As amplified in *Hispanic* Magazine, Lo Nuestro attracts 2.899 million homes versus 1.427 million homes watching the Academy Awards, and 2.606 million Latino homes tuned in to the grandest sports spectacle, the Super Bowl.

In April of 2004, the 15th *Billboard* Latin Music Awards honor 65-year-old Mexican band, Banda El Recodo with a Hall of Fame trophy and vocalist Soraya with its Spirit of Hope Award for her efforts on behalf of cancer awareness. She is herself a cancer survivor having lost three close relatives to the disease.

The nationally televised gala from the Miami Arena features performances by Paulina Rubio (who opens the show by lip synching while she bounds around the stage), Gloria Estefan, acoustic guitarist

Luis Fonsi, romantic balladeer Alejandro Fernández, Arturo Sandoval dueting with vocalist Alicia Keys, La Ley and especially impressive turns by Banda El Recodo, Pilar Montenegro and David Bisbal. The inaugural Telemundo broadcast posts an 8.2 household rating and a 4.9 among 18- to 49-year-olds, a major increase over last year's telecast by 78 percent and 113 percent, respectively, according to Telemundo's analysis of the Nielsen data.

Three artists win triple awards, the late Celia Cruz, Ricky Martin and Juanes. Cruz, who is also given a musical tribute, wins top Latin albums artist of the year, top Latin greatest hits album (*Hits Mix*) and top female tropical album of the year (*Regalo De Alma*). Martin wins male Latin pop album of the year for *Almas Del Silencio* plus Hot Latin track of the year and Latin pop airplay track of the year. Juanes' awards are for songwriter of the year for his album *Un Dia Normal*, hot Latin track of the year and pop airplay track, the latter for *Fonographia*, on which he duets with Nelly Furtado, the Canadian singer/songwriter. Three acts win dual awards: salsa singer India's album, *Sedúceme*, earns her top female tropical airplay track and Latin dance club play track; Reggaeton duo Luny Tunes wins top tropical album for *Más Flow* and new artist, and Akwid's debut album, *Proyecto Akwid*, snares top Latin rap/hip-hop album of the year and regional Mexican new artist album of the year.

The telecast offers some unusual moments. The first two awards presented to the national TV audience are Akwid's hip-hop trophy followed by Arturo Sandoval winning the top Latin jazz award for his album, *Trumpet Evolution.* Andres Cantor, the veteran soccer play-by-play specialist know for his trademarked long goooalll calls, uses this technique to announce the jazz winner with a long Arturrrooooo Sandoval. The broadcast includes an A-list of sponsors pitching their products in Spanish, the exclusive language for the event.

The third annual MTV Video Music Awards Latinoamérica is a mixture of international stars, traditional and alternative bands and the outlandish dresses worn by hostess Mexico pop star Paulina Rubio, culminating with a gold sparkly dress and no back, which intentionally shows off her naked buttocks and a red thong. For viewers of the telecast from the Jackie Gleason Theater in Miami Beach October 21 live on MTV2 in the U.S. and on MTV channels in Mexico, Central and South America, and rebroadcast domestically on flagship MTV nine days later, the accolades barrage honors winners in 18 categories. Mexican singer/accordion player Juliet Venegas steals the music spotlight with three awards: artist of the year, best solo artist and best Mexican artist. Her 2003 BMG album, *Si*, helps catapult her into the mainstream spotlight. Two groups earning two awards are Mexico's alternative music denizens Café Tacuba and the U.S' light rockers Maroon 5. Tacuba's trophies are for best alternative artist and video of the year for the tune *Eres*. Maroon 5's achievements are as best new international artists overall and best new international rock artists.

Spain's La Oreja De Van Gogh walks away with best group title while fellow countryman Alejandro Sanz is named best pop artist. Chile's La Ley earns the best rock artist title; Belinda Peregrin is named best new Mexican artist; Diego Torres best Argentine artist while countrymen Airbag win best new Argentine artist. Two American acts gain key nods. Avril Lavigne repeats as best international pop artist while Black Eyed Peas is named best international hip-hop/R&B act.

Artists performing besides Rubio include: Venegas, Molotov, Juanes, Beto Cuevas, Cartel De Santa, La Ley, Black Eyed Peas, Lenny Kravitz, the Beastie Boys, and Pitbull (the last four from the U.S.) fusing with musicians whose global roots encompass Mexico, Chile and Colombia.

Not to be out done by the music accolade shows, the film community has four festivals all its own. The 20th annual International Film Festival offers 65 films from 24 nations this year in addition to a new feature, *Miami Encuentros* (*Miami Encounters*), designed to allow new filmmakers from Spain and Portugal to run their works before potential U.S. distributors HBO, 20th Century Fox and Sony Pictures Classics. The festival's new director, Nicole

Guillemet, formerly managing director at Sundance for 15 years, says she's attempting to program films that appeal to a wide, diverse audience. She's hired by Florida International University, which runs the festival, after attendance drops at last year's event. In 2004, it presents 67 titles over its 10-day run at five different theaters and report 50,000 paying customers, up somewhat from 2003. One of its more unusual titles is *Havana Suite*, Cuba's official entry for a 2004 Academy Award. It neither wins this competition or an Oscar nomination. This is also the first year the festival is under the direction of Miami Dade College, which takes over the operation from Florida International University, which operates the event from 1999 through 2003. FIU, as it's called, provides the needed cash to keep the event going after its 1983 original founder and film exhibitor Nat Chediak finds his funding drying up from governmental sources.

In addition to this major event, the city plays host to the seventh annual Miami Latin Film Festival (which attracts upwards of 25,000 people), the University of Miami's new twice monthly Latin Film Series, the seventh annual Brazilian Film Festival and two international events which provide exposure for Spanish-language films, the Fort Lauderdale festival and Miami Gay and Lesbian festival. All these film festivals prompt the *Herald* to tag Miami "the U.S. epicenter for Latin American films."

Miami's two leading radio morning shock jocks, WXDJ-FM's Enrique Santos and Joe Ferrero, retain their informal title of on-air outrageous pranksters. The *El Zol* duo create a series of headline-generating negatives for their *El Vacilón De La Mañana* program, which in one instance, Raul Alarcón, chairman and owner of the SBS station is among the callers who express distaste for their stunt of the day. Using taped portions of a 2001 conversation between Fidel Castro and Mexico's president, Vicente Fox, the duo use Castro's edited phrases during calls to unsuspecting persons. In January, the segment titled *Fidel Te Llama* (*Fidel's Calling You*) ensnares Venezuelan president Hugo Cháves, a close friend to Castro, who is informed his ally is calling, hears Castro's voice and believes he's on the phone. Only after a few confused exchanges does Santos reveal it's not Castro.

According to the *Herald* story depicting this latest prank, Santos, who along with Ferrero are second-generation Cuban Americans, starts shouting at Cháves: "terrorist, animal, murderer." Angered listeners light up the station's switchboard, including SBS' Alarcón, described by Santos as not being "very happy" over the incident. SBS operates two other Miami stations, WCMQ-FM, which plays Spanish oldies and WRMA-FM, which airs Spanish adult contemporary tunes.

In June, the duo makes a crank call to Castro, using Cháves' voice, and gets through to someone they believe is the Cuban dictator. Ferrero calls Castro an "assassin" and also boasts that "all of Miami is listening." Castro responds with several expletives, including a crude remark about Ferrero's mother, according to a story in the *Los Angeles Times.*

Santos and Ferrero earlier create non-political havoc on April Fool's Day of 2002 when they state the first people in line for a Julio and Enrique Iglesias concert at the AmericanAirlines Arena will be given free tickets. When scores of people show up for the bogus offer, the station suspends the duo with pay for three days.

But things get real down and literally dirty in February of 2004 when the WXDJ duo go beyond the bounds of good taste by airing the supposed voices of a masturbating priest and a marijuana smoking welfare recipient. During another attempted prank, they try to call the beleaguered Haitian president Jean-Bertrand Aristide's office. When they cannot get through, the *Herald* reports that they call Aristide's secretary gay.

The increased use of vulgarity among Spanish radio disc jockeys in cities with large Latin populations, like Miami, New York and Los Angeles, is emerging as an issue at the Federal Communications Commission, which grants licenses and has regulatory power over radio and TV stations. The *Herald* indicates the use of raw language and bad taste stunts are generating complaints from the Hispanic community including the influential Washington headquartered National Council of La Raza, whose president, Raul Yzaguirre, admits to the paper "Spanish-language radio is raunchier than English (radio), and there is no accountability whatsoever."

This swelling tide of concern is reflected by Washington solons clearing a measure that will significantly boost the fines the FCC can issue for offending Spanish and English broadcasters. One problem the FCC admits, is that of the 20 investigators in its obscenity enforcement bureau, only one speaks Spanish. Complaints anent crude language on Spanish radio, involving taped dialog, are turned over to a company which translates the tapes into an English transcript, which is then reviewed by the enforcement staff. The problem with this system, according to the *Herald*, is the difficulty in literally capturing the actual vulgarity in the language transference.

Despite the various pranks by the WXDJ morning duo, the FCC in late April of 2004, focuses on the bogus call to Fidel Castro and fines the station $4,000. The fine is cotton candy compared to the huge fines the FCC will levy against Anglo stations in 2004. Citing an "informal complaint" from some unidentified person, the federal agency fines WXDJ for not informing participants in phone conversations their comments will be broadcast. According to a *Herald* story, the station argues against the fine by claiming the rules do not cover a leader of a government unfriendly to the U.S. The FCC rejects that argument, stating the regulation is meant to prevent someone on the phone from being embarrassed, and recognizes "the intent and result of WXDJ's actions to fool and surprise the recipients of the call."

While Miami in 2003 has 12 Spanish radio stations, up from six in the fall of 1990, the number drops to 11 in 2004, a year in which there are 626 Spanish radio stations throughout the nation, based on figures in the newsweekly *Broadcasting and Cable*. In 2005, SBS' WXDJ enters the record books by becoming the city's first-ever Hispanic station to best all radio stations with more than $23.3 million in revenue, according to the Los Angeles accounting firm of Miller, Kaplan, Arase & Co.

Miami, already the acknowledged center point for Spanish-language network television, gains a powerful new company in March of 2004 when Televisa, Mexico's largest producer of programming, Univision's exclusive source for novelas and an 10.9 percent shareholder, opens what it calls an executive operations center. The center will coordinate new projects for domestic Latin viewers. Moving to Miami are Emilio Azcárraga, Grupo Televisa's chairman/CEO and the company's largest single shareholder and two other executives. Speculation is that Azcárraga's move to the U.S. with his new bride clears him to apply for citizenship and bypass FCC regulations limiting foreign ownership in broadcasting companies.

It also opens the door for a possible move to acquire a larger equity position in Univision, whose exclusive pact with Televisa runs until 2017. In its fourth quarter earnings statement released in late February, Televisa reports earnings of $96 million of its $2.14 billion total revenue from its Univision deal, according to the *New York Times*. Azcárraga holds the top executive slot in the company founded by his grandfather following the death of his father, Emilio Azcárraga Milmo, in 1997. The company also announces it will open a Los Angeles outpost in May for its film distribution company, Televisa Cine, which will release its current movies, catalog titles and TV films for the domestic Hispanic market. First product distributed in the U.S. will be the comedy *A Day Without Mexicans*.

The addition of these new programming producers to the local scene, underscores the importance of Miami's expanding role as the home for original news, talk, entertainment shows and scripted novelas aimed at domestic Latinos emerging from Univision, Telemundo and Venevision International, the three leading companies using Miami-based actors and production support. Telemundo completes two original novelas using some of last year's $30 million original programming budget: *Amor Descarado and La Prisionera*. Earlier, President/CEO McNamara predicts his original programming expenditure will rise this year to $60 million. In addition, Telemundo continues to obtain soap operas from its three overseas suppliers, Mexico's Argos, Colombia's Caracol and Brazil's Globo. Nonetheless, Ramón Escobar, Telemundo's executive vice president of programming, tells *Weekly Variety* that "three quarters of its primetime programming is now being produced in Miami."

In a very competitive move, Telemundo reportedly spends $10 million on the *La Prisionera* novela just to help leading man Mauricio Islas out of his contract with Televisa, Univision's principal novela producer. Five months after Islas signs with Telemundo, Televisa files a $1 million lawsuit against the actor in Mexico City, charging him with breaking his contract, and also seeking 40 percent of his salary for working under that name which it claims is on his contract. Islas' attorney claims Televisa has not registered the name with Mexico's National Institute of Author's Rights. Initially, after Islas signs with Telemundo, Televisa files an injunction in the U.S. against the network, alleging its negotiations with the actor are unauthorized, which the court overrules. In the new action, Televisa claims Islas is still bound to his contract.

While Univision's latest soap from Televisa is *Mariana De La Noche*, it commissions 13 episodes of the legal drama, *Al Filo De La Ley*, from Plural Entertainment, a local firm, in exchange for exclusive U.S. airtime.

Venevision International is presently producing upwards of 1,200 hours of TV programming from its headquarters here, a marked increase from the 240 TV hours it creates four years ago. Its current novela is *Angel Rebelde*, a co-production with another local firm from Venezuela, Fonovideo, which airs on Univision, its main U.S. connection. Venevision's other shows include two daily talkers: *Casos De Familia and Quien Tiene La Razon* plus *Camera Candida*. Fonovideo has also signed to work on Televisa's new immigration novela, *Inocente De Ti*, which will be shot here and in Mexico.

Following Televisa's entry into Miami, another television firm, New York-based but little known outside the TV advertising industry, National Cable Communications, opens a two-person Miami outpost to sell local Latin ad agencies on the value of cable television spot advertising. Working with Noeli Sanchez, the director of sales, hired away from NBC/Telemundo national sales in Miami, is regional account manager Kim Fabian, who shifts southward from NCC's Gotham office, where she's an account executive. No more cold winters for her. NCC has 14 other sales offices nationwide, including three which also deal with the Hispanic market: New York, Dallas and Atlanta. "A vast majority of Hispanic only business comes through Miami agencies," notes Dean Diltz, NCC's manager of corporate communications. Within the Dallas staff, one person, Robert Getz, is assigned to exclusively deal with Hispanic agencies in that city and San Antonio. NCC is the nation's largest spot cable TV advertising rep firm in the country, whose owners are Comcast Cable Communications, Time Warner Cable and Cox Communications.

On a level of personal significance is the granting of U.S. citizenship to 43-year-old Kike Santander, the three-time Latin Grammy winning Colombian songwriter/producer. He is among 5,500 new citizens sworn in during morning and afternoon ceremonies at the Miami Beach Convention Center. His appearance naturally attracts extra media coverage, and he tells the *Herald*, "This country opened many frontiers for me and allowed me to grow professionally. Becoming a citizen makes it official how much I appreciate what this country has done for me." Among the artists Santander works with is Spaniard David Bisbal, last year's best new artist Latin Grammy winner.

The city's creative zestiness inculcates two new musical styles. The first is a revitalized appreciation of trova, a former popular romantic ballad style inculcated by Cuban troubadours pre-Castro, during his reign and in the late '80s when the genre includes cries for greater freedom. A number of clubs in the area feature trova nights, ranging from Hoy Como Ayer in Miami's Little Havana, Havana Dreams Café in Doral, and the Centro De La Trova at Coral Gables' Spanish Cultural Center, for example. Singer/songwriting artists are both local proponents and visitors from Latin America, who weave their stories to the accompaniment of their own guitars.

The second musical wave blends together such cultural cornerstones as Colombian vallenato and cumbia, Cuban son and timba, Puerto Rican salsa, Brazilian samba, Jamaican reggae, and American funk and rap. Propelling this amalgamated sound are Latin

American immigrant musicians whose fusion is saluted at the Miami Funk Festival, which Tanya Bravo, one of the festival's four female founders tells the *Herald* is the "evolution of Latin music in today's urban culture." Bravo and partner Liz Easton form their own record label, Soulas, and a production company bearing their last names, to help artists in the genre gain wide exposure. First artist on the label is Itagui Correa, the 25-year-old piano playing leader of polycultural bands Suenalo Sound System, Xperimento, and Los Por Juana, whose musical education begins in his native Medellín, Colombia, where he lives until his family moves to Miami 10 years ago.

Javier Garcia is a musician mixing nationalities and musical styles who has the good fortune to be signed to Surco/Universal Latino, which will release his debut CD produced by hit maker Gustavo Santaolalla next January. Garcia's father is from Cuba, his mother from Ireland, so he grows up in Spain and Ireland and then as a teenager moves to Miami with his family where his musical mixing results in blending elements from Cuba, Argentina, Haiti, Jamaica, and the U.S. This blending of music from all over the Latin world, not just from Cuba, is what differentiates this musical experimentation.

JD Natasha is a bilingual 16-year-old singer, who makes her debut on EMI Latin with the album, *Imperfecta/Imperfect*, which is designed to attract other Spanish and English-speaking teens. Eleven tunes are in Spanish; three in English. The Miami resident, whose legal name is Natasha Janeth Dueñas, plays piano and guitar and writes lyrics which reflect anger and the angst of her generation.

Bacilos, the local multinational hit and hip trio, shifts direction on its new Warner Music Latina album, *SinVerguenza* (*Shameless*), to counter what lead singer Jorge Villamizar claims is a "culture of shame" among Hispanic musicians who prefer to toss aside their Latin roots in favor of American musical styles, which he chides during an interview with the *Los Angeles Times* during a stop on its national tour. Accompanying the Colombian vocalist/composer and trio mates Brazilian bassist André Lopes and Puerto Rican drummer José Javier Freire on the road are three Cuban musicians playing electric guitar, violin and percussion. The sound of the album with its more serious themed tunes and mixture of Caribbean rhythms, uncomplicated pop melodies and rock elements, is overseen by two new producers, Miami's Juan Vicente Zambrano and the late Brazilian whiz Tom Capone, who replaces Sergio George, co-producer of the band's last hit album.

The plight and reputation of local record labels are enhanced by the commercial success attained by three companies and the addition of a company aiming at older listeners. Perfect Image, which specializes in urban Latin sounds, is driven by Tribales, Los Ilegales, Top 4 and Fito Blanko. SGZ, formed this year by former WEA Latina president George Zamora and hit making producer Sergio George to specialize in tropical music, clicks with its first artist Tito Nieves. Vene Music, formed last year by parent Venevision International to release compilations, shifts into new works this year with its first artist, Juan Luis Guerra. Klasico Records, formed by producer Roberto Livi, takes aim at what he perceives are older neglected consumers with his first release planned for next year featuring Venezuelan singer José Luis Rodríguez. Livi hopes to attract other acts based on his history of producing and writing hit tunes for artists ranging from Julio Iglesias to José Jose to Rocio Durcal and Camilo Sesto and Rodríguez himself, he tells *Billboard.* Livi's last label association is Megamusic, a joint venture formed last year with Raul Alarcón, Sr., founder and chairman emeritus of Spanish Broadcasting System, with whom he's no longer connected.

When Coral Gables hosts the 20th annual International Hispanic Theatre Festival which presents 12 plays from four other South Florida communities: Miami, Miami Beach, Homestead and Fort Lauderdale, its entry is *El Hombre Immaculado* (*The Immaculate Man*). Countries represented besides the U.S. are Mexico, Spain, Argentina, Colombia, Venezuela and Bolivia. While most of the plays are in Spanish, several have what's called "supertitles" which appear on a screen above the stage.

The eighth annual Brazilian Film Festival of Miami, which runs for seven days at the Lincoln Theatre, offers 13 films and nine shorts, all in Spanish with English subtitles. Adding a musical sound to the festival, Olodum, an Afro-Brazilian carnival band performs on the closing day. Formed in Salvador, Bahia, Brazil, in April 1979 following 15 years of military rule and the return of democracy, the band begins with drums and voices and adds horns, synthesizers and longer singing arrangements. Its music celebrates black history in Brazil and is featured on Paul Simon's 1991 album, *The Rhythm of the Saints.*

Not to be outdone, the second annual Flamenco in the Sun 2004 festival offers a month-long extravaganza of music, dance and workshops built around the fiery music of Spain. There's a mix of international stars and local devotees attempting to regenerate the local scene's romance with the music born in Andalusia in southern Spain. It's been 30 plus years since flamenco is popular here, so the fledgling festival's challenge is to rekindle the fires of fanaticism and it hopes to accomplish this with its co-sponsors, the Bailes Ferrer Flamenco Dance Company of Broward County, the Miami-Dade College Cultural Affairs department and a new cultural events promoter, FUNDarte. "We are trying to bring back the true art form, so that we can forget about the street rumba stuff they were calling flamenco," stresses Damaris Ferrer to the *Herald.* He's the founder and artistic director whose group is among the local acts performing. The festival's hopes are buoyed on the earlier acceptance this year of flamenco-flavored performances by classical guitarist Paco De Lucia and Barcelona's Ojos De Brujo group, which marries flamenco with Cuban salsa, rap and rock rhythms.

The music of Colombia literally arrives in Miami when Codiscos, a leading tropical music label opens an office here in August of '05. The 55-year-old formally named Compañia Colombia De Discos, based in Medellín, specializes in vallenato and salsa acts.

Miamians, including a number of resident musicians, pitch in to raise money for victims of Hurricane Katrina, which ravishes New Orleans and the Gulf Coast area August 27, 2005, in the nation's worst natural disaster in history. Hosting the Miami-Dade County Relief

Concert September 25 at the AmericanAirlines Arena in Miami are actor/producer Andy Garcia (who initially lives in Miami after arriving with his family from Cuba) and Emmy-award winning actress/dancer Debbie Allen. Among the artists performing are trumpeter Arturo Sandoval (who also escapes from Cuba and establishes permanent residence here), Jon Secada (who moves here from Havana with his family in 1971 when he's nine years old and changes his name from Juan to Jon in 1990), Jack Jones, Jose Feliciano, Vikki Carr, Luny Tunes, Los Temerarios, Ed Calle, and Ana Cristina, a 19-year-old Cuban American, and Sony Music artist, who becomes the first Latino artist in history to sing the national anthem at a presidential inauguration, president George W. Bush's swearing in on January 20, 2005. During the concert, Sandoval performs his *The Motherland of Jazz* composition honoring New Orleans arranged by Calle and co-produced by Grammy-winning Rudy Pérez. A Spanish version of the relief tune is also recorded by Cristina and Michael Angelo.

Secada, who gains audiences for his 1992–'94 English and Spanish-language albums, seeks to resurrect his career after recently terminating his relationship with Crescent Moon Records and his former manager/label owner Emilio Estefan, for whom he starts recording in 2002, following his work for Epic two years earlier. Known for his initial writing for Gloria Estefan, Ricky Martin, Jennifer Lopez, Shakira, and Cher, among others, Secada finds a groove for himself by mixing R&B, pop and Latin elements on his albums, and these are the ingredients on his new CD released in October of '05. A greatest hits compilation due in '06 will feature Secada warbling songs he's written for other artists.

The CIFALC School for the Performing Arts, which opens here in 2003 to train semi-pro actors and actresses for a career in Spanish TV telenovelas, expands its training program to include non-pros in the fall of 2005. The school founded by Aquiles Ortega, claims to be the first of its kind utilizing TV and recording studio training facilities.

Articles

"Miami Stations Makes Radio History." Billboard, Feb. 11, 2006
"Steering A Growing Ship." Latin Notas, Billboard, Nov. 26, 2005
"Another Day For Jon Secada." Latina, October, 2005
"Ana Cristina Chosen To Perform And Record Theme Song For Relief Concert." HispaniaNet.com, Sept. 21, 2005
"Codiscos On The Go." Latin Notas, Billboard, Sept. 3, 2005
"Special Olympics Bows Latin Xmas." Billboard, Aug. 20, 2005
"The Nation's First Acting School Dedicated To The Telenovela Industry." HispaniaNet.com, Aug. 6, 2005
"Labor Loses May Increase PAC Costs." Miami Herald, Aug. 4, 2005
"Telemundo's Top-Tier Switch." Daily Variety, April 7, 2005
"Telemundo Prepares For Change At Top." Hollywood Reporter, April 6, 2005
"New Latin Music Fuses Many Styles In A Polycultural Jam." Miami Herald, Nov. 22, 2004
"Livi's New Label Targets Older Music Fans." Billboard, Nov. 20, 2004
"Recap: Notable Latin Chart Bows." Billboard, Nov. 20, 2004
"Switching Gears But Staying True." Los Angeles Times, Nov. 13, 2004
"Teen Singer JD Natasha Puts Accent On Bilingual." Houston Chronicle, Aug. 12, 2004
"Dance Of The Gypsies." Miami Herald, Aug. 6, 2004
"Breathing New Life Into An Old Musical Tradition." Miami Herald, July 23, 2004
"Music Men Hope Success Is Easy As SGZ." Billboard, July 3, 2004
"11 Productions, Seven Countries, One Fabulous Festival." Miami Herald, June 4, 2004
"Televisa Files Suit Over Thesp's Ankling." Daily Variety, May 11, 2004
"Bash Honors Latin's Best." Billboard, May 8, 2004
"Miami Station Fined For Its Castro Prank." Miami Herald, April 24, 2004
"Inside Miami: Se Habla Telenovelas." Weekly Variety, April 19, 2004
"So Far, Just An Idol In Making." Los Angeles Times, April 4, 2004
"Biz Reacts To Warner Cuts." Billboard, April 3, 2004
"El Recodo, Soraya Honored." Billboard, April 3, 2004
"Premio Lo Nuestro Beats Oscars, Super Bowl." Hispanic Magazine, April 2004
"Mixing It All Up Jorge Moreno Sings A Tune All His Own." Hispanic Magazine, April 2004

"Latin Songwriter Becomes Citizen." Miami Herald, March 24, 2004

"Bono, Stern Feel FCC Slap." Daily Variety, March 19, 2004

"Performing Arts Center Is Facing More Delays." Miami Herald, March 13, 2004

"Latin Music's Hottest Stars Highlight Calle Ocho." Miami Herald, March 12, 2004

"FCC Won't Budge On Infinity Indecency Fine." March 8, 2004

"Clear Channel Pays FCC 'Bubba' Fine." Daily Variety, March 5, 2004

"KCRW Fires Loh Over Obscenity." Los Angeles Times, March 4, 2004

"What The F——?!" Los Angeles CityBeat, March 4, 2004

"Hola To Hollywood." Daily Variety, March 2, 2004

"Marc Anthony, Marco Antonio Solis Among Big Winners At Premio Lo Nuestro." Hispanic PR Business Wire, March 2, 2004

"Serious Issues At The Core Of Radio's Off-The-Air Antics." Los Angeles Times, March 1, 2004

"Mexico Media Mogul Follows The Money." New York Times, Feb. 27, 2004

"Broadcasters Promise Their Own Clean Air Act." Los Angeles Times, Feb. 27, 2004

"Top Televisa Brass Set For Miami Move." Daily Variety, Feb. 27, 2004

"Clear Channel Yanks Stern Show Over Smut." Daily Variety, Feb. 26, 2003

"Clear Channel To Stop Airing Stern Show." Los Angeles Times, Feb. 26, 2004

"A Clean-Air Initiative From Clear Channel." Los Angeles Times, Feb 25, 2004

"Shock Jocks Rock Spanish Radio." Miami Herald, Feb. 15, 2004

"Miami Film Fest Boosts Slate, Auds." Daily Variety, Feb. 11, 2004

"Miami Nice For Hispanic Surge." Hollywood Reporter, Jan. 6, 2004

"Nilo Cruz Steals All The Limelight." Miami Herald, Dec. 21, 2003

"Next Film Festival to Offer 64 Entries from 34 Countries." Miami Herald, Dec. 12, 2003

"TV Ratings." Miami Herald, Nov. 29, 2003

"Break Out The Cigars." Time, Nov. 3, 2003

"Thought Pac Has Woes, Future May Be Bright." Miami Herald, Nov. 3, 2003

"Facing a $2.7 M Yearly Deficit, Trust Seeks To Increase PAC Revenue." Miami Herald, Nov. 3, 2003

"Respondents Ask: What Performance Center?" Miami Herald, Nov. 3,

2003

"Performance Postponed." Miami Herald, Nov. 3, 2003

"MTV Latin At 10." Billboard, Oct. 25, 2003

"Mexico's Molotov Explodes At MTV Latin America Nods." Hollywood Reporter, Oct. 24, 2003

"The Winner Is…" Miami Herald, Oct. 22, 2003

"Miami Grows Live Music Scene." Billboard, Oct. 11, 2003

"Roberto Livi, SBS Founder Start Label." Billboard, Oct. 11, 2003

"Problems With Visas Create Roadblock For Cuban Artists." Miami Herald, Oct. 8, 2003

"Latina Starlet Mendes Gets Hotter And Hotter Roles." Houston Chronicle, Oct. 2, 2003

"Rock Acts Lead Latin VMA Nods." Billboard, Sept. 20, 2003

"Latin Grammys." Latin Notas, Billboard, Sept. 20, 2003

"Juanes Sweeps With 5 Latin Grammys." Los Angeles Times, Sept. 4, 2003

"Miami Sparkles With Star-Studded Awards Show." Sept. 4, 2003

"Cubans Unlikely To Attend Grammys." Los Angeles Times, Sept. 3, 2003

"Politics Spoil Grammy Party For Cuban Stars." Daily Variety, Sept. 2, 2003

"Latin Grammys Bring Untold Local Profits." Miami Herald, Aug. 30, 2003

"Grammy Business Is Music To Their Ears." Miami Herald, Aug. 29, 2003

"Pro-Castro Activists To Join The Fray At Latin Grammys." Miami Herald, Aug. 29, 2003

"Velasquez Wed To 'Zapata' Bio." Hollywood Reporter, Aug. 5, 2003

"Latin Grammy Street Parties Get Started Today." Miami Herald, Aug. 3, 2003

"Latin Grammy Protest An Issue Again." Miami Herald, Aug. 1, 2003

"Beach Oks Deal Paving Way For Symphony Hall." Miami Herald, July 31, 2003

"Gloria Gets Personal." Billboard, July 26, 2003

"2 Exiles Add A Condition For Backing Grammys." Miami Herald, July 24, 2003

"Urban Rumba Has Miami Moving." Miami Herald, July 23, 2003

"HMO Primes 2nd Feevee." Daily Variety, July 7, 2003

"Venevision At Home In U.S." Hollywood Reporter, July 1, 2003

"Fox And Venevision Pact For DVD Distrib." Daily Variety, June 30,

2003

"Is Your Humidor Running?" Los Angeles Times, June 20, 2003

"Mexican Hit 'Law' Courting U.S. Auds." Daily Variety, June 16, 2003

"Latin Sizzles, Chayanne, Pilar Top Billboard Awards." Billboard, May 17, 2003

"Miami Has Message For Latin Grammys." Miami Herald, May 9, 2003

"A Funny Opportunity." Los Angeles Times, April 21, 2003

"Cuban Artists Face Miami Vice." Daily Variety, April 15, 2003

"Latin Clubs reflect Ever-Evolving Melting Pot." Miami Herald, April 15, 2003

"Cuban Playwright Wins Pulitzer Prize." Miami Herald, April 8, 2003

"Latin Film Fests Center On Miami." April 6, 2003

"In Its 25th Year, Calle Ocho Has Grown Beyond Its Founders' Dreams." Miami Herald, March 7, 2003

"Dead Air? Music Fans Decry Lack Of Variety In Local Radio." Miami Herald, March 2, 2003

"New Director Sets Ambitious Course." Variety, Feb. 17, 2003

"Spools Of Cool." Miami Herald, Feb. 16, 2003

"Cruz Wins Four Awards At Premios Lo Nuestro." Billboard, Feb. 15, 2003

"Cuban Exiles Shifting Hard-Line Position." Miami Herald, Feb. 12, 2003

"Mongo Santamaria, 80; Percussionist, Bandleader In forefront Of Latin Jazz." Los Angeles Times, Feb. 4, 2003

"S. Florida Hoping To Lure The Latin Grammys." Jan. 30, 2003

"Film Fest Puts Accent On Spanish." Miami Herald, Jan. 15, 2003

"Plea For Unity Among Cuban Exiles." Los Angeles Times, Jan. 14, 2003

"No Caller ID? Chavez Falls For Castro Prank 'Call.'" Miami Herald, Jan. 7, 2003

"New Sound Machines." Los Angeles Times, Dec. 29, 2002

"Hispanic Niche Itch." Daily Variety, Dec. 9, 2002

"Payola Called Fixture In Latin Music." Miami Herald, Dec. 8, 2002

"South Florida: Branching Out." Billboard, Nov. 16, 2002

"J&N 20th Anniversary." Billboard, Nov. 9, 2002

"Mexico's Stones At Latin Rock Fest." Miami Herald, Nov. 6, 2002

"MTV's Next Generation." Miami Herald, Oct. 23, 2002

"Latin Grammy Singer Comes Full Circle." Miami Herald, Oct. 2, 2002

"We're Number One." Miami New Times, Sept. 26, 2002

"Harsh Critic's Vulnerable Side Shows In 'Master Class.'" Miami

Herald, Sept. 24, 2002
"Ballet Stretches Out." Miami Herald, Aug. 31, 2002
"'La Lechuga' Raises Spanish-Language Theater." Miami Herald, Aug. 19, 2002
Cultural Renaissance." Hispanic Magazine, July/August 2002
"It's Rock En Español From Miami." Miami Herald, July 30, 2002
"Tampa Mayor Part Of Controversial Delegation To Cuba." Miami Herald, July 30, 2002
"Czech Dodges Miami Politics." Miami Herald, July 21, 2002
"Candidates In Race For Governor Woo The Hispanic Vote." Miami Herald, July 8, 2002
"A Study Of Latin Studios." Billboard, June 29, 2002
"Guerra's Music Mirrors Dominican Republic." Miami Herald, June 21, 2002
"Dance Rhythms Come With Subliminals." Latin Notes, San Antonio Express-News, June 16, 2002
"Miami Picked For MTV's Latino Awards." Los Angeles Times, June 11, 2002
"Miami Rocks. No, really." Miami Herald, June 6, 2002
"Bush Visit Sign Of Exiles' Influence." Miami Herald, May 20, 2002
"Love Of Country: Cuba's Centennial." Miami Herald, May 17, 2002
"Putting Miami On Stage." Miami Herald, May 11, 2002
"Latin Music Conference Aims To Keep Momentum Going." Miami Herald, May 5, 2002
"Latin Radio Cuddling Up To Bachata." Miami Herald, April 27, 2002
"The Return Of Wack Radio." Miami Herald, April 15, 2002
"Cuban Radio Spat Is Just A Sideshow." Miami Herald, March 25, 2002
"Castro's Daughter Is A Quiet Rebel." Miami Herald, March 8, 2002
"He's Numero Uno." Electronic Media, Jan. 21, 2002
"To The Network Born." Broadcasting & Cable, Oct. 1, 2001
"Find A 'Muy Friquiado' Way To Speak." Los Angeles Times, Aug. 8, 1997

Chapter 14
CAPITULO 14

New York: Energy Central 2002–2004/2005
NUEVA YORK: CENTRAL DE LA ENGERIA
2002–2004/2005

• SBS exec Carey Davis claims radio audience larger than for Latin TV.

• WPIX-TV uses far-off Buenos Aires interpreters for 10 p.m. news simulcast.

• NY1 News channel debuts its Noticias news spin-off network.

• Blue Note's Bruce Lundvall maintains his Cuban connections.

• Dominican Republic provides the most players for Major League Baseball.

• LPMs, PPMs, APMs: While they're Nielsen's new TV ratings technologies, Local People Meters cause a furor.

• Arbitron adds language weighting to build radio survey databases.

• Lincoln Center honors Latin music with its newest resident ensemble, the Afro-Latin Jazz Orchestra.

New York City is the energy magnet which attracts artisans from all over the Latin world to join homegrown Nuyoricans in the pursuit of stardom. While the borough of Manhattan is the home base for Hispanic radio and TV stations, the top concert venues and the melting pot for Latin recording activities, the city's neighboring boroughs with large Latino communities create a showcase circuit within the metro region. New York's Latin entertainment community, combined with the city's other branches of show business, and its role as the nation's media and financial centers, earns it the sobriquet of America's Energy Central.

In 2002, the International Latin Music Hall of Fame holds its fourth annual induction and awards ceremonies at the Hostos Center for the Arts and Culture in the Bronx. Celia Cruz and Johnny Pacheco are awarded lifetime achievement awards, while posthumous inductees include Noro Morales and Santitos Colón. Manhattan venues, of course, are the primo locales which help keep the Latin music flowing. Mexico's hot rock band, Jaguares, plays Town Hall. Lincoln Center houses its in-house Afro-Latin Jazz Orchestra led by pianist/composer Arturo O'Farrill, son of the late legendary composer Chico O'Farrill, who passes away last year. The new orchestra is part of the Jazz at Lincoln Center program, whose 21 Latin flavored concerts date back to 1991. Smaller venues like El Flamingo, La Maganette, the Bubble Lounge, Metronome and the Wild Palm, provide exposure for Gotham's coterie of second-tier Latin groups. The downtown Joyce Theater is where Ballet Hispanico performs three works tributing Havana's romance with Cuban jazz and American swing music, Argentina's tango and Latin America's love songs. On Broadway, Rosie Perez and Joe Pantoliano make their theatrical debuts on the Great White Way in the revival of Terrence McNally's *Frankie and Johnny in the Claire De Lune*. The duo replaces the show's original stars, Edie Falco and Stanley Tucci.

One local band, pianist Wayne Gorbea and his Salsa Picante, with its trombone laden Afro-Caribbean sound, catches the ear of Shanachie, the New Jersey-based jazz label, which issues two of the bands CDs, the most recent being *Fiesta En El Bronx*.

The Bronx, with its large Hispanic population, is the spawning ground for educator/percussionist/bandleader Bobby Sanabria, born to Puerto Rican parents, who's Ascension ensemble works together 20 years. This year he records *¡Quarteto Ache!* with a quartet for Khaeon World Music. It's a major departure, he tells *Latin Beat*, from his Grammy-nominated 2000 CD, *The Afro-Cuban Dream...Live and in Clave* recorded with a big band.

DG, a new world music label from Deutsche Grammophon, releases the soundtrack from the film *Frida*, with a score by Elliot Goldenthal, which is both adventurous and authentic. The tempestuous love affair between painter Diego Rivera and bisexual Frida Kahlo is a blending of acoustic guitar intertwined with other stringed instruments strumming through the music of not only the lead character's native Mexico but also the endemic sounds of Brazil, Argentina, Spain, and Cuba for a truly Latin American experience.

Tommy Mottola, chairman and chief executive at Sony Music Entertainment—known formerly as Thomas D. Mottola, after he replaces the ousted Walter Yetnikoff in 1990, and as the ex-husband to Mariah Carey—is hard at work restructuring the company after losing $132-million, according to its latest fiscal report. Among his major Latin acts are the super-hot Jennifer Lopez, who records for the Epic label, and has the highest visibility, thanks to the efforts of Mottola and her manager, Benny Medina (whom she dumps in 2003). Mottola is also the exec credited with building the careers of Latino artists Gloria Estefan, Ricky Martin, Marc Anthony, and Shakira as well as a handful of mainline artists. Although he's now married to another Latino thrush, Thalía, she's on the EMI, not Sony roster. After 13 years as head of Sony Music, Mottola exits the company in January of 2003 and reemerges as head of the relaunched disco label of the '70s Casablanca Records. Before joining CBS Records as president in 1988 he's the manager for such acts as Hall & Oates, Carly Simon, and John Mellencamp.

One of the promising developments in New York Spanish radio is the debut of an hour on WSKQ to play new records. The show, *La Música Nueva*, airs Sundays, starting in June from 11 p.m. to midnight, arguably not the best time to attract large audiences, but safe enough not to affect the station's overall ratings. The Spanish

Broadcasting System station is the city's leading Hispanic station, ranking sixth in the ratings, in October, for example.

New York's three Hispanic TV stations, Univision's WXTV and its TeleFutura WFUT plus Telemundo's WNJU, all report increased viewership. Citing Nielsen Station Index sweeps periods data, Univision claims overall Hispanic viewing increases by 127 percent during November alone. WXTV remains the Latino powerhouse, especially in the 6 p.m. news battle with the Anglo stations, especially among viewers 18 to 34, 18 to 49, and 25 to 54. WXTV also claims a major scoop by obtaining the world's first interview with the sister of accused terrorist Jose Padilla. Olga Alvarez, anchor/reporter, conducts the interview on the 6 p.m. *Noticias 41* news in June.

It's cold and rainy with threats of snow. It's the last few days in March and the first week in April of 2003 and I'm hoping my interview schedule in Manhattan won't be hampered or hindered by this dismal weather I've arrived in from sunny and warm Los Angeles, my home since leaving New York in 1962. I've brought a warm coat and umbrella to combat any storms I may encounter while walking or taxiing to a series of interviews with New York City-headquartered companies adding their own creative voices to the germinating Latin entertainment industry.

I've lined up interviews with the head of Spanish Broadcasting System's two radio stations, the general manager of Anglo TV station WPIX which offers some Spanish-language programming (on the SAP separate audio program channel of stereo sets); the general manager of NY1 News, the 24-hour all news channel which is debuting a Spanish-language channel in June, veteran Latin musician Larry Harlow, whose interview appears in Chapter 11 along with other artists, executives with Major League Baseball, the two major broadcasting ratings services, Arbitron, for radio and Nielsen, for TV, the head of Blue Note Records, Bruce Lundvall, who sets up Havana Jam in 1979 when he's president of CBS Records and which is the focal point for Chapter 2 of the book, plus officials at two advertising agencies, María Cueva, vice president/director of MediaCom's

Hispanic media buying operations, which creates commercials in Spanish, and Jean Pool, executive vice president of North American Operations at Universal McCann, which places its Anglo clients in Spanish media. Some of these interviews will appear in a series of articles I'll write for *TelevisionWeek*, the business newsweekly for which I do features.

After spending the weekend on Long Island with my brother Joseph (who promises me it won't snow during my time in New York), his wife Barbara, their son Howard, his wife Paula and their precocious two-and-a-half year-old daughter Brianna, as the relaxed buffer between Los Angeles and the intense research journey I'm about to begin in Manhattan, with or without snow, I head into "the city" as suburbanites call Manhattan Sunday evening via the Long Island Rail Road. It's 40 degrees and it snows twice and rain dampens the streets most of the time. A flash of sunshine one morning and afternoon brightens the colors of Manhattan. While the weather may be inclement, the mood among the people I interview remains cheery and upbeat despite the grayness of the days outside.

During my stay in the Big Apple, I walk to a number of interviews weather permitting, or take cabs along traffic-clogged main streets. One afternoon after exiting a lunch at the Friar's Club en route to my next appointment, I encounter snow flurries which feel damp against my face and cover my head with white flakes. My vision is clouded by snowflakes which melt when they meet the ground, leaving it damp but passable. Look up and it's snowing; gaze down and there's no trace of anything. Even though everyone is dressed in winter clothes, these masses of humanity still walk briskly along Broadway, Seventh, Sixth, Fifth, Madison, and Park Avenues. There is the unique and distinct sound of people's shoes brushing against the sidewalk as they hurry to their jobs or appointments. It's a sound I grow up with when I'm a native New Yorker and work in bustling Manhattan. It's a sound unheard in the Brentwood section of Los Angeles where I now live. The Time Life building is down the street from the New York Hilton where I'm staying and located between

53rd and 54th streets on Sixth Avenue. So at night I'm able to walk past the street level CNN studios and watch live evening news updates. NBC and Rockefeller Center are also close by, affording me an opportunity in the evening to peek into the empty *Today* show set in its street level studio and even spot *Saturday Night Live*'s exec producer Lorne Michaels exiting the NBC building into a waiting cab.

Since I'm interviewing people from different industries who are all inexorably tied into Hispanic show business in some fashion, I find myself adjusting to each new interview where the lingo may be different from what I've just heard. After chatting with María Cueva about creating Spanish-language commercials for Spanish media, for example, I shift gears and head to Larry Harlow's apartment on 86th Street and Columbus Avenue off Central Park, where we chat about his career as a Caucasian Jew specializing in Latin music. I've seen his credit on scores of albums and he turns out to be as prolific a storyteller as he is a pianist and bandleader.

Carey Davis is the Spanish Broadcasting System executive with whom I've done phone interviews in the past for several broadcasting publications and I'm looking forward to finally meeting him. He's always been cordial and gracious and a wealth of information. Since the SBS offices on 56th Street between Sixth and Fifth Avenues are close to the Hilton, it's a short walk to his office. Our 9 a.m. meeting starts off friendly, and things are going smoothly until I ask my final question and then things get real frosty. Carey's office is toward the rear on the first floor of a small office building, SBS' home for 15 years and the former locale for several British clothing manufacturers. He's distinguished looking and full of energy and dramatic flavor as he answers my questions. He, like all the other people I will interview, is dressed in business attire unlike the casually dressed executives in Miami. Carey is the vice president/general manager of SBS' two FMs, *WSKQ* (*Mega 97.9*) and *WPAT* (*Amor 93.1*), who's studios are on the second floor. With outlets in Miami, Los Angeles, San Francisco, Chicago, San Antonio, and Puerto Rico, the company owns and operates 16 stations, down from the 25 it previously owns in 2002. This is Davis' seventh year with SBS; he is the former general sales manager for five years at New York's first all news station WINS-AM, the first rock 'n' roll station to can pioneer rock jock Alan Freed in 1958 after four years and on April 16, 1965, drop the music and start its new news format.

WSKQ's format is salsa and merengue, reaching men and women in all age demographics. WPAT plays Spanish adult contemporary romantic ballads for its target audience of women. "New York," Carey says, "is the most diverse Hispanic market in the U.S. with immigrants from long ago and yesterday and from every Spanish-speaking country in this hemisphere and from the mother country of Spain."

Davis is absolutely resolute about the future for Hispanic radio based on the average age of the region's Anglos and Hispanics. "The average here in the market is 37; the average age of the Hispanic is 27. So we're naturally going to be younger-skewing radio stations. WSKQ is the number two 25 to 54 radio station in New York and WPAT is the tenth radio station with the same demographic following." Why does SBS keep the WPAT call letters for the instrumental music station, which I used to listen to regularly? "The call letters are a heritage for soft easy listening music and since we're going to do that in Spanish, it seems a good idea to keep the call letters."

SBS' two stations compete against Hispanic Broadcasting Company's two outlets, WCAA-FM (which plays tropical music) and WADO-AM (one of the city's oldest stations and one I used to listen to in the 1950s for its Latin music, which is now into news/talk) and Mega Communications' WLXE-AM, which plays regional Mexican for that emerging nationality in what is the nation's No. 1 radio market with 88 stations listed in the *New York Times*—35 AMs, of which five are Spanish, and 53 FMs of which only two are Latin and both are SBS properties. WSKQ's off-the-wall, raunchy morning show since 1993, *El Vacilión De La Mañana*, is hosted by Puerto Rican-born Luis Jiménez and his first partner, Junior Hernández, who dies in 1998 and is replaced by Ramon "Moonshadow" Broussard. The show's popularity between 6–10 a.m. helps the station become the city's No. 1 outlet. Later this year, ABC Radio Networks signs a deal with SBS to syndicate the show along with several others to heavily populated U.S. Latin cities, broadening the exposure for tropical music and the hosts' salty humor.

With Puerto Ricans the largest Hispanic group in the area, what role do they and play in your programming? Answers Davis: "Puerto Ricans are not only the largest Hispanic group, but they've been here in New York the longest." Davis calls Puerto Rico "the trendsetter in music. It dominates the Caribbean music that our listeners want. We get a lot of our music from Puerto Rico, especially salsa. The music is always changing and we're now playing reggaeton, (a mixture of reggae and hip-hop with salsa) at night as well as bachata from the Dominican Republic which I'd liken to country and western love songs on WSKQ. WPAT plays music by Luis Miguel, Ricky Martin and Chayanne; it's a combination of ballads and Spanish pop."

Puerto Ricans begin their migration to New York in the 1940s, followed by the next wave from the Dominican Republic in the '60s, with the large arrivals from Mexico occurring in the '90s to meet up with the early Mexican pioneers to New York of the '80s. 2000 Census figures estimate the Puerto Rican population as 789,172, down from 1990s 861,122. Dominicans counted for the new census number 406,806, with Mexicans at the 186,872 level, miscellaneous and other Latinos 430,108, South America with 236,374, Central America with 99,099 and Cuba with 41,123. Collectively, the Census claims there are 2.2 million Latinos representing nearly 27 percent of the region's population—and growing. Robert Smith, a Barnard College sociologist, who tracks undocumented aliens in the Northeast, estimates the city's true Mexican population, including illegals, is closer to 300,000. In 15 years he predicts Mexicans will supplant Puerto Ricans and Dominicans, of which there are 107,000, as the city's largest Hispanic community. The city's transnational composition is truly remarkable, with neighborhoods for the aforementioned plus Colombians, Nicaraguans, El Salvadorans, Chileans, and Peruvians.

While WSKQ's DJs are from the Caribbean, the station is obviously appealing to the all-important Mexican population, which is broadening its musical tastes to encompass tropical music.

When I ask if his stations draw bilingual listeners, Davis says "yes" and strengthens the point by asserting that "80 percent of the Hispanics in the city are bilingual and the SBS stations have larger audiences than the market's Spanish TV stations. That's a heavy claim," he admits. "Why is that? It's because of the music. You can be Spanish-dominant, bilingual or even an English-dominant fifth-generation Puerto Rican, but you want the music that both takes you back and also unites you with your brethren here."

Interestingly, the two SBS stations run around 15 percent of their commercials in English "because our audience understands them." Davis explains that companies with a well-known product like Mobil find the transition easier to make with English commercials. "The basic rule of thumb is that while our audience understands the English in the head, to reach the heart, el corazon, es mucho mejor en Español." Spanglish, the blending of English and Spanish words is heard more often on WSKQ's morning drive time.

Despite all the media coverage of the explosion of the Hispanic population in New York, Davis says national advertisers are still weary about buying Spanish radio. "Our rates are discounted around 25 percent of what the general market stations charge for a 60-second spot," he points out. "For argument's sake," he says leaning forward, "we'll say if it costs $1,000 on WSKQ, it should probably be in the area of $1,500, and my job is to close the gap."

Davis says it's a "fun sell" rather than a hard sell with advertising agencies, stressing: "Every month we see corporate America realizing they've got to embrace the Hispanic market. Today, we have the Men's Warehouse, which never used to advertise with us. We have supermarkets, Pepsi, McDonald's, Mercedes Benz, Hyundai, and Toyota. We should be doing better with investment firms and computer manufacturers and pharmaceuticals. When I first got here, it was seldom you would have any politician advertising in Spanish. Now, they wouldn't dare do a campaign without a Spanish counterpart."

Davis notes his two stations' music playlists combine input from its local program directors, the corporation's national program director Bill Tanner and through research. "Radio," Davis opines, "works best when people realize it is a balance of art and science."

Referring to the political clout the Miami Cuban exile community asserts over Spanish radio and TV, I ask Davis if there's any similar pressure from New York Cubans or any other ethnic group. "No, there isn't," he replies. "We're not just radio formats, we're advocates for Hispanics in New York. We're fighters for the community."

I've saved my most emotionally explosive question for last, with this preamble: "Last December, the *Miami Herald* ran a story about payola in radio and alleged that WSKQ employees had been taking money to play music. And Ruben Estrada, a former employee was quoted as mentioning names and talking about how rampant payola was in Spanish radio, especially here. What are your comments?"

Davis' expression dramatically changes and I sense I've put him on the defense with a topic which has no relationship to anything we're discussing. "Well, in that article was a response from our attorney Jason Shrinsky, and I'll let it stand there." "He denied the charges," I pipe in. "I'm going to let it stand as what our corporate attorney said," Davis responds quickly and obviously uncomfortable with the confrontation. "I'm just going to stay with what Jason said, which was a denial," he repeats.

My follow-up question is: "Other than this station, have you heard anything about payola at other Spanish stations around the country?" He starts to say something but never finishes his thought and my departure for my next interview is not a smooth and comforting experience.

Three months later on June 28, SBS celebrates its 20th anniversary with a concert in Madison Square Garden. Among the artists paying homage to the radio network are Ricky Martin, Carlos Vives, Sin Bandera, and Soraya.

One year later, Carey graciously sends me a season's greetings card.

My next interview is at WPIX-TV, the Tribune-owned Channel 11, a WB Network affiliate, which launches a Spanish-language version of its 10 p.m. news on the SAP channel February 3, so it's obviously a situation I need to check into. In going bilingual with its news, WPIX becomes the first English-language TV station in the city to offer this service to the city's Hispanic population. WPIX, one of the city's first independent stations not affiliated with either of the three major networks before becoming a WB affiliate, is located in the New York Daily News building on 42nd Street, so it's a quick taxi drive from SBS. It's a beautiful sunny day, with no indication the weather will turn cold and nasty. I've set up an interview with Betty Ellen Berlamino, the station's vice president/general manager, who I discover previously works for the Tribune station in Los Angeles, KTLA, as its local sales manager from 1988 to '94, when she moves East to join WPIX as its general sales manager until being promoted to vice president/station manager from 1998 to 2000, the year she ascends to her present position.

In setting up the interview with Berlamino, her press rep Ted Farone tells me she has a tight schedule and can see me for half an hour and no longer right after my meeting with Carey Davis. So I'm very conscious I have to be out of the SBS offices by 9:45 the latest in order to get to the Daily News building. Even though the cab driver is new to the city and is unfamiliar with the historic Daily News building, traffic flows smoothly and I arrive at my next destination in time for the 10 a.m. meeting.

Berlamino and I chat in her large office with a wide view onto 42nd Street with the morning's bright sun illuminating the room. When I learn that WPIX originally starts offering Spanish-language SAP broadcasting in October 2000 with two off-network syndicated shows which come with a Spanish audio track, *Friends* and *Suddenly Susan*, and then expands the list to include *Fresh Prince of Bel-Air*, *Dharma & Greg*, *Will & Grace*, and *Everybody Loves Raymond*, I ask

Berlamino why she waits until this year to offer a Spanish translation for the 10 p.m. news—a move which increases the station's bilingual programming to five-and-a-half weekly hours, or 23 percent of its schedule on a typical weekday. "We were unable to find a partner to translate the news. It's an expensive proposition and we didn't want to employ someone fulltime like KTLA in Los Angeles has for its 10 o'clock news," she explains. "When we finally decide on Caption Colorado, we believe it's time to make this service available. Then we ask how will we tell everyone about the Spanish service? If we had decided to start the new service several years ago, it would have been costly to advertise on Spanish radio and TV. With Tribune starting up *Hoy*, a daily Spanish newspaper that makes it economically feasible to promote the SAP service through a series of ads."

Berlamino admits the exploding Hispanic population in the tri-state area of New York, New Jersey, and Connecticut, is causing the station to look for more Spanish SAP programming. Notes the executive: "More and more syndicated shows have a Spanish audio track, and we're looking for other syndicators to provide these audio tracks. We've added *Greetings from Tucson* on Fridays. Weekends we offer a translated version of *Mucha Lucha* during our Saturday morning cartoon block and several of our weeknight sitcoms also run on the weekend. We just bought *My Wife and Kids* from Disney which becomes available in the fall of 2005." Despite all the bilingual programming, Berlamino admits Spanish advertisers haven't started using the SAP channel for their commercials.

The VP/GM also informs that she has four Hispanic on-air reporters among its staff and "lots of Hispanics working behind the scenes." The station's morning shows employ Mat Garcia, the helicopter traffic reporter, field reporter Marysol Castro, and Rosemary Gomez, the Long Island correspondent. Lolita Lopez is the nighttime newscast's reporter.

While Berlamino acknowledges the station has no way of knowing how many people are using the SAP simulcast, she does point out that WPIX provides a "10 p.m. alternative to Univision and Telemundo's 11 p.m. newscasts. The 10 p.m. news covers events in the

Hispanic community for a highly assimilated population which has been in New York a long time and speaks Spanish and English. This is not an immigrant city like Los Angeles where people don't often speak English."

When the executive starts explaining that Caption Colorado's WPIX-assigned translator is in Buenos Aires and there's lots of technology employed to transmit the scripts to Argentina and have the voice translation sent back live to New York, I know I need to speak to the company and get the inside look at how this long distance connection works. Berlamino admits at first there are technical glitches. "It's rare now more than its commonplace," she says. WPIX partners with General Motors and Pontiac to sponsor the Spanish translation for the first year, "but it doesn't cover the entire cost," adds Berlamino, explaining the on-screen broadcast carries an animated notice which reads "Gracias Pontiac for bringing us the WB News at 10 on 11." The closed caption portion of the broadcast carries a Dodge credit.

After chatting with Berlamino, who I observe is not looking at her watch to send me on my way after a half hour, but warmly chats with me for nearly an hour, I depart for several other interviews. Returning to my hotel, I call Caption Colorado in Englewood, Colorado, and speak with Lindsay Polumbus, an account executive, who walks me through the process. The first thing she tells me is that the company doesn't employ "translators, who translate the written word." It employs "interpreters because they translate the spoken word." Actually, there are three interpreters in the company's Buenos Aires office, all of whom have "neutral accents." Three interpreters are used, Polumbus explains, because "there's a lot of pressure on the spot to translate the words in real time as they're spoken. It's a simultaneous interpretation."

First step in the process is for WPIX to send a copy of the script over the Internet several hours before the 10 p.m. newscast. Then the actual audio feed of the newscast is sent to Argentina on what's called an "ISDN high-quality phone line which is transmitted through a decoder at the station. The interpreters work in a sound booth with high-quality microphones and earphones through which they hear the broadcast. When they speak into the microphone, they use their free hands to make emphasis points in the sound booth.

"Argentina is two hours ahead of New York, so it's midnight when the interpreters speak into the microphone which is connected to the same ISDN line which sends their interpretation back to the station's decoder which is hooked into the live outgoing feed to the SAP channel." While this transatlantic technology sounds complicated, in reality it works.

NY1 News, the Time Warner Cable's 24-hour all-local news channel, will have no long distance problem in reaching its Hispanic viewers in New York's five boroughs when it debuts its NY1 Noticias June 30. I've read that NY1 News is located in the famous downtown Chelsea Market, so I'm looking forward to going down there to see first-hand a television channel located in a building with food stores. It sounds very unusual. In fact, Edward Pachetti, the channel's public relations coordinator, e-mails me a warning that it may be a bit confusing finding the elevator that goes to the sixth floor newsroom, in space previously occupied by the gritty HBO series *Oz*.

The Chelsea Market is somewhat of an oddity itself, having been a Nabisco cookie factory—where the Oreo cookie, originally named the Oreo biscuit and the Oreo cream sandwich is produced in 1912—before its conversion into a retail and wholesale, and now TV network complex. Nabisco, formerly the National Biscuit Company, is established in 1898 through the merger of three companies, the first of which is formed in 1889. It departs Manhattan in 1958 for a new bakery in Fair Lawn, New Jersey, in 1958. The market's 800-foot long food concourse opens to the public in 1996. There are 28 retail businesses on the ground floor and Ed has given me the tip to look out for Ruthy's Cheesecake and then look across the corridor to the elevator to NY1 News.

While walking slowly past Amy's Bread and Buon Italia Imports and Chelsea Wholesale Flowers and Chelsea Thai, Elena's Cookies, Frank's Butcher, Hale & Hearty Soups, the Juice Factory, Sarabeth's Bakery, the Lobster Place, Souk Café, Imports from

Marrakesh, the Fat Witch Bakery, and the place with the catchiest title, the Unbagelieveable, an indoor waterfall creates a smoothly strong background sound. After looking at all these food stores, I head back in the direction I've come from, spot Ruthy's, turn to my left and there's the elevator which takes me to the network's sixth floor, 55,000-square foot facility. It's 11 a.m.

After Ed comes out to greet me, he takes me on a tour of the 10-year-old local news channel, in which Time Warner invests $30 million in renovations, including state-of-the-art digital equipment for its four studios. Before moving downtown into West Chelsea, NY1 News is headquartered uptown on 42nd Street and 10th Avenue.

In walking around the large, open-spaced news room and empty sets, I notice two things: corridors are named after famous, New York City streets: there's Broadway, Flatbush Avenue, Park Row and Woodhaven Avenue, and there's a dearth of people in view, which seems odd for a news channel which operates around the clock. Where's the hustle and action within the newsroom? I'll find the answer to this question when I learn how NY1 News and its Noticias sister will operate. When Noticias launches on June 30 as the city's exclusive Spanish news channel, it'll pattern itself on the NY1 News operation. The Spanish network will be part of Time Warner's digital tier of Hispanic services. Before meeting with Steve Paulus, NY1's senior vice president/general manager, who'll hold the same title for the Spanish sibling, Maritza Puello, hired as the executive producer for Noticias from the Fox News Channel, fills me in on how the new operation will operate as it follows the same half-hour news clock formula utilized by its Anglo parent.

"Our plan is to provide news about community issues and day-to-day life in New York. Half-hour segments are taped, so if you watch one hour, you get all the day's news," she says. Rail and road traffic reports run every 10 minutes. Live events are inserted with the anchors at the desk to provide live information. When they're not on live, the anchors are preparing for the next broadcast. With NY1

News employing 150 people in the newsroom, including anchor/producers, reporter/writers, we'll share resources, including its two live microwave trucks."

Those half-hour taped segments are the reason there's no visible energy being expended in the newsroom when I pass through: everything seen on the air is a pre-taped report.

NY1 has around 30 on-camera reporters including several who are bilingual. "We'll use these bilingual reporters, who will do two stories, one in English and a second in Spanish for us. I'll also hire a fully bilingual staff of three anchor/producers, one writer, one reporter, and two news assistants. Our operations staff will include our own and NY1 personnel. We'll shoot our own stories. If it's a big story, we'll send out a NY1 news assistant to accompany the reporter and operate the camera." Since this is a non-union shop, all the reporters operate their own videotape camera and sound equipment, setting up the camera on a stand, and then moving in front to do their report. Back at the studio, their multi-tasking includes writing, editing, and producing their stories.

By the time of the June 30 launch, Puello's hires include: anchor/producers Philip Klint, Adriana Hauser, and Adhemar Montagne; reporter Juan Manuel Benitez; writers Cristina Maldonado and Silvina Sterin-Pensel; researcher Cynthia Maldonado; and desk assistant Luz Plascencia.

While NY1 News' anchors do the weather, handling weather in Spanish for Noticias is WSI Studios, a company which provides weather graphics and a voiceover to Time Warner Cable's Tampa Bay, Florida, Bay News 9 En Español local service, launched in March of 2002 by the company's Anglo service Bay News 9. Time Warner Cable claims the Tampa Bay Spanish channel is the nation's first and only local 24-hour Spanish-language news service. So NY1 Noticias will become the second around-the-clock local Hispanic news service with its own news set within the NY1 enclave.

When I meet with Steve Paulus in his office overseeing the newsroom, he points out that the company's New York digital tier has 500,000 subscribing households, of which he estimates 100,000 are Hispanic homes. By contrast, NY1 News is available to two million subscribers.

Paulus spends 13 years with CBS' owned and operated Gotham TV station WCBS in various news positions before joining NY1 News as news director for its September 8, 1992 debut, is named vice president for news in 1993 and moves up to his current position in 1999. "The key for the Spanish operation," he tells me "is to offer New York City news in Spanish aimed at the Puerto Rican, Dominican and Mexican communities. This is a multi-cultural community and the challenge is to develop communication with all the different communities and cover all the issues that affect New York City and the issues that affect these subsets. A lead story about New York in English, will probably be the lead on NY1 Noticias. Second section stories will cover different topics. If you look at what Univision and Telemundo do, they mirror the English network affiliates to some degree. NY1 Noticias will be a mirror unto itself.

"One of our mandates for Noticias," he continues, "is not to be a crime channel. We celebrate New York, telling the good and the bad." Paulus believes the local Hispanic community benefits when it has access to local coverage. Among the beats Paulus envisions for Noticias are immigration, politics, mass transit, health care, and education, topics one may also encounter on NY1. "Our reporting," notes Paulus, "is modeled on newspapers, but we don't have as many reporters."

It expressly doesn't have any sports reporters. The channel airs a daily sports highlight segment in the morning written by someone on that shift. NY1 on the other hand, has a seven-person sports staff, a daily segment during the morning along with a nightly sports call-in show airing weeknights from 11:30 to 12:30 a.m.

As for its local news competitors, Paulus is benevolent towards WPIX's 10 p.m. news in Spanish. "It's a smart business proposal because no one is doing Spanish at 10 o'clock. I like to think we'll pull audience away from WPIX, but it'll take a while to accomplish that.

People are accustomed to news at 10 and 11 p.m., but in every other time period we win. The way the Hispanic audience is growing, Noticias could be as big or bigger than NY1 News."

One area in which both news channels will cooperate is in bundling advertising. "We'll be doing some packaging," says Joanne Tombrakos, NY1 News' director of ad sales. "There'll be lots of show sponsorship and entitlement opportunities at Noticias. She points to Sleepy's, a mattress company, a major NY1 News advertiser, sponsoring the "In the Papers" segment, which has a similar deal with the newspaper *Hoy*. "We're transferring that idea to Noticias. We're also developing Verizon, an entitlement sponsor on NY1's 'Community Calendar' segment to do the same thing on Noticias. With an entitlement, the company's name appears with the event, so you have 'Community Calendar by Verizon' or 'Traveler's Weather by General Motors.'"

By March of 2004, Noticias doubles its staff, changes the look of its set, anchor desk and on-air graphics. Maritza Puello's editorial staff now totals 16, including freelancers, from its original eight-person nucleus on launch day. Puello is now the executive editor, with Daniel DeJesus replacing her as exec producer.

My appointment with Bruce Lundvall, chief executive officer of EMI's three major American labels, Blue Note, Manhattan, and Angel, is set for 4 p.m. on a rather gloomy afternoon. The company has moved from its midtown Park Avenue location to a downtown locale at Fifth Avenue and 21st Street. When I arrive at the Bruce's office, he greets me with a serious look, informs me an emergency meeting has come up with two Washington, D.C., executives with Jazz Lines International, who are flying in to meet with him and apologizes for the delay. "I'll try to be done as soon as possible," he says, inviting me to read some of the magazines in his reception area before closing the door when the duo arrives. So I read and re-read several of the periodicals, periodically asking his executive assistant of four years, Astrid Hepner, to check on how the meeting's progressing. "It won't be too long." she tells me. Around 5 p.m. Bruce's door opens, the two men exit and he beckons me in. I've read in this morning's *New York Times* that Bruce is to be honored tomorrow with a Beacon in Jazz Award from the New School University's Jazz Program, along with Les Paul, the jazz guitarist and inventor and Jay McShann, the blues pianist.

The first thing I notice about Bruce's office are the photos on the walls of current Blue Note artists and musicians he respects, including Miles Davis, Dexter Gordon, Cassandra Wilson, Lester Young, Thelonious Monk, Lena Horne, Michel Petrucciani, and both a painting and photo of Clifford Brown. There's also a photo of comic film actor WC Fields. "Why a photo of Fields?" I ask. "You don't have to mention that," he says. "No, I'd really like to know why he's on your wall with all those famous musicians," I parry. "He's my idol, he was a great artist," Bruce explains, expressing admiration for his improvising skills and quick wit.

Although Blue Note is one of the nation's oldest and most respected jazz brands, and pop singer Norah Jones, in her debut this year wins five Grammy awards and is the hottest new name in music, I'm here to discuss Lundvall's involvement with Latin music and the after effects of his creating Havana Jam in 1979. Bruce's career dates back to 1960 when he joins Columbia Records marketing department, staying with the CBS company 21 years as vice president of marketing, vice president/general manager of the Columbia label and president in 1976 following the removal of Clive Davis for supposed personal financial transgressions. In 1982, he moves to Elektra as president of the newly created Elektra/Musician label and two years later joins EMI to revive the suspended Blue Note operation and create Manhattan, a pop imprint. In 1988, he's appointed East Coast general manager for Capitol and president of Blue Note, followed by his new CEO responsibilities in May of 2002.

"With Havana Jam taking place 26 years ago, has this bridge-crossing event been relegated to a quiet place in music history?" is my opening question to Bruce now that we're sitting next to each other on the couch across from his desk, both of us in our business attire.

"I don't think so," he responds. "I think the repercussions have perhaps been quiet but very real and very much felt," he answers. "I had signed Irakere with Chucho Valdés, Paquito D'Rivera, and Arturo Sandoval before we did Havana Jam. This was during the Carter Administration when it was okay to open a cultural passage for Cuban music. It takes a while but we're able to release two Irakere albums and Irakere arrives here to do limited tours. It causes a lot of curiosity and that's followed by Havana Jam and everything that happens subsequently. So I suppose as a sequence of events, you could trace back principally to Havana Jam, but I think there's been a long-term curiosity with Cuban culture. The Cuban Ballet was coming to America and later Orquestra Aragon and other Cuban artists came here with special visas to perform. The cumulative effect has made Cuban music a very important part of the American music scene.

"Chucho Valdés, was sort of an anomaly along with Irakere in the years following Havana Jam. Now he comes here constantly and he's revered as the new Art Tatum. Gonzalo Rubalcaba, whom I signed later, continues to be a Cuban citizen, which is highly unusual, and yet he lives in Florida and is signed directly to us. He's completely an anomaly. He's the only Cuban who's allowed to live and work in the U.S., without defecting. And then we have the commercialization of Cuban music through the Buena Vista Social Club records."

Having signed the most Cuban musicians during his career, I ask Bruce to explain the reasons for signing Irakere, Paquito D'Rivera, Chucho Valdés, Gonzalo Rubalcaba, and Rubén Blades. "Irakere is the most inventive band I've heard in years. It's a true fusion of jazz with Latin music, contemporary pop and classical music elements. I first hear Chucho with Irakere during a trip to Havana a year before Havana Jam, and I'm astonished by his playing, his arranging and his compositions. He's a major, fully formed, extraordinary musician. I sign Paquito because I'm wildly impressed by his style, his passion and his saxophone playing. He is very unhappy and trying to leave Cuba. I found out from some Cuban contacts that if he tries to leave he could be put right in jail. I thought maybe the best way for him to get out of

Cuba is to go on tour with Irakere and sort of run away. So I guess that's what he does. He ends up in Spain and then goes to America. I was still at Columbia Records and I hadn't seen him in two years when he finally comes to my office and I immediately sign him. And we release his first four albums. Gonzalo is a good example of a Cuban artist that's very well versed in all of Cuban music, classical music, and dance music. That impresses me. Since he's come to the U.S., he's integrated his music into the mainstream of jazz and his style, as a result, has actually changed a bit."

In what way has his music changed? "There's the Cuban machismo thing of playing more notes than any one else and playing harder, faster, louder, higher. It's the Cuban sense of playing. That's out of his music now; there's a lot of space and delicacy and a lot of depth and it's still Cuban. On the other hand, Chucho is a great virtuoso player. He plays with such intensity and speed, and lots of notes in a brilliant technical manner. And he's broadened his style tremendously, using lots of standards and other influences. These two are very opposite now in terms of their approach to playing.

"I got to know Rubén Blades when he's with the Fania All Stars and we record two albums with the band for Columbia. And by the time I leave to go with Elektra, we've become friends and we talk about a record he wants to do called *Buscando America* (*Discovering America*), which really has to do with the disappearance of people in Chile and all through Latin America where there are reigns of terror going on. So I sign him and he takes the entire Elektra staff through the album cut by cut. It's all in Spanish and he explains the meaning of each song and people are in tears at the end of the meeting. When the album comes out in 1983, he's compared to Jackson Browne and Bob Dylan."

Would he ever do another Havana Jam? "You don't need to do it now because there's a jazz festival every year in Havana and American artists go there and play with Cuban artists. Havana Jam was an amazing moment because at that time nothing of that sort was going on. Now, would that be an event today? I suppose if you did it right, but then it might be too commercial."

Lundvall doesn't surprise me when he says that the nation's Hispanic population, now numbering an estimated 37 million persons, hasn't made a major impact on the sale of Blue Note's Latin releases, since the majority of Latino immigrants have no connection in their native lands to jazz. The increase, he points out is in the Latin pop area, citing Enrique Iglesias, Gloria Estefan, Jennifer Lopez, Marc Anthony, and Ricky Martin, as the kinds of "integrated artists" who are benefiting.

Among the Latin jazz artists Blue Note releases in addition to Valdés and Rubalcaba are Bebo Valdés, Chucho's father, Canadian flautist/soprano saxophonist Jane Bunnett "who has built her career on integrating her music with Cuban artists in Havana," the late blind pianist Frank Emilio and Los Van Van, the popular dance band released on the Metro Blue label "We also released the *Calle 54* film soundtrack which embraces the entire culture of Cuban and Latin jazz," Lundvall points out, adding: "The film should have been in theaters a lot longer than it was."

What, in his opinion, does the American record industry need to do to stimulate sales of Latin jazz records? His mind is obviously focused exclusively on Cuban musicians rather than the specific question when he answers: "The problem with Cuban artists particularly," he begins, "is they really can't come here and play that easily because of the U.S. embargo. The real issue seems to be if you're a booking agent or manager, you're subject to all the politics of the day. Very recently Chucho was not allowed to come here because of visa problems. He's a Cuban national and if there's some issue going on in the government that we may or may not know about, issues like this can lead to revoked visas, causing concert dates to be cancelled. So you can imagine how frustrating that is for a manager of booking agent who has to cancel dates." Or a record company seeking to utilize personal appearances to promote that artist's new or current release.

Lundvall admits being envious of Sony with its roster of crossover artists Marc Anthony, Ricky Martin, and Jennifer Lopez. "I was beside myself because they're all on Sony. I though where is EMI? How did we miss out?"

Does record industry veteran Lundvall sense the Latin pop crossover phenomenon is peaking? "I bet not," he replies, "because some other artist will pop up. I think there are going to be a lot of artists that live here, absorb this culture and can sing in Spanish and English. And there's a huge potential for that music."

There's almost a fanatical interest among Latinos for professional baseball, as anyone who regularly follows the sport knows, a result of the increase in Hispanic players, many of whom are the superstars of the sport. The super super of the superstars is Alex Rodriguez, known affectionately as "A-Rod," signed by the Texas Rangers in 2003 to a record-shattering $252-million, 10-year contract to play third base. In 2004, the Rangers trade him and his huge salary to the New York Yankees, where he'll play second base.

So on a sunny morning I head to the Office of the Commissioner of Baseball (who's Bud Selig) to chat with Matthew Gould, manager of media relations for Major League Baseball (MLB), in the company's Park Avenue headquarters to gain some understanding about baseball's historic love affair with Hispanic athletes.

The Dominican Republic provides baseball with the most players over the years and I want to know if this is still the case. "Yes it is," Gould responds, handing me the most recent breakout report of foreign players, which lists the Dominican Republic leading all Latin nations with 79 players, followed by Puerto Rico with 38 and Venezuela with 37 as of opening day rosters. One year later, the Dominican is represented by 79 players, followed by 45 from Venezuela and 36 from Puerto Rico, according to the commissioner's office.

Why is the Dominican always the leading Latin nation feeding players into MLB? "There's a passionate fan base there as well as very talented players like Sammy Sosa (the Chicago Cubs homerun hitting phenomenon) and Miguel Tejada (the Baltimore Orioles 2002 American League's most valuable player)."

Of baseball's 30 teams, the hapless Montreal Expos lead all teams with 14 players, followed by the Baltimore Orioles with 12, while 11 Latinos grace the lineups of the Texas Rangers, Los Angeles Dodgers, and San Francisco Giants.

Overall, among the 30 teams, 230 players are born outside the U.S., representing 16 foreign countries and Puerto Rico. The other Latin nations following the three aforementioned leaders sending players to the pros are Mexico (17), Cuba (10), Panama (7), Colombia (3), and Nicaragua (2). The commissioner's report for 2004 reveals a slight decline in foreign-born players: in addition to the aforementioned three leaders, the Dominican Republic, Venezuela and Puerto Rico, Mexico is represented by 16, Cuba by 9, Panama by six, Colombia by 3 and the Nicaragua Antilles by one.

The minor leagues over the decades have a larger number of Hispanics, which portends additional players possibly moving up the ladder to the majors, with the Dominican Republic providing 1,437, an astonishing number to lead by a very wide margin the 13 other Latin countries which include alphabetically Argentina (1), Brazil (7), Colombia (38), Costa Rica (2), Cuba (20), Curacao (13), Ecuador (2), El Salvador (2), Honduras (2), Mexico (95), Nicaragua (36), Panama (60), and Puerto Rico (130). Overall, 32 nations are home to 2,851 players in the minor leagues.

Of the 30 major league teams, 12 provide local Spanish radio coverage for the Arizona Diamondbacks, Colorado Rockies, Florida Marlins, Houston Expos, Los Angeles Dodgers, New York Mets and Yankees, Anaheim Angels, Boston Red Sox, Seattle Mariners, Tampa Bay Devil Rays, and Texas Rangers. Television really does a job providing Hispanic coverage. Major league clubs license 700 plus local broadcasts in Spanish via the secondary audio program (SAP) channel on stereo TVs. More than 130 local games from the New York Mets, Milwaukee Brewers, San Diego Padres and Arizona Diamondbacks are seen on Spanish-language networks in their locales. ESPN's Sunday night feature called *Deportes*, simulcasts in Spanish all of the 26 nationally televised "Games of the Week" covered by ESPN.

Additionally, MLB International broadcasts more than 30 games per week into Latin markets in Central America, South America and the Caribbean, as part of its pact with more than 50 overseas broadcasters which transmit games to 224 nations around the world.

So baseball is truly an international favorite activity. But how is the nation's foraging Hispanic population impacting the game's fan base and ticket sales? "We definitely see growth in our Latin fan base," says Gould. "We were just in Mexico City this past March where the Dodgers–Mets played two exhibition games and we nearly doubled our attendance there." In 1996, MLB begins playing its games in foreign countries. The Mets play San Diego three regular season games in Monterrey, Mexico. In 1999, exhibition games take place between the Mets and Montreal twice in Santo Domingo, and Baltimore versus the Cuban national team in Havana, while Colorado meets San Diego in a regular season match in Monterrey. In 2000, exhibition games pair Boston versus Houston twice in Santo Domingo; Arizona versus Anaheim in Hermosillo, Mexico; and Atlanta versus Tampa Bay twice in Caracas, Venezuela.

Things start to expand in 2001, with nine games in Latin countries, eight of which are exhibitions. Cleveland plays two with Houston in Valencia, Venezuela; Colorado plays San Diego in Culiacan, Mexico; Pittsburgh plays Tampa Bay twice in Mexico City; Oakland plays Arizona in Hermosillo, Mexico; Toronto meets Texas in an exhibition and the lone regular season game in San Juan. The year 2002 sees one game outside the U.S.: San Diego versus Arizona in an exhibition in Hermosillo.

The year 2003 is the breakout year, with 25 games outside Mainland U.S. While the Mets meet the Dodgers in two exhibitions in Mexico City, the financially ailing and fan-depleted Montreal Expos schedule 23 regular season games in San Juan, which becomes its second home to games against the Mets, Atlanta Braves, Cincinnati Reds, Anaheim Angels, Texas Rangers, Florida Marlins, and Chicago Cubs.

Since 1999, Major League Baseball opens its season outside the continental U.S., with the 2001 opener taking place in San Juan,

Puerto Rico, between the Toronto Blue Jays and the Texas Rangers. Exhibition games are also played in Venezuela and Mexico, with fans in the Dominican Republic, Mexico, Puerto Rico, and Venezuela, taking part in the voting for the 2001 All Star game.

During April of 2001, which MLB labels "Month of the Americas" in honor of baseball's Latin heritage, spring training exhibition games are played in Valencia, Venezuela, between the Cleveland Indians and Houston Astros; and in three Mexican cities, Culiacan between the San Diego Padres and the Colorado Rockies; Mexico City between the Pittsburgh Pirates and Tampa Bay Devil Rays, and Hermosillo between the Arizona Diamondbacks and the Oakland A's.

The Cleveland–Houston contest is the second consecutive MLB series in Venezuela; the Boston Braves versus the Devil Rays having played in Caracas in 2000. The San Diego–Colorado game marks the debut of American pro baseball in the Mexican city of Culiacan, while the Tampa Bay–Pittsburgh contest marks the first MLB games in Mexico City in 20 years. For the Diamondbacks, it's the fourth straight year the team travels to Hermosillo for an exhibition game.

What's the long-term effect of playing games outside the U.S.? "People become fans," Gould responds. "And they can watch the regular season games we broadcast on television, they buy products advertised, maybe even attend the games we bring to their country, or maybe if they come to the States, they'll come to the games here as well."

As far as building audience for games carried on Spanish radio and TV, Gould says, "We definitely think there's been an increase in the audience foundation, which goes along with the increase in the success of the Latin players like Sammy Sosa, Manny Ramirez, Juan Gonzalez, Ivan Rodriguez, Pedro Martinez, Miguel Tejada, and Magglio Ordonez."

When I ask Matthew who the first Hispanic big leaguers are, he does some research which claims Colombia's Luis Manuel Castro is the pioneer in 1902 with the Philadelphia Athletics, followed in 1911 by Cuba's Rafael Almeida and Armando Marsans with the Cincinnati Reds. Then there's a time lag until 1933 when Mexico's Mel Almada joins the Boston Red Sox; Venezuela's Alejandro Carrasquel becomes a Washington Senator in 1939; Puerto Rico's Hiram Bithorn joins the Chicago Cubs in 1942, and Venezuela's Alfonso "Chico" Carrasquel signs with the Chicago White Sox in 1950. Ten years after World War II ends in 1945, Panama's Hector Lopez joins the Kansas City Athletics and Humberto Robinson becomes a Milwaukee Brave in 1955; one year later, the Dominican's Osvaldo Virgil is added to the New York Giants roster and another Venezuelan, Luis Aparicio, signs with the Chicago White Sox.

There's another span of blank years until 1976 when Nicaragua's Dennis Martinez joins the Baltimore Orioles; Honduras' Gerald Young becomes a Houston Astros in 1987; Curacao's Hensley Meulens becomes a New York Yankee in 1990; Belize's Chito Martinez becomes a Baltimore Oriole in 1991 and Aruba's Gene Kingsale is added to the Orioles in 1996. After '96, Cuban players begin arriving after defecting or establishing residences in another country like Costa Rica or the Dominican Republic, which allows them to sign as a free agent. "If they establish residency in the U.S.," Gould points out, "they are subject to our rule 4 draft, which is basically our amateur draft where college players and anyone who resides in the U.S., or a U.S. territory or Canada is subject to the draft. They can't just sign a free agent contract."

Hispanic team managers? "The first one is believed to be Al Lopez with the Cleveland Indians in 1951," says Gould. In 2003, Felipe Alou manages the San Francisco Giants; Tony Pena the Kansas City Royals and Carlos Tosca the Toronto Blue Jays. Ozzie Guillen joins the list in 2004 with the Chicago White Sox, after starting his playing career in 1985 with the White Sox, Baltimore Orioles, Boston Braves, and Tampa Bay Devil Rays in 2000. He is the first Venezuelan to manage a major league team. One year later, with the White Sox leading the central division of the American League in May, 41-year-old

Guillen's contract option is picked up for 2006, is extended two years and includes an option for the 2009 season.

The first Hispanic umpire to work in the Major Leagues is Armando Rodriguez, assigned to the American league in 1974, notes Gould, adding: "Current Hispanic umpires include Laz Diaz, Angel Hernandez and Alfonso Marquez."

In 1951, White Sox shortstop Chico Carrasquel becomes the first Latino to start in an All Star game and in his first time at bat, singles off Robin Roberts, the Philadelphia Phillies pitcher.

In 1977, Yankee pitcher Mike Torres becomes the first Mexican American to win a World Series game. He accomplishes this against the Los Angeles Dodgers on their home field, according to Roger Kahn's excellent book about the 1978 World Series winning Yankees, *October Men.*

History is also made in 2003 when Arturo "Arte" Moreno, a Phoenix outdoor advertising executive turned billionaire, becomes the first Latin owner of a major league team, the Anaheim Angels, acquired for $183.5 million from the Walt Disney Company. And in a move to make his an "L.A." team, and attract Southern California fans to a "major market" team, Moreno drops Anaheim from its name in 2004.

Regarding Latino players, Gould notes, "The number of foreign-born players has consistently been rising since we started compiling numbers in 1997." Over the years, the broadening number of Latino ballplayers specifically, provides an international flavor to the game, and a growing number of millionaires whose Spanish last names are no longer hard to pronounce.

One year later, while watching a Food Network special on baseball stadium food, the impact of Hispanics on the game is reflected among the vittles offered at a number of stadiums. Pro Player Field, home in Miami to the Florida Marlins, has a strong emphasis on Latin food, with a special area where a salsa band adds its infectious rhythms for dancers while others feast on the spicy offerings. The program names the venue as having the best spicy food.

As if that's not enough Latin recognition, the Marlin's official tune for the new season is the Spanish *Vienen Al Son* by Rey Ruiz. The Houston Astros' Minute Maid Park is named stadium with the best Tex-Mex food. And outside the Boston Red Sox's venerable Fenway Park, former Cuban star Luis Tiant, operates a stand which specializes in a legendary Cuban sandwich.

The Los Angeles Dodgers' eponymous named stadium is lauded for its famous Dodger dogs rather than it's Mexican favorites. Totally missing from the national report is the San Diego Padres longtime food connection with Hispanics from Tijuana who cross the border in special busses, and mingle at special Latino food booths along with hometown Hispanics.

Great restaurants aside, one of the joys of being in Manhattan is that it's such a wonderful place to walk from one appointment to the next. And that's the situation in which Major League Baseball and my next appointment at Nielsen Media Research are a few buildings apart. Nielsen is the dominant—and only—surveyor of public television viewing, and Arbitron, is the equally powerful radio ratings survey source, with both companies since the 1980s caught in the middle of the exploding Hispanic population which creates a conflagration between English-language broadcasters and Spanish-language competitors. It's an explosion I first notice in Los Angeles where Spanish radio stations are emerging as the city's most popular and certain newscasts on Univision's local station are beating the Anglo network affiliates.

Ratings are one of the most acrimonious areas of show business to begin with, and since the emergence of large Latino populations in sundry major U.S. cities, nasty rifts emerge between the Anglo stations who claim Nielsen surveys are inaccurately giving the Spanish TV stations larger viewing audiences which diminishing their own ratings power. These disputes pitting the English versus Spanish broadcasters far exceed the chasm between Spanish-language record companies' desires for getting new records played and what Spanish radio stations choose to put on their playlists.

In TV, the two cultural mediums do not coexist as friendly neighbors, and that's the reason I'm headed next to Nielsen to learn what the company, part of the Dutch VNU media empire, is doing to bring harmony—if that's possible—to a contentious situation, and a sense of justice to the charges lobbed against its technology used in both languages. Ratings results are fraught with political and economic issues and consequences, and that's why the radio and TV ratings services are under pressure to right industry perceptions and beliefs.

The person I'm going to meet with at Nielsen is Jack Loftus, senior vice president of corporate communications, the former respected television editor at *Weekly Variety* and former editor of the biweekly *Television/Radio Age*, to whom I report when I'm that magazine's Los Angeles correspondent. When I arrive at the Nielsen's office building, getting entry requires going through a complete September 11 terrorist examination. It's the only time during all my New York interviews that my bag carrying my tape recorder, pad, and pens is searched, I have to fill out a form listing who I'm going to meet and then I wait until some representative from Nielsen comes down to the lobby to escort me up in the elevator. Its almost two years after the World Trade Center Twin Tower debacle, and the security mood at this office building is professionally tense and on the alert for suspicious people and their belongings.

In addition to Loftus, I also chat with Karen Plount, the vice president of Hispanic Services, about how Nielsen is addressing the needs and concerns of Hispanic broadcasters who are concerned that national advertisers see the full picture of how important the Hispanic market has become.

In addition to its general market service, the Nielsen Station Index (NSI), which includes Hispanic viewers, the company also services Hispanic TV with its own national daily Nielsen Hispanic Television Index (NHTI) and its local Nielsen Hispanic Television Stations Index (NHSI). It's obvious Nielsen faces several major problems: how to measure this targeted audience in the company's general market and separately specific Hispanic surveys, defining who's watching by language preference within the home environment and how to increase the number of families participating in the survey, especially since newly arrived immigrants have never heard of Nielsen and its TV ratings. General market station managers feel Nielsen is been overemphasizing Spanish-language proponents to the detriment of English-speaking viewers.

Loftus, like Matthew Gould at Major League Baseball, comes prepared with copious statistics, policy statements and plans for dealing with the Hispanic market. In assessing Nielsen's 2003 statistics for the two worlds of television—the top 10 general markets and how they compare with the top 10 Hispanic cities—some marked differences emerge. The nation's top 10 general markets by rank and their number of TV homes are New York (7,282,320), Los Angeles (5,318,040), Chicago (3,351,330), Philadelphia (2,830,470), San Francisco (2,436,220), Boston (2,353,500), Dallas/Ft.Worth (2,195,540), Washington, D.C. (2,169,230), Atlanta (1,971,180), and Detroit (1,899,910). That's a total of 31,807,740 TV homes.

The Hispanic market listings are different in several ways. Los Angeles and New York swap the top two positions, Chicago is in fifth place not third, Dallas/Ft. Worth is ranked sixth, not seventh. Miami/Ft. Lauderdale, plus five other cities on this list, are not included in the general market listings. So the top 10 Latino cities and their TV households are Los Angeles (1,585,390), New York (1,100,030), Miami/Ft. Lauderdale (550,190), Houston (399,220), Chicago (384,140), Dallas/Ft. Worth (324,120), San Antonio (317,810), San Francisco/Oakland/San Jose (317,200), Phoenix (246,160), and Brownsville, McAllen, Harlingen, Texas (232,270). Cumulatively, that's 5,456,530 TV homes.

Although Nielsen plans introducing a new research system, the Local People Meter overnight service during the next three years in the nation's top 10 TV markets, it will not incorporate Hispanic measurements into the National People Meter system until 2006. Local People Meters, already in operation in Boston, will replace the current combination of meters and diaries in the first 10 cities.

While the general market survey represents all television stations, Spanish-language station sell advertising based primarily on the Spanish sample which focuses on Spanish-language viewing. This is the world of multiple surveys in which Nielsen exists, a world neophytes may find foreboding. A core element Nielsen is working on is to provide what Susan D. Whiting, Nielsen's president/CEO calls "a unified base for planning and buying of all national television media, including Spanish-language television, into the general market sample by 2005."

The present National People Meter sample of around 5,000 households will be expanded to nearly 10,000 homes, of which 1,000 will represent Hispanic households. This number, Whiting says during a national client meeting in Phoenix earlier in March, "will be sufficient to provide stable audience estimates for the various Hispanic programmers" (meaning TV networks).

To accomplish the goal of reflecting the nation's changing demographics, Nielsen will add what it calls "weighting," or categorizing a population's characteristics, to the National People Meter sample starting this September. Since February of 2002, the company has used subsets of Spanish-speaking people to define the Los Angeles market, notably people who mostly or only speak Spanish, are bilingual or speak mostly or only English. When Nielsen begins introducing its Local People Meter service in the top 10 markets, the company will include these homes, on a weighted basis, into its national sample, starting with the 2004–'05 season.

In addition to this national project, Nielsen also employs Boston as the test market since last year for its Local People Meter technology. Next year, the company will add Los Angeles, New York, Chicago and San Francisco, with Philadelphia, Washington, D.C., Detroit, Dallas/Ft. Worth joining in 2005 and Atlanta coming on board in 2006.

In addition to switching technology from diaries and meters to exclusive electronic meters, Nielsen is also working with Arbitron in its development of a Portable People Meter which can be used outside the home.

On a more current basis, Karen Plount, the Hispanic services VP, talking to me from the phone in her office, indicates the company is increasing "its national Hispanic sample this year by 25 percent. So we're going from an 800 people meter sample to a 1,000 sample, and in Los Angeles, where we have a 200 People Meter sample, we're going to a 250 sample this year." In New York, the company uses meters to measure households and diaries to measure people. In fact, dual survey methods are in use in a number of markets, Plount explains. "L.A. is a people meter service while New York, Chicago, Miami and San Antonio are meter/diaries. The remainder of our NHSI markets are diary only."

With both a general market and Hispanic survey, I ask Plount to explain how they differ. Nielsen has been providing a Spanish-language service since 1992 in New York and then adds Los Angeles two years later. "Our general market samples (the NSI or Nielsen Station Index) report both Spanish and English stations, or what the whole market is viewing. In our NHSI (Nielsen Hispanic Station Index), we define homes on five tiers: homes that speak only Spanish, mostly Spanish, Spanish–English equally, mostly English and English only. And we weigh these language groups so we get the right proportion by language. Starting this year, our general market reports are now weighted by language as well."

The growing number of mixed-heritage Hispanics underscores the complexity of finding the proper weighting mix. According to the 2000 Census, among the seven million people who belong to more than one race, Hispanics account for six percent of the multiracials. Additionally, in its story on new Hispanics in America, the April 2004 *Hispanic* Magazine quotes the Tomás Rivera Policy Institute at the University of Southern California as projecting that "over 52 percent of the grandchildren of Latin immigrants—or the third generation within that family—will intermarry someone who is not Hispanic."

How does Nielsen deal with a Hispanic community which is so split by different cultures, and does that create a problem in getting these people to participate in the sample? Explains Plount: "We've been using bilingual phone surveyors for a long time. You have to make sure that your translators are using words that are generally understood. If you don't, you can end up using a word that means something different to the different cultures. Now, we hire people from the area in which we're recruiting, so that works out well because they go to the door to recruit people from the same culture as they are."

In dealing with the general market sample, there are several problems in lining up Hispanic participants. Plount stresses that while the goal is "to have a representative sample of all types of homes in the market in the right proportion, Hispanics cooperate at a lower rate in general and Spanish-language dominants at an even lower rate." Why is that? "It may be trust of who's at the door, the procedures you use to get them to cooperate, including what they get paid, and the language you approach them in which has a lot to do with it as well." When I ask her what people get paid to fill in diaries or use meters, she defers to Loftus, noting remuneration "is not going to change your standard of living. Generally I consider it proprietary."

So when the discussion switches over to Jack, in white shirt and tie in his spacious office, he is a goldmine of helpful information, including "$5 a week for a diary home and for a metered home, a couple hundred dollars a quarter." He also provides historical perspective to Nielsen's rating services.

Under the guise of the general market service are two categories, he explains: the National People Meter service using 5,000 metered homes which measure viewing of broadcast and cable networks and syndicated programs, and the local meter and diary services that cover the nation's 210 television market. The national service provides overnight information from its 5,000 households which broadcasters and advertisers scour each morning. This is also the data the television industry lives on during the four so-called sweeps periods of November, February, May, and July, when it sets its advertising rates.

"Ten years ago, Univision and Telemundo tell us they need a separate measurement because the existing sample in cities like Chicago is not big enough for them to pull out Spanish-language people and sell advertising on that figure. They feel the sample would be indicative of just the general market and not of the various demographics like Spanish-language dominant or bilinguals or Mexican, Cuban, and other cultural groups. So we start a Spanish service, first in Los Angeles as the test market, using the same People Meter methodology we use to collect national data, but not the same methodology we use to collect local data, and it works. Univision and Telemundo like it, so we roll it out as a national service. We have between 800 and 1,000 metered Hispanic homes representing the entire U.S."

Conflicts and friction between Anglo and Hispanic broadcasters begin to emerge as the nation's Hispanic population grows. Notes Loftus: "As more Hispanics come into the marketplace over the past 10 years, their viewing of Spanish-language stations begins to show up more and more in both our Hispanic and general market samples. You begin to see sizable dents in the general market station audiences, with viewers moving over to Spanish-language television. Three years ago, the Spanish stations begin looking at the general market ratings books and begin to say, 'we're doing pretty good in the general market ratings, especially in the major markets,' so that's where they want to see more of our focus.

"In Miami and Los Angeles, for example, among adults 18-to-34, citing one demographic group, a Spanish-language station would outperform an English-language station. Anglo stations take notice of this change, and Spanish media tells us our sample should more accurately represent the composition of the marketplace in terms of specific demographic breakouts, because we both know that language has a major influence on what people watch on television. A household that speaks mostly or only Spanish has viewing habits that are different from a household that speaks mostly or only English. So because we know that, we make adjustments to our sample and our recruiting to match the changing population, and we began to see some complaints from the English-language stations.

"So a few years ago, we introduce two procedures into the way we recruit homes in the general market sample in Los Angeles and New York. We began bringing homes into the sample in conformity with where the areas where the sample is most out of whack. It's called structured prioritization."

What do you mean by out of whack? "That's when the characteristics of the sample don't conform to the population you're trying to measure. Let's say we're under represented in homes where Spanish is mostly or only spoken, and that's where the sample is out of conformity with the universe, so the person in the field prioritizes those homes first. It could be homes with cable, or homes with working women or homes with children. You pick your category to prioritize.

"The other thing we do as we began to recruit homes, is look at the composition of our samples in the general marketplace. Years ago, when we recruit a home in Los Angeles, for example, we knock on the door and said 'we're from Nielsen' and they said 'yes or no.' And in that random sampling, our survey reflects a category called 'Hispanic.' But it doesn't reflect whether or not that category of Hispanic is mostly or only English, bilingual or mostly or only Spanish. So the sampling does not conform to the language strata. Now it does. As you look at how we measure general market television, you find that in trying to conform the sample to the universe of people under the category of Hispanic who speak mostly or only Spanish, you're getting a lot of people who are watching Univision and Telemundo and other Spanish-language television. Anglo stations start asking, 'Where did my audience go? What's wrong with the sample?' Well, the sample is better reflecting the Hispanic population in Los Angeles and New York in terms of language spoken in the home." And that is what's causing "all the brouhaha in the general market research category."

When a family signs up to be a Nielsen home, how long are they committed to be part of the sampling? "For a diary, it's one week. For a set metered household, it's five years and for a People Meter home, it's two years. With the diary, which is the oldest form, people write down what time, station and program they are watching. The meter is attached to the television set and tells us if the set is turned on, the time, the channel and what program is watched or tuned. Tuned is the word we use. But we don't know who's watching. So every night between 3 and 5 a.m. those meters phone in to our technical operations center in Dunedin, Florida, outside Tampa, the tuning status of those samples in 60 metered markets, including L.A. and New York. During the four sweeps periods, we send diaries to different people in those same markets. We ask them to fill out information for one week and tell us what they watch. That's where we get our demographic information. You combine the demographic information from the diary with the tuning information from the meter and report the total data.

"The new People Meter is also used for a national audience measurement and will be used for local measurement as well. This is a remote attachment to the set tuning meter which allows people to press a button to say they're in the audience and watching a specific channel." It fills in the void of the set tuning meter which does not identify who is watching. "We put the two pieces of information together and every night when that meter calls in to Dunedin, it brings in both the tuning information and who is watching as well. Everyone in the home is given a button number. Press your number and the meter recognizes you're in the room watching television."

During 2002, Boston becomes the test market for the Local People Meter technology. First, Loftus says, "We call it a demonstration market as opposed to a test market because we know the People Meter works. So we use a diary panel (of several thousand people) and also a set meter panel (400 homes) like we have in 55 other markets and then we put in our People Meter panel, first in a couple of hundred homes, then 400 and then 600 homes and we run the data in parallel for one year.

"At the end of the year, we shut off the diaries and set meters and rely on People Meters for the audience data. That's when we announce plans to use People Meters for local TV audience measurement in the top 10 markets as the only source for collecting viewing data. We're not sure whether we'll be introducing People Meters for Hispanics in the local markets. They are used with Hispanics for the general market service." The Local People Meters provide continuous information which advertisers can use to make programming decisions with, rather than waiting for the sweeps periods to obtain demographic ratings.

While it may seem that Nielsen has the nation wired, make way for yet another device, the Portable People Meter (PPM). It's a technology jointly being tested by Nielsen and Arbitron in Philadelphia. It's different from Nielsen's People Meter, Loftus explains, "in that it picks up audio from both encoded television and radio signals. It reads those codes being received by the meter that people wear and take with them wherever they go."

For the first time, a device is being tested that records what a person is watching on a TV screen outside the home, creating the potential for a mobile survey audience in all kinds of locations. The Philadelphia test is drawing criticism from the Hispanic community which claims Philadelphia, which is not a major Hispanic TV market, is the wrong city to gauge how Latinos will respond to this technology.

Responds Loftus: "That's a fair criticism if that was our intent. Our intent is to make sure the technology works and then the next level is recruiting people to participate, and at this point, different recruiting techniques are required for different demographic groups."

Following testing in Philadelphia and Houston of the PPM, Nielsen in March of '06, said it will not jointly develop the technology with Arbitron as the single national ratings source for all of broadcasting. Nielsen indicated it doesn't believe PPMs are the correct way to measure TV viewership, claiming early testing produced larger TV viewing than it could explain. Shortly thereafter, Arbitron announces it will bow PPMs in the top 50 U.S. markets, starting in July of '06 with Houston. It will then bring the technology to the top 10 American cities by October 2008, with the remainder by October 2010.

Just about the time I'm in New York, the issue of Nielsen's Hispanic representation in the general market survey surfaces in Los Angeles, where the February local ratings results indicate boosts for Spanish TV to the detriment of English-language programming. Since February of 2002, Nielsen successfully uses subsets of Spanish-speaking viewers to define the overall L.A. audience. This could play a role in Univision's KMEX, for example, emerging the winner in the 11 p.m. news battles with the network affiliates in the 18 to 49 age category. Last year, the station is third in this demographic. And in the 25- to 54-year-old category, KMEX sees a 55 percent increase while rival KVEA, the Telemundo/NBC station, has a 10 percent increase among those viewers.

NBC, in a major seven-year deal, signs with Nielsen for audience measurement services for its broadcast and cable television properties including Telemundo and its 13 owned TV stations. Nielsen claims it is the most comprehensive media research agreement of its kind. As part of the deal, NBC will support the expansion of Nielsen's national People Meter survey from 5,000 to nearly 10,000 homes. NBC is also going to implement Nielsen's new digital encoding methodology for generating TV ratings, the Active/Passive metering system, set to be introduced in 2004. The A/P Meter will identify programs, stations and networks via electronic codes embedded in programs and received in sample homes, Anglo and Hispanic alike.

In the months to come, however, NBC will test its relationship with Nielsen by challenging its methodology and charging too much Hispanic representation is the reason for the overall drop in broadcast network primetime viewing. In October, Nielsen notifies TV officials that its data shows men 18 to 34 are watching primetime shows between 8 to 12 percent less than they did last year. Nielsen says it first notices the drop in July during pre-season NFL games. Then in September, when the networks launch their new season shows, they start complaining when these programs don't earn the ratings figures they anticipate. In November, NBC's research president Alan Wurtzel claims the decline is based on Nielsen's push to increase its Hispanic representation by adding more 18- to 34-year-old Latino males to its sample of 5,000 TV homes. Wurtzel claims that while adding more Hispanics makes the sample more representative of the population, these new viewers do not watch as much TV as members of other demographic groups do.

NBC claims Hispanic men in the spring represent 74 percent of the total universe of 11.8 million Hispanic males, and that by October the number rises to 94 percent. It also asserts the viewing decline among Hispanic males 18-to-34 drops from an average of 60 minutes per day to 47 minutes, whereas during the first two weeks of last season, overall viewing among all men in the same age category is 56 minutes a day which drops to 54 minutes this year. Drawn into the numbers imbroglio, Loftus concedes the male Hispanic sample may be a factor, along with other issues, in the decline of overall male viewership.

This matter of the lost legion of male viewers fades from the headlines in 2004 as the Local People Meter, the digital era Active/Passive meter and audience weighting become hot ticket subjects, especially in March. That's when Nielsen announces a delay in phasing in the A/P Meter, claiming the early model is unable to measure viewing of digital video recorders like TiVo. So the introduction is now set for a mid-2005 phase-in.

Nielsen also announces the delay in introducing Local People Meters in Los Angeles and Chicago, while going ahead with its New York City launch in April. The company says it's holding back the two city introduction because of concerns that its samples correctly reflect the demographic composure of these markets. Los Angeles is now pegged for a July bow from its original March start, while Chicago is now scheduled for August from its June debut.

In commenting on this matter, Loftus wards off criticism from broadcasters, including News Corp., which owns the Fox Television Network, whose chairman, Lachlan Murdoch (son of owner Rupert Murdoch), issues a statement of concern. The TV network chieftain claims the People Meters may "undercount viewership by as much as 25 percent." Loftus counters the company backs the quality of the New York sample, but admits concern about quality issues in the other two cities. Loftus also stresses that the Local People Meter technology and procedures are the same used by the company for its national ratings sample, which is not under fire. The use of weighting to improve its audience ratings databases, additionally generates a firestorm from a report by the Media Ratings Council which believes weighing ratings by households, rather than by individuals, has serious shortcomings. Many Hispanic households are not homogeneous at all, with older members speaking Spanish, their younger children speaking English and some members switching back and forth.

The switchover from paper diaries sent in four times a year to Nielsen's data collection center in Central Florida to Local People Meters generates such a flurry of disapproval that it becomes the company's largest crisis since it begins measuring television ratings in 1950.

One month later, in April, a firestorm of additional criticism from a number of different organizations, including lawmakers and advocacy groups joins the Fox Television Group in opposing the new technology. The public outcry prompts Nielsen to halt the New York debut. In a reversal of its plan to bow the new technology in New York April 8, Nielsen now sets the debut for June 3. The company responds to a request for an audit of its LPM system by creating a task force of industry and community leaders to study the complaints and guarantee that all viewers are counted correctly.

Among the diverse organizations and individuals in opposition to the New York introduction are the National Association of Broadcasters, the National Association for the Advancement of Colored People (which claims the LPM also undercount African-Americans), the Hispanic Congressional Caucus, the Hispanic

Federation and the National Hispanic Media Coalition. Politicians also see the advantage of being part of the public outcry and media blitz. They range from a majority of the New York City Council, the New York state legislature to members of Congress, including New York Senator Hillary Rodham Clinton, Michigan Representative John Dingell, Massachusetts Representative Ed Markey, California Representative Hilda Solis, and Texas Representative Charles Gonzalez.

Their collective concern for an external audit of the LPM technology is countered by Nielsen president Susan Whiting who states its audience measurement services "do not undercount Latin viewers."

Nielsen makes a major public pronouncement to the TV industry in a two-page ad titled "Everyone Counts" in the April 12 issue of *TelevisionWeek*, stating its position on Hispanic television ratings and its conclusions about a National Hispanic Media Council report on Latin TV it commissions by the research firm of Rincon & Associates. On the first page, Nielsen makes these points about its ratings history:

"It beings measuring TV audiences in 1950. It measures all Hispanic viewing on both English- and Spanish-language TV. It begins its separate Hispanic TV viewing People Meter ratings service in 1992 and uses People meters to measure Hispanic viewing nationally. It has a Local People Meter survey in Los Angeles as a service to Spanish-language media. It uses language spoken in the home to ensure that all Hispanics are represented accurately and then weighs these samples to ensure that both Spanish and English speakers are represented fairly. Its measurement services are audited annually by an independent accounting firm and accredited by the industry-supported Media Rating Council."

On the second page, the company offers "facts about the National Hispanic Media Council's Report on Latino TV": "The NHMC is a public interest group that promotes diversity in the TV industry. Its study was conducted by Rincon & Associates, which did not claim to have any expertise about how TV ratings are collected, processed, and reported. Rincon conducted a phone survey of Latinos in Los Angeles, Miami, New York, and San Antonio. This is not a representative sample of Latino households in the entire U.S. Rincon relied on listed phone numbers in four markets, thus substantially excluding Latinos with unlisted numbers or all Latinos with no telephones. Fewer than one in nine Latinos identified for sampling agreed to participate in the first wave of the phone survey, while only one in 50 participated in the second and third waves of interviews. By Rincon's own admission, it over sampled Latinos who watch a lot of TV and under sampled Latinos who don't watch a lot of TV. By its own admission, Rincon began the study with a built-in bias that the Nielsen TV ratings undercount Latino audiences."

Nevertheless, Nielsen's bowing to pressure to delay the New York debut and study the technology, produces a full page ad in the *New York Times* on April 15 from a long list of organizations and individuals, headlined "New York to Nielsen: Thank You for Hearing Our Concerns. Now, It's Time to Address Them." It's signed the Don't Count Us Out/Queremos Ser Contados Coalition. One month later, The National Hispanic Media Coalition and other members of Don't Count Us out focus on halting Nielsen's plans to introduce LPMs in Los Angeles and Chicago July 8 until it's tested in another city to the pressure group's satisfaction.

A news conference by the Don't Count Us out coalition in May on the steps of Los Angeles' city hall hardly draws the kind of media attention the group's protest garners in New York City. The omnipresent Alex Nogales of the National Hispanic Media Council, injects civil rights into the subject of LPMs undercounting minorities. "If Nielsen gets it way, minority viewership could be dramatically undercounted and the civil rights of Latinos and African Americans will be shortchanged with less programming, economic opportunities and less influence in the media marketplace," he says.

Nielsen, as part of its reaction to the criticism and pressure, hires an outside public relations firm and the Tomás Rivera Policy Institute to review a study which questions its measurement techniques of Latinos in its viewing survey.

One branch of TV which does welcome the people meters to New York City is the cable industry. Why is it going against all the opposition? Simple. The trade organization, the Cabletelevision Advertising Bureau, cites Local People Meters in Boston since 2002 as having "the effect of increasing the reported audience from cable while...decreasing the reported audience from broadcast television," stresses Kevin Barry, the CAB's vice president of local sales and marketing to *Multichannel News*, a cable TV newsweekly. One major cable systems operator, Comcast Corp., which has systems in Northern New Jersey, says it also supports the New York entry and will additionally subscribe to LPM surveying in all initial 10 cities where Nielsen will utilize them.

In May, the Media Ratings Council, an industry group, declines to accredit the LPMs in New York following the release of a critical audit by the firm of Ernst & Young citing problems with the composition of the sample audience and a high fault rate in determining which programs are being watched. CBS responds to the MRC's concern by asking Nielsen to delay the New York rollout. CBS says that while it supports the technology, it is concerned about flaws in the samples and Nielsen's rush to introduce the methodology.

Among cities in the top 10 markets, Boston, the sixth largest, is the first to receive LPMs in 2002. Despite pressure from opponents, Nielsen says it'll debut the LPMs on schedule in New York June 3, two months after the original launch date, and introduce the technology in Los Angeles July 8 and in Chicago August 5. But in a conciliatory move, Nielsen says it will maintain the old meter/diary system along with the new people meters in New York, so stations and ad agencies may use either source for ratings information. Critics believe Latino and black households have been undercounted for years using the old methodology and they will again be underserved by the new technology. At stake are the $25-billion annual reaped by local TV stations, where a ratings point can make a big difference in a station's revenue income, plus Nielsen's own $200 million investment in the new technology.

Despite the negativism against the LPMs, there are boosters as well. Two black TV networks, BET, owned by Viacom and the new TV One partially owned by cable giant Comcast, support the rollout of LPMs. WNBC-TV, the NBC local station, and WNJU, Telemundo's Gotham outlet, also support the LPMs. However, Univision Communications isn't so accommodating and it files a suit against Nielsen Media Research in Los Angeles Superior Court in June of '04, charging the technology undercounts minority viewers. The suit alleges that Nielsen's L.A. sample contains too few young Hispanics and too many who speak mostly English. Univision also charges Nielsen will be releasing flawed and deceptive TV ratings. The network believes the LPMs will produce lower ratings for its flagship KMEX which would result in less advertising revenue, a source needed to fund new programming.

Nielsen counters with its own filing in Superior Court, charging Univision "seeks to prevent the L.A. market's use of a modernized, improved and more accurate system that is already in use across the U.S. and locally in Boston and New York because it results in lower ratings for some of Univision's programs."

One month later in July, a Los Angeles Superior Court judge denies Univision's petition for a preliminary injunction to the introduction of the LPMs in L.A., claiming the network fails to provide sufficient evidence the LPMs would cause irreparable damage to Univision and the city's Spanish-speaking Hispanics. By November, animosities are cooling off; Univision Communications withdraws its suit against Nielsen, which then drops its counter suit. This same month, a new seven-year contract is restructured between Nielsen and the merged NBC and Universal, now operating as the NBC Universal conglomerate. Seven months after Univision and Nielsen drop their suits, the two companies announce a non-specific multimillion dollar deal for Nielsen to provide ratings for the TV network's 34 stations for at least five years, with a Univision research official indicating in the *Los Angeles Times* the two firms have been working on a few issues to improve the methodology and include more Spanish speakers in the audience sample.

Once the LPMs are in service in New York, all of the New York TV stations register ratings declines, according to Nielsen figures. The sharpest ratings dips are registered by Univision and the Fox stations WWOR and WNYW. In Los Angeles, Nielsen installs the people meters in 794 homes, a third of which are Hispanic. Overall, it says Spanish is the principal language in 15.5 percent of the sampling homes. While Nielsen says the sampling reflects the makeup of the city, critics claim Nielsen has signed up too many older viewers and Latinos whose primary language is English.

As if Nielsen isn't drawing enough flack, two U.S. Senators, Barbara Boxer (D-California) and Conrad Burns (R-Montana), set a hearing before the communications subcommittee in Washington for July, following the deployment of the LPMs in Los Angeles. Nielsen's president Susan Whiting defends her company for two hours of what is called "serious grilling" by representatives from Fox Television, Univision and the Media Rating Council. The hearings, however, fail to provide any resolution to the dispute. The only good news Nielsen receives is that both solons believe the federal government will not become embroiled in this imbroglio. Following the hearing, Nielsen issues an optimistic statement which reads: "Clearly it is the view of the committee that the private sector should work out any issues related to TV ratings, and we are fully committed to working within the media industry to resolve any outstanding issues, just as we have in the past." Just when smoke from fired guns begins to dissipate, the powerful American Federation of Television and Radio Artists (AFTRA), representing 80,000 members, joins those voices against the LPMs. In a statement, AFTRA asserts: "Because our members' interests are directed impacted by the ratings, it is essential that data collection be conducted in a manner that correctly reflects all viewers and listeners, especially in recording the viewing and listening habits of Latinos, African Americans, and others who appear to be under reported in Nielsen Media Research's new Local People Meter ratings system."

With Nielsen gaining conditional accreditation from the Media Research Council, the audience and research measurement oversight organization in August, following its having introduced LPMs in Boston in 2002, it proceeds with its scheduled debuts in 2004 in Los Angeles August 30, followed by New York and Chicago on September 27. And once LPMs are introduced in Washington, Philadelphia, San Francisco, Dallas, Detroit, and Atlanta in 2005, the number of sampling homes will double to 10,000.

Cities utilizing the LPM technology are among the elite markets out of the 210 local regions Nielsen surveys which are given overnight results for the first time during the 2004 November sweeps period. Information using the diary method on age, gender, racial/ethnicity, and program preference in diaries is previously available four weeks after the sweeps period ends.

Seeking additional support, Nielsen forms an alliance with the William C. Velasquez Institute, a Latino research firm to evaluate and make recommendations regarding all aspects of the new audience measurement technology as it affects Hispanics. It's Nielsen's first such affiliation in its 54 year history. It also lands the support of the Rev. Jesse Jackson, who cites the use of LPMs raises the number of African-American TV viewers shifting from broadcast to cable niche networks.

In March of 2005, the Independent Task Force on Television Measurement, created in April of last year to study Nielsen's audience measuring methods as they pertain to minorities, releases a 62-page report compiled over eight months to Nielsen's CEO Whiting, who responds positively to its recommendations. They include over-sampling people of color in all the LPM markets; collecting individual characteristics on household members, including the race and language of each person in the sample household; providing recruitment material in Spanish and Asian languages and improving cultural awareness among the company's representatives.

The report notes that "beyond the issue of minority measurement, the continued inadequate representation of persons of color on television or in positions of authority remains a significant problem within this industry." While the recommendations have to be approved by Nielsen's clients, CEO Whiting stresses in her official response: "The task force's first priority was to understand the science of television audience measurement, and then make practical recommendations about how to improve the service and help Nielsen do a better job of measuring America's highly diverse and changing population. We are committed to working with our clients to implement these recommendations."

However, dark clouds appear once again for Nielsen, putting it on the defense when stations in Washington protest the introduction of LPMs in their market on June 2, causing Nielsen to delay the rollouts in D.C. and Philadelphia until June 30 to provide stations time to study data from the LPM service in operation in other markets. The protesting D.C. stations, ABC affiliate WJLA, CBS affiliate WUSA, Fox-owned WDCA and WTTG and Tribune-owned WBDC, issue a statement asserting the new technology is being applied "over the strong reservations of local broadcasters" and without meeting "the minimum standards of the Media Rating Council," the federal ratings and research oversight agency. The stations also charge LPMs fail to provide usable information from ethnic groups in the survey. Nielsen's counter offensive statement before it decides to delay the entry of LPMs in the nation's capital, stresses, "Local People Meters are making Washington, D.C.'s, local television ratings more accurate and representative of the local population than ever before." Of the markets using LPMs, only Boston and San Francisco receive full accreditation from the Media Rating Council, while New York, Los Angeles, and Chicago receive conditional accreditation. Following the Washington protest, 19 major TV station groups, including those involved in the D.C. complaint, warn the ratings provider of "flaws in the system which must be repaired before LPM service is expanded," reports

TelevisionWeek. These concerned giants include CBS; NBC Universal TV Stations; Tribune Broadcasting; Gannett Broadcasting; Post-Newsweek Media, Inc.; Hearst-Argyle Television, Inc.; EW Scripps Company; Belo Corporation, LIN-TV Corp., Barrington Broadcasting Company, LLC; Liberty Corporation; Fox TV Stations (Fox Broadcasting); Cox TV (Cox Broadcasting); Allbritton Communications Company; Fisher Communications, Inc.; Emmis Communications Corporation; Media General Broadcast Group; and Dispatch Broadcasting.

The controversy over LPM's effectiveness is the subject of a Senate Commerce Committee hearing in July. It focuses on legislation introduced by Sen. Conrad Burns (R-Montana) titled the Fairness, Accuracy, Inclusivity and Responsiveness in Ratings Act (FAIR). The bill requires all ratings services to receive mandatory accreditation from an independent source before they become the industry standard. Currently ratings overview by the Media Rating Council (MRC), formed in 1964 at the urging of Congress, are voluntary. Susan Whiting, Nielsen's president, testifies Nielsen will agree to follow a new voluntary audit and accreditation code by the Media Rating Council as opposed to the federal ratings regulations as proposed in FAIR. George Ivie, MRC's executive director, testifies the voluntary audit and accreditation code will be ready by October. Whiting also claims Nielsen feels pressure from advertisers to get the LPMs operational as expeditiously as possible. Another witness, Pat Mullen, CEO of Tribune Broadcasting, says broadcasters are upset with the ratings giant for rolling out LPMs in several cities without MRC accreditation. One ad agency official, Kathy Crawford of MindShare Worldwide, Inc., testifies advertisers have been waiting 15 years "for a service to tell them the next day how well their spot did the night before," reports *Daily Variety*. The battle rages on.

Following my interview at Nielsen and before heading to Arbitron to discuss its Hispanic radio coverage, I have lunch at the Friar's Club on 57th Street between Fifth and Sixth Avenues with Ted Farone, the public relations representative for WPIX and Univision's

New York station WNJU. Arbitron is also on 57th Street, a short brisk walk away from the Friar's, and since Ted's got an appointment near where I'm headed, we walk together through a light snowfall. I've got two meetings at Arbitron, first with Thom Mocarsky, the communications vice president, who's flown in from his Columbia, Maryland, office and with David Lapovsky, executive vice president of worldwide research. Thom directs me to a conference room where he makes my day with his largess of invaluable studies and information on the company's separate Hispanic radio ratings samples. Then he drops me off at David's office with its expansive view of 57th Street where I notice the snow has stopped falling. He's seated at a small table munching on a late lunch.

Arbitron has been measuring general market radio audiences since 1964 and in 1966 begins its telephone recruitment of participants from what it calls "High Density Hispanic Areas" for its weekly mail-in dairy surveys of their radio listening patterns. These are regions which have one or more zip codes and at least a 25 percent Hispanic population base from which to choose from.

Of the nation's 13,000 plus radio stations in 2003, 650 plus are now Hispanic formatted, according to Arbitron's 2003 edition of its study titled "Hispanic Radio Today How America Listens to Radio." In a subsequent story in *Billboard* anent this report, the newsweekly quotes "13,685 stations of which 699 are Hispanic programmed, up from 564 four years ago." When I query both parties on the number discrepancies, Arbitron's Thom Mocarsky replies: "The *Billboard* estimates are theirs, not ours. They sound reasonable and you should source accordingly." In turn when I query Leila Cobo, the magazine's Miami bureau chief (who I interview during my 2002 Miami sojourn), she responds: "The numbers are from Arbitron" but she can't recall from whom she receives them. "We don't keep tallies on numbers of stations. They do."

Arbitron begins researching Spanish-language radio usage among Hispanics in 1995. Why is this important? The answer, Lapovsky explains, "is there is a correlation between the shares of Spanish-language radio stations and Hispanics' ability to speak

Spanish. Since 1974, we've had a Hispanic phone question concerning are you of Hispanic origin or a descent, which is what the Census Bureau asks. But they don't ask whether you speak Spanish or not. So since 1995 we've had our research program find the best way to ascertain which Hispanics speak Spanish and what their listening habits are. As the Hispanic population has become more assimilated, there clearly are Spanish speakers and non-Spanish speakers among the Hispanic population. Our focus is on those people who speak Spanish.

"If you look at the share of audience in Spanish radio, you see it divided into groups of Spanish-language, Hispanics who are Spanish-language dominant or English-dominant and everybody else. Everybody else and English-dominant Hispanics are more similar in their listening habits than they are similar to each other and Spanish-dominant Hispanics. Given the fact there is a relationship between language spoken and Spanish-language radio, we've begun adding language weighting," which Arbitron material says won't be completed until the Winter 2006 survey. Weighting is a statistical technique which helps compensate for any over or under sampling of a population segment based on that market's total residency and in this case, the percentage of Hispanics residing there.

Three major Hispanic networks, Hispanic Broadcasting Corp., Spanish Broadcasting System and Radio Unica are concerned that it's going to take until the winter of 2006 to fully implement the language preference weighting. According to the *Radio and Records* newsweekly, the three networks hold conference calls to discuss how to react to Arbitron's announcement delaying the language weighting to its quarterly surveys. Bill Tanner, SBS' executive vice president of programming calls it "too little too late."

Arbitron announces an interim plan for weighting, prompting the question to Lapovsky of how will this plan coming out much sooner assuage negative comments from programmers? "We believe we've presented them with an alternative that meets many of the objectives of language weighting. It gives them estimates they can use to show their audience under language weighting. It gives them an indication of the degree to which there is or isn't bias in the estimates, and it provides them with something they can use to show the strength of their audience and strength of their advertising to advertisers." A spin-off service specifically for advertisers is the company's Hispanic Market Service which is based solely on combining its Hispanic diaries from winter/spring and summer/fall. The report, Arbitron boasts, "is used by more than 250 advertising agencies" in planning their Hispanic radio campaigns.

For its Winter 2002 survey, Arbitron, in consultation with broadcasters modifies the way it collects and classifies language preferences. It switches from a three-part question in the diary to four-part questions during the diary recruitment phone call.

Arbitron surveys 286 separate markets with the percentage of Hispanics in each varying. Lapovsky notes that while Arbitron and the Census are "right on" with each other's population estimates, "we may tend to be slightly over representative."

How are the surveys for Anglo and Hispanic radio different? "We have tailored the system which is the same for both markets, to the needs of the groups of respondents. So a Hispanic respondent today receives different incentives, a higher amount of money and more telephone calls during the week to help them do the task of filling in a bilingual diary in Spanish and English. We use bilingual phone interviewers to make that initial call. If a Hispanic person appears in the middle of Des Moines, we might not have Spanish speakers standing by to make that call."

The basic survey method is a seven-day radio listening diary which the respondent sends back to Arbitron in a prepaid-postage self-mailer. The participant receives a token $1 for filling out the diary. During the ratings periods of winter, spring, summer and fall of 2003, for example, Arbitron utilizes a total of 119,633 diaries to survey Hispanic listening patterns. Qualifying Hispanics, who are part of a "Differential Survey Treatment" plan, are treated differently from general market survey participants. They are paid $2, are given two additional follow-up calls during survey week and after the survey concludes, an additional follow-up $2 and bilingual survey materials.

I once receive an unsolicited diary in the mail during the 1990s despite the fact I'm writing about radio. I mark in my favorite stations, pocket the $1, and mail it back. I remember being surprised by the measly $1 this multimillion dollar company pays to have people take the time to fill out the diaries which provide it with the vital information is uses to make or break radio station's standings in their community, as well as being the data upon which the advertising industry relies in making decisions to spend millions of dollars for their clients.

The company uses an expanded diary in small and medium markets, except that the questions include socioeconomic and consumer behavior topics. That's called the qualitative diary. There's also a bilingual diary for standard and qualitative diaries.

The surveys are conducted over four 12-week spans during winter, spring, summer and fall seasons. Interviewers attempt to make 13 phone calls to reach sample households during the period prior to each survey week. The calls are made at different times of the day and evening and on different days of the week.

Arbitron's ratings surveys cover the most popular formats within Spanish-language radio: Mexican regional, contemporary (the Spanish version of Top 40), tropical (salsa and merengue) news/talk, variety (various music styles), and Tejano (a confluence of styles from Mexico and Texas). Its 2003 report indicates Hispanics spend 46.6 percent of their radio listening time with Spanish formats. In a breakdown by format popularity, Mexican regional leads with 17.7 percent followed by: contemporary 13.4 percent; tropical 6.1 percent; news/talk 4.2 percent; variety 3.1; Tejano 1.4 percent, and religious 0.7 percent. Formats are also popular by region of the country.

To wit: Mexican regional listeners are usually found in the East North Central, South Central, Mountain, and Pacific regions. The music appeals to 58 percent of Hispanic men 18 years and older more than it does women of the same age comprising 42 percent of the audience. The format is especially popular with 18- to 44-year-olds who comprise 73 percent of the format's audience.

Contemporary is popular in the New England, West North Central and Mountain regions. More than 80 percent of the music's fans are under 35, with teens accounting for almost one-third of the audience.

Tropical listeners are found in the South Atlantic, Middle Atlantic and New England regions. The audience splits almost evenly between men and women aged 25 to 44.

News/talk is especially popular in the Middle Atlantic, South Atlantic, East and North Central regions. The format is most popular with people 65 and over, who comprise more than 25 percent of the audience.

Variety is strongly favored in the West North Central region as well as in the Mountain, Pacific and South Central regions. The format's popularity focuses on listeners 25 to 44, with more women than men tuning in.

Tejano is favored in the South Central region than in any other part of the nation. It appeals mostly to adults 25 to 44, attracting more female listeners than male.

Two English-language formats are the most favored by Hispanic Americans. Contemporary hits radio, known as "CHR," is the favorite Anglo format among Hispanic teens and young adults. It's most popular among Hispanic listeners in New England, West North Central and Mountain regions.

Adult contemporary is favored mostly by 25- to 44-year-old Hispanics, with more women than men in the audience. Its Hispanic audiences are in the South Atlantic, New England, West North Central and Mountain regions.

Arbitron's top 25 Hispanic radio markets in 2002 in numerical order reflect the nation's expansive Latin population: Los Angeles, New York, Miami/Ft. Lauderdale/Hollywood, Chicago, Houston/ Galveston, San Francisco, Dallas/Ft. Worth, San Antonio, McAllen/ Brownsville/Harlingen, Phoenix (10), San Diego, Riverside/San Bernardino, El Paso, Washington, D.C., Denver/ Boulder, San Jose,

Austin, Fresno, Las Vegas, Albuquerque (20), Atlanta, Boston, Nassau/Suffolk (Long Island), Orlando, and Sacramento (25).

Having introduced its new surveying technology the Portable People Meter in Philadelphia months ago, with the intention of using it in both its general market and Hispanic surveys, what has the company learned from the City of Brotherly Love? Lapovsky's answer corresponds to complaints from Hispanic broadcasters: "The reality," the executive begins, "is that Philadelphia is not a dominant Hispanic market, so the findings are based on a very small number."

Why then use Philadelphia? "The primary reason is the distance from our facilities in Columbia, Maryland, which is where our technology lab and our public relations people are. We did not want to use New York because it is a very daunting medium research situation and Philadelphia is easier to do since the city is able to demonstrate what our estimates will look like for radio stations not specifically Spanish-language."

Lapovsky says the new portable meter uses an "encoding system of audio codes you can't hear in the most common frequencies transmitted by the station. People carry it around all day and at the end of day, they place the encoder into the base component and the information about what stations they've been listening to come to us. The meter hears every radio station that has an encoded signal."

Since Arbitron's partner in the PPM is Nielsen, the two companies have to determine when they'll roll the system out nationally. "The beauty of the PPM is that the encoder has no biases. You can encode a Hispanic television station as readily as you can an English or Spanish radio station. We've done a supplementary study in more heavily Hispanic markets to judge how readily Hispanics would be wiling to accept the task, and we've got some positive results."

Although he doesn't mention it, Arbitron has developed a "National Media Lifestyle Survey" based on results from its trial in Philadelphia which explores the ways people use radio and TV in their daily routines. For example, in facts published in *Broadcasting and Cable*, 77 percent of home radios are in the bedroom, with 68 percent in the living room. Eight-eight percent of cars and trucks have a radio. Ninety-three percent of TVs are in the living room, with 68 percent in the bedroom.

During the summer of 2002, I notice the ratings for Los Angeles Spanish radio significantly decline. Why does this happen? I ask a year later. "There is always some degree of sampling errors, or bounce between surveys," Lapovsky says. "Bounce," what's "bounce?" "It's a change in audience. Whether it is merited by actual events in the marketplace, a change in format or the natural sampling error, it's the bounce-downs that are focused on," he opines, adding: "Bounces up are brilliant programming strategies."

Arbitron's plans for using portable people meters takes on a surprising shift in direction in December 2004. The company announces that instead of using the technology as a ratings service, it will instead use it to develop an advertising industry planning aid called "Project Apollo" with Nielsen's Home Scan service which utilizes the Uniform Product Code bar-coding technology to track consumer purchases within a special nationwide household panel. Arbitron says it will need financial commitments from advertisers of between $50 million to $100 million for the planning aid system, reveals *TelevisionWeek*.

Two years after its Philadelphia PPM introduction, Arbitron brings the technology to Houston in July of '05. The new round of testing comes on the heels of new questioning about the accuracy of Arbitron's current system of manually filling out weekly diaries. Clear Channel Communications, the nation's largest radio chain with 1,270 stations, wants a new rating system to replace the manual handwritten diaries. Arbitron is among the companies Clear Channel invites to make a proposal, giving it an opening to push the PPM system. The radio giant is concerned about the totality of the diaries being filled out. In its response to Clear Channel, spokesman Thom Mocarsky says the company welcomes the request for more accurate listenership data while also stressing its promotion for its electronic measurement technology.

What's happening on the streets of New York in 2003? The International Latin Music Hall of Fame's fifth annual awards ceremony and concert at the Hostos Center for the Arts and Culture in the Bronx, is filmed by WABC-TV's *Puerto Rican Panorama* and by New Jersey Public Television program *Images/Imagenes*. Inductees include Juan Gabriel, Trini Lopez, Arturo Sandoval, Juan Luis Guerra, Henry Lee "Pucho" Brown, Roberto Roena, Ismael Quintana, Flaco Jiménez, Alberto Beltrán, Nelson Ned, Ray Santos, Manny Oquendo, José Luis Monero, and Justi Barretto. Desi Arnaz is among those inducted posthumously.

Vocalist Jon Secada plays the central role of the master of ceremonies in the off-Broadway version of *Cabaret* at Studio 54. Following his three-month appearance from June to August, he returns to vocalizing on a holiday tour with singer Jaci Velasquez and trumpeter Arturo Sandoval. Secada's premier stage appearance dates back to 1995 when he plays the role of Danny Zuko in the Broadway production of *Grease*.

The late Tito Puente's life is celebrated in a three-hour concert at Avery Fisher Hall in Lincoln Center on April 21, a day after he would have been 80 years old, and nearly three years following his death. His 20-piece orchestra conducted by Angel "Cucco" Peña, performs his best-known works, with guest musicians including Puente protégés and former band members Dave Valentin, Hilton Ruiz, Giovanni Hidalgo and vocalist Domingo Domingo Quiñones. One segment of the concert features performances by Tito Puente Jr., Rubén Blades, Jon Secada and percussionist Sheila E. The second half puts the spotlight on female vocalists Melinda León, Roselyn Sanchez and Ednita Nazario. The concert is later telecast as a two-hour special on both Telemundo and its NBC parent. Puente is among the bands in 1955 which help strengthen the mambo craze of 1951 along with Machito, Tito Rodriguez, Joe Loco, Noro Morales, Jose Curbelo, and the La Playa Sextet, among others.

One month later, the 18-piece Afro-Latin Jazz Orchestra led by pianist Arturo O'Farrill, Jr. makes its debut at Lincoln Center's Alice Tully Hall. Arturo is the son of the late legendary Cuban musician/composer/arranger Chico O'Farrill. Wynton Marsalis, artistic director of the Jazz at Lincoln Center project, guests with the orchestra on trumpet. "The idea behind the orchestra is to perform the very best compositions in the Afro-Latin genre," says the young O'Farrill, who grows up in Mexico, when his Cuban-born father who arrives in New York City in 1948 moves there in the '50s due to the decline of the big bands for whom he's been a much requested arranger. Arturo, who grows up in New York City upon his father's return there in the '60s, is conservatory trained and becomes a much-desired pianist for Latin jazz record dates and concerts in addition to leading his own quintet.

New York City in '05 honors his late father almost four years to the day he passes away on June 27, 2001, by naming the intersection of West 88th Street and West End Avenue after him on June 19. Nine days later, Arturo and the Afro-Latin Jazz orchestra debuts on Palmetto Records with *Una Noche Inolvidable* (*An Unforgettable Night*), recorded last January 28 during the inaugural season at the Frederick P. Rose Hall, the new home for Jazz at Lincoln Center. Appearing with the 18-piece orchestra are guest vocalists Claudia Acuña and Herman Olivera. The ensemble becomes a resident orchestra at Lincoln Center in 2002. The release is the second in the Jazz at Lincoln Center series, following *A Love Supreme* with Wynton Marsalis and the Lincoln Center Jazz Orchestra. Arturo branches out on his own with his piano trio album, *Live in Brooklyn* on Zoho Music accompanied by Andy Gonzalez and Dafnis Prieto.

Local record companies are turning to hometown favorites for new releases. High Note Records pairs Brooklyn's modern jazz pianist Cedar Walton, a devotee of Latin music since 1964 when he's a member of Art Blakey's Jazz Messengers, with Bronx-born congero Ray Mantilla, and Venezuelan-born bassist Cuco Martinez on the album *Latin Tinge*. Yerba Buena, a two-year-old septet, releases its second CD, *President Alien*, which combines rhythmic elements from Afro-Cuban, cumbia, merengue, calypso and hip-hop on the Razor & Tie label. The band's creation is the result of the independent label's owner, Venezuelan-born Andres Levin putting together musicians for the earlier produced album *Red Hot + Riot*. Current band members are from New York, Nigeria and Havana and include Levin, the guitarist, songwriter, producer; percussionist Pedro Martinez, saxophonist/flutist Ron Blake, trumpeter Rashawn Ross, drummer Terreon Gully and vocalists Xiomara Laugart and CuCu Diamantes.

Saxophonist Paquito D'Rivera, one of the first Cuban musicians from Irakere to defect to the U.S. and set up residence in New Jersey, is expanding his recorded repertoire to include the first Spanish-language interpretation of Stravinsky's *Histoire De Soldat*, as well as recording an all-Brazilian album, *Brazilian Dreams* for MCG and his first all-clarinet disc, *The Clarinetists* for Peregrina Music. When the new Canadian owners of New York's 90-year-old Spanish newspaper, *El Diario/La Prensa* announce plans to have Fidel Castro as well as other Latin nation presidents write columns, D'Rivera, one of 70,000 Cuban Americans residing across the Hudson River in Union City, New Jersey, strongly protests via e-mail the paper giving Castro exposure. Even though the column is heavily promoted, it is killed by the owners. By 2004, Paquito turns his attention to a big band setting by recording with Germany's noted WDR Band for the Universal/ Pimienta album, *Big Band Time*, which features trumpeter Claudio Roditi and bassist Oscar Stagnaro.

A law suite involving Rubén Blades and his former record label and its publishing company, draw attention to the often contentious relationships within show business. Blades files his federal suit against Fania and Vaya Records and their publishing firms, charging failure to pay record and publishing royalties and copyright infringement. Originally filed in 1984 and settled in '85, the new suit alleges the defendants have not fulfilled those court-ordered terms. In the 1970s, Blades signs with Fania, owned at the time by Gerald Masucci for records and publishing. His new suit also alleges that several of the defendant firms unlawfully exploit his compositions.

A number of local labels go on a signing spree. Latin Cool expands its roster by signing Andrea Brachfeld and her Son Charanga band, vocalist Debbie Resto and releasing a second CD by Cintron, a 13-piece ensemble featuring bilingual harmony vocals. Already on the label are Larry Harlow, and ensembles Latin Jazz Coalition and Cintró. Flauta Records tributes the Orquestra Broadway's 40th anniversary with its first new recording in 21 years, titled appropriately *40th Anniversary*.

Radio personality Ernesto "Chico" Alvarez Peraza also has a special birthday. He celebrates 15 years hosting *The New World Gallery* on Pacifica's WBAI-FM Sundays from 4–6 p.m. The bilingual program hosts a live jam session as part of the birthday celebration.

In August, the first Latin New York Festival provides a musical smorgasbord of 100 events at venues in Manhattan and the Bronx, culminating with the 27th annual Salsa Festival at Madison Square Garden. Headlining are Oscar D'Leon and his orchestra, featuring Johnny Pacheco, Bobby Valentin, Papo Lucca, and Gilberto Santa Rosa and his band. The festival, dedicated to Celia Cruz, who dies one month earlier, also features poetry and paintings. One year later, the 28th annual Salsa spectacular at the Garden headlines the hometown favorite Fania All Stars led by Pacheco.

Upstate in Syracuse, the Festival Latinoamérica celebrates its 11th anniversary over two days in October. Despite rain, some 6,500 persons attend the outdoor shows at Clinton Square, where the music is provided by the Paquito Guzmán orchestra plus 10 other bands performing salsa, merengue and bachata stylings, including Grupo Provocativo from nearby Buffalo and Reguetón, a New York hip-hop band and the local Latin jazz ensemble Folklore Urbano.

During 2004, New York City initiates a plan to attract additional Hispanic media to the city to join such firms like MTV Español, VH1 Uno and the Hispanic Information and Telecommunications Network, which are all headquartered in Manhattan. Mayor Michael Bloomberg forms the Latin Media and Entertainment Commission to recruit new Hispanic media firms as well as attract high-profile Hispanic events to the city that are obviously from Miami and Los Angeles. Attending the announcement ceremony at City Hall is the ubiquitous Jennifer Lopez, named honorary chairwoman.

Latin jazz's Nuyorican heritage is equally represented at the 31st annual International Association for Jazz Educators Conference held at the Hilton and Sheraton hotels in midtown Manhattan. The four-day event in January, with its panels and musical showcases, draws the participation of the Lincoln Center Afro-Latin Jazz Orchestra, Paquito D'Rivera and the New York Voices, Michel Camilo Trio, David Sánchez Sextet, Caribbean Jazz Project, and Susie Hansen Latin Jazz Band. The fourth annual Latin Jazz Pro Jam features an all star ensemble focusing on the rhythms of Cuba, Brazil and Latin America. Two clinics also deal with rhythm instruments: One deals with how to assimilate Brazilian rhythms, melodies and harmonics into jazz, while the other probes the evolution of the bass in Afro-Cuban music. One panel in particular, "The Contributions and Influence of Latin Musicians in Jazz: A Supreme Oversight," reaffirms the influence and contributions of Hispanics to the music.

Three of the city's top cable system operators, Time Warner, Comcast Corp. and Cablevision Systems Corp., provide Hispanic digital tiers of programming aimed at the targeted 27 percent of the city's population, or 2.2 million people.

One of the city's pioneering salsa DJs, Polito Vega celebrates 45 years in New York radio, 15 with WSKQ-FM (*La Mega*), Spanish Broadcasting System's tropical station, which is the city's most favored Spanish-language outlet. Six years ago, WSKQ becomes the first Spanish station to hit No. 1 in the overall ratings. This year, its morning show, *El Vacilon De La Mañana* becomes the market's leading radio show, according to Arbitron. Polito's weekend show, *Salsa Con Polito*, especially the Sunday noon to 8 p.m. stanza, is a popular favorite of fans of traditional salsa.

As part of the tribute celebration for the 66-year-old personality, the Fania All Stars headline a concert for Vega at the Continental Airlines Arena in East Rutherford, New Jersey. The event is being coordinated by promoter Ralph Mercado and John Sepulveda, a former concert promoter, now head of SBS' entertainment division, which builds concerts in tandem with SBS stations in New York, Los Angeles, Chicago and Puerto Rico. The reunited Fania All Stars performing at the concert include Johnny Pacheco, Bobby Valentin, Papo Lucca, Yomo Toro, Ray Barretto, Roberto Roena, Richie Ray, Bobby Cruz, Jimmy Bosch, Alfredo De La Fé, Domingo Quiñones and vocalists Ismael Miranda, Cheo Feliciano, and Adalberto Santiago. Guest artists include Tego Calderón, La India, Oscar D'Leon, and José Alberto "El Canario." One original All Star missing from the concert who cannot come to financial terms with concert promoters Spanish Broadcasting System (SBS), Fania and Ralph Mercado Productions is Larry Harlow. He tells SalsaPower.com: "I feel personally very bad that I cannot play for Polito Vega's 45th anniversary. He has been a big force in keeping our music alive." The four-and-a-half hour concert is taped by Sony Discos in CD and DVD forms for the holidays. It's the first live Fania release in many years. One rainy night later, the Fania All Stars celebrate their 40th anniversary by performing in concert at the James L. Knight Center in Miami, headquarters for SBS which operates three radio stations in this market. Guesting with the band is vocalist Albita Rodriguez, who like La India in New York, performs a tribute to Celia Cruz. Among the alumni missing this gig are Willie Colón, Ray Barretto and Junior González.

Vega and Fania have a connection dating back to the early '60s when he supposedly becomes the first New York DJ to play a Fania record, Johnny Pacheco's single, *El Campeon*, which Fania Records owner Jerry Masucci personally delivers to him, according to a *Billboard* spotlight section on Vega.

Born in Ponce, Puerto Rico, but raised in New York, Vega begins his radio career in 1960 at two stations which broker time for Latin music, WEVD-AM and WWRL-AM, and then joins WBNX-AM, which along with WHOM-AM are the city's only Latin stations. At WBNX, Vega initially does the midnight to 6 a.m. shift for two years and is switched to daytime by program director Raul Alarcón, Sr., who buys WEVD-FM in 1989 for the new SBS, changes the call letters to WSKQ and hires Vega away from WBNX.

With more Hispanics in New York City, performance venues reach out to tap into this market of music lovers. The six-year-old nonprofit Jazz Gallery has been providing new Latin jazz bands with an exposure platform in the downtown South Village area for the past two years. The newest musician gaining an exposure booking at the club is Dafnis Prieto and his band. He's the latest Cuban drummer to arrive in New York who plays a full set of drums, not just Latin percussive instruments. Prieto also works with several other groups at the venue. He arrives in the city in 2000 on a work visa while performing with Canadian Jane Bunnett's Spirits of Havana band at various U.S. festivals, applies for permanent residency and settles in the Washington Heights section of Manhattan. Prieto, 27, draws the attention of Eddie Palmieri and 14 other groups, which hire him before he sets out with his own ensemble. He is the newest Cuban drummer to hit New York since 1947 when the pioneering Chano Pozo arrives to infuse Afro-Cuban elements into Dizzy Gillespie's band. A *New York Times* profile calls his playing style "a collaboration of various Afro-Cuban percussion sounds, from old religious music to modern music" all produced by one set of trap drums.

In the borough of the Bronx to the north of Manhattan, the flow of Latinos into the Southern portion of the area, is reason enough for the creation of a first-time entertainment enclave. It's an uplifting improvement for this section of the city made infamous in the 1970s by its abandoned buildings and lost sense of hope, drawn into the national spotlight by a visit by then president Jimmy Carter. Now the Hispanic community can be drawn together by the Hostos Center for the Arts and Culture, which opens in 1994 as part of Hostos Community College. In addition to a 900-seat concert hall, there's also an art gallery and repertory theater. Among the name groups performing this year are Cuba's Orquestra Aragón, Larry Harlow and his salsa band, Puerto Rican reggaeton rapper Daddy Yankee, the Alvin Ailey American Dance Theater and the Dance Theater of Harlem. Mexican mariachi and Puerto Rican bomba bands also find a place at the Hostos to perform. It's obviously doing well by its patrons:

during the 2002–'03 season 85,000 people attend nearly 300 events there, according to the *New York Times*. Also in the area are local eateries which cater to the Puerto Rican community by booking local bands. The Bronx, like other boroughs of New York City with large Hispanic populations, sways to the beats of its Latin heritage.

In a separate move, nine men who play for the late Tito Puente in his orchestra, form the Latin Giants Big Band. It provides an outlet for José Madera, Bobby Porcelli, Lewis Kahn, Johnny Rodriguez, George Delgado, Pete Miranda, Mitch Frohman, John Walsh, and Mario Rivera, to keep working together.

Fantasy Records, mining its rich catalog, reissues eight titles by Harlem-born timbalero Henry "Pucho" Brown and his seminal Latin Soul Brothers, originally released on Prestige between 1966 and '69. Significantly, the Soul Brothers are mainly Anglo musicians. When the boogalu Latin movement begins to fade in the early '70s, Pucho says adios to his soul brothers, only to reform the band in 1995 and record the album, *Rip a Dip*, for sister label Milestone and begin touring again. The newest addition to the Pucho collection is *The Hideout*, named after a Berkeley, California, club in which Pucho appears, and which operates from the '40s through the late '60s. The album, due this fall, explains Pucho, is in part "a tribute to the musicians who played there." Pucho's albums feature the infectious fusion sound of the boogalu as well as English lyrics.

Three albums with interesting themes are released by percussionist Andy Durán, the bicultural band Cordero and trombonist Conrad Herwig. Durán and his Latin Jazz Band continue their series of concept albums with *Formats & Concepts* which tributes both TV themes New York City, including three tunes honoring the Big Apple featuring Tito Puente and La Lupe, the Joe Cuba Sextet and Bobby Rodriguez Y La Compañia. Cordero, named after lead vocalist/guitarist Ani Cordero, performs half its tunes in Spanish and English on their Daemon CD, *Somos Cordero*. Also adding musical diversity is the guest horn section of the New York-based Antibalas Afrobeat Orchestra.

Half Note Records releases a special Miles Davis tribute CD, *Another Kind of Blue: The Latin Side of Miles*, recorded live at the parent Blue Note club last year, which features trombonist Herwig, pianist Eddie Palmieri and saxophonist Paquito D'Rivera. The club is also the locale this year where Herwig and band perform as part of the promotional efforts for the recording. Herwig previously wins plaudits for his recording of the *Latin Side of John Coltrane* on Astor Place Records.

One record executive who sees promising days for Latin music is Thomas "Tommy" Mottola, former head of Sony Music, now head of the revived Casablanca label, a former disco specialist in the '70s. "The Latin audience is growing by leaps and bounds and as a base for Latin artists, it is stronger than ever," he tells the *Hollywood Reporter*. If, he emphasizes, an artist wants to cross over into the megabuck market, "you need a hit record in English." During his tenure, Sony strikes gold in the Latin crossover field with Ricky Martin, Marc Anthony, and Jennifer Lopez. Mottola tells the *Reporter* he helps create the term "Latin explosion" by introducing Lopez and Anthony.

While there are those who feel the Latin explosion occurs much earlier in outbursts by various artists of differing musical complexions before Marc Anthony and Jennifer Lopez, the growth of Latin rappers is contained within the past three years. So it's appropriate that Latin rappers and reggaeton regulars recognize their commercial heat by meeting in New York for the third annual Latin Rap Conference September 20 at the Latin Quarter. With a plethora of plethora of record companies, radio stations group owners and artists in attendance, the event encompasses panel discussions, a talent showcase, and a Latin youth meets the executives session.

Articles

"Arbitron To Launch Portable Radio-Ratings Meter In July." Los Angeles Times, March 15, 2006

"Nielsen: 'Portfolio' Over PPM." Hollywood Reporter, March 2, 2006

"Latin Rap Conference Attracts Latin Music Pioneers & Top Music Executives." HispaniaNet.com, Aug. 30, 2005

"Nielsen OKs Voluntary Code." Daily Variety, July 28, 2005

"NAB, Comcast Weigh In On LPM." Hollywood Reporter, July 22, 2005

"Clear Channel Seeks New Rating System." Los Angeles Times, June 14, 2005

"Univision, Nielsen Reach Deal Amid Ratings Rift." Los Angeles Times, June 9, 2005

"Nielsen Says No To Demand To Halt LPMs." TelevisionWeek, June 6, 2005

"Nielsen Delays Launch Of 2 LPMs." Hollywood Reporter, June 2, 2003

"Nielsen Delays Rollout Of Meter Amid Opposition." Los Angeles Times, June 2, 2005

"White Sox Reward Guillen." Los Angeles Times, May 31, 2005

"D.C. Latest Battle Zone For Nielsen." TelevisionWeek, May 30, 2005

"Chico Carrasquel, 77; Was 1st Latino To Start In A Major League All Star Game." Los Angeles Times, May 27, 2005

"Nielsen Proceeds With LPMs In D.C." Multichannel News, May 23, 2005

"Luis Jimenez: La Mega 97.9 Morning Man Turns Movie Star." Billboard, May 14, 2005

"Nielsen Agrees To Task Force Plans." TelevisionWeek, March 28, 2005

"Minority Report Rips Nielsen Tools." Daily Variety, March 24, 2005

"Nielsen Plans Changes In Audience Tracking." Los Angeles Times, March 24, 2005

"PPM Could Launch As Planning Tool." TelevisionWeek, Dec. 13, 2004

"KNBC-TV Newscast Loses Ground." Los Angeles Times, Dec. 3, 2004

Univision Drops Suit." Los Angeles Times, Nov. 30, 2004

"Nelsen, NBC Universal Sign Seven-year Deal." Hollywood Reporter, Nov. 22, 2004

"Sweeping Change Afoot." Hollywood Reporter, Nov. 3, 2004

"For Nielsen, Fixing Old Ratings System Causes New Static." Wall Street Journal, Sept. 16, 2004

"Jackson's Endorsement A Boost To LPMs." Multichannel News, Sept. 13, 2004

"Latino Group To Aid Nielsen In Refining Measurements." Hollywood Reporter, Sept. 9, 2004

"40th Anniversary Of The Fania All Stars With Special Guests at James L. Knight Center Miami." SalsaPower.com, Aug. 10, 2004

"Nielsen Clears Hurdle In L.A." TelevisionWeek, Aug. 9, 2004

"Tribute to Polito Vega, 45 Years On The Radio, Fania All Stars And Special Guests." SalsaPower, Aug. 9, 2004

"Larry Harlow Is Missing From The Fania All Stars Reunions In New Jersey And Miami." SalsaPower.com, Aug. 9, 2004

"Polito Vega: New York DJ Celebrates 45 Big Ones At La Mega." Billboard, Aug, 7, 2004

"AFTRA Joins Coalition Against Nielsen System." Daily Variety, Aug. 4, 2004

"Rating Fight Abates." Daily Variety, July 16, 2004

"LPM Clash Heading To Senate." Multichannel News, July 12, 2004

"Nielsen Rolls Out 'People Meters." Los Angeles Times, July 8, 2004

"Univision Loses Request To Halt Nielsen System." Los Angeles Times, July 2, 2004

"Pair Of Senators To Enter Melee On People Meters." Daily Variety, June 28, 2004

"Nielsen Counting On Court Battle." Daily Variety, June 23, 2004

"Big Apple Count." Broadcasting & Cable, June 21, 2004

"LPMs Find Favor." TelevisionWeek, June 21, 2004

"Nielsen Meters Faulted In Audit." Los Angeles Times, June 15, 2004

"Univision Sues Nielsen Over Ratings System." Los Angeles Times, June 10, 2004

"Political Opposites Costar In A TV Drama." Los Angeles Times, June 3, 2004

"CBS Joins Battle Against Nielsen's People Meters." Daily Variety, June 3, 2004

"Nielsen Plays By N.Y. Book." Hollywood Reporter, June 2, 2004

"Nielsen Offers A Compromise." New York Times, June 2, 2004

"Watchdog Rejects Nielsen Plan." Hollywood Reporter, June 1, 2004

"Black Nets Back LPMs." Multichannel News, May 24, 2004

"Nielsen Sticks To Rollout Of N.Y. Meters." TelevisionWeek, May 17, 2004

"Nielsen Allies Band Together For Battle." Daily Variety, May 11, 2004

"People Meter Pulls In Protesters." Hollywood Reporter, May 11, 2004

"Nielsen Protest Shifts To L.A." TelevisionWeek, May 3, 2004

"New York To Nielsen: Thank You For Hearing Our Concerns. Now, It's Time To Address Them." Paid ad in the New York Times, April 15, 2004

"Everyone Counts." Paid ad in TelevisionWeek, April 12, 2004

"Most Valuable Franchise: Yankees." Los Angeles Times, April 9, 2004

"NAB, Advocates Pan People Meters." Multichannel News, April 5, 2004

"N.Y. Braces For People Meters." TelevisionWeek, April 5, 2004

"The Songs Are The Heart Of The Band." Los Angeles Times, April 4, 2004

"His Devilish Vision." Los Angeles Times Magazine, April 4, 2004

"Viva Marlins." Latin Notas, Billboard, April 3, 2004

"Nielsen Delays People Meter Bow." Daily Variety, April 2, 2004

"Critics Urge Metering Delay." Hollywood Reporter, April 1, 2004

"What's In A Name?" Hispanic Magazine, April 2004

"IAJE The World's Greatest Jazz Hang." Latin Beat, April 2004

"Dialogue With Thomas Mottola." Hollywood Reporter, March 31, 2004

"Cable Welcomes People Meters To N.Y.C." Multichannel News, March 29, 2004

"Nielsen Delays 2 People Meters." Hollywood Reporter, March 23, 2004

"People Who Don't Need People." Broadcasting & Cable, March 15, 2004

"New York To Latin Media: Take A Bite." Multichannel News, March 15, 2004

NewsLine: Ruben Blades Suit." Billboard, March 13, 2004

"In The South Bronx, The Arts Beckon." New York Times, Jan. 30, 2004

"Ernesto Chico Alvarez Peraza." Latin Beat, December 2003

"Diablo In Details?" Daily Variety, Nov. 11, 2003

"NBC Attacks Nielsen Methodology." Hollywood Reporter, Nov. 11, 2003

"New York Mayor Is All Aquiver Over J. Lo." USA Today, Oct. 30, 2003

"Nielsen's Feud With TV Networks Shows Scarcity Of Marketing Data." Wall Street Journal, Oct. 29, 2003

"In Urban Media War, It's Canadians Vs. Latinos." Los Angeles Times, Oct. 20, 2003

"Mexicans Finding A Place In A City Of Immigrants." Los Angeles Times, Oct. 6, 2003

"Festival Latino Americano 2003." Latin Beat, October 2003

"Year Buena: Alien Music." Down Beat, September 2003

"Fiesta Brings New York Best Of Latin Culture." New York Daily News, Aug. 24, 2003

"Mexican Immigrants Are Transforming New York City's Latino Presence, Even As They Cope With The Usual, And Some Unexpected, Pitfalls." Los Angeles Times Magazine, Aug. 3, 2003

"Exciting 20th." Latin Notas, Billboard, July 12, 2003

"Viva Puente!" Down Beat, July 2003

"Acting Is A 'Cabaret' For Secada." Billboard, June 28, 2003

"Mottola Takes U Turn." Daily Variety, June 8, 2003

"Traditions: That Latin Tinge!" Jazziz, May 2003

"Spinning Connections In A Worldwide Groove." New York Times, April 26, 2003

"Latin Notas: Viva Puente." Billboard, April 26, 2003

"Paquito D'Rivera: The Multiple Facets Of The Most Creative Cuban Jazz Defector." Latin Beat, April 2003

"International Latin Music Hall Of Fame." Latin Beat, March 2003

"NewMethods Shift Scores In L.A. Demo." Daily Variety, March 28, 2003

"A Music Man's Mantra: Let's Make A Deal." New York Times, Dec. 15, 2002

"When Celebrating Havana, Why Not Share A Cigar?" New York Times, Dec. 13, 2002

"Spanish-Lingo Nets Mark Si Change." Daily Variety, Dec. 3, 2002

"'Frankie And Johnny' To Get New Leads." New York Times, Nov. 23, 2002

"Bobby Sanabria." Latin Beat, November 2002

"Historians Are Doing The Mambo." New York Times, Oct. 24, 2002

"Scoring 'Frida'." New York Daily News, Oct. 18, 2002

"NY1 News Eyes 2003 Spinoff For Spanish Speaking Viewers." Multichannel News, Oct. 14, 2002

"A Bite From The Apple." Latin Beat, October 2002

"Wayne Gorbea Y Salsa Picante." Latin Beat, October 2002

"At A Bronx Church, New Latinos Meet Old, And Tension Ensues." Wall Street Journal, Aug. 8, 2002

"A Bite From The Apple." Latin Beat, August 2002

"Mega 'Musica.'" Latin Notas, Billboard, June 15, 2002

"New York's WXTV Secures Padilla Scoop." Hollywood Reporter, June 14, 2002

"WPIX Translates Newscast Into Spanish." Electronic Media, Feb. 3, 2002

"Turning 10, NY1 Gets $30M New Home." Multichannel News, Jan. 28, 2002

"From Cuba, With Rhythm, Taking Jazz By Storm." New York Times, Jan. 17, 2002

Chapter 15
CAPITULO 15

Puerto Rico: The Cultural Commonwealth 2002–2004/2005
PUERTO RICO: EL ESTADO CULTURAL
2002–2004/2005

• Puerto Rico sends 38 players to the Major League Baseball.

• ASCAP and BMI hold their awards ceremonies in Puerto Rico for the first time.

• Telemundo's WKAQ celebrates its 50th anniversary.

• Rekindled Menudo in the works.

• Reggaeton challenges salsa as the top sound of the day.

• Yankee Daddy is reggaeton's chart-busting Mainland champion.

• Mainland Spanish-language labels sign local rappers.

• Tego Calderón signs historic pact with Atlantic Records.

• LIN-TV and NBC set Puerto Rico channels for the Mainland using programming from their local stations.

Puerto Rico is a vital, creative cauldron with a rich history of providing Mainland America with its cultural riches. Separated from New York City by 1,611 air miles and from Miami by 1,400 air miles, the U.S. territory sees an estimated 2.7 million of its citizens migrate to the U.S. in search of jobs to create its own diaspora, carrying with them a musical heritage which enriches, integrates and innovates much of this nation's Latin music history. Today, Puerto Ricans are established in Los Angeles, in Cuban-dominated Miami, in Hawaii, where they arrive in the early 1900s to work in the sugar cane fields, and in a growing number of other U.S. cities, besides those situated along the Eastern seacoast.

A beautiful Caribbean nation of 3.9 million people (as of 2005) who speak Spanish and English, the Island's two official languages since 1993, they are serviced by 54 radio stations, nine of which are not Spanish-formatted. Bounded on the north by the Atlantic Ocean and by the Caribbean Sea on the south, Puerto Rico spawns a long list of celebrities in music, film and sports who depart for the Mainland where they achieve their star status.

Its music reflects its history of 400 years as a Spanish colony, of becoming a territorial possession of the U.S. after the Spanish-American War of 1898 and of achieving local self-government in 1952 as a commonwealth, thus solidifying its interest in the core elements of American pop music.

Today, there are copious local bands which make a good living by principally performing before local audiences in San Juan and in their own municipalities. They are the Island's true home-grown successes.

In the Miramax/Lionsgate film, *Dirty Dancing Havana Nights*, released in 2004, filmmakers use the capitol city of San Juan and Ponce, the second largest city, to replicate Havana in November 1958 prior to and during the early hours of the Castro takeover. Old San Juan's narrow cobblestones and pastel buildings are a perfect match for their counterparts in Old Havana. Located 900 nautical miles from Cuba, Puerto Rico's music utilizes that nation's Afro-Cuban musical characteristics.

I recall the cobblestones, multicolored buildings and visiting the famous fort, El Morro—built in 1589 and expanded during the 1760–1780 period—during my 1962 sojourn to San Juan to attend a Columbia Records convention there in July. The white sandy beach outside our hotel is as scalding as the blazing sun, while the music in the hotel and clubs is just as hot. Cuba's Afro-Cuban musical mixture as well as the Dominican Republic's merengue, are among the outside musical strains which meld into the endemic music created by Puerto Rican musicians which are as varied as the bolero, rumba, bomba, bolero, danza, cuatro, plena, salsa, and in recent years reggaeton. Puerto Rico's long tradition of folk music and romantic ballads are based on African and Spanish rhythms.

Much of Puerto Rican music is linked to instruments devised on the Island, including the guiro (a hollowed out gourd) found in Columbian music; four different instruments adapted from the six-string Spanish guitar, with the 10-stringed cuatro, the most popular and often revered as Puerto Rico's national instrument; percussion instruments maracas, tambours, and African-style drums. Drums played by hand are a key component in the African-inspired bomba music. Instruments used in plena music, which is built around Puerto Rico's wide cultural heritage, include the guiro, the dried-out gourd with parallel grooves which are scrapped with a stick, the 10-stringed cuatro and tambourines, known as panderos and brought here from Africa. While bomba and plena are the key forms of folk music, salsa or "sauce" in English, is the sound imported around the world, first from New York City to San Juan and then back out into the Latin world. Salsa bands require a plethora of percussion instruments: bongos, timbales, congas, gourds, claves, maracas and cowbells.

Puerto Rico's musical styles and trends easily traverse the ocean to infiltrate and influence the domestic U.S. Latin scene in the areas of pop and jazz. One area of music often overlooked is classical, headed by the late, world-renowned cellist Pablo Casals, who settles in Puerto Rico in the 1950s from his native Spain and becomes the director of the Puerto Rico Symphony and Conservatory of Music. In 1957, he founds the Casals Festival, an annual two-week concert series which takes place in San Juan's Fine Arts Center. His concerts on the Mainland are always sellouts and his recordings are cherished by his fans. His mother is from Puerto Rico and that's where he dies in 1973 at age 97. He is acclaimed as the 20th century's greatest cellist.

By the late 1990s, some 3.1 million Puerto Ricans are residents of the U.S. Mainland, following the earlier immigration waves of the 1940s–'50s and '60s, all of which ease economic struggles on the Island. Between the decades of the '60s and '80s, Puerto Rican musicians are influenced by musical ideas generated from New York, the Caribbean and Latin America. During the mambo craze of the '50s before Castro, Cuban bands perform in Puerto Rico alongside local groups fusing the bolero, mambo and elements of New York Latin jazz within Afro-Cuban rhythms.

During the '60s, bands led by Bobby Capó, Chucho Avellanet and Danny Rivera help alter the sound of the bolero by infusing rock music instruments and increased sound levels to affect the subtle rhythmic undercoat of the music.

Historically, among the Island's popular long-running groups are the Rafael Muñoz Orchestra, formed in 1934 and La Sonora Ponceña, founded by pianist Enrique Lucca in Ponce, in 1954. The Muñoz aggregation, led from May 12, 1934 until the leader's death on September 2, 1961, makes its mark via a long association with RCA Victor Records. The band's slow rather than traditionally rapid boleros, strengthened by a flowing string section, remains his musical legacy in a catalog still available in 2005. Muñoz's son Monchito, who's a drummer, leads one of several tribute bands. Former Muñoz Orchestra vocalist, José Luis Monero, leads another.

Ponceña features two pianos played by Lucca's son Papo and Rafael Ithier, an array of trumpets and three vocalists. It is followed by two of the leading bands modernizing the local bomba and plena traditional musical styles, Rafael Cortijo's band and a spin-off from that band, El Gran Combo, whose leader, pianist Rafael Ithier, after leaving his former employer, creates a modern 13-piece salsa ensemble including two pianos, two saxophones, two trumpets and three lead vocalists. El Gran Combo eschews the jazzier, improvised styles of New York-based groups led by Puerto Rico's Eddie Palmieri and Tito Puente's 70's ensembles. Two other popular salseros, of the '60s–'70s salsa era in New York, Willie Colón and Hector Lavoe, help Fania Records build its salsa catalog and are also members of the high-flying Fania All Stars. Lavoe, born in Ponce, moves to New York in

1963 and is known as "El Cantante" for his distinctive high nasal voice and ability to improvise. In 1973, Lavoe splits from Colón, forms his own band and then runs into hard times, fighting drug addiction and a downward slide into poverty. In 1993, he reportedly dies of AIDS in New York. He's three months shy of his 47th birthday. His life will be depicted in a major movie starring Marc Anthony with his wife Jennifer Lopez the film's producer. The movie is discussed in Chapter 11 along with other facets of the professional/married life of Lopez and Anthony.

During the early '80s, the Island's hard-driving salsa morphs into what's called salsa romantica, led by vocalist Lalo Rodriguez, who influences a number of other balladeers including Frankie Ruiz, Jerry Rivera and Eddie Santiago. But it's the salsa style which percolates in Puerto Rico, which drives the Island's musical identity into the 21st century, when new musical influences and idioms begin to take shape...and have a profound influence on New York and other Eastern cities where tropical music, as it's called on Spanish radio, is a favored format.

There's even an evolution in the sound of the merengue as vocalist Elvis Crespo and his former band Grupo Manía, both restructure the Dominican import in the early '90s.

Among musicians achieving crossover success are two well-known locals: Jose Feliciano and Ricky Martin. Vocalist/guitarist Jose Feliciano, born blind in Lares, moves to southern California, sings in English, wins six Grammys, earns 14 Grammy nominations, gains 40 gold and platinum albums during his popularity heydays of the '70s when he's a resident of Orange County, and is making his presence known again in 2004. Ricky Martin, born in San Juan as Enrique Martin Morales, breaks into show business in 1984 with the Island's new teenage pop group, Menudo. After five years, he heads out on his own and becomes 1999's breakout and crossover solo artist and Grammy winner for his best Latin pop performance on *Living La Vida Loca* from the album *Vuelve*, his fourth Spanish-language LP for Sony since 1992. On the periphery of breakout success in the U.S. is romantic crooner Chayanne, born in San Lorenzo, who gains Latin market success in the late '80s–early '90s and then after a slump, rebounds in 1996, when he starts cooking in the domestic Latin market on the Mainland.

Among the Island's musical forms, it's the tropical salsa/merengue sound, reflecting the Island's geographical heritage that remains the most popular form of radio programming here. In fact, within San Juan's 54 radio stations, of the 45 in Spanish, nine are tropical exponents, lead by market leader WPRM-FM and followed by WKAQ-FM in fourth place and WZNT-FM in fifth position during the summer of 2003. The other tropical formats can be heard on these other FMs: WZAR, WIVA, WXYX, WCMN, WUKQ, WRIO, WZMT, WHOY and WZET.

By 2004, a growing array of local Spanish-lingo rappers clicks with the new sound of reggaeton and beings to attract attention on the Mainland.

Puerto Rico's list of acclaimed celebrities includes names regularly seen in both the sports and film worlds, especially jockey Angel Tomás Cordero, Jr., born in Santurce, who wins 7,057 races before retiring after 22 years in 1992; golfer Juan "Chi Chi" Rodriguez, born in Rio Piedras, who comes to the foreground in the 1960s and during his 40-year career wins eight Professional Golfers Association tours and 22 senior PGA tours and a place in the PGA World Golf Hall of Fame in 1992. He also presents the Island on 12 World Cup teams; baseball legend Roberto Clemente, born in barrio San Anton in Carolina, August 18, 1934, plays 18 seasons with the Pittsburgh Pirates from 1955 to 1972, appearing in two World Series. On New Year's Eve 1972, the plane he charters to fly supplies to earthquake victims in Nicaragua crashes into the sea after taking off. Roberto is on board and his body is never found. In his honor, a 304 acre sports complex is named after him as is the Roberto Clemente Coliseum in San Juan.

In the film industry, Benicio Del Toro is among the most sought-after dramatic protagonists; José Vicente Ferrer, born in

Santurce, is an Academy Award winner and respected stage headliner, who's married to vocalist Rosemary Clooney until his passing in 1992; Raul Julia (Raul Rafael Carlos Julia Y Arcelay), born in San Juan, maintains a career in films and stage productions from 1964 until his death in 1994, and actress Rita Moreno, born in Humacao, who conquers film and Broadway, becomes the first woman to win entertainment's four top awards: the Oscar, for films, the Tony for Broadway theater, the Emmy for television and the Grammy for recordings. Her role in the 1961 film adaptation of the Broadway musical, *West Side Story*, depicting Puerto Rican life in New York City, establishes her acting credentials.

Multimedia actress Rosie Perez digs deep into her Puerto Rican heritage in 2005 to write and produce the documentary, *Yo Soy Boricua, Pa' Que Tu Lo Sepa* (*I'm Puerto Rican For Your Information*), which focuses on New York City's annual Puerto Rican Day, for cable's Independent Film Channel. Perez's career seems as hot as a chili pepper: after appearing in HBO's *Lackawanna Blues*, PBS drama *Copshop* and the feature film *All The Invisible Children*, and costarring in the Broadway production of *Fearless* with Mary-Louise Parker, she's signed to a show development deal with Fox Broadcasting.

Musical alterations to Puerto Rico's musical landscape are noticeable in 2002. As salsa starts to fade in popularity, resulting from what critics call record labels releasing almost identical sound alike discs, rap, or reggaeton, which blends spoken word dialog with the rhythm of Jamaica's reggae dancehall style, is on the ascension. The folkloric categories of bomba and plena are being modernized by a number of local bands in addition to several festivals spotlighting the genre. And backup bands are being replaced in clubs by recorded music as the accompaniment for singers and solo musicians. It appears to be a tumultuous period on the Island, which measures 100 miles by 35 miles. Nevertheless, Puerto Rican bands, which ply the local concert circuit exclusively in 2002, provide salsa, merengue, rock en Español and rap devotees with a menu of choices. Local management firms and booking agencies often keep their insular clients working year-round on the Island. With 78 municipalities scattered throughout the commonwealth, artists can tour these locales and play before audiences who choose not to travel into the capital city of San Juan. Management firms seek out sponsors to help foot the bill. Edwin Medina of Skandalo Music, which manages several bands, emphasizes to *Billboard* in a story about touring in Puerto Rico that "sponsors are crucial to an artist." He points out that of the 145 dates Skapulario, one of his rock bands plays, around 100 are sponsored events. Among the bands working the entire year at public and private events is Algarete, according to Peter Cruz, owner of his eponymous 24-year-old booking agency.

If a band doesn't ply its trade elsewhere, as some do by playing in Central and South America, it remains a local success story without any international buzz. Limite 21, a 12-year-old merengue band can play 200 dates within Puerto Rico's borders, including 97 dates between May and July, while also venturing to Colombia, Panama, Costa Rica and Orlando, Florida, according to DME booking agent Edwin Covas.

An emerging rap artist colony, despite a hard struggle for mass attention, captures the ear of Mainland Latin labels Sony Discos, EMI Latin and Universal Latino. Buddha's Productions Records links with Sony; Night Man signs with Universal and EMI signs the group 3-2 Get Funky. Along with Buddha's Productions, other local labels spearheading the rap revolution are Pina Music, BM and Fresh Productions. 3-2 Get Funky's Mickey Perfecto and one-named partner Bimbo initially record four albums for RMM and are heard rapping on Celia Cruz's current hit, *La Negra Tiene Tumbao.* Pina Music's chief rap acts are Master Joe and Og Black and Lito & Polaco.

Puerto Rico is one of three stops for El Banco Popular De Puerto Rico's 10th annual *Encuentro* (*Encounter*) music special featuring the Island's Robi Rosa, along with Panama's Rubén Blades and the Dominican Republic's Juan Luis Guerra. The 90-minute concert to be released on three formats, CD, DVD and VHS, is taped at the Mario "Quijote" Morales Coliseum, with additional segments in the two other nations. Each vocalist performs five tunes and then sings together on a composition by Island singer/songwriter Antonio Cabán Vale. The three vocalists represent 30 years of popular Latin music.

In addition to an annual folkloric festival in the village of Loiza Aldea, other bomba and plena gatherings take place around the Island, with a number of young bands seeking to upgrade the music, including using modern instruments, contemporary arrangements and adding the cuatro guitar for its distinct sound. Pedro Guzmán, a cuatro expert, infuses traditional music with a jazz influence. Other bands in the upgrade movement include William Cepeda, Plena Libre and Edwin Colón Zayas.

One of Puerto Rico's hippest imports is alto/tenor saxophonist David Sánchez, who combines bomba and plena rhythms within Latin jazz on his 2002 Columbia release, *Melaza* (*Molasses*). The New York resident says including the two folk music rhythms is a salute to the Puerto Rican musicians who germinate the music which he grows up hearing. His father even plays in a bomba/plena band, providing additional exposure in which to soak up the two rhythms and apply them when he decides to become a fulltime jazz artist. Sánchez is signed by the label in the mid-'90s. His debut recording, *The Departure*, is followed by *Sketches of Dreams*, *Street Scenes*, *Obsesion*, *Melaza* and *Travesia*. Two years later, the 35-year-old native of Hato Rey explores nine Latin classical works on *Coral*, his seventh album for Columbia. Two years in the making, it's his first recording with a symphony orchestra, the City of Prague Philharmonic Orchestra, recorded in the Czech Republic. Relatively known compositions are by Brazilians Heitor Villa-Lobos and Antonio Carlos Jobim, Argentinean Alberto Ginastera, the orchestra's conductor Carlos Franzetti and Sánchez himself. Working with the saxophonist are his associates, pianist Edsel Gomez, bassist John Benitez and drummer Adam Cruz, plus guest alto saxman Miguel Zenón. The mood and tempo of this album—a hybrid jazz/classical mixture which is more mellow than combustible—is a marked departure from his previous fiery Latin excursions.

Local bands working in the non-folk music areas are plentiful and include: El Gran Combo, Son By Four, Angel López, Son's former lead singer who's striking out on his own, Circo, Olga Tañon, Andy Montañez, Cheo Feliciano, Willie Rosario, Papo Lucca, Roberto Roena, Humberto Ramírez, Luis "Perico" Ortiz, Limite 21, Domingo Quiñones, Tony Tun Tun, Jerry Rivera, Victor Sanabria, Skapulario, Malas Mañas, Fuga Alterna, La PVC, Giselle, Grupomania, Victor Manuelle, La Secta Consejo, Cultura Profética, Lito & Polaco, Wisin & Yandel, Sal Pa' Fuera, Algarete, and Bartolo & The Heartbreakers.

While the majority of these musicians never cause a ruckus on the Mainland, El Gran Combo, Son By Four, Circo, and Olga Tañon, are among those who do reach out for a broader audience.

Angel López, the former lead singer with Son By Four, who's replaced by Luis Damón, a New York vocalist, certainly causes a major ruckus by splitting from the group consisting of brothers Jorge and Javier Montes and cousin Pedro Quiles who formed the backing chorus behind him. Adding salt to the wound is that both López and the group are signed to Sony Discos. While the band, founded by the Montes brothers, records an album on the Island, López is completing his debut for Sony, *En Mi Soledad* (*In My Loneliness*) at the Miami studio owned by Oscar Llord, who happens to be president/CEO of Sony Discos and also executive producer on the album. Sony avoids making public the split in the group until a lawsuit contesting who owns the group's name is awarded to its founders. López, who tries once before for a solo career in the early '90s before joining the quartet, makes a second attempt at a solo career while in Miami at a Sony Disco's showcase at BillboardLive as part of the festivities surrounding the *Billboard* Latin Music Awards.

For Santurce-born Olga Tañon, who's merengue's top female artist, with two straight Grammy-winning albums on Warner Music Latina, being a devotee of the Dominican Republic's chief musical export is not enough. She's looking to build her next album around pop ballads, working with Marco Antonio Solís, who produces her hit

1995 album *Nuevos Senderos*. Two years later, she wins two awards at the Premio Lo Nuestro awards in Miami to add to her two Latin Grammys, including best female pop vocalist. Now a native of Orlando, she and her husband purchase a Mexican restaurant and plan building a fast-food chain in Puerto Rico. In 2005, the "queen of meringue" switches labels from Warner Music Latina after 10 plus years to join the new Sony BMG imprint. Her first album for her new label, *Una Nueva Mujer*, is released in April of '05 and combines a mixture of Puerto Rican cultures with personal message songs. Her new CD is the four-time Grammy winner's first studio session since *Sobrevivir* is released in 2002, according to *Billboard*. Warner Bros. bids farewell one month earlier with the CD/DVD *Como Olvidar…Lo Mejor De Olga Tañon*. She gains Mainland exposure April 7 by performing with an array of other stars at a Selena tribute concert airing live on Univision from the Reliant Stadium in Houston.

For Circo, which means circus, the Island's leading alternative rock or rock en Español band, its reputation has been slow in crossing the ocean to the Mainland. Last year, it's an obscure band to Mainlanders. This year, with two Latin Grammy nominations for best new artist and best rock album by a duo or group with vocal, both for its first-time recording, the very lengthy titled *No Todo Lo Que Es Pop Es Bueno* (*Not Everything Pop Is Good*), the quintet is dead center in the national spotlight. Unfortunately, it's shutout in both categories by Jorge Moreno and La Ley, respectively. Circo's albums are distributed throughout the U.S. by Miami-based independent DLN. José Luis "Fofé" Abreu, the band's lead singer, is also its most flamboyant member in his persona and dress, while several other members sport Mohawk haircuts. Circo is an outgrowth of El Manjar De Los Dioses, a local fusion band formed in 1994, in which Abreu, keyboardist Edgardo Santiago and drummer José David Pérez are all members. When Abreu chooses to split in 2000, he takes his two associates with him, adds bassist Nicolas Cordero and guitarist Orlando Méndez, and the band makes its debut in New York at the second Latin Alternative Music Conference in 2001. The band's electronic music, its offbeat lyrics and Abreu's on stage theatrics, attract followers of rock en Español at home and along the music's accessible club scene on the Mainland.

Venezuela's three-year-old Latin World Entertainment label has obvious eyes for the U.S. market by opening offices here and in Miami. It releases a double CD by local rock band and former EMI act Fiel A La Vega with accompaniment by the Puerto Rican Symphony Orchestra with whom it previously performs.

Rock en Español acts lose a major radio outlet when WCOM-FM, owned by SBS Puerto Rico, drops the music after one year and returns to Spanish contemporary music under the new call letters of WODA (*Onda 94*). It's the latest format switch for *Cosmos 94*, whose previous format is rap. Besides being Puerto Rico's first rock en Español station, during its year of existence, it helps local and global rock bands gain the attention of hardcore listeners. At the time of the format switch, Miami-based SBS owns three other stations in this market.

In 2003, Spanish Broadcasting System boosts the number of its local properties to 11 outlets in its 24-station universe. One year later, SBS owns and operates a total of 25 stations here and in New York, Los Angeles, Miami, Chicago, and San Francisco. Rival Hispanic Broadcasting Corporation, prior to being purchased by Univision Communications, enters this market by purchasing El Mundo Broadcasting and its four stations-three FMs and one AM-for $32 million in cash from Fundacion Angel Ramos Inc. HBC presently owns or operates 63 stations on the Mainland.

Three of SBS' stations here are tropical formats. During my trip to New York in 2003, while discussing that city's Latin radio business, Carey Davis, the company's vice president/general manager of its two prime Gotham outlets, tells me that salsa still leads the music parade on his tropical station and market leader, WSKQ. "Salsa from Puerto Rico dominates the Caribbean music industry that our listeners want," he says, adding: "some merengueros come from Puerto Rico, but mostly they're from the Dominican Republic." Puerto Rican record labels are the prime source for salsa, which shows signs of fading off the radio dial on the Island in favor of the melding of hip-hop, reggae and salsa into reggaeton. "This is a music with a strong urban feel," says Davis. "You might say that in Puerto Rico, which does not have an African-American population per se, reggaeton is the replacement for hip-hop. It has legs, as we say. It's a popular thing there." Reacting to the reggaeton rage, SBS in June of '05 switches WOND, its meringue station, to the popular sound, notes *Billboard*; in September, WCMA flips from its English-language adult contemporary style to old and new Spanish pop hits by name acts, differentiating it from the contemporary ballad sound of WIOB, another SBS outlet.

Four local rock en Español bands are signed by Mainland record companies, even though there's no local radio outlet for their music. Following the lead of Universal Music Latino which signs the duo Vivanativa last summer, EMI Latin signs Algarete and Orbe Azul, while Sony Discos lands Skapulario and Puerto Raices. EMI's president, Jorge Pinos, tells *Billboard* that with the decline in tropical music, "we are focusing more on alternative music."

The Island's romance with rap/reggaeton receives a major boost with the release in 2003 of Tego Calderón's debut album, *El Abayarde*, on White Lion Records, which BGM acquires for distribution, a move which lands the album on *Billboard*'s Top Latin Albums chart. Unlike other rap acts which rhyme in angry tones, Calderón chooses a less frenzied style, which adds spice by sprinkling in elements of reggaeton, salsa, bomba and DJ vinyl scratching. These ingredients generate enough heat locally to exceed 150,000 copies of the album sold here and 70,000 copies on the Mainland to where BMG Latin picks up its national distribution. What's remarkable is that Calderón is 31, senses the changing tastes of his fellow Islanders and is able to fuse multiple ingredients into a contemporary sound. During the three years his family lives in Miami Beach, he's exposed to rap in English and begins dabbling in that genre. It's only when he returns home does he begin rapping in Spanish, combing that with traditional vocals riding over a bevy of Caribbean rhythms.

Two years later, Calderón and his Jiggiri label make history by becoming the first Spanish-language artist signed to English-language Atlantic Records, which will release his primarily Spanish album *The Underdog* with its Spanish title *El Subestimado* in October. The album will include minimal English lyrics by some unnamed artists in addition to guest appearances by Don Omar and Eddie D, according to *Billboard.*

Calderón credits Luis Armando Lozada, whose professional name is Vico C, with inspiring him to rap in Spanish. Lozada, 32, who leads a trouble life including battles with drugs, which are reflected in his lyrics, is often called the godfather of reggaeton since he scores his first local hit 15 years ago when he's 17. Last year, he wins a Latin Grammy for his EMI U.S. Latin album *Vivo.*

One other local rapper joining Calderón on the Latin chart several months later is Don Omar, legal name William Omar Landrón Rivera, whose *Last Don* album is released on the VI Music label.

While Calderon has his link with Atlantic, White Lion and its acts, Volito, Calle 13 and Lisa M. are distributed in 2005–'06 by Sony, half of the giant merged company called Sony BMG.

Reggaeton/rap artists exert such a major influence on the Island's record sales that Robi "Draco" Rosa, an artist on his own Phantom Vox label, suggests the music now accounts for 60–70 percent of all record sales during a *Billboard* panel on rap in Miami. Reggaeton duo Baby Rasta & Gringo, who debut in 1997 on local label New Records with their hit album, *Live Desde El Más Allá*, crack the *Billboard* Top Latin Albums chart at No. 10 this year with *Sentenciados*, which gains the national muscle of new distributor Universal Music Latino. By 2004–2005, there's a major reggaeton revolution underway on the Mainland as Puerto Rican artists, led by Daddy Yankee, make the nation's best-selling album listings.

Two festivals, one honoring salsa, the other jazz, draw top name artists from the Mainland. For the 20th straight year, radio station Z-93 presents its annual National Salsa Day concert, featuring this year's local favorites and alumni of the Fania All Stars from New York at the Estadio Juan Ramón Lubriel De Bayamón before an estimated crowd of 25,000 salseros. The third Sunday in March is legally designated as the Dia Nacional De La Salsa in honor of the Island's salsa legacy. Honored this year are Johnny Pacheco and Roberto Roena. The bands of Moncha Rivera, Bobby Valentin, Tito Rojas, and Tommy Olivencia precede the Fania All Stars during its three-hour nostalgic trip through the ensemble's '70s hits. Twenty-three New York members of the Fania band make the trip to San Juan for the concert. Among them is honoree Johnny Pacheco. Special guests with the all stars are Ricardo "Richie" Ray and Bobby Cruz.

During the 13th Puerto Rico Heineken JazzFest at the Tito Puente Amphitheater in Hato Rey, the endemic bomba rhythm is uncorked by reedman Paquito D'Rivera's sextet; pianist extraordinaire Chick Corea's New Trio romps through several Latin-flavored tunes while vibist Gary Burton and pianist Makoto Ozone indulge in some Latin jazz improvisations. D'Rivera and associates add the folkloric beat to *Paquito*, written by Corea, whose trio explodes on his own *La Fiesta* and *Anna's Tango*. Burton and Ozone lift *Afro Blue* with lilting Latin jazz figures during their set, with the vibist joining D'Rivera's ensemble on a tango as well.

Catalino "Tite" Curet Alonso, one of Puerto Rico's revered salsa and bolero composers passes away August 5 in Baltimore where he resides for the last three weeks of his life. He'd been moved there from his native land by his daughter Angie, a nursing instructor, with burial taking place several days later on the Island. Cause of death for the 77-year-old, according to the daughter, are complications from heart disease and poor circulation. Alonso, a prolific composer, writes for Fania Records during the '70s and '80s. One of his best-known works is *La Tirana* recorded in 1968 by Cuban vocalist La Lupe. Alonso is renowned for crafting his tunes to match the voice and personality of the intended artist.

Batacumbele, a band with Puerto Rican-New York City roots, dating back to its formation in the late 1970s as a leader in fusing various cultural ingredients, returns to the Tito Puente

Amphitheater September 19 to honor the memory of one of its founders, trumpeter extraordinaire Juancito Torres who dies July 27. Called "Puerto Rico's national trumpeter," Torres also performs with a number of groups ranging from the Puerto Rico All Stars, the Fania All Stars to bands led by Machito, Eddie Palmieri, and Dave Valentin. Batacumbele's leader, Angel "Cachete" Maldonado, reunites some of the original members for the memorial concert. He forms the band while living in New York and adds Puerto Rican members when the New York contingent returns to San Juan, where they come up with the official name which is based on three local terms, bata for drum, cumbele, a derivative of kum for knee, and bele for bending your knees. The band's sound is an amalgam of Afro-Cuban tunes, a dash of Latin jazz improvisation topped with Puerto Rican and African folk rhythms.

Two Puerto Rican bands based in New York, Yerba Buena and Antibalas, are blending their multicultural backgrounds into musical heat waves. Yerba Buena, a sextet which debuts on the Fun Machine/Razor & Tie label, blends New York Puerto Rican bred boogalu with Cuba's rumba, Colombia's cumbia, Nigeria's Afro-beat, and America's soul and hip-hop on the CD *President Alien*. While touring, the band seems to appeal the most to non-Latinos, Andres Levin, the band's producer/leader/guitarist tells *Billboard* its multicultural sound helps land it opening spots for such groups as Willie Nelson, the Dave Matthews Band, Café Tacuba, and the late Celia Cruz.

Antibalas, whose 15 members have ethnicities embracing a wide array of nationalities along with a musical mixture of rock, jazz, Brazilian, and Cuban, mixes all these ingredients on their first two albums for Ninja Tune. The two albums featuring the blending of traditional African sounds with jazz and funk with lyrics in Spanish, English, and Yoruba, are *Liberation Afrobeat* and *Talkatif*.

Waving the flag of feminism during the last week in December, romantic/dramatic vocalist Ednita Nazario's 20th album, *Por Ti* on EMI Latin USA, becomes the first women's recording since

January to debut at No. 1 on *Billboard*'s Top Latin Albums chart. Her pop album, primarily written by women, features acoustic instruments and a rock undercoating. The last female to top the survey earlier in the year is Celia Cruz. Her 21st album, the summer 2005 Sony BMG Norte release, *Apasionada*, rises to second place on *Billboard*'s Latin Pop Albums chart, affirming her strong connection with the public after nearly 30 years of recording for Melody, EMI Latin, Sony Discos, and the recast Sony BMG Norte, touring (and appearing in the ill-fated Broadway musical *The Capeman*). In fact, buoyed by her record-breaking three consecutive sold out concerts at the José Miguel Agrelot Coliseum the weekend of November 20, the Ponce resident will embark on a concert tour of the Mainland in 2006, appearing in an untitled English-language movie, and recording her next album which includes a number of duets with Julieta Venegas and La Oreja De Van Gogh, notes *Billboard.*

While there's a plethora of Puerto Rican heritage musicians in New York, including the two Titos, bandleaders Puente and, Rodriguez, Puerto Rican baseball players establish their own home base in the major leagues in the 1950s, starting with Vic Power, a seven-time winner of the Gold Glove Award, and the late Roberto Clemente, who plays his entire career in right field with the Pittsburgh Pirates from 1955-1972 to become the first Latino elected to baseball's Hall of Fame. The 37-year-old is killed when his chartered DC-7 crashes off Puerto Rico on Dec. 31, 1972 while flying emergency supplies to earthquake-devastated Nicaragua. Two years after his passing, the Ciudad Deportiva Roberto Clemente sports center is opened and a coliseum is renamed after him. The sports city, however, runs into financial problems with bank loans and government grants in 2003, which halts future growth of the sports city as it's called here.

San Juan's Hiram Bithorn Stadium is the site for the opening game of the 2001 season between the Toronto Blue Jays and the Texas Rangers. It's also the second home for Montreal, which schedules 22 of its regular season games in 2003 there since its hometown fan base is seriously disappearing due to its dismal team record. Baseball's reliance and romance with Latin players is one of the topics discussed in Chapter 14.

At the start of the 2003 season, Puerto Rico places 38 players in the major leagues, the second largest contingent behind the Dominican Republic with 79, and 130 in the minor leagues. Puerto Rican major leaguers scattered throughout the nation include Bernie Williams and Jose Posada of the New York Yankees, Juan Gonzalez of the Texas Rangers, Roberto Alomar and Rey Sanchez of the New York Mets, Alex Cora of the Los Angeles Dodgers, Ramon Vasquez of the San Diego Padres, brothers Bengie and Jose Molina of the Anaheim Angels, Javier Lopez and Jose Hernandez of the Colorado Rockies, J.C. Romero of the Minnesota Twins, Javier Valentin of the Tampa Bay Devil Rays, Carlos Beltran of the Kansas City Royals, Jose Vidro of the Montreal Expos, and Carlos Baerga of the Arizona Diamondbacks. By the start of the 2004 season, 36 Puerto Ricans are playing in the major leagues. Since Hiram Bithorn begins pitching for the Chicago Cubs in 1942, Puerto Rico sends more than 200 players to the big leagues.

The Expos, called *Los Expos* here, open their new home away from home series at Hiram Bithorn Stadium by whipping the New York Mets 10-0. Despite the lopsided score, local fans greet three homegrown Mets stars, Jose Vidro, Roberto Alomar, and Rey Sanchez with standing ovations. Among those in the stands is Vidro's mother who has never before seen her son play in a major league game. And when the California Angels destroy Montreal 15-4, as part of a three-game match-up, it's the first time Angels brothers and catchers Bengie and Jose Molina play before family and friends. Among Bengie's four hits, which drives in three runs, is a homer in the eighth inning resulting in his pointing to his family in the stands as he rounds the bases. The brothers have only been home one time for the funeral of their grandmother since 1993 when they make their minor league debuts.

Prior to the umpire's call of "play ball," Chi Chi Rodriguez, the Island's notable golfer, selects to chip the ceremonial first pitch rather than throw it out.

For its first season in San Juan, the Expos end up with 13 wins and nine loses. One of the loses occurs when the Dominican Republic's Moises Alou hits a tie-breaking two-run single to help the Chicago Cubs defeat Montreal 4-3. Although hit in the helmet by a pitch, Sammy Sosa remains in the game to the delight of locals who cheer Chicago more than they do *Los Expos* during this game.

2004 marks the year romantic multimedia star Chayanne celebrates his 25th year in show business. Born Elmer Figueroa Arce in Rio Piedras, he first breaks into music with the boy quartet Los Chicos when he's 10 in 1979 and records five albums with the group. He's also the band's most famous alumnus who uses the nickname his mother bestows upon him based on the 1950's pioneering TV western *Cheyenne* when he goes solo as a teenager and makes his mark on the international Latin scene in the late '80s–early '90s. However, his career spirals downward in the '90s and breaks open again in 1996 with the release of the album *Volver A Nacer* (*To Be Born Again*). Currently promoting his latest Sony Norte album, *Sincero*, on a tour of South America and the U.S. from March through October, the 35-year-old vocalist remains true to his Latino fans by recording 12 albums in Spanish for Sony Discos. On stops in Los Angeles and Miami, his new hard-edged sound is a stark contrast to his past romantic persona, highlighted by his starring with Vanessa Williams in the 1998 film *Dance With Me* and appearing on the Fox TV series *Ally McBeal* in 2001.

With the Miami resident considering a stab at the lucrative crossover English-language market, his new sound, amplified by an eight-piece electric band, may be testing the waters with a new style, while retaining his romantic electricity for female followers. One reason for his growing success is the radio play he garners on romantic ballad stations like New York-New Jersey's WPAT-FM. Tony Luna, the program director, calls him "one of the station's core artists" in a *Billboard* spotlight, adding: "He has what we call 'lágrima' (or tears) in his voice."

One year later, Chayanne's career is highlighted on the Azteca America TV network in *Especial Musical: Chayanne*. The special includes footage of a concert in Mexico City which reportedly attracts 140,000 spectators, plus an overview of his hits and an exclusive interview. His latest Sony album, *Desde Siempre*, compiles his romantic hits, and is his 13th album since 1984.

During the summer of '05, Chayanne teams up with fellow stars Marc Anthony and Alejandro Fernández for a historic 15-city tour of the Mainland, the first time these three different musical stylists perform together. Additional tour information is covered in Chapter 19.

Among the hallmarks in 2004 is the 50th birthday of the Island's first TV station, Telemundo's WKAQ (Channel 2), launched by founder Angel Ramos on March 28, 1954, and marked by a four-hour special April 1.The broadcast is attended by 1,800 guests who walk down a red carpet leading into San Juan's Centro De Bellas Artes Luis A. Ferré. The special telecast highlights the station's novelas and original programs spanning the last five decades. Among San Juan's four TV stations, Telemundo's chief competitor Univision operates WLII and sister network TeleFutura's WSTE.

During WKAQ's initial year, it broadcasts from 3 to 10 p.m. Among its achievements: in 1968 its entire programming is in color and it broadcast its first program, the World Series, via satellite. The next year in September, the Telemundo network is formed when United Atmosphere Productions Corporation agrees to carry Telemundo's programming already seen on Channel 2, on its Channel 20 in Ponce and Channel 22 in Mayaguez. Two months prior to forming the network, WKAQ carries man's first steps on the moon via satellite. In 1983, Ramos sells the station to John Blair & Company for $55 million. In 1987, Blair sells Telemundo to Reliance Capital Group for an unspecified price. The new owner's initial purchases include WKAQ and stations in Miami, New York, San Jose/San

Francisco, Chicago, and Hartford, Connecticut, to expand the network within the Mainland.

WKAQ's current president/general manager is Luis Roldan, who begins his career at the company's New York WNJU in sales in 1984, shifts briefly to NBC's WNBC-TV and rejoins WNJU in 1991. He moves to WKAQ in 1998. The station's local programming grows to 50 hours of news and entertainment. In his bio, Roldan prophesizes that a key lesson he's learned while working here is that "sometimes the popular thing to do isn't always right and the right thing to do isn't always popular."

There's two additional firsts recorded for the Island when the two leading music performing rights organizations, the American Society of Composers & Authors (ASCAP) and Broadcast Music Inc. (BMI), hold their Latin Awards one night apart here at the same hotel, the Ritz Carlton San Juan.

The 12th annual El Primo ASCAP Awards names Joan Sebastian and Rudy Pérez songwriters of the year and Sony/ATV publisher of the year. The song of the year winner is *Tal Vez*, composed by Franco De Vita and published by Warner Bros. The rock song of the year goes to *Eres Mi Religion*, composed by José Fernando Olvera Sierra and published by EMI/April Music; the hip-hop/reggae top tune goes to *Masucamba*, composed by Tego Calderón and published by El Abayarde. Yerba Buena, the New York Afro-Latin fusion sextet, comprised of saxophone, trumpet, bass, guitar, drums and conga, is named the top independent group of the year.

Among BMI award recipients at its 11th annual celebration is Colombia songwriter/producer Estéfano as Latin songwriter of the year for the third straight time. He also shares this honor in 2000 with Marco Antonio Pérez, Mario Quintero, Kike Santander, and Shakira. Estéfano's World Deep Music Publishing Corporation, which holds the rights to four hit tunes on BMI's list of the top 50, is also named publisher of the year.

In addition to Estéfano, other multiple winning songwriters include Juanes and Kike Santander with three songs and Emilio

Estefan, Jr., Lester Mendez, Mario Quintero, Jorge Villamizar, and Teodoro Bello Jaimes with two tunes.

The song of the year trophy is presented to *Perdóname Mi Amor* (*Forgive Me My Love*) written by Ramón González Mora, published by Sony-Seg Music and performed by norteño band Conjunto Primavera. Last year, Mora wins the same award for another Conjunto Primavera hit, *Morir De Amor.*

On a reflective note, a musical tribute to the late Rafael Hernández, a BMI composer who passes away in 1965, features Andy Montañez, Rafi Escudero and Chucho Avellanet. Hernandez is known for his prolific body of works exceeding 3,000 compositions.

A third first occurs when ballad stylist Ednita Nazario opens the new 20,000 capacity José Miguel Agrelot Coliseum in May as part of a tour backing her Sony Norte CD, *Por Ti.* She's already performed four soldout concerts at the Roberto Clemente Coliseum in March and has toured Mexico, Panama, New York, Miami, Orlando, and Los Angeles.

Another happy moment for Islanders watching the *Billboard* Latin Music awards on Telemundo in May occurs when local favorites Luny Tunes & Noriega win the tropical album and new artist awards for their album *Más Flow*.

Sadness follows the death of 47-year-old bandleader/percussionist Ivan Cáceres in a car accident on March 12, 2004. Known for his bongo playing, he's often called "Mr. Bongolandia." He had recently released his first self-produced album, *Roots of Acid Salsa*.

Jazz and salsa are showcased respectively at the 2004 Latin Jazz Symposium and the 21st Años Dia Nacional De La Salsa festival.

The four-day Latin jazz event in April is presented by the Puerto Rico Federal Affairs Administration and *Latin Beat* magazine first at the Universidad Del Sagrado Corazon in Santurce and then at California State University, Long Beach. Artists performing locally are the Humberto Ramirez Group, the Gabriel Rodriguez Band, plus guest musicians Paquito D'Rivera, Ralph Irizarry, Ben Lapidus, and Jesús Caunedo.

The salsera festival at El Estadio Roberto Clemente features its own power lineup of local bands, notably Conjunto Chaney, Tipica 73, Salsa Fever, and La Sonora Ponceña.

A mixture of local and internationally-known jazz artists helps make another jazz bash, the Heineken JazzFest De Puerto Rico a rousing success. Appearing at the June event at the Tito Puente Amphitheater are pianist Monty Alexander, saxophonist Gato Barbieri, trombonist Jimmy Bosch, jazz/pop band Spyro Gyra, the Lincoln Center's Afro-Latin Jazz Orchestra, and vocalist Dianne Reeves. Local bands offering their own Latin jazz spin include the ensemble led by saxophonist Edgar Abraham and the Tony Pérez Quintet.

A historic coming together in 1982 of established and emerging Latin jazz artists from Puerto Rico, Cuba, Brazil, Argentina, and the Mainland makes its appearance this year on the two DVD set, *Tierrazo Jazz Live In Puerto Rico 1982*. The Tierrazo Music release captures the first-ever appearance by this blending of artists at San Juan's Centro De Bellas Artes. Disc one features Cuba's Irakere led by pianist co-founder Chucho Valdés and New York flutist Dave Valentin and his group. Disc two showcases the Island's own Batacumbele, New York's Tito Puente, the "king of the timbal," plus several supporting timbale players and Brazil's superstar vocalist, Tânia Maria.

In a most adventurous concept, trumpeter Humberto Ramirez sets his interpretation of Miles Davis recordings for the first time within a host of tropical Latin rhythms. The San Juan-based AJ Records *Miles Latino* features homegrown bassist John Benitez, Cuban drummer Horacio "El Negro" Hernandez, New York percussionist Richie Flores, Venezuelan pianist Ed Simon, and guest saxophonist Michael Brecker. Ramirez tells *Jazziz*, he selects rarely or never recorded tunes within a Latin mode for the album. His other A.J. releases include *Dos Almos* with Eddie Gomez and Gonzalo Rubalcaba and *Best Friends* with congero Giovanni Hidalgo.

Flutist Nestor Torres, who grows up in the city of Mayaguez, moves with his family to Flushing, New York, where he begins his professional career, eventually settles in Miami in 1981 and is today the leading jazz flutist in smooth jazz. During his musical matriculation, he studies at the New England Conservatory of Music and the Berklee College of Music, plays flute in New York area bands which popularize the Cuban charanga sound and is exposed to Latin jazz in the Big Apple. His new album, *Sin Palabras* (*Without Words*) on the Heads Up label, is his latest example of a pop instrumental sound which is favored by the nation's smooth jazz radio stations. The album includes R&B, rap and Latin ingredients, all designed to generate crossover jazz acceptance. It's a reflection of his musical openness, dating back to 1989 when he's signed by PolyGram and debuts under his own name with *Morning Ride*, which features guest pianist Herbie Hancock.

Following a near-death experience in a boating accident in Miami, and the collapse of his marriage, Torres discovers that PolyGram is now disenchanted with Latin jazz. After the release of *Dance of The Phoenix*, which he is unable to promote, he's dropped from the roster, but his growing reputation lands him a two album deal with Sony, where he records *Burning Whispers* in 1994 and *Talk To Me* in '96, before shifting to Shanachie, where his CDs reflect his Latin roots on the LPs *Luna Latina*, *This Side of Paradise* and *Mi Alma Latina/My Latin Soul*. *This Side of Paradise*, earns him a Latin Grammy as the best pop instrumental album. Despite his success, Torres admits to *Jazziz*, he's piqued by the writers who dismiss his playing as being a Latin version of Kenny G, the ultra successful soprano saxophonist whose music is a mainstay on smooth jazz stations, and is detested by many music critics but loved by his pop music fans.

Remember Menudo, Puerto Rico's hot and sexy boy band which captivates teenage girls from its founding in 1977 through the '90s? It's coming back. Menudo Entertainment, a new company, will hold talent searches here, on the Mainland and in Latin America this summer to find five bilingual, bicultural 10- to 14-year olds, who will be replaced as they get older, just like the original band was structured to change partners when they hit 16. The company's three principals are Jeff Weiner, a former talent business manager,

Barry Solomon, a former NBC executive, and promoter Jerry Brenner. The Williams Morris Agency will handle the new company in its talent search, production of a TV special centered on the auditions and its efforts in acquiring product endorsements and merchandising. Miami-based Ole Music, the new label owned by former Sony Discos president Oscar Llord, will release the first new Menudo album.

These hyped plans never materialize, like many show business projects, albeit one year later, in February of 2005, reality TV producer Ben Silverman and Menudo Entertainment owners Weiner and Solomon are promoting an American Idol style TV competition encompassing the band auditions and the recording of the new group's debut album, which the William Morris Agency is packaging.

Of the 30 kids who filter through the original Menudo, only Ricky Martin achieves solo stardom. Robi Rosa, a former lead singer with the group, is also working as a solo, recording two Portuguese-language albums in Brazil when he's 17, and when he's older, cutting two albums in Spanish and one in English in the States and also quietly writing tunes for Martin, Julio Iglesias, and Ednita Nazario. After leaving the teeny bopper Menudo, Rosa creates a character named Draco, who wears pink hair, mascara, and arms-length black leather gloves. He's still seeking his breakout album, with his latest on Columbia titled *Mad Love.*

One singer who decides to switch from pop ballads to a tropical salsa format setting is local-bred Victor Manuelle. His *Travesia* CD on Sony Discos, becomes the first tropical album to hit No. 1 on the *Billboard* Latin album chart since Celia Cruz's passing last summer. Although he's heading in a new direction, Manuelle hangs onto his pop image by recording the single, *Tengo Ganas*, in pop and tropical versions. While working with producer Emilio Estefan, Jr., who generally doesn't do salsa albums, Manuelle writes or co-authors seven of the album's 12 tunes which meld with the Afro-Caribbean rhythms.

Two leading salsa artists are set for summer releases: Marc Anthony's next Sony release will be in Spanish while Elvis Crespo brings his merengue sensibilities to new label Ole Records. Anthony also plays a major role in the R-rated, bloodstained film, shot against a Mexican setting, *Man On Fire*, starring Denzel Washington, Dakota Fanning, and Christopher Walken, and released on the Mainland in mid-April.

A septet calling itself Puerto Rican Masters records the album, *Present La Historia De La Salsa*, at the Tito Puente Amphitheater. Its members include Luis "Perico" Ortiz, Elias Lopes, Pedro Brull, Luisito Carrión, Wichy Camacho, Papo Sánchez, and Henry Santiago, who perform tunes by the masters of salsa ranging from Celia Cruz to Puente himself.

In one of the most heated and unusual legal actions, Ricky Martin's filing of a $2.5 million suit against his manager of 12 years, Angelo Medina, in New York Supreme Court, is answered in San Juan Superior Court by Medina, who files a $63.6 million counter suit. Martin's initial action seeks to gain "unearned management commissions based on unjust enrichment, breach of agreement and breach of fiduciary duty," resulting from unspecified advances Martin receives from Sony Music Entertainment for additional albums, for which Medina, as his manager, is entitled to his commission, according to *Billboard*'s coverage.

Medina, who handles Martin during his early years and helps build his career, alleges "breach of contract, unjust enrichment and pain and suffering" in his suit. Both manager and artist amicably part ways last September, with Medina continuing to handle Martin's concerts here. Medina's breach of contract stipulation is based on the allegation that Martin did not honor that portion of their departure agreement.

Several months later, in mid-October, the two reach a confidential settlement in San Juan. Judge Oscar Davila prohibits both parties from releasing details of the settlement, followed by Martin and former manager Medina hugging each other during a news conference.

In a separate action—prior to the settlement of Martin's legal battle with Medina—encrusted with advocacy for a good cause, Martin establishes the People For People Foundation and launches a campaign against sexual exploitation and the sale of children into prostitution in Latin America and Asia. The vocalist cuts TV commercials in Spanish, Portuguese, and English for airing here, on the Mainland and in Latin America.

And in a move to gain entry into the reggaeton derby, EMI Music U.S. Latin signs a multiyear distribution pact with Guatauba Productions, which specializes in compilation albums. The first album under the deal and EMI's first reggaeton product is *Sazón Con Flavor* featuring a bevy of new, untested artists. Founded by Manolo Guatauba, the company also maintains an office in Miami which facilitates marketing and promotional activities with EMI.

Ignacio Pena, a local pop/rock guitarist, records five tunes on his second Universal Music Latino album, *Anormal*, in English, thus seeking general market radio play. Thematically, the songs deal with timely political and social issues. It's a marked departure from his previous all-Spanish CD *Mundo Al Reves*, whose focus is on Hispanic radio exposure.

Sticking to his traditional style, Gilberto Santa Rosa, 42, a major sonero, or improvisational vocalist with links to the purebred '70s style of salsa, retains both these ingredients on his Sony Discos release, *Auténtico*. Utilizing songs by Puerto Rican and Cuban composers and performed by two separate groups of studio musicians, Santa Rosa's improvised riffs as well as the potpourri of Afro-Caribbean tempos, brings the past into the present. During Mainland appearances in 2005, Santa Rosa hews closely to the native salsa traditions he embraces during his 28 years in show business. Backed in concert by a 12-piece band, which includes trumpeter Rebecca Zambrana, the show emotes energy from its heated mambos, warm-hearted boleros and the leader's improvised riffs.

Local favorite Samuel Hernández, as a result of two popular locally released Christian music albums and a radio played single on his own label, SH Productions, is catapulted into the Christian music showcase during *Billboard*'s 15th annual Latin Music Conference in Miami. *Faltan 5 Para Las Llegó*, his 2000 CD, remains No. 1 among local Christian album sales for more than a year, while 2003's *Jesús Siempre Llega A Tiempo* spawns the top local radio airplay single, *Levanto Tus Manos*, and a music video which incongruously airs on local music video channels.

Sparked by the acceptance in 2003 of such Christian music artists as Marcos Witt, Roberto Orellana, Jaci Velasquez, and Hernández, religious music branches out this year from its Christian base to encompass young non-religious music fans. Among the Christian music acts gaining favor locally are according to *Billboard*, Juan Luis Guerra, León De Judá, Abraham Velázquez, René González, and Daniel Carveti, all of whom produce high-quality albums which are promoted with the same zeal as secular albums. Initially helping to promote the message of God are FM's WKAQ, a Spanish contemporary music outlet and Nueva Vida (WNNV), a Christian music station, the oldest of the Island's five religious stations.

One year after reggaeton sweeps ashore on the Mainland in 2004 (covered in Chapter 19), its infectious reggae rhythmic base is modified to include more tropical and pop rhythms. This Caribbean fusion produces a better-produced, more mainstream sounding CD which certain tropical radio stations in New York and Miami regularly mix in their playlists. It's a big deal break for local proponents Don Omar (William Omar Landrón Rivera), Daddy Yankee (Raymond Ayala), Tego Calderón, Vico C, Robbi Draco Rosa, Baby Rasta & Gringo, Luny Tunes (Francisco Saldana as Luny and Victor Cabrera as Tunes), Noriera, the Trebol Clan, Pilar Montenegro, Gizelle D'Cole, Don Dinero, Bimbo (Jesus Otero), Angel & Khriz, Zion & Lennox, Enemigo, Gloria, and Tony Touch, for example. One reggaeton tune miraculously lands on the nation's best-selling list, the bilingual *N.O.R.E.* featuring Daddy Yankee, Nina Sky, Gem Star, and Big Mato.

Two new disc companies—Flow Music and New Records—join Raymond Ayala's *El Cartel* label in cracking through the dicey playing field of commercial success on the Mainland. Ayala, Daddy

Yankee's star is assuredly ascending. Reggaeton specialist Flow Music's major acts are DJ Nelson and Noriega, who also appears on an album with Luny Tunes on its sister label Mas Flow, which is also the name for the group's album. Neophyte New Records finally hits the commercial mark this year after four years with its reggaeton efforts by Baby Rasta & Gringo. All three labels are distributed by Universal Music & Video Distribution (UMVD), a major reason these two companies gain national recognition and land on the best-selling charts.

Daddy Yankee is undisputedly Puerto Rico's hottest reggaeton artist, with hit albums which transfer reggaeton to the more generally accepted rap or hip-hop terminology on the Latin Albums and general market Top 200 charts and boosting his importance as a concert and television show guest. He bypasses Don Omar, whose first album, *The Last Don*, hits the Top Latin Albums survey in 2003, with the VI/Machete follow-up, *The Last Don: Live Vol. 1, bowing on Billboard*'s Top Latin Albums chart in 2004. By 2005, only *The Last Don: Live Vol. 1* remains on the chart.

Daddy Yankee's commercial status based on last year's breakout album, *Barrio Fino*, which sells 750,000 copies as of July 2005, earns him a recording contract with Interscope and an overseas publishing administration deal with EMI Music, excluding Puerto Rico and Mainland U.S., which he'll continue to oversee and reap the profits. The record deal, according to *Billboard*, involves a compilation DVD and his five previous *El Cartel* CDs distributed by UMVD. Coinciding with the new label association is a 21-city tour involving cities in the U.S. and Latin America. This first ever reggaeton arena tour aptly tagged "Who's Your Daddy?" is being promoted on both Spanish-language and Anglo radio stations which seek to entice Latin teenagers. Launched August 27 at New York's Madison Square Garden, the tour's Mainland stops include Los Angeles, San Diego, Houston, Washington, D.C., Orlando, Miami, and Chicago on October 8, with visits interspersed in Ecuador, Colombia, and Venezuela. Veteran concert maven Henry Cárdenas' company, Cárdenas Marketing Network, is handling the project. Colombian-born, U.S.—raised Cárdenas has over the years through his previous firm Cárdenas, Fernández & Associates and CMN formed in 2004, worked with such artists as Ricky Martin, Marc Anthony, Enrique Iglesias, Carlos Vives, Alejandro Fernandez, Vicente Fernández, Juan Gabriel, and Maná.

Daddy Yankee's career comes full circle as a teenager rhyming words in the slums of San Juan's Villa Kennedy housing project to becoming a pioneer in the '90s in the growth of Jamaican-fed reggaeton following its arrival on the Island from its origins as a hybrid music encompassing dancehall tempos and Spanish lyrics originally developed in Panama, which is heard by Jamaican workers and subsequently brought home, to its invasion on the Mainland to his return home to appear in a major concert on Showtime with Usher in March.

The impact of the hit album results in the 28-year-old rapper appearing along with Don Omar on Univision's hit music awards show *Premio Lo Nuestro* at the AmericanAirlines Arena in Miami in February followed two days later with his performance at the city's Bob Marley Caribbean Festival and food drive at the Bayfront Amphitheater. While in Miami, he also headlines a concert produced by radio network Spanish Broadcasting System and its local station, El Zol 95.7 (WXDL), called appropriately "Reggaetonzol." Mainland media goes bonkers over Daddy Yankee's multicultural marriage of musical styles, with the *New York Times* labeling it one of the top hip-hop titles of the year, and *Vibe* magazine effusing that Daddy Yankee's "changing the perception of reggaeton," which is quoted by the *Miami Herald* in a large feature. Fourteen years after he begins his musical journey, he's the opening act for Usher's March concert special on Showtime which also features Beyoncé in a surprise appearance following her singing three of the five nominated tunes for the best film song on the recent Oscar telecast.

Daddy Yankee draws a similarity between the raps by Mainlanders Dr. Dre, Run-DMC, NWA and Big Daddy Kane to his own homeland inspirations for the *Herald* when he says they are all street smart observers of the ills of their respective communities.

The Island's hot musical import also has enough sizzle to motivate Sirus Satellite Radio, one of the Mainland's two satellite subscription services to launch *El Rhumbon* Sundays from 10 p.m. to midnight. Ayala's popularity also propels *Barrio Fino* back on the nation's best-selling list, Dec. 10, 2005 in 138th position.

Raymond Ayala's third release on *El Cartel*, *Barrio Fino*, features guest salsa sonero Andy Montañez on one tune. Originally assigned to VI Music, which is distributed by UMVD, the distributor's domestic clout enables it to garner greater Mainland sales to add to the artist's local fan base, resulting in the LP debuting on the Top 200 on Nov. 27, 2004 and 31 weeks later it's in 75th place. It also bows at No. 1 July 31, 2004 on the *Billboard* Top Latin Album chart, remaining in that slot until it drops to No. 2 after 48 weeks on June 28, 2005 when it's replaced by Shakira's Epic disc *Fijacion Oral Vol. 1.* Ayala's first two CDs, *El Cangri.Com* (released is 2002) and 2003's *Los Homerun-es Vol.1*, both distributed by *El Cartel*, make the *Billboard* Top Latin Albums chart for brief periods. A new Ayala release, *Ahora Le Toca Al Cangri! Live*, also makes the Latin Albums list.

By 2007, Daddy Yankee is a major force in urban Latin music. His newest album, *El Cartel*: *The Big Boss*, featuring English-language artists is geared for crossover stardom, and is the followup to his 2005 bilingual effort, *Bario Fino En Directo*, the best-selling Latin album of 2006, notes *Billboard.* The new June release will spearhead a 40-city world tour, including 18 U.S. stops starting in Chicago on August 31 and ending in Houston October 14. Next year, he's scheduled to tour the U.S., Latin America, Europe, and Asia.

VI Music's success attracts Machete Music, Universal Music Group's new so-called urban label, which comes calling with dollars in hand, and acquires a 50 percent ownership in the label in April. VI's releases through UMVD will now be labeled Machete/VI Music. Juan Vidal, VI's founder/CEO, retains his position while Machete, itself launched one month ago in March by Gustavo López, is now responsible for sales, marketing, and publicity.

There's nothing loony about Luny Tunes. Luny Tunes & Baby Ranks' *Mas Flow 2* on Universal Latino cracks the Top 200 albums chart as well as the Latin chart in '05. Luny Tunes & Noriega's debut VI album, *Más Flow*, has enough momentum to wind up on *Billboard*'s top Latin Albums chart. It also earns the wacky named act two awards on the magazine's 2004 televised Latin Music Awards (see Chapter 19). In addition to these two titles, another 2004 Top Latin Albums entry, *La Trayectoria* has its own longevity. And the flow keeps moving: *Mas Flow: Platinum Edition* also finds a home on the Latin Albums chart briefly in March of '05 before fading away. *Mas Flow 2* fades from the general market chart after 14 weeks while remaining in the top 10 of the Latin Albums chart for the same period of time. In addition to performing as Luny Tunes, Saldana, and Cabrera maintain a highly successful second career as reggaeton producers. The duo, often referred to as the architects of the new sound of reggaeton for their installation of changing drum patterns and synthesized riffs (created by Saldana) and sympathetic melodies (by Cabrera) to upgrade the music's sound, are transplanted Dominicans who first meet in the Boston suburbs where they are exposed to reggaeton. They move to Puerto Rico in 2000 and establish a recording studio in the city of Carolina.

La Secta, the Island's stellar rock band signs with the Universal Music Group for Mainland release of its debut CD release, *Consejo*, in May. The band's first four albums are released on its own No Little Fish imprint, with its last release in 2003, *Tunel*, tied to two concerts at the Roberto Clemente Coliseum in San Juan.

La Secta's local appeal attracts major corporations which see dollar signs in the band's mass appeal. Budweiser signs up as a financial/promotional angel in 2003 to promote the album and fund the cost for a music video and the production costs to rent the Clemente Coliseum for the band's two gigs. In 2005, it's Verizon Wireless PR offers a host of promotional support activities prior to the band's CD release and a special phone number allowing its customers to call a special number and hear a preview of the album.

Vico C, the 33-year-old veteran rapper, finds energized success in 2005 as his EMI release, *Desahogo*, which is more rap than reggaeton, hits the *Billboard* Top Latin Albums chart in 8th position and then its downward slide. It's a late coming of age for the Island's veteran purveyor of raps about life's values, based on his reformation following a period of drug abuse and a jail term for violating his parole condition to avoid drug use. The album is the nucleus of a special on MTV Puerto Rico, which airs on the Mainland on MTV Español. Released as a dual disc, the album features guest appearances by reggaeton act Ivy Queen, reggae/rap mixer Cultura Profética and salsero Gilberto Santa Rosa. A single from the album, *Se Escaman*, is done in two colorations: rap on the A-side; reggaeton on the flip side. A born-again Christian, Vico C seems more socially conscious than unconscious, utilizing the reggaeton rhythm as the background foundation for his foreground word pictures.

El Gran Combo marks 42 years in the salsa business by joining Sony Discos from RCA International. The 13-piece ensemble, which suffers numerous personnel changes during its highly charged career, stresses danceable music on its new CD, *Aqui Estamos y De Verdad!* Its current lineup includes piano, trumpet, saxophone, two trombones, bass, congas, timbales, bongos and two vocalists. Born in the aftermath of the breakup in 1962 of Combo De Rafael Cortijo, the band gains international acceptance and in 1982 celebrates its 25th anniversary with a historic concert in New York's Madison Square Garden.

Tito Nieves celebrates 30 years as a salsa singer with a 16-city tour starting June 4 of '05 in Miami and concluding in New York November 23 at Carnegie Hall. Nieves goes into the recording studio in June to cut his debut album for Miami's SGZ Records, reports *Billboard*. The CD's planned release in September is designed to be a key element in promoting the tour.

A compilation CD/DVD combination featuring salsa sounds recorded during a 2003 concert at the Tito Puente Amphitheatre in San Juan, captures many gems from the 1970s when the music is king in the Caribbean and New York City. Released this year, *Viva La Salsa* on Gold Star/Universal, features 18 acts performing time-stopping salsa classics. For many of today's salsa buffs, it's a welcome look backward in time.

The achievements of Fran Ferrer, a multitalented composer/ arranger/ musician/producer are covered in the Tierrazo anthology recording, *Puerto Rico 2010-Descarga Boricua Pá Qué Te Cuento*, spanning 1972 to the present. The five CD package reflects Ferrer's evolving style as a composer building his music on his nationalistic fervor. Puerto Rico 2010 is the futuristic name of Ferrer's first group formed in 1970 and is featured on the first disc in 1972, *Fran Ferrer Puerto Rico 2010-Hemos Dicho ¡Basta!*. The second disc, *Fran Ferrer-Yerbabruja*, is recorded in 1976 and reflects the battle for Puerto Rican political and social freedom of the '70s. The third record, 1993's *Descarga Boricua-¡Esta Si Va!* features 25 musicians enmeshed in the roots of Afro-Caribbean music augmented by salsa and Latin jazz trappings. The 1996 sequel, *Descarga Boricua II*, features an enlarged ensemble performing memory lane selections. The fifth CD, 1998's *Descarga Boricua III—Somos Uno*, again features the all stars expressing the full power of a Latin big band.

Romantic balladeer Luis Fonsi, alters his musical direction during the summer of 2005 with a dramatic shift to a harder rockish sound on his Universal Latino album *Paso A Paso* which is produced by Argentina's hit-making Sebastian Krys at the Hit Factory studio in Miami. Rock guitar riffs and hard beat drumming replace the gossamer feeling of strings previously utilized, notes the *San Antonio Express-News*. A single written by Amaury Gutiérrez, *Nada Es Para Siempre*, carries a special message of positive love and living for the moment for the 26-year-old Fonsi whose girlfriend is battling breast cancer. The sound alteration works since the CD rises to No. 2 on *Billboard's* Latin pop album chart and hits the mainstream Top 200 Albums survey as well. A single, *Nada Es Para Siempre*, cracks the mainstream Hot 100 chart a few weeks later.

Fonsi's commercial success lands him his first major music publishing pact with Sony ATV Music Publishing Latin America, according to *Billboard*. The singer/composer's Fonsi Music Publishing previously handles administration of his copyrights, including tunes for other artists. Sony ATV additionally signs an administration deal with reggaeton label Pina's publishing arm, Mafer Music, whose writers include Lito & Polaco and Nicky Jam.

Deciding to resurrect the roaring big band classic sound of '70s–'80s salsa, N'Klabe, a 10-piece ensemble fronted by a trio of male singers, finds this groove in its *Amor De Una Noche* Nu/Sony Discos CD and *I Love Salsa* single released in the fall of '05. Vocalists Félix Javier, Ricardo Porrata, and Héctor José Torres grow up listening to the sound of the salsa bands which stress horns and jazzy harmonics, Torres tells the *San Antonio* Express-News. Following chart success with the single and album which hits No. 1 on *Billboard*'s tropical album chart, Sony Discos releases the album in October in the dual disc CD/DVD format which includes four additional songs, three of which are duets with Victor Manuelle, Gilberto Santa Rosa and Voltio.

Michael Stuart, a salsa sonero from San Juan, stars in a six-city Mainland tour titled "Homenajaes" which begins in New York at the Copacabana and winds through Philadelphia, Miami, Chicago, Las Vegas, and Los Angeles and then heads for South America and Europe. The tour is produced by Stuart's home-based The Real Thing Corporation and includes a 15-piece band. The vocalist's *Sin Miedo* RMM album is in contention for this year's best tropical album at the Latin Grammys airing live November 3 on Univision.

The Montreal Expos return for a second season at Hiram Bithorn Stadium in '04. When I query Elias Markos of the team's media relations department as to the number of games to be played, and the number of Hispanics and Puerto Ricans on the roster, he promptly e-mails me back the statistics. "There are supposed to be 22 games, but the May 23 game versus San Francisco was rained out and the game rescheduled for Montreal's Olympic Stadium on August 9, so this year's total will be 21 barring any more rainouts." In April, the team plays six games, winning one against the New York Mets, 1-0. In May, the Expos win one of five games, this time against Milwaukee, 3-2. In July, the team wins half of its 10 games, three against

Pittsburgh and two versus Toronto. The team closes out its second Puerto Rico stand with a 7 win, 14 loss record.

Markos notes there are nine Latinos playing for the Expos this year, versus 12 last season. Puerto Rico is represented by Jose Vidro and Endy Chavez and first base coach Jerry Morales.

In its series against the Toronto Blue Jays, Canada's more successful team, Expos hurler Liván Hernández wins the two games and third baseman Tony Batista drives in a career record five runs to help defeat the Blue Jays before 23,875 fans, the most in attendance for the Expos winning games. In its three games against their next "visitors," the Atlanta Braves, the Expos lose all three of the contests, but manage to win three of its four games against Pittsburgh during their final series in San Juan. During its lone loss to the Pirates, 11-0, Expos third baseman Tony Batista snares his 1,000 career hit, while left-handed batter Chad Bentz socks his first Major League hit, a single to left field in the seventh inning. He's one for two thus far. And when left-handed pitcher Scott Downs beats the Pirates, 2-1, he becomes the first left-handed starter to win a game for the Expos since June 21, 2001. With the victory, the Expos finish the first half of the season with a 31-56 record. In 2005, the team moves to Washington and becomes the Nationals, the latest incarnation of the old Washington Senators.

One of the Commonwealth's rising film stars is sultry Roselyn Sanchez, who after a series of film roles on the Mainland, returns home to film *Cayo* her first Spanish-language feature this year. After breaking into local show business as a comedic actress, she moves to New York in 2001 to pursue a career as an actress, enrolling in acting classes while improving her English. Her perseverance pays off with her first film role, that of a sexy secret agent in *Rush Hour 2*, which leads to playing different types of roles in *Boat Trip*, *Chasing Papi* and this year *Edison* in Vancouver, Canada, and *Cayo*. She then departs the Island for her next film, *Rave Train*.

Sanchez's upward mobility places her in the company of Cuba Gooding in *Boat Trip*, Kevin Spacey, Morgan Freeman, Justin

Timberlake, Dylan McDermott, and LL Cool J in *Edison* and Freddie Prinze, Jr. in *Rave Train.*

Having moved away when she's 21, she's elated over returning to do *Cayo*, telling *Hispanic* magazine: "It's great to be able to work at home again...I love going back home and seeing my family and friends from high school. It brings me back to reality."

Although *Chasing Papi* is designed to appeal to English-speaking Hispanics in the U.S., the film's poor performance at the box office rankles the actress, who laments to the magazine, "We just have to support our projects more." Audiences will have another chance to support her newest project, *Yellow*, which she announces in 2005 will film here and in New York. In addition to starring in the drama about the death of her father, Sanchez is also the film's producer and script co-author with Nacoma Whobrey. Her cast associates include D.B. Sweeney, Sully Diaz, Jaime Tirelli, and Manny Perez, according to the *Hollywood Reporter*. She's also signed for the CBS TV series *Without A Trace to* play a New York City police officer.

Puerto Rico is in the spotlight in 2004 at AmericArtes, the Latin American festival at the Kennedy Center in Washington, D.C., which showcases the eclectic blending of regional cultural influences of Africa, Spain, and Portugal within Latin America. This fall's *Espiritu De Puerto Rico* takes place, September 7–26. Each year the event spotlights a different Latin American culture with dance, music, theater, film, and literary arts presentations. Among the Puerto Rican artists appearing at various venues within the Center are the Orquestra Sinfónica De Puerto Rico, singers Ednita Nazario, Olga Tañon, Gilberto Santa Rosa, percussionist Frank Colón, the Miguel Zenón Quartet (featured on David Sànchez's Columbia album *Coral)*, Chucho Avellanet and Lucecita Benítez, known as Tres Voces, D.C. salsa band Son De Aqui, Andanza, the Island's first contemporary dance company, the Nuyorican Poets, and Puerto Rico's Teatro Del Sesenta.

Among the performing artists, the Orquestra Sinfónica, founded by Pablo Casals in 1958, is directed by Guillermo Figueroa and features soprano Ana María Martínez and tenor César Hernández. Santa Rosa, known as *El Caballero De La Salsa* (*The Gentleman of Salsa*), is the first Puerto Rican singer of tropical music to perform at New York's Carnegie Hall. Tañon, called *La Reina Del Merengue* (*The Queen of Merengue*), is honored each year at home on November 9 which is designated *El Dia De Olga Tañon*. Nazario is nominated for a Latin Grammy in 2002 and appears in Paul Simon's ill-fated Broadway musical *The Capeman* along with Marc Anthony. Tres Voces, known as the "national voices of Puerto Rico," perform romantic, socially conscious and political tunes.

This year's event is coordinated with the Commonwealth and bolstered by funding from the Puerto Rican Tourism Company, the Puerto Rican Federal Affairs Administration and Rums of Puerto Rico.

The Commonwealth plays a key role during the 2004 Summer Olympics in Athens as local vocalist Michael Angelo is the featured voice on Telemundo's exclusive Spanish-language theme song *Que Viva La Unión* written by writer/producer Rudy Pérez. The TV network uses the theme for its first-ever live coverage of contests of special interest to Latinos like soccer and boxing. Angelo will also record for Pérez's new record company, Upfront Music Group, located in Miami.

While adults have ample musical milestones to enjoy, younger Islanders don't have to cry "I want my MTV" anymore. The music channel with a Spanish accent, MTV Puerto Rico, debuts August 11 on LIN-TV Corporation's San Juan WJPX which feeds the signal to three other Island stations also owned by LIN. MTV Puerto Rico starts off with programs running between 6 p.m. and 6 a.m. daily, with music videos in tropical, rock en Español, reggaeton, pop and rap aimed specifically at the local audience, augmented by Spanish-dubbed series from the parent English network. By November, the music channel hires male and female VJs after a local talent search, and then begins expanding its programming to include more original shows from its own studio. With LIN's WAPA connection added to the three cable systems carrying MTV Puerto Rico, the signal is able to reach 85 percent of the Island's 1.2 million TV homes, according to MTV.

One local vocalist who can benefit from the new MTV is Melina León, who starts out singing in the merengue style and shifts into a Latin pop mode on her new eponymous Sony Discos album. The record features 10 romantic ballads, with nary a tinge of merengue. Known for singing the song *Qué Será De Ti* on the Telemundo novela *El Clon*, León is appearing at several Latin Grammy street parties on the Mainland prior to the September 1 telecast on CBS by singing...merengue tunes.

Utilizing the local program content from its San Juan TV stations here, LIN and NBC create Spanish-language cable networks on the Mainland catering to Stateside Puerto Ricans. LIN gets the jump on NBC by starting September 1, 2004, to simulcast programming from WAPA, one of its San Juan stations, on its new Mainland network titled WAPA America via DirecTV. The network simulcasts the local station's news programming blocks from 5 a.m. to 11 a.m. and from 4 to 6 p.m., with the station providing other content from its library between 7 and 9 p.m.

NBC's plan involves its top-ranked Telemundo outlet WKAQ as the heart of the new Telemundo Puerto Rico Network offering 35 hours of weekly news plus talk, boxing, music videos, and film programming starting February 1, 2005. The new network debuts in 1.3 million homes on Cablevision Systems Corporation's digital tiers in New York and New Jersey, with an estimated one third of the Mainland's Puerto Rican population living in New York City. Puerto Ricans overall comprise an estimated 10 percent plus of the nation's Mainland Hispanics.

Both companies see a void for Puerto Rico-oriented programming on the major Hispanic networks, Univision and Telemundo, whose content is heavily Mexican and Latin American. LIN believes transplanted viewers from Puerto Rico, the Dominican Republic and the Caribbean, who watch WAPA, will welcome the station's signal in their new homes in New York, Miami, Boston, Chicago, and Orlando or wherever. LINs' television vice president

Paul Karpowicz tells *Multichannel News*, "There are more Puerto Ricans living in New York than there are in San Juan."

In still another major transaction, LIN's major stockholder, Dallas-based private-equity firm Hicks, Muse, Tate & Furst, sensing potential in the local cable industry for digital video and high-speed data services, acquires Centennial Communication's Puerto Rico Cable TV Corporation for $155 million in cash. The company has nearly 305,000 subscribers in Ponce and Mayaguez (the Island's second and third largest cities) plus San German and Aguadilla. The purchase ends the Wall, New Jersey, telephone company's search for a buyer. Centennial originally buys into the local cable market in 2000, spending $170 million in cash for Pegasus Communications Corporation's 55,000 subscribers, and one year later acquiring 37,000 subscribers from Teleponce Cable TV Inc. for $107 million. Hicks Muse intends to expand the system's already built capabilities for digital TV to make it a more popular and profitable branch of programming.

A locally produced talent contest, *Objetivo Fama*, airing on Univision's leased station WLII and airing every Saturday for 13 weeks in the first quarter, does so well in the local ratings that TeleFutura, Univision's sister network on the Mainland, broadcasts the show as well. The first three winners receive cash prizes and contracts with Univision Records. First place winner Janina wins $25,000 while second place winner Sheila and third place finisher Ektor both win $10,000. All three will have debut albums released next year. Janina's debut LP is released in March of '05. ES Television, which produces the show, has grandiose plans for a second version involving auditions on the Mainland in the fall, with the show airing simultaneously locally and on the TeleFutura network around the nation, with viewers voting for the winners in both locales. The show's second season from January to May of '05 attracts around one million voting viewers who select New York City's Anais Martinez, the champ and winner of a contract with the Univision Music Group. Janina, last year's champ has her debut album released in March of '05.

Exercising its option, Univision acquires WLII in Caguas and WSUR in Ponce, its signal repeating second leased station, for an estimated $190 million in December of '04. With its local radio stations, WKAQ-AM/FM and WUKQ-AM/FM, Univision can now offer advertisers radio/ TV package deals as it strengthens its presence in the Island's broadcasting industry. However, since taking over the two stations, relations between management and the local employee's union Upagra, the Union of Journalists, Graphic Artists and Related Occupations, become contentious. The union claims Univision cuts the number of locally produced programs in favor of its high content of network shows from Mexico and Venezuela and reduces the opportunity for work by local talent and production crews. These key hot spots are among the items holding back the signing of a new three-year contract. On the Mainland, most of Univision's employees are non-union. In January, Upagra files a complaint with the Federal Communications Commission in Washington contesting Univision's right to the two station's licenses. In a counter move, Univision files a complaint against the union with the National Labor Relations Board.

With no rancor or political agenda, cable's popular Food Network visits the Island to tape a segment of Rachael Ray's quirky series *$40 A Day*. The Commonwealth's storied history is reflected in the locales and restaurants she visits, ranging from San Juan's cobble-stoned streets to the historic Castillo De San Felipe Del Morro (El Morro fortress) built in 1539 on the San Juan Bay from which local soldiers fight off attacks by colonial powers England and Holland to eateries La Bombonera, opened in 1902 for breakfast; La Casita Blanca (little white house) for lunch, the Bacardi Rum distillery and Aguaviva for dinner, voted one of the world's 75 best restaurants in 2003 by travel magazine *Conde Nast Traveler*.

From Caguas to the Big Apple, that's the success story for one Puerto Rican radio star. Although he's long been on the Mainland and a leading radio personality at New York's WSKQ-FM, Luis Jiménez traces his career back to growing up in Caguas where he starts as a non-salaried 15-year-old news reader. He's also friends with George Mier, whose dad is an engineer at the Caguas station. When the Mier family moves to Orlando, Florida, the two pals are separated until Jiménez's family moves to the same city in the late '80s where Mier is working as the program director at his dad's radio station, WONQ and he hires Jiménez to do on-air work. Years later, when Mier makes a major leap to New York to become the program director at Spanish Broadcasting System's tropical music station WSKQ-FM, he opens the door for his friend who becomes the host of the morning show in 1993. As a result of his brand of risque humor, Jiménez becomes a hot New York radio personality, helping his station become the city's most listened to outlet in 1998. In addition to being a top radio personality, Jiménez and his second sidekick, Ramon "Moonshadow" Broussard, are syndicated in 2004 by ABC Radio Networks with Boston, Philadelphia, Tampa, Orlando, and Hartford, Connecticut, coming on board as of Oct. 1, 2005. The two hosts of *El Vacilón De La Mañana* are also the stars of the film *El Vacilón: The Movie*, a fictitious recreation of incidents listeners phone in, slated for release in '05.

Film production takes on a new role as three movies are shot here during 2006, two of them paying homage to the Islands spawning reggaeton music. They include: *Legal Tender*, John Singleton's first urban Latin story with a soundtrack dominated by reggaeton. Shooting for the $3 million drama begins here in May and then shifts to New York City. The next film *Mal De Amores*, also shooting in May, will be 80 percent financed by the Puerto Rican Film Fund, with Benicio Del Toro, one of the three executive producers. The third film, set to shoot in June, is *Reggaeton*, co-produced by Sony/BMG and Jennifer Lopez's Nuyorican Productions. Its musical title reflects the commercial feel of this genre, launched here, imported through the Mainland, and now returning as a theatrical release.

Articles

"White Lion's Reggaeton Roar." Billboard, Feb. 18, 2006

An Island Unto Itself." Multichannel News, Feb. 13, 2006

"Ednita Nazario: Puerto Rico's Pop Queen Is More 'Passionate' Than Ever." Billboard, Dec. 10, 2005

"The Conquest Of America (North And South)." New York Times,

Dec. 4, 2005

"Stars: Henry Cardenas." Billboard, Oct. 8, 2005

"Grammy Nominee Michael Stuart Stars In 'Homenajes.' HispaniaNet.com, Sept. 28, 2005

"Perez Signs With Fox For One-Year Deal." Daily Variety, Sept. 26, 2005

"Changing Stations." Billboard Latin Notas, Sept. 24, 2005

"N'Klabe's 'I Love Salsa' Hits No. 1 On Charts." San Antonio Express-News, Sept. 18, 2005

"The Faces Of Urban Regional." Billboard, Sept. 10, 2005

"Puerto Rico's Rafael Munoz." Latin Beat, September 2005

"Yankee Is Coming, And Coming Strong." Los Angeles Times, Sept. 7, 2005

"Sony's Pina Play." Latin Notas, Billboard, Sept. 3, 2005

"Sony ATV Signs Fonsi." Billboard Latin Notas, Aug. 13, 2005

"Sanchez On 'Yellow' Road Back To Roots." Hollywood Reporter, Aug. 8, 2005

"Fonsi Takes Different Sonic Path On His New CD." San Antonio Express-News, Aug. 8, 2005

"Home Run For Yankee." Billboard, Aug. 6, 2005

"Food network Experiences Puerto Rico On $40 A Day." HispanicAd.com, July 29, 2005

"Reggaeton Star Calderón Leaps To Atlantic." Billboard, June 18, 2005

"Puerto Rico Rumpus." Weekly Variety, May 30, 2005

"Happy Anniversary." Latin Notas, Billboard, May 28, 2005

"Luis Jimenez: La Mega 97.9 Morning Man Turns Movie Star." Billboard, May 14, 2005

"Machete Buys Into VI Music." Billboard, April 16, 2005

"Tañon A 'New Woman.'" Billboard, April 13, 2005

"Vico C Rides Reggaeton's Wave." Billboard, March 26, 2005

"Witty, Vibrant Salsa Santa Rosa Style." Los Angeles Times, March 7, 2005

"La Secta Calls On Telephone Co. For Support." Billboard, March 12, 2005

"Reggaeton Gets Rich: And Rapper Daddy Yankee's Street Sounds Lead The Way." Miami Herald, March 6, 2005

"Latin Music May Be Evolving, But It Can Never Grow Old." Miami Herald, March 6, 2005

"Telemundo Cable Reaches Out To U.S. Puerto Rican Community." NBC Universal Media Village.com, Feb. 10, 2005

"Cooking Up Menudo." Daily Variety, Feb. 9, 2004
"NBC Uni Says Si To Spanish Cable Net." Hollywood Reporter, Feb. 1, 2005
"Christian Acts Build Following In Puerto Rico." Billboard, Jan. 15, 2005
"Univision To Buy Puerto Rican Stations." Los Angeles Times, Dec. 29, 2004
"MTV-LIN Expand Island Venture." Multichannel News, Dec. 6, 2004
"Reality Sets In." Latin Notas, Billboard, Dec. 11, 2004
"Recap: Notable Latin Chart Bows." Billboard, Nov. 20, 2004
"Radio Finally Ready For Reggaeton." Billboard, Nov. 6, 2004
"Ricky Martin Settles Lawsuits." Los Angeles Times, Oct. 15, 2004
"'Barrio' A Big Deal For Daddy." Billboard, Sept. 28, 2004
"Centennial Sells Its Puerto Rico Subscribers." Multichannel News, Sept. 13, 2004
"Puerto Rican Cable Firm Sold." Multichannel News, Sept. 13, 2004
"Where's The Love?" Jazziz, September 2004
"NBC Eyes An Island Import." Multichannel News, Aug. 30, 2004
"Leon Leans Toward Pop." Billboard, Aug. 28, 2004
"MTV In Puerto Rico," Latin Notas, Billboard, Aug. 28, 2004
"Perez Up Front With Olympics Song, New Label." Billboard, Aug.14, 2004
"Pop/Rocker Pena Looks Beyond Earthly Values." San Antonio Express-News, Aug. 1, 2004
"Heineken Jazzfest De Puerto Rico." Latin Beat, August 2004
"Pick Of The Month: Pa Que Te Cuento." Latin Beat, August 2004
"AmericArtes Festival 2004: Espirit De Puerto Rico." HispaniaAd.com, July 23, 2004
"Expos Edge Pirates." MLB.com, July 11, 2004
"Chayanne: 25 years Of Stardom At The Peak Of Latin Pop." Billboard, July 10, 2004
"EMI Signs Licensing Deal With Guatauba." Billboard, July 10, 2004
"A Night Of Milestones In San Juan." MLB.com, July 9, 2004
"No Halladay For Expos In San Juan." Major League Baseball.com, July 3, 2004
"On The Move With Roselyn Sanchez." Hispanic Magazine, July 2004
"Distribution Deal Lifts Baby Rasta & Gringo." Billboard, June 5, 2004
"Spanish Harlem Orchestra." Latin Beat, June 2004
"Talent, Versatility, Class." Hispanic Magazine, June 2004
"2004 Jazz Symposium Puerto Rico." Latin Beat, June 2004
"21 Anos De Tradicion Salsera." Latin Beat, June 2004

"Ricky Martin Launches Anti-Abuse Campaign." Miami Herald, May 28, 2004

"Godfather Of Puerto Rican Rap Hasn't Stopped Fighting." Miami Herald, May 25, 2004

"Saxophonist David Sanchez Explores Latin Classical Masterworks." Columbia Records press release, May 24, 2004

"Menudo Mania." Latin Notas, Billboard, May 22, 2004

"Olga Tañon Singer, Mother, Wife And Restaurateur." Hispanic Magazine, May 2004

"Chayanne's New Looks Fool No One." Los Angeles Times, April 20, 2004

"Telemundo Celebrates 50 Years Of Broadcasting In Puerto Rico." Telemundo Website, April 6, 2004

"Improvisation Gives Spice To Salsa." Los Angeles Times, April 4, 2004

"The Many Voices Of Robi Rosa." New York Times, April 4, 2004

"Chayanne: Scandalously Nice Guy." Miami Herald, April 2, 2004

"Manuelle Expands Repertoire Into Pop Arena." Houston Chronicle, April 2, 2004

"Menudo Returns: Hunt For New Members Begins." Billboard, March 27, 2004

"Sony/ATV Nabs Latin ASCAP Nod." Hollywood Reporter, March 16, 2004

"Estefano Holds On To Songwriter Crown At 11th Annual BMI Latin Awards In Puerto Rico." BMI Website, March 16, 2004

"Medina Countersues Martin." Billboard, March 13, 2004

"Most Valuable Franchise: Yankees." Los Angeles Times, March 9, 2004

"A Latin Miles." Jazziz, February 2004

"Nazario Breaks Jinx On Billboard Latin Albums Chart." Dec. 13, 2003

"Batacumbele Once Again." Latin Beat December 2003

"Multi-Ethnic Music Flourishes In Puerto Rico." Billboard, Sept. 27, 2003

"Cubs Feel At Home In Puerto Rico." Los Angeles Times, Sept. 10, 2003

"Corea Main Attraction At Hot Puerto Rico Jazz Fest." Down Beat, September 2003

"Puerto Rican Singer Wraps His Rap In Traditional Salsa." Miami Herald, July 1, 2003

"Rap Rocks Charts." Latin Notas, Billboard, June 28, 2003

"Conference Panelists Rally Around Rap." Billboard, June 21, 2003

"The Rise Of Rap." Billboard, June 21, 2003

"Giving It Their All." Los Angeles Times, June 20, 2003

"Baseball As A Partime And A Metaphor." Los Angeles Times, June 15, 2003

"San Juan Has Plenty Of Atmosphere." Los Angeles Times, June 4, 2003

"Molina Enjoys Nice Reunion." Los Angeles Times, June 4, 2003

"P.R. Is Good For The Molinas." Los Angeles Times, June 3, 2003

"Clemente Legacy Is Told In Human Terms." Los Angeles Times, June 3, 2003

"Dia Nacional De Salsa In Puerto Rico." Latin Beat, June 2003

"Island Ball." Los Angeles Times, March 12, 2003

"Hispanic Takes El Mundo." Daily Variety, Feb. 18, 2003

"Calderón Appeals To Rap And Non-Rap Fans." Billboard, Feb. 15, 2003

"Signings Boost Fortunes of Rock En Español." Billboard Jan. 12, 2003

"Touring Puerto Rico: Big Business For A Tiny Isle." Billboard, Oct. 19, 2002

"Latin Rock Loses WCOM Support." Billboard, Oct. 19, 2002

"What's Become Of Latin Music?" Latin Beat, October 2002

"In The Center Ring." Los Angeles Times, Sept. 9, 2002

"Circus Act: Puerto Rico's Colorful But Classy Circo May Be The Best Latin Pop Band In North America." New Times Los Angeles, Sept. 12, 2002

"New Act Circo: It's A Wonder!" Miami Herald, Aug. 28, 2002

"Banco Popular Promotes Unity." Billboard, July 20, 2002

"Merenguera Will Stir Some Pop Into Her CD Mix." Latin Notes, San Antonio Express-News, July 7, 2002

"Rap On The Rise In Puerto Rico." Billboard, May 11, 2002

"Lopez's Musical Equation Subtracts 1 From Son By Four." Miami Herald, May 7, 2002

"Latin World Opens Up." Latin Notas, Billboard, May 4, 2002

Chapter 16
CAPITULO 16

Broadcast's Airwave Dynamics 2003–2004
ONDAS DE RADIO/TELEVISION DINAMICAS 2003–2004

Radio and television executives live in an environment of uncertainty, sparked by the adrenalin rush of the latest ratings revelations or how their newest program enticements are attracting the public away from their competitors. Or simply how the public is reacting to their current on-air offerings. In this chapter, a number of radio and TV executives reflect on how they compete in their markets to function in this frenzied world of Hispanic broadcasting.

KWKW-AM Los Angeles has a historic connection with Spanish broadcasting dating back to 1941, when as an English-language station, its Pasadena owner begins partial broadcasting of news about the war to Hispanic listeners. Gaining its government license on March 10, 1922, the station switches ownership and call letters several times before becoming KWKW and a Spanish-language broadcaster in 1957 under its then owner William Beaton. Lotus Communications Corp., which acquires the station in 1962, continues with its regional Mexican music format called *La Mexicana* until it switches to news/talk in January of 1998 and then adds sports to the mix in January of 2003.

Although listeners in Los Angeles in 2003 may not realize it, KWKW is the flagship station for Lotus, which owns and operates 24 stations of which 10 are Spanish-language in Fresno, Bakersfield, and L.A., with the others offering music or talk in Las Vegas, Reno, San Antonio, and Tucson. Lotus' two other L.A. market stations are KWKU-AM in nearby Pomona, which simulcasts the KWKW programming, and KIRN-AM, licensed to the suburb of Simi Valley, which broadcasts in Farsi to L.A.'s large Iranian population. "We've always been told we're the oldest Spanish-language station in the country," says Jim Kalmenson, the station's general manager/president and son of Howard Kalmenson, Lotus' founder who purchases the station in 1962. "I'm aware there are several other stations which also claim to be the oldest, so I tell people we were the first Spanish station in Los Angeles."

Kalmenson joins his father's company in 1986 as sales manager, having worked for two years in a similar position with the South Carolina Radio Network. He becomes KWKW's general manager in 1990 and gains the presidency in 1996.

KWKW traces its history back to March 10, 1922, when as an all-religious station operated by the Bible Institute of Los Angeles, it debuts under the call letters KJS at 1300 on the dial. In the summer of 1925, the call letters change to KTBI. In 1931, the Bible Institute sells the station to Errett Lobban "E.L." Cord, a car manufacturer/car dealer who renames the station KFAC, for Fuller, Auburn, and Cord. Auburn and Cord are the cars Cord's company sells at Fuller Motors. In March of 1941, the station moves to its present 1330 dial setting under the ownership of Los Angeles Broadcasting Inc., which holds the license until the next buyer.

KWKW is a bit of an oxymoron. Despite its vintage, it often ranks outside the top 20 stations in the Arbitron ratings, yet its owners claim it is the highest billing Spanish station in the city because its audience of 25- to 54-year-olds is loyal to its talk/sports format featuring coverage of the Los Angeles Dodgers and Lakers, the Chivas (Club Deportivo Guadalajara) soccer team from Mexico and NFL football.

When I visit the station in 2004, its offices and studios are in the Hollywood Plaza Building at the corner of Hollywood Boulevard and Vine Street on the second floor. Its neighbors are the world-famous Pantages Theater across the street on Hollywood Boulevard and Capitol Records, known around the world for its circular building design, which stands on Vine Street starkly against its Hollywood Hills backdrop and the James Doolittle Theater in the opposite direction on Vine. The building where KWKW is located is the former home for a May Company department store, now merged with another chain operation. Within the year, the company moves to its own $6 million building, custom-designed offices and six studios, a few blocks away on Barham Boulevard.

A banner in the station's reception area proudly proclaims, "Los Angeles Lakers En Español KWKW 1330 AM." The receptionist answers the phone with "Good morning, KWKW" in English and then switches to Spanish when the caller is a Latino. Employees greet the receptionist with "buenos dias" and switch to English when they greet me as a non-Hispanic. This bilingual banter, I discover, represents the station's mix of Hispanic and Anglo employees, many of whom sell advertising.

Each time Jim Kalmenson looks out his window onto Hollywood Boulevard, he's confronted with a large billboard for KSCA-FM, a leading Spanish station, heralding its morning superstar personality Reñan Almendarez Coello.

With 19 Spanish stations in town programming to various Latino communities, led by the majority from Mexico, Kalmenson says the station's objective is to "provide responsible programming. We know we serve a large ethnic community that has a lot of issues adjusting to society here, so we call our station 'the station that improves your life.' Our slogan is 'Los Programas Que Mejoran Tu Vida.'

"While sex and vulgarity are pretty prominent in Spanish radio, we don't want to be branded that way. To us it doesn't serve a meaningful purpose. We are local owners, so we interact in the community in a different manner. Other stations report to their stockholders rather than to their conscience."

Programming-wise, KWKW believes its talk and sports combination is the proper mix for L.A. Explains Kalmenson: "Sports is one of a few programming concepts which bridge all Latino cultures. If you program music, you have to narrow your identity, but here with talk, you can cover many areas. Our new morning sports, with emphasis on soccer, is very international in scope. Midday we have a show *Gracias Doctor* (*Thank You Doctor*) which has been on six years and in the afternoon the featured show is *Nuestos Cuidad* (*It's Our City*)."

It takes a while for station to add sports talk to its format. "It was on my wish list for years," admits Kalmenson, "but I couldn't find the right people. That changed when we hired Rolando 'El Veloz' (the voice) González and Edú Villamar to host the morning drive time sports show, *Deportes Por La Mañana*. There were three fulltime English sports talk stations here, but none in Spanish before we started. I think Latinos are more compulsive about sports than Anglos. The Lakers, for example, have been a phenomenon in the Latin market here without a Hispanic star."

When Kalmenson pulls the plug on what he calls "a very good, happy talk show hosted by Carlos Magaña and Tonia Castro" after five years and replaces it with the sports chatter program, "we had a strong, negative response from callers," he admits, adding: "It was not an easy move to make." Two years later, the station's sports and talk programming will greatly expand, with the two morning sports chat talents now doing an afternoon stint as well. In 2005, the station becomes the flagship for the new 24-hour ESPN Deportes radio sports network.

KWKW's first foray with sports is in 1958 when it begins covering Dodger béisbol. According to the Dodgers broadcasting history, the first announcing team consists of René Cárdenas, Miguel Alonzo, and Milt Nava. One year later, Dodger records show Jaíme Jarrín replaces Nava on the live broadcast, and has been with station ever since. In numerous published reports, Jarrín is listed as reporting Dodger games in 1958. He does this from a studio, where equipped with a pair of headphones, he interprets Vince Scully's English account of the action into Spanish. His bio says that after migrating to Los Angeles from Ecuador in 1955, he becomes the station's sports director and since 1973 is the lead Dodger play-by-play announcer. One fact is not in dispute: in 1998 Jarrín is awarded the Ford C. Frick Award and is voted into the broadcaster's branch of Baseball's Hall of Fame.

The station builds its sports roster by adding the Lakers in 1997 and the NFL's *Monday Night Football* in November of 2003 from distributor Westwood One. "We carry all the Dodger games," says Kalmenson, noting that if a Dodger game conflicts with a Lakers playoff game, "we'll run the playoff game." The station also secures Latin coverage of the World Series provided by a Miami company, "regardless of who's in it."

Lakers' home and away games are broadcast by Jose "Pepe" Mantilla and Fernando Gonzalez. The station has carried Chivas soccer for 20 years and Atlas competition two years, all designed to appeal to futbol fanáticos.

With the station's key age demographic 25-to-54, does this create a problem selling ads, since its the 18 to 49 age audiences that advertisers usually seek? "I don't see it as a problem," Kalmenson says. "While the Lakers do very well with younger demographics, we're the No. 1 billing Spanish station in Los Angeles without getting the 18- to 34-year-olds." Arbitron, the ratings service, claims KWKW attracts the oldest and wealthiest Spanish speakers as well as attracting such blue-chip advertisers as car manufacturers and real estate firms, in addition to traditional food favorites. A 30-second spot on a Chivas soccer match costs $900; the same length spot on a Laker game goes for $500. This is the first year the Dodgers are selling their own in-game advertising for KWKW. "We sell all immediate adjacencies before and after the game at $300 a spot," explains Kalmenson, "so we do okay." To the extent that billing a reported $10 million for a 30th placed station is okay. During the previous ratings periods, the station is in 43rd place with a 0.5 and a 0.3 rating, which will inch upward to a 0.4 rating during the winter of '04.

The Dodgers, Lakers, and Chivas attract different age groups. "If you're looking for younger people, the Lakers draw 18-to-34. If you want the 25- to 35-plus audience, it's the Dodgers. But since this is a young market, the Lakers in totality reach more people. Soccer is 18 to death. But soccer is only played once a week. So its net impact on the station is less than the Lakers who might be playing three or four times a week."

Kalmenson says he doesn't concern himself with the station's position on the rating listings. "We usually have a 1.2 rating and in the 30th ranking." The major problem with Arbitron ratings, he believes is measuring language preference and weighing language preference, two factors Arbitron will address in the next year. "I subscribe to Arbitron, but I'm not in love with it. My feeling about Arbitron," he tells me, "is they're like the Jews. Everybody blames them for all their problems. All the Spanish broadcasters do," and then he laughs at the analogy, which makes me uncomfortable with his phraseology.

Kalmenson finds the Los Angeles marketplace "peculiar" in that if "you ask people what they listen to there's a strong prejudice to answer in a way that seems correct. Everybody recognizes that it's cool to listen to FM. It's not for AM. There's a great need to do what's accepted and correct in this country. So ratings are skewed horribly wrong, but I don't make an issue out of it. I don't hire and fire show hosts based on their ratings. I do it based on the result pattern our advertisers get. It's a very unusual manner for managing a radio station, but it works. We talk to advertisers. They cancel if they're not getting results. We pay attention to their concerns."

On the day I'm visiting the station, Jim's dad Howard is also on the premises, so I have the good luck to meet this visionary broadcaster and chat with him about how he gets into Spanish-language radio. Prior to this endeavor, he's an ad salesman for ABC-TV for five years and then joined CBS where he's the general manager of its TV affiliate in Las Vegas, KLAS.

In 1962, no longer associated with KLAS, he says he's in Los Angeles walking along Hollywood Boulevard "and right outside from where we're sitting at the corner of Hollywood and Vine, there's a big billboard with Carmen Miranda's picture and the words 'Spanish radio KWKW.' I look up at it and think, 'My God, that's a good idea,' and I decided I'd inquire about buying the station. I call up the station's broker, Jack Stoll, and he says the station is for sale by its owners Les Malloy and Stan Breyer. In those days, you could only own 14 stations, so every station owner is important in his own right and has his own dynasty. I have Jack call them and he comes back and says they want a million-and-a-half dollars and $500,000 down. I've got fifty grand I've earned over the years.

"My father is Benjamin Kalmenson, vice president of Warner Bros. Pictures and a very successful man, who later becomes president of the company. I said to him, 'Dad, I've got this wonderful idea about Spanish radio, but I don't have the money to buy the station I'm looking at.' I am 30 years old at this time. He says to me, 'Schmuck, offer them $250,000 down, plus a million.' I said, 'They'll laugh at me and throw me out.' He says, 'Do as I say.' So I make the offer and they accept it." And then he laughs. "So I take out a loan from the Bank of America for $200,000 and he cosigns and I pay it off."

Kalmenson is well prepared to enter Spanish radio and speak the language since he says he learns Spanish while a student at Riverside Military Academy in Gainesville, Georgia, from his Cuban roommates. That in itself is fascinating. What's more intriguing is that when he takes over the station, "it's billing $30,000 a month, the format is heavy Mexican ranchera, norteno, and some ballads, announcers earn $100 a week, I make about $200 a week as the general manager and salesman, on commission. The first year the station makes a fortune because the guys who owned it before don't know how to run it. But they also don't know how to count. They're making more money than they thought."

KWKW has only one other Spanish competitor, KALI-AM. "They have better personalities than we do, including Elena Salinas, who's the top personality in Spanish radio. But we have a great sales force and we out-bill them. Spanish radio is in its infancy and our problem is our ad rates are terrible. We have a $12 a minute rate while the Anglo stations are getting $100. There couldn't have been more than 30–35 Spanish stations in the U.S. at this time, and we all belong to the Spanish Language Broadcasters Association. Today, there are hundreds of Spanish stations and no association, no cohesion, and no unity. (Arbitron says there are 650-plus Hispanic stations on the air this year.) We bill $200,000 to $300,000 a year and we think we're doing great. It's pre-Spanish television, so we have an enormous amount of retailers advertising on the station. I could walk into any store along Whittier Boulevard and Brooklyn Avenue in East Los Angeles and I know the owner and his customers. We have lunch and dinner together. I go to bar mitzvahs, weddings, and funerals. Their business is in my hands and my business is in their hands as well."

Kalmenson, now 71, recalls that the station moves several times. "We've been in this building one year and we're about to go into our own building. It'll be the first one we've ever owned." Regardless of its address, recording artists know where to find the station and make personal appearances. Recalls Kalmenson: "We are very important to record companies at that time. Every star would come here to do interviews. They know our announcers and they'd dine with us. Today, it would be like seeing Madonna, or Rod Stewart, or Bruce Springsteen, or KISS sitting in the lobby. Today, radio is too much of a business. It's corporate and they don't have the relationship or the fun we once had."

With 19 Spanish stations in Los Angeles, how does all this competition affect your business? "Let me put it this way. In 1962, with one competitor we billed $300,000. There were no Spanish FMs. Today, there are only a few Spanish AMs. Now we bill $10 million a year and have 18 competitors and we don't have any ratings because we're AM and the FMs with ratings bill $35 million. But because of our Lakers and Dodgers and soccer, we're in a new world unto itself.

The greatest boon to radio is competition because it brings in new accounts. And there is no end to it."

Is he still involved in the station? "Yes and no," he responds." I don't have anything to do operationally; my ideas and point of view are different. What I offer our company is stability, continuity of ownership, and good fellowship. We're billing around $60 million a year for all our stations and we're not one dollar in debt."

If any one Hispanic media company parallels the nation's merger mania, it's the marriage between radio networks Tichenor Media System and Heftel Broadcasting Corporation into the Hispanic Broadcasting Corporation (HBC) in 1997, followed by its acquisition by Univision, the leading Hispanic television network in 2003 to become Univision Radio. The birth and death of individual companies into a national giant is a natural result of the enticing appeal of the nation's exploding Hispanic population, with the potential for greater listenership and national advertising revenue.

When I first chat with McHenry "Mac" Tichenor, Jr., president of Tichenor Media System in 2002, the company owns 60 stations in 13 cities, plus five in Mexico, and is reacting to the influx of newly arrived Hispanics by expanding its reach into new markets. "The exploding Hispanic population has had a big effect on us, especially in areas which weren't previously regarded as large concentrations of Hispanics. We and others have gone in and started Spanish-language operations in cities like Las Vegas that was never on our radar as a big Hispanic market," he says. "It's just been a fabulous market for us (with some 250,000-plus Latinos working in the hotels and construction fields) and has opened our eyes to the potential of smaller markets outside of the normal Los Angeles/Miami/New York type areas that we've been focused on. But we've also moved into well establish Hispanic areas like Arizona and New Mexico. We're also looking at Sacramento and Austin, and we'd like to add stations in almost all of our markets, particularly where we've only got one or two stations like Fresno, El Paso, and McAllen (Texas)."

Within the next 10 years, Tichenor sees Spanish radio growing alongside the Hispanic population. "I think you see more Hispanic markets like Raleigh-Durham, Washington D.C., Montana, Connecticut, and Vermont. You see not just our company but others go in and serve this growing market. We've already seen the number of Spanish-language radio stations grow from under 200 seven years ago to over 600 today, and I think you'll see this same trajectory continue."

Tichenor is the grandson of the company's founder, McHenry Tichenor, and the son of the Dallas-based company's former president McHenry Taylor Tichenor. The company's history in Spanish radio dates back to 1949 with its purchase of KGBT-AM in Harlingen, Texas. Mac, as he's known within the radio industry, joins the acquisition-minded company in 1979, working his way up the corporate roster, and when his dad retires in 1981, he assumes the presidency of Tichenor Media System. It's in this power position that he persuades the company's board of directors two years later to totally focus on Spanish radio. By July 10, 2003, HBC owns or programs 65 radio stations in 17 of the nation's top 25 Hispanic markets. It's also the exclusive Spanish programmer for the XM Satellite Radio Network, so Mac's gut feeling is paying off.

With the acquisition by Univision on the horizon, Tichenor ticks off the benefits. "The main effect we're looking at is being able to effectively team up radio and television which can be helpful in going after those national advertisers who have not tried Spanish media or who have only stuck their toe in the water, and get them to make a full-fledged commitment to address the U.S. Hispanic population with their marketing messages in Spanish."

Before being wooed by Univision, HBC and the nation's second Spanish radio network, Spanish Broadcasting System, are in a merger mood, which then dissipates into SBS filing a lawsuit against HBC and Clear Channel Communications for halting their intended marriage. Notes Tichenor in business legalese: "We were in serious discussions with them and had some threshold issues that we could just never resolve, particularly in the form of corporate governance issues. The main reason we went with Univision is it was a good deal for our stockholders, because we think we can work with that asset base to build the market."

As for the lawsuit, Tichenor notes, "there have been motions for dismissal and answers filed and discoveries going on. I think it's got a life of its own and it will probably go well into 2003." In February of 2003, a federal judge dismisses SBS' antitrust suit against HBC and Clear Channel, its biggest shareholder. The suit, filed in U.S. District Court in Miami in June of 2002, charges HBC and Clear Channel, a 26 percent owner of HBC, with trying to injure SBS by hindering its access to capitol, depress its stock, interfere with its advertisers, and stop it from buying radio stations.

HBC receives a second wave of good news in September when the FCC clears Univision's purchase of HBC for $3.25 billion, ending a fractious fight among politicians who find fault with the merger or see it as a healthy competitive melding of two companies. This groundbreaking merger is covered in Chapter 17.

In addition to focusing on future expansion, Tichenor is also keyed to the present status of how Arbitron measures Hispanic radio audiences. His biggest complaint is that Arbitron "is not getting a representative sample of Spanish speakers in the survey. They do not control how many Spanish speakers are in the sample versus English or bilinguals. If they have a target of 1,000 Hispanic diaries in the market and if they want two-thirds of them to be Spanish speakers, if that's the percentage of the market, and if they get one-eighth who are Spanish speakers, they still publish the results if they were reflective of the market."

As a network, HBC offers very little national programming for its stations, "because there's not much Spanish-language programming that translates across the country. But we do use the network as a sales tool so an advertiser can get nationwide coverage. Format-wise, regional Mexican is the category heard the most, but there are also geographical differences reflected in Mexican music. So our three major formats are regional Mexican, the romantic ballad amor format, and the tropical format, which encompasses salsa and merengue, which is most popular on the East Coast."

During the past five years, of the 27 stations HBC buys, Tichenor says, "all have been English stations that we have converted to Spanish, except one or two. All of our English-language acquisitions have been in New York, all over Texas, Chicago, Phoenix, Los Angeles, and San Diego." It's usually failing stations that standout as acquisition prime. In 1997, it acquires low-rated adult album alternative or Triple A formatted KSCA-FM from Gene Autry, which quickly turns into one of Los Angeles' top-rated Spanish stations.

How does Tichenor assess the inequity of the ad rates Spanish stations charge versus what Anglo stations rate cards demand? "Our issue on this point," he says, "is not that our rates are lower than for the general market. Our problem is that there are not enough advertisers in Spanish radio, so it's not a pricing issue; it's a volume issue. And that's why we're so focused on this merger to put teams in place to go land some of those advertisers not yet using Spanish radio."

HBC has the unique distinction of employing four female general managers of multiple stations in their cities. In Miami, it's Claudia Puig; in New York it's Stephanie McNamara; in Phoenix it's Michelle Hohman, and in San Francisco/San Jose it's Ali Shephard.

Three of the company's on-air personalities reach beyond their local communities. Rick Sanchez's *Buenos Tardes America* airs in Miami on WQBA and in New York on WADO weekdays from 3 p.m. to 5 p.m. It's a show that deals with topical issues. Reñan Almendarez Coello's No. 1 rated morning show since 1997, *El Cucuy De La Manaña*, a blend of risqué comedy with life-improving assistance to listeners on Los Angeles' KSCA, is syndicated into San Francisco/San Jose, Phoenix, Las Vegas, and Chicago. Raúl Brindis' morning show on KLTN Houston also airs in Dallas, San Antonio, and San Francisco. Coello, known as "El Cucuy," spells trouble for HBC. After shifting from mornings to afternoons in February 2003, and boosting the station's ranking from 24th to second, he gets into a battle with HBC one year later in February over its refusal to increase the pay and working conditions for his on-air "Tropa Loca Crew" and walks out February 20 in protest during his live show. Univision suspends him and SBS quickly hires him and his team to be KLAX-FM's new morning show, which debuts one month later. Univision fills Coello's vacated afternoon slot with David "El Gatillero" Palacios, the former popular midday host on its KHOT-FM in Phoenix. Palacios' show is also being beamed by Univision back into Phoenix, as well as to its stations in San Francisco/San Jose, Fresno, Sacramento, and Las Vegas.

HBC operates three stations in Chicago in 2002 and picks up a fourth in 2003. Chicago native Jerry Ryan is HBC's vice president/general manager of all these stations, and when I chat with him in 2003, he mentions one major market situation that on the surface sounds strange but actually makes sense. "This is the second largest Mexican market in America; only Los Angeles has more Mexicans. How about that?" he says on the phone. "All the old Eastern European neighborhoods are now Mexican," adds Ryan, whose been in Chicago with HBC a little over one-and-a-half years, arriving from Phoenix where he helps put the company's KHOT on the air in 1999. The city's population of 7.4 million in 2003 is 12.9 percent Hispanic; by May of 2004 it's risen to 17 percent of the 12-million-plus population.

Why would people from a hot climate nation migrate to Chicago with its bone-chilling winter temperature and powerhouse winds, which vocalist and former native Lou Rawls dubs the "Hawk." Says Ryan: "They come here for the great blue collar manufacturing jobs. This is a manufacturing town with a lot of factories. There's only about a 14 percent difference between the Hispanic and African American populations. How about that? That's what really stuns people."

With Mexicans accounting for 75–80 percent of Chicago Latinos, Puerto Ricans represent 12 percent of the community, prompting Ryan to boast: "This is the second largest Puerto Rican population behind New York. And from 26th Street all the way to

79th Street, it's solid Mexican. On Mexican Independence Day, September 16, there are Mexican flags on the street and guys driving around with flags on their cars. It's unbelievable. "

Ryan oversees WOJO-FM (regional Mexican); WIND-AM (news/talk); WLXX-AM (tropical but changing to Latin pop); and the new kid, WXXY-FM (contemporary Latin) but slated to simulcast WLXX's Latin pop format once Univision acquires HBC, which it does this year. In 2004, the company acquires WVIV-AM and renames it WRTO with a news/talk format, shifting former news station WIND to Spanish adult contemporary.

How does he juggle his time to handle all the stations? It's his staff that enables him to wear so many hats, he admits, citing two examples. "I've got an operations guy for regional Mexican, César Canales who's called Mexicanos hasta las gachas, Mexican to the bone. That's how people describe Chicago: Mexican to the bone. One of my account executives, Pepe Saldivar, has lived in San Antonio and Brownsville, Texas, and he likes living here because he feels closer to Mexico in Chicago than he did in any other city. This is a very proud Mexican city. What makes it so different from Los Angeles is that it's so isolated."

Of all its stations, WOJO is a 23-year veteran of Spanish radio, followed by WIND 25 years and WLXX 24 years. WIND is a former Westinghouse English-language news/talk outlet.

Opines Ryan: "This is a tough town in which to play new acts. It's got to be a hit. While HBC provides, "programming guidance, we develop our own playlists. If you're a Spanish station that's appealing to new immigrants, you're not playing rock en Español; you're playing regional Mexican artists like Joan Sebastían who's from Zacatecas and Los Razos who are from the state of Michoacan." Ryan knows his customers. "The bulk of the Mexicans here are from Michoacan, Jalisco, Guanajuato, San Luis Potosi, Mexico City, Zacatecas, Guerrero, and Puebla," he says.

Is he concerned about the Hispanic population becoming so Americanized that Spanish radio might lose some of its audience?

"For the new immigrants, that's not going to happen." What about their children? "It depends on how much they've been exposed to their culture. Mexicans are people who hang onto their culture. I do admit that by the time the third generation matures, it's going to be a little tough for them to hang onto the culture their parents promote. They have a stronger preference for English while the first and second generations have a strong affinity for Mexican music."

How's Ryan's Spanish? "I wouldn't say I'm fluent," he says candidly. "But I know enough to understand and speak it. I had Spanish in high school and I've been to Mexico several times. When you're around it every day, you pick it up. When I visit English and Spanish advertising agencies, 90 percent of the transactions are in English. When I go out on the street I communicate with people in Spanish."

With a background in general market radio for such companies as Pough (WJJD-AM-FM Chicago), ABC (for its Chicago powerhouse WLS-AM-FM and KTKS-FM Dallas), and the Phoenix companies Duff (KESZ-FM), Mac America (KESZ/KOAZ), and Bryson (KBZA), Ryan is hired by HBC to put its Phoenix Spanish station KHOT-FM on the air. Three years later he moves back to his Chicago hometown to oversee the company's three stations.

HBC's main competitor, Spanish Broadcasting System, which has one station, WLEY-FM competing in the regional Mexican area in Chicago, acquires three from Big City Radio in 2003 to come even with HBC. SBS' new properties include former English programmers WKIE, WKIF, and WDEK, all flipped to Spanish adult contemporary. Other competitors in the market are formidable networks Entravision and Radio Unica.

Bill Tanner, Spanish Broadcasting Systems executive vice president for programming, is the complete radio executive, starting out in English-language radio as a disc jockey and program director, most often handling these two jobs simultaneously for such stations as Hicks Broadcasting's WJDX-AM in Jackson, Mississippi; Heftel Broadcasting's WHYI-FM and Beasley-Reed Broadcasting's WPOW-FM, both in Miami at different times, and at Metromedia's WASH,

Washington, D.C. The Vicksburg, Mississippi, native's resume also includes functioning for a brief period as vice president of programming for Heftel Broadcasting Corporation and helping launch Cox Communication's WHQT-FM in Miami. So he's been involved in adult contemporary, Top 40, and rhythm 'n' blues radio by the time he enters Spanish radio in 1992 with SBS to start WXDJ-FM in Miami.

Two years later, Heftel hires him as its programming VP, a position he holds through the merger with Tichenor Media System into Hispanic Broadcasting Corporation, until he joins SBS in 2000 as its executive vice president for programming, operating from Los Angeles, a continent away from SBS' Coral Gables, Florida, headquarters.

As SBS' programming maven, Tanner exerts a lot of power over the Latin record industry. Although he doesn't put it exactly that way, he does tell me during my phone interview that he "supervises the programming on all of our 22 stations, and that means I work as sort of an advisor and counselor to the individual stations' program directors. I hire the program directors in consultation with the people who own the company, but whatever shows up on the air is my direct responsibility."

How does he determine which records and artists get played? "It's largely a function of the individual station program directors who come to me and say they think this is a really good record, and I listen very closely to their recommendations. If they don't have any particular record they think is a standout during the week, we then look at the track record of an artist especially in terms of previous popularity. In New York, you're certainly going to play a new record by Marc Anthony real quick or a new artist that everyone loves like Juanes. You're always listening to the sound of the record, whether it's memorable and whether it's something that will hit the popularity meter. You do have to understand Spanish to understand the lyrics, but you also have to have an ear for how catchy the song is. How's the melody? How's the interaction between the musicians? Is it the sort of tune you can't get out of your head? If it is, then it's probably going to be a hit."

Since SBS' stations are in scattered major cities, Tanner travels a lot, and interestingly speaks to his executives in English, noting: "I do have some understanding of Spanish, but what I speak is radio. My English-language friends say to me, 'What the hell do you know about Spanish radio?' And I always say, 'it ain't Spanish they need help with. It's the radio."

There are some obvious differences between programming English-language and Spanish-language radio stations. "The similarity is that we are all measured by the same Arbitron yardstick. But then music and culture are the fundamental bedrock of Spanish-language radio and every little thing is subject to the subtleties of the culture. Cubans don't sound like Mexicans who don't sound like Guatemalans or Central Americans or Puerto Ricans or Dominicans. They all have their different accents. One of the wonderful things about Spanish culture is that it's not all monolithic; it's very diverse."

This diversity in the nation's continually expanding Hispanic community "is pulling us more into the center stage of American radio," Tanner tells me. "We're now focused on the largest markets. The number of listeners that can be reached in Los Angeles, New York, Miami, Chicago, and Puerto Rico is vast. If you take the next 20 markets, they don't add up to those top markets."

In November of 2000, SBS sets a national price record of $250 million to buy the 79-year-old KFSG-FM, a Los Angeles Christian music and talk station owned by the International Church of the Foursquare Gospel, which continues to broadcast until its license for the 96.3 FM slot expires in March of 2003, when SBS converts the dial position to 93.5 and the call letters to KZAB La Sabrosa (The Flavorable One) featuring a musical menu of cumbia, punta, roca, merengue, and salsa, designed to appeal to listeners from Colombia, Nicaragua, and El Salvador. The new station joins SBS' other L.A. properties, adult contemporary KXOL-FM (El Sol) and regional Mexican formatted KLAX-FM (La Raza).

While with HBC, Tanner helps take its two L.A. stations, KLVE-FM and KSCA-FM to the top of the ratings chart. Now working with KLAX and KXOL, "we've got parity with HBC," he enthuses.

In programming for a national chain, Tanner takes into account the differences in audience. "Los Angeles is a particularly young market," he explains. "Miami is definitely older and dominated by the Cuban community, which has been there since the early sixties. New York has a well-entrenched Puerto Rican community, but there are two new immigrant waves, Dominicans and Mexicans. We even have a Mexican music show Saturday mornings on WPAT, which is our pop and ballad station while WSKQ is our tropical music station that appeals to both Puerto Ricans and Dominicans. The Mexican immigrants, who comprise about 80 percent of the Hispanic population in Los Angeles, have an average age in the early thirties. Both of our stations in Los Angeles appeal to the broad age group of 25 to 54. What we've found is that as people get married in their early twenties, they begin to have more of a fondness for their native language, so that people who wouldn't be caught dead at 17 chattering in Spanish, suddenly get very close to Spanish when they begin to develop a family."

When Tanner arrives in L.A. in 1994, "there are two Spanish stations on FM, (SBS') KLAX, which starts in 1992, and (Heftel's) KLVE. KLAX is the first station to go to No. 1 with a Spanish-language format. By 1995, KLVE has run away with the ratings by playing beautiful Spanish ballads. We call it Musica Romantica and it's very successful until 1997 when Heftel acquires KSCA-FM (with its adult album alternative music from Gene Autry), and changes it to regional Mexican with a very high profile morning personality, Reñan Almendarez Coello."

Having worked for both Heftel/Hispanic Broadcasting Corp. and SBS, what are the differences between the two companies? "HBC is a very well run company operated by Mac Tichenor and his staff that operates like a bank. Its people are very comfortable in the world of the stock market. SBS is owned by Hispanics, Raul Alarcón and his family, who are originally from Cuba. I'd say SBS sees its ties as blood ties to the Spanish-language community and culture than HBC, which is more of a group of businessmen who own a big company. Raul Alarcón, Sr. started the company and his son Raul, Jr. is the chairman of the board and president. He's a very hands-on owner who believes his mission is to provide a Hispanic presence in the American media."

Regardless of whom he's working for in Spanish radio, Tanner stresses Hispanic broadcasters help new arrivals who only speak Spanish integrate into the U.S. "by entertaining them in Spanish, and giving them tips on the air, including local news on our stations in the morning. In Los Angeles, we consider our role to be a friend and help people acclimate to a culture they're not used to. You have a lot of people who've lived on ranches and they have their difficulties getting along in Los Angeles. So we go out and meet people at events and we sponsor health symposiums and other events designed to help them in their new home."

Do Spanish-language radio and TV stations keep people isolated in their cultural communities by broadcasting to them exclusively in Spanish? I keep thinking of the term "cultural ghettos," but I somehow shy away from that term. "No, it's not a trap, it's a velvet glove," Tanner responds. "I think there are other pressures and opportunities in the community, which determine whether people are going to assimilate into the English-language culture. The whole basis for the appeal of Spanish-language media is that people who grow up in a Spanish-speaking environment don't lose their taste for it."

What does Tanner envision for the future? "Our company is very good at running big markets stations and that's where we've chosen to concentrate our firepower." In 2004, SBS owns and operates 25 stations. Its speedy hiring of superstar personality Reñan Almendarez Coello one day after he and HBC part company on March 17 produces a ratings bonanza for SBS, which returns him to morning drive time on March 22. After only nine days on the air as KLAX's morning host, his fan base propels him into the No. 1 morning slot among Spanish stations. Tanner tells the *Los Angeles*

Times that Coello's presence raises the station's audience share from 2.2 percent in February to 4.8 percent, which translates into a jump for the station's morning show from fourth place in February to numero uno. The next week his share of audience rises to nine percent. "We thought he'd be No. 1 almost immediately. But I didn't think we'd see it to this degree," Tanner philosophizes to the paper.

Seeking to reduce its debut in 2004, SBS agrees in August to sell two of its LA-area stations, KZAB-FM and KZBA-FM to Styles Media Group for $120 million to reduce its negative financial position. Since last September, the company has been selling off six stations in Chicago, San Francisco, and San Antonio, to also obtain cash with which to pay off its senior subordinated notes coming due after November 1 of this year. The sales obviously diminish the number of stations on Tanner's watch. In September of 2005, he leaves SBS to focus on his freelance consulting for several English-language radio station groups that he's been doing in addition to his responsibilities for SBS, which may retain him as a consultant as well.

Although it's often overshadowed by other Hispanic radio and TV networks, Entravision Communications Corporation of Santa Monica, California, is a well delineated media conglomerate. In 2003, it syndicates four music formats-down from seven available a few years ago-to its 58-owned radio stations plus affiliates, owns 21 Univision and 14 TeleFutura affiliated TV stations among its 39 TV properties, owns an outdoor billboard agency that targets Los Angeles and New York Hispanics, and the 90-year-old New York newspaper *El Diario/La Prensa*, which it will sell in 2003 to a private investment group for $18 million in cash and a $1.9 million note.

Its headquarters take up the entire sixth floor of a swanky six-story building in the media section of the city on trendy Colorado Boulevard. While I'm waiting to chat with Walter F. Ulloa, its chairman/CEO, the receptionist speaks English on the phone—unlike Miami where every business call at a Spanish entertainment company is answered in Spanish—and there seem to be lots of Anglo employees scampering around. I'm directed by his secretary to a large, empty conference room, where shortly a door opens and in strides Ulloa, apparently from his adjacent office. He's dressed in a blue suit, white blue-striped shirt with a blue tie, and with nary a greeting or shaking of hands, he sits down on the opposite side of the table from me and says, "What is it you need to know?" I'm a bit taken by his formality, directness, and lack of any greeting, which hasn't been the case with my other interviews with heads of corporations. Nevertheless, Ulloa and Entravision are powers within Hispanic media. Before getting involved with Entravision, Ulloa works for Univision's Los Angeles station, KMEX, from 1976 through 1989 in a variety of positions.

Entravision's operation center in Campbell, California, near San Jose, satellites the radio formats to affiliates. There's Tricolor (regional Mexican), which is the most popular format; Radio Romantica (adult contemporary), Super Estrella (pop rock), and the newest format, La Consentida (classic oldies). "Through our technology," explains Ulloa, "using a back channel, we provide local news and weather to our stations, which are in middle to small markets, whereas HBC and SBS are in the big markets. But we do compete with HBC in Phoenix, San Francisco, Las Vegas, El Paso, Dallas, and Chicago, and with SBS in some of those markets as well. Our strategy has been to concentrate on the Southwest with our radio stations. The increasing Hispanic population also increases the population base in every one of our markets. We're looking to add to our existing station clusters in 23 markets as well as looking at new emerging markets like Oklahoma City and Raleigh/Durham (North Carolina).

"While most of our stations are satellite-fed, in Los Angeles we program the stations locally because of the size of the market. Because there's so much at stake here (with 20 Spanish stations), we feel it's probably better to program locally."

In an unusual and complicated move for a principally Spanish-language radio network, Entravision switches two of its three Super Estrella formatted stations, KSSC-FM (Santa Monica) and KSSD-FM

(Newport Beach), to an English-language disco dance station renamed "The Party Station KDL" in January. A third station in this cluster, KSSE-FM Riverside, continues airing the Super Estella format, while the dance music format is simulcast on retitled KDLD and KDLW. The formula is based on Entravision's Dallas dance station, KKDL-FM, which launches the format in August of last year and is one of the Anglo radio stations the company owns. Upbeat dance music is designed to attract bilingual 18- to 34-year-olds as well as non-Hispanics. Both KDLD and KDLW are former dance stations under 1998 owner Clear Channel when they are known as KACD and KBCD and promoted as "Groove Radio."

Super Estrella moves to three California stations that the company acquires last Christmas Eve from Big City Radio for $137 million, KLYY-FM (Arcadia), KVYY-FM (Oxnard), and KSYY-FM (Fallbrook), all of which are on the dial at 107.1 in their respective cities. Ulloa says the format is "99 percent Latin artists but also artists who've crossed over to English like Ricky Martin, Shakira, and Enrique Iglesias." One key advantage to the "trimulcast" is the combined signals fill in coverage areas the company lacks in Southern California.

Among the company's expansion moves is the purchase of the Latin Communications Group in 1999 for $252 million, which includes New York's premiere newspaper *El Diario*; the launch in 2001 of Spanish TV stations in Santa Barbara, California, and Tampa and the added muscle in San Diego when it takes on the operation of two general market TV stations, XUPN, a UPN Network affiliate and XETV, a Fox Broadcasting affiliate. The company already operates two Spanish stations, KBNT, an Univision outlet, which it owns and XHAS, a Telemundo affiliate, whose owner is Mexico's Televisa. At this juncture, Entravision's 21 Univision affiliates represent the largest station group associated with the Miami network.

Ulloa says the company's TV plans focus on adding outlets for Univision and its new sister network, TeleFutura, in such cities as San

Diego, Laredo, Seattle, Portland, and Salt Lake City. "The challenge with the TeleFutura stations is getting them to a cash flow positive position, which we expect to do within the next 12 months.

"Generally it's more economical to buy a construction permit for a radio or TV station and build it from the ground up," says Ulloa. "But," he stresses, "we don't see them anymore, so we're buying existing stations and converting them to Spanish."

Do Entravision radio and TV stations attract second and third generation Hispanics? Parries Ulloa: "They absolutely attract second and third generation bilinguals. The Hispanic market is growing at such an incredible rate that reliance on Spanish-language media by Latinos will be there into the future. I'm second generation Mexican-American. My parents and I are born here. My grandfather came here in the early 1900s. I watch and listen to English-language radio and television. I also watch and listen to Spanish-language radio and TV. Both offer me something that's important; I can connect with both socially and emotionally.

"When I start in the business in 1976 with KMEX, the entire Spanish-language electronic media is doing around $30 million. Today, the business exceeds $2 billion." During his KMEX tenure, Ulloa writes editorials for the general manager, is the station's production manager, and for the last seven years handles ad sales. This well of diverse experiences becomes invaluable when Entravision debuts in 1996 and begins trading on the New York Stock Exchange in 2000.

When we discuss the nation's cultural diversity, Ulloa becomes circumspect. "One of the beautiful aspects of this country is we're able to continue to grow as a people and a producer of consumer products because of our diversity. "We're all immigrants," I chime in. "Exactly, we're all immigrants, and that's what the majority, if there's such a thing, has had trouble adjusting to. With the growth of the Latin, Asian, and African-American markets, this is not about one dominant culture. This is about the United States and it's incredible diversity, and isn't it magical and beautiful what's been created here?"

One of the first general market TV stations in the nation to reach out to touch and ensnare Hispanics is Tribune Broadcasting's KTLA in Los Angeles, which creates a Spanish interpretation of its 10 p.m. hourly news in 1984 to pull viewers away from watching Univision and Telemundo's newscasts, whose slants are more foreign than local. In a story I write about the station's prescient bilingual endeavor for *Television/Radio Age*, both Steve Bell, the station's vice president/general manager and Jeff Wald, its news director, strongly state KTLA is the nation's only station offering a news show in Spanish via the second audio program channel, the so-called SAP channel, available on new stereo sets. Wald amplifies this point in 2003 when he tells me, "We were the first Tribune station to have the SAP translation because at the time we had the largest Spanish-speaking population on the West Coast."

Other stations which follow KTLA's lead in introducing a Spanish SAP service, include WRAL Raleigh-Durham, North Carolina (which bows out after two years for financial reasons); WOOD Grand Rapids, Michigan, KCST San Diego, and WCIX Miami, which drops its simulcast in May of 1987 after almost three years for both economic reasons and because the city's two Hispanic stations, WSCV and WLTV, launch 10 p.m. newscasts. Besides WRAL and WCIX, ABC drops simulcasting of its *Nightly News* one year after it begins the SAP service in 2000.

Over the years, other Los Angeles TV stations add Spanish SAP programming, but for KTLA, the city's oldest TV station, it's all a matter of the competition catching up. Tribune's New York outlet, WPIX, starts its SAP service in 2003, and when I'm in the city that year, I discuss this topic with the station's general manager, whose comments are recorded in Chapter 14.

Ten years later in 1994, Univision's L.A. station, KMEX's *Noticias 34* will become the No. 1 watched newscast in Los Angeles at 6 and 11 p.m. causing shock waves to vibrate through the world of Anglo television.

In 2003, Jeff Wald returns to KTLA as its news director after working for another local station, KCOP, which hires him to build up its news operation. I'm interested in Wald's thoughts on the station's pioneering SAP efforts, which also include offering several off-network situation comedies, which the studios provide with a Spanish voice track.

Why does the station specifically launch its SAP service in 1984? "The SAP technology has just come out and our research indicates a lot of people are watching our news who don't speak English. They want to know what's going on in the general community, so we decide to have someone provide them with a Spanish translation, someone with the ability to read a script and translate it on the fly and then listen in the other ear to unscripted reporters and translate what they said."

"We always want to be on the cutting edge of new technology and the SAP button opens up this new market for us. The job requires someone with an international background who understands news. We hold auditions and I select whom I think is the right person. But she speaks Castilian Spanish and we receive calls from viewers who say she's speaking a dialect not common in Los Angeles. They know she isn't familiar with local speech. So less than one month later I found Analia Riggle, who wasn't in the first set of auditions."

When she joins the station fulltime, the Argentine native, who's lived in L.A. nine years, brings to the position 18 years as a translator and nine years as an interpreter. She uses what she calls "neutral Spanish" when I chat with her in 1988. Fifteen years later, she's still KTLA's Spanish news voice. "There's no way to gauge whether the simulcast adds to our ratings," Wald admits. "But it's added to the station's goodwill in the community." While two other general market L.A. stations, KTTV and KCAL also offer Spanish translations, Wald points out that when KTLA first begins with using Riggle there "are serious concerns about hearing a female voice when you push the SAP button while on the screen you see several different male/female anchors" (especially Hal Fishman, who, with a few slight departures, starts with the newscast in 1964). The public today accepts that you don't need to have male-female voices, you can have one voice it can relate to."

During the early years when stereo TV prices drop from $1,000 to an affordable $200, which makes them available to Hispanics, there are awkward moments for viewers and broadcasters. Some set owners are apparently not familiar with the SAP button, or they press the wrong button and see Hal Fishman on the screen and hear Analia speaking Spanish. Fishman relates this confusing state to me during my initial visit to the station: "I've gotten letters from people who say they can't understand what I'm saying and that I have a female voice."

During my observation visit to watch Analia at work, I observe a woman in a very tense work environment. Seated in his small sound booth, her eyes concentrating on the printed script, she jabs at the air with her left hand to emphasize words. She has five small black and white monitors that display the in-studio teleprompter with the script, individual shots of the three anchors, Fishman, Jann Carl, and Larry McCormick, and the picture going out over the air. In 1995, Carl leaves KTLA for a featured reporting/hosting role on *Entertainment Tonight*.

KTLA, like the other Anglo stations, has a number of Hispanic on-air news staffers: Giselle Fernandez, a former CBS correspondent is now one of the anchors on the station's *Morning News*, while its *News At 10* staff includes co-anchor Lynette Romero, reporters Patricia Del Rio, who's been with the station three years and Ted Garcia, who's also been covering general assignment stories for six years. Romero is elevated from reporter after three years to sit next to Fishman. Fernandez will leave the station after a few years into the new millennium.

Like all the Anglo station news directors in L.A., Wald is cognizant of the bilingual Hispanic audience and growing importance of the market's Latino power. "We make a concerted effort to cover all our communities, but it's a hard job," he admits. "I don't think we can leave the Hispanic-type stories to the Spanish TV stations exclusively anymore."

Sponsors obviously savor the Spanish simulcast since the English-language broadcast proudly announces that the Spanish translation "is sponsored by... ."

TV Azteca, Mexico's powerful television company has a grand idea for entering the U.S. with a third network designed for domestic Hispanics. In July of 2000 it creates a joint partnership to form Azteca America with Pappas Telecasting Company of Visalia, California, which operates 30 stations around the country. When the stock market plunge dissipates Pappas' plans to obtain the funding to buy stations in major Hispanic centers, including 13 stations owned by Barry Diller's USA Network as the launch pad for Azteca America, Univision, acting aggressively and obviously aware of Azteca's intention of building its network, snaps up the stations for $1.1 billion in December 2002 and uses them to launch its second network, TeleFutura in January of 2003.

Once Pappas fails to raise the capital for the network, the original partnership split of 80 percent Pappas/20 percent Azteca, is restructured with TV Azteca owning 100 percent of the new venture. Nonetheless, the network debuts in July 2001 with one station, Pappas' KAZA in Angeles. It begins adding other stations to the fledgling network: Reno in November followed in January by stations in San Francisco, Sacramento, and Houston. Non-Pappas stations are added in Orlando, Las Vegas, and Salt Lake City in June of 2002.

However, by October of 2002, the two parties are in a full-blown legal battle over terms of the affiliation agreement and Azteca's desire to buy into Pappas' Los Angeles flagship station. Within months, TV Azteca agrees in principal to resolve its legal disputes with Pappas and will seek additional station affiliates from the company.

In July of 2003, Azteca America signs a three-year local marketing agreement worth $15 million a year to the Harry Pappas-owned company to operate KAZA. In addition to Pappas, other station groups aligning themselves with the new network include TVC Television, Cocola Broadcasting Companies, and Una Vez Más.

A few weeks after I meet Luis J. Echarte, president/CEO of Azteca America at a reception in honor of the network in Beverly Hills, we set a date to speak on the phone about the network's plans for America. He's got a strong background in finance and banking and joins TV Azteca as chief financial officer in 2000 until 2001 when he becomes the architect for the formation of Azteca America. Born in Cuba, Echarte calls himself "a Cuban of the world right now." He arrives in the U.S. with his family in 1960, attends school in Philadelphia, settles in Miami, becomes a citizen and attends Memphis State, University of Florida, Georgia State, and Stanford.

By the time I do my phone interview with Echarte from Mexico City in July of 2003, the network has 26 affiliates, covering 63 percent of Hispanic households. He says the company is signing affiliates "because we're a foreign company and not allowed to buy stations. We can only have a 25 percent minimum investment in any U.S. company." Parent TV Azteca operates two national TV networks in Mexico, Azteca 13 and Azteca 7 comprising 300 owned and operated stations throughout Mexico.

Programming beamed from Mexico City is carried by Azteca America's affiliates in Los Angeles, New York, Miami, Houston, San Antonio, Phoenix, Tucson, San Francisco/Oakland/San Jose, Albuquerque, San Diego, Fresno/Visalia, Sacramento/Stockton/Modesto, Orlando, Austin, Las Vegas, Monterey/Salinas, Bakersfield, West Palm Beach/Ft. Pierce, Salt Lake City, Santa Barbara, Palm Springs, Naples/Ft. Myers, Wichita, Oklahoma City, Reno, and Victoria, Texas. The network shares advertising revenue with its affiliates who broadcast its news, soap operas, and Mexican soccer.

When the network makes its first sales and programming presentation to national advertising agencies in New York in 2003, Echarte announces 10-plus hours of live programming a day, ranging from variety shows, novelas, comedy series, children's programs, soccer, and news. Of all its programming originating from Mexico, only one, *Hechos America*, a newscast airing weekdays from 5–5:34 p.m. is designed exclusively for U.S. Hispanics with both an international flavor and some U.S. coverage. It debuts in November of 2002. In fact, Echarte says, "80 percent of Azteca 13's programs are transmitted to the U.S. (from Mexico)."

A news staff of 350 operates out of Mexico City with U.S. correspondents in L.A., New York, Washington, Miami, Houston, and San Antonio, while overseas correspondents are in Guatemala City, Madrid, Buenos Aires, Paris, and Tel Aviv. News staffers work on three programs, all with hechos (facts) in their titles: the 7 a.m. *Hechos AM*, anchored by Ramón Fregosa; the 10 p.m. *Noticiero Hechos*, anchored by Javier Alatorre; and *Hechos America*, anchored by José Martín Sámano and Rebeca Sáenz.

When I ask Echarte how his newscasts differ from those at Univision and Telemundo, he responds confidently, "We are probably more geared toward Mexican Hispanics than they are, and with 67 percent of Hispanics from Mexico, we claim we represent more of the market than our competitors."

While Azteca's novelas are done in Mexico City for a Mexican audience, Echarte says "some elements, or pieces" are added to the soap operas which will appeal to American viewers. "If a show is 50 minutes, you add 10 minutes which offers some connection for the U.S. viewer. The novelas are also focused more on contemporary stories."

Two other programs also have a U.S. connection. *Ventaneando*, the top celebrity entertainment show (which means peeping), does a broadcast from Caesars Palace in Las Vegas in which Celine Dion is interviewed. "The value of going to the U.S. with this show," notes Echarte, "is it brings the program closer to its American audience." And its community outreach show, *A Quien Corresponda* (*To Whom It May Concern*), accepts calls from the U.S.

With the dominant amount of Azteca America's programming coming from Mexico, why would the multi-cultural U.S. Hispanic population be interested in Mexican-flavored shows? Explains Echarte: "The country which produces the largest amount of Hispanic programming in a language that speaks to the ears of most Hispanics is Mexico. Televisa and us are the first and second largest producers of Hispanic programming. Hispanics in the U.S. are used to the Mexican language. It's a friendly language to them versus Argentinean or

Chilean, which are difficult Spanish to understand. Televisa, through its deal with Univision, has made the U.S. market used to the kinds of programming we do, so it transcends beyond just Mexicans."

Since it creates is own programming for its own network, Echarte hawks the network as being a "fully integrated" U.S. Hispanic TV company. How does this enable the new company to attract national advertisers, the life's blood of television? "If you're fully integrated," he explains, "you can deliver ratings because you're more attuned to the market, produce shows for that market and make changes if the production doesn't work. We offer various integrated advertising tools like product mentions, casual product usage and product placement which allows advertisers to be more involved in show production." In three different novelas, a box of Procter & Gamble's Gain detergent is added to a scene of people unpacking groceries; a segment is shot inside a McDonald's, and a virtual Kmart shopping bag appears conspicuously in the background.

Among the network's prized shows are its the primetime reality series *La Academia*, designed for young viewers, and its soccer coverage of eight of 20 teams in Mexico's First Division League, which appeals to all futbol fanáticos. The network is a mixture of high-power and low-power transmitting stations, albeit the low-powers outnumber the stronger signals. It's not something Spanish networks with a combination of high- and low-power stations boast about.

While Echarte predicts the network will increase its Latin household penetration to 83 percent by year's end, it misses its distribution mark and in January of 2004 announces it's now reaching 73 percent of Hispanic households with the addition of affiliates in Dallas and Corpus Christi. This now places the network in 33 markets. "Passing the 70 percent clearance mark is another milestone in our build out," boasts, Echarte, obviously overlooking his earlier distribution projection. The company does have something tangible to crow about: in February it acquires exclusive transmission rights to the Chiapas Jaguares of Mexico's First Division soccer league, boosting Azteca's license to nine of the 20 teams in the league. This means Azteca America and TV Azteca will increase their soccer coverage from 71 to 84 regular games.

In a major distribution move in August of 2004, Azteca America signs with its first cable systems operator, Time Warner Cable, for coverage in the New York-New Jersey area. Its arrangement covers 900,000 Hispanic cable subscribers. When the network begins operation in mid-2001, its first affiliates are local UHF broadcast stations. All told, the network is now in 38 markets covering around 78 percent of the Hispanic population.

Although it's not directly affected, Azteca America's parent, TV Azteca, is being investigated for possible violations of securities laws by the U.S. Securities and Exchange Commission and in Mexico for an alleged fraud by Mexico's version of the SEC, the National Banking and Securities Commission. Although TV Azteca denies any wrongdoing by several individuals, two American members of its board of directors resign. They are Gene Jankowski, former president of the CBS Broadcasting Group and James Jones, a former U.S. Ambassador to Mexico. The financial imbroglio, begun in '04, stretches into '05 and seems to have a life of its own. This complex cross-border situation, which involves a debt financing deal and profits for several corporate officials, is covered in Chapter 19. (In a matter involving full disclosure, another of Azteca America's directors is Michael Viner, owner of Phoenix Books, which publishes this book.)

One of Azteca America's early affiliates is Pappas Telecasting's Houston station, KAZH, which joins the network in late February of '03 and whose general manager/general sales manager, Emilio Nicolás, Jr., is a third generation Hispanic broadcaster following his grandfather and father into the industry. Those are two engrossing reasons to chat with him. So on a clear day in Los Angeles in July, I call Nicolás at home because he can't get to the station. Hurricane Claudette, a 300-mile-wide storm, and the nation's first hurricane of the season, is raking Texas and Nicolás is stuck at home without any electricity or phone service. I reach him on his cell phone, but he says its battery is running low, so I should call back on his wife's cell.

He downplays the severity in Houston by telling me, "it's just a heavy rain here with power outages." Then, in an up-tempo mood talks about the important things happening at the station, which Pappas purchases two years ago when it airs only paid programming and is located 45 minutes south of downtown Houston. The station is moving within three months into Houston proper, has doubled its transmission power to 5,000 watts to become a full-power station, and is planning to introduce what he calls "a truly Hispanic newscast rather than a general market newscast."

"We're preparing to introduce our local news early next year," Nicolás says. "In some Spanish markets, it's local news at 5 and national news at 5:30. We'll have our local news at 10 p.m. followed by the national broadcast at 10:30. Spanish primetime runs from 6 to 10 p.m." The executive speaks of a news studio design encompassing digital technology and a new news slant.

Several of Nicolás' projections do not happen on time, I discover in May of 2004. Responding to questions about updating these developments, Nicolás e-mails me: "We have been delayed in building our permanent home. The station is currently in temporary quarters in Houston. This has resulted in the delay for launching our local news and bringing our local shows in-house for production. The current time table is for late this year." The executive also notes a new local show, *Latin US*, airing Sundays at 9:30 a.m., which provides information on immigration, starting a business as well as obtaining small business loans.

Nicolás joins KAZA in March as general manager/general sales manager with three years experience as vice president/general manager of Telemundo's' KVDA in San Antonio and 10-and-a-half years as general manager with Univision's KMEX in Los Angeles, WXTV, New York, and KDTV San Francisco, the latter for eight-and-a-half of those years. So he brings to Houston an understanding of how Spanish TV operates in three other competitive markets. "News formats in Spanish have very little differences from general market stations other than language. It's the same format with two anchors, sports and weather segments. With KAZA, I want to find ways to make the newscast different and very Latino-oriented. It will be a newscast with emphasis on civic journalism and effective positive social change. Our audience will not just be informed of the news, it will know how to take action to improve their conditions when necessary. When I was at KVDA (one of five Hispanic TV stations in Houston), we found that cameras could help us effect positive social change. We were the first station to use Web cameras situated in different locations. We'd get instant reaction from the people affected by the news story. If a championship school band didn't receive new uniforms, cameras pursued the story."

The station airs six shows produced by local companies encompassing children's, a music/interview show aimed at the city's 120,000 Salvadorans, an interview show focusing on Latin American entertainment personalities, and a music video show spotlighting regional Mexican acts. It also carries a weekly news program hosted by a local Azteca news service correspondent. Once it's in its new facilities, KAZH expects to bring the shows in-house.

Having savored life in several major cities, Nicolás finds Houston a different experience, principally on an economic level. "There's a remarkable economic vibrancy here because 25 percent of the city's small businesses are Hispanic," he says. Of the city's 5.5 million residents, 1.7 million are Hispanic, with people of Mexican descent 65 percent of the population, followed by the 150,000 Salvadorans and 100,000 Colombians. Seventy-eight percent of the city's Hispanic population, Nicolás points out, arrived in the last 10 years. Growing up in San Antonio, he says he "was conditioned from childhood to avoid Houston and Dallas because they were rough places for us. Prejudice was horrific outside Dallas and Houston. It's a whole different world today, where Spanish is spoken throughout Houston."

Among his accomplishments is winning an Emmy Award as executive producer for San Francisco KDTV's coverage of the September 1985 8.1 Mexico City earthquake, for which he was the executive producer. "We landed the first U.S. crew in Mexico, consisting of four people, and beat the American networks by eight hours by sending our video back first." Within one hour of the quake at 7:19 a.m. Mexico City time, KDTV, then an affiliate of the Spanish International Network (SIN), airs the first satellite-fed images of the disaster from Imevision, the Mexican government's TV station.

Nicolás' broadcasting bloodline traces back to his grandfather, Raúl Cortez, who arrives in San Antonio in 1930 from Jalapa, Veracruz, Mexico with his parents and begins his show business career in 1935 by operating a theatrical booking agency that brings in some of Mexico and Latin America's top musical acts. In 1945, he moves into radio and launches regional Mexican music format KCOR-AM, which claims to be the first full-time Hispanic radio station in the nation. Cortez's pioneering company is named Pan American Broadcasters. Ten years later, he starts KCOR-TV, channel 41, now owned by Univision. KCOR radio is eventually sold to Hispanic Broadcasting Corporation, which in turn is acquired by Univision in 2003, which retains the Mexican music flavor.

Initially, KCOR-TV broadcasts Mexican movies and programs and live local shows in the evenings to viewers who purchase a UHF converter to pick up stations beyond channel 13. After several years of red ink, due to advertising hesitancy and the need to acquire all its programming since it's not aligned with any network, Cortez sells the station to an Anglo group of investors who rename it KUAL and maintain its Spanish programming. KUAL changes its call letters to KWEX in 1961 when Emilio Ascárraga, the powerful Mexican owner of Televisa Broadcasting, and a group of U.S. investors, including Emilio's dad, Emilio Sr., purchases the station and begin to build the Spanish International Network (SIN). Emilio, Sr. leaves his family in Coahuila, Mexico, in 1949 when he's 19 to come to San Antonio where he obtains his citizenship in 1959.

In 1971, Cortez dies of a heart attack at age 66 in San Antonio. Five years later, SIN reportedly becomes the first network to satellite its programs to affiliates.

In 1988, Azcárraga and his group—which operates SIN stations in New York, Miami, Fresno, San Francisco, Phoenix,

Albuquerque, Chicago, Corpus Christi, Houston, and Sacramento—sells both stations and the network to Hallmark Cards and First Chicago Venture Capital for 301.5 million dollars. It is renamed Univision. Federal courts force Azcárraga to sell because his Televisa owns 75 percent of SIN, a greater share than the 20 percent of a TV station the company is allowed by law. Hallmark in turn sells the package in 1992 to A. Jerrold Perenchio, its present owner, who will sell Univision in 2006 to an investment group, an action covered in Chapter 19.

When Emilio, Sr. joins KCOR-TV at the behest of Raul Cortez in 1965, he has a master's degree in biology and plans to enter medical school. But with Texas medical schools discriminating against Latinos, Nicolás switches directions, becomes a research biologist and takes a part-time job at the TV station. By 1981, he's the senior vice president of Spanish International Communications Corporation (SICC), the licensee for Spanish-language TVs in the U.S. and general manager of KWEX.

In 1986, he becomes president of SICC when Rene Anselmo, SICC's and SIN's former president, resigns following a 10-year legal suit by shareholders and licensing problems with the Federal Communications Commission. Shareholders charge his dual role is a conflict of interest. A federal judge in California supports the shareholder's claim that Anselmo made decisions in favor of SIN to the detriment of SICC. And since SICC uses SIN for nearly 50 percent of its programming under Anselmo's dual responsibility, an FCC administrative law judge rules in January of '86 that KWEX and nine of SICC's stations, in addition to several others in which Anselmo is involved, should not have their licenses renewed. The FCC suggests that if the corporation restructures itself, that will open the way for license renewals. Anselmo's departure appears on the surface to diminish the corporation's license problems.

Following the sale of Univision in 1992, Emilio, Sr. departs SIN and starts a new business, Nicolas Communications Corporation to manage its TV stations, KNIC Houston, KCPR, and KXCC

Corpus Christi (both started in 1990), followed by KXLK Austin, launched in 1998. In 1991, Emilio, Sr.'s youngest son Guillermo joins the company right out of college as its treasurer. All the stations are subsequently sold; KCPR in the spring of 2003 to Univision for its TeleFutura network, KXLK and KXCC to Pappas in the third quarter of '03.

"On December 31 of 2003, the company goes out of (the TV) business," says Guillermo, who notes in our phone conversation that brother "Emilio is the only one still in television." The family now operates a real estate management company.

America's three main Hispanic TV networks generally compete programming-wise in the same areas. It's in the genres of news and soccer that Univision, Telemundo and Azteca America often go toe-to-toe and story-to-story. So when I'm assigned to do stories on both topics for *TelevisionWeek*, I find myself looking inside their news and sports operations and chatting with the heads of these departments as well as executives from several other Latino sports networks.

When the second Gulf war breaks out in Iraq in 2003, Jorge Ramos and María Elena Salinas, Univision's co-anchors of its *Noticiero Univision* national newscast at 6:30 p.m., lead the news division's on-location coverage, which draws a 17.0 Hispanic household rating for the first week of the conflagration. The duo also appear on the network's morning entertainment/news show, *Despierta America*, which remains the No. 1 morning show with Hispanics since November 1992. A total of seven on-air reporters plus technical staff, totaling nearly 20 people in the Persian Gulf region, provide coverage for Univision's other network newscasts, *Primer Impacto*, *Ultima Hora*, and *Agui Y Ahora*, points out Sylvia Rosabal-Ley, the network's news director from her Miami headquarters. Univision also feeds back raw video footage from ABC and edited reports from CNN En Español.

Ramos, who spends the first three weeks reporting live from Kuwait and Iraq, while Salinas reports from Kuwait and Baghdad during a two-week period, tells me the network newscasts, "provide the global adjunct to Univision affiliates local news emphasis. Our world and perspective are much wider than that of ABC, CBS, and NBC, and that's what we've been doing the last 17 years."

There's also another major difference he cites, attributable to the nation's surging Hispanic population, legal and illegal. "We're seeing an incremental increase in our audience on a year-to-year basis, which is the opposite of what's happening with the English-language networks which see decreasing viewership." Citing a study by the Tomás Rivera Policy Institute of Claremont, California, he indicates "nine out of 10 Latinos speak Spanish at home; eight out of 10 are bilingual and 57 percent of that studied group chooses to watch the news in Spanish. This is a major attitude change. Ten years ago, one in four bilinguals watched the news in Spanish."

As for the undocumented, estimated by the U.S. to total eight million, the majority Hispanic, Ramos says these people "have no voice in the English-language newscasts, for obvious reasons. They speak Spanish and are afraid of being interviewed. For us, they are part of our life. If they are interested in finding out what's going on in Venezuela or Peru on a regular basis, they won't find anything on the three networks."

While Univision's 19-owned stations and affiliates carry the network newscasts, TeleFutura, the year-old sister network, aimed at a younger audience and encompassing its 21-owned stations and affiliates, provides 45-second news briefs from 10 a.m. through the primetime evening hours. A separate staff, under the direction of Univision's news department, prepares the briefs. Univision's news legacy dates back to June 1, 1981 when the company, then known as the Spanish International Network, debuts its first network newscast. Univision network news currently employs 303 full and part-time employees.

What's different about Univision network news is its change in attitude and content. Notes Ramos: "We've moved over the years from concentrating on Latin America to now focusing on the Hispanic community in the United States, and also covering major news stories like the anthrax scare in Maryland, the Laci Peterson murder in California. And with more than 50 percent of our audience Mexican Americans or of Mexican origin, we cover Mexico like we cover Washington."

Ramos, a native of Mexico, joins the network's Los Angeles station, KMEX in 1984 as a reporter. Two years later, he moves to Miami to host the morning show, *Mundo Latino*. Several months later, he changes hours and programs to anchor the network's nightly 6:30 to 7 p.m. *Noticiero Univision*. Since he and Maria Elena Salinas have been together 17 years, he quips, "We are probably the oldest news couple in the business."

With news bureaus in Los Angeles, New York, Miami, Chicago, Washington, San Antonio, San Francisco, Mexico, El Salvador, Peru, and Columbia augmented by freelancers in Guatemala, Nicaragua, Venezuela, Argentina, and Brazil, news director Rosabal-Ley notes the newscasts look for socio-economic issues from these areas that are relevant to U.S. Hispanics. "We never set out to do a program and measure content by country. Obviously the audience is mostly Mexican, so we keep an eye on that community, but issues for other Hispanics are also covered. There are no pre-set notions about story ratios." She has been news director for the past year and with Univision 18 years in various news positions.

One topic not being covered by Univision News is the acquisition by parent Univision Communications of Hispanic Broadcasting Corporation, the leading Spanish radio network. Why isn't this merger being covered? "We have more important things to cover," is Rosabal-Ley's answer. "The only broadcast coverage we've had is HBC's competitor, Spanish Broadcasting System's aggressive campaign against the purchase."

Once an also ran in news, now part of the NBC family, Telemundo is reaping the benefits of long-time NBC News, first during the War in Iraq and next year during the Summer Olympics in Athens, Greece, and the presidential elections. Telemundo's present full force news operation in Hialeah, Florida, is the result of Joe

Peyronnin, a 35-year TV journalist being hired by the then Sony-owned company in April 1999 as executive vice president of news and information programming. He gets the network operation operational in February 2000. Up to that point, Telemundo's news presence centers on a half-hour newscast provided by CBS-owned TeleNoticas, which is ironically purchased by CBS' Westinghouse parent from Telemundo in 1996.

"We know we need a strong news presence," Peyronnin tells me on the phone, adding: We also know Univision has a 10-year start with a strong news presence and an anchor team in place on its 6:30 news." By the time NBC acquires Telemundo in April 2002, the division employs nearly 200 and has representation in key domestic cities, Mexico and throughout all of Latin America.

During the second Iraq war, 11 Telemundo staffers work alongside NBC personnel, and the network even broadcasts stories by two of NBC's high-profile correspondents, David Bloom, who dies of an embolism while on assignment and Kerry Sanders, NBC's Miami correspondent. While Sanders speaks in Spanish, Bloom's narrative is translated by either morning anchor José Díaz-Balart or Pedro Sevcec later in the day. Telemundo also preempts its daytime programming to add news from 2 to 4 p.m. and expands it's 6–6:30 p.m. news to run until 7 or 8 p.m. A late night show, *Punto Final*, is created which also dispenses war news.

The joint effort pays off with strong household ratings. From an average of 19 percent of Hispanic households watching the network, its war coverage generates a 28 percent viewing in Hispanic homes during the first week of its war coverage to 32 percent for the second week, according to Nielsen data provided me by Telemundo.

As an operating company within NBC and considered part of NBC News, Peyronnin reports to NBC News president Neal Shapiro. A native New Yorker, Peyronnin commutes home to his family on weekends and every two weeks appears at NBC headquarters in 30 Rockefeller Plaza in Manhattan "to attend the NBC News staff meetings and discuss our mutual plans."

Based on his 35 years with CBS from 1970–'95 in various news positions and as president of Fox News and also creator of its network operation, Peyronnin uses this experience in 2002 to launch a series of newscasts on Telemundo, starting with the morning block of *Hoy En El Mundo* (7–9 a.m.) and *De Mañanita* (9–10), followed by the afternoon *Al Rojo Vivo Con Maria Celeste* (5–6) and *Noticiero Telemundo*, the seven day 6:30 p.m. newscast. The weekend edition of *Noticiero* starts three days before September 11, hosted by Ilia Calderón, reportedly the first black Hispanic on Spanish-language TV. During the summer, the network's first public affairs show, *Sin Fronteras*, makes its debut. These shows are satellite fed to Telemundo's 13 full-power and 10 low-power owned stations, plus 32 affiliates. The owned and operated full-power stations are in Chicago, Denver, Dallas, Houston, Los Angeles (which has two), Miami, New York, Puerto Rico, San Antonio, San Francisco, Phoenix, and Tucson. The low-powers are in Colorado Springs, Denver (which has two), Monterey/Salinas, Phoenix, Pueblo, Reno, Salt Lake City, Santa Maria, and San Luis Obispo.

When it comes to soccer on Spanish TV, I discover in 2004 an overload of hyperbole from the networks all claiming they carry the best and most matches. But there's one little known channel, Gol TV, which only carries soccer and does broadcast the most matches. The company is a creation of Tenfield, a Uruguayan company that starts operations in 2003. Located in North Bay Village, outside Miami, the channel offers soccer from around the world plus daily newscasts. Three of its directors, president Francisco Casal, vice president/executive director Enzo Francescoli, and vice president Nelson Gutierrez, are all former professional soccer players. The channel offers more than 1,000 games per year in either English or Spanish, depending on which distribution service you sign up for.

Gol TV, plus other newcomers ESPN Deportes and Azteca America, along with Fox Sports En Español, Univision, and Telemundo, provide domestic Hispanics with a window into the world of international soccer. The result of all the coverage creates, "a very competitive push for licenses," admits Jorge Hidalgo, executive vice president of sports for Telemundo, who recalls when soccer was a two network competition starting in 1992.

"Soccer is the passion for Hispanics," says Andrés Cantor, the best-known soccer announcer for his signature long goooall calls. "It's part of the culture of Latin America and it's the game we're brought up with," he tells me on the phone from the Miami offices of the company he co-founds in 1989, Futbol De Primera, which provides soccer coverage and news for radio. (Cantor is among the talent profiled in Chapter 11.)

When Gol TV debuts on February 14, 2003, it has close to three million subscribers from the Dish Network, which is a small distribution number, but a comparable one for a niche cable or satellite-delivered network. "We're focused on the 40 percent of the Hispanic population in this country which is not Mexican," says Constantino Voulgaris, the company's director of business development. "And we're the only network to broadcast in both English and Spanish. Our main objective is to be a reference for soccer regardless of nationality."

To achieve this goal, Gol TV's distributors offer different language preference subscription packages. Eileen Montalvo, its director of marketing/communications, notes that Dish Network, for example, "offers two audio packages, 'Dish Latino,' which is only Spanish and 'AT150' which is exclusively English. Cable distributors provide a service involving the SAP channel option, in which you can hear the commentary in a different language on the SAP channel. Adelphia offers both English and Spanish with the SAP option in California and Miami. Comcast, in its nationally available Hispanic digital tier of programs, has Spanish first with English an SAP capability. Cablevision in New York offers Spanish first with an English SAP choice."

The company has four English narrators and five interpreting in Spanish along with the video pictures it receives from the originating TV company in the host nation. "We do try to carry the original content games," says Voulgaris, "so that people from Colombia, Nicaragua, and Guatemala can hear their native accents."

Gol TV has an agreement with Telemundo to carry 40 Mexican League World Cup qualifying matches. It also carries "the countries with the best soccer, Italy and Spain," emphasizes Voulgaris. So that soccer buffs can enjoy football, futbol, fussball, or voetbal.

ESPN Deportes, the Spanish-language sports network which debuts January 7, 2004, is the outgrowth of a four-hour Sunday night block that runs for two-and-a-half years on multi-use cable channels. Its hallmark soccer attraction is the Union of European Football Association's (UEFA) Champions League competition. "It's the best soccer outside the World Cup competition. These are the top 32 European teams which have been narrowed down to England, Spain, France, and Portugal which meet in Germany May 26 for the league championship," says Lino Garcia, ESPN Deportes' general manager since June of 2003. It's his first job running a sports network, having previously dealt with Hispanic marketing for 15 years with Universal Television, Sony Entertainment Television, and HBO, including help launch HBO En Español. UEFA licenses 77 matches to the company, with 64 exclusive to ESPN Deportes and the other 13 to ESPN2 that broadcasts them in English. "We'll offer some European World Cup qualifying matches this year as well in 2005, with ESPN Deportes' Sunday evening hour show covering the day's results," notes Garcia. Seven matches are broadcast this season, 10 are slated for next year. Among the national teams competing are Germany, England, Spain, Italy, France, Portugal, and Holland, with ESPN Deportes hoping to feature at least one of these teams during the run up to the championship. Why would Hispanics want to watch European soccer teams? "A lot of the European teams include 70 players from Latin America," explains Garcia.

The synergy between Deportes and ESPN2 dates back to the Spanish network's debut when ESPN2 simulcasts several editions of the Spanish version of *SportsCenter* from January 8 to 14, introducing hosts Michele LaFountain, Heriberto Murrieta, Fernando Palomo, and Jorge Eduardo Sanchez Perez to ESPN2's nearly 87 million households. Garcia calls the ESPN2 exposure "a sampling opportunity" which starts up again April 25 and runs through the end of June.

The network airs three soccer news shows for its futbol fanáticos: *Futbol Picante*, a half-hour devoted to Mexican soccer; the twice weekly *Fuera De Juergo*, which recaps international results and *Goles De España*, a weekly highlight of Spanish league action. There's also a weekly magazine hour, *UEFA Champions League Weekly*, which airs during the season and covers all aspects of league play.

Has ESPN Deportes entry into Spanish sports TV affected the cost for league licenses? "Absolutely not," responds Garcia. "We don't look at it to be beneficial to all to force rights fees to go higher than they are now." ESPN Deportes is available in one million Hispanic cable households during its initial months.

Soccer is especially popular among men 18-to-49. It is the cornerstone of Fox Sports En Español since the News Corporation network debuts in November of 1996. "Soccer is close to 50 percent of our hours," declares David Sternberg, the network's Los Angeles-based general manager, one of several titles he holds within the Fox Cable Networks Group. The network averages 540 matches annually from division one national leagues in Argentina, Brazil, Costa Rica, El Salvador, Honduras, and England, as well as from six tournaments, InterLiga, Copa Libertadores, Copa Sudamerica, Recopa Sudamericana, Champions World Series, and the UEFA Cup. The network also airs one game a week from the U.S. pro league, Major League Soccer (MLS) Saturdays at 7:30 p.m. during its season of April through November. Soccer has two seasons, generally January through June and August through December, so the action is available almost all-year round.

"Virtually all our games are live, with an occasional tape delay," says Sternberg. "If you look at the demographics of Hispanics in the U.S., a huge number are of Mexican origin, so Mexican clubs draw the largest audience. The games also attract strong following among Salvadorians, Colombians, and Argentineans. In many cases we take the original feed from the country of origin. When events are played in the U.S., we have our own commentators, Samuel Jacob, a Mexican, for the Mexican league, MLS and InterLiga, while Luis Rodriguez, from El Salvador, handles Salvadoran games. We have our own commentators in Argentina, Fernando Niembro and Enrique Macaya Márquez, who report for our sister channel Fox Sports Latin America," he explains during our phone interview.

Top soccer matches attract enough adults 18-49 to earn a 1.6 national Hispanic household Nielsen rating and a five or six "coverage" rating for households in the Fox viewing universe, points out Tom Maney, the network's senior vice president of ad sales. Car manufacturers are the top advertising genre at this audience, followed by beer and telecommunications. "Sixty percent of our ad business is focused on adult males, while on the broadcast network's Spanish programming skews more towards females."

Sternberg, like all sports networks officials is guarded when discussing license fee costs. He does tell me they are "significant, but when compared to U.S. sports licenses, we're not talking about the same order of magnitude." The network is available to six million U.S. Hispanic households.

Although Univision and its sister networks, TeleFutura and Galavision (on cable), collectively offer 600 hours of soccer, or 40 percent of the sports coverage, the arrival of ESPN Deportes and Gol TV has a tempering effect on David Downs, president of New York-based Univision Sports. "They and Fox Sports En Español are in the marketplace competing for events, and this does make all of our lives a little tougher. Sports is an unusual place. It contains events important to us and not as important to English-language television. So fees paid by sponsors are lower for soccer than are paid for the NFL by the English-language networks."

Downs allocates soccer games to the various networks "where it makes sense," he explains during our phone chat. "Sports are a niche on Univision and we'd never preempt a hit novela at night for a soccer game," he says. "TeleFutura, which skews slightly more male, seeks the more attractive sports events, even during primetime. Galavision has the most flexible schedule for any first-class sport we offer them.

"The games vary in performance by network because of their distribution, the competition each faces and the time period in which they're placed," explains Downs, who formerly toils 21 years with ABC Sports, his last position being senior vice president of programming. Among the events he negotiates for Univision are the 1994 and 1998 World Cups, when they are held in the U.S. and France, respectively. "Liga Mexicana, arguably the best league in North and Central America, is the No. 1 rated sports property on Univision and TeleFutura and the best rated program on Galavision. It averages a 6.4 Hispanic household rating on Univision, a 4.0 on TeleFutura and a 1.0 on Galavision. Soccer is primarily seen on weekends, 4 to 6 p.m. and 8 to 10 p.m. on Saturdays and 10 a.m. to 3 p.m. on Sundays."

Since 2000, when long goooall caller and play-by-play announcer Andrés Cantor departs Univision for Telemundo, Univision's replacement is Pablo Ramírez assisted by Ricardo Mayorga as the color commentator.

Even without Cantor, 205 games from Liga Mexicana, Mexico's Division One league are shown on the three networks. Univision owns the rights to 10 of these teams. "This league is enormously successful because the vast majority of the U.S. Hispanic population is of Mexican descent or recent arrivals. While 75 percent of its players are from Mexico, the other 25 percent are from other Latin American nations," says Downs.

The World Cup is one of Univision's prime ratings hotspots. It has been airing them every four years since 1978 when it was the Spanish International network. The 1994 Cup earns an average 11.3 household rating, according to Nielsen. During its 2002 run prior to the championship, the U.S. versus Mexico is its most watched match ever among 18- to 49-year-olds on Spanish-language TV, and garners an average 10.0 rating. The U.S. triumphs 2-0, much to the chagrin of sundry U.S. Mexican residents, who view the broadcast at 11:30 p.m. on the West Coast and at 2:30 a.m. in the East.

Rights for the 64 matches in both the 2002 and 2006 World Cup cost Univision $150 million, a figure Downs admits is a record amount for either U.S. English or Spanish-language soccer.

Another top attraction on Univision is the Copa América competition. This summer for the first time, 17 games will air on TeleFutura, while its older network carries nine contests. "The last time in 2001, 10 games air on Univision and 16 on Galavision."

When NBC-owned Telemundo tackles the Athens Olympic Games this summer in Spanish for the first time as part of NBC's exclusive coverage, "two thirds of our 130 hours of programming will be soccer," notes Jorge Hidalgo, Telemundo's executive vice president of sports. And with Mexico's national men's and women's teams qualifying for the Olympics, he envisions super ratings. "Since they qualified," he quips to me on the phone from his Hialeah, Florida, headquarters, "I sleep better." Hidalgo also tells me, "We'll make a conscious effort to cover every Hispanic athlete and country." Heading Telemundo's overall on-air coverage are Andrés Cantor and Jessi Losada, with Alejandro Blanco handling the soccer color. Prior to the actual Games, Telemundo runs a series of specials on Hispanic Olympic hopefuls.

How do the Olympics compare with the World Cup? Parries Hidalgo: "It compares quite a bit. If you take the Mexican team, we'll cover it the same way we would if they were in the World Cup. Between the two events, the Olympics have greater viewership, although the World Cup is a major international attraction and does very well in the U.S."

On a regular basis, Telemundo airs the Mexican Division One league and claims an exclusive pact with two of its teams, Atlante and Chiapas, as well as with the Mexican national team. Its other exclusives include the U.S. men's and women's national teams. Of the 94 matches it carries, 10 are with the American teams. The Mexican league runs from January through June and then starts up again from August to December." Hidalgo says soccer league schedules are unpredictable. "They're made up at the 11th hour and there are times when two or three or four weeks go by with no soccer." Seventy percent of Telemundo's weekends are dedicated to soccer content.

It sounds repetitive, but Mexico is everyone's top draw. Telemundo knows this first-hand. Last year, according to the network's news spokesman, Gerardo Oyola, when Mexico plays Colombia, the match earns a 10.9 rating among men 18-to-49 and an 8.9 among all adults the same age. When Mexico plays Costa Rica, Telemundo's broadcast earns a 5.7 rating among adults 18-to-49, and when Mexico plays the U.S., the contest rates a 9.8 among men 18-to-49 and an 8.2 for adults overall 18-to-49.

Azteca America's coverage is really Mexican-laden. TV Azteca, the parent company of the U.S.' newest year-old Spanish network beaming out of Mexico City, owns Monarcas Morelia, a Mexican Division One league champion. TV Azteca purchases the 43-year-old team in 1993 and sees its investment pay off with the league title in 2000. During the 2002 season, it finishes second. David Faitelson, Azteca America's dual-positioned sports director and on-air commentator for several programs, lays claim to being the leader in Mexican soccer.

"Our 180 broadcasts are the most Mexican soccer matches on any network," he proclaims during our phone conversation. Faitelson, who's been in his post since 2001, says the network's license covers home games for nine of the league's teams, last season's winner Pachuca, Jaguares (the current first place leader), Queretaro, Cruz Azul, Veracruz, Irapuato, Santos, Tecos, and the aforementioned Monarcas Morelia. By early April, Azteca America boasts it "broadcasts 59 Mexican League soccer matches, versus 18 for TeleFutura, 12 for Univision and nine for Telemundo," according to spokesman Daniel McCosh.

Faitelson, born in Israel, moves to Mexico with his parents when he's nine years old. He starts covering sports for three of Mexico City's daily papers and moves into TV with Imevision, the government-owned network, which later becomes TV Azteca, where he handles major competitions. He covers three World Cup tournaments, 1994 in the U.S., France in 1998, and Korea/Japan in 2002; four Olympics in Seoul 1988, Barcelona in 1992, Atlanta in 1996, and Sidney in 2000 and several Pan American Games. He also maintains a busy on-air schedule. His commentaries are heard on *Los Protagonistas*, which airs on Azteca America at 1 a.m.; for the parent network, he hosts the *Los Protagonistas* edition which airs at 11 a.m. Monday through Friday; the daily sports report during *Noticiero Azteca America* at 6 p.m. weekdays and finally hosts the weekly soccer special, *El Color*.

Azteca America covers soccer since its inception in 2001, with four to six matches carried live on weekend afternoons to its 33 affiliates.

Articles

"Tanner Leaves Spanish Broadcasting System." HispanicAD.com, Sept. 2, 2005

"Spanish Broadcasting To Sell 2 Southland Stations." Los Angeles Times, Aug. 18, 2004

"Azteca's Making Inroads." Daily Variety, Aug. 17, 2004

"Azteca America Adds 5 Affils." Hollywood Reporter, May 21, 2004

"TV Azteca Shares Fall On Board Changes." Los Angeles Times, May 11, 2004

"'El Cucuy' Tunes In Higher Ratings For SBS." Hollywood Reporter, April 27, 2004

"Univision Radio's Popular Midday Host Named Afternoon Drive-Time Disc Jockey." HispaniaNet.com, March 28, 2004

"SBS Tunes In L.A. Radio Star 'El Cucuy.'" Hollywood Reporter, March 19, 2004

"'El Cucuy' Returning To Morning Radio." Los Angeles Times, March 18, 2004

"KSCA-FM's 'El Cucuy' Suspended For Walkout." Los Angeles Times, Feb. 26, 2004

"Azteca Chief Target Of Probe." Hollywood Reporter, Feb. 11, 2004

"TV Azteca Denies Wrongdoing." Hollywood Reporter, Jan. 28, 2004

"Univision Gets Approval For Radio Merger." Los Angeles Times, Sept. 23, 2003

"Claudette's Surprising Force Jars Gulf Coast." Los Angeles Times, July 16, 2003

"L.A. Gets New Format." Latin Notas, Billboard, April 5, 2003

"Breaking The Language Barrier." TelevisionWeek, April 7, 2003

"Spanish On Sap Just Hasn't Caught On." Broadcasting & Cable, March 23, 2003

"Format Ventures Beyond Mexico." Los Angeles Times, March 7, 2003

"KFSG Switch Represents A Changing Southland." Los Angeles Times, Feb. 28, 2003

"U.S. Judge Dismisses Spanish Broadcast Suit." Wall Street Journal, Feb. 3, 2003

"Switch To Spanish Signals Industry Growth." Los Angeles Times, Jan. 17, 2003

"Rare Radio Lingo Swap In L.A." Daily Variety, Jan. 23, 2003

"TV Azteca Trades Suits With Partner Over Joint Venture." Wall Street Journal, Oct. 28, 2002

"Control Key To Azteca America." Hollywood Reporter, July 19, 2002

"Mac Tichenor: Hispanic Radio It's A Matter Of Pride." Radio Ink Magazine, May 27, 2002

"Azteca, U.S. Partner Establish Terms For Joint Venture." Wall Street Journal, Oct. 23, 2001

"Entravision's San Diego Move." Electronic Media, Oct. 22, 2001

"Entravision Launches 2 Spanish TV Stations." Los Angeles Times, March 30, 2001

"It's All About The Audience." Los Angeles Times, March 2, 2000

"Entravision Buys Latin Group." Hollywood Reporter, Dec. 23, 1999

"Senor Dodger (Sports Announcer Jaime Jarrin Translates Vic Scully's Play-By-Play Report Of Los Angeles Dodgers Baseball Games)" Los Angeles Magazine, August 1998

"The New Signal." June 16, San Antonio Express-News, June 16, 1991

"New TV Channel Targets Hispanics." San Antonio Express-News, May 21, 1991

"Manager At KWEX-TV Takes Control At SICC." San Antonio Express-News, May 3, 1986

"SIN Pioneers Changed TV For Everyone." San Antonio Express-News, Sept. 23, 1995

"Local Spanish TV Goes To The Rescue." San Francisco Examiner, Sept. 22, 1985

"KWEX President Pioneered Spanish Language TV." San Antonio Express-News, Dec. 5, 1982

"Raul Cortez Is Dead At 66." San Antonio Express-News, Dec. 17, 1971.

Chapter 17
CAPITULO 17

Changing Landscape...Again 2003
CAMBIANDO EL PAISAJE 2003

• Univision, through its acquisitions, becomes more powerful in the record and radio industries.

• In death, Celia Cruz's albums remain best sellers.

• Library of Congress includes Tito Puente in its new list of treasured recordings.

• As sales of Latin albums continue to shrink due to piracy, the Recording Industry Association of America allocates $2.5 million to exclusively confront the problem.

• Major global labels, facing declining revenues, streamline stateside operations.

• Telemundo and Univision push originally developed novelas reflecting life in the U.S.A. that viewers can connect with.

• English-language TV opens door wider for talent, but not enough to satisfy lobby groups.

• Latino films garner record 10 Academy Award nominations.

• Arturo "Arte" Moreno buys the Anaheim Angles to become the first-ever Hispanic owner of a U.S. major league sports team.

Restive, intransitive and seeking to break barriers, Latin entertainment is a kettle of fiery explorations as the new millennium moves forward. Records, broadcasting, and films are all exploring new creative endeavors.

With the U.S. now the world's largest market for Spanish-language record sales, outranking both Spain and Mexico, artists from all over the Latin world focus on domestic Hispanics with a potpourri of musical genres.

Traditional salsa is in a slump with new forms such as reggaeton, a combination of rap and reggae, and electronic music, fusing into the Afro-Caribbean mothership. Although the music from a variety of catalog artists is still heard on tropical formatted radio stations in the East, there are no new influential salsa labels generating fresh excitement in New York City, the acknowledged home for salsa on the Mainland, since the genre's two main generators, Fania Records fades following the death in 1997 of co-founder Jerry Masucci, and RMM and its owner, Ralph Mercado, declare bankruptcy in 2001.

Rap's cause is being aided this year by such major labels as Universal, EMI and Sony looking to strengthen their representation since the genre continues to gain recognition, with the Latin Grammys bestowing its own blessing on the music with a rap award category. A good percentage of the rap artists are from Puerto Rico, where reggaeton is gaining a solid foothold as salsa diminishes in popularity.

A distant relative to reggaeton is the genre called Latin dance music, or disco, which might sound simplistic, but is a mixture of various dance beats with tropical rhythms like merengue, salsa and bachata, which allows the music to gain airplay on general market stations which specialize in rap and on Latino radio which plays pop and tropical artists.

The mixture of styles and rhythmic patterns also encompasses the blending of Caribbean tempos with pop and rock ingredients, as exemplified by the success of newcomer Juanes, who blends rock, funk, and R&B within his Colombian music. His debut in America in 2001 based on his debut album, *Fijate Bien* on Surco/Universal, results in six Latin Grammy nominations and helps catapult him to stardom. The next year, his CD, *Un Dia Normal* (*A Normal Day*), exceeds 500,000 sold copies in the U.S. alone and this year he really comes into his own, winning five Latin Grammy awards including record and song of the year for *Es Por Ti.*

Many of the tropical-pop-rock hyphenated artists like Juanes, are singer-songwriters whose numbers are increasing. They include Luis Fonsi, Alejandro Sanz, Jorge Moreno, Sin Bandera, Bacilos, Donato Poveda, Diego Torres, Shakira, Obie Bermúdez, Ednita Nazario, Soraya, and La Oreja De Van Gogh.

Sin Bandera is the vocal duo of Noel Schajris from Argentina and Leonel García from Mexico, which mixes strains from the bossa nova and rhythm'n'blues into its signature sound. Bacilos is a Miami-developed multinational folk-pop trio whose members are from Colombia/ Ecuador, Brazil, and Puerto Rico, which earns six Latin Grammy nominations and wins two last year including best Latin pop album and top tropical song.

Record labels rely on male romantic ballad singers as their fundamental hit-makers since Latin radio is more open to melodic ballads, which appeal to females. Among the new heartthrobs are Universal's David Bisbal (winner of the best new artist Latin Grammy), Luis Fonsi (Universal); Juan Gabriel, José José, Cristian Castro, and Alexandre Pires (BMG); Luis Miguel and Ricardo Montaner (Warner Bros.); Ricky Martin and Chayanne (Sony) and Marco Antonio Solís and Los Temerarios (Fonovisa).

Hit-generating producer Kike Santander, whose latest efforts are for Bisbal and Alejandro Fernández, explains the cultural ingredient which propels romantic music to *Billboard* thusly: "Latins are more emotional. They get depressed, they cry more. And they need songs to beg forgiveness, to get drunk to, to propose to. That's part of their essence."

Part of Mexico's apparent new essence is its successful rock en Español/alternative music bands: Molotov, El Gran Silencio, Café Tacuba, Kinky, and Control Machete, which are one million miles from the traditional mariachi sound and none to sorry about the distancing. Their music, as well as the tremors created by other

Mexican ensembles like Nortec Collective, Nopal Beat, as well as singer/songwriters Natalia Lafourcade and Ely Guerra, who favor electronics, ska, heavy metal, rap sensitivities, and politically caustic lyrics—a reflection of how they perceive their native land amidst the global universe. Café Tacuba offers perhaps the most radical musical experience when it collaborates with the Kronos Quartet, an avant-garde classical music ensemble.

Three of these-better known new sound bands, El Gran Silencio, Control Machete, and Kinky, as well as lesser-known Inspector and Plastilina Mosh, are from Monterrey, 150 miles from the U.S. border, which has a rich tradition for musical experimentation. Machete's forte is rap; Kinky favors electronica, or electronic music; El Gran Silencio combines reggae and ska from Jamaica with its cumbia and norteño beats; Plastilina Mosh favors experimental sounds while Inspector probes a ska and cumbia connection.

Despite the acceptance of these Mexicans rockers, the Spanish authors and publishers society, Spanish Society of Authors Composers and Publishers (SGAE), which since 2000 sponsors "Rock En¡," an artist tour through the Americas, cancels the U.S. leg for the first time, alleging a lack of interest in the genre by the Miami major labels as well as its own budget problems.

Several socio-political reasons are proffered for the recent emergence in the U.S. of these often radical musical aggregations. A more open Mexican society plays a role in allowing these bands, previously relegated to underground status, to emerge in the spotlight of public acceptance, a radical departure from the repressive attitude within the government and the media monopolies, which stifled creative free expression in Mexico. And with the advent of satellite television and the Internet, Mexico's musicians are gaining first-hand exposure to the influential styles of other Latin American and U.S. groups.

Non-Mexican new wave artists finding acceptance among U.S. Latins include a coterie from Colombia: Aterciopelados, which connects electronica with cumbia and vallenato rhythms from the country's Atlantic Coast; Carlos Vives, who fuses rock with the vallenato rhythm and Juanes and Shakira, who crack the domestic market last year; Guatemala's Ricardo Arjona, Argentina's Diego Torres, and Cuba's Jorge Moreno.

There are diverse influences affecting the music of Colombia, which Shakira points out in the *San Antonio Express-News*: "The Caribbean region of the country is mostly influenced by African rhythms while the interior is more influenced by Andean sounds" which include flutes and percussion. Her music also prominently incorporates her Lebanese ancestry.

Following the success of Spain's romantic vocalist David Bisbal, a number of additional Spanish acts are geared for domestic exposure, including La Oreja De Van Gogh on Sony and David Bustamante, Sergio Dalma and Ismael Serrano on Universal Music Latino. None come to the U.S. with the kind of exposure Bisbal gains. Initially he appears on the reality TV series *Operacion Triunfo* that catches the attention of record label Vale Music, which hires Kike Santander to produce Bisbal's debut CD, *Corazón Latino*, for Universal Music Latino. Bisbal's vocal style embroiders the note-quavering style of the flamenco singer onto his powerful voice, dramatically spotlighted during his performance at the 2004 *Billboard* Latin Music Awards in Miami. All are hoping to emulate the success of Alejandro Sanz, who cracks the American market in 1997 with his single, *Corazón Partio*, and leaves an opening in the ensuing years for Spaniards to follow suit.

Two events are tinged in historical nostalgia. Among the first 50 recordings selected by the Library of Congress for its National Recording Registry is Tito Puente's 1958 release, *Dance Mania*. Puente is the solo Hispanic among the recipients who represent all forms of repertoire. The storied Smithsonian Institution, another Washington, D.C., educational landmark, in mid-January launches a four-year, 11-city tour across America for its *Latin Jazz: La Combinacion Perfecta*, multimedia, bilingual exhibition which opens in its Arts And Industries Building in the fall of 2002. This is the first show ever presented by the Smithsonian that focuses on Latin jazz, which gains a major boost with the addition of a Latin jazz Grammy award during the last decade. The exhibition's main focus is on the contributions of the U.S.' Latin communities and the overpowering impact of Cuba's contributions dating back to the 1940 emergence of the seminal Latin jazz band, Machito and his Afro-Cubans, with the exhibition crediting Machito's 1943 signature song, *Tanga*, as the genre's first original Latin jazz tune. Born Frank Grillo, Machito, a singer and maracas player, moves to New York in 1937 as vocalist with La Estrella Habanera before forming his own band and hiring his brother-in-law Mario Bauzá as music director, who signs a galaxy of American soloists from 1948 to 1960 to guest with the ensemble. While playing Ronnie Scott's club in London in 1984, Machito suffers a fatal stroke.

The Cuban influence is also reflected in the exposure for percussionists Mongo Santamaria, Candido, Chano Pozo, Patato Valdés, Armando Peraza, and Francisco Aguabella and the platitudes given to Irakere, the Cuban-funded jazz fusion band which gains national attention during the "Havana Jam" cultural exchange concerts between CBS Records and the Cuban government in Havana in 1979. Among the band members who gain prominence in the U.S. are pianist Chucho Valdés, saxophonist Paquito D'Rivera and trumpeter Arturo Sandoval, the latter two defecting and living in the U.S.

While the exhibit pays tribute to musicians of Puerto Rican ancestry (Tito Puente's signed timbales are among the instruments on display for example), the program downplays the contributions of Brazil and Argentina.

On a level of historical significance, D'Rivera, the multi-talented saxophonist, composer and staunch anti-Castroite makes history when he becomes the first artist to win Latin Grammys in two categories. He snares the classical accolade for the album, *Historia Del Soldado* and the Latin jazz trophy for *Brazilian Dreams*.

On a lesser level, but nonetheless still significant, Juanes is shut out in the 45th annual regular Grammy Awards competition, ending his streak of accolade achievements. Entered in the best Latin rock/alternative album category, his Universal Music Latino CD, *Un Dia Normal*, loses to Maná and its *Revolución De Amor* Warner Bros. CD. Bacilos, whose career is on the ascendancy, wins the best Latin pop album award for *Caraluna* on Warner Bros. All told, the Recording Academy bestows seven Latin Grammys, with Celia Cruz winning the salsa album with *La Negra Tiene Tumbao* (Sony Discos; three veteran names in Latin music, Bebo Valdés, Israel López "Cachao," and Carlos "Patato" Valdés, comprising the Bebo Valdés Trio, win the best traditional tropical album with *El Arte Del Sabor* (Blue Note); Groupo Mania wins the best merengue album for *Latino* (Universal Music Latino); Joan Sebastían snares the Mexican album for *Lo Dijo El Carazón* on Balboa/Discos Musart, and Emilio Navaira wins the Tejano album for *Acuérdate* on BMG U.S. Latin. In the jazz category, the Caribbean Jazz Project's *The Gathering* on Concord Picante wins the Latin jazz award. In the world music competition, Rubén Blades snares the prize for *Mundo* on Columbia. And in the pop category, Carlos Santana makes an appearance on the winning pop collaboration with vocals album, *The Game of Love*, featuring Michelle Branch on Arista. Two months after her brain surgery, Celia Cruz accepts her award with her usual broad smile.

One of the lesser covered areas of music is Latin Christian, which in 2003 gains several important distribution breaks, designed to increase its retail exposure in the English and Spanish markets. CanZion Productions of Houston and Vida Music of Miami enter into a partnership both companies view as leading to greater growth. Vida, which is distributed by the powerful Zondervan company, will distribute CanZion's top 15 titles to both Christian bookstores and to general market mass-merchant retailers. A major enticement in the deal is CanZion's top artist Marcos Witt. In turn, Vida's top-selling albums will be distributed by CanZion to specialty Hispanic Christian bookstores.

Aiding strength to this expansionist movement, Word Distribution, the leading Christian record purveyor, joins with publishers Broadman & Holman and Editorial Unlit in a campaign titled *Su Mundo Latino*, designed to stimulate the sale of Spanish-language books and records in Christian bookstores nation-wide. The goal is to cover 500 bookstores this year.

One powerhouse Latin Christian artist who's branching out into the general market is Jaci Velasquez, with two recordings and a film debut. Her new releases are *Unspoken* on Warner Bros. Christian Records in English and *Milagro*, a Latin pop effort on Sony Discos in Spanish. Her big screen debut is in *Chasing Papi* in which she plays an unflattering rich girl. One of her tunes from the *Milagro* album, *I Don't Need A Man*, is the film's title tune. Her buildup includes doing radio and TV ads for Pepsi as well as touring 23 major markets to promote her recordings. There's one interesting aside to this 23-year-old's career. When she's 14 years old, she signs with Word Records of Nashville, which is subsequently acquired by Warner Bros. and rechristened Warner Bros. Christian Records.

Celia Cruz, while recovering from last December's surgery to remove a cancerous tumor, plans recording her third album for Sony this spring. In July, she passes away while working in Miami. By the end of the year, a frenetic response from her fans to keep her music alive, results in three of her discs on *Billboard*'s list of the year's top records. The albums on the tropical music chart include: *Hits Mix* and *Regalo Del Alma* (both on Sony Discos) and *Exitos Eternos* (Universal Latino). *Regalo* is both her last studio recording and her lone No. 1 disc this year. Her album output, including several for Vene/EMI Latin and Lideres Entertainment Group, also positions her as the top tropical and Latin album artist.

Regional Mexican music continues its dominant sales position in the U.S., accounting for more than 60 percent of all Latin music sales, with the top sellers Intocable, Los Bukis, Los Tigres Del Norte, Conjunto Primavera, Bronco, Pancho Barraza, Limite 21, Pepe Aguilar, and Los Temerarios.

While the English-language record industry's sales continue to dip 3.6 percent to around 656 million units, total sales by all Latin artists singing in Spanish and English amount to 27.5 million units, up from 23.7 million units sold the previous year, according to Nielsen SoundScan, which electronically measures album sales in major retain chains, but not in small mom and pop operations. And according to the Recording Industry Association of America (RIAA), the record industry's main trade and lobbying organization, shipments of Latin albums total 38.6 million units, a six percent decline from 2002's 41.1 million units shipped to retailers. The RIAA, responding to industry estimates that between 30 to 40 percent of all Latin records sold are counterfeit, and that 28 percent of all illegal CDs seized in its raids are of Latin content, commits $2.5 million in new anti-piracy funds. The money will also fund the hiring of eight fulltime Latin music field investigators. The RIAA claims two million pirated albums are seized this year in the Mainland and Puerto Rico; the majority of the discs seized outside Puerto Rico are regional Mexican.

On the corporate level, several major companies assert dominance in new roles. For the first time, the new Univision Music Group, consisting of the Univision, Fonovisa, and Disa labels, displaces longtime pacesetter Sony as the top Latin distributor. Sony finishes second with an 18.58 percent share of the market. In business three years, the Univision Group's market share percentage hits 28.18 percent (up from 10.86 percent last year), according to Nielsen SoundScan. In a breakdown by labels, Fonovisa accounts for 12.83 percent (up from 10.41); Univision for 6.91 (up from 4.01) and Disa for 8.45 percent over last year's 6.85. Disa and Fonovisa's strength are both in regional Mexican music, while Univision offers a broader range of styles.

Parent company Univision Communications becomes the power in Latin radio by acquiring Hispanic Broadcasting Corporation and its 68 stations for $3.2 billion. Sony changes its name to Sony Music Norte, a division which will cover the U.S., Mexico and Central America. And Universal Music Video Distribution becomes the leading distributor of Latin product in the U.S.

The Latin U.S. retains its growth pattern, sticking peccadilloes into rural America where Hispanics move and change the color and complexity of these communities. According to the U.S. Census post 2000 national headcount, Georgia tops the list of states with the fastest-growing Latino population, with a 17 percent rise to an estimated 516,000 Hispanics, followed by North Carolina, Nevada, Kentucky, and South Carolina. California has the most Hispanics, 11.9 million, followed by Texas, New York, Florida, Illinois, New Jersey, and Pennsylvania. The nation-wide Latino population is now an estimated 38.8 million, according to the Census, which reveals one interesting statistic: 60 percent of the Latin population is now born in the U.S., advancing the possibility of more bilinguals for the general market entertainment industry to romance.

Mexico accounts for 67 percent of the U.S. residing Latinos followed by Central and South America with 14 percent. Mexico also accounts for around 60 percent of the estimated eight to 11 million undocumented immigrants who regularly sneak across the nation's porous borders. The Immigration and Naturalization Service in January pegs the number of illegals living in California at around 2.2 million.

12 California cities are among the nation's top 20 Latino communities with the highest percentage of foreign-born residents in 2003: Miami, Santa Ana, Los Angeles, Anaheim, San Francisco, San Jose, New York, Long Beach, Houston, San Diego, Oakland, Boston, Dallas, Sacramento, Honolulu, El Paso, Stockton, Riverside, Fresno, and Chicago.

With the Spanish population tripling between 1990 and 2000 in Alabama, Arkansas, Georgia, Nevada, North Carolina, South Carolina, and Tennessee where blue collar jobs beckon to migrants and transplanted Latinos from California, New York, and Illinois, new opportunities arise for artists to tour these and other ancillary markets and for radio station groups to add affiliates in new small to large-size communities.

Two markets, El Paso, Texas, and Fresno-Visalia, California, offer stark proof of how their Hispanic populations generate Hispanic radio and TV.

El Paso, which sits on the border with Juarez, Mexico, is 73 percent Hispanic, producing a rich trove of bilingual listener/consumers for Entravision, Univision, and TeleFutura TV affiliates and Hispanic Broadcasting Corporation and Council Tree Communication's radio stations. These U.S. broadcasters compete with Juarez's nine TV signals. Entravision's KINT, an Univision station, is the market's top advertising biller. El Paso, along with San Diego, are the nation's two busiest crossing points for immigrants, resulting in regional Mexican and Spanish adult contemporary music being the most popular of the local Spanish formats which compete against the 20 Juarez radio stations which beam into the community.

If you look at the Fresno-Visalia community in Central California, you find that 42 percent of its population is Hispanic, providing the self-proclaimed "Raisin Capitol of the World" with five Spanish TV outlets (Univision and its TeleFutura and Galavision operations, Telemundo and Azteca America) and five Spanish radio stations from the networks of Infinity Broadcasting, Lotus Communications, Radio Unica, Hispanic Broadcasting Corporation, and Entravision.

Two veteran artists, Jose Feliciano and Vikki Carr, who achieve major success in the general market during the '60s and '70s, obviously have a loyal fan base in 2003. Feliciano, best known for his *Light My Fire* pop hit, explodes onto the *Billboard* top Latin albums in second place with his Universal Latino album, *Senor Bolero 2*, a major breakthrough in the Latin market. Carr, a mainstay of Liberty Records when it's a hot Hollywood independent label, and best known for her pleading ballad, *It Must Be Him*, receives the San Antonio Hispanic Heritage Society's third annual Tito Guízar Award. The San Antonio resident earns a Grammy in 1995 for *Recuerdo A Javier Solis*, her tribute album to the late ranchera singer.

Responding to the importance of the Hispanic market, the Disney Company, in a first for its Walt Disney Records division, releases its first two Spanish-language children's albums, *Favoritas De Las Princesas De Disney* (*Disney Princess Favorites*) and *Disney Presenta*

Cantar Y Jugar (*Disney Presents Sing and Play*). *Princesa* features songs from a myriad of hit Disney animated films, while *Cantar Y Jugar* is a collection of favorite playtime tunes from Latin America performed in a variety of different dance tempos. English versions of both recordings are among the company's most popular titles. The Spanish albums are being distributed in the U.S. by Universal Music & Video Distribution. The CDs are an adjunct to Disney's line of read-along DVDs, available since 2002, which have a Spanish-language option feature. Recent DVDs include *El Rey Lion* (*The Lion King*), *El Libro De La Selva* (*Jungle Book*), and *La Vida Mickey 11*.

A number of new recordings add new flavors to the dollar-rich Hispanic music mart.

Mezzo-soprano opera star Denyce Graves, in a major artistic change in direction, goes Latin on her new RCA Red Seal release, *The Lost Days*. She performs with Cuba's Chucho Valdés and José María Vitier, Brazil's Eliane Elias, and Argentina's Pablo Ziegler, all of whom perform their own original compositions. The New York recording session is produced by Ettore Stratta for RCA's venerated classical label.

Brazilian percussionist Airto Moreira, a top-selling artist of the '70s, releases his first album in the U.S. in 20 years, *Life After That*, on NARADA.

Tenor saxophonist David Murray's trips to Havana in 2001 and 2002 to record with Cuban musicians, produces *Now Is Another Time* on Justin Time Records, the Montreal label, with an interest in Latin music. The recording features members of his U.S.-based band and the Cuban musicians and arrangers all focused on the Afro-Cuban connection.

Pete Escovedo, one of music's best-known timbale players, releases his first live album in 15 years, *Live!* on Concord Picante, which features his percussionist children, Sheila E and her brothers Peter Michael and Juan performing with his all-star band. Escovedo, at 67, is one of the remaining elders of Latin jazz now that Tito Puente, Chico O'Farrill, and Mongo Santamaria have since passed on.

The album carries the flavor of the band Azteca, which Escovedo co-leads with his late brother Coke in the early '70s. During its short lifespan, it's known for its multi-cultural fusion of Brazilian and Latin tempos with rock and funk elements.

Concord, in another move to attract new customers, signs its newest multi-cultural phenomenon Ozomatli, which uses Afro-Cuban and Latin rhythms as the base for its inclusions of Middle Eastern, rap, R&B and jazz improvisations. And usually gets its audiences up on their feet and dancing to its overpowering energy and cacophonously discordant sounds. The band's two previous albums are on Almo Sounds, the label owned and formed by Herb Alpert and Jerry Moss, following their sale of A&M, the wildly successful company they form in the early '60s—which features Alpert and the Tijuana Brass and Julius Wechter and the Baja Marimba Band, two ersatz Latino combos which gain stardom around the world—to PolyGram in 1989 for $500 million.

Also showing recognition for the Latin alternative scene is this year's South By Southwest music festival in Austin. The annual event, generally focuses on new rock bands, devotes four showcases to Latin acts during its four days of talent presentations at various nightclubs as well as panel discussions. The Hispanic contingent spans nationally established artists and new regional acts. Name-power performers include Molotov, Jorge Moreno, and Tejano veterans David Lee Garza Y Los Musicales. Adding breadth to the showcases sponsored by the Texas chapter of the National Academy of Recording Artists (NARAs) and the Latino Rock Alliance of Austin are: Austin's Del Castillo sextet, which blends flamenco with rock and which is named the event's band of the year; Long Beach, California's Jenni Rivera, a neo-banda singer who specializes in risqué corridos and controversial narco-corridos; Brownsville's Big Circo norteño hip-hop septet; Mexico's Panda quartet, which supports a hard punk rock style and Peru's energized Libido quintet.

The expansion of the Hispanic population across America prompts major name Latino acts with drawing power to draw in customers to a growing number of large seating arenas. Maná, arguably Latin rock's superstar act, is being booked by the powerhouse Creative Artists Agency into the Miami Arena and the city's AmericanAirlines Arena, the Mandalay Bay Hotel in Las Vegas, New York's Madison Square Garden, San Diego's Sports Arena, and the Patriot Center in the nation's capital. Additionally, touring Latin acts are also playing the new Kodak Theater in Hollywood, the Hollywood Bowl and Greek Theater in Los Angeles, the Universal Amphitheater in Universal City in the San Fernando Valley section of L.A., the Home Depot Center in distant Carson, Caesars Palace in Las Vegas, and the Gwinnett Center in the Atlanta suburb of Duluth which launches its Latin initiative with two bookings by Los Temerarios.

This year, the initial Latin acts playing the Kodak Theater (home to the Academy Awards) are Pepe Aguilar and Alejandro Sanz, who both do sellout business. In 2002, Aguilar is the first regional Mexican performer to play on the same Hollywood Bowl stage with the Los Angeles Philharmonic. Sanz's 20 shows in two months this year doubles the amount of gigs he plays last season.

Propelling these Latin tours are three major concert promotion firms, Clear Channel, House of Blues, and AEG, all of which provide professional expertise for these grinding experiences with the artist's manager, record company, publicist, and tour sponsor when there is one.

One event sponsored by McDonald's, the "LoMcXimo Tour" stars rock en Español bands Molotov and El Gran Silencio, with stops in Houston at the Verizon Wireless Theater, New York at the Hammerstein Ballroom, in Miami at the James L. Knight Center and in Universal City at the Universal Amphitheater. One artist picking up a sponsor is Enrique Iglesias, whose 2004 world tour will be under the aegis of PepsiCo.

One major figure that contributes to the growth of the Latin concert business, Ralph Hauser, III, 41, dies of an apparent heart attack in Whittier, California, February 14, while playing racquetball. The Montebello, California, born businessman becomes THE man in

Latin touring by becoming the exclusive U.S. representative for many of the biggest attractions in domestic Latin entertainment through his Hauser/CIE Entertainment. In 1985, after working with his father booking rodeos and Mexican music acts into the Pico Rivera Sports Arena, he opens his own concert promotion firm. In 2001, he forms a partnership with CIE, another concert promotion firm, which acquires a majority position in the new firm. At the time of his death, he's the company's CEO and is known for bringing Mexican artists into major venues like Madison Square Garden and the Universal Amphitheater. Among the artists he works with are Vicente and Alejandro Fernández, Joan Sebastían, Luis Miguel, Rocio Durcal, and Juan Gabriel, with whom he's in the midst of a legal dispute when he dies. The company averages more than 100 concerts annually to rate eighth among the top 50 concert promoters in trade magazine *Polstar*'s ranking of firms achieving more than $1.1 million in global ticket sales.

On a more upbeat level, a number of Latin music's big guns fire volleys in different directions. For the first time in five years, Ricky Martin releases a Spanish-language album, *Las Almas Del Silencio* (*Souls of Silence*) on Sony Discos from which the fast-rising pop/rock single *Tal Vez* (*Perhaps*) emerges. It's his first Spanish studio recording since 1998's breakthrough *Vuelve*. Buoyed by strong sales, the album debuts on *Billboard*'s influential top 200 album chart at number 12, which ties Enrique Iglesias' *Quizas* as the highest Spanish-language debuting album. Originally working on an English-language album, which is nearly complete, Martin changes course and decides to go Spanish based on his need to go back to his roots and beginning. The 31-year-old singer has been out of the public spotlight for the past two years and the new LP is also a musical diversity from his upbeat party records. It's reflective lyrics and longing for love are paired with rhythms from his native Puerto Rico, Colombia, the Andes, and the Middle East. While these ingredients are designed to support his cultural roots, his follow-up album out next March will be the English one he stopped doing for the crossover market.

Café Tacuba, Mexico's sizzling, quirky rock en Español quartet, switches from Warner Bros. to MCA owned and distributed Geffen Records, the longtime English-language proponent of heavy metal rock bands, which has no Latin music department. Nonetheless, the group releases its *Cuatro Caminos* CD emphasizing rock dynamics, employs a real drum instead of a drum machine, and lyrics in Spanish for its new label, which discovers it's no party promoting a Latin alternative music group since there's little or no radio play. Of the new release, Emmanuel Del Real, the band's keyboardist and one of its composers tells the *LA Weekly*: "I find it surprising that after 14 years of playing together, we finally made the kind of record that we liked listening to when we were teenagers."

Spain's Alejandro Sanz, who writes his own material, acts as his own producer on his new release, *No Es Lo Mismo*, which features one tune excoriating Fidel Castro and another featuring the more welcomed Cuban rapper GQ on the R&B flavored *Try To Save Your Song*. Sanz expresses hope for a better Cuba on the tune *Labana*, a slang expression for Havana, explains the *San Antonio Express-News*, which quotes this line of Sanz's lyrics: "Cuenta 1,2,3,4 que ta vas Fidel," which translated means, "count 1,2,3,4, you're leaving Fidel." The author additionally explains in the story: "I tried to recount the drama experienced by people who leave the island in a balsa wood boat and risk their lives over 90 miles of sea to escape a very hard political situation."

One Cuban artist, 84 going on 85-year-old bassist Israel "Cachao" López, long credited as the creator of the mambo along with his older brother Orestes in their native land in the late '30s and currently a Miami resident, flies to Los Angeles to record his latest album, *¡Ahora Si!* in Capitol Records historic Studio A. The new album features an array of veteran Latin musicians, none in the same age bracket as "Cachao." It will be distributed by the Univision Music Group, and is the second album produced by Andy Garcia, himself a respected Cuban American film star and working musician. It is Garcia who jump starts "Cachao's" new career in 1989, elevating him from only playing in local Miami clubs and working in the band of the charanga duo of Hansel Y Raúl. That year, the two meet in San Francisco where the acoustic standup bassist is performing. Garcia is so impressed he winds up producing a tribute concert and a film documentary on the legendary Cuban musician. In 1993, Garcia and "Cachao" collaborate on their first album together, *Master Sessions, Volume 1*.

How is "Cachao" connected to the mambo? Looking to create a new rhythm, the López brothers compose a fast-paced danzón they name *Mambo*. The tune and the new dance fail to inspire Havana's dancers, so the brothers slow the tempo down to fit the Island's accepted romantic mood and the mambo gains acceptance. Ten years later, a Cuban bandleader adds horns and a commercial flavor and the mambo explodes in the Latin world and then the U.S. The bandleader's name is Dámaso Pérez Prado.

In the 1980's it's Julio Iglesias whose name sparks a global explosion. By 2003, the Iglesias show business clan is led by first son Enrique, who explodes onto the bilingual scene in 1995 and is now being followed by son number two, Julio, Jr., 30, who makes his professional debut with the album *Tercera Dimension* (*Third Dimension*) which he co-produces. Julio, Enrique, 28, and older sister Chabeli, 31, who works in Spanish-language TV, have lived in Miami 20 years since leaving Spain in 1982 following the kidnapping of their grandfather and their mother's concern for their safety. Initially the plan is for the kids to live in Miami one year. She remains in Spain while Julio tours the world and a nanny brings up the children. The parents get divorced in Spain three years before the children head to the safety of Miami.

Julio, Jr.'s new album sports a mid tempo rock pulse under his songs of frustrated love experiences. In 1995, he records a soft pop album, *Under My Eyes*, which is not released in the U.S. Between albums, he's busy writing songs and waiting for the right opportunity to record again. This is the right climate, he feels, since there is a growing acceptance of rock en Español bands.

In between his recording activities, Enrique, 28, signs a one-year pact with PepsiCo to place him in its commercials and sponsor his 2004 world tour following the release of his next English-language Interscope album later this year. He previously represents Doritos, a division of PepsiCo, for a year. In eight years, Enrique releases six hit albums and makes his film debt this summer in *Once Upon A Time In Mexico* with Johnny Depp and Antonio Banderas. In 1993, to please his father, Enrique enrolls at the University of Miami to study business, but this rock'n'roll fan of U2 and Bruce Springsteen rather than his father's romantic Latin music, drops out a year later and makes a demonstration tape under the name Enrique Martinez, which he offers various record companies without telling his parents. Fonovisa, the Mexican label is impressed enough to sign him in 1995 to a $2 million, three-album deal. Months later, so the story goes, Julio, Sr. finds out about the contract and the two have a major fight in which Enrique leaves home and the two do not speak. In 1999, Enrique signs a six-album deal with Universal/Interscope worth a reported $44 million. Enrique's success in music is accomplished without his father's assistance.

Seeking a respite from recorded music? Festivals offer the creative enticement to enjoy live Latin music.

The Playboy Jazz Festival's 25th anniversary bash at the Hollywood Bowl showcases the diversity of Latin jazz styles, from Poncho Sanchez's jazz and blues flavored octet with James Moody guesting on tenor saxophone and flute to the Bobby Rodriguez Salsa Orchestra to Los Hombres Calientes which solidifies the bridge between New Orleans and Afro Caribbean music to the marginal jazz-R&B-rap meldings of Ozomatli. Over the years, I've attended many of these sold out festival parties at the Bowl in which the Latin bands really ignite the audience. So during the 25th anniversary party I ask Bill Farley, the festival's vice president of marketing to detail the event's relationship with Latin jazz. "Six years ago it becomes evident that Latin music and Latin jazz in particular are experiencing a burst of popularity. We found Latin jazz to be a tremendous crowd pleaser," he says. "Each year its popularity grows but it'll never be the Playboy Latin Jazz Festival. We feel we have to include Latin with all forms of jazz because patrons who come here to see their favorite Latin acts will be exposed to other forms of jazz. We've presented three or four Latin jazz acts for the past several years."

After checking his files, Farley sends me the following historical information: "Playboy was a forerunner in bringing Latin jazz to the public, starting with the festival's inception in 1979 when both Flora Purim and Willie Bobo perform. Willie also appears in 1981 and teams with Mongo Santamaria and his band in 1983. In 1984, Tito Puente makes his debut performance. In 1990, Tito is a special guest with the Poncho Sanchez band on the bill with the Elaine Elias trio. In 1997, we have two Latin acts on each day of the festival: Gato Barbieri and Cuba's Los Van Van and Tito Puente with India and Roy Hargrove's Cristol band. In 2000, Los Van is back along with Rubén Blades, Celia Cruz, and Ozomatli."

The annual Sedona Jazz on the Rocks bash in the Sedona Cultural Park ("America's Red Rock Showcase" as it promotes its unique natural assets) in Sedona, Arizona, spins off a separate Hot Latin Jazzfest. Its top lining attractions: saxophonist Paquito D'Rivera, flutist Nestor Torres, and vocalists Carmela Ramirez and Claudia Villela.

The 12th annual week-long San Jose International Mariachi Festival at the Mexican Heritage Plaza, features a mixture of pros and student groups. The pros include the all-female Mariachi Reyna De Los Angeles from East L.A., Mariachi Sol De Mexico De José Hernández from Los Angeles, and local favorites Mariachi Santa Cecilia, Los Cenzontles with Julián González, Mariachi Azteca, and Los Lupeños De San Jose.

San Francisco's Hispanic scene spawns festivals and local favorite bands. Women In Salsa III at La Peña Cultural Center in nearby Berkeley showcases Cha Cha Boom, Orquesta D'Soul and La Familia. SFJAZZ, the acronym parent non-profit organization that presents the annual San Francisco Jazz Festival, includes an array of

Latin performers during its fourth season. The opening event, Latin New York: A Salsa Dance Party, features Eddie Palmieri and La Perfecta II, vocalist India and the Spanish Harlem Orchestra performing before 3,000 fans at the Bill Graham Civic Auditorium. Other events feature Ibrahim Ferrer and his orchestra, Chucho Valdés with the Gonzalo Rubalcaba trio and Joe Lovano and bossa nova's exemplar João Gilberto. During the start of the actual Jazz Festival, a benefit to aid the Mission Neighborhood Centers features Cuba's 64-year-old Orquestra Aragón at the Roccapulco dancehall. Two of the Bay Area's leading groups are John Santos & The Machete Ensemble, an 18-year-old ensemble, which expands out of the Bay Area to play gigs in distant places like Madison, Wisconsin. Jesús Diaz is a local favorite and Cuban-born leader of the four-year-old, nine-man salsa band Jesús Díaz Y Su QBA. He plays percussion and writes most of the band's compositions, which carry the flavor of both life in Havana and America.

Columbus, Ohio, not normally recognized as a major Hispanic community, has a thriving Latino populace, which the eighth annual Ohio Festival Latino addresses. The downtown event, billed as "the largest Hispanic/Latino event in Ohio," projects 200,000 people attending this year's two-day event of music, employment and health issue information and lots and lots of food.

The new Latino Cultural Center in Dallas, and its 300-seat performing arts theater, will be utilized by such local groups as Teatro Dallas, the Anita N. Martinez Ballet Folklorico (ANMBF) and Cara Mia Theatre Company. Its first year operating budget is $492,718, according to Betty Switzer, director of the city's Office of Cultural Affairs, which operates the center. Switzer tells the *Dallas News* the budget "is enough, most especially for the first year." She hopes to raise funding through a membership drive to augment the city's budget with which "we will be able to produce a really good season of events."

In show business, when you're hot, people gravitate to your glistening flame. Universal Music Group represents this axiom. It's deal to exclusively distribute and manufacture three labels from Univision Communications, catapults the company's distribution wing, Universal Music & Video Distribution (UMVD), from last among major distributors 18 months ago to first place because of the artist power it acquires. By the end of the first quarter of 2003, Universal Distribution's share of the Latin market is up to 32.5 percent from the same period last year when it controls 18.8 percent of the marketplace resulting from its three Univision label deal as well as a pact with VI Music, the Puerto Rican rap and reggaeton specialist label.

Univision, during its own power-seeking actions, acquires two regional Mexican powers: half of Disa Records in 2000 and Fonovisa last year in a $240 million stock deal, to add to its own Univision label and expand the new Univision Music Group's influence. When Univision acquires 50 percent of Monterrey, Mexico-based 32-year-old Disa for $75 million from its Chavez family owners, it beats out competitors Sony and Universal.

Under terms of the deal, Universal receives a distribution fee on all sales from Fonovisa, which reportedly earns around $100 million in sales from its hot acts including Marco Antonio Solís, Los Tigres Del Norte, and Banda El Recodo. The Univision Music Group, headed by José Behar, gains an estimated $20 million in sales during its initial year of selling albums by hot acts including Jennifer Peña and Pilar Montenegro. Mexican superstar band Los Tigres Del Norte, incidentally, has been together 33 years, accumulating 125 gold and 130 platinum albums.

Universal's stellar sellers include vocalists Enrique Iglesias, Molotov, Juanes (on the Surco label which Universal distributes), Paulina Rubio, David Bisbal, Alicia Villarreal, Beresuit, and Luis Fonsi. Rubio returns to Spanish on her 2004 release, *PauLatina*, her first Spanish release since the smash *Paulina* in 2000 and her English release in 2002. Universal also handles tropical music TV compilation sets from Lideres Records and catalog albums by Marc Anthony and Tito Puente, plus other name acts which record for RMM, the troubled New York tropical label Universal acquires in May of 2002 for $10 million. RMM is undergoing bankruptcy proceedings as a result of a songwriting dispute when Universal beats out Sony for the catalog. Universal reaches outside the normal music channels to sign former Miss Universe Alicia Machado, who's from Venezuela. Her pop album debut is slated for the spring of 2004. Tejano star Bobby Pulido also jumps on board the fast-moving Universal train after eight years with EMI Latin.

The company is an integral part of the movement to sign up hot producers to joint venture record label deals. Among its stalwarts operating under this agreement are Omar Alfanno (Alfanno Music), Gustavo Santaolalla and Anibal Kerpel (Surco), and Oscar Guitán and Don Dinero (Guitián Brothers Music) for rap.

Universal's Music Publishing Group snares all the music publishing companies owned by Gloria and Emilio Estefan, Jr. It's the first time the husband and wife consolidate all their copyrights in one company. Under terms of the exclusive pact, which takes two years to complete, the L.A. publisher will manager, the international rights and usage to the 3,000 titles in the Estefan Enterprises, two publishing companies, Foreign Imported Productions & Publishing and Estefan Music Publishing, previously administered by Sony/ATV, while Gloria Estefan releases her tunes through EMI Music Publishing. The Estefan's catalogs include sundry hits by Gloria and the Miami Sound Machine including *Conga*, *Don't Wanna Lose You*, *Live for Loving You*, *Words Get in the Way*, and *Cuts Both Ways*.

Adding to its management team, Universal Latino hires the controversial Jesus Gilberto Moreno, as head of regional Mexican music in December. Three years ago, Moreno, then head of promotion for Fonovisa, is successfully prosecuted by the federal government on a single charge of payola by paying an unnamed radio station programmer $2,000 to favor Fonovisa acts. Moreno pleads guilty. His attorneys tell the court that Moreno is following the "social mores in Mexico where such payments are legal," explains the *Los Angeles Times*. Fonovisa's then president, Guillermo Santiso, later pleads guilty to a felony payola connected tax count of writing checks amounting to $425,000 to a bogus company to launder the payola funds. The label also admits to a felony tax count for falsely reporting its promotional expenditures. Moreno joins the team led by Jesus Lopez and John Echeverría, hired 18 months ago. During my 2002 trip to Miami, I chat with both of them about the domestic and international markets and their comments are contained in Chapter 13.

Univision Records, in its first major artist signing, nabs Pepe Aguilar, a Grammy winning vocalist, after his contract expires with Los Angeles regional Mexican label Musart/Balboa in January and is in the studio two months later to record his first album for his new label, *Y Tenerte Otra Vez* (*And Having You Again*). It reaches No. 1 on Billboard's Top Latin album chart in April, something he's never accomplished during his 12 years in show business and 22 albums. His last album for Balboa, *Por Mujeres Como Tú* (*Because a Woman Like You*), is released in 1998, but lacks the national impact he enjoys on Univision with its UMVD distribution, which places the recording in major retail chains where his music isn't previously available. Univision television features Aguilar on all its major programs as well as on its Website. Besides Aguilar, Univision's other top sellers include Los Bukis and Los Temerarios, with the addition of regional Mexican specialist Lupillo Rivera, formerly with Sony Discos and merengue/pop vocalist Giselle, who shifts from BMG U.S. Latin, adding diversity to the roster. The label also has the firepower of producers Robert Livi with whom it forms a joint venture label called Megamusic Records and Rudy Pérez whose label's nomenclature is simply RPE.

Julio Iglesias Sr., now 59, releases what is being called a "negative" themed album, *Divorcio* on Sony Discos, albeit there's sufficient romantic pastiche to ensure sales. After 35 years in the glow of stardom on the global stage, Iglesias believes the new CD, with its romantic ballads and inclusion of Caribbean and South American ingredients, packs just the right ingredients for today's Latin market. The album is nearing sales of one million copies after four months. While he admits to the *Miami Herald* that he doesn't have a "daily relationship" with sons Enrique and Julio, Jr., he also takes a cutting swipe at some of the top young Latino vocalists. "You can't compare me to Enrique or Shakira or Ricky Martin. They are not Latin artists. They are artists who happen to have Latin genes but who perform American music, universal pop music. My son is not a Latin artist... Latin is cha-cha-cha, mambo, guaracha, son, vallenato, and merengue. I am a Latin artist." For young people steeped in today's Latin pop scene, it's Enrique, the bilingual superstar, not his father, who represents the fire and soul of the Iglesias musical empire.

Warner Music Latina, looking to strengthen its image in Latin pop, sees Julio's son, Julio Iglesias, Jr. and his debut album, *Tercera Dimensión*, as a new force in fusing Latin pop and rock. His brother Enrique, who's established himself as a Latin heat wave on rival Universal, assists in the production of the CD along with Luis Fernando Ochoa, whose clients include Shakira, Ricky Martin, and Bacilos and Pete Masitti, who works with Hootie and the Blowfish.

Warner's current success in Latin pop is a result in part to the sound of Bacilos, a quartet consisting of Jorge Villamizar of Colombia, the lead vocalist; André Lopes, the Brazilian bassist; José Javier Freire, the Puerto Rican percussionist, and Pedro Alfonso, the Cuban violinist/arranger. The band's debut WB album, *Caraluna*, wins this year's best Latin Pop Grammy, which elevates the Miami-based group into the realm of top dollar-earning ensembles. Among artists on its roster, Olga Tañon, has several distinctions. She's been with the company since 1992, building a fan base for her fiery merengue sound, which earns her the sobriquet of *Mujer De Fuego* (*Woman of Fire*) according to the *Miami Herald.*

Her latest album, *Sobrevivir* (*Surviving*), is an amalgam of pop, flamenco and tango ingredients added to the ballad format. During the recent Orange Bowl halftime show, broadcast by CBS, Tañon is among the artists performing, an obvious booking as a result of her winning English and Latin Grammys for her album, *Yo por Ti* (*I'm for You*), five Premio Lo Nuestro accolades and one *Billboard* plaque. Born in Puerto Rico, the vocalist is an Orlando resident, living with her six-year-old daughter Gabriela, fathered by Puerto Rican major league baseball star Juan Gonzalez, to whom she's no longer married.

Roselyn Sanchez, another Puerto Rican vocalist, now living in New York, signs a joint venture album deal with BMG for her company, Tres Erre Música, whose two partners are producers Raymond Castellón and Roy Tabaré. Sanchez maintains a second career as a film actress with roles in two new features, *Chasing Papi* and *Boat Trip*. But no singing.

In one of the most dramatic moves in the record business, the heart of BMG U.S. Latin, is cut by its international parent, which switches the label from being a creative outpost for signing artists to becoming a marketing/promotional/distribution vehicle. The goal is to emphasize its catalog and deal with artists without having its own A&R department. Maarten Steinkamp, BMG's International president, based in New York, and controlling the U.S. operation since last year, trims the Miami staff from 44 to 30, following the reassignment of Rodolfo López-Negrete from senior vice president of international and chairman of BMG U.S. Latin to overseeing the U.S., Mexico, and South American operations. Steinkamp, in addition to heading the Miami operation, also supervises the company's operations in Mexico, Brazil, Chile, and Argentina. A key reason for the downsizing is the label's reduced market share, attributed to a lack of hits since the peak year of 2001 when it owns 10.64 percent of the market, according to Nielsen SoundScan. For the first nine months of this year ending September 30, the company's market share is 7.4 percent, down from 8.8 percent during the same period last year.

Among the artists on the domestic roster whose fates are undetermined are Jerry Rivera, Pablo Montero, Juan Gabriel, Cristian Castro, and Alexandre Pires. The plan, according to *Billboard*, is to build artists from BMG's labels in Mexico, Spain, and Argentina, sign local acts for promotion or distribution on a project basis, increase its regional Mexican act roster and help develop acts from Jive Records and Arista, two other BMG-owned labels.

One of BMG's top acts, the Latin rock band Los Fabulosos Cadillacs are on "hiatus" after 18 years. Vocalist Gabriel Fernandez, whose solo album, *Vicentico*, is released by BMG, tells the *Los Angeles Times* after all these years, "We're meant to develop stuff on our own."

Amidst shakeups in its parent EMI Music Latin America's operation, EMI Latin USA, the domestic wing of the parent company, seeks to secure distribution deals with independent labels for niche artists it needs. Having signed a distribution and marketing pact with Gogo Music of Puerto Rico for its alternative and tropical acts for the Island and Mainland markets late last year, EMI Latin USA's president/CEO Jorge Pino signs distribution pacts with Arias Music for its regional Mexican and rap acts, Max Mex Records, Inc. for its regional roster, and Vene Music, owned by Venevision International, a Miami firm that produces and distributes movies and videos. Vene's first two albums are tropical compilations, which will be advertised on Univision. During my 2002 Miami trip, I interview Venevision's Jose Antonio Espinal, its international marketing director, whose comments are found in Chapter 13. EMI also reaches into the artistic community to create a joint venture label, King of Bling Music, with Kumbia Kings members AB Quintanilla, III and Cruz Martinez.

On the creative level, EMI has ample reasons to smile. Thalía receives gold and platinum awards for four albums: *Thalía*, *Arrasando*, *Grandes Exitos Con Banda*, and *Hits Remixed*. In a battle of new bands sponsored by Budweiser and alternative music magazine *La Banda Elástica* in Los Angeles, L.A. bilingual quartet Los Abandoned wins first prize and a contract with EMI Latin. The new group joins EMI's alternative roster of El Gran Silencio, La Mosca Tsé Tsé, Manú Chao, and Enrique Bunbury.

Two of the label's new CDs debut at No. 1 on *Billboard*'s Top Latin Album charts. Intocable's greatest hits CD/DVD compilation, *La Historia*, debuts there, while its CD-only version bows in the number five slot, joining its recent studio album *Sueño* which is at number 32. *The Kumbia Kings 4*, its fourth entry for the label, follows suit several weeks later. Bandleaders Quintanilla and Martinez create a bilingual LP with Spanish cumbias and English R&B ballads, and collaborations with such major acts like Juan Gabriel, El Gran Silencio, Ozomatli, Limite 21, and Aleks Syntek.

Quintanilla, incidentally, is the brother of the late Tejano rising star Selena, leader of her band, Los Dinos, and writer/producer of many of her hits. EMI reissues its 10 album Selena catalog in August, seven years after her murder by the president of her fan club in Corpus Christi. The LPs will be released in chronological order with a new hits complication, *Ones*, added to the release schedule to commemorate her 20 years in music. The albums include the 1995 *Live: The Last Concert*, originally released two years ago. Notes president Pino in his comments to *Billboard*: "We wanted to put out these 20 years of music as a legacy for a new generation of fans and in a way that is truthful and reflects her love of life and her desire to succeed." Tying in with the potential of new Selena dollars, Image Entertainment releases the DVD version of her last concert, *Selena: The Last Performance*, which features footage of her February 26, 1995 concert at the Houston Livestock Show And Rodeo. The DVD also includes a 44-minute documentary on the making of the 1997 Selena film and includes an interview with Jennifer Lopez, who portrays the vocalist.

Like other major labels, EMI's Miami office is among those hit by a corporate job slashing at all its Latin American labels. Among those departing is Rafael Gil, head of all Latin American divisions for the past seven years and with the company since 1970. He's replaced as president/CEO by Marco Bissi, who shifts over from Universal Music Mexico, where he's been the president seven years.

Sony Discos undergoes its own updating. Parent Sony Music International consolidates all its Latin music operations in the U.S., Mexico, and Central America under one Miami located division called Sony Music Norte. Kevin Lawrie, formerly president of Sony Music Mexico for the last four years, moves to Miami to oversee the operation. He's been with Sony since 1993 and replaces Oscar Llord, who while holding the title seven years, owns several apparent conflict of interest businesses, including a publishing company, Ventura Music Group, which contains sundry tunes recorded by Sony acts and a recording studio where many of Sony's acts record. Translated, that means in addition to his record company salary, he pockets the cash from publishing songs his artists record and from steering them to his own recording studio to cut their singles and albums. This is not the kind of arrangement generally found in the mainstream record industry, although there have been situations involving publishing royalties and producing fees. Once outside the Sony empire, Llord opens Ole Music in Miami.

Sony Music Entertainment, under which the record labels operate, offers no official reason for Llord's departure, which follows the exiting of Tommy Mottola, the division's chairman/CEO. Among the acts Llord helps market are Ricky Martin, Marc Anthony, Shakira, and Chayanne; among the acts he signs are Elvis Crespo, Son By Four, India, and Brenda K. Starr. One of Llord's most unusual deals is with Telemundo for an album featuring tunes by the 14 original contestants on the TV music talent show *Protagonistas De Le Música* (*Music for Protagonists*) and its follow-up *The Best of…*, which showcases the contest's finalists. Sony also plans releasing albums by the segment's two winners.

In a boastful statement following his departure, which *Billboard* publishes, Llord notes: "We made more hits and crossover success stories, established more chart records and produced more profits than any other Latin label in U.S. music history." Last year, Sony is named *Billboard*'s top Latin albums label for the fourth consecutive year since 1998.

And in a major acquisition, Sony Music Entertainment buys Crescent Moon Records, Gloria, and Emilio Estefan's label formed in 1994 and places its imprint within Sony Norte. Gloria is nearing completion of her first English-language LP in seven years for Sony's Epic Records imprint. She does not record for Crescent Moon. The sale is seen as a result of label president Mauricio Abaroa's departure to open his own music management firm, Earth Town Entertainment, whose clients include Crescent Moon artist Gian Marco. Estefan, reaching out to expand his TV operations, forms a 50-50 joint production company called Plural Luna with Grupo Prisa, Spain's largest media company. The new entity is a partnership between Estefan Television Productions and Plural Entertainment, Prisa's film/TV production subsidiary. The new company is focused on producing TV dramas, sitcoms and other forms of entertainment shows for the U.S. Hispanic market. It's seen as a stop gap action to counter the decline in Latin record sales. Estefan's early TV forays have been in the specials area.

Radio's national Spanish news voice, financially troubled Radio Unica, files for bankruptcy protection in U.S. District Court for the southern district of New York in October with a prepackaged reorganization plan and asset sale, so it can proceed with its sale of 15 owned stations to MultiCultural Radio Broadcasting Inc. for $150 million. The transaction provides MultiCultural with 15 stations to add to its 34-owned outlets.

The already charismatic Los Angeles Latino scene adds new hot ticket enticements throughout show business.

For the first time, the outdoor John Anson Ford Amphitheatre's performing arts series includes a heavy dose of multicultural events. During the Hollywood venue's largest series of concerts ever, seven Latin events are scheduled, of which four are American premieres and two L.A. debuts. The U.S. premieres include Madrid's Vivian Acosta's one-woman show; Barcelona's Compañia Marta Carrasco; Cuba's El Ciervo Encantado, and the screening of a Mexican silent gangster film enhanced by two off-screen actors and a pianist. The local premieres involve the Brazilian dance troupe Fundo De Quintal and Cuba's Orquesta La Modern Tradicion, which specializes in classic forms of Cuban dances. In addition, Panama's national dance company, Ballet Folklorico Panameno De Elisa De Céspedes, celebrates the country's centennial with its first appearance here in years.

The fifth annual West Coast Salsa Congress presented by Albert Torres at the Hollywood Park Casino for five nights in May attracts salsa fanaticos from all over the world. Despite a decline in salsa's popularity, a reported 4,000 dance fans attend each of the evenings presentations to enjoy the music of Ray Barretto, Oscar D'Leon, Richie Ray and Bobby Cruz, Jimmy Bosch, Herman Olivera and Ray De La Paz, Johnny Polanco Y Su Conjunto Amistad, and Freddie Crespo Y Su Mambo Revue, among others. Fans also marvel at the routines of a bevy of professional quality salsa dance performers. L.A. is just one stop in the 14-city circuit of congresses Torres and wife Maya sponsor. Salsa fans indulge their urges by dancing along with the Afro-Caribbean beats. A contingent from Japan numbers 300, indicating just how global salsa music is. One of the more unusual acts is Latin Madness, a 35-member musical comedy dance troupe from New York, whose act traces the development of Latin dance in the U.S.

While another major event is the fifth annual Puerto Rican Parade & Festival in Montebello, California, City Park, which features a bevy of bands for two days in June and is "dedicated to preserving Puerto Rican culture," the overriding event is the arrival in L.A. in August of the Latin Alternative Music Conference after three years in New York. Among bands performing are Las Ultrasónicas (the all girl group from Mexico), Los Amigos Invisibles, Sidestepper, Nortec Collective, Volumen Cero, Plastilina Mosh, Los Abandoned, and Go Betty Go.

A reported 1,200 persons attend the seminars and performances at the Beverly Hilton, which draws local criticism for their lack of name power acts. Tomás Cookman, co-founder of the event, counters these charges by stressing to *Billboard* the event "is about recognizing and bringing attention to the music, not selling concert tickets." Despite the lack of strong broadcast support for alternative bands, several exceptions surface, including MTV Español's *A Todo Volumen* alternative music show as well as exposure on KCRW-FM L.A.'s *Morning Becomes Eclectic* and on New York's WFUV-FM and WCAA-FM, all English-language stations.

Cookman, who manages La Ley and vocalist Vicentico of the band Los Fabulosos Cadillacs, decries the lack of exposure on

Spanish-language radio for rock en Español bands in favor of regional Mexican and pop formats. L.A.'s lone radio station providing rock acts with an hour at 10 p.m. Monday through Thursdays is KSSE-FM (Super Estrella). Elias Autran, the station's promotions/marketing director, places the role of alternative bands within the station's programming arc when he tells the *Los Angeles Times*: "Super Estrella is a Top 40 station. We'll play rock artists like Maná, Jaguares or Juanes, as long as they have hits that make it to the Top 40...I think Latin rock is still an underground force."

In the topsy-turvy world of L.A. Hispanic radio, the market's most powerful personality shifts time periods and several of the leading stations lose audience and ratings positions. KSCA starts the year off by revealing Reñan Almendarez Coello is leaving his 5 to 11 a.m. slot Monday through Saturday after six years to work weekday afternoons from 3 to 7 p.m. With the time shift comes a name alteration for the program, from *El Cucuy En La Mañana* (*The Boogeyman in the Morning*) to *El Cucuy De Los Tardes* (*The Boogeyman in the Afternoon*). He cites working mornings 16 years, including his KSCA stint, takes its toll physically and he needs a change. Eddie "Piolin" Sotelo, the morning host at KLOK-AM San Jose, California, takes over the weekday morning shift, raising concerns at Hispanic Broadcasting Corporation that he'll be able to retain Coello's No. 1 A.M. spot over both Spanish and Anglo personalities, including comic Steve Harvey on R&B/rap KKBT-FM.

In the bounce back and turnaround ratings battles, rankings for last summer revealed months later, KSCA drops from second to ninth place; KLVE drops from seventh to 10th and KXOL slips from 13th to 23rd, while KBUE jumps from 16th to 12th. In the fall Arbitron survey released in January, KSCA rebounds to third place, KLVE jumps upward to sixth, KBUE rises one notch to 11th and KXOL improves to 20th place. Spanish Broadcasting System bows *La Sabrosa* aimed at the market's one million Central Americans in March which plays cumbia, merengue, salsa, punta, and soca styles of music on two stations found at 93.5 on the FM dial, KZAB Torrance and

KZBA Ontario. It competes to a degree against Entravision's KLYY-FM, which targets listeners from Mexico, Central America, and South America. Entravision, as noted in Chapter 16, drops its dance music format simulcast on KDLD Santa Monica and KDLE Newport Beach in favor of alternative rock music, the fourth format switch in five years.

One of L.A.'s pioneering Hispanic journalists, Pete Moraga, who works for CBS' KNX and Univision's KMEX-TV, passes away in his retirement home in Mesa, Arizona, September 23, 2003 of a heart attack. He's 77 and his journalism career spans 1949 to 1992 when he retires, principally with KNX all-news station and its sister KCBS-TV. After spending most of the '70s at KNX, he joins KMEX in 1981 as its news director, returning to KNX in 1988 as a reporter and commentator for KCBS-TV. His first job in radio is in 1949 with KIFN in Phoenix, the state's first fulltime Spanish station.

One of L.A.'s homegrown homeboy acts, Akwid, is a major Latin rap act, whose Univision debut album *Proyecto Akwid*, is a national phenomenon, and the result of Sergio and Francisco Gomez adapting the music of black South Central L.A. with their own Hispanic roots. Explains their manager Guillermo Santiso to the *Los Angeles Times*: "These guys came up with exactly what I wanted to hear, which is a mix of cultures."

Latin music's dominating retail chain, Tinton Falls, New Jersey-headquartered Ritmo Latino operates 44 outlets across the nation in Latino heavy cities, while eyeing further expansions. Known for discounting to attract customers and its elimination of cassettes to open more room for DVDs, 25 of its stores have book sections and since 1999, five are named Ritmo Rock for its stock of Latin and non-Latin rock bands. In August of 2004 as it celebrates its 15th anniversary in Los Angeles, a work force of 400 operates 45 stores, three in Santa Anna, California, where the first Ritmo Latino outlet opens in 1989.

Lots of L.A. music fans tune to LATV, the local bilingual cable channel which programs original music to English-dominant Latin 12–34 years old listeners since 2001 on broadcast station KJLA, and expands nationally with a satellite signal December 1. While the current 7–11 p.m. programming is available to four million L.A. area homes through cable systems and direct broadcast satellite providers DirecTV and Dish Network, LATV plans providing 24 hours of programming for its national audience, six daily hours repeated four times a day to create a 24-hour cycle. Name acts are a feature of the network as well as providing TV exposure to bands that cannot obtain airplay anywhere else. Nine hours of LATV's 20 hours a week are live from the studio as opposed to music videos.

While LATV's principal language is English, interviews with music acts may be conducted in Spanglish, the mixture of Spanish and English words to germinate a new word or phrase within a sentence. Flavio Morales, LATV's program director, calls the use of Spanglish a spontaneous outpouring. The use of two languages by the station's 13 hosts, production staff and studio audience exemplifies the growth in Los Angeles, and other major Latin cities, of two meshing cultures. Daniel Crowe, the music channel's president, wants to compete with the likes of MTV, Univision, and Galavision by offering a broad range of programming, including fashion, lifestyle, films with Latino stars or themes or Spanish-language films with English subtitles. LATV is founded by Walter Ulloa, the co-founder and CEO of Entravision, the Santa Monica-headquartered Spanish-language radio/TV/ billboard conglomerate. My interview with Ulloa, who discusses the radio network, appears in Chapter 16.

On the national television level, Univision and Telemundo are both focusing on creating original telenovelas about life in the U.S., which domestic Hispanics can relate to. While it's a major dual alteration of their programming which heretofore arrives from overseas sources, these distant Latin American production entities continue providing the two majors with tear-jerking stories. Come September, the first of the homegrown drama series make their debuts.

The year begins for Univision with its live coverage of the Rose Parade followed by a novela adapted from an old Cuban radio serial and retitled *Entre El Amor Y El Odio*, whose story plot contains such current theme as the rash of kidnappings and everyday violence in Mexico.

Both networks during their upfront programming presentations in May to advertising agencies in New York, find Madison Avenue more amenable to spending money on Spanish television. Telemundo's owner, NBC, does its part to make advertisers aware of Spanish-language TV, especially since Telemundo will for the first time, broadcast 169 1/2 hours of events of interest to Hispanics during the 2004 Summer Olympics from Athens. NBC's total coverage for all its broadcast and cable networks and a separate high-definition service, amounts to 1,210 hours, 350 more than originally announced. Remarkably, NBC's total coverage of the Atlanta Olympics eight years ago totals 171-1/2 hours.

Univision, during its sales presentation at which the majority of ad dollars are allocated for new programming well in advance of when the shows premiere, stresses that 95 of the most watched 100 shows on Spanish-language TV in the past year are on its air. Its namesake and year-old TeleFutura broadcast network and Galavision cable service are accepted by 35 percent of Hispanic households between 7 and 11 p.m., the company stresses. The network's president, Ray Rodriguez, tells the audience during Univision's seventh annual presentation that the year-old TeleFutura counter programs its older brother network while troubled Galavision, which overhauls its format last year to break away from young adults, will refocus its efforts in news, sports, and entertainment for viewers of all ages. Among its new shows are *Accion*, a Sunday evening sports news show; *Los Reporteros*, a news magazine; *Más Deporte*, a live sports magazine, and *Por La Puerta Grande* an entertainment variety show. The network reaches 5.7 million Hispanic cable homes, for coverage of 90 percent of Hispanic cable households.

Among the crop of Univision's in-house produced novelas is *Te Amare En Silencio* to be shot entirely in Los Angeles. The $6 million plus production features Mexican actor Eduardo Yañez, formerly a major player in novelas for Mexico City's Televisa, which provides Univision with its soap operas until 2017, and is currently a 15 percent owner in the U.S. company. The soap will feature scenes shot in Hollywood, along Beverly Hills' most famous street, Rodeo Drive, and on the area's many beaches, now frequented in mass numbers by Hispanic families. The in-house production looks to duplicate the successful Televisa formula of conflicts, affirmations, and passion all within the story arc. In a sense, the decision by Univision to create its own primetime novelas is a smart business move to break away from relying so heavily on Televisa for this kind of highly popular programming.

A second original telenovela about a U.S. law firm handling immigration cases, *A Filo De La Ley* (*At the Edge of the Law*), will be produced in Miami at Univision's production facilities. Moving in another first area for the network is the interactive novela, *Rebeca*, with viewers voting via the Internet on the soap opera's ending.

TeleFutura, seeking to program differently from Univision, will premiere the first adult animated series in Spanish-language TV history, *Betty Toons* plus a newsroom comedy, *Noticias Calientes* (*Hot News*), a game show/reality combination, *Armas De Seduccion* (*Weapons of Seduction*), a sex therapy/talk show *Quien Tiene la Razón?* (*Who's Right?*) and five novelas: *La Costeña* (*The Girl from the Coast*), a love story; *Juana La Virgen* (*Juana's Miracle*), a 17-year-old virgin who becomes pregnant; *De Pocas Pocas Pulgas* (*Just a Few Fleas*), a 12-year-old boy and his bonding with a lonely old man; *La Mujer De Judas* (*The Wife of Judas*), a 20-year-old murder mystery, and *La Niña De Mis Ojos* (*The Girl of My Eyes*), a mother chooses her son's bride. The network is also tapping into the Hollywood studios' catalogs of 400 films dubbed in Spanish for airing in primetime as an alternative to novelas. Within a month, Univision buys two TV stations, KFTL in Stockton, California, and WKFT in Raleigh, North Carolina, bringing its total number of owned outlets to 53.

Univision's acquisition of Hispanic Broadcasting Corporation's 68 stations for $3.2 billion in stock is one of the year's most contentious events. Federal antitrust regulators in March agree to the merger so long as Univision divests itself in the company's 27 percent ownership of conglomerate Entravision Communications whose holdings include 52 radio stations, 18 TV stations and a major outdoor billboard company. Univision agrees to reduce its staked to 10 percent over six years. The government is concerned the Entravision stations combined with HBC's creates extraordinary clout and influence. During the 14 months between the acquisition announcement, shareholder approval in February, a Justice Department review and approval in March and the Federal Communications Commission's 3-2 clearance for the merger in September, a heated battle unites 20 Democrats in Congress with rivals Spanish Broadcasting System (which loses out in its bid to merge with HBC), NBC/Telemundo and the National Hispanic Policy Institute in their opposition to the marriage. They claim the mega-giant company could severally reduce competition for advertising dollars. Democrats are also concerned that Univision CEO A. Jerrold Perenchio, whose control of the company dates back to 1992, is a staunch Republican, and will use the power of the radio network to recruit Hispanics to the Republican Party.

Supporting the merger are some Republicans plus New Mexico's Democratic governor Bill Richardson, Henry Cisneros, a former Univision president and Housing secretary under President Bill Clinton and the National Council of La Raza. Several opponents place ads in newspapers. The National Hispanic Policy Institute goes national while Democratic Representative Bob Menendez of New Jersey advertises in Capitol Hill publications. Menendez's concern is the merger will affect the ability of rival stations to remain in business. Ads placed by Univision countering the monopolistic charges appear in newspapers including the *New York Times*, *Washington Post* and *Washington Times* and keep the vitriol alive. Despite all the hyperbole and political nitpicking, the historic merger takes place, HBC becomes the Univision Radio Group and the din of dissent fades.

Telemundo, despite the prestige of being part of General Electric's NBC division since its $2.7 billion purchase in April of 2002, is still looking to improve its second-place programming position behind Univision following poor showings by Hispanic versions of *Temptation Island* and the Spanish airing of NBC's violent drug-dominated miniseries *Kingpin*. Last year, audiences tune out big time to several of its newer offerings. New telenovelas with themes more attuned for domestic Hispanics are an area for optimism, and which will support GE chairman/chief executive officer Bob Wright's prosaic comment in the *Wall Street Journal* that Telemundo "is one of the biggest opportunities" for growth. Advertising-wise, Telemundo hopes to improve over last year's upfront sales of around $220 by stressing its new primetime programming, funded by an additional $50 million from NBC to do battle against Univision and its ace novelas acquired from Mexican partner Grupo Televisa. Telemundo's primetime budget last year is $24 million. Jim McNamara, Telemundo's president for the past two years, tells the biannual Television Critics Association gathering in Hollywood, that during this time period, the network's overall programming budget rises from $85 million to $140 million. NBC sets Telemundo's sales projection this year at $500 million.

NBC's impact on Telemundo is omnipresent, especially with several NBC executives now having oversight in several areas. Jeff Zucker, president of NBC News, entertainment and cable, oversees Telemundo's primetime programming; Randy Falco, NBC Television Network president, handles its financial matters and Jay Ireland, head of NBC's 14 TV station group, is also responsible for Telemundo's 15 TV stations. NBC also elevates Don Browne, president/general manager of its Miami WTVJ, to Telemundo's chief operating officer. A 24-year NBC veteran, Browne oversees the integration of Telemundo's Miami outlet, WSVC, into WTVJ's offices and studios in Miramar. Handling double assignments for NBC/Telemundo in Miami is José Díaz-Balart, who co-anchors WTVJ's 5 p.m. news with Jennifer Valoppi, while continuing to co-anchor Telemundo's national morning newscast, *Hoy En El Mundo*.

Programming-wise, NBC resurrects boxing after an 11-year hiatus, with Telemundo airing the three Saturday afternoon bouts in

May. The matches are presented by Main Events, which shares ad revenues with the two networks after taking out the costs for televising the fights. Telemundo entices Univision weatherman John Morales to join the party by also offering him exposure on NBC's *Weekend Today*. For two years running, Telemundo simulcasts the historic Macy's Day Parade from New York with NBC's English-language coverage. It also joins NBC in televising the Golden Globes for the first time where two off-screen hosts announce the nominees in English and the winner in Spanish. Commercials are also bilingual; spots for Telemundo's soaps are in Spanish. Spain's *Talk To Her* wins the best foreign film award, while Elliot Goldenthal's music for *Frida* is named best original film score.

NBC, in an effort to promote its cable channels, MSNBC, CNBC and Bravo, launches *Más* a promotional campaign designed to help cable system companies expand and retain their Latin customers. The $1 million campaign coincides with National Hispanic Heritage Month in September and consists of three low-key ads running on Telemundo and mun2. Despite the nation's broadening Hispanic population, NBC's research indicates that just 54 percent of the nation's 15 million Hispanic homes have cable, that many Hispanics are happy with the three Spanish broadcast networks and that for many newly arrived immigrants, cable TV is an unfamiliar commodity.

The synergy between NBC and Telemundo is a major accomplishment in Los Angeles. Among several first time events, NBC's KNBC and Telemundo's KVEA and KWHY and its 250 staffers relocate from Glendale and are all housed on NBC's huge Burbank studio lot. Additionally in March, KNBC and KVEA simulcast the L.A. Marathon in English and Spanish with separate anchors and production crews. Jodie Mena, KVEA's news operation manager, tells me KVEA has its own camera crews at the start and finish and four microwave trucks along the course. Its coverage is anchored by Mauricio Cardenas and New York City marathon winner German Silva. "We pick locations where events are happening, like in the Guatemalan and Mexican communities and each truck and its three-person crew hop-scotch to predetermined locations during the race," says Mena. "We also share camera positions with KNBC. Since there are so many Latino runners, we start profiling around 20 of the top runners almost two months before the race; we insert them during the race and some are dropped into our pre-race show." The joint efforts continue when both stations cover "Fiesta Broadway" on April 27, reportedly the world's largest Cinco De Mayo celebration in downtown L.A., which draws crowds of 500,000 to the daylong performance and food celebration. Both stations' taped coverage airs as separate one-hour specials on May 3.

Later in the year, Telemundo wins a court battle against Univision to cover the Mexican Independence celebration at Los Angeles City Hall. Telemundo's KVEA and KWHY sue the City of Los Angeles, charging it violates their 1st Amendment rights to cover the event, which Univision covers exclusively for the past 20 years. Telemundo claims it tries for four months to convince L.A. officials to provide its cameras access to the event. Univision not only has front-row access to the annual *El Grito* celebration at City Hall, but also produces the event and provides the talent for a concert it broadcasts.

In its complaint in U.S. District Court, Telemundo charges Univision secures the broadcast rights without competitive bidding and that Alex Padilla, the City Council president, claims it's too late to change the broadcast plans so that Telemundo will be confined to a separate area with cameras from other networks. According to Telemundo, Padilla informs the network that Univision is willing to provide it with its live audio and video feeds, and for the two networks to work out a deal. That's when the two stations seek their injunction and Judge Audrey B. Collins rules in their favor, ordering the city to provide Telemundo's stations with the same access to the event. In her 15-page ruling, from which the *Los Angeles Times* extracts comments, Judge Collins writes: "Defendants have not presented one reason, compelling or otherwise, why they initially decided that KMEX's cameras should be granted access to the official ceremony while Telemundo's should be required to use a video feed from KMEX."

Telemundo scores another hit on Univision when its lures away KMEX's chief news anchor, Eduardo Quezada to its KVEA to co-anchor that station's 6 and 11 p.m. newscasts. For 27 years Quezada is a main draw at KMEX.

When the second Gulf War breaks out, Telemundo is the first Spanish-language network to break the news. It's two L.A. stations air special reports on how the war is affecting Hispanics in Southern California. All of Telemundo's stations, in addition to receiving the network's news coverage, receive video from NBC and MSNBC. Interest is high because of the large number of Hispanics in the Armed Forces. The war, relates Manuel Abud, general manager of the two stations to the *Los Angeles Times*, "is so relevant to our people, and that's why we've been so totally committed and so aggressive." The growth of Telemundo's news operation is covered in a series of interviews I do which appear in Chapter 16.

Aiming to create a new avenue for viewers accustomed to the formulaic pattern of novelas produced overseas, the network launches the first novela starring a black leading man, *Adrián Está De Visita* (*Adrian Is Visiting*), introducing Walter Díaz to American viewers. This show, produced in Colombia, casts a spotlight on the practice in Latin America of hiding one's African heritage, and prompts Manny Martinez, Telemundo's programming vice president, to point to Latin America's large black population which is hardly seen on Spanish television and tell the *Miami Herald*: "We should reflect that mix more often. Not all of our grandparents are from Spain." *Adrián*, features a love interest from a white woman and follows Telemundo's airing in 2000 of the Brazilian saga, *Xica*, which breaks the color line by featuring a black female in the title role who has romances with white men. Both shows are obviously sexually charged.

Among the novelas focusing on the lives of Hispanics living in the U.S. is one filmed in Houston, *La Ley Del Silencio* (*The Vow of Silence*), a story about a priest and a social worker dealing with the local Latin community's desires for a better life. Another show, *Amor Descarado* (*Love Unleashed*), is a story of confused identity with Jose Angel Llamas playing the dual roles set in the South Florida Hispanic community. It's the first novela produced in Telemundo's newly constructed Miami studio.

Entering the realm of reality series with *La Cenicienta* (*Cinderella*), a dating show with twists, the lead 23-year-old Latina is courted by 20 bachelors of different nationalities. She's also a single mother. NBC places Eva Tamargo Lemus, an actress on its daytime *Passions* soap opera in the cast in a major role. For the first time, Telemundo will provide English-language captioning for *La Cenicienta* and *Amor Descarado*. The network's strategy is designed to attract Spanish speakers and English-dominant viewers who will boost the show's viewership. NBC does its part to attract bilinguals by running promotional spots promoting the closed captions during episodes of *Fear Factor* and *For Love or Money* on August 25, prior to both show's September 8 start. *Amor* branches out from its domestic perch by debuting on MVS, Mexico's pay TV channel 52 in November. It's the first American-produced Spanish-language novela to play in Mexico in recent years.

The Peacock Network (NBC) also adds to its historical firsts by offering Spanish captions for its top-rated *The Tonight Show with Jay Leno* in September.

Whether it's a competitive move or just a coincidence, Telemundo and Univision debut locally produced novelas on the same night. Telemundo's *El Alma Herida* (*The Wounded Soul*) and Univision's *Te Amaré En Silencio* (*I Shall Love You in Silence*), both debut on December 15, prompting McNamara, Telemundo's president, to candidly inform the *Miami Herald*'s Spanish edition *El Nuevo Herald*: "This is a crucial moment in the history of Spanish-language television in the United States. For the first time, the audience can choose between two home-grown telenovelas."

Despite all the money thrown into original programming and the hoopla anent, the continually growing U.S. Hispanic market, Spanish-language TV faces the razor sharp conundrum of assimilated Latinos turning to mainstream media and tuning in less to Spanish broadcasting which is the language of choice of their parents. Several media executives offer cogent reasons why Spanish TV needs to worry. "As the younger generations become more acculturated (meaning they are equally or more comfortable speaking English as Spanish), they may not tune to either Spanish network," David Joyce, an analyst with Guzman & Co., tells *Forbes.com.* The Academy of Television Arts & Science's Todd Leavitt, tells the *Forbes* Website: "You have a noticeable and strong demographic shift as Hispanics evolve from first-generation immigrants to a second generation that's assimilated. The kids are bilingual and educated…and looking to be a part of society."

It's towards this youthful demographic that Telemundo aims two programs: *El Beso Del Vampire* (*The Vampire's Kiss*) and *Los Teens*, its first teen novela. *El Beso* is a story about modern vampires with a comedy ingredient from Brazil's Globo Productions, one of Telemundo's major program suppliers. *Los Teens* is filmed at a Miami high school by Falcon Productions and follows the lives of six teenagers who deal with such treacherous situations as virginity, teen pregnancy, AIDS, drug use, and divorced parents. The show incorporates the practice among Anglo networks called "product placement" in which sponsor's merchandise is prominently used or displayed within the show. It replaces reality talent search *Protagonistas De La Música*-which includes product usage-once its 14-week run ends with the two top winners emerging from Cuba and the Dominican Republic.

Telemundo obviously believes in the reality genre. Besides these new shows, it launches volume two of its pioneering 2002 hit series, *Protagonistas De Novela*, Spanish TV's first reality show. The second edition maintains the formula in which a group of aspiring actors are locked in a Miami studio for two months while they compete for roles in a Telemundo-produced novela. A third new series, *Protagonistas De La Fama*, expands on the formula by including actors, singers, and dancers living together who will be voted off the show by viewers.

Seeking to strengthen its programming department, the company makes a series of executive changes, culminating in August with Ramón Escobar, former senior vice president of local news and local programming for the station group, elevated to executive VP of programming and production, replacing Manuel Martínez-Llorián, who departs six months earlier. Previous hires adding hoped for strength to the department include: Mauricio Gerson (formerly with USA Networks Latin America) as senior VP overseeing Mexico productions; Alejandro García (formerly with Sony Pictures International TV) as senior VP handling Miami productions; Adriana Ibañez (former with Colombia's TV Caracol) as senior VP of programming and scheduling (a new position) and Perla Farías (formerly with Venezuela's RCTV) as director of novela development. Mimi Belt, already with the network, is promoted to VP of program development, specifically for reality shows.

Despite its focus on generating U.S. produced programs, Telemundo acquires 26 films by Mexico's beloved late comic actor Cantinflas, whose legal name of Mario Moreno Reyes is hardly known or referred to. Nonetheless, for the majority of Telemundo's viewers who are of Mexican extract, the exclusive deal covers five years, enough time to air the comic's output from the 1940s through the early '80s. He passes away in Mexico City of lung cancer on April 20, 1993, three months shy of his 79th birthday.

Whether Jennifer Lopez, whom Telemundo signs to develop and executive produce shows through her Nuyorican Productions, can add program power, is a matter of this busy superstar finding the time and actual commitment—between movies, records, clothes lines, marriages, divorces, and romances—to do the work. Her first project centers on a girl from the barrio who wants to become a star.

Mun2, Telemundo's young adult, male-oriented, bilingual targeted network, enters the reality world with two music shows, *NY Underground* and *La Familia Perfecta* (*The Perfect Family*). *Underground* focuses on aspiring Hispanic rap artists as they prepare for that magic moment when they're discovered and gain entry into show business. Yolanda Foster, mun2's programming vice president, justifies the weekly series by noting: "There are many young U.S. Latin musicians that are well known in the streets of New York, but are not yet on the radar screen of most record companies." *Perfecta*, a daily hour planned for a first quarter 2005 debut, will focus on six different neophyte artists who leave home to pursue their dreams of stardom. Artists from Texas, New York, Los Angeles, and the Caribbean, whose styles favor reggaeton, rap, pop or bachata, will be followed by camera crews for behind-the-scenes glimpses of their crusades. The final episodes brings all six together to discuss their musical experiences. The channel dates back to when it's GEMS, a female network which NBC acquires along with Telemundo.

Its two new programs fit in smoothly with mun2's array of on-air music shows including *FuZion*, an entertainment magazine which zeros in on music from the Caribbean to Puerto Rico; *Roof*, a two-hour nightly extravaganza mixing live performances, interviews, videos, and listener call-ins; *Adrenolina*, which matches music to the uptempo sports of surfing and snowboarding on weekends. A second weekend feature, *SpeedLogic*, covers two motor sports popular with Latin males: street racing and low-riders.

New to the lineup are *Lugar Heights*, an animated series; *Twisted Novela Theater*, a soap opera parody; *Chat*, the first talk show designed for domestic Latinos, produced in partnership with Miami Dade College where the weekly half-hour show is taped and *Off the Roof*, a nightly newsmagazine targeting West Coast Latino culture as it relates to sports, fashion, music, politics, and lifestyle and produced in L.A. by Miami's Perfect Image, which handles several other shows for the network.

Although the growth of the U.S. Latino market now reaches 37 million (excluding illegals), according to 2001 estimates by the U.S. Census, Hispanics remain fairly low on Anglo television's visibility screen, a soporific situation which seems to befuddle and anger Hispanic media bashing groups and rights organizations. According to a projection by major advertising agency, Initiative Media North America, a little over five percent of all series on the six English-language TV networks feature Latinos at the beginning of the 2002-'03 season, way below the percentage of Hispanics in the U.S.

In spite of this gloomy situation, the Screen Actors Guild (SAG) finds the number of minority members working in general market TV hits the highest level in its history. Latinos are cast in 379 roles, a 1.2 percent increase to bring their share of the jobs to six percent, primarily in episodic TV. Three programming genres that largely attract Hispanics are family friendly, children's and reality shows. According to Initiative Media, *American Idol*, *Joe Millionaire*, *Fear Factor*, *The Simpsons*, *King of the Hill*, and *Malcolm in the Middle* are favorites among younger Hispanics who tend to be bilingual or English-language dominant.

Despite this inchoate situation, I find an impressive, albeit small list of Latinos playing before national audiences. Perhaps the best known is Martin Sheen (who eschews using his Estevez last name), star of NBC's *The West Wing*. By network, here are many of the lucky personalities and shows gaining national exposure this year:

Broadcast

ABC: George Lopez, star of his eponymous hit ABC comedy series starts its third season this fall on Fridays. It's the first major network sitcom to feature a Latino family since NBC's *Chico and the Man* (1974–'78 which features comic Freddie Prinze, who dies by shooting himself in the head one year before the series is terminated). Members of Lopez's family include Constance Marie, Belita Moreno, Masiela Lusha, and Luis Armand Garcia. Bruce Helford, the show's executive producer, tells *Weekly Variety* the show is designed for a "universal audience" in a similar light the way *The Cosby Show* attracted viewers of all ethnicities. The success of this show re-energizes the 41-year-old comic's career in standup and launches him in the comedy record field...Cleto Escobedo, Jr. leads the band on *Jimmy Kimmel Live* the network's late night talk entry...Lisa Guerrero adds her sexy personality and show business expertise to *Monday Night Football* as the sideline reporter, replacing Melissa Stark after three years. She is the first Hispanic member of the show's broadcast team...*L.A. Dragnet* features detectives Eva Longoria and

Roselyn Sanchez...The cast of cop drama *10-8* features Miguel Sandoval and Danny Nucci...*Threat Matrix*'s ensemble includes Kurt Caceres while the comedy *Married to the Kellys* includes Kiele Sanchez as the female lead.

CBS: Cheech Marin rejoins *Judging Amy* in a recurring role. Adam Rodriguez joins *CSI: Miami* as a crime investigator...Enrique Murciano plays a New York FBI agent in *Without a Trace*...The network signs several actors to series deals, notably comics Jackie Guerra and Freddy Soto. (One of the truisms in show business is a signing does not necessarily produce a job.)

Fox: Luis Guzman stars in his own series *Luis*, whose cast includes Jaclyn DeSantis and Diana-Maria Riva...Cheech Marin and Al Madrigal top line *The Ortegas*...Joaquim De Almeida and Vincent Laresca are among the ensemble at *24*...D.J. Cotrona is among the cast of *Skin*, an intercultural drama. After just four of its 10 episodes, Luis is given his walking papers. Fox and ABC, it should be noted, beat the other broadcast networks in employing the highest number of Hispanic actors in primetime, 11 percent, according to Initiative Media, the ad buying agency.

NBC: Yancey Arias heads the cast of the Mexican drug cartel drama *Kingpin*, aided by Bobby Cannavale, Miguel Sandoval, Rubén Carbajal, Angela Alvarado Rosa, Maria Conchita Alonso, and Jacob Vargas. Series creator David Mills ensures the show features Latin music from such known acts as Café Tacuba and Kinky plus a number of lesser known acts ranging from rap to rock to flamenco. After its limited run of six episodes over three weeks on Sundays and Tuesdays, which draws strong criticism from within the Latin community for its glorified portrayal of violence and drug dealing and negative stereotypes of Latinos, NBC ends its connection with the show...Bobby Cannavale also appears on *Third Watch*.

PBS: *American Family*, Gregory Nava's saga of an East Los Angeles Mexican family, is renewed for a second season. Its stars include Edward James Olmos, Raquel Welch, Sonia Braga, Constance Marie, and Esai Morales. For Welch, the role is only her third in her career in which she receives screen credits as a Latina. Her first two works include playing a Mexican in 1968's *Bandolero* and a Mexican Yanqui Indian in 1969's *100 Rifles*. First pitched to CBS in 2000, which passes on what would have been the first network Latino drama, PBS acquires the first 22 episodes for its 2001–2002 season and it becomes the first ever drama series on broadcast TV with an all-Latino cast and the network's first original primetime drama in decades. Following disappointing ratings, the show goes on hiatus for a year.

In the first of two firsts, *The Misadventures of Maya and Miguel*, a story about the lives of 10-year-old Latino twins, becomes the network's first animated comedy for six- to eight-year-olds, utilizing bilingual off-screen voices. Originally designed by Scholastic Entertainment, Inc. (SEI) for commercial TV, the show heeds PBS' interest in funding a new children's program and shifts direction. It's offered in English and Spanish. The second first centers around the U.S. showing of *Mariachi: The Spirit of Mexico* extracted from Guadalajara's International Mariachi Festival. Guest starring with sundry mariachi bands is opera tenor Plácido Domingo.

PBS also offers two Hispanic-themed specials, *Encuentro* which features vocalists Rubén Blades from Panama, Juan Luis Guerra from the Dominican Republic, and Robi "Draco" Rosa from Puerto Rico discussing their upbringing and how their native lands affect their music through the songs they perform, and *Race Matters* which details what happens to the small town of Silver City, North Carolina, when Latinos move in, including illegals, to work in furniture and clothing factories, and some of its white residents rebel with great anger. A racial unity rally seeks to unite the city's black, white, and Hispanics. Among the Hispanic businesses catering to the new arrivals is radio station WNCA.

This autumn marks the fifth year anniversary of Latino Public Broadcasting (LPB), which provides PBS with films dealing with issues of interest to domestic Latinos. Funding for LPB's endeavors comes from the Corporation for Public Broadcasting from which PBS also obtains funding. Each year, LPB accepts story submissions and culls them down to a select few for funding from aspiring and professional Latino filmmakers in all genres of expression, explains LPB's executive director Luca Bentivoglio, a former programming vice president at Telemundo, in *Hispanic* magazine. Among its offerings this year are *Visiones*, a three-hour documentary anent Latino art and culture, produced in Austin by Hector Galán; *Foto Novelas*, a half-hour fantasy anthology series by Los Angeles producer Carlos Avila, and *The Blue Diner*, a two-hour drama from Boston producer Natatcha Estebanez.

LPB's first film for 2004 will be Phillip Rodriguez's *Mixed Feelings*, which explores the differences in urban development between San Diego and Tijuana its cross-border neighbor. Bentivoglio, who works with LPB's chairman, Edward James Olmos, indicates all told there will be more than 23 hours of LPB programming available to PBS' 300 independent stations, which choose which of the network's programs to air in their cities.

WB: *The Help* features Camille Guaty and Al Santos, while the network's Kids WB! cartoon block renews *Mucha Lucha* for a second season. The story centers around the famed masked Mexican wrestlers and features a simulcast in Spanish through the SAP channel. First season episodes will begin airing on the Cartoon Network next year.

Syndication

Two superstars look for career expansion in syndicated TV. Cristina Saralegui, star of her own Univision weekly talk show, signs with Touchstone Television, a Disney company, to create an English-language sitcom based on her life, possibly for ABC, which Disney also owns. She's already appeared in a number mainstream shows. She discusses her career with me in Chapter 11...Jennifer Lopez signs with Universal Domestic Television to executive produce a daytime hour ensemble chat show co-hosted by her sister Lynda, a New York TV reporter for Anglo and Hispanic stations. One year later, however, Universal cancels plans for the Lopez show...*Urban Latino*, a weekly English-language half-hour devoted to the diversity of Hispanic culture in this country, gains a renewal for a second season by distributor Artist And Idea Management. The show appears in 45 markets with Celines Toribio, Johnny Salgado, and recording artists Noemi hosting.

Cable

Fox Sports En Español: The network bows its first awards show, Premios Fox Sports, honoring Hispanic and Latin American athletes in soccer, baseball, motor sports, tennis, and golf December 17. The show, hosted by Geraldo Rivera, emanates from the New Radisson hotel in Miami and airs two nights later in the U.S. and throughout Latin America and the Caribbean of Fox Sports Latin America.

FX: In its second season, the Emmy-winning gritty cop series *The Shield* pairs up David Aceveda as the supervisor to lead actor Michael Chiklis. New to the cast is Danny Pino as a nasty drug lord.

HBO: A Latino mortician in a key role? Absolutely. That's the role played by Freddy Rodriguez in *Six Feet Under*, currently in its third season as Federico Diaz, the ambitious mortician/embalmer/ partner in the business. His equally ambitious wife Vanessa is played by Justina Machado. Both actors are from Chicago and include similar Chicago theater and film/TV credits.... Films with Latino themes are gaining exposure on the pay service. Actor John Leguizamo scores a triple play in the *Undefeated*, a boxing film, which he co-authors, stars in and for the first time directs. The film details the struggles of a second generation Puerto Rican kid from a barrio in Jackson Heights Queens where Leguizamo grows up, who uses boxing as ticket to a better life. It's shot in Leguizamo's old neighborhood and in Madison Square Garden. Leguizamo is also hired by Spike TV, the male-directed network to create *Zilch And Zero*, a half-hour animated special about two film buffs for 18- to 34-year olds...Antonio Banderas stars as Pancho Villa, the Mexican revolutionary, in *And Starring Pancho Villa As Himself*, a film about the actual filming in 1914 of his exploits by pioneering American silent filmmaker D.W. Griffith's Mutual Film Company called *The Life of General Villa*. HBO's budget of $23 million sets a record as its most expensive cable movie.... Seeking additional Latino films, the company signs with Maya Pictures for six low budget films about U.S. Latinos which will be directed by new Latino filmmakers with Moctesuma Esparza executive producing. Among his credits is producing the film *Selena*...A gritty documentary about New York City's largest Puerto Rican gang, the Latin Kings, is the explosive subject for a segment in the channel's *American Undercover* series titled *Latin Kings: A Street Gang Story*. At the core of the documentary is the story of the rise and fall of its leader, Antonio "King Tone" Fernandez whose sentencing to a federal prison weakens the gang's position among the Puerto Rican community which venerates him.... In a lighter vein, standup comic Rick Gutierrez is signed to develop and star in a comedy series.

Local news: Time Warner Cable launches NY1 Noticias, its all-Spanish 24-hour news channel as an adjunct to its successful NY1 News general market station. (This major happening is covered during my visit there in Chapter 14.) NY1 Noticias follows the successful path taken by two other local news channels, Time Warner Cable's Tampa Bay News 9 En Español which bows last year and Phoenix's ¡Mas! Arizona, a veteran since 2000. ¡Mas! Arizona also includes coverage of the city's pro teams, the basketball Suns, starting in the fall of 2000 and the baseball Diamondbacks in the spring of 2001. The channel is a spin-off from the Arizona News Channel, a partnership between Cox Communications and Belo Corporation, which operates KTVK, an independent station...Natalie Morales works her way up the TV ladder from marketing/public affairs at Court TV to News 12, a Bronx, New York, cable channel, where she's its first morning anchor, to NBC affiliate WVIT, Hartford, Connecticut, where she's a weekend anchor/reporter to national exposure on MSNBC as an anchor and correspondent.

Playboy TV En Español: The four-year-old, pay-TV, softcore adult entertainment service aims its programs at men, women and couples aged 18 to 65. Programming, including six new series, covers the gamut of sexually stimulating topics. Programs originally shot for Playboy TV, are culled from its library and dubbed in Spanish.

Its other series, mostly hours, are provided by the Claxson Interactive Group, Inc., with offices in Miami and Buenos Aires. These shows run the gamut from *Erotika*, offering a guide to unusual places in the U.S., Latin America and Europe to *Las Fronteras Del Placer* (*The Borders of Pleasure*) in which couples participate with an on-screen duo in specially designed games. Shows from the English-language library include: *Playboy's Playmates* who share exotic moments with viewers and *Sex Under the Lights*, which provides a behind-the-scenes look at how adult entertainment is made. The overseas produced shows are also seen on Playboy TV Latin America and Iberia, which debuts in 1996.

Sci-Fi: Edward James Olmos plays the lead role of Commander Adama, originally portrayed by Lorne Greene in the 1978–'79 ABC hit *Battleship Galactica*, in a remake of the series, which features Spanish closed captioning. It's the first time the science fiction channel provides this second language feature as part of its initiative to reach more Hispanics. Olmos also narrates a half-hour documentary in English and Spanish about the series for Cable in the Classroom (CIC), an industry informational effort. It's also the first time a non-Spanish network offers CIC a feature in Spanish.

Showtime: Timed for Hispanic Heritage Month in October, the pay service airs *The Original Latin Kings of Comedy*, a 90-minute special starring George Lopez, Paul Rodriguez, Cheech Marin, Joey Medina, and Alex Reymundo…Salma Hayek makes her directorial debut on *The Maldonado Miracle*, a story about a dying town in which the blood of an 11-year-old illegal immigrant may be the source for the blood discovered on a statue of Jesus. Rubén Blades plays a central role in the cast.

¡Sorpresa!: The three- to 14-year-old targeted kids' network debuts on March 14 in South Florida and other Hispanic communities with a lineup of Spanish-language games, cartoons, talk and variety shows from Puerto Rico, Mexico, Spain, Argentina, and Chile. Mornings are devoted to younger children, afternoons and evenings to the older kids. The network, which means surprise in English, is headquartered in Hialeah, Florida, and is owned by Firestone Communications, a media company in New York. The channel is using the production studios and satellite uplink facilities Firestone acquires from the creditors of the four-year-old Hispanic Television Network of Fort Worth, Texas, which is in Chapter 11 bankruptcy restructuring, but goes off the air when ¡Sorpresa! comes alive with shows it believes will service an underserved age group. The new entity also acquires HTVN's cable systems agreements, so it starts off reaching 400,000 subscribers on 350 different systems.

The advertising industry is cautiously altering its insouciant attitude towards Hispanic TV, propelled by propitious estimates of Hispanic buying power, now set at $764 billion within two years by the Selig Center for Economic Growth. Ad agencies are creating Hispanic divisions, top name artists are headlining commercials and the recorded music by hit acts is playing under the on-screen visuals. Commercials are also being shot outside the U.S. for economic reasons, just like "runaway" films are shot in other nations where costs are considerably less than they are in this country.

A survey by the Association of National Advertisers, Inc. (ANA) indicates 50 percent of its members maintain separate multicultural marketing departments, of which 32 percent have their own budgets. Two years later in '03, the ANA reports 86 percent of respondents to its domestic Hispanic marketing study are now advertising to Latinos, a 10 percent gain over a previous study in 2002, according to *Advertising Age*. Also, half of the agencies surveyed have separate multicultural departments, with budgets of $4.8 million out of an average client's $225 million budget. The study reveals an interesting trend: 52 percent of survey participants develop bilingual ads, with 22 percent using Spanish-language ads in the general market to obviously reach Hispanics who tune into mainstream media.

Among the high-profile agencies offering multicultural services are Starcom MediaVest Group (SGM), MediaCom, Young & Rubicam, Inc., Publicis Group, MindShare, and the Interpublic Group of Companies.

While the top Hispanic media advertisers include powerful brands like Procter & Gamble, AT&T, General Motors, Sears, Kraft, Wells Fargo Bank, McDonald's, Carl's Jr., Burger King, Continental Airlines, Sprint, Avon, Honda, and beer companies, among others, the Association of Hispanic Advertising Agencies, the trade group for 65 Spanish-language agencies in 29 locales including San Juan, reflects in the *Wall Street Journal* in 2004 that in 2003 5.1 percent of all national advertising budgets impact Hispanic media, a rise from 4.6 percent in 2002. The trade group also reveals that of the nation's 671 major advertisers, representing 80 percent of all ad dollars spent in this country in 2003, $3 billion is spent in Hispanic TV and print outlets, a third increase over 2002's figure of $2.3 billion, which means there's still a long journey Hispanic marketers must traverse before they reach parity with Anglo market budgets.

The competing Spanish-language agencies, which provide their own expertise for marketers seeking a foothold in the Hispanic market, come in all sizes across the U.S. Of this group, I've had occasion to interview executives at La Agencia De Orci & Associados in Los Angeles, Anita Santiago Advertising in Santa Monica, California, Bromley Communications in San Antonio, The Bravo Group in New York City, and Del Rivero Messianu DDB in Miami.

During my trip to New York, I meet with several ad agency executives to discuss their involvement in Hispanic TV. Jean Pool, executive vice president and director of North American operations at Universal McCann, tells me that in major Latin markets like New York, Los Angeles, Miami, and San Antonio, "Spanish stations are so important, they've become the general market, not the separate Hispanic market. Retailers don't look at a market as Hispanic. They look at places like Texas, Florida, and California as trading areas that have heavy Hispanic populations."

María Cueva, MediaCom's vice president/director of Hispanic media buying, points to the growing trend among clients to use their general market budgets to buy special events like the Super Bowl "because they're trying to reach Anglo and Hispanic consumers."

Other special events she mentions are the Grammys, Latin Grammys, Miss Universe contest, Golden Globes, and the Olympics. "Procter and Gamble running a first-time commercial for Crest in Spanish during the regular Grammys this year is unique."

Jose Aybar, vice president and managing director of media services for MediaCom's Wing Latino Group, checks in from San Juan, Puerto Rico, via speakerphone to discuss runaway commercials. "In the past few years," he tells me, "the trend among multinational clients is to produce commercials in Argentina, Uruguay, Colombia, Mexico, and Spain using local actors, with the U.S. production companies traveling to where they're filming. A 30-second spot, depending on its sophistication and whether it's filmed outdoors in the U.S. can run to hundreds of thousands of dollars. In Latin America, it costs half of that."

"Hispanic networks in this country want an original Spanish commercial done in Spanish for the Spanish culture," interjects Cueva. "People involved in creating Spanish spots must be sensitive to colloquialisms, since words have different meanings in different nations."

When McDonald's sets its Big Mac sights on the young Latin market, it assigns the job to Miami-based agency Del Rivero Messianu, which integrates rap music, English, Spanish, and Spanglish lyrics with a cast of Hispanic, black and white actors and actresses for the 30-second commercial which runs on Univision, Telemundo and its mun2 network as well on ABC, CBS, NBC, BET, and in syndicated shows. Agency co-owner and chief creative officer Luis Miguel Messianu tells me via phone, "We use close to 100 actors on the two-day shoot in Los Angeles featuring a wide range of colors from light to dark Hispanics and people who look more Mexican or Caribbean." The cost for the job? "Close to half-a-million dollars," responds Messianu. How close I ask? "Close," he parries, laughing at his answer. The commercial obviously works. "There's a 32 percent increase in sales in July and an increase of 45 percent for July and August," he says, not laughing.

With the growth of the Hispanic media, record companies are increasingly licensing their top acts' discs for commercials as well as releasing Latin film soundtrack albums. These synchronization rights are additional revenue for record companies and artists, especially in light of declining retail sales. Among the artists involved in national ad campaigns: Enrique Iglesias (for Doritos); Kinky (Honda, Motorola, Smirnoff and for such series as *Kingpin*, *Six Feet Under*, and *Alias*); Bacilos (GM's Corvette); Shakira (Pepsi); Thalía (Dr. Pepper); Maná (Coors), and Fito Páez (Coca-Cola). Feature films with soundtrack CDs include: *Y Tu Mamá También* (Volcano); *Frida* (Universal Classics); *Chasing Papi* (Sony Discos' first soundtrack project of its own contains 50 percent Latin music including Jaci Velasquez's English and Spanish singles for *No Necesito Un Hombre* (*I Don't Need a Man*). Next year, J-Records releases the soundtrack for *Havana Nights: Dirty Dancing* with authentic Cuban music of the '50s and rap-flavored versions of older Cuban tunes.

By the fall, voices of discontent are uttering their frustrations over lack of greater representation on Anglo TV in spite of minority job showcases at ABC, CBS NBC, and Fox for Latinos and African-American actors/actresses, writers and directors. These showcases are the result of pressure from Hispanic and black groups anent the lack of ethnic diversity, and the expanding, albeit, small presence on-air of Hispanics in broadcast, cable and syndication projects.

NBC, the first network to sign a diversity intention agreement, claims it employs a minority writer for each sitcom and drama it airs. Fox says as a result of dealing with the Directors Guild of America, it employs Linda Mendoza to direct episodes of *Mad TV*, *Bernie Mac*, and *Grounded for Life*. With this experience, she's hired to direct her first feature film, *Chasing Papi*. ABC speaks of hiring six out of seven writers in last year's writing program for series this season. CBS culls 800 candidates from its second talent showcase to select two finalists, Lourdes Colón and Veronica Diaz to "talent holding" deals for next year's season.

The National Latino Media Council grouses that Hispanics remain proportionately the least represented minority on TV and The

National Association of Hispanic Journalists asserts the networks are not increasing their coverage of the Hispanic community. For the eighth year, the journalist organization's *Network Brownout Report* reveals that of around 16,000 stories airing last year on the major newscasts, only 120 are about Latinos. Two-thirds of all evening newscast stories on ABC, CBS, NBC, and CNN about Latinos involve crime, terrorism, and illegal immigration. On the positive side, eight stories about politics and the growing Latino voting base air on the networks, which increase the length of Latino-stories from two minutes and 25 seconds in 2001 to two minutes, 51 seconds in 2002. "This year's report once again highlights the dismal progress the networks have made in their coverage of the nation's Hispanic community," proclaims the organization's president Juan Gonzalez, a columnist for the *New York Daily News*. The report includes qualitative analysis of the aired stories, which concludes the coverage portrays Latinos as a dysfunctional class, living on the fringes of mainstream American society, in poverty as criminals, with illegals a security threat to the nation. The organization blames a lack of Hispanics working in network newsrooms and in management for the community's poor image.

One lone organization that finds progress in TV diversity is the Multi-Ethnic Media Coalition, which tracks how well the broadcast networks are doing in honoring a 1999 agreement. Of the organization's three members, the National Latino Media Council awards Fox a B-plus; a B to ABC, and C-plusses to CBS and NBC.

The 75th annual Oscars have a Latin flavor this year, as Hispanics earn 10 nominations, six for *Frida*, including a best actress nod to Salma Hayek for her portrayal as Frida Kahlo, the surrealistic Mexican painter whose life with that nation's leading painter Diego Rivera is a tempestuous affair. The film also earns nominations for art direction, costume design, makeup, original score, and original song. Spain's Pedro Almadóvar receives nominations for original screenplay and directing *Hable Con Ella* (*Talk to Her*). The remaining nominations go to Mexico's *El Crimen Del Padre Amaro* for best foreign-language film and to brothers Carlos and Alfonso Cuarón for their original screenplay for *Y Tu Mamá También*.

During the ABC telecast March 23, Hayek loses out to Nicole Kidman in *The Hours* while composer Elliot Goldenthal's original score for *Frida* tops film Academy favorite Elmer Bernstein's score for *Far From Heaven* and Philip Glass' entry for *The Hours*. *Frida*'s second and final win is in the makeup category. The best foreign film award goes to Germany's *Nowhere In Africa*.

Latin entries achieve several firsts: Two Spanish-language titles compete in the best original screenplay category, and Almodóvar's effort becomes the first Spanish-language entry to win the screenplay statue. Ironically, his film is not eligible for a best foreign film nomination since Spain submits *Mondays In the Sun* instead. The same fate befalls the Cuarón brothers' film, which is ineligible since it's released in 2001, so it too lands in the best screenplay category. And in another first, Lila Downs, who makes her acting debut in *Frida* and sings several tunes on the soundtrack album, becomes the first Latina to perform a nominated tune, dueting with Caetano Veloso on *Burn It Blue*. The tune loses to *Lose Yourself* from *8 Mile*.

Several months before the Oscars are announced, Hayek blasts Hollywood's stance on Hispanic actresses in a feature in *Vanity Fair*, asserting she's told by one anonymous studio executive: "It doesn't matter how good you are. You can never be a leading lady because we can't take the risk of you opening your mouth and people thinking of their maids because that's what you sound like."

The potential for high grosses for Hispanic films prompts several overseas companies to enter the domestic market. Mexico's Televisa Cine and Spain's Prisa Group team with U.S. company Latin World Entertainment to create a domestic distributorship for Latin films. Initial releases will focus on films from the three companies. Televisa Cine and Prisa's New York-based Plural Entertainment have already released several titles in Mexico and are working on their first English-language film, the comedy *Un Dia Sin Mexicanos* (*One Day*

Without Mexicans), which will create a controversial stir when it's released in 2004 because of its theme that when there are no Latino workers in California, life becomes intolerable.

Also joining the rush to the U.S. is Madrid's Phoenix World Investments, which establishes an L.A.-located domestic distribution firm PWI USA. The U.S. entity plans acquiring films for theatrical and DVD release as well as producing its own films at Mexico City's Estudios Churubusco.

Arenas Entertainment, with partnership ties to Universal Pictures since 2001, signs deals to make films with the regional Mexican band Los Tigres Del Norte, KSCA's popular personality Reñan Almendarez Coello and best-selling author Victor Villasenor. Los Tigres will co-develop and co-produce movies based on their experiences or those of other Latino musicians; Coello's autobiography, *En La Cumbre De La Pobreza* (*At the Summit of Poverty*), will provide the nucleus for a film about the Honduran immigrant's impoverished childhood and his arrival and success in U.S. radio. The company has also acquired film rights to Villasenor's book, *Macho!*, about a young Mexican immigrant working as a fruit picker in California.

One American studio, 20th Century Fox's specialty film imprint, Fox 2000, enters the domestic Hispanic market with the comedy *Chasing Papi* which features a cast of rising names in Hispanic TV and music, which the studio hopes will entice business at the box-office. These names, unfamiliar to mainstream America, include vocalist Jaci Velasquez, Roselyn Sanchez (who co-stars in the short-lived ABC series *L.A. Dragnet*), Sofia Vergara (a show host on Univision), and Eduardo Verástegui in the lead role of Papi Chulo. The story line is also designed to appeal to the diverse Hispanic community, with the central male character being engaged to three women with a different cultural background. Two months after its release, *Chasing Papi*'s box office return is a reported $6.1 million. Industry estimates are that *Papi* cost $10 million to make.

In a big screen version of the life of Emilio Zapata, titled *Zapata*, the 1909 Mexican revolutionary, singing star Alejandro Fernandez plays the lead role in his film debut with Patricia Velazquez cast as Zapata's wife.

Although there have been previously released Spanish-themed films which have done well like *La Bamba*, *Selena*, *Frida*, *Empire*, and *Y Tu Mamá También*, others have not been so well received, including *Woman On Top* and *Price of Glory*, with Hispanic stars Jimmy Smits and Penélope Cruz. One criticism leveled at Hollywood studios is their lack of understanding on how to market films to Hispanics.

Among the films being distributed this year by Venevision International of Miami, which it acquires from Mexico's NuVision, is the controversial political satire *Herod's Law* about Mexico's previous ruling party, PRI. When it's originally shown in Mexico, it so infuriates government officials, they try to halt its release. They do not and it becomes one of Mexico's highest-grossing films following its release in February of 2000 and seen by a reported two million people. But up until this year, no U.S. distributor is interested in releasing the movie despite its tying for the Sundance Film Festival's Latin American Film award in 2000.

Among the notable achievements of Hispanics in film, the late José Ferrer is honored by the Directors Guild of America as the first Latino director to join the union in 1956. Six years earlier, he achieves another first by becoming the first Latin to win the best acting Oscar for *Cyrano De Bergerac* in 1950. Of the 28 films he appears in, he directs five: *The Shrike*, *Cockleshell Heroes*, *The Great Man*, *I Accuse*, and *The High Cost of Living*. The Puerto Rican-born actor/director, whose real name is José Vicente Ferrer De Otero Y Cintrón, dies in 1992 at age 83.

Cameron Diaz is pronounced the top-grossing female movie star by the *Guinness Book of World Records*. Her $40 million take tops Jennifer Lopez's $39.4 million. Among her roles that contribute to her largess are *Charlie's Angels: Full Throttle*, *Gangs of New York*, and *Shrek*. She continues her voiceover work in *Shrek 2* in 2004.

A variety of topics, some involving Hispanic themes, provide work for major names and production companies. Penélope Cruz joins Halle Berry in *Gothika*, a story about clashes in a mental institution. The Spanish actress stars in her first English-language film, *Hi-Lo Country*, in 1998. A very busy Benicio Del Toro plays an assassin in *The Hunted*, his first major role since winning an Oscar in 2001 for his role of a Mexican narcotics cop in *Traffic*, and a troubled ex-con and born-again Christian in *21 Grams*. This film is also the first English-language film for Mexican director Alejandro González Iñárritus.

Antonio Banderas, Salma Hayek, Eva Mendes, and Enrique Iglesias (in his film debut) add their passion along with Johnny Depp to *Once Upon A Time In Mexico*, director Robert Rodriguez's third and final film about the exploits of the lead character El Mariachi, a Mexican guitar player-crime avenger played by Banderas. Rodriguez is also helming *Spy Kids 2* and *Spy Kids 3-D: Game Over*. Mendes appears on the fast rack to national recognition through her work in two films with Denzel Washington, *Training Day* and *Out of Time*. In *2 Fast 2 Furious* and *Stuck On You* she costars respectively with Matt Damon and Greg Kinnear. The sultry Cuban American actress' film debut five years ago is a result of a music video she does for Aerosmith which leads to small parts in *Urban Legends: Final Cut*, *A Night at the Roxbury*, *All About the Benjamins*, and *Exit Wounds*.

Rita Moreno plays her first Spanish-language role in *Casa De Los Babys* (*The House of Babies*), director John Sayles' 14th film, in which Moreno plays the proprietor of a motel where six women from the U.S. come to adopt babies from a local orphanage in an unidentified Latin country.

Javier Bardem, one of Spain's busiest actors, appears in his second English-language film, *The Dancer Upstairs*, playing a police officer chasing a terrorist in Latin America. In 2000, his performance in his first English-language film, *Before Night Falls*, earns him an Oscar nomination, but he loses out for the best actor trophy to Russell Crowe in *Gladiators*.

John Leguizamo is committed to three projects. In *Sueño*, he's a struggling Mexican immigrant in L.A. who enters a singing contest. Others in the cast include Elizabeth Peña (a regular in the Showtime Latino drama *Resurrection Blvd.*) and Ana Claudia Talancón (whose recent work includes *Ladies Night* and *El Crimen Del Padre Amaro*). Leguizamo will also appear in the Spanish-language thriller *Cronicas* and work on an animated series, *Freaky's World*, for Nickelodeon, the children's cable network.

Diego Luna, fresh from his role in *Y Tu Mamá También*, joins the cast of the English-lingo western, *Open Range*, starring Robert Duvall and Kevin Costner. America Ferrera, the emerging star from the surprise hit, *Real Women Have Curves*, next moves to star in *How the Garcia Girls Spent Their Summer*. One actress gaining a presence in the Anglo industry is Michelle Rodriguez, with roles in *S.W.A.T.* (toplined by Samuel L. Jackson) and including Oliver Martinez; *Control* (starring Matt Dillon and Willem Dafoe) and in *Sian Ka'an*, the first reported Hispanic themed and produced animated feature, who's other voices include Salma Hayek, Alfred Molina, Plácido Domingo, and Cheech Marin. The film will have Spanish and English voice tracks, another first. Marin is also working in *The Underclassman* as an undercover cop with Roselyn Sanchez as his love interest.

In yet another crime story, the life of the late Colombian billionaire drug czar Pablo Escobar will be explored in *Killing Pablo*, based on the book, *Killing Pablo: The Hunt for the World's Greatest Outlaw*. Escobar is killed in 1993 by U.S. and Colombian police who finally track him down. Involved in the as yet uncast project are Gregory Nava's and Antonio Banderas' production companies.

Perhaps one of the most riveting documentary films ever released is *Balseros*, a film by Carlos Bosch, a reporter for Spain's Catalonian Public Television show *Trenta Minuts*, who travels to Havana in 1994 with his cameraman to record the plight of Cuban rafters who construct wooden rafts of questionable durability for a journey to freedom in the U.S. Bosch and cameraman Josep María Domènech send back several stories via satellite to the network in

Barcelona and upon their return they assemble a story for *Trenta Minuts*. Following being picked up by the U.S. Coast Guard and sent to the U.S. Naval base at Guantanamo Bay, Cuba, Bosch flies there to interview the rafters. Months later, after the detainees are allowed to immigrate to Miami, Bosch meets them there before they're relocated to various parts of the U.S. The subsequent film follows seven Cubans over a seven-year time span living in their new homes in Connecticut, Pennsylvania, New Mexico, and Texas.

In perhaps an only in L.A. story, a company called Suspect Entertainment provides all sorts of Latinos from tattooed former inmates to gangbangers to lowriders, all from the East L.A. barrio for films and commercials. The company also provides consultation services covering script, dialog and gangster behavioral characteristics, all designed to add authenticity to projects in which Chicanos are central to the storytelling. It also scouts locations and provides all sorts of vehicles and clothing as well as an available array of people available as extras. Its two owners are Manny Jiminez and a woman using the one name of Stella, who form the company one year ago and often call upon people recently released from prison or on parole, for whom this work is their first legal job.

Jiminez tells the *LA Weekly* that after getting out of prison, and trying to land a job with the film studios, he connects with someone who is looking for Mexicans for a film. Jiminez lands a job and when no one takes "your fingerprints, I said, 'Fuck it.' I'm going to work in the movies." Stella is the youngest and lone girl among 11 children. She works for her family's construction company 17 years as a demolition engineer before meeting Jiminez. Among the company's credits are *Training Day*, *S.W.A.T.*, *Charlie's Angels*, *The Fast and the Furious* and the FX series *The Shield*. Among the actors its "clients" work with are Denzel Washington, Michelle Pfeiffer, Faye Dunaway, Jennifer Tilly, and Robert Wagner.

On Broadway, Latinos appear in three of the American Theatre Wing's Tony-nominated plays, while in L.A. the local Latino theater scene struggles for recognition. Tony nominated performances are recognized for Antonio Banderas and Chita Rivera in *Nine*; John Selya in *Movin' Out*, and Marian Seldes in *Dinner At Eight*. Rosie Perez appears for four months in one of the nominated revival plays, *Frankie and Johnny in the Claire De Lune*, replacing Edie Falco, but does not snare a nomination. Her costar is Joe Pantoliano. None of the other nominees win trophies either. Perez, born in Brooklyn to parents from Puerto Rico, develops a broad-sounding New York accent, which doesn't halt her stage debut in 1999 in *A Midsummer's Night Dream* following movie roles starting in 1989 with Spike Lee's *Do the Right Thing*, followed by *White Men Can't Jump*, *It Could Happen to You*, and *Fearless*. Her previous stage work encompasses *The Vagina Monologues*; *Borrowed Light* (with Glenn Close and Joanne Woodward) and José Rivera's drama *References To Salvador Dali Make Me Hot*.

The theater loses one of its Tony-winning Latino directors when Gerald Gutierrez, 53, is found dead in his Brooklyn apartment by his brother in late January of complications following the flu. Gutierrez wins consecutive Tonys in 1995 and 1996 for directing revivals of *The Heiress* and *A Delicate Balance*.

Ricardo Montalban, the 83-year-old veteran film actor, is honored in L.A. in May when the Jimmy Doolittle Theater in Hollywood is renamed for the actor, whose eponymous named foundation owns the 76-year-old, two-story building. The Montalban Foundation raises $2.3 million to acquire the building four years ago. It is the first-ever Hispanic owned and operated theater in the U.S. The Mexican-born actor, recovering from back surgery appears in a wheelchair during the renaming ceremonies. He appears in 50 plus films during his career, which includes his lead role in the hit TV series *Fantasy Island*. The theater plans launching a regular season in 2005. Three years ago it hosts the road show production of *Selena*, which does not fare well with Angelenos.

Despite the availability of the Montalban Theater, the second annual International Latino Theatre Festival chooses to use the downtown Los Angeles Theatre Center to present its 10-day event featuring plays by 10 visiting theater groups from such nations as

Argentina, Chile, Ecuador, and Cuba, among others. The festival is also offering a Los Angeles Theater Scene Showcase of local performers at various locales around town. In its second season, it focuses not only on Mexican descendants, but also on residents from Central and South America, Cuba, and Puerto Rico. Its three directors reflect that expansive concept: Jorge Folgueira is from Cuba; William Flores is from El Salvador and Flavia Saravalli is from Spain and Argentina.

Ballet remains a quiet zone for Latinos. Mexico City-born Domingo Rubio is finding life dancing in films and with the Joffrey Ballet of Chicago forces one to make decisions as to where the future lies. For Rubio, who starts dancing when he's 18, his future includes leaving the ballet troupe he joins in 1999 after this engagement since he's cognizant of the physical pressures of professional ballet dancing, especially now that he's 37. While appearing here with the Joffrey, he dances the role of the half-man, half-goat in *Afternoon of a Faun* and the Christ figure in *IDNA*, an anti-death penalty statement created by the Joffrey's artistic director Gerald Arpino, who spots Rubio at Cal State Los Angeles in East L.A. performing with Mexico City's Taller Coreográfico de la UNAM in 1997. This Christmas, Rubio appears in Robert Altman's ballet-themed film, *The Company*, providing the kind of national exposure artists dream of.

Two dancers with the Boston Ballet, the husband and wife duo of Gianni DiMarco and Adriana Suárez, born in Caracas, Venezuela, are solidly entrenched in Bean Town. The two meet in Boston in 1994 when DiMarco, living and working in Montreal with Les Grands Ballet Canadiens, visits a friend at the Boston Ballet where Suárez is the prima ballerina, but on leave for a year after left knee surgery to repair a torn ligament. Three months after meeting, DiMarco injures his left knee and Suárez flies to Montreal to lend him her support. In the spring of '95, when an audition in the Boston Ballet opens, DiMarco wins the competition and the heart of his lady love, whom he marries. During the Boston's down period they dance with other companies and in 1998 return to the Boston where she subsequently dances the lead in *The Sleeping Beauty*, *The Nutcracker*, and *Dracula*. DiMarco's leads include *Don Quixote*, *Romeo And Juliet*, and *The Four Temperaments*. After the birth of their daughter, Gianna on December 15, 2000, the couple continue with their professional lives.

Professional baseball's ownership ranks take on a decided Latin flavor when the Walt Disney Company-owned Anaheim Angels sell the franchise to Arturo "Arte" Moreno, a Phoenix business millionaire for $183.5 million in April. Moreno becomes the first Hispanic owner of a U.S. major league team in any sport. Disney's sale marks the culmination of its four-year search to sell last year's World Series championships. Their poor financial performance of a reported $100 million in loses, during the seven years Disney owns the team, motivates the sale. Baseball's 30 owners approve the sale shortly thereafter. Media mogul and former cowboy actor Gene Autry founds the team in 1961 and sells it to Disney in 1996. Moreno, 56, is the former co-owner of Outdoor Systems, a billboard advertising firm he and his partner Bill Levine form in 1984, subsequently acquire 70 other outdoor firms, and then sell the company to Infinity/CBS in 1999 for $8.3 billion. He begins working in outdoor advertising in 1973 for Eller Outdoor in Tucson and then joins the giant Gannett Outdoor firm in '79 in Kansas City and two years later moves to the company's New Jersey headquarters as president/general manager.

Moreno's interest in sports encompasses minority ownerships in the Class A Salt Lake Trappers baseball team in 1986, the National League Arizona Diamondbacks in 1995 and the NBA Phoenix Suns in 2000. At the time of the Angels sale, Moreno retains his minority sales in the Suns.

A fourth-generation Mexican American, Moreno grows up the oldest of 11 children in one of Tucson's working class neighborhoods. Based on his billboard company's success and sale, his net worth is estimated at $940 million by *Forbes* magazine, which ranks him 246th among the nation's 400 richest people.

On his first day in office May 23, Moreno makes several decisions that will please Angels fans and the large Orange County Latino population. He cuts beer prices after discovering on a visit to

Edison Field that a large imported beer cost $8.50; gives 35 visitors from Mexico free tickets to an Angels game and promises to have more of the games on television and to boost the number broadcast in Spanish. He also shows up at the corporate offices with red sombreros bearing the Angels logo for his management team. During the 2004 season, he drops the Anaheim identity in favor of calling the team the Angels to attract fans from outside the city's boundaries, especially from Los Angeles. He will later create havoc by renaming the team the Los Angeles Angels of Anaheim and winds up in a legal battle with the city over the name alteration.

Moreno's history-making status follows one year after Omar Minaya of the Montreal Expos becomes the first Latino general manager in major league baseball.

Moreno's ascension is perfectly tied to the growing ranks of Latin ballplayers in the major and minor leagues. At the start of this season, 230 players in the majors represent 16 foreign nations and Puerto Rico, the majority Hispanics. The Dominican Republic leads all Latin nations with 79 players. This is one of the topics, along with the historic impact of Latins on the sport, I address during my trip to New York in 2003 when I meet with an official in the corporate offices of Major League Baseball, which is contained in Chapter 14.

Big money starts showing up in players' contracts early in the year, a portent of what'll happen once the season ends.

Yankee second baseman Alfonso Soriano renews his contract with an increase of $170,000 to raise his earnings to $800,000 for his third year in the majors. The club says Soriano is now the highest-paid player with two to three years of big league experience who wasn't eligible for arbitration or didn't have a prior multiyear agreement. With this signing, the Yankees become the first major league team with a $150 million payroll, which will move upwards when it signs baseball's highest-paid player Alex Rodriguez next year.

St. Louis home run slugger Albert Pujols agrees to a $100 million, seven-year pact. It's a compromise over the $10.5 million yearly salary he seeks, which the team counters with $7 million before agreeing to the new figure.

Dodger pitcher Odalis Perez, traded by the Atlanta Braves last winter, starts off with his new team by winning 15 games and losing 10, which earns him a $3.4 million one-year contract, up from his previous salary of $625,000.

The Montreal Expos acquire two players from the San Francisco Giants, Liván Hernández, and Edwards Guzman and $3.2 million in a swap for pitcher Jim Brewer and a player to be determined. Hernandez is now playing on the same team as his half-brother, Orlando Hernández, acquired from the Yankees during the off-season.

Prior to the opening of spring training, and as a result of the post September 11 war policy against terrorism, the U.S. Immigration scrutinizes documents of foreigners entering the U.S. And as a result, Major League Baseball discovers 550 cases of ballplayers using false birth dates or names in the last two years. The Dominican Republic accounts for 99 percent of the fraudulent identities.

It becomes a new concern for the league, which continues its outreach program to foreign nations begun in 1996. During an exhibition game this year at Mexico City's Foro Sol Stadium, the New York Mets beat the Los Angeles Dodgers, 16–11. In addition to this contest, the Kansas City Royals play the Arizona Diamondbacks in Hermosilio, Mexico.

The downtrodden Montreal Expos, who hardly draw any crowds at home, schedule 22 home games in San Juan, Puerto Rico's Hiram Bithorn Stadium. Moving locations does not guarantee a winning season. Among its second home games against the Chicago Cubs, the Expos lose 4-3, with the Cubs' Moises Alou hitting a tie-breaking two-hit single in the seventh inning. Alou tells the *Los Angeles Times* the team is "distracted and nervous" about playing its first game in San Juan. Nevertheless, the crowd of 15,632 cheers every run by the Cubbies.

So pervasive are Latinos in the majors, that both the American and National League All Star Game rosters include 10 Hispanic stars. The starting lineups for the 74th classic feature four Hispanics for the National League and five for the American League, which wins 7–6.

The Nationals include: Edgar Renteria and Albert Pujols of St. Louis, Javy Lopez of Atlanta, and Jose Vidro of Montreal, while the Americans include: Alfonso Soriano and Jorge Posada of New York, Carlos Delgado of Toronto, Alex Rodriguez of Texas, and Edgar Martinez of Seattle.

The All Star Game is the first of several select baseball games, which will be broadcast in Spanish by two Disney companies, ABC Radio Networks under the banner of ESPN Deportes Radio. Play-by-play and analysis of this game as well as league championship playoffs and the World Series will be provided by Jaíme Jarrín, the voice of the Los Angeles Dodgers Spanish-language radio coverage and Roberto Clemente, Jr., whose work is heard in Spanish on sister network ESPN and for the Yankees, who are not owned by the Disney Company. Among the cities carrying the ABC Spanish feed are New York, Miami, Los Angeles, Houston, Dallas, Phoenix, and San Diego. ESPN Deportes is the Sunday evening block of Spanish programming carried on ESPN since 2001, and heading for a formal full network launch in 2004.

In one of the most unusual "comebacks," 12 years after leaving the Los Angeles Dodgers as one of its pitching aces, Fernando Valenzuela is back at Dodger Stadium June 5, this time as part of the KWKW Spanish-language radio broadcasting team. He sits between Jaíme Jarrín, who's been with the Dodger broadcast team 45 years and Pepe Yñiguez, who's in his six year, as the team's color commentator. KWKW's historic position within Hispanic radio is discussed by its owners in Chapter 16 during my visit to thc station this year. Prior to making his broadcasting debut, Fernando throws out the ceremonial first pitch prior to the Dodgers-Colorado Rockies game. In his first season with the team in 1981, the left-handed Valenzuela pitches five shutouts in eight starts and is responsible for creating "Fernandomania" among L.A. fans which heightens when he helps the team win the 1981 World Series, and becomes the first rookie to snare the prestigious Cy Young and rookie of the year awards.

On March 28, 1991, prior to the start of spring training, the team releases him, apparently because he's unable to keep the magic going. He is bitter about being dropped. His record during his 10 seasons is 141 wins and 116 losses. While playing for Anaheim, Baltimore, Philadelphia, San Diego, and St. Louis, he winds up with a 32-37 record before ending his U.S. career in 1997, followed by four years in the Mexican winter league. Under this three-year contract, Valenzuela, 42, works all home games and road games with National League West rivals. He's also only required to work from the top of the second inning to the bottom of the seventh. Since this is his first broadcast job, he admits to the *Los Angeles Times*, "I'm a rookie all over again."

Seasoned players, not rookies, set records during the season.

Alex Rodriguez, while still the shortstop with the Texas Rangers before being wooed by Boston and winding up with New York's Yankees, hits his 300th home run of his career in March in a game against the Anaheim Angels which beat the Rangers 11–5 at Anaheim. At 27, he's the youngest player in baseball to reach that plateau after playing 249 games. He exceeds Jimmie Fox, also 27, who in the 1930's hit his 300th after 328 games. The megabuck player hits his three-run homer in the fifth inning off Ramon Ortiz. The historic home run ball is tossed back onto the field by a fan.

Texas Ranger Rafael Palmeiro and Chicago Cubs Sammy Sosa both hit their 500th home runs. Sosa hits his in April against the Cincinnati Reds. Palmeiro's power blast which follows against the Cleveland Indians, marks him as the 19th player to reach this pinnacle. Sosa, from the Dominican Republic and Palmeiro from Cuba, are thus far reportedly the only players born outside the U.S. to reach that magic number. Sosa will subsequently hit 537 home runs to exceed Mickey Mantle and become the 10th player in baseball to reach this status.

With the season coming to a close, the Minnesota Twins acquire the oldest player in the major leagues, 46-year-old pitcher Jesse Orosco, from the Yankees. He originally plays for the Twins in 1978 and is then traded to the New York Mets that year where he stays until 1985. He plays in 15 games for New York after being acquired from San Diego. During his 24 seasons in the majors, Orosco pitches in 1,244 games, the most in major league history.

When the season ends, five Hispanics have set league records. In the American League, Texas' Alex Rodriguez hits 47 home runs while Boston's Pedro Martinez earned run average is 2.22 and Toronto's Carlos Delgado achieves 145 runs batted in. In the National League, St. Louis' Albert Pujols attains a 359 batting average and Atlanta's Russ Ortiz wins 21 games. Rodriquez is not only named the American League's most valuable player for the first time in his career, he's also the first player from a last place team to win the honor, Texas finishing last in the American League West four straight years.

Ortiz, acquired in a trade with San Francisco last December, becomes the first major leaguer to win 18 games when he bests the Colorado Rockies, 12-6 in Denver. His win helps the Braves sweep the three-game series. The victory in August matches his career high set in 1999 against San Francisco.

Carlos Delgado hits four homers to lead the Toronto Blue Jays 10-8 victory over Tampa Bay in Toronto in September to become the first Latino to achieve this level of performance. His first homer in the game is also his 300th of his career. He's the fifth American Leaguer to homer four times in a game and the 15th player to reach this mark. The last time anyone hits four homers in the same game occurs in 2002 when teammate Shawn Green accomplishes the feat against the Los Angeles Dodgers.

Florida's Marlins, with an impressive lineup of Hispanics, wins its second World Series since its seventh-game victory against the Cleveland Indians in 1997, shockingly upsetting the favored New York Yankees in six games, for a 4-2 series. The final embarrassing 2-0 game takes place on the Bronx Bombers home field of Yankee Stadium. Among Hispanics on the 11-year-old champion's roster are Michael Tejera, Ugueth Urbina, Luis Castillo, Miguel Cabrera, Alex González, Juan Pierre, Juan Encarnacion, and Ivan Rodriguez, the catcher who is named the National League's most valuable player. Rodriguez, a 10-time All Star catcher, is acquired from the Texas Rangers for $10 million as part of a one-year contract.

Once the World Series is history, forthcoming honors draw attention to the achievements of Latinos. The American League's Golden Glove awards go to Angels' catcher Bengie Molina who wins for the second straight year, Oakland third baseman Eric Chavez and Texas shortstop Alex Rodriguez. The league's rookie of the year goes to Kansas City shortstop Angel Berroa. While the league's Cy Young Award goes to Toronto pitcher Roy Halladay, the Chicago White Sox Esteban Loaiza finishes second with the Boston Red Sox Pedro Martinez finishing third.

Once the season concludes, the money boys take over, exploiting the axiom that when you're hot, you're worth a lot. In one of the most complex headline-grabbing deals, the Boston Red Sox pursue Texas Ranger Alex Rodriguez, he of the 10 year, $252 million contract signed in December 2000. He averages $25.2 million a year, including a signing bonus of $20 million. In the deal, A-Rod as he's called, will be swapped for Manny Ramirez, whose salary is $160 million over eight years, the second highest in baseball. The Rangers are demanding the Red Sox pick up all of the $179 million remaining on A-Rod's contract through 2010, while chipping in with $5 million a year for five years towards the $97.5 million a year remaining on his contract through 2008.

A few days later in an effort to expedite the deal, the Rangers tell the Red Sox to forget contributing to the remaining $97.5 million. Texas also drops its demand for the additional $25 million, lowers it to $15 million and then cancels this amount out. As the talks stall, Commissioner Bob Selig steps in with a deadline to complete or end the trade. The players' union also steps in to voice its protest to the salary, which it feels would be reduced rather than restructured in violation of its labor pact with organized baseball. Enter the Yankees in February of 2004 to clean up the imbroglio by signing Rodriquez in a swap for second baseman Alfonso Soriano. Under terms of the deal, the Yankees will pay A-Rod $112 million, while the Rangers pay $67 million of the $179 million remaining on his $252 million pact. This is the most cash involved in a trade in major league history.

Rodriguez shifts from short to second base. His paycheck elevates the Yankees payroll to the highest in baseball, around $200 million.

In other less stupendous deals, but still very respectable ones, the Baltimore Orioles sign free-agents shortstop Miguel Tejada and catcher Javy Lopez. Tejada lands a $72 million, six-year deal. He last plays for the Oakland Athletics where he's named the American League's most valuable player in 2002. Lopez, formerly with Atlanta, is signed to a $22.5 million, three-year deal.

The Angels acquire free-agent pitchers Bartolo Colon and Kelvin Escobar. Colon, formerly with the Chicago White Sox, signs on for four years at $48 million. It's the second most expensive contract in the team's history, exceeded only by the $80 million paid to first baseman Mo Vaughn in 1998. Escobar, formerly with Toronto, signs a three-year pact paying him $18.75 million.

Former Florida outfielder Juan Encarnacion receives $8 million from the Dodgers to bolster their offense for two years.

The Tampa Bay Devil Rays sign San Francisco outfielder Jose Cruz, Jr. to a $6 million, two-year deal. Seattle picks up infielder Carlos Guillen for $2.5 million and a one-year contract.

On the low end of the salary scale, pitcher Armando Almanza signs with Atlanta for one year at $500,000 after being released by Florida.

U.S. national soccer team coach Bruce Arena, after opening the season with a 4-0 victory over Canada, names 23 Major League Soccer players to his squad for games against Argentina and Jamaica. Six are Hispanics. Arena says by adding the MLS players, the team will be stronger for upcoming international tournaments during the summer. When the U.S. team meets Mexico at Reliant Stadium in Houston, a record crowd of 69,582 sees the two rivals play to a 0-0 tie. It's the largest crowd to ever see a soccer match in Texas. It's the first meeting of these two titans since June of 2002 when the U.S. beats Mexico 2-0 in South Korea to advance to the quarterfinals of the World Cup, signifying to many soccer fans the shift of power from Mexico to the U.S.A.

Major League Soccer achieves a sense of upgraded class with the opening on July 1 of the new $240 million, 85-acre Home Depot Center, a multi-event facility that is the new home for the Los Angeles Galaxy. The center, on the campus of California State University Dominguez Hills in Carson, California, includes the 27,000-seat outdoor specifically built soccer field which will also be used for the MLS All Star game, the United States Soccer Federation's 11 national teams, including men's and women's World Cup teams, and concert events. There's also a track and field stadium with seating for 20,000, an indoor velodrome, baseball and softball fields, and volleyball courts. Philip Anschutz, the Denver billionaire, and his Anschutz Entertainment Group (AEG) fund the project. The company owns the Galaxy, NHL Kings and the Staples Center where the Kings play in downtown L.A. The company's interests also include five of the league's 10 teams: Chicago Fire, Colorado Rapids, New York/New Jersey MetroStars, (Washington), D.C. United, and the San Jose Earthquakes. AEG plans to build stadiums for the MetroStars in Harrison, New Jersey, opening in 2006, with venues for its Chicago and Washington teams to follow.

In September, Anschutz sells the Colorado Rapids to Stan Kroenke, whose Kroenke Sports Enterprises owns the NBA Denver Nuggets and the NHL's Colorado Avalanche and promises to construct a soccer-specific stadium in the Denver area by the 2006 season. With the Rapids playing in its own stadium, the MLS will have four teams with their own venues: The Rapids, The Galaxy, Columbus Crew, and Dallas Burn, the latter scheduled to have its stadium operating in Frisco, Texas, in 2005. The Galaxy's previous home since 1996 is the Rose Bowl in Pasadena.

The Galaxy, last year's MLS champions, inaugurate the sold out soccer stadium June 6 by defeating the Colorado Rapids, 2-0. At the end of the season, despite its new home and new uniforms, the team blows a four goal lead and loses the two game, first-round MLS playoff series to the San Jose Earthquakes, 5-4. So it's adios to dreams of a second straight championship. The champions' season-starting roster includes 11 Hispanics of which six are born in Mexico, El Salvador, Venezuela, Colombia, and Guatemala.

Since AEG is among the groups operating multiple teams in the league, a situation unheard of in any other American professional sport, the question arises: who do you root for if you own multiple teams and they to do battle against each other?

The MLS may have its first foreign-owned expansion team. Jorge Vergara, owner of the Chivas De Guadalajara in the Mexican National League, wants to bring his team before U.S. fans by the spring of next year, moving up the debut from an earlier announced 2005 debut. Four cities are being considered: San Diego, Houston, Los Angeles, and Chicago.

When Vergara does decide in May of 2004, the *Los Angeles Times* reports it's L.A. as the home for his Chivas USA team which will alternate weekends with the Galaxy at the Home Depot Center, starting in 2005. Among L.A.'s Hispanic community, Chivas and Mexico City's Club America are both popular attractions.

A study by AEG as to what effect Chivas USA will have on Galaxy attendance indicates there are enough local fans to support both teams. Club America's owner, Televisa, the nation's leading media company, is discussing its entry into the league possibly in 2006, according to the *Times*, which also quotes MLS commissioner Don Garber in November of 2003 that Bert Wolstein, an Ohio businessman, signs a letter of intent to become an "MLS investor-operator of a team in Cleveland where he'll build a 20,000 seat soccer stadium for the 2005 season." While the paper also reports two other cities are interested in expanding the league: Rochester, New York, where public funding for a stadium is approved, and Oklahoma City, where the University of Central Oklahoma begins a renovation of its Wantland Stadium in the suburb of Edmond, a later report in July of 2004 announces Salt Lake City as its newest expansion franchise joining Chivas USA in 2005.

The Salt Lake investors are led by Dave Checketts, former president of the both the New York and the Utah Jazz in the National

Basketball Association. The new team will play at Rice-Eccles Stadium, also the home for University of Utah football.

Founded in 1906, Chivas is the only team in the Mexican league, which exclusively employs Mexican players, while other league members hire top stars from Central and South America. When the team joins the MLS, it will have to abide by league rules that require American player participation. Ivar Sisniega, Chivas' executive president, tells the *Times* the U.S. team will consist of "eight or nine Mexican players and the others will be Americans...mostly Mexican American or Hispanic players to the extent that's possible. The coach will be Mexican and the team will communicate in Spanish." Sisniega also stresses that American players will need to learn Spanish if they don't already know it. The last time the L.A. area has two professional soccer teams occurs 20 years ago when the Los Angeles Aztecs and the California Surf compete in the short-lived North American Soccer League.

In the MLS' eighth championship playoffs in November of this year, the San Jose Earthquakes defeat defending champions the Galaxy to advance to the finals where they prove victorious over the Chicago Fire, 4-2, before 27,000 fans at the Home Depot Center, the first league championship held in the new venue. Of both teams 22 players, the champions sport four Latinos, the losers three.

Soccer coverage on the Spanish TV networks is a topic explored in Chapter 16.

Of the handful of Latinos in the National Football League, estimated to be two percent, the Tampa Bay Buccaneers' place-kicking expert, Martin Gramatica, produces one of the most dramatic achievements when he hits the mark three times during the team's 48-21 victory over the Oakland Raiders in Super Bowl XXVII. Oakland, incidentally, is the seventh team and the third in the last five years to kick for the first score of a Super Bowl and then wind up the losers.

As part of Super Bowl Week activities prior to the game, the NFL reaches out to the Latino community in San Diego and Tijuana with its first-time Super Bowl Latino Leadership Initiative, which encompasses in San Diego, a Youth Leadership Clinic in connection with the Chicano Federation in which speakers, including San Diego linebacker Zeke Moreno, discuss educational goals and leadership skills; a Women's Leadership Clinic in conjunction with the local chapter of MANA, a national Latina organization; a Leaders of Tomorrow Workshop with the Chicano Federation, in which celebrity speakers including Pro Football Hall of Fame recipient Anthony Muñoz, discuss leadership skills before Latin business, community and government officials. The league, through its NFL Latino Scholarship Program, also donates $50,000 in scholarships for Latino students in the San Diego area. NFL will also sponsor a Chicano Youth Leadership Camp during the summer. In Tijuana, the league donates $25,000 to help Esperanza International, a humanitarian organization, build classrooms for a new school; donates $18,000 worth of computer supplies to the Tijuana Educational Linkage Committee, and contributes $36,000 to fund two computer labs in Tijuana schools as part of Fundacion Televisa, the Mexican media conglomerate's charity organization.

In terms of athletic prowess, a player who emerges from behind the reputations of previous San Francisco 49er quarterbacks is Jeff Garcia, who leads the team to a 38-22 victory over the New York Giants in one of the biggest wins and his first playoff victory this year. The victory sparks the second biggest comeback in NFL history, when he leads the march to overturn a solid Giants' lead. Up until this win, Garcia remains in the shadows of more coruscating 49er quarterbacks Steve Young, who precedes him as the team leader, and Joe Montana and his Herculean exploits in getting the team past the NFC championship game in 1981 and into Super Bowl XXIII.

In addition to Gramatica and Garcia, other members of the elite Hispanic footballers fraternity are, according to *Hispanic* magazine, Tony Gonzalez of Kansas City, Adam Archuleta of St. Louis, Donnie Edwards and Zeke Moreno of San Diego, Bill Gramatica of Green Bay, Marco Rivera of Green Bay, Victor Leyva of Cincinnati, and Roberto Garza of Atlanta.

Basketball is undergoing its own international flavor adaptation, with players from 34 nations and territories generating interest overseas as the National Basketball Association expands its fan base. Among the standout Latinos are the Memphis Grizzlies seven-foot Paul Gasol from Spain, the Dallas Mavericks Eduardo Najera from Mexico, the Denver Nuggets Nene Hilario from Brazil, and the San Antonio Spurs Emanuel "Manu" Ginobili from Argentina.

Gasol, in winning the rookie of the year honor last year, is the first European to do so, while Hilario is among the third of the 18 players from overseas chosen this season for the league's All Star Weekend's rookie-sophomore game, and the only Latino making the first team. Among his achievements is setting a Nuggets rookie record for field goal accuracy. Ginobili's seacoast hometown of Bahia Blanca is referred to as the nation's basketball capital, with its unique sports facility, the Club Bahiense Del Norte, run by Manu's father Jorge, which specializes in turning out basketball players, including his three sons. Ginobili's two brothers are also basketball-bred. Leandro is a retired player with an Argentine team while Sebastian plays for a team in Northern Spain. The city traces its love for basketball to the 1970s, according to the *San Antonio Express-News*, when three of its local sons make the Argentine national team and play in global competition.

While these and other Hispanic players are generating home-grown fans among Hispanics, there's no denying that with a record 65 players from outside the U.S. representing 16 percent of the athletes this year, basketball is the new playground for foreign talent, the majority from Europe, albeit the NBA knows, hoopball is very popular with Hispanics in this country and around the globe.

Despite not having a Latin superstar on the Los Angeles Lakers, or for that matter any Latin player, the team draws heavily from the Hispanic community. Although not sitting in the $1,800 courtside seats, Latinos are nonetheless well represented throughout Staples Center where the team plays, and when it wins a championship, young Latinos are very evident on the street exuding their enthusiasm for the accolade. Overseas, the game's appeal is bolstered by young and middle class urban fans following the exploits of their national teams. In a story on the NBA's international expansion, *Time* reports that close to 15 percent of its $900 million in annual television revenue is now derived from its 148 overseas licenses.

One year later, of the 67 foreign players from 33 countries and territories, nine are Hispanic, with Brazil contributing three and Puerto Rico and Spain each represented by two players. Brazil's reps are Alex Garcia (San Antonio) and Nene Hilario (Denver) and Leandro Barbosa (Phoenix). Puerto Rico's stars are Carlos Arroyo (Utah) and Daniel Santiago (Milwaukee) while Spain's duo includes Paul Gasol (Memphis) and Raul Lopez (Utah). Mexico's lone rep is Eduardo Najera (Dallas) and Argentina's solo player is Emanuel Ginobili (San Antonio).

Boxing, long favored by Hispanics, is turning pugilists into businessmen. Former junior middleweight champion Fernando Vargas, who joins Oscar De La Hoya in the boxing-business circle, is being romanced to corporate America as a new connection to the Hispanic market. Rolando Arellano, his co-manager, is working with Miguel Gutierrez, founder of the G3 Group, which does marketing, event planning and branding for major companies, including Allstate and Colgate-Palmolive Peet. The objective with Vargas is to enhance his image and create a brand that will sell goods for advertisers. The Oxnard, California, resident, already owns apartment houses in Bakersfield, California and works with the satellite TV distributor Dish Network.

De La Hoya and his two-year-old Golden Boy Promotions, which presents boxing cards including HBO Latino's *Boxeo De Oro* series and the new *Fiesta De La Hoya* pay-per-view TV series when he's not fighting, is also a spokesman for Visa, Nestle, Miller, and Gateway. His company is designed as his second career when his boxing career ends. After winning three matches but being defeated for a second time by Shane Mosley in the junior middleweight division in October, De La Hoya begins throwing verbal punches against Bob Arum and his Top Rank promotion firm. The spiff occurs following Arum's promoting four fights featuring Latino boxers at Staples Center in

L.A. on the same night De La Hoya presents a competing match in Las Vegas. Arum suggests his audience will not be affected by the competing heavyweight bout. De La Hoya counters that attitude by telling the *Los Angeles Times* "audiences prefer good fights, regardless of ethnicity. I say it is selling the Latino fighter short...who shouldn't be exposed to just the Latino crowd." The highlight of De La Hoya's card is James Toney's defeat of Evander Holyfield.

Among the Latino boxers punching their way to popularity in the U.S. are Mexico's Erik Morales, the World Boxing Council champion in the super-featherweight category; Carlos Hernandez of Bellflower, California, the International Boxing Federation's (IBF) junior-featherweight champion (the first world champion with El Salvadorian roots); Rafael Marquez of Mexico City, the IBF's bantamweight champion; Edgar Cardenas of Mexico, the IBF's light-flyweight champion, and Mike Anchondo of La Puente, California, in the featherweight division.

Horse racing's most successful jockey, Laffit Pincay Jr. retires from the sport after 37 years of competition in the U.S. in April 29, 2003 as a result of a horrendous fall at Santa Anita on March 1. The native of Panama suffers serious fractures in his neck from a fall after his mount, Trampus Too, clips the heels of Rainman's Request, resulting in their fall at the California track. In February of 2006, the 59-year-old settles a suit against the track, alleging negligent treatment following his accident. He claims the fractures weren't discovered until four days after the spill, when he has X-rays taken as a result of constant pain and his doctors warn him it's too dangerous to continue racing. The settlement is reportedly for more than seven figures, reports the *Los Angeles Times*. Pincay receives a $2.7 million judgment in a second suit against Huntington Ambulance on May 7, 2007 for improper care following his fall. Instead of being put in a body and neck brace, the suit claims the jockey is simply transported to the track's first-aid station, treated and released.

During his career he rides to victory 9,530 times, surpassing Willie Shoemaker's world record of 8,833 wins on December 10,

1999. In 1985, he becomes the first jockey to earn $13 million in one year.

Jose Santos, almost makes history by riding Funny Cide to victory in the Kentucky Derby and Preakness, but fails to win the Belmont Stakes, the third leg of the fabled Triple Crown when Funny Cide finishes third. Had he won, Funny Cide would have been the first Triple Crown winner since Affirmed achieves that distinction in 1978. Santos is on board for 12 of the horse's major races. During his Kentucky Derby ride, Santos is suspected of carrying an illegal electrical device to stimulate Funny Cide's winning performance. The controversy is a result of a newspaper photo that appears to show a black object in Santos' hand. After an investigation by Churchill Downs stewards, he is cleared when the black object is deemed an "optical illusion."

Articles

"Jury Awards Pincay $2.7 Million." Los Angeles Times, May 9, 2007
"Pincay, Santa Anita Settle," Los Angeles Times, Feb. 15, 2006
"Finally, Some Due." Los Angeles Times, July 19, 2005
"Marketers Hone Focus On Minorities." Advertising Age, Nov. 1, 2004
"Miller Turns Eye Toward Hispanics." Wall Street Journal, Oct. 8, 2004
"Multicultural Issue Divides Ad Industry." Advertising Age, Aug. 23, 2004
"BK Taps C.O.D. For Latin American Biz." Advertising Age, Aug. 9, 2004
"MLS News." Los Angeles Times, July 15, 2004
"'I Want Hispanic People To Be Comfortable In My Stores.'" Billboard, June 19, 2004
"L.A. Will Get Second Pro Soccer Team." Los Angeles Times, June 5, 2004
"Who Found Success In '03 And How." Billboard, May 1, 2004
"RIAA Latin Sales Slide Slowed In 2003." Billboard, April 10, 2004
"International Players In The NBA." NBA.com, March 15, 2004
"Nod To A-Rod." Feb. 17, 2004
"Yankees Go With The Cash Flow." Los Angeles Times, Feb. 16, 2004
"Univision Is Top Latin Label In U.S. For 2003." Billboard, Jan. 31, 2004
"Sales Up, Shipments Down: So What's The Story?" Billboard, Jan. 24,

2004

"Latin Music Enjoyed Success In 2003." Billboard, Jan. 17, 2004

"Mexico A-Go-Go." Miami Herald, Jan. 4, 2004

"San Francisco Artist Of The Year." Latin Beat, January 2004

"Tribute To Jose Ferrer." Latin Beat, January 2004

"Year In Music." Billboard, Dec. 27, 2003

"The Top Stories." Billboard, Dec. 27, 2003

"Youth, Experience Mingle Atop Latin Charts." Billboard, Dec. 27, 2003

"A Hybrid Tongue Or Slanguage?" Los Angeles Times, Dec. 27, 2003

"CBS Signs Discoveries Colon, Diaz." Hollywood Reporter, Dec. 24, 2003

"Red Sox Blink And Miss Out." Los Angeles Times, Dec. 24, 2003

"Lopez And Orioles Finalize Deal." Los Angeles Times, Dec. 23, 2003

"Clearing Out Bad Data On Illegal Immigrants." Los Angeles Times, Dec. 22, 2003

"Musicians, Take A Lesson From Celia Cruz: Move Forward." Miami Herald, Dec. 21, 2003

"Mexican Bands Stage Resurgence." Los Angeles Times, Dec. 21, 2003

"Geraldo Rivera To Open Inaugural 'Premios Fox Sports' On December 17." HispaniaNet.com, Dec. 21, 2003

"Latin Fans Love Romance." Billboard, Dec. 20, 2003

"KDL To Change Music Format Again." Los Angeles Times, Dec. 20, 2003

"Blockbuster Remains On Critical List." Los Angeles Times, Dec. 19, 2003

"Union's Reservations Block The Blockbuster." Dec. 18, 2003

"Selig Steps Into Talks." Dec. 17, 2003

"NBC's Zucker Takes Reins Of News, Creative Content." Los Angeles Times, Dec. 16, 2003

"New Telenovelas Focus On Lives Of Hispanics In the USA." Miami Herald, Dec. 16, 2003

"Angel Fans Could See A New Face In Right." Los Angeles Times, Dec. 16, 2003

"Baltimore Signs Tejada For 6 years, $72 Million." Los Angeles Times, Dec. 15, 2003

"Rival Novelas Lather Up." Daily Variety, Dec. 15, 2003

"Latinos Remain Marginalized By Network News Coverage." HispanicAd.com, Dec. 15, 2003

"Dodger Trade Could Be A Hit." Los Angeles Times, Dec. 14, 2003

"A Telenovela With The Sights, Sounds Of L.A." Los Angeles Times, Dec. 12, 2003

"Latinos Rare On The Air." Los Angeles Times, Dec. 12, 2003

"Speed Pays Off For Anchondo." Los Angeles Times, Dec. 12, 2003

"Colon's In Town, More To Come?" Los Angeles Times, Dec. 10, 2003

"Red Sox Continue Pursuit Of Rodriguez." Los Angeles Times, Dec. 9, 2003

"Colon Joins The Angel Armory." Los Angeles Times, Dec. 9, 2003

"Alphabet Laps Up 2 More 'Lopez'" Segs. Daily Variety, Dec. 8, 2003

"Battle Lines." TV Guide, Dec. 6, 2003

"LATV Launches Nationwide." Billboard, Dec. 6, 2003

"LATV Shifts To 24-Hour Schedule." Los Angeles Times, Dec. 1, 2003

"LATV Makes Leap To National Stage." Multichannel News, Dec. 1, 2003

"Two Brothers, Two Cultures, One Sound." Los Angeles Times, Nov. 28, 2003

"Turkey Day Tradition." Electronic Media, Nov. 24, 2003

"Mexico Bows U.S. Novela." Daily Variety, Nov. 24, 2003

"Holes In The Heart." Newsweek, Nov. 24, 2003

"Earthquakes Win MLS Cup." Los Angeles Times, Nov. 24, 2003

"Fights Change For De La Hoya." Los Angeles Times, Nov. 22, 2003

"Rodriguez Is MVP In A Cellar's Market. Los Angeles Times, Nov. 18, 2003

"GE, Eager To Take On Univision, Pushes Telemundo On Programs." Los Angeles Business Journal, Nov. 17, 2003

"'Galactica' Soars In Spanish." Multichannel News, Nov. 17, 2003

"No Spanish Rock For U.S." Billboard, Nov. 15, 2003

"Latino Festival Looks To Define Its Mission." Los Angeles Times, Nov. 14, 2003

"BMG Latin Retools Its Operations." Billboard, Nov. 15, 2003

"Maqrin Back At Eye's 'Amy'." Daily Variety, Nov. 12, 2003

"Hayek Joins Cast Of Bilingual Toon 'Sian.'" Daily Variety, Nov. 11, 2003

"Berra, Willis Are Top Rookies." Los Angeles Times, Nov. 11, 2003

"Galaxy Really At A Loss." Los Angeles Times, Nov. 10, 2003

"Latin Producers Launch Labels." Billboard, Nov. 8, 2003

"Latin Retailers Ahead of Curve." Billboard, Nov. 8, 2003

"Chivas Aim For Early MLS Entry." Los Angeles Times, Nov. 6, 2003

"Latin Touring Heats Up." Billboard, Nov. 4, 2003

"Diversity In TV: Progress Seen At Big 4." TelevisionWeek, Nov. 3,

2003
"Expansion Plans Are Revealed." Los Angeles Times, Nov. 2, 2003
"Decline In Album Sales Slows In 2003." Los Angeles Times, Nov. 1, 2003
"Natalie Morales." Hispanic Magazine, November 2003
"Eva." Hispanic Magazine, November 2003
"Marlins' Magician." Hispanic Magazine, November 2003
"Cracking The Top Ten." Hispanic Magazine, November 2003
"Red Sox Play Some Hardball." Los Angeles Times, Oct. 31, 2003
"Thousands Play Hookey To Party At Three Parades." Miami Herald, Oct. 29, 2003
"Miami Hooked Again On Marlins." Los Angeles Times, Oct. 29, 2003
"Dade Offers A Plan To Help Build Stadium." Miami Herald, Oct. 29, 2003
"Fox Hands 'Luis' Walking Papers." Hollywood Reporter, Oct. 28, 2003
"HBO Grows Latino Market." Hollywood Reporter, Oct. 27, 2003
"Going Local." Multichannel News. Oct. 27, 2003
"The Fish That Ate New York." Los Angeles Times, Oct. 26, 2003
"Ferrera Sets Her 'Summer' Plans For Indie." Hollywood Reporter, Oct. 22, 2003
"PBS Facing Crisis." TelevisionWeek, Oct. 20, 2003
"Universal Takes Aim At Daytime." TelevisionWeek, Oct. 20, 2003
"Singer Sanz's Latest CD Takes On Castro." San Antonio Express-News, Oct. 19, 2003
"De La Hoya Likes The Competition." Los Angeles Times, Oct. 15, 2003
"Coalition Laments The Invisibility Of Asians, Native Americans On TV." Los Angeles Times, Oct. 14, 2003
"Hispanics Favor Family Shows." TelevisionWeek, Oct. 13, 2003
"Universal Music Latino Pacts With Guitian." Billboard, Oct. 11, 2003
"Hayek Has A Directing Hand In Her First TV 'Miracle.'" Los Angeles Times, Oct. 10, 2003
"Latin L.A. Story 'Sueno' Lands At El Camino." Hollywood Reporter, Oct.10, 2003
"The 24 Seven." TV Guide, Oct. 18, 2003
"Guerra, Soto Prep CBS Sibling Sitcom." Hollywood Reporter, Oct. 10, 2003
"Radio Unica Bought." Hollywood Reporter, Oct. 7, 2003
"Hernandez Ends Two Cuts Above." Los Angeles Times, Oct. 6, 2003
"No Doubt For Morales This Time." Los Angeles Times, Oct. 5, 2003

"Staples Center Card Is The Latest From Arum." Los Angeles Times, Oct. 4, 2003

"FCC Approves HBC/Univision Merger Amid Dissension." Billboard, Oct. 4, 2003

"Latin Grammys: Another First: Classical & Latin Jazz." Hispanic Magazine, October 2003

"Cameron Diaz: Screen Queen." Hispanic Magazine, October 2003

"Leap For Love." Hispanic Magazine, October 2003

"Casa De Los Babys." Latin Beat, October 2003

"San Francisco Mariachi Power." Latin Beat October 2003

"Pete Moraga, 77; Bilingual L.A. Newsman Boosted Latinos' Image." Los Angeles Times, Sept. 29, 2003

"Final Leaders." Los Angeles Times, Sept. 29, 2003

"'Balseros' A Tale Of Cuban Survivors." Los Angeles Times, Sept. 28, 2003

"Ritmo Latino's Growth Starts At Its L.A. Confab." Billboard, Sept. 27, 2003

"Delgado Puts On A 4 Show." Los Angeles Times, Sept. 26, 2003

"Anschutz Unloads The Rapids." Los Angeles Times, Sept. 24, 2003

"Univision Ok'd For Radio Buy." Hollywood Reporter, Sept. 23, 2003

"Networks Are Catching Friday Night Fever." Los Angeles Times, Sept. 22, 2003

"Census: Hispanic Growth Continues." Miami Herald, Sept. 18, 2003

"'Latin Kings Of Comedy.' Hollywood Reporter, Sept. 15, 2003

"Latino Cultural Center Gets A Director And Plans For Its Future." Dallas Morning News, Sept. 12, 2003

"Debut Of 'Amor Descarado' Gets Warm Reception." Houston Chronicle, Sept. 12, 2003

"Big Bangs, But Is That Enough For Your Buck?" Los Angeles Times, Sept. 12, 2003

"FCC Republicans Appear Set To Clear Univision Acquisition." Wall Street Journal, Sept. 11, 2003

"Telemundo Wins Greater Access To Festival." Los Angeles Times, Sept. 11, 2003

"Rodriguez, Molina Voice Hispanic Ani." Hollywood Reporter, Sept. 11, 2003

"Hispanics Finally Break The TV Barrier." USA Today, Sept. 10, 2003

"Telemundo Seeks Parody With Rival At L.A. Gala." Los Angeles Times, Sept. 10, 2003

"Marin Cops Role As Police Boss In 'Underclassman.'" Hollywood

Reporter, Sept. 10, 2003
"Cubs Feel At Home In Puerto Rico." Los Angeles Times, Sept. 10, 2003
"NBC Goes Bilingual With 'Leno,' Telemundo Titles." Variety.com, Sept. 9, 2003
"Mas Promotions Aim To Widen Latino Base." Electronic Media, Sept. 8, 2003
"HBO Unit Laughs With Gutierrez." Hollywood Reporter, Sept. 8, 2003
"Hispanic TV Special Report." TelevisionWeek, Sept. 8, 2003
"Mana Makes It Back To U.S." Billboard, Sept. 6, 2003
"Telemundo Caps Revamp Of Its Programming Unit." Daily Variety, Sept. 5, 2003
"Cristina Crosses Over." Daily Variety, Sept. 5, 2003
"California Leads U.S. In Foreign Born." Los Angeles Times, Sept. 4, 2003
"English Twist For Latin Aud." Daily Variety, Sept. 3, 2003
"Hispanics Will Be A Bit More Visible This Fall." San Antonio Express-news, Sept. 3, 2003
"Twins Get Orosco From The Yankees." Los Angeles Times, Sept. 2, 2003
"Where Are The Latinos?" Hispanic Magazine, September 2003
"John Sayles' La Casa De Los Babys." Hispanic Magazine, September 2003
"Sounds Of Violence." Premiere Magazine, September 2003
"Having A Ball," Hispanic Magazine, September 2003
"Two To Watch Among New Breed of Tropical Pop/Rockers." Billboard, Aug. 30, 2003
"LAMC Gets Down To Business." Billboard, Aug. 30, 2003
"Hot For The Game." TV Guide, Aug. 30, 2003
"Ortiz Is First To Reach 18 Victories." Los Angeles Times, Aug. 25, 2003
"His Big Risk Paid Off." Parade, Aug. 24, 2003
"Viva La Revolucion." LA Weekly, Aug. 22, 2003
"Immigrants Head For Less Crowded States." USA Today, Aug. 22, 2003
"New Selena DVD Spotlights Her Final Show." Houston Chronicle, Aug. 22, 2003
"NBC To Promo Telemundo." Daily Variety, Aug. 21, 2003
"Reggaeton Growing On U.S. Music Fans." New York Daily News,

Aug. 18, 2003
"EMI Fuels Selena Legacy With Reissues." Billboard, Aug. 17, 2003
"Giselle Returns To Merengue Base." Billboard, Aug. 16, 2003
"Estefan In Long-Term Sony Pact." Hollywood Reporter, Aug.15, 2003
"Latin Music On The Rise." Los Angeles Times, Aug. 14, 2003
"ABC Radio, ESPN Pitching Spanish Baseball B'dcasts." Daily Variety, Aug. 14, 2003
"Out Of The Blue, Fernando's Back." Los Angeles Times, Aug. 11, 2003
"The Fit Club." TV Guide, Aug. 9, 2003
"Say Cheesecake." TV Guide, Aug. 9, 2003
"SAG Marks Historic High." Hollywood Reporter, Aug. 8, 2003
"Versatile Guerro Gets Sideline Role For 'MNF.' HispaniaNet.com, Aug. 4, 2003
"A Wild Ride Into Revisionism." Los Angeles Times, Aug. 3, 2003
"Café Tacuba Taps Geffen For Spanish Album." Billboard, Aug. 2, 2003
"San Francisco Aragon Aragon." Latin Beat, August 2003
"'S.W.A.T.' Goes Splat: Team Of Cliched Cops Turns TV Remake Into Major Bust." Wall Street Journal, Aug. 8, 2003
"Univision, HBC Are Still Waiting." Miami Herald, July 31, 2003
"FCC Approval Seen For Bid By Univision." Los Angeles Times, July 30, 2003
"Packing A Marketing Punch." HispaniaNet.com, July 29, 2003
"Telemundo Plans Dating Show With 'Cinderella' Story. Houston Chronicle, July 28, 2003
"Rodriguez Takes 'Control.'" Daily Variety, July 25, 2003
"Leguizamo Makes HBO Boxing Film Real And Inspirational." Houston Chronicle, July 25, 2003
"Leguizamo Set In Cuaron Pic." Daily Variety, July 17, 2003
"Stunned Zito Scratched From Stars To Make Room For Rocket." USA Today, July 16, 2003
"Extended 'Family' At PBS." Daily Variety, July 15, 2003
"Sanchez On Road To 'Kansas.'" Hollywood Reporter, July 14, 2003
"'American Family' To Be Revived." Los Angeles Times, July 12, 2003
"WB Flips Over 'Mucha Lucha!'" Los Angeles Times, July 12, 2003
"Special Report: Multicultural." Advertising Age, July 7, 2003
"Music That's Heard Everywhere Except On The Radio." Los Angeles Times, July 7, 2003
"Miami Dade College Partners With mun2 To Produce 'Chat.'" HispaniaNet.Com, July 6, 2003
"NBC, Telemundo Oppose Merger Univision Plans." Wall Street

Journal, July 3, 2003

"Broadcasting Battle." Hispanic Magazine, July 2003

"Spy Kids 3." Hispanic Magazine, July 2003

"Pincay Jr Retires." Hispanic Magazine, July 2003

"Business Punch." Hispanic Magazine, July 2003

"Latinos Get Leverage." Weekly Variety, June 30, 2003

"Spanish Acts Seek To Conquer U.S. Market." Billboard, June 28, 2003

"Bissi Begins EMI Latin Tenure." Billboard, June 28, 2003

"Michaels, Leguizamo Will Get Into Nick Mix." Daily Variety, June 26, 2003

"Powerful And Passionate, Domingo Rubio Is Looking For New Challenges." Los Angeles Times, June 26, 2003.

"Bilingual And Busy." Broadcasting & Cable, June 23, 2003

"Market Profile: El Paso, Texas." MediaWeek, June 23, 2003

"Univision Sparks Heated Debate In Two Languages." Miami Herald, June 22, 2003

"UMVD Nearly Doubles Latin Share." Billboard, June 21, 2003

"Latinos Now Top Minority." Los Angeles Times, June 19, 2003

"Telemundo Acquires 26 Cantinflas Films." Daily Variety, June 18, 2003

"Spanish-Language Films Take Aim At U.S. Market." Los Angeles Times, June 11, 2003

"LATV Hums National Rollout Tune En Espanol." Multichannel News, June 9, 2003

"Sopresa! Joins Race For Latino Youth." Advertising Age, June 9, 2003

"Ricky Still Packs Star Sales Punch." Billboard, June 7, 2003

"Absolutely No Place Like Home For Galaxy." Los Angeles Times, June 7, 2003

"Galaxy As Good As New Again." Los Angeles Times, June 7, 2003

"Two Latin Labels Get New Leaders." Billboard, June 7, 2003

"Charting Pepe." Latin Notas: Charting Pepe." Billboard, June 5, 2003

"Univision Lobbies Pols On Hispanic Merger." Daily Variety, June 5, 2003

"Univision Makes Eleventh-Hour Push To Seal Hispanic Radio Deal." Los Angeles Times, June 4, 2003

"Dems Object To Univision Buy." Electronic Media, June 2, 2003

"Sitcom On Latino Kids Speaks PBS' Language." Los Angeles Times, June 2, 2003

"GE's Telemundo Hasn't yet Met Expectations." Wall Street Journal, June 2, 2003

"Fresno-Visalia, Calif." MediaWeek, June 2, 2003

"Latino TV Waves U.S.—Made Flag." Multichannel News, June 2, 2003

"Mun2's 'Roof' Tilts To West." Daily Variety, June 2, 2003

"Cachao, King Of Cuban Swing, Is Still Kicking Up The Temp." Miami Herald, June 2, 2003

"San Francisco: Women In Salsa III, Jardinero: Latin Beat, June 2003

"Palmeiro, Sosa In '500 Club.'" Hispanic Magazine, June 2003

"Spring Things In San Francisco." Latin Beat June 2003

"Going For The Crown." Hispanic Magazine, June 2003

"Vikki Carr To Receive Guizar Award." San Antonio Express-News, May 30, 2003

"EMI Latin Topper Exits." Daily Variety, May 30, 2003

"Goal Oriented." Hollywood Reporter, May 30, 2003

"Sony Music Groups Latin Ops." Daily Variety, May 29, 2003

"Univision Defends Buying Hispanic Station." Washington Times, May 29, 2003

"L.A.'s Spin On Salsa." Los Angeles Times, May 27, 2003

"Phoenix Rises In U.S." Daily Variety, May 27, 2003

"It's Still All Work, No Play." Los Angeles Times, May 23, 2003

"Angels' New Owner Puts Fans At The Top Of The Order." Los Angeles Times, May 23, 2003

"Telemundo makes History With The Premiere Of 'Los Teens.'" Telemundo.com, May 21, 2003

"Martin Tones Down 'La Vida Loca.'" Miami Herald, May 21, 2003

"WTVJ's Browne Named Telemundo Chief Officer, Miami Herald, May 21, 2003

"Ricky Martin To Release Album In Spanish." Associated Press May 18, 2003

"Spanish-Language TV Hits Stride At Upfront Market." Electronic Media, May 16, 2003

"Moreno Dream Comes True." Los Angeles Times, May 16, 2003

"Third Iglesias Reaches Out For The Stars." Miami Herald, May 15, 2003

"Love Of The Game Brings Angels' Buyer To Baseball." Los Angeles Times, May 15, 2003

"BMG U.S. Latin Quits A&R." Billboard, May 15, 2003

"Univision's Upfront About Its Dominance." Daily Variety, May 15, 2003

"Univision Unveils Complementary Programs For Networks." Miami Herald, May 15, 2003

"'Movin' Out' And 'Hairspray' Rack Up Tony Nominations." Los Angeles Times, May 13, 2003

"Spanish-Language Networks Have Plenty To Offer Viewers." Houston Chronicle, May 14, 2003

"Lopez Connects With Telemundo For Prod'n Deal." Hollywood Reporter, May 14, 2003

"Telemundo Targets Mexican Americans." Miami Herald, May 14, 2003

"Leguizamo To Create Spike Special." MediaWeek, May 12, 2003

"U.S. And Mexico Tie In Mexico." Los Angeles Times, May 9, 2003

"Hilario Named To NBA's All-Rookie First Team." May 9, 2003

"Placido Domingo To Emcee Guadalajara's International Mariachi Festival." HispaniaNet.com, May 8, 2003

"Telemundo Poaches Univision's Quezada." Los Angeles Times, May 6, 2003

"2 Deals Boost Univision's Portfolio To 53 Stations." Los Angeles Times, May 1, 2003

"Staying Grounded." Hispanic Magazine, May 2003

"Iglesias Jr. Dreams In 3-D." San Antonio Express-News April 27, 2003

"In Step With Justina Machado." Parade Magazine, April 27, 2003

"Joint Venture Broadens Christian 'World.'" Billboard, April 19, 2003

"Synch Deals Boost Latin Acts." Billboard, April 19, 2003

"Latino Studio Signs Majors." Houston Chronicle, April 18, 2003

"EMI 'Fine-Tuning' Has Little Effect On Deal-Making." Billboard, April 17, 2003

"Phoenix Businessman Agrees To Buy Angels." Los Angeles Times, April 16, 2003

"Disney Is Closer To Selling Angels." Los Angeles Times, April 15, 2003

"Martin's No. 1 Debut First For Latin Tracks In 5 Years." Billboard, April 12, 2003

"Sanchez Sings." Latin Notas, Billboard, April 12, 2003

"Telemundo Facing Reality Of Sluggish Ratings." Miami Herald, April 11, 2003

"'Papi' Chasing Latinos." Hollywood Reporter, April 11, 2003

"Living La Vida Lopez." TV Guide, April 5, 2003

"U.S. Biggest Latin Market Amid Regional Slump." Billboard, April 3, 2003

"Aspiring Young Urban Latino Artist In Reality Show @ mun2 Television." HispanicAd.com, April 4, 2003

"Topple Kingpin." Hispanic Magazine, April 2003

"Becoming Raquel." Hispanic Magazine, April 2003

"Christian Alliances." Latin Notas, Billboard, March 29, 2003

"As Time Goes By." Miami Herald, March 29, 2003

"EMI Latin USA Signs Distribution Deal With Venevision International." Billboard, March 29, 2003

"Univision Plan Ok'd." Daily Variety, March 27, 2003

"Ambitious New Season At Ford Theater Has A Latin Zing." Los Angeles Times, March 26, 2003

"Telemundo Turns To Aggressive Reporting To Attract New Viewers." Los Angeles Times, March 26, 2003

"Arenas Bags 'Los Tigres' And 'Macho!'" Daily Variety, March 26, 2003

"Latino Studio Signs Big Names." Los Angeles Times, March 26, 2003

"Salsa Sings The Blues As It Hits A Big Slump." Los Angeles Times, March 25, 2003

"Hernandez Joins Brother With Expos After Trade." Los Angeles Times, March 25, 2003

"What A Niche Audience!" Broadcasting & Cable, March 24, 2003

"Victories Cap A Turbulent Year In Screenwriting Categories." Los Angeles Times, March 24, 2003

"Kings Ready For Radio's Crown." Billboard, March 22, 2003

"Telemundo, Mun2 Tackle Titans." Multichannel News, March 17, 2003

"More Players Spice Up the Game." TelevisionWeek, March 17, 2003

"Local Latino Beat Warms Up." Multichannel News, March 17, 2003

"The NBA's Global Game Plan." Time, March 17, 2003

"Big League Beisbol Is A Solid Hit In Mexico." Los Angeles Times, March 16, 2003

"Latinos Rock SXSW Venue Vibe." San Antonio Express-News, March 16, 2003

HBC Set To Become Univision Music Group." Billboard, March 15, 2003

"Thugs On Film: Suspect Entertainment Helps Hollywood Keep It Real. LA Weekly, March 14, 2003

"All-Spanish Kids TV Channel Set To Launch." March 13, 2003

"Distribution Deals," Latin Notas, Billboard, March 12, 2003

"SBS Debuts Cumbia FM." MediaWeek, March 10, 2003

"Beyond Cute Faces, To The Lyrics." March 9, 2003

"Latinos Well Represented In Music Festival Lineup." Houston Chronicle, March 8, 2003

"Intocable Campaign Makes 'History' Via EMI." Billboard, March 8,

2003

"Germ Of An Idea." Los Angeles Times, March 6, 2003

"Yankee Payroll Is $150 Million." Los Angeles Times, March 5, 2003

"Rodriguez Youngest To Hit 300 Home Runs." USA Today, March 4, 2003

"New Latin Markets Emerge." Billboard, March 1, 2003

"The Language Of Synergy." Los Angeles Times, March 1, 2003

"Latin Music Mourns Mainstay Hauser." Billboard, March 1, 2003

"Latin Madness." Latin Beat March 2003

"Making Inroads In Public Broadcasting." Hispanic Magazine, March 2003

"Latinos Score Big With Oscar Nods." Hispanic Magazine, March 2003

"Will Crime Pay?" Hispanic Magazine, March 2003

"Broadway Rosie." Hispanic Magazine, March 2003

"Feds OK Univision Deal For Hispanic." Daily Variety, Feb. 28, 2003

"Juanes' Streak Ends." Los Angeles Times, Feb. 24, 2003

"I Can Push Myself." Parade, Feb. 23, 2003

"¡Vamos A Bailar!" Billboard, Feb. 22, 2003

"Ralph Hauser, III, 41; Promoter Of Latin Music." Los Angeles Times, Feb. 19, 2003

"Pujols Agrees To 7-Year Contract." Los Angeles Times, Feb. 19 2003

"Film Trio Targets U.S. Hispanics." Hollywood Reporter, Feb. 18, 2003

"Latin Notas: Disney Discs." Billboard, Feb. 15, 2003

"Exposure From Behind The Scenes." Los Angeles Times, Feb. 15, 2003

"New You See Them, Now You Don't." Hollywood Reporter, Feb. 14, 2003

"NBC Gets Back In Rings With Telemundo's Help." Daily Variety, Feb. 14, 2003

"Is 2003 Oscar's Year Of The Latino?" USA Today, Feb. 12, 2003

"Hispanic Group Criticizes 'Kingpin.'" HispaniaNet.com, Feb. 8, 2003

"Sounding Dramatic." Daily Variety, Feb. 6, 2003

"Role Call." TV Guide, Feb. 1, 2003

"Even With A Scorecard, You Can't Tell The Players." Los Angeles Times, Feb. 1, 2003

"Smithsonian Offers Introduction To Latin Jazz." Down Beat, February 2003

"Gerald Gutierrez, 53; Broadway Director Won 2 Tony Awards." Los Angeles Times, Jan. 31, 2003

"'El Cucuy' Hits The Snooze Button, Eyes Film And TV." Los Angeles

Times, Jan. 29, 2003
"Radio Host To Quit A.M. Show." Jan. 28, 2003
"Sounds Like America." Los Angeles Times, Jan. 28, 2003
"Olga Tanon: Sultry Siren Of Merengue." Miami Herald, Jan. 28, 2003
"Turf War." Time, Jan, 27, 2003
"Jimmy Kimmel: Super Sunday," TV Guide, Jan. 25, 2003
"Aguilar to Univision." Latin Notas, Billboard, Jan. 25, 2003
"Estefan Deal Consolidates Copyrights Under UMPC Umbrella." Billboard, Jan. 25, 2003
"Prize Protagonists." Latin Notas, Billboard, Jan. 25, 2003
"Ivan Rodriguez, Marlins Reach $20-Million Deal." Los Angeles Times, Jan. 23, 2003
"Four Galaxy Players Join U.S. Team." Los Angeles Times, Jan. 23, 2003
"Super Bowl XXVII Reaches Out To Latino Community." HispaniaNet.Com, Jan. 23, 2003
"Colombia's Musical Diversity Gains Fans." San Antonio Express-News, Jan. 22, 2003
"Plot Twist: Telenovelas Casts 1st Black Leading Man." Miami Herald, Jan. 21, 2003
"Spanish-Language Programming: B'casters Eye Bigger Share Of U.S. Auds." Weekly Variety, Jan. 20, 2003
"Los Abandoned Are Alone No More." Los Angeles Times, Jan. 18, 2003
"Universal Music To Manage Estefan Songbook." Miami Herald, Jan. 17, 2003
"Del Rio Becomes Jaguars' Coach." Los Angeles Times, Jan. 17, 2003
"Argentine Fans Love Spurs' Ginobili." San Antonio Express-News, Jan. 17, 2003
"Walt Disney Records Debuts Spanish-Language Versions Of Its Children's Titles." HispaniaNet website, Jan. 16, 2003
"Telemundo's Tricky Transition. Forbes.com, Jan. 16, 2003
"Par, Carnahan High Over 'Killing Pablo." Daily Variety, Jan. 14, 2003
"EMI Latin USA Makes Deal-A-Gogo." Billboard, Jan. 13, 2003
"Picks And Pans: The Shield." People, Jan. 13, 2003
"Universal Aims To Translate Latin Music Into Profits." Los Angeles Times, Jan. 12, 2003
"The Good, The Bad, The Funny." Los Angeles Times, Jan. 12, 2003
"Returning To The Top Of The Charts." Los Angeles Times, Jan. 12, 2003

"Mun2 Television Launches Reality TV Music Show Featuring Young Aspiring Artists." HispaniaNet.com, Jan. 12, 2003

"Telemundo Still Flirting With Younger Latino Audience." Houston Chronicle, Jan. 10, 2003

"Berry Locks Up Criminal Shrink Pic." Jan. 19, 2003

"Perez Earns A Big Raise To $3.4 Million." Los Angeles Times, Jan. 17, 2003

"Universal To Sell Latin Record Label's Albums." Jan. 8, 2003

"Hayek Tells Of Struggle Against Hollywood's Latino Slurs." HispaniaNet.com, Jan 8, 2003

"The Networks' Crime Wave Of Antiheroes." Los Angeles Times, Jan. 6, 2003

"Garcia Takes His Place In 49er Line." Los Angeles Times, Jan. 6, 2003

"'Entre El Amor Y El Odio' An Old Love Story Told Differently." Houston Chronicle, Jan. 3, 2003

"The Fabulosos Cadillacs Finally Run Out Of Gas." Los Angeles Times, Jan. 2, 2003

"NY1 Spins Off A Spanish-Language Channel." Electronic Media, Dec. 16, 2002

"Setting Frida Kahlo's World To Music." Wall Street Journal, Nov. 7, 2002

"United In Their Love Of The Outsider." New York Times, Oct. 27, 20002

Chapter 18
CAPITULO 18

Mexico's American Imprint 2003-2004/2005
IMPRESION AMERICANA DE MEXICO 2003-2004/2005/2006

• Artists chip away at traditional regional genres with a taste of rap and R&B.

• Independents Freddie emphasizes roots music; Balboa stresses low-priced CDs to counter piracy.

• Regional Mexican radio remains the most listened to Hispanic format as a result of Mexican migration around the U.S.

• Chicago's "Durango" dance music craze gains a national following.

• Death halts career of rising teen idol Adán Sánchez, 19; pioneers Don Tosti and Isidro López also pass away.

• Univision TV/Univision Records combine on first-ever CD showcasing Norteño styles combined with DVD focusing on immigration.

While regional Mexican music is covered in previous chapters, this chapter focuses on the two years where artists are making dramatic efforts to alter and redirect the music to embellish it with elements from mass market musical styles that appeal to young people.

The general rule in show business is that nothing stays the same. The exigencies of a fickle public's changing tastes and attitudes, coupled with the emergence of aggressively devised new trends, often helps topple to a degree what's hot and popular at the moment. One segment of Latin entertainment seemingly immune to total change over the years is regional Mexican music, the roots connection for newly arrived immigrants from Mexico as well as the link within Mexican American families where the children grow up to favor American music, but retain a respectful appreciation for the endemic music of their parents and grandparents.

Of all the forms of Latin music in this country, regional Mexican, with rare exceptions where it's covered regularly by media in the Southwest, reaps the least national coverage in the general market media, despite its dominant position accounting for close to 70 percent of all domestic Hispanic records sales to the nearly 70 percent of this nation's Mexican heritage citizens now spread across the country. The music is blithely dismissed by tropical music formatted stations even though there probably are Mexican immigrants living in their communities

Despite a droop in overall Latin albums in 2003, regional Mexican is the lone branch of the industry that shows growth, with total album shipments to retailers reaching 22.9 million units from last year's 22.8 million units shipped. Of course, shipments and actual sales of these albums are two totally different situations. Record companies like to publicly espouse the shipment numbers, but fail to announce the number of albums returned for lack of sales.

Of all the categories of Mexican music heard in the U.S., the most popular and familiar is the mariachi, once called the national music of Mexico in the first two decades of the 20th century, whose sound is transformed by cornets and then trumpets. When Mexican immigrants flood into Los Angeles in the '70s, the "City of Angels" becomes the center of mariachi.

While Mexican-flavored music rules in terms of Spanish-language radio formats, the 21st century image of young artists chipping away in some instances at the traditional forms of mariachi, ranchera, norteño, grupo, conjunto, corrido, banda, and Tejano styles to include rap, rock, rhythm 'n' blues, and Latin pop stylistic influences in 2003, reflects a desire to contemporize the music.

Nevertheless, the lasting quality of traditional regional Mexican music propels record companies in 2003 to retread their catalogs while they also boost their investments in building their regional Mexican rosters to feed the dominant Mexican American audience. Regional Mexican labels keeping the flame alive include Freddie, Balboa/Musart, Fonovisa, Disa, Joey Records International, Univision, MusiMex, EMI Latin, WEA Mex Records, Procan, Universal Latino, BMG Latin, La Sierra Records, and Platino Records, for example. Following a number of major executive changes at BMG U.S. Latin, the Miami-based company turns its focus on strengthening its bottom line by strengthening its regional Mexican roster.

For copious veteran regional Mexican artists there's a bond with their fan base. Artists like the legendary Vicente Fernández, plus Los Temerarios, Pepe Aguilar, Joan Sebastían, Los Tigres Del Norte, José José, and La Banda El Recodo, for example, remain powerful forces in the music after lengthy careers.

Aguilar, San Antonio's native ranchera star, causes ripples among traditionalists by including two electric keyboards, electric guitar, flute, saxophone amidst strings, acoustic guitar, and trumpets as he straddles tradition and modern sounds dressed in his traditional western Mexican outfit with his huge sombrero.

Although the rock en Español movement seems to have generated its cavalcade of publicity, Latin rap artists appear to be gaining favor to the point where some industry pundits believe it can surpass Latin rock as the hot, new fusion sound. The list of bands melding rap lyrics in Spanish with regional Mexican styles encompasses Akwid, consisting of brothers Sergio and Francisco Gomez, born in Mexico but raised in South Central L.A. to fellow Angelinos Jessie Morales and Lupillo Rivera to Brownsville, Texas,' Big Circo to Houston's Lil J to Corpus Christi, Texas' Kumbia Kings to Monterrey, Mexico's, girl band La Conquista, and accordionist

Celso Piña with guest rapper Blanquito Man, to Los Jardineros, Grupo Límite, Los Razos with rapper El Chavo Farruco, Chicos De Barrio, Los Capi, Imán, and Siggno to cite a few examples.

The Kumbia Kings are the creation of A.B. Quintanilla, III, the brother/writer/producer of slain Tejano superstar Selena, murdered in 1995. Two years after this tragedy, Quintanilla debuts the eight-member Kumbia Kings with the EMI Latin album *Amor, Familia Y Respecto*, which introduces it's melding of Tex-Mex cumbia with rap and R&B and sells a reported 650,000 copies. The McAllen, Texas, resident, stocks the band's newest single, *No Tengo Dinero* (*I Don't Have Money*), a Juan Gabriel early hit, in its new album *4*, with a mixture of powerhouse guests, including Gabriel, guitarist Chris Perez, Selena's husband at the time of her death, rock en Español band El Gran Silencio and Ozomatli, L.A.'s 10-piece multicultural cauldron of musical styles. It's a mix designed to appeal to rock-leaning young adult bilinguals and their more traditional Mexican roots music-leaning parents. The album contains eight tunes in Spanish and four in English, earmarking the recording as a crossover effort the way it's 2000 release, *Think'n About You*, is all-English.

Since rap remains the big moneymaker in the general market, it's only natural that Latin labels seek to produce their own version of the talk style, but without the violence and hatred spewed by sundry Anglo acts.

Of the spectrum-spanning bands, Akwid's debut Univision album, *Projecto Akwid* in 2003, is a runaway success, selling 200,000 copies after four months for its blending of rap with banda and norteño tempos. José Behar, Univision Records president, asserts to Ramiro Burr, the *San Antonio Express-News*' excellent Hispanic music reporter, who naturally focuses on regional Mexican acts, "There is absolutely no doubt that Akwid has revolutionized Latin music by fusing two cultures and two music genres in a transcending way." Behar calls this emergence of rap into Latin music "a new urban regional movement. The marriage of styles is a result of the brothers Gomez listening to traditional Mexican music at home and to rock and rap when with their English-speaking pals at school."

The current romance with rap is not the first time spoken word appears on regional Mexican records. Pioneering efforts date back to the early '90s. In 1991, Tejano bands Tierra Tejano and La Sombra utilize the rap concept on *Las Hijas De Don Simón* and *El Sancho*, respectively. In 1994, Selena combines cumbia with rap on *Techno Cumbia*, while Los Reyes Locos utilizes falsetto rap on *El Llorón*.

In addition to altering the sound of traditional regional Mexican, some acts are transforming their on-stage personas away from charro suits with their bejeweled western shirts, vests and slacks, boots, cowboy hats or sombreros and omnipresent mustaches.

Sparx, a quartet of sexy looking sisters from Albuquerque, New Mexico, supplement their tight harmonies on their Fonovisa CD, *Lo Dice Mi Corazón*, with figure-revealing tops and slacks for a contemporary fashion statement.

Grupo Límite tosses off its traditional Western clothes in favor of an "urban" look. Notes the band's Alicia Villarreal in the *Express-News*: "We just thought our dress should be consistent with what we're expressing musically."

La Conquista takes on the hip-hop culture's penchant for colored hair and eye-catching clothing in addition to its addition of R&B ingredients to its Mexican cumbia sound.

Replacing matching Western clothing with more non-traditional outfits are male groups Imán, Intenso, Siggno, Sólido, and La Costumbre.

Big Circo goes one step beyond clothing by wearing Kabuki makeup during its gig at the South By Southwest Showcase in Austin, reminiscent of '70s flamboyant rock band KISS.

Banda balladeer Rogelio Martínez, born in Sinaloa, Mexico, but raised in L.A., appears on the cover of his new CD, *Atrévete A Olvidarme*, with spiky hair and fashionable clothes, eschewing the western garb of the banda brigade he's worn in the past. He tells the *Express-News* he tries to "project a new image" on his recordings.

Amidst the whirlwind of stylistic alterations going on in Latin music, Freddie Records, the 34-year-old Corpus Christie, Texas, Martinez family-run independent, remains a steady exponent of traditional regional Mexican music. When I chat on the phone with Freddie Martinez, Jr., the company's vice president of operations and son of founder Freddie Martinez, Sr., who's the label's first artist, he stresses that the company's "bread and butter is the regional Mexican market. It's where our knowledge and marketing expertise is." Even with more Hispanics arriving in the U.S. from Central and South America, Martinez, Jr. says the label's norteño, banda and Tejano music "appeals to people from El Salvador and Venezuela and other parts of South America besides Mexicans, who obviously enjoy it because that's where the roots of the music come from." Martinez, Sr. is a seasoned vocalist who's recorded for several regional labels in the South Texas area, while playing the dance circuit by the time he starts singing for his own label. After 34 years, the company's catalog is rich with the roots music of Mexico and includes the first album Selena records, *Mis Primeras Grabaciones*, released in 1984, plus Intocable, Conjunto Bernal, Grammy winners the Latin Legends, Jimmy Gonzalez Y El Grupo Mazz, Sólido, Ramon Ayala Y Sus Bravos Del Norte, up through the current "Norteño King," Ramon Ayala. Martinez, Jr.'s comments concerning the background behind Selena's debut on Freddie and the effect of her subsequent death in 1995 are discussed in Chapter 3.

Norteño is the label's top selling category, Martinez points out, explaining the music from the north of Mexico is played by four or five piece conjuntos or groups, consisting of accordion, drums, bass and the 12-stringed bajo sexto Spanish bass guitar with "maybe a saxophone added like you find with two of our artists, Los Tigres Del Norte and Ramon Ayala." As for Tejano music, Martinez says the early pioneers in the '50s and '60s are influenced by big bands with 12–15 pieces and lots of saxes and trumpets and rhythm instruments. As the music evolves in the late '70s and '80s, the bands start incorporating keyboards, synthesizers, and electrical instruments with pop, rock, and country influences which come into play because most Tex-Mex musicians are bilingual, he points out. Growing up in Texas speaking fluent English and Spanish, musicians are exposed to these other types of music, which they include along with accordions and the bajo sexto.

"We've seen a decline in Tejano in the last couple of years," Martinez notes. "A lot of the newer artists growing up in South Texas are incorporating a lot more of norteño roots to appeal to a wider audience base. A lot of the new music falls into the gray area between norteño and Tejano. Some Tejano bands use trumpets and saxes and the feel of their music is a little more contemporary. Some bands are even mixing in a little rap as well."

Banda is typically like a big brass band, with the key exception of including a tuba that provides the distinctive umpah umpah sound. Fernandez doesn't sense any change in this genre's characteristics.

One of Freddie's most unusual projects is its joint venture with Warner Music Latina to market an album of Ramon Ayala singing and playing the accordion and dueting with the late Pedro Infante, whose catalog is owned by Warner. All the tunes on the album are by Infante. Freddie and Warner jointly release the CD, *Pedro Infante Y Ramon Ayala, Dos Voces Unidas Por Primera Vel* late last year.

"We share responsibility 50-50 in the marketing, promotion and profits," explains Martinez, Jr. "We've both put out several compilation albums and we want to do a high-profile project, so we developed this project." Ayala incidentally releases his 100th album for the label, *El Número Cien* (*Number 100*), prior to the duet compilation release. This recording is similar to the pop hit Natalie Cole achieves when she sings a duet with her late, great father Nat King Cole 12 years ago. "Capitol put a new music bed underneath Cole's original track for *Unforgettable* and it appears they're singing together. It's the same concept here with us using the original Pedro tracks, the majority of which are recorded in the '40s and early '50s for Peerless, whose catalog Warner bought several years ago."

Martinez, Sr., the album's producer and Ayala listen to more than 360 of Infante's tunes before selecting the repertoire. Notes

Martinez, Jr.: "Ramon hand-picks the songs that mean the most to him and he feels comfortable doing. His band, Sus Bravos Del Norte, comes in and recuts all the original music tracks. We're able to put Pedro's voice onto the new music track and make it appear they're singing duets together."

This is the label's first joint distribution deal for the U.S. "We have a distribution deal with Sony for Mexico and 10 years ago we did a compilation which includes six tracks from Ramón and Vicente Fernandez which has a limited release in the U.S."

How does he feel about the narco-corrido movement in which drug trafficking is sometimes condoned and even romanced? "We've had groups in the past that have recorded those types of songs. We don't have any now. And we don't have a policy in place where if a band wants to record a narco-corrido song we wouldn't be completely opposed to it. But at the same time, we're not encouraging it either or actively seek artists that'll record that particular style. There's an audience out there for it, and we're in the business to sell records, but it's not something we actively seek." In 2004, Freddie signs a number of artists who choose to switch from major labels, including Jimmy Gonzalez Y El Grupo Mazz, Michael Salgado, and La Tropa F, the latter having earlier recorded for Freddie. The label also snares the reformed and reunited La Fiebre, a formidable Tejano band of the early '90s, which disbands eight years ago and reemerges with its new *Reunidos* CD.

Balboa/Musart, the Culver City, California-based regional Mexican specialist, has its own rich catalog of albums. It loses one of its premiere artists, mariachi balladeer 34-year-old Pepe Aguilar this year to Univision Records, which has greater national distribution. Having started to freshening up his style with electric keyboards and guitars as adjuncts to the traditional strings, trumpets, and guitarron in the waning years of his Balboa relationship, his final Balboa album, *Lo Mejor De Nostros*, reaches No. 10 on the *Billboard* Top Latin Album charts. With Univision securing space in major retail chains, Aguilar's first album for his new label, *Y Tenerte Otra Vez*, debuts on the best-selling chart at number two. One year later, Aguilar changes labels again, shifting this time to Sony Music.

In a move to stimulate catalog sales, Balboa sells 130 plus three CD sets at the phenomenal low budget price of $9.99 in an attempt to set the price so low that there is no profit for pirate firms to duplicate these products. Valentin Velasco, Balboa's president, boasts to *Billboard* that he doesn't "know of a single falsified three-pack in the market." With these three-packs translating to $3.33 a CD, Frank White, the label's vice president of operations and director of promotions, further tells the newsweekly that price is lower than what the pirates charge, which translates into selling "close to 250,000 copies per month of these special three-packs."

The label's lowball price for these special CDs is indicative of the low prices the regional Mexican albums are sold for because of the competition from pirates who sell their products at flea markets and swap meets at very low prices. Piracy is one of two factors especially injurious to regional Mexican product. The second impact occurs in California, the largest market for regional Mexican goods, from cheaper priced Mexican imports.

Among its artists being offered in single CD collections at $5.99 budget prices is Joan Sebastian, whose CD is *Colección De Oro*. Sebastian is a recent winner of two Latin Grammys this year for best banda album and best banda song, both from the album *Afortunado*. Balboa's roster also includes Grammy-winning Banda Cuisillos plus Adan Cuen, Paquita La Del Barrio, Pancho Barraza, Axé Bahia, and José Julian among others. One year later, the low-price strategy helps sell the single dance music CD *Za Za Za* (*Mesa Que Mas Aplauda*) by Veracruz, Mexico's Climax Club DJ Osskar Lobo and his similarly titled Grupo Climax trio. One of Disa's hot acts is Mexico's 24-year-old sextet Patrulla 81, which in 2004 lands two albums on *Billboard*'s Top Latin Albums chart, *Cómo Pude Enamorarme De Ti* and the live date *En Vivo Desde: Dallas, Texas*. One year later, its *Divina* reaches the number two spot on the survey.

One English-language blues specialty label, Arhoolie of El Cerrito, California, has a strong Tejano catalog because its owner, blues aficionado Chris Strachwitz is steered towards the work of San Antonio accordion player Flaco Jiménez by Genie Wolf-Miri, who operates the Rio Record store in that city. Jiménez is represented in Arhoolie's Tejano catalog with seven albums. Strachwitz also records Flaco's brother Santiago Jiménez, Jr. and their father Don Santiago Jiménez, along with a long list of Tejano artists, and a smattering of other Mexican genres. His slogan for the company, "Down Home Music Since 1960," reflects the year he starts in business and its emphasis on roots music of America and other world nations, including Mexico.

While blues buffs recognize Arhoolie's achievements, they might be surprised by how strong its links are with regional Mexican music. But it's only through my research for this book that I uncover Chris' history with Tejano, Tex-Mex and regional Mexican music.

As a reporter and jazz and blues buff myself at *Billboard*, I've done a number of interviews with owner Chris Strachwitz focusing on his blues endeavors for the label.

As he explains in his Website history of his company: "Over the years I had stopped in San Antonio because I had become very fond of Mexican music, but wasn't sure if I could sell it to the blues lovers around the world who were my prime audience. I would often drop by to visit Genie Wolf-Miri whose late husband produced Rio Records. She operates the Rio Record shop and tells me that of all the fine accordionists in San Antonio, Flaco Jiménez is the one who has the charisma to become a star. She was right and Flaco has since taken conjunto/norteño music around the world. He won us a Grammy with the album *Ay Te Dejo En San Antonio*."

Arhoolie's roots series of Tejano albums include the first songs Flaco records for Rio, which Strachwitz acquires and releases in 1995. The label also introduces historic 78 and 45 r.p.m. discs in a series devoted to Mexican American border music on its Folklyric Records imprint. *Pioneer Recording Artists 1928–1958* is the first in a series of

CDs initially released in 2002, featuring 26 tunes from Strachwitz's own collection of 78s and 45s which are transferred to CD. The majority of the discs reflect the norteño and conjunto music created on either side of the Rio Grande in San Antonio and Monterrey, Nuevo Leon, Mexico, the creative centers for this music.

Among the Tejano artists on Arhoolie are several with historically slanted titles: Lydia Mendoza, and her *First Queen of Tejano* CD, one of six albums in the catalog in addition to appearing on volume one of *Pioneering Recording Artists*; Narciso Martinez, labeled the *Father of Texas-Mexican Conjunto* on one of his albums; Valerio Longoria with *Texas Conjunto Pioneer* and Chris Sandoval with his *Pioneer of Tejano Music* CD. Freddie Fender has no pretenses in any of his three Tejano record titles. All told, there are 49 regional Mexican titles in the Arhoolie catalog.

This masterful collection of vintage regional Mexican and Tex-Mex albums, purportedly the world's largest collection of recorded music for these two genres, finds a public home in 2005 when the recordings are transferred digitally to UCLA's Digital Library Program, explains the *Los Angeles Times*. In a collaborative effort involving 73-year-old Strachwitz, UCLA Spanish professor Guillermo Hernandez, the UCLA Chicano Studies Research Center Project, the New Mexico Fund for Folk Culture, Los Tigres Del Norte Fund at UCLA and its Fonovisa record label, both of whom are financing the project, the first 16,000 78 r.p.m. recordings representing the first half of the 20th century will be available during the summer via Internet access. Phase two will involve transferring 14,000 45 r.p.m.s and 3,000 albums spanning the 1950s–1990s. The digital transferring is being done at the label's headquarters by employee Antonio Cuellar before the watchful eye and ear of Strachwitz, whose fascination with Mexican roots music prods him into acquiring and developing a collection of what are historical gems of Mexican culture.

In a phone conversation with Strachwitz (in 2005), he tells me he's still finding records to go into the digital collection and "likes regional Mexican music, preferring mostly rural stuff from the country, cantina music, which in English is honky tonk. Its low-class music and I feel it like I feel the blues." "How's your Spanish?" I ask. "It's pretty bad," he admits, adding, "I feel it more than I speak it. You let your imagination tell you what you're hearing; you kind of feel the soulfulness." He eschews today's Mexican pop, stressing, "it doesn't do much for me. They're pop schlock singers who could be from any place but they happen to sing in Spanish." I ask him how his fondness for Mexican music turns into first a commercial enterprise and then a benevolent gesture. And he unravels his early life's journey, which takes him from his native Germany to Santa Barbara, California where he hears his first Mexican music on the radio, first on a powerful Mexican station and then on a low wattage station from a nearby city.

Chris, his mother, four sisters and brother migrate from German to Reno, Nevada, in 1947 where his great aunt lives. He's 16 at the time his family arrives two years after the end of World War II, with his father following one year later. The family lives in Reno until the late '60s when he travels to California and attends private school near Santa Barbara. "That's when I hear Mexican music for the first time on two radio stations, XERB-AM Rosarito Beach in Baja, Mexico, and a 250-watt station in Santa Paula which plays rancheras in the afternoon," he explains.

After attending Pomona College, the University of California at Berkeley, going in the U.S. Army and then teaching German at a high school in Los Gatos, he starts Arhoolie in that city and then shifts to El Cerrito in the 1970s. Presently residing in Berkeley, which is next to El Cerrito in Northern California, the venerable aficionado is "constantly listening to Mexican music on three Bay Area Spanish-language stations. His 50 year record hunting escapade begins in the '60s when he starts traveling to Texas, Louisiana, Arizona, and New Mexico exploring for blues records. In Texas "while looking through jukebox stacks looking for blues records, I find Mexican records which I'd heard on the radio." These early forays produce "tons of records including early mariachi records by the Cuarteto Coculense, which records on a cylinder for Edison in 1908 in Mexico City. It's the only cylinder I own. Edison, RCA Victor, and Columbia are the three American companies recording in Mexico City, where they all record the same artists."

Strachwitz points to the '70s when he starts to sense collecting Mexican discs could become a major enterprise. "It became noticeable to me," he recalls, "when I was contacted about buying enormous quantities of those discs. Through a collector of Hawaiian music I was able to acquire the Vocalion 8000 series of pure Mexican music.

"It's very important you understand that all the first Mexican artists are recorded on this side of the border by American companies, some of whom record them in New York and Los Angeles. They also go to Mexico City from 1904–1908 to make all acoustic recordings. Around 1925 electrical recording is introduced and by 1928, American companies are taking their equipment into the field to record Mexican music. The Mexican companies are recording well-to-do singers appealing to people who can afford to buy records."

Can he suggest a financial value for his collection? "I can't put a price tag on it because a lot are one of a kind, including several hundred early Vocalions and Victors."

As Chris Strachwitz learns, the key to selling records is inexorably tied to using conventional regional Mexican radio stations, generally found in communities with large Mexican populations. Regional Mexican stations attract 17.7 percent of Latino listeners, the largest number of all the Spanish-language radio formats, according to the Arbitron ratings company's 2003 edition of "Hispanic Radio Today, How America Listens To Radio." Regional Mexican listeners are 58 percent men 18 years and older, while women in the same age group represent 42 percent of the radio audience. Specifically, persons in the 18-to 44-year old bracket, account for 73 percent of the format's listeners. This subject of Hispanic radio is explored in Chapter 14, which covers my research trip to New York in 2004 and my meeting with Arbitron executives.

One of the regional Mexican stations which specializes, even loves, playing music by new, non-traditional regional Mexican bands is Liberman Broadcasting's Burbank located KBUE-FM (La Quen Buena). Previously playing romantic ranchera music by established singers, the station switches to cutting edge music with the hiring in 1998 of songwriter/music publisher Pepe Garza as program director by Liberman's vice president of programming Eduardo León, who admits the station is playing a brand of music already available on other stations with a stronger signal. So the duo begins researching the tastes of the Hispanic community where they discover young people are interested in corrido artists not being played on L.A. radio. During its first five years, the station provides exposure to the narco-corridos movement in which bands extol the exploits of drug dealers; provides airplay in 2004 for the trendy music developing out of Durango, Mexico, called música Duranguense (the music of Durango) but popularized by Mexican bands living in Chicago—go figure the geographical logic in this—and the rap en Español movement. Program director Pepe Garza tells *Billboard* the prime listeners for this music are 18-to-43-year-olds, an audience void which traditional regional Mexican stations currently eschew. He also notes many Hispanics live in neighborhoods also populated by African Americans, so they are exposed to rap music.

For the past four years KBUE honors these trendy artists with its Premios Que Buena annual regional Mexican Music Awards at the Universal Amphitheatre. Winners are selected by the public, which votes at participating business locations and on the Internet. Among the artists performing this year: Ramon Ayala, Los Razos De Sacremento, and award-winning Akwid.

The 2004 winners: Conjunto Primavera with three awards for artist of the year, best norteño band and best norteño song for its hit *Una Vez Más*; Akwid and Adán Sánchez with two trophies each, Akwid named artist of the year and top song recipient in the urban regional field (which combines rap with banda), while Sánchez wins as both solo and best looking artist of the year. Single awards also go to La Banda El Recodo, Grupo Montéz De Durango, Tucanes De Tijuana,

Jenni Rivera, Valentin Elizalde, Dueto Voices Del Rancho, and El Coyote Y Su Banda Tierra Santa.

Despite its niche format, or because of it, the station is ranked either 10th or 11th in the Arbitron ratings, behind three other Spanish formats, including two traditional regional Mexican proponents, KLAX and KSCA and KLVE, which features adult contemporary artists.

Four Mexican acts celebrate significant anniversaries in 2003: La Banda El Recodo, formed 65 years ago in 1938; José José 40 years; Conjunto Primavera 25 anniversaries and Intocable reaching the 10-year mark. La Banda El Recodo, formed in Mazatlán, Mexico, is unique in that in addition to being the oldest band still working, it's also the largest, employing 17–18 members whose fiery trumpets, trumpets and clarinets, trombone, tuba, percussion, and tight vocal harmonies, set sparks flying during its appearances in domestic Latin markets, Australia, Japan and South and Central America and on the 2003 and 2004 Latin Grammy Awards telecasts. In fact, when I catch the band for the first time during the 2004 broadcast, its unique acoustic instrumental sound and stage presentation jolt me out of my seat, they are that engaging…and good.

While the term banda refers to a big, brass band sound usually played by 10 to 15 members, El Recodo's history dates back to the Mexican state of Sinaloa, with the current ensemble maintaining the tradition of melding Mexican and German polka and waltz influences (brought to Mexico in the middle of the 19th century) used by its founder and first leader clarinetist Don Cruz "Crucillo" Lizárraga. Lizárraga passes away on July 17, 1995, at age 77, with his son Germán taking over as leader until 2002, when brother Alfonso takes over the baton. Alfonso and brother Joel, along with Luis Antonio "Mimoso" Martinez, are the vocal front line for the band, one of Fonovisa's top touring acts. Since 1991, it records for RCA, ARO Music, La Sierra, Sony Discos, and WEA. During its career, it records more than 160 albums, dating back to its initial hits during the 1940s. During the 1940-'50 era, it also records the soundtracks for a number of Mexican films, broadening its appeal throughout Mexico from its Sinaloa base. During the '60s and '70s, the band boosts its vocal prowess while remaining a Western area Mexican favorite. During the '80s when the dance craze called quebradita is popular and bands are adding keyboards and electric guitars, boosting a strong vocal presence while trimming their woodwind sections, El Recodo retains its acoustic sound. By the time the quebradita techno-banda craze fades in the mid-90s, El Recodo's style encompasses rancheras, waltzes, boleros, and cumbias. Throughout its history, the band's brass, tuba and clarinet sound remains its basic sound, albeit with the addition of bongos, congas, and guira. Within *Billboard*'s anniversary special, Joel Lizárraga calls the brass the band's "essence, the percussion the filling, the clarinet and tuba the defining sound, with the tuba the bass of the harmony."

The band's musicality touches the U.S. in 2001, when a sing-along ranchera single, *Y Llegaste Tu* from the album *Contigo Por Siempre* catches the ears of Hispanics in Texas and winds up on *Billboard*'s Regional Mexican Airplay survey for 47 weeks, winding up at No. 1. The album is named best banda record during the 2001 Latin Grammys. Among its sundry recordings, in addition to its basic instrumental albums are ranchera tributes to legends Juan Gabriel in 1997 and Vicente Fernández in 2002. The band will emerge as an explosive force following its spectacular performance during the 2004 Latin Grammys, which provides a national platform for its version of a modern Mexican swing band. One year later, it returns to its traditional Mexican roots with the album *Hay Amor*, which focuses on rancheras and romantic melodies from its home state of Sinaloa. An accompanying DVD recasts the band's history as well as the town of El Recodo, which provides the ensemble with its name.

Conjunto Primavera is Ojinaga, Chihuahua, Mexico's musical ambassador. The sextet is formed on the first day of spring 1978 and features singer Tony Melendez, accordionist/keyboardist Felix Contreras, saxophonist Juan Dominguez, bajo sextoist Rolando Perez, bassist Oscar Ochoa, and drummer Adan Huerta. Its first 20 albums are issued on the small Joey label, followed by an affiliation with AFG Sigma starting in 1995, where it gains its first gold record for *Me Nortie*. In later years, Juan Ramirez joins on saxophone and the band becomes a Fonovisa act and continues recording hit albums.

It blends tinges of ranchero, norteño, bolero, and cumbia to create a diverging sound on its 31st album, *Decide Tú* (*Decide Yourself*). Its impact on the musical genre results in its gaining two Latin Grammy nominations this year, best norteño album for *Perdoname Mi Amor*, and best regional Mexican song for the title cut. Two additional albums, *Necesito Decirte and Ansia De Amar*, are also big sellers, which in turn helps rank the band along with Los Tigres Del Norte and Los Tucanes De Tijuana as the top-selling norteño bands in the U.S., according to the *San Antonio Express-News*.

Intocable, located in Zapata, releases its anniversary album, *10* on EMI Latin, which expands the national audience for the Tejano norteño specialists, initiated with its 1999 release, *Contigo*. Today, the band's amalgamation of sounds, ranging from rancheras, boleros, and rock undercoatings, ensures large crowds for its public appearances.

On a local level, San Antonio favorite Linda Escobar Y Su Conjunto, celebrates her 40th year in show business and her 47th birthday. She's been singing professionally since she's seven years old.

One artist who doesn't turn pro that young is José José, whose legal name is José Rómulo Sosa Ortíz, and the son of famous Mexican opera tenor turned concert pianist José Sosa Esquivel and concert pianist Margarita Ortiz De Sosa. When his father passes away in 1968, he takes his father's similar first name as a memorial tribute and becomes José José. The current 55-year-old vocalist, who starts singing with a trio on the streets of Mexico City as a teenager, returns to the trio format this year with three CDs under the El Principe Con Trio banner on BMG U.S. Latin. The romantic balladeer is often referred to as El Principe De La Canción (The Prince of Song) because of his pioneering efforts in combining love songs built around mariachi, bolero, and American pop tunes for three decades, starting in the '60s through the '90s.

While his career is marked by three marriages and bouts with alcoholism, his musical style remains dominant through his initial recordings for Discos/Orfeon (1963), RCA (1967), Ariola Music (1976) and subsequently BMG, now the parent company that includes RCA as one of its labels. By 1983, the artist is holding his own with the likes of Julio Iglesias, Roberto Carlos, and José Luis Rodríguez, according to a *Billboard* profile. His popularity earns him nine Grammy nominations between the mid-'80s and early '90s. In 1987, he salutes one of his American idols, Frank Sinatra, by performing two of his signature songs, *New York, New York* and *I've Got You Under My Skin*, during a Radio City Music Hall concert in New York City. In 1986, he gets together with another Sinatra-inspired vocalist, Paul Anka, for the duet *Déjame Conocerte* (*Let Me Get to Know You*) on Anka's *Amigos* Latin-flavored album. Shifting gears in 200l, he records his first mariachi album, *Tenampa*, which Juan Gabriel produces and plays a major role in writing or collaborating on all the songs.

His influence on other singers is recognized in 1998 when a plethora of alternative stalwarts like Molotov, El Gran Silencio, Moenia, vocalist Juliet Venegas, and members of La Ley produce a rock salute to his non-rock compositions on the album, *Volcán: Tributo A José José* and in 2002 by the San Antonio Hispanic Heritage Society which awards him its Tito Guízar Award. Future plans include a possible duets album in 2005 and sitting on the other side of the control room glass to produce albums by his son José Joel, 27, and daughter Marysol, 21, his children from his second marriage.

On a more conventional level, José León (Hernandez, who does not use his last name professionally) and his quintet Solitario perform traditional cumbias, the 18-year veteran's vocals and accordion leads producing dance infectious rhythms. Growing up in Washington State to parents working the migrant labor fields, he performs with area bands and when he arrives in San Antonio in 1995, is signed to a contract by Catalina Records owner Arthur Cadena.

Bronco El Gigante De América, one of the top regional Mexican norteño bands formed in 1978 by four friends in Apodaca, Nuevo León, Mexico, disbands in 1996, and returns this year as the quintet El Gigante De America. During its hot run in the '90s, the band records six albums for Fonovisa, has a comic book named after it, appears as themselves in a Mexican TV soap opera, and after deciding to pack it in, visits 11 countries during its "Gira De Adios (Goodbye Tour)," culminating in Mexico City's huge Estadio Azteca venue. Of the group's members, José Guadalupe Esparza (vocalist/bassist), Javier Villarreal (guitar), José Luis Villarreal (drums) and Ramiro Delgado (accordion/keyboards), Delgado and Esparza go out on their own; Delgado with BMG U.S. Latin and Esparza with Fonovisa. When they reform, the band adds a fifth member, Aurelio Esparza on percussion. He's José Guadalupe's brother. The quartet's grupera sound is rekindled on its new Fonovisa recording *Siempre Arriba*, which features ballads and danceable cumbias.

Grupo Montéz De Durango of Chicago, a heretofore local regional Mexican septet, bursts onto the national scene this year with its second album on Disa, the indie label half-owned by Univision, which uses its TV network to promote the band's Duranguense music and its Universal Music & Video Distribution to obtain radio play and secure shelf space in such mass market retainers like Wal-Mart, Best Buy and Kmart, augmented by in-store appearances in Chicago, Los Angeles and Las Vegas. Chicago's WOJO (La Que Buena), is the first station to play the band and other groups on small independent labels. As a result of this multi-platform exposure, the album, *De Durango A Chicago*, not only lands on the *Billboard* Top Latin Albums chart in the second position November 1, but also debuts on the magazine's top 200 album chart in 88th place. The band's connection to the popular dance style called El Pasito Duranguense (The Durango Step), created originally by another Chicago band, La Raza De Chicago, is a key factor in building its reputation in Chicago and the surrounding areas.

Formed seven years ago by Jose Luis Terrazas as a band which morphs into playing trendy Duranguense dance music built around a combination of merengue and ranchera elements, the group's debut is on the Terrazas label, which in turn leads to BMG Latin where the group records one uneventful album. Despite this lack of sales success, the band signs with Disa whose initial CD, *El Sube Y Baja*, in 2002 makes enough noise to remain on the Top Latin Albums chart for more than 23 weeks and peak at No. 43.

Following the band's first acceptance in the Midwest, its infectious sound next breaks in the Southwest, notably Texas and then in California.

Terrazas, a percussionist, is a native of Durango, Mexico, and grows up in Chicago, where traditional Mexican banda groups headline dances in the area. So forming his own band that includes two of his sons, Terrazas and cohorts join other Chicago bands playing the dance music, including label mates Braceros and Los Horóscopos De Durango, Univision's Alacranes Musical, and Universal's Conjunto Atardecer, according to a *Billboard* feature on Durangoish music.

Another Chicago band blending Duranguense influences with regional stylistic ingredients from Mexico's Zacatecas and Michoacán regions is Prófugos De Chicago, which accomplishes this fusion replete with fiery trumpets and trombones on *A Poco No*. Albums by Grupo Montéz and Prófugos are the forerunners of 2004's explosive breakout from "The Windy City" of a full-blown Duranguense movement on Disa.

By May of 2005, this trendy sound reaches the *Billboard* Top Albums chart, fuelled by Disa's Patrulla 81, a Mexican, not Chicago band, and its *Divina* CD. Other genre bands on the survey include Grupo Montéz De Durango and Los Horóscopos De Durango.

San Antonio is home to two awards events saluting Tejano artists in '03. The National Hispanic Music Hall of Fame honors six artists at the organization's annual induction ceremony taking place at Randy's Ballroom. Lauded are Domingo "Mingo" Saldivar, the late Valerio Longoria, Paulino Bernal, Martin Macias, Mariachi "Art Lopez" Chapultepec, and Narciso Martinez. Sam Zuniga, the organization's founder and president, lauds the inductees in the *Express-News* as a "continuous pillar of Tejano musicians who have made major contributions," adding: "With these six individuals, we now have 116 people who have been recognized since the start of the Hall of Fame at the beginning of the Tejano Music Awards in 1980."

The 23rd Annual Tejano Music Awards moves from the Alamodome after nine years to Freeman Coliseum, where the Texas Talent Musicians Association (TTMA) hands out its accolades. Top winners include Jimmy Gonzalez Y El Grupo Mass, with three awards and Jennifer Peña with two trophies. Gonzalez and cohorts win the best crossover song for *Ahora Que Hago Sin Ti* (*Now What Do I Do Without You*), best album group for *Si Me Faltas Tu* (*If You're Not Here*), and best song for *Yo Te Voy A Amar* (*I'm Going to Love You*). Peña's honors are for best female vocalist and entertainer. In other categories, the Kumbia Kings are named best show band; A.B. Quintanilla III, its leader, is named best male entertainer; the Chris Perez Band walks away with the most promising band honor; while the conjunto progressive plaque goes to David Lee Garza Y Los Musicales for its album *Estamos Unidos* (*We're United*). Awards are presented in 14 categories with the winners chosen by fans who contact the awards organization for ballots.

In San Antonio, Hispanics represent 49 percent of the population, with Hispanic Broadcasting Corporation's KXTN-FM, which plays Tejano, in ninth place in the morning and afternoon drive time hours. It is one of HBC's six Spanish stations in the market and the biggest money-earner among the city's FM stations, according to the BIA Financial Network.

In 2004, regional Mexican albums continue to pace the Latin record industry, accounting for 59 percent of all Spanish-language album purchases in this country, according to the Recording Industry Association of America's latest statistics covering the mid-year period. Regional Mexican labels Fonovisa, Disa, and Balboa/Musart help the domestic Latin record industry's first half-year sales rise 28 percent over last year's similar period, reports Nielsen SoundScan, which tracks retail sales at mass merchant chains. While Univision-Fonovisa and Disa sales rise 33 percent over last year's 28.3 figure, Balboa's sales rise 25 percent over last year. Balboa's president Valentin Velasco credits its sales rise in *Billboard* to its increased presence in major retail outlets and its low-priced merchandise, including three CD packs for $7.50. One album selling for $5.99 is *Za Za Za* by Veracruz, Mexico's, Grupo Climax. DJ Osskar Lobo, owner of the Climax Club, writes several of the album's dance tunes which garner local radio play and club sales, resulting in Balboa offering Lobo a contract, with the album and a similarly titled single landing on Billboard's national Latin charts. The band additionally winds up being Balboa/Musart's surprising hit artist of the year, with its album winding up No. 1 on *Billboard*'s year-end recap of Regional Mexican albums.

Several regional artists alter their styles to seek broader audience acceptance (covered in Chapter 19), while urban regional music, the euphemism for a fusion of norteño, banda and rap, enlarges into various offspring styles which ignite the continued transformation of regional Mexican into new grooves. Young rappers en Español, eager to control their careers, and destinies, start their own record companies. The Chicago-based música Duranguense dance style continues its trendy expansion following its initial breakout last year. The Univision Music Group of labels maintains its leadership position as the home for best-selling albums.

While a number of new independent record labels join the traditional regional Mexican community: Dope House Records, Urbana Records and F.O.G. in Houston; ARC in San Antonio; Hacienda Records and Crown Records in Corpus Christi, and Thumb Records of Pomona, California, for example, the growth of urban regional music within the broad spectrum of traditional regional Mexican music is a major happening, chronicled by *Billboard* and the *San Antonio Express-News*. At the core of the urban regional growth is an impressively growing list of believers joining the Kumbia Kings and Akwid, who either add rap and rap/R&B flavored tunes to their different regional Mexican styles to attract young ears. These adventurers include Mexiclan, ATM, Lil J, Yolanda Perez, DJ Kane, Chingo Bling, SPM (South Park Mexican), Brown Boy, Don Cisco, Hispanic MC, Baby Bash, Amanda Perez, Los Razos, Big Circo, Quinto Sol, Kingz One, La Conquista, La Sombra, Grupo Chevere, and Stefani Montiel.

Stefani, who previously records for Sony Discos, admits to *Billboard* that while her main stress is on cumbia dance tempos, she includes R&B and hip-hop on her new World album, *Takin' on the World*, "because we are really trying to appeal to the youth." The inclusion of multi-elements, she stresses, continues the tradition of music and culture reflecting society's evolving tastes.

With Spanish-language regional Mexican and pop radio taking an almost hands-off approach to playing urban regional artists, Tejano stars seek to recapture young fans who grow tired of the traditional sound on Tejano-formatted stations and seek enrichment through bilingual rap acts. Some Anglo radio stations slowly add these bilingual rap records to their playlists to attract young Hispanics. This uneven radio exposure forces record company boosters of the subgenre to circumvent the lack of radio exposure by going "to the street" with promotional efforts at flea markets, low-rider shows and music festivals.

Not only are Latinos rapping in Spanish, but also their attire and appearance apes the hit Anglo rappers in terms of large sized casual shirts and pants, backward baseball caps, lots of dangling jewelry and obvious body tattoos.

This year, música Duranguense, gains a respected place among the hybrids, thus expanding the reach of regional Mexican music. Led by the pioneering breakout band, Grupo Montéz De Durango and its Universal Music & Video distributed hit Disa albums, *Durango A Chicago*, followed by its first live recording, *En Vivo Desde Chicago*, a number of other Duranguense groups also gain positions on *Billboard*'s Top Latin Albums chart, notably K-Paz De La Sierra, Conjunto Atardecer, Patrulla 81, Los Horóscopos De Durango and four artist compilations on Disa. The magazine's regional Mexican airplay survey also reflects the music's popularity, with three Duranguense bands represented among the top five slots, especially Los Horóscopos De Durango's tune, *Dos Locos*, in the top position.

With the exception of Conjunto Atardecer, which records for MusiMex/Universal, all the other groups are on the Procan imprint which is distributed by Disa through Universal Music & Video Distribution. While K-Paz is formed by former Grupo Montéz members, the other novice bands gain experience on independent labels well below the national publicity spotlight prior to Grupo Montéz's debut last year.

Not content to build on its original sound, Grupo Montéz De Durango's next album contains urban regional ingredients, according to Disa's executive vice president of sales and marketing Jeff Young. The label also releases a children's album pairing the character El Moro with the music of Durango.

The success of Univision Music Group labels, Univision, Fonovisa, and Disa, the latter a partnership with its Mexican founders, the Chavez family, provides Universal Music & Video Distribution with strong product, which enables it to place nine of its album in the top 10 slots on *Billboard*'s Top Latin Albums chart for two weeks in June. Artists in this unheard of situation, which Univision Music Group's president/CEO Jose Behar labels "unprecedented," are Univision's Lupillo Rivera in first place for two weeks with *Con Mis Propias*; Jennifer Peña's *Seduccion* which starts at the top and drops to number five and Los Huracanes Del Norte's *Con Experiencia Y Juventad* in sixth place; Fonovisa's Conjunto Primavera at number two with *Dejando Huella* and Banda El Recodo's *Exitos Con Tradición* at number seven. Disa has four albums in the top 10: Los Horóscopos De Durango in third place, Groupo Montéz De Durango in fourth, and various artist compilations, ninth and tenth. Although Disa's 2001 half-ownership with Univision calls for the U.S. company to buy out its remaining assets by June of 2006, according to *Billboard*, when the sale is not completed, Disa files a breach of contract suit on July 18 in U.S. District Court in the Central District of California. The suit, according to *Daily Variety*, alleges Univision employs "heavy handed legal tactics" to sidestep buying the remaining shares of Disa.

In an aggressive move to build its regional Mexican presence, Sony Music Norte aligns itself with two new labels, Serca Music, owned by manager Servando Cano and music publisher Serca, located in Monterrey, Mexico, and Mexa Music, owned by Miguel Trujillo, formerly EMI Latin USA's vice president/general manager of its regional Mexican/Tejano division. Now here's a convenient twist: Trujillo, who'll act as a consultant for Sony, is a former Serca U.S. marketing/promotion maven, and it's through this connection that he brings Serca to Sony.

Mexa is a branch of Mexa Entertainment, with offices in Los Angeles and McAllen, Texas. The two deals are for three years. While Mexa is searching for new and established acts to sign, Serca's roster includes Los Herederos De Nuevo Leon, Pancho (former lead singer with Los Tigrillos), and El Rey De La Cumbia Nortena.

A note of sadness hallmarks the death of rising teen idol Adán Sánchez in a car crash in Sinaloa, Mexico. The 19-year-old Los Angeles-born son of the late corrido vocalist Chalino Sánchez is on a promotional tour throughout Northwestern Mexico, March 27 when a tire blows on his 1989 Ford Crown Victoria causing it to overturn, killing him instantly from severe head injuries, according to Mexican authorities. The irony in the rising star's death is that his father, a narco-corridos song specialist, was slain execution-style in Sinaloa 12 years ago. He was 32; Adán was eight at the time.

The death of Sánchez, who helps build the Los Angeles regional Mexican artist community, and is on the cusp of stardom, draws the kind of attention on the West Coast and on Spanish-language TV and radio garnered by major celebrities.

Prior to his passing, Univision releases his album *Un Soñador* (*A Dreamer*), which contains Adán's tribute tune to his dad, *Arriba Chalino Sánchez* (*Long Live Chalino Sánchez*). And a week before his death, Sánchez headlines and sells out the prestigious 3,650-seat Kodak Theater in Hollywood, becoming the youngest performer to play the three-year-old venue. During his career, Chalino dramatically alters traditional corridos utilizing accordion-led polkas and waltzes when he starts assertively singing about the drug criminals. Following a concert in Sinaloa, the vocalist and his brother Espiridion, according to reports, are stopped in traffic by armed men in a federal police car and taken away. The brother is released and the next morning Chalino's body is found by an irrigation canal, blindfolded, his wrists contain rope marks and he's been shot twice in the back of his head, according to the *LA Weekly*.

Chalino starts out recording for a small L.A. label Cintas Acuario and then graduates to Sony, EMI, and Univision, which re-release his albums or sign new singers influenced by his narco-corridos. One of these South-Central L.A. copycat singers, Edgar Aguilar, who starts listening to Chalino three years after his death, makes the frightening observation to the *LA Weekly* that life in the Los Angeles barrio is "about selling dope, smoking dope, shooting people."

Unlike his father, Adán's music eschews narco-corridos in favor of love ballads and up tempo songs built around banda and norteño arrangements. Known to his fans as *El Compita* (*Little Buddy*), his recording career spans 11 years with Rosalino, Musart, Luna Music, and Univision and produces eight albums, his national breakout occurring last year when he signs with Univision Records and his debut album, *Un Soñador*, lands on the *Billboard* Top Latin Album chart.

Abel De Luna, whose Luna Music independent label releases six albums by Adán, plans releasing a CD of previously unreleased material by the performer on April 15, the day the singer would have turned 20. Univision has three finished songs for the album Sánchez is working on at the time of his death. Jose Behar, EMI Latin's president, says there are no immediate plans for a memorial album. Having signed Selena to the label prior to her being murdered in

1995, Behar tells the *Los Angeles Times*: "I've been through this experience before. The one thing we are not going to do is exploit his death. Anything we do will be with the blessing of his mother and manager."

As the leading young voice within Los Angeles' Mexican music community, Adán's death takes on Herculean proportions. On Sunday, the day following the death announcement, thousands of fans gather at Lincoln Park in East L.A. Other fans bring flowers and candles to the Burbank studios of KBUE-FM, which conducts an Adán music marathon over the weekend. A massive response by an estimated 15,000 people at an evening memorial service in Norwalk on April 2 turns ugly when they are denied a glimpse of the singer's body. After tossing white roses and ribbons on the passing hearse escorted by Los Angeles County sheriff's patrol cars en route to the St. John of God church, the boisterous crowd prompts relatives to cut short the planned public viewing of the body after 9 p.m.

The size of the crowd, which overwhelms surprised law enforcement and the funeral director, forces the public showing to be moved back to 6 p.m. from 9 p.m. Some of the public is allowed into the church until 8 p.m. so a private service for the family can begin. As a result of the over-emotional reaction by fans, the family sets the next day's funeral at an undisclosed site. Fans flock to the church after learning about the memorial service on Spanish-language radio stations.

Eerily, Adán is heard dueting with rising banda star Yolanda Perez on the tune *Bueno Bye* from her debut Univision album *Dejenme Llorar* released in May, almost three months after his death. Perez, a 21-year-old bilingual singer mixes Spanglish, rap, and norteño rhythms on the song *Estoy Enamorada* which reflects the cultural chasm separating a bicultural American teenage girl and her traditional Mexican father.

Although Los Tigres Del Norte is known for helping create the narco-corrido stories about the violent Mexican drug scene in the 1972 with the Fama single, *Contrabando Y Traición*, based on the exploits of a drug dealer named Camelia La Tejana, the socially conscious norteño superstar group fuses its ballad stories within the blue collar sound of accordion-driven polkas and waltzes. Its newest Fonovisa album, *Pacto De Sangre* (*Blood Pact*), sets off an additional controversy with one of its timely topics. *Las Mujeres De Juárez* (*The Women of Juarez*), a story song about the Mexican government's inability to solve the more than 350 murders of women since 1993, many working in the border assembly plants for American firms called maquiladoras, is one of two tracks on the album which confronts explosive situations within Mexico and is the song which creates a controversy on the Mexican side of the border. The other song, *José Pérez León*, deals with the actual instance of 18 people, including León, who suffocate in a truck while being smuggled into the U.S. in May of last year. During its 35-year career, the band records 30 plus albums whose collective sales top 32 million copies.

In a *Billboard* article covering the band's history and the release of this album prior to the negatively reactive comments, band member Hernán Hernández offers the group's prescient belief that its corrido about the grisly homicides "is telling the government that people deserve to have these murders solved. Maybe a song can't resolve a problem, but you can at least let people know about what's not being done." Following the album's release March 30, it debuts at the top of the *Billboard* Top Latin Albums chart, its fifth album since 2000 to reach No. 1. During its 35-year career, the band records 30 plus albums whose cumulative sales top 32 million copies.

Arriving from Mexico in San Jose in 1968, the teenage quintet's powerful connection with the public begins in 1978 when it begins discussing immigration to this country on the tune *Vivan Los Mojados* (*Long Live the Wetbacks*), a new newsy topic mixed within its repertoire of stories about people and their heroic actions. So when it tackles the imponderable subject of the unsolved murders and disappearances of the women in Juarez in the state of Chihuahua across the border from El Paso, the hot light of their song generates critical fireworks. Their outrage at the murders of the women, many of them raped, also contains accusatory lyrics over police complicity in the serial-style murders. Two groups in Chihuahua strongly disapprove of the band's coverage of the murders, reports the *Los Angeles Times*, citing other media reporting on the emerging controversy, including some family members who feel the band is milking the situation for commercial gain. Victoria Caravelo, who heads the Chihuahua Women's Institute, tells *Reuters*, the British news agency, "The mothers say it's profiting from a tragedy" and they additionally don't want the song aired on the radio, according to the news service story. Taking a colder, economic business stance, Victor Valencia, who heads the Chihuahua state assembly, tells the Mexico City newspaper *El Universal* the tune fuels "an atmosphere of terror" which "generates a negative image of Ciudad Juarez."

Jorge Hernández, leader of the band which includes brothers Hernán, Jorge, Luis (who replaces brother Raúl), Eduardo, and cousin Oscar Lara, responds to Valencia's strident comments by telling the *Times*: "He says he wants to clean up the name of Ciudad Juarez and let's hope he does it. But it defies logic to think a song by Los Tigres would spur his concern at this late date. If he really wanted to defend his city, he should have started a long time ago."

Mexico's Los Temerarios (the fearless) has taken that adage to heart, aiming at the American market and scoring decisively since 1993, when its Fonovisa albums begin cracking the Top Latin Album charts. This year, brothers Gustavo and Adolfo Angel Alba transform their romantic grupo sound into their first ranchera album to commemorate their 27th year in show business. The band is on fire, with top-selling albums *Tributo Al Amor*, *La Mejor…Coleccion* (an earlier Disa best of collection) and its newest CD, *Veintisiete*, which consists of hits Adolfo recalls from his childhood rather than original songs he usually writes for the group. The CD's focus is on volatile love stories that resonate with average people.

The Fresnillo, Zacatecas, Mexico, band builds its ranchera sound by adding traditional instruments, including trumpets and violins, not normally connected to its keyboard propelled sound, which focuses on upscale romances. *Veintisiete*, released in 2004 and focusing on mariachi and ranchera music, features duets with two of the band's favorite singers, Javier Solis and Vicente Fernández, the latter appearing on *Las Llaves De Mi Alma*. The duet between the band's Gustavo and Solis on *Sombras* is a result of a technological pairing, not the two performing together in the studio, indicates the *San Antonio Express-News*.

The LP debuts at No. 2 on *Billboard*'s Top Latin Albums chart, vastly superseding its earlier Fonovisa release, *Tributo Al Amor*, which languishes in the middle number range. The new album also spawns a single, *Qué De Raro Tiene*, which is released to Spanish radio in ranchera, bolero, and pop versions, which helps garner airplay on stations that normally avoid regional Mexican music. By 2005, *Veintisiete* sales reach two million copies. Adolfo is recording three albums on his own, one focusing on ballads, the other two have strains of the double platinum album. The band, which becomes a power in grupo music in 2003 when regional Mexican favorites Bronco and Los Bukis are no longer working units, wins a *Billboard* Latin Music award in '05. The band starts out in 1977 as Conjunto La Brisa, then changes its name in 1982 to its present identity. Initially signing with CBS Mexico in 1983, the group switches to Disa in '88, which leads to its 12-year affiliation with Fonovisa. In addition to Adolfo on keyboards, Gustavo on guitar and lead vocals, cousin Fernando Angel on bass, the rhythm section is staffed by Jonathan Amabiliz on percussion and Karlo Vidal on drums.

Ranchera singer Graciela Beltrán hits pay dirt when she involves Conjunto Primavera on her Univision CD *Mi Otro Sentimento*. Band member Tony Melendez also duets with the Mexican singer on the single *Corazon Encadenado*. The album lands on *Billboard*'s regional Mexican best-seller list. Recorded in the San Antonio studio owned by Conjunto Primavera's manager, it's a mixture of norteño, cumbia, banda polkas, and some Latin pop influences.

In an effort to rekindle his lackluster recording career, Luis Miguel turns to his native roots on *Mexico En La Piel* on Warner Music Latina to recapture the excitement of his 1990's cascade of hits with a package of ranchera standards. Enlisting the backing of Mariachi Vargas De Tecalitlán, Miguel offers 13 time-tested tunes made famous by equally famous mariachi greats like Vicente Fernández and José Alfredo Jimenez in a musical gumbo of energetic orchestral arrangements. It takes a while, but Miguel's latest CD is spotlighted on TV network Azteca America's popular *Especial Musical* series January 25, 2005. The hour special, beamed to the network's 38 U.S. Hispanic markets, features the vocalist discussing the album, music videos, a number of which are played, and his personal life.

Fourteen years ago, a commercial enterprise creates a festival to celebrate Cinco De Mayo in Los Angeles. The 15th version of Fiesta Broadway this year, arranged by All Access Entertainment to encompass 11 blocks along downtown Broadway, a popular Hispanic shopping area, draws an estimated 500,000 persons who listen to a plethora of regional Mexican stylists and other musical genres on four stages, and visit copious food and gift stalls in the 80-degree heat. While Mexican pop singer/actress Lucero and mariachi vocalist Pedro Fernandez are named the festivals queen and king, the main musical attractions include Mariachi Divas, an all-female group, Tex-Mex accordionist Flaco Jimenez, norteña vocalist Jimena plus merengue singer Elvis Crespo, pop singer and former Miss Universe Alicia Machado, flamenco pop duo Andy & Lucas, salsa singer Rey Ruiz, and Cuban vocalist Albita Rodriguez. There are also regional Mexican dance companies and high school mariachi bands adding their own musical ingredients.

Miguel Chacon, the festival talent coordinator indicates to the *Los Angeles Times* that regional Mexican groups that are family-oriented are favored since the prime audience for the free event is working class Mexican.

San Antonio and Tejano music build on their vintage, interlocked relationship. Despite a reported decline in Tejano sales, the San Antonio-based Tejano Music Awards provides a happy environment for this branch of regional music during its 24th annual presentation. Taking place the first time at the Alamodome and at the Graham Central Station nightclub, the awards pay tribute to Jay Perez, Jimmy Gonzalez Y El Grupo Mazz, Marcos Orozco, Los Desperadoz, and Michael Salgado.

Perez nabs male entertainer, male vocalist and crossover tune for *Together* and vocal duo along with Ramiro Herrera for *No Me Volvere Enamorar*; Gonzalez wins best song and best album for *Te Llevo En Mi Alma* and *Live En El Valle*, respectively; Orozco is named most promising artist; Los Desperadoz wins best conjunto album for *Lucky 13*, and Salgado wins best norteño album for *Tu Musica Sin Fronteras*.

The National Hispanic Music Hall of Fame, also located in the city, inducts 12 musicians and groups during its third annual ceremonies. Included are pioneers Tito Guízar, Los Alegres De Terán and Los Relampagos Del Norte, along with Pedro Ayala, Paco Betancourt, Los Donnenos, Eligio Escobar, Eva Garza, Steve Jordan, Armando Marroquin, Raul Moreno, and Rita Vidaurri. The event's founder is Sam Zuniga, Tejano researcher and former historian for the Tejano Music Awards.

Conjunto artists in San Antonio honor one of their own, the late Valerio Longoria at a memorial festival at Rosedale Park in July organized by Rodolfo Lopez, president of the Conjunto Heritage Taller, a fairly new organization dedicated to preserving conjunto music. A dozen local bands appear at the event, which is being considered for an annual happening. One month later, the Conjunto Stampede Festival features five local groups at Mission County Park.

San Antonio's own, Jennifer Peña, seeks to broaden her audience with the Univision CD *Seducción* which combines ballads along with pop and salsa versions on the tune *Vivo E Muero En Tu Piel* and a number of cumbias to keep her loyal fan base content. The album works and becomes a No. 1 seller and is among the Univision Music Group's record-setting nine albums in the top 10 positions on the best-selling Latin album chart.

Two of the city's leading mariachi bands, Mariachi Campanas De America and Mariachi Las Altenas, are off to Hollywood to perform at the Mariachi USA Festival at the Hollywood Bowl June 26. Campanas, celebrating 25 years in show business, will also perform at the Hispanic Heritage Awards at the Kennedy Center for the Performing Arts in Washington in September. The Festival organization also hosts San Antonio's annual mariachi bash and plans to take the show on tour in the U.S. next year. Rodri J. Rodriguez, who is involved with Mariachi USA and heads up Rodri Entertainment, is planning to launch a mariachi tribute show in Las Vegas at the Planet Hollywood Hotel and Casino titled Mariachi Passion & Tribute. Already entrenched in the city is the 14th annual Las Vegas Mariachi Festival, Noche De Mariachis, at the Aladdin Theatre of the Performing Arts. Featured this year are headliners Mariachi Vargas De Tecalitlán, Mariachi Sol De Mexico De José Hernández, Mariachi Los Camperos De Nati Cano and the San Juan Folkloric Ballet. Special guests on the show's Telemundo telecast are Vikki Carr and José Luis Rodríguez.

The strength of Texas' Hispanic music industry is reflected in the lineup of 15 acts playing the 2004 Hispanic State Fair in San Antonio's Rosedale Park and the 2004 South Texas Conjunto Association Awards that same Sunday in July at the Municipal Auditorium in Harlingen. The Fair's musical attractions include Jimmy Gonzalez Y El Grupo Mazz, Grupo Vida, Los Palominos, Elida Reyna, La Fueza, Milagro, Stefani Montiel, Chente Barrera, Grupo Bryndis, Los Invasores, and Juan Tavares, among others. Performing at the Conjunto Awards Ceremony, which inducts Gilberto Lopez of Los Dos Gilbertos and Fidel Perez Y Su Conjunto into its Hall of Fame, are Joe Gonzalez, Los Volcanes, Jimmy Lee Y Tentacion, Ricky Naranjo Y Los Gamblers, Badd Boyz, Grupo Invasion, and Tina Y Los Gallitos.

A number of local San Antonio bands wage musical combat in the city's 20th annual Conjunto Shootout during two nights of competition at the Market Square. Among the bands vying for the audience's enthusiasm are Grupo Vida, Mingo Saldivar, Rodeo, Jaime Y Los Chamacos, Ricky Ruiz Y Los Escorpiones, Flaco Jimenez, Nick Villarreal, Los Astronautas, and Los Dorados Del Norte.

Although San Antonio is regional Mexican heaven, contemporary salsa fans are the targets at the Salsarengue-Reggaeton Festival in Eisenhower Park. Participating groups espousing the rap/salsa marriage include Andy and His Banda Mambo, Laly and His Rumba Orchestra, Tropicante Orchestra, Louis Shati and His Orchestra, and the Mayunbe Dance Company.

Headlining the 75th national convention in San Antonio of the League of United Latin American Citizens at the SBC Convention Center in July are an expanded Bronco quintet plus former Kumbia Kings vocalist DJ Kane (Houston's Jason Cano) and Poder Del Norte, the 15-year-old band from Monterrey. Monterrey is also the creative launch pad for such other acts as the El Gran Silencio quartet and vocalist Alicia Villarreal.

El Gran Silencio, with its blending of regional styles interspersed with some rap and rock, lands a slot at the House of Blues in Los Angeles. Comprised of brothers Tony and Cano Hernández (vocals and guitars), drummer Ezequiel Alvarado and accordionist Isaac "Campa" Valdéz, the Latin alternative band's dynamism lands it a live, acoustic six-tune performance guest shot the next morning on Los Angeles KCRW-FM's popular *Morning Becomes Eclectic* show hosted by station program director Nic Harcourt, who uses the band's manager to help translate his comments and questions into Spanish.

Vocalist Villarreal, formerly with the hit norteño band Grupo Límite two years ago, sets off on a solo career, with Universal Latino releasing her debut mariachi recording, *Por Lo Prohibido*, followed by *Cuando El Corazon Se Cruza* which is aimed at appealing to both norteño and mariachi fans. The album is a pastiche of norteño, mariachi, cumbia, flamenco, and R&B elements. It also introduces her upgraded non-regional Mexican appearance, consisting of a revealing blouse, torn jeans and long, flowing blond hair, all of which replaces many of her Grupo Límite accoutrements of cowboy hat, undamaged jeans and long braided hair.

On the opening tune, *Ausencia*, Villarreal duets with hot Spanish heartthrob David Bisbal, with the melody riding over strains of flamenco and mariachi. Cruz Martinez, her husband and current member of the Kumbia Kings, both produces and co-writes the songs on the album. Martinez is among the musicians working on Grupo Límite's 2002 hit album, *Soy Asi*. Villarreal informs the *San Antonio Express-News* she is "fortunate" that her record company suggests "Cruz Martinez to produce the album. The idea was to fuse mariachi and grupero norteño with the accordion and give it a Latino touch to appeal to new audiences."

By mid-year, all the albums on *Billboard*'s Regional Mexican chart are also on the broader appealing Top Latin Albums survey. Sharing this dual exposure are Los Temerarios, Marco Antonio Solís/Joan Sebastían, Akwid, Patrulla 81, Grupo Bryndis, Vicente Fernández, Grupo Climax, Duelo, Los Rieleros Del Norte/Adolfo Urias Y Su Lobo Norteño, Ana Bárbara, Conjunto Primavera, Los Horóscopos De Durango, Ramon Ayala Y Sus Bravos Del Norte, Los Tigres Del Norte, Liberacion, and four various artist compilations. Of this group, Los Temerarios and Grupo Climax are among the Latin acts also on the more impressive mainstream *Billboard* Top 200 Albums chart, notably Los Lonely Boys, Bronco, Marc Anthony, Marco Antonio Solís, and Joan Sebastían, an indication Hispanic albums are drawing enough sales to make the general market chart.

Two members of this aforementioned group, Joan Sebastían and Marco Antonio Solís, embark on their first-ever "Gira De Los Grandes" concert tour together, in which they'll perform 12 shows from July through October in California, Texas, Nevada, and Illinois. Their duet album on Fonovisa, *Dos Grandes*, is a major hit on the Top Latin Albums chart, while Solís' Fonovisa title, *La Historia Continua* and Sebastían's *Coleccion De Oro* on Musart are also listed.

Don Tosti and Isidro López, two pioneering stylists whose influence escapes the boundaries of time, pass away.

Tosti, a pioneer songwriter whose *Pachuco Boogie* in 1948 mirrors the emerging Los Angeles fashion trend among young Hispanics for wearing zoot suits and favoring American pop music, dies at 81 of cancer in his Palm Springs home, August 2. Pachuco music has a minor revival in 1978 as a result of the play *Zoot Suit*. Tosti's *Pachuco Boogie* is also the title of a 2002 Arhoolie Records compilation of pachuco songs, including the title tune. The music is an amalgam of swing, jump and boogie woogie tunes spiced with Spanish lyrics by bands in Los Angeles from 1948 to 1954.

Tosti, born Edmundo Martinez Tostado in El Paso, is a musical prodigy, playing violin and piano and adding standup bass when he moves to L.A. as a teen. When he's 19 he's hired by Jack Teagarden to play trombone, his latest musical conquest, in the jazz trombonist's band, one of the few Mexican Americans to play in such swing bands of the '40s and '50s as Jimmy Dorsey, Les Brown and Charlie Barnett. After this band education, he forms his own ensemble, the Pachuco Boogie Boys and in the '60s moves to Palm Springs where he leads his orchestra at local area hotels.

Tosti's musical influence is felt in Houston where Los Skarnales combines pachuco boogie with Jamaican ska and reggae and other world music influences on its own Megalith album *Pachuco Boogie Sound*. The sextet's bilingual effort includes guest artists who solidify its two cultural approaches, enhanced by having toured with 1999 and 2000 versions of the "Watcha Latino" rock tour. Nick Gaitan, the band's bassist tells the *San Antonio Express-News* the band's music "is a hybrid of different types of world music that is full of an urban element" and includes "early Jamaican ska and reggae, soul, danzon, conjunto, punk rock, and rockabilly." Other band member believers include Chris LaForge, guitar; Robert Rodriguez, accordion; Ryan Scroggins, organ; Beans Wheeler, drums, and Felipe Galvan, vocals. A Tosti tribute album surfaces in 2004, *Aka El Tostado*, which casts an additional spotlight on Tosti's prescient development of Chicano rock and his inclusion of jazz, cha cha cha and mambo ingredients. Pianist Eddie Cano is among the musicians on this original 1980s LP that concludes with a remake of Tosti's signature tune, *Pachuco Boogie*.

Isidro López, called the padre of modern Tejano, dies August 16 in Corpus Christi from complications from an earlier massive stroke. The 75-year-old saxophonist/vocalist achieves Texas musical history when he adds accordions to his big band blending of ranchera, mariachi, and rock elements during the new music's development in the mid-1950s in South Texas. López suffers a stroke April 11, which results in several hospital stays, ending with his condition worsening the week prior to his death. While his family works the cotton fields in the '30s and '40s, López listens to norteño music on Mexican border radio stations as well as American country artists. He learns to play the tenor saxophone while in high school in Corpus Christi and as a teenager during the end of the 1940s decade he begins playing with several conjunto bands, whose accordion sound characterizes the flavor of the Mexican American folk music genre. López eventually forms the Isidro López Orchestra, which records several regional hits and becomes a favorite on the Southwest tour circuit.

Two years after Mexico's Grupo Televisa sells its Fonovisa label to Univision Communications for $235 million, and a year after Univision demands the return of some of this money back for alleged over charging for some assets, the two parties reach a financial agreement. Grupo Televisa forks over $16.5 million to end the dispute. News of the financial settlement appears in a notice Univision files with the U.S. Securities Commission in Washington.

The synergistic reach of Univision TV and Univision Records combines to produce a CD focusing on various styles of norteño music while its accompanying DVD zeros in on the plight of immigration between the U.S. and Mexico. The album, *Mi Homenaje A La Musica Norteña/A Tribute To Norteño Music*, contains 13 tracks including performances by Los Tigres Del Norte, Conjunto Primavera, Bronco El Gigante De América, Graciela Beltrán, Los Huracanes Del Norte, Jenni Rivera, Polo Urias, Raza Obrera, and Diego Martinez. Univision's Mario Kreutzberger (better known as Don Francisco) who hosts two shows, *Sabado Gigante and Don Francisco Presenta*, sings on four songs and joins in duets with other artists on the album. The CD lands on *Billboard*'s Top Latin Albums chart. A portion of the proceeds from the CD's sales is earmarked for two charities that assist men and women struggling through illegal immigration problems.

The DVD, which Univision claims is a Latin music industry first, covers the struggles of immigrants, with Francisco traveling to Tijuana to visit the two organizations, to San Jose to discuss the topic with Los Tigres Del Norte and to Monterrey, Mexico, to chat with other musicians regarding their personal experiences as immigrants traveling across the border into the U.S.

Jay Perez is the top winner in The Texas Talent Musicians Association's 24th annual Academy of Tejano Artists and Musicians music awards, snaring three honors and sharing a fourth, while Shelly Lares and Jimmy Gonzalez Y El Grupo Mazz each win two accolades in ceremonies at San Antonio's Villita Assembly Building. Perez is named top male vocalist, male entertainer of the year, his tune *Together* is named top crossover song and he and Ramiro "Ram" Herrera win the top vocal duo honor. Lares' two awards are the female versions of the top vocalist and entertainer. Gonzalez and his group win song of the year for *Tu Uevo En Mi Alma* and group album of the year for *Live En El Valle*. Perez and Gonzalez are repeat winners from last year in the male vocalist and group album of the year categories, respectively.

Among the other winners, Michael Salgado's *Tu Musica Sin Fronteras* snares the conjunto norteño LP of the year; Los Desperadoz's *Lucky 13* earns the conjunto Progressive award; Grupo Vida is named show band of the year and Marcos Orozco, the most promising band.

As part of the festivities, which reaches out to include conjunto, grupo, and Christian music, an array of familiar musicians performs, including winner Ramiro Herrera, Eddie Perez, Adalberto, and the Tejano Academy Orchestra, consisting of Academy members.

Ranchera specialist Alejandro Fernández, who maintains a separate career from when he's working with his genre-leading father Vicente, strikes out for a younger following with his newest Sony Disco release, *A Corazón Abierto*, which concentrates on acoustic pop ballads with a stronger percussive feel. While the tunes are of lost love and its accompanying sadness, it's also a marked difference from two previous pop albums with their mixture of lush string accompaniments and emotion laden Mexican ballads. The challenge for Sony in marketing this recording's appeal to younger listeners who eschew the traditional sound of ranchera is working: the CD debuts on the general market *Billboard* Top 200 albums chart September 25 at number 125 and becomes the second Latin LP behind Los Lonely Boys on the best-seller list. After four weeks, it drops off the survey after sliding to number 186. The "new" Alejandro's efforts in attracting a younger audience, especially Latinas, also pays off during his concerts. His pop-flavored songs intertwined with traditional mariachi strains, his modernistic dress ranging from both tight leather and charro pants to his sexual body movements, cast him as a modern romantic figure.

Alejandro and his legendary father Vicente are selected to open and close New York City's six-week long MexicoNow festival in December with sold out concerts at Madison Square Garden. The duo is not only the biggest names in regional Mexican music to appear, but they're also among the most expensive tickets of the dozens of events taking place in 36 venues throughout the city's five boroughs. Vicente and his band open the festival; Alejandro is the closing act. MexicoNow is focused on New York's Mexican population, the fastest growing immigrant group in the city, with 186,872 persons being counted by the 2000 census, with an additional estimated 100,000 or more undocumented Mexican immigrants living in the Bushwick and Sunset Park sections of Brooklyn, East Harlem in Manhattan and in Elmhurst and Jackson Heights in Queens. This big push occurs over the past 10 years, resulting in Mexicans representing 17 percent of all Latinos in the Tri-State area of New York, New Jersey, and Connecticut, and in many cases creating assimilated Latinos who jam clubs in Brooklyn, Harlem, and Queens which specialize in sonidero Mexican entertainment shows or reggaeton, the Puerto Rican mixture of rap and reggae. Closing the festival is the culmination of the Mexico City to New York City Lady of Guadalupe Torch Relay involving 7,000 runners and culminating with a ceremony in Central Park, a concert in midtown and a mass at St. Patrick's Cathedral. Azteca America's New York station WNYN, hooks into the New York leg of the relay.

For new pop singer Betzaida, being part of the Univision family enables her to gain national TV exposure prior to the release of her eponymous debut ballad album with its mixture of rhythmic textures ranging from rockish guitar patterns to vallenato accordion breaks to upbeat reggaeton moods. Signed to Fonovisa in 2000, she's caught up in the transition at the label when it's purchased by Univision for it's growing record group and has to wait until this year before her album is released. While waiting, the Chicago native who's raised in Mexico, is signed by the Univision TV network to sing the theme for the Copa America soccer championships in Latin America which it televises from Peru in July.

Mexican ranchera and pop vocalist Juan Gabriel is back on the concert circuit following a two-year legal battle with Hauser Entertainment, his former booking agency, over commissions. The complex matter of Gabriel suing the agency, which files its own counter suit, is decided by a Los Angeles Superior Court judge ordering Gabriel to pay the agency $1.9 million. That amount will come from splitting his concert earnings over the next two years from 45 appearances.

Mexican vocalist Ana Gabriel is also on the concert circuit with Vicente Fernández, the ranchera king, who plays a major role in her 30-year career that spans 20 albums. Her newest Sony release, *Tradicional*, is a collage of ranchera, mariachi and banda standards and one Fernandez classic, *Volver, Volver*. Gabriel, whose legal name is Lupita Araujo, develops the theme for the new LP two years ago when she performs with Fernández at the Grammy Awards, she explains to the *Houston Chronicle*.

Pepe Aguilar makes his debut on Sony Discos with *No Soy De Nadie* after leaving Univision in a dispute over "creative differences." The CD is a mixture of rancheras, boleros, and electric guitar fuelled pop ballads, not the normal strong point for the veteran Mexican vocalist. Aguilar seems bent on finding himself; his first two recorded projects in 2005 are a mariachi album and an Italian pop LP for overseas release. The inspiration for that offbeat idea is his debut duet performed on *Mi Credo* with Italian vocalist Tiziano Ferro for a Mexican TV reality show. The cut is included in *Big Hits*, a compilation album EMI Latin USA releases in April.

With the 10th anniversary of slain Tejano star Selena looming next year on March 31, her family announces a tribute concert April 7, 2005 at Reliant Stadium in Houston, the last city she appears in at the Astrodome before 69,000 fans before being murdered in her hometown of Corpus Christi. The anniversary is commemorated on TV by Univision and its sister network, TeleFutura, which devotes three hours to the slain singer on the evening of her death, starting with a Corpus Christi-based special, *Recordano A Selena* (*Remembering Selena*) hosted by the network's Charytín Goyco. In the hour-long program, TeleFutura's cameras recall her childhood, entry into show business and capture her fans' gravesite vigil. The emotional special is followed by the film *Selena* starring Jennifer Lopez and Edward James Olmos.

The 70,000-seat Reliant stadium is converted into a 55,000-seat venue for the concert, *Selena ¡Vive!* (*Selena Lives!*), broadcast live by Univision from 8 to 11 p.m. Brother A.B. Quintanilla, III and his Kumbia Kings perform along with Gloria Estefan, Thalía, Banda El Recodo, Intocable, Pepe Aguilar, Alicia Villarreal, Carlos Vives, Paulina Rubio, Olga Tañon, Jay Perez, Aleks Syntek, Lucero, Ana Gabriel, Ana Bárbara, Los Dinos, Alejandra Guzman, India, Pablo Montero, Grupo Montéz De Durango, Bobby Pulido, and Mariana Seoane. The telecast garners a 35.9 Nielsen Hispanic Television Index rating, the highest ever achieved by a Spanish-language special, attracting 3.9 million households. EMI Latin releases a CD/DVD of the concert, which helps revitalize Selena's album catalog, which is greedily milked ad nauseam, following her murder. EMI alone in '05 celebrates Selena's legacy by releasing four albums: *Unforgettable: Special Edition*, *Unforgettable: The Live Album*, *Momentos Intimos* and *Selena Remembered: Her Life, Her Music, Her Dream*. They all land on *Billboard*'s April 23 Top Latin Albums chart. Several other non-EMI

Selena packages are also in the mix, including Univision Records *Mexico Recuerda A Selena* (*Mexico Remembers Selena*), featuring regional Mexican acts signed to the Univision Music Group interpreting some of her hits.

By June 4, only the *Studio Album* remains on the Latin chart in 73rd place, two from the bottom and is gone the following week. However, another EMI Latin title *Selena Vive!*, a various artists tribute bows on the chart May 28 in 15th place and by June 18 it slips to 23rd and rebounds the next week to 19th place.

According to *Billboard*, five of her albums reach No. 1 on the magazine's Top Latin Albums chart since her death. One of these, the English-language *Dreaming of You* also remarkably bows in the top position on the Top 200 albums survey, giving the artist the posthumous distinction of being the first Latin singer to hit No. 1 on the general market survey.

On his own, Quintanilla and his Kumbia Kings are doing quite well this year, having broken through commercially in 2001. Three of its EMI Latin albums are Latin chart makers, including the most recent *Fuego*, which also lands on the general market Top 200 list. The eight-member instrumental band, which specializes in a modernized version of cumbia, is spearheaded by bassist Quintanilla, guitarist Chris Perez and keyboardist Cruz Martinez. On *Fuego*, two Mexican pop acts, teen singer Belinda and Noel Schajris of Sin Bandera, make guest appearances, adding their vocal prowess to the Texas band's own powerful instrumental mix of R&B and rap.

The Mariachi Vargas Extravaganza, a four-day festival of workshops, local competitions and a closing concert, celebrates its 10th anniversary in San Antonio in December with the world's oldest reputed mariachi band, Mariachi Vargas De Tecalitlán, heading the closing concert at the Municipal Auditorium. The 107-year-old band intersperses music from its new RCA International CD, *Boleros Romanticos*, comprised of bolero classics, within its program. Pepe Martínez, the band's musical director/arranger for nearly 30 years, boasts to the *San Antonio Express-News* that all the tunes on the CD "are identified with Mexico....these are songs of the pueblo, of the people."

The music is indeed the music of the people in Texas, where an estimated 10,000 students are enrolled in mariachi music education programs throughout the state. Festival organizer Cynthia Muños tells the newspaper mariachi "is one of the few musics that connect kids with (their) grandparents."

Seeking to connect with Mexican and Latin dance styles, Austin's Michael Ramos combines acoustic and digitally created sounds to energize traditional Mexican music on *Charanga Cakewalk Loteria De La Cumbia Lounge* on Artemis. Looking for a connection to Tejano devotees, guitarist/singer Carlos Maldonado and Grupo Fuerte invoke accordion and polka rhythms on *The Tough Boys of Texano* on Discos Tica.

As the year ends, Los Temerarios and Marco Antonio Solís emerge as the top-selling regional Mexican and romantic Mexican artists, respectively, in *Billboard*'s year-end recap analysis. Los Temerarios, consisting of brothers Gustavo Angel and Adolfo, winds up in the top slot on both Regional Mexican and Top Latin Album lists as a result of their hit CDs *Veintisiete* and *Tributo Al Amor*. Solis, whose base is in regional Mexican, shows he's capable of successfully crossing over into Latin pop when his Fonovisa CD, *La Historia Continua*, earns dual awards as the Top Latin Album and Top Latin Pop album categories.

Following Los Temerarios as the top Regional Mexican album artist are Los Tigres Del Norte, Grupo Montéz De Durango, Grupo Climax, Vicente Fernández, Joan Sebastían, Akwid, Conjunto Primavera, Adán Sánchez, and Los Bukis.

Shifting from artistry to economics, the top dollar earning companies in the genre are Univision Music Group, Disa, Sony Discos, Balboa, and EMI Latin. Balboa/Musart's Grupo Climax heads the list of best sellers with *Za Za Za*, followed by Los Temerarios' *Veintisiete* and *Tributo Al Amor* on Fonovisa; Marco Antonio Solís/Joan Sebastían's *Dos Grandes* on Fonovisa; Grupo Montéz De Durango's *En*

Vivo Desde Chicago on Disa; Los Tigres Del Norte's *Pacto De Sangre* on Fonovisa; the various artists' compilation *Agarron Duranguense* on Disa; Bronco/Los Bukis' *Cronica De Dos Grandes* on Fonovisa, and Conjunto Primavera's *Dejando Huella* on Fonovisa.

When the 2004 regular Grammys are announced in December, San Antonio's role as the wellspring for Tejano music is reinforced as five of its bands vie for the genre's top album trophy. The five nominees hoping to be the lucky winner on the CBS telecast next February 13 are: David Lee Garza, Joel Guzman, and Sunny Sauceda's *Polkas, Gritos Y Acordones* on Guzman Fox; Stefani Montiel's *Takin' on the World* on World; Emilio Navaira's *Entre Amigos* on BMG U.S. Latin; Jay Perez's *Mi Destino* on La Voce, and Grupo Vida's *Vivo* on Tejas Records. And the winner is *Polkas, Gritos Y Acordones.* In the Mexican/Mexican American album race, Intocable's *Intimamente* on EMI Latin is the top choice.

As 2005 begins, one San Antonio conjunto not vying for national honors, but remaining a top local act, is Los Aguilares, which celebrates 45 years in show business January 28. Consisting of teenage brothers Emilio, Genaro, and Frank Aguilare, the band gets started in the early 1950s and undergoes several personnel changes over the years.

Disa Records' signing of Chicago-based Duranguense-devoted bands the last two years, germinates into sales successes, which propel the Univision Music Group label to seek additional American bands. Starting off the new year buoyed by its record 13.05 percent of the 2004 American Latin record market, according to Nielsen SoundScan figures, which are greater than three of the major labels, BMG, Warner and EMI, Disa in February releases its next highly anticipated album by the first Duranguense band it signs in 2003, Grupo Montéz De Durango's *Y Sigue La Mata Dando.* Two other similar genre groups, according to *Billboard*, Los Horóscopos De Durango and Patrulla 81, are set for release in the next two months. Following Univision Music Group's 2001 purchase of a 50 percent ownership in the Monterrey, Mexico, Disa company, Domingo Chavez, a member of the family which owns the other 50 percent, moves to the U.S. and after striking gold in Chicago, begins building the roster with other U.S. acts to where half of the talent currently is U.S. based, with the other half Mexican groups. Disa's sales are aided by the cross-promotion it gains on Univision's TV networks.

In addition to building its association with the music from the Mexican state of Durango, which blends acoustic banda with synthesizers, Disa is now focusing on introducing new bands from what it's calling tierra caliente, which is a spin-off from Duranguense.

Running neck and neck with Grupo Montéz De Durango's new album release date, are two highly popular regional Mexican bands, Conjunto Primavera and Intocable. Primavera's Fonovisa album is *Hoy Como Ayer*; Intocable's double CD EMI release, *X*, celebrates the band's 10th anniversary. With Fonovisa also owned by the Univision Music Group, it gains national distribution from the powerful company-owned Universal Music & Video Distribution. Although two of the three CDs go on sale at the same time, Intocable's double CD follows two weeks later and has an edge since its Tejano/norteño music combination of polkas, august folk rhythms and pop ballads is far field from the danceable music of the Duranguense bands. One of Intocable's albums contains all new songs and is the band's first studio session in 18 months. The other CD subtitled *Xtra* features 11 of the band's songs recorded by various artists saluting the group's anniversary.

Smithsonian Folkways Records introduces a new a series of albums to its three-year Latino series. The initial new CD released in March is *Llegaron Los Camperos* featuring 10 tunes performed by Nati Cano, a pioneer in mariachi music from Los Angeles, with his group, Mariachi Los Camperos De Nati Cano, and is a companion to the label's 2002 *Viva El Mariachi* release. Three additional releases spotlight Los Camperos De Valles' *El Ave De Mi Soñar: Mexican Sones Huastecos*; compilations by Los Pieneros De La 21's tribute to Puerto Rican sounds, and a retrospective of Chicano and Afro Colombian marimbas. Daniel Sheehy, the label's recordings director, tells the *San*

Antonio Express News 25 additional releases are planned for the next six years.

Long known for its leadership position in norteño music since 1994 and its emphasis on topical, serious story themes, Los Tigres Del Norte takes a new creative direction into lighter fare with its Fonovisa album *Directo Al Corazón*, which combines cumbias, corridos, and norteño ballads. Jorge Hernández, the group's leader infers to *Billboard* the band's intention to "make a happier, more youth-driven album." The band's concerts in Latin America and Spain during the past 18 months, have exposed its brand of regional Mexican music new listeners. As part of its international push, the new CD is released simultaneously in the U.S., Mexico, Spain, and Central and South America.

Univision's live broadcast of the 17th annual Premio Lo Nuestro A La Música Latina Awards February 24, covers a broad scope of musical categories and is followed by three award shows honoring Tejano musicians. The first, the Tejano Music Industry Awards March 17 at the Civic Center in Del Rio, Texas, will be followed two days later by the (TTMA) Texas Talent Musicians Association's 25th annual Tejano Music Awards at the newly constructed Kickapoo Lucky Eagle Casino in Eagle Pass. The third ceremony is the first Premio A La Música Awards March 29, a spin-off from the La Musica Latina Fan Fare in San Antonio, spotlighting new bands. The three awards presentations honor both Tejano's 50-year history of traditional conjunto accordion-propelled polkas with the electric keyboard infusion found in the orquestra movement which are advocated by new traditional bands like Fiel A La Vega, Carlos Maldonado Y Grupo Fuerte and Los Tavares to newer blendings of cumbia, hip-hop and R&B, exemplified by the Kumbia Kings and Tabu.

Marc Anthony is the top multiple winner in the 17th annual Premio Lo Nuestro A La Música Latina music awards from Miami's AmericanAirlines Arena. His accolades are all in the tropical competition for best male artist, salsa artist of the year, best album for *Valió La Pena* on Sony and song of the year for *Ahora Quién*. Other multiple winners: Paulina Rubio and Sin Bandera with three each and Alicia Villarreal with two trophies. Rubio is honored for best pop female and video artist and legendary young artist. Sin Bandera's trophies are all in the pop category as top group or duo, and for having the top album, *De Viaje* on Sony and song of the year, *Que llora*. Alicia Villarreal's accolades are in the regional Mexican genre as best female artist and grupero artist of the year. Also in this grouping, artist of the year awards go to Intocable in norteño and Pepe Aguilar in ranchero music. Tropical artists Carlos Vives is named artist of the year and Elvis Crespo, merengue artist of the year. In the pop category, Chayanne is named best male artist and in rock, Juanes is named artist of the year, with Maná's *Esenciales Luna* on Warner Latina, the top album. Two deceased artists are honored: Celia Cruz is named best tropical female artist and Adán Sánchez, the best regional Mexican male artist. Two rappers from Puerto Rico, Daddy Yankee and Don Omar hit gold in urban music, the former for *Barrio Fino* as best album and the latter as artist of the year.

Performing live are Chayanne, David Bisbal, Sin Bandera, Paulina Rubio, Alejandro Sanz, Don Omar, Daddy Yankee, Juliet Venegas, and Los Tigres Del Norte.

The Tejano Music Industry accolade show honors individual musicians, songwriters and rising male, female and group, with voting done by musicians themselves. The silver anniversary Tejano Music Awards, produced by the San Antonio-headquartered TTMA, which votes on its winners, presents lifetime achievement trophies to award founders Rudy Trevino and Gilbert Escobedo. Among the artists performing are Jimmy Gonzalez Y Mazz, a Grammy winner, along with Grammy nominees Jay Perez, Ram Herrera, Stefani Montiel, and Grupo Vida, plus Los Desperadoz and K1, formerly the Kumbia Kings, among others.

Top multiple winners at the Tejano Music Awards include Grammy winner David Lee Garza with three and Jay Perez and Shelly Lares with two trophies. Garza Y Los Musicales walks away with best song *No Puedo Estar Sin Ti*; best progressive conjunto album *Solo Contigo* and best crossover song *Who's That Gringo?* Perez's honors are as top male vocalist and male entertainer. Lares' duo wins are similar as female vocalist and entertainer. Grammy winner Jimmy Gonzalez E El Grupo Mazz nabs the top Tejano album for *Para Mi Gente* while Oro Solido wins the traditional conjunto album for *En Vivo Contigo* and DJ Kane wins the top urban Tejano album for his self-titled package. K1 is named the most promising group.

Winners at the Tejano Music Industry Awards include David Lee Garza Y Los Musicales who sweep the top instrumental honor with *Azucar Polka Medley*. Local favorites are Jorge Alejandro keyboards; Steve Roth, bass; Chente Barrera, percussion and male rising star; Al Gomez, bajo sexto; Art Guillermo, trumpet; Max Baca, saxophone; Joel Guzman, guitar, and Val Maltos, accordion. Single named artist Sesi wins as female rising star while La Fueza is the group rising star.

The first Premios A La Musica ceremonies honor musicians in 22 categories and are organized by KWEX, Univision's San Antonio TV affiliate, March 29 at the Charline McCombs Empire Theater. Inaugural winners include: Intocable, best norteño group; Michael Salgado, best Tejano artist; Ramiro Garza, best male vocalist; Jennifer Peña, best female artist; Latin Breed, best Tejano orchestra; David Lee Garza, best conjunto progressive group; Mariachi Campanas De America, best mariachi band; Kumbia Kings, best Latin urban band; Salsa Del Rio, best merengue band; top album, tie between Jennifer Peña and Kumbia Kings.

Laura Canales, 50, at one time the leading female Tejano vocalist and eight times Tejano Music Awards recipient, dies April 16, 2005 in Corpus Christi of complications from an unexplained surgery. From 1975 through 1985 the singer born in Kingsville, Texas, records 17 albums for Freddie Records and then continues with releases on GP, CBS, Capitol, EMI, and Fonovisa, where she cuts her final album in 1996. With the exception of six months as a DJ at KYST in Houston in 1988, the majority of her career is spent as a vocalist, first with Snowball & Co. then with El Conjunto Bernal and finally with drummer husband Balde Munoz in Laura Canales & Encanto. Among her Tejano Music Awards are plaques as top female vocalist of the year, top female entertainer of the year and top album and single winner.

Banda/narco-corrido artist Lupillo Rivera splits his musical personality in two in an experiment that could be a Latin music industry first. He records banda and mariachi versions of the same songs for two versions of his new *El Rey De Las Cantinas* Univision album that are designed as a dual package selling for $14.98. Released in June, it takes three months to record each individual CD, explains *Billboard*, the banda version featuring Banda Aires Del Pacifico with its brass and clarinet undercoatings within the large ensemble, while his first foray into mariachi on the accompanying CD features Mariachi Internacional De Mexico's reliance on violins and trumpets, showcasing this traditional Mexican music highly popular in the U.S. As part of its blanket promotional efforts, Univision services all Latin radio music formats with the single *Ya Me Habian Dico*. Rivera, whose popularity with bicultural banda fans dates back to 2001, launches a tour in late June in which he performs half the concert with a banda band dressed in conventional suit and cowboy hat and the other half with a mariachi band in which he's attired in a traditionally colorful mariachi outfit.

Lupillo Rivera is one of the artists of Abel De Luna, former head of Sony Discos regional Mexican and Tejano division oversees during his stay with the company from 2000 to 2003. During that period De Luna sells his Luna Music label to Sony, and upon leaving the company, starts up a second version as an independent label, signing with the Univision Music Group for distribution in July of 2005. Among his artists, according to *Billboard* are regional Mexican acts Banda Los Lagos, Los Hermanos Higuera, Altarosa Villa, and Yesenia Flores. In addition to his music interest, De Luna also owns 15 Spanish-language radio stations, many in secondary markets.

Celebrating 30 years in music, Polo Urias along with his band of 10 years, Maquina Norteña, release their first live recording, *En Vivo Maquina Norteña* recorded at the Far West Club in Dallas. Prior this first live performance album on Fonovisa, all of Urias' previous 30 plus norteño albums are done in the studio. Interestingly, Fonovisa releases the entire evening's show rather than selecting songs from the gig as has been its previous modus operandi when preparing live albums, notes *Billboard*. The new release, which includes Urias' two sons, Erik and Aarón, is aimed at reaching several age groups with its brand of romantic music. Prior to forming his current ensemble, Urias is the lead singer with two other aggregations, Los Jilgueros Del Arroyo, and Los Rieleros Del Norte.

Maintaining its tradition of bringing the past into the present, the 16th annual Mariachi USA Festival brings to the stage of the Hollywood Bowl in June respected names in Mexican music, Trio Los Panchos (which gains wide awareness for its Columbia recordings with Eydie Gorme in the 1905's) and Jose Feliciano, an early crossover artist who returns to his Mexican roots in 2004 with his Universal Latino hit album *A Mexico Con Amor* (*To Mexico With Love*). They join Cuban-born, New Mexico-raised producer Rodri J. Rodriguez's lineup of Mariachi America De Jesus Rodriguez De Hijar from Mexico, Mariachi Los Arrieros from McAllen, Texas, and two female groups, Mariachi La Altenas from Texas and Mariachi Mujer 2000 from California. Rodriguez, whose producing career spans 20 years, first becomes exposed to mariachi music while touring Mexico with some American artists.

Just when regional Mexican is bursting with stylistic genres, a new subgenre emerges under the moniker Música De Tierra Caliente. This sound is a combination of cumbia, banda, and synthesizers, all melded into a danceable style in the Chicago-developed Duranguense dance music mode and takes it name from Mexico's especially warm southern region. Its early proponents are Triny Y La Leyenda, signed to Universal Music Latino and Toño Y Fredy and Beto Y Sus Canarios signed with Disa, the label which plays a key role in bowing the Duranguense movement. Canarios' newest CD, *Ardientes*, is the 10-man group's fourth for the label. González Garcia, the band's lead singer/writer, tells *Billboard* the key to gaining airplay in the U.S. is to combine romantic lyrics with a danceable beat. The combination obviously works as the CD cracks both the general market Top 200 Albums survey and the Top Latin Albums chart, debuting at No. 2.

Sensing the germination of a possible sonic movement, Disa, Universal and Fonovisa add fuel to the fire. According to *Billboard*, Disa will release Toño Y Fredy's second album along with debut albums by several new artists as well as compilation and greatest hits packages; Universal, which issues the 12-CD low-priced series *Clásicos De Tierra Caliente*, adds to its catalog with titles by Grupo Exito and La Dinastia De Tuzantla, while Fonovisa breaks into the genre by signing Los Remis and La Flama.

With the nation's Mexican population invading new regions on a regular basis, two of Mexico's dynamic performers set separate tours with separate goals. Neither Alejandro Fernández nor Luis Miguel are following the weathered circuit of fairgrounds, clubs, and convention centers which superstars like Vicente Fernández, Joan Sebastían, Juan Gabriel, and others inhabit to maintain contact with their loyal fans at an average of $30 a ticket. The venues may be off the main street, but the prices are wallet bending just the same. Both artists are focused on mainstream venues.

Vocalist Fernández—along with co-headliners, Marc Anthony and Chayanne—blend their ranchera, tropical and pop influences during their 18 arena summer shows in 16 U.S. cities, starting with Houston's Toyota Center August 17. The three Sony BMG artists alternate opening and closing each show. The tour marks the first time they perform on the same stage as headliners offering a different brand of music. The label will use the tour to promote new albums and singles by Fernández and Chayanne.

Luis Miguel's concerts are 100 percent Mexican-flavored and built around his first-ever all mariachi album, *Mexico En La Piel*, released by Warner Music Latina in 2004. While mariachi tunes are also found on his other albums and at his concerts, his non-mariachi hits are naturally being showcased during the 40 "Mexico En La Piel" tour stopping in both major and secondary markets starting September 13 in Fresno, California. Among the venues are several presented by House of Blues Concerts. Following the American dates, Miguel plays 10 shows in Argentina, Chile, and Uruguay, notes

Billboard, before moving to Mexico to fulfill 17 engagements on the final leg of the tour.

One year following the death of 19-year-old rising star Adán Sánchez in a car accident in Mexico, another 19-year-old singer, Ulises Quintero, also of Los Angeles, emerges with uncanny links to the late singer. Not only is Sánchez Quintero's main vocal influence, but the norteño stylist has some physical facial resemblances, and is handled by Sánchez's former manager, Rodolfo Portillo, notes the *San Antonio Express-News*. Quintero's debut Sony BMG Music Norte album, *Tengo Un Corazon*, stresses cumbias, corridos, and bolderos. Quintero cites his dad, an upright bass player and lead singer with a band in Durango, Mexico, plus Ramon Ayala, the norteño superstar, Antonio Aguilar, the venerable ranchera specialist and Lupillo Rivera, the currently hot narco-corrido singer, for helping build his appreciation of various forms of Mexican music. His plans are to form a band and hit the tour circuit.

Aguilar, the 86-year-old romantic vocalist and film star, is honored by his singing sons, Pepe and Antonio, Jr. and wife Flor Silvestre, during his farewell concert at the Pico Rivera (California) Sports Arena September 4. His family provides the music for the 30-year show business veteran, who enjoys the tribute seated to the side of the stage on a leather couch, notes the *Los Angeles Times*. Antonio, Jr. continues his dad's tradition of singing while riding a horse being put through a series of moves to the strains of mariachi music.

San Antonio's Academy of Tejano Music presents its second annual awards to working musicians September 18, with David Lee Garza and Los Desperadoz each winning two trophies. Garza wins in the grupo and accordion categories; Los Desperadoz walks off with the conjunto and group vocal prizes. Among the 22 music awards presented at the Villita Assembly Hall, Ramiro Herrera is named best male vocalist while Stefani Montiel wins as the top female singer. In the individual instrumental awards the bajo sexton goes to Max Baca; bass: Stanley Revillas; drums: Chente Barrera; guitar: Gilbert Velasquez; keyboards: Art Guillermo; percussion:

Jorge Alejandro; saxophone: Joe Posada; trombone: Rene Garcia, and trumpet: Al Gomez.

With board members also vying for awards, and winning some, double winner Garza attempts to deflect criticism by telling the *San Antonio Express-News* the board has discussed whether members should be in the running for awards, adding: "The nomination and voting process is very important to us...and we see the peer recognition system as the best way to recognize other artists."

Vocalist Montiel, a third vice president on the board, and this year's top female warbler, also performs in the new group Las Tres Divas which includes Elida Reyna and Shelly Lares, who lose to their bandmate in the top vocal category. Other groups performing: the Latin Breed, Jesse Serrata, and Crossroads.

If there's any branch of music dramatically boosted by all the new Mexican immigrant population centers developing in untapped states and cities during the last five years, it's the regional Mexican concert field which achieves grandiloquence status as hundreds of firms cater to artists in the areas of management, booking and promotion. Not only are these musicians playing the traditional neighborhood venues, but they're also headlining in major concert halls and arenas. Check out your local newspaper listings for time and location.

Mexican artists in 2006 alter the sound of music from south of the border. Two of these groups, Rebelde, or RBD, a teen-flavored pop band, and Belanova, which stresses electronics as an electro-pop group, both find favor with U.S. audiences for their differing musical approaches. At its inaugural U.S. tour launch in Los Angeles in March, Rebelde, whose actor-singer members portray a high school band on the similarly named Univision novela, attracts 60,000 plus fans to its gig at the Los Angeles Coliseum. Belanova, led by singer Denisse Guerrero, bassist Ricardo Arreloa and keyboardist Edgar Huerta, are a favorite of Southern California's Spanish-language radio stations, including L.A.'s KSSE-FM, which signs the six-year-old group for its "Reventón" concert series July 29.

In addition to these two groups, both veteran and up-and-coming female vocalists are cracking the male-dominated regional Mexican music fraternity, in what is being labeled a cultural change in attitude towards female singers by female fans, who generally have favored male singers. Two of the gal warblers, newcomer Jenni Rivera and veteran Ana Gabriel, join RBD and newcomers Horoscopes De Durango (which features two female singers) on the *Billboard* Latin Albums chart. Other new artists the magazine cites as gaining fan favor include Diana Reyes, Graciela Beltrán, Alicia Villarreal, Ana Bárbara, La Chido, Lidia Avila, and Anais.

Articles

"Univision Faces The Music." Daily Variety, July 19, 2006.

"Regional Mexican Girl Power." Billboard, April 22, 2006

"Bringing Latin Pop To Life." Orange County Register, April 21, 2006

"Tejano Winners Include Montiel, Garza." San Antonio Express-News, Sept. 21, 2005

"An Emotional Farewell To Mexico's Roy Rogers." Los Angeles Times, Sept. 6, 2005

"Tierra Caliente Heats Up." Billboard, Aug. 13, 2005

"Quintero Has A Youthful Take On Norteno Tradition." San Antonio Express-News, July 31, 2005.

"Disa Act Leads Tierra Caliente Charge." Billboard, July 23, 2005

"Urias Live Set Took Time." Billboard, July 9, 2005

"Luna, Univision In Label Venture." Billboard, July 9, 2005

"Los Temerarios Mexico's Superstars Of Melody & Romance." Billboard, July 9, 2005

"Brothers In Music." Billboard, July 9, 2005

"Luis Miguel Gets Road Ready." Billboard, June 25, 2005

"Regional Mexican Acts Hit The Road." Billboard, June 25, 2005

"Rivera Offer Two (Genres) For The Price Of One." Billboard, June 4, 2005

"Mariachi USA Festival." Hispanic Magazine, June 2005

"Banda El Recodo Honors Its Tradition." Billboard, May 28, 2005

"Patrulla 81 Shows What Duranguense Can Do." Billboard, May 21, 2005

"Mariachi USA Festival Celebrates Sweet Sixteen At Hollywood Bowl."

HispaniaNET.com, May 19, 2005

"Laura Canales Dead At 50." Billboard, April 30, 2005

"Selena's Appeal Still Strong." Billboard, April 23, 2005

"Los Tigres Lighten Their Message On New CD." Billboard, April 2, 2005

"Premios A La Musica Debuts At The Empire." San Antonio Express News, March 30, 2005

"'Recordana A Selena' Kicks Off Primetime Tribute To The Queen Of Tejano Music On TeleFutura." Univision.net, March 28, 2005

"Still In Love With Selena." Billboard, March 26, 2005

"Agular Plans One-Two Punch." Billboard, March 26, 2005

"Grammy Winners Among Victors At Tejano Awards." San Antonio Express-News, March 20, 2005

"Llegaron Los Camperos National Treasure." San Antonio Express-News, March 20, 2005

"Artists Added To Roster Of Superstars To Perform At Univision's 'Selena !Viva!" HispaniaNet.com, March 17, 2005

"Univision Records Releases Selena Tribute Album: Mexico Recuerdo A Selena." Univision.net, March 17, 2005

"Despite Changes, Tejano Has Returned To Its Roots." San Antonio Express-News, March 6, 2005

"Marc Anthony, Paulina Rubio and Sin Bandera Top Winners At 'Premio Lo Nuestro 2205'" Univision.net, Feb. 24, 2005

"25th Annual Tejano Music Awards Show Highlights Unveiled." HispaniaNet.com, Feb. 16, 2005

"In A Mexican Groove." Los Angeles Times, Feb. 1, 2005

"Shift To U.S. Signings Drives Disa's Sales." Billboard, Feb. 5, 2005

"Retail Awaits Rush Of CDs from Trio Of Hit Latin Acts." Billboard, Feb. 5, 2005

"S.A. Group Marking 45 Tuneful Years." San Antonio Express-News, Jan. 27, 2005

"Selena Memorial Concert In April." Los Angeles Times, Jan. 26, 2005

"Emilio Hyped About Grammy Nomination." San Antonio Express-News, Dec. 30, 2004

"Mariachi Vargas Goes Classic, Four Days." San Antonio Express-News, Dec. 2, 2004

"Mariachi Vargas Extravaganza's Popularity Reflects A Rise In Cultural Pride." Dec. 1, 2004

"Miguel Makes A Ranchera Misstep." Los Angeles Times, Nov. 28,

2004

"Kumbia Kings Continue Their Reign." Billboard, Nov. 27, 2004

"The GQ Mariachi." Los Angeles Times, Nov. 22, 2004

"Tribute Planned For Fallen Star." San Antonio Express-News, Nov. 19, 2004

"Hispanic Honors Friday Night." San Antonio Express-News, Oct. 28, 2004

"Latin Singing Legend Ana Gabriel Knows Her Limits." Houston Chronicle, Oct. 15, 2004

"Kumbia Kings Bring Tejano To The Future." Houston Chronicle, Oct. 15, 2004

"Juan Gabriel Is Back On stage." Los Angeles Times, Oct. 4, 2004

"Mariachi Rings Up 25 Years." San Antonio Express-News, Sept. 23, 2004

"Latino Pop Singer Ready To Tackle New Challenges." San Antonio Express-News, Sept. 19, 2004

"For Fernandez, Less Is More." San Antonio Express-News, Sept. 17, 2004

"New Salute To Tejano Musicians." San Antonio Express-News, Sept. 16, 2004

"Tiff's Settled On Latin Label." Daily Variety, Aug. 24, 2004

"Los Temerarios Embrace Rancheras." San Antonio Express-News, Aug. 22, 2004

"Tejano Pioneer Lopez Dies At 75." San Antonio Express-News, Aug. 17, 2004.

"Sony Adds Two Latin Allies." Billboard, Aug. 21, 2004

"Singer Grows With New Duet." San Antonio Express-News, Aug. 15, 2004

"Los Skarnales' New CD An Eclectic Mix Of World Music." San Antonio Express-News, Aug. 8, 2004

"10 Is The Key Number As Intocable Celebrates." San Antonio Express-News, Aug. 5, 2004

"Don Tosti, 81; Inspired Latin Music Craze." Los Angeles Times, Aug. 4, 2004

"The Return Of Los Chuntaros." Latin Beat, August 2004

"Lupillo Rivera" El Toro." LA Weekly, July 30, 2004

"Los Temerarios Reaching Mainstream." Billboard, July 31, 2004

"Villarreal Calls Solo Move Challenging But Rewarding." San Antonio Express-News, July 25, 2004

"Hot Releases, Discounting Boost Latin Music Sales." Billboard, July 24, 2004

"Mexico Says 'Yeah Yeah Yeah' To 'Za Za Za.'" Billboard, July 24, 2004

"Conjuntos Aim To Claim Top Spot At Shootout." San Antonio Express-News, July 22, 2004

"Music Plentiful At Hispanic Fair." San Antonio Express-News, July 15, 2004

"Bronco, Others To Help LULAC Celebrate." San Antonio Express-News, July 8, 2004

"Los Tigres Del Norte: Music With A Social Conscience." Hispanic Magazine, July 2004

"2004 Hispanic Magazine Achievement Awards, Rodri J. Rodriguez." Hispanic Magazine, July 2004

"Eclectic Music Mixes," Hispanic Magazine, July 2004

"Urban Regional Digs In." Billboard, June 26, 2004

"Independents On The Rise." Billboard, June 26, 2004

"The Distrib Landscape." Billboard, June 26, 2004

"Conjuntos Paying Tribute To Longoria." San Antonio Express-News, June 24, 2004

"Univision Goes Nine For 10 Again On Chart." Billboard, June 19, 2004

"The Durango Gang Busts Out Of Chicago." June 12, 2004

"Rising Star Perez Has Much In Common With Selena." San Antonio Express-News, May 16, 2004

"Marketing Outdraws Mariachs At L.A. Festival." Los Angeles Time, April 26, 2004

"Outrage Begets Outrage." Los Angeles Times, April 24, 2004

"Fista Leans Toward Family Fare." Los Angeles Times, April 23, 2004

"Los Tigres Take Their Stories From Real Life." Billboard, April 17, 2004

"Death Of Adan Sanchez Draws Widespread Grief." Billboard, April 10, 2004

"RIAA: Latin Sales Slide Slowed In 2003." Billboard, April 10, 2004

"To His Fans, Sanchez Was Family." Los Angeles Times, April 3, 2004

"Fans Jam Streets To Mourn Teen Idol." Los Angeles Times, April 2, 2004

"Adan Sanchez, 19: Latino Singer Was Rising Teen Idol." Los Angeles Times, March 28, 2004

"Despite Downturn, Tejano Awards Remain Upbeat." Billboard, March

27, 2004

"Arriba Chalino Sanchez." LA Weekly, March 19, 2004

"Los Chalinillos: The Next Generation." LA Weekly, March 19, 2004

"Changes At BMG U.S. Latin." Billboard, Jan. 24, 2004

"Premios Que Buena Toast Top Regional Mexican Acts." Billboard, Dec. 27, 2003

"KBUE PD Pepe Garza: Billboard Q&A." Billboard, Dec. 27, 2003

"José José Mexico's Prince Of Song." Billboard, Nov. 29, 2003

"Banda El Recodo: Six Decades Of Making Music & History." Billboard, Nov. 15, 2003

"Durango's Surprise 2-Step." Billboard, Nov. 1, 2003

"Latin Indies' Pricing Strategy Also Fights Piracy." Billboard, Sept. 27, 2003

"Like Father And Mother And Son." Los Angeles Times, Aug. 25, 2003

"Bronco Moves, Carefully, Back Up The Charts." San Antonio Express-News, Aug. 24, 2003

"Daring Artists Radically Alter The Sound Of Mexican Music." San Antonio Express-News, Aug. 24, 2003

"Primavera Uses Success To 'Pay Back' Community." San Antonio Express-News, Aug. 17, 2003

"Hall Of Fame To Induct Longoria, 5 Others." San Antonio Express-News." Aug. 15, 2003

"Jose Leon Finds A Hook In 'Las Cositas." Houston Chronicle, July 25, 2003

"Regional Mexican Radio Tops Among U.S. Hispanics." Billboard, June 6, 2003

"Urban Mexican Music Is His Rule." Miami Herald, June 4, 2003

"Pepe Aguilar Takes Mariachi In A Fresh New Direction." San Antonio Express-News, June 1, 2003

"Rap And Hip-Hop Fusion Fuel Regional Mexican Scene." Billboard, May 24, 2003

"José José's Trio Album Pays Tribute To His Roots." San Antonio Express-News, May 11, 2003

"Surging Interest Ignites Regional Mexican Scene." Billboard, May 10, 2003

"La Conquista's New CD Reveals Its Real Image." San Antonio Express-News, April 20, 2003

"Winners Unveiled At Tejano Awards." Billboard, April 19, 2003

"Singer Looking, Sounding Different." San Antonio Express-News,

April 4, 2003

"Border Music." Hispanic Magazine, April 2003

"Kumba Kings Leader Ready To Give Up His Crown." March 14, 2003

"San Antonio." MediaWeek, Jan 20, 2003

"Latin Music Successes Span Spectrum." San Antonio Express-News, Jan. 4, 2003

Chapter 19
CAPITULO 19

Historical Backdrop: Olympics & Elections 2004/2005/2006 Music/Records, Radio/Television
CONTEXTO HISTORICO: OLIMPIADAS Y ELECCIONES
2004/2005/2006
MUSICA/DISCOS, RADIO/TELEVISION

• Spanish media's importance underscored as presidential candidates court Latino voters, with record amounts spent on political advertising.

• Radio giant Clear Channel clears way for switching more stations to Spanish formats.

• ABC Radio Networks signs first-ever pact with Spanish Broadcasting System to syndicate 3 of its top-rated morning shows.

• Cuban music/dance troupe makes historic appearance in Las Vegas. 49 members subsequently defect.

• Spanish-language albums provide an impressive presence on the nation's best-selling mainstream chart.

• Rap En Español and reggaeton are hot, hot, hot.

• Galavision celebrates its 25th anniversary.

• Telemundo's president Jim McNamara resigns after six years.

• Univision Radio's head Mac Tichenor resigns one year after Univision Communications acquires Hispanic Broadcasting Corporation, the network his family owns for 23 years.

• Latin Grammys shift from CBS to Univision.

• ABC becomes the first English-language network to offer primetime shows in Spanish, while Fox Sports En Español offers English-language coverage to broaden its audience.

• ABC, CBS, NBC and Fox start converting novelas into English.

• Univision Communications sold to Saban Capitol Group, which bests Televisa offer.

Amidst the excitement of 2004's quadrennial year in which the Olympics and the presidential elections at home occur every four years, Spanish-language media reaps the financial rewards of the Democrats' and Republicans' political propaganda ads amidst a nation split by the George W. Bush Administration's unilateral invasion of Iraq and the subsequent revelations that the reasons given by the government for going to war against Saddam Hussein are dead wrong. The chasm between the incumbent president and his opponent John Kerry fuels the increase in specially targeted Spanish-language commercials aimed at Hispanic voters.

One year later, when 84-year-old Pope John Paul II dies in his apartment in the Vatican's Apolostic Palace in Rome at 9:30 p.m. April 2, following his public suffering from a number of debilitating illnesses, the world unites in sorrow and Spanish media meld with the world's communications companies in covering his death and funeral live from Rome.

One topic blisters the political dialog on local and national levels: what to do about the constant influx of illegals flooding across the porous U.S.–Mexican border. While no one knows the accurate number of undocumented aliens in the U.S., a *Time* magazine investigation for a cover story on the breaching on America's borders places the estimate this year at around 15 million, with a record three million entering the country this year alone from a host of non-Latin and Latin nations, including Mexico, El Salvador, Guatemala, Nicaragua, Brazil, and Venezuela.

Addressing the controversial topic of undocumented immigrants, President Bush tells leading Spanish-language network Univision during a White House interview 13 days before the election that he supports legal status for immigrants who fill jobs unwanted by Americans. The president says he's comfortable with a temporary worker program and a card that gives these guest workers legal status, while rejecting the idea of amnesty for those illegals already in the country. In a second interview with Telemundo, Bush pushes his plans for security, education and healthcare as the reasons Latinos should cast their votes for him.

On the presidential campaign front, Univision snares Democratic president candidate John Kerry for an interview with the network's news anchor Jorge Ramos. It's Kerry's first face-to-face interview on Spanish-language TV. Ramos says Kerry's appearance (in May) "demonstrates that politicians and presidential candidates need to speak to Spanish-language media to attract the Hispanic vote," he tells this to the French news service Agence France Press (AFP). During his interview, Kerry supports easing new travel restrictions to Cuba by Cuban exiles imposed by the Bush administration and supported by some in Miami's exile community. He also tells Ramos he believes all Americans should be able to travel to Cuba without any restrictions.

Three days before the election, both President Bush and Senator Kerry appear in separately taped 10-minute, primarily English interviews on the network's long-running and popular three-hour *Sábado Gigante* (*Gigantic Saturday*) audience participation variety show with host Mario Kreutzberger. During the hour devoted to the upcoming elections, Kreutzberger, known as the comical Don Francisco, chats with the president in Washington and with Kerry in Scranton, Pennsylvania. The topics discussed are of interest to the show's reported 100 million viewers in the U.S. and Latin America: immigration, amnesty for illegals, religion, and family values.

This year's presidential elections target four swing states with huge Hispanic populations, with projections by financial analysts that

Spanish-language television will be the prime recipient of a record $12 to $17 million in advertising, all aimed at the estimated seven to eight million Latinos nationwide who are expected to vote on November 2. The key states gathering the most attention and ad dollars this year are New Mexico, Nevada, Arizona, and Florida. These four states contain 1.4 million Hispanic voters and represent 47 of the 270 electoral votes needed to win the presidency.

This year, the record budgets by the two parties are being fueled in part by the Democratic Party, which is aware it cannot take the Hispanic vote for granted, especially in the swing states, since President Bush's 2000 campaign captures Nevada and Florida. Close to 60 percent of the nation's Hispanics reside in California, Texas and New York. While Hispanics traditionally vote Democrat, except in Florida, the Republicans make a strong push to change the perception of their candidate across the nation.

The 2000 Census estimates there are 16.1 million adult Hispanics eligible to vote, an enticing voting block for the political parties to pitch their messages on Spanish radio and TV. One dissenting media voice charging Spanish broadcasting is not garnering its fair share of presidential advertising is Entravision Communications. Head of its broadcast group Philip Wilkinson notes in the *Hollywood Reporter* that "Spanish-language media get less than three percent of political ad spending." He feels that amount should be two or three times greater.

In fact, following the election Univision does report a surprisingly low figure from political advertising in its third-quarter report, which paradoxically reveals a major increase in its net income for this period. The network claims its take from political advertising is $2 million for its TV stations and $1.3 million for its radio stations. Chief financial officer Jeffrey Hinson opines to the media the low figures are a result of most of its stations being outside of the battleground states where the majority of the ad spending occurs.

Telemundo, working in conjunction with parent NBC, handles convention coverage starting with its morning newscast, *Hoy*

En El Mundo, continuing throughout the day with news briefs and closing with the network's *Noticiero Telemundo*. It also serves up a Spanish translation for the two candidate's acceptance speeches. Pedro Sevcec is the key anchor, with Lori Montenegro the chief political reporter and other field reporters adding to the coverage.

Sevcec also leads Telemundo's live commercial-free coverage of the three 90-minute presidential debates featuring simultaneous Spanish translations. Two Hispanic congressmen, Bob Mendez (D-NJ) and Lincoln Diaz-Balart (R-FL), are among the guest commentators providing post-debate reactions.

On election day, the network operates as part of the NBC News team headquartered in "Democracy Plaza" in Rockefeller Plaza in New York, with Sevcec anchoring the coverage that involves eight other on-air reporters. Election coverage begins with its 7 a.m. news show, *Hoy En El Mundo*, continues on its 5 p.m. newsmagazine, *Al Rojo Vivo Con Maria Celeste* and on its 6:30 p.m. newscast, *Noticiero Telemundo* and then throughout the night beginning at 7 p.m.

Joe Peyronnin, Telemundo's executive vice president of news and information programming, indicates being part of the GE-NBC News family provides Telemundo's presidential election night coverage with facilities in Rockefeller Plaza, video from some locations, graphics, technical assistance and exit poll data. When I ask him if the election provides his viewers with "exciting television," Peyronnin responds: "I think so because it's a very interesting race and there is higher interest among Hispanic voters this year than in the last election. There's more at stake: immigration, the war in Iraq, terrorism all resonated with our audience." These topics are of concern to the network that lands a White House sit-down interview with President Bush in the waning days of the campaign.

Telemundo correspondents produce live interviews with the two winning Hispanic Senate candidates, Mel Martinez in Miami and Ken Salazar in Denver, in addition to also carrying their acceptance speeches. The network also carries John Kerry's concession speech followed by President Bush's victory speech.

During the three presidential debates Telemundo employs three translators—two for the candidates and one for the narrator. "In order to make sure no one has an advantage, we rotate them during the debates," says Peyronnin.

Univision's coverage of the Democratic and Republican national conventions is carried live on its *Noticiero Univision* newscast starting at 6:30 p.m. and its *Ultima Hora* at 11:30 p.m. with anchors Jorge Ramos, María Elena Salinas and Enrique Gratas. Both Bush and Kerry's acceptance speeches are broadcast live with simulcast Spanish translations. The next day, *Despierta América*, the network's early morning news/variety program, provides convention wrap-up coverage.

As for the three debates, they run live and commercial-free on the Galavision cable network, utilizing the feed footage, as do all the English and Spanish networks.

Election day coverage commences with Univision's live morning news/variety show, *Despierta América*, which includes correspondent Enrique Teutelo reporting from Crawford, Texas, where the president votes and then returns to the White House to follow his reelection hopes. TeleFutura's coverage includes continuous updates on *Noticias Al Minuto* (*News Updates*) leading up to its primetime coverage from 7 to 9 p.m., during which time Univision runs its popular novelas, followed by its election reporting. Anchoring the coverage from Univision's election headquarters in Miami are Jorge Ramos and María Elena Salinas who are joined by anchor Enrique Gratas in Miami, focusing on key Senate and House races; anchor Maria Antonieta Collins in Miami, correspondent Jaime Garcia in Los Angeles covering any voter irregularities, chief Washington correspondent Lourdes Meluza and correspondent Martin Berlanga tracking events at the White House and at Republican party headquarters.

Covering the Democratic Party headquarters in Boston are Blanca Rosa Vilchez and Luis Megid. Additionally, correspondent Lourdes Del Rio follows voting in Florida; anchor Sergio Urquidi follows the race in Florida between Cuban-American Republican Mel

Martinez, who departs Bush's cabinet as secretary of Housing & Urban Development to run against Democrat Betty Castor for the state's Senate seat vacated by Democrat Bob Graham, while correspondent Victor Hugo Saavedra follows the heated battle in Colorado between fifth-generation Colorado rancher and two-term Democratic state Attorney General Ken Salazar and Republican beer magnate Peter Coors.

The company's news department provides primetime live coverage under the banner *Noticiero Univision: Destino 2004* (*Univision Network News: Destiny 2004*) to its broadcast networks, Univision and TeleFutura and its Galavision cable outlet.

Galavision's election day coverage spans five hours of primetime and late night programming. Reporting live from Washington on *Elecciones Presidenciales 2004* are Televisa news anchors Joaquín López Dóriga and Leonard Kourchenko from 7 to 11:30 p.m., augmented by correspondents in New York, Los Angeles, Miami, Boston, San Diego, McAllen-Brownsville, and El Paso.

The historic victories by Ken Salazar in Colorado and Mel Martinez in Miami give the Senate its first two Hispanic senators since the first Hispanic Senator Joseph Montoya, the Democrat from New Mexico retires in 1977. Salazar is also Colorado's first-ever Hispanic senator. And in a non-political first, Sony Discos' 19-year-old Ana Cristina becomes the first Hispanic in history to sing the national anthem, performing the venerated *Star Spangled Banner* at the inauguration of the reelected president.

While election night coverage on broadcast and cable networks draws 55 million viewers, according to Nielsen Media Research, Univision dominates Spanish-language coverage, reaching 2.7 million viewers, followed by Telemundo with 700,000, and TeleFutura with 600,000 viewers. Telemundo's 18-1/2 hours of coverage contains high and low viewing periods. By comparison, NBC reaches 15.2 million viewers, followed by ABC with 13.2 million, CBS with 9.5 million, Fox News Channel with 8.1 million, CNN with

6.2 million, Fox Broadcasting with 4.7 million, and MSNBC with 2.8 million.

The power of Spanish-language TV on the elections is plain to see as Bush attracts 45 percent of the Latino vote to Kerry's 53 percent, especially in the highly populated Hispanic states of New Mexico, Nevada, Arizona, and Colorado. The Bush figure is seven percent higher than the 2000 percentage, reports the *Los Angeles Times*, citing exit poll data. It's the highest share of Latino votes garnered by a Republican presidential candidate since the late Ronald Reagan scores 46 percent of the Latinos in 1984.

The reach of the TV medium is easily reflected in the windfall of advertising for Telemundo's coverage of the summer Olympics in Athens, the first-ever Spanish language coverage of any Olympics on American TV as part of the NBC family of broadcast and cable networks. While Telemundo does not break out its ad revenue, NBC reports its windfall from the Olympic totals $1 billion, generating $460–$470 million in profits. Prior to the Olympics, Telemundo's advertising sales rise 34 percent this year to $300 million during its May sales presentation to Madison Avenue agencies, according to an unnamed NBC spokesman quoted by the *Hollywood Reporter*.

During the 17-day summer Olympics in Athens in August, Telemundo offers 174 hours of coverage of sports it deems of prime interest to Hispanics, notably men's soccer (with tournament coverage on Mexico, Costa Rica, Argentina, Puerto Rico, Paraguay), women's soccer (U.S., Brazil), boxing, men's basketball (Puerto Rico, Argentina), track and field, baseball, and men's beach volleyball.

Telemundo's coverage along with NBC and its cable networks, CNBC, MSNBC, Bravo, USA, and a first time, special NBC high-definition TV network, produces 1,210 hours of programming, three times more than NBC's coverage of the 2000 summer Games in Sydney, Australia. Athens is the most watched non-U.S. Summer Games in history, attracting 203 million viewers. The collective coverage is more than the combined total of the last five Summer Olympics, according to NBC.

While NBC averages a 15.0 household rating and a 26 share of the total TV viewing, viewership numbers and ratings for Telemundo's coverage of the 28th Summer Games alone are not released by NBC or Telemundo. I try to obtain the ratings results but they're not forthcoming; they are obviously embarrassingly and disappointingly low. A report in *Multichannel News* indicates ratings for Telemundo's Olympics coverage from 1 to 8 p.m. drops 25 percent from its regular programming during those seven hours. Anchoring the network's coverage are Jessi Losada and Andrés Cantor, with Cantor also reporting on soccer with mate Alejandro Blanco. As for the other sports, Edgar Lopez and Adrián García Márquez cover baseball and basketball; Lopez and María Montero, beach volleyball and race walking; René Giraldo, Raul Marquez, and Claudia Trejos, boxing, with Leticia Coo at the main sports desk.

"Every Hispanic athlete that has excelled has been on our broadcast," boasts Jorge Hidalgo, the network's executive vice president of sports.

Turning from elation to tragedy, Pope John Paul's final weeks in 2005, in which he is publicly seen struggling to breathe and speak, necessitating a hospital stay and recuperation at home, alerts the media to the impending tragedy. Telemundo commences April 5 to broadcast live a number of special news programs on the Pope's failing health. Univision focuses its Pope coverage on five of its popular programs, including its late night newscast, *Noticiero Univision Ultima* (11:30–midnight).

Azteca America assigns reporters Javier Alatorre and Jorge Zarza to cover the Pope's failing condition and funeral. Their reports are featured on *Cobertura Especial Juan Pablo II*, April 1–7 which runs at different times around the clock, with varying lengths for the eight special reports, starting with a high of 8-1/2 hours and diminishing to 30 minutes.

Against this backdrop, the Latin recording industry in 2004, suffering its own losses, seeks solutions to drooping retail sales, the stagnant problem of piracy in Latin America, where an estimated 69 percent of CDs sold are illegal copies, by initiating tightened budgets and reductions in both label staffs and talent rosters. The Recording Industry Association of America reports that Latin music albums constitute a third, or 1.98 million copies, of all illegal CDs seized in anti-piracy raids in the U.S. last year, with the West Coast accounting for 62 percent of all the Latin CD seizures.

Among the areas of solvency being looking at by record companies are less expensive means of marketing and distribution, including downloads off the Internet and signing less expensive acts with pizzazz which can generate the kind of buzz which forces conservative Latin radio to think past its shrinking playlists.

Amidst this field of gloom, one area of optimism is the growth of national tours across America by major name acts in various musical genres, bringing together major talent agencies like William Morris and Creative Artists Agency, with national and local concert promoters to build a circuit beyond the traditional big-city venues with established Hispanic communities. Unlike four years ago, when tours are confined to the usual top 10 cities with large Latin fan bases, this year acts are additionally playing in second- and third-tier locations like Hartford, Connecticut; Raleigh, North Carolina; and Minneapolis, the William Morris Agency's Miami vice president, Michael Vega, tells *Billboard*. Tours are also planned for the Spanish-speaking and bilingual or English-language markets to avoid an act playing before an unappreciative audience.

One of the major venue chains, House of Blues, says Latin acts comprise 25 percent of its touring business. Since many of the acts travel here from Latin America, travel costs can eat up any marginal profits. Another hurdle facing concert promoters is the competition from Spanish radio stations which, like their English-language counterparts, present top talent in free promotional concerts or with a minimal ticket price, which is a no-win situation for a promoter charging $50 and up for a show by that same artist who plays that city earlier for a radio station.

The top record industry story, the merger of two giants, Sony (formerly CBS Records) and BMG (formerly RCA and Arista

Records) into BMG Music Entertainment, results in a restructuring of both company's Latin operations. Sony executive Frank Welzer, named chief of the new Latin operations, taps Kevin Lawrie, formerly president of Sony Music Norte, as president of Sony BMG Norte. He'll supervise the company's activities in the U.S., Mexico, and Central America from an office in Miami.

Two of the major labels the previously named BMG U.S. Latin and Warner Music Latina cut their Miami-based staffs, set adrift their presidents, reduce their staff payrolls and trim their artist rosters. Anticipating the merger of BMG and Sony (which occurs in the summer), BMG's A&R vice president Adrian Posse departs in January, followed three months later by the termination of BMG president Rodolfo López-Negrete and 16 other staffers. Juan Carlos Bernardez is now chief operating officer BMG U.S. Latin. George Zamora, Warner Music Latina's president, departs in June along with 12 staffers. These firings follow the termination of Sony Discos chairman Oscar Llord and EMI Latin America chieftain Rafael Gil last year.

And while the majors are looking to cut into the lead the independent labels apparently have in signing alternative music groups in the reggaeton and rock and rap en Español fields, they are nonetheless aware of the difficulties in breaking a new act whose music does not fit any of the restrictive radio formats. In today's environment, radio consolidation results in greater concerns for ratings, ad revenue, and researching how a new record resounds with the public—a modus operandi that looks askance at the promotional efforts by the labels to pitch anything new and chancy. Except if the talent has some name value or hook, either as a member of another band, or appears in a Spanish TV novela, or lands a slot on the playlist of an influential radio station in a major city, all of which can be exploited by the record company in its promotional pitches with stations hesitant to air something new and untested. This is the same problematic situation Anglo labels must overcome in their efforts with mass appeal radio.

Amidst this mélange, the crossover movement, which explodes in 1999 led by Ricky Martin, who leads the new effort by Spanish-speaking artists to record in English and snare the big bucks and big audiences, is on the decline this year. When an artist does try to appeal to English speakers, he or she usually records several tunes in Spanish to appease their Latino fans and not lose that traditional consumer base. The dual concentration also involves separate music videos and promotional campaigns—all of which run up the costs for marketing that project, and in today's cost-conscious environment, is a major investment. Artists signed to a major label have the advantage of their English-language album being released on the major imprint, while their all-Spanish LP is released on the company's Latin affiliate. For example, Enrique Iglesias' English albums are released on Interscope, with Universal Music Latin issuing his Spanish CDs. His recent English effort, 7, sells around 260,000 copies, good for a Spanish release, but shows slippage among his Anglo fans. Despite only selling 270,000 copies of her 2002 English debut album *Border Girl*, a figure below sales predictions, Paulina Rubio has her English contract renewed by Universal, which anticipates larger sales for her next Spanish release, *Paul-Latina* which will be promoted during a national tour. She's set to release another English album in 2005.

Tropical music benefits from a surge of power unleashed by the heat generated by Victor Manuel's hit Sony Norte CD, *Travesia*, followed by the arrival of new albums by Elvis Crespo on Ole, Marc Anthony, Rey Ruiz and Grupo Niche on Sony Norte and Melina León on Universal.

Anthony, whose earlier albums are either salsa in Spanish on Sony Discos or pop tunes in English on Columbia, and whose musical career is oftentimes overshadowed by his private escapades, including his marriage to Jennifer Lopez in June, bows his first Spanish pop release with *Amar Sin Mentiras* (*To Love Without Lies*) on Sony Discos which includes the duet, *Escapémonos*, with his new wife. The couple initially pairs vocally in 1999 on Lopez's *On the 6* album. Anthony's new album hits the *Billboard* Top Latin Albums, rising to No. 3.

Of Sony's four major crossover acts—Martin, Marc Anthony, Jennifer Lopez, and Shakira—only Anthony is among the Latino artists of different musical schools who make the *Billboard* Top 200 general market album chart in midyear. This in itself is a major breakthrough, an indication that Hispanics this summer have enough sales clout to make the all-important survey.

The leading act is a relatively unknown rock en Español band from West Texas, Los Lonely Boys, whose self-titled Epic album reaches the ninth position after 24 weeks and then begins to decline slowly, only to gain momentum throughout the rest of the year and into 2005. Its compatriots on the survey include Bronco El Gigante De America, Grupo Climax, Marco Antonio Solís & Joan Sebastían, Los Temerarios, Amanda Perez, Akwid, and Ozomatli.

Later in the year, two other Los Temerarios albums make the best-selling list as do single titles by Alejandro Fernández, Juan Luis Guerra, Los Tigres Del Norte, Los Bukis, Kumbia Kings, Brazeros Musical, Ryan Cabrera, Juanes, K-Paz De La Sierra, Le Tigre, Marco Antonio Solís, and Luis Miguel. The appearance of these Spanish-lingo albums is sufficient proof that Latin product is denting the mainstream best-seller list with alacrity and are not a fluke happenstance.

Also showing signs of appropriateness are the upstart independent labels formed by former heads of major record companies in 2004, who trade in the all-encompassing services of a major company which seeks to satisfy broad audience appeal with different genres of music for the total freedom to make their own decisions and specialize in a certain kind of music. And after years of being part of a corporate mentality, they are free to set up their own limits and goals and use their corporate expertise for their own individual aggrandizement.

Former Warner Latina president George Zamora and his partner, producer Sergio George, focus their new SGZ Entertainment label on urban tropical artists like Tito Nieves, Charlie Cruz, Ciclón, Frankie Negron, and India. Distribution is through Sony, which handles SGZ's first release, Ciclón's eponymous CD in April of 2005. In January of 2005, SGZ signs top salsa star La India, who'll have her own label. India is reunited with George, who works on production of her 1994 RMM album, *Dicen Que Soy*. Originally singing in English on disco discs, she switches to Spanish when joining Sony, until her contract expires in 2004. One year later, the partners sell a major unspecified share of the company to the Univision Music Group while retaining their titles of president and A&R vice president, respectively. The first album release on November 22 under the new ownership is Tito Nieves' *Hoy, Mañana Y Siempre*. It will be followed by the debut CD from Anais Martinez, winner of TeleFutura's *Objetivo Fama* reality series competition.

Former Sony Discos chairman Oscar Llord's Ole Music label, formed in partnership with financial angel Lideres Entertainment, owned in turn by the Cisneros Group, is a combination of known talents like Elvis Crespo and Charlie Zaa, and neophytes Teen Tick and Tommy Torres. Llord's modus operandi is to break acts regionally and then grow their appeal on a national basis. His company also operates management, music publishing, and concert promotion firms which helps keep all these functions coordinated in-house, while distribution is handled through Universal Music & Video Distribution.

By 2005, Llord's partner acquires majority ownership of the company, whose roster now includes besides Crespo and Zaa, Tommy Torres, Alvaro Torres, and Angelica Maria, with regional Mexican artists next to be signed.

Former vice president/general manager of EMI Latin's regional Mexican operation Miguel Trujillo's Mexa Music label naturally specializes in that brand of top selling music, with distribution by Sony. His first releases are due next year.

Former BMG U.S. Latin's managing director Francisco Villanueva stresses cumbia music on his Mock & Roll Record label. With the exception of Mexa, which is Texas based, all the other independents are in Miami.

Rap en Español, led by Mexican-born, L.A.-raised brothers Sergio and Francisco Gomez performing as Akwid are the impetus for the growing category of music called urban regional, a gumbo of styles ranging from norteño to cumbia incorporating bilingual lyrics. Besides Akwid (the name is a combination of the hermanos' earlier DJ nicknames AK and Wikid) in promulgating the fusion of cumbia with the spoken word, are such well-known groups as the Kumbia Kings, Control Machete, Vico C, ATM, and Yolanda Perez, followed by the soft styles of DJ Kane, a former member of the Kumbia Kings, Frankie J (Francisco Javier Bautista) and Baby Bash, and the harder-edged groups like Juan Gotti, Mexiclan, Chingo Bling, Los Delinquents, Kemo the Blaxican, and Don Abusivo.

While rappers gain attention due to the nation's acculturated bicultural population, and are making their way into the general market, the early lack of reggaeton artists from Puerto Rico on the general market survey, reflects the difficulty in crossing over this brand of alternative music which blends Puerto Rican salsa spiced with Afro-Caribbean rhythms, reggae, rap, and dancehall influences. Having outgrown its Puerto Rican roots built during its close to 10-year gestation on the Island, the music's popularity is reflected on the *Billboard* Top Latin Album chart, not the general market listing. Artists espousing reggaeton are usually found on independent labels that are distributed by the majors.

One area where reggaeton is catching on is in Southern California, with Ritmo Latino, the leading Hispanic record retailer reporting impressive sales in a number of its locations, especially among Central Americans. There's even an attempt to add Mexican banda elements to create a new reggaeton fusion sound. Tego Calderón on White Lion distributed by BMG is a major force in the music whose other proponents include Daddy Yankee (Raymon Ayala) on El Carte/VI, Ivy Queen (Martha Ivelisse Pesante) on Real Music distributed by Universal and Don Omar (William Omar Landrón Rivera) and Magnate & Valentino on VI Music, among others. One reason the music achieves some inroads on the Mainland is the alternation of the music's raw, gritty lyrics to be less caustic, and the watering down of the music to include more pop and tropical rhythms to the basic reggaeton beat, resulting in some tropical formatted radio stations instituting reggaeton programs to their schedules or adding tunes to their playlists.

With reggaeton albums producing commercial sales successes during the year, cautious Spanish radio stations throw their support to Puerto Rico's hottest musical import, which gains its first exposure on Puerto Rico's pioneering WVOZ-FM, which converts from former English-language Top 40 WODA-FM.

Tropical stations WSKQ-FM and WCAA-FM New York and WRTO-FM and WXDJ-FM Miami, reports *Billboard*, are among the leading outlets supporting the music by playing tracks from top-selling CDs by Daddy Yankee, Don Omar, Baby Rasta & Gringo, Zion & Lennox as well as songs featuring multiple artists like Pilar Montenegro, Gizelle D'Cole and Don Dinero on *Tómalo Suave*. The bilingual tune *Oye Mi Canto* by N.O.R.E. (Victor "Noreaga" Santiago) which cracks the magazine's Hot 100 best-selling singles survey, results in national exposure for its participants performing with N.O.R.E.: Daddy Yankee, Nina Sky, Gem Star, and Big Mato.

The music's coming of age is seen in its being included in the fifth Latin Grammy awards presentation in September, along with a number of alternative Latin acts up for awards in the new category of urban, music which includes Tego Calderón and Vico C, both from Puerto Rico, and L.A.'s banda rapping Akwid. Two Mexican rock acts, Café Tacuba and vocalist Juliet Venegas, are also among the nominees.

Also apparently coming of age a second time is the reintroduction in the New York music scene of indigenous Puerto Rican elements by a core group of Latin jazz musicians, led by percussionist Ralph Irizarry, a Nuyorican with a Puerto Rican heritage. This turning away from the influence of Cuban music which helps fuel the New York Latin scene for many years is highlighted by the U.S. government's 40 plus years trade embargo against Cuba, which prompts local musicians to keep the Cuban influences alive and dominant over their Puerto Rican instincts. Irizarry and his group Timbalaye are now using Puerto Rican rhythms like plena, danza, and bomba on their three BKS Records releases. In the past, he tells *Jazziz*, he emphasizes Cuban rhythms like the mambo, cha cha cha, and son montuno.

Nuyorican conga player Chembo Corniel who fronts his own band, Group Chaworo, says local players are hooking into the world music scene as well to include elements from other Latin nations like Spain and Argentina. Irizarry cites the growth of musicians from the Dominican Republic, Colombia, Venezuela, and Peru, who are also altering the sound of music in New York.

Is Latin alternative music, the graduated cousin of rock en Español at the crossroads of its existence? The topic is on the minds of participants at the fifth annual Latin Alternative Music Conference held at the Beverly Hilton Hotel for five days in August where they attend panel discussions and perform free concerts around Los Angeles. While the music receives scant radio play and obtains below potential commercial sales, its musicians continue to receive critical acclaim, including sundry nominations for Latin Grammy Awards. Sponsored by Cookman International of North Hollywood—whose owner Tomás Cookman manages Paulina Rubio and Volumen Cero and operates his own record label, Nacional Records—the conference regularly spotlights the changing sound of alternative Latin music to those people who believe in its cause.

To Cookman's credit, the event attracts a plethora of diverse performers who are in the vanguard of the movement. Appearing in concert settings are L.A.'s Yerba Tribe, San Diego's B-Side Players, singers Ely Guerra, and Andrea Echeverri, formerly of Colombia's Los Aterciopelados, Los Abandoned, Bajofondo Tango Club, a seven-piece band, Kevin Johansen, and Superlito.

While Cookman scores the major multinational labels for their hesitancy to invest in breaking new acts, especially the alternative bands which receive little radio play, he's signed four acts to his label: Tijuana's Nortec Collective, Colombia's Aterciopelados and two of its players, Héctor Buitrago, and Andrea Echeverri.

A number of new and established alternative acts not participating at the conference are nonetheless vying for Latin Grammys. They include Mexico's breakout rock song writer/vocalist/accordion playing Juliet Venegas; new singer-songwriter Kevin Johansen, born in Alaska, raised in Argentina and living in New York; Mexico City's veteran rockers Café Tacuba; and founding member Emmanuel Del Real. Award winners are covered later in this Chapter.

Whether they're called Rock en Español or Latin Alternative, U.S.-born multicultural rock-based bands are surfacing beyond the Mexican hotbeds of Monterrey and Tijuana, Miami, and Los Angeles spawning grounds, many taking their inspirations from Mexico's Café Tacuba, Aterciopelados, La Ley, Molotov, El Gran Silencio, Kinky and Nortec Collective, and Miami-based Volumen Cero. The latter hit Warner Latino quintet is an ideal exemplar of how cultures blend, not clash. Its members from Colombia, Chile, and Peru combine the rock'n'roll elements they grow up listening to on Miami radio with a host of Latin cultural ingredients. This confluence of sounds is what drives several New York bands like Yerba Buena, whose members are from Cuba, Venezuela, Virgin Islands, and the U.S.; Los Amigos Invisibles, consisting of all Venezuelans; Soulsa, whose members reflect their Puerto Rican, Cuban, and Dominican backgrounds; Barra Libre, whose players are from Mexico, Ecuador, Puerto Rico and the U.S.; and Los SuperKarma, whose brothers are of Ecuadorian heritage. Helping grow the New York scene is the growth of the Mexican immigrant community whose young members transport to their new home a familiarity and appreciation for the energy and intertwining of ethnic elements with American rock'n'roll.

Before the holiday selling season commences, statistics from two major sources—the Recording Industry Association (RIAA) and Nielsen SoundScan—reflect the interest in sundry forms of music. Nielsen SoundScan, which tallies sales from major retailers, indicates 14.1 million Latin units are sold at retail, up from 12 million for the same period last year. The research company projects this will be the strongest sales year ever if sales continue to hold up during the final half of the year. According to the RIAA's midyear report, shipments of Latin recorded music grow by 21.5 percent over the same period last year. It's the first time in four years the record industry trade group reports an increase in overall music genre shipments, expressly CDs, which rise to 21.2 million units from 17.7 million during the first half of 2003. With DVDs following next, the total number of units shipped to retailers comes to 21.9 million.

One of salsa music's new players breaking into the market is Libertad Records, founded in the Philadelphia suburb of Wynnewood by Latin music maven Aaron Luis Levinson in 2000. His creation, the 13-piece Spanish Harlem Orchestra including three male vocalists, displays its Puerto Rican roots by specializing in the music heard in New York City's primarily Puerto Rican community of Spanish Harlem in Manhattan, specifically salsa from the 1940s to the '70s. The band's second LP and first for Libertad, *Across 110th Street*, clicks with salseros and winds up on the *Billboard* Top Latin Albums chart.

The ensemble makes its formal debut in 2002 with *Un Gran Dia En El Barrio* (*A Great Day in the Neighborhood*) on Ropeadope Records for which it earns a Grammy nomination for the recording and a *Billboard* Latin Music Award the next year for the top tropical salsa album by a new artist. Its follow-up CD is this year's, *Across 110th Street*, a reference to part of the barrio that encompasses Spanish Harlem. Libertad, co-owned by Levinson and his partner John Robertson, Jr. in Libertad Entertainment, has the major advantage of being handled by Red Distribution, the Sony-owned company since January of 2003, which handles independent labels and whose retail and radio muscle helps produce the band's first national hit. The album lands on the *Billboard* Top Latin Albums in 43rd place July 3, rising to 55th place, dropping down to number 70 and departing the survey after seven weeks. Nevertheless, it remains on the best-selling tropical albums chart for 12 weeks before dropping off September 18.

The new album features four tunes performed by Rubén Blades, who, along with Oscar Hernandez, the Spanish Harlem Orchestra's pianist/director, performs in the Ray Barretto band in

1976. That's their musical connection. Attesting to its commercial and artistic prowess, the album lands a Grammy nomination in the salsa/merengue album category, which it wins when the results are announced February 13, 2005, on CBS.

My connection with Libertad occurs while driving in my car one Sunday afternoon and listening to the bilingual radio show, *Alma Del Barrio* on KXLU-FM Los Angeles, which plays one of the fiery band's new tracks, *Un Gran Dia En El Barrio*, in which Blades is heard in front of the band's three vocalists.

The tune catches my attention, which results in chatting with Levinson on the phone and being brought into his world of building a new pathway to salsa lovers. "We are identifying a more sophisticated and underserved adult audience that commercial Latin radio does not address," he says. "Everyone is looking for that 14- to 17-year-old female. I don't care if they buy an album. I'd love them to, but I'm marketing Latin music to adults, and surprisingly enough, that's a novel idea. We're looking to sell to both Hispanics and Anglos who love Latin music."

During the summer, the band, with Blades, tours Europe. Boasts Levinson: "We have Ruben's swan song for the foreseeable future since he has the cabinet position of Minister of Culture with the Panamanian government starting in September."

Levinson, a former singer with an R&B band called Gutbucket, is first exposed to Latin music in his native Philadelphia and then is really enmeshed in the music when he's attending the New School for Social Research in New York in 1981 and living there until 1985. He says the Spanish Harlem Orchestra is "an alternative to the conventionally produced pop salsa records." Several elements go into this claim of being different from the city's other salsa aggregations. "This is a band comprised of guys in their thirties playing music that stretches all the way back to the 1940s. I felt there was a hole in Latin music for a group that not only draws its repertoire from original songwriting but from the grand tradition of the music stretching back half a century."

There's also a basic difference in the way the band sounds and the way it's recorded. Explains Levinson: "The entire orchestra is in the studio all at one time playing live," which he claims is not the norm in salsa music. Levinson says his producing style is to avoid overdubs and individual section-by-section recording. "The arrangements feature a bit of jazz inflected harmonies that you'd never get in a commercial salsa arrangement. So I'd say we are musically more sophisticated."

Is that a reason why a lot of tropical radio stations don't play the orchestra? "Absolutely."

Are stations boycotting the record because the music's too sophisticated? "Yes, or it's too much like the great Latin music of the past and isn't influenced enough by the way modern records are recorded and sound. So if program directors play the album, they would say 'this record will stick out and it doesn't sound like the rest of what we're playing.'" Which is a no-no for commercial radio.

While the Spanish Harlem Orchestra is Libertad's breakout hit act, its first Puerto Rican band, the 17-piece Truco Y Zaperoko, gains a best salsa album nomination for *Musica Universal* in the regular Grammy competition in 2003. The Spanish Harlem Orchestra, despite radio's negative attitude, earns a regular Grammy nod in 2004 for best salsa album. Both CDs lose to Celia Cruz, prompting Levinson to parry: "It's hard to beat Celia Cruz" to which I interject "dead or alive." "Dead or alive" Aaron repeats.

Levinson musical pathway leads him to several record companies before launching Libertad. In 1997, with a collection of albums notably focusing on the Nuyorican salsa of the '60s and '70s, he senses "the music I'm listening to which is both an ethnic niche and considered pretty obscure, begins to change and evolve, and I realize this is no accident. It's reflecting the dramatic changes in the demographics of the United States. Today, you walk down the streets of Philadelphia and one out of every five Philadelphians probably speaks some Spanish. My attorney Brad Rubens and I see a hole in the market for a quality Latin label now that Fania no longer produces records while RMM, another dominant force, is starting to exit the tropical Latin market as well."

"So Brad drafts a detailed business plan and we present it to Rykodisc, which is already in the Latin market." The company buys the idea, RykoLatino is born in 1997 and operated by Levinson, Rubens, Arthur Mann and producer Joe Boyd and during its short run releases 12 albums including reissues from the '90s and new titles by Jimmy Bosch and Plena Libre, among others. "While I'm operating RykoLatino from Philadelphia, a friend from Philadelphia, Andy Hurwitz, is running the Knitting Factory label." When Andy leaves that company, he forms rope-a-dope in Brooklyn in 1998 and lands a distribution deal with Atlantic Records, a Time Warner company, for U.S. distribution.

"Andy tells me the guys at Atlantic are looking to do a Latin album and I should go talk with them. So I go there and pitch the idea that I have a band called the Spanish Harlem Orchestra and they're kind of interested. We cut the album, *Un Gran Dia En El Barrio*, and then the Time Warner-AOL merger happens. And an enormous amount of cost-cutting takes place and the Atlantic label called Division One for whom I make the record closes down. I receive a phone call telling me they aren't putting out my album. So I call Andy and ask him to listen to it and he's kind of sitting on the fence because rope-a-dope records jazz, funk, and groove-based music and this is a salsa album." But he decides to release it in 2002. One year later, Levinson reaches for broader distribution muscle and signs with Red Distribution.

Although his Latin album collection from his Philadelphia days is pretty impressive, Levinson says he experiences a musical epiphany when he's living at 122nd Street and Amsterdam Avenue in Manhattan, "which 20 years ago is entirely Puerto Rican. "Without exaggeration, I hear salsa music in my building every day on records and on the radio from seven o'clock in the morning until four o'clock the next morning."

Los Lonely Boys are a trio of brothers from San Angelo, Texas, who seem to have exploded unannounced on the nation's best-seller album list with their self-titled Epic album. In fact, the Garza brothers—Henry, 26, on guitar, JoJo, 24, on bass, and Ringo, 22, on drums—have been gigging on the Texas and Southwest circuit since the 1990s, with their brand of Mexican-Tejano-country-rock'n'roll fusion, and the album first appears on the independent Or Music label which is distributed by Sony-owned Red Distribution, and is then upgraded by Sony to its Epic label.

This is the imprint Los Lonely Boys are on when the band makes the *Billboard* Top 200 best-selling album chart with its eponymous CD, which gains strong radio play initiated by Austin's KGSR. The exposure translates into national retail sales, with the single, *Heaven*, from the album, cracking the general market Hot 100 best-seller list. For a new act, they will have an amazing run on the best-selling albums list, remaining there 75 weeks and dropping off the chart as of August 27. The single, however, lasts 30 weeks on the national listing, ends up in 42nd place the week of December 4 and then fades from memory. The group's popularity ensures them a highly visible slot on ABC's *New Year's Rockin' Eve*, the lone Hispanic presence among the performers on the show hosted this year by Regis Philbin, substituting for Dick Clark, the 75-year-old regular host for the past 32 years, who is recovering in a hospital from a stroke suffered December 6. The bilingual trio also receives a spotlight showcase during the opening segment of the 47th annual Grammys February 13, 2005, when it performs its hit single, *Heaven*, principally in English, with the final chorus in Spanish.

The tune catapults the group to win the Grammy for pop vocal performance by a duo or group. Sony decides to cash in by releasing two albums in February of 2005. The first is a so-called DualDisc version of their debut album, with the original audio on one side and video features on the back side, including footage of an acoustic performance. The second release a few weeks later is the band's first concert LP, *Live at the Fillmore*, the relished home for some of the great rock, blues, and jazz concerts during San Francisco's psychedelic era of the late '60s, which I cover for *Billboard*.

I'd never heard of the group until I receive an excited phone call from my wife one morning from her office at *Entertainment Tonight* where TVs are always on, while I'm working on the book, telling me to "quickly turn on channel seven, there's a band playing you ought to see."

What I observe are three musicians bathed in blue lights with a smoke machine filling the area in which they're playing some hard-driving rock en Español music. The show is ABC's *The View*, whose female panel of disparate pals, including executive producer Barbara Walters, normally tackles items of interest to their female audience. What's this band playing Latin music with a rockish twist doing on this show? And who are they?

The answer comes as this bilingual trio finishes up and the credits roll. It's Los Lonely Boys, and the reason they're booked on this morning show is because they're on a promotional tour for their first hit album in July. Earlier this year they appear on the late night TV talk/variety shows (Jay Leno, Conan O'Brien, Jimmy Kimmel) and open on the road for several acts including George Thorogood and the Allman Brothers.

Like all quirky things, the brothers have a swell story behind their explosive emergence. Their father, Ringo Garza, Sr. along with his seven brothers, plays in the conjunto group, the Falcones, in the '70s and '80s, which mixes the Mexican style with country. At home, he teaches his sons to play music and as they grow their interest spans Tex-Mex, country, R&B, and rock music. This background enables them to accompany their dad when his band breaks up, resulting in the family relocating to Nashville where the sons hope their vocal harmonies and songwriting will land them a recording contract. It doesn't. So they return home to West Texas and their work as a trio catches the attention of Willie Nelson, who invites them play at his Farm Aid concert last year and to record their first album in his Pedernales Studios in Austin.

The band is a hit during this year's 17th annual South By Southwest Music Conference in Austin, drawing a large crowd to its concert and winning album and song of the year awards, which helps spike the album's sales. The band's surprise hit album propels it onto the national TV screen where it's paired in a duet with Carlos Santana during the fifth annual Latin Grammy Awards CBS telecast September 1 from the Shrine Auditorium in Los Angeles. One year later, the group's Latin/rock fusillades are showcased among the nine all-star collaborator tracks on Santana's new Arista album *All That I Am. The Heaven* single along with a number of other crossover type discs reflects the growing integration of Hispanic artists into the mainstream music market, fueling the drive for this kind of financial success for future artists so inclined.

Two established artists, Julio Iglesias and Gloria Estefan, go in opposite directions with their careers in 2004. Iglesias, 60, tours the world in support of his new Sony *Divorcio* release, by his account, his 76th album during his 35-year career. He shows no signs of retiring and passing the baton to Enrique and Julio, Jr. his sons more in tune with younger Hispanics than he is. The LP is his latest since 2001's *Noche De Cuatro Lunas.* A recipient of a star on the Hollywood Walk of Fame, Iglesias' new release focuses on dispensing with worldly possessions and bad relationships and memories, all couched in upbeat and ballad tempos spiced with accordion fills. It seems like another era of regenerating his adult fan bass for the handsome, romantic figure, who becomes a crossover star in 1984 through his duet with Willie Nelson on the single *To All the Girls I Loved Before.*

Crossover superstar Estefan decides to curtail touring to spend more time with her family in Miami, but not before launching her 27-city "Live & Re-Wrapped" summer tour which starts July 30 and concludes at home in Miami September 25, stressing material from her new Epic *Unwrapped* album, her first English album since 1996's *Destiny.*

This year is a memorable one for the venerable nine-man multicultural, bilingual volcano called Ozomatli. While appearing opening night at the South By Southwest conclave's showcase of alternative Latin music in Austin's the Exodus Club on March 18, the band closes its set with its traditional conga-line exit, only this time the musicians wind up outside the club at 2:30 a.m. A passing policeman claims he fears the music could "incite a riot," and tells the band members they cannot play in the street and should return to the club. Following an altercation with officer Justin Owings, two band members, bassist Willy Abers and percussionist Jiro Yamaguchi, and the group's manager, Sue Blackman-Romero, are arrested and charged with two misdemeanors and one felony. They are taken into custody and released the next morning. Abers is charged with failure to obey a lawful order, a class C misdemeanor and a possible $500 fine; Blackman-Romero is charged with interfering with police duties, a class B misdemeanor, punishable by up to 180 days in jail, and drummer Yamaguchi is charged with assault on a police officer, a third-degree felony punishable by up to 10 years in jail.

With these charges yet to be resolved, the band releases its debut Concord album *Street Signs* on June 22 as the follow-up to its September 11, 2001, CD *Embrace The Chaos* on Interscope, which acquires the band from its original label, Almo Sounds. In July, the three individuals plead no contest and are given probationary sentences ranging from three to six years. By July 10, the album debuts at No. 2 on the *Billboard* Top Latin Album charts and at 125 on the Top 200 chart and then begins its exit off the pop chart while remaining on the Latin survey 18 weeks.

The seven-year-old L.A. band which mixes Latin rhythm with Middle Eastern influences and rap and jazz ingredients, adds other influences to the new album through a number of guest appearances by pianist Eddie Palmieri, the string section of the City of Prague Philharmonic Orchestra, French violinists Les Yeux Noir and Los Lobos singer/guitarist David Hidalgo. The band's multicultural adventuring earns it a Grammy as best Latin rock/alternative album for *Street Signs*.

Riding the wave of commercial success, the band launches its 22-stop "Rock Prendido" domestic tour August 5 through September 4. Concord president John Burk tells *Billboard* the band is "the next generation of combining Latin music with other art forms." Members of this next generation ensemble include in addition to Yamaguchi and Abers, Justin "Nino" Porée, Asdrubal Sierra, Raúl Pacheco, Ulises Bella, Mario Calire, Rene "Spinobi" Dominguez, and Jabu.

The heat generated by Ozomatli and Los Lonely Boys recent 2004 Grammy awards assuredly pays off at the box office when Oz guests on Los Lonely Boys' first national tour in 2005. It's also the year Ozomatli celebrates 10 years in show business. Of the 43 dates on Los Lonely Boys' tour from April to October through the U.S. and Canada, Ozomatli appears on eight, including six with another group, Calexico. Santana guests with the headliners on 21 dates. During the tour, Oz releases its first concert recording, *Live at the Fillmore*, taped at the famed San Francisco venue last winter.

Another popular band, East Los Angeles' most famous ensemble, Los Lobos, celebrates 31 years together and enters its fourth decade in 2004 with its most adventurous album, *The Ride*, on Hollywood/Mammoth, which features an eclectic lineup of guests, 11 songs in English and two in Spanish. It's the former Garfield High School student's 12th album and the first it self-produces since David Hidalgo, Cesar Rosas, Conrad Lozano, and Louie Pérez hook up in 1973, form Los Lobos Del Este De Los Angeles, and add saxophonist Steve Berlin in 1983 to the name shortened group. That quintet's first release on Slash, *And a Time to Dance*, sets traditional Mexican and Anglo rock tunes to a danceable beat. That signature sound is the hallmark of the new CD whose guests include Mexico City's leading rock band, Café Tacuba plus Rubén Blades, Quetzal vocalist Martha Gonzalez, Elvis Costello, Bobby Womack, Mavis Staples, Tom Waits, Richard Thompson, Dave Alvin, and Little Willie G (Garcia), an early East L.A. rock legend. With only two songs sung in Spanish, both featuring guests Blades and Café Tacuba, the CD is obviously aimed at the crossover market. While dealing with pained love, spiritual, and social issue-themed songs, many of the collaborations are new versions of tunes the band recorded years earlier.

The band from the City Terrace section of East L.A. is set to spend much of 2004 on the road. Although it's been 27 years since the band records *La Bamba* for the similarly titled film about the late Ritchie Valens, the same fire and intensity displayed on that seminal album release is what keeps this aggregation alive and alert to the changing sound of Latin/rock fusion music.

Criss-crossing language borders and musical genres also seems to be the goal of a growing number of performers who see the domestic market in terms of multicultural opportunities.

Paulina Rubio releases *Pau-Latina*, her second Spanish-language album for Universal Music Latino since her debut in the U.S. in 2001. She tells *Hispanic* magazine "it's the new generation of rancheras," utilizing a combination of traditional Mexican country music, reggaeton, batucada, the Brazilian folk rhythm, and hip-hop. The album solidifies her Mexican roots by including two powerhouse regional Mexican acts, Banda El Recodo and a tune by Marco Antonio Solís. She plans to also release her second English-language CD later this year. *Paulina*, her first U.S. CD in 2001, follows its original release in her native Mexico in 2000 and sells nearly two million copies globally, according to Nielsen SoundScan. Its follow-up in 2002 is her debut English-language crossover effort, *Border Girl*, which sells 270,000 copies domestically, according to SoundScan figures.

Spain's David Bisbal, fresh from his breakout exposure last year at two major TV telecast award shows, the *Billboard* Latin Music Awards and the Latin Grammy Awards where he's named best new artist, releases *Buleria* on Vale Music/Universal, which fuses his Spanish culture with a strong American pop Latino influence. The 24-year-old's debut CD, *Corazón Latino* (*Latin Heart*), cobbled together in Miami by producer Kike Santander two years ago, establishes his bona fides in his native country and then spreads slowly throughout Latin America and the U.S.

Jennifer Peña, best known for singing cumbia norteña material, seeks to broaden her Tejano and regional Mexican base into Latin pop with both her new album, *Seduccion* and its 2002 *Libre* predecessor, her first CD for Univision Records. Peña, 20, is bent on maintaining her two cultural bases as evidenced by her inclusion in the new title of several cumbias and norteña tunes among the pop-driven songs.

One of the leading voices in ranchera music, Alejandro Fernández, shifts gears and heads in the crossover direction with *A Corazón Abierto* (*With an Open Heart*) on Sony Discos, emphasizing songs of romance and passion. Although he's done pop material on three of his previous 14 albums, including the half-million selling *Me Estoy Enamorando* in '97, this is the first time his record label is focusing on the mainstream Latin market. A 15-city domestic tour is sponsored by McDonald's and Cingular, and promoted by concert giant Clear Channel Entertainment.

Using traditional ranchera and banda music as her musical base, 21-year-old Yolanda Perez aims her Fonovisa albums, *Dejenme Llorar* and her latest, *Aqui Me Tienses*, at young American Latinos, utilizing bilingual lyrics, English phrases, R&B-flavored tunes and songs which connect with U.S.-born Hispanic teens. The vocalist raps in English with her Spanish-speaking duet partner Don Cheto on the track *La Reyna Del Mall*. The CD's title tune by Perez comes in both Spanish and English versions, providing another opportunity for bilingual exposure for the U.S.-born singer whose parents are from Mexico.

Colombia's hit maker Carlos Vives adds a fusion feel to his new EMI Latin release *El Rock De Mi Pueblo* (*The Rock of My Land*). There's the native folk rhythm vallenato mixed with cumbia, rock, and pop elements, indicating Vives' evolving musical stance as he seeks a contemporary image. His vocals and instrumental parts are all recorded live in the studio to recreate the sound of his stage shows. Having released his first LP, *La Gota Fria* in 1992 featuring the blending of vallenato with pop and rock textures, Vives' follow-up recording on PolyGram Latino, *Clásicos De La Provincia*, remains on the *Billboard* Top Latin Albums for 86 weeks, peaking at No. 2. In

2000, *Déjame Entrar* hits No. 1, and one year later also collects two Latin Grammys and one regular Grammy.

John Arthur Martinez, born in Marble Falls, Texas, focuses on country music for Latino fans with his Dualtone album, *Lone Starry Night*. While Martinez believes there are generations of Hispanics who enjoy country music, but have no Latino role model in this field, Dualtone's co-president Scott Robinson opines to *Billboard* that "country music is slow to accept anything different" and if this barrier can be breached there are opportunities for Mexican American artists like Martinez, who gains notoriety as both a participant, special radio station correspondent, and first runner-up on last year's *Nashville Star* on cable's USA Network.

Marcos Witt, already an established Latin Christian star whose 22 CanZion albums are distributed to Christian Bookstore Association retail outlets, lands a second distribution deal with Sony Music Norte, which places his music in secular outlets. So last year's winner of a Latin Grammy for best Christian album has all his bases covered. First release by Sony is the live concert he does at the Los Angeles Sports Arena last November titled *Recordando Otra Vez*. While he's the founder of CanZion in 1986, Witt does not impact the radar of major labels until Sony Norte's president Kevin Lawrie sees Witt perform at this concert and signs the artist who's brought to him by Mauricio Abaroa, the former president of Crescent Moon Records in Miami last year.

This year Witt embarks on a 10-month tour of the U.S., Latin America, and Spain ending in November, which hooks up nicely with the album's release in March. Born in San Antonio to a family of missionaries, the one-month-old infant moves to Durango, Mexico, with his parents where his religious family life guides him into the world of Christian music in Spanish.

Juan Luis Guerra, the Dominican Republic's tropical music ace, is also moving into Christian music in Spanish. His first religious work is *Para Ti* on Vene Music distributed by Universal Latino. Guerra's name power powers the CD onto the No. 2 slot on *Billboard*'s

Top Latin Albums chart, a record mark for a debuting Christian album. It also re-enters the general market Top 200 albums survey. Powering the album's chart positions are several factors: the merengue-driven single, *Las Avispas*, which gains acceptance on tropical formatted radio stations, and the placement of the record in not only Christian record outlets, but in secular stores which normally stock his romantic bachata records.

Later in the year, an array of top name artists ranging from Linda Ronstadt and Marco Antonio Solís to Christian singers Jaci Velasquez, Fernando Ortega and Kaci add their stylistic distinctions to *Amor Sagrado*, the Univision two-CD, 30-track collection of Christian and inspirational songs.

Velasquez, who records for Word Records, bows her own Christian label, Apostrophe Records, whose first two artists are singer/songwriter Michael Cook and Idaho band Grand Prize. Domestic distribution is handled by Word Records.

On his own, Solís, one of Mexico's top grupero stars, delves deeply into lushly arranged pop material on *Razón De Sobra* on Fonovisa, which is designed to appeal to U.S. and overseas fans, with whom he originally connects in 1999 with his first pop LP, *Trozos De Mi Alma*. The album follows his departure in '95 from Los Bukis, Mexico's top romantic song act where he's the lead singer/songsmith to go out on his own. Since Fonovisa is part of the Univision Music Group, Solis' new release is promoted on the Univision, TeleFutura and Galavision TV networks. Solís' self-penned compositions and his empathy for romantic ballads are augmented by arranger Pablo Aguirre's melding of strings with accordion to gain the desired "international sound."

One of Mexico's leading rap trios, Control Machete, which hasn't had an album in four years, following the departure of one of its members, attempts a come back as a duo on *Uno, Dos* on Universal Latino. Originating at the University of Monterrey in the mid-'90s, Antonio Hernández, Raul Chapa and Fermin Caballero create a group which discusses hot ticket social issues like the U.S.' immigration policies, especially against Mexican illegals. After two hit albums, Caballero splits to go solo. The duo's return release is strengthened by its widened song themes and musical sophistication.

One of Brazil's leading artists, vocalist/acoustic guitarist Caetano Veloso, records his first all-English album on Nonesuch, *A Foreign Sound*, in which he interprets a bevy of American pop hits ranging from Cole Porter's *Love for Sale* to Elvis Presley's *Love Me Tender* to Nirvana's *Come As You Are* to Stevie Wonder's *If It's Magic.*

Ely Guerra, the Mexican alternative rock vocalist known for her songs of social concern, focuses on love and sexuality on her first studio album in five years with the enticingly sensual title, *Sweet & Sour, Hot & Spicy* on Higher Octave. Her last studio session, *Lotofire*, is recorded when she's 27 and thinking differently musically.

José Alberto, born in the Dominican Republic, raised partially in Puerto Rico and emerging as a major salsa vocalist in New York, celebrates 25 years in show business with the release of his 27th career album, *Then and Now*, on the Pina label. The LP is a compilation of his top hits and includes four newly arranged and digitally remastered tracks from the three LPs he records with his band for SonoMax starting in 1983 for which he acquires the rights. It's his 16th release as a solo artist, having earlier recorded with several bands including Tito Rodriguez and Tipica 73. Known by the nickname *El Canario* (*The Canary*) for employing whistling as an instrument on his records.

Brazilian vocalist/composer Caetano Veloso releases his first all-English LP of his 40-year career, *A Foreign Sound* on Nonesuch Records, which explores the works of 20th century writers ranging from Cole Porter to George Gershwin to Bob Dylan to Stevie Wonder to Kurt Cobain. Veloso, 62, tells the *Miami Herald* there's an inexorable connection between the music of Brazil and the U.S., which validates his idea for an all-American album. "Bossa nova connects better to the tradition of American good beautiful songs than does rock'n'roll."

Veloso's niece, Belõ Velloso, is among the three vocalists making their U.S. debut on the tour "Latinas! Musical Divas of Latin

America," sponsored by New York record company Putumayo World Music to promote a new compilation CD. Also making U.S. bows are expatriate Chilean singer Mariana Montalvo and revue headliner Colombia's Totó La Momposina.

Monchy and Alexandra, proponents of their Dominican Republic's bachata rhythmic style, upgrade their music by infusing the sounds of rock with Latin pop ingredients on their new J&N album *Hasta El Fin*, which debuts on *Billboard*'s Top Latin Albums chart at No. 7, the highest positioning achieved by an album from the duo, Ramón E. Rijo and Alexandra Cabrera De La Cruz (Monchy and Alexandra).

Miami-based Bacilos peppers its new Warner Music Latina release, *SinVerguenza*, with timely political topics during this year of political discourse. The follow-up to last year's top pop Latin Grammy album, *Caraluna*, is spiced with songs anent immigration, biculturalism, drug use hypocrisy, and class confrontations. The trio of Jorge Villamizar, the lead singer and tunesmith, Andre Lopes on bass and José Javier Freire on drums, selects two producers for the project, Colombia's Juan Vicente Zambrano and Brazil's Tom Capone, who will die in a motorcycle accident following the presentation of the Latin Grammys in L.A.

Spain's hit group, La Oreja De Van Gogh keeps its focus on '80s-'90s resonating Latin pop on its new Sony Discos release, the very long titled *Lo Que Te Conte Mientras Te Hacias La Dormida* (*What I Told You While You Pretended to Be Asleep*) which accompanies its previous album, *La Oreja De Van Gogh En Directo: Gira*, to the Top Latin Albums chart. The San Sebastian-based quintet admits feeling comfortable playing in the U.S. with its large and expanding Hispanic population. A contrast from playing in France, a 30-minute drive by car from their home, where member Xabi San Martin tells the *South Florida Sun-Sentinel*: "They don't understand a word we say."

Certainly the LP with the weirdest trajectory is Septeto Rodriguez's blending of Cuban Jewish and intrinsic music on !Baila Gitano Baila!. The Tzadik Records release focuses on Cuban drummer/arranger/composer Roberto Juan Rodriguez's efforts to highlight Cuba's Jewish heritage on a number of the 10 tracks, which naturally are propelled by both Jewish and Caribbean rhythms. Adding to the unorthodoxy of the CD is the utilization of accordion, organ, clarinet, trombone, violin, and cello to the septet's musical spectrum.

Rodriguez's blending of Latin rhythms, Jewish melodies klezmer-style and jass improvization, reflects his upbringing in Miami where his father, a trumpet-playing Latin bandleader lands the then-15-year-old a gig in a band playing Yiddish theater music for Miami's retired elderly Jewish community. That job opens Rodriguez to Jewish music with which he solidifies a strong emotional tie and helps feed the recorded klezmer movement of 2005.

Far afield from Yiddish music, singers Claudia Acuña from Chile, Luciana Souza from Brazil, Marta Gómez from Colombia and instrumentalists Ray Mantilla and Conrad Herwig from New York and John Santos from San Francisco infuse Latin jazz with their own cultural influences.

Acuña, a U.S. resident since the mid-'90s, emphasizes Spanish on *Luna*, her third MaxJazz Records release, reversing her language preference for English on her first releases. Sousa, also a U.S. resident since the '80s, and a Grammy nominee during the last two years, stretches her musicality on her new *Neruda* on Sunnyside. Gómez, a native of Cali who moves to Boston to study jazz at the Berklee College of Music, debuts on Chesky Records with *Cantos De Agua Dulce* (*Sweetwater Songs*). This collection of primarily her tunes is the backbone for her jazz-flavored interpretations of popular folk music of Latin America utilizing son, cumbia, and zamba rhythmic textures.

Herwig, a very busy trombonist, continues his forays into Latin rhythmic tributes to jazz's super stylists with *Another Kind of Blues: The Latin Side of Miles Davis* on High Note, as the follow-up to his 1996 release *The Latin Side of John Coltrane*. The new release is recorded live at New York's Blue Note club, featuring Paquito D'Rivera, Dave Valentin, Brian Lynch, Edsel Gomez, John Benitez, and Ronnie Cuber.

Percussionist Ray Mantilla reemerges as a leader after several years out of the spotlight with his new Space Station septet's tribute to 1950's bebop on the Savant Records release, *Man-Ti-Ya*. Among the 10 tunes is the George Gershwin classic, *The Man I Love*, performed as a bolero.

The Latin Giants of Jazz, a 17-member band formed in 2002 by members of the late Tito Puente orchestra, honors its namesake on its debut release, *The Latin Giants Play the Music of the Palladium: Tito Lives* on Gigante, a Denver label. The band is also featured on the DVD, *The Latin Giants of Jazz With Eddie Palmieri Live at the San Sebastian Jazz Festival: July 2003*. In addition to recasting the music of Puente (born Ernesto Antonio, Jr. April 20, 1923), the ensemble also performs the music of two other jazz and dance bands who make the Palladium the home for Latin music, Machito and Tito Rodriguez.

Following Puente's death in New York City May 31, 2000, the Puente family attempts to keep the band alive, finally closing it down until percussionist member Johnny Rodriguez, Jr. in 2002 decides to reactive it and finds willing acceptance among other former members. Helping to get it going is saxophonist Stew Jackson, who becomes CEO of Latin Giants of Jazz Inc. in Denver. Rodriquez becomes the band's executive director. The new orchestra varies in size from 12 to 21 players depending on the job; the debut album lists 21 players: six saxes, five trumpets, four trombones, piano, bass, timbales, conga, bongo, and lead vocalist.

Another version of a "ghost band" featuring the music of departed leaders, is The Big 3 Palladium Orchestra, which keeps alive the memories of Machito, Tito Puente, and Tito Rodriquez, three of the hottest bands to play New York's fabled Palladium during the 1950's mambo mania. Formed four years ago by Mario Grillo, Jr., son of Frank Raul Grillo, best known simply as Machito, Tito Rodriguez, Jr, and Tito Puente, Jr., the band's soul is the music of these three orchestras, which hones its playing edge at showcases and festivals before recording its debut Big 3 Enterprises, Inc. CD, *Live at the Blue*

Note March 6 of this year for the Rumba Jams Music label. The three sons take turns leading the 23-member orchestra and playing timbales all under the direction of José Madera.

Also interpreting the music of Machito and Tito Puente along with Pérez Prado is Chicago's Angel Meléndez & The 911 Mambo Orchestra, a 20-piece big band that concentrates on the mambo rhythm, which shakes the New York Palladium during the 1950s on its debut eponymous Latin Street Music release. In addition to classic cuts by these bands, the 911 crowd led by its trombone-playing leader also offers several original tunes and an offbeat merengue of the well-known Hebrew tune *Havah Nagilah*.

On his own, Tito Puente, Jr. records *In My Father's Shoes* for HispaniX Records, which Universal Latino distributes.

Very much on its own is the Jazz on the Latin Side All Stars, a stellar group put together by José Rizo, an L.A. area DJ who hosts a similarly titled Friday night show for 14 years on KKJZ, which means he has no problem getting airplay on the station. The band's third disc and first studio session for Saungú Records is *The Last Bullfighter*, featuring a mixture of jazz classics and original tunes co-written by Rizo, who also co-produces the album with trombonist Francisco Torres.

Mexican tenor saxophonist Diego Maroto, a name familiar to New York jazz fans but relatively unknown in other parts of the U.S., is featured during New York City's "Mexico Now" month-long multimedia festival in November. Maroto and his sextet, which patterns its sound after the East Coast school of 1960s hard bop, appear at Dizzy's Club Coca-Cola at the Frederick P. Rose Hall on Broadway on the bill with Mexican-born drummer Antonio Sanchez and his group. Mexico is generally not known for developing jazz musicians, so for Maroto and Sanchez to gain footholds in the New York jazz scene is a major accomplishment.

Several New York bands stress the endemic music of the Dominican Republic and Puerto Rico. A collage of Dominican groups are heard on *Quisqueya En El Hudson* on Smithsonian Folkways exploring merengue, bachata (featuring guitar style ballads), salve (utilizing the call and response pattern) and palos (which utilizes heavy drum solos). The Smithsonian label is also home for Viento De Agua's *Unplugged: Material Prima*. The CD focuses on two drum styles, the plena, developed in Puerto Rico and featuring single head drums and narrative story-telling lyrics, and bomba, a West African/Puerto Rican musical style. These two musical styles are also the hallmark for Plena Libre's *Estamos !Gonzando!* on Times Square records. The album honors several pioneering plena musicians, going back to the 1960s when the instrument is utilized by big dance bands.

The world of opera, especially the Spanish kind, makes a welcome appearance in this country when the Dallas Opera offers a double presentation of works by that nation's renowned composer Manuel De Falla: *El Amor Brujo* and *La Vida Breve*, a composition celebrating its 100th anniversary this year. While mezzo-soprano Denyce Graves stars in both operas, flamenco dancer Maria Benitz is spotlighted in *El Amor Brujo*, a hybrid with dancing, spoken dialog and singing. In this work, Graves and Benitz portray the same character, dressed similarly with each performing their specialty. It's the story of a Gypsy woman who loses her lover and tries to recapture his attentions by throwing a spell over him. The second opera is also a story of betrayed love between a poor woman and her lover from a higher class in society.

Ironically, the Santa Fe Opera, which last presents De Falla's *La Vida Breve* in 1975, plans its second Spanish opera in 30 years in 2005: Argentine Osvaldo Golijov's *Ainadamar*. It's based on the life story of poet-playwright Federico García Lorca.

Mexico seems to be a spawning ground for opera singers. The latest tenor to emerge on the international stage is 32-year-old Rolando Villazón, originally from Mexico City, now a Paris resident. Buoyed by the acclaim for his debut 2004 CD, *Italian Opera Arias* on Virgin Classics, Villazón stops in Los Angeles in January of 2005 to sing seven performances of *Romeo and Juliet* with Russia's emerging soprano Anna Netrebko for the Los Angeles Opera. The tenor is booked airtight through 2009 with appearances around the world.

According to a *Los Angeles Times* feature, Villazón follows such renowned Mexican opera singers as Francisco Araiza and Ramón Vargas, who are among a coterie of singers being hyped as the replacements for Plácido Domingo (artistic director of the L.A. Opera) and Luciano Pavarotti. Two key events propel Villazón's career, his finishing second in 1999 at Domingo's opera competition in Puerto Rico and his 2001 televised performance in the New York City Opera's production of *La Boheme*.

The world of the Internet, fast gaining as a source for music downloading, is used heavily by Hispanics, according to a study by America Online and research firm Roper ASW. The study indicates Latinos use the Internet more often than the general population, prompting two new Latino targeted firms, emepe3.com and emusiclatino.com to enter the field, notes *Billboard*. Emepe3.com is launched first out of Miami by founder Andy Kleinman as a music news source in 1999 and then shifts into music downloading sales last April. Despite lacking titles from the major U.S. labels, Kleinman calls his operation "the world's first all-Spanish-language digital music store."

EmusicLatino is also a Miami-headquartered firm that licenses material by new and untested artists. The site is run by the Sierralta Entertainment Group, whose president/CEO is Miguel Sierralta. The company offers individual tunes as well as complete albums through middleman Liquid while amazon.com handles shipping. Yahoo Music in April of 2005 launches Latin stations for rap, reggaeton, and classic oldies, reflecting an increase in Yahoo En Español users and the growing popularity of reggaeton.

Latin music maintains its role as festival industry energizer on both sides of the language barrier. The 26th annual Playboy Festival at the Hollywood Bowl in June presents Yerba Buena, Horacio "El Negro" Hernández, Katia Moraes and Sambaguru and KKJZ's José Rizo and his 18-piece Jazz on the Latin Side All Stars. The Bowl also presents its own Jazz evening series featuring Willie Colón and his orchestra, Los Hombres Calientes and the Lincoln Center's Afro-

Latin Jazz Orchestra. Its neighboring John Anson Ford Amphitheater presents Latin dance troupes, a tribute to Peru's noted percussionist Alex Acuña who performs with his own folk/jazz ensemble and the 11th annual Brazilian Summer Festival produced by Brazilian Nites Productions, formed in 1989 by husband-wife Gilberto and Patricia Leao. This year's bill, which celebrates Brazilian Independence Day September 5, features As Meninas, the all-female band from Bahia; Bayú, which blends Jamaican and American influences into its bossa nova/sambas, and the Oya Brazil Samba Show. Spain is represented at the venue with a dance bill featuring *Sonidos Gitanos/Gypsy Flamenco* starring director/dancer Maria Bermudez, dancers Enrique Pantoja and Andrés Peña and a supporting cast of singers, guitarists, drums, and viola.

The L.A. region's Colombian/Peruvian Latin Music Festival in Long Beach by the Queen Mary museum/resort attracts a reported 5,000 fans to hear the music of Grupo Gale, Grupo Niche and Fruko Y Sus Tesos.

Salsa festivals proliferate in Los Angeles, New York, and Philadelphia.

The sixth annual West Coast Salsa Festival continues attracting fans to the Hollywood Park Casino in Inglewood like horse racing fans are drawn to the racetrack during its season. The Albert Torres Production's five-day event combining dancing, music seminars, and talent performances, draws a reported average 4,500 persons per day to the marriage of dance (with teams from Puerto Rico, New York, Los Angeles, Chicago, San Francisco, Colombia, France, and Italy), and music featuring Johnny Pacheco and his band, Africando with its French singers from Senegal, Roberto Roena Y Su Orquesta, the Spanish Harlem Orchestra, El Gran Combo De Puerto Rico, Johnny Polanco Y Su Conjunto Amistad, and Nora & Orquesta De la Luz from Japan.

New York's own fourth annual Salsa Congress at the Hilton, hosted by founder David Melendez, honors two of the Palladium's mambo dance stars, Mike Ramos and Freddy Rio. During the three-day event, salsa buffs dance to recorded music in the hotel's grand ballroom and also attend exhibitions and workshops. Appearing in-person to keep the dancers swaying are Wayne Gorbea Y Su Salsa Picante, Conjunto Imagen and Johnny Polanco Y Su Conjunto Amistad.

Philadelphia's first annual Salsa Congress produced by Willie Torres and Juanito Santiago, features the music of Willie Colón, India, Jimmy Bosch, Conjunto Clásico, and the Lebrón Brothers. The dance bash at the downtown Loew's Hotel sets a *Guinness Book of World Records* record when 4,250 individuals participate in a choreographed dance.

Chicago's first Latin Jazz Festival, held over five days features panels and performances at venues around the city. Musicians participating are Eddie Palmieri Y La Perfecta II, Bobby Sanabria, Eliane Elias, Dos Claves Orquestra, John Santos Quintet, Manny Oquendo Y Libre, Nelson Gonzalez, Victor Parra, and Andy Gonzalez and unannounced friends.

The fourth annual International Accordion Festival in San Antonio features performers from Argentina, Brazil, Texas, Ireland, Albania, and the Middle East. Argentina's Rubén Rodriguez and his three accordion infused band introduces one of his country's lesser-known folkloric musical styles, the chamamé at La Villita's Arneson River Theater. The chamamé blends rhythms of Argentina's Mbya-Guerani Indians with Africa and Creole-Spanish immigrants, he explains to the local *Express-News*, which senses the music is similar to South Texas conjunto.

Brazil's upbeat forró music is performed by a band inspired to call itself Forro in the Dark, while the San Antonio accordionist Ponty Bonc and The Squeezetones cement together elements of conjunto, Cajun, zydeco, and American blues.

Death takes Peggy DeCastro, 82, the eldest of the Latin singing trio, the DeCastro Sisters, commonly called the "Cuban Andrew Sisters" March 6 in Las Vegas of lung cancer. Her last appearance is February 14 performing in a wheelchair with her surviving sister Cherie at the Las Vegas Boulder Station. The sisters,

Peggy, Cherie, and Babette, move with their family from Havana to Miami in 1945 and are brought to Hollywood to appear in Carmen Miranda's film, *Copacabana* and provide animal voices to Disney's animated *Song of the South*. The sisters gain fame by appearing in 1947 on the first telecast by Los Angeles' first TV station, KTLA, and then performing at the Las Vegas Sahara and Desert Inn hotels during the 1950s. It's during this decade they start recording a string of hit tunes ranging from *Teach Me Tonight* to *Boom Boom Boomerang* to *Cowboys Don't Cry*. She's survived by her son Gene Lilley and sister Cherie.

On a regional level, Roberto Zenteno, 76, a one-armed Houston bandleader for 50 years, passes away July 29 in a local hospital after complaining of chest pains. Born and raised in Monterrey, Mexico, to parents who are actor/dancers, he loses an arm in an accident when he's five, but starts playing trumpet when he's 13 and tours with a popular Monterrey band. Moving to Houston in the 1950s, he picks up local gigs at private clubs and the Rice Hotel, and becomes probably the first Hispanic trumpet player performing in front of Caucasian audiences, son Javier Zenteno, informs the *Houston Chronicle*. He's one of five children and the drummer in his dad's band, which appears at the downtown Sambuca Jazz Café. Roberto is survived by his wife, Elsa, a daughter and four sons.

The Santana name gives birth to the new generational Salvador Santana Band, led by the 21-year-old keyboard playing son of music legend Carlos and his wife Deborah. The sextet features Salvador's musical pals from his home in San Rafael and the L.A.-based California Institute for the Arts, where he's a student. The band makes its debut at San Francisco's Warfield Theater in June and then tours Europe with his father's group. His piano style is drawn from such individualists as Chick Corea, Herbie Hancock, McCoy Tyner, and Keith Jarrett, he tells *Latin Beat*, while Jimi Hendrix, John Coltrane, and Billy Cobham are the models for his arrangements, which augur a band which melds jazz with Latin, rap, and rock elements. Obviously seeking his own identity, Salvador's seven-piece ensemble eschews a lead guitar, substituting a saxophone for his father's electric instrument.

The 2004 major accolades season begins with the regular Grammys at the Los Angeles Staples Center in February followed by *Billboard* Latin Awards in Miami in April and the Latin Grammys at the Shrine Auditorium in Los Angeles in September.

The secular 46th annual Grammys offers a sprinkling of Latino acts performing on the CBS telecast and in seven awards categories with a Hispanic flavor. Disparate Latin acts are paired during the three-hour broadcast, so you have trumpeter Arturo Sandoval trading fours with Justin Timberlake on piano on *Señorita* and Chick Corea playing implausibly with the Foo Fighters on their *Times Like These*. Jorge Calderon is among the eight artists warbling a tribute to the late Warren Zevon, who passes away from cancer last year and wins two Grammys this year for rock duo and contemporary folk album.

In a surprise win, Christina Aguilera snares the female pop vocal performance honor for *Beautiful*, a tune from her double platinum, English-language RCA album *Stripped*, which she dramatically performs earlier in a dark pants suit on her knees while bathed in bright lights. She changes into a wide-open plunging neckline dress to accept her statue and indicates she's working on another Spanish-language LP to follow *Stripped*, whose theme she conveniently almost accomplishes with her breast-baring dress.

Competing in the pop instrumental album category, Ry Cooder and Manuel Galbán win for *Mambo Sinuendo* on Nonesuch, while in the seven Latin categories themselves, Alejandro Sanz wins the Latin pop album with *No Es Lo Mismo* on WEA International; Michel Camilo with Charles Flores and Horacio "El Negro" Hernández cop the Latin jazz album title for *Live at the Blue Note* on Telarc Records; Café Tacuba cops the Latin rock/alternative LP for *Cuatro Caminos* on MCA; Ibrahim Ferrer captures the traditional tropical crown for *Buenos Hermanos* on Nonesuch; Celia Cruz captures the salsa/merengue crown with *Regalo Del Alma* on Sony

Discos; Joan Sebastían tops in the Mexican/Mexican American combination category with *Afortunado* on Balboa/Musart, and Jimmy Gonzalez Y El Grupo Mazz nabs the Tejano category for *Si Me Faltas Tu* on Freddie.

The *Billboard* presentation, televised in April on Telemundo, is the culmination of the publication's 15th annual Latin Music Conference at the Eden Roc Resort, with the awards held in the Miami Arena. Talent reigns at both events, and taking an approach, which helps the Academy Awards sparkle, the Diamond Information Center, provides $5 million worth of jewelry artists can loan and wear on the April 29 telecast. During the four-day conference, a bevy of new acts are showcased for industry leaders from a number of record companies. New label Ole offers up two veterans Elvis Crespo and Oscar D'Leon, and new faces K1, Angel López, Tommy Torres, and Charlie Zaa. Universal Music Latino's spotlight shines on Alih Jey; Warner Music Latina promotes Volumen Cero; Revolu, a rap specialist, presents Pearl and Julio Acosta; Dimelo! Records features Mellow Man Ace, while a Christian music showcase features *American Idol* finalist RJ Helton plus Karina Moreno, Samuel Hernández, and Jez Babarczy.

Of the actual awards themselves, the 10th annual presentation's top honors go to Sony Discos as the top pop tropical label and the Universal Music Group as the top regional Mexican label. The late Celia Cruz, rappers Akwid and Luny Tunes & Noriega win two trophies each: Cruz for top Latin album artist of the year and for her top tropical female LP of the year, *Regalo Del Alma* on Sony Discos; Akwid as new regional Mexican artist and Latin rap album winner, both for *Proyecto* on Univision, and Luny Tunes & Noriega as top tropical group album and new tropical artists, both for *Mas Flow* on VI Music.

Juanes is named songwriter of the year; Rudy Pérez producer of the year. Ricky Martin's *Almas Del Silencio* on Sony Discos earns him the top male Latin pop LP honor; Ednita Nazario's *Por Ti* on Sony Discos gains her the Latin pop female honor; Kumbia Kings wins the category's group award for its EMI Latin title *A.B. Quintanilla, III Presents Kumbia Kings*, and David Bisbal wins the new artist pop album title for *Corazon Latino* on Vale/Universal Latino.

The tropical album of the year is won by Ibrahim Ferrer for *Buenos Hermanos* on World Circuit/Nonesuch, while Ozomatli wins the rock alternative title for *Coming Up* on Concord Picante.

Marco Antonio Solís earns the regional Mexican album of the year for *Tu Amor O Tu Desprecio* on Fonovisa; Grupo Montéz De Durango wins the category's male group title for *De Durango a Chicago* on Disa, while Ana Gabriel wins the female nod for *Dulce Y Salado* on Sony Discos.

Arturo Sandoval, winner of the Latin jazz album title for *Trumpet Evolution* on Crescent Moon/Columbia, performs a duet with R&B singer Alicia Keys on the telecast which also highlights performances by Gloria Estefan, Alejandro Fernández, Paulina Rubio, Pilar Montenegro, La Ley, and Banda El Recodo, the subsequent recipient of the magazine's 2004 Hall of Fame award.

Despite being crammed with non-Hispanic presenters and performers, and the broadest array of category nominees, the fifth annual Latin Grammys salute more familiar, traditional artists than newcomers. The two-hour CBS telecast September 1 from the Shrine Auditorium in Los Angeles, continues its viewership decline from the initial 2000 telecast which sets the show's high watermark of a 5.2 rating and a nine share equaling 7.5 million viewers to this year's 2.4 rating, a four share reaching 3.3 million viewers, a decline from last year's 3.4 rating, a six share equaling 5 million eyeballs.

While CBS and the Latin Recording Academy keep their disappointments to themselves, the broadcast on an English-language network, rather than on any of the giant Spanish-language networks, does provide a glimpse inside the splintered Spanish and Portuguese-language music industries, whose members vie for accolades in 43 categories, seven of which are honored during the broadcast with the remainder scrawling down the screen during the commercial breaks by an impressive array of national sponsors pitching their products in English, Spanish, and in a few exceptions in both languages.

Repeat host George Lopez is funnier and cleaner than his last assignment and more political in this election year, arriving on stage riding a white horse and dressed in a spiffy traditional Mexican mariachi charro suit with a large sombrero, following the show's explosive bilingual opening duet between Spain's romantic hero David Bisbal dressed in an open white shirt and pants and MTV's own sensuous Jessica Simpson attired in a gray sequined tight dress, surrounded by hip-shaking male and female dancers. It's an indication of the kind of sex-laden image the Latin Grammys portray to the general audience. All the dancers display the same bump and grind routines, indicating a similarity of style by the choreographer.

Spain's Alejandro Sanz is the evening's top winner, with four trophies but is on tour in his native country and unable to acknowledge his winnings of best album, best male pop album, record of the year and song of the year, all from the Warner Music Latina CD *No Es Lo Mismo*. In his absence, co-producer Lalo Pérez makes the trek to the stage, and upon accepting the album of the year award, thanks God "for giving us the gift to hear things that no one else can." With these four awards, Sanz now has 11 Latin Grammys, the most of any individual since these gramophones are presented.

Among the other multiple winners are new Brazilian vocalist Maria Rita and Mexico's Café Tacuba. Rita wins best new artist, best popular Brazilian album for her self-titled Warner Music Brazil CD and best Brazilian song, Milton Nascimento's *A Festa* from the same album. Alternative band Café Tacuba wins the best alternative music album for its Universal Music Mexico CD, *Cuatro Caminos*, while member Emmanuel Del Real wins best rock tune for *Eres* from the same album.

The highly touted and publicized multiple-nominated *Lágrimas Negras* on Calle 54/BMG by 85-year-old Cuban pianist Bebo Valdés and 35-year-old Spanish flamenco singer Diego "El Cigala" Jiménez Salazar wins only one accolade as best traditional tropical album.

Host Lopez takes aim at President Bush, California Governor Arnold Schwarzenegger, and Jennifer Lopez. "You can call me G-Lo," he says. "People are always asking me if Jennifer Lopez and I are related. I hope not because I'm next in line to marry her. She's already got the dresses. But we don't need to walk down the aisle; she can meet me at the priest."

Among other key winners: song of the year: *Más Y Más* by Robi "Draco" Rosa from the *Mad Love* Columbia LP; female pop vocal album: *Ednita Nazario*, Sony Discos; male pop group album: Sin Bandera's *De Viaje*, Sony Discos; best rock solo vocal album: Juliet Venegas' *Si* on BMG Mexico/Ariola; best group rock album: La Ley's *Libertad*, Warner Music Mexico; best salsa album: Celia Cruz's *Regalo Del Alma*, Sony Music; best merengue album: Johnny Ventura's *Sin Desperdicio*, Musical Productions; best contemporary tropical album: Albita's *Albita Llegó*, Angels' Dawn Records; best ranchera album: Vicente and Alejandro Fernández's *En Vivo Juntos Por Ultima Vez*, Sony Discos; best banda album: Banda El Recodo's *Por Ti*, Fonovisa/Univision; best grupo album: Alicia Villarreal's *Cuando El Corazón Se Cruza*, Mercury/Universal; best Tejano album: Jimmy González Y El Grupo Mazz's *Live En El Valle*, Freddie Records; best norteño album: Los Tigres Del Norte's *Pacto De Sangre*, Fonovisa/Univision; best Latin jazz album: Chucho Valdés' *New Conceptions* on Blue Note; best instrumental album: Yo-Yo Ma's *Obrigado Brazil Live in Concert*, Sony Classical; best Brazilian contemporary pop album: Carlinhos Brown's *Carlinhos Brown Es Carlito Marrón*, Ariola/BMG Music Spain; best Brazilian rock album: Skank's *Cosmotron*, Epic; producer of the year: Javier Limón.

Carlos Santana, named the Latin Recording Academy's person of the year, and Los Lonely Boys, the year's breakout bilingual act, are among five duets peppering the ceremonies and offer a bilingual *La Bamba* and *I Don't Wanna Lose Your Love*. The others include rock bands Café Tacuba and Incubus (whose bilingual set is bleeped three times by CBS for questionable lyrics); L.A.'s Akwid and Puerto Rico's Roselyn Sanchez (performing in English and Spanish), and the aforementioned pairs of Valdes/El Cigala, Bisbal/Simpson, whose hot opener portends the evening's sensual heat quotient.

The solo spotlight shines on Mexico's Paulina Rubio and Marco Antonio Solís, Puerto Rico's Robi "Draco" Rosa and L.A.'s Ozomatli, of whom Lopez says: "This is a group so ethnically diverse, they get pulled over no matter who's driving."

Tom Capone, one of the losing producer of the year nominees who does produce winning LPs by Maria Rita and Skank, is killed in a traffic accident hours after leaving the downtown Shrine and attending several parties. He is the competition's most nominated Brazilian talent thus far. The 37-year-old dies when his rented motorcycle collides with a car at a Ventura Boulevard intersection in the San Fernando Valley and is thrown from the cycle onto a roadway and into a building. He is pronounced dead a little after 3 a.m. His body is returned to Rio De Janeiro where he's buried September 6.

Capone, whose real name is Luis Antonio Ferreira Gonçalves, is nominated for album of the year, producer of the year, best pop Brazilian album, with whom he shares the honor with singer Maria Rita for his engineering, and two nominations for record of the year for Rita's *A Festa* and Skank's *Dois Rios*. He is the first Latin Grammy nominee to die in an accident following the ceremonies. He is survived by his wife and one-month old son and by two children from a previous marriage, ages 11 and five. Besides being director of A&R for Warner Music Brazil, he's also able to function as an independent producer.

Apparently having had enough of low ratings on CBS, which is supposed to air the Latin Grammys in 2005, the sponsoring Latin Recording Academy in May of 2005 announces the awardcast will shift to Univision, and the sixth annual event will he held on November 3 at the Shrine Auditorium in Los Angeles rather than in its previous September slot. The show will run three, not two hours and switch from Wednesday to Thursday. The Academy affirms its decision by noting that while English-language awards show viewing among domestic Hispanics 18–34 is down 28 percent, viewership among this same age group for Spanish-language award shows is up 58 percent. Univision will promote the show on its air and on its TeleFutura and Galavision sister networks and on its Univision Radio Network and its Univision Website. Gabriel Abaroa, the Miami-based president of the Latin Recording Academy tells *Billboard* its membership questions why the show is in English and aimed at the wrong market. "We have the opportunity to create a deal at the right time," Abaroa says, "with the right network for the right market."

Among honors announced prior to the Latin Grammy's September telecast, Mexico's 57-year-old singing legend José José (legal name José Rómulo Soza Ortíz) is awarded the person of the year Grammy for his 36 years in show business. Six musicians are also awarded lifetime achievement awards: Sergio Mendes, Johnny Pacheco, Spain's Rocio Durcal, Brazil's Jorge Ben Jor, Cuba's Generoso Jiménez and Argentina's Sandro De America.

During the telecast which features English-language subtitles for non-Spanish-speaking viewers, Colombian rock singer Juanes is the top multiple winner with three trophies for rock solo album (*Mi Sangre*), best rock tune (*Nada Valgo Sin Tu Amor*), and best music video (*Volverte a Ver*). Dual winners include Spain's singer/songwriter Alejandro Sanz; Dominican vocalist Juan Luis Guerra and Brazilian composer Ivan Lins.

Sanz's awards are for *Tu No Tientes Alma*, which wins the prestigious record and song of the year; Guerra's honors are for best tropical song (*Las Avispas*) and best Christian album (*Para Tí*); Lins' *Cantando Histórias* walks away with both the album of the year and best Brazilian album.

In recognizing the broadcast's first carriage on a Spanish-language network, Mexican actor co-host Eduardo Santamarina proclaims, "The Latin Grammys have come home." Amidst this comfortable setting devoid of any English-language TV or music personalities, three upsets highlight the presentations. Italian vocalist Laura Pausini tops Spain's alternative singer/songwriter Bebe for female pop vocal album with *Escucha*; Obie Bermúdez's *Todo En Ano* wins the best male pop vocal album, the Puerto Rican from New Jersey besting Marc Anthony, Alejandro Fernández, and Marco Antonio Solís, while Los Angeles multiethnic, multicultural rock/jazz band Ozomatli's *Street Signs* nabs the best alternative album. Bebe, nominated in five categories, earns one Gramophone for best new artist, while Anthony is vindicated with the best salsa album for *Valió La Pena*. In the urban album category, Puerto Rico's hot reggaeton act, Daddy Yankee snares the trophy with *Barrio Fino*. The high-strung Bebe causes the only controversy during the straitlaced telecast when her edgy lyrics in her anti-domestic violence hit *Malo* are bleeped out, as are some comments during her acceptance speech.

In other categories, Elvis Crespo's *Saboréalo* wins best merengue album and Carlos Vives' *El Rock De Mi Pueblo* wins best contemporary tropical album. Two Cuban artists are honored: bassist Israel "Cachao" López 's *¡Ahora Si!* as best traditional tropical album and pianist Bebo Valdés *Bebo De Cuba* as top Latin jazz album. In the regional Mexican competition, Luis Miguel's *México En La Piel* is named best ranchera album; Banda El Recodo's *En Vivo* best banda album; Intocable's *Diez* best norteño album; Ana Bárbara's *Loca De Amar* best group album and *Polkas, Gritos Y Acordeónes* by David Lee Garza, Joel Guzman and Sunny Sauceda best Tejano album.

The switch to Univision attracts 5.1 million viewers, up from last year's 3.3 million viewers for the CBS broadcast, according to Nielsen Media Research. With its improved ratings as a backdrop, the Latin Recording Academy sets its seventh annual ceremony in New York for the first time, with the November 2 event from Madison Square Garden airing live on Univision.

The John K. Kennedy Center for the Performing Arts in the nation's capital, is the locale for the Hispanic Heritage Awards Foundation's 18th annual Hispanic Heritage Awards taped September 20, 2004 for airing on NBC eight days later and then on Telemundo. Of the six honorees, two are from the entertainment world, actor John Leguizamo and TV/radio sports soccer announcer Andres Cantor.

NBC is the second major TV broadcast network this year to carry a bilingual program in primetime, following CBS' recent coverage of the fifth annual Latin Grammys. The Heritage show's no-frills format moves the honors show along, featuring performances by Paulina Rubio, Karia Pasian, Mariachi Campanas De America, and an array of Latin film and TV actor presenters. TV personalities include Telemundo's Maria Celeste Arrarás, PBS' *NewsHour With Jim Lehrer*'s Ray Suarez, plus actresses Candela Ferro, Nia Long, Judy Reyes, and actor Nicholas Gonzalez; film actress Lacey Chabert, actor Gael García Bernal, and vocalist Carlos Vives. Andres Cantor, in accepting his award, says, "I want to be a role model for kids wanting to get into Spanish television. Kids can look up to me as their standard." There is a mixture of Spanish and English commercials-another first for NBC-by some of the nation's top brands.

As fall 2004 commences, Ryan Cabrera, a 21-year-old Dallas-raised, Colombian American rock guitarist breaks onto the *Billboard* Top 200 albums chart in September with his debut Atlantic album, *Take It All Away* at No. 8 and then slowly slides downward right through the early months of the new year, until it hits 188 on May 7 of 2005 and is gone the next week. For a while in the early months of 2005, Cabrera has two singles on *Billboard*'s Hot 100, the prophetic *On the Way Down* (which is the direction it's going) and is gone after 26 weeks by January 22, and *True*, which debuts December 11 at No. 52 and remains on the survey 29 weeks until May 14 of 2005 and is then history. A follow-up CD, *You Stand Watching*, shows a shorter chart presence, bowing in 24th place and by the middle of November it's in 177th place and heading south.

His first English-language CD is a genuine hit for the singer who starts off playing in a high school punk rock band and learns to speak Spanish with his grandmother's assistance by watching Telemundo and its soap operas. Although he becomes a bonafide recording star, his career is somewhat clouded by his on-again, off-again friendship with his next-door Dallas neighbor Ashlee Simpson, whose dad winds up managing them as well as older sister and MTV personality Jessica.

One artist seeking to broaden his appeal, and not see fans defect, is Colombian vocalist Juanes, born Juan Esteban Aristizabal, whose third Surco/Universal album, *Mi Sangre* (*My Blood*) faces a daunting task. Can it surpass or equal the record sales of his second LP, *Un Diá Normal*, which is last year's top-selling Spanish-language album in the U.S. with 559,000 units sold, according to Nielsen SoundScan, out of a total of 1.8 million copies sold worldwide, according to the record company. Like most things in music, figures are malleable, with the label claiming domestic sales of 800,000, 241,000 more than the independent SoundScan reports. Juanes is so hot during 2003 that *Un Diá Normal* wins the Latin Grammy album of the year award, plus five other titles.

His heat carries over to 2004 where *Mi Sangre* debuts in the No. 1 slot on the Top Latin Albums chart and cracks the Top 200 albums survey that same week in October in 33d place, the newest Latin artist to hit the mass-market chart. The CD spends nine weeks on the Top 200 list, dropping to 178 and then exiting the survey. However, the LP remains on the Top Latin albums list as the year ends.

Percussionist Henry "Pucho" Brown, one of the key figures in the 1960s Latin boogalu movement in New York City which cements Latin, jazz, and soul into a funky dance music with a sound all its own, emerges with an album on Milestone which recalls those fusion sounds all but forgotten in Latin music today. *The Hideout* CD, named after a notorious bar in Harlem, the section of Manhattan where Brown is born, features Pucho and His Latin Soul Brothers septet whose reeds, brass, and violin create an infectious spicy ingredient for songs ranging from Stevie Wonder's *Superstition* to Bebo Valdés' *Guajeo En Dominante* to Les Baxter's *Quiet Village* to Brown's own title tune.

Brown forms this band in 1966, disbands it three years later and reforms it in the mid-1990s with its first new release, *Rip a Dip*, appearing in 1995 on Milestone Records. Following single album releases for different labels in ensuing years, including his last recording in 2000, *How'm I Doin'?* on Cannonball Records, Brown is out of the record business, working personal appearances instead. From 1966 through 1969, Pucho and associates release eight albums on Prestige Records, acquired in the 1970s by Fantasy Records of Berkeley, California, which also owns Milestone, the former New York-based jazz independent.

One of the pioneering East L.A. Chicano rock bands from the 1950s, The Armenta Brothers, makes its long delayed debut on the Brown Bag Records CD, *Lifetime Achievement*. Known as the "Pride of East L.A." and as the house band at the El Monte Legion Stadium where touring bands from Mexico and the U.S. perform, this is the group's first album in its 55 years as an L.A. favorite group. It is also its first-ever studio session, which revives some of its repertoire including *Pachuco Hop* and *Corrido Rock*.

Brown Bag, in operation since 1998, uses as its slogan "America's Music From East of the L.A. River." Its initial releases include two Tierra titles originally released in 1973 and '75 by two different labels and combined in a two-disc set, *Tierra/Stranded*. The label follows that with *Si Se Puede!*, an anthology of tunes honoring Cesar Chavez and the United Farm Workers of America union featuring various Chicano bands including Los Lobos.

El Chicano, one of the seminal Latin/rock crossover bands of the '70s, which has been out of the limelight for years despite playing some 100 dates around the world, pops up with its MCA reissue disc, *The Best of El Chicano*. The band is also scoring a documentary on the life of the late union organizer Cesar Chavez. It makes a rare L.A. appearance in October at the John Anson Ford Amphitheatre on the bill with songwriter Mark Guerrero & Radio Aztlán. These two groups along with Tierra, another former hit Latin crossover ensemble, are among the groups performing at last year's Latin Oldies Festival in San Bernardino, California. El Chicano, formed in 1968 in East L.A. as the V.I.P.s, blends bilingual lyrics with Latin and rock tempos and some R&B tossed in for diversity. Its transformation of jazz bandleader Gerald Wilson's *Viva Tirado* instrumental homage to

Mexican matador Jose Ramon Tirado in 1970 on its debut MCA album as El Chicano, becomes its ticket onto the general market best-selling singles and album charts. Between 1970 and '76, the band records seven LPs for MCA and is the first reported Chicano band to play the world-renowned Apollo Theater in New York's Harlem. Following its departure from MCA, the band records an album for CBS in 1982, with MCA issuing a collection of its tunes under the title, *Chicano Chant* in 1997, and a greatest hits collection in 1988, *Viva! El Chicano, Their Very Best* and licensing five other titles to Bomba Records in 1995. The band starts its relationship with L.A.'s Thump Records in 1995 with *Latin Legends Live*, which includes performances by Malo and Tierra, followed by *Painting the Moment* in 1998. Thump is a repository for oldies and Chicano bands.

While the band's original lineup for its debut album includes Bobby Espinoza on organ, Mickey Lespron, guitar; Freddie Sanchez, bass; Andre Baeza, congas, and John De Luna drums, its personnel changes with the years. When guitarist Lespron performs on *Painting the Moment*, his return marks 20 years away from the El Chicano lineup.

While Chicano bands have the taint of other era, a number of record companies are targeting the Latin teenybopper market—a population looming as a new source of revenue, especially since the rigidity of Latin radio is opening up a bit as a growing number of stations program for this teen audience born in the U.S. and acculturated. Among the labels signing teen-oriented acts in the pop, rock and urban regional categories who can write about salient youth-oriented, dual cultural topics are Sony, BMG, EMI, Universal and Univision. In fact, Univision Music Group senior vice president of national marketing Lupe De La Cruz boasts to *Billboard* that young age Latino artists are connecting with fans who buy Anglo rap acts 50 Cent, Black Eyed Peas and Jay-Z. "Now they have music that is relevant to them," he says. In addition to teenage consumers, labels are also targeting the 17–25 group, which likes its flavors of the month young, spunky, and relevant to today's world.

Among Hispanic broadcasters eyeing the 12–17 demographic, Telemundo's youth-oriented mun2 network and Entravision Communications radio stations which air its teen-flavored Super Estrella format, are joined by industry giant Clear Channel Radio, which plans to convert 20–25 of its English-language stations to Spanish within 18 months. Of its 1,270 U.S. stations, 18 currently are Spanish formats geared for older listeners.

Acts helping build the youth movement vary in age and may be home-grown or from Mexico or Puerto Rico where youth is more readily accepted. For example, EMI Latin's JD Natasha is 16, Univision's Jae-P is 19; Sony's Reik is a trio of teens while its Ha-Ash are teen sisters; Universal's Angels are preteen girls while Alih Jey is 21 and focused on the older demographic. Other acts building a base for the youth movement include: Akwid, Flakiss and Crooked Stylo (EMI), Yolanda Perez (Univision), Kalimba, and La Sinfonia (Sony); Belinda and brothers Andy & Lucas (BMG). JD, whose complete name is Natasha Jeannette Dueñas, writes and sings her own tunes in Spanish and English on her debut CD, *Imperfecta-Imperfect*. Growing up in Miami, the singer/guitarist is exposed to the bilingual world, resulting in this language mixture on the 14-song album, which relies on hard rock arrangements for its contemporary, mainstream appeal.

Rock en Español bands in Houston struggling for respect, are starting to percolate on a new level of awareness. The nascent movement is being recognized by two Hispanic FM radio stations, KROI and KLOL, and the 25-year-old Anglo Numbers nightclub which sets aside two evenings each month to showcase local Latin rock bands. Among the groups benefiting from this attention are the bilingual quartet Volátil plus two groups, Los Gallos and Triple, which maintain a collegial attitude, like working gigs together and sharing members when necessary rather than trying to cut each other out of jobs.

Citing the potential of the Latin music industry and the need to push for greater marketing budgets to gain greater domestic album sales, veteran talent managers Irving Azoff and Alejandro Asensi form AA Music Management in Los Angeles to foster the careers of their current Latin clients and also build a boutique agency with a small client roster.

Azoff's initial Latin client is Christina Aguilera while Asensi represents Mexican superstar Luis Miguel. Azoff also represents Jewel, Seal, the Eagles, Van Halen, and Babyface through his agency, azoffmusic management.

The new agency's first client is Miguel whose next release on Warner is due in November. It will also handle Aguilera for the Latin market and help promote her second Spanish-language Sony BMG release due next spring.

The new partners join a small coterie of name mangers working with Latin artists, notably Tommy Mottola with Marc Anthony, Benny Medina with Ricky Martin, and Ceci Kurzman with Shakira after years with Freddy DeMann.

New Mexico, known as the "Land of Enchantment," boasts of an enchanting new concert venue in Albuquerque, the $22.8 million Roy E. Disney Center for the Performing Arts, located on the 51-acre National Hispanic Cultural Center in the Barelas low-income suburb outside the city. Funding for the Disney Center is a combination of private and federal dollars. Opened four years ago, the National Hispanic Cultural Center (NHCC) and its foundation support "cross-cultural appreciation and understanding" of Hispanic culture and achievements.

Originally a nonprofit organization, it's now a state agency which operates a research library, art museum, restaurant and store. The new performing arts center contains the 691-seat Albuquerque Journal Theatre, the 288-seat Bank of America Film Theatre and the 97-seat Wells Fargo Auditorium, large and small rehearsal halls, four star dressing rooms, four chorus dressing rooms, and the Graciela Katarina Gonzales Green Room.

Under the banner of *Maravilla*, the Disney Center formally opens its doors to the public with a series of events September 17–30. The first concert program September 18 features trumpeter Arturo Sandoval, tenor Daniel Rodriguez, mezzo-soprano Suzanna Guzmán, the New Mexico Symphony, the pop group Soluna, the Francisco Martinez Dancetheatre, flamenco guitarist Chuscales, vocalist Rebekah Del Rio, and flamenco dance troupe Yjastros.

Other evening activities include:

Screenings in the Bank of America Film Theatre of the Roy E. Disney produced, Salvador Dali inspired animated short, *Destino*, and Nancy De Los Santos' *The Bronze Screen* documentary which celebrates 100 years of Latino Hollywood history, and a performance in the NHCC's Plaza Mayor by San Francisco Latin funk band Los Mocosos.

An evening of hip-hop, dance, and poetry in the Albuquerque Journal Theatre featuring Zimbabwe Nkenya, Echetal Danza Azteca, and the National Flamenco Conservatory.

Five Latina comics are showcased during a taped concert in the Journal Theatre.

Screenings of film shorts, documentaries, and the hit theatrical film, *Real Women Have Curves*, along with appearances by several of its cast members, highlight daylong activities at the Bank of America Film Theatre.

Zoot Suit night at the Journal Theatre offers a staging of the Luis Valdez written play, the first ever by a Chicano playwright to run on Broadway and then become a film starring Edward James Olmos with direction by Valdez.

The nascent Latin music digital video disc business shows signs of turning Christmas into a green-colored holiday of flowing dollar bills. DVDs are catching on with the public as a greater number of titles are released this year. According to the Recording Industry Association of America, a record number of Latin music DVDs, 726,000 are shipped to stores during the first half of this year. Last year, during the same midyear period, 208,000 DVDs are shipped to retailers. In a lot of instances, CD/DVD combinations, first introduced last year, are gaining status as the hot item to buy. Especially since the roster of artists releasing these combo discs keeps expanding to include Alejandro Fernández, Maná, Marco Antonio

Solís, Los Temerarios, Shakira, Luis Fonsi, La Ley, and Ricardo Arjona, among others. DVDs provide the visual augmentation of a band performing live. Maná's package, for example, includes concert and documentary footage as does Shakira's, while La Ley's offers the band's 23 videos. The market's additional growth in 2005 is covered later in this chapter.

When the closing year's top products of 2004 are released in *Billboard*'s final recap issue, one of the surprise results centers around Marc Anthony, who debuts at No. 1 on the Top Latin Albums list twice with his first pop release, *Amar Sin Mentiras*, and then a salsa version of the album under the title *Valio La Pena*. Both are on Sony Discos. In addition to Anthony, 18 other acts reach No. 1 on the Latin Albums listing, notably: Los Temerarios, Marco Antonio Solís, A.B. Quintanilla, III & Kumbia Kings, Bronco/Los Bukis, Paulina Rubio, Intocable, Victor Manuelle, Grupo Montéz De Durango, Los Tigres Del Norte, Adán Sánchez, Conjunto Primavera, Jennifer Peña, Lupillo Rivera, Daddy Yankee, Bronco El Gigante De América, Grupo Climax, Juanes, and Luis Miguel.

In order of importance, the top 25 Latin album artists include a swath of familiar money-earners: Los Temerarios, Marco Antonio Solís, Grupo Montéz De Durango, Los Tigres Del Norte, Marc Anthony, Juanes, Maná, Vicente Fernández, Grupo Climax, La Oreja De Van Gogh, Joan Sebastían, Don Omar, Intocable, Akwid, Conjunto Primavera, A.B. Quintanilla, III, Kumbia Kings, Los Bukis, Paulina Rubio, Pepe Aguilar, Adán Sánchez, Sin Bandera, Alejandro Fernández, K-Paz De La Sierra, and K-Paz El Gigante De America.

The five top Latin album companies are Univision Music Group, Sony Discos, Disa, Universal Latino, and EMI Latin. The top 10 Latin pop acts are Juanes, Marco Antonio Solís, Maná, La Oreja De Van Gogh, Marc Anthony, Paulina Rubio, A.B. Quintanilla, III, Kumbia Kings, Sin Bandera, and Thalía. The number uno record producer is Rudy Pérez, followed by Estéfano, Aureo Baqueiro, Jose Luis Terrazas, Emilio Estefan, Jr., Jesus Guillen, Sebastian Krys, Pepe Aguilar, Sergio George, and Luis Fernando Ochoa.

2004 is a good year for the sale of Latin albums, which are up 23 percent over last year, according to year-end Nielsen SoundScan statistics, which shows 32.3 million units gobbled up by the public, but offers no dollar value for their purchases. One major reason for the increase in sales is the availability of product at large national chains to the detriment of small family-owned record shops which heretofore are the main source for recorded entertainment. The leading distributor of Latin records continues to be Universal Music & Video Distribution, with 48.1 percent of all album sales, followed by the new Sony BMG with 23.6 percent of the sales.

When the general market 47th annual Grammy nominations are announced in mid-December, Latin artists or compositions are represented in 20 of 107 categories. The eventual winners in their categories are: Los Lonely Boys, pop vocal performance by a duo or group; Charlie Haden, Latin jazz album, *Another Kind of Blue: The Latin Side of Miles Davis* (Verve International); Marc Anthony, Latin pop album, *Amar Sin Mentiras* (Sony Discos); Ozomatli, Latin rock/alternative album, *Street Signs* (Concord); Israel "Cachao" López, traditional tropical album, *¡Ahora Si!* (CineSon/Univision); Spanish Harlem Orchestra Featuring Rubén Blades, salsa/merengue album, *Across 110th Street* (Libertad); Intocable, Mexican/Mexican-American album, *Intimamente* (EMI Latin); David Lee Garza, Joel Guzman and Sunny Sauceda, Tejano album, *Polkas, Gritos Y Acordeónes* (Guzman Fox); Paquito D'Rivera, instrumental composition, *Merengue* from *Obrigado Brazil* (Sony Classical), and guitarist David Russell, instrumental solo performance, *Aire Latino* (Telarc).

During the three-and-a-half hour telecast on February 15, 2005, three Latin artists perform out of a total of 29. In addition to Los Lonely Boys, who include some Spanish in their performance, Jennifer Lopez and husband Marc Anthony sing together for the first time anywhere. The couple reprises the dramatic ballad, *Escapémonos* (*Let's Escape*), sung entirely in Spanish, which first appears on his current hit Epic album, *Amar Sin Mentiras*, and is their follow-up to *No Me Ames* which they sing on her 1999 Epic album, *On the 6.*

Escapémonos could mirror their real life goal of not being scrutinized and finding a safe haven. "Let's hide from the crowd/from the day to day absurdities/where all those disturbing things are/no longer in our lives" is the repetitive thought performed in a bedroom setting, where Jennifer takes off her satin robe to reveal an unbecoming gown from another era, a stark contrast to Mark's contemporary white shirt, tie and black suit. Hand-in-hand they depart their boudoir setting. While some in the audience at the Staples Center in downtown Los Angeles audibly disapprove of their singing entirely in Spanish, their highly hyped duet together is obviously designed to appeal to those bilingual Hispanics CBS hopes are tuning in. Unfortunately, she sings off-key several times while he's sturdy and follows the score correctly. Show host Queen Latifah, in introducing the pair, calls Lopez Anthony's "partner in music and in life." Lopez will later explain throat problems cause her faulty singing.

Good news continues in April of 2005 when the Recording Industry Association of America, the trade organization for major record companies, reports that during 2004 shipments of Latin recordings jump 25.6 percent to 48.5 million units shipped to retailers over last year's 38.6 million units. The value of the music shipped is placed at $650.7 million, a record amount since the organization begins tracking Latin product in 1997. The caveat here is that these figures are for recordings shipped, not sold.

The newest Latin fusion sound to emerge from the West Coast that shows signs of elasticity in 2005 is urban regional music, a subgenre of Latin urban, featuring regional Mexican elements mixed with rap. In some instances it's competing for attention with the reggaeton rap crowd and the Latin alternative rockers. Labels seeing dollars in both urban Latin and the new urban regional music's future start to proliferate. In the urban Latin field, EMI Latin introduces its New Element logo; Warner Music Latina bows Mic Discos and the Universal Music Group launches Machete Records, which acquires 50 percent of Puerto Rico's reggaeton specialist label VI Music. With a few exceptions, like Univision's Daddy Yankee and Vico C on New Element, urban Latin acts are not receiving exposure on most Latin radio stations. Univision's Fonovisa Records jumps into the competition by signing David Rolas, Locura Terminal, and Enemigo. Urban regional's flag-waver is L.A.'s Akwid leading the charge for Univision Records and gaining strong airplay.

When Warner Music Latina signs a distribution/marketing deal with Dope House Records in 2005, it gains not only an imprint specializing in urban Latin music, but also a company whose English/Spanish CDs will be handled in-house by Atlantic Records. With a name like Dope House, one wonders if there's a hidden message imbedded in its moniker which will inspire radio play and consumer sales. Its two owners are brothers Arthur, Jr. and Carlos Coy, who record under the name SPM. The label's other act is Juan Gotti, first out with the Warner Latina album *John Ghetto* in April, which includes a guest appearance with Grupo Pesado, a regional Mexican band and label mate.

Miami-based EMI Latin and Mexico's Grupo Televisa partner in the formation of a new U.S. record company, EMI Televisa Records, as part of a Mexico City-based joint venture that debuts September 1 following its July announcement. The label will include established acts like Thalía, Intocable, Vico C, and A.B. Quintanilla and the Kumbia Kings.

Three years ago, Televisa sells its Fonovisa label for around $235 million in stock to Univision, which includes the label in its Univision Music Group. Now, with Televisa's non-compete clause having run out in April, the conglomerate freely re-enters the record industry to develop projects with its U.S. partner for both the U.S. Hispanic and Mexican markets. Televisa, locked in a nasty legal feud with Univision TV, for whom it provides the majority of its primetime novelas (reported on later in this chapter), can now compete against Univision's record label empire.

A historic joint venture between two major companies is not, however, without extracting its human toll. Jorge Pino, EMI Latin's president/CEO for four years is forced out and replaced by Rodolfo López-Negrete, BMG U.S. Latin's former chairman, who brings along BMG's former A&R vice president Adrian Posse.

Sony Discos sees potential in the Bronx, New York, quartet Aventura, which specializes in the traditional music of the Dominican Republic called bachata, by signing a distribution pact with Platinum Music, the act's record company. The group's first release under the new distribution arrangement is *God's Project*, it's third for Platinum. The CD features guest appearances by reggaeton acts Don Omar and Tego Calderón and singer Nina Sky. What's unusual about this group is that lead singer Anthony Santos' tune, *Obsesión* (*No Es Amor*), from its first album, *We Broke the Rules* (released in 2002), becomes a hit in Russia, France, Germany, Spain, Italy, and Norway in Spanish, while the English version by unknown Frankie J cracks the American singles charts.

Frankie J is one of 2005's surprise new breakout stars, who vaults from his backup singing position with the Kumbia Kings to become a chartbusting solo artist on the general market singles and album chart. The 26-year-old, born Francisco Javier Bautista Jr. in Tijuana, who moves with his family to San Diego, bows on the *Billboard* Hot 100 with his Columbia Spanglish single, *Obsession* (*No Es Amor*) featuring Baby Bash in January and then makes an impressive debut on the Top 200 albums survey in third place with his *The One* CD April 9. It's the singer's first solo album since going off on his own in 2003 with his debut CD *What's a Man to Do?* While the new album is principally in English, there's a Spanish version of *Obsession* and a reggae version as a bonus track.

While *The One* CD remains on the Top 200, *Obsession* is no longer anyone's obsession and is replaced on the singles survey in June by the new *How to Deal* and by September is working its way down and off the chart. *The One* also begins its decline and by December 3 is 194th.

Shakira joins the singles sellers' list in May with her Sony Discos *La Tortura* featuring Alejandro Sanz which precedes her Sony BMG Norte June album release, *Fijación Oral, Volumen 1*. In a reactive action to the singer's inability to make an in-store promotional visit to promote *Fijación*—her first Spanish album in seven years—the powerful

42-store Ritmo Latino chain cancels its initial five figure order for the chain and orders a lesser amount for a small group of its new stores. The record company tells *Billboard* a scheduling conflict prevents the singer from appearing at a Ritmo Latino outlet. She does, however, draw a mob to appearances at a New York Virgin Megastore and a FYE outlet in Miami. Ritmo takes that to indicate Sony and Shakira are focusing on her crossover audience rather than her Latin followers. One week later, all is forgiven as the singer agrees to a fall in-person appearance at an undisclosed Ritmo outlet, and the retailer begins selling the CD throughout its chain. In its first week, the album sells close to 157,000 copies, according to Nielsen SoundScan, doubling the amount ever sold by a Spanish-language album in its first week in this country, skyrocketing to the No. 4 slot on the Top 200 mainstream chart and the No. 1 position on the *Billboard* Top Latin Albums survey.

Oral Fixation, Vol. 2, an all-English follow-up slated as her next release, features along with all new tunes, a collaboration with Carlos Santana. It's her first English-language LP in four years and it debuts on the best-selling list at No. 5, which along with her previous No. 4 slotted *Fijación Oral Volumen 1*, makes her the year's lone artist to have two albums in dual languages land in the top five. Her crossover popularity also earns her the favorite Latin award during the nationally televised American Music Awards in November. One month later, she wins the Billboard Music Awards Latin pop album artist of the year. In addition, her video for the hit single, *La Tortura*, becomes the first Spanish-language music video in regular rotation on MTV and its sister VH1. Following an appearance on Saturday Night Live, she is slated to perform on *MTV's New Year of Music* New Year's Eve telecast from Times Square. By June 3 of '06, after 25 weeks on the chart, the CD is in 25th place and dropping.

Mariah Carey launches her comeback career, returning to the best-selling singles chart with her Island single, *We Belong Together*, which debuts in 81st place April 16, a far cry from her previous year's performances. Six weeks later the single is in third place and on June

4 it hits No. 1, the 35-year-old's 16th career chart topper and the most for any female vocalist. Sixteen weeks later, it's still No. 1.

Amazingly, Carey's reenergized status results in her sustaining three singles on the best-selling list on December 3: *Don't Forget About Us*, *Shake It Off* and *We Belong Together*. In crafting her return to hit status, her studio-produced hybrid sound of R&B with rap undercoating rhythms echoes the dominant sound of the blues genre.

The No.1 single is obviously the path setter for the five-octave singer's Island album *The Emancipation Of Mimi*, which is her nickname, which debuts on *Billboard*'s April 30th top album chart in the No. 1 slot, as a result of selling 404,000 copies in the week prior to the chart's publication, according to Nielsen SoundScan statistics. Five weeks later, the CD remains in second place for the fourth straight week, and after bouncing back to No. 1 and dropping to fifth, by September 10, it's back to No. 3, and then begins its yo-yo decline...again. The album is so popular for the comely comeback queen that it sells four million copies, going platinum four times since being released. A follow-up CD, appropriately titled *The Emancipation of Mimi: The Platinum Edition*, is released November 15 in two separate formats, CD and CD/DVD, the former containing the original 14 songs plus new tracks, while the dual version contains videos of four songs.

When the general market 48th annual Grammy nominations are announced December 7, Mariah's remarkable comeback produces eight nominations (along with a similar number for rapper Kanye West and new R&B singing sensation John Legend) prior to the February 8 televised ceremonies from Los Angeles. They include album of the year and best contemporary R&B album for *The Emancipation of Mimi*; record of the year, song of the year, best female R&B vocal performance and best R&B song for *We Belong Together*; best female pop vocal performance for *It's Like That*, and best traditional R&B vocal performance for *Mine Again*. While she is stymied in the major categories, she does walk away with three honors in the R&B field, all from her *Emancipation* album: top female vocal, song, and contemporary album. Her previous Grammy was in 1990 as the year's new artist. The Grammy-winning album helps land her a starring role in the interracial film drama *Tennessee*, which shoots in New Mexico and Tennessee in the spring of 2006. It's her third role following *WiseGirls* in 2002 and *Glitter* in 2001.

And when *Billboard* announces winners of its 18th annual Music Awards December 6 at the MGM Grand Garden Arena in Las Vegas, Carey is named five times during the Fox TV telecast. She wins top female album artist, top female R&B/hip-hop artist, Hot 100 song of the year, Hot 100 airplay tune of the year and rhythmic Top 40 title, all for the single *We Belong Together*. She is also scheduled to end the year by closing out *Dick Clark's New Year's Rockin' Eve 2006* on New Year's Eve from Times Square.

Carey ends her concert and tour hiatus after three years in the summer of '06. Following a July 29 concert at the Kodak Theater in Hollywood, she embarks on a 30-city U.S. tour commencing August 15 through October 10. Titled "The Adventures of Mimi: The Voice, The Hits, The Tour," the sojourn features a compilation of tunes from her latest CD plus hits from her 15 album catalog, along with surprise guest artist appearances. The smash album, after 58 weeks on the survey as of June 3 of '06, is in 58th position following a resurgence up from No. 95.

The *Emancipation* title reflects her seeking distance from her failed five-year marriage to Columbia Records chieftain Tommy Mottola, who signs her to the label in 1988 and several disappointing albums including *Charmbracelet* and her first album for EMI/Virgin, *Glitter* in 2001. On January 24, 2002, Virgin releases her from her contract with an astonishing $49 million payoff broken down into two parts $28 million plus $21 million she receives when signing in April of 2001, citing disappointing reviews of both the CD and a similarly titled film. In its Mariah cover story, *Parade*, the Sunday newspaper supplement, notes the new album's title also reflects failed romances with New York Yankees star Derek Jeter in 1998 and Argentine vocalist Luis Miguel the next year. Mariah's previous top debuting album, 1999's *Rainbow* sells 323,000 copies. The new rap-laden *Emancipation* project features guests Snoop Dogg, Twista, and Nelly. It's the 14th album for the Long Island born singer since her self-titled LP in 1990, and whose multinational background includes Venezuelan, African American, and Irish American traces.

Two brothers from San Bernardino, California, Bobby (28) and Isaiah "Iz" (27) Avila, who initially break into the music business as writers and producers in 1993 and work for such powerhouse acts like Usher, Janet Jackson, and Mary J. Blige, emerge from their behind-the-scenes roles with their own record label, ABX Records in 2005 and their debut CD, *The Mood: Soundsational*, an English mixture of rap and R&B.

Two record company partners parting ways and going their separate paths are Anthony Perez and Jorge Guadalupe of Perfect Image Records. Guadalupe's new partner is Ivy Queen, the reggaeton star and former Perfect Image artist, who form Filtro Musik. First release is a reggaeton compilation *Cosa Nostra* followed by Ivy Queen performing with various female singers in other styles of music on *Drama Queen*. Perez's company is Roof Records, reflecting the similarly named mun2 TV series that he produces, which is supposedly leaving that Telemundo-owned network for the all music videos little know seven-year-old Más Música TeVe channel. Among the label's artists are Big Boy and Tribales, a reggaeton group that compliments the label's series of *Jamz* reggaeton compilations.

Colombia's Estéfano after spending his time writing songs for other artists, records his first solo singing album, *Código Personal: A Media Vida*, a mixture of acoustic and electronic sounds, which Universal Music Latino releases September 20. Born Fabio Alonso Salgado in Cali, he arrives in the U.S. in 1989 and after stints in New York and Los Angeles winds up in Miami where the money he earns by writing songs for Gloria Estefan, Jon Secada, Julio Iglesias, Chayanne, Shakira, Paulina Rubio, Marc Anthony, and Thalía, enables him to establish Estéfano Productions Group and Midnight Blue Studios. In 1995, Estéfano and Donato Poveda become recording artists for Sony Discos, where they enjoy several hits before disbanding one year later.

Lou Pearlman, the wizard behind the success of the Backstreet Boys and *NSYNC, decides to bring his expertise to the Latin market via his new Trans Continental Latino label, with his first signing C Note, another boy band. C Note, which previously records for Epic, will sing in English, Spanish and Spanglish on its debut EP released September 27. In 2007, Pearlman's music empire is nonexistant and as of January, he leaves the country with Florida and federal officials chasing after him for perpetuating what could be one of the largest Ponzi fraud cases in the state's history, according to *USA Today*.

When the 16th annual *Billboard* Latin Music Awards airs live on Telemundo April 28, 2005, from the Miami Arena, recipients are basically well-known artists with a few new names reflecting contemporary musical styles. The star appeal produces a record two million viewers and an 11.6 rating, up from last year's 8.2, thus giving the network its highest rating since it begins airing the show in 1999. The top album winners of the year include: Latin pop-Juanes, male album for *Mi Sangre* (Surco/Universal Latino); Paulina Rubio, female album for *Pau-Latina* (Universal Latino); A.B. Quintanilla, III/Kumbia Kings duo or group for *Fuego* (EMI Latin); Juliet Venegas, new artist for *Si* (Ariola/BMG Latin); Sony Discos as top album label.

In individual categories, Los Temerarios wins as Latin album artists (Fonovisa/UG); Ozomatli wins rock/alternative album for *Street Signs* (Concord Picante); Marco Antonio Solís and Joan Sebastían, greatest hits album for *Dos Grandes* (Fonovisa/UG); Univision Music Group as top Latin album label; Paco De Lucia, jazz album for *Cositas Buenas* (Blue Thumb/GRP); Akwid, rap album for *KOMP 104.9 Radio Compa* (Univision/UG); Rudy Perez top producer and Leonel Garcia top songwriter.

In tropical music-Juan Luis Guerra, male album for *Para Ti* (Vene/Universal Latino); Omara Portuondo, female album for *Flor De Amor* (World Circuit/Nonesuch/Warner Bros.); Monchy & Alexandra, duo or group album for *Hasta El Fin* (J&N/Sony Discos);

Michael Stevan, new artist for *Recordando Los Terricolas* (Fonovisa/UG); Universal Latino as top album label.

In regional Mexican-Luis Miguel, male album for *Mexico En La Piel* (Warner Latina); Grupo Climax, male duo or group album for *Za Za Za* (Musart/Balboa); Los Horóscopos De Durango, female group album for *Locos De Amor* (Procan/Disa); Grupo Climax, new album artist for *Za Za Za;* Univision Music Group as top album label.

Award-reaping Akwid, fast becoming L.A.'s hottest Spanish rapping commodity, does what many artists with notoriety and new-found riches do, the brothers Francisco and Sergio Gomez start their own record company, Hefes Records, a joint venture between Diwka, their company and Headliners Records, their current label, which Univision Records distributes. The new label's initial release aimed at the youth audience during the summer of 2005, notes *Billboard* features Kuky, a Mexican American rapper/vocalist/tunesmith. Two tracks by Akwid add additional promotional power to the release.

Three show business personalities, P. Diddy, rapper Pitbull (Armando Christian Perez), and Emilio Estefan, become partners in Bad Boy Latino, a record company focusing on urban Latin music. Perez of Cuban descent, born and raised in Miami by his mother, is a popular force in Spanish rap, whose appearance on MTV2's *Hip Hop Connection* bridges what network executive Amy Doyle tells *Latina* magazine is the "cultural gap" by encompassing various musical elements including reggaeton with his Spanish-language dialogs.

Reggaeton's infectious beats and lyrics continue gaining the ears of some English-language radio stations who find the commercialized Puerto Rican-inspired music appeals to bilingual, acculturated young listeners in 2005. These Top 40/contemporary hits stations in large markets are adding Spanish tunes by a growing number of Latin rappers led by Yankee Daddy, Don Omar, Luny Tunes, and Ivy Queen. Arguably the leader in adding Spanish tunes to its programming is Miami's prescient WPOP-FM, followed by city mate WRMA-FM, plus WKTU-FM, and WHTZ-FM in New York, KISS-FM in Los Angeles, KZZA-FM Dallas/Ft. Worth and WIOO-FM Philadelphia. In addition, many English programmers converted by Clear Channel to Spanish programming are also expanding the exposure for a variety of Spanish formats, including reggaeton tracks.

Adding impetus to the music's apparent steady growth in 2005 are Spanish stations converting to the catchy "hurban" sound featuring rap and bilingual DJs or adding individual song titles to their playlists, with *Billboard* pointing out that Nielsen Broadcast Data Systems is tracking a growing number of stations that play hurban-driven reggaeton. They all follow Puerto Rico's SBS outlet which flips its English-language Top 40 WODA-FM to reggaeton specialist WVOZ-FM, followed in June of 2005 by the switch of another of its Puerto Rican stations, WOND from meringue to reggaeton. Among the other format switchers are Univision Radio's KCOR-FM San Antonio and New York's WCAA-FM, which both promote themselves as "La Kalle (The Street)." WCAA competes against rival Spanish Broadcasting System's market leader WSKQ-FM, which spices its tropical format with reggaeton and rap. The same music mix occurs at KXOL-FM, its former Latin pop station in Los Angeles, which promotes itself as "Radio Reggaeton Y HipHop Too" and features bilingual Spanglish DJs aimed at attracting coveted 12- to 24-year-olds. The music switch results in KXOL bounding from 18th in the spring into a tie for second place in the summer Arbitron survey with Latin programmer KLVE-FM. In other switches, SBS' Miami's alternative rock KZLA-FM changes its call letters to WMGE and Clear Channel's KLOL-FM in Houston shifts from rock to a bilingual format combining reggaeton with rap.

Univision Radio follows its WCAA New York switch on May 27, 2005, by additionally adding eight more converted markets to the music mix targeting second- and third-generation bilingual Hispanics: Chicago's simulcasting WVIX-FM/WVIV-FM; Las Vegas' KQMR-FM; San Francisco's simulcasting KWF-FM/KWZ-FM; San Antonio's AMOR-FM (formerly KCOR-FM); Dallas' KFZO-FM; and Miami/Ft. Lauderdale's WRTO-FM on August 2.

Additional conversions occur at Sun City Communications KFMR-FM Phoenix which promotes itself as Club 95: Latino Vibe; Infinity's WYUU-FM in Tampa, which drops its country rock format to become La Nueva FM 92.5, and Entravision's Dallas KZZA-FM which becomes Casa 106.7.

By the fall of 2005, around 30 stations have changed formats, some from one Spanish format to hurban, others switching from faltering English-language formats. In most instances, the music change produces better ratings. According to *Billboard*, this is the case with KRZZ-FM San Francisco (shifting from adult contemporary to regional Mexican); KSJO-FM San Jose (shifting from classic rock to regional Mexican); WZTA-FM Miami (shifting from alternative rock to hurban as WMGE-FM); WHFS-FM Washington, D.C., going from rock to tropical as WLZL-FM; WKKB-FM Providence dropping English for tropical music; and at Atlanta's first Spanish station WWVA-FM.

There's also a Spanish version of the "Jack," the non-stop Top 40-style format minus DJs gaining popularity among English-language rock stations converting to the constant play format. Entravision Radio shifts five of its 54 Hispanic stations to the non-stop format under the slogan "José: Toca Lo Que Quiere (José Plays What You Want)." These stations include Albuquerque's KRZY-AM, Denver's KMXA-AM, Sacramento's KRCX-FM, Stockton's KCVR-AM, and Modesto's KCVR-AM.

As 2006 unfurls, several station groups introduce still another format: Latin oldies hits from the '70s through the '90s. Clear Channel, the first chain to play oldies in 2003 under the format "La Preciosa," says it will link its 13 oldies stations (formerly playing English formats) into a new La Preciosa network and offer the music to other radio companies, notes *Billboard*. It is joined in the oldies brigade by Univision Radio which switches KCOR San Antonio from reggaeton and its Dallas station KLNO-FM from regional Mexican to its new "Recuerdo" format. Entravision's "José" format launched in October of 2005, and patterned after English-language radio's "Jack" style of non-stop hits, includes oldies titles at its seven José outlets. While Latin stations tinker with new formats in 2006, several either drop their reggaeton programming or see declining listenership, as a cooling off system descends during the spring. Cities affected include Los Angeles, Miami, Dallas, and Las Vegas, notes the *Los Angeles Times*.

In another forward moving development, a number of Puerto Rican-based reggaeton producers are being hired by mainstream rappers, R&B and pop singers to create reggaeton remixes of their songs or original songs to tap into the music's growing acceptance. Artists seeking to tap into the music's growing popularity among young Latinos who may also produce an expanded fan base include Alicia Keys, Jay-Z, Ja Rule, and Sean Paul as well as familiar Latin pop acts like Ricky Martin, Jennifer Lopez, and Enrique Iglesias, notes *Billboard*. Francisco Saldana (Luny) and Victor Cabrera (Tunes), collectively known as Luny Tunes and Bimbo are the ace producers landing these money-making assignments.

Reggaeton's trendy acceptance in 2005 is one factor fueling the Latin population's powerful sales impact on the record industry as reflected by the number of Spanish-language albums being sold which wind up on the mainstream top albums listing. During the first six months of 2005, the sales of Latin albums grows 17.6 percent over the same time frame last year, according to Nielsen SoundScan, with the No. 1 CD rapper Daddy Yankee's *Barrio Fino* on *El Cartel/VI*, selling 525,700 copies. His panache helps land a new single, *Rompe*, on the chart in 90th place December 3. That same month the LP approaches one million copies sold, while an earlier crossover single, *Gasolina*, becomes the genre's first platinum disc for 200,000 copies shipped. *Barrio Fino* to lasts 49 weeks on the chart, dropping to 175, but rebounds to 138 as of December 10, '05 and the disappears to be replaced in January by *Barrio Fino: En Directo*, which is in 119th place on June 3 of '06 after 23 weeks on the survey.

Far a field from reggaeton's growing popularity, Concord Picante, Concord's Latin jazz imprint, celebrates its milestone silver anniversary in May with a four-CD, 50-track box set, the *25th Anniversary Collection*, which recasts its own popularity roster. The aural documentary encompasses the distinctiveness of Afro-Cuban, salsa, rhumba, samba, charanga, and calypso through the artistry of Cal Tjader, Tito Puente, Eddie Palmieri, Poncho Sanchez, Laurindo

Almeida, Charlie Byrd, Tânia Maria, Mongo Santamaria, Ray Barretto, Pete Escovedo, Monty Alexander, the Caribbean Jazz Project, Ray Vega, Ozomatli, and Jeff Linsky, along with a strong list of guest artists on many of these recordings.

Ry Cooder, having helped popularize the vintage music of Cuba in his series of 2000 and 2001 Grammy-winning recordings focused around the Buena Vista Social Club, sets his sights on the Chicano music of a section of Los Angeles made famous by the Los Angeles Dodgers. Chavez Ravine is the Hispanic community torn asunder by the Brooklyn Dodgers who choose the community for its new stadium where the transplanted team plays its first game in 1962 following four years at the 100,000 plus seating Los Angeles Memorial Coliseum starting in 1958. That's the year owner Walter O'Malley deserts the New York borough after 68 years for greener pastures in L.A. And instead of green pastures, his Dodger Stadium sits atop a hill overlooking downtown L.A.'s staid skyline. *Chavez Ravine* is now the title of the June 2005 Nonesuch/Perro Verde release which is sung in English and Spanish and is a mixture of conjunto, corrido, carló, a vintage Mexican American dialect and jazz and blues. The album quickly lands on both the top Latin Albums charts and the Top 200.

The LP is steeped in history and musical wonders, including the last song by the late Don Tosti, and Lalo Guerrero, who records three tunes. Other guest artists include Little Willie G, accordionist Flaco Jimenez and singers Erzi and Rosella Arvizu (Guerrero's nieces). Dodger Stadium, which displaces Mexican American families from various neighborhoods, is memorialized in two closing songs on the CD: *3rd Base*, *Dodger Stadium* and *Soy Luz Y Sombra*, which reflects positive thoughts for the future.

Thalía is also in a state of mind mode with her *El Sexto Sentido* (*The Sixth Sense*) EMI Latin album, her 11th studio session which includes English-language versions of three tunes in the all-Spanish release. It's the follow-up to her 2003 eponymous titled English-language debut CD. In a departure for EMI, the new CD will be released concurrently in the U.S., Latin America and Japan, followed by Europe, Canada, Australia and the remainder of Southeast Asia, reports *Billboard*. In the past, EMI first releases Spanish-language discs in the U.S. and Latin America, and then goes into non-Latin nations. And in another first, EMI is working with Apple Computer's iTunes online store to provide digital distribution orders for the CD, which earns the buyer free downloads of two special singles.

The music of the late composer Antonio Carlos Jobim highlights a spring two-day business and cultural symposium in Ft. Lauderdale, Florida. With the state's estimated 250,000 resident Brazilians as the cornerstone for the gathering, the Symphony of the Americas led by Claudio Cruz, the conductor of the São Paulo State Symphony, performs the North American premier of *Jobim Sinfonico* at the Broward Center for the Performing Arts. The work premieres and is recorded in Germany in 2002 and wins a 2004 best classical Latin Grammy. Paulo Jobim, the guitar-playing son of the composer who passes away 10 years ago, is among the 75 musicians performing the work, which includes his father's classic tunes *A Felicidade* and *the Girl From Ipanema* and some earlier works prior to the bossa nova craze of the early '60s.

The 12th annual Brazilian Summer Festival is set a blaze by Beth Carvalho, Brazil's "Queen of Carnival" at Los Angeles' John Anson Ford Amphitheatre in June. The 40-year-old samba legend attracts a full house of resident Brazilians, who, according to the *Los Angeles Times*, sing along with her and are motivated to dance along with the on stage dancers and musicians in her quartet, the Quinteto Em Branco E Preto, augmented by guest musicians Chocolate, yes that's the trumpeter/drummer's name, saxophonist/flutist Dirceu Leite, and guitarist Carlinhos 7 Cordas.

Three superstars, Marc Anthony, Chayanne, and Alejandro Fernández, perform together for the first time on their history-making summer tour of large seating venues in 15 U.S. cities. Their blending of Anthony's English-language pop and Spanish salsa, Fernández's ranchera and Chayanne's Spanish pop ballads is designed to appeal to an audience which accepts all forms of Latin music. The three contemporary Sony artists will alternate who's the opening act and even work together if they choose to. Launching August 17 in Houston, the tour encompasses locales in Texas, Arizona, California, Illinois, New York, Washington, D.C., Georgia, and Florida, terminating in Miami September 16.

As fall unfurls, Eduardo Cruz, Jr., brother of actress Penélope Cruz, and John Santos, an Oakland-based conguero, celebrate milestones. Cruz is signed to Warner Music Latina where he'll record his debut album in Los Angeles in 2006; Santos celebrates the 20th anniversary of his Bay Area group, the 10-piece Machete Ensemble, whose pan-Caribbean style blends salsa, plena, jazz, and Afro-Cuban ingredients.

Ricky Martin, absent from the music scene since 2002, releases his first all-English Columbia album in five years, *Life*, in October. It's a personal reflection of his life, his humanitarian work and his travels to Puerto Rico, Egypt, Thailand, and Brazil, which inspires musical elements from these journeys woven into the recording. It doesn't do well, bowing at 31 and then dropping to 111 by December 11 as it heads off the survey. A single, *I Don't Care* featuring Fat Joe and Amerie, cracks the Hot 100 on October 15 at 88, drops to 98, rises to 65 and then drops out of sight. While his three-year absence obviously affects his record-selling power, Martin will be touring in the U.S. next spring following dates in Latin America.

Another crossover star, Carlos Santana, fares better than Martin with his new Arista album, *All That I Am*, debuting at No. 2 November 19. The disc features duets with 12 artists including Steven Tyler, Mary J. Blige, Sean Paul, Los Lonely Boys and Bo Brice. A companion DVD, *Live By Request*, features performances from Santana's two previous Arista LPs *Supernatural* and *Shaman* mixed in with other Santana performances.

Juelz Santana, no relation of Carlos, breaks onto the nation's best-selling album chart with his second Diplomat/Def Jam album, *What the Game's Been Missing!* On December 10 in ninth place. A single, *There It Go! (The Whistle Song)*, hits the top singles survey eight weeks earlier. The artist, a Honduran/African American rapper, born Laron Louis James on February 18, 1982, previously recorded with the groups Draft Pick and the Diplomats. The Harlem resident's debut album, *From Me to You*, comes out in 2003. Santana's earlier lyrics extolling the "courage" of Mohammed Omar Atta, a September 11 terrorist and pilot of one of the planes that crashes into the Twin Towers, draws angry criticism. He counters those comments with a lyric that shows empathy for the victims of the World Trade Center disaster.

As 2005 concludes, regional Mexican remains the dominant genre of salable Latin music, notes *Billboard* in its year-end sales recap. Univision Music Group's hit regional Mexican acts result in its becoming the top-selling Latin label for the second consecutive year. Disa, one of the Univision labels (along with Univision and Fonovisa), is the genre's top label. Sony BMG is the dominant imprint in the Latin pop and tropical categories. Individually, Daddy Yankee and Shakira are the two top-selling Latin artists.

In 2005, death takes Eduardo "Lalo" Guerrero, 88, the pioneering barrio singer with a comedic and socially conscious eye on his bicultural experiences March 17 in a nursing home in Palm Springs, California, where he'd been suffering with prostate cancer. It's a long way from his home in Tucson where his mother teaches him to sing and play guitar. His music captures the Chicano world during World War II that is at the core of the 1977 stage musical, *Zoot Suit* set in the barrios of Los Angeles. Among his 1940's hits is *Marijuana Boogie*; his comedy parodies covering pop tunes span four decades: 1955's *Pancho Lopez*, a take off on the hit pop tune *Davy Crockett; No Chicanos on TV*, and 1990's *Mexican Mamas, Don't Let Your Babies Grow Up to Be Bus Boys*. In its obituary, the *Los Angeles Times* mentions Guerrero performs on Los Lobos' 1995 Grammy-nominated bilingual children's album, *Papa's Dream* and in 1997 becomes the first Chicano honored with the National Medal of Arts, which he receives from President Clinton. A television documentary is in preparation by his son Dan and filmmaker Nancy De Los Santos. Its title: *Lalo Guerrero: The Original Chicano*.

Bandleader Jose Melis, arguably the second most recognized Cuban on U.S. television behind Desi Arnaz in the 1950s, passes away April 7 in a hospital in Sun City, Arizona, of a respiratory infection at age 85. During the mid-1950s, the piano-playing musician is the musical director for a series of Jack Paar shows on CBS from 1953–'56, followed by NBC's *The Tonight Show* from 1957–'59 when the program is renamed *The Jack Paar Show* until it goes off the air in 1962 and becomes *The Tonight Show* again under Johnny Carson. Born in Havana as Jose Melis Guio and trained as a classical pianist at the Havana Conservatory of Music and at New York City's Julliard School of Music, Melis is drafted into the U.S. Army during World War II in 1943 and becomes a naturalized citizen in 1944. It's during his Army days that he meets Paar and is named leader of a 40-piece Army band that plays at various USO venues.

As a result of his *Tonight* show exposure, Melis records eight albums starting with Latin label Seeco Records and then for Mercury Records. During his career, Melis also works with a number of top names including Frank Sinatra and Tito Puente and appears as a guest soloist with several symphonies including the Boston Pops Orchestra.

Jamie Mendoza-Nava, 79, a classically trained musician from La Paz, Bolivia, who turns to film composing in the U.S. in 1953, dies May 31 of complications from diabetes at the Kaiser Permanente Medical Center in Woodland Hills, California. In addition to writing for the Walt Disney Company's TV series *The Mickey Mouse Club* and *Zorro*, he also works on the *Mr. Magoo* theatrical cartoon series for United Productions of America. After stating his own firm, he composes music for more than 200 films in the horror, sci-fi, and adventure fields. He is survived by his wife, four children, two brothers, and four grandchildren.

Ibrahim Ferrer, the longtime Cuban tenor, whose career is resurrected when he becomes a member of the Buena Vista Social Club recording group in 1998, dies in Havana, August 7 after completing a month-long European tour, and entering the hospital for treatment of gastroenteritis. The 78-year-old is also suffering from emphysema. He is the third member of the Buena Vista Social Club to pass away: singer Compay Segundo and pianist Rubén González die in 2003. After a long career as a singer with various Cuban bands in the '40s, '50s and '60s, including supplementing his musician's income during the early years of the Castro government by working various jobs, Ferrer finally retires in 1991, only to be discovered by Ry Cooder and Cuban bandleader Juan De Marcos González in 1997. They record him first with the Afro-Cuban All Stars debut album *A Toda Cuba Le Gusta* and then as a member of the Buena Vista ensemble whose eponymous album features him on the cover, sells six million copies and wins a Grammy award that year as well. The band is featured in the 1999 Wim Wenders documentary anent the band and the Cuban music of the 1940s era, the same year Ferrer records his solo debut album, *Buena Vista Social Club Presents Ibrahim Ferrer*, which sells 1.5 million copies. In 2000, Ferrer wins the best new artist award at the first Latin Grammys. This new artist is 73. His follow-up album, *Buenos Hermanos*, is released in 2003 and wins a Latin Grammy and a regular mainstream Grammy the next year as the best traditional tropical Latin album.

A proponent of Cuba's pre-revolutionary musical style called son, which blends African and Spanish rhythms, Ferrer gains a reputation as a sonero, or improvising vocalist. He's born in the city of Santiago, the home of the son movement. His survivors include his wife Caridad Diaz.

Ray Barretto, the conguero who mastered the worlds of salsa and Latin jazz during a career spanning nearly 50 years, dies February 17, 2006, of complications following quadruple bypass surgery at an unnamed hospital in New Jersey. The 76-year-old musician of Puerto Rican ancestry, born in Brooklyn and raised by his mother in the Spanish Harlem section of Manhattan, gains notoriety with the 1963 hit *El Watusi*, which earns him a place on the Fania Records roster. During the salsa heat spell of the '60s through the '80s, he records close to two dozen albums for the company, segueing to Latin jazz when the salsa movement faded. As a sought-after percussionist, he plays with both jazz and rock bands ranging from Cal Tjader, Cannonball Adderley, Dizzy Gillespie to the Rolling Stones, and the Bee Gees. During the latter years of his life, he records three albums for Concord. His last, *Time Was-Time Is*, released in September of 2005, is nominated for a Grammy in the best Latin jazz category. Prior to being hospitalized in January of 2006, he is given one of the nation's highest jazz honors by being selected one of the National Endowment for the Arts' Jazz Masters of 2006. He is survived by his wife Annette Brandy Rivera, children Raun, Ray Jr., Kelly, Christopher, and four grandchildren.

Pio Leyva, 88, another member of the Buena Vista Social Club, dies March 23, 2006, in Havana of a heart attack following a stroke suffered four days earlier. Although not on the 1997 original hit album, Leyva appears in the ensuing film documentary anent the group and on its international tour. During his career, he sings with the bands of Bene More and Bebo Valdes, makes records for RCA Victor in the 1950s, and works later with another Buena Vista Social Club member, the late Compay Segundo.

Rocio Durcal, 61, the popular Spanish film star who developed a second hit career as a recording artist performing traditional Mexican music, passes away March 25 in her home outside Madrid following a five-year battle with cancer. Born Maria De Los Angeles De Las Heras Ortiz, she begins her film career in 1961, shifting to music in 1977 and, the year she meets Juan Gabriel, whose songs she records on copious albums, including her theme song, *Amor Eterno* (*Eternal Love*). She is survived by her husband and three children. Gaining fans in the U.S. for her music, she was the first Latina to headline at the Universal Amphitheatre in the San Fernando Valley section of Los Angeles in 1984, following that with additional gigs at the venue until her last concert there in 2002, one year after her first cancer surgery, according to the *Los Angeles Times*.

Soraya, the 37-year-old pop singer born in New Jersey, and partially raised in Colombia, her parents' native land, dies of breast cancer May 11 in Miami. She'd been diagnosed with the disease in 2000, putting a halt to her career to undergo various treatment including a mastectomy, breast reconstructioan and 12 months of chemotheraphy, according to the *Los Angeles Times*. A video she records about her cancer is aimed at telling Hispanic women there is no shame in having cancer. Her career begins in 1996 with the release of her debut album, *On Nights Like This* in English on Island Records and in Spanish *En Esta Noche* on the Polygram Latino U.S. label. The album is dedicated to her mother who dies of breast cancer in 1992. In 2004, after resuming her career, she wins a Latin Grammy for her eponymous CD in the best singer/songwriter category. In 2005, her album *El Otro Lado De Mi*, is also nominated for a Latin Grammy. Her survivors include her father, brother, and extended family.

Pianist/composer Hilton Ruiz, a child prodigy who performs at New York's Carnegie Hall when he's eight, dies June 6 in a New Orleans hospital following a fall May 19 in the French Quarter which leaves him comatose. The New York-born Latin jazz musician of Puerto Rican parents, and a resident of Teaneck, New Jersey, was working on a Hurricane Katrina benefit project. The 54-year-old is survived by his wife and daughter, both named Aida. Several weeks after her father's death, the daughter sues a Bourbon Street dance club, charging he was attacked and beaten there, with the club's bouncers offering no protection during the assault and assistance following the attack, according to the *Hollywood Reporter*.

Sergio Mendes, the tireless leader of crossover act Brasil 66 and 67, emerges in February of 2006 with *Timeless*, his first album in eight years combining multiple musical styles. The Concord/ Starbucks Hear Music CD cements samba with R&B and rap and includes guests Will.I.Am of Black Eyed Peas, Justin Timberlake, India.Arie, Erykah Badu, and Stevie Wonder. The CD encompasses new renditions of past hits like *Mas Que Nada* and *Fool on the Hill* (which he performs in the White House for President Richard Nixon, and whose irony is not lost on the growing anti-Vietnam war movement).

Amidst the 48th annual general market Grammy Awards February 8, the following Latin album awards are proffered: Latin Jazz: Eddie Palmieri for *Listen Here* on Concord Picante; Latin pop: Laura Pausini for *Escucha* on Warner Music Latina; Latin rock: Shakira for *Fijacion Oral Vol. 1 on Sony*; tropical: Bebo Valdes for *Bebo De Cuba* on Calle 54; salsa: Willy Chirino for *Son Del Alma* on Latinum Music; Mexican/Mexican American: Luis Miguel for *Mexico En La Piel* on Warner Music Latina; and Tejano: Little Joe Y La Familia for *Chicanisimo* on TDI.

Christina Aguilera, the Grammy-winning, bilingual sex siren for her English-language crossover hits, focuses on recording both English- and Spanish-language albums in 2006 for RCA. Her English-lingo CD, *Back to Basics*, features a mixture of soul, blues, and jazz-tinged elements, five of which are produced by rap specialist DJ Premier. Her duet with Andrea Bocelli on *Somos Novios* from his hit CD *Amore* (released in February of 2006), follows earlier duets with Ricky Martin and Justine Timberlake on her multi-platinum album *Stripped*. The multicultural singer with an Ecuadorian/Irish heritage first gains popularity when her 1999 eponymous album debut earns her a Grammy for new female artist.

The Latin explosion prods Time Life to expand its release of Hispanic-themed specialty albums. Its latest venture in April of 2006 is a 10-CD set, *El Canto De Sirenas* (*The Sirens' Song*). The series highlights popular tunes from the 1930s to the 1980s performed by top torch singers like, according to *Billboard*, Lola Flores, Libertad Lamarque, and Lola Beltrán, among others. A 30-minute infomercial running on Spanish-language TV is hosted by Daniela Romo, who also performs on the compilation.

RBD, Univision's hot young adult Mexican stars of its *Rebelde* musical series, while on the heels of a U.S. concert tour of 39 arena shows in the spring of 2006, releases its newest album, *Live in Hollywood* on April 4. The album by the sextet is recorded at the Pantages Theater in Hollywood. It's the winsome group's third album since its premiere *Rebelde* in January of 2005 and its *En Vivo* and

Nuestro Amor follow-ups several months later. What's unusual about this popular group of 19- to 24-year-olds is its being signed and managed by Mexican TV giant Televisa. The group's CDs are released on the joint EMI/Televisa label. RBD plans recording another Latin pop CD following the end of the soap opera's run in the U.S. in December. The TV series begins on the U.S. Mainland in March of 2005, following launches in January in Puerto Rico, Brazil in September, and Mexico in 2004. By 2006, the group's domestic popularity results in the three albums making the *Billboard* Top Latin Abums chart, with *Rebelde* winning two *Billboard* Latin Music Awards and the sextet voted the Telemundo Viewer's Choice Award.

A number of top Latin artists, led by Gloria Trevi and Ivy Queen, record a Spanish-language version of the National Anthem, *The Star Spangled Banner*, in April of 2006. *Nuestro Humno* (*Our Anthem*) on Urban Box Records is designed to show support for migrants in the U.S. Sung primarily in Spanish with some English words, the tune also appears on the album *Somos Americanos*. The song, with some altered lyrics, debuts on Hispanic radio April 28 as a prelude to May Day demonstrations May 1 against immigration reform laws. It produces a backlash ranging from President Bush to conservative radio talk show hosts on Anglo stations. The president tells reporters: "I think people who want to be a citizen of this country ought to learn English and they ought to learn to sing the National Anthem in English," reports the *Los Angeles Times*.

Sales figures for 2005, released in April of 2006, are up 12.6 percent over 2004, reports Nielsen SoundScan, which tracks retail sales. According to *Billboard*, major factors contributing to the rise, besides the nationally expanding Hispanic population, include major retail chains Wal-Mart, Kmart, Borders, and Barnes & Noble stocking Latin albums to accommodate customers in both big and small cities. And with secondary markets attracting touring regional Mexican acts, more people are attending concerts and then purchasing CDs at both the big chains and small family-owned record stores. There's also the phenomenon, according to NPD Group, a

Port Washington, New York-based research firm, of non-Latins buying close to 30 percent of all Latin recordings since 2003.

The explosive news that Clear Channel—the largest, most revered, envied and often despised radio network because of its tightly controlled formats and ancillary artist promotional activities—is converting upwards of 25 lower-rated English stations from its 1,270 station group to Spanish-language formats in 2004–'05, is another major indicator of the appeal and potential the rising Hispanic population offers. Already operating 18 Spanish formats, the new additions will only bring the company's Spanish properties to around two percent of its stations. The San Antonio-based division of Clear Channel Communications, sensing the sluggish growth for English-language radio, gears up for its latest push into Latino radio by hiring Alfredo Alonso as its senior vice president of Hispanic radio. He's the former president/CEO of Mega Communications, which owns 20 radio stations, and has a reputation for turning around losing formats and introducing new ones.

The company plans finding openings in mid-sized markets in the West and Southwest where the Hispanic population may be underserved by the other behemoths of Spanish radio like Univision Communications, which owns 68 stations; Entravision Communications with its 53 stations; Spanish Broadcasting System which used to own 27 stations and is winnowing down its properties to 19 on the Mainland and Puerto Rico, and Liberman Broadcasting with its 15 stations. The first Clear Channel stations switched over in September are Atlanta's low-rated talker, WMAX-FM and its suburban simulcaster, WHEL-FM, which become contemporary pop WWVA and WVMA (*Viva Atlanta*).

The next switchover occurs in San Jose October 28, where rock station KSJ0-FM is converted to regional Mexican hits *La Preciosa*, aimed at 25–54 listeners. In February, Clear Channel switches Orlando's WEBG-FM from oldies to become "Rumba 100.3." During 2005, in addition to shifting its Houston station to the hurban Hispanic format, Clear Channel also converts Albuquerque's KZPR-FM, Miami's WZTA-FM, and Denver's KMGG-FM to the hurban community.

KMGG's slogan "Latino and Proud" is representative of the chain's focus on attracting 18-34-year-old bilinguals at all these locations. By February of 2006, Clear Channel has switched the desired 29 stations to Spanish. The hurban switchover is a small but trendy movement within the nation's 678 Spanish radio station community.

While Clear Channel focuses on building its Spanish empire, one of its English-language 50,000 watt stations, KLAC-AM in Los Angeles, is experimenting with a Latin music themed Sunday show, *Viva the Rhythm*, from noon to 3 p.m. during 2004–'05. The hybrid show, which features both pure Latin music by Latin artists and Anglo singers warbling songs with Spanish titles or sparked by Latin tempos, is initially hosted by Gil Avila, co-founder and past president of Nosotros, and Jon Denny and co-produced by Denny and José "Pepe" Molina. It's focused on bilingual listeners and includes in-studio interviews and performances by both local and nationally known musicians, and phone-in interviews with major names from other cities. By 2005, Denny is the show's lone host.

Brad Chambers, KLAC's program director, says he's not aware of any other English-language station in the nation offering a hybrid Latin music show. The adult standards station which plays music from the "Great American Songbook" includes many of these artists in its mix of music, which ranges from 9 to 10 tunes per hour, he informs me. "We're focusing on English-speaking Spanish households, the same people who like the music we ordinarily play and the traditional English-language audience which is our core and probably doesn't listen to Latino radio at all. But appreciates the historic significance of the Latin contribution to American music," says Chambers, who's been the station's program director since December of 2002 when the station drops its talk format and returns to music. He's also the host of the morning drive-time show.

The station's principal listeners are 35 years and up, which also covers *Viva the Rhythm*, which debuts June 6 in place of the regular middle-of-the-road music heard during that time period. Although I regularly tune in the station, I'm stopped cold one Sunday in August when I hear the Fania All Stars on KLAC and discover the program.

For co-producer/host Denny, the show is designed to "reflect the sounds and spirit of 21st century Los Angeles where 50 percent of the population is Latino. It's the music of their lives. If you aren't speaking English and recognizing Spanish, then you're living in another place all together."

Denny feels the show provides "an opportunity to reach out to a vibrant and real audience that major English-language stations are not recognizing." (Spanish-speaking Latinos have 17 Hispanic radio stations in the L.A., market which program for the dominant Mexican majority first and then to immigrants from other Latin nations. None, however, has the 50,000-watt signal KLAC possesses, which enables it to cover a broad range of terrain outside of the L.A. area.)

The music mix is designed to be "both exciting and palatable to people who are just learning and hooking into Latin music as well as to those who may live and breathe it for the last 30 years. The way we wean people into Spanish-speaking artists is to let them hear Eydie Gorme doing *Blame It on the Bossa Nova*. It's walking that line but being true to the rhythms." The music mix includes such artists as Pérez Prado, Machito, Tito Puente, Tito Rodriquez, Willie Bobo, Eddie Cano, Willie Colón, Eddie Palmieri, Jose Feliciano, Astrud Gilberto, Trio Los Ponchos, Gloria Estefan, Susie Hansen, and Eliane Elias, among others. The show averages two guests per stanza. By 2005, the show is being syndicated to 170 stations across the country by programmer Music of Your Life.

A former New Yorker, Denny, says he got hooked on Latin music fairly late in 1999 when he attends his first Latin concert at Carnegie Hall starring Celia Cruz, Tito Puente, and Arturo Sandoval. What prompts him to see that concert? I ask. "A half Latina girlfriend," he answers and then laughs.

Denny and Jose "Pepe" Molina meet socially three years ago. In the summer of 2003, Molina brings the concept for *Viva the Rhythm*, which he and Denny discuss to Greg Ashlock, Clear

Channel's regional vice president. The premise is that English-dominant Hispanics are a "very underserved community in Los Angeles." "He tells me the station would like to get involved because of the sheer size of the population," Molina recalls, "and because he wants the station to be inclusive and reach everyone."

In January of 2005, Clear Channel breaks the news it will switch the music format from KLAC's 570 dial position to its 690 AM Tijuana-based station XTRA, which will drop its sports talk format on February 3. As 2005 concludes, Clear Channel plans unloading 690 to Grupo Mexicana, a Madrid company with studios in Tijuana, which reformats the station as Spanish talk on February 6, 2006. *Viva the Rhythm* will have to find an L.A. outlet since Music of Your Life does not have an affiliate there.

Spanish Broadcasting System (SBS), located in the Miami area of Coral Gables, is in a retrenching mood, and in need of cash to pay down its debt. So it sells Chicago stations WDEK, WKIE, and WKIF for $28 million in cash to Newsweb Radio Group and two of its L.A. outlets, KZBA and KZAB, to Styles Media Group for $120 million in cash, leaving it with 19 stations.

SBS initially creates a stir when it bows KZBA and its suburban cousin in March 2003 as *La Sabrosa*, which concentrates on playing tropical music from Central America to ensnare that location's growing L.A. population. In a formal statement, SBS president/CEO Raul Alarcón notes the sales from these two Los Angeles transactions plus earlier station sell-offs "totaling approximately $230 million will be available to reduce outstanding debt and strengthen our balance sheet." SBS' KLAX-FM (*La Raza*), with its new morning personality, Reñan Almendarez Coello, whom it hires away from Univision's KSCA-FM last March after Coello leaves that station in a labor dispute, is No. 2 in the market.

Then in a dramatic move in October, Viacom International, Inc., the giant media conglomerate, announces it is "merging" its low-rated Infinity Broadcasting San Francisco English-language radio station KBAA-FM (ranked 37th out of 44 stations Arbitron rates) into

SBS in exchange for a 15 percent ownership stake in the company, 10 percent now, five percent at a later date. The value of the radio station and Viacom's initial stake in SBS is estimated to be worth $75 million. The arrangement also gives Infinity the right to purchase an additional five percent of the company. SBS surprisingly keeps the station's English-language adult contemporary music, simulcasting this format with its sister station KBAY-FM.

As part of the groundbreaking deal with Viacom—which owns and operates 185 stations in 22 of the nation's largest markets—SBS and Viacom divisions including CBS and Viacom Outdoor advertising will jointly market their properties to Hispanic consumers. The connection with SBS and its 22 stations is significant for Viacom since its earlier interest in getting into Hispanic broadcasting by taking over Telemundo is overshadowed by NBC's acquisition. Les Moonves, Viacom's co-president, indicates to the *Wall Street Journal* the possibility exists of Infinity and SBS striking similar deals in smaller cities with expanding Hispanic populations.

True to Moonves' word, Infinity reformats its low-rated Washington, D.C., alternative rocker WHFS-FM to El Zol 99.1 with a mixture of music from the Caribbean and Latin America in January of 2005. The interfacing of salsa with merengue and bachata dance tunes is designed to attract 25 to 54-year-olds from the D.C. metropolitan area's 400,000 plus Hispanics, a 25 percent rise in Latinos during the past four years, according to 2002 Census figures. SBS acts as a consultant/advisor in the switch to Spanish music.

Joel Hollander, Infinity Broadcasting's newly promoted chairman/CEO, calls the D.C. format change "a tremendous opportunity to launch a Spanish-language format where 10 percent of the population is not being directly served."

In a third major multicultural transaction in November, SBS signs a five-year distribution deal with ABC Radio Networks for the syndication of its three top-rated morning shows in New York, Los Angeles and Miami. Shows ABC will syndicate and sell advertising on are KLAX-FM Los Angeles' *El Cucuy De La Manaña* with Reñan Almendarez Coello; WSKQ-FM New York's *El Vacilón De La Mañana* with Luis Jiménez and Ramon "Moonshadow" Broussard (which also airs in Puerto Rico) and WXDJ-FM Miami's *El Vacilón De La Mañana* with Enrique Santos; and Joe Ferrero.

Darryl Brown, executive vice president of ABC Radio Networks, indicates these three programs will attract Mexican, Cuban and Puerto Rican listeners. ABC Radio, which provides English-language programming to 4,700 affiliates, also syndicates parent Disney's ESPN Deportes radio version of the similarity titled Spanish-language TV network. In February 2005, ABC announces the formal formation of the Hispanic Advantage Network with a fall premiere as the first Spanish radio network owned by an Anglo company. Programming will consist of several SBS syndicated morning shows acquired in its recent five-year deal with the Spanish network, ABC Radio's Hispanic Major League Baseball coverage and programs from sister radio network ESPN Deportes.

Already heavily entrenched in radio, SBS in July of 2005 makes its first foray into Spanish-language TV with a $37.5 million purchase of Miami's WDLP (Channel 22) from William De La Pena, according to the *Hollywood Reporter*. The Coconut Grove-based company's new station called Mega TV, also covers nearby Ft. Lauderdale, while its three radio stations in Miami, WCMQ-FM, WRMA-FM, and WXDJ-FM, provide it with the initial opportunity to sell commercials and cross-promote its programming on both radio and TV, similar to the way Entravision and Univision Communications utilize their radio and TV properties across the nation. In addition to offering 75 percent original programming, Mega TV plans syndicating its shows to other U.S. stations in the summer of 2006, with international sales by the fall.

SBS also makes radio history by bowing its first all-English music countdown show on KXOL-FM, its bilingual Los Angeles station in March of 2006. The Sunday show, *The Rick Dees Weekly Top 40 Con Sabor*," airing from 6 a.m. to 10 a.m., features former longtime KISS-FM morning personality Dees, whose other countdown show is his nationally syndicated *Rick Dees Weekly Top 40*. For KXOL, the music mix contains reggaeton, rap, urban and top 40 hits.

Four of L.A.'s popular Latin radio personalities help spur 500,000 marchers to a historic pro-immigration downtown rally March 25, 2006. The call to march is prompted by KSCA's Eddie Sotelo, KBUE's Reñan Almendarez Coello, Ricardo "El Mandril" (The Baboon) Sanchez, and KHJ's Humberto Luna. They follow up their initial clarion call to protest on March 25 by appearing together in front of City Hall on March 20 to further stimulate protest over proposals in Congress to tighten immigration laws, which could affect the estimated 11 to 12 million undocumented aliens in this country. Police claim it's one of the largest demonstrations in the city's history. Prior to radio's support, KMEX, the Univision TV station covers the ground roots buildup on March 13.

In a surprise announcement in December of 2004, as Univision Radio makes major changes in a number of cities around the country, its president McHenry Tichenor reveals his resignation at the end of this year to "pursue other interests," one year after Univision purchases the 68 station Hispanic Broadcasting Corporation, which Tichenor's family owns for 23 years, and renames it Univision Radio. Tichenor remains as a consultant and director with the company. My earlier wide-ranging interview with this erudite Spanish-language radio network pioneer is contained in Chapter 16.

Entravision communications is also involved in selling its stations in Chicago, WRZA-FM and WNDZ-AM to Newsweb for $24 million and WZCH-FM for $5 million to NextMedia Group.

Soccer, a major attraction on Spanish-language TV, enters the L.A. radio market as Entravision's KLYY-FM regional Mexican cumbia music specialist (*La Cumbia Caliente*) signs a two-year pact with 16-year-old Fútbol De Primera of Miami to carry its exclusive soccer coverage and news programs. Primera is co-owned by renowned soccer announcer/personality Andres Cantor, whom I interview in Chapter 11, and has its own network of radio stations that carry its soccer coverage, including Cantor's daily two-hour news/commentary show. Commencing October 11, KLYY airs Cantor weekdays from 7 to 8 p.m. KLYY's general manager Karl Meyer, who also oversees Entravision's two other L.A. cluster stations, KSEE-FM and the KLDL-FM/KDLE-FM combination, calls the addition of soccer "the perfect compliment to the station's format" since the Los Angeles market is home to eight million Hispanics, the vast majority with Mexican roots and a passion for music and soccer."

As the year ends, Entravision switches three stations from its *Radio Romantica* Spanish adult contemporary format to its *Super Estrella* network aimed at 18 to 34-year-olds. The "flipped" stations (the radio industry term for a format change) include KJMN Denver; KRRE Sacramento and KLOB Palm Springs, California, which are now hearing music by the likes of Shakira, Maná and Paulina Rubio. The company also acquires syndication rights in February of 2005 to SBS' Los Angeles morning personality Reñan Almendarez Coello, which it sends to its Radio Tricolor Network, including outlets in 13 Hispanic markets.

In late July of 2005, Entravision sells its two San Francisco stations, KBRG-FM and KLOK-AM, to Univision for $90 million. The addition gives Univision Radio six stations covering the San Francisco/San Jose market, including KSOL-FM/KSQC-FM which simulcast its Spanish adult contemporary music and KWZ-FM/KWF-FM, which equally share a regional Mexican format. KBRG broadcasts Spanish contemporary music while KLOK, a Spanish tropical music outlet, switches to Univision's RadioCadena new/talk/sports format.

Knocked off the air amidst the horror and destruction wrought by Hurricane Katrina on New Orleans August 29, 2005, during the nation's worst natural disaster, Univision's tropical station KGLA-AM returns to work September 4 to provide continuous news coverage about Katrina's aftermath and new damage inflicted by Hurricane Rita, which adds to the misery along the Gulf Coast region. The Big Easy station acts as a conduit for the Hispanic community searching for relatives and friends and work opportunities.

MultiCultural Radio Broadcasting Inc. of New York, acquires the financially troubled Hialeah, Florida, headquartered Spanish news/talk network Radio Unica and its 15 stations for $150 million in cash. The network ceases to exist and the time is leased to independent producers for their own multi-ethnic programming. MultiCultural Radio, formed in 1972 as the first multi-language media company, operates 48 stations, all of which offer leased time foreign language formats, including Spanish. A company official in New York tells me he has no idea how many brokered Spanish stations there are.

Los Angeles' KXLU-FM's bilingual *Alma Del Barrio* celebrates its 30th anniversary March 21. The public station licensed to Loyola Marymount University broadcasts Latin music weekends from 6 a.m. to 6 p.m. and is the longest running show of its genre in the nation. (see Chapter 9). The show celebrates its birthday with a dance at the Queen Mary Exhibit Hall in Long Beach featuring L.A.'s Johnny Polanco Y Su Conjunto Amistad and New York's Los Soneros Del Barrio and Manny Oquendo Y Libre. Once only heard on the low-powered local station, today its wide range of Latin musical styles are available worldwide on the website www.kxlu.com. Nina Lenart, one of the show's popular hosts from 1982 to December of 2004 when she leaves because of lingering health problems, subsequently diagnosed as cancer, passes away quietly on July 15, 2005.

While KXLU's bilingual series gains national recognition, an impressive array of public radio stations across the nation feature Latin music shows ranging from jazz to tropical styles to regional Mexican to Cuban artists who may not be able to appear in-person in the U.S.

During the baseball season when the Boston Red Sox are in second place behind the hated New York Yankees in the American League, the tiny Spanish Beisbol Network beams the Beantown favorites in Spanish to six New England stations, two of which are English-language broadcasters. The brainchild of 43-year-old Bill Kulik, the network begins broadcasting to New England's growing Hispanic population in 2002, fueled by the $500,000 his investors invest in what they see as a golden opportunity to tap into the estimated $700 billion a year spent by Latinos. Boston's Hispanic population is comprised of Puerto Ricans, Dominicans, and Central Americans, so with the Red Sox roster including three stars from the Dominican Republic, notably Pedro Martinez, David Ortiz, and Manny Ramirez, it's a match of unbounded opportunities.

One year after several of Miami's radio personalities are called to account for their raunchy on-air comments, and the Federal Communications Commission (FCC) expresses its concern over the 2004 MTV produced Super Bowl halftime show in which Janet Jackson's right breast is bared for a worldwide TV audience because of a "wardrobe malfunction," Spanish radio networks, Univision, SBS, and Liberman, claim they have tightened or reasserted their decency standards for on-air personalities, prohibiting blatant sexual and other off-color innuendos.

The FCC has only two investigators who speak Spanish out of its force of 20, creating an unsettling major problem since the number of Spanish radio stations continues to grow and apparently is out of the grasp of the governmental agency's investigative force when it does receive complaints about malfeasance in Spanish broadcasting.

If that sounds unsettling, here's a real puzzler to ponder. Where have all the Latin radio listeners gone in the nation's No. 1 Hispanic radio market Los Angeles? Spanish-language stations, which dominate the top of the ratings in the 1990s as a growing Hispanic population boosts the positioning of Latino stations in the Arbitron standings, lose their ratings prestige in 2004 and 2005. Nevertheless, there are 18 Spanish stations in 2006, and several are back in key popularity positions. No other mainland U.S. city has as many Spanish outlets.

Satellite radio, slowly expanding its paying customer base, led by the two key services, Sirius and XM, directs its signals toward potential Hispanic listeners.

Sirius Satellite radio, itself on a slow growth path, reaches out to the Hispanic community with three Latin music stations, *Mejicana*, a voice for regional Mexican and Tejano music; *Universal Latino* which specializes in pop and rock acts; and *Tropical* which obviously plays tropical sounds. The commercial free subscription service also offers three talk channels in Spanish. Sirius expands its Latin inventory into sports in the fall of 2005 with Spanish-language broadcasts of 31 National Football League contests provided by CBS Radio Sports/Westwood On. The *NFL Futbol Americana* coverage encompasses Monday Night Football, Thanksgiving Day games, NFL playoffs, the AFC and NFL championships leading into Super Bowl XL on February 5, 2006.

XM goes after Latino beisbol fans, signing a $650 million pact with Major League Baseball for exclusive rights to broadcast its games in English and Spanish for 11 years. XM will broadcast every regular season game in English and some in Spanish as well as the playoffs and World Series commencing in 2005. XM will pay MLB $50 million the first year and $60 million for each additional year through 2012, when it has the option for three additional years. XM indicates it needs to sign up 700,000 new subscribers to cover the cost of this licensing deal. XM goes full-bore with Spanish programming in August of 2005 with the introduction of XM Deportivo, a 24-hour all sports channel, shifting its Spanish-language baseball coverage to the new network. An array of recognized Hispanic sports broadcasters are hired as show analysts/commentators.

Aside from the impact of Hispanic television on election coverage, Spanish-language TV receives kudos and criticism in three national reports in '04. In its fourth report on race and gender diversity, the Oakland-based child advocacy lobby Children Now, after reviewing primetime entertainment programming on ABC, CBS, NBC, Fox, UPN, and WB, surmises Latinos account for more than six percent of the actors during the 2003–'04 season. That's an increase from four percent for the previous TV season. However, the study also reports that Latinos remain underrepresented when compared with the overall Hispanic population. With the exception of the hit *George Lopez Show* on ABC, the study says Latinos continue to be depicted as working menial jobs or as criminals.

Hispanic viewers are increasingly switching between Spanish- and English-language news programs, a result of the growing number of acculturated U.S.-born Latinos. According to the Pew Hispanic

Center, 44 percent of its survey respondents during a month-long period switch between both mediums, while just over half watches more news in English and than in Spanish. It seems Hispanics are a channel switching dual cultural community.

Spanish-language TV's main networks, Univision and Telemundo are severely criticized by the Parents Television Council (PTC) for their high levels of sexual content between 8 and 11 p.m. following the examination of 99 programs, comprising 104 hours of programming during a three-week period last year. The two networks' sexual content is comparable with that of all the English-language broadcast networks, but there is less profane content on Spanish TV during the prime hours than on the Anglo networks, the report points out.

The report also indicates there's less violence than on the major English-language broadcast networks. It obviously does not monitor unregulated cable TV where anything goes. One shocking statistic: the highest levels of sexual content are found in the popular and long-running family show, *Sabado Gigante* hosted by Don Francisco on Univision and Telemundo's 26-episode teen drama *Los Teens*, which airs last summer.

PTC analyst and study author Lucia Alzaga warns that the highly charged sexual content should be a major concern, and "is extraordinarily degrading toward women and sets a horrible example for young girls watching these programs with their families."

Both networks respond to the study. Univision's statement, according to the *Los Angeles Times*, calls attention to its efforts "to responsibly provide high quality news, entertainment, and public interest programming and to do so within all applicable laws and regulations." Telemundo's programming vice president Mimi Belt, says its series about a Miami high school is designed to bring attention to a list of critical issues affecting teens encompassing HIV, pregnancy, drug and alcohol use, suicide, obesity, homosexuality, racism and divorce, and not just sex. She also points out that each episode contains public service announcements designed to provide assistance to teens and their parents in need to help.

Despite new fall shows on ABC, the WB and UPN providing employment for Hispanics, National Hispanic Foundation for the Arts chairman Felix Sanchez laments the paucity of Hispanic actors in major roles on the networks, telling *Hispanic* magazine: "We're still on the sidelines, but there's just more of us on the sidelines."

While there may not be lots of starring roles for Hispanics, lots of Hispanics apparently like watching lots of commercials. A separate Nielsen study for Univision indicates 36 percent of Hispanics watching Spanish TV watch commercials in their entirety as opposed to 17 percent of Hispanics who sit through commercials on Anglo TV. The study also indicates that 75 percent of the nation's Hispanic TV watchers view both Spanish and English programming, while two-thirds remain loyal to their endemic language.

Regardless of what English-language networks Hispanics watch, the number of Latino actors working in TV and movies remains disappointingly low, according to a survey by the Screen Actors Guild. Based on employment in 2003, acting roles for Latinos falls 10.5 percent, with male leading roles in primetime shows dropping 31 percent. Overall acting jobs for SAG members declines 1.6 percent. SAG's president Melissa Gilbert believes producers are still reluctant to broaden the ethnicity of cast members. SAG also cites the rash of reality programming and the alleged undercounting of Latino and African American TV viewers by Nielsen Media Research as additional reasons for the droop in employment for its ethnic members.

Univision, the seventh largest station group in the nation as ranked by newsweekly *Broadcasting & Cable*, during its sales pitch in New York in May of '04, announces its first three reality series, *Apostando Al Amor*, *Historias Para Contar*, and *Lo Veremos Todo Con Niurka & Bobby* which features Cuban cabaret dancer turned novela actress Niurka Marcos and her Mexican husband Bobby Larios, whose troubled personal life sets the stage for this series.

Galavision, Univision's fulltime cable network, celebrates its 25th anniversary in November of 2004 with some impressive audience increases, according to the Nielsen Hispanic Television Index. During the third quarter of the year, the network points to increases in its 18 to 49-year-old viewers, 11 percent during the daytime period and 43 percent during the 3–7 p.m. hours, compared to the same period last year. It also has 48 of the top 50 programs on Spanish-language cable. Its coverage of Fútbol Liga Mexicana, Mexico's premier soccer league, and its major newscast, *Noticero Con L. Ayala*, also see major increases in audience size among the 18–49 demographic.

The network's fortunes turn when it switches in 2002 from a mix of English and Spanish shows to all Spanish under the tutelage of its current ownership which buys the channel from Hallmark in 1992, which acquires the channel from its original founder/owner Rene Anselmo, who makes it part of his Mexico City-based Satellite International Network as a pay TV service in 1979. Along the way, Galavision programs Mexican feature films and miniseries, first-run shows from Mexico's Televisa (under Hallmark) and more sports and novelas under its latest ownership consortium of A. Jerrold Perenchio, Televisa and Venevision.

In addition to its weekly 45 hours of news, sports, and entertainment shows during the daytime and novelas at night, the network will be covering five major soccer tournaments next year. It currently reaches 40 million viewers, translating into 83 percent of domestic Hispanic TV households.

Galavision holds a distinct historical place in U.S. television, starting out as a pay service, then switching to a broadcast outlet and then converting to a cable network.

Televisa, Univision's longtime program supplier, which opens a Miami office last year and moves its president Emilio Azcárraga Jean there to oversee its expansion move in the U.S., begins production of its first telenovela, *Inocente De Ti* (*Innocent You*), with an all-Mexican cast, at the city's Fonovideo studios. The move places Televisa closer to Univision's Miami production center.

In the area of news and awards shows, Univision excels.

News anchor María Elena Salinas is named outstanding news anchor by the National Hispanic Media Coalition. Univision News wins two Edward R. Murrow awards for excellence in journalism from the Radio-Television News Directors Association. The accolades are for best videography for its religious special *Noticias Univision Presenta: En Busca De Un Milagro* (*Univision News Presents: In Search of a Miracle*) and for a series on its daily newsmagazine *Primer Impacto* about child abuse in Mexico titled *Mis Padres, Mis Verdugos* (*My Parents, My Abusers*).

Seeking to solidify itself with the youth market, the network airs the first *Premios Juventud* awards which target music, film, sports, pop culture, and fashion figures in an irreverent and humorous setting September 23 from Miami's James L. Knight Center.

Besides bestowing honors in 22 categories, the event features a top line of musical acts including A.B. Quintanilla and Kumbia Kings, Juanes, Akwid, Jennifer Peña, Paulina Rubio, Fulanito, Ivy Queen, Aleks Syntek, and Ana Torroja.

Winners selected in a nationwide poll of 1,000 Hispanic TV viewers aged 12–34 include triple winners Thalía and Chayanne and double winner Jennifer Lopez. Single winners include Paulina Rubio, Liberacion, Juanes, and New York Yankees superstar Alex Rodriguez. These awards are Spanish-language TV's first ever allowing Hispanic youth to pick their idols in various categories.

The unconventional program is a ratings hit. The show scores a 23.3 rating among Hispanic households and a 12.8 rating among adults 18–49, according to the Nielsen Hispanic Television Index. It's seen by nearly 4.4 million viewers. Univision claims the first-ever event easily bests the more established awards shows, including the Academy Awards, Grammy Awards, Golden Globes, and *Billboard* Latin Music Awards in all the key Hispanic audience age and sex demographics.

The network also hits a goldmine when it secures a $100 million, three-year advertising contract with the Miller Brewing Company, its largest single ad contract in its history, calling for Miller to advertise on Univision, TeleFutura, Galavision, and the Univision Radio Network. Miller also becomes the exclusive sponsor of several of Univision's programs, notably primetime novelas and exclusive beer sponsor for Univision's first half coverage of the World Cup games in 2006. It will additionally sponsor Mexican League soccer games and as the title sponsor for the primetime boxing show *Solo Boxeo*, the name is changed to *Solo Boxeo De Miller*. Both of these sports events run on the parent network.

In its third quarter report, Univision indicates its 18–49-age audience grows 23 percent during its primetime novela block. When the final episode of the novela, *Amartes Es Mi Pecado* airs on October 22 from 9 to 11 p.m., the episode finishes second in primetime among all the broadcast networks. It's a first, the network claims, based on Nielsen figures that show the program attracts 3.11 million viewers 18–49, followed by NBC's *Third Watch* with 3.9 million viewers. The telenovela also outdraws shows during that time period on ABC (2.98 million), CBS (2.52 million), WB (2.42 million), Fox (2.0 million) and UPN (1.16 million).

Univision's 28-owned stations plus affiliates reach 98 percent of domestic Hispanic households, while its TeleFutura network, launched in 2002 with a $1.4 billion purchase of the old USA Broadcasting stations owned by mogul Barry Diller, reaches 79 percent of Hispanic TV viewers through its 33-owned and operated stations.

TeleFutura's focus on building its 18–49 demographic appears to be working, especially during the early morning and daytime periods with talk and variety programming. In a formal statement released to the financial community in October based on Nielsen Hispanic Television Index statistics, the network lays claim to becoming the nation's second Spanish-language TV network behind parent Univision in four key day parts, early morning, daytime, early fringe (4–5 p.m.) and weekend daytime among Hispanics 18–34. It's also number two among 18 to 49-year-olds in early morning, daytime and weekend daytime programming.

In the third quarter of this year, the network claims gains of 22 percent in primetime and 29 percent in total day viewing among 18 to 49-year-olds. Since debuting in January of 2002, the network says its 18–49 audience grows 120 percent in primetime and 157 percent from sign-on to sign-off. Boasts Alina Falcón, TeleFutura's executive vice

In late October, Univision closes its L.A. office that handles program acquisitions and shifts its film division into its Miami programming department. Although Univision plans airing two Hollywood films, *Frida* and *The Crime of Father Amaro*, TeleFutura runs a larger number of films during its weeknight *Cine De Las Estrellas* 9 p.m. slot and on weekends in the afternoon *Cineplex* block.

Also debuting in October is the series TeleFutura labels "one of the most ambitious projects in the history of novelas," *Amor Real* (*True Love*), a tale set in 19th century Mexico with a cast of more than 1,000 actors, extras and technicians during the two years it takes to film this epic. A proven hit in Mexico and Latin America, the series airs weeknights at 9 p.m.

When results of the November sweeps book are in, TeleFutura gains some boasting rights. It claims reaching its highest primetime audience levels among Hispanics in the 18–34 and 18–49 brackets during any sweeps period since its debut in January of 2002.

Despite its leading position in Spanish TV, or because of it, Univision Communications is known for its policy of selectively allowing its executives to talk to the media. So when I almost walk into Chairman/CEO/majority owner/billionaire Jerry Perenchio at a Bette Midler concert at L.A.'s Staples Center, I reintroduce myself to him and mention we used to have regular story meetings when I was *Billboard*'s L.A. bureau chief many years ago and he headed up Chartwell Artists. I ask him if he'd chat with me about Univision and Spanish-language TV and he says to contact him, which I do via e-mail. The next day I receive the following e-mail response: "It was fun running into you the other night. As you probably know, I don't do interviews. I am sorry if I misled you the other night at the concert but you caught me somewhat off guard. We kind of prefer to stay out of the spotlight because 'it fades your suit' like my old mentor Lew Wasserman (head of MCA and then Universal Pictures) used to say, and let our results, hopefully, make our case for us. I hope you understand. Warmest regards, Jerry Perenchio."

In an alignment in the executive suite of Perenchio's Univision Communications Inc., Ray Rodriguez is promoted by Perenchio in February of 2005 to president and chief operating officer of the parent company from president of the company's three networks. Rodriguez fills the vacancy left by Henry Cisneros, who departs in August of 2000 to form a joint venture company, which plans building inner-city housing. Cuban-born Rodriguez begins his career with Univision in 1990 as vice president/director of talent relations, and is subsequently given responsibility for all the networks.

Rodriguez's promotion positions him as the heir apparent to Perenchio upon his retirement. The promotion also results in Mexico City-based Televisa-which owns 10.9 percent of the company and is its primetime supplier of three hours of telenovelas-being displeased with being left out of the decision by Perenchio to upgrade Rodriquez, and in a recriminatory action bans all its talent from appearing on Univision. The Mexican company's talent often hosts Univision's variety shows. Immediately affected is Univision's February 24 broadcast of the 17th annual music spectacular *Premio Lo Nuestro 2005* and its need to replace 23 Televisa artists, including host Eugenio Derbez, presenters and sundry novela stars.

Facing the daunting task of quickly assembling replacements two days before the show is Alina Falcon, newly named executive vice president/operating manager to replace Rodriquez, but not with his title of president of the Univision TV Networks. Falcon's promotion raises her from head of Univision's sister TeleFutura network.

The live three-hour show from Miami's American Airlines Arena, with its international cast of musical talents, awards multiple honors to Marc Anthony with four, Paulina Rubio and Sin Bandera each with three and Alicia Villarreal and Intocable with two trophies each. Anthony's awards are in the tropical music category for salsa artist of the year, best male artist, best album, *Valio La Pena* (Sony), and song of the year, *Ahora Quién*. Rubio's accolades are for best pop female artist, top video artist, and legendary young artists award. Sin Bandera's honors are as best group/duo, best album, *De Viaje* (Sony), and song of the year, *Que lloro* (Sony). Villarreal's pair are for best regional Mexican female artist and grupero artist of the year. Intocable's wins are for best album with *Intimamente* (Warner Bros.) and norteño artist of the year.

The other category winners include rock: Juanes, artist of the year; Kalimba, best new soloist/group of the year; Maná's *Esenciales: Luna* (Warner Bros.), best rock album; tropical: Carlos Vives, traditional artist of the year; Celia Cruz, best female artist; Aventura, best group/duo; Luna Llena, best new soloist/group of the year; regional Mexican: Adán Sánchez, best male artist; Grupo Montéz De Durango, best group/duo; Marco Antonio Solís's *Más Que Tu Amigo* (Fonovisa), song of the year; Banda El Recodo, banda artist of the year; Pepe Aguilar, ranchero artist of the year; Mariana Seoane, best new soloist/group of the year; urban: Don Omar, artist of the year and Daddy Yankee's *Barrio Fino* (VI Music), best album.

As for the Rodriguez promotion imbroglio, in addition to Televisa's chairman/CEO Emilio Azcárraga Jean, Gustavo Cisneros, head of the Cisneros Group of Venezuela, whose Venevision TV wing provides Univision with additional primetime programming and owns 13.4 percent of Univision, is also upset over not being consulted. Officials from both companies express their ire in a four-hour face-off meeting in Los Angeles with Perenchio. According to the *Los Angeles Times*, Perenchio is criticized for running Univision like a private enterprise, not a publicly held company and for not setting up a plan to select his successor, where upon he says he plans to stay on indefinitely as the company's top executive, a claim he later makes to Wall Street analysts. This feud is marked by a historical footnote: Perenchio, along with Azcárraga Jean's father (Emilio Azcárraga Milmo) and Gustavo Cisneros, are the founders of Univision.

In what's shaping up as a generational battle between 74-year-old Perenchio and the 37-year-old Emilio Azcárraga Jean, whose father founds what is today the world's largest Spanish-language media empire, Grupo Televisa, Perenchio faces severe over his shoulder scrutiny from U.S. resident Emilio, who joins the family business when he's 20. In 1997, one month before he dies, Azcárraga Milmo promotes his son, then 29, to head the family business. Azcárraga Jean, who is presently vice chairman of the Univision board, apparently seeks a greater role in the company's future. Although he has homes in Miami and San Diego, where his wife gives birth to a son, making the child an American citizen, U.S. law prohibits foreigners from owning more than 25 percent of an American broadcasting company.

Nonetheless, Azcárraga Jean floats the idea he may apply for U.S. citizenship. Meanwhile, he's stuck with the 1992 pact his father signs with Perenchio guaranteeing the U.S. network exclusive Televisa programming until 2017. In an effort to show Univision can create its own hit novelas, Perenchio in 2003 has the network produce *Te Amare En Silencio* (*I Will Love You in Silence*) only to discover a major casting flaw: the lead character is a male, rather than the traditional female, and this miscue results in a major loss in audience. This faux pas adds fuel to Azcárraga Jean's negative attitude regarding Perenchio's indefinite leadership. Also exasperating the situation is the failure of many of Univision's own produced novelas.

However, three months after the rift between Perenchio and Azcárraga Jean over Rodriguez's promotion, Azcárraga Jean, and his board alternate, Alfonso De Angoitia, resign from Univision's board of directors. At the same time, Televisa files suit May 9 in U.S. District Court in Los Angeles, charging Univision with breach of contract, copyright infringement and $1.5 million in royalty fees it fails to pay in the first quarter for the popular primetime awards show *Premio Lo Nuestro*. The suit also asks for protection from paying Univision $5.2 million in royalties previously asked for by the U.S. network. Univision calls the suit "baseless" and says it will "vigorously defend against it."

Two months later, Televisa adds two additional claims to its lawsuit. The first claim, according to Televisa executive vice president Alfonso De Angoitia, in a call to analysts, centers around Univision's altering the rebroadcast of soccer matches "in ways not permitted." The second charge is that Univision failed to make part of its unsold advertising time available to Televisa. Univision files a counter suit August 15 in Los Angeles District Court alleging bad faith actions like, according to *Daily Variety*, over billing production costs, barring Univision reporters from Televisa events, revealing the results of telenovelas on Televisa talk shows, refusing to edit its shows to conform to U.S. TV standards and refusing to eliminate product placements that violate Univision's broadcast guidelines

Kid power is on display when Univision's Premios Juventud youth awards bestow 30 unconventionally named honors during its second annual live telecast September 28, 2005, from the University of Miami. Leading the array of winners, chosen by fan voting online are reggaeton king Daddy Yankee and vocalist Shakira, each with five statues. Daddy's dandies are in the categories for "Catchiest Tune," "I Hear Him Everywhere," "My Favorite Concert," "Favorite Urban Artist," and "He's Got Style." Shakira walks away with "Best Moves," "I Hear Her Everywhere," and the more straitlaced "Favorite Pop Artist," "Favorite Rock Artist," and "Best Duet."

In November of 2005, Univision encounters a new executive shapeup, when Tom Arnost, co-president of its Television Group, resigns, with cohort Michael D. Wortsman named the sole president of the 62 Univision and TeleFutura station groups. Wortsman, the previous executive VP of corporate development for the Univision TV Group, has a background in English-language TV with stations in San Diego, Washington, Los Angeles, and San Francisco. Earlier in the month, Univision announces acquiring 2010 and 2014 U.S. rights to World Cup soccer tournaments and 26 other Fédération Internationale De Football Association (FIFA) sponsored events for ($325 million), and a drastic cut in its TV division of around 275 workers, despite third quarter TV revenue of $343.3 million, up from last year's $328.1 million.

Univision's secure financial position as the nation's fifth largest TV network is undoubtedly in play as Univision Communications Inc.'s board of directors, led by Perenchio, votes to sell the TV, radio, and record company in February of 2006. Financial analysts suggest if there's a bidding war, the winning price could top $13 billion, according to the *Los Angeles Times*. Among the possible suitors with deep pockets: News Corp., Viacom, CBS Corp., Walt Disney Company, and Time Warner, with a consortium consisting of two firms that own shares in the company, Mexico's Grupo Televisa and Venezuela's Venevision, and buyout companies Providence Equity Partners, and Madison Dearborn Partners also analyzing its purchase participation. Among the interested buyers, Time Warner, the Walt Disney Company, CBS Corp., and News Corp. subsequently change their minds. Televisa, which currently owns more than 11 percent of Univision, aligns itself with four U.S. investment firms since U.S. law forbids foreign firms from holding more than 25 percent of a U.S. company.

By the June 20 auction deadline after a number of suitors have dropped out, Televisa and a consortium led by entertainment mogul Haim Saban are the remaining parties. On June 27 Univision accepts an offer of $36.25 a share from the Saban consortium which consists of private equity firms Providence Equity Partners, Madison Dearborn Partners, Texas Pacific Group, and Thomas H. Lee Partners. The deal is valued by Univision at $13.7 billion, which assumes $1.4 billion in debt, according to the *Los Angeles Times*. The winning amount is the second from the Saban group, whose initial bid is 25 cents under the $35.75 a share offered by Televisa and its remaining partners, Bill Gates' Cascade Investment and Bain Capital. Told of its shortcoming over the weekend of June 24–25, Saban raises its offer to $36.25. The Saban offer contains a provision that allows Televisa to increase its equity stake to more than 19 percent. The sale, which must be approved by Univision Communications shareholders and the Federal Communications Commission, could be a done deal by the close of first quarter 2007. If the deal goes through, Perenchio collects $1.3 billion for his 11 percent ownership. Televisa issues a statement expressing "disappointment" and indicates it is considering alternatives to entering the U.S. TV market. On September 18, 2006, Televisa chooses to end its bid for the company.

Univision Communications consists of two broadcast TV networks, a cable channel, 62 TV stations, 69 radio stations, and a music division with record record companies. Perenchio calls the deal a "blockbuster transaction" in a press release and then heads to a European vacation on his private jet, notes the *Times*. On March 27, 2007, the Federal Communications Commission clears the sale to the group of private investors led by billionaire Haim Saban. Perenchio will earn around $1.3 billion for his 11.5 percent stake in the company.

Prior to the sale closing, Perenchio's decision elicits two prompt, separate class action suits June 27 and 28 filed in Los Angeles Superior Court by two San Diego law firms on behalf of shareholders. Both actions claim board of directors, rather than shareholders, receive the best financial deal. And then on July 6, Televisa files a motion with the Securities and Exchange Commission asserting it wants to sell its 11.4 percent ownership in Univision so it can pursue its intentions to compete in the U.S. market. By selling its stake, Televisa is not bound by its 1996 participation agreement which prohibits it from starting any business in the U.S. that would compete with Univision. However, Televisa is still bound by its 1992 programming pact with Univision which expires in 2017.

Prior to the auction in March, Univision Communications reveals a sharp drop in fourth quarter earnings as it disposes of around $70 million in charges to make any sale more appealing. One of those disposed of fees is the nearly $6 million it pays "under protest" to Televisa over the disputed programming fees, reports the *Los Angeles Times*. Also revealed is the conglomerate's intention to file a counterclaim to recover the money.

Despite its legal battles with Televisa, Univision signs a long-term pact in March of 2006 for continued programming for its Puerto Rico TV stations with Televisa and its other supplier, Venezuela's Venevision, through 2017. The deal mirrors the exclusive through 2017 in effect on the Mainland.

What begins in January of 2007 as a local drive by Univision's L.A. station, KMEX, to register Hispanic green card holders to become U.S. citizens, expands into a national campaign by parent

Univision Communications stations months later in New York, Miami, Phoenix, Dallas, Houston, and San Antonio to join the "Ya Es Hora" (It's Time Already) bandwagon, with other cities also planning to promote the idea. The target audience are the more than 8 million legal Hispanic permanent residents whose voting power could impact the 2008 elections on the presidential and state levels, reports the *Wall Street Journal.* The Univision campaign, utilizing its TV and radio stations, is the largest effort ever to stimulate Hispanics to become citizens and voters, according to the National Association of Latino Elected and Appointed Officials Education Fund, which spearheads the drive. A second phase of the campaign in 2008 will emphasize getting new citizens to polling places. The KMEX campaign encompasses information on all newscasts, public service announcements, and a half-hour Saturday show devoted to teaching viewers how to become a citizen. During newscasts, anchors offer questions found on civics tests applicants must pass. As a result of the station's campaign, the number of applicantions filed in the L.A. area jumps 123 percent versus a 59 percent increase for the nation for the first the three months of the year, according to the article.

Even though it loses out to Univision in 2005 for the two World Cups, Telemundo, unlike its competitor, has no pressures or bans limiting its hiring of actors and actresses to stifle its benchmark decision in 2004 to air all originally produced shows during primetime in the fall, a move begun last year when it begins airing original telenovelas at a cost of $40 million, according to the network. Cost for the new shows could run $10 to $20 million more.

Of all its new shows, two set record marks. The premiere of *Anita No Te Rejes* (*Anits Don't Give Up*) is the network's highest rated show at 8 p.m., earning a 4.5 Nielsen rating among the coveted 18–49 demographic, while *Gitanas* (*Gypsies*) is the network's biggest production ever, shot in various locales throughout Mexico and featuring the creation of an entire city built by Telemundo and Argos Productions, its production partner, on 20,000 square meters of land in Xochitla Ecological Park, north of Mexico City.

Product placement, the growing practice in English-language TV, where products are integrated into a show's storyline, is utilized by Telemundo in 2004 and 2005, with a number of advertisers signing up to have their merchandise placed within the sets or used prominently by the actors in soap operas. They include the insertion of Procter & Gamble and Nissan Motor America products in its novela, *Amor Descarado* (*Brazen Love*) and in its morning reality show *De Mananita* which spawns a segment called *Camino a Casa* (*The Way Home*) in which Century 21 realtors help a young married couple purchase their first home. Other shows embracing branded product content are the network's first home improvement show, *Asi Se Hace* (*That's How It's Done*), with merchandise from Big Lots and the novela, *La Prisonera*, with two cell phones from Verizon Wireless.

In the past, when soaps arrive from overseas, all the commercials are already in place. With shows locally produced and content control guaranteed, that's no longer the case.

When Telemundo announces the six-part miniseries *Zapata: Amor En Rebeldia*, the story of Mexican revolutionary Emiliano Zapata, starring Mexican actor Demián Bichir in the title role, Ramón Escobar, the network's executive vice president of programming and production, believes the story "resonates with everyone who believes in freedom and justice." The show is taped in 25 locations in Central Mexico to cover the 10 years of the storyline, starting in 1910 with the onset of the revolution that topples dictator Porfirio Díaz, who flees to Europe.

During the assault by Hurricane Frances swirling through South Florida in September, Telemundo's local station, WSCV teams with sister NBC station WTVJ to provide a hurricane help line for people affected by the disaster. WSCV's hurricane coverage throughout the broadcast day of September 3, draws an 8.2 rating, 13.7 share, a record for the station, whose 11 p.m. news outdraws all English TV stations and Univision's WLTV news at that hour, according to the network.

The sixth annual El Premio De La Gente, Latin Music Fan Awards, presented in 14 categories October 21 at the Universal

Amphitheater in Studio City, California, and televised by the network October 30, shines brightly on three award-winning Paulina Rubio, for both artist and pop artist of the year and for song of the year (*Te Quise Tanto*). Dual winners include David Bisbal, best new artist and contemporary artist of the year and Chayanne, in the pop male artist of the year and best music video categories. Album of the year goes to Sin Bandera's *De Viaje*. Olga Tañon wins the best tropical act; Los Temerarios the best pop music group and Banda El Recodo the urban, corridos or norteño group of the year.

Winners are voted on by fans either through ballots available at various retail outlets or at show title sponsor Chevrolet dealers or via mailed ballots to Hispanic households across the country by a direct mail company. One of the show's unique features is the utilization of audience members to announce the winners.

Special tribute awards are presented to radio personality Reñan Almendarez Coello as the Citizen of Radio; vocalist Paquita La Del Barrio as Star of the People, cumbia/vallenato star Aniceto Molina with the Glory of the Music accolade, and Chihuahua, Mexican singer Gloria Trevi, upon her return to freedom after jail terms in Brazil and Mexico dating back to 2000, as the Soul of the People recipient. Show executive, Luis Medina, days prior to planning out the event, tells the *New York Times* he's besieged by phone calls from people asking if Gloria is going to be on the show and whether she'll perform. Since the awards are selected by fans from working artists and Trevi is not on the ballot since she's in a Mexican jail, her unexpected acquittal on rape, kidnapping, and corruption charges six weeks before the show, sets her free. So Medina books the singer known as Mexico's sexy rebel called *La Atrevida* (*The Daring One*) and makes up the honor he bestows on her. He also adds her to the acts performing.

The popular singer/movie actress, born Gloria De Los Ángeles Treviño Ruiz, who's known as the "Mexican Madonna," vanishes in 1999 along with her mentor, Sergio Andrade, after they're charged in Mexico with sex crimes and are captured in Brazil in

January 2000 and incarcerated. She returns to Mexico in December 2002 to stand trial and he follows a year later. Following her acquittal, Trevi, now 37, rejuvenates her recording career aimed at appealing to Mexican fans and her potentially domestic fan base of Mexicans who've migrate to the U.S. by releasing the album, *Cómo Nace El Universo* (*How the Universe Is Born*) for BMG U.S. Latin, signing with Miami-based talent agency World Entertainment Associates, and planning a tour for the CD which will start in Mexico City and then move to the U.S. sometime in March of 2005. The new album, her sixth, is a mixture of serious-themed pop and rock tunes and is her first since being jailed in January. It contains eight of her compositions.

Her apparent legion of patient fans scoops up the album and places it on *Billboard*'s top Latin Albums list December 25, where it remains until March 12, 2005, in 71st place and then disappears. By March of 2005, the CD racks up sales exceeding 150,000 copies, the majority sold in the U.S. The 23-city "Trevolution" tour as it's called, commences March 3 in her hometown of Monterrey, Mexico, and begins its U.S. sojourn April 8 in Texas, with planned stops including Los Angeles, Miami, Chicago, Cleveland, and Detroit. However, since the dynamic diva is six months pregnant with her third child by the time she regales fans in L.A., the tour featuring an eight-piece band is cut short until later in the year. Prior to hitting the Mainland, Trevi stops in San Juan to promote the album and appear on the live TeleFutura program *Objetivo Fama*.

Amid all this "Trevimania," Andrade, her ex-manager, is sentenced in Chihuahua to close to eight years in prison for rape, kidnapping and corruption of minors. But he's allowed to go free based on time already served after he pays financial remunerations to his accuser plus a small fine.

On an equally serious level, the highly-charged subject of Hispanics sneaking into the U.S. is given a harsh searchlight in the Telemundo series *Tres Fronteras* running in the newsmagazine *Al Rojo Vivo Con Maria Celeste* airing weekdays at 5 p.m. The expose airing in

November, is compiled and reported by Francisco Cuevas, Telemundo's Los Angeles correspondent and cameraman Carlos Huazano, who spend eight days with a group of Central and South American immigrants as they capture their dangerous endeavors to cross the border between El Salvador and Guatemala, Guatemala and Mexico and then into the U.S.

Mun2, Telemundo's young and bilingual cable network (with shows in English and Spanish with English subtitles), geared for a major programming expansion push, targets potential new voters with coverage on two shows and public service announcements, all designed to explore issues of concern to young Latinos like the war in Iraq, abortion, and gay marriage.

As a spin-off to its *The Roof*, a bilingual music/entertainment show introduced in December 2002, the network launches a touring talent show, *Roof on the Road: El Reventón Urbano*, to Miami, New York, San Antonio, and Los Angeles. Every three months the roadshow visits another U.S. city to present urban alternative acts that appeal to the three-year-old network's targeted audience.

The Roof allows the network to play major U.S. cities "with a Latin celebration targeting young Hispanics," explains Yolanda Foster, the network's programming vice president. Artists performing at the Grand Avenue Night Club in downtown L.A., for example, feature a variety of musical stylists geared for alternative music fans: Ilegales, Monchy & Alexandra, BandaHood, Trivales, Chuly, Fulanito, Kinto Sol, Flakiss, and La Factoria.

The Roof touring show is one of five specials mun2 broadcasts during Hispanic Heritage Month running from September 15 through October 15 on Saturdays from 10 to 11 p.m.

Overseeing the network's overall growth strategy is Antoinette Zel, lured away in December from MTV Networks Latin America where she'd been the president since 2001. She'll also oversee any new cable business in the U.S. and Latin America. Six months later, she's named senior executive vice president of network strategy and shortly thereafter announces the relocation of mun2 from Miami to Los

Angeles by October 1. The move for the four-year-old bilingual, youth-oriented cable network is designed to tap into the Hollywood creative community and even utilize the facilities of parent NBC Universal's local Universal Studios theme park. Zel, who oversees mun2, tells the *Los Angeles Times* she wants to broaden the channel's programming for bilingual Hispanics to more aggressively compete with other popular networks catering to young viewers including MTV, WB, and UPN. In October of 2005, she relaunches the network with new graphics and programming including *WWE Raw*, a popular professional wrestling funfest, which includes Latino favorite Eddie Guerrero. The show will be broadcast in Spanish on Sunday and in English the following Wednesday. Also introduced is expanded musical coverage to encompass regional Mexican and reggaeton in addition to its Caribbean sounds.

In April of 2007, the actual move of mun2 to the Universal City Walk on the NBC Universal lot is complete and a new 16,000 square foot multimillion dollar open studio complex is in operation broadcasting an array of live programming focussing on the desired bilingual 18–34 demographic. Mun2's ratings shoot upward with the move and new programming including reality and documentaries. Mun2's move to L.A. reflects the city's growing bilingual creative center along with LATV and Si TV. In April of '07, the 6-year-old Spanglish LATV cable network finally becomes a national network through digital satellite transmission to a growing number of markets including Miami, Las Vegas, and Houston, reports the *Los Angeles Times*. Si TV, the pioneering 3-year-old English-language cable network continues increasing its national distribution as a booster of Latino culture/English programming.

At the end of 2004, financial news is good for Telemundo and discouraging for Univision. While posting double-digit ad revenue growth over recent years, Univision's fourth quarter ad revenue slips 20 percent from last year's similar period. One reason for the decline in ad revenue is linked to cutbacks by telecommunications giants AT&T and MCI, film studios and retailers.

Telemundo credits its 14 percent upbeat financial status in part to its Olympics coverage. Of the company's 14 full-power and nine low-power owned stations on the Mainland who reap the dollar benefit, four of the full-power stations, WNJU New York, WSNS Chicago, WSCV Miami and KTMD Houston, report major ratings increases.

Carbon copying the success of Fox TV's *American Idol* talent search, Telemundo begins tryout auditions in New York, Miami, Los Angeles, and Puerto Rico for its own *Nuevas Voces De America* (*New Voices of America*) set for a February 2005 debut. The 20 finalists will live in Miami Beach and be coached and guided in both their musical and personal appearances. The winner of the series from Estefan Television Productions will receive a recording contract from an unnamed major label.

In 2005, the network moves into home makeover programming, the hot rage on Anglo TV, and sets an internal writing program to find scribes for its novelas. When it introduces one of two homemaker shows, *Lo Dejo En Tus Manos* (*I Leave It in Your Hands*), it snares the Lowe's home improvement chain as the main sponsor.

Politics and music are the programming mix with which Telemundo entices audiences during the first months of 2005. The network's Miami-based *Sin Fronteras* Sunday show co-host Ana Patricia Candiani ventures to Mexico for an exclusive interview with President Vicente Fox and his wife, First Lady Martha Sahagún, in the official residence in Los Pinos.

The network also bows the new 15 segment Sunday music reality series *Nuevas Voces De América*, created and produced by Emilio Estefan, Jr. in which Universal Music will sign the winner to a recording contract and have the option to sign additional singers for two compilation albums. All the show's competitors will sing songs written for them by Estefan's publishing companies. Preceding *Nuevas Voces is Objetivo Fama*, a similar new show on TeleFutura from 7 to 9 p.m., whose competition winner lands a contract with the Univision Music Group.

Telemundo also broadcasts the 2005 *Billboard* Latin Music Awards airing April 28 from the Miami Arena, and continues its devotion to original telenovelas with three series set for the spring of 2005. The initial show, *La Ley Del Silencio* (*Law of Silence*), is set in the Dallas Hispanic neighborhood of Oak Park and produced by Fremantle Productions Latin America of Miami. The show, in addition to being the first from Fremantle, is also the network's first in high-definition TV.

Despite expensive efforts to create domestically themed novelas during the past three years through a series of co-productions at a reported cost of $120 million, Telemundo lags behind Univision, casting a shadow over president Jim McNamara's reign. On April 6, 2005, McNamara resigns his six-year tenure and is replaced by Don Browne, NBC News' Miami bureau chief starting in 1979 and the 10-year president/general manager of NBC's Miami station WTVJ, who is brought over to become Telemundo's chief operating officer in May of 2003. McNamara's contract is up for renewal and disagreements over a number of issues are involved in his departure. He remains in Miami and where he'll develop entrepreneurial-type projects, according to published reports. Randy Falco, president of the NBC Universal TV Group, which includes Telemundo, lauds the departing executive "for a remarkable job leading Telemundo through a period of impressive growth."

McNamara plays a key role in 2001 in helping influence NBC to purchase Telemundo from Sony and Liberty Media Corporation, its co-owners for $2.7 billion. For his efforts, when NBC takes over in 2002, McNamara is given a three-year contract, and according to the *Los Angeles Times*, he also receives a bonus "of close to $50 million" from the two owners for closing the acquisition. Despite setting up production operations in Miami and Dallas, and co-production deals in Mexico City, Buenos Aires and Bogotá, Colombia, to create original programming to counter Univision's stronghold on top Latin shows, the effort fails. Telemundo attracts 25 percent of the U.S. Spanish audience while Univision controls the other 75 percent. In 2002, I interview McNamara in his office and our in-depth conversation appears in Chapter 13.

Two-and-a-half months after replacing McNamara, Don Browne steers Telemundo towards more Mexican-originated programming, signing a deal with Argos, an independent production company, for novelas, while also looking for reality and news shows created by Mexican companies, all aimed at the U.S' 40 million Hispanics.

The strength and popularity of Spanish-language primetime programming results in Univision's novelas outranking a number of Anglo stations who see their audiences drop during the summer of 2005. During this period, Univision becomes the No. 1 network overall with 18 to 34-year-olds, attracting an average of 1.2 million nightly viewers for its first-run novelas, explains *Entertainment Weekly*, to overtake No. 2 Fox in that demographic. Riding this Hispanic explosion, fuelled by the 12 percent growth since 2002 of the number of Hispanic TV households in the nation which now totals 10.9 million, Univision's New York station, WXTV strikes its own historical stake when it becomes the first Spanish-language station in the Big Apple to win a sweeps period during primetime, besting all stations regardless of language. WXTV becomes No. 1 during the July sweeps among the 18–49 and 25–54 demographic groups. Two months later, WXTV for the first time wins the 11 p.m. local news race among viewers 18–49 on August 2 with a 1.5 ratingh/4 share of audience.

Univision's three-year-old sister network TeleFutura also shows aggressive signs it's serious anent overtaking NBC's Telemundo as the No. 2 Spanish network, gaining viewership among 18 to 34-year-olds with its game show and sports programming during daytime and primetime hours, while Telemundo's young adult viewers decline during the September 20, 2004–June 19, 2005 period, according to the *Wall Street Journal*. The domestic Spanish TV networks are all in the sights of ad agencies who are sending more dollars towards this branch of show business, the *Journal* quoting a rise in ad expenditures of 19.6 percent in the first quarter of 2005 over the same period last year.

On Thanksgiving Day, 2005, Telemundo simulcasts along with NBC the 81st annual Macy's Thanksgiving Day Parade from New York. Not only is this the fourth year Telemundo provides Spanish-language coverage with its own on-camera hosts, but it's also the first time Telemundo personalities Maria Celeste Arrarás and Maria Antonieta Collins ride on NBC's float alongside NBC stars. History is also made by the inclusion of the first-ever Latino-themed balloon, with *Dora the Explorer* generating media attention for the popular and pioneering bilingual children's TV series.

Telemundo stands to gain by NBC Universal (NBCU)'s decision in January of 2006 to sell four of its small market stations as part of a plan to invest in additional Telemundo stations and gain duopolies (two owned stations in the same city) in markets with growing Hispanic communities where it already owns NBC stations. The stations up for sale are in Columbus, Ohio; Providence, Rhode Island; Raleigh, North Carolina, and Birmingham, Alabama. In a separate transaction, NBCU acquires KDEN-TV Denver from Longmont Broadcasting that operates Channel 25. The new full-power station, a former Home Shopping Network outlet, will become the company's 17th Telemundo owned outlet, replacing two low-power Telemundo stations KMAS and KSBS in the market.

Seeking to secure its own foothold for Mexican-produced novelas, Telemundo's deep-pocket parent, General Electric, announces in February of 2006 it will construct a studio in Mexico to produce these primetime gems. An earlier effort by GE to acquire Mexico City's bankrupt Canal 40 UHF station as a source for programming falls through. Although Telemundo's deal with Mexico's Argos production company remains intact, the network wants tighter control of the shows, according to *Daily Variety*. Canal 40 is now under the control of TV Azteca, parent to Azteca America. During a visit to Mexico City in April, Telemundo president Don Browne reveals the network and Grupo Xtra are partners in the new studio, with Telemundo investing $25 million to form the joint venture Estudios Mexicanos Telemundo, which will open in the fourth quarter of 2006.

First production will be a novela, with other programming genres being explored including mini-dramas, games, variety, and talk. In addition, the two companies are partners in Palmas 26, a new entity seeking to enter Mexico's TV industry, presently dominated by the Televisa and TV Azteca networks, according to the *Hollywood Reporter*.

Azteca America, the third Spanish network, adds station affiliates in Brownsville/McAllen, Texas; Tampa, Florida; Hartford, Connecticut, and Boise, Idaho, increasing its reach to 70 percent of the domestic Hispanic TV audience in 38 markets. The Mexican-owned network, in a move to appeal to its U.S. audience, begins Americanizing its reality series *La Academia*, its new novela *La Heredera* and inserting U.S. products into its Mexican-based shows which air in this country. It also revamps its late night schedule.

In the case of *La Academia*, participants from the U.S. are chosen along with those from Mexico where the show is produced to compete in this contest among aspiring singers living together and performing a weekly live concert. One third of the songs are in English by the American cast members.

One member of this show's cast, single-name singer Yahir, so impresses the network that he's signed as the lead in the new youth-oriented daytime new novela, *Soñarás*, which depicts the struggles of a 20-year-old singer to find success in his drive to become a star. Six members of the *La Academia* cast, Raúl, Estrella, Nadia, Erika, Suzette, Ricardo, and Toñita, star in a four-city "Estrellas De La Academia" tour to capitalize on their new-found notoriety. In 2005, the show will exclusively use aspiring singers from the top U.S. Hispanic markets, a step taken to further Americanize the show's content.

The idea pays off for the four-year-old series when a Mesa, Arizona, teenager, Yuridia Gaxiola finishes second in the voting in 2005 and wins $92,000 and a car. The winner is a 27-year-old teacher from Guerrero who lands $320,000 and an SUV. As a result of its hit status, TV Azteca launches a spin-off, *La Academia America* in November, completing the circle for Americanized TV.

The network begins utilizing product insertion and integration as a means of customizing its programming and enticing

American advertisers by offering this capability, reveals *Advertising Age*. In one instance, a box of Gain detergent from Procter & Gamble is among the products being unpacked in a novela seen in this country. In a second instance, a Kmart shopping bag is inserted into another novela.

Of the two new primetime soap operas added to strengthen evening programming, *La Heredera* is the network's first novela to feature U.S. Hispanic characters in leading roles portrayed by Silvia Navarro and Sergio Basañez.

During the summer of 2004, the network continues its coverage of Mexican League Soccer, offering exclusive coverage of eight of the 18 teams during the 2004–'05 season, representing 150 matches. With this coverage, the network reasserts its position as the leading domestic Spanish TV network offering the most Mexican league games.

During the fall, the network tackles the emotionally charged unsolved murders involving rapes of by now 370 young women, with scores of others unaccounted for in Cuidad Juarez in northern Mexico along the Texas border dating back to 1993 in the five-part miniseries *Tan Infinito Como El Desierto*. The series follows various governmental investigations into the killings dating back to 1993, a sad moment in the border state which reverberates across all of Mexico as the crimes continue unabated.

In October, the parent company, TV Azteca, Mexico's second TV network, with 39 percent of the nation's TV stations, behind Grupo Televisa controlling 56 percent of the TV stations, is given notice by the U.S. Securities and Exchange Commission that it may impose fines or penalties in possible civil suits against chairman Ricardo Salinas Pliego and an outside partner, Moises Saba, for their involvement in a financial deal with telephone company Unefon, which owns a minority stake in the company. The SEC claims the two fail to report $218 million they make in a 2003 debt refinancing, which may be a securities violation. As a result of the SEC action, Wall Street investment firm Morgan Stanley downgrades the company's ratings.

TV Azteca is hit on January 4, 2005, by the SEC's filing its lawsuit in Federal District Court in Washington, D.C., which it first hints at last October, which now includes expanded charges of civil fraud against TV Azteca, chairman Salinas Pliego and two directors including Azteca America's president/CEO Luis J. Echarte. Salinas Pliego is accused by the SEC of purchasing the debt of Unefon, the mobile phone company, at a discount and then selling it back to the company at the full price through an investment firm, Codisco, he owns with Saba. Ricardo Salinas and family own 56 percent of TV Azteca, which at the time of the transaction also owns close to half of Unefon. In 2007, Unefon separates from TV Azteca and merges into Grupo Iusacell. In its first filing against a Mexican company, since TV Azteca is listed on the New York Stock Exchange, the SEC charges Salinas Pliego, followed by Pedro Padilla Longoria, a board member and former TV Azteca CEO, and Echarte with allegedly steering $109 million to Salinas through a debt transaction deal.

The filing claims the defendants "engaged in an elaborate scheme to conceal Salinas Pliego's role in a series of transactions through which he personally profited" and also filed periodic reports that did not disclose his involvement in transactions between TV Azteca's wireless phone subsidiary Unefon and Codisco, the private firm Salinas Pliego co-owns. The SEC also seeks court orders to bar Salinas Pliego and Padilla Longoria from serving on any U.S. traded public company. Salinas issues a statement which calls the charges "false, in bad faith and discriminatory" and he slams the cooperation Mexico's stock market regulatory agency, Comision Nacional Bancaria Y De La Valores, provides to the SEC, calling it "absurd for the SEC to use a Mexican company and Mexican citizens to try to impose U.S. regulations in an extraterritorial manner, unilaterally ignoring international laws."

Following TV Azteca's request for more time to respond to the U.S. charges of securities fraud, the Federal District Court in Washington in February grants it a four-month extension which is extended again in May until July 11, with the possibility of the trial starting shortly thereafter.

Mexico's securities watchdog agency strikes back in February of 2005, when it states it believes TV Azteca executives committed fraud in the refinancing debt deal, and will allow the company an opportunity to state its case during a hearing before the agency. With its stock down 15 percent since the SEC files its charges in January, TV Azteca in April reveals it is considering a number of options to boost is share price on the New York Stock Exchange, including a merger, reorganization, private negotiated transactions and tender offers. Two months later, the Mexican Banking and Securities Commission fines TV Azteca $2.4 million for what it labels its fraudulent actions in the debt financing deal at Unefon, in which chairman Salinas Pliego and several business associates reap personal profit at the expense of stockholders. The securities regulator levies an additional $82,500 to the fine, this time against Unefon. Three days after Azteca sues Mexico's finance minister Francisco Gil Díaz for "abuse of authority, intimidation, attempted extortion and censorship," the official files criminal charges against Salinas Pliego "for unlawful use of privileged information." Concerned how this is all impacting the company's financial posture in the U.S., Salinas Pliego says he's considering delisting its stock on the New York Stock Exchange, due to what he claims are the high costs of "over-regulation" in the U.S. He cites several high-profile cases ranging from WorldCom to Enron to Adelphia Cable, which are responsible for creating what the company calls this over-regulated environment that requires increased costs and expenses. Following news of Salinas Pliego's plan to delist the stock, its price drops to $7.46 per share.

At a special stockholder's meeting June 1, an overwhelming majority votes to delist TV Azteca and two other Salinas-controlled companies, retailer Grupo Elektra and phone company Iusacell, from the New York Stock Exchange (NYSE) which lists the Mexican firms since 1997. On June 9 TV Azteca formally notifies the NYSE and the Bank of New York to terminate their American Depositary Receipt (ADR) programs for the three companies. Trading on the three firm's ADRs will terminate within 30 days, with delisting occurring in 60 days. On July 18, TV Azteca is no longer listed on the NYSE, and holders of its ADRs have 60 days to exchange them for certificates on the Mexican Exchange. So Salinas Pliego's earlier consideration is supported by the stockholders, freeing the troubled company from jurisdiction by U.S. regulators while allowing traders to invest in its stock on the Mexican Exchange, the Bolsa Mexicana De Valores.

On September 14, 2006, the SEC and Salinas Pliego reach a settlement in the lawsuit. Salinas Pliego agrees to pay $7.5 million to settle accusations of fraud involving the concealment of the deal between the TV Azteca subsidiary and the cell phone company Codisco secretly owned by him and a partner. Salinas Pliego neither admits or denies any wrongdoing. Board member Pedro Padilla Longoria agrees to pay $1 million. Echarte settles his involvement by paying a $200,000 fine without admitting any wrongdoing. According to a network spokesman, Echarte's involvement was he "sent an e-mail to shareholders announcing that the Codisco transaction had come to public light."

In November, Adrian Steckel, former CEO of Unefon, one of the Salinas' mobile phone companies, is appointed president/CEO, replacing Luis Echarte, who becomes chairman of Azteca America. Michael Viner, an original member of TV Azteca's board, is no longer affiliated with the company.

During the months the legal turmoil unfurls and engulfs its parent, Azteca America maintains an independent position by creating new programs and acting as if nothing is happening on both sides of the border. In a move which obviously helps improve its standing in New York City, the network's WNYN affiliate hooks up with the Asociación Tepeyac De New York's fourth annual Lady of Guadalupe Torch Race, starting in Mexico City October 10 and culminating in Manhattan at St. Patrick's Cathedral on Fifth Avenue on December 12. The 7,000 runners navigating across America, holding a torch as a symbol of unity between the two nations, are videotaped by WNYN during the New York leg of the run and aired on a delayed basis in its newscasts.

And in an effort to strengthen its bridge to music fans which already can satiate their appetites with the *Especial Musical* hour series, the network announces a new magazine show, *Billboard Latino*, which debuts Saturdays at 9 p.m. commencing February 5, 2005. Jorge Jaidar, the network's COO, calls music a key ingredient for its audience. The weekly hour show is a co-production by the network with Miami-based 13th Floor Television and New York-head quartered *Billboard*. The show reviews the newsweekly's top Latin charts and features artist news, interviews and performances conducted at recording studios around the country. Show hosts Efrain Barrera, Angelica Del Rosal, and Sascha Allendes, along with correspondents in New York and Los Angeles, travel to recording studios to attend taping sessions.

During the first quarter of 2005, EchoStar Communications Corporation's DISH Network signs an agreement to include Azteca America among its Latino programming package and include the U.S. network's *La Academia 4* musical variety show on another Echostar channel.

During the first months of 2005, when the network's distribution reaches 70 percent of U.S. Hispanic homes in 39 markets (compared to Univision's 98 percent and Telemundo's 92 percent), the little network that could cracks the top 25 primetime ratings rankings for the first time five times. Among these happy moments is the 13th place finish May 30 for its exclusive Mexican Soccer League's championship, which draws a 7.2 rating and translates to 1.3 million viewers, its best-ever numbers performance during its brief four-year existence.

Parent company TV Azteca's total revenue in 2006 in U.S. dollars is $887 million, debt is $814 million, while Azteca America's revenue is $44 million.

Despite some good experiences with Azteca America, Pappas Telecasting, citing what it calls a lack of strong ratings and programming growth after six years, announces in April of 2007 it will end six of its seven station affiliations with the network on June 30, '07. Pappas and Mexico's TV Azteca form the U.S. network as a joint venture which debuts in August of 2001. Azteca America says it is looking initially for replacement affiliates in Houston and San Francisco, two of the departing cities. Pappas' L.A. station, KAZA, has a local market agreement ending in June of '08. However, Harry Pappas, chairman/CEO, indicates that deal could end earlier. Pappas owns 27 stations, including many English-language plus the seven Azteca America affiliates in Los Angeles, Houston, San Francisco, Sacramento, Reno, Omaha, and Sioux City, Iowa. At its current high point Azteca America is available in 55 markets.

Liberman Broadcasting, the independent Burbank-based broadcaster with four Spanish TV and 16 radio stations around the country, is hardly in the national media spotlight. However, that changes in 2004 and 2005. When it debuts a new reality series, *Gana La Verde* (*Win the Green*) weeknights from 7 to 8 p.m. starting July 1, 2004, in which contestants vie for assistance in gaining a residency green card, it faces the heat of negative publicity.

Legal advocates and three members of Congress protest the show which airs on Liberman's stations in Houston (KZJL), Dallas (KMPX) Los Angeles (KRCA), and San Diego (KSDX), claiming it exploits and possibly endangers participants. Contestants must accomplish extraordinarily distasteful and gross stunts. The winner's prize is a year's work by immigration lawyers to help the individual gain his/her green residency card. Many of the show's contestants have either student or work visas and are in the process of becoming U.S. residents. Some are apparently undocumented aliens, whose real names are used on the program.

Six organizations involved with immigration legal and advocacy causes who are upset with the 14-year-old TV network's L.A. produced show, and demand it be taken off the air, include, according to the *Los Angeles Times*, which breaks the page-one story in August: the American Immigration Lawyers Association, California La Raza Lawyers Association, Central American Resource Center, Coalition for Humane Immigration Rights of Los Angeles, Latina Lawyers Bar Association and the Mexican American Bar Association.

Leonard Liberman, KRCA's vice president/general manager, repels all the complaints, telling the newspaper all contestants sign a 20-page release which specifically says there's no guarantee of a green card. He also says the show does not require people use their real names on the program. Despite the heat, the show continues its run.

Ian Stoilkovic, the show's executive producer, tells me in late October there are no other complaints since the hullabaloo begins. "When people understand the concept of the show, there's no problem." Stoilkovic says there's a winner every show who gains legal services for a year from the immigration lawyers hired by the network's Beverly Hills attorney Richard Sherman to obtain the green card, which legalizes their presence in this country. "A few people are very close to getting their cards," notes the exec producer.

And when KRCA unveils a 75-billboard campaign in Los Angeles, Orange, Riverside, and San Bernardino counties in April of 2005 promoting itself to Mexican viewers, its thematic overture turns into another cause célèbre, which draws in California Governor Arnold Schwarzenegger. The billboard shows two of its newscasters in front of a photo of the downtown skyline with the headline "Los Angeles, CA" in the sky. An X goes through CA with the word Mexico in red obviously replacing the California abbreviation. In the middle of the photo is a reference to the station's newscast, *Noticias 62* airing at noon and 9 p.m. At the bottom of the ad are the words "Tu Ciudad. Tu Equip" (Your City. Your Team). The hyperbole is seen by Members of Americans for Legal Immigration as promoting a welcoming feeling for illegal immigrants, one of the nation's hot button topics. Liberman officials tell the *Los Angeles Times* the outdoor advertising billboards and posters (owned by Clear Channel Communications) are not designed to create controversy, but rather to tell Spanish-language viewers that *Noticias 62* news is the place to turn for important news and information affecting their lives. Network and station official Leonard Lieberman calls the newscast a popular program in L.A. where residents of Mexican descent make up a major portion of the city, so the news covers both L.A. and Mexico. He tells the newspaper, "You just have to drive around L.A. to know that this is a Hispanic city."

Governor Schwarzenegger, an advocate of closer scrutiny of the nation's borders, tells L.A. radio station KFI that he's asking

KRCA to remove the billboards since he believes the wording of "Los Angeles Mexico" implies the city is part of Mexico and can encourage illegal immigration. Bowing to pressure, the station shortly alters the now-controversial billboard to eliminate the Los Angeles Mexico inference, with the two newscasters now appearing in front of the skyline with only the name of the newscast plus the "Your City, Your Team" in Spanish and English remaining at the bottom of the artwork. KFI-AM, an English talk station, takes advantage of the imbroglio by positioning a billboard on a busy street in the San Fernando Valley which sarcastically reads: "Just to clarify. You are here." with an arrow aimed at "Los Angeles, CA. USA." The salutation reads "Gracias, KFI-AM 640."

During the fall 2004 season, English-language broadcast TV continues to be lambasted, this time by three probes for its lack of Latinos in central roles. In the first instance, Felix Sanchez, chairman and co-founder of the National Foundation for the Arts, in a guest commentary in *TelevisionWeek*, points to the disparity in the number of programs centered in major cities with large Hispanic populations and the lack of an equal representation of Hispanic actors in the casts of these series.

Citing New York City, where "2.2 million Hispanics represent 27 percent of the population, Latinos comprise 28 percent of the city's police department and nearly one-quarter of Latino law school graduates go into public service law, none of the New York-based shows, CBS' *CSI: NY* and NBC's *Law & Order*, *Law & Order: SVU* and *Law & Order: CI* includes a single Latino lead role, while plenty of Latino victims and criminal characters appear briefly from episode to episode."

Sanchez also points to shows shot in other cities with large Hispanic populations where the same shortcomings are true, notably Los Angeles, home for NBC's *LAX*; Las Vegas, home for CBS' *Dr. Vegas*; Chicago, home for NBC's *ER*, and Boston, home for *The Practice* and *Boston Legal* on ABC.

A second study, this time by the National Association of Hispanic Journalists, titled "Network Brownout 2003" and carried by the *Los Angeles Times*, has both good and bad news regarding TV coverage of Hispanics in the U.S. First the good news: news coverage is more favorable towards Latinos last year due mostly to coverage of Latinos fighting in the war against terrorism. The bad news carries an old complaint that the nation's fastest-growing minority "remains mostly ignored." The study of more than 16,000 stories on the nightly newscasts of broadcast networks and CNN reveals that a total of 131 stories, or 0.82 percent, are about Hispanics, a rise above 2002's 120 stories, or 0.75 percent. Of 639 hours of news, four hours involve Hispanic stories. Positive human interest stories about Hispanics total 15 during 2003, a sharp rise from the three the previous year.

Of the networks surveyed using Vanderbilt University's Television News Archives, CNN has the most Hispanic stories: 47, for a total of nearly 90 minutes, followed by CBS with 30 stories representing a little more than 48 minutes. ABC's coverage declines from 35 stories in 2002 to 27 in 2003.

The third annual probe by the UCLA Chicano Studies Research Center looks at the 2004 fall primetime lineup on the six English-language broadcast networks for both regular and recurring characters in TV series and unearths shortcomings for both Latino and Asian-American actors and actresses. Citing eight series set in Los Angeles, the center of Los Angeles County in which 45 percent are Hispanic and 12 percent are Asian-American, the report claims Latinos are seen in 14 percent of the total regular roles and comprise the entire cast on one series (obviously *George Lopez*). Asian-Americans are not cast in any regular roles. In Miami, where 57.3 percent of the population are Latinos, Hispanics comprise 27 percent of the characters in shows set in the city, while in New York, with its 27 percent Hispanic population, eight percent of the actors employed on shows filmed there are Hispanic. Appraising the overall composition of all show regular cast members, the report finds a four percent decline in Latino characters over previous seasons. ABC winds up looking good, employing 13 of 26 Hispanic characters in primetime, with Fox, WB, and UPN cited for the lack of Hispanics during that critical programming period. States the report: "If television presents a microcosm of our society, it is a distorted one at odds with our nation's changing demographics."

Across the nation, several TV station groups target bilingual Hispanics with Spanish-language interpretations of their local news, utilizing closed-caption technology from two-year-old Ohio firm Translate TV, which utilizes the closed-caption space on one of the station's two signal channels designed for that purpose. Among station groups providing this service to their Hispanic viewers are Hearst-Argyle in Boston at WCVB; LIN TV in Connecticut, Michigan and Texas, Dispatch Broadcast Group in Indianapolis, Indiana and Columbus, Ohio and Tribune's WGN in Chicago. Viacom's Sacramento UPN station KMAX uses interpreters to translate the station's five-hour *Good Day Sacramento* program via the SAP channel. What's unusual about this arrangement, which begins in late November, is that vice president/general manager Bruno Cohen incorporates lead interpreter Martha Garcia, and several assistants as on-air personalities along with the show's English-language hosts. The interpreters work in tandem pairs in their own sound booth. The hosts and interpreters informally banter several times an hour during the broadcast, usually asking how a story is being translated.

Direct Broadcast Satellite market leader Dish Network, and its vaunted competitor DirecTV, aggressively continue to entice Hispanics in 2005. DirecTV, for example, which begins targeting Hispanics in January of 2004 with its Para Todos service, seeks to overtake Dish Network's Latino tier of programs first offered in the late '90s-early 2000s. Para Todos executive Mark Ryan tells *Multichannel News* that by the end of 2005, "We will have programming from every Spanish-speaking country in the world except Cuba."

When the Imagen Foundation's 20th annual awards honor 11 television and six film categories in addition to three special honorees at the Beverly Hilton in June, a handful of Latinos walk away with trophies. Among film nominees: *The Motorcycle Diaries* is the top multiple winner as best film, Walter Salles as best director, Rodrigo De

La Serna as supporting actor and José Rivera earning the special Norman Lear Writer's Award. There is no film actor category since there is only one qualifier, *Diaries'* Gael García Bernal. *Maria Full of Grace* star Catalina Sandino Moreno wins the best actress trophy. Shelbie Bruce wins the supporting actress nod for *Spanglish*. Underscoring the lack of positive roles for Latins, *Maria Full of Grace* is about a Colombian drug smuggling "mule" while *Spanglish* focuses on an illegal immigrant working in the U.S. household. The film documentary award goes to *Visiones: Latino Art & Culture* while *Cuco Gomez-Gomez Is Dead* prevails in the theatrical short or student film category. In the TV competition, Jimmy Smits wins top honors for his role on *West Wing*; Freddy Rodriguez wins the supporting actor role for the third straight year as a funeral home official on HBO's *Six Feet Under*, while Argentina's Mía Maestro wins supporting actress honors for her portrayal of an FBI agent on ABC's *Alias*. *Yo Soy Latina* nabs the live theatrical production. Among the special honorary awards, CBS Entertainment president Nina Tassler is lauded as the first Hispanic female to head the programming department at a major network in winning the Creative Achievement Award; George Lopez wins the Hennessy Privilege Award for his contributions to the Latin community; the film *Innocent Voices* wins the Humanitarian Award for its true story of 12- and 13-year-olds being conscripted into the El Salvador army, and the *Hollywood Reporter* earns the President's Award for its editorial coverage of Latin show business accomplishments.

In a long-overdue acknowledgement of the achievements of domestic Hispanic TV, the National Television Academy—previously known as the National Academy of Television Arts & Sciences—which presents the annual Emmy Awards for achievements in English-language TV, unveils its Emmys En Español June 3, 2005. The awards to individuals—not programs—are presented at San Antonio's McNay Art Museum.

Five on-camera personalities and one network executive receive honorary Emmys: Jorge Ramos, a Univision news anchor; Maria Celeste Arrarás, a Telemundo newsmagazine host; Mario Kreutzberger, Univision's *Sabado Gigante* show host known as Don

Francisco; Andres Cantor, Telemundo's soccer play-by-play commentator; Verónica Castro, Univision novela star, and Ray Rodriguez, new president/COO at Univision Communications.

In a major power move for a greater presence in Spanish-language TV, media giant Viacom—which owns CBS, Paramount and a number of cable networks including MTV and its MTV Español spin-off—acquires the seven-year-old Más Música TeVe Network and 10 Caballero TV stations in Northern California and central Texas owned by Eduardo Caballero for an undisclosed price in October of 2005. The acquisition is a Spanish-language music video and entertainment channel that is carried on 10 of Caballero's 12 stations, according to *Multichannel News*.

Of prime importance to Spanish TV are the additions of four major networks to the Nielsen Media Research's national ratings survey alongside the six English-language networks, the Nielsen Television Index (NTI). Univision is the first to sign in December of 2005, followed by Telemundo and Azteca America the next month and TeleFutura, Univision's counter-programming network in February. With all the key Latin networks now being graded in the national ratings service, the exclusive National Hispanic Television Index (NHTI) will be phased out in September of 2007.

The move marks the end of the separation between English and Hispanic networks begun in 1992 with the separate Latino ratings service, which the Hispanic companies lobby for. With their entry into the NTI, Hispanic networks anticipate gaining millions of dollars in advertising since some of their news, soccer, and primetime novelas rate higher than programs on the English-language TV networks.

With Spanish TV networks copying programming trends of the Anglo networks, it's only a matter of time before the latter start adapting successful programming concepts from their Hispanic competitors. That time arrives in mid-December of 2005. ABC, CBS, and syndicator Twentieth Television reveal plans to bring the telenovela format to English-language audiences during primetime in the summer of 2006. NBC joins the novela conversion crowd in February of 2006.

Nina Tassler, CBS' Entertainment president, indicates the network is developing five original 13-week series, from which at least one would be selected to air at least twice a week in the first year. She is especially keen on the genre, which runs from start to finish over several months on the Spanish networks, since she sees firsthand her Puerto Rican grandmother watching these romantic/dramatic soap operas, she tells *Daily Variety*. Viacom sister company, Paramount Network Television, is developing three of these sagas.

ABC is seeking already-produced novela themes to air up to five nights a week; it is also developing a remake of the Colombian novela *Yo Soy Betty La Fea* titled *Ugly Betty*, featuring America Ferrara in the lead role and Salma Hayek as an actress and a co-executive producer, to air Thursdays at 8 p.m. The network also signs with Mexico's Televisa to produce an English-language novela based on a series from its library of soaps. In addition, ABC is teaming with producers Endemol USA to bring the hit Spanish reality/competition TV series *Operacion Triunfo* to the domestic market. NBC in January of 2006 joins the novela transformation parade by charging sister network Telemundo with producing an English-language version of its hit series *El Cuerpo Del Deseo* (*Body of Desire*) for possible airing in the summer of 2006.

Fox TV's parent, News Corp., joins the novela parade with the announcement on February 22 of 2006 it is forming a new venture, My Network TV, which will include two novelas within its 12 hours of weekly primetime programming beginning September 5. The new network consists initially of 10 former Fox-owned UPN affiliates, displaced when both the UPN and WB networks are combined in a new CW Network in September. Both of its series, *Desire* at 8 p.m. and *Secrets* at 9 p.m. are produced by company-owned syndicator Twentieth Television, which will offer the series to stations in non-competing markets outside New York, Los Angeles, Chicago, and Dallas, for example.

Each of the steamy Spanish melodramas, translated into English by Twentieth, will encompass 65-hour episodes airing over 13 weeks. Both series are acquired from Colombian company Caracol Televisión. Normally novelas run five nights a week for three to 18 months on Spanish TV. In a move to attract bilinguals, English-speaking novela stars from the original dramas will occasionally be featured. Twentieth originally plans to sell *Desire* as a syndicated show, but scraps that plan when the CW Network is announced; a second plan to have the Fox Network introduce the series in June on its stations at 10 p.m. is also cancelled in favor of premiering the program on its new network.

The NBC Universal Television Group signs a two-year pact with Galan Entertainment to produce English versions of novelas from its Telemundo network in February of 2006. The first conversion involves the soap *Body of Desire*, which begins production in mid-2006. Galan is owned by namesake Nely Galan, Telemundo's former entertainment president from 1998 to 2000.

Seeking to get into the Hispanic market, two successful English-language production companies sign up to provide Telemundo and competitor TeleFutura with Spanish versions of their popular hit shows. Endemol USA, which produces NBC's 2006 super hit, *Deal or No Deal*, in June forms Miami-based Endemol USA Latino to create a Spanish version titled *Vas O No Vas* for Telemundo, NBC's Latin network as well as TV and film projects for other clients. Former Galan executive Stephanie Fisch is named senior vice president of the new operation. Also in June, FremantleMedia begins producing a Spanish version of its long-running game show *Family Feud* for Univision's sister broadcast network TeleFutura.

The habit-forming nature of novelas sparks a new emphasis on Spanish-language TV shows being transferred to DVDs in 2005. Key to the success of this move is the availability of these DVDs in major retailers like Wal-Mart, Target Stores, Best Buy, and Hollywood Video, reports the *Wall Street Journal*. Vital to the DVD movement are suppliers Televisa Home Entertainment, Univision Communications, and Venevision International. Normally novelas air over several months and can last up to 150 hours. On DVD, they are condensed to between five and 15 hours. Sales of 30,000 copies are a success for Spanish titles, whereas English-language titles can reach in the millions. Despite DVD's growth potential, overall, broadcast, cable and syndication minimize the opportunities for Hispanic lead actors...again, although Latinos are gaining a foothold in isolated instances. Here's how the spectrum looks by medium in 2004/2005:

Broadcast

ABC: When Barbara Walters steps away from her co-anchor chair on *20/20* after 20 years in October, the prized spot is awarded to Elizabeth Vargas, 42, an NBC and ABC veteran who becomes the first Latina to host a major primetime newsmagazine. Prior to joining ABC in 1996, the Emmy-winning journalist with a Puerto Rican/Irish heritage, is a correspondent for NBC's *Dateline* and *Today* during a three-year period. Prior to being promoted to ABC's flagship show, she hosts ABC's *World News Tonight* when Peter Jennings is not on the broadcast up until his death from lung cancer on August 7 of 2005. Then in December, along with Bob Woodruff, the two are named co-anchors of the newscast effective January 3, 2006. Woodruff, who also joins ABC in 1996, works on the broadcast as the Saturday anchor and before that as the Justice Department and a foreign correspondent. When Woodruff and his cameraman are seriously injured in Iraq on January 29 of 2006, Vargas has the emotionally challenging job of informing viewers about their scrape with death. She also works with a number of substitute hosts. In March, she announces she is expecting her second child due sometime in late summer. On May 23, ABC announces *Good Morning America* veteran Charles Gibson will join *World News Tonight* on May 29 as its sole anchor, following Vagras' last day on May 26 after which she departs to go on maternity leave. During June, Gibson will continue appearing as a co-anchor of *Good Morning America*, Monday through Wednesday. When Woodruff is fit to return to work, he'll probably function as a correspondent. Vargas plans returning in the fall to co-anchor *20/20* and host special programs.

One year after its debut in 2003, *Extreme Makeover: Home Edition* signs Eduardo Xol as its resident landscape designer. The former singer/novela actor/landscape design company owner, son of Mexican immigrants who grows up in East Los Angeles, impresses the show's casting producers via a series of on-camera tests to snare the job in October of 2005. One year later, his role expands to room designing as he gains his own star status alongside the show's exuberant host Ty Pennington.

In the drama department, among *NYPD Blue*'s handful of female detectives, Jacqueline Obradors remains the lone Hispanic in the cast, Esai Morales having left the show as the 15th squad's lead detective this year. When the series concludes its run after 12 years on March 1, 2005, the network schedules a one-hour retrospective prior to the final episode (number 261), highlighting all the cast members. Jimmy Smits, who plays detective Bobby Simone from 1994–'98, a partner to cantankerous lead character Andy Sipowicz (played by Dennis Franz), is the retrospective's major on-screen narrator. Clips of his emotionally draining deathbed scene reflect the gripping power of the show and mark a sharp contrast to Esai Morales' emotionless squad leader Lt. Tony Rodriguez from 2001 to 2004.

Two new shows with Latinos in the cast spearhead ABC's revival. *Lost*, the network's new drama hit, includes Jorge Garcia, the lone Hispanic among the 14 survivors on a plane enroute from Sidney, Australia to Los Angeles, which crashes on an unidentified island. Garcia, the son of a Cuban mother and Chilean feather who grows up in San Juan Capistrano, California, plays Hugo Reyes, who's raised in California. The show adds a second Latino for its second season, Michelle Rodriguez, following her appearance as Ana-Lucia Cortez in a flashback scene. *Desperate Housewives*, the primetime sexy soap opera, features Eva Longoria as one of the four featured on-camera wives, whose husband played by Ricardo Chaviro is business-driven and inattentive to her sexual needs, which are fulfilled by the couple's young macho gardener. Her scheming mother-in-law is played by 62-year-old veteran actress Lupe Ontiveros until she's killed off in an accident in an episode in April 2005. Longoria's TV popularity (and good looks) ignites interest within the film community which signs her for two features, *The Sentinel* with Michael Douglas, Kiefer Sutherland, and Kim Basinger and *Harsh Times* with Christian Bale, playing serious roles anathema to her sex-starved housewife on the hit ABC series, whose other female stars are all nominated for a dramatic Emmy while she is bypassed.

Longoria, who grows up on a ranch in Corpus Christi, the youngest of four sisters, breaks into TV on such daytime soap operas as *The Bold and the Beautiful*, *General Hospital*, *The Young and the Restless* and the primetime *Beverly Hills, 90210*. She also lands a role in the CBS movie of the week, *The Dead Will Tell.*

Continuing its love affair with the *George Lopez Show* for a third year, the Alphabet network adds six additional episodes to the Warner Bros. Television comedy skein to bring its season total to 28, up from the original order for 22 shows. The show about the plant manager of a Los Angeles airplane parts factory whose run-ins with his family constitutes a major plot line, averages 8.6 million viewers since moving to its Tuesday 8:30 p.m. slot from Fridays in 2004.

During the Christmas holidays, Lopez stars in *Naughty or Nice*, an ABC television movie in which he plays a repugnant sports radio show host. Lopez makes the TV film a family affair since his wife Ann is the executive producer…and Sofia Vergara, a Univision show host, makes her acting debut in the new fall 2005 situation comedy *Hot Properties* as one of four female real estate agents.

ABC, in addition to the dramatic adaptation of the telenovela *Yo Soy Betty La Fea*, also acquires the Emilio Estevez-starring Warner Bros. TV family comedy *Long Island Sound. Yo Soy Betty La Fea* (*Ugly Betty*) is a partnership between Salma Hayek's Ventanarosa Productions and Ben Silverman's Reveille Productions.

Seeking to upset traditional Hispanic TV viewing patterns, ABC on September 8, 2005, announces it will offer its entire fall primetime entertainment schedule with either dubbed Spanish dialog or subtitles. The Alphabet network thus becomes the first Anglo network to dramatically focus on luring Hispanic TV viewers away from their beloved novelas and tune in instead to its returning super hits *Lost*, *Desperate Housewives* and *George Lopez* and its new sci-fi thriller *Invasion* and *Freddie* comedy series starring Freddie Prinze, Jr., the son of the late comic, and co-starring Jacqueline Obradors. These shows will have dubbed dialog by hired actors available on the SAP channel of TV sets. The Lopez series, incidentally, offers dubbed dialog since bowing in 2001. The subtitles will be available on the closed caption channel. After a short run, *Freddie* is cancelled.

In addition, ABC is dubbing what's called "long form programming" which encompasses TV movies *Have No Fear: The Life of John Paul, II*, *Pirates of the Caribbean: The Curse of the Black Pearl*, and *Catch Me If You Can*, plus Charlie Brown Thanksgiving and Christmas specials.

In 2006, after a three-year absence from TV, ABC acquires rights to The Alma Awards, which honor Latinos in positive role model positions in show business. The taped show, co-produced and hosted by *Desperate Housewives*' Eva Longoria, airs June 5 from the Shrine Auditorium in Los Angeles.

Henry Alfaro, one of the nation's pioneering Mexican American reporters with ABC's Los Angeles KABC-TV for 35 years from 1970 to 2005, is inducted into the National Association of Hispanic Journalists Hall of Fame on June 17, 2006. A reporter with the station's *Eyewitness News*, he covers local, regional, and national events as one of the nation's first bicultural reporters and hosts *Vista LA*, the first half-hour show on L.A. TV in 1994 to focus on positive aspects of Hispanic life for English-speaking viewers.

CBS: John Leguizamo is signed to star as a sports agent/father and his uncast working wife in a new untitled drama series from 20th Century and Paramount TV. He'll also be one of the show's producers.

NBC: Jimmy Smits, the *NYPD Blue* alumnus, is among the new cast members hired to infuse new interest in *The West Wing*'s sixth season. He plays Texas Democratic congressman Rep. Matthew Santos, the former Houston mayor who's a presidential contender for the office soon to be vacated by Martin Sheen's character President Bartlet. During the show's final season in 2006, Smits' character wins a tight presidential election, becoming the nation's first Hispanic president-a harbinger of possible future events? Smits, with a Puerto Rican and Suriname heritage, spends much of 2004 working in stage productions in New York City. He appears in seven films since 1986, including 2002's *Star Wars Episode II* and *Episode III* in 2005. The key Latina in *Will & Grace* is 68-year-old veteran Shelly Morrison, whose Rosario character is a strongly opinionated woman.

Trial By Jury hires Kirk Acevedo to play a New York detective assigned to the Manhattan District Attorney's office in the latest *Law & Order*-spawned show which debuts in the spring of 2005. The actor of Puerto Rican ancestry previously stars in the HBO series *Oz* and will also be seen in the forthcoming film *The New World*.... *Law & Order: SVU*'s co-producer is Jose Molina, a powerful behind-the-camera position, who gains his entry into television as a result of participating in the internship program of the Academy of Television Arts & Sciences, which eventually lands him his current position.

Benjamin Bratt, who's been concentrating on his film roles (covered in Chapter 20), signs on for a major role in NBC's fall 2005 dramatic series *The E-Ring* which explores the inner workings of the Pentagon, Hollywood-style...John Leguizamo takes a break from his film roles to join the long-running drama *ER* as a controversial new supervising physician. He'll appear in at least 12 episodes during the 2005 season.

The Serranos, airing for two seasons on Spain's Telecinco network, is acquired by NBC for development in this country as a family drama. *Serranos* is the story of two former high school sweethearts who meet 20 years later when they both are married and have families. The Buenos Aires-owned company, Promofilm, which operates out of Miami, sells the rights to Reveille Productions in L.A. to develop the show at the Peacock network. It's the first fiction series sale by Promofilm to land at an English-language TV network; the company's earlier dealings are with Telemundo, NBC's Hispanic cousin, in the reality and soap opera genres.

In April of 2005, Telemundo's L.A.-based KWHY plays a key role in the launch by NBC Universal's San Diego station KNSD of an independent Spanish-language station called *Mi San Diego TV 43* on low-power KBOP. Since KNSD already reaches a large group of English-speaking Hispanics, and there is a corporation-owned Telemundo outlet in the market, KNSD launches the Spanish station to reach that portion of the market that speaks Spanish exclusively, and is not tuned to KNSD, explains *Multichannel News*. The new outlet utilizes KWHY's 38 hours of local programming each week, including morning and evening film packages, along with the first Padres baseball games in Spanish. During the summer it plans a 7 p.m. Spanish local newscast prepared by KNSD.

Fox: Gloria Estefan joins the ranks of guest judge/composer whose work is sung on an episode of the top-rated *American Idol*. She's the only Latino proffered this honor…John Leguizamo, riding a hot streak with multiple media offers, signs for an untitled comedy series built around his life as a film and TV personality. He'll also hold an executive producer's title along with writer Peter Murrieta…. Joining the cast of the hit sexy primetime soap *O.C.* is the omnipresent Nicholas Gonzalez, cast in the ensemble role of a love interest. His resume includes roles in *Anaconda*, *Resurrention Blvd.*, *American Family* and *The Brothers Garcia*.

Oscar De La Hoya's low-rated boxing reality series, *The Next Great Champ*, which airs on both the Fox TV Network and Fox Sports En Español three nights later, gets knocked out after four episodes. The remaining five episodes are shifted to the Fox Sports Network on cable. The show draws 5.2 million viewers for its debut episode, landing in fourth place in its Tuesday at 9 p.m. slot. The concept is to place 12 unknown boxers living together in house who vie against each other for a chance at a pro-boxing contract with De La Hoya's Golden Boy Promotions and a shot at a title fight with the World Boxing Organization. *The Champ* debuts before NBC's previously-announced *The Contender*, a similar boxing reality series involving *Rocky* film star Sylvester Stallone, hits the airwaves.

Lauren Sanchez, known for her sexy persona and plunging cleavage on camera, hosts Fox TV's 2005 hit reality summer series *So You Think You Can Dance*. The Albuquerque native is regularly seen co-hosting the freewheeling 11 p.m. news on KCOP-TV Los Angeles, the Fox-owned UPN affiliate along with Rick Garcia, who walks over to the UPN set from covering sports for Fox-owned KTTV's 10 p.m. news. Along with weathercaster Maria Quiban, who's Filipino, and Sanchez and Garcia, both Mexican American, the Channel 13 news features an all-minority cast doing an English-language news at that hour. Sanchez's previous TV credits include anchoring/reporting for *Fox Sports News Tonight* on the Fox Sports Network and appearing on *The Best Damn Sports Show Period*, *Goin' Deep* and *Extra*.

Geraldo Rivera, a war correspondent for the Fox News Channel since November 2001, debuts his own *Geraldo at Large* syndicated newsmagazine show October 31, 2005, airing on Fox TV Network stations week nights at 11 p.m. It's the latest challenge for the award-winning, self-effacing, controversial journalist who breaks into TV in 1970 as a reporter for WABC-TV in New York. Born Gerald Michael Rivera to Allen Rivera of Puerto Rican ancestry and Lillian Friedman of Russian Jewish ancestry in Babylon, New York, Rivera's strong muckracking personality enables him to stand out during his career at ABC News on *Good Morning America* and *20/20* during the 1980s, 11 years as host of his *Geraldo* syndicated talk show, three years with *Rivera Live* on CNBC from 1994–97, four years with NBC, leaving in 2001 for the Fox News Channel and an upgrade to his own newsmagazine series. His syndicated show is cancelled after January 26 of '07, with Rivera shifting to the Fox News Channel with his program, and also appearing as a special correspondent for breaking news and as a guest on Bill O'Reilly's *The O'Reilly Factor*.

PBS: *American Family-Journey of Dreams* is the expanded title for the highly acclaimed series in its second season airing Sunday evenings. Among the subjects covered is the Iraq war in the series produced by PBS outlet, KCET Los Angeles. The cast of returning principals includes Edward James Olmos, Constance Marie, Yancey Arias, Raquel Welch, Esai Morales, Rachel Ticotin, Lynn Whitfield, and Sonia Braga. The series is singled out by the Hollywood Foreign Press Association's Golden Globes for a nomination in the miniseries or TV movie category in its 62nd annual competition, the lone all-Hispanic cast among the five contenders. During the NBC awards telecast on January 16, 2005, the El Norte Production loses to HBO's *The Life and Death of Peter Sellers.*

During its celebration of Hispanic Heritage Month from September 15 and October 15, the network honors the talents of Hispanics in the arts in the six-part series *Visiones: Latino Arts and Culture*, all produced and directed by Texas filmmaker Hector Galán.

The network also reaches out to youngsters with *Maya & Miguel*, a half-hour animated series from Scholastic Entertainment that highlights the adventures of Hispanic twins and their bilingual parrot, which airs during a two-hour afternoon school programming period. A second series, *Los Niños En Su Casa*, designed to assist parents in preparing their children for school, is produced by KCET, for airing on PBS stations throughout the state.

During the two months of the celebration, PBS offers a variety of encores for Latino-themed documentaries and specials. In another KCET production, *PBS Hollywood Presents*, the two-part *Cop Shop*, whose cast includes detective Richard Dreyfuss and Rosie Perez playing a prostitute named Heaven in a brothel whose madam is played by Rita Moreno. What makes the miniseries different for a TV drama is its being shot live to tape non-stop, so it gives the actors the feel of live theater as well as recalling the way early live TV scripted shows are done before videotape.

The network is the principal repository for shows from Latino Public Broadcasting (LPB), created in 1998 in Los Angeles by Edwards James Olmos and Marlene Dermer as part of the National Minority Consortia, itself a division of the Corporation for Public Broadcasting. LPB provides funding for independent filmmakers. Among its features airing on PBS in 2004 are *Farmingville*, the story of the attempted murders of two Mexican laborers in Farmingville, New York, which runs in June; and two fall programs, *Visiones: Latino Art & Culture* and *The Life and Times of Frida Kahlo*, the renowned Mexican painter. In 2004, the non-profit LPB produces 30 hours of programming, up from 23 last season.

PBS airs its third documentary by Cuban American filmmaker Adriana Bosch, a two-hour profile of Fidel Castro on its *American Experience* program in January of 2005. The Castro project utilizes archival footage she collects. Born in Santiago, Cuba, in 1955, she flees with her family in 1968 to Spain and then to Elizabeth, New Jersey, Boston in 1977 and settles in Miami in the summer of 2004.

The network adds Daisy Martinez to its array of cooking shows in 2005. The 46-year-old Brooklyn-born professional chef of Puerto Rican ancestry hosts *Daisy Cooks!* which features family recipes as well as other favorites from the Caribbean, Latin America, and Spain.

During the fall of 2006, PBS introduces a new network, PBS Kids Go! which includes two hours a day of programs in Spanish with English subtitles. A companion channel for preschoolers introduced in October of 2005, PBS Kids Sprout, airs several shows with Latin characters during its unusual 24-hours-a-day, seven-days-a-week schedule.

Following protests by Latin advocacy groups that the contributions of Hispanic solders are excluded from his Word War II PBS series, *The War*, documentarian Ken Burns reverses his grevious decision on May 10, 2007 to now include Hispanic solders in his 14 hour series which debuts in September of '07. Burns says he will add stories about Hispanic veterans between segment breaks or after each installment.

UPN: *Kevin Hill*, the network's new breakout hit legal series, counts Jon Seda of Puerto Rican heritage among its six starring characters, led by film actor Taye Diggs. Seda's extensive film and TV experience includes NBC's *Homicide: Life on the Street* and the film *Selena* in which he plays husband Chris Perez to Jennifer Lopez as the slain singer.

Lopez and her obvious magnetic appeal is lured to UPN to executive produce *South Beach*, a primetime soap opera set in South Miami Beach, one of her favorite haunts. The series will shoot some scenes with entire Spanish dialog and English subtitles to appeal to a bicultural audience. The actress and partner Simon Fields' Nuyorican Productions are among the participants in developing the show which Paramount Network TV will produce. This is the third production deal for Lopez, following deals to develop a sitcom for NBC based on her growing up in the Bronx and a first-look arrangement with Fox TV Studios and Regency TV.

WB: *The Mountain* casts Alana De La Garza as the central figure in a love triangle between two brothers in the resort of Boundary Mountain. Her character is half Irish, half Mexican. She's the director of special events at the resort favored by wealthy tourists and sports buffs. Prior to this nighttime soap, she stars in the longtime daytime soap *All My Children* and appears in guest roles on *Las Vegas* and *JAG*.

As of the fall of 2006, the UPN and WB networks will no longer exist, as their parent companies, CBS and Warner Bros. join together in a new network, the CW, which will include programs from both failed operations as well as new, original series.

Syndication

Bob Vila, who pioneers home renovation TV 25 years ago, celebrates 15 years of syndication for *Home Again*, his own production following his 10-year run on PBS with his original series, *This Old House*. The 58-year-old Boston-area homebuilder paves the way for the current rash of home improvement programming on the broadcast and cable networks. In April of '07, CBS Television Distribution cancells his show, ending 28 years on broadcast TV, with Vila solely appearing on several home improvement cable TV network shows.

Tribune Entertainment signs Mario Lopez to host the news series *Real People* for the 2005–'06 season. The current host of *Pet Stars* on Animal Planet, Lopez's credits include co-hosting *The Other Half* on NBC, starring in NBC's *Saved By The Bell*, USA Network's *Pacific Blue*, and series *You Win Live*, *America's Most Talented Kids*, and *Will You Marry Me?*

Twentieth Television signs 10-year Florida Circuit Court Judge Alex Ferrer to preside over its entry in the crowded courtroom genre, where justice is meted out for a variety of minor offenses, not the type Ferrer is used to, ranging from murder to rape, armed robbery and drug dealing. The show is planned for the 2005–'06 fall season. Ferrer, a Cuban-American, becomes at 19 the youngest member of the Coral Gables police department as well as the youngest cop in Miami-Dade County. And when he's 34, he becomes the youngest judge in Miami-Dade County as well.

Scholastic Entertainment's bilingual children's series *Maya & Miguel* on PBS is built around 10-year-old twins, whose mother is from Mexico, the father from Puerto Rico and a parrot, which speaks English and Spanish. The series debuting October 11 is built around a cast of well-known Latin stars and behind-the-scenes voiceover experts including Candi Milo, who voices Maya and her Mexican cousin Tito. As one of the busiest Latina voiceover actresses, Milo is also the voice of the flea on *Mucha Lucha* on the Kids WB Saturday block. Her compatriots on the new show include Nika Futterman who's the voice of Miguel; singer/actor Carlos Ponce is the voice of the twin's father Santiago Santos; Elizabeth Peña is the voice for mother Rosa; Lupe Ontiveros is the voice for the twins' grandmother Abuela Maggie; Erik Estrada is the voice for the neighborhood mailman Senor Felipe and Lucie Liu plays Maggie, a best friend to Maya.

AIM Tell-A-Vision, the New York production company, whose initial two-year-old show, *Urban Latino TV*, targets U.S. born Hispanics with English-language programming, adds two new half-hours in 2004 aimed at this demographic. *American Latino Television* is a lifestyle show aimed at second- and third-generation Hispanics, while *Kulture Shock TV*, is a pop culture show designed to appeal to Latino and general market youth. America's emerging romance with Hurban music, blending reggaeton with rap and Latin rhythms, allows the company to bow its third season of *Sonidos*, its quarterly hour series with *Volume 9: Latinos in Hip Hop* during August and September of 2005. The program not only features such artists as Akwid, Pitbull, Kinto Sol, Frankie J, but also analyzes the Chicago and Cuban rap movements. The next segment, *Volume 10: Latin Divas* airs in November.

Cable

Comedy Central: Seeking to further its connection with Carlos Mencia, the East Los Angeles-bred, Honduran Mexican comic who tours with the Three Amigos comedy package in 2001 and performs standup specials for the network and HBO, the laugh channel signs the comic to a 10 episode series debuting in July of 2005. The half-hour show, *Mind of Mencia*, features staged segments and is co-executive produced by Mencia and Robert Morton, former producer of David Letterman's late night shows on NBC and CBS. The breakout hit series is renewed for a 13-episode second season in 2006.

CNN: Drooping ratings for the three-year-old *American Morning* see co-host Soledad O'Brien losing her original partner Bill Hemmer, a 10-year vet with the network, who's replaced by Miles O'Brien, shifting from CNN's *Live From* series. The moves are designed to "improve the chemistry between Soledad and her male counterpart," as well as make the broadcast a stronger outlet for hard news, according to the network. Soledad has been with the show since June of 2003. The 38-year-old, who's formal name is Maria De La Soledad O'Brien is the fifth of six children of Estella, a black Cuban who comes to the U.S. in 1958 to go to college and meets her soon-to-be husband Edward at Johns Hopkins University. Like all her siblings, Soledad is a Harvard graduate whose broadcast career encompasses KIIS-FM and WBZ-TV Boston; NBC News in New York; the Peacock Network's KRON-TV in San Francisco; the Discovery Channel (where she wins a local Emmy for *The Know Zone*); hosting MSNBC's *The Site* science show, and a series of NBC gigs on the *Today Show*, *Weekend Nightly News* and *Weekend Today* before landing her current co-anchoring slot.

CNN's eight-year-old Spanish service, CNN En Español, with three million domestic subscribers, including resident Mexican citizens, will focus on the 2006 Mexican presidential election, which for the first time in history, will include votes from these out-of-country residents, the majority living in Texas and California. Carmen Aristegui, host of her self-titled half-hour primetime news talk show originating in Mexico City, will cover the feelings of Mexican residents by broadcasting her show from key Hispanic market cities, according to the *Los Angeles Times*.

Disney Channel: *Handy Manny*, a cartoon featuring bilingual characters, debuts in early 2006 within the channel's seven-year-old *Playhouse Disney* preschoolers' block of shows. Wilder Valderrama is the voice of the lead character, while the title theme is sung by Los Lobos.

Food Network: Juan-Carlos Cruz, who drops 100 pounds to tip the scale at 180, champions healthy eating and weight loss to counter the nation's obesity epidemic on *Calorie Commando* and *Weighing In*. The Los Angeles resident/chef previously hosts *Cruising in the Kitchen* on PBS.

Fuse TV: Argentinian-born, U.S.-raised Marianela Pereyra co-hosts *Daily Download* on the all-music, audience interactive channel aimed at 12 to 34-year-old music fans. Originally launched in the U.S. as MuchMusic in 1984, the struggling Canadian channel is acquired in 2000 by Rainbow Media Holdings, Inc., which changes its name in May of 2003. Marianela, who credits Daisy Fuentes for her pioneering work as MTV's first Latina VJ, handles a series of broadcasting jobs prior to landing her Fuse gig. She hosts a show on KLSX-FM in Los Angeles, appears on *ElimiDate*, a WB reality series and UPN's *Half & Half*, and during 2005 covers the Grammys for both Fuse and the syndicated *Access Hollywood*.

FX Network: Bruno Campos plays one of the magical plastic surgeons, Dr. Quentin Costa, in the 2005 hit series, *Nip/Tuck*. The former resident of Rio De Janeiro breaks into American show business in 1995 with the Brazilian film *O Quatrilho*, which gains an Oscar nomination for best foreign language film. Three years later he cracks TV with a starring role opposite Christina Applegate on the NBC series, *Jesse*, which runs until 2000.

HBO: For the first time, an HBO Latin America original series (produced in Argentina), airs in the U.S. in December of 2005, first on HBO Latino, the domestic Spanish-language channel and then on HBO's Signature channel with English subtitles. The 13-episode thriller, *Epitafios* (*Epitaphs*), is a story of a tormented love affair amidst a criminal investigation. The historical 1968 Chicano high school student walkout in East Los Angeles protesting inequalities in the system is reexamined in the March 2006 drama *Walkout*. The stellar lineup of cast members includes executive producer Moctesuma Esparza, who helped organize the event, and is played by Bodie Olmos, son of director Edward James Olmos. Among the film/TV actors in key roles are Michael Peña, Alex Vega, Victor Villasenor, and Efren Ramirez.

Lifetime Network: The women's channel signs comedienne Debi Gutierrez to star in a project based on her real-life experiences as a working mother raising three children with the assistance of her husband and her ex for 2005. In addition to doing specials for Lifetime and Showtime, she also appears at various comedy festivals in the U.S. and Canada.

MTV: Susie Castillo, Miss USA 2003, is the featured host starting in January of 2005 of the hit series *Total Request Live* from New York and *Weekend Dime*, the Los Angeles-based weekend video countdown show. She also hosts a third music video show from MTV's Beach House in Las Vegas. As a result of her beauty and popularity, the former Methuen, Massachusetts, resident, also lands parts in ABC's *My Wife and Kids* and UPN's *Half & Half*.... Wilmer Valderrama, the Venezuelan/Columbian/American actor born in Miami who plays Fez on Fox TV's *That '70s Show*, is signed to host *Yo Momma*, being labeled a "trash-talk" contest show next year.

In April of 2006, MTV reveals a major revamping of its MTV Español channel, launched in 1998. The channel will be retitled MTV

Tr3s (MTV Three) and reintroduced in the fourth quarter as a programmer for U.S.-born Latinos. MTV Tr3s will feature music programming and lifestyle and cultural documentaries, notes *Daily Variety*, in which a mix of Spanish with English subtitles, complete English or a mix of both will be offered per show. The new network will be manned by execs in programming and news from MTV, headed by Lucia Ballas-Traynor, former general manager of MTV Español and VHUno, its sister Latin service, whose fate will be evaluated following MTV Tr3s' makeover.

By May of '07, Tr3s is available to around 48 percent of the Hispanic TV-watching audience (28 million plus homes) following its debut last September. It achieves this distribution by adding copious broadcast stations, among them Los Angeles and Phoenix, and satellite service DirecTV, to avoid being exclusively lumped in among cable's Latin digital packages for which there is an additional fee. The service to bilingual 12 to 34-year-olds is creating original series to aument music videos, while airing shows from parent MTV custom recast for Latinos, notes weekly *Variety*.

Nickelodeon: Five years after launching the now hit animated series *Dora the Explorer*, which incorporates Spanish words, the network introduces to its fall 2005 schedule a spin-off, *Go, Diego, Go!*, centering on Dora's 10-year-old equally bilingual cousin, replete with Spanish expressions.

With Univision's Galavision and Telemundo's bilingual mun2 established outposts on cable, a plethora of new networks turns the quotidian equation into one of aggressive action within the 75 Spanish-language network universe available to Latino cable customers.

While ESPN Deportes, the History Channel En Español, Voy Network, and Si TV provide new alternatives, they also have to compete for viewers with the popular MTV Español and its older skewing VH Uno, the obvious spin-off from VH1. While MTV Español plays various Mexican forms of music plus programming from MTV Latin America, VH Uno targets Caribbean musical styles and gains long form programming from its partnership with VH1 Latin America, also launched this year.

History Channel En Español, part of the A&E Television Networks, celebrates its first anniversary in June of 2005, with a combination of original shows and Spanish-language versions of signature shows from the parent History Channel. One year after its launch, its first original monthly series, *Panorama Mundial*, a global perspective of Latin America hosted by historian Alberto Coll debuts in April. Celebrating Cinco De Mayo, the traditional Mexican May celebration of its victory over France in 1862, the channel airs the weeklong daily series *¡Viva Mexico Week!* Its segments range from the Mexican American war of 1848 to profiles of boxer Oscar De La Hoya, rebel leader Pancho Villa, Selena, the slain Tejano star, the pyramids of Mexico, the story of the Aztecs, and the Mexican revolution of 1910.

Voy and Si TV are specifically targeted towards acculturated Latinos. It's a market underrepresented albeit a potential growth area, as statistical research from the Simmons National Consumer Study in *Advertising Age* indicates. Some 76 percent of U.S.-born Hispanics watch Anglo TV as compared to 29 percent of that group that watches Spanish-language TV. Amongst foreign-born Latins, 81 percent favor Spanish-language TV.

Si TV, which starts out as a production company in Los Angeles five years ago, and then seeks to raise the capital to become a cable network, finally achieves its goal in late February of 2004. Its English-language general entertainment programming is geared towards 18- to 34-year-olds.

Voy, which follows in July, targets 18- to 49-year-old Hispanics with a wide array of entertainment and lifestyle programming.

Si TV's founder Jeff Valdez and his partner, San Antonio venture capitalist/real estate developer Bruce Barshop initially launch Si Productions, Inc., whose first shows include *The Latino Laugh Festival* for Showtime, *The Brothers Garcia* for Nickelodeon and two syndicated series, *Café Ole* and *Funny Is Funny*, which wind up as reruns on Si TV. Among the network's original offerings are the talk show *The Rub*, the reality series *Urban Jungle*, the fashion show *Fly Paper: Style That Sticks*; the syndicated series *Urban Latino* and *Malcolm*

& Eddie, reruns of *New York Undercover* and *Queen of Swords*. With carriage on Cox Communications, Time Warner Cable, EchoStar's Dish Network, Si TV now reaches eight million homes, a good start for its investors who provide $70 million in funding, according to *Multichannel News*.

Seven months after its network introduction, Si TV expands its programming with three new original series in the music video, reality, and food genres. Five hours of its original shows are consolidated into a new Saturday night block called "The O-Si." While Valdez shows a propensity for comedy shows to fill the hole he sees for Hispanic-themed comedy programming, the network shoots for big film titles by licensing five titles from Universal Pictures. In a separate deal, Si TV acquires a series in which foreign films are redone with new plots.

As it celebrates its first anniversary on February 25, 2005, Si TV offers 70 percent of its original programming in high-definition TV, 10 original programs (up from five) and its first scripted comedy show, *Circumsized Cinema*, which revises Mexican B films into 22-minute mini movies with altered plots. Si TV also says yes to airing three evergreen series, *American Family*, *Resurrection Blvd.*, and *Dark Angel*, a two-hour showcase for independent and multicultural films, seven additional original series in the games, sketch comedy, and reality genres, plus 90-second film news interstitial segments.

In April of 2006, Valdez relinquishes programming responsibilities while retaining his chairmanship of the channel. It's part of a management shake-up, which sees former EchoStar executive Michael Schwimmer named the channel's chief executive. EchoStar is a major investor in Si TV.

Voy, which debuts in July as a digital channel from its L.A. base, features English-language lifestyle and entertainment fare. Andrew Thau, its president/CEO, says he's targeting "sophisticated Hispanics" who are not being satisfied by the programming on English-language TV. Thau is a veteran of cable TV, previously serving as senior vice president of operations and network development for the Fox Cable Networks and Fox Sports International.

All the participants in Spanish sports coverage face the competitive clout of Univision and Telemundo, which hold rights to many of the leading soccer and basketball competitions. Cognizant of the growing interest among Hispanics for professional basketball, Telemundo bows the third season of 15 NBA games under the banner "La NBA En Telemundo" starting January 23 of 2005 with play-by-play Saturdays by Edgar Lopez and the second season of *NBA Max* November 7 with a one-hour special which recaps previous season's highlights. This regular Sunday half-hour hosted by Lopez and Claudia Trejos is a youth-oriented lifestyle/entertainment show centering on NBA players on and off the court.

In 2004, cable's role as the dominant appointment TV locale for Spanish-speaking sports fans expands with the entry of a third network, ESPN Deportes, the fulltime digital spin-off of Disney's 25-year-old money machine ESPN. Initially starting out in 2000 carrying some pro baseball Sunday nights and then expanding in 2001 to a Sunday evening programming block offering baseball, football, and boxing, the 24-hour network debuts January 7 with exclusive coverage of 70 regular season Major League Baseball games on Sunday and Monday evenings, and then expands its reach to coverage of the National Basketball Association and the National Football League as well as soccer and boxing. In 2003, the network offers 13 Sunday nights of NFL football on *La NFL Dominical Por ESPN* that are preceded by a Spanish hour version of *NFL Prime Time*.

ESPN Deporte's entry along with eight-year veteran Fox Spots En Español, and the all-soccer all the time year-old Gol TV, ensures that sports buffs have access to what Fox Sports En Español's president David Sternberg labels the big three: soccer, baseball, and boxing.

ESPN Deportes hires Lino Garcia, a former vice president at Universal Television as general manager for its 24-hour debut. The new network creates its own version of the parent's popular *SportsCenter* newscast, naming Michele LaFountain, Heriberto Murrieta, Fernando Palomo, and Jorge Eduardo Sanchez Perez as its hosts.

The network plans airing more than 200 live events from Major league Baseball, the National Basketball Association, Wimbledon, the French Open, and soccer from the UEFA Champions League, Major League Soccer and the Copa Del Rey competitions, winter baseball from Mexico's Liga Del Pacifico league and motorcar racing from the Indy Racing League's Indy Car Series.

As ESPN Deportes celebrates its first anniversary in January of 2005, it's signal reaches seven million cable homes of which close to one million are Hispanic households in major Hispanic markets like Los Angeles, New York, and Miami.

Parent network ESPN and its ESPN International strengthen their positions within the soccer world by signing exclusive distribution pacts for the U.S. and overseas with rights holder Soccer United Marketing, which grants them coverage of U.S. men's and women's National team home matches including the men's World Cup qualifiers in 2005 leading up to the championship in 2006, and women's qualifying matches prior to the women's cup in 2007.

Fox Sports En Español enters 2004 with the foundation of 300 new hours of programming in soccer, boxing, and Caribbean World Series baseball from Puerto Rico prior to Major League Baseball's spring training period. The network's daily 3 p.m. newscast, *Fox Sports Noticias*, on August 17 celebrates its 5,000th consecutive program dating back to July 27, 1997, when Martin Liberman and Fernando Pacini co-anchor the launch. Liberman's current co-anchor is Adrian Puente. One week later, the network announces its exclusive two-year contract with the Mexican Soccer League for 26 regular season matches, 13 from mid-August to late November, and the remainder from January to May 2005. Mexico now gives the network coverage of five leagues including the U.S., Argentina, Brazil, and El Salvador. Combined with these leagues plus year-round championship tournaments, including the Copa Sudamericana quarter-final, semi-final and championships, the network's soccer programming now exceeds 1,000 hours.

During baseball's postseason playoffs, the network covers the division series, the American and National League championship series and the World Series. It's the fourth year the network offers exclusive Spanish-language coverage of the run up to the baseball title.

The World Series between Boston and St. Louis does well in the ratings, averaging a 1.23 among adults 18–49 and a 1.33 among men in the same age category. But during the seventh game of the American League Championship between the faltering Yankees and the come from behind Red Sox, the telecast earns a 4.74 average household rating, the highest figure Fox Sports En Español attains for any league championship series since it acquires rights to the Major League Baseball postseason competition.

For the second straight year, the network covers *La 2da Edición De Premios Fox Sports*, the awards ceremony which recognizes the achievements of U.S. Hispanic and Latin American athletes in soccer, baseball, boxing, basketball, motor sports, tennis, and golf which takes place December 15 at the Jackie Gleason Theater in Miami Beach and airs January 9 of 2005 to viewers in the U.S. and Latin America.

Among key winners are the Dominican Republic's Manny Ramirez, the World Series champion Boston Red Sox's slugger, named most valuable Series player; Albert Pujols, the St. Louis Cardinals Dominican born but raised in the U.S. first baseman named baseball's outstanding Latin American player; Mexican American Oscar De La Hoya, outstanding boxer; Argentina's Emanuel Ginobili, San Antonio Spurs guard, outstanding Latin American basketball player; Argentina's Paola Suarez, outstanding Latin American tennis player; Mexico's Pumas, outstanding Mexican soccer team; Honduras' Amado Guevara, outstanding U.S. Major League Soccer player; Mexico's Ana Gabriela Guevara, female athlete of the year and the Dominican's Felix Sanchez, male athlete of the year.

In addition to these national services, regional networks also keep local fans in touch with their favorite teams in Spanish. Some key examples: Cox Communications in San Diego provides a Spanish service for Padres baseball; the Madison Square Garden Network in New York offers Spanish play-by-play on the SAP second audio programming channel for New York Knicks NBA action but not for the NHL Rangers which are involved in the players-league salary standoff which kills the 2004 season; and Comcast Corporation in Atlanta airs Falcons football in Spanish on its Comcast Sports Southeast channel through a tie-in with the originating local NBC station.

Paralleling the growth of the programming networks, cable systems operators further develop packages to entice new Latin customers. For example, powerhouse Cox Communications introduces *Pacquete Latino* which provides 35 channels for $34.95 a month, including the less known TuTv, a joint venture of Univision and Mexico's Grupo Televisa, which offers two film, one music, and two lifestyle networks. Several cable systems lower their previous $50 or higher pricing for digital Spanish networks to under $30 include Time Warner, Adelphia, Insight, and Charter, whose Charter Latino cost $24.95 and is available in the West, Northwest, and Southeast.

In its battle between cable companies and satellite providers to sign up new customers, two systems operators, Comcast, for example, adds 100 hours of free Spanish video-on-demand (VOD) programming to its Cable Latino program package launched last year, while Charter will add free VODs to lure immigrant customers who may not want to sign up for an entire package of networks.

With soccer's World Cup—the equivalent of the World Series and Super Bowl combined for futbol fanatics—set for Germany in 2006, U.S. Spanish-language TV networks begin mapping their plans for this herculean event which will be shown in the morning and midday to projected larger audiences than view the 2004 World Cup from Japan and Korea during the early morning hours. Leading up to the championship, domestic Latino networks, general entertainment, and sports, offer select coverage of 2005 playoff games.

Cable's Anglophile networks efficaciously embrace a variety of Hispanic causes in 2004/2005.

Striking a note for realism on broadcast TV as far as Hispanics are concerned, the January 13, 2005, episode of CBS' drama *CSI: Crime Scene Investigation* includes for the first time a Spanish song whose narco-corrido lyrics perfectly suit the storyline for the Las Vegas-situated show and the city's escalating Hispanic population.

Extremo, a Los Angeles-based group, and actor Yancey Arias perform two songs written expressly for the segment by show scribe Dustin Lee Abraham.

Discovery Networks launches two new Hispanic channels in June, Discovery Kids En Español and Discovery Travel & Living (Viajar Y Vivar). Both networks feature programming from Discovery's Latin American networks plus dubbed shows from Discovery's other U.S. channels. In addition, the kids channel will offer original educational preschool, preteen, and family oriented series, while the Travel channel gains programming from Discovery's Latin American travel and living channel.

MSNBC's *Ultimate Explorer*, which debuts in June, provides correspondent Mireya Mayor with a national platform. The child of Cuban parents who grows up in Miami, she's the lone Latina among the show's four on-camera world-traveling personalities.

Nickelodeon spins off a new series, *Go, Diego, Go!* from its hit *Dora the Explorer* series. Set for the fall of 2004, the new show spotlights the exploits of Dora's eight-year-old cousin Diego.

Showtime airs the winners of the 2004 Los Angeles Latino International Film Festival as part of its five-year-old *Latino Filmmaker Showcase*, which runs during National Hispanic Heritage Month, September 15–October 15. Two shorts and three features are presented on the broadcast.

Spike TV, the "men's channel" sees tennis and baseball as the means for attracting Hispanics during Latin Heritage Month in September with two original documentaries. Its first ever documentary, *Pancho Gonzalez, The Latino Legend of Tennis* airs September 16 from 10 to 11 p.m. and focuses on the late Mexican American stars domination of the sport for 30 years up until his 5-1/2 hour triumph in Wimbledon's center court against Charlie Pasarell in 1969. Gonzalez, 67, passes away of stomach cancer in Las Vegas in 1995. The film is followed two days later by *Viva Baseball*, a 90-minute film about Hispanic players in Major League Baseball, a very timely topic, for a fall airing. The documentary probes discrimination felt by early Latino players like Roberto Clemente once they crack the big leagues in 1958 and include interviews by director Dan Klores ranging from pioneers like Manny Minoso and Juan Marichal to today's successful superstars like Alex Rodriguez and Sammy Sosa.

The real life spectacle of Michael Jackson going on trial in Santa Maria, California, in February of 2005 for allegedly molesting 13-year-old Hispanic cancer victim Gavin Arvizo in 2003, attracts more than 50 TV crews and 1,000 journalists from around world. Stationed in the media village are Univision and CNN Español, with Telemundo using the pictures provided by parent NBC's network news crew and selectively having its own reporter at the courthouse.

In a probable first for a broadcast TV network series, the March 23 episode of ABC's hit *Alias* is broadcast almost entirely in Argentine Spanish with English subtitles. The network is hoping the episode will attract a new Latino audience. Although the series has included some non-English dialog, this is the first time the show airs an almost entire foreign-language stanza. Set in Argentina, the script is originally written in English, reports the *New York Times*, and then translated into Argentine Spanish, the native language of actress Mia Maestro, who's born in Buenos Aires. Spanish is also the native language for the other actors in the episode.

Bolstering the cause for English-language shows, a research report by ad agency ODM Latino, whose client is McDonald's, indicates that Hispanic kids 2–11 spend around 80 percent of their TV viewing with English-language shows, reports *Multichannel News*. Univision disputes the English domination, claiming its weekend kid show *Complices Al Rescate* ranks among the top five broadcast TV shows viewed by Hispanic kids 2–11.

The major Anglo broadcast networks, watching Univision rank No. 1 among 18- to 34-year-olds during 19 primetime nights of the 2005 season, are on the offensive to lure that advertiser-desired audience, especially in major cities where they own local stations, reports the *Wall Street Journal*. NBC, whose Telemundo consistently trails Univision in audience and ad revenue, adds Spanish dialog to its *Passions* soap opera and begins signing popular actors appearing in

Telemundo novelas for primetime projects, starting with actress Genesis Rodriguez who appears in the primetime novela *Prisionera*.

During all the television networks' annual program presentations to advertisers in New York in May called the "upfronts," Univision, Telemundo, and Azteca America all stress new product, upbeat audience projections and some new dressing on the cake, while still bemoaning their shortfall in gaining more national advertising dollars.

Univision announces its first late night variety show, *¡Ay Qué Noche!*, which Televisa and Fonovideo will produce in Miami weeknights from midnight to 1 a.m. featuring performing acts and celebrity interviews before a studio audience. Also hyped are its acquisition of the Latin Grammy Awards, switching from CBS and airing November 3, and continued coverage of soccer's World Cup 2006 in which 64 matches will be spread over Univision, TeleFutura, and Galavision.

Under the banner "Hecho Para Ti (Made for You)," Telemundo reports four new original primetime hour novelas, two weekend dramas and a weekday miniseries patterned after the Rubén Blades hit tune *Pedro Navaja* and set within a Spanish community in New York City. The NBC Universal-owned company will also revamp its mun2 network aimed at the 12–34 audience, with new graphics and new programming including a weekly variety series, *VivoLive*, filmed at the Universal CityWalk at Universal City, California, and the animated series *Huevocartoon*, featuring savvy speaking eggs. The youth-oriented network will also split coverage of World Wrestling Entertainment's highly popular *Raw* series with English-language USA Network, the company-owned highly ranked cable service.

In a separate growth move unrelated to its sales pitching, Telemundo ups its company-owned full-power station count to 15 in May with the purchase of KBLR in Las Vegas from Summit Media Limited Partnership for an undisclosed price.

Azteca America's presentation stresses its 70 percent U.S. distribution into 39 markets, a new boxing series, *Julio César Chávez*

Presenta, hosted by the famous Mexican boxer and a new domestic version of the parent network's hit musical reality series, *La Academia*, currently in its fourth season in which three contestants are from the U.S. The network also stresses an increase in live sports and music programming, its 8,000 annual hours of programs from its Mexican parent plus 1,000 plus hours of exclusive programming for domestic consumption, including a U.S. version of its celebrity news series *Ventaneando*.

In other key developments:

ESPN Deportes TV lands its own version of ESPN's popular reality series *Dream Job* in which aspiring Latino sportscasters from New York, Los Angeles, Miami, Dallas, and Chicago audition for a job covering the 2006 World Cup in Germany.

The network also debuts two sports competition firsts: live coverage of the X Games 11 for three days in August and 17 regular season Monday Night Football games in 2006.

ESPN Deportes Radio in partnership with ABC Radio Networks and Lotus Communications, also announces the launch of the first domestic 24 hour Spanish-language sports network in September of 2004. Lotus' Los Angeles talk station KWKW-AM, will be the network flagship with other initial affiliates in Las Vegas, Reno, Tucson, Bakersfield, Fresno and Pomona, California. Advertising and affiliate sales and marketing will be handled by ABC. KWKW is the longtime radio outlet for the Los Angeles Dodgers. The network will offer talk and events including baseball's All Star game, league championship series, the World Series and Mexican Soccer home matches of the Chivas team, the latter starting with the 2006 season.

Fox Sports En Español adds 1,500 new live hours to its 5,000 hours of programming in 2004. Of the new additions, 500 focus on soccer from four club competitions plus a series linked to its World Cup 2006 coverage. Also hyped: its reportage of Major League Baseball's All Star game and postseason playoffs. In September of 2005, the network aggressively moves to attract more English speakers and bilinguals by offering 70 percent of its programming in

English, joining Gol TV which earlier offers an alternative language service. Earlier in the year the network adds the two-hour live interactive soccer show, *Jorge Ramos En Vivo!*, to its Monday night lineup commencing August 1. This Jorge Ramos is known as *El Relator De America* (*The Commentator of the Americas*) and is not to be confused with the similarly named Univision newscaster. Along with co-host Hernan Pereyra, a longtime radio sports figure, the show discusses concluded and upcoming matches, particularly from the Mexican National League, the Copa Toyota Libertadores and Copa Nissan Sudamericana competitions.

Gol TV, the compleat soccer bilingual network, in its initial push before advertisers stresses its 1,500 matches of which half are live and its intention to create instructional shows for youngsters. Gol TV's coverage in soccer-heavy TV features action from top futbol leagues around the world encompassing Mexico, Europe, and South America. It's TV's one-stop soccer shopping center.

The National Association of Hispanic Journalists (NAHJ) 23rd annual convention in June of 2005 at the Fort Worth Convention Center attracts newly elected Los Angeles mayor Antonio Villaraigosa as its opening speaker. Its earlier released "Network Brownout" report which reveals the poor coverage of Latinos on four national TV networks is augmented by the strong comments of actor John Leguizamo who decries the lack of roles for Hispanic actors and actresses. While Villaraigosa is asked about his plans beyond Los Angeles, notably Washington, a key focal point of the gathering centers around the organization's 2003 Parity Project initiative designed to increase the number of Hispanics in English-language TV from the current 5.2 percent to nine percent by 2008. An NAHJ database of Hispanic journalists is designed to assist general market stations looking for Latino broadcasters in front of and behind the camera.

Actor Leguizamo lashes out at the roles proffered to Latinos, telling the NAHJ he's become "disillusioned by the stereotypical gang member and handymen roles offered to Latin actors. We have to tell the whole plethora of our stories (since) we have the whole spectrum in our culture."

ESPN2, the sister channel to ESPN, as part of a move forward with original programming, signs veteran TV personality Mario Lopez as the co-host with Thea Andrews for *ESPN Hollywood*, its daily half-hour show which covers the pop culture link between sports and entertainment debuting August 15 of 2005. Andrews, a Canadian actress, is the former co-host of ESPN2's *Cold Pizza* morning show and also plays a sports reporter in the ESPN original movie about pro football titled *Playmakers*.

During May of 2007, major Spanish- and Engish-language TV networks unfurl their new season lineups. Among the high-profile endeavors:

ABC signs Salma Hayek and Jose Tamez, coproducers of the hit ABC series *Ugly Betty* to develop new series for the network through their Ventanarosa productions.

CBS signs Jimmy Smits to head a cast of Hispanic actors in the drama *Cane* focussing on a Cuban American family in business in Miami. The show, with occasional subtitles and reggaeton music, includes in its ensemble: Hector Elizondo, Rita Moreno, Paola Turbay, Nestor Carbonell, Eddie Matos, Michael Trevino, Lina Esco, Sam Carman, Alona Tal, and Polly Walker.

Telemundo, among its long lineup of new shows, will provide exclusive Hispanic coverage of the 2008 Summer Olympics in Beijing, along with parent NBC. It will air 28 events spread over 17 days. It will also bow five internally produced novelas, and a weekly late night variety show (broadcast from its new facility at the Universal Studios City Walk Hollywood). The network will also launch a campaign to encourage Latinos to vote in the 2008 presidential elections. Its mun2 bilingual youth-oriented network will bow a half-hour weekly magazine show based on its popular website, and two weekly 30-minute reality shows.

Univision will introduce among its 30 new shows two original scripted series, *Como Amar Una Mujer* (*How to Love a Woman*), based on Jennifer Lopez's latest CD of the same title. She is creative director and executive producer of the five-part series. The second show is a Spanish version of the hit ABC series *Desperate Housewives* (*Amas De Casa Desperadas*). The network is also heralding its new Sunday morning news show *Al Punto*, anchored by Jorge Ramos, designed to focus on the 2008 presidential race, and garner its share of political ad dollars.

Articles

"CBS Is Going Out On A Limb." Los Angeles Times, May 17, 2007

"Univision's New Image Is Star Of Party." Los Angeles Times, May 17, 2007

"Univision Makes Foray Into Originals." Daily Variety, May 17, 2007

"Hayek Sits Pretty With ABC Deal." Daily Variety, May 15, 2007

"Telemundo Presents New Original Programming Grid For 2007-2008." Telemundomv. com, May 15, 2007

"Univision Gives Citizenship Drive Unusual Lift." Wall Street Journal, May 10, 2007

"Burns Will Add Latinos To War Series." Los Angeles Times, May 11, 2007

"Televisa Ends Attempts to Take Over Univision." Los Angeles Times, September 19, 2006

"At ABC, A Hopeful Bet on 'Betty.'" Los Angeles Times, August 14, 2006

"Univision's Buyout Deal Draws Shareholder Suits." Los Angeles Times, June 29, 2006

"Televisa Cashes In Chips." Daily Variety, July 6, 2006

"Televisa Could Battle Its U.S. Partner." Los Angeles Times, July 6, 2006

"Univision OKs Saban Bid." Hollywood Reporter, June 28, 2006

"Televisa Mum On Future." Hollywood Reporter, June 28, 2006

"How Televisa Lost Univision Bid." Los Angeles Times, June 28, 2006

"Ruiz Plea." Hollywood Reporter, June 20, 2006

"Endemol Hip To Hispanics." Daily Variety, June 20, 2006

"Career Of Firsts Distinguishes Henry Alfaro." TelevisionWeek, June 12, 2006

"Hilton Ruiz, 54; Jazz Musician Known For His Versatility." Los Angeles Times, June 7, 2006

"Televisa In ABC's Family." Daily Variety, June 6, 2006

"So Hot, So Fast." Billboard, May 27, 2006

"Charles Gibson Named Sole Anchor Of ABC's 'World News Tonight.'" ABC. Com, May 23, 2006

"Soraya, 37; Singer Raised Breast Cancer Awareness." Los Angeles Times, May 12, 2006

"Televisa Teams Up In Bid For Univision." Los Angeles Times, May 12, 2006

"'Nuestro Himno' Foes Say U.S. Song Should Be Sung In English." Los

Angeles Times, April 29, 2006

"Latin Rising." Billboard, April 29, 2006

"National Anthem Gets Latinized." Los Angeles Times, April 25, 2006

"When The Fad Goes Fizzle." Los Angeles Times, April 16, 2006

"Manhattan Latin." Hollywood Reporter, April 12, 2006

"Red Hot RBD." Billboard, April 8, 2006

"Telemundo Sets New Studio." Hollywood Reporter, April 6, 2006

"MTV In Latin Makeover." Daily Variety, April 4, 2006

"Si TV Co-Founder Out As Programming Head." Los Angeles Times, April 1, 2006

"Time Life's Latin Leap." Latin Notas Billboard, April 1, 2006

"Rocio Durcal, 61; Spanish Actress, Singer Evolved From Teen Idol To Musical Stylist."_Los Angeles Times, March 30, 2006

"How DJs Put 500,000 Marchers In Motion." Los Angeles Times, March 28, 2006

"Pio Leyva, 88; Cuban Singer Appeared With Buena Vista Social Club." Los Angeles Times, March 26, 2006

"Miami Gets Mega TV." Billboard, Latin Notas, March 25, 2006

"Rick Con Sabor." Billboard, Latin Notas, March 25, 2006

"Worlds Collide." Billboard, March 25, 2006

"Univision Boosters." Daily Variety, March 24, 2006

"Long Hard Climb." Multichannel News, March 20, 2006

"'Walkout' In Step With 1968." Los Angeles Times, March 18, 2006

"Televisa Denying Univision Group Effort." Daily Variety, March 14, 2006.

"50 Latino Impact Players." Daily Variety, March 9, 2006

"Televisa, Private Equity Firm May Bid Jointly For Univision." Los Angeles Times, March 10, 2006

"Univision's Earnings Depressed By Charges." Los Angeles Times, March 3, 2006

"NBC, Galan Sign Deal To Make English Telenovelas." Los Angeles Times, Feb. 28, 20006

"TV For Kids Courts Spanish Speakers." Los Angeles Times, Feb. 28, 2006

"Carey Tunes Up Indie Film." Daily Variety, Feb. 27, 2006

"GE Making Mexico Plans." Daily Variety, Feb. 23, 2006

"The Hurban Sprawl." Newsweek, Feb. 27, 2006

"News Corp. Fights Back With New Network." Los Angeles Times, Feb. 23, 2006

"Fox Has A Sixth Sense." Daily Variety, Feb. 23, 2006

"Ray Barretto, 76; Conga Player Noted In Worlds Of Salsa And Latin Jazz." Los Angeles Times, Feb. 18, 2006

"Nielsen Speaks Spanish." Daily Variety, Feb. 16, 2006

"Univision Board To Consider Sale." Los Angeles Times, Feb. 9, 2006

"Grammy Awards." Daily Variety, Feb. 9, 2006

"Pop Goes The Alphabet." Daily Variety, Feb. 7, 2006

"Good Sports." Billboard, Feb. 4, 2006

"ABC Relaunches Alma Kudos." Daily Variety, Jan. 30, 2006

"Latin Radio Formats Keep Flipping For Oldies." Billboard, Jan. 28, 2006

"NBCU Agrees To Buy Longmont's KDEN-TV In Denver." TelevisionWeek, Jan. 23, 2006

"Ides Of March Augurs NBC Change." Hollywood Reporter, Jan. 23, 2006

"NBCU Stations Up For Sale." TelevisionWeek, Jan. 16, 2006

"Reggaeton Broke Out But Regional Mexican Acts Drove Latin Biz." Billboard, Dec. 24, 2005

"Telemundo, Too, To Join Nielsen Ratings Ranks." Daily Variety, Dec. 22, 2005

"Nielsen Bows To Latino Viewers." Los Angeles Times, Dec. 20, 2005

"Shakira Now More Famous." Billboard, Dec. 17, 2005

"Billboard Music Awards." Billboard, Dec. 17, 2005

"Summer Sudsers Nets Taking Radical Soap Approach." Daily Variety, Dec. 15, 2005

"CBS Eyes Summer Lovin'." Hollywood Reporter, Dec. 15, 2005

"Twentieth Has U.S. 'Desire.'" Hollywood Reporter, Dec. 14, 2005

"Times Square Will Be Crowded." Los Angeles Times, Dec. 13, 2005

"'Now' No. 1 Again; A First For Shakira." Los Angeles Times, Dec. 8, 2005

"Grammy Nominations." Grammy.com, Dec. 8, 2005

"Thriller In Any Language." Los Angeles Times, Dec. 7, 2005

"ABC Picks Duo For New Format." Los Angeles Times, Dec. 6, 2005

"The Conquest Of America (North And South)." New York Times, Dec. 4, 2005

"La Reina Del Crossover Hit." Los Angeles Times, Nov. 26, 2005

"Mendes' Sweet Return." The Beat: Billboard, Nov. 26, 2005

"A No-Nonsense Voice For Latin America." Los Angeles Times, Nov. 20, 2005

"Univision TV Co-Prez Exits." Daily Variety, Nov. 16, 2005

"Univision Names Michael D. Wortsman President, Univision Television Group." Univision.net, Nov. 14, 2005

"Latin Radio Flips Boost Ratings." Billboard, Nov. 12, 2005

"Jose Is The Latin Jack." Latin Notas Billboard, Nov. 12, 2005

"Right Audience And More Of It For Latin Grammys." Los Angeles Times, Nov. 7, 2005

"It's Pure Spanglish At This L.A. Radio Estacion." Los Angeles Times, Nov. 5, 2005

"Latin Grammy Awards: Playing To A Familiar Audience." Los Angeles Times, Nov. 4, 2005

"Univision To Cut Payroll Despite Increased Profit." Los Angeles Times, Nov. 3, 2005

"Viacom Buying 'Mas Musica' Assets." Multichannel News, Oct. 31, 2005
"Ricky's World." People, Oct. 24, 2005
"SGZ, Univision Move Forward." Billboard, Oct. 22, 2005
"'Prince Of Song' Continues To Charm." Billboard, Oct. 22, 2005
"Latin Grammys Set Fetes." Daily Variety, Oct. 18, 2005
"KXOL's Format Switch Wins, In Any Language." Los Angeles Times, Oct. 18, 2005
"Latin TV Leader Retools Lineup." Billboard, Oct. 15, 2005
"New Cruz On The Scene." Billboard, Oct. 15, 2005
"Carey Is Looking Golden With 'Mimi: Platinum.'" USA Today, Oct. 14, 2005
"No Strings Attached For Younger Santana." Los Angeles Times, Oct. 10, 2005
"Santos Celebrates 20 Years Of Machete." Down Beat, October 2005
"Extreme Makeover: Xol Edition." Tu Cuidad, October 2005
"KGLA 1540 AM Back On The Air In New Orleans." HispanicAd.com, Sept. 28, 2005
"Night Of Stars And Premier Performances In 'Premios Juventud Awards." HispaniaNet.com, Sept. 28, 2005
"Redirecting DirecTV." Multichannel News, Sept. 19, 2005
"For Reggaeton, Unlikely Newcomers." Billboard, Sept. 17, 2005
"2005-06 NFL Games In Spanish @ Sirius." HispanicAd.com, Sept. 13, 2005
"Target Demos: Moms, Youths." TelevisionWeek, Sept. 12, 2005
"Fox Sports En Ingles." Multichannel News, Sept. 12, 2005
"Networks Have An Ear For Spanish." Los Angeles Times, Sept. 11, 2005
"Radio Flips For Reggaeton." Billboard, Sept. 10, 2005
"ABC Spells Español." Daily Variety, Sept. 9, 2005
"ABC Speaks Spanish In Primetime." Hollywood Reporter, Sept. 9, 2005
"XM Deportivo Set To Launch On XM Satellite Radio August 15." HispaniaNet.com, Sept. 2, 2005
"3 For The Road." Latina, September 2005
"The Story Behind Television's Latin Star." Hispanic, September 2005
"Daisy Cooks," Hispanic, September 2005
"The Calorie Commando." Hispanic, September 2005
"Leguizamo Scrubs Up For 'ER' Duty." Daily Variety, Aug. 31, 2005
"Univision Flagship Makes Nielsen History In NYC." HispaniaNet.com, Aug. 30, 2005
"Televisa Tube Tussle." Daily Variety, Aug. 26, 2005
"In Macho Contest, We Have A Winner." Los Angeles Times, Aug. 26, 2005
"New Names Rule At Latin Grammys." Los Angeles Times, Aug. 24, 2005
"'Telenovelas' Become A Vibrant New Niche In The DVD Market." Wall Street Journal, Aug. 22, 2005
"Pearlman Sees Future For Latin Boy Bands." Billboard, Aug. 20, 2005

"Stars Estéfano." Billboard, Aug. 20, 2005

"Valderrama To Host Trash-Talk Show." San Francisco Chronicle, Aug. 18, 2005

"Showbiz On Center Court As ESPN Goes 'Hollywood.'" Hollywood Reporter, Aug. 15, 2005

"Ibrahim Ferrer, 78; Found Fame In Buena Vista Social Club." Los Angeles Times, Aug 8, 2005

"Radio Lured By Latino Clout." Los Angeles Times, August 6, 2005

"No Hablo Ingles." Entertainment Weekly, Aug. 5, 2005

"Third Season Of Sonidos Music Specials Debuts With Exploding Latinos In Hip Hop Special." Hispanic PR Wire News, Aug. 2, 2005

"Jorge Ramos En Vivo!" To Debut On Fox Sports En Español." HispanicAD.com Aug. 2, 2005

"A Runaway Hit." Hispanic, August 2005

"Miami Kingpin." Latina, August 2005

"Say It Again, Omar." Los Angeles Times, July 31, 2005

"Latin Albums Surge Amid Industry Decline." Billboard, July 30, 2005

"Reggaeton Rules." Latin Notas Billboard, July 30, 2005

"Univision Makes $90M Radio Deal." Los Angeles Business Journal, July 26, 2005

"A Spanish-TV Upstart Nips At Heels Of No. 2 Telemundo." Wall Street Journal, July 25, 2005

"Pino Out At EMI Latin." Billboard, July 23, 2005

"Televisa Sings U.S. Tune," Hollywood Reporter, July 20, 2005

"Televisa Cues Music Again With EMI." Daily Variety, July 20, 2005

"New EMI Venture Will Focus On Growing Latin Music Market." New York Times, July 20, 2005

"Televisa, EMI Latin Join Forces." Miami Herald, July 19, 2005

"Mexico's Azteca Exits NYSE." Hollywood Reporter, July 18, 2005

"Televisa Heats Up Feud With Univision." Daily Variety, July 18, 2005

"Spanish Broadcasting System Hits The Wall On The Street." HispanicAd.com, July 18, 2005

"SBS Making Television Debut." Hollywood Reporter, July 14, 2005

"Nets Score Early In Soccer World Cup." Weekly Variety, July 11, 2005

"Telemundo's Major Makeover." Weekly Variety, July 11, 2005

"Thalía's 'Sixth Sense.'" Billboard, July 9, 2005

"Reggaeton Contracts Replace Handshakes As Genre Explodes." Billboard, July 2, 2005

"'Jobim Sinfonico' Highlights Florida-Brazil Forum." Down Beat, July 2005

"Hot New TV Star…Carlos Mencia." Latina, July 2005

"Brazilian Festival Brings The Crowd To Its Feet." Los Angeles Times, June 28, 2005

"Two New Labels Emerge." Billboard, June 25, 2005

"Sony, Ritmo Latino Settle Shakira Dispute." Billboard, June 25, 2005

"Telemundo Puts Emphasis On Telenovelas From Mexico." Hollywood Reporter, June 24, 2005

"Leguizamo Decries Hollywood's Latino Roles." HispaniaNet.com, June 20, 2005

"Imagens Ride With 'Diaries.'" Hollywood Reporter, June 20, 2005

"Latinos Fete 'West,' Smits." Daily Variety, June 20, 2005

"Telemundo To Relocate Its Youth Channel To L.A." Los Angeles Times, June 20, 2005

"Ritmo Refuses Shakira Set." Billboard, June 18, 2005

"Latino Coverage Is Still Scant." Los Angeles Times, June 17, 2005

"Jaime Mendoza-Nava, 79; Used Classical Training, Bolivians Roots In Composing For TV And Film." Los Angeles Times, June 16, 2005

"Telemundo Shuffles Studio Exec Suite." Daily Variety, June 17, 2005

"Noms Reflect Slow Change." Daily Variety, June 17, 2005

"Renewed Commitment For Hispanic Journalists." TelevisionWeek, June 13, 2005

"Hispanic TV Heats Up Major Markets." TelevisionWeek, June 15, 2005

"Mariah Celebrates A Sweet 16." People, June 13, 2005

"Embracing San Diego." Multichannel News, June 13, 2005

"Radio Riding Reggaeton Wave." Billboard, June 11, 2005

"Hemmer Bolts CNN's 'Morning.'" Daily Variety, June 7, 2005

"Azteca Reaches Rating Mecca." Weekly Variety, June 6, 2005

"I Didn't Feel Worthy Of Happiness," Parade, June 5, 2005

"Songs Of The Uprooted." LA Weekly, June 2, 2005.

"Azteca To Delist From NYSE." Daily Variety, June 2, 2005

"TV Azteca Leaves Wall Street." Hollywood Reporter, June 2, 2005

"Running With The News." Hispanic Magazine, June 2005

"Akwid Readies New Label Venture." Billboard, May 28, 2005

"ShakiraX2." Billboard, May 28, 2005

"Azteca Fraud Trial Delayed." Daily Variety, May 25, 2005

"Hispanic Network Upfront Likely To Surge." Multichannel News, May 23, 2005

"Latin Grammys Swap CBS For Univision." Billboard, May 21, 2005

"New Latin Charts Bow." Billboard, May 21, 2005

"Univision Lineup Leans On Televisa Shows." Daily Variety, May 19, 2005

"Univision Adds Novelas, Variety." Hollywood Reporter, May 19, 2005

"ESPN Deportes Lands Its Own 'Dream Job." Daily Variety, May 19, 2005

"ESPN Deportes Unveils Programming & Showcases Media Platforms." HispanicAd.com, May 18, 2005

"Univision, TeleFutura, Galavision 2005-2006 Line-Up." HispanicAd.com, May 18, 2005

"Telemundo Schedule Heavy On Original Programming." Hollywood Reporter, My 18, 2005

"Telemundo Pumps Up Novelas." Daily Variety, May 18, 2005
"Univision Grows Vid Arm." Daily Variety, May 17, 2005
"Hispanic B'Casters Ready For Primetime." Daily Variety, May 16, 2005
"Spanish Soap Opera." Weekly Variety, May 15, 2005
"Awards Heat Up TV." Billboard, May 14, 2005
"Televisa Head Quits Univision Board." Wall Street Journal, May 11, 2005
"Resignation Intensifies Univision Battle." Los Angeles Times, May 11, 2005
"Hispanic Nets Feud." Daily Variety, May 11, 2005
"Latin Grammys Find New Beat On Univision." Hollywood Reporter, May 10, 2005
"Hispanic Nets Keep Eye On The Prize." Advertising Age, May 9, 2005
"Tottering Topper's Legal Woes Hit Azteca." Weekly Variety, May 9, 2005
"Azteca Chief Makes Legal Move." Daily Variety, May 6, 2005
"Cable TV Stations Revamping Ads That Created Stir." Los Angeles Times, May 5, 2005
"Azteca Down On NYSE Talk." Hollywood Reporter, May 4, 2005
"Azteca's Game." Hollywood Reporter, May 3, 2005
"Additional Azteca Fine." Daily Variety, May 3, 2005
"Azteca's Salinas Draws New Charges." Daily Variety, May 2, 2005
'Big Four' TV Networks Get A Wake-Up Call-In Spanish." Wall Street Journal, May 2, 2005
"Latin Music Is Alive And Well On Public Radio." Latin Beat, May 2005
"Latin Shipments Up, Up & Up." Billboard, April 30, 2005
"Adventura's Adventure." Billboard, April 30, 2005
"Latin Rap Makes Its Move." Billboard, April 30, 2005
"Mexican Gov't Fines Azteca." Hollywood Reporter, April 29, 2005
"Gov. Praises 'Minuteman' Campaign." Los Angeles Times, April 29, 2005
"Clear Channel To Dismantle Media Empire." Wall Street Journal." April 29, 2005
"An Ad Putting L.A. In Mexico Called Slap In Face." Los Angeles Times, April 27, 2005
"Two Stations Challenge Radio Leader." Los Angeles Times, April 26, 2005
"Illegal Immigration Fears Have Spread." Los Angeles Times, April 25, 2005
"Trevi Triumphant." Los Angeles Times, April 25, 2005
"Road To The Unfront: Univision." Advertising Age, April 25, 2005
"Univision: Come To Where The Ratings Are." TelevisionWeek, April 25, 2005
"Jose Melis, 85; Bandleader For Jack Paar's Variety Shows." Los Angeles Times, April 21, 2005
"Mariah Breaks Out." Daily Variety, April 21, 2005
"Mariah Soars To No. 1." USA Today, April 21, 2005
"Border-Watch Group To Stop Patrols." Los Angeles Times, April 21,

2005
"Frankie J's Second CD Worth The Wait." San Antonio Express News, April 17, 2005
"Original 'Reali-mentaries,' Games, Yuks On Si TV Slate." Hollywood Reporter, April 14, 2005
"Emancipation Proclamation." Newsweek, April 18, 2005
"Spotlight R&B Singer Frankie J." People, April 18, 2005
"Latin Notas: Closer Quarters." Billboard, April 16, 2005
"Comcast Cites Hispanic Gains." Multichannel News, April 11, 2005
"Discovery, Nickelodeon Offer More Than Soap Operas To Hispanic Viewers." Advertising Age, April 11, 2005
"Telemundo Chief Quits, Is Replaced By NBC Veteran." Los Angeles Times, April 7, 2005
"Browne Takes Telemundo Helm." Hollywood Reporter, April 7, 2005
"Telemundo's Top-Tier Switch." Daily Variety, April 7, 2005
"Radio Hooked On Latin." Billboard, April 9, 2005
"Telemundo News Offers Unique Minute-To-Minute Coverage From The Vatican." Telemundomv.com, April 5, 2005
"TV Azteca Keeping Options Open." Hollywood Reporter," April 4, 2005
"Pope John Paul II Dies." Los Angeles Times, April 3, 2005
"Are These Latinos Becoming The Most Powerful Men In Music?" Latina, April 2005
"Discovery Set For Spanish Immersion." Hollywood Reporter, March 31, 2005
"First Time Ever Spanish TV Station Leads Tucson." Univision.net, March 28, 2005
"Leguizamo, Elfman Join CBS Pilots." Hollywood Reporter, March 24, 2005
"Pop Star's Ex-Manager Sentenced In Rape Case." Los Angeles Times, March 23, 2005
"Closed-Captions Translate News Into Spanish." Broadcasting & Cable, March 23, 2005
"Si TV Marks Anniversary With Success." Hollywood Reporter, March 21, 2005
"'Alias' En Español." New York Times, March 20, 2005
"Coming On Strong Again." Los Angeles Times, March 20, 2005
"Billboard To Honor Pair Of Latin Icons." March 19, 2005
"Latin Notas: That's Dope." Billboard, March 19, 2005
"Lalo Guerrero, 80, Pioneering Barrio Singer." Los Angeles Times, March 18, 2005
"Hope Floats At SXSW Festival." Los Angeles Times, March 16, 2005
"Azteca America Launches Fundacion Azteca America." HispanicAd.com, March 15, 2005
"The Great Kids Debate." Multichannel News, March 14, 2005
"Texas: Deep In The Heart of The Hispanic Market." Multichannel

News, March 14, 2005

"Academy Sets Spanish-Language Honors." Hollywood Reporter, March 14, 2005

"Latin Rocker Juanes." People, March 14, 2005

"The Old Versus El Nuevo." Los Angeles Times, March 10, 2005

"KMAX Reaches Out To Hispanic Viewers." Broadcasting & Cable, March 7, 2005

"MTV's On The Lookout For Latin Viewers." Daily Variety, March 4, 2005

"Looking Back Over The 'Blue' Years." USA Today, March 1, 2005

"Q&A Kirk Acevedo." Latina Magazine, March 2005

"The Paq-Man's Half-Century." Hispanic Magazine, March 2005

"Latinos In Hip Hop To Reggaeton." Latin Beat, March 2005

"Telemundo Preps U.S. Telenovelas." Weekly Variety, Feb. 28, 2005

"'Boys' Just Keep Their Hits Comin'." Los Angeles Times, Feb. 28, 2005

"History En Español Gains Birth In Miami." Multichannel News, Feb. 25, 2005

"Telemundo Bets On Las Vegas Station." Hollywood Reporter, Feb. 24, 2005

"Falcon Flies To Top Post At Univision." Daily Variety, Feb. 23, 2005

"Varied Field Vies For Billboard Latin Honors." Billboard, Feb. 19, 2005

"Trevi On Comeback Trail." Latin Notas, Billboard, Feb. 19, 2005

"Latin's New Voices." Billboard, Feb. 19, 2005

"Mexico's Trevi Announces Tour." Los Angeles Times, Feb. 15, 2005

"El Cucuy Ratings Debate Rages." Hollywood Reporter, Feb. 14, 2005

"Talent In Crossfire." Daily Variety, Feb. 14, 2005

"The Complete List Of (Grammy) Winners." Los Angeles Times, Feb. 14, 2005

"'Lost' Takes An Odd Path To Diversity." Los Angeles Times, Feb. 13, 2005

"Univision Has New President." Los Angeles Times, Feb. 10, 2005

"Jackson Media Circus Descends On Courthouse." Los Angeles Times, Feb. 10, 2005

"Univision Says Hola to New Prexy-COO." Daily Variety, Feb. 10, 2005

"U.S. Gives Azteca Reprieve." Daily Variety, Feb. 10, 2005

"Emmys Seek To Honor Hispanics En Español." Daily Variety, Feb. 9, 2005

"Stand Up Guy Getting A Gig." Daily Variety, Feb. 8, 2005

"An ESPN Rookie With Room To Grow." Multichannel News, Feb. 7, 2005

"'Possible Violations' For TV Azteca." Hollywood Reporter. Feb. 3, 2005

"Fresh Options Infuse Hispanic TV." Advertising Age, Jan. 31, 2005

"India Takes Indie Turn." Billboard, Jan. 29, 2005

"Exile's Documentary On Castro Lets Her Confront Feelings." Miami Herald, Jan. 29, 2005

"Latin Notas: 'CSI' Runs With Corridos." Billboard, Jan. 29, 2005
"Peacock Touts Parity Position." Daily Variety, Jan. 24, 2005
"The Voice To Watch." Los Angeles Times, Jan. 23, 2004
"Air America Flies Back To Southland." Los Angeles Times, Jan. 20, 2005
"Spanish Album Sales Surge In 2004." Billboard, Jan. 22, 2005
"Velasquez Ready To Make Her Mark With Label." Billboard, Jan. 22, 2005
"Spanish Album Sales Surge In 2004." Billboard, Jan. 22, 2005
"Latin Notas: Sanz Branches Out." Billboard, Jan. 22, 2005
"Battle Intensifies Over Control Of Mexican TV." Los Angeles Times, Jan. 17, 2005
"Viacom Names New CEO Of Infinity." Wall Street Journal, Jan. 14, 2005
"Hollander Names CEO At Infinity." Hollywood Reporter, Jan. 14, 2005
"A Change That Finally Makes Sense At XTRA." Los Angeles Times, Jan. 14, 2005
"Bien! Infinity, SBS In Harmony." Hollywood Reporter, Jan. 13, 2005
"Univision Sales Sputter." TelevisionWeek, Jan. 10, 2005
"Music Industry Deal Consolidates Firms Of 2 Talent Managers." Wall Street Journal, Jan. 7, 2005
"An Azteca Crusade." Daily Variety, Jan. 5, 2005
"SEC Charges TV Azteca With Fraud." Hollywood Reporter, Jan. 5, 2005
"In Step With Jimmy Smits." Parade, Jan. 2, 2005
"NBC's Other Language." Broadcasting & Cable, Jan. 3, 2005
"Judge Alex The Latest Hispanic To Take On TV Court Cases." Hispanic Magazine, January, 2005
"SBS In Bay Area." Hollywood Reporter, December 28, 2004
"Entravision Makes Triple Play With 'Super Estrella' Flips. Radio & Records.com, Dec. 27, 2004
"Gutierrez Fills Maternal Role For Lifetime." Hollywood Reporter, Dec. 27, 2004
"Winning Combo: romantic, Regional Mexican." Billboard, Dec. 25, 2004
"The Chart-Toppers." Billboard, Dec. 25, 2004
"Year In Music & Touring (Top Latin Product)." Billboard, Dec. 25, 2004
"KHOM-TV Goes Spanish In Phoenix," HispanicAd.com, Dec. 16, 2004
"TeleFutura Shatters Primetime Record In November Sweeps." HispanicAd.com, Dec. 16, 2004
"Study Cites Lack Of TV Diversity." Los Angeles Times, Dec. 15, 2004
"TV Skeins Don't Reflect City Diversity." Daily Variety, Dec. 15, 2004
"Study: News Coverage of Latinos Is 'Dismal.'" Los Angeles Times, Dec. 14, 2004
"U.S. Networks Big Winners Of Awards." Houston Chronicle, Dec. 10, 2004
"President To Leave Univision Radio." Los Angeles Times, Dec. 9, 2004
"Univision Sweeps Clean With Sudsers." Daily Variety, Dec. 8, 2004
"Miami Spice For UPN." Daily Variety, Dec. 8, 2004

"Programming Focused On Hispanic Local Interests Is On The Rise." Multichannel News, Dec. 6, 2004

"Operators Are Using A Variety Of Strategies To Lure A Wider Base Of Latino Subscribers." Multichannel News, Dec. 6, 2004

"Latin Execs Take An Indie Turn." Billboard, Dec. 4, 2004

"Music DVD Sees Year-End Surge Of Releases." Billboard, Dec. 4, 2004

"Mexican Pop Star Trevi Launches New Album." Miami Herald, Dec. 3, 2004

"Latin Music, Groups Moving Into Houston Mainstream." Houston Chronicle, Dec. 1, 2004

"Maya & Miguel." Hispanic Magazine, December 2004

"Slug: Latin Alternative Music." Latin Beat, December 2004

"Stripped Down And World Weary." Los Angeles Times, Nov. 28, 2004

"Jazzy, Rhythmic, Sublime." Los Angeles Times, Nov. 28, 2004

"Galavision At 25." TelevisionWeek, Nov. 22, 2004

"RIAA, SoundScan: Latin Sales Up." Billboard, Nov. 20, 2004

"Telemundo In 'Idol' Gear." Daily Variety, Nov. 15, 2004

"ABC Radio Speaks Spanish." Daily Variety, Nov. 15, 2004

"The Martyred 'Mexican Madonna.'" New York Times, Nov. 14, 2004

"Fusion Feels Fine To Monchy & Alexandra." Latin Notas, Billboard, Nov. 13, 2004

"Stav Talking Money For Univision." Hollywood Reporter, Nov. 12, 2004

"SBS & ABC Radio Networks To Syndicate Morning Shows." HispanicAd.com, Nov. 10, 2004

"55 Million Watched Election Night Coverage." HispanicAd.com, Nov. 10, 2004

"'Latinas!' Offers Continental Style." Los Angeles Times, Nov. 8, 2004

"Decades Of Sounds Reveal A Musical Treasure Island." Los Angeles Times, Nov. 7, 2004

"Natasha Rocks Like Joan Jet, But Stands On Her Own." San Antonio Express-News, Nov. 7, 2004

"Univision Sends Out Mixed Picture." Los Angeles Times, Nov. 5, 2004

"Bush Snags Much More Of The Latino Vote, Exit Polls Show." Los Angeles Times, Nov. 4, 2004

"They Won't Touch This Hot Potato." Los Angeles Times, Oct. 31, 2004

"ESPN Deportes Launches Cronometro" HispaniaNet.com, Oct. 30, 2004

"Univision Telenovela Beats Rivals In English." Miami Herald, Oct. 30, 2004

"KSJO/San Jose Flips To Spanish." Radio And Records, Oct. 29, 2004

"Univision Tries To Boost Share Of Political Ads." Wall Street Journal, Oct. 25, 2004

"Translating Faith Into Spanish." Time, Oct. 25, 2004

"Branded Content Hits Hispanic TV." Advertising Age, Oct. 25, 2004

"Strong Sales For Latin Tours." Billboard, Oct. 23, 2004

"Latin Extends Its Reach." Billboard, Oct. 23, 2004
"Solis' Pop Appeal." Billboard, Oct. 23, 2004
"Young Soap Star Carries Soundtrack To The Charts." Billboard, Oct. 23, 2004
"Academia Tours." Latin Notas, Billboard, Oct. 23, 2004
"Bush Tells Spanish TV He Backs Guest-Worker Program." Los Angeles Times, Oct. 22, 2004
"Univision Shuts Off L.A. Buyers." Daily Variety, Oct. 21, 2004
"XM Goes To Bat With MLB Deal." Hollywood Reporter, Oct. 21, 2004
"Spending Passes $1 Billion Mark, More To Come." Los Angeles Times, Oct. 21, 2004
U.S. Elections Are To Set Record For Spending At $3.9 Billion. Wall Street Journal, Oct. 21, 2004
"'West Wing' In A New Campaign For Ratings, Respect." USA Today, Oct. 20, 2004
"TV Ad Spending Soars As Messages Turn Shrill." Los Angeles Times, Oct. 19, 2004
"WCVB Speaking Spanish." MediaWeek, Oct. 18, 2004
"Market Profile: Los Angeles." MediaWeek, Oct. 18, 2004
"Accordion Proves Its Worth At Festival." San Antonio Express-News, Oct. 18, 2004
"No Excuse For Lack Of Latinos In TV Roles." TelevisionWeek, Oct. 18, 2004
"Turning A Chance Into A TV Career." TelevisionWeek, Oct. 18, 2004
"Young Singer Finds Balance In Two Styles, Two Cultures." San Antonio Express-News, Oct. 17, 2004
"Azoff's Latin Link." Billboard, Oct. 16, 2004
"For Bacilos, Being Different Makes The Difference." Billboard, Oct. 16, 2004
"Argentine Music Is More Than Tango." San Antonio Express-News
"La Oreja De Van Gogh Shows An Ear For Music." South Florida Sun-Sentinel, Oct. 14, 2004
"It's Miller Time." Daily Variety, Oct. 11, 2004
"Fox Knocks 'Champ' To FSN." Multichannel News, Oct. 11, 2004
"'Maya & Miguel' Hablan A Kids In Two Languages." Houston Chronicle, Oct. 11, 2004
"The Latino Playing Field." Multichannel News, Oct. 11, 2004
"Telemundo Sets Sights On The Young And The Bilingual." HispaniaNet.com, Oct. 10, 2004
"Univision's 'Premios Juventud," A Hit With Youth Of All Ages." HispaniaNet.com, Oct. 10, 2004
"Small Hispanic Record Producer Wins Verdict Over Univision In Trademark Case." HispaniaNet.com, Oct. 10, 2004
"Vives Finds Some Folk In The Rock Of His People." San Antonio Express-News, Oct. 10, 2004

"A Brazilian Tribute To America." Miami Herald, Oct. 10, 2004
"Sony, BMG Tackles Sales, Latin." Billboard, Oct. 9, 2004
"Guerra Gets Religion." Billboard, Oct. 9, 2004
"Young Yolanda Strikes Up The Banda." Billboard, Oct. 9, 2004
"Calling For Puente." Latin Notas, Billboard, Oct. 9, 2004
"SEC Issues Downgrade Of Azteca." Daily Variety, Oct. 8, 2004
"Azoff, Aseni Team For Latino Tunes." Daily Variety, Oct. 8, 2004
"Los Lobos Cruises Past 30." Honolulu Advertiser, Oct. 8, 2004
"Miller Turns Eye Towards Hispanics." Wall Street Journal, Oct. 8, 2004
"Show Targets DIY Crowd." Houston Chronicle, Oct. 8, 2004
"Acting Jobs Decline For Latinos, Asians." Los Angeles Times, Oct. 7, 2004
"TeleFutura Takes #2 Spanish-Language Network Spot In Four Major Dayparts." Business Wire, Yahoo.com, Oct. 7, 2004
"Televisa Soaps To Bow On DVD." Daily Variety, Oct. 6, 2004
"Off Duty But On Camera." Los Angeles Times, Oct. 6, 2004
"Peacock Sitting Pretty." Daily Variety, Oct. 6, 2004
"Viacom To Take Up To 15% Stake In Spanish Broadcast System." Wall Street Journal, Oct. 6, 2004
"Viacom Targets Hispanic Audience." Hollywood Reporter, Oct. 6, 2004
"Product Placement A Telenovelas Plot Twist." Miami Herald, Oct. 5, 2004
"'Champ' Is Defeated." Los Angeles Times, Oct. 5, 2004
"Futbol De Primera @ KLYY-FM 'La Cumbia Caliente' In LA." HispaniaNet.com, Oct. 5, 2004
"Univision Radio Flip-Flops Radio Stations." HispanicAd.com, Oct. 5, 2004
"Esparaza Inks Deals With Net Quartet." TelevisionWeek, Oct. 4, 2004
"Latin Biz Sets Sights On Teens." Billboard, Oct. 2, 2004
"El Matador Scores A Goal With ESPN." Hispanic, October 2004
"Jose Alberto El Canario." Latin Beat, October 2004
"The Ride 30 Years Of Los Lobos." Latin Beat, October 2004
"'Ugly Betty' Getting An ABC Makeover." Daily Variety, Sept. 29, 2004
"Gotti Raps About Barrio Life And Having A Good Time." San Antonio Express-News. Sept. 26, 2004
"CCR Speaks More Spanish." Billboard, Sept. 25, 2004
"Latino Vote Still Lags Its Potential." Los Angeles Times, Sept. 25, 2004
"El Premio Awards For The Fans." Billboard, Sept. 25, 2004
"Viva El Chicano! '70s Latin Rock Legend." HispanicAd.com, Sept. 24
"Telemundo Taps Vet Zel." Daily Variety, Sept. 24, 2004
"Files Show How Celia Overcame 1960s Blacklist." Miami Herald, Sept. 23, 2004
"Estevez Tops 'Long Island' Pilot For ABC." Hollywood Reporter, Sept. 23, 2004
"Lopez Flows To Dimension's 'Lava.'" Daily Variety, Sept. 23, 2004

"Mun2 Television Celebrates Hispanic Heritage Month." HispanicAd.com, Sept. 21, 2004

"New Mexico's Vision, L.A.'s Dream." Los Angeles Times, Sept. 21, 2004

"Maria Bermudez Supplies A Hearty Evening Of Flamenco." Los Angeles Times, Sept. 21, 2004

"Cox Courts Latinos With Channel Pack." Hollywood Reporter, Sept. 21, 2004

"Kerry Seeks Cuban-American Beachhead." Wall Street Journal, Sept. 20, 2004

"Winning The Latino Youth Market." Multichannel News, Sept. 20, 2004

"Industry Remembers Capone." Billboard, Sept. 18, 2004

"Juanes Puts His Heart Into 'Mi Sangre.'" Billboard, Sept. 18, 2004

"Clear Channel To Grow In Spanish." Los Angeles Times, Sept. 17, 2004

"Clear Channel: Spanish Revolution." Hollywood Reporter, Sept. 17, 2004

"Clear Channel Plans To Expand In Spanish-Language Market." Wall Street Journal, Sept. 16, 2004

"Flamenco From Spain." Los Angeles Times, Sept. 16, 2004, HispanicAd.com, Sept. 16, 2004

"Hispanamericanos: The Third Culture Study In The Works." HispanicAd.com, Sept. 15, 2004

"'El Gringo Malo' Wins Fans Airing Spanish Baseball." Wall Street Journal, Sept. 14, 2004

"Hispanic TV networks Faulted With High Levels Of Sexual Content." HispanicAd.com, Sept. 14, 2004

"The Latin Grammys." Billboard, Sept. 11, 2004

"A Panoramic Survey Of Latino Culture." Los Angeles Times, Sept. 11, 2004

"A Bilingual Quandry." TelevisionWeek, Sept. 9, 2004

"Rough Opening Round For Fox." Los Angeles Times, Sept. 9, 2004

"Leguizamo, Murrieta Land In Fox Family." Hollywood Reporter, Sept. 7, 2004

"Telemundo 51: Viewers' Choice During Hurricane Frances." NBCmv.com, Sept. 7, 2004

"NBC Reached Olympic Heights." Multichannel News, Sept. 6, 2004

"PBS Sets Diversity Curve." TelevisionWeek, Sept. 6, 2004

"He's Turning Back The Dial To TV's Golden Age." Los Angeles Times, Sept. 5, 2004

"Fernandez Opens Up To Broader Audience." Billboard, Sept. 4, 2004

"Capone Puts Brazil Atop Latin Grammy Nods." Billboard, Sept. 4, 2004

"Producer Tom Capone Dies In Crash." Hollywood Reporter, Sept. 3, 2004

"Sanz Sets The Pace." Daily Variety, Sept. 2, 2004

"Sanz Is A Big Winner At The Latin Grammys." Los Angeles Times, Sept. 2, 2004

"PTC Looks At Content On Spanish Stations." Los Angeles Times, Sept. 1, 2004

"World Beyond Salsa." Jazziz, September 2004

"Latinos On TV This Season, A Vanishing People." Hispanic, September 2004

"The Mambo Kings Remembered." Jazziz, September 2004

"Latin Giants Of Jazz: Tito Lives." Latin Beat, September 2004

"Los Santana: And The Beat Goes On." Latin Beat, September 2004

"1st Annual Philadelphia Salsa Congress." Latin Beat, September 2004

"Athens Is Most-Watched Non-U.S. Summer Games." Los Angeles Times, Aug. 31, 2004

"World-Class Olympics For NBC Uni." Hollywood Reporter, Aug. 31, 2004

"Reality 'Joke' Is On Si TV." Hollywood Reporter, Aug. 31, 2004

"NBC's Athens Games Attracts 203 Million Unique Viewers, Most Watched Non-U.S. Summer Games In History." NBCmv.com, Aug. 30, 2004

"Spike Swings At Doc." Daily Variety, Aug. 30, 2004

"Majors Bring Priorities To Confab." Billboard, Aug. 28, 2004

"Telemundo Wins New Viewership With Its Historic Olympic Coverage." NBCmv.com, Aug. 27, 2004

"Telemundo Premieres 'El Mundo De Mariana,' A New Friend For Today's Hispanic Women." NBCmv.com, Aug. 27, 2004

"Video Of Tiger Attack On Magician To Stay Private." Los Angeles Times, Aug. 26, 2004

"Rounding The Bend." Hollywood Reporter, Aug. 26, 2004

"2 Carriage Deals En Español." Hollywood Reporter, Aug. 24, 2004

"Peacock Tubthumps Its Olympic Platform Perfs." Daily Variety, Aug. 24, 2004

"Networks Gear Up For Convention." Houston Chronicle, Aug. 21, 2004

"Celebrate Hispanic Culture On PBS." HispaniaNet.com, Aug. 21, 2004

"AIM Tell-A-Vision & Maximas Announce Launch of American Latino TV." HispaniaNET.com, Aug. 21, 2004

"Can They Say That?" Los Angeles Times, Aug. 20, 2004

"Acuna And His 2 Bands." Los Angeles Times, Aug. 19, 2004

"Telemundo Completes Primetime Block Of Original Productions With The Premiere Of 'Te Voy A Ensenar A Querer.'" NBCmv.com, Aug. 19, 2004

"Latino Kudeocasts Set." Daily Variety, Aug. 18, 2004

"An Exquisite Fusion Of Tango And Electronica." Los Angeles Times, Aug. 16, 2004

"Pols Spend Big To Court Hispanic Vote." Advertising Age, Aug. 16, 2004

"1999 Was The Year Of The Latin Explosion. Ricky. Enrique. JLO. But the High-Gloss Boom Went Bust-With Lessons For The Next Wave." Los Angeles Times, Aug. 15, 2004

"Alt-Latin Lacks Women." Billboard, Aug. 14, 2004

"Cookman Goes Nacional." Billboard, Aug. 14, 2004

"Stunts For Green Card Aid Criticized." Los Angeles Times, Aug. 13, 2004

"Super-Tuff." Los Angeles CityBeat, Aug. 12, 2004

"Changing Face Of Alt-Latino." Los Angeles Times, Aug. 12, 2004

"Mun2 Television Hits Los Angeles By Storm With 'The Roof On The Road: El Reventon Urbano.'" MBCmv.com, Aug. 12, 2004

"Lopez Signs On To 'Real People.'" TelevisionWeek, Aug. 8, 2004 "Vives' Roots Run Deep." Billboard, Aug. 7, 2004

"Cachao Says 'Finally'" Latin Notas, Billboard, Aug. 7, 2004

"Ely Guerra Likes To Keep Changing Her Style." San Antonio Express-News, Aug. 5, 2004

"Telemundo Presents 'Zapata: Amor En Rebeldia' An Unprecedented Event In Spanish Language Television." NBCmv.com, Aug. 5, 2004

"Crossing The Line For A Chance At Legal Status." Los Angeles Times, Aug. 4, 2004

"Salsa Meets Jazz Again." Jazziz, August 2004

"Salsa Regains Its Stature At The 6th Annual West Coast Salsa Congress." Latin Beat, August 2004

"New York 4th Annual Salsa Congress." Latin Beat, August 2004

"Brazilian Nites Productions." Latin Beat, August 2004

"Zenteno, 76, Prodigy In trumpet, Band Leader." Houston Chronicle, July 30, 2004

"Telemundo Offers Olympic Coverage." Houston Chronicle, July 30, 2004

"Sweet On 'Serranos.'" Daily Variety, July 28, 2004

"New Telemundo Series Set In World Of Gypsies." Houston Chronicle, July 23, 2004

"Probation For Band Members." Los Angeles Times, July 22, 2004

"He's The Boogeyman Of Morning Radio." Los Angeles Times, July 21, 2004

"Parties Target Hispanics In 4 Battleground States." USA Today, July 20, 2004

"Los Lonely Boys Keeping Good Company." San Antonio Express-News, July 19, 2004

"Hispanic TV Ad Growth Seen Waning." Hollywood Reporter, June 17, 2004

"Latin Grammys' Broader Strokes." Los Angeles Times, July 15, 2004

"Strong Shift In Rhythm For Latin Grammys." Los Angeles Times, July 12, 2004

"Reality Takes A Novela Turn." Los Angeles Times, July 12, 2004

"DirecTV Gives HITN A Life." Multichannel News, July 12, 2004

"Ozomatli's 'Street' Heat." Billboard, July 10, 2004

"Bio Marks Cruz Anniversary." Billboard, July 10, 2004

"Univision Picks Up Two Edward R. Murrow Awards." Houston Chronicle, July 9, 2004

"Mun2 TV Sells Bilingual 'Roof'." Daily Variety, July 7, 2004

"He's Tex-Mex And Pure Country." Billboard, July 3, 2004

"Making His Marc." Billboard, June 19, 2004

"NBC To Air 'Mummy' Ride Special." Los Angeles Times, June 19, 2004

"They're An American Band." Los Angeles Times Magazine, June 6, 2004

"New Telemundo Reality Includes Star Contestants." Houston Chronicle, June 4, 2004

"Networks Give New Voice To Hispanic Households." Advertising Age, May 31, 2004

"SBS Talks Up El Cucuy As Ratings Soar." Hollywood Reporter, May 26, 2004

"Smooth Choice: Latin Academy Salutes Santana." Hollywood Reporter, May 25, 2004

"Televisa Lending Its Stars To Univision." Daily Variety, May 25, 2004

"Jennifer Pena Polishes Her Pop Appeal." Billboard, May 22, 2004

"Univision Slate Stresses Growth." Hollywood Reporter, May 20, 2004

"Univision Bets On 'Reality'." Miami Herald, May 20, 2004

"Telemundo Loads Fall Sked With Originals." Daily Variety, May 19, 2004

"A Foreign Sound." People, May 17, 2004

"Standup Guy Lopez Inks Showtime Deal." Daily Variety, May 14, 2004

"Santa Fe Plans Opera In Spanish." Los Angeles Times, May 7, 2004

"White House Tightens Travel Limits, Financial Squeeze On Cuba." Los Angeles Times, May 7, 2004

"Cultural Plate Getting Crowded." Advertising Age, May 3, 2004

"Not Just Another 'Ride.'" Los Angeles Times, May 2, 2004

"Latin Talent Suffers." Billboard, May 1, 2004

"Web Site & Label Sells Latin Product Exclusively Online." Billboard, May 1, 2004

"Billboard Latin Conference Events Preview." Billboard, May 1, 2004

"Advertisers Aim To Connect With Hispanics." Billboard, May 1, 2004

"Banda El Recodo Honored." Billboard, May 1, 2004

"New Acts Will Shine At Confab." Billboard, May 1, 2004

"Los Lobos: More Than La Bamba." Hispanic Magazine, May 2004.

"Thalía's Cinderella Story." Miami Herald, April 30, 2004

"Teledrama 'Inocente De Ti' Made Solely In U.S." Houston Chronicle, April 30, 2004

"Latin Music Business In Spotlight, Losing A Beat." Miami Herald, April 26, 2004

"TV Still At A Loss For Words With Latinos." Daily Variety, April 26, 2004

"LPB Funds TV, Film Projects For Latinos." TelevisionWeek, April 26, 2004

"Hispanic Sports Market Widening." TelevisionWeek, April 26, 2004

"New Download Site Targets Latin Market." Billboard, April 24, 2004

"Discovery, Televisa Will Open 'Sesame.'" Daily Variety, April 22, 2004
"Air America Seeks L.A. Home." Daily Variety, April 21, 2004
"More Latinos In Prime Time." Los Angeles Times, April 21, 2004
"Telemundo, Argos Talk Novelas." Hollywood Reporter, April 20, 2004
"Peggy DeCastro, 82; Part Of Hit Latin Singing Trio." Los Angeles Times, April 19, 2004
"Brazilian, Chilean Expand Boundaries Of Latin Jazz." Los Angeles Times, April 18, 2004
"Los Lonely Boys Make New Friends." Billboard, April 17, 2004
"Afro-Cuban Tsunami Sweeps Mainstream Shores." Billboard, April 17, 2004
"Air America Grounded In L.A." Daily Variety, April 17, 2004
"A Left Turn In Chicago." Hollywood Reporter, April 16, 2004
"Network Hopes To Attract Hispanics By Speaking English." HispaniaNet.com, April 13, 2004
"Si TV Adds Backing." Multichannel News, April 12, 2004
"U.S. Blocks Tour Of Cuban Band." April 9, 2004
"Not A Laugh Riot." Los Angeles Times, April 8, 2004
"Univision Keeps Steady Aim On Youth Market." Houston Chronicle, April 2, 2004
"Latin Music Antipiracy Efforts Pay Off." Daily Variety, April 1, 2004
"Rough Radio Takeoff." Daily Variety, April 1, 2004
"No Rules." Hispanic Magazine, April 2004
"Gay Rights Group Angry At Univision Show." Digitalspy.co.uk Website, March 31, 2004
"Telemundo Premieres 'Historias Y Testigos,' An Original Mini-Series Full Of Mystery, Drama & Suspense." NBCmv.com, March 30
"Proliferating Nets Chase Big Market." TelevisionWeek, March 29, 2004
"Manuelle Ends Dry Period For Tropical Music." Billboard, March 27, 2004
"Rap & Roll: Mexico's Control Machete Is Back." Miami Herald, March 26, 2004
"Not Quite 'Ya Se Fue!'" Austin Chronicle, March 26, 2004.
"Gloria Estefan Rocks The House On Telemundo." NBCmv.com, March 26, 2004
"Hispanic B'Casters Eye Pols' Ad Dollars." Hollywood Reporter, March 22, 2204
"Soul Of Salsa In L.A. Turns 30." Los Angeles Times, March 19, 2004
"Latin Sports Nets Gain." Multichannel News, March 15, 2004
"Operacion David Bisbal." Billboard, March 13, 2004
"Salinas Wins." Hollywood Reporter, March 10, 2004
"Adios Anglo." Broadcasting & Cable, March 8, 2004
"Parties Seeking To Speak Language Of Latino Voters." Los Angeles Times, March 6, 2004
"Rubio Rules Charts." Billboard, March 6, 2004

"Thalía's Greatest." Latin Notas, Billboard, March 6, 2004

"Reggaeton Acts Rise Up On Indie Labels." Billboard, March 6, 2004

"Latinos Heed A Spanish Call To Action." Multichannel News, March 8, 2004

"History Channel Readies Spanish-Language Net." Multichannel News, March 1, 2004

"Wild At Heart." Hispanic, March 2004

"Si TV Launch Now A Reality." Hollywood Reporter, Feb. 24, 2004

"TV Boosts Univision Q4." Daily Variety, Feb. 23, 2004

"Si TV Heads To Launch Pad With 7M Homes" Multichannel News, Feb. 23, 2004

"LEN Media Expands Representation." MediaWeek, Feb. 9, 2004

"MultiCultural Radio Acquires Radio Unica For $150M." San Antonio Business Journal, Feb. 6, 2004

"ABC Laps Up More 'Lopez.'" Daily Variety, Feb. 2, 2004

"CD's Mix Mirrors World, Rubio Says." San Antonio Express-News, Feb. 1, 2004

"Latin Ballad Master Julio Has A New Album." Miami Herald, Feb. 1, 2004

"Adios, Chicago." Latin Notas, Billboard, Jan. 31, 2004

"BMG U.S. Latin Makes Cuts; Sirius Gets Serious." Billboard, Jan. 30, 2004

"Label Acts tread Carefully With Crossover Bids." Billboard, Jan. 24, 2004

"Christian King Sets Sights On Secular World." Billboard, Jan. 24, 2004

"Univision To Offer, Regain Shares." Los Angeles Times, Jan. 7, 2004

"A Rarity On stage: Spanish Opera." Dallas Morning News, Jan. 2, 2004

"Young Actor Stars On PBS Show." Hispanic Magazine, January 2004

"Amid Op Ire, ESPN To Launch Deportes." Multichannel News, Dec. 22, 2003

"Deportes Delivers." Daily Variety, Dec. 3, 2003

"Latino-Themed Si TV Loves L.A." Daily Variety, Nov. 13, 2003

"Cablers Agree to Si TV." Daily Variety, Sept. 26, 2003

"Cable Channel Si TV Going 'Underground.'" Hollywood Reporter, July 22, 2003

"ESPN Deportes Launches On ABC Radio Networks." HispaniaNet.com, July 13, 2003

"ESPN Deportes Taps Garcia." Daily Variety, June 10, 2003

"On The Stump For Si TV, Valdez Finally Hears Yes." Hollywood Reporter, Feb. 3, 2003

"Boxeo De Campeones And Copa Toyota Libertadores To Contribute Live Programming." HispaniaNet.com, Jan. 17, 2003

Chapter 20
CAPITULO 20

Film, Theater, Dance, Sports 2004/2005/2006
PELICULAS, TEATRO, DANZA, DEPORTES 2004/2005/2006

• Major Hispanic film stars spearhead surge of studio and independent projects, often crossing from English to Spanish languages.

• Newly emerging Latino movie actor/actresses draw attention to foreign films, even generating Golden Globe, Oscar buzz.

• Oscar snub to Uruguayan best song nominee creates wave of resentment.

• Spanish films find receptive home on digital videodiscs.

• GALA, the nation's leading Spanish-language theater group in Washington, D.C., finds a permanent home after nearly 30 years.

• Documentary film focusing on Cuba's ballet heritage attracts two international stars who return to their homeland to perform.

• Hispanics represent 85 percent of foreign players in Major League Baseball.

• Baseball tainted by growing steroid scandal.

• 16 Latinos represent the highest number of players in the NBA.

• Major League Soccer's expansion adds Chivas USA spin-off from Mexico.

• Jockey John Velasquez heads racing's top money earning list.

The royalty of Hispanic actors appearing in major theatrical films reinforces the box office power and appeal these artisans possess in attracting consumers to spend money on movies. This is the time, familiar names and new faces appear in a growing number of major releases in both English and Spanish. Seeking their piece of the money machine, new production companies scramble for projects while film festivals wave their banners of something new, something controversial, something from another culture that deserves to be seen in this country.

Two major trends emerge in the film industry: Spanish-language films marketed to the general population featuring unknown actors and actresses strike a chord of acceptability and go on to gain nominations for major awards; and the growth of a hardcore group of females behind the cameras as writers–producers–directors seeking to counter the depiction of Latinas as maids and sexual bait with more substantive roles.

Within the royalty ranks this year, Antonio Banderas, Benicio Del Toro, Andy Garcia, Benjamin Bratt, Salma Hayek, Penélope Cruz, Jennifer Lopez, Cameron Diaz, Alfred Molina, and John Leguizamo are all involved in big ticket items as they spearhead the new Latino movement. Rising stars Diego Luna, Gael García Bernal, Marc Anthony, and Catalina Sandino Moreno are finding their own film niches. Directors Robert Rodriguez and Alfonso Cuaron are established links to major English-language projects, while Pedro Almodóvar and Walter Salles deal in high profile, dramatic Spanish-language films.

Raquel Welch, the film sex goddess, who at age 63 is a much-tempered active actress in her 40th year, is the subject of a film retrospective at the Los Angeles County Museum of Art. The former Jo Raquel Tejada, seen recently in the PBS series *American Family* and in the theatrical release *Legally Blonde*, shows through her work that she possesses dramatic and comedic skills as well as a beautiful face and curvaceous body, the latter two characteristics that most often are associated with her demeanor. The day-long screening of her films includes such campy early works as 1966's sci-fi mind-bender *Fantastic Voyage*, 1967's *One Million Years B.C.* (in which she appears in what's called "the first bikini"), *Bedazzled* (based on the work by Faust), the notorious 1970 X-rated *Myra Breckenridge* (based on the novel by Gore Vidal), and 1973's *The Three Musketeers* for which she wins a Golden Globe award from the Hollywood Foreign Press Association.

Antonio Banderas works in two worlds, as the voice for the Puss-in-Boots character in the animated *Shrek 2* and the desperate husband whose wife disappears in the drama *Imagining Argentina*, an updated version of the horrors of 1976 Argentina when a military junta takes over the country and tens of thousands of people are rounded up, disappear, and are never heard from again, creating the tragic category of Desaparecidos (The Disappeared). Among members of the cast are film veteran Rubén Blades, Leticia Dolera, and Maria Canals. Banderas also costars with Catherine Zeta-Jones in the sequel, *The Legend of Zorro*, filming in Mexico, which comes out in the fall of 2005. It's an update of their troubled marriage since the 1998 original, *The Mask of Zorro*, in which the pair are the central characters. Mexico is also the locale for his next film, *Bordertown*, in which he costars for the first time in a film with Jennifer Lopez. The story is one of a number focusing on the unsolved murders of 370 Mexican women along the U.S.–Mexican border since 1993. Gregory Nava, who directs Lopez in the 1997 feature *Selena*, is the film's director and co-producer. He and Banderas first work together on *Zapata* in 2001. In 2006, Banderas works in Spanish and English. He stars in the English-language *Take the Lead* as a teacher of ballroom dancing to delinquent students at a Manhattan high school, and is signed to star in *Conquistador*, the story of 16th century explorer Hernán Cortés. Filming in Spain and Mexico, *Daily Variety* calls the $40 million production the highest ever for a Spanish-language film. Banderas is also signed to return to Broadway in 2007 in *Don Juan Demarco*, an adaptation of the 1995 film.

Salma Hayek, 38, and a resident of Veracruz, Mexico, follows her dramatic achievement in last year's Oscar-nominated *Frida* by playing the girlfriend and jewel thief partner to Pierce Bronson vacationing in the Bahamas following a successful heist in *After the Sunset*. Her next film is the outlaw comedy *Bandidas*, set in 1888 Mexico and filmed there with costar Penélope Cruz. It's the first time the two friends appear together in a film.

On her own, Hayek appears as a fiery Mexican waitress in L.A. who is romanced by writer Colin Farrell in *Ask The Dust*, written and directed by Robert Towne (released in March of 2006) and then plays half of a 1940's murdering duo with Jared Leto in *Lonely Hearts*, filming in Florida in April of 2005.

In April of 2007, Hayek, her production company, Ventanazul, and MGM unite to produce two to four broad-appeal Latin-themed films for an unspecified number of years. MGM will finance the English-language venture.

Penélope Cruz, a 32-year-old established actress from Madrid, Spain, who makes her U.S. film debut in 1998's *The Hi-Lo Country*, appears in two films this year: *Head in the Clouds*, a World War II drama/love story co-starring Oscar-winning Charlize Theron, followed by *Noel*, a made-for-TV movie airing on Turner Network Television (TNT) involving Christmas Eve relationships whose cast includes Susan Sarandon, Paul Walker, and Alan Arkin.

Cruz and Hayek, the sexiest, crossover, bilingual Latina actresses, in their movie *Bandidas* play two land owners who unite to seek vengeance against railroad toughs who steal their land and murder their loved ones. The Twentieth Century Fox film is scheduled for release in 2005.

Cruz will also be seen in three additional films in 2005: co-starring with Matthew McConaughey in Paramount's action feature *Sahara* (filmed in Morocco) as the only female in this poorly acted saga with two parallel plots; the release by Spain's Casa Nova Films in selected L.A. theaters of the subtitled *Bendito Infiero* (*Blessed Inferno*), costarring Gael García Bernal in a disjointed, contrived heaven-versus-hell allegory, and the Italian sexual drama *Don't Move* (*Non Ti Muovere*). For her performance in the latter film she wins the People's Choice prize in the 17th annual European Film Awards presented by the European Film Academy in December, followed by a David Di Donatello Award, the Italian Oscar as best actress.

Benjamin Bratt appears in four films, with major roles in *Catwoman* opposite Halle Berry, and *The Woodsman* with Kevin Bacon and Kyra Sedgwick, and a cameo in *Thumbsucker* with Vince Vaughn and Keanu Reeves. The actor, of Peruvian–German extraction, also stars in *The Great Raid*, based on the Word War II effort to rescue 500 American POWs from a Japanese prison camp in the Philippines, due for release in 2005. Bratt's last major portrayal is in 2001's gritty *Piñero,* in which he portrays New York poet/playwright Miguel Piñero. Breaking into TV in 1988, his career takes off during his 1995–99 role as detective Reynaldo "Rey" Curtis on the hit TV drama series *Law & Order*. In making the transition to the big screen, he accumulates a long list of film credits including *Follow Me Home*, *Abandon*, *Traffic*, *Miss Congeniality*, *Red Planet*, *The Next Best Thing*, *The River Wild*, *Clear and Present Danger*, and *Bound By Honor*.

Jennifer Lopez, following her key role as a hotel maid being romanced by Ralph Fiennes as a political candidate in *Maid in Manhattan*, does better at the box office than her final disastrous films with love interest Ben Affleck, *Gigli* and *Jersey Girl*. However, she is mired in another disappointing film, *Shall We Dance?* in which she costars with Richard Gere in the remake of the 1996 Japanese ballroom dancing romance. Her newest completed film, *Monster-in-Law*, pairs her with Jane Fonda, making her return to movie-making after 15 years. The film is released in early 2005.

Alfred Molina plays the evil scientist Dr. Otto Octavius in 2004's *Spider-Man 2*, starring Tobey Maguire in the lead role. It's a marked departure from his portrayal in 2002 of the great Mexican painter Diego Rivera in *Frida*, in which he has a tempestuous on-screen romance with Salma Hayek. The English-born actor of Spanish–Italian parentage tackles the role of Bishop Manuel Aringarosa, president-general of the controversial Catholic organization Opus Dei, which plays a central role in the film *The Da Vinci Code* set for a May 19, 2006 release. During his career, Molina appears in 50 film, TV, and theater productions.

Benicio Del Toro lands roles in two films, *Guerrilla*, in which he plays the Cuban revolutionary hero, Ernesto "Che" Guevara, during the final years of his life and *Sin City*, the screen version of the Frank Miller novel series, in which he appears in the final segment of the film featuring a large ensemble cast, including Latinas Jessica Alba, Rosario Dawson, and Alexis Bledel. Of the films, only *Guerrilla* is shot outside the U.S. in Veracruz, Mexico, starting in May of 2006.

John Leguizamo is an equally busy thespian, with seven projects spanning 2004–'05. The most historical is the drama *Tlateloco*, retelling the 1968 massacre of Mexican students by the government in Tlateloco, Mexico City, on the night before the Mexican Summer Olympics. The film will be shot in both Mexico and the U.S. in English and Spanish. Leguizamo's other projects include reprising the voice of the character Sid in *Ice Age 2*, appearing in a remake of the 1976 thriller *Assault on Precinct 13*, and in 2005 headlining *Sueno* (which means dream), appearing in *The Honeymooners* and *Land of the Dead*, and starring in his Spanish-language film *Crónicas*. The 40-year-old, New York-raised actor, whose roots include a Colombia mother and Puerto Rican father, plays a journalist in this newest film shot in Ecuador and seeking answers to the murders of hundreds of children throughout Latin America. During his 20-year career, he stars in hit Broadway plays *Freak* and *Mambo Mouth* and in 40 films, notably *Carlito's Way* (1993), *to Wong Foo Thanks for Everything, Julie Newmar* (1995), *William Shakespeare's Romeo & Juliet* (1996), *Summer of Sam* (1999), *King of the Jungle* (2000), *Empire* (2002), and *Undefeated* (2003).

Andy Garcia's schedule includes both acting and directing challenges. He's in the ensemble cast of *Ocean's Twelve*, the follow-up to *Ocean's Eleven*, has roles in two independent films, *The Lazarus Child* and *Modigliani* and stars, produces, and makes his feature film directorial debut in his own independent film, *The Lost City*.

Eva Mendes, the Cuban-American actress and new face for Revlon cosmetics, costars with Will Smith in the Colombia Pictures romantic comedy, *Hitch*, which comes out in February of 2005. Her next film is *Trust the Man* being shot in New York. Following its completion, she'll costar in Colombia's *Ghost Rider*, an adaptation of the Marvel Comics title with Nicolas Cage. The two films continue her pattern of working in pictures with major names like Johnny Depp in *Once upon a Time in Mexico*, Matt Damon in *Stuck on You*, both in 2003, and Denzel Washington in 2001's *Training Day*. Born in Miami March 5, 1976, following her parents' departure from Cuba, she grows up in Los Angeles and launches her film career in 1998, which spans 13 films.

Among the new faces, Diego Luna, 23, following his triumph in the 2001 release, *Y Tu Mamá También*, shot in his native Mexico, plays the lead romantic role with Romola Garai, 20, in *Dirty Dancing: Havana Nights*, the remake of 1987's *Dirty Dancing*. Set in 1958 Havana, prior to the dawning of the Castro revolution, the movie utilizes the streets of San Juan and Ponce, Puerto Rico, to simulate Havana. The music is as much the star of the film as are the dance sequences and romance between Luna and his newfound American friend with whom he enters a dance contest. Playing Luna's brother is Cuban-born actor René Lavan, with a large cast of Hispanic actors/actresses and technicians working on the project. There's English and Spanish dialog with some English subtitles, a new happenstance for a mainstream audience film.

The music is not totally authentic pre-Castro Afro-Caribbean/Afro-Cuban, albeit it does explore its fiery Latin roots. It is, nonetheless, watered down by the addition of rap and rock tunes, since the soundtrack is released on J-Records, a 50-50 partnership between BMG and music master Clive Davis, whose expertise is in creating commercial hits. Of the 27 songs in the film, 13 are Latin and include performances by known acts Carlos Santana, Jorge Moreno, Aterciopelados, Yerba Buena, and Christina Aguilera. The soundtrack CD contains 11 of these tunes, plus a bonus track of Santana with Moreno performing a Spanish version of *Satellite* (*Nave Espacial*). This hybrid mix of musical styles, in which hip-hop rides over Latin rhythms, creates a contemporary Americanized sound rather than a truthful style of Cuban music popular prior to the change of governments and the rushed departure of American businessmen and tourists.

Following *Dirty Dancing: Havana Nights*, Luna appears in two other American films, *The Terminal*, alongside Tom Hanks, and *Criminal*, before returning home to star in the thriller *Nicotina*. The film wins six Mexican Ariel Awards, the equivalent of the U.S. Oscars.

Luna's final feature of the year is *Criminal*, a bilingual, con artist, caper film, which is a takeoff on the 2000 Argentinean film *Nueve Reinas* (*Nine Queens*) with the action switching from Buenos Aires to Los Angeles.

Attracting equal critical buzz is Gael García Bernal, the 25-year-old Mexican actor with two major Spanish-language releases almost on top of each other. *The Motorcycle Diaries* chronicles the 1951 journey across Argentina, Brazil, and Peru on a troublesome 1939 Norton motorcycle with traveling cycle owner Rodrigo De La Serna, a 28-year-old Argentinean. The film illustrates the early political awareness of the then 23-year-old medical student Ernesto "Che" Guevara. *Bad Education* (*La Mala Educación*) focuses on a sex-abuse scandal within the Catholic church as the backdrop for this Pedro Almadóvar-directed drama filmed in the director's native Spain in which Bernal plays three roles, including a transvestite drag queen. The film's sexual content results in its being rated NC-17 by the Motion Picture Association of America, the current designation for what was formerly an X rating, indicating adults only.

The Motorcycle Diaries wins two British Academy of Film and Television Arts (BAFTA) for Gustavo Santaolalla's score and best non-English film in February of 2005. The BAFTAs are England's equivalent to the American Oscars.

The *Diaries*' score is written by Argentina's Gustavo Santaolalla and is his third major work, enabling him to become the hottest new Latin composer working in American films. The composer's guitar leads his musical travelog through South America, which intersperses acoustic and electric instruments,

Brazilian percussion, and Peruvian woodwinds. Santaolalla plays a number of different stringed instruments as well as vibes, pipes, and flutes. It's a major musical shift for the musician who starts his career in the Argentinean rock band Arco Iris. Prior to catching the attention of Hollywood studios, he moves to Los Angeles in 1982 and discovers and produces four acts: Café Tacuba, Molotov, Juanes, and Maldita Vecindad. Incidentally, Molotov is the first breakout act on Santaolalla's Surco Records, a 1997 joint venture rock en Español label with Universal financing, of which he's its president.

Since branching out from record production to film scoring, Santaolalla has also done *21 Grams* and *Amores Perros.* Santaolalla's next film project is Ang Lee's controversial 2005 *Brokeback Mountain*, a romance between two gay cowboys, in which he's collaborating on the score with Bernie Taupin. Their tunes will be sung in the film by Willie Nelson, Emmylou Harris, and Rufus Wainwright. The film earns eight Academy Award nominations in 2006, including Santaolalla's original score and best film song, *A Love That Will Never Grow Old*. He also pens the score for *North Country*, which is bypassed in the music categories. However, he does win for his *Brokeback Mountain* score, dedicating his victory to Argentina and all Latinos. His next project in 2006 is *Babel* starring Brad Pitt, Gael García Bernal, and Cate Blanchett.

Gael García Bernal's next appearance on American screens is in *Dot The I*, whose cast in the R-rated drama includes Argentine neophyte Natalia Verbeke. This British-Spanish production initially screened at the 2003 Sundance Film Festival is scheduled to open in theatres in 2005. In addition to his two recently released films plus *Amores Perros*, *The Crime of Father Amaro*, and *Y Tu Mamá También.* Bernal's *Bad Education* experience enables him to join such budding actors like Antonio Banderas, Penélope Cruz, and Javier Bardem whose careers are boosted by working with Pedro Almodóvar.

In 2006, Bernal makes his directorial debut as well as starring in an untitled drama for Canana Films of Mexico City, the firm he co-owns with fellow actor Diego Garcia and producer Pablo Cruz. Bernal also stars in the sci-fi drama *The Science of Sleep*, a hot property shown at the Sundance Film Festival.

In an act of political contrition, *The Motorcycle Diaries* executive producer Robert Redford visits Cuba earlier in the year to privately screen the film, directed by Brazilian Walter Salles, for the widow and children of Guevara, the late guerrilla fighter who joins Fidel's Castro's forces and is subsequently tracked down and killed by the CIA in the jungles of Bolivia in October of 1967. While in Havana, Castro visits Redford at this hotel to discuss the film. The two figures apparently have a cordial visit.

Argentina's Mia Maestro, who costars in *The Motorcycle Diaries* and plays a major role in the hit ABC TV series, *Alias*, is seen next in the big screen Spanish-language *Secuestro Express*, which opens in August of 2005 in a limited number of cities. Filmed in Caracas, it's a story about kidnappings in Venezuela, made all the more surreal by a civil war and a nationwide oil strike, requiring onsite security and bodyguards. During her first season on *Alias*, she works with Brazil's Sonia Braga, and during one episode a large portion of the dialog is in Spanish.

Making her film debut in the low budget, $3 million controversial all-Colombian drug smuggling film *Maria Llena Eres De Gracia* (*Maria Full of Grace*) portraying a 17-year-old "mule" who smuggles drugs into the U.S. is 23-year-old Colombian actress Catalina Sandino Moreno. During production of the all Spanish-language film, the fledgling actress has to ingest five shot-glass size pellets, telling *USA Today*: "I can't believe that people swallow 100 of these." While mules receive upwards of $10,000 per trip to swallow the packets, one leak can cause death.

Columbian-born Orlando Tobon, a resident of New York City for 40 years, is given a role in the film that reflects his real-life work. Tobon deals with Spanish-speaking immigrants as a travel agent/accountant in the Colombian section of Jackson Heights and has actually dealt with some of these dead couriers. He is hired by writer/director Joshua Marston to play a character based on his life, which includes raising money to send back to Colombia the bodies of those whose packets have burst during their air journey. The HBO/Fine Line film receives critical acclaim at the Sundance and Berlin film festivals, helping to kick start Moreno's career in this country, while Tobon continues in his role as "the mayor of Little Colombia." In December, the movie is named best first film by the New York Film Critics Circle (NYFCC), a respected award-presenting organization.

Javier Bardem, Spain's first Academy Award nominee as best actor (for *Before Night Falls* in 2000, in which he plays Cuban poet and dissident Reinaldo Arenas), and the central figure in its 2002 foreign-language Oscar entry, *Mondays in the Sun*, also plays both supporting and starring roles in two dramatic endeavors. In the DreamWorks/ Paramount release *Collateral* starring Tom Cruise (as a hired assassin) and Jamie Foxx (as the woe-begotten cab driver who picks him up at the L.A. airport), Bardem plays a magnetic drug lord. The 34-year-old Bardem's spellbinding performance in *The Sea Inside* (*Mar Adentro*) from Fine Line Features, is the true story of 55-year-old quadriplegic Spanish poet Ramón Sampedro, confined to bed for 30 years following a diving accident, who wishes to end his life. In the end, on January 12, 1988, Sampedro gains his wish and freedom from his confining existence and reliance on others when a female associate (not revealed in the film) participates in his assisted suicide.

The all-Spanish cast, directed by co-producer Chilean-born Alejandro Amenábar, 32 (who also writes the screenplay, edits it, and composes the music), includes Belén Rueda, Lola Dueñas, and Mabel Rivera, who portray three critical females impacting Sampedro's life-or-death struggle.

For Bardem, this is his second role as a paralyzed person, having portrayed a policeman in 1977's *Live Flesh*, directed by Almodóvar. Bardem's latest riveting performance in *The Sea Inside* earns him the best actor prize in the 17th annual European Film Awards, with Amenábar winning as best director. Although nominated in seven categories in this competition, director Pedro Almodóvar is surprisingly and completely shut out from winning a trophy for *Bad Education*, but which is named the best foreign film by the 69-year-old New York Film Critics Circle. Based on his riveting performance in *The Sea Inside*, Bardem is signed to star in three films for Anglo studios: *Goya*, *Love in the Times Of Cholera*, and *No Country for Old Men*.

Despite being critically acclaimed, *Maria Full of Grace*, *The Motorcycle Diaries*, and *Bad Education*, are ruled ineligible for the top foreign-language Academy Award at next February's ceremony presented by the Academy of Motion Picture Arts and Sciences. Each film is bypassed for a different reason set within what some film critics call the Academy's outdated rules, which fail to acknowledge the intertwining globalization of the movie industry.

The three films can now only compete in the best actor/actress, screenplay, and best overall picture categories.

Since a country can only enter one film as its official Oscar entry, and Spain has two strong contenders, *Bad Education* and *The Sea Inside*, it goes with the latter. Sony Pictures Classics is now focusing on *Bad Education*'s writer/director Pedro Almodóvar for the best original screenplay award.

In the case of *Maria Full of Grace*, the Academy rules the film isn't sufficiently Colombian, despite its Colombian actors, since an American writer/director (Joshua Marston) and U.S. financing (HBO Films) are also involved. Allowed to submit another entry, Colombia chooses *El Rey*.

As for *The Motorcycle Diaries*, with its cast and crew from around the world including Mexico, Puerto Rico, Argentina, and France, no nation can claim and enter the film, since there are multiple participants and submissions are by single nations.

Since 2000, foreign-language films are nominated once for best picture, three times for top director, and six times for either best original or adapted screenplay.

Following the lead of Salma Hayek to successfully pursue her goal of bringing to the screen the story of Frida Kahlo, a group of relatively unknown females are seeking their place in the film firmament, where they hope to produce films that cover the entire spectrum of the human experience. Among the growing array of filmmakers devoted to this process are Elisha Miranda, a triple hyphenate (writer-producer-director) and co-founder of Chica Luna Productions; Tricia Creason Valencia of Flaca Films; writer-director Susana Tubert; director Maria Escobedo; writer-producer Karen Torres; and writer-producer-director Cyn Cañel Rossi, all of whom have had small films released domestically, according to *Hispanic* magazine. Cañel Rossi's *Rhythm of the Saints* is the only Latina film shown at the Sundance Film Festival in 2003. Torres' *Pleasant Dreams* is released in 1996 and is supposedly the first film created by a New York Puerto Rican hyphenate. Escobedo's *La Cocina* is aired on PBS. Tubert's debut is with the short, *Gypsy Girl*. This slowly building movement for reality in Latin-themed films by females is underscored during the 2004 New York International Latino Film Festival when nearly 50 percent of the films shown are by Latinas, notes Calixto Chinchilla, founder and director of the festival. The overall growth of Latin-themed films released in the U.S. is emphasized during the 2005 Miami International Film Festival, which has 118 entries, of which director Nicole Guillemet says 40 percent are Spanish-American productions.

Three major Latin film projects do receive nominations for the 77th annual Oscar presentation, which airs February 27, 2005 on ABC. *The Sea Inside* gains two nominations for best foreign film and makeup; *Maria Full of Grace*'s neophyte Catalina Sandino Moreno is the surprise nominee in a field of well-known figures for best actress, and *The Motorcycle Diaries* gains nods for adapted screenplay by José Rivera and original song *Al Otro Lado Del Rio* (*To the Other Side of the River*) by Jorge Drexler. In addition, *In the Morning* (*7:35 De La Mañana*) is a nominee in the live-action, short film category. Moreno is up against one key statistic: Italy's Sophia Loren is the only woman to win best actress for a foreign language film role.

Prior to the Oscars being announced, *The Sea Inside* sweeps 14 of its 15 nominations for Goya statues at the 19th annual Spanish

Academy Awards in Madrid on January 30, 2005, to become the most honored film ever. Alejandro Amenábar wins four of these honors as executive producer, director, screenwriter, and composer; Javier Bardem and co-star Lola Dueñas win their respective best acting categories.

Four of the top-rated Latin films are also nominated for the 20th annual Independent Spirit Awards, which are presented at an informal luncheon in a large tent in a parking lot in Santa Monica State Beach the Saturday afternoon prior to the formal Oscars the next evening. Of the four, *Maria Full of Grace*, lands four nods: for producer Paul Mezey, director and first screenplay Joshua Marston, actress Catalina Sandino Moreno, and supporting actress Yenny Paola Vega. *The Motorcycle Diaries* follows with three: director Walter Salles, the debut performance of Rodrigo De La Serna, and cinematography Eric Gautier. Single nods are given to two Spanish entries in the foreign film category, *Bad Education*, directed by Pedro Almodóvar and *The Sea Inside*, directed by Alejandro Amenábar.

Under sunny skies after weeks of rain-damaging weather, the Spirit Awards honor *Maria Full of Grace*'s Catalina Sandino Moreno as best female lead and director Joshua Marston for best first screenplay; *The Motorcycle Diaries* with trophies for actor Rodrigo De La Serna and cinematographer Eric Gautier; and *The Sea Inside* for best foreign film.

Each year the Spirit Awards gain in stature as more major name actors and actresses and film studios fill the ranks of the independent film community. Since the event is televised live on the Independent Film Channel and then rebroadcast by Bravo later that evening, the festivities attract top name participants who in turn attract media coverage, which in turn beckons hardcore film fans.

Since the hullabaloo takes place at the beach location where my wife and I are usually found on weekends, I generally walk over to watch the limos and sports cars arrive with stars, starting between noon and 1 p.m. It's a carnival-like atmosphere with fans shouting out the names of the talent as they emerge from their vehicles and head for the event's version of the red carpet. Fans with cameras (separated some distance from the movie stars) shout out their names along with "over here, over here" as they try to gain their attention for a photo or enthusiastically proclaim, "we love you" prior to the talent walking past the eager lineup of TV and print media cameras and interviewers. Half the actors turn to acknowledge the public adoration with a wave, a smile, or actually standing still to have their photo taken.

Standing there under the warm sun and clear blue sky, watching how excited this crowd gets with each arrival, the more knowledgeable fans informing the less aware, who openly ask, "Who's that?" I'm struck by how this unpretentious awards ceremony, with its participants in casual attire-compared to the formal wear of the next evening's Oscar glam fest at the Hollywood Kodak Theater-fits right in with the beach setting of people sunning or surfing, dolphins swimming past, pelicans diving straight down into the water to find food, and a parade of people walking, rollerblading, and bicycling past the hardcore fans focused on the stars and the massive tent which fills an entire parking lot and forces the general public to park someplace else.

The 77th annual Oscars in 2005, with edgy comic Chris Rock the host and a reconfigured format designed to attract younger viewers and reverse a ratings decline, offers a Spanish-language simulcast for the fourth consecutive year using the SAP channel on stereo TVs. Once Nielsen releases the show's ratings, the desired goals are half achieved. The three-hour, 14-minute show attracts 41.5 million viewers, down from last year's 43.5 million viewers, but it's up three percent among 18- to 34-year-olds. More people watch the Oscars than do the Golden Globes (16.8 million) and the Grammys (18.8 million).

Latinos tuning in are rewarded for their diligence as Spain's *The Sea Inside* is named top foreign language film, the fourth Spanish film to win an Oscar and the 19th nominated from that nation, while a tune from *The Motorcycle Diaries* is the surprise winner for original song. It's also the first time a non-English tune wins the Oscar, the first time a Spanish-language song is ever nominated, and the first time a Uruguayan is nominated and wins. Salma Hayek introduces Spanish actor and non-singer Antonio Banderas and Mexican American electric guitarist Carlos Santana who perform the tune, *Al Otro Lado Del Rio* (*To the Other Side of the River*). When the tune is named the category winner, Jorge Drexler, the 40-year-old Uruguayan composer of the music and the lyrics mounts the stage and sings some of his lyrics in Spanish, ending with "gracias" and "thank you" in English. The reason Banderas sings the song is explained a few days later when press reports in Uruguay and the U.S. reveal the behind-the-scenes drama previously unknown in this country.

It's political payback time for Drexler. The reason he sings rather than thanking everyone involved in the film is to show Oscar officials that he can sing, especially since he warbles the tune in the movie. Nonetheless, Oscar producer Gil Cates refuses his request to perform his own tune during the telecast, inviting teen pop idol Enrique Iglesias instead. When he declines, Banderas accepts and is accompanied by Santana's soaring electric guitar. Banderas, tapping his knee to simulate a flamenco feel, does a commendable job as a vocalist. It's also the first Oscar performance for both.

The Oscar exposure results in Warner Music Latina rushing out Drexler's first album release in the U.S., *Eco*, which naturally contains the Oscar-winning song. His earlier output includes seven albums—none released in the U.S. because he's an unknown performer from a Latin nation not known for its musical strengths—plus assignments to write music for four films, a Latin Grammy nomination and an MTV Latin America award.

The faux pas by Cates resounds negatively in Uruguay and the U.S. Hayek, it turns out, winds up introducing the song because Gael García Bernal, who stars in the film, backs out in protest to the snub. Two weeks before the Oscars, the Uruguayan media is reporting on Drexler's disappointment in being passed over, even after he speaks with Cates. Director Walter Salles labels the exclusion "unethical and ignorant of the cultural diversity that exists in Latin America" and is supported by a number of other film luminaries from Mexico, Spain, and Brazil, including actor Javier Bardem. Robert Redford, the film's producer, plans filing a protest with the Academy of Motion Picture Arts and Sciences. Following the telecast on ABC, the Uruguayan media is united in its outrage over the slight. Newspapers laud Drexler's a capella singing "as an act of revenge." The influential daily *El Pais* publishes a six-page section honoring Drexler, the 40-year-old former physician who changes careers 10 years ago to become a singer/composer. Uruguayans are upset that the song is performed in an up tempo mood, with Spain's flamenco flavor rather than in a slower Uruguayan folk style.

Cates defends his action by telling the *Wall Street Journal* he chose Banderas because he's a "bigger star" and big stars attract viewers. Drexler's unknown status in the U.S. results in his walking down the red carpet and not being interviewed during ABC's pre-show telecast. The *Los Angeles Times* also reveals he's not invited to any of the post-Oscar glitzy parties, but does gain entry to the *Vanity Fair* party after showing a guard his Oscar statuette. Although embarrassed, Drexler is humbled by his victory and tells the *Times* the Academy "voted for a totally unknown person who had no type of lobby behind him and who made no move to get nominated."

In the best actress category, Catalina Sandino Moreno, the least-known candidate up for an Oscar, loses to Hilary Swank, the favorite in *Million Dollar Baby*. Had Moreno won, she would be the fifth Latin to nab an Oscar following José Ferrer in 1951 for best actor in *Cyrano De Bergerac*; Anthony Quinn in 1957 for best supporting actor in *Lust for Life*; Rita Moreno in 1962 for best supporting actress in *West Side Story;* and Benicio Del Toro in 2001 for best supporting actor in *Traffic*.

Latin artisans will in 2006 help make the Oscars a foreign affair. Penélope Cruz wins best actress for *Volver* while Gustavo Santaolalla's original score wins for *Babel*. Latinos also walk away with crafts awards in three categories for *Pan's Labyrinth* while a Latina scores with her costume design in *Marie Antoinette*.

Oscars aside, a number of name Latino personalities appear in English-language productions that do not generate any Academy Award buzz.

Marc Anthony, the salsa/pop crossover singing star and latest husband to Jennifer Lopez, appears in the good company of Oscar-winning Denzel Washington and Christopher Walken in *Man on Fire*, a story set amidst real-life abductions in Mexico.

Anthony, born Marco Antonio Muniz in New York to Puerto Rican parents, also signs to play salsa singer Hector Lavoe in *El Cantate*, a joint production between Lopez and partner Simon Fields Nuyorican Productions and David Maldonado, Lavoe's former tour manager. Anthony will sing Lavoe's tunes in the film to be shot in Puerto Rico and New York. He's found supporting acting roles in earlier films *Bringing out the Dead*, *Big Night*, *Hackers*, and *The Substitute*, the latter dating back to 1996.

In an example of a proven musical star crossing over into film, Mexican ranchera/mariachi/pop romantic idol Alejandro Fernández makes his big screen debut in *Zapata*, playing the lead role, under the direction of Alfonso Arau.

Spain's 28-year-old Paz Vega seeks breakout status with appearances in two films, director James L. Brooks' first film in eight years, the comedy *Spanglish*, starring Adam Sandler and Tea Leoni for Columbia, which is mainly in English with Spanish spoken at appropriate dramatic moments, and her upcoming starring role in Sony's Spanish-language *Di Que Si*. Having established her acting credentials at home in two exotic films, Paz makes her American screen debut in the 2001 art house film *Sex and Lucia* before being signed by Brooks for her domestic saga debut this December, which required learning her lines phonetically since her English skills need mucho work. The film's score by Hans Zimmer underscores Paz's presence through Brazilian guitarist Heitor Pereira. During her first 45 minutes on screen, Paz speaks no English and the acoustic guitar represents her presence in the family.

Cameron Diaz, 33, is working on her 21st film, *In Her Shoes*, since she launches her film career in 1994 with *The Mask*. The new project, for which she's paid a reported $25 million, is released in 2005, and pairs her with Shirley MacLaine, Toni Collette, and Mark Feuerstein. Diaz's last film is the 2003 hit *Charlie's Angels: Full Throttle*, the sequel to 2000's *Charlie's Angels*. In between *Angels'* projects, she appears in *Gangs of New York* and *The Sweetest Thing*, and does a voiceover for *Shrek*. In 2001, she wins an Oscar nomination for *Vanilla Sky*.

When the 62nd annual Golden Globes nominations are announced by the Hollywood Foreign Press Association in December prior to the awards presentation on NBC January 16, 2005, three previously acclaimed films are listed among the nominees: Javier Bardem for best dramatic actor in *The Sea Inside*, which along with *The Motorcycle Diaries* are among the foreign film candidates, while Hans Zimmer's *Spanglish* score competes in the original score category. *The Sea Inside* asserts itself when it's awarded the best foreign film Golden Globe in January. Bardem is shut out for best actor, which goes to Leonardo DiCaprio for *The Aviator*.

In a switch from drama to comedy, Dania Ramirez goes from Spike Lee's *She Hate Me*, *The Subway Stories*, and *25th Hour* to *Fat Albert*, the comedy based on the Bill Cosby created character in 1970's animated TV series. She plays the love interest to the main character in the Fox Pictures release. Her extensive TV career also includes roles in *The Sopranos* and *Buffy the Vampire Slayer*.

A number of major studio projects infuse a diversity of topics and talent to the confluence of releases.

Touchstone Pictures/Imagine Entertainment's *The Alamo*, sets a possible historical film industry record in recasting the historic 1836 battle to defend the fort outside Houston for 13 days by approximately 184 Texans standing against the estimated 2,500 troops led by Mexican dictator General Antonio Lopez De Santa Anna. Touchstone claims it has created the largest freestanding set ever built in North America, involving 70 individual structures spread over 51 acres on a private ranch west of the state capitol.

The historical battle is worth retelling. On the morning of March 6, Santa Anna's troops storm the fort and kill all its defenders including James Bowie and Davy Crockett during the 90-minute battle. On April 12, General Sam Houston and 910 pioneers surprise Santa Anna and with the cry of "Remember the Alamo" ringing in the air and destroy his army at nearby San Jacinto. The general's surrender to Houston leads to the Treaty of Velasco, resulting in Texas gaining its independence from Mexico. On December 29, 1845, Texas becomes the 28th state in the Union. This film's cast of well-known American actors and its large supporting cast of Mexican actors, led by Emilio Echevarría as Santa Anna and Jordi Mollà as a Tejano (Texas Mexican American), retells the epic history of this dramatic battle.

Californians' reliance on Mexican help is one of the key points in the satirical *A Day Without Mexicans* look at life in the Golden State when all 12 million of the state's Latinos suddenly disappear one day. Shot mainly in English in the U.S. and Mexico, Anglos are left to their own survival as the state's 57 percent of construction workers, 58 percent of its cooks and 53 percent of its janitors (figures based on the 2000 Census) all vanish in this first-time effort by Mexican director Sergio Arau.

Topical films are also being developed.

An inside glimpse of Brazil's antiquated penal system is the subject of *Carandiru*, a Sony Pictures Classics/HB Filmes release with its all-Brazilian cast portraying the horrors and light moments inside São Paulo's men's Casa De Detencáo (House of Detention). Built in 1956 to house 3,000 inmates, the center is home to 7,500 instead, all of whom are tried or convicted and are waiting for a judge's ruling on their cases, a process which can take years to complete. Among the key players are Antonio Grassi, Ivan De Almeida, Luiz Carlos Vasconcelos, and Milton Gonçalves.

Beisbol, the story of Latino baseball players cracking the ethnic barrier in this country in 1948, films interviews with past and present Hispanic Major League stars for the Rhino Film documentary slated for release next year. Working with producer/director Alan Sawyer are executive producers actor Esai Morales and Rhino's Steve Nemeth. Major League players being interviewed are retired Juan Marichal and

Orlando Cepeda, and active players Adrian Beltre, Edgardo Alfonso, and Liván Hernández.

The plight of the unsolved deaths of at least 370 women, some raped or terribly mutilated or unaccounted for in Ciudad Juarez, Mexico, in the northern Mexican state of Chihuahua along the Texas border going back to 1993, is the subject spurring *The Virgin of Juárez*. Minnie Driver costars as a Los Angeles reporter investigating the murders with Ana Claudia Talancón, who plays a woman who survives an attack and begins having troubling visions and develops stigmata.

In a much lighter vein, *The Latin Divas of Comedy*, being produced by Payaso Entertainment, receives a $1.3 million loan from the State of New Mexico as an incentive to film in the state, which is what happens in September in Albuquerque during the opening week of the Roy E. Disney Center for the Performing Arts. The film will be distributed by Paramount as the follow-up to its 2003 DVD, *The Original Latin Kings of Comedy*. The loan comes from an $85 million fund created by the state to attract films to shoot mostly in the state and hire crews encompassing 60 percent New Mexico residents.

On the directorial level, Robert Rodriguez continues his pace-setting position with two projects, *Sin City*, for Dimension Films and *A Princess of Mars* for Paramount. Benicio Del Toro and three other Latins, Jessica Alba, Rosario Dawson, and Alexis Bledel, are among the cast appearing in the three-part *Sin City*. Rodriguez, who writes the script, will co-direct the film based on a series of Frank Miller novels. He follows this assignment by directing Edgar Rice Burrough's *A Princess of Mars*, a science fiction adventure based on Burrough's 11-volume series *John Carter of Mars*. Shooting and post-production for *Princess* next year will be based at the director's Austin, Texas, Troublemaker studios. Rodriguez's previous works include *Spy Kids*, *El Mariachi*, *Desperado*, and *Once upon a Time in Mexico*.

Antonio Banderas dons his director's cap for the second time, following his initial *Crazy in Alabama*, to helm an unnamed Spanish novel, which he'll shoot in Spanish in his hometown of Malaga in

Spain. The film is set in 1978 following the 40-year reign of Dictator Generalissimo Francisco Franco and reflects the freedom that teenagers on a holiday enjoy along with the rest of the populace.

Spain's Pedro Almodóvar signs Penélope Cruz and Carmen Maura for the comedy, *Volver*, set to begin filming in July of 2005 in Madrid and in the area of Castilla-La Mancha, where he grows up. Maura works with Almodóvar in a number of films including 1988's *Women On the Verge of a Nervous Breakdown*.

Mexico's Alfonso Cuaron is dealing with two projects. He tackles the sensitive subject of the violent student uprising in Mexico City in *Mexico '68* and the sci-fi thriller *The Children of Men*. This year he scores with *Harry Potter and the Prisoner of Azkaban*, following his earlier notoriety for *Y Tu Mamá También*, *Great Expectations*, and *A Little Princess*.

Brazil's Walter Salles follows up his work on *Dark Water* with *Linha Do Pase*, which will be shot in his native country.

Mexico's Luis Mandoki completes two projects in his homeland: *Casas De Carton*, his initial effort involving children in El Salvador based on screenwriter Oscar Torres childhood experiences and *Amapola*, which deals with the narcotics trade.

Two neophytes making their directorial debuts are actress Rosie Perez, with a documentary about New York's annual Puerto Rican Parade in which she also serves as on-camera narrator, which will premiere in 2005 on the Independent Film Channel, and Lance Rivera, a hip-hop director and record company owner, who debuts with the comedy *The Cookout* starring Queen Latifah.

They are followed in 2005 by Fernando Meirelles, who directs his first major English-language film, *The Constant Gardener*, based on John Le Carré's novel. Meirelles, 50, last directs the Argentinean documentary *City of God*, which wins a 2004 Oscar nomination. Between films, he directs TV commercials, an area he'll probably be spending less time in now.

Writer/director Rodrigo García, who specializes in exploring the delicate world of American females, utilizes nine 10-minute vignettes shot in real time in *Nine Lives*, his newest film opening in October of 2005. The 46-year-old filmmaker of Colombian ancestry grows up in Mexico and lives in Los Angeles for 20 years. His earlier works include *Things You Can Tell Just by Looking at Her* and *Ten Tiny Love Stories.*

Christina Milian, the 23-year-old composer/singer/actress emerges in 2005 with back-to-back films, *Man of the House*, opposite Tommy Lee Jones and *Be Cool* starring John Travolta and Uma Thurman in which the hit R&B vocalist of Cuban descent who's born in Jersey City, New Jersey, plays an aspiring singer in this saga of the dark underside of the music business. Born Christine Flores, she changes her name to her mother's maiden name to gain roles other than those offered exclusively for Latina characters, reveals the *Los Angeles Times*. It obviously works.

She's steadily making films since doing a voiceover character in 1998's *A Bug's Life*, which is followed by on-camera roles in *American Pie* and *Durango Kids*, both in 1999; *Love Don't Cost a Thing*, 2003; and *Torque* in 2004.

Milian's debut eponymous album in 2003 is released on Universal International and is followed by 2004's *It's About Time* on Island Records/Def Jam Recordings, blending urban, pop and Latin influences. A single with rapper Fabolous, *Dip It Low*, earns her a 2004 Grammy nomination in the rap collaboration category. In *Be Cool*, she performs four songs including one with Steven Tyler and Aerosmith. None show her Hispanic heritage. The film's varied score includes Sergio Mendes, leader of the hit group Brazil '66 and '67, playing piano in a club scene with the Black Eyed Peas. One of her compositions, *Play*, winds up on Jennifer Lopez's 2001 CD *J. Lo*.

Sofia Vergara, a Colombian actress best known for her work in Spanish-language TV while being relatively unknown to mainstream viewers for her acting, gains media awareness in March of 2005 when she's seen with Tom Cruise following his breakup with Penélope Cruz. The publicity helps put her in the spotlight for her voiceover role in the animated feature *Robots*. She's also done two other films for release, *Pledge This!*, the National Lampoon comedy and a skateboard action picture, *Lords of Dogtown*. She's also signed to work with Ray Romano in the comedy *Grilled* and with Mark Wahlberg in *Four Brothers*, an action revenge film directed by John Singleton.

Joining the list of Latin film actors in 2005 are Rick Gonzalez, Lynda Carter (Linda Jean Cordova Carter), Alexis Bledel and America Ferrera. Of the four, Gonzalez and Carter are cast in sure-fire Summer releases: Gonzalez in *War of the Worlds* starring Tom Cruise and directed by Steven Spielberg, and Carter in the surprise Summer delights *Sky High* and *The Dukes of Hazzard*. For Gonzalez, the 26-year-old raised in Brooklyn, whose heritage includes Dominican and Puerto Rican strains, this film elevates him to the top tier of film works, having previously appeared in *Coach Carter* and *Old School*.

Carter, 54, and best known for playing the vivacious crime-fighting Wonder Woman in the hit TV series from 1976 to '79, makes her big splash screen comeback in the Disney Summer release *Sky High*. She also plays the object of Willie Nelson's heart in *Dukes*. She also appears in several episodes of NBC's *Law and Order: SVU*. The Mexican American actress traces her roots back to Chihuahua, Mexico, and is born and raised in Phoenix by her Mexican American mother and Anglo father. She admits in *Hispanic* magazine that since she doesn't look Latin, people are surprised when they learn she is half Latina, even though she says she talks about her heritage throughout her career.

Bledel (who has a sustaining role in the TV series *The Gilmore Girls*) and Ferrera both star in *The Sisterhood of the Traveling Pants*. Ferrera is also seen in the skateboard saga, *Lords of Dogtown*.

Gina Torres, first seen in the second and third *Matrix* films, makes her starring debut in the fall's *Serenity* the sci-fi film set 500 years in the future. The 36-year-old Cuban American married to actor Laurence Fishburne, draws attention for her role as a Russian intelligence agent in the hit ABC TV series *Alias*.

Emilio Estevez, in his role as writer/director for *Bobby*, his film about the assassination of Robert F. Kennedy, includes Freddy Martinez in the cast for his independent production shooting in Los Angeles in the fall of 2005.

Estevez's brother Charlie Sheen and Eva Longoria (the breakout star in ABC's hit series *Desperate Housewives* are among the voiceover talents working in *Foodfight!*, a 3-D cartoon comedy aiming for a fall 2006 release.

Pedro Gonzalez Gonzalez, one of the busiest Mexican-American character actors in film and TV, dies February 2, 2006 of natural causes in his home in Culver City, California. The Aguilares, Texas, native was 80. His first TV appearance in 1953 as a contestant on the hit Groucho Marx quiz show, *You Bet Your Life*, leads to acting roles in numerous film and TV series. These include such John Wayne films as *The High and the Mighty* and *Rio Bravo* and TV series *Wanted: Dead or Alive* and *Gunsmoke*. He is survived by his wife Leandra, son Ramiro, daughters Yolanda and Rosie, seven grandchildren, and three great-grandchildren.

Spanish films on digital video disc (DVD), once a rarity, are now a growing commodity, with an increasing number of aware companies catering to this after market audience, notably Columbia TriStar Home Entertainment, Universal Studios Home Video, Twentieth Century Fox Home Entertainment, Maverick Entertainment, and Ground Zero Entertainment. In addition, Ventura Distribution, Urban Vision Entertainment, and Desert Mountain Media, are among the DVD releasers whose products span what's called the "Golden Age" of Mexican cinema from 1936 to 1956 through both Spanish-dubbed versions of English titles, English titles with a story of particular appeal to Latinos, and current imported films from Mexico and other corners of the Spanish-speaking world. Of this group of companies, Ventura Distribution of Ventura, California, is the kingpin company, handling distribution for a host of companies with Spanish-language product. Among its clients are Cozumel Films, formed 15 years ago by Yolanda Machado, which specializes in

Mexican classics from the "Golden Age" and from Desert Mountain and its array of contemporary Mexican and Latin American films and Spain's Lola Films, including the 1994 Academy Award-winning best foreign film, *Belle Epoque* (*The Age of Beauty*).

Fox starts its specialty company, Cinema Latino, in 2003 to distribute films on DVD from Mexico, Spain, and Venezuela, the latter through the powerful Venevision International that provides the new brand with nine films. Maverick, a Deerfield Beach, Florida, company, has its eye on the young urban Latino with some its releases.

One of the most unique DVD releases is Phoenix-based Desert Mountain Media's story of two Jewish women in Mexico City in the 1960s, one of European descent, the other with a Turkish heritage, who go their own ways and defy their family's traditional expectations. The release, *Nova Que Te Vea* (*Like a Bride*), marks a first for the DVD industry since it's shot in Ladino, which blends Hebrew and Yiddish in with the Spanish dialog. Directed by Guita Schyfter, the cast features novela actor, Ernesto Laguardia, and film figures Claudette Maillé, Angélica Aragón (*Havana Nights* and *The Crime of Padre Amaro*), and Emilio Echevarría (*The Alamo* and *Amores Perros*).

Three movie distribution companies join the Hispanic DVD movement.

Oxxo Films and Venus Pictures, both in Los Angeles, team to distribute classic and contemporary family films. Oxxo, which already distributes films from Mexico's Televisa Cine, is co-producing a 12 film series on the life of Mexican women. Venus has a working relationship with Mexican producer Alfredo Ripstein and his grandson Daniel Birman's Alameda Films.

1211 Entertainment, formed by Steven Bauer, the Cuban-American actor who stars in *Traffic* and Frank Aragon of Mexican-American heritage, will produce films and TV programs. Upcoming projects include *Ninety Miles*, the saga of a Cuban man's flight to freedom across the 90 miles that separates Cuba from the U.S. In 1999, the two produce and Aragon directs *My Father's Love* which explores a single mother raising her children in the Latino community of East L.A. Bauer's most recent acting project is *The Lost City* with Andy Garcia as star, producer, and first-time director.

Cinema Management Group of Los Angeles acquires exclusive international distribution rights to Chile's *B-Happy* drama anent a 14-year-old girl's struggle to overcome adversity. The company is also handling the Venezuelan drama *Punto Y Rara* (*Step Forward*), which deals with anti-government guerrilla activities in Venezuela and Colombia. It wins the top picture award at this year's Los Angeles International Latino Film Festival.

The Los Angeles Festival, along with similar events in Miami, Chicago, New York, and San Diego, encapsulates the works of Hispanic filmmakers. The International Latino Cultural Center of Chicago's 20th annual Chicago Latino Film Festival in April of 2004 presents a retrospective of 100 past favorite films from the U.S., Latin America, Spain, and Portugal.

Among the past films gaining a second showing are two with now well-known actresses: Penélope Cruz in the Spanish release, *La Niña De Tus Ojos* (*The Girl of Your Dreams*) and Sonia Braga in the Brazilian drama *Tieta Do Agreste*. In the "Made in the U.S./Chicago" segment, four films are representative of different aspects of Latino life. Films from Spain reflect the political and social conflict in the Basque country. Other program segments focus on film music, Haiti's troubled history, Andalusian movies, and a Chilean comedy.

The fourth annual New York International Latino Film Festival has grown to where this year it's now presented by HBO and supported by the New York City Latin Media and Entertainment Commission. Calixto Chinchilla, the festival's 27-year-old founder/director, lines up 60 plus films including two U.S. premieres: *Imagining Argentina* starring Antonio Banderas, Rubén Blades, and Emma Thompson and *Nicotina* with Diego Luna, along with the world premieres of *107 Street* from director Antonio De La Cruz, and *Mission Movie* which explores the changing composition of San Francisco's Mission District.

San Diego's 11th annual Latino Film Festival, originally established as a student film festival, is now a West Coast repository for films from both sides of the border, attracting 15,000 patrons of Hispanic films to view the 100 features and shorts.

While the Miami festival is discussed in Chapter 13, the eighth annual Los Angeles Latino International Film Festival features 100 plus short, feature-length and documentary titles from all regions of the Latin world. Founded by a number of filmmakers led by Edward James Olmos, this year's 10 day Festival includes the American premiere of *Ladies Night*, the first production from the Disney Company's Miravista Latin film label. The Venezuelan entry, Elia Schneider's *Punto Y Raya*, which depicts the guerilla wars in Venezuela and Colombia, wins the best picture award. Three films from Argentina, however, walk away with major accolades. *Hoy Y Manana* wins the top debut nod, *India Praville* the top screenplay and *Conversaciones Con Mama*, an Argentinean–Spanish co-production, the audience award. The top director award goes to the U.S.' Nancy Savoca for *Dirt*. This year's lifetime achievement award goes to Rita Moreno, the lone Latina as of 2004 to win an Academy Award for her role in *West Side Story* 40 years ago.

A five-film retrospective on the emotional and satirical works of Spanish director Pedro Almodóvar is a highlight of the 18th annual American Film Institute's Los Angeles International Film Festival, which features 136 films from 42 nations, 28 U.S. premieres, 24 world premieres, and 11 North American premieres. Almodóvar's works being showcased are *Women on the Verge of a Nervous Breakdown*, *Live Flesh*, *All about My Mother*, the Oscar-winning *Talk to Her* and his latest work, *Bad Education*.

Three fairly low-profile Hispanic actors gain broader recognition in 2005. Enrique Murciano gains a major romantic role in Sandra Bullock's *Miss Congeniality 2: Armed and Fabulous* FBI agent sequel. The 31-year-old Cuban-American resident of Miami is cast as an agent in the film, a role he portrays in the hit CBS TV drama series *Without a Trace*. Prior to his TV gig, he's generally known for his stints in dark, tragic dramas like *Traffic* and *Black Hawk Down*.

Look close and that's Zofi Saldaña portraying Bernie Mac's daughter, introducing Ashton Kutcher to her father in the interracial comedy *Guess Who*, a reverse take-off on the 1967 hit *Guess Who's Coming to Dinner* in which Katharine Houghton brings home fiancé Sidney Poitier to meet her parents Spencer Tracy and Katharine Hepburn (who in real life is Houghton's aunt). Saldana, 26, has a mixture of Dominican, Lebanese, and Puerto Rican in her background, and is one of a few Latinas hired to play non-Hispanic roles, including her latest as the dark-skinned beauty in *Guess Who*. She also appears with Tom Hanks in 2003's moderate successful *Terminal*. Her first film role in 2000 is *Center Stage*, a drama centered on the world of ballet.

Rosario Dawson, who plays the heavy role of a submachine gun-carrying prostitute in the dark film noire *Sin City*, next appears in the film version of the hit Broadway musical *Rent* in 2005. The 25-year-old New York actress, whose bloodlines include Puerto Rican, Cuban, African-American, Irish, and Native American, starts her career in *Kids* in 1995 when she's 15, followed by *He Got Game* in 1998 and *Men in Black II* in 2002. In 2006, she's signed for the sequels to *Sin City* and *Clerks*, as well as the original films *Killshot*, and *Descent*. She also forms her own production company, Trybe Films.

Two U.S. film studios, Walt Disney and Warner Bros., join Columbia Pictures Productions Mexico, Twentieth Century Fox Mexico, and Columbia TriStar, in opening offices in Mexico City to facilitate the flow of Mexican movies into the U.S. The Walt Disney Company operates Latin film firm Miravista, while Warner Bros. launches Warner Bros. Pictures Mexico. While all satellite offices plan their own releases, they still have to obtain clearances from their home offices across the border. Mexico's state-owned funding agency, Fidecine's, Victor Ugalde, the agency's head, informs *Weekly Variety* it expects upwards of 45 films to be shot this year, up from 36 in 2004. Among Mexico's movie companies planning to add to this optimistic projection, is the oddly named Canada Films owned by actors Gael García Bernal and Diego Leon.

A new multi-functional company formed by Latin film producer Moctesuma Esparza joins the ranks of entrepreneurs tapping into the still untapped domestic Hispanic market. His movie theater firm, Maya Cinemas, opens eight multiplex screens in Salinas, California, in July of 2005, in which one of the screens is reserved for Hispanic-focused films. The company plans to open eight theaters in California, New Mexico, Chicago, Dallas, and the New York borough of the Bronx, all playing first-run Hollywood films and one Spanish-language movie by the end of 2006. Esparza's second firm, Maya Pictures, is designed to create and distribute films that appeal to young Latinos. The first of these films is *Walkout* starring Edward James Olmos, which will air on HBO. It's also working on a scripted series for Si TV, *Circumcized Cinema*. An investor in Si TV, according to the *Hollywood Reporter*, Esparza, is involved in creating a one-hour TV series of the film *The Milagro Beanfield War* for Touchstone Television. The producer's credits include the film *Selena* and the made-for-television movie *Introducing Dorothy Dandridge*.

In perhaps 2005's most unusual film venture, the traveling Hispanic Film Heritage Tour visits five cities with free shows of classic Mexican films from August 18 to September 20. Utilizing an 18-wheel mobile movie theater, the 95-seat theater offers five Mexican "golden era" movies starring legendary actor Pedro Infante, all made by producer/director Ismael Rodriguez. The mobile cinteca or theater will visit supermarkets around Washington, D.C., including Silver Springs, Falls Church, and New Carrollton, Maryland, and Woodbridge and Manassas, Virginia.

During 2006, a number of Latinos add additional luster to the film medium both in front of and behind the camera. In addition, a major American independent film company plans to distribute Spanish-language movies in the U.S.

Talent includes Jessica Alba, Alexis Bledel, and actor Michael Pena. Alba's growing resume of recent appearances in *Sin City*, *The Fantastic Four*, and *Into The Blue* follows work on the hit Fox TV series *Dark Angel*. Bledel's movie roles in *Sin City*, *Tuck Everlasting*, and *The*

Sisterhood of the Traveling Pants follow her title role in the hit WB Network's *Gilmore Girls*. Pena lands the major role in the emotional film *World Trade Center*, about a New York/New Jersey Port Authority policeman who, along with fellow officer Nicolas Cage, are rescued from the wreckage of the Twin Towers following the September 11, 2001 attacks. The Chicago-born Mexican-American actor earlier appears in the 2005 Oscar-winning film *Crash* and is seen in such TV series as *CSI*, *The Shield* and *ER*.

Screenwriters active include Guillermo Arriaga, José Rivera, and brothers Alfonso and Carlos Cuaron. Arriaga's credits include *21 Grams*, *Babel* (with Brad Pitt and Cate Blanchett), and *The Three Burials of Melguiades* (with Tommy Lee Jones). Rivera grabs the gold ring as the first Puerto Rican to earn an Oscar-nomination for his script for *The Motorcycle Diaries*, which earns him the assignment for Jack Kerouac's classic *On the Road*.

While the duo is responsible for *Y Tu Mamá También*, Alfonso handles both *Harry Potter and the Prisoner of Azkaban* and the forthcoming 2006 release, *Children of Men*.

Directors directing are Simon Brand, Alejandro González Iñárritu, and Fernando Meirelles. Brand, with a background in commercials and pop music videos, advances to big screen gigs *Unknown* and *Paraiso Travel*. Iñárritu graduates from the Spanish-language *Amores Perros* to the English-language *21 Grams* and *Babel*. Meirelles advances from commercials and films in Brazil to the 2005 Oscar-nominated *The Constant Gardener*.

Cinematographers peering through lenses include Emmanuel Lubezki, Rodrigo Prieto, and Cesar Charlone. Lubezki's work encompasses Spanish (*Y Tu Mamá También*) and English films (*Sleepy Hollow*, *Like Water for Chocolate*, *The New World*), and his latest project, *The Children of Men* with Clive Owen and Julianne Moore. Prieto's work on *Brokeback Mountain* gains him a 2005 Oscar nomination, following work on *21 Grams*, *Alexander*, and *Frida*. Charlone's camera work is behind *The Constant Gardener* and the earlier Oscar-nominated Brazil feature *City of God*.

Lionsgate Films, fresh from its best film Oscar win for *Crash*, releases the first of a series of films made in Latin America on April 14 aimed at bilingual novela and soccer buffs. The movie, *La Mujer De Mi Hermano (My Brother's Wife)* starring Univision telenovela stars Barbara Mori, Manolo Cardona, and Christian Meier, was purchased by Panamax Films, the company created by former Telemundo president Jim McNamara and signed by Liongate's president Jon Feltheimer last year to tap the Latin market for movies for U.S. release. The project reunites the two executives, Sony official Feltheimer having hired McNamara to head Telemundo in 1999 while under Sony Corporation ownership. The duo hopes to release six to eight movies a year, including its second release in October '06, *Pretendiendo*, also starring Mori, as well as build a video library of other Spanish-language movies for sale at major retail chains, notes the *Los Angeles Times*. This newest venture is the latest attempt by Hollywood studios in recent years to triumphantly crack the domestic Hispanic movie-going market. Efforts by New Latin Pictures, LLC, Latin Universe, Venevision International, and Universal Pictures deal with Arenas Entertainment and Samuel Goldwyn Films were all under achieving.

While stage productions featuring Hispanics generally are at the low end of show business activity, there are several notable high-points around the country, ranging from the opening in Washington, D.C., of the GALA Hispanic Theater to Chicago's 14-year-old Aguijón Theater Company to touring troupes to several New York City plays which salute the Latino experience in America.

GALA, the acronym for Grupo De Artistas Latino Americanos, is often called the nation's leading Spanish-language theater, which for nearly 30 years produces nearly 150 plays in Spanish and English as well as presenting music, dance, and poetry at a number of temporary sites around the nation's capitol. On January 7 of 2005 it opens its permanent home in the Tivoli Theater, a 1920s-style movie house, following a fundraising drive that raises more than $3 million. Hugo Medrano, the Argentine actor/director who is GALA's producing artistic director, opines in *Hispanic* Magazine the theater will "fulfill the longtime mission of establishing a national center for Latino performing arts."

First production in the newly refurbished 2,000-seat Tivoli is *Yerma*, a play by Spain's Federico García Lorca, with Medrano the director. It will be followed by *Poet in New York* and *Real Women Have Curves*.

Chicago's Aguijón Theater Group, founded by Rosario Vargas, who migrates to the Windy City from her native Colombia, is designed from the start to fill the void for theater for the 750,000 Spanish-speakers, representing 25 percent of the city's population, according to the U.S. Census. The theater group is the city's lone permanent company presenting plays almost entirely in Spanish. In its current home surrounded by neighborhoods reflecting Chicago's varied Hispanic mix of Mexican, Puerto Rican and Central Americans, the theater provides English subtitles to purportedly make it the only bilingual permanent theater company in the Midwest. One night the play may be entirely in Spanish; the next night it'll be done in English, Vargas explains to *Hispanic* Magazine, adding casts are drawn from actors from 11 nationalities.

The Theater presents upwards of four productions annually, each running for around four months. In 2003, Aguijón participates in the first annual Goodman Latino Theater Festival along with such other groups as the Theater of Mexico, Certain Inhabitants, and Compañia Marta Carrasco of Spain. Among this assemblage, the latter group is the only one performing entirely in Spanish, while the others use subtitles or perform in English. For her work in Chicago, Vargas is honored by the Mexican Fine Arts Museum of Chicago with its Sor Juana achievement award, named after the 17th century Mexican writer Sor Juana De La Cruz.

Austin, a city with five Latin theater groups, gains national attention as its 10-member Latino Comedy Project launches its first national tour. The five-and-a- half-year-old sketch comedy troupe, which last year celebrates its fifth annual Latino Comedy Festival at the city's Paramount Theatre, is known for skewering ethnic stereotypes, cultural figures, and cultural presumptions. It keeps its sarcastic skills honed by also playing at various sketch comedy festivals around the country.

During the fall of 2004, Austin's newly formed Latino Theater Alliance, consisting of the five Latino theater artists groups, combines to present the yuletide traditional *La Pastorela* pageant of the shepherd's journeying to see baby Jesus which includes old carols, modern gospel music, jokes, and dancing angels and devils. The last year the play is presented is in 2001, which prompts Verónica Castillo-Pérez, executive director of one of the groups, LUPE Arte, to help motivate the city's four other theater companies to band together and present the Christmas story for 16 days in December at the Tillery Street Theater, operated by Austin Latino/Latina Lesbian, Gay, Bisexual and Transgender Organization (ALLGO).

New York provides a launch platform for the off-Broadway debuts of three Cuban-Americans from Miami and the Broadway premiere of a musical with a Latina playing the lead role.

The three 21-year-old Miamians, Marco Ramirez, Rebecca Delgado, and Alejandro H. Fumero, make their off-Broadway debuts in *A Place Without Seasons* as part of the eighth annual New York International Fringe Festival in August at the Access Theater in the downtown Tribeca section of Manhattan. All three attend NYU's Tisch School of Dramatic Arts. Ramirez is the author of the drama; the other two are producer/actors. The Fringe Festival is known as the largest multi-arts event of its kind in North America, with companies from all over the world participating. The Miamians are among those selected to perform from among 800 applicants.

Chosen for the lead role of Brooklyn in the 11-character play *Brooklyn The Musical* on Broadway is Eden Espinosa, who lands the choice slot at its initial staging two years ago at the Signature Theater in Arlington, Virginia, followed by its move one year later to the new Denver Civic Theater prior to its opening on Broadway at the Plymouth Theatre in September. *Brooklyn* is more than just a musical; its story deals with such somber topics as homelessness, drug addiction, and returning Vietnam veterans. Espinosa's previous

Broadway appearance takes place last year in *Wicked* in which she plays two roles. The native of Anaheim Hills, California, develops her acting skills with jobs at both Disneyland and Universal Studios in Southern California.

In an action similar to giving a gift with one hand and talking it away with the other, the South Coast Repertory of Costa Mesa, California, unveils an Emerging Artists Initiative, designed to expose works by lesser-known playwrights while closing down for budgetary reasons its Hispanic Playwrights Project. This is an annual festival in operation since 1985 that brings national attention to works by unknown Latino writers. Under the new program, the theater group plans to commission four to six new plays by newcomer writers of different ethnic backgrounds and cultures including Hispanics, explains David Emmes, the organization's producing artistic director.

Hispanic actors, despite respectable nominations in the Tony and Emmy awards, are almost invisible in the winners' circles. Naturally they shine in the Imagen Awards, which honor achievements by Latinos in film and TV.

The lone Hispanic winner in the 58th annual Tony Awards broadcast live by CBS June 6, 2004 are composers Robert Lopez and Jeff Marx for *Avenue Q*. Nominees include: Pulitzer recipient Nilo Cruz's *Anna in the Tropics* (best play); Daphne Rubin-Vega (featured actress for *Anna in the Tropics*); Alfred Molina (leading actor in a musical category for *Fiddler on the Roof*), and Raúl Esparza, (featured actor in a musical for *Taboo*).

The 56th annual Primetime Emmy Awards aces out Antonio Banderas in the outstanding lead actor in a miniseries or movie for his portrayal of Pancho Villa in the HBO feature film *And Starring Pancho Villa As Himself*. The accolade goes to Al Pacino as Roy Cohn in the HBO presentation, *Angels in America*. *Pancho* loses out in the made-for-TV movie category to another HBO entry, *Something the Lord Made*.

When it comes to the 19th annual Imagen Awards, Banderas wins two trophies, one for the Emmy neglected *And Starring Pancho*

Villa As Himself as the best actor in a TV drama (which wins the best TV movie honor) and as best actor in a film for *Once upon a Time in Mexico*.

Other Imagen winners include: George Lopez and costar Constance Marie as best actor and actress in a TV comedy (*The George Lopez Show*), with cast mate Belita Moreno named best supporting actress. The PBS series *American Family* wins best primetime drama; HBO's *The Kidnapping of Ingrid Betancourt* wins best TV documentary; Freddy Rodriguez lands the best supporting actor for HBO's *Six Feet Under*; Tia Texada is named the best supporting actress for NBC's *Third Watch*; and Rosa Blasi is named best actress in a TV drama for *Strong Medicine*.

Although the 34th Nosotros Golden Eagle Awards draw ample star power, the star of the evening at the Beverly Hilton Hotel is 84-year-old founder Ricardo Montalban, who appears in his wheelchair to recognize this year's winners. The packed house rewards Montalban's surprise appearance with hearty applause as he takes a front row position to observe Hector Elizondo receive the Life Achievement Award named after him. Other accolades from the oldest Latin entertainment advocacy organization include outstanding acting awards to *Desperate Housewives*' Eva Longoria; *CSI: Miami's Adam Rodriguez*; *That 70's Show*'s Wilmer Valderrama and *Six Feet Under*'s Freddy Rodriguez. Luisa Leschin of *The George Lopez Show* wins the outstanding writing award. Music is provided by Mariachi Tierra Del Sol.

Although the awards are presented amid a festive mood, trouble brews under the surface for the Ricardo Montalban Foundation, which purchases the former 1,200-scat Doolittle Theatre on Vine Street in Hollywood for $2.4 million and changes the marquee to the Ricardo Montalban's Theatre. The venue, unveiled in May of 2004, aims to become the central point for Hispanic theater in the city. Unknown to the public, until the *Los Angeles Times* breaks a story in June of 2005, is the fact that the Foundation is suspended in April of last year by the California Franchise Tax Board for failing to file financial status reports dating back to its founding in 1999. Although it has a federal tax exemption as a non-profit organization, the Foundation fails to file for the same status in California, which wants the organization to address its tax problems immediately. The money brouhaha also puts into question the theatre's ability to fulfill its promise of generating Latino stage productions.

Latinologues, the 10-year traveling excursion into contemporary Latino life in the U.S, after touring 20 plus cities, settles into Broadway's Helen Hayes Theatre, October 23 to December 4, with previews beginning September 13. The creation of Mexican-American comedy writer and actor Rick Najera, the English-language show takes no prisoners in its humorous depiction of Hispanic lifestyles and peccadilloes, combined with critical headline-generating events to smack home Najera's proclaimed mission "to make people laugh, think, and touch them," he tells *Latina* magazine. The Broadway cast will be directed by Cheech Marin and include Mexican comic legend Eugenio Derbez, film/TV actress René Lavan, local TV show host Shirley A. Rumierk, and Najera. Najera hones his comedic skills writing for two hit Fox TV series, *In Living Color* and *Mad TV*, the latter still on Saturday nights.

The Mambo Kings, a 1992 movie, is short-circuited in its August journey to Broadway after being lambasted by critics in San Francisco during its four-week tryout ending June 19, 2005. The $12 million musical starring Esai Morales, David Alan Grier, Christiane Noll, vocalist Albita, actress Justina Machado who spends five seasons on HBO's *Six Feet Under*, and telenovela star Jamie Camil, is the story of two Cuban brothers moving to Manhattan from 1950s Havana. The music is by Carlos Franzetti, with lyrics by Arne Glimcher, the play's director (the same role he plays in the film version which stars Armand Assante and Antonio Banderas in his English-language debut along with musicians Tito Puente on timbales and Desi Arnaz, Jr. on congas). Glimcher additionally co-authors the book with Oscar Hijuelos, whose 1989 Pulitzer Prize-winning novel, *The Mambo Kings Play Songs of Love*, is the basis for the play. *Mambo Kings* would have been the first Latin Broadway musical since Paul Simon's *The Capeman* with its almost all-Latin cast debuts and closes rather quickly in 1998.

Among theater productions, *Avenue Q*, the 2004 Tony-winning musical, which combines puppets with real grownups discussing life on their street in Manhattan, hits the thespian lottery in 2005. The unique play about inner-city life, which is still attracting theatergoers to the 800-seat John Golden Theater, will open a production this Fall at the new Wynn Las Vegas resort in a specially-built 1,200 seat theater during its open-ended run. Lopez and Marx are also developing a flurry of projects for the theater, films, and TV.

Raúl Esparza, a Cuban-American actor from Miami, maintains his favorite status among Broadway producers by landing the leading character of Caractacus in the 2005 stage production of *Chitty Chitty Bang Bang*, a role played by Dick Van Dyke in the 1968 film. Esparza, a New York resident for five years, earns a Tony Awards nomination in 2004 for his featured role in *Taboo*. His other lead credits are *Evita* and *Sunday in the Park*.

Sara Ramirez is the female lead in Broadway's 2005 runaway hit comedy musical, *Monty Python's Spamalot*, which garners 14 Tony Award nominations, including one for Ramirez as featured actress in a musical. The 29-year-old Mexican actress, who's raised in San Diego, is the lone Latina in the cast featuring David Hyde Pierce, Tim Curry, and Hank Azaria. She initially makes her stage debut in Paul Simon's 1998 musical, *The Capeman*, starring Marc Anthony and Rubén Blades, which tanks within two months. When the 59th annual American Theatre Wing's Antoinette Perry Tony Awards telecast from New York's Radio City Music Hall are announced on CBS June 5, Ramirez wins the featured actress in a musical statue for her standout performance of the Lady of the Lake, a character developed for the stage adaptation. Her triumph is one of the three the play wins as best musical and best musical direction by Mike Nichols, who snares his ninth Tony and first for directing a musical. The hit play is an adaptation of the British cult comedy troupe's movie *Monty Python and the Holy Grail.*

Chita Rivera, the iconic 72-year-old Broadway and film luminary, stars in *Chita Rivera: The Dancer's Life*, a stage production headed for Broadway in November of 2005. The musical's out-of-town workout opens September 22 at San Diego's famed Old Globe Theater. The Puerto Rican dancer/actress born Dolores Conchita Figueroa Del Rivero in Washington, D.C., is supported on stage with 10 dancers, including a number of men who work with her in previous shows. The book is written by Terrence McNally, author of the book for three earlier musicals in which she stars, *The Rink*, *Kiss of the Spider Woman* and *The Visit*. Her achievements include eight Tony nominations—the most recent for the 2003 revival of *Nine*, starring Antonio Banderas and victories for *The Rink* and *Spider Woman;* She also earns a prestigious 2002 Kennedy Center Honor.

Freddy Soto, a comic on the cusp of breaking out as a national figure, dies in his sleep at home in Los Angeles July 10 of undetermined causes. Soto, 35, had performed hours earlier at the Laugh Factory in Hollywood. Among his recent credits: a part in the 2004 film *Spanglish*, opening for Marc Anthony on a 30-city tour, and appearing along with Pablo Francisco and Carlos Mencia on the "Three Amigos" tours in 2001 and 2002, captured on a DVD release by Miramax last May. Born in El Paso, he moves to Los Angeles in 1990 to seek his place in the comedy world. He's survived by his wife Cory and Cruz, his three-year-old daughter.

The exploits of Latin dancers are given prominence in two major events, New York's J.P. Morgan Chase Latino Cultural Festival and in the release of a documentary film, which screens at the Miami Film Festival and the Los Angeles Latino Film Festival.

Appearing at the New York event at the Queens Theater in the Park, the seven-year-old Producciónes La Lágrima of Hermosillo, Mexico, performs a new work, *Canciónes Para El Camino* (*Songs for the Road*) created by co-founder Adriana Castaños that delves into the happy and sad relationship between two lovers. She and her co-founder David Barrón are the featured duo in this number while cast members Manuel Ballesteros, Claudia Carrillo, and María

Luisa Solares appear in *Frágil Paraiso*, a dance about wandering animals, with the two ladies also performing in *Azul Cobalto* as fish/women.

The documentary, *Dance Cuba: Dreams of Flight*, is a major look into the depleted state of highly accomplished classical dance in Castro-controlled Cuba. The 105-minute film in English with Spanish dialog, details how Alicia Alonso, Cuba's dance matriarch, and head of the Ballet Nacional De Cuba, contacts Septime Webre, the Cuban-American artistic director of The Washington Ballet with an invitation to perform at the October 2000 Havana Dance Festival. Cynthia Newport, the film's New York-based producer/director, also secures another international name, Carlos Acosta, a former star in Cuba's national ballet, who's been a featured dancer with the Royal Ballet in London for seven years, for the second featured performance in the documentary. Chucho Valdes, Cuba's leading jazz pianist provides the music for this terpsichorean escapade.

Two sisters, Lorena and Lora Feijoo, alumni of the Ballet Nacional De Cuba who's mother is a ballerina and teacher at Havana's Escuela Nacional De Ballet while they're growing up, obtain U.S. work visas and become principal dancers at two key ballet troupes. Lorena, 34, dances with the San Francisco Ballet and also acts in Andy Garcia's independently produced film, *The Lost City*, while Lorna, 30, dances with the Boston Ballet and also appears in the *Dance Cuba: Dreams of Flight* documentary. The attraction of dancing and earning U.S. dollars stimulates Lorena in 1990 and then Lorna to leave their homeland and bring their art to new audiences. An estimated 20 other Cuban dancers also defect including Nelson Madrigal who'll marry Lorna while working in Boston, José Manuel Carreño who joins the American Ballet Theatre (ABT), and Carlos Acosta. Another ABT member is Argentina's Julio Bocca, while the Miami City Ballet's ensemble includes Venezuela's Mary Carmen Catoya, notes *Time*.

The United States Postal Service celebrates Latin dance during 2005's National Hispanic Heritage Month from September 15 to October 15 with mambo, cha-cha-cha, meringue, and salsa stamps. Dedication ceremonies take place in New York, Miami, and Milwaukee. The mambo and cha-cha stamps are designed by

Cuban-American artists Sergio Baradat and Edel Rodríguez, respectively; the salsa stamp is the work of José Ortega of New York and Toronto, and the meringue stamp is designed by Rafael López, a Mexican who resides in San Diego.

You don't need to speak Spanish to realize that in professional baseball, soccer, and boxing, and to a lesser extent, in football and basketball, Hispanic stars continue generating much of the headline-making news. In fact, of the 227 foreign players on baseball rosters on opening day of the 2004 season, Hispanics represent 85.9 percent of those athletes, or 37 percent of the players on team rosters, according to two reports in the *Los Angeles Times*.

One player missing from any team's roster is Jesse Orosco, the 46-year-old left-handed pitcher, who decides to retire in January after 24 years in the major leagues. Offered a minor league contract by the Arizona Diamondbacks worth $800,000 if he makes the team, last year's oldest player in baseball decides to retire instead, three months before his 47th birthday. During his career starting in 1979 with the New York Mets and including terms with the Los Angeles Dodgers, Cleveland Indians, Milwaukee Brewers, Baltimore Orioles, St. Louis Cardinals, San Diego Padres, New York Yankees, and Minnesota Twins, he sets two major league records for 1,252 games pitched and relief appearances in 1,248 games. During his career, the Santa Barbara, California, hurler gives up 1,055 hits and 512 runs. In 1988, he's a member of the World Series winning Dodgers. During 2003, his last season, he plays for San Diego, New York, and Minnesota.

The 2004 baseball season highlights the achievements of Latino superstars during the season in the All Star game, the World Series playoffs, the actual championship games and the post-season awards which glide into winter's player trades.

This year, baseball players' salaries drop for the first time since 1995. And despite a cut of 2.5 percent from the start of last season, opening day average salaries are $2,313,535, according to the *Los Angeles Times*. The New York Yankees, with their record $183 million payroll, counter the trend as a result of signing Alex Rodriguez to the largest pact in baseball history, $252 million spread over 10 years, which breaks down to $21.7 million a season, the most earned by any player for the fourth straight year. Rodriguez, traded by the Texas Rangers in February, naturally tops the list of the top 20 money-earning players, including four Hispanics. In second place is Manny Ramirez of the Boston Red Sox with $20.4 million. Boston's payroll is $130 million, second behind the Yankees. Carlos Delgado of the Toronto Blue Jays follows in third with $19.7 million, with Pedro Martinez of Boston in sixth with $17.5 million and Sammy Sosa of the Chicago Cubs eighth with $16.8 million.

Prior to the new season, money deals for re-signing players or landing new ones, shows fans what a million dollars can buy. Some examples:

Juan Gonzalez, the American League's twice-named most valuable player, and free agent, re-signs with the Kansas City Royals for one year for $4.5 million. The pact includes $2 million in incentives; an option for $7 million for 2005, which if not accomplished, earns Gonzalez a $500,000 buyout.

Orlando Cabrera, the Montreal Expos most valuable player two years running at shortstop, signs a $6 million, one-year pact with the team, up from last season's $3.3 million contract.

In one of the strangest twists, Ivan Rodriguez, a 10-time all-star catcher leaves the World Series champion Florida Marlins for the Detroit Tigers, whose 119 loses versus 43 wins last season, sets the American League record for defeats. The lure is a $40 million, four-year deal, which breaks down to $7 million this year, $8 million in 2005 and $11 million for 2006 and 2007.

Arte Moreno, the Angels' first Latin owner, as part of his pledge to reach out to Latinos in Los Angeles and Orange Counties, signs four Latino free agents. Vladimir Guerrero, the star outfielder with the New York Mets, jumps to the Anaheim Angels for $70 million and a five-year contract; former Toronto Blue Jays pitcher Kelvin Escobar signs a three-year deal worth $18.75 million; former Chicago White Sox hurler Bartolo Colon inks a four-year deal worth $51 million; and former Oakland A's outfielder Jose Guillen, signs for

$6 million for two years. One local sports writer reflects that these players are now able to communicate for the first time with an owner who speaks their language.

Last fall, in his first year of ownership, during the 2003 to 2004 off-season, Moreno starts marketing the Anaheim Angels as "L.A.'s Team" on television and in its outdoor advertising and deletes the city's identity off the uniforms, schedules, and website. In the spring of this year, Anaheim is also eliminated from Angel Stadium, despite the 1996 lease agreement requiring the team to be called the Anaheim Angels as part of the city's contributing $30 million to ballpark renovation in 1997. Created in 1961 by Gene Autry as the Los Angeles Angels, the team's name changes to California Angels when it moves to Anaheim in 1966 and to the Anaheim Angels in 1997 when the Walt Disney Co. is the new owner. As the season progresses, the name change becomes a politically contentious issue, and by the end of 2004, it starts coming to a boil.

The Anaheim City Council says it rejects the name change and will take legal action to enforce the stadium lease that mandates the team be called the Anaheim Angels right through the term of the lease that expires in 2029, but has a one-time escape clause in 2016. While stating he's not certain whether he'll rename the team the Los Angeles Angels prior to the opening of the 2005 season, Moreno does indicate to the *Los Angeles Times* he'll "eventually sit down with the city of Anaheim and try to resolve the issue." In a subsequent letter, the city contends the team violates its stadium lease by removing the city's name from all tickets, merchandise, and publicity notices during Moreno's 18 months of ownership.

As 2005 unfurls, Moreno decides to call the team the "Los Angeles Angels of Anaheim," stressing this moniker will help attract new national advertisers to the team's radio and TV broadcasts and elevate the team from a secondary market to a major market with a potential audience of 16 million people. Anaheim counters by suing the team, asking the Orange County Superior Court to disallow the L.A. moniker and require the team to prominently restore the

Anaheim identity in its merchandise and marketing. In a meeting with team officials, the city rejects the new, lengthy two-city name, which is a first for major league baseball. The team asserts it is not in violation of the lease agreement since the city's name is included in the new identification. Following its resolution last November by the Los Angeles City Council opposing the name switch, the city of Los Angeles files a legal brief arguing the Orange County Superior Court should reject "the Angels' attempt to profit from the Los Angeles name they abandoned long ago," reports the *Times*.

The state Court of Appeals sets a hearing for March 28, eight days prior to the call "to play ball." The all-important hearing results in Justice David Sills, the presiding justice of the 4th District Court of Appeal urging both parties to try again to solve their dispute. Anaheim's co-counsel Andy Guilford and Angel attorney George Stephan agree to talk, but city officials staunchly believe there can be no deal unless team owner Moreno removes Los Angeles from the team's moniker. Although the two sides meet in late April to arbitrate their differences, nothing is resolved.

As the legal battle continues, Orange County Superior Court Judge Peter Polos twice rejects the city's request for a preliminary injunction to stop the team from modifying its name. In May, the Angels file a suit in Orange County Superior Court against the city asking once again for clearance to play as the Los Angeles Angels of Anaheim, even though the team no longer uses Los Angeles in its team name. An earlier petition by the Anaheim City Council in March of 2005 asking the State Court of Appeal to order the team to drop Los Angeles from its name is denied on June 27. The appellate court urges a renewal of mediation. Since no resolution is reached, a January 9, 2006 trial will hear this matter. A few days before the trial starts, the city of Anaheim says it will not refurbish Angel Stadium if the team continues to incorporate Los Angeles in its name. The city also projects the Angels moving to L.A. in 11 years. Following nearly five weeks of testimony, a seven-woman, five-man jury decides nine to five that team owner Moreno is legally entitled to use his two-city name.

The panel, which deliberates a little over four hours, says the city should have written a stronger contract to guarantee that the team remained the Anaheim Angels.

In an action parallel with the trial, Moreno in February of 2006, along with unnamed investor partners, acquires 50,000-watt radio station KXME-AM for $42 million. The Spanish talk/sports station will become the bilingual home for the Angels with the new season. The station's signal, strongest of all the market's 17 Latin stations, ensures the team broad-ranging coverage regardless of its name.

When the team takes the field on opening day of 2005, 81-year-old Cuban-born Preston Gomez begins his 25th season as the team's special assistant to Angel's general manager Bill Stoneman and manager Mike Scioscia, responsible for being the middleman between the two and the club's roster of Latin players. The *Times* calls him "the liaison" in its feature on his career in professional baseball, one among the pioneering Cuban players who blaze the path for other Latinos in later years. These early Cuban players include Mike Gonzalez and Dolph Luque, who debut in the 1920s and are followed in later years by such familiar and unfamiliar names as Minnie Minoso, Cookie Rojas, Luis Tiant, Tony Perez, Camilo Pascual, Pedro Ramos, Mike Cuellar, Zoilo Versalles, and Tony Oliva.

Gomez is a 21-year-old shortstop with the Havana Sugar Kings in 1944 when he's signed to the Washington Senators, where he only plays eight games and is sent to the minors because of his lack of hitting ability. His major league playing career over, he remains in baseball, where he manages in the Mexican Winter League, coaches a Dodgers minor league franchise, becomes the first manager of the expansion San Diego Padres, and after three seasons manages the Houston Astros and Chicago Cubs, followed by coaching slots with the Dodgers, St. Louis Cardinals, and Anaheim Angels.

During the 2004 season, individual players achieve notoriety for a diversity of reasons, mostly with their personal élan.

Toronto's Carlos Delgado protests the war in Afghanistan and Iraq by refusing to stand during the playing of *God Bless America* at ballparks around the country following the September 11 attacks on the U.S. While playing in Yankee Stadium in July, he's booed by fans in the seventh inning stretch during a moment of silence prior to the song being played on the public address system.

Edgar Martinez, the American League's two-time batting champ, announces his retirement prior to the conclusion of this season, his 18th with the Seattle Mariners as its designated hitter (DH). Martinez, 41, bats more than 300 in 10 of his seasons and leads the league in hitting in 1992 and 1995. Of his 7,060 times at bat, close to 5,000 are as a DH. He holds the record for DH home runs and runs batted in. During his career up to this point in August, he has 305 homers and 1,244 runs batted-in.

Cleveland's Omar Vizquel gets six hits to tie the American League record for a nine-inning game as the Indians go on a 22-0 rampage against the New York Yankees on their home field. It's the Yankee's largest massacre in its 101-year history. Previously, the Bronx Bombers have never been beaten by more than 18 runs, losing to Detroit 19-1 in 1925 and 24-6 to Cleveland in 1928.

Former San Francisco first base slugger, 43-year-old Venezuelan Andres Galarraga, who has beaten non-Hodgkin's lymphoma (a form of cancer) in 1999 and in 2003, is signed by the Angels in August to its Salt Lake Triple-A team and one month later is brought up to the Angels as a probable designated hitter. During his 25 games with Salt Lake, he bats .304.

The redoubtable Angels' 22-year-old right-hander Francisco Rodriguez, in his second full season in the major leagues, amasses 110 strikeouts by September 18 to set the club's record by a relief pitcher. He's also holding opponents to a .170 batting average with his 95-miles-per-hour fastball and two breaking pitches. Two years ago, his pitching helps the Angels win their first-ever World Series title. That same month, the team suspends left fielder Jose Guillen for the remainder of the season and the postseason without pay for a specific disruptive incident—one of several throughout his career—citing a violation of the appropriate conduct clause in each player's contract.

Los Angeles Dodger third baseman Adrian Beltre breaks the club's single-season record for runs batted-in for that position by whacking a three-run double in the seventh inning of the team's 7-6 victory against the Colorado Rockies in Denver to rack up 111 RBIs. His achievement overtakes the previous record holder Ron Cey's 110 RBIs achieved in 1977.

Chicago Cubs 35-year-old superstar Sammy Sosa can't seem to get away from trouble. He is fined a day's salary, $87,400, out of his $16.15 million bonanza, for arriving 70 minutes before the opening pitch of the team's final game of the regular season at Wrigley Field, and apparently departing 15 minutes into the game. The team is also miffed that Sosa never puts on his uniform. Sosa claims he's in the clubhouse until the seventh inning; the team claims its security cameras in the parking lot show otherwise. It's obvious Sosa's glory days are coming to an end in 2004. That one-day's fine is in sharp contrast to the $3,500 he receives in 1985 for signing with the Texas Rangers when he's 16 years old. Four years later, he's on the Rangers active roster and then after playing 25 games, is traded to the Chicago White Sox in 1990 where he stays for two-and-a-half seasons before shifting to the Cubs.

Historically, Sosa and his other Latino brothers turn the 1990s into the era of Hispanics, becoming the sport's dominant minority; in 1998 he becomes the symbol for Latin baseball because of his competitive role against Mark McGwire of the St. Louis Cardinals, his prime opponent in the home run derby seeking to overtake Roger Maris' single season 61 homers record of 1961, 33 years after Babe Ruth set the mark in 1928. In 1998, Sosa and McGwire are nip and tuck smacking homers in a home run race, which fires the public and the media following the devastating players' strike in 1994. McGwire finishes the year with 70 homers to Sosa's 66.

Also at work is the revelation that McGwire is discovered using androstenedione, a pill that produces a hormone designed for building muscle mass, explains Howard Bryant in his book on steroids in baseball aptly titled *Juicing The Game: Drugs, Power and the Fight for the Soul of Major League Baseball.* Sosa, who is not yet suspected of taking steroids, displays a flamboyant reaction to his home run assault, starting with a hop to launch him around the bases where upon returning to the dugout he taps his heart, flashes a peace sign and blows a kiss to his wife and mother which is duly recorded by the cameras. Between Sosa and McGwire, they create what Bryant calls "a multicultural home run derby."

Heading into the new season, fans in Boston and New York are especially keen for a battle between these two legendary rivals for a World Series championship playoff, with the Red Sox determined to rid themselves of the "Curse of the Bambino," the sale of 19-year-old pitcher/outfielder George Herman "Babe" Ruth to the Yankees on January 5, 1920, for $125,000 plus a $350,000 loan to the team's new owner Harry Frazee to finance his Broadway production aspirations. With the Babe as one of the Yankees' home run sparkplugs during his 15 years with the team from 1920 to 1935, the team goes on to win 39 American League pennants and 26 World Series titles.

The Yankee roster, in addition to Alex Rodriguez at third, boasts pitchers Javier Vazquez from the Montreal Expos and Cuban defector Jose Contreras, returning ace Mariano Rivera, center fielder Bernie Williams, and catcher Jorge Posada.

The Red Sox are pinning their hopes on the likes of pitcher Pedro Martinez, left fielder Manny Ramirez, shortstop Nomar Garciaparra, and designated hitter David Ortiz to add firepower to their drive for the American League East title and entry into the Series playoffs. The last World Series the Sox win is in 1918; this year, the Sox will dominate the Yankees in the Series playoffs and make it to the World Series where they defeat St. Louis for the title.

In the heat of the regular season, several emotional events occur. Jose Contreras, who defects from Cuba in December 2002 and is signed by the Yankees to a $32 million, four-year contract, is reunited with his wife and two daughters who defect in June of this year after being apart 20 months. Contreras learns of his family's arrival in the U.S. from his lawyer/agent, Jaime Torres, who hears the news from a *Miami Herald* reporter. One day after arriving on U.S. soil, the family is released into Torres' custody and Contreras flies from Baltimore to Miami for his long overdue reunion. Five days after the family's

90-mile trip from Cuba with 18 other freedom-seekers in a 31-foot, 1980 Chris-Craft powerboat which runs aground off Big Pine Key, 108 miles southwest of Miami, and is captured by the U.S. Border Patrol, the family watches Contreras pitch his best game of the season on June 27.

He strikes out a career-high 10 batters during six shutout innings as the Yankees beat their neighborly rivals the New York Mets 8-1 in the first game of a double header in Yankee Stadium. During a press conference between games accompanied by wife Miriam, 11-year-old Naylan and three-year-old Maylenis, Contreras dedicates his victory on the field to his family and "to the people of Cuba who support me."

Right before the August trade deadline, a flurry of actions sees the following switches: Boston sends its star shortstop Nomar Garciaparra, a five-time all star shortstop and two-time American League batting champion, who's been plagued with an injured Achilles' tendon, to the Chicago Cubs; The Yankees trade inconsistent pitcher Contreras (now 8-5 in 18 games), despite his earlier emotional reunion with his family, to the Chicago White Sox for hurler Esteban Loaiza with a 9-5 record in 21 starts. Nomar joins former Yankee hurler Orlando Hernández, traded in 2004 after two seasons with the New Yorkers where he posts a 61-40 regular season mark and goes 9 and 3 in the post season. Montreal trades Orlando Cabrera, its Golden Glove shortstop to Boston and picks up Chicago Cubs shortstop Alex Gonzalez and pitcher Francis Beltran.

Struggling Toronto, with a 47-64 slate and a record 17 games under .500 late in the season, fires manager Carlos Tosca after two years. Tosca, 50, is the fifth Cuban to manage a major league team. The team's former third base coach, he finishes with a 189 and 191 record as manager. The four Cuban managers preceding him are Tony Perez, who helms Cincinnati in 1993 and Florida in 200l; Cookie Rojas, California in 1988 and Florida in 1996; Preston Gomez, San Diego from 1969 to 1972, Houston from 1974 to 1975 and the Chicago Cubs in 1980, and Mike Gonzalez, St. Louis in 1938 and 1940.

By the time the rosters for the 75th All Star game are announced in July, the prowess of Hispanic players accounts for 25 of the 64 selections, with the American League (AL) sporting 15 Latinos, the National League (NL) 10.

The AL's starting lineup includes: Ivan Rodriguez, Detroit, catcher; Vladimir Guerrero, Anaheim, right field; Manny Ramirez, Boston, left field; Alex Rodriguez, New York, third base; and Alfonso Soriano, Texas, second base. Position reservists include: Victor Martinez, Cleveland, catcher; David Ortiz, Boston, first base; Carlos Guillen, Detroit, shortstop; and Miguel Tejada, Baltimore, shortstop. Pitchers include: Esteban Loaiza, Chicago; C.C. Sabathia, Cleveland; Javier Vazquez, New York Yankees; Francisco Cordero, Texas; Mariano Rivera, New York Yankees, and Francisco Rodriguez, Anaheim.

The NL's starting lineup sports: Edgar Renteria, St. Louis, short stop; Albert Pujols, St. Louis, first base; and, Sammy Sosa, Chicago Cubs, right field. Position reservists: Johnny Estrada, Atlanta, catcher; Moises Alou, Chicago, outfield; Carlos Beltran, Houston, outfield; Miguel Cabrera, Florida, outfield; and Bobby Abreu, Philadelphia, outfield. Pitchers include: Liván Hernández, Montreal, and Armando Benitez, Florida.

In the stranger than fiction category, Carlos Beltran becomes the first player to be selected for one All Star team, the American League, and winds up playing for the National League. The switch occurs after Beltran, selected while a member of the Kansas City Royals, is traded to the Houston Astros and is picked to fill the center field position when Cincinnati's Ken Griffey, Jr. is placed on the team's 15-day disabled list with a torn right hamstring injury.

Among the sluggers competing in the All Star Home Run Derby, Baltimore Orioles Miguel Tejada wins the competition with 15 and becomes the fifth Latino to win the title since 1990. Previous winners: 2001—Luis Gonzalez, Arizona Diamondbacks; 2000—Sammy Sosa, Chicago Cubs; 1997—Tino Martinez, New York Yankees; and 1993—Juan Gonzalez, Texas Rangers.

Who wins the game? The Americans League, 9-4 in Houston. During the first inning, Seattle's Ichiro Suzuki doubles and comes home on Detroit's Ivan Rodriguez's triple. Boston's Manny Ramirez's blasts a two-run homer, followed by Texas' Alfonso Soriano's three-run blast. It's the first time in All Star history that a team's starters all bat in the same inning. For Angels' relief pitcher Francisco Rodriguez, the game has its own special emotional significance. His appearance in the eighth inning in which he gets two batters out to end the stanza, is the first time he's ever pitched while his grandmother is in the stands. The victory is the AL's 20th against the NL's 30 wins, with two ties dating back to 1933. Soriano is awarded with the game's most valuable player trophy, the seventh Hispanic thus honored since 1962. The others are 1999—Pedro Martinez, Boston Red Sox; 1998—Roberto Alomar, Baltimore; 1997—Sandy Alomar, Jr., Cleveland; 1982—Dave Concepcion, Cincinnati; 1967—Tony Perez, Cincinnati; and 1965—Juan Marichal, San Francisco.

Amid fiercely fought skirmishes leading to the World Series, St. Louis and Boston emerge as the top teams having both battled seven games to win their respective league titles. St. Louis overcomes the Houston Astros in the best of seven series, 4-3 while Boston overpowers the Yankees in an amazing comeback, 4-3. Hispanic players on all four teams play key roles.

The Bronx Bombers get to play Boston after winning the best of five AL division series against the Minnesota Twins, 3-1, spearheaded by the home run power of Ruben Sierra and Alex Rodriguez, and the relief pitching of Mariano Rivera.

In getting to the World Series, St. Louis defeats the Los Angeles Dodgers in the five game series, 3-1, 8-3, 8-3, and 6-2 in the fourth game. The Dodgers lone win is in game 3, 4-0, in which Jose Lima throws a five-hit shutout.

The Astros earn the right to meet St. Louis after vanquishing the Atlanta Braves in five games of the NL division series, sparked by Carlos Beltran's two home runs in the fifth game, giving him four homers for the series, which are instrumental in helping him tie Barry Bonds' postseason eight homer mark.

During the Astros versus Cardinals series, homers by Albert Pujols, Scott Rolen, Carlos Beltran, and Jim Edmonds help St. Louis earn its first trip to the World Series since 1987.

Obviously keyed by their defeat of the Yankees, the Red Sox rout St. Louis in the World Series in four games, 11-9, 6-2, 4-1, and 3-0 to finally win their first Series championship since 1918. Boston's Manny Ramirez, who bats .412 during the World Series, is named the most valuable player, even though he commits two eighth-inning errors in game one which leads to two Cardinal runs. Orlando Cabrera and David Ortiz help in this victory. Cabrera also helps the Sox secure game two with a two-run single in the sixth inning. Pedro Martinez's change-up pitches in game three helps keep the Cardinals scoreless over seven innings by only allowing three hits. He retires 14 straight batters before being relieved in the eighth inning. He also throws out a runner at home and contributes a run-scoring single. Manny Ramirez's first inning homer set the pattern for the victory. The Sox 3-0 shutout in game four is sparked by the entire team and ends an 86-year World Series drought.

What's amazing about the Red Sox victory is how they rebound in their playoffs with the Yankees, down 3-0, they become the first baseball team to overcome this shortcoming and win the seven-game series. The series is arguably the most dramatic, fingernail biting competition. In game one, which New York dominates 10-7, Mariano Rivera ensures the victory with the final outs in the top of the eighth to save the game for Mike Mussina.

Rivera's appearance in the game is one of the series' emotional moments and one of the most difficult in his nine-year career. On the morning of this opening game, he's in his native Panama attending the funerals of two of his wife's cousins, Victor Avila, 35, and his 14-year-old son Victor Dario Avila, who are electrocuted in a freak accident in his home pool the day before. The Yankees provide Rivera with a private jet for the five-hour return flight to New York after the service. He arrives at Yankee Stadium around 9 p.m. during the top of the third inning. In game two, it's Rivera saving the victory, 3-1. New York wins game three 19-8. Game four lasts 12 innings with Boston playing at home and winning its first game 6-4.

Orlando "El Duque" Hernández, the Yankee starter, holds the Sox in check for four innings, allowing only a second inning single as the team scores two runs on Alex Rodriguez's two-run homer to left center in the third inning. In the fifth, the Sox hit Hernández for three runs.

Hernández, who signs with the Yankees in 1998 for $4.3 million, defects from Cuba the following year, and is one of the team's wizards until 2002 when his career starts faltering as a result of a shoulder injury which requires surgery. During the 2002 off-season he's signed by Montreal but doesn't play during the 2003 season. The Yankees sign him in March of this year for $500,000 and send him to the minors until he's brought back to the majors before the All Star game in July and joins the pitching rotation the next month, which lands him his slot in the World Series.

David Ortiz's, the Sox cleanup hitter, and homerun maven in game four, whacks a two-out, run-scoring single to center against reliever Esteban Loaiza in the bottom of the 14th inning to give Boston its 5-4 victory in game five. The game runs 5 hours, 49 minutes, the longest in post-season history.

The series shifts back to New York for game six with the Yankees leading three games to two. The Sox win the game, 4-2, on second baseman Mark Bellhorn's three-run homer off starter Jon Lieber in the fourth to force a game seven after being down three games. After the Sox score four runs in the fifth to take the lead 4-0, Yankee Bernie Williams blasts a solo homer in the seventh off Curt Schilling, playing with a blood-soaked bandage and sock on his right ankle covering a dislocated tendon, who's replaced in the eighth by Bronson Arroyo who gives up a one-out double to Miguel Cairo. Derek Jeter's single to left scores Cairo to bring the score to 4-2 in favor of the Yanks. Alex Rodriguez then knocks a grounder towards first, which draws both first baseman Doug Mientkiewicz and Arroyo in towards the ball. With no one covering first, Arroyo picks up the ball, places it in his glove and attempts to tag Rodriguez as he runs past. Rodriguez hits Arroyo's left forearm with his left hand and the ball pops out of his glove and into foul territory as Jeter scores and Rodriquez goes to second.

The six-man umpiring crew responds to protests from Boston and calls Rodriquez out for interfering with Arroyo and sending Jeter back to first. The hotly contested play results in a three-minute delay as fans pepper the field with bottles and trash. With Arroyo getting the next batter out to end the inning, police officers in riot gear are instructed by a league official to position themselves along each foul line to protect the umpires in the top of the ninth inning. It's a sight rarely seen in a World Series game.

In the highly charged seventh game, Boston's dramatic 9-3 comeback victory affirms its dominance this year over the Yankees, led in part by two homers by Johnny Damon and single homers by David Ortiz and Mark Bellhorn. Damon's two home runs in the second and fourth innings are against Javier Vazquez. His first is a grand slam, followed by a two-run blast, which gives Boston an 8-1 lead. Vazquez replaces Kevin Brown after Ortiz hits the Yankee starter for a two-run homer in the first inning. Bellhorn taps Tom Gordon in the eighth with a homer off the right field foul pole for the 9-3 victory.

Once the ground stops vibrating in Boston and the World Series is a historical fact, the post-season awards add their own glitter.

Vladimir Guerrero, the Anaheim Angel's right fielder, is named the American League's most valuable player. In his first season with the Angels after leaving the Montreal Expos, Guerrero leads the team to the American League West title. The Dominican resident is honored at home for his achievement in a ceremony at the presidential palace, flanked by President Leonel Fernandez and Jay Payano, the national sports minister. Guerrero receives 21 of 28 first place votes by the Baseball Writers Association of America, finishing ahead of countrymen Manny Ramirez and David Ortiz, both with the Red Sox.

In the voting for the National League MVP, San Francisco's Barry Bonds wins the title for the fourth straight year, earning 24 of 32 first place ballots, with the Dodgers' third baseman Adrian Beltre finishing second and St. Louis' Albert Pujols in third place. Bonds and

Ramirez also pick up Hank Aaron Awards as the most outstanding hitters in their leagues. It's the third consecutive year for Bonds, the first for Ramirez who ends Alex Rodriguez's three-year streak.

Johan Santana, the Minnesota Twins 20-6 pitcher, receives all 28 first place votes by the baseball writers to win the American League Cy Young Award. Santana is the first Venezuelan to win the award and the first unanimous winner since Arizona's Randy Johnson's achievement two years ago and the first American Leaguer since Boston's Pedro Martinez in 2000. Coming in second is the Yankees' Mariano Rivera, who leads the majors with 53 saves, a career high.

National League managers and coaches award Dodger shortstop Cezar Izturis and center fielder Steve Finley Gold Glove honors. Izturis is both a first-time honoree and the team's first Gold Glove shortstop since Maury Wills wins the honor in 1962. Third baseman Adrian Beltre wins the Silver Slugger award as the best offensive player at that position.

Edgar Martinez, the Seattle Mariner's designated hitter, who retires after the season, wins the Roberto Clemente Award, presented to a major league player for his skills on the field combined with his charitable work in his community, which involves Martinez's working to find a cure for muscular dystrophy in Seattle.

Once the World Series symbolizes the conclusion of on field competition, fierce competition begins for signing the 207 free agent players as well as re-signing team stalwarts or going after other heavy hitters.

A hot, new pitching rivalry emerges in New York for the 2005 season, pitting two new arrivals in the city: the Mets' Pedro Martinez versus the Yankees' Randy Johnson acquired from the Arizona Diamondbacks. Martinez, 33, eight years younger than Johnson, 41, achieves a 19-6 record in 2004, while Johnson's record is less impressive, 16-14. Nevertheless, Johnson's 17-year career record is 246 wins while Martinez's is 182 wins during his 13 years in the majors.

Anaheim's owner Arte Moreno goes on a signing spree, which includes agreements with seven Latinos, foremost of whom is free agent Boston shortstop, 30-year-old Colombian Orlando Cabrera to a $32 million, four-year contract.

During the off-season, Baltimore signs former Cubs slugger Sammy Sosa to a complicated salary agreement, despite a decline in his hitting over the past four years and some recent troubling behavior during his 13-year career with the Cubbies. Since his highly watched home run derby with Mark McGwire in 1998, Sosa's at bat average begins declining, batting .253 last season and hitting 35 homers while playing in only 126 games. In fact, in addition to his batting average and home runs, Sosa's hits, runs scored, and RBIs all decrease every year starting in 2001. To make matters worse, on June 3, 2003, playing against Tampa Bay, Sosa shatters his bat on a ground ball out to reveal cork in the barrel for which he's suspended eight games. Initially, the 36-year-old right fielder's Chicago contract sounds like a Wall Street money matter: according to published reports, the Cubs will pay $16.15 million of the $25 million Sosa is still owned as part of his $72 million, four-year contract. However, since Sosa already receives $1,307,692 of his salary for the new season, based on a monthly payout, that amount is deducted from what the Cubs owe the Orioles, reducing the amount Baltimore receives to $6,842,308. Baltimore will have to pay $8.85 million of Sosa's $17 million salary for the new season.

During his 17th season in 2005, his on-field performance falls below his better days as the Orioles drop from first place to fourth in August. On a lesser scale, the team re-signs slugger Rafael Palmeiro to a $3 million, one-year pact and signs free agent Toronto shortstop Chris Gomez to an $825,000 minor league deal. In 2005, Sosa and Palmeiro will be engulfed in a massive steroid scandal covered later in this Chapter.

Sosa and Palmeiro both achieve home run records once the 2005 season is well underway. In hitting his 583rd home run at home June 18 in the Orioles' 7-3 victory over the Colorado Rockies, Sosa ties McGwire for sixth place on the all-time career list. The blast is Sosa's ninth of the season. One day later, Palmeiro hits his 560th home run for 10th place. On July 26, Sosa smacks number 586 as Baltimore defeats the Texas Rangers 5-4 to tie Frank Robinson for fifth, while Palmeiro ups his ante to 568 to move into ninth place. The next day, Sosa hits number 587 in the Orioles 11-8 loss, to move him momentarily into sole ownership of fifth place. It's his third homer in four games and his 13th of the season. After his final season with Baltimore in 2005, and not playing in '06, he resurfaces in '07 with his original Texas Rangers where he's expected to be the regular designated hitter and a parttime oufielder.

In a strange footnote to Dodger activities, former pitching ace Fernando Valenzuela turned team Spanish radio commentator this year, tries his hand as a player with Mexicali's Aguilas late in the regular season of the Mexican Winter Pacific League where he accumulates a 2-2 record. While the Winter League draws major leaguers, it's an oddity for a prime former superstar like Valenzuela to be playing in this minor league. His name and reputation attracts fans from cities along Mexico's Northwestern coast to see him pitch. The 44-year-old from Navajo, Mexico, pitches five innings as his team defeats Los Mochis, 2-1 to face Mazatlán in the best of seven championship series in the Triple-A league in January of 2005. Valenzuela loses one of the first two playoff games, 3-2 in 10 innings. Mazatlán bests Mexicali by winning the final four games and advances to the Caribbean World Series on its home field which Fox Sports En Español televises. In the championship game, Mexico defeats the Dominican Republic, 4-3, before 15,000 at Teodoro Stadium. It's Mexico's first title since 2002 and its fifth since 1970. The Dominican Republic comes into the championship with 13 titles to its credit.

Among the major leaguers playing in the title game for Mexico are Vinny Castilla (who's 303 career home runs is the most of any Mexican in the major leagues), Erubiel Durazo, Daniel Cortes, and Trenidad Hubbard, a 38-year-old center fielder who has played for nine major league teams during his career, while Miguel Tejada (the American League's most valuable player in 2002), Alberto Castillo, Rafael Furcal, Ronnie Belliard, Miguel Batista, and Daniel Cabrera play for the Dominican Republic.

In 1979, Valenzuela joins the Dodgers, spends that year and 1980 in the minor leagues, and in 1981 begins his major league career. On opening day, April 9, 1981, the 20-year-old lefthander pitches a five-hit shutout against the Houston Astros, one of four shutouts during an eight-game winning streak, which helps create the pitcher's "Fernandomania" craze that inspires strong devotion from fellow countrymen during his career in L.A., which ends in 1990. It's estimated that every time he pitches, attendance rises by around 9,000 Fernando fans. In 1981, when the team wins the World Series, he becomes the first pitcher to earn the National League's rookie of the year and Cy Young Award in the same year. After 10 years of throwing 90 miles-an-hour plus screwballs, Valenzuela begins a series of trades to St. Louis in 1991, Baltimore in 1993, Philadelphia in 1994, San Diego in 1995 to 1997, and St. Louis in 1997, where he ends his major league career.

San Francisco, the Dodgers' prime rivals, signs 70-year-old manager Felipe Alou's son Moises to a $13.25 million, two-year pact that includes an option for the 2006 season. Moises, 38, joins the oldest outfield in baseball; left fielder Barry Bonds is 40 and center fielder Marquis Grissom is 37. Alou bats-in a career-high 39 homers to drive-in 106 runs for the Chicago Cubs last season. This will be the second time the senior Alou will manage his son, overseeing him at Montreal from 1992 to 1996. During their stay in Canada, both father and son are rookies: Felipe as the team's manager, his son the neophyte right fielder. Starting out with the Pittsburgh Pirates in 1986 through 1990, the year he's traded to Montreal where he stays until 1996, Moises plays for the 1997 World Series champion Florida Marlins and the Houston Rockets from 1998 to 2001 before joining the Cubs in 2002 through last year.

And when 42-year-old veteran pitcher Roger Clemens chooses to play a second season in 2005 with his hometown Houston Astros rather than retire, his $18 million salary—the highest the team ever pays a pitcher—places him on the list with 10 other players, including six Hispanics, whose annual paycheck is worth $17 million or more.The wealthy Latinos in this elite circle include: New York

Yankee Alex Rodriguez, $25.2 million; Boston's Manny Ramirez, $20 million; Toronto's Carlos Delgado, $19.4 million; Chicago Cubs' Sammy Sosa, $18 million; Boston's Pedro Martinez, $17.5 million; and New York Met's Carlos Beltran, $17 million.

The excessive wealth tossed at the players during the off-season, draws the ire of Pittsburgh and Baltimore team officials, who criticize their fellow owners for their free spending excesses. Pittsburgh's managing general partner Kevin McClatchy notes that giving "an average pitcher $7 million" prompts other average pitchers to require the same amount. Orioles' owner Peter Angelos specifically cites Florida's paying Toronto's traded Carlos Delgado $52 million to play first base as "fiscal insanity."

Once baseball's follow-the-money escapades cease, and teams head to their spring training camps, the sport's image over illegal substance use is tarnished further in February of 2005 by claims in a book by Havana-born Jose Canseco of steroid use by a number of major names in the sport. Admitting steroid use himself, Canseco claims in *Juiced: Wild Times, Rampant 'Roids, Smash Hits and How Baseball Got Big*, he injects the banned body-building substance into homerun sluggers Mark McGwire when they play together with the Oakland A's and Jason Giambi and Texas Ranger teammates Rafael Palmeiro, Juan Gonzalez, and Ivan Rodriguez. He claims to also personally inject two of his Tampa Bay Devil Rays teammates Wilson Alvarez and Dave Martinez. He also suspects other stars of using steroids including Barry Bonds, Sammy Sosa, Miguel Tejada, and Roger Clemens. Canseco reiterates these charges during an interview on CBS' *60 Minutes*. All deny using steroids except the Yankees' Giambi. Former A's manager Tony La Russa, while telling the *Los Angeles Times* he suspects four or five of his players with using performance-enhancing drugs, including Canseco, McGwire is not one of them. Canseco and McGwire play for the A's under La Russo from 1986 to 1992, the period in which time the team wins the World Series from 1988 to 1990. McGwire issues a statement saying, "Once and for all, I did not use steroids or any other illegal substance" during his years with Oakland and St. Louis. Canseco, who plays pro baseball 17 years, is named an all star six times and the most valuable player (MVP) in 1988, also has a troubled private life including two divorces and several run-ins with the law.

The growing brouhaha over steroid use in baseball reaches the House of Representatives, whose Committee on Government Reform, sensing an opportunity for its members to be in the national spotlight chasing down a public health concern, calls a hearing for March 17th. Canseco promptly says he'll testify. Initially the players are defiant against appearing voluntarily, so subpoenas are served to all involved, including baseball commissioner Bud Selig, Canseco, Sammy Sosa, Rafael Palmeiro, Mark McGwire, Jason Giambi, Curt Schilling, and Frank Thomas. Giambi, who reportedly admits steroid use before a 2003 federal grand jury investigating steroid distribution by the San Francisco based Bay Area Laboratory Co-Operative, a nutritional supplement company, is excused.

During the nationally televised hearing Palmeiro, Sosa, and Thomas deny taking steroids, McGwire refuses to answer any questions and will not implicate "my friends and teammates." Schilling joins Palmeiro in blasting Canseco and assails his book as "glorifying steroid use." As someone who has read the book, he's correct on that point. Canseco, given the cold shoulder by the other players at the hearing, admits his usage and sarcastically tells the committee that after listening to the denials, "I was the only individual in Major League Baseball to use steroids. That's hard to believe." Members of the committee after 11 hours of testimony, question the league's new anti-drug policy and indicate Congress needs to step in and clean up this mess if baseball doesn't do it itself.

After all the hoopla about steroid use and Major League Baseball defending its new steroid testing plan, which the congressional committee finds lacking, the unimaginable happens on the eve of opening day April 3. Alex Sanchez, the Tampa Bay Devil Ray's center fielder is suspended for 10 days after testing positive for steroids under the league's new drug policy. He claims he doesn't intentionally use steroids, but rather uses over-the-counter supplements. The Cuban athlete joins Tampa Bay on March 19 after being released by the Detroit Tigers. He is followed several weeks later by five additional suspended players: Jorge Piedra, Colorado outfielder (April 11); Agustin Montero, Texas pitcher (April 20); Jamal Strong, Seattle outfielder (April 26); Juan Rincon, Minnesota Twins relief pitcher (May 2); and Rafael Betancourt, Cleveland pitcher (July 8). Rincon, reported to be "devastated" to learn he tests positive for performance-enhancing drugs, asks the players' union to file a grievance over his 10-day ban. These players are very fortunate. Six weeks after the House holds its steroid-use hearings and calls the league's new steroid policy covering an initial 10-day suspension "dismal," commissioner Selig notifies players' union head Don Fehr of its proposed tougher, new rules, starting with a 50-game suspension for a first offense, 100 games for a second offense, and a lifetime ban for a third positive test.

Four of the eight owner members of Baseball's Executive Council endorse Selig's new plan and ask the Players Association to also accept the new policy. Don Fehr says he's willing to discuss modifications with the league's negotiators.

Apparently spurred on by the recalcitrant and defiant attitude of several of the players subpoenaed to testify at the House hearing in March, two separate House committees approve steroid testing bills. The House Energy and Commerce Committee approves a bill in June that sets steroid testing rules and penalties for Major League Baseball, the NFL, NBA, and NHL. The Drug Free Sports Act calls for a suspension of half the season for a first offense, a full season for a second, and a lifetime ban for a third violation. The committee also creates a U.S. Boxing Commission. This bill follows similar legislation passed in May by the House Government Reform Committee. Rep. Henry Waxman, a member of the panel hearing testimony into widespread steroid use, and a member of the Energy and Commerce Committee, urges the two committees to come up with a bill that can be brought to the floor of the House.

Once the spotlight is off Washington, the steroid epidemic continues to unravel, infecting the minor leagues where Wilson Delgado and Luis Ugueto are among four players given 15-game suspensions. They join a group of unnamed minor leaguers who are quietly suspended this season for violating the minor league anti-steroid program. Infielder Delgado plays for Triple-A Albuquerque, part of the Florida farm system, while utility player Ugueto is with the Kansas City minor league system.

On August 1 baseball snares its biggest fish in superstar Rafael Palmeiro. Four and a-half months after he tells a Congressional hearing that he's never used steroids, he is suspended for 10 days for violating baseball's steroid policy agreed upon by the Players Association and Major League Baseball. The suspension costs the Baltimore first baseman $165,746 from his $3 million 2005 contract. He is the biggest star to be newly tainted by steroid use; the previous six major leaguers are not in the same status league with the 3,018 hit/569 homerun champion. The announcement of his suspension is made prior to the Orioles home game against the Chicago White Sox, which the Orioles lose 6 to 3.

Following his suspension, Palmeiro denies any intentional steroid use in a conference call to reporters, asserting in the *Los Angeles Times*: "I have never intentionally used steroids. Never." In fact, he uses the word intentionally two additional times in his statement: "I have never intentionally used a banned substance, but I unfortunately wasn't careful enough" and "Ultimately, although I never intentionally put a banned substance into my body, the independent arbiter ruled that I had to be suspended under the terms of the program." He additionally stresses, "Why would I do this in a year when I went in front of Congress and I testified and I told the truth? Why would I do this during a season where I was going to get to 3,000 hits? It just makes no sense." The inference in Palmeiro's comments is that he consumed over-the-counter dietary supplements that contain a banned performance-enhancing drug, albeit he never names the questionable supplement. Published reports in two New

York newspapers, the *New York Times* and *Newsday* indicate the steroid is stanozolol, known by its brand name of Winstrol. It's the same steroid that causes Canada's Ben Johnson to lose his gold medal in the 100 meters during the 1988 Olympics.

The next day, August 2, Seattle Mariner pitcher Ryan Franklin becomes the franchise's second player along with Jamal Strong to be suspended for 10 days for steroid use. Franklin's suspension will cost around $133,333 of his $2.4 million salary. Franklin, the eighth player suspended, asserts in the *Seattle Post-Intelligencer*, "Until the day I die, this is hard for me to believe." Franklin says he is taking a multivitamin and a protein shake at the time in early May he provides a urine sample which is analyzed at a World Anti-Doping Agency lab in Montreal and comes back positive, according to the newspaper. The player provides his supplements to the players' union for testing and inclusion in its appeal. Both come back negative following testing at a Nashville lab. Baseball's Health Policy Advisory Committee chooses to hold a hearing and passes the matter to Major League Baseball's arbitrator, Shyam Das.

Three days after baseball's public announcement on August 1 of Palmerio's positive test and his suspension—a fact it withholds for two months—Congress announces it will investigate whether Palmeiro commits perjury in March when he denies taking steroids before the House Government Reform Committee. Through a statement by his agent, Arn Tellem, the tainted player says he will cooperate fully with the committee. The revelation of which drug Palmeiro is alleged to have used is attacked by Don Fehr of the players' association, who cites the joint drug agreement between the league and the players prohibits disclosure of the specific ingredient used beyond informing the public of the suspension.

Following Congress' announcement to investigate Palmeiro's suspension, Thomas A. Davis, III (Republican, Virginia) and Henry Waxman, the ranking Democrat from Los Angeles, send commissioner Selig a list of questions about the suspension and when MLB first learns about his misstep. MLB responds to the request by turning over its documents. In September, the House Committee begins quietly speaking to several unnamed active players who know Palmeiro anent whether he lies under oath about any steroid use. A few weeks later, following subsequent published reports that Palmeiro tells an arbitration panel on the Health Advisory Committee that teammate Miguel Tejada unknowingly provides him with vitamin B-12 that contains steroids, Tejada is reported to be in "shock" over the allegation, reports the *Los Angeles Times*. Disturbed by this latest headline-attracting development, the Orioles put Palmeiro on paid suspension for the remaining 10 games of the season. Once the season ends, Palmeiro is among the first 54 players filing for free agent status. On November 9, Congress announces it will not prosecute Palmeiro on perjury charges, citing a lack of evidence he lies when denying under oath that he's never used steroids.

When the Senate's Commerce Committee holds its hearing September 28, the commissioners of the four major pro sports, their union leaders, and five baseball Hall of Famers hear the solons threaten legislation if baseball fails to upgrade its current discipline rules that mandate a lifetime ban for third-time offenders. Baseball commissioner Selig warns if the players don't agree to his five-month-old proposal involving a first-time suspension of 50 games, a second-time offense of 100 games, and a lifetime ban for a third offense by the conclusion of the forthcoming World Series, he will endorse federal proposals for a two-year suspension for a first offense and permanent expulsion for a second violation. Chairman John McCain (Republican, Arizona), quoted in the *Los Angeles Times* as referring to Rafael Palmeiro's denial of steroid use before the House committee in March and his 10-day suspension in August, notes: "The patience of this body, reflective of its constituents, has reached an end."

There appears to be no end to the number of players testing positive for steroids. Following the end of the regular season, the commissioner's office reveals three additional players in trouble: Texas pitcher Carlos Almanzar, New York Met pitcher Felix Heredia, and New York Yankees outfielder Matt Lawton, who files for free agent status.

With his baseball career mired and tainted by the controversy over steroids, Canseco, who retires in 2001, seeks a new career as a movie action hero. In September, he hires little known but aggressively eccentric producer Bob DeBrino to influence Hollywood power brokers that he's the newest entry into the action genre.

The power of Congress' intent on regulating steroid use in professional sports results in both Major League Baseball and its players' union in November agreeing to stricter penalties, including testing for the first time for amphetamines. In a major reversal for the powerful players' union, it agrees to a 50-game suspension without pay for a first-time violation, 100 games for a second offense, and a lifetime suspension for a third. An expelled player could seek reinstatement after two years. First-time amphetamine offenders will have to undergo mandatory evaluation and follow-up testing. A positive test will carry a suspension of 25 games, 80 games, and ultimately a lifetime ban. The plan mirrors commissioner Selig's recommendations he proposes one month after appearing before the House committee. The new rules are much harsher than baseball's current first time 10-day suspension, second time 30-day suspension, and 60 days for a third failed test, and a lifetime ban after a fifth offense. Players will be tested twice a year, starting in 2006 and overseen by an independent administrator, with the actual tests conducted by the World Anti-Doping Agency's laboratory. In addition to penalties for steroid use, players convicted of possession and/or distribution will be suspended, facing anywhere from a 15- to 60-game suspension to a lifetime ban depending on the number of offenses. Two days after the MLB and the players' union accede to the new rules, the team owners unanimously approve the tough new drug policy.

Baseball is again rocked in March of 2006 by another alleged steroid scandal that snares several Latin players. According to the book *Game of Shadows*, which focuses on homerun slugger Barry Bonds, seven other players are also named, including Benito Santiago, Bobby Estalella, and Armando Rios. Baseball commissioner Bud Selig responds several weeks later by naming former U.S. Senate Majority Leader George Mitchell to lead an inquiry into the alleged use by the players. Mitchell previously served on a panel in 2000 analyzing the financial status of the sport. His part ownership of the Boston Red Sox and chairmanship of the Walt Disney Company, which owns ESPN, are questioned by Hall of Fame pitcher and now Republican Senator from Kentucky, Jim Bunning, because of his closeness to the sport. Drug tampering emerges again on May 7, 2007, after Juan Salas, a Tampa Bay relief pitcher flunks a drug test as part of Major League Baseball's testing program. He is suspended for 50 games after becoming the sport's first player in '07 to be cited for a performance-enhancing substance, according to the commissioner's office.

While steroid-use remains a hot media subject and is at the core of Canseco's book, *Juiced*, the edition however, is not totally about steroid-dominated baseball. He also veers away to discuss other baseball-related inside topics. One which is of interest to this history report centers on 2004 World Series champion Boston Red Sox World Series bullpen coach Euclides Rojas. Rojas is a name clouded over during the hysteria of Boston's come from behind victory over the New York Yankees. In October 1994, the year of the infamous player's strike, while visiting Cuban refugees staying at the U.S. military base at Guantanamo Bay, Canseco writes he meets Rojas, who attempts to flee Cuba with his wife and son along with other disgruntled Cubans in a raft which is found floating at sea and rescued by the U.S. Coast Guard which brings its passengers to Guantanamo. Rojas, a pitcher with the Cuban national team, and his family finally make it to the U.S. six months later, and in 1995 he starts playing in the minor leagues, first for Palm Springs in the Independent Western League and then with the Florida Marlins Triple-A franchise in Charlotte, North Carolina. Injuries to an elbow while pitching for Cuba halt his career, so he turns to coaching for the Marlins, then the Pittsburgh Pirates, and in 2003 is hired by the Red Sox as bullpen coach. Writes Canseco: "Rojas, the same proud, brave man I met as a refugee at Guantanamo, wearing flip flops, now has a World Series ring and will always be part of baseball history for helping the Red Sox win the

World Series for the first time since 1918." In surfacing Rojas name, Canseco offers readers one of the happier stories in the book.

One casualty of spring training is New York Mets hopeful first baseman Andres Galarraga, who decides to retire. The 43-year-old plays 17 games for the Mets during spring training, hits .235, smacks three home runs for seven runs batted in. Still, it's a disappointing spring training. He leaves the pros after 19 seasons with seven teams and one home run short of reaching 400 during his career. He had signed a minor league pact with the Mets during the off-season and was hoping to make the home team. Among the teams he plays for are Montreal (twice), St. Louis, Colorado, Atlanta, Texas, San Francisco (twice), and Anaheim. "The Big Cat" as he's called, is a five-time All Star and twice named Gold Glove winner who hit 444 doubles and batted-in 1,195 runs.

During mid-season play, St. Louis first baseman Albert Pujols creates some happy, boastful news for baseball by becoming the first major leaguer to hit 30 homers in each of his first five seasons in the big leagues. He accomplishes this feat with a two-run homer in the first inning of the Cards' at home 11-3 victory over the Atlanta Braves, his 190th home run since joining the Cardinals in 2001. His 160 home run total for his first four seasons is second to Ralph Kiner's 168 four-baggers from 1946 to 1949 while with the Pittsburgh Pirates.

Three pioneering Latino players pass away, Bobby Avila, the lesser-known Cesar Gutierrez, and Alfonso "Chico" Carrasquel.

Roberto "Bobby" Avila, who joins the American League's Cleveland Indians in 1949 and becomes the first Mexican to win the league's batting championship in 1954 while with the Indians, dies October 26, 2004 in his home in Veracruz, Mexico. His death at 78 is attributed to complications from diabetes and a lung problem. His signing salary as a second baseman is $17,500 and he comes through for his team as a three time American League all star in 1952, 1954, and 1955. In 1954, the year he wins the AL's batting crown, he hits 0.341, blasts a career-setting 15 homers, which drives in 67 runs, also a career high, and leads the team to the league championship. During the World Series against the New York Giants, Cleveland loses in four games. During the race for the league title, he plays half the season with a broken thumb. After nine seasons with Cleveland, in 1959 he plays for the Baltimore Orioles, Boston Red Sox, and Milwaukee Braves, it's his final year in pro ball. During his 11-year career, he plays in 1,300 games, landing 1.296 hits for a batting average of .281. In 1960, he returns to Mexico and plays for that city's Tigers in the Mexican league. A few years later, he becomes president of the league.

Cesar Dario Gutierrez, the Venezuelan-born shortstop, dies January 22, 2005, in his home in Maracaibo of a heart attack at age 61. He's best known for tying the ancient 1892 American League record set by Baltimore's Wilbert Robinson during a nine-inning game. While with Detroit in 1970, he connects for seven consecutive hits, six singles, and one triple, in a 12th inning game against Cleveland, which the Tigers win.

Gutierrez starts his major league career when he's 24 with the San Francisco Giants from 1967 to 1969 and becomes the 11th Venezuelan to play in the majors. He's then traded to the Detroit Tigers where he stays from 1969 to 1972 when he's sent to the Montreal Expos. Before joining San Francisco, he's signed as an amateur free agent by the Philadelphia Phillies in 1960, and is subsequently sent to the Pittsburgh Pirates who then upgrade him to the majors by trading him to San Francisco.

Alfonso "Chico" Carrasquel, another Venezuelan who makes history in 1952 by being the first Hispanic player to appear in an All Star game, dies in his native Caracas of cardiac arrest May 26, while being transported to a hospital, following several years of battling diabetes. He's a four-time all-star with the Chicago White Sox from 1950 to 1955. Originally signed by the Brooklyn Dodgers in 1949 to play shortstop, but with Pee Wee Reese holding down that position, Branch Rickey, the team's general manager sells Carrasquel's contract to the White Sox prior to the opening of the 1950 season for $35,000. He and Nellie Fox become one of the game's best double-play tandems. Following the 1955 season he's traded to the Cleveland

Indians in a swap for Larry Doby and then plays for the Kansas City Athletics and the Baltimore Orioles.

During his career, he has a .258 lifetime batting average, hits 55 home runs, and has 474 runs batted in. He's also the first of three Venezuelans to play in the majors at the shortstop position. His compatriots are Luis Aparicio and Ozzie Guillen, the current manager of the Chicago White Sox. Following his playing days, Carrasquel stays with the game as a Spanish-language play-by-play announcer for White Sox telecasts and also works for the team in community relations.

Luis Aparicio starts his career in 1956 with the White Sox; is traded to Baltimore in 1963; and helps the Orioles beat the Los Angeles Dodgers in the 1966 World Series, where upon he returns to the Sox in 1978 and completes his career with Boston in 1973.

Jose Guillen starts his career at age 21 with the White Sox. He also plays for Baltimore and Boston in the late 1990s, with the Tampa Bay Devil Rays in 2000, and then lands the manager's post with the White Sox in 2004. During his career, he plays shortstop, left field, first, and second base.

Prior to his steroid scandal, Rafael Palmeiro makes the history book when the first baseman becomes the 26th player to achieve 3,000 hits during his 20-year career on July 15 by doubling in a run off Seattle pitcher Joel Pineiro in his team's 6-3 victory in Seattle. The 40-year-old Cuban-born left-handed hitter's double to the opposite field ties him briefly with Roberto Clemente for 25th place, until he smashes a single in the next inning, and jumps ahead of Clemente, who moves into 26th place. Clemente achieves his milestone in 1972. With his 3,000th hit, Palmeiro joins the elite club of Hank Aaron, Willie Mays, and Eddie Murray who have 3,000 hits and 500 career home runs. During his career Palmeiro plays for the Chicago Cubs (1986 to 1987), Texas Rangers (1989 to 1993, and 1999 to 2003), and Baltimore (1994 to 1998, and 2004 to 2005). Following his return, Palmeiro is booed by fans at home and on the road. He has two hits in 26 times at bat, notes the *Los Angeles Times*, when he's sent home September 5 to tend to knee and ankle injuries.

Kendry Morales, a 21-year-old member of the Cuban national baseball team, finally gets to play ball for an Angel minor league team almost one year after he defects and travels a circuitous route to become a pro in the U.S. He's supposedly removed from the Cuban team in 2003 by officials who fear he's planning to defect. One of Morales' agents, John DiManno, tells the *Los Angeles Times* Kendry attempts to defect several times and "on three occasions is caught and jailed for up to five days." In June of 2004, he indeed defects along with 18 other people who flee by boat and arrive in Miami. From there he travels to Nicaragua and then to the Dominican Republic, the home away from home for many ex-Cubans, where he's granted citizenship and free-agent status.

Following tryouts by the Angels, he's signed to a six-year contract with a $3 million bonus and assigned to the team's class-A Rancho Cucamonga franchise in Southern California, but remains in the Dominican Republic awaiting his work visa which needs to be signed by the Dominican president, thus missing spring training, reports the *Times*. The first baseman, who speaks no English, makes an auspicious debut May 21, 2005, when he smashes a home run on the second pitch he's thrown, past the right-center field fence. His homer, two singles, and three runs driven in aren't enough to thwart the team's 10-8 loss to Visalia. In June, he's promoted to the team's double-A Arkansas franchise in time to celebrate his 22nd birthday.

A switch-hitter, Morales plays several positions for his club team, Industriales, and the Cuban national team, which he joins when he's 19. During the 2003 World Cup, his grand slam in the final game enables Cuba to defeat Taiwan 6-3. Morales joins a growing list of Cubans playing in the majors before and after Fidel Castro's takeover in 1959. The early pioneers include, according to the *Times*: Dolph Luque, 21 seasons from 1914 to 1935 with the Boston Braves, Cincinnati Reds, Brooklyn Dodgers, and New York Giants; Martin Dihigo, who plays in the Negro League because of segregation and is elected to the Hall of Fame in 1977; and Minnie Minoso from 1949 to 1980 with Cleveland, Chicago White Sox, St. Louis, and

Washington Senators. Players leaving after the revolution: Tony Perez, who signs with Cincinnati when he's 17, plays 22 seasons in the majors from 1964 to 1986 with Cincinnati, Montreal, Boston Red Sox, and Philadelphia Phillies, and is elected to the Hall of Fame in 2000; Luis Tiant, from 1964 to 1982 with Cleveland, Minnesota, Boston Red Sox, New York Yankees, Pittsburgh, and California Angels; and Rafael Palmeiro, who arrives with his family in 1971 when he's five, and plays 19 seasons starting in 1986 with the Chicago Cubs, Texas, and Baltimore as of 2005. Players defecting: pitching brothers Liván Hernández in 1995, who plays for Florida, and in 2005, with the new Washington team, who's followed by Orlando in 1998 who plays for the Yankees and the White Sox in 2005, among others.

One day prior to the All Star contest, Major League Baseball, stunned by the International Olympic Committee's eliminating baseball from the Summer Games after 2008, announces its own global competition, the 16-team World Baseball Classic, with the inaugural event set for the first three weeks in March 2006. Players from U.S. teams will play for their national squads rather than for the U.S. prior to the start of the regular season. ESPN, ESPN2, and ESPN Deportes sign on in 2006 to provide exclusive U.S. TV coverage. The second tournament, according to the *Los Angeles Times*, will take place in 2009, and then be held every four years. Among the international players attending the announcement conference in Detroit who will play for their home teams are Carlos Beltran of Puerto Rico and Miguel Tejada of the Dominican Republic. By December, 177 players sign up to play in the inaugural tournament, including Alex Rodriguez, Derek Jeter, Bernie Williams, Eric Gagne, Albert Pujols, Ivan Rodriguez, Bartolo Colon, Miguel Tejada, Alfonso Soriano, David Ortiz, Duaner Sanchez, Jose Cruz, Jr., Oscar Robles, Ricky Ledee, Rafael Furcal, and Francisco Rodriguez. Named manager of the U.S. team is Buck Martinez, the former Toronto Blue Jays manager. Among players signing up who drop out are Manny Ramirez, Pedro Martinez, and Vladimir Guerrero.

Teams slated for the 18 days of competition are being broken into four groups of four teams each. The U.S. team will compete against Mexico, Canada, and South Africa in Phoenix. Japan, South Korea, Taiwan, and China will compete in Tokyo and in Anaheim during round two. Puerto Rico, Cuba (the three-time Olympic gold medallist), Panama, and the Netherlands will vie against each other in San Juan. And the Dominican Republic, Venezuela, Australia, and Italy will compete in Orlando. Puerto Rico will play host to the first and second rounds in San Juan's Hiram Bithorn Stadium, the same venue used by the visiting Montreal Expos in 2003 and 2004. The semifinals on March 18 will be held in San Diego and Latin America, with the championship also taking place two days later in San Diego, which beats out Anaheim, Los Angeles, Phoenix, Houston, and Seattle to host the championship round. Each 27-man team will be selected by that nation's national federation. Major league owners and the U.S. players association will govern the competition. The *Times* indicates 47 percent of the net proceeds will be spent on team prize earnings. The remainder will principally go to MLB, the players union, and the International Baseball Federation. Players may be paid by their national federations while U.S. pros will be paid their regular spring training per diem.

Cuba, first denied entry into the tournament by the U.S. based on its economic embargo against the Castro government, gains permission to play in January of 2006 when the U. S. Treasury Department sets aside the ban to allow the team to compete. In the championship game on March 20, Japan defeats Cuba 10-6 at San Diego's Petco Park before 42,696 fans. The U.S. team, with Derek Jeter and Alex Rodriguez among the starters, while eliminated in the preliminary round, beats Japan 4-3, South Africa 17-0, and Mexico 2-0. It also loses to Canada 8-6, Korea 7-3, and Mexico 2-1 in its second meeting. Japan's march to victory includes wins against China, Taiwan, Mexico, Korea, and loses to the U.S., and Korea twice. Cuba, after losing to the Dominican Republic, beats them in their re-match to reach the finals. It also defeats Panama, the Netherlands, Venezuela, and Puerto Rico, with whom it loses in an earlier game.

Earlier, Latin players comprise 24 of the 64 athletes selected for the 2005 All Star Game, won by the American League 7-5 at Detroit's Comerica Park. Baltimore shortstop Miguel Tejada, in addition to hitting a home run, is also named the game's most valuable player. The victory is the American League's eighth victory over the Nationals, along with one tie, since 1997.

In an example of how uncertainty can rule an athlete's career, Jose Cruz, Jr. is traded in August for the seventh time in eight years. The switch-hitting outfielder's latest shift occurs in mid-August from Boston to the Los Angeles Dodgers. Since breaking in with Seattle in 1997, the 31-year-old plays for Toronto, San Francisco, Tampa Bay, and this year for both Arizona and Boston. The Dodgers are the 2003 Gold Glove winner's sixth team in four years. This season, a bulging disc in his lower back keeps him on the disabled list for one month with Arizona, which trades him to Boston on July 30, where he plays in four games before being traded to Los Angeles, details the *Los Angeles Times*.

Why do the Dodgers want a player who is hitting .215 this year, down from his career batting average of .248? The team believes Cruz has the potential to strengthen its left handed hitting capability.

The Seattle Mariners find their decision to sign 16-year-old Venezuelan pitcher Felix Hernandez three years ago for a $27,000 bonus is paying big dividends this year. The right-hander makes his major league debut August 4 with a 98 mile an hour fastball which earns him 11 Kansas City strikeouts to become the first teenager to achieve 10 or more strikeouts in a game since Dwight Gooden hits that level in 1984, reports *USA Today*. The Mariners believe they have another potential superstar in the now 19-year-old Hernandez. He's brought to the Mariners Class-A Northwest league franchise when he's 17, going 7-2 with 73 strikeouts in 55 innings. Last year, he plays for the team's Class-AA San Antonio franchise with a 5 and 1 record, and this season he again moves up the class ladder to Triple-AAA Tacoma where he goes 9 and 4 before being called up to the Mariners.

The Angels' Vladimir Guerrero hits his 300th home run September 2 in his team's 4-1 victory over the Seattle Mariners at

Angels Stadium. The blast on a 1-0 pitch from Jamie Moyer in the eighth inning, follows his previous homer August 14, and places him on the list of baseball's highest career home run hitters in 24th place.

Angels' pitcher Bartolo Colon also lands in the history book by becoming the American League's first 20-game winner during the final days of the season with his team's 2-1 victory over the Texas Rangers at Angel Stadium September 19. Not only does the 32-year-old Dominican athlete pitch seven solid innings, but he's also the team's first 20-game winner since Hall of Famer Nolan Ryan achieves this milestone in 1974, 31 years ago, by defeating the Texas Rangers by the same 2-1 score. Colon is a year old when Ryan sets his mark. He's been with the Angels since last year, having left the Chicago White Sox for a $50 million, four-year deal in December of 2003.

Major League Baseball, seeking to compensate for its error six years ago in not acknowledging Hispanic players on its All-Century Team, conducts fan balloting in 2005 to select a Latin legends team. Fan votes from August 29 through October 10 are announced before game four of the World Series. The Legends include: first baseman Albert Pujols; second baseman Rod Carew; shortstop Alex Rodriguez; third baseman Edgar Martinez; outfielders Roberto Clemente, Manny Ramirez, and Vladimir Guerrero; pitchers Fernando Valenzuela, Pedro Martinez, Juan Marichal, Mariano Rivera, and catcher Ivan Rodriguez. This year, a record 29.2 percent of opening day players are born outside the U.S., according to *USA Today*, which notes 91 are from the Dominican Republic, which continues to send the most players to American baseball, with 46 from Venezuela, 34 from Puerto Rico, and 18 from Mexico.

Following the conclusion of regular season play, first round match-ups in the playoffs pit the Yankees versus the Angels and Boston versus Chicago in the American League and San Diego versus St. Louis and Houston against Atlanta in the National League. In the division championships, the Los Angeles Angels of Anaheim meet Chicago while St. Louis battles Houston. The victors set to meet in the Fall Classic are the White Sox, who top the Angels

4-1 to play in their first World Series since 1959 (where they lose 4-2 to the former Brooklyn now Los Angeles Dodgers) and the Houston Astros, who eradicate the St. Louis Cardinals 5-1 in game six to win the series 4-2 to earn their first World Series appearance in the franchise's 44-year history.

Ending an 88-year drought, the White Sox sweep the series in four games, with a 1-0 triumph in the final game at Houston. The winning run comes home in the eighth inning. Diehard White Sox fans break into an elated "ole, ole, ole, oo-le, oo-le" after the reality sets in. Along the way, the series sets several records. The Sox's five-hour, 14th inning 7-5 victory in game three sets a record for the longest game in the Series history. It's also the first time the championship team is managed by a Venezuelan, the irascible Ozzie Guillen, while Freddy Garcia becomes the first Venezuelan starter to win a World Series game. Unfortunately for Fox TV, the series registers the lowest viewership on record, averaging 17.2 million viewers, according to Nielsen Media Research, a 32 percent decline from last year's Boston-St. Louis series. Offsetting the national decline, the series plays well in both hometowns. No surprise there.

Four days after the series ends, the baseball world is saddened by the death of Al Lopez, 97, the enervating catcher-turned-manager of the White Sox and Cleveland Indians, October 30 in a hospital in Tampa, Florida. He'd been hospitalized two days earlier when he suffers a heart attack. Born Alfonso Ramon Lopez in Tampa, he plays catcher 19 years for Brooklyn, Boston, Pittsburgh, and Cleveland, setting a record of playing in 1,918 games, a mark which lasts until 1987. He's elected to the Baseball Hall of Fame in 1977 as the manager of the Indians from 1951 to 1956 and the White Sox from 1957 to 1965 and from 1968 to 1969, when he resigns for health reasons with a career winning record of 1,422 wins and 1,026 loses. During his tenure, he leads both Cleveland and Chicago to American League titles. He is survived by a son, three grandchildren, and nine great-grandchildren.

Vic Power, an award-winning first baseman, the first black Puerto Rican to be signed by the New York Yankees in October of

1953, traded to the Philadelphia Athletics two months later in a 10-player trade, and who plays for six teams during his 12 years in the majors, dies of cancer November 29 in Bayamón, Puerto Rico. He's 78. Power, along with Ruben Gomez, a New York Giants pitcher, are the first Puerto Rican players in the majors in 1953. A native of Arecibo, the Yankees bring him up from their Kansas City Blues minor league team after he bats 0.349 that season. During a career in which he's known for always catching the ball with a one-handed swipe, he plays for the Kansas City Athletics when the Philadelphia team moves to that city in 1955, the Cleveland Indians from 1958 to 1961, the Minnesota Twins, 1962 to 1964, the Philadelphia Phillies in 1964 and the California Angels from 1964 to 1965 after which he retires. A winner of seven straight Golden Glove awards from 1958 to 1964, he also becomes the first player in the American League since 1927 to steal home twice in the eighth and tenth innings in the Indians 10-9 victory over the Detroit Tigers.

On a happier note of achievement, Angel pitcher Bartolo Colon is named the American League Cy Young Award winner, the team's first recipient since Dean Chance wins the honor in 1964. Finishing second in the voting by the Baseball Writers Association of America is Yankee relief pitcher Mario Rivera, followed by Minnesota Twin left-hander Johan Santana, the 2004 Cy Young winner. The scribes also name Alex Rodriguez, the Yankees' third baseman, the American League's most valuable player. His 48 homers breaks Joe DiMaggio's 68-year-old team record of 46 home runs by a right-handed batter. It's Rodriguez's second MVP, having won the award in 2003 in his final season as shortstop with the Texas Rangers. Coming in second is David Ortiz, the designated hitter with the Boston Red Sox, followed by Vladimir Guerrero, an Angel outfielder. Named the AL's manager of the year is Ozzie Guillen of the World Series champion Chicago White Sox. In National League voting, Albert Pujols, the St. Louis Cardinals first baseman, wins his first most valuable player award.

In 2006, the New York Mets, the runaway champions in the National League Eastern Division, sparked by a Latino general manager and a bevy of Hispanic players, are poised to face off against the American League East's champions, the dreaded New York Yankees crosstown rivals in the playoff battle leading into the World Series. The Met's lineup is a result of general manager Omar Minaya's talent searches during the past two years turning the perennial last place finishers into the hottest team in the National League in '06, notes *Time* magazine. Having become baseball's first Hispanic general manager in 2002 with the dismal Montreal Expos, Minaya, 47, goes on a talent buying spree when he joins the Mets and in 2003 snares Toronto's Carlos Delgado, and in 2004 signs two players to top dollar contracts, free agent pitcher Pedro Martinez ($53 million in a four-year deal) followed by Carlos Beltran of the Houston Astros ($119 million for seven years). Minaya also brings to the New York market three players performing below their potential, leadoff hitter Jose Reyes, second baseman Jose Valentin and outfielder Endy Chavez. If the Mets win the World Series, it'll be their first title in 20 years.

Looking to the future end of the 46-year-old U.S. trade embargo against Cuba, the *New York Times* reports on April 26, 2007, that Major League Baseball is contemplating a multi-pronged program to re-establish relations between the two nations. Baseball is looking at building training schools similar to those in the Dominican Republic leading to the signing of players, and possibly moving a minor league team to the Island nation 90 miles from Miami. Cuba operates a 16-team national league whose 90 game season runs from November to April. Pro baseball's ties to Cuba go back to the 1900s, including the Brooklyn Dodgers training there in the '30s and '40s and the Washington Senators forming a minor league team there in 1946, according to the paper.

Major League Soccer, sensing growth potential, stretches its tentacles throughout the year to meet the potential of new Hispanic fans in new locations in the U.S.

With 10 teams comprising the league in 2004, MLS announces two additions, Chivas USA, a new team formed expressly for the U.S. by the powerhouse Chivas club of Guadalajara, Mexico, and its owner Jorge Vergara, which will play at the Carson, California, Home Depot locale of the L.A. Galaxy on alternate weekends and a franchise for Salt Lake City to be operated by a group of investors, including the former president of the Utah Jazz and the New York Knicks of the NBA, Dave Checketts. The Real Salt Lake team will play its first several seasons at Rice-Eccles Stadium, home to the University of Utah's football squad. Both teams will debut in 2005, picking up the void left by the closure in 2002 of the financially troubled Miami and Tampa Bay teams.

In a flurry of new construction in 2004, the Chicago Fire, D.C. United, FC Dallas, New York/New Jersey MetroStars, and San Jose Earthquakes all plan to build new stadiums. While they are all operated by the Anschutz Entertainment Group (AEG), both D.C. and San Jose are also up for sale. In December of 2005, AEG relocates San Jose to Houston, with the hope of finding a new owner. The team's new name, Houston 1836, doubly offends Hispanic fans. The date reflects Texas' secession from Mexico, while the team's logo shows Sam Houston leading his attack on horseback against Mexican troops, notes the *Houston Chronicle* and the *Los Angeles Times*. Bowing to public displeasure the league renames the team the Dynamo, which will play its first three years at the University of Houston's Robertson Stadium.

The Chicago Fires' $70 million, 20,000 to 25,000 seat venue in suburban Bridgeview, Illinois, should be completed by the start of the 2006 season. The 60-acre site located 12 miles southwest of downtown Chicago, will be the permanent home for the Fires but will also be used for international and National Collegiate Athletic Association (NCAA) matches. The team continucs to use Soldier Field until its new stadium, team offices, and training fields are ready.

The renamed FC Dallas, formerly the Dallas Burn, is scheduled to move into its soccer-specific stadium in Frisco in 2005, being built by its owner the Hunt Sports Group. D.C. United also plans constructing a 24,000 seat with luxury boxes, training fields, and facilities one mile from RFK stadium along the Anacostia River. It'll use RFK with the transplanted Montreal Expos, now the Washington

Nationals, until its own stadium is completed by the 2007 projected date. AEG plans building a stadium in Harrison, New Jersey, for the MetroStars as part of an entertainment/shopping complex, with a completion date of 2006.

AEG completes its $150 million Home Depot Center in Carson, California, in 2003, which houses the Los Angeles Galaxy and U.S. national teams and will now be the home for the new Chivas USA franchise.

While baseball seems the favorite sport for defecting Cuban athletes, two former members of Cuba's national soccer team, Alberto Delgado and Rey Angel Martinez, are today stars with the Colorado Rapids. In 2002, while in Los Angeles for an international Gold Cup competition, the pair travel to Miami where Martinez has relatives. In 2004, Martinez, 23, tries out first for the Rapids and makes his debut last June, to become the first Cuban player in the league. Two weeks later, Delgado, 26, his pal in Havana, joins him on the team. MLS teams field both American and foreign Hispanics.

When the MLS All Star game takes place in July and is televised by ABC, Hispanics comprise only four starting positions of the 22 fielded by the East and West teams. These elite starters include Carlos Ruiz and Andreas Herzog of Los Angeles for the West and Jaime Moreno of D.C. and Amado Guevara of New York/New Jersey for the East.

As for Chivas USA, its management stresses the team will reach out to Mexican-American fans. However, because of MLS rules limiting the number of foreign players each team can have, Chivas USA will have a Mexican coach and fill its foreign player needs exclusively with Mexicans while the rest of the roster will consist of Americans. The team also notes all players will speak Spanish. Founded in 1906, the parent Mexican team is the only one in its Mexican league whose roster is comprised exclusively of Mexican players, while other clubs employ players from Central and South America.

In a surprise move, Chivas USA eschews Mexico and names instead as coach 47-year-old Dutch-born Thomas Rongen, former coach with the Tampa Bay Mutiny, New England Revolution, D.C. United, and the United States' Under-20 men's team. Rongen's shortcoming of not speaking Spanish fluently is noted by the Spanish media.

Chivas USA's entry into the Los Angeles area market is cleared by the Galaxy-owned AEG, which commissions a study indicating there are enough Mexicans to support two teams and thus create a rivalry.

The American team's first signings, Mexican soccer legend Ramon Ramirez, Martin Zuniga, and Francisco Palencia are all from the parent club. Fellow countrymen Isaac Romo and Alonso Sandoval add additional Mexican flavor.

During the league's expansion draft, Rongen's signings include Arturo Torres and Ezra Hendrickson from the Galaxy; Orlando Perez from Chicago; Francisco Gomez from Kansas City; Antonio De La Torre from Colorado; Thiago Martins from D.C. United (a Brazilian who speaks Portuguese, not Spanish); and English speakers Matt Taylor from UCLA and Craig Ziadie from Jamaica. Joining the team in 2005 are Costa Rican Douglas Sequeira, whose Saprissa club loans him to the upstart unit for one year, and two Mexican players from the Galaxy, Jesus Ochoa and Antonio Martinez.

In February of 2005, when the league makes a historic move to expand team rosters to 28 players by adding 10 reserves, Chivas USA's signings include Javier Barragan, a California State Dominguez goalkeeper. It's the first roster expansion in the league's 10-year history. One month later, it appears Chivas USA is not getting off to a healthy start. With two players injured, three decide to leave including Ramon Ramirez, named the team's captain and defensive midfielder. He leaves the team because of visa problems in timely bringing his children's nanny to the U.S.

With three players gone, Chivas signs Ryan Suarez, a defender with the Galaxy only to discover that one week after leaving the team, Ramirez regrets his decision and wants to be reinstated. A meeting is held with co-owner Antonio Cue, recognizing Suarez will help sell tickets, welcomes him back.

Team maven Cue is a Mexican millionaire with real estate holdings, and no soccer experience. His partner, Jorge Vergara, 50, is equally wealthy. He's born in Guadalajara, and knows the excitement of competition by playing goalie, succeeds enough financially to own a soccer team in Costa Rica and buys out the majority of the 196 investors in the financially troubled Guadalajara-headquartered Chivas team for an estimated $120 million, reveals the *Los Angeles Times Magazine*.

Vergara's purchase of the Chivas USA's franchise costs $26.5, with $12 million going to the AEG for territorial rights to the L.A. market and the remainder for its expansion fee. The team is his latest foray into entertainment. He forms Anbelo Productions in 1999 with director Alfonso Cuaron. Their collaboration produces the hit Spanish-language film, *Y Tu Mamá También*. Cuaron's successes also include *Harry Potter and the Prisoner of Azkaban*. In 2004, Anbelo releases the *The Assassination of Richard Nixon* starring Sean Penn, which is followed by *Crónicas*, starring John Leguizamo in his initial Spanish-language film.

Vergara's optimism anent his U.S. soccer project is based on Major League Soccer's projection that Hispanics comprise 50 percent of its fans. Among immigrants, soccer represents a link to their past, as evidenced by the huge turnouts at the Los Angeles Coliseum for matches between Latin teams, especially from neighboring Mexico. Chivas USA promotes its presence with a slogan which substitutes fútbol for soccer, asserting its presence in words all Hispanics can appreciate: Adios soccer, el fútbol esta aqui. Which translated may be anathema to kids playing the game, their parents and U.S. born soccer fans: "Goodbye soccer, fútbol is here."

The second expansion team, Real Salt Lake, signs one Hispanic, Pablo Brenes from the New York/New Jersey MetroStars, among its 10 choices.

When the league's ninth season ends, Amado Guevara of the MetroStars is named most valuable player one day prior to the MLS ninth Cup championship contest in November in which D.C. United defeats the Kansas City Wizards, 3-2 before 25,797 at the Home

Depot Center. It's the fourth win for D.C. United. D.C.'s 24-man championship roster is led by 15-year-old rookie phenomenon Freddy Adu.

Previous MLS Cup winners include: San Jose, 2003; Los Angeles, 2002; San Jose, 2001; Kansas City, 2000; D.C. United, 1999; Chicago, 1998; and D.C. United, 1997 and 1996.

In what's called a groundbreaking TV deal by AEG, both Chivas USA and the L.A. Galaxy matches will be televised locally next year on the Fox Sports Network's FSN West and FSN West 2.

A labor dispute between U.S. Soccer and the U.S. National Team Players' Association which is mediated by the federal government in January of 2005, results in the players agreeing not to strike in return for an immediate wage hike, which also clears the way for the U.S. coach Bruce Arena to select his 25 players for the final round of qualifying play of the North and Central American and Caribbean (CONCACAF) competition for the 2006 World Cup against Trinidad and Tobago, Mexico, Guatemala, Panama, and Costa Rico between February 9 and October 13. On the U.S. national team, which knocks out Panama and Jamaica, six of the players are competing for the first time on the national team, while all 11 have never played together as a unit. Mexico shows its favored status among U.S. resident Mexicans by beating Ecuador, 2-1 before an ecstatic crowd of 41,812 at Giants Stadium in East Rutherford, New Jersey, and Guatemala, 2-0 before an appreciate crowd of 21,000 at the San Antonio Alamodome. Mexico's coach Ricardo Lavolpe uses many players from 2004's Athens Olympic team to secure victory in the two matches.

In 2005, the U.S. continues its winning ways, beating Colombia 3-0, at California State Fullerton's Titan Stadium and then Honduras 1-0 at University Stadium in Albuquerque in the final warm-up matches. In its World Cup qualifying games, the USA defeats Trinidad and Tobago 2-1 and loses to Mexico in Mexico City, 2-1 in the thin 7,200-foot altitude at Azteca Stadium before close to 110,000 fans. On the more oxygen-available Legion Stadium in

Birmingham, Alabama, and with coach Arena reshuffling his lineup after the embarrassing loss to Mexico, the U.S. shuts out Guatemala 2-0.

The Americans also face a second shot at Costa Rica, Panama, Mexico, Guatemala, and Panama and a single match against Trinidad and Tobago between June and October in additional qualifying matches. In the winnowing-out process, the U.S. triumphs over Costa Rica 3-0 in Salt Lake City, Panama in Panama City 3-0 and Trinidad and Tobago 1-0 in Hartford, Connecticut, while Mexico defeats Guatemala and Trinidad and Tobago 2-0 and Costa Rica 2-0 to lead the six teams in the CONCACAF regional playoffs. And when the USA and Mexico meet in their crucial showdown September 3 in Columbus, Ohio, in what's being called the most important match between the two teams since the 2002 World Cup, the USA shuts out Mexico 2-0. The victory qualifies the Americans for the World Cup for the fifth straight time.

In its next game, the U.S. and Guatemala play to a 0-0 tie in Guatemala City. Rebounding from its loss to the U.S., Mexico shuts out Panama 5-0 in Mexico City to clinch its World Cup slot.

Although the spotlight is naturally focused on the U.S. and Mexican teams' travails, Costa Rica's 3-1 defeat of Cuba in Seattle in July, produces the first political firestorm of the competition in this country. After playing in two games, Cuba's Maikel Galindo begins the process of asking for asylum in the U.S. Following Cuba's 4-1 loss to the U.S., Galindo scores a tying goal against Costa Rica two days later, but it's not enough to fire up his team to victory. Costa Rica advances to the Cup by defeating the U.S. 3-0 at San Jose to join the U.S. and Mexico as CONCACAF's qualifiers for the 2006 World Cup.

On the league level, as MLS teams gear up for the 2005 season, Costa Rican national team member Pablo Chinchilla joins the L.A. Galaxy and is reunited with Steve Sampson, his coach with the Costa Rican team from 2002 to 2004. With the media spotlight shining on Chivas USA, the team loses its first exhibition game to the

San Jose Earthquakes, 3-0, March 5, 2005, on its home field, the Home Depot Center. A few weeks later, the team trades its leading player, Carlos Ruiz, a Guatemalan striker to FC Dallas to make room for Landon Donovan, a star on the U.S. national team, who's been playing in a German league and was previously the MLS' U.S. player of the year for three of his four seasons with San Jose during its championship years of 2001 and 2003.

Ruiz is the Galaxy's leading scorer during his three seasons with the club, accounting for the lone goal in the team's 1-0 victory over the New England Revolution to gain its first league championship in 2002.

Reflecting on the new season, commissioner Don Garber feels the league is in the best shape of its existence, he boasts to the *Los Angeles Times*. In August, FC Dallas opens its soccer-designed stadium on time in Frisco, Texas, where the league's championship cup match will be played November 13. MLS' reserve league utilizing players not on their first team's roster will play a six-home, six-away schedule. With the addition of Chivas USA and Real Salt Lake, the Kansas City Wizards move to the Eastern Conference from the Western League. The realignment now has the Eastern Conference consisting of the Chicago Fire, Columbus Crew, D.C. United, Kansas City Wizards, MetroStars, and New England Revolution. The Western Conference conferees include Chivas USA, Colorado Rapids, FC Dallas, Galaxy, Real Salt Lake, and the San Jose Earthquakes. Title defenders D.C. United will play its games at RFK Stadium along with the Washington Nationals new baseball team until each team's own stadium is constructed.

During the new season, MLS games will be given the greatest TV coverage in its history. ESPN2 will air 26 games, ESPN Deportes 11 to 12; ABC TV 3; 20 to 30 on Fox Sports En Español; 25 to 30 on the renamed Fox Soccer Channel (formerly Fox Sports World); and 28 on the HD Network. International matches will also come into American homes via Univision, Telemundo, Azteca America, Gol TV,

ESPN2, ESPN Deportes, and ABC, the latter three offering World Cup coverage. ABC and its ESPN and ESPN2 sister cable channels will televise all 64 Gold Cup games from Germany live from June 9 to July 19 and in high definition television. The games will be shown at better times than in the past since Germany has a six-hour time difference with the East Coast.

The Chivas expansion team with its Mexican pedigree is looked upon by the league as the door opener for other international teams. Garber indicates MLS is looking further beyond U.S. borders. In November of 2005, the league admits Toronto as its 13th team and its first Canadian franchise, with play commencing in 2007.

On opening day of 2005, the two expansion teams defuse all the hype; Chivas USA loses 2-0 to champions D.C. United, while Real Salt Lake plays to a 0-0 tie with the MetroStars in New Jersey on a rainy, wind-swept field. In its home field debut, Real Salt Lake gains its first league win, 1-0 over the Colorado Rapids. A disappointingly low crowd of 18,493 fills the 27,000-seat Home Depot Center to watch Chivas USA lose to D.C. United 2-0 on April 2, the day Pope John Paul II dies, and the parent club's Mexican National League match against Puebla is televised on Univision one hour before the American expansion team's contest begins. These are two possible reasons for the low attendance at the Chivas match. Looking for its first victory, Chivas USA faces the San Jose Earthquakes on its home turf at Spartan Stadiums and winds up with a 3-3 tie and its first goal in the team's short history after three minutes of play.

When Chivas USA finally meets the Galaxy three weeks later on both their home field at the Carson Home Depot Center, L.A. dominates 3-1. After four games, Chivas has a dismal 0-3-1 record while the more seasoned Galaxy is 2-1-0. In its next match against the Eastern Conference leading New England Revolution, Chivas USA loses again, 1-0, at Gillette Stadium in Foxboro, Massachusetts. To its credit, Chivas USA holds the league's highest-scoring team scoreless until the 88th minute of the 90-minute contest when the winning goal is recorded. Chivas finally tastes victory against the league's other expansion team, Real Salt Lake, 1-0 before 10,893 home fans at the Home Depot Center. The goal is recorded on a penalty kick by Hector Cuadros at the 39-minute point in the contest. Following loses to the Colorado Rapids 2-1 at Denver and Western conference leader FC Dallas, 5- 2 at home, Chivas remains in the loss column with an 1-7-1 record.

Despite free ducats to fans 50 and older at the Dallas game, attendance keeps dropping for the third straight home match. The loss coupled with the attendance of 8,977 results in a meeting between the club's president and co-owner Cue and coach Rongen. And when Chivas meets its L.A. neighbors, the Galaxy on their dual home field for the second time, Chivas loses 2-0 before 20,916, its highest home crowd of the season. With a record of 1-8-1, team co-owner Cue replaces coach Rongen in June with another veteran Dutch coach, 56-year-old Hans Westerhoff, who remains the director of football for all three of Chivas co-owner Jorge Vergara's three teams, Chivas De Guadalajara, Chivas USA, and Saprissa, the Costa Rican champions. He is also the former coach of the parent Mexican Team as well as four teams in the Netherlands. Rongen, who formerly coaches the Tampa Bay Mutiny, New England Revolution, and D.C. United, is named the club's sporting director.

One day after the coaching change announcement, but without Westerhoff, Chivas, playing at home ties the Kansas City Wizards 1-1 before 7,558, to improve its record to 1-8-2. The tying goal is made on a free kick by Ramon Ramirez, a former member of Mexico's national team, who scores his first goal in the MLS. In its next match under the direction of Westerhoff, the team loses to the Chicago Fire 5-2 at Chicago's Soldier Field to alter its record to 1-9-3. Following the debacle, Westerhoff is downtrodden by the team's overall performance, and admits he's working on bringing in new players. But not before the team ties San Jose 1-1 at home. It's the two teams' second tie since April when the game ends 3-3. Then the Colorado Rapids take Chivas for a bumpy ride, 3-1 on its home field, followed by FC Dallas' 2-1 home victory.

Following losses to the Kansas City Wizards 3-0 and to the Chicago Fire 1-0, the hapless newcomers record is 1-13. After 17 games of the 32-match season, Chivas has given up a league high of 39 goals and remains entrenched in last place in the Western Conference. Amidst this dismal environment, the team releases two defenders, Ryan Suarez and Alfonso Loera. Suarez is dropped after a verbal exchange with coach Westerhoff following the team's 3-0 whitewash by Kansas City. He is quickly signed by the MetroStars. Loera, one of the original Mexican players sent to the team by its parent club, departs in a contract renewal dispute, according to the *Los Angeles Times*. In its second match against Salt Lake, Chivas romps again, 5-1 for its second victory of the season, which ends its 11 winless game streak to up its record to 2-13-3. Unfortunately in its next game against the Galaxy on their joint home field, Chivas loses 2-0 while the Galaxy ends a six-game losing streak. In its next match, Chivas edges past the New England Revolution 1-0 at home to raise its record to 3-14-3, but its key midfielder, Hector Cuadros is injured when he collides with the Revolution's Joe Franchino, receives a head injury, collapses after the game and is removed on a stretcher and taken to a nearby hospital by ambulance. He is subsequently diagnosed with a grade two concussion and undergoes a CT scan. This latest win is Chivas' first against an established league team, following its two victories over Real Salt Lake, the second new franchise. In their third match-up, Salt Lake edges past Chivas 2-1 to improve its mark to 5-11-4 while Chivas falls to 3-15-3.

In a bit of clever planning aimed at really luring Southern Californian Hispanics who are losing or have already lost faith in the new Chivas USA franchise, there will be two Chivas teams on the same bill. Instead of playing its final game against the Galaxy October 8 at the Home Depot Center, the MLS game will be the opening match August 10 at the Los Angeles Coliseum, followed by Chivas' parent, Chivas of Guadalajara, facing its rival, Mexico City's Club America. The doubleheader attracts a crowd of 88,816—the second largest for an MLS game—in which the Galaxy defeats Chivas USA

1-0 in the opening game on Landon Donovan's conversion of a penalty kick into the winning score after 83 minutes. In the all-Mexican nightcap exhibition, Club America bests the Mexican Chivas 2-1. The largest crowd to view an MLS game is the 92,216 that crams into the Rose Bowl in Pasadena to view a doubleheader featuring the Galaxy versus Tampa Bay and the U.S. against Mexico on June 16, 1996, according to the *Los Angeles Times*.

Following its defeat by the Galaxy, Chivas drops its match against D.C. United 3-0 at RFK Stadium in Washington in 119-degree heat, to lower its record to 3-7-3. Chivas has now been shutout nine times, including its opening 2-0 loss to D.C. United April 2 and remains winless on the road. It does, however, tie its next two consecutive games against the MetroStars (3- 3) at Giants Stadium in East Rutherford, New Jersey, to end the Stars' eight-game winning streak, and FC Dallas (2-2) in Fresno, Texas. But in its next two games, it continues its losing ways on the road with similar 3-0 white washes by the Columbus Crew and by the San Jose Earthquakes. Playing its next two games at home, Chivas loses 2-1 to the first place Earthquakes on late goals by the visitors, and is stymied for the second time by the Colorado Rapids 3-1. As the season nears its end, Chivas, entrenched in last place in the Western division, edges past Columbus, the Eastern division's bottom team, 1-0 in Ohio, ties Colorado 1-1 in Denver and loses its final game at home, 2-0 to the MetroStars to close its first season at 4-22-6, the worst record in the league. In a postmortem, Antonio Cue, the team's chief honcho admits to the *Los Angeles Times* he will change "30 percent of the team" and seek "physically and mentally strong players" to aggressively compete in the "very physical league."

In his first major postseason reshuffle, Cue hires MLS veteran coach Bob Bradley, 47, to replace Holland's Hans Westerhoff. Despite hiring an American coach, Cue says the team "is going to continue having a Mexican heart and a Mexican identity," according to the *Times*, with the caveat, "We are going to look at players from Mexico, from MLS and from other countries as well" as part of his plan to be more competitive.

Salt Lake, besides being bested twice by Chivas, is also having problems in its fledgling season. After debuting with a 0-0 tie against the MetroStars in New Jersey, losing at Los Angeles to the Galaxy 3-1 and winning its home debut 1-0 against the Colorado Rapids, the team goes on a downward skid. After losing at Dallas 3-0, tying San Jose 2-2 at home, losing at Los Angeles to Chivas USA 1-0, it then beats both the Los Angeles Galaxy 2-1 and Chivas 2-0 at home. And then loses five straight, to Columbus 2-0, Chicago 3-0, FC Dallas 2-0, Los Angeles 1-0, and San Jose 3-0. Another meeting with the Galaxy produces a 1-1 tie, followed by 3-1 loss to Chicago, and a 2-2 tie with the MetroStars. With its second loss to Chivas and a 3-2 defeat by Kansas City, its record stands at 3-11-4, but it improves when it beats FC Dallas 3-0 at home to end its 10—game losing streak, and improve its record to 4-11-4. With a 2-1 victory over Chivas and 10 straight losses to New England 4-1, Kansas City 4-2, San Jose 1-0, D.C. United 5-1, New England 1-0, FC Dallas 2-1, Colorado 2-0, Columbus 2-1, Colorado again 2-1, D.C. United 3-1, a 2-2 tie with San Jose, and a 1-0 loss to Colorado, Salt Lake's debut record closes out at 5-22-5. The team ends up in fifth place, one level ahead of Chivas USA.

One possible factor contributing to the Salt Lake losses is the absence of two key players who are competing for their U.S. and Jamaican national teams in the CONCACAF Gold Cup playoffs. This is a major problem impacting the league, which sees the depletion of team rosters as top players join their national squads playing through the playoff rounds leading up to next year's World Cup in Germany.

The MLS' championship in November is a rematch of the 2002 title battle between the Los Angeles Galaxy and the New England Revolution, with the same result: a 1-0 overtime victory for the Galaxy, giving it its second league title. In the match contested at Pizza Hut Park in Frisco, Guatemala's Guillermo Ramirez comes off the bench to score the winning goal in the 67th minute of the game, or 17 minutes into overtime. For his efforts, the 27-year-old is named the MLS Cups' most valuable player. During regular season play, the

Revolution finishes with a 17-7-8 record to the Galaxy's 13-13-6 mark. The team's two regular season games end in 1-1 ties. In the playoffs, the Galaxy defeats the Colorado Rapids to win the Western Conference title while New England bests the Chicago Fire to snare the Eastern Conference crown.

The further internationalization of the MLS is underscored in July by the revelations of Don Garber, the league's commissioner, who says in his state of the league address prior to the All Star game that the 12-team league is looking to expand to 18 teams, starting in 2007 with its Toronto franchise, according to the *Los Angeles Times*.

Running almost parallel to the MLS season, the Lamar Hunt U.S. Open Cup, the nation's oldest soccer tournament for pro and amateur teams, winds its way towards the championship. The L.A. Galaxy playing at home, defeats FC Dallas 1-0 for the title, following its MLS loss to Dallas 4-1 one week earlier. Herculez Gomez's decisive goal in the championship gives the Galaxy its second Cup title since 2001. He also scores two goals in the quarterfinal victory over San Jose 2-1 and in his team's 5-2 romp over the Minnesota Thunder in the semifinals. The Galaxy advances to the quarterfinals by whipping Chivas USA 3-2, which earlier beats the Charlotte Eagles of the United Soccer League 3-2 in initial Open Cup competition.

As the league prepares for its 11th season opener April 1, 2006, its sights are set on new franchises and the construction of soccer stadiums. Multiple club operator, AEG sells its MetroStars franchise to an Australian businessman for $50 million plus, who renames the team the New York Red Bulls. AEG still operates the L.A. Galaxy, Chicago Fire, D.C. United, and the Houston Dynamo. The MetroStars sale is part of the MLS plan to have multiple team owners decrease their holdings, league commissioner Don Graber informs the *Los Angeles Times*, adding the plan is to have single team owners in the years to come. Two additional expansion teams are planned for somewhere in the Midwest in 2008 and in the Philadelphia suburb of Glassboro, New Jersey, in 2009, with a possible team returning to Northern California to replace the San Jose Earthquakes which moves to Houston in 2006. New soccer-specific stadiums will bow this year in Chicago, followed by new venues in Colorado and Toronto in 2007, New York in 2008, and Salt Lake by either 2008 or 2009.

Following a dramatic 2006 MLS Cup championship won by the new Houston Dynamo 4-3 against the New England Revolution on penalty kicks following the teams 1-1 tie in regulation and overtime, the league opens its 12th season in April of 2007 with both optimism and uncertainty. Optimism because of the presence of European superstar David Becckham signed to the L.A. Galaxy, major national and regional TV coverage for the first time of its 195 games and seven of the now 13 teams, including new entry Toronto, playing in their own soccer stadiums. Uncertainty for the new season due to the reported 10 of last year's 12 teams having lost money.

In the world of boxing, crucial victories are overshadowed by critical injuries and death in 2005, following a deathless 2004.

Oscar De La Hoya, the "Golden Boy" as he's called, loses a lot of his luster in his attempt to dominate the middleweight division while a number of lesser-known Latino fighters win championships in lesser weight divisions.

De La Hoya, heavily involved in his boxing promotion career and also delving into a boxing reality series for Fox TV, which turns out to be an utter failure, is the World Boxing Organization's (WBO) middleweight champ when he goes up against the undisputed 160-pound World Boxing Council (WBC) middleweight title holder Bernard "Bernie" Hopkins, who knocks him out in the ninth round at the Las Vegas MGM Grand Arena in September of 2004.

Still smarting from this defeat, De La Hoya in February of 2005 tells the *Los Angeles Times* he seeks one more fight because: "I can't go out with that defeat," he says. Following a 20-month layoff, De La Hoya wins the World Boxing Council super-welterweight title May 6, 2006 by stopping defending champ Ricardo Mayorga at 1:25 in the sixth round at the MGM Grand Garden Arena in Las Vegas.

Seeking to retain his World Boxing Council super-welterweight championship against unbeaten Floyd Mayweather Jr. on May 5, 2007, 34-year-old De La Hoya loses a split decision to the 30-year-old before a sellout crowd of 16,200 at the MGM Grand Garden in Las Vegas. The loudly booed decision based on Mayweather's winning four of the last five rounds in the 12-round contest, earns the new champ an unblemished 38-0 record, while De La Hoya emerges with a 38-5 resume, and five loses in his last 10 bouts after 15 years as a professional. In what's called a Cinco De Mayo battle, a Latin aura permeats the event, with Mayweather entering the arena wearing a Mexican sombrero, a robe emblazoned with the Mexican red, green, and white colors, while his handlers wear T-shirts with the slogan "Mayweather loves Mexico"; De La Hoya makes his entrance to the sounds of Mexican music, and crossover star Marc Anthony sings the National Anthem.

As the defending champ, whose Golden Boy Productions promotes the fight, De La Hoya earns $50 million plus based on his share of the gate, pay-per-view, closed-circuit and sponsor merchandising. Mayweather's take is around $20 million. In addition, the fight's gate is a record $19 million, based on tickets costing $150–$2,000, with an additional 28,000 closed-circuit seats sold at $50 at seven MGM–Mirage-owned hotels in Las Vegas, plus an additional 2,000 locations around the U.S. And if that's not enough, the HBO pay-per-view telecast to 176 countries generates a record $120 million based on a record 2.15 million buys. According to the *Los Angeles Times* the previous PPV buy record for a single fight is 1.99 million in 1997 for the second Mike Tyson-Evander Holyfield match, while the previous PPV revenue record is $112 million for the 2002 Mike Tyson–Lennox Lewis battle.

According to final punching statistics, De La Hoya throws 587 and lands 122, while Mayweather throws 481 punches and connects with 207. After the fight, De La Hoya is uncertain of his fighting future, while Mayweather says he's retiring, a status some writers question since a rematch will be a goldmine event.

Boxing, while important for his ego, is one aspect of the budding Golden Boy business empire for the son of Mexican immigrants who settle in East Los Angeles. Among its activities are the four-year-old Golden Boy Promotions, which has 18 fighters under contract, and will present 30 cards in six states this year, including 24 on TV; Golden Boy Partners, a real estate investment company which allocates $100 million over three years with partner John Long for projects in inner city Latino communities principally in California; interests in Spanish-language newspapers in Los Angeles, New York, and Chicago, and the Oscar De La Hoya Foundation, which provides financial assistance to charities dealing with the Los Angeles Hispanic community.

The 31-year-old fighter from East L.A. who turns pro after winning a gold medal in the 1992 Olympics, subsequently wins the super lightweight (130 pounds), super welterweight (135), welterweight (140), junior middleweight (147), and middleweight (154 pound) titles. During his journey, De La Hoya triumphs over Wilfredo Rivera, Hector Camacho, Jr., Julio Cesar Chavez (in his 100th professional fight), Pernell Whitaker, Arturo Gatti, Javier Castillejo, Felix Sturm, and loses to Felix Trinidad, Sugar Shane Mosley, and Bernard Hopkins.

In other key events:

In the peaceful environment of the International Boxing Hall of Fame, two-time World Boxing Council featherweight champion Bobby Chacon is among its 15 inductees. His crowns are attained in the featherweight category from 1974 to 1975 and as the super-featherweight champion from 1982 to 1983. The California-born fighter's attempt at a third title in 1984 is squashed by World Boxing Association lightweight titleholder Ray "Boom Boom" Mancini. Chacon's career-ending record is 59 wins, seven losses, one tie, and 47 knockouts.

After two years out of the ring, Puerto Rican former welterweight, junior middleweight and middleweight champion Felix "Tito" Trinidad's comeback sees him knock out Nicaragua's Ricardo Mayorga in the eighth round at Madison Square Garden. Trinidad's followers wave Puerto Rican flags during the match while shouting his nickname.

Jose Luis Castillo, the World Boxing Council lightweight champion, gains a split decision over Joel Casamayor at the Mandalay Bay Events Center in Las Vegas in December. In defense of his World Boxing Council lightweight title on March 5, 2005, Castillo defeats Julio Diaz, who incurs injuries to both eyes, resulting in a technical knockout in the 10th round at the Mandalay Bay Events Center in Las Vegas. With the victory, the Mexicali, Mexico, fighter's record stands at 52-6-1 with 46 knockouts, and his next opponent stands to be Diego Corrales, the World Boxing Organization's lightweight titleholder. When the two meet in a punching battle for the unified lightweight championship May 7, 2005, Corrales emerges from a devastating punishment in the 10th round by Castillo to rally and counterpunch his way to victory as the referee stops the fight at 2:06 of the round at the Mandalay Bay Events Center. Entering the battle, Corrales is 40-2-33 while his opponent's record is 52-7-1. In the semi-main event, Mexico's Juan Manuel Marquez, the defending World Boxing Association (WBA) and International Boxing Federation (IBF) featherweight titleholder, wins a unanimous decision over Colombia's Victor Polo.

In their follow-up slugfest on October 8, Castillo, who weighs in three-and-a-half pounds overweight, stops Corrales 47 seconds in the fourth round of their 12-round battle at Las Vegas' Thomas Mack Arena. In an odd way, Castillo's weight allows Corrales to retain his World Boxing Council and World Boxing Organization lightweight titles since the match is reduced to non-title status.

Fernando "Ferocious" Vargas, the former junior middleweight champion who loses his crown to Oscar De La Hoya in an 11th round TKO in Las Vegas September 14, 2002, returns to the ring after a 15-month break because of a bad back and scores a unanimous 10-round decision over Raymond Joval of the Netherlands in Corpus Christi March 26, 2005, during his HBO televised bout. After his victory, Vargas indicates he wants to return to the light middleweight class and seeks a match with Javier Castillejo, the World Boxing Council's champion. In choosing to fight Vargas in August, Castillejo is stripped of his super-welterweight title by the World Boxing Council for refusing to earlier face challenger Ricardo Mayorga.

In their second bout August 20, Vargas scores a unanimous 10-round decision against Castillejo at the Allstate Arena in Rosemart, Illinois. Following the fight, Vargas admits his loss of 20 pounds to make the 154-pound super-welterweight limit leaves him "sluggish."

Vargas' career is a checkered one. After losing his IBF junior middleweight title to Felix Trinidad on December 2, 2000, in Las Vegas by a TKO in the 12th round, Vargas wins the WBA's junior middleweight crown with a seventh round TKO against Jose "Shibata" Flores in 2001, but loses it to De La Hoya one year later. He's also suspended by Las Vegas boxing officials for testing positive for steroids following the fight.

During 2003, he rebounds from his loss to De La Hoya by beating less formidable opponents Fitz Vanderpool and Tony Marshall, signs that a number of severe body injures inflicted in the ring have healed.

By 2005, Vargas, who grows up in Oxnard, California, sets up his own non-punching business empire, similar to Oscar De La Hoya's out-of-the-ring business enterprises.

Vargas cobbles together a number of business activities in concert with his manager and business manager, which include, according to the *Los Angeles Times*: a clothing company, real estate investment firm, a record label whose first artist is Samuel Hernández, and a boxing management firm handling Daniel Cervantes, a Mexican junior-welterweight. Vargas is also testing the acting waters with a part in the action film *Alpha Dog*.

In his return to the ring on February 25, 2006, Vargas is pummeled enough in his left eye by Shane Mosley that the fight is stopped after one minute, 22 seconds of the tenth round of the junior-middleweight bout at the Mandalay Bay Events Center in Las Vegas. For his TKO loss, and battered shuteye, Vargas earns $4 million.

In a battle for the heavyweight title, before a half-filled Madison Square Garden in New York April 30, 2005, defending World Boxing Association champion John Ruiz loses to James Toney in a unanimous decision after 12 rounds. The loss sends the 33-year-old Ruiz into retirement. There's a strange fiction-to-reality twist to this fight. Four years ago, Toney plays a victorious Joe Frazier defeating Muhammad Ali portrayed by Will Smith in the 2001 hit movie *Ali*. With this real battle, Toney adds his new belt to those already won as middleweight, super-middleweight and cruiserweight champion. Eleven days after he defeats Ruiz, Toney tests positive for the anabolic steroid nandrolone and is suspended for 90 days and fined $10,000 by the New York State Athletic Commission, which declares the bout a no decision. While Toney denies taking the drug, his promoter Dan Goosen is quoted in the *Los Angeles Times* that Toney takes a legal form of cortisone, pregnenolone, that metabolizes into nandrolone, to help with the healing process following surgery for a torn left bicep last September and that he ceases taking the drug in January.

Twelve days later, Toney declines his right to appear before the New York State Athletic Commission. Under World Boxing Association rules, the championship must be given back to Ruiz while Toney is disallowed from fighting for the WBA title for two years. It now appears that Ruiz, who decides to override his retirement decision after his loss and stay active as a boxer, may have made the right call as he is reinstated as the WBA heavyweight champion. Hang on a minute, on July 20 Toney's suspension is lifted by the New York State Athletic Commission when results of his latest urinalysis test come back negative. Asked for a comment on his reinstatement, the *Los Angeles Times* quotes the 36-year-old boxer as saying: "I just want to get into the ring and smash someone."

Dr. Anthony F. "Tony" Daly, a renowned Los Angeles-based sports medicine specialist for nearly 30 years, who's the L.A. Clippers' doctor, the medical director for the U.S. Olympic Committee, and our family orthopedist, is the physician who performs the biceps surgery on Toney. Daly tells the *Times* he's "not surprised to learn he (Toney) tested positive, but I am disappointed. I'm not surprised because of the big weight gain" (he weighs a career record 233 pounds for this fight), adding: "And he looked pretty darn muscular to me." During a coincidental visit to his office a short time later, I ask Daly if he thinks there's steroid use in boxing. "Steroids bulk you up and fighters wouldn't be able to make their weight if they did," he responds while adding, "with the possible exception of heavyweights."

Daly, a member of the California State Athletic Commission, also explains following Toney's surgery that he does a lot of work with boxers, including those signed to Bob Arum's Top Fight Promotions. And that's the reason he's seated with Arum in the front row at the recent Corrales-Castillo slugfest in Las Vegas. In the reception area of his office hangs a large autographed poster of Oscar De La Hoya's December 15, 1997, Madison Square Garden match against James Leija, emphasizing the caliber of athlete he tends to. The poster's tag line reads: "His looks will charm you/his hooks will harm you." "I've seen almost all of Oscar's fights," Daly says, adding: "Now that he's a promoter, I'm seeing his boxers as well." Daly sees around six fights a year in various cities. "If a boxer is hurt I'll see them after the fight," Daly explains, "otherwise they come to me in my office." Daly's first foray into sports medicine occurs in 1962, when as an Army doctor he's assigned to West Point to take care of the football team during its Fall season.

At another fight Dr. Daly attends a few weeks later in L.A., one fighter is critically injured, a legendary father wins his "farewell" match and his son is triumphant on a card at the Staples Center on May 28.

Mexico's revered Julio Cesar Chavez, 42, who has fought only three times since being knocked out in 2000 by Kostya Tszyu, defeats fellow super-lightweight Ivan Robinson, 34, in a unanimous decision to boost his 25-year career record to 107-5-2, including 88 knockouts.

Chavez's son, 19-year-old Julio, Jr., shows his mettle in a preliminary bout with a first round knockout of fellow lightweight Adam Wynant to boost his career record to 20-0, including 14 knockouts. Wynant is so pounded by Chavez, Jr. in the first 42 seconds of the opening round of the scheduled six rounds, that he voluntarily drops to the canvas and the referee ends the contest.

In a late afternoon second match on the 10-fight card seen by a few of the crowd of 17,692 who will eventually cheer Mexico's greatest fighter the senior Chavez in victory, 32-year-old Ruben Contreras from Ciudad Juarez, Mexico, suffers a seizure moments after being pummeled by Hawaii's rising star Brian Viloria, 24, in the sixth round. Contreras stops fighting, according to the *Los Angeles Times* coverage and walks to his corner 55 seconds into the round of the scheduled eight-round match, with bleeding from his mouth and nose. After indicating to the referee he cannot go on, the unbeaten Viloria is awarded a technical knockout victory. While still in his corner, Contreras complains in Spanish of double vision and of a headache in the back of his head, and while leaving the ring tells his trainer Ruben Gomez, according to the newspaper, "I feel like I'm going to pass out."

And then he suffers the seizure, is treated by paramedics stationed at the venue as required by the State Athletic Commission and rushed to nearby California Hospital Medical Center where trauma surgeon David Duarte performs the two-and-a-half-hour hour surgery to remove a blood clot around his brain, and is put in a medical induced coma for 72 hours to allow his brain to heal. Dr. Duarte credits the action by the paramedics with keeping Contreras alive en route to the hospital. To Dr. Daly sitting in the front row, "It seemed he wasn't seriously hurt; he just went to his corner and quit." Ten days after the surgery, Contreras is starting to come out of his comatose state. At a news conference, Dr. Duarte says progress is being made, but how extensive his injuries are cannot yet be determined, albeit he will need extensive rehabilitation. Three weeks later on June 17, Contreras awakes from his coma, is responsive but unable to speak and is moved out of intensive care. Five weeks later, he's sitting up and making "very good progress," which allows him after a month at the California Hospital Medical Center to be transferred to the noted Rancho Los Amigos National Rehabilitation

Center in Downey, where he is expected to remain two months before returning home to Ciudad Juarez, Mexico.

Five weeks after undergoing rehabilitation, Contreras is released and plans living for a while with relatives in Los Angeles before returning home. Physician Ziyad Ayyoub tells the *Los Angeles Times* the fighter has made "significant progress…and will continue to improve over the year to two years." While he suffers from a weakness on his left side and requires a walker and a wheelchair, he is able to handle a number of personal activities including eating, showering, and dressing himself.

Here's the irony in this tragic situation: had Contreras, who's training for a May 28 fight against Austreberto Juarez in the farming community of Oxnard, California, kept to that schedule and not filled in on four day's notice for Cuidad Juarez boxer Alejandro Moreno, who is unable to make the required weight for his fight that same night, his life would not be in danger. For his appearance in the ring against Viloria, he's paid $4,000, double his normal fee, plus travel expenses. Contreras, who has a wife and two young sons and a daughter in Cuidad Juarez, has worked in El Paso for the past six years as a kitchen cabinet carpenter. His post fight medical expenses are being paid for by promoter Bob Arum's Top Rank company's insurance, which also pays for rooms for the family at a nearby hotel. Contreras' wife Nancy Maldonado, whose dislike for boxing results in her seeing only one of his 29 fights, according to the *Los Angeles Times*, is at his bedside along with the boxer's father. Among the many concerned messages received by the hospital is one from Mexico's president Vicente Fox.

With his victory, Viloria's record of 18-0 elevates him to face WBC light-flyweight champion Eric Ortiz. The next day, Viloria, a sorrowful Waipahu resident, tells his hometown newspaper, the *Honolulu Advertiser*, "I just went to church and prayed all day. That's pretty much all I can do right now." Returning to the Staples Center September 10 in his first fight since his tragic sixth-round knockout over Contreras on May 28, Viloria wastes little time in defeating Ortiz with a knockout in two minutes, 59 seconds of the first round of the 12-round battle. This fight is ringed in emotion. Not only is Contreras, who is regaining his mental acuity and muscle control, an invited guest seated near ringside, but Viloria dedicates the fight to him and embraces his former foe prior to entering the ring. It's a scene rarely, if ever, seen in boxing. After his quick victory, Viloria is candid about his feelings seeing Contreras at the match: "I was choked up to see Ruben in the stands," reports the *Los Angeles Times*. "I almost cried and held it back. I'm fighting for the world championship. I couldn't look like a crybaby."

Four days after Viloria's victory sends Contreras to the hospital, the California State Athletic Commission states it will conduct an investigation and requests a copy of the fight tape from Top Rank Boxing to check for any subtle signs that the fight should have been halted earlier. The commission's departing executive director Dean Lohuis tells the *Los Angeles Times*: "We are not saying there was any wrongdoing whatsoever, but you can't let something like this go without an investigation."

Five weeks after the Contreras near-death experience, Martin Sanchez, a super lightweight from Mexico City dies one day after being knocked out in his fight July 1 against Rustam Nugaev, a Russian fighter at the Orleans hotel in Las Vegas. He is the fifth fighter to die in Las Vegas since 1994.

Sanchez, 26, is knocked out by a right-hand punch at 2:09 of the ninth round of the scheduled 10-round bout. Two physicians examine Sanchez in his corner and later in his dressing room and despite bleeding from the nose and mouth, declare he's okay. A short time later, a Nevada Athletic Commission inspector observes Sanchez "walking strangely" and summons one of the doctors who earlier said the fighter was fine. Observing Sanchez's pupils are greatly enlarged, according to the *Las Vegas Review Journal*, he is summarily rushed by ambulance to Valley Hospital where neurosurgeon Jason E. Garber performs emergency surgery to a massively swollen brain and removes a large subdural hematoma. Sanchez is placed on a ventilator but dies after 11 a.m. the next day. In August, the WBC launches an investigation into the death.

During a triple card at the MGM Grand Garden Arena in Las Vegas on September 17, a title is won following a bout in which a fighter is so badly beaten he undergoes surgery to relieve pressure on his brain, but dies later. In the tragic bout, Jesus Chavez severely beats up Leavender Johnson, the International Boxing Federation's lightweight champion, with the referee stopping the fight 38 seconds into the 11th round of their 12 round fight. Following his departure from the ring, Johnson shows signs of a medical problem, and falls into a state of semi-consciousness, according to the *Los Angeles Times*, and is taken by ambulance to University Medical Center where he undergoes brain surgery to relieve the pressure caused by a subdural hematoma. Following surgery by Dr. William Smith, the 35 year-old boxer is listed in critical condition.

Two days after surgery, Johnson is improving "dramatically" and remains in a medically induced-coma, reports the *Times*. He will be slowly brought out of the coma during the next week. However, his condition worsens and five days after his pummeling, he passes away on September 22. Dr. Smith notes the force of the blows shifts Johnson's brain from one side of his head to the other and the survival rate for this kind of injury is 15 percent.

Among the people initially visiting him in the hospital in addition to his father and two brothers are Chavez, boxer Shane Mosley and the fight's promoters Bernard Hopkins and Oscar De La Hoya. Chavez expresses "shock" over what happens, noting, "I sure as heck didn't expect this to happen," reports the *Times*. Johnson's father Bill frees the concerned fighter of any guilt, stating, "Don't feel you are to blame. This is just the state of the game."

De La Hoya tells the paper there should be "stricter neurological exams" before a fighter enters the ring, with the cost, possibly several thousand dollars, incurred by the promoters. "What's a few thousand dollars," he asks, "if it saves lives?" Following Johnson's death, his promoter, Lou DiBella, echoes the concern for greater oversight of the sport, noting in a statement reported in the

Times: "National uniform health and safety regulations must be instituted and enforced for boxing."

Latino boxers dominate deaths in Las Vegas. The last boxer to die in the ring prior to Johnson is Pedro Alcazar in his fight against Fernando Montiel June 22, 2002, at the MGM Grand. Alcazar collapses in the shower in his hotel room two days later and passes away later that day. The death debacles during this period begin with Robert Wangila dying July 28, 1994 from injuries inflicted six days earlier by David Gonzalez in their fight at the Aladdin. Two weeks after his fight with Gabriel Ruelas on May 6, 1995, at Caesars Palace, Jimmy Garcia passes away. And two days after his September 26, 1997, fight with James Crayton at the Orleans, Johnny Montantes dies of his injuries.

On a happier note, Alfonso Zamora, 51, a former 1975 WBA bantamweight champion, is inducted into the World Boxing Hall of Fame in August of 2005, the lone Hispanic among eight new additions. He competes from 1973 to 1980 when he retires with a career record of 33 victories, of which 32 are knockouts, and five losses. His pro-career is preceded by his winning a silver medal in the 1972 Munich Olympics.

In horse racing, among Hispanic jockeys working with thoroughbreds at tracks across the nation, John Velasquez, Edgar Prado, Victor Espinoza, and Rafael Bejarano shine the brightest. Velazquez is named the top money earner for 2004 and Bejarano the top rider of winning horses, according to Equibase Company LLC, which compiles the official North American racing results. Hispanic jockeys also dominate the industry's Eclipse Awards.

Velasquez rides 1,327 horses, wins 335, and has mounts that earn $22.2 million. The New York-based jockey replaces Jerry Butler as the top money earner, Butler finishing fifth with $14.5 million. New York jockey Prado finishes second with $18.3 million and California-headquartered Espinoza is third with $15.9 million, according to the *Los Angeles Times*. Bejarano accumulates 455 wins out of 1,922 races for a 24 percent victory record.

In voting for the industry's Eclipse Awards, Velazquez is named the year's top jockey, besting Bejarano and Prado; Brian Hernandez, Jr. is voted the best apprentice jockey, outscoring Pablo Fragoso and Angel Quinones, and Ghostzapper is named the 2004 horse of the year by members of the National Thoroughbred Racing Association, the National Turf Writers Association and the *Daily Racing Form* in ceremonies January 24, 2005, at the Regent Beverly Hills Hotel in Beverly Hills.

Ghostzapper, with only four wins in four starts and Javier Castellano, the 27-year-old Venezuelan in the saddle, is the least run horse to win the title since Native Dancer's three for three record in 1954.

The year is marked by a serious internal labor dispute involving some of the 1,200 nationwide riders and their Jockeys' Guild Union, which since 2002 does not provide catastrophic accident insurance to its members following its policy lapse. Individual tracks insure riders with up to $100,000 coverage, but the seriousness of the matter causes a number of riders to announce a two-day boycott on November 10 and 11 during the Fall meet at the 130-year-old Churchill Downs, Louisville home of the Kentucky Derby. A number of jockeys with serious illnesses are at the background of the current concerns among riders, including a broken collarbone Martin Pedrosa suffers earlier in the year at Santa Anita, a recent accident at Churchill Downs resulting in a punctured lung, fractured collarbone, and four broken ribs for jockey Tony D'Amico and a fractured vertebra and three broken ribs for Alex Solis incurred July 23 during a spill at the Del Mar Racetrack in Del Mar, California.

Among the 15 boycotting riders are leading money earners Rafael Bejarano and Robby Albarado; their refusal to work results in their being banned during the Fall meet ending November 27. Agreeing to participate are 26 jockeys including apprentices Brian Hernandez, Jr. and Juan Molina, Jr.

Steve Sexton, president of Churchill Downs, expresses the jockeys' concern and calls the insurance coverage "a legitimate issue," in the *Los Angeles Times*. Sexton says since riders are independent contractors, they must "accept the cost of their insurance coverage." The National Thoroughbred Racing Association, reacting to the situation, says it will form a working group to study jockey insurance needs. Jockeys are covered by workers' compensation insurance in New York, New Jersey, Maryland, California, and Idaho, but in Kentucky, as in other states, they are not covered by these benefits.

A few days after the jockeys' refusal to ride at Churchill Downs, 14 unnamed riders refuse to race at Churchill Downs-owned Hoosier Park in Anderson, Indiana, forcing the track to cancel its 12-day card on November 12. The next day, the track resumes racing with 14 unnamed jockeys willing to work. Hoosier Park, like other small tracks claims it cannot afford coverage for riders that can total $10,000 a year per rider.

Underscoring the potential danger of personal injury, four jockeys are hospitalized, three November 20 at Golden Gate Fields in California, and one the next day at Hollywood Park in Inglewood, California. Following a four-horse accident during the second race at Golden Gate, Alfredo Miranda, and David Lopez both receive mild concussions and Francisco Duran suffers a broken right collarbone. The fourth rider, Iggy Puglisi is not injured. The seven-horse race for two-year-olds is declared a no-contest.

During the sixth race at Hollywood Park, jockey Goncalino "GF" Almedia is involved in a spill that sends him to the hospital complaining of lower back pain. Almeida is thrown to the ground when his mount, Sparkling Ava, suffers a fatal leg injury. Three months later in February of 2005, 40-year-old jockey Ron Warren, Jr. is injured during a fall at Bay Meadows Race Course in San Mateo, California, and undergoes four hours of surgery to repair a broken right leg and left hip. Also during February, Alex Bisono, David Flores, and Julio Garcia are all injured in a chain-reaction spill at Santa Anita Racetrack, resulting in two of the horses dying. All three are hospitalized. Indiaman, ridden by Bisono dies from a broken neck while Glen Canyon, ridden by Garcia suffers a compound fracture of the left front cannon bone and is put to sleep. Flores' mount, Bornwithit, trips over Glen Canyon but is not injured.

Trying to avoid a potential jockey walkout that could impact the 2005 Kentucky Derby, Churchill Downs Inc. sues the Jockeys' Guild in federal court in Louisville, March 3. The suit seeks an injunction to prohibit jockeys from boycotting races at the company's tracks similar to the Guild's actions last November at Churchill Downs and at sister track Hoosier Park in Anderson, Indiana. Andy Skehan, CEO of Churchill Downs Inc., in the suit cites the union stating its action is to pressure tracks to provide additional on-track medical insurance. In the suit he also says the company is seeking to increase its accident insurance at its tracks from $100,000 to $1 million. He also claims his company is paying the guild around $375,000 annually as an industry contribution for jockey's insurance. "Since the guild will not explain where the money is going, we are withholding this funding and exploring possibilities for redirecting it in a manner that would be beneficial to the jockeys," continues the action. The suit also contends tracks spent more than $5 million in premiums to jockeys' insurance in 2004 in addition to paying fees of around $2.2 million annually to the guild, so the union's allowing its accident coverage to lapse in 2002 is not justified.

Injuries continue to happen in 2005. Patrick Valenzuela is hurt when he falls at the start of a race at Hollywood Park May 9, incurring a concussion and knee injury which requires some cartilage removal and is out several weeks, returning to race in the Spring–Summer meet June 11. Russell Baze breaks his left collarbone June 8 in a spill at Golden Gate Fields in Albany, California, when his horse, Cowboy Badgett falls and breaks his left front ankle and has to be euthanized. During the July Fourth weekend, two jockeys take spills at Texas tracks and are in critical condition. Akili Gray, thrown from his mount at Fredericksburg's Gillespie County Fairgrounds July 2, suffers head injuries and is taken to University Hospital in San Antonio. Two days later, Casey Lambert is involved in a three-horse fall at Lone Star Park in Grand Prairie and is taken to a Dallas hospital with a punctured lung, a broken jaw, and several broken ribs.

Valenzuela, 41, and one of the nation's leading jockeys, who finishes fifth nationally in 2003 when his mounts earn $15.6 million, is in the center of a major drama in 2004 involving drug use, refusal to undergo drug testing, two suspensions, including a goof by the California Horse Racing Board, and a final resolution of the situation which leaves him inactive from July 2 through January 13, 2005. During his 25 plus year career, Valenzuela wins some of the biggest races, ranging from the 1989 Kentucky Derby with Sunday Silence to seven Breeders' Cup winners. But he's also missed years of racing due to drug-related problems that result in 11 suspensions or license revocations.

On July 1, although he's suspended for a year for failing to show-up in January for a urine test at Santa Anita Park racetrack in Arcadia, California, the length of the suspension is later changed to a month's time and he rides two winners at Hollywood Park in Inglewood, California. The next day, he's suspended again when he's unable to produce enough hair for a drug test since he's supposedly shaved his head and other parts of his body. Valenzuela's conditional license of recent years contains an amended agreement that he submit to hair follicle testing.

During his hearing at the Del Mar track in August before the track's stewards, a California Horse Racing Board (CHRB) toxicologist from Las Vegas, Dan Berkaville, testifies about the difference between using hair and urine to test for drugs. Mike Kilpack, the supervising investigator for the CHRB, testifies he relays the information to Hollywood Park stewards that Valenzuela, with his head shaved, also doesn't have sufficient strands of hair on his body with which to do a drug test. The jockey's urine is tested three times on July 1, with two tests negative and the third inconclusive. Valenzuela's attorney, Neil Papiano, submits a photo taken on July 7 that shows groin hair, rebutting Kilpack's testimony. One week later, Valenzuela is suspended for the rest of 2004 by the three steward panel, which also stipulates that the jockey not be considered for a future license.

Just when things seem really gloomy for Valenzuela, an administrative law judge in January of 2005 overrules the steward's suspension on the technicality that there's a difference between a strand and a follicle of hair.

This splitting of hairs, so to speak, prompts the CHRB to revoke its ban and admits its error in stating Valenzuela is subject to "hair follicle test" rather than "hair strand testing." On Wednesday, January 12, Valenzuela is granted a conditional license, which makes him eligible to race at Santa Anita. Valenzuela agrees to tests whenever he rides in other states as well as in California. On January 23, in his first stakes appearance atop Saint Fleet, he wins the $150,000 Palos Verdes Handicap. Valenzuela's last stake victory is May 31, 2004 atop Designed For Luck in the Shoemaker Mile at Hollywood Park. The race is named after the late, great Bill Shoemaker, who sets the world's record for winning 8,833 races and earning $100 million during his 40-year career, including the Kentucky Derby four times, the Belmont Stakes five times and the Preakness Stakes twice before retiring in 1990. Following an accident in which his Ford Bronco rolls down a 50-foot embankment, he's paralyzed from the neck down and confined to a wheel chair. He then works as a horse trainer until retiring in 1997 and dies of natural causes on October 12, 2003.

Valenzuela again shows his popular appeal by being selected to compete in the third annual Sunshine Millions Classic, an eight-race card split between Santa Anita in California and Gulfstream Park, its sister track in Hallandale Beach, Florida, which is exclusively for horses bred in either state. Riding Classic Endeavor—a seven-year-old, with a five race-winning streak, including three in a row since last August—at Gulfstream on January 29, 2005, Valenzuela finishes third behind a 70 to 1 shot, Musique Toujours, ridden by Jorge Chavez. Valenzuela does better during Santa Anita's rain-soaked meet in February, riding six stakes winners.

In July of 2005 riding Lava Man, Valenzuela wins his first Gold Cup at Hollywood Park in Inglewood, California. The featured 66th annual $750,000 signature race is his first win in nine attempts, in which he bests six other Latin jockeys including New Yorker and

Eclipse winner John Velazquez, who finishes fifth on the favored Limehouse.

Valenzuela's past catches up with him on July 22, 2006 when he enters a Pasadena, California, hospital that treats substance abuse and mental health problems following his decision four days earlier not to ride on opening day at Del Mar. Prior to his hospitalization, he passes two urine tests and once released from the hospital after six weeks, also passes a hair follicle test, all conducted by the California Horse Racing Board. The CHRB nonetheless wants him to explain why he admitted himself into rehab before he can race in the state. In the interim he starts racing and winning in Toronto. Returning to California in late September, he takes a physical requested by the CHRB and agrees to provide additional medical information so he can resume riding in the state.

Martin Pedrosa, bouncing back from a broken collarbone suffered in an accident at Santa Anita which keeps him out of action for five weeks, rides in two of Southern California's back-to-back meets. He finishes sixth in victories at Del Mar with 18 firsts and then wins a record 51 races during the 17-day Fairplex Park meet at the Los Angeles County Fair at Pomona. The 39-year-old Panamanian jockey thus bests David Flores' Fairplex record of 48 wins in 1991. It's Pedrosa's sixth straight year of being the top rider. His career record win total of 431 dates back to his start at Fairplex in the 1980s.

Pedrosa rides a 6 to 1 shot, Truly a Judge, across the finish line first in the $100,000 Native Diver Handicap December 11 at Hollywood Park. Also on the card that day, Victor Espinoza rides Fusaichi Samurai's winning debut in the fourth race at the park.

The importance of Latin jockeys is underscored during the eight race Breeders' Cup card at Lone Star Park in Grand Prairie, Texas, on October 30 when seven of the mounts are ridden by familiar Hispanic names.

The Classic race is won by Ghostzapper ridden by Javier Castellano, besting 12 other horses of which four are also ridden by Latins: John Velazquez atop Roses In May; Edgar Prado atop Birdstone; Jose Santos atop Funny Cide; and Cornelio Velasquez atop Bowman's Band.

Velazquez is in the saddle for two other winning races: the Distaff won by Ashado and the Sprint won by Speightstown; the Mile is captured by Singletary ridden by David Flores while the Turf race goes to Better Talk Now carrying Ramon Dominguez.

Several days later, Castellano rides 8 to 1 shot Mass Media to victory in the $111,200 Sport Page Handicap at Aqueduct in Jamaica, New York. Also during the Aqueduct season, Velazquez rides Megascape, a 9 to 2 shot to victory in the $106,500 Valley Stream Stakes. And in December at Calder Race Course in Florida located at the Dade and Broward County lines, Velazquez wins two of the four stakes races: the $100,000 My Charmer Handicap atop Something Ventured and the $100,000 Tropical Turf Handicap atop Host.

Another winning jockey, 28-year-old Ramon Dominguez, who's primarily been working in Delaware, Maryland, and at Saratoga Race Course in upstate New York, makes his first visit to Hollywood Park and wins both of his races. The Venezuelan scores atop Louvain in the first division of the $75,000 Miesque Stakes and with favored Cajun Beat in the $150,000 Hollywood Turf Express.

Look closely at the horses working out mornings at Santa Anita in late January of 2005, and you'll see Alex Solis, 40, in the saddle preparing for his comeback in February after recovering from a fractured back vertebra and three broken ribs in a spill at Del Mar last July 23. The back injury requires surgery and keeps the veteran rider inactive until January 20. At the time of his fall, he's leading the nation in purses with $11.5 million and winds up ninth in the standings for 2004. Unfortunately, when he does race after his six-and-a-half half month absence on February 5 in the $300,000 Strub Stakes, which he last wins in 1995, he finishes second atop Imperialism to Rock Hard Ten in a photo finish. In two other races, Solis finishes fifth and second in the sixth and ninth races, respectively. He finally wins a race the next day on Indian Flare, a three-year-old first-time starter.

In one of the top races leading up to the Kentucky Derby, Bellamy Road ridden by Javier Castellano captures the $500,000 Wood Memorial Stakes at New York's Aqueduct in March by 17-1/2 lengths, completing the 1-1/8th miles in 1 minute 47 seconds and 16, to equal the track record set in 1973 by Riva Ridge in the Stuyvesant Handicap.

Castellano is among eight other Latin jockeys riding three-year-olds in the 20-horse, 131st running of the fabled Kentucky Derby, May 8 at the $121 million renovated Churchill Downs. Of the nine, Cornelio Velasquez atop Closing Argument finishes in the money in second place behind 50 to 1 long shot Giacomo, ridden by Mike Smith. The other Latin jockeys in the race: Rafael Bejarano, Jorge Chavez, Ramon Dominguez, Edgar Prado, Jose Valdivia, Jr., Patrick Valenzuela, and John Velasquez.

At the 103rd annual Preakness, the second leg of the Triple Crown of Thoroughbred Racing May 21, Ramon Dominguez atop Scrappy T finishes second in a controversial race won by Afleet Alex ridden by Jeremy Rose. The morning after the race in Baltimore, Scrappy T's trainer Tim Ritchey criticizes Dominguez for causing his mount to veer into Afleet Alex's path on the final turn toward the finish line. Afleet Alex has his heels clipped, stumbles and almost touches the ground with his nose. But he regains his footing and wins by 4-3/4 lengths. After viewing film of the race one week later which shows Dominguez sharply hitting Scrappy T from the left side causing the horse to veer to the right and Afleet Alex running onto Scrappy T's heels, Pimilco Race Track stewards decide Dominguez has not broken any rules and therefore no fine or suspension is appropriate. The other six Latin jockeys in the Preakness are David Flores, Cornelio Velasquez, Rafael Bejarano, Edgar Prado, Robby Albarado, and Jose Santos.

Six Hispanic riders are also competing in the 137th Belmont Stakes at Belmont Park, Elmont, New York, the final leg of racing's fabled Triple Crown. While Afleet Alex is the runaway victor, he's followed in second place by Andromeda's Hero ridden by Rafael Bejarano and in third by Nolan's Cat with Norberto Arroyo, Jr. in the saddle. Edgar Prado in fourth finishes out of the money along with Javier Castellano, Jose Santos, and John Velazquez.

Not all the name Latinos are at Belmont. Alexis Solis, competing at financially troubled Hollywood Park, purchased for $260 million in July from owner Churchill Downs by the Bay Meadows Land Company, guides Sweet Return across the finish line to win the $350,000 Charlie Whittingham Memorial Handicap. During the track's spring–summer season, Garrett Gomez is the leading money finisher. He finishes second in the featured Gold Cup in July atop Borrego behind Pat Valenzuela on Lava Man. During the 10-race program, he wins one race, has two seconds and one third to boost his record to 315 starts including 53 first, second and third place finishes. On the final day of the 64-day meeting, Gomez rides two winners and three-second place finishers to retain his leading rider status, which includes 62 first place victories.

When the circuit next shifts to Del Mar, California, Gomez, 33, makes his first appearance at this fabled track in two years following drug-related problems, according to the *Los Angeles Times*, and on opening day rides long shot Becrux to victory in the Oceanside Stakes. Gomez also finishes second and third in two other money-paying races. Alex Solis, who finishes five races behind Gomez at Hollywood Park, wins one race and finishes second in another, an indication he and Gomez will compete for the riding crown at Del Mar during its 43-day meeting.

At the conclusion of the meet, Espinoza edges out Gomez 53 to 50 in the winning jockey standings. Gomez, however, is in the saddle in six stakes winning races, accounting for around $3 million in earnings, notes the *Los Angeles Times*.

In a race wrapped in nostalgia, Hall of Famer Angel Cordero, Jr., who hasn't raced since 1995, comes out of competitive retirement at age 73 to compete in the Cotillion Handicap at Philadelphia Park Racetrack October 1. Riding the 2-5 favorite Indian Vale, Cordero finishes fifth. The Santurce, Puerto Rican, is the first and only Commonwealth rider to win the Triple Crown's Kentucky Derby (1974, 1976, and 1985), Preakness (1980 and 1984) and Belmont Stakes in 1976. In 1988, Cordero who's legal name is Angel Tomás Cordero, Jr., is inducted into the National Museum of Racing and the Hall of

Fame, to become the only Puerto Rican in the Hall of Fame. A near fatal accident in 1992 forces his retirement and he closes out his career third on the all-time list with 7,037 wins in 38,646 starts. He comes out of retirement in 1995 to ride unsuccessfully in the Breeders Cup and then steps out of the spotlight again. During his career he wins the Breeders Cup four times. He's currently active in racing as the agent for another hot Puerto Rican rider, John Velazquez.

During the 22nd running of the Breeders' Cup at Belmont Park in Elmont, New York, October 29, Hispanic jockeys win six of the seven races. In the main Breeders' Classic Cup race, Cornelio Velasquez finishes second on Flower Alley behind Jerry Bailey and his victorious Saint Liam, but wins the Breeder's Cup Distaff race with Pleasant Home, a 30 to 1 long shot. Edgar Prado and Garrett Gomez (who leaves the meet at Santa Anita in California) both win two races: Prado the juvenile fillies with Folklore and the sprint atop Silver Train, while Gomez snares the juvenile race atop Stevie Wonderboy and the mile with Artie Schiller. For Prado, it's his first Breeders' Cup win in 42 tries. In the filly and mare turf race, Rafael Bejarano leads Intercontinental to victory.

John Velasquez, the Eclipse winner in 2004 and 2005 as the nation's leading jockey, is injured and out of action indefinitely after falling April 20 at Keeneland in Lexington, Kentucky. Riding Up An Octave, he breaks his right shoulder when the horse falls and rolls on top of him. He spends one day in the hospital; his animal is euthanized on the track.

Although it's hardly noticed or exploited, the National Basketball Association has a record 16 Hispanic players on 13 of its 30 teams during the 2004 to 2005 season. Of the 16, six are acquired in the June draft. Seven years ago, the entire NBA has two Latino players. The current Latino heading toward superstar status is Emmanuel "Manu" Ginobili of the San Antonio Spurs, who helps guide his team to the NBA championships in June of 2005 against the defending Detroit Pistons. Despite a lack of Latin superstars, the league's fan base is increasingly snaring bilingual Hispanics, a result of the growing number of Latin players, 10 NBA teams which start broadcasting their games in Spanish on the radio three years ago, and are subsequently joined by TV networks Telemundo and ESPN Deportes which air pre-season and regular season games.

Arturo Nuñez, the Miami-based NBA vice president/ managing director of Latin America and U.S. Hispanic activities since October 2003, who's been with the league since 2000, says 65 percent of the nation's growing Hispanic population are NBA fans. "And that's 15 percent of the total NBA fan base," he tells me during our phone interview. Why is the sport so popular with Latinos? "The advent of the Latino player in the league helps tremendously. We see each Latino player as a bridge to his particular community of origin. The 16 Latino players are roughly three percent of our players." While he credits Spanish radio coverage as another factor, "the most landmark thing that's happened is that Telemundo and ESPN Deportes broadcast in Spanish."

The NBA–Telemundo connection dates back to 2002 when it starts airing a 15-game schedule, while ESPN Deportes begins its NBA coverage with the 2003 to 2004 season. During its third coverage season, Telemundo makes history by elevating Claudia Trejos to *La NBA En Telemundo* to become the first female of color commentator on any professional U.S. men's sports broadcast, working in the broadcast booth with Edgar Lopez. Since joining the network in 2002 from KTLA in Los Angeles, where she is the English-language sports anchor for its 10 p.m. newscast, Trejos is also a sports reporter for newsmagazine *Al Rojo Vivo Con Maria Celeste* and co-host for *NBA Max*, a half-hour weekly youth-oriented program.

Teams currently offering their games in Spanish on radio include: New York Knicks (WADO-AM); Dallas Mavericks (KFLC-AM); Houston Rockets (KYST-AM); San Antonio Spurs (KCOR-AM); Los Angeles Lakers (KWKW-AM), Miami Heat (WQBA-AM); Orlando Magic (WONQ-AM); Phoenix Suns (KSUN-AM); Sacramento Kings (KRCX-FM); and Portland Trail Blazers (KRMZ-AM).

The six new draftees are Rafael Araujo with Toronto; Peter Ramos with Washington; Luis Flores with Golden State after initially being selected by Houston, then traded to Dallas which passes him onto Oakland; Anderson Varejao with Cleveland after originally being drafted by Orlando; Andres Nocioni with the Chicago Bulls; and Carlos Delfino with the Detroit Pistons, A seventh player, Alex Garcia, drafted by the New Orleans Hornets is waived due to a torn knee ligament and returns home to Brazil for six months of rehabilitation. He'll have to wait until he's fully healed before he can be hired by another team.

What is there about basketball that attracts Hispanic players and fans? Responds Nuñez, who explains the seven-year-old Miami office, called NBA Latin America, spends ample time on domestic and overseas Latin activities: "In the early 1990s you had the 1992 'Dream Team' consisting of the U.S. Men's Olympic team featuring Michael Jordan, Larry Bird, Earvin 'Magic' Johnson, and Charles Barkley and other NBA A-list players and commissioner David Stern's vision of globalizing the NBA. We've taken 21 games to Latin America, 16 to Mexico, one to the Dominican Republic and four to Puerto Rico during the last 10 years. That includes exhibitions and four regular season games that were played in Mexico or Puerto Rico. We also have sponsorship programs, like the Gatorade three-on-three player league in Brazil that lets kids play in a variety of cities and develop a yearning and desire to continue playing basketball. We do three-on-three and five-on-five programs in Mexico, Argentina, Puerto Rico, and Venezuela. We also take players on tours, conduct camps and clinics in many of the countries in Latin America.

"We have a program called 'Basketball Without Borders' where last year we brought 50 of the best players from 14 Latin American countries to Rio De Janeiro, Brazil, to play for a week with NBA coaches and players to develop and hone their skills. This year, we're doing the same thing in Buenos Aires, Argentina. A spin-off of this program is our 'Legacy Project' where we leave a reading and learning center behind in an impoverished community in those two countries, with computers donated by Dell, which provide an

Internet connection. The money to fund this activity comes from our partners, Dell, Gatorade, TAM Airlines in Brazil, and Aerolineas Argentinas in Argentina.

"So kids in Latin nations are exposed to the league's international community activities and its Latino players. A kid in Mexico sees Eduardo Najera, who's from Chihuahua, Mexico, playing with the Golden State Warriors. And thinks if I work hard I could be one of those guys. The same thing is happening in Brazil and Argentina and Puerto Rico."

Why do these locations provide the most players to the league? "It's because of the strength of their leagues," answers Nuñez. "Puerto Rico has a great league, Argentina has an excellent professional basketball system, Brazil has a pretty good one while Mexico has a weaker league."

Then the executive, a native of Harlem, New York, the son of Venezuelan and Cuban parents, with a background in product development with various companies starting in 1994, credits the league's international players, including European and Hispanics with "revolutionizing our game." How so? "The major difference between the traditional NBA player and these international players is they're more well-rounded (in their skills). If you watch Manu Ginobili, Leandro Mateus Barbosa, or Carlos Arroyo, these guys are fast, they drive, they make things happen, they're scrappy players who hustle for the ball, they get down on the floor. They speed up the game. Ginobili is not a position player he dribbles, shoots, passes, and rebounds. Whatever you need him to do on the floor, he can do it. These European and a lot of the Latin American players are taught to do it all."

Of the current roster of Latino players, Nuñez says, "30 percent probably don't speak good English, particularly the Brazilians who speak Portuguese. What the teams do is provide an interpreter to help them with the English so they understand the plays and what the coach is doing. Little by little, they get in classes and learn the language."

One player who does speak English well is the Spurs' new super-player Ginobili, the Argentine guard of Italian descent, who is a dynamic player in all situations especially when driving through a team's defenses to score an unscoreable lay-up. A 57th draft pick in 1999, Ginobili plays three seasons in Italy before joining the Spurs in the fall of 2002. During the summer of 2004, he leads his Argentinean team to the Olympic basketball gold medal. During the 2004 to 2005 season, he's the team's second highest scorer behind Tim Duncan.

To get to the 2004 NBA championships, San Antonio bests the Phoenix Suns in the playoffs 4-1 while Detroit eliminates the Miami Heat, 4-3 despite its new center, ex-Los Angeles Laker Shaquille O'Neal. San Antonio starts the title battle by romping to victories, 84-69 and 97-76 at home, shifting to Detroit for three games, losing 97-79 and 102-71, then slipping past the Pistons in overtime 96-95 on Robert Horry's three-pointer with 5.8 seconds remaining to lead the series 3-2. Back home for the possible final two games, San Antonio loses to Detroit 95-86, forcing the first seventh game final since 1994's Houston victory over New York. When the Spurs triumph 81-74 before their ecstatic home fans, it's their third title since 1999.

During the Phoenix playoffs, Ginobili averages 22.3 points; during the finals, he averages 26.5 points, affirming the yearlong calls by fans of "Ma-Noo, Ma-Noo, Ma-Noo."

Following the championship series, the NBA's draft includes four Latinos out of 60 chosen players in the first and second rounds. Toronto picks Charlie Villanueva from the University of Connecticut; Orlando selects Fran Vazquez from Spain who elects to say in Europe; Sacramento selects Francisco Garcia from Louisville and Portland picks Ricky Sanchez from Florida's IMG Academy.

In August, prior to the player-signing deadline, a historic five-team, 13-player trade, including three Hispanics takes place, according to the *Los Angeles Times*. The teams involved are Miami, Boston, Memphis, Utah, and New Orleans. Miami receives draft rights to Spain's Roberto Duenas; Boston obtains draft rights to Spain's Albert Miralles; and Memphis obtains Raul Lopez from Utah. In a separate deal, San Antonio signs Argentina's Fabricio Oberto, who is on the Argentine team with Manu Ginobili which wins the gold medal at the Athens Olympics.

For the high-riding Ginobili, this is his second championship season having played on the Spurs NBA title team two years ago. It's also the first season he plays in the NBA All Star game. He is only the second Latino to play on an NBA All Star team, following Panama born U.S. raised Rolando Blackman who plays in the 1985 and 1986 All Star games while with the Dallas Mavericks from 1981 through the 2000 to 2001 season.

Do U.S. Hispanics who follow baseball and soccer also automatically follow basketball? "As a result of a 2003 study in which we asked teens what sport was the most popular," says the NBA's Nuñez, who is conversant in English, Spanish and Portuguese, "76 percent said basketball, 55 percent said football, 46 percent baseball, and 46 percent soccer. That statistic shocked me, given immigration patterns. But the reality is you only need a ball and a basket to play the game, so much more people participate in the sport. And we believe as a league that those people who play the sport at a young age eventually become fans who attend the games and viewers of the sport on TV and listeners on the radio, all parts of the base of the business."

Of the current 16 Latinos in the league, four are from Brazil; three from Argentina and Puerto Rico; two from Spain and one each from Mexico, the Dominican Republic, and Belize. They play for cities with varied Hispanic populations like Phoenix, San Antonio, Chicago, Washington, Salt Lake City, Oakland, Detroit, Denver, Cleveland, Milwaukee, New Orleans, Memphis, and Toronto. Interestingly, there are no Latinos on New York, Los Angeles, Miami, and Orlando teams, even though these are among the cities with Spanish radio coverage for their large Latino constituents.

The Brazilians are Rafael Araujo with Toronto; Anderson Varejao with Cleveland; Leandro Mateus Barbosa, Phoenix; and Nenê (Maybyner Rodney Hilario), Denver. The Puerto Ricans are Carlos Arroyo, Detroit; Daniel Santiago, Milwaukee; and Peter John Ramos, Washington. The Argentineans include: Carlos Delfino, Detroit; Manu Ginobili, San Antonio; and Andres Nocioni, Chicago. The two Spaniards are Raul Lopez, Utah and Pau Gasol, Memphis.

Golden State (Oakland) has two players, Mexico's Eduardo Najera and the Dominican Republic's Luis Florez, while Belize's Milt Palacio is with Toronto.

Pau Gasol finds himself facing a family adversary when the Memphis Grizzlies visit Spain in October of 2003 to play against the FC Barcelona team of the national league, for whom Gasol once plays. His brother Marc is now on the team, resulting in a competitive battle, won by the Grizzlies, 91 to 80.

Among current players, five are nominated in the outstanding Latin American basketball player category in the second annual *Premios Fox Sports* awards televised by Fox Sports En Español December 15 from the Jackie Gleason Theater in Miami Beach. The Spurs' Manu Ginobili is awarded the honor, besting Dallas' Eduardo Nájera, Utah's Carlos Arroyo, Detroit's Carlos Delfino and Chicago's Andres Nocioni.

The first two pioneering players in the league are Alfred "Butch" Lee and Carl Herrera. Lee, of Puerto Rican descent, is the first Hispanic to play in the NBA, joining Atlanta during the 1978 to 1979 season as a guard and then playing for Cleveland and Los Angeles from 1979 to 1980, the year he retires. Herrera, a Venezuelan, plays for the Houston Rockets during the 1992 to 1995 seasons, coming to the pros from team Real Madrid in Spain.

Herrera's pre-NBA background includes stints overseas playing for his native Venezuelan national basketball team and its 1992 Olympic team, Real Madrid of Spain and attending Jacksonville, Texas, Community College (1987 to 1989) and the University of Houston (1989 to 1990). He's the first Venezuelan in the NBA, drafted in 1990 in the second round by the Miami Heat, which trades his rights along with another player to the Houston Rockets. Instead of starting with Houston, he is signed by Real Madrid of Spain for whom he plays one season before returning to the U.S. in 1991 and the Rockets, where he plays forward and stays until 1995, becoming the first Latin American player to win NBA titles with Houston in the 1992 to 1994 and 1994 to 1995 seasons. He's next traded to the San Antonio Spurs where he stays from 1995 to 1998, and is traded in 1999 to Vancouver. He plays four games for the Grizzlies before being signed by the Denver Nuggets where he plays 24 games before the team releases him and he goes into retirement.

Lee and Herrera are followed by Rolando Blackman, Dallas, 1981 to 1992; Milt Palacio, Toronto Rapters, 1999 to 2000; Eduardo Najera, Golden State, 2000 to 2001; Daniel Santiago, Milwaukee Bucks, 2000 to 2001; Pau Gasol, Memphis Grizzlies, 2001 to 2002; Carlos Arroyo, Detroit Pistons, 2001 to 2002; "Manu" Ginobili, San Antonio Spurs, 2002 to 2003; Raul Lopez, Utah Jazz, 2002 to 2003; Nenê, Denver Nuggets, 2002 to 2003, and Leandro Mateus Barbosa, Phoenix Suns, 2003 to 2004.

Among the league's other Latin pioneers are Tommy Nuñez, Rolando Blackman, and Ginobili. Nuñez is the league's first Hispanic referee, working the hardwoods from 1973 until his retirement towards the end of the 2002 to 2003 season after three decades. Born in Santa Maria, California, he's raised in Phoenix where he begins refereeing club teams and in 1970 gets a shot at referring a Phoenix Suns game which results in his being signed as a league ref in 1973. Nuñez is the only Mexican-American among the NBA's 28 referees. During the off-season, he directs his National Hispanic Basketball Classic, an annual tournament for Latino youths. His accomplishments earn him a place in volume one of the book *Hispanic Heroes of the U.S.A.*, an induction into the Latin American International Sports Hall of Fame and the 1992 Roberto Clemente Award for Excellence by the National Council of La Raza.

In 1990, Blackman, a Panamanian, becomes the first Latin player to be selected for an All Star Game. He begins his NBA career in 1981 with Dallas, where he plays until 1992 and is then traded to New York where he remains until retiring in 1994. Ginobili is the second Latino to be selected for an All Star Game, the 2005 edition in Denver where he scores eight points as a reserve player for the Western conference team which loses to the East, 125 to 115.

In addition to its attractive player roster, NBA En Español utilizes its corporate élan to ingratiate itself with the U.S. Hispanic community by launching a smattering of outreach programs with benefits for all ages, beginning with its celebration of Hispanic Heritage.

While the number of Latin players continues to grow, along with other international hotshots, numbering close to 80 men in baggy shorts, the number of Hispanic team owners is stuck at one with the sale of the Phoenix Suns to an investment group for $401 million in April, earning Arte Moreno, an eight percent limited partner, an estimated $32 million. Moreno is now focusing fulltime on his ownership of the Anaheim Angels baseball team. The lone NBA minority owners are brothers Juan and Carlos De Céspedes and Felix Sabates in the new Charlotte Bobcats, whose majority owner is Robert Johnson, founder and former owner of the Black Entertainment Network (BET) cable network. Sabates also runs NASCAR racing teams. Included in the ownership transaction in Bobcats Basketball Holdings are management of the new Charlotte Arena in which the team plays and the Charlotte Sting of the WNBA, the NBA's nine-year-old 13-team women's' league.

The WNBA has two Latinas, Argentina's Diana Taurasi with the Phoenix Mercury and Brazil's Janeth Arcain with the Houston Comments during the 2004 to 2005 season. Why so few players? Aren't there top Latinas on U.S. college teams and overseas? The NBA's Nuñez says there have been as many as 10, mainly from Brazil, but they left to return to play with their national teams, or their contracts are not renewed, depleting the ranks of the U.S. pros. Since its inception in 1997, the WNBA draws foreign players from 40 nations, including Brazil, Colombia, Portugal, and Spain.

But with the addition of Chicago in the league in 2006, raising the team number to 14, the opportunity for signing more female Latin players is promising, Nuñez believes. The teams are broken into two seven-team conferences. The Eastern Conference consists of Chicago, Charlotte Sting, Connecticut Sun, Detroit Shock, Indiana Fever, New York Liberty, and Washington Mystics. Competing in the

Western Conference: Houston Comets, Los Angeles Sparks, Minnesota Lynx, Phoenix Mercury, San Antonio Silver Stars, Seattle Storm, and the Sacramento Monarchs.

During the WNBA's next seasonal draft, five Brazilians are signed: Janeth Arcain to Houston; Ericka DeSouza to Los Angeles; Kelly Santos and Adriana Moises to Phoenix; and Helen Luz to Washington.

Cognizant of the 40 million domestic Latinos, the majority of whom are from Mexico, NASCAR, the vastly popular stock car race league, stages its first competition in Mexico City, the Telcel Motorola Mexico 200, March 6, 2005. It's the first international competition in its Busch Series division and features a number of Latino drivers as a lure for hometown fans and the 17.5 percent of its U.S. fan base that is Latino and African-American. The majority of racecar fans are white and U.S. born. NASCAR is the acronym for National Association for Stock Car Auto Racing. The Telcel Motorola race is an outgrowth of NASCAR's union with Mexican financial interests last year to create NASCAR Mexico to launch its own stock car series, Desafino Corona (Corona Challenge). Competing for Telco Motorola 200's $2.3 million purse and championship points are Adrian Fernandez, 41, Mexico's leading race car driver, steering his first stock car, a Chevrolet sponsored by Hendrick MotorSports of North Carolina; Michel Jourdain, Jr. 28, who's competing in the 2005 Busch Series in a Ford Taurus for the Ford Motor Company's racing division; Carlos Contreras, 34, driving a Dodge Charger for FitzBradshaw Racing, also of North Carolina; and Jorge Goeters, a local favorite also driving a Ford. The race is won by defending Busch Series champion Martin Truex, Jr. driving a Chevrolet, with two Americans finishing second and third. Goeters, who leads for the first 24 laps, makes a pit stop, and is in 10th place when he encounters smoke on the 66th lap and pulls off the track. None of the Mexican drivers finishes in prominent positions.

Prior to racing before hometown fans, Jourdain competes in two Busch Series races in the U.S., finishing in the middle of the pack in both contests. He's the first Latino signed in 1999 by American company HRT Motorsports of Miami to race in the full 35-race Busch Series schedule. Contreras, signed in 1999 by HRT Motorsports of Miami, becomes one of the first Hispanics competing in NASCAR, driving for three seasons, first in the Craftsman Truck Series and then in some Busch Series races, two of the sport's key national circuits along with the granddaddy, the Nextel Cup Series.

Luis Diaz, a Mexico City driver, teams up with veteran drive Scott Pruett to win the Grand American Road Racing Association's "Grand-AM" at the California Speedway in Fontana, California. Diaz, who wins the pole position the previous day, turns over his CompUSA Ganassi Racing Lexus Riley car to Pruett on the 21st lap while he's in fourth place, with his teammate gaining the checkered flag on what turns out to the final 86th lap, after officials cite a two-hour, 45-minute time limit on the race.

NASCAR's TV ratings in the U.S. are huge for Fox TV, parent News Corp's FX, NBC, and the TNT cable channel. America's Fortune 500 companies are among the sport's sponsors with their sprightly logos adorning the modified closed interior vehicles as well as having exclusive name identity on the racing circuits.

One of the major West Coast races is the Toyota Grand Prix of Long Beach, California. In the 3lst edition with a field of two-car teams whose drivers are from the U.S., England, Canada, Australia, Sweden, Mexico, Spain, Brazil, and France. The twosome of France's Sebastian Bourdais and Brazil's Bruno Junqueira prevails during the 1.97-mile, 81-lap, 11-turn street course. Bourdais finishes first and Junqueira third among the Champ Car drivers from the dual car teams, presenting car co-owner and veteran actor Paul Newman with the championship trophy. Bourdais and Junqueira have been competing in the U.S. in Champ Car races going on three years. Champ Cars are single-driver, tight chassis, no-roof racers, which compete on major circuits along with three other vehicle models: Formula One and IRL (both single driver chassis without roofs and NASCAR (souped-up sedans).

In auto racing's most prestigious competition, the Indianapolis 500's 89th edition run May 29, 2004, on the Memorial Day weekend, which England's Dan Wheldon wins driving a Dallara-Honda, Brazil's Vitor Meira finishes second steering the David Letterman/Bobby Rahal team's Honda-powered Panoz.

Among the other Hispanic drivers in the 200-lap competition on the Indianapolis Motor Speedway's two-and-a-half miles rectangular oval, Mexico's Adrian Fernandez finishes 14th after completing 197 laps and Brazil's Bruno Junqueira ends up 30th after an injury sustaining crash on the 76th lap.

Competing in the Toyota Indy 400 on October 16, controversy engulfs the finish when Tony Kannan of Spain inexplicably slows down a few yards from the finish line to allow teammate Dario Franchitti from Scotland to pass him and win the 400-mile, 200-lap race at the California Speedway in Fontana, California. The two racing with Dallara–Hondas battle through the final 49 laps of the Toyota Indy 400 before Kannan takes the lead and then relinquishes it to Franchitti. Afterwards, Kannan tells the *Los Angeles Times*, "I really don't know what happened. Either I missed a shift or pressed the wrong button." Finishing third is Vitor Meira, the second place finisher at the Indy 500 last May.

With its TV ratings declining, the key for NASCAR's success in 2007 is luring greater Latino fans beyond its current fan base of 8.9 percent, notes *USA Today*. Four years after beginning its Drive for Diversity, the program's current shining light is Colombia's Juan Pablo Montoya, the Indianapolis 500 winner in 2000, who joins NASCAR in 2006. However, he's only finished twice in the top 15 of eight Nextel Cup races in '07. Aric Almirola, born in Tampa and of Cuban descent, makes his Nextel debut in March in Las Vegas where he crashes and finishes 41st out of 43 drivers. However, in the Craftsman Truck Series he finishes five times in the top 10. Across the border, NASCAR's developmental Corona Mexico Series, begun in '06, attracts 33 drivers in '07 for the first two of 15 scheduled events. It's hoped these drivers will compete in the U.S. and act as a magnet to help snare those desired Hispanic fans.

Professional golf's roster since the men's Professional Golf Association (PGA) is founded in 1916, followed by the women's counterpart, the Ladies Professional Golf Association (LPGA) in 1950, consists of such Hispanic stalwarts as Lee Trevino, Juan "Chi Chi" Rodriguez, Severiano "Seve" Ballesteros, Angel Cabrera, Nancy Lopez, Laura Diaz, Pat Perez, Robert Gamez, Paula Marti, Miguel Angel Jimenez, Vicente Fernandez, and lesser-known Joe Jiminez, Joe Jimenez, Miguel Jimenez, Homero Blancas, Jose Maria Canizares, and Camilo Villegas. Sergio Garcia and Lorena Ochoa are the new emerging Latin breakout players, Garcia bypassing Cabrera, now 36, who's been a pro for 16 years since 1989, while Ochoa has hopes of being touted as the next Latina Nancy Lopez, whose competing days appear to be over. It'll take a while, however, before any new Latin achieves the grandiloquence of Trevino, Rodriguez, and Lopez, the great Hispanics who've left their strong footnotes in golf history.

Spain's Sergio Garcia helps power the six-member European team to victory over the U.S. in the 2006 Ryder Cup in Ireland 18 1/2–9 1/2, September 24. It's the same score and result the last time the two teams face each other in 2004. Over three days, 28 matches are played with Garcia winning four straight. Garcia also shows strong resiliency during 2005, following years of difficulty, including at age 25, regularly trailing in the shadow of No. 1 ranked Tiger Woods and Vijay Singh. Shooting a six under 65 to finish with a 14 under 270 total, Garcia wins the Booz Allen Classic in Bethesda, Maryland in June of 2005. It's his sixth PGA Tour victory of his career and one in which Woods and Singh do not compete. Nevertheless, his 270 score ties the course record at the Congressional Country Club. Competing against Tiger and Singh in the 134th British Open in July at St. Andrews, Scotland's, Old Course, which Woods wins, Garcia finishes seven under par with a 181 along with four others including Singh. Thirty-nine-year-old Jose Maria Olazabal qualifies for the tournament when countryman Seve Ballesteros drops out due to a back problem. During his career, Olazabal wins the U.S. Masters Golf Championship in 1994 and 1999 as well as 24 other worldwide tournaments and plays on six European Ryder Cup teams.

Competing in the PGA Championship in August, Garcia finishes three over par along with four others at the Baltusrol Golf Club in Springfield, New Jersey. In his next major tournament, the NEC Invitational at the Firestone Country Club in Akron, Ohio, August 21, Garcia ties for sixth with four others, all finishing one under par. Garcia finally wins a major tournament, the Omega European Masters Crans-Montana "European Masters" in Switzerland in September. Returning to the U.S., he finishes in a tie for third in the American Express Championship at Harding Park Golf Course in San Francisco.

Prior to these performances, Garcia, in May of 2005, is ranked sixth in the world in earnings with $7 plus million, with Argentina's Angel Cabrera 15th with $4 million plus, and Spain's Miguel Angel Jimenez 20th with $3 million plus. As of May 15, Garcia is the lone Hispanic in the elite 300 club among the 21 players who drive a ball 300 yards during a season. He accomplishes this feat in 2003 with a drive of 300.9 yards. He is also rated ninth in the 50 world golf rankings, with Miguel Angel Jimenez in 18th place.

During the Wachovia Championship at Charlotte, North Carolina, in May of 2005, Garcia shoots a one-under par and a seven-under 137 total during the second round of play in blustery winds, giving him a two-shot lead. After three rounds, he's a six-shot leader, but collapses on the final round and is eliminated on the first extra hole of a three-man playoff, when he misses a 6-foot shot for par to finish with a 72. This three-man shootout televised by CBS draws a 5.5 rating, the highest in the three-year history of the tournament.

Garcia's growing status is utilized by the New York Stock Exchange when he's given the honor of ringing the opening bell May 23 to commence trading, and to also draw attention to the PGA Tour and to boost the visibility of its players. His visibility is raised when he finishes in a three-way tie for third place in the 105th U.S. Open Championship at the Pinehurst No. 2 course in Pinehurst, North Carolina. Garcia, who turns pro in 1999, is a flashy, 19-year-old charismatic player who generates a wave of "Sergiomania" among

American teenagers, following his third place tie in his premiere PGA appearance at the Byron Nelson Classic near Dallas. The native of Borriol, Spain, becomes the youngest Ryder Cup participant that year when he represents his homeland. In 2000, he finishes third in PGA Tour driving statistics, which combine distance and accuracy and in 2001 his power propels him to No. 1. He also wins four tournaments, two in the U.S. and one each in Europe and South Africa and is elevated from 16th to sixth in the world rankings, earning him $5.5 million.

Pat Perez emerges the top Latino in a small contingent competing in the PGA Championship in August of 2005 by finishing one under par with three other players for fourth place at the Baltusrol Golf Club in Springfield, New Jersey. It's a good showing for the 29-year-old Perez, a pro since 1997 and a skilled player whose temper tantrums in the early years of his career generate enough heat to label him the PGA Tour's "most tempestuous rookie" in 2003. And when he's labeled the "hottest player on tour" writers not only mean he's good, but he's also a hothead who curses, throws his clubs in anger over a missed shot, or tries to break them, and bad mouths features on renowned courses like Pebble Beach Golf Club and the Westchester Country Club. The Phoenix-born Mexican American athlete ties for fifth at the Western Open at Lemont, Illinois, in July of 2005. He also ties for fifth at the Cialis Western Open and ties for sixth at the Buick Invitational. During 2004, he ties for third at the 84 Lumber Classic, one of 32 tournaments he enters, finishing in the money 18 times.

In 2003, he ties for second in the Buick Invitational and his paycheck of $261,333 escalates his earnings to $1,006,341, making him the eighth rookie on the Tour to pass $1 million in earnings. During this season, he also ties for second at the Bob Hope Chrysler Classic, ties for 10th at the Bay Hill Invitational, and sets the course record of 11 under par 61 at the Bermuda Dunes Country Club. In 2002, he finishes second at the AT&T Pebble Beach National Pro-Am.

For Robert Gamez, September 26, 2005, is a historic moment in his 15-year career as a pro. That's the date he wins the Valero Texas

Open and ends his 394 event-losing streak dating back to 1990 when he finishes first at the Bay Hill Invitational, 15 years and six months ago. That year, he also wins the Touchstone Energy Tucson Open and the Nestle Open. In winning at San Antonio's La Cantera Golf Club's Resort Course, he closes with a six under par 64 for a three-stroke victory worth $630,000. With this emerging from the shadows victory, Gamez, born in Las Vegas and a resident of Orlando, ranks 89th in career earnings on the PGA Tour. In 2004, among the 10 tournaments he enters, the 37-year-old finishes in the top 10 one time, coming in ninth at the Sony Open in Hawaii, while tying for 11th at the AT&T Pebble Beach in California. Last year, he enters 31 tournaments, with two top 10 finishes and two records at the Bob Hope Classic at the Indian Wells Country Club; in the third round he finishes 12 under 60 and on his back nine he has seven birdies and an eagle to finish with an eight under par 27, which sets the nine hole tournament record.

Lorena Ochoa, the 25-year-old native of Guadalajara, Mexico, in 2007 is hot on the heels of overtaking Annika Sorenstam, 37, as the leading female pro in the early months of competition. She enters the new year as last year's player of the year, winning the Vare trophy for lowest-scoring average and earning the most money: $12.59 million, all accolades previously owned by Sorenstam. However, a faltering performance in the $2 million Kraft Nabisco Championship in Rancho Mirage, California, at the end of March, finds her tied for 10th place after four rounds.

Ochoa starts 2006 off in spectacular fashion at the same Kraft Nabisco tournament in California March 31. At the end of the first round, she shoots a 10-under par 62 to land in the record books. Not only does she set a tournament record, she also equals the best round in the history of LPGA major championships. The next day she shoots a 71-one-under-par to retain her lead. On the final round, however, fast-moving 31-year-old Australian Karrie Webb forces Ochoa into a playoff, which Webb wins with a birdie on the first hole. Webb earns $270,000; Ochoa $168,226. Two weeks later, she rebounds by winning her first tournament of the year, the Takefuji Classic at the Las Vegas Country Club, with a 19-under par 197 for the 54 holes.

After a slow start in 2005, Ochoa wins her first LPGA tournament, the Wegmans Rochester International (New York) LPGA in June following three runner-up finishes earlier in the year. The victory is worth $225,000 and keeps her in third place among top money earners with $762,268. She next ties for sixth in the U.S. Women's Open Championship with a 72 whole score of 291, seven over par, due to faltering play in the second and third rounds of the tournament at Cherry Hills Village, Colorado.

In 2004, Ochoa wins her first pro event, the inaugural Franklin American Mortgage Championship in Franklin, Tennessee, with a four under par 68 and follows that by becoming the first Mexican-born player to win the LPGA Wachovia Classic, where she crosses the $2 million mark in career earnings. She also scores her first LPGA hole-in-one at the CJ Nine Bridges Classic in South Korea, and racks up 18 top 10 finishes to become the fastest rising player in Ladies Professional Golf Association history.

Ochoa starts her career off smartly on the college level. During her two years playing for the University of Arizona, she sets a record of 12 collegiate victories out of 20 tournaments and is named the National Collegiate Athletic Association's player of the year in each of her two seasons. Her eight straight wins during the 2001 to 2002 season are an NCAA record. That's also the year she becomes the first golfer and youngest recipient of Mexico's National Sports Award, presented to her by Mexico's president Vicente Fox. In 2002, her fledgling year as a pro, she makes an impressive start, winning several tournaments.

During 2003, she finishes in the top 10 eight times and is named the rookie of the year, becoming the first Mexican-born player to capture the accolade. For her stunning achievements as an amateur golfer, the Tucson, Arizona, resident is the recipient of the fourth annual Nancy Lopez Award, the first Latina thus honored.

Laura Diaz, a pro from Scotia, New York, since 1997, is tied for third in the first round of the Michelob Ultra Open at the Kingsmill Resort & Spa in Williamsburg, Virginia, in May of 2005.

She fails to win a tournament in 2005, finishing 11 over par for a score of 295 after 72 holes in the Sybase Classic at New Rochelle, New York's famed Wykagyl Country Club.

For 30-year-old Diaz, formerly known as Laura Philo, playing golf is a family affair; her father is pro Ron Philo who teaches her to play and her husband Kevin is a teaching professional. In 2003, she hits the $2 million earnings level. In 2004, she recovers from ankle surgery to post seven top 10 finishes. During 2002, she enjoys her best season on the Tour with 10 top 10 finishes, including a tie for second at the Welch's-Circle K Championship in Tucson, Arizona. During her college competition for Wake Forest, she wins the 1995 Athletic Collegiate Conference championship and is a first-team All American in 1996 and 1997. In 1998, she's named the rookie of the year on the Women's Pro Golfers European Tour. She wins her first LPGA Tour tournament in 2002 at the Welch's/Circle K championship, followed by winning the LPGA Jamie Farr Owens Corning Classic in Toledo, Ohio.

Spain's 25-year-old Paula Marti is a top 10 player since turning pro in 2000. The Barcelona-born athlete moves to the pro ranks after winning the Spanish amateur championship in 1996 and playing on the junior Ryder Cup team in 1995 and 1997. In 2004, she shoots two career low 65s, during the final round of the Franklin American Mortgage championship (tying for sixth) and during the third round of the Welch's/Fry Championship in Tucson. She also ties for seventh at the Wegmans Rochester International tournament. Her best finish in 2003 is a tie for 12th at the Weetabix Women's British Open. In 2002, she wins the Australian LPGA Tournament of Champions, ties for second at the Weetabix, following four straight rounds in the 60s. In 2001, she wins two tourneys on the Ladies European Tour, La Perla Italian Open and the Kellogg's All-Bran Ladies British Masters.

Argentina's Angel Cabrera turns pro in 1989. He's 20 when he joins the PGA tour in 2001. During his early years, he concentrates on tournaments in South America, winning the Paraguay Open in 1995 and the Volvo Masters of Latin America in 1996. He represents Argentina five times in World Cup competition, finishing third in 1998 with Ricardo Gonzalez and second in 2000 with Eduardo Romero behind the U.S. team. In 1995, he joins the European tour and in 1999 finishes second to Sergio Garcia in the Murphy's Irish Open. One year later, he finishes second on the European Tour. In 2001, he wins his first European title, the Open De Argentina in Buenos Aires and then begins concentrating on the PGA Tour in the U.S. that year, winding up seventh at the U.S. Open and 10th at the U.S. Masters. In 2002, he nabs his first European tour tournament, the Benson and Hedges International Open; the next year attempting to play on both the European and PGA circuits, his scoring lacks consistency and he admits playing in both major competitions is difficult for him. In 2004, he snares two tournaments in Argentina and finishes second at the European Masters and the Volvo PGA. He completes the year ranked 31st in the world ratings; in mid-2005 he's ranked 33rd and his $4.37 million earnings ranks him 15th in the world money-wise.

Lee Trevino, born in Garland, Texas, on December 8, 1939, joins the professional golf circuit in 1967 and finishes in 45th place. The next year, the 28-year-old unknown wins the U.S. Open and in 1971 repeats as the titleholder. Among his four other major championships are the PGA championship in 1974 and 1984 and the British Open in 1971 and 1972. In 1971, he also wins his first of three Canadian Opens to become the first player to win the U.S., British, and Canadian Opens in the same year (1971). Playing on the Champions Tour, he racks up 29 victories and is inducted into the World Golf Hall of Fame in 1981. During his PGA Tour competitions he wins 32 times, his last victory occurring in 1984. At the time of his retirement from the pro tour one year later, he's second on the career earnings list. He plays on the U.S. Ryder Cup team six times against its British opponents and is named captain of the team in 1985. He's also active on the seniors' tour, winning his first title in 1992 and his second two years later and in 1995 breaks a year-long draught by winning the Northville Long Island Classic.

Trevino, called "Supermex," is indeed one lucky golfer. During the PGA Tour in 1975, he's stuck by lightning on June 27 during the Western Open in Chicago, and while being jolted pretty good, survives with severe lower back problems that necessitate a series of operations. Two years later, he's recovered enough to win his second Canadian Open, an accomplishment he repeats in 1979, and in 1984 at age 44 wins the second of his PGA championships.

Juan "Chi Chi" Rodriguez places his native Puerto Rico on the pro golf map. Born in Rio Piedras in 1935, he's a pro player for 40 years, winning eight PGA tours and 22 senior tours. For some one who grows up helping his dad in the sugar cane fields, golf is really good for Rodriguez, whose earnings as a pro golfer exceed $7 million. During both the 1990 and 1991 seasons, he wins four PGA tournaments in each of those years. He's known for consistently hitting the ball 250 yards or more during his career. He is also known for his colorful personality traits on the links, especially when he holes a putt. He is a member of the Puerto Rican World Cup team 12 times. In 1987, he wins the senior's championship and in 1992 is inducted into the PGA's World Golf Hall of Fame. His last victory occurs in 1993 when emerging health problems affect his game. While competing on the senior tour in 1998, he suffers a heart attack in October due to what turns out to be a blocked artery for which he has an angioplasty procedure. Through his Chi Chi Rodriguez Foundation in Clearwater, Florida, he's able to house and assist troubled and abused youngsters.

Severiano "Seve" Ballesteros is Spain's most famous golfer who turns pro when he's 16, plays on six PGA Tours, 56 European Tours, wins the Masters in 1980 and 1983 and the British Open in 1979, 1984, and 1988 and is elected to the World Golf Hall of Fame. In 2000, he's named both the European Player and Spanish Sportsman of the Century. He's also an eight-time member of the European Ryder cup team and non-playing captain of the team in 1997. In 1980, he wins the U.S. Open to become the first European to wear the green jacket at Augusta. He repeats the achievement in 1983 and 1984 to gain recognition in some quarters as the best player in the world. Splitting his time between the U.S. and Europe comes with a costly price: In 1981, he's voted off the European Ryder Cup team for playing too much in the U.S. Then in another dispute, this time with the PGA Tour, his request to play part-time in the U.S. is denied, so he remains in Europe fulltime. In 1984, 1985, and 1988 he wins the British Open, the latter his last major victory of his career.

But he remains an active player in Ryder Cup competition in 1989, 1991, 1993, and 1995, which marks his last tournament victory. His achievements prompt the European Tour in 2000 to initiate the Seve Ballesteros Trophy for teams from England/Ireland competing against teams from continental Europe similar to the way they do battle in the Ryder Cup. In that inaugural event, Seve, the European team captain beats Colin Montgomerie, the undisputed top European golfer in their singles match as the European team wins the match overall. Known for using fencing stokes when he holes a long putt, Ballesteros' play in recent years slackens off, with some speculation he'll hold off on competition until 2008 when he can join the Seniors Tour, replete with major names and lesser-known competitors.

In addition to PGA Senior Tour champs Trevino and Rodriguez, Joe Jiminez wins the Senior's title in 1978. In 2005, the 25th anniversary of the champions tour, Jiminez at 80, is still competing, pairing with 81-year-old Charles Sifford in the Demaret Division of the tour near Savannah, where they finish second to the team of Orville Moody, 71, and Jimmy Powell, a spry 70. Between 1998 and 2000, Jiminez and Safford win the division at this event. Formed in 1993, the Demaret division is for golfers 70 and above.

Joe Jimenez, with a similar name but spelled differently with an "e" instead of a second "i", is 65 when in 1991 he makes senior championship tour history at the Inglewood Country Club near Seattle by firing a nine under par 63 in the second round to best his age for the first time in his career. In doing this, he becomes the "youngest" senior player to accomplish this feat. In 1995, when he's a mere 69, he shoots a 62 to tie for seventh place at the Ameritech

Senior Open. Homero Blancas also competes on the senior tour but is not a standout competitor.

Nancy Lopez's domination of the Ladies Professional Golf Association (LPGA) circuit is being challenged by Sweden's Annika Sorenstam since her retirement from active competition in 2002. In 2005, the 47-year-old is named captain of the U.S. Solheim Cup team, which will attempt to regain the cup from the European team in September at the Crooked Stick Golf Club in Carmel, Indiana. The American team has never lost at home. "Women's golf didn't exist before Nancy Lopez," strongly asserts Donna Lopiano, chief executive officer of the Women's Sports Foundation in *Hispanic* Magazine, which presents her with its Billie Jean King Contribution Award, the most recent of her accolades since the Torrance, California-born, Albany, Georgia resident turns pro in 1978. In her rookie year, she wins nine tournaments, including a record-setting five in a row and wins the rookie of the year, player of the year, and the Vare Trophy, becoming the only player to win these honors in the same season. She continues burning up fairways the next year, capturing eight tournaments, being named player of the year, and Vare Trophy recipient for the second time.

During her active years, she wins 48 LPGA tournaments and nine league awards, is inducted into the LPGA's World Golf Hall of Fame in 1989, and in 2000 during the LPGA's 50th year, is named one of the league's top 50 players and teachers.

In 2002, she announces she'll play in 14 events as part of her farewell tour after 24 years on the circuit. In 2000, she plays a limited number of events due to gall bladder problems, but the year is highlighted by the Chick-Fil-A-Charity Championship in Stockbridge, Georgia, adding, "Hosted by Nancy Lopez" to its title. The tournament also creates the annual Nancy Lopez Award to be presented during the tournament to the world's top female amateur golfer. It's at this event in 1997 that she wins her 48th career title and also becomes the first player to record four rounds in the 60s at the U.S. Women's Open. It's also the year she hits $5 million in career earnings. She becomes the second player in league history to achieve

$3 million in 1990, up from $2 million in 1988 and $1 million in 1983. She lands her first hole-in-one in 1982 at the Peter Jackson Classic.

The National Football League, following the lead of other professional sports which play games outside the Continental U.S., schedules its first regular season game between the Arizona Cardinals and the San Francisco 49ers in Mexico City, October 2, 2005. Since 1978, the NFL plays seven exhibition games in Mexico. At the time of the game at Estadia Azteca, 7,200 feet above sea level, the combatants are at the bottom of the four team Western Conference. League officials anticipate a larger crowd in Mexico than regularly attends the Cardinals home games. The NFL expects this good turnout based on its research which indicates there are 20 million pro football fans in Mexico compared to the 25 million Mexican-American football buffs, notes the *Los Angeles Times*. The Arizona squad includes guard Rolando Cantu, born and raised in Monterrey, who is the first Mexican national to make an NFL roster in a position other than a kicker, according to the *Times*. The game, won by the Cardinals 31 to 14, draws the largest regular season crowd in NFL history: 103,467, which is 68,398 more than watches last season's meeting at Sun Devil Stadium, notes the *Times*. Especially appealing to the fans is Cardinals player Robert Griffith leading his team onto the field waving a Mexican flag.

Professional tennis, overseen by the United States Tennis Association, the name successor for the U.S. National Lawn Tennis Association formed in 1881, is a sport, which in comparison to others does not have a strong Latin presence in recent years. Nor a leader like the late Pancho Gonzalez, a poor boy from the barrio of Los Angeles who matures into a worldwide figure during his 30-year career. The ranks of the pros include a large number of Spaniards in both the men's and women's ranks, followed by players from Argentina, Chile, Ecuador, Brazil, Peru, Mexico, Puerto Rico, Colombia, Paraguay, and Mexico. Among the contingent of Latinos on the tour, Marcelo Rios from Chile and Juan Carlos Ferrero from Spain are among the handful of younger players drawing attention to themselves in a sport made exciting by a long list of Anglo legends and the U.S. Pancho Richard Alonso Gonzalez, Peru's Alex Olmedo (Luis Alejandro Rodriguez Olmedo), and Spain's Jordi Arrese.

And among women, the legacy players include an equally impressive list of Anglos and Brazil's Maria Bueno, the Dominican's Mary Joe Fernandez, and Argentina's Paola Suarez.

In 1968, organized tennis establishes the "open era" of competition, allowing players to compete in all tournaments and make their living as a tennis pro.

Pancho Gonzalez is one of the sport's all time champions, competing in the open era and winning the U.S. pro singles title eight times and the U.S. national singles title in 1948 and 1949. In 1969, at age 41, he's the oldest seeded player in Wimbledon Championship history, besting America's top player Charlie Pasarell in 112 game match, 22-24, 1-6, 16 -14, 6-3, and 11-9 which lasts 5 hours and 12 minutes spread over two days on the center court. It's the longest tournament match until 1992 when Michael Chang and Stefan Edberg exceed it by 14 minutes in the U.S. Open. Gonzalez dies of stomach cancer in Las Vegas in 1995 where he's a teaching pro; he's 67.

During his career, he's a very intense competitor who faces the discrimination of being a Chicano from L.A. and an outsider to the so-called upper-class tennis establishment. He turns pro in 1954 and is credited with a serve that is clocked at 112 miles per hour. In 1948 he wins the U.S. Open Championship at Forest Hills, New York and the next year he turns pro at the age of 21 and plays on the victorious U.S. Davis Cup team which defeats Australia. After several lean years, at age 42, he reaches the quarterfinals of the U.S. Open. In 1972, three months before his 44th birthday, he's the oldest player to win a tournament, the Des Moines. He's also the oldest player that year to rank ninth in the nation and land on the world top ten player list in 1948, 1949 (finishing first), 1968, and 1969. In 1968, he's named to the Tennis Hall of Fame. After retiring in 1969, he becomes an instructor and non-playing captain of the U.S. Davis Cup team.

Marcello Rios, a 30-year-old from Santiago, Chile, who starts training for a career in tennis in 1988, travels with his family to Florida in 1990 to meet with famed coach Nick Bollettieri, who accepts him for tutelage. Two years later he's on the pro circuit, and along with countryman Gabriel Silberstein, they get to the finals of the U.S. Open. The next year, Rios wins several tournaments including the U.S. Open and is ranked No. 1 among junior players. In 1997, he's the first Chilean during the open era to reach the quarterfinals of both the Australian and U.S. Open. He's also the first Latin American ranked No. 1 in the world and during his career wins 18 titles.

Juan Carlos Ferrero, born and raised in Onteniente, Spain, in 1980, has dual nicknames: "Mosquito" due to his speed and small physique and "chavalito" (little kid). He begins his pro career in 1998, winning several tournaments in his native country, is named the ATP Tour newcomer of the year in 1999 and by 2000 is ranked Spain's No. 2 player. That year he makes the quarterfinals of the Sydney Olympics. By 2001, he finishes fifth in the year-end rankings, the highest by a Spaniard since Alex Corretja finishes third in 1998. He also compiles a career best 16-match winning streak that year as well. By 2002, he's ranked fourth in the world and becomes the first Spaniard to appear in the top two consecutive years since Sergi Bruguera accomplishes that feat from 1993 to 1994. In 2003, he moves up to No. 3 worldwide and is again the first Spaniard to achieve that position since Alex Corretja holds it in 1998. In winning 33 matches on clay and 30 on hard courts in the same season, he matches Ivan Lendl, who wins at least 30 matches on both surfaces in 1980. For his efforts, he's awarded his nation's 2003 National Sportsman of the Year Award, which he receives the next year from King Juan Carlos. It's the Spanish government's highest sports honor. In 2004, he becomes the first Spaniard to reach the U.S. Open finals since Manuel Orantes wins the title in 1975. He helps Spain defeat Argentina 3-2 in the Davis Cup semifinals and for the year he earns a career-high $3,026,760.

One of Latin America's early stars is Peru's Alex Olmedo, born in 1936 and a student at USC in 1956 where he wins intercollegiate titles for the school in singles and doubles in 1956 and 1958. The next year he is a finalist for the U.S. singles indoor title and wins the Wimbledon and Australian titles. Called "Chief" at USC because of his Incan features and six-foot height, Olmedo is at the center of a controversy when he's selected for the U.S. Davis Cup team by the 1958 to 1959 captain Perry Jones, who lobbies for his inclusion based on Olmedo being a U.S. resident whose native country has no Davis Cup team. After he wins his semifinal match over Italy's Nicola Pietrangeli, his presence on the U.S. team as a non-citizen generates a rash of criticism, which continues during the Cup round when American Ham Richardson is benched in favor of Olmedo in the singles competition, which he wins against his Australian opponent in Brisbane. In the Cup championship at Forest Hills, the U.S. loses to Australia 3 to 2. In 1960, he turns pro having been ranked No. 2 in the U.S. in 1958, and No. 1 in the U.S. and No. 2 in the world in 1959. He is elected to the Hall of Fame in 1987.

Argentina's Paola Suarez, born in 1976, turns pro when she's 18 and accumulates 354 wins with 223 losses in singles competition; 454 wins with 161 losses in doubles play during her career, which translates into earnings of $4,837,968 by the time she's 29 in 2005.

The Dominican Republic's Mary Joe Fernandez, born in 1971, wins more than she loses, racking up 437 singles wins versus 203 losses and 344 doubles wins against 141 loses worth $5,258,471 leading into 2005. In 1996, with Lindsay Davenport, she wins the French Open doubles title and in late 1997, she undergoes arthroscopic surgery on her right wrist.

Articles

"A Real Heavyweight In Pay-Per-View Stats." Los Angeles Times, May 10, 2007

"Mayweather Defeats De La Hoya, Floyd Picks Up The Split." Los Angeles Times, May 6, 2007

"Baseball Looks To Create A Possible Portal To Cuba." New York Times, April 26, 2007

"How The Mets Got Red Hot." Time, Oct. 2, 2006

"Europe Pours It On With U.S. In Ryder Cup Blowout." Los Angeles Times, Sept. 26, 2006

"Valenzuela Returns, Prevails In Toronto." Los Angeles Times, Sept. 18, 2006

"Valenzuela Must Pass Hair Test." Los Angeles Times, Sept. 7, 2006

"Velenzuela In Hospital As Testing Sought." Los Angeles Times, Aug. 15, 2006

"Romance in Spanish." Daily Variety, July 25, 2006

"Towering Tribute." Hispanic, August 2006

"Top Jockey Velazquez Out With Injury." Los Angeles Times, April 22, 2006

"This Time, Ochoa Gets To Enjoy Finish." Los Angeles Times, April 16, 2006

"Banderas Is The 'Juan.'" Daily Variety, April 10, 2006

"Banderas Conquers Epic." Daily Variety, April 5, 2006

"Rising Stars Fall As Webb Rallies For PGA Victory." Los Angeles Times, April 3, 2006

"For Ochoa, 71 Is The New 62." Los Angeles Times, April 1, 2006

"Ochoa On Mark With 62." Los Angeles Times, March 31, 2006

"Mitchell's Baseball Ties Raise Questions." Los Angeles Times, March 31, 2006

"Searching For Movies That Speak To Latinos." Los Angeles Times, March 30, 2006

"Mitchell To Lead Steroids Inquiry." Los Angeles Times, March 30, 2003

"MLS Looks Way Down The Field." Los Angeles Times, March 29, 2006

"Guevara Movie To Film In Mexico." Los Angeles Times, March 28, 2006

"Sheffield Implicated In Book." Los Angeles Times, March 23, 2006

"Japan Is Classic Winner." Los Angeles Times, March 21, 2006

"Cubans In Midseason Form." Los Angeles Times, March 19, 2006

"Japan's Win Counts Most." Los Angeles Times, March 19, 2006

"A Classic Fall For U.S. With Loss To Mexico." Los Angeles Times, March 17, 2006

"U.S. Gets To Second Standing Up." Los Angeles Times, March 11, 2006

"Canada Hangs U.S. To Dry." Los Angeles Times, March 9, 2006

"Houston Team Gets Renamed The Dynamo." Los Angeles Times, March 7, 2006

"From Mets' Perspective, Classic Is A Glass Half Full." New York Times, March 6, 2006

"Classic Win For The U.S." Los Angeles Times, March 6, 2006

"Garcia Bernal Takes 1st Shot At Directing." Hollywood Reporter, March 2, 2006

"Psst! The Cubans Are Coming." Time, March 6, 2006

"Mosley Gets Swell TKO In 10." Los Angeles Times, Feb. 26, 2006

"Santaolalla Goes To The Movies." Billboard, Feb. 25, 2006

"NL Books Bardem For 'Cholera.'" Hollywood Reporter, Feb. 17, 2006

"Pedro Gonzalez Gonzalez, 80; Comedic Entertainer And Character Actor Who Starred In Movies And TV." Los Angeles Times, Feb. 15, 2006

"Anaheim Strikes Out Against Angels." Los Angeles Times, Feb. 10, 2006

"Key Word Is 'Include' For Angel-Anaheim Jury." Los Angeles Times, Feb. 10, 2006

"MLS Goes Backward, All The Way To 1800s." Los Angeles Times, Feb. 6, 2006

"Moreno Leads Group As It Buys Radio Station." Los Angeles Times, Feb. 5, 2006

"Cuba Gets Approval To Compete In Classic." San Diego Union Tribune, Jan. 21, 2006

"Anaheim May Plan On Angel Move." Los Angeles Times, Jan. 4, 2006

"MLS Gets A New City." Los Angeles Times, Dec. 16, 2005

"U.S Gets A Tough Draw." Los Angeles Times, Dec. 10, 2005

"Major League Stars Sign Up For World Baseball Classic." Los Angeles Times, Dec. 6, 2005

"World Baseball Classic Is Value Laden." USA Today, Dec. 6, 2005

"Vic Power, First Baseman With Flair, Is Dead at 78." New York Times, Nov. 30, 2005

"Vic Power." www.baseballlibrary.com, Nov. 30, 2005

"Bradley To Coach Chivas USA." Los Angeles Times, Nov. 22, 2005

"Baseball Owners Approve New Steroid Policy." Los Angeles Times, Nov. 18, 2005

"Owners Unanimously Approve Baseball's New Steroids Policy." Sportsnetwork.com, Nov. 17, 2005

"2006 FIFA World Cup." ESPNsoccernet.com, Nov. 16, 2005

"Baseball Backs Stiffer Penalties For Steroid Use." New York Times, Nov. 16, 2005

"Baseball Adds Muscle To Steroid Punishment." Los Angeles Times, Nov. 16, 2005

"Pujols Wins A Narrow Vote Over Jones For NL MVP." Los Angeles Times, Nov. 16, 2005

"Rodriguez Edges Ortiz For AL MVP." Los Angeles Times, Nov. 15, 2005

"Galaxy Is The Biggest Fish Again." Los Angeles Times, Nov. 14, 2005

"MLS To Add Toronto, But Others May Move." Los Angeles Times, Nov. 12, 2005

"Congressional Panel Doesn't Charge Palmeiro." New York Times, Nov. 10, 2005

"Tough Task Ahead For Galaxy." Los Angeles Times, Nov. 10, 2005

"After Pain Comes A Cy." Los Angeles Times, Nov. 9, 2005

"Lawton Draws Drug Suspension." Los Angeles Times, Nov. 3, 2005

"Al Lopez, 97; Hall Of Famer Led White Sox, Indians To Pennants." Los Angeles Times, Oct. 31, 2005

"It's A Classic Finish For Saint Liam." Los Angeles Times, Oct. 30, 2005

"De La Hoya-Mayorga Fight Tentatively Set For May 6." Los Angeles Times, Oct. 28, 2005

"Fox Needs A Ratings Rally." Daily Variety, Oct. 28, 2005

"Valenzuela Rides Five Winners." Los Angeles Times, Oct. 28, 2005

"White Sox Get Their Fix." Los Angeles Times, Oct. 27, 2005

"Guillen, Garcia Share Pride For Country." USA Today, Oct. 27, 2005

"Estevez Adds Three Stars To 'Bobby' Cast." Los Angeles Times, Oct. 27, 2005

"Late-Inning Reserve Gives The White Sox A Lead In The 14th As Chicago "Takes A 3-0 Edge in Longest Game In Series History." Los Angeles Times, Oct. 26, 2005

"Theps Bite On Food Toon." Daily Variety, Oct. 25, 2005

"Valenzuela Scheduled To Return Wednesday." Los Angeles Times, Oct. 24, 2005

"Houston, You Have Liftoff." Los Angeles Times, Oct. 20, 2005

"Stewards Ask Valenzuela To Meet With Them." Los Angeles Times, Oct. 20, 2005

"Gomez Can Pad His Lead." Los Angeles Times, Oct. 19, 2005

"Chivas Ponders A Lost Season." Los Angeles Times, Oct. 19, 2005

"Franchitti Edges Suddenly Slow Kannan." Los Angeles Times, Oct. 17, 2005

"Nine Thick Slices Of Life." Los Angeles Times, Oct. 13, 2005

"Anaheim Legal Bill: $1.1 Million." Los Angeles Times, Oct. 12, 2005

"Castillo's Punches Are Heavy As Well." Los Angeles Times, Oct. 9, 2005

"Mexico Embraces Game." Los Angeles Times, Oct. 3, 2005

"It's Another $1-Million Upset Win For Borrego." Los Angeles Times, Oct. 2, 2005

"Mexico Game Inaugurates A New Era." Los Angeles Times, Oct. 2, 2005

"Palencia's Goal Is Enough For Chivas." Los Angeles Times, Oct. 2, 2005

"Cameron Diaz: In Her Shoes." Star, Oct. 10, 2005

"Baseball Put On Notice On Steroids." Los Angeles Times, Sept. 29, 2005

"Anaheim Could Share World Baseball Classic." Los Angeles Times, Sept. 29, 2005

"Gomez Is At The right Spot At The Right Time." Los Angeles Times, Sept. 29, 2005

"Gamez Ends His Drought." Los Angeles Times, Sept. 26, 2005

"Chivas USA Still Gets Little Help." Los Angeles Times, Sept. 25, 2005

"Angels Tell Palmeiro Not To Bother Returning." Los Angeles Times, Sept. 24, 2005

"Boxer Dies From Injury." Los Angeles Times, Sept. 22, 2005

"Latin Dances Unveiled On New U.S. Postage Stamps." HispaniaNet.com, Sept. 21, 2005

"Colon Is 20-Something." Los Angeles Times, Sept. 21, 2005

"Congress Asks Players For Input On Palmeiro." Los Angeles Times, Sept. 20, 2005

"Injured Boxer Shows Fight." Los Angeles Times, Sept. 19

"Dancer, Your Life Is Calling." Los Angeles Times, Sept. 18

"Another Loss Plays Out." Los Angeles Times, Sept. 18

"Boxer Johnson In Critical State After Brain Surgery." Los Angeles Times, Sept. 18, 2005

"Mosley's Win Over Cruz Is Unanimous But Not Pretty." Los Angeles Times, Sept. 18, 2005

"Gomez Propels Galaxy To Final." Los Angeles Times, Sept. 15, 2005

"Viloria Is A Knockout In Return." Los Angeles Times, Sept. 10, 2005

"De Rosario Gives Chivas The Boot." Los Angeles Times, Sept. 10, 2005

"Mexico Secures German Spot." Los Angeles Times, Sept. 8, 2005

"Taking Some Mighty Swings." Los Angeles Times, Sept. 7, 2005

"Palmeiro Sent Home To Rest Knee." Los Angeles Times, Sept. 6, 2005

"Anaheim Is Finalist To Stage New Event." Los Angeles Times, Sept. 6, 2005

"U.S. Clinches Spot In World Cup." Los Angeles Times, Sept. 4, 2005

"Crew Spoils Fun For Chivas USA." Los Angeles Times, Sept. 4, 2005

"Guerrero Has A Crush On Mariners." Los Angeles Times, Sept. 3, 2005

"Driven To Be Diverse." Los Angeles Times, Sept. 3, 2005

"La Divina Gina." Latina, September 2005

"Latinologues On Broadway." HispaniaNet.com, Aug. 30, 2005

"Traveling Movie Theater Features Mexico's Golden Age Of Cinema." HispaniaNet.com, Aug. 30, 2005

"Chivas Gets A Point On The Road." Los Angeles Times, Aug. 28, 2005

"Gomez Makes The Most Of It." Los Angeles Times, Aug. 27, 2005

"Mariners Dream Teen: The Next Generation Pitcher?" USA Today, Aug. 25, 2005

"MLB Launches Vote For 'Latino Legends Team.'" USA Today, Aug. 24, 2005

"Real Madrid Breezes To 5-0 Win Against Team Of MLS Stars." USA Today, Aug. 24, 2005

"Borrego Comes From 9th To Win." Los Angeles Times, Aug. 22, 2005

"Imperialism Wins Late Burst." Los Angeles Times, Aug. 22, 2005

"Disappointing Tie For Chivas." Los Angeles Times, Aug. 22, 2005

"Vargas Eyes De La Hoya." New York Times, Aug. 22, 2005

"Vargas' Win Is Scaled Down." Los Angeles Times, Aug. 21, 2005

"Earthquakes Increase Lead In West." Los Angeles Times, Aug. 21, 2005

"U.S. Mexico Soccer Stakes Grow Ever Higher." New York Times, Aug. 19, 2005

"U.S. Nears World Cup Berth." Los Angeles Times, Aug. 18, 2005

"ABC, ESPN To Broadcast All World Cup Games." Los Angeles Times, Aug.18, 2005

"Early U.S. Score Holds Up 1-0." Los Angeles Times, Aug. 18, 2005

"Borgetti's Goal Lifts Mexico, 2-0." Los Angeles Times, Aug. 18, 2005

"Superhero Redux." Los Angeles Times, Aug. 14, 2005

"Chivas USA Gets Walker's Payback." Los Angeles Times, Aug. 14, 2005

"Congress Gets Documents On Palmeiro." Los Angeles Times, Aug. 13, 2005

'Latinologues' To Play Broadway." Los Angeles Times, Aug. 11, 2005

"Galaxy Beats Chivas, 1-0, In Front Of 88,816." Los Angeles Times, Aug. 11, 2005

"Club America Rallies To Win." Los Angeles Times, Aug. 11, 2005

"Outfielder Cruz Acquired In Trade." Los Angeles Times, Aug. 10, 2005

"Chivas Feels The Heat In 2-1 Loss To Salt Lake." Los Angeles Times, Aug. 7, 2005

"Pujols' 30th Homer Makes History." Los Angeles Times, Aug. 6, 2005

"Boxer Who Nearly Lost Life In Bout Headed Home Friday." Los Angeles Times, Aug. 4, 2005

"Palmeiro Faces More Scrutiny." Los Angeles Times, Aug. 4, 2005

"Galaxy Pours It On, Beats Chivas USA Again." Los Angeles Times, Aug. 4, 2005

"Franklin Denies Steroid Use Despite Positive MLB Test." Seattle Post-Intelligencer, Aug. 3, 2005

"Doubt Shadows Palmeiro." Los Angeles Times, Aug. 3, 2005

"Heat Gets Walker In 5-Team Deal." Los Angeles Times, Aug. 3, 2005

"Drug Rules Catch Baseball Star." Los Angeles Times, Aug. 2, 2005

"Suspensions." Los Angeles Times, Aug. 2, 2005

"Ahora (Mia Maestro)." Latina, August 2005

"Palmeiro Suspended For Steroids Policy Violation." USA Today.com, Aug. 1, 2005

"Velazquez Adds To Saratoga Wins." Los Angeles Times, July 31, 2005

"Late Goals Help Beat Fulham, 4-1." Los Angeles Times, July 31, 2005

"League Aims For Expansion, Development," Los Angeles Times, July 30, 2005

"Sosa's Milestone Homer Not Enough." Los Angeles Times, July 28, 2005

"Lopez Finishes Night To Remember For Sosa." Los Angeles Times, July 27, 2005

"U.S. Makes Panama Pay The Penalty." Los Angeles Times, July 25, 2005

"A Winless Streak Ends For Salt Lake." Los Angeles Times, July 24, 2005

"Cloud Over Chivas' Win." Los Angeles Times, July 23, 2005

"Esparza Has New Plan for Latin Venture." Hollywood Reporter, July 21, 2005

"Toney's Suspension To Be Lifted." Los Angeles Times, July 21, 2005

"Gomez Keeps Comeback Going Strong At Del Mar." Los Angeles Times, July 21, 2005

"Real Madrid's Visit Might Set Stage For Others." Los Angeles Times, July 19, 2005

"Galaxy Does Itself Proud." Los Angeles Times, July 18, 2005

"British Open Tiger's Double Major." Los Angeles Times, July 18, 2005

"Madrid Mystique." Los Angeles Times, July 18, 2005

"Colombia Eliminates Mexico." Los Angeles Times, July 18, 2005

"Royal Visit." Los Angeles Times, July 17, 2005

"Beasley At His Best As U.S. Advances." July 17, 2005

"Gomez Quite A Pillar Of Scoring For Galaxy." Los Angeles Times, July 17, 2005

"Palmeiro Hits It Big." Los Angeles Times, July 16, 2005

"Mexico Forges Ahead By Stopping Jamaica." Los Angeles Times, July 14, 2005

"Rally Gives Chivas A 3-2 Victory." Los Angeles Times, July 14, 2005

"Freddie Soto, 35; Latino Comedian's Stand-Up Act Had Universal Appeal." Los Angeles Times, July 13, 2005

"U.S. Looks Lackluster But Still Wins Group." Los Angeles Times, July 13, 2005

"AL Keeps Its Edge." Los Angeles Times, July 13, 2005

"It's A Record Effort for Phillies' Abreu." Los Angeles Times, July 12, 2005

"Out Of Olympics, Baseball Plans A Real World Series." Los Angeles Times, July 12, 2005

"Mexico Is Just Fine After Win." Los Angeles Times, July 11, 2005

"O'Brien's Play Good As Gold In U.S. Victory." Los Angeles Times, July 10, 2005

"Lava Man Runs Hot In Gold Cup Romp." Los Angeles Times, July 10, 2005

"Chivas USA Ends Its Misery In Grand Style." Los Angeles Times, July 10, 2005

"Spanish Accented." Los Angeles Times, July 10, 2005

"'Mambo's' New Problemo." Weekly Variety, July 10, 2005

"Frustrating First Game For Mexico." Los Angeles Times, July 9, 2005

"Goal Oriented." Los Angeles Times, July 8, 2005

"Gomez Tries To Extend Lead." Los Angeles Times, July 7, 2005

"Velazquez Searching For Gold." Los Angeles Times, July 6, 2005

"U.S., Mexico Ride Collision Course." Los Angeles Times, July 5, 2005

"Boxer Sanchez Dies After Bout At The Orleans." Las Vegas Review Journal, July 3, 2005

"Present Still Bleak For Chivas USA." Los Angeles Times, July 3, 2005

"Injured Boxer Is Making Progress." Los Angeles Times, July 2, 2005

"Panel OKs Sports Bills." Los Angeles Times, June 30, 2005

"ABC Scores With NBA, But CBS Wins." Los Angeles Times, June 29, 2005

"Chivas Releases Defenders." Los Angeles Times, June 28, 2005

"'Mambo Kings' Ends N.Y. Bid." Los Angeles Times, June 28, 2005

"Anaheim Loses Its Battle For Now." Los Angeles Times, June 28, 2005

"Birdie Lives Up To Name." Los Angeles Times, June 27, 2005

"Chivas USA Still Half Bad." Los Angeles Times, June 26, 2005

"Lawyers give Anaheim A Break In Angel Case." Los Angeles Times, June 25, 2005

"Finals Ratings Strong In L.A." Los Angeles Times, June 25, 2005

"Duncan Is MVP As San Antonio Wins Title, But Horry Is There Again." Los Angeles Times, June 24, 2005

"Real Madrid Is Making Its Way To The U.S. Soon." Los Angeles

Times, June 24, 2005
"Galaxy Lacking Inspiration." Los Angeles Times, June 23, 2005
"Late Dallas Goal Beats Chivas." Los Angeles Times, June 23, 2005
"A Diva Is Born." Latina, July 2005
"String Of Late Birdies Helps Ochoa Take Title." Los Angeles Times, June 20, 2005
"Campbell's Up To Par." Los Angeles Times, June 20, 2005
"Sosa's Homer In Victory Ties Him With McGuire." Los Angeles Times, June 20, 2005
"Cunningham Chews Up Chivas USA For Rapids." Los Angeles Times, June 19, 2005
"He's Defect Free." Los Angeles Times, June 17, 2005
"Montalban Foundation Out Of Business, For Now." Los Angeles Times, June 15, 2005
"Spur Of The Moment." Los Angeles Times, June 14, 2005
"Manu Making His Mark In Finals." USA Today, June 14, 2005.
"Garcia's 65 Wins Booz Allen." Los Angeles Times, June 13, 2005
"Afleet Alex Is Back For Seconds." Los Angeles Times, June 12, 2005
"Sweet Return Keeps Head Up." Los Angeles Times, June 12, 2005
"'Fog Clearly Wins Again." Los Angeles Times, June 12, 2005
"Donovan Gives Galaxy A 1-0 Win In Return." Los Angeles Times, June 12, 2005
"Chivas USA Gets Even After Its Near Misses." Los Angeles Times, June 12, 2005
"U.S. Takes Care Of Business." Los Angeles Times, June 9, 2005
"Russell Baze Suffers Injury." Los Angeles Times, June 9, 2005
"Argentina Earns Spot With Win Over Brazil." Los Angeles Times, June 9, 2005
"Contreras Still Critical, But Condition Improves." Los Angeles Times, June 8, 2005
"U.S. Takes A Cautious Approach On Panama." Los Angeles Times, June 8, 2005
"B'Way Pets Its Python." Daily Variety, June 6, 2005
"Chivas USA Can't Keep Up With The Fire." Los Angeles Times, June 5, 2005
"Mexico Handles Guatemala, 2-0." Los Angeles Times, June 5, 2005
"For U.S., It Turns Into A Marquee Event." Los Angeles Times, June 5, 2005
"Journeyman In A Fight For His Life." Los Angeles Times, June 4, 2005
"Tie Is A Nice Gift For Chivas." Los Angeles Times, June 2, 2005
"Contreras Fight To Be Reviewed." Los Angeles Times, June 2, 2005
"Keepin' It Cool." Latina, June 2005

"Who's Hot, Ahora...Rick Gonzalez." Latina, June 2005

"Ham-A-Lot!" Latina, June 2005

"Still Flying High." Hispanic Magazine, June 2005

"Westerhoff Will Become Coach Of Chivas USA." May 31, 2005

"Boxer Remains In Critical Condition." Los Angeles Times, May 30, 2005

"Shocked Viloria Praying For Foe." Honolulu Advertiser, May 30, 2005

"His-And-Her Victory." Los Angeles Times, May 30, 2005

"Now You Know." Los Angeles Times, May 30, 2005

"Patrick Eyes Piece Of History." Los Angeles Times, May 29, 2005

"Chavez Is A Unanimous Winner." Los Angeles Times, May 29, 2005

"Boxer Has Seizure, Then Brain Surgery." Los Angeles Times, May 29, 2005

"Same Old Tune For Chivas USA." Los Angeles Times, May 29, 2005

"Jockey Dominguez Is Cleared." Los Angeles Times, May 27, 2005

"Chico Carrasquel, 77: Was 1st Latino To Start In a Major League All-Star Game." Los Angeles Times, May 27, 2005

"Argentina Stops Mexico, Sets Up Final With Brazil." Los Angeles Times, May 27, 2005

"Boxing Fans Get Discount Special." Los Angeles Times, May 25, 2005

"Real Madrid Is Making Its Way To The U.S. Soon." Los Angeles Times, May 24, 2005

"Jockey Is Criticized After Stumble-Causing Intrusion." Los Angeles Times, May 23, 2005

"No Answers For Chivas USA." Los Angeles Times, May 23, 2005

"Angels' Morales Hits Homer In First At-Bat." Los Angeles Times, May 23, 2005

"Afleet Alex Gets Up And Goes." Los Angeles Times, May 22, 2005

"The 300 Club." Los Angeles Times, May 15, 2005

"Colorado Quiets Chivas, 2-1." Los Angeles Times, May 15, 2005.

"Galaxy Doesn't Help Itself." Los Angeles Times, May 15, 2005

"More Suspensions For Minor Leaguers." Los Angeles Times, May 14, 2005

"Toney Won't Dispute His Drug Test Result." Los Angeles Times, May 13, 2005

"Owners Endorse New Drug Policy." Los Angeles Times, May 12, 2005

"Toney Is Knocked Out By Positive Drug Test." Los Angeles Times, May 12, 2005

"Long Last Day Gets Away." Los Angeles Times, May 9, 2005

"Garcia Collapses, Singh Wins." Los Angeles Times, May 9, 2005

"Giacomo's Golden Gait." Los Angeles Times, May 8, 2005

"Chivas' 1-0 Victory Is Better Late Than Never." Los Angeles Times, May 8, 2005

"Corrales Climbs Off The Ropes." Los Angeles Times, May 8, 2005

"Dressing Up Churchill Downs." Los Angeles Times, May 6, 2005

"Kentucky Derby Capsules." Los Angeles Times, May 6, 2005

"Sorenstam (76) Must Make Cut Before She Can Make History." Los Angeles Times, May 6, 2005

"Six Shooter." Los Angeles Times, May 5, 2005

"Baseball May Revisit Its Derided Steroid Policy." Los Angeles Times, May 3, 2005

"Selig Wants To Give Steroid Offenders 50 Games To Life." Los Angeles Times, May 1, 2005

"Chivas Falters At The Finish." Los Angeles Times, May 1, 2005

"Toney Finally Relives His Favorite Scene." Los Angeles Times, May 1, 2005

"Stars Of The Show." Hispanic Magazine, May 2005

"Dot The I." Hispanic Magazine, May 2005

"Toney Vs. Ruiz Is A Fight For Title, Attention." Los Angeles Times, April 30, 2005

"Almodovar Names His Next Stars." Los Angeles Times, April 30, 2005

"De La Hoya Turns Eye To Real Estate Projects." Los Angeles Times, April 28, 2005

"Banderas In 'Bordertown' With Lopez." Hollywood Reporter, April 28, 2005

"Mediation Fails For Angels, City." Los Angeles Times, April 27, 2005

"Galaxy Owns The Town." Los Angeles Times, April 24, 2005

"Amazin' Inroads By Mets." Los Angeles Times, April 18, 2005

"Real Salt Lake Wins Home Opener." Los Angeles Times, April 17, 2005

"A Cool Hand Prevails." Los Angeles Times, April 11, 2005

"Chivas USA More Than All Talk." Los Angeles Times, April 11, 2005

"Barrera Wastes No Time, Stops Fana." Los Angeles Times, April 10, 2005

"Bellamy Road Rules In Wood Memorial." Los Angeles Times, April 10, 2005

"In Racing, Teamwork Is In The Eye Of The Beholder." Los Angeles Times, April 10, 2005

"Around The Majors." Los Angeles Times, April 7, 2005

"Big Deal For Indian Catcher." Los Angeles Times, April 6, 2005

"Committee To Compare Drug-Testing Policies." Los Angeles Times, April 6, 2005

"Baseball Makes First Steroid Bust." Los Angeles Times." April 4, 2005

"Pruett Holds Fast For Fontana Win." Los Angeles Times, April 4, 2005

"It's A Disappointing Day For Chivas USA." Los Angeles Times, April 3, 2005

"For Starters, Real Salt Lake Gets The Point." Los Angeles Times, April 3, 2005

"Q&A Enrique Murciano." Latina, April 2005

"Zoe-Ology." Latina, April 2005

"The Performance Of A Lifetime." Hispanic Magazine, April 2005

"U.S. Soccer Victory Lack Home Equity." Los Angeles Times, March 31, 2005

"Outlook Is As Bright As It Can Be." Los Angeles Times, March 30, 2005

"Galarraga Retires One Homer From 400." Los Angeles Times, March 30, 2005

"Court Urges Anaheim, Angels To Negotiate." Los Angeles Times, March 29, 2005

"Mexican Biz Bulks Up." Weekly Variety, March 28, 2005

"Mexico Refuses To Let U.S. Come Up For Air." Los Angeles Times, March 28, 2005

"Vargas Wins In His Return." Los Angeles Times, March 27, 2005

"Galaxy Tries A Star Swap." Los Angeles Times, March 25, 2005

"Open-Door" Los Angeles Times, March 22, 2005

"Kicking Soccer Even Higher." Multichannel News, March 21, 2005

"Johnson In Good Position Again." Los Angeles Times, March 20, 2005

"Alomar May Announce Retirement." Los Angeles Times, March 19, 2005

"Williams, Morales Head To Broadway." Los Angeles Times, March 19, 2005

"Players Balk On Steroid Use." Los Angeles Times, March 18, 2005

"'Don't Move,' My Dearest Love." Los Angeles Times, March 18, 2005

"House Panel's Steroid Inquiry To Play Before A Sellout Crowd." Los Angeles Times, March 16, 2005

"Ruling Favors Anaheim." Los Angeles Times, March 16, 2005

"Selig Is Willing To Testify." Los Angeles Times, March 15, 2005

"Ramirez Says He Wants To Return To Chivas USA." Los Angeles Times, March 13, 2005

"Conquistador In Cleats." Los Angeles Times Magazine, March 13, 2005

"No Castaway." Los Angeles Times, March 12, 2005

"USA's Other Aging Boomers." USA Today, March 11, 2005

"Father And Son Delighted To Be Reunited." USA Today, March 11, 2005

"Angels Claim Anaheim Can't Justify Fast Appeal." Los Angeles Times, March 10, 2005

"U.S. Is Heard Loud And Clear." March 10, 2005

"U.S. Mexico Share The Spotlight." Los Angeles Times, March 9, 3005

"Nov. 7 Trial Date Set In Angel Case." Los Angeles Times, March 9, 2005

"Congress To Call Players." Los Angeles Times, March 9, 2005

"Ramirez Leaves Chivas USA." Los Angeles Times, March 9, 2005

"'Hearts' In Right Place For Hayek." Daily Variety, March 8, 2005

"Crise's Deli Dalliance Serves Up Curiosity." USA Today, March 8, 2005

"Truex Is A Winner In Mexico." Los Angeles Times, March 7, 2005

"Race To The Border." Los Angeles Times, March 6, 2005

"Diaz Doesn't See Loss Coming." Los Angeles Times, March 6, 2005

"Jockeys' Guild Sued By Churchill Downs." Los Angeles Times, March 4, 2005

"As This Moon She Rises Higher." Los Angeles Times, March 3, 2005

"Judge Rules Angel Names Case Can go On." Los Angeles Times, March 3, 2005

"Uruguay Is Asking Why The Oscars Snubber Jorge Drexler." Wall Street Journal, March 2, 2005

"A Tone-Deaf Oscar Snubbed The Best Song Winner." Los Angeles Times, March 2, 2005

"Opening Doors." Los Angeles Times, March 2, 2005

"Oscars Hit Sour Notes." Daily Variety, March 2, 2005

"Youth Was Served." Daily Variety, March 1, 2005

"Anaheim Files Appeal." Los Angeles Times, March 1, 2005

"Barrel Of Barrio Laughs." Latina Magazine, March 2005

"Sister, Sister." Latina Magazine, March 2005

"Two Horses Die, Jockeys Hurt In Spill." Los Angeles Times, Feb. 27, 2005

"In Step With Christina Milian." Parade, Feb. 27, 2005

"Spirit Awards Toasts 'Sideways' With Sweep Of Six Major Categories, Los Angeles Times, Feb. 27, 2005

"A Songwriter's Dream Has Disappointing End." Los Angeles Times, Feb. 27, 2005

"Earning Their Stripes." Los Angeles Times, Feb. 26, 2005

"Their 'Q' Ratings Keeps Going Higher And Higher." Los Angeles Times, Feb. 23, 2005

"Mild Upset For Grand Appointment." Los Angeles Times, Feb. 21, 2005

"License To Run Is No Flop In The Slop." Los Angeles Times, Feb. 20, 2005

"Golden Touch." Los Angeles Times, Feb. 18, 2005.

"Twins Give Santana Big Deal." Los Angeles Times, Feb. 15, 2005

"McGwire Responds To Canseco." Los Angeles Times, Feb. 14, 2005

"'Aviator' Takes Flight With 4 BAFAs." Hollywood Reporter, Feb. 14, 2005

"Canseco Throws Book At Baseball." Los Angeles Times, Feb. 13, 2005

"Canseco Suspected Clemens, Bonds, Sosa." Los Angeles Times, Feb. 12, 2005

"Canseco's Claims Keep On Ticking." Los Angeles Times, Feb. 11, 2005

"In Oscar's Spotlight-But Who Is She?" Los Angeles Times, Feb. 11, 2005

"Pair To Chair Spirit Awards." Daily Variety, Feb. 9, 2005

"Chicago To Join WNBA." Los Angeles Times, Feb. 9, 2005

"It Takes A Little While, But Mexico Wins Title." Los Angeles Times, Feb. 8, 2005

"Ordonez, Tigers Agree To Deal." Los Angeles Times, Feb. 8, 2004

"Mendes Rides With Cage On Col's 'Ghost.'" Hollywood Reporter, Feb. 7, 2005

"Rock Hard Ten Shows He Has An Edge." Los Angeles Times, Feb. 6, 2005

"A Series Of Muy Grande Events." Los Angeles Times, Feb. 5, 2005

"Solis All Set To Get Back On The Horses." Los Angeles Times, Feb. 4, 2005

"'Bendito Infiero' Is Beyond Salvation." Los Angeles Times, Feb. 4, 2005

"With The Trade Official, Sosa Is Ready For Orioles." Los Angeles Times, Feb. 3, 2005

"Goyas Swept Out To 'Sea'." Hollywood Reporter, Feb. 1, 2005

"In Step With Eva Mendes." Parade, Jan. 30, 2005

"Orioles May Save Face With Sosa." Los Angeles Times, Jan. 30, 2005

"Great Scott! What A Winter." Los Angeles Times, Jan. 30, 2005

"Millions Favorites Face The Musique." Los Angeles Times, Jan. 30, 2005

"Pirate Boss Blasts Owners." Los Angeles Times, Jan. 29, 2005

"Sosa May Become An Oriole." Los Angeles Times, Jan. 29, 2005

"Sunshine Event Sheds Light On Weather." Los Angeles Times, Jan.

29, 2005
"Delgado Is Biggest Catch For Marlins." Los Angeles Times, Jan. 26, 2005
"Domestic Forwards Get Their Chance." Los Angeles Times, Jan. 25, 2005
"Ghostzapper Ends Up The Smartest Money." Los Angeles Times, Jan. 25, 2005
"Temporary Solution Problematic." Los Angeles Times, Jan. 24, 2005
"Valenzuela Is Working His Magic In Mexico." Los Angles Times, Jan. 24, 2005
"Valenzuela Gets First Stakes Win Since Return." Los Angeles Times, Jan. 24, 2005
"Double-Barreled Firepower." Los Angeles Times, Jan. 23, 2005
"Judge Won't Block Angel Name Switch." Los Angeles Times, Jan. 22, 2005
"Rocket decides He's The Re-Firing Type." Los Angeles Times, Jan. 22, 2005
"Solis Begins His Comeback After July Spill At Del Mar." Los Angeles Times, Jan. 21, 2005
"This Time, L.A. Has Problems With The Angels." Los Angeles Times, Jan. 20, 2005
"Gagne Picks Up A Two-Year Deal." Los Angeles Times, Jan. 19, 2005
"Cleveland And Cora Reach Deal." Los Angeles Times, Jan. 19, 2005
"Washburn Agrees To Deal." Los Angeles Times, Jan. 19, 2005
"Soriano, Rangers Agree To Deal For $7.5 Million." Los Angeles Times, Jan. 18, 2005
"Dodgers Swing for Big Triple." Los Angeles Times, Jan. 18, 2005
"Chivas Stocks Up, Galaxy Overhauls." Los Angeles Times, Jan. 15, 2005
"Valenzuela Receives OK To Ride." Los Angeles Times, Jan. 13, 2005
"'Moneyball' Is Hard To Figure." Los Angeles Times, Jan. 12, 2005
"Cash On Delivery." Los Angeles Times, Jan. 11, 2005
"DePodesta's Puzzle Is Almost Complete." Los Angeles Times, Jan. 11, 2005
"Beltran Is New King Of Queens." Los Angeles Times, Jan. 10, 2005
"Astros Fail To Sign Beltran Before Midnight Deadline." Los Angeles Times, Jan. 9, 2005
"Board Admits Mistake; Valenzuela To Return." Los Angeles Times, Jan. 8, 2005
"Judge Overrules Stewards' Suspension Of Valenzuela." Los Angeles Times, Jan. 7, 2004

"Johnson, Yankees Agree To Extend Contract." Los Angeles Times, Jan. 7, 2005

"Chacon, Fraser Join Hall Of Fame Class." Los Angeles Times, Jan. 7, 2005

"Anaheim Sues The Angels." Los Angeles Times, Jan. 6, 2005

"Trio Is Up For Two Eclipse Awards Each." Los Angeles Times, Jan. 6, 2005

"Angels To Be Team Of 2 Cities." Los Angeles Times, Jan. 4, 2005

"Pas De Duex Is At Heart Of Cuban Dance Film." Los Angeles Times, Jan. 4, 2005

"It's A Beautiful Day For O'Neill." Los Angeles Times, Jan. 3, 2005

"The Emerging Latina Voice In Filmmaking." Hispanic Magazine, January 2005

"And The Oscar Went To…" Hispanic Magazine, January 2005

"A Legend Returns." Hispanic Magazine, January 2005

"Major League Baseball Free Agent Signings." Los Angeles Times, Dec. 26, 2004

"City Moves Toward Suit Against Angels." Los Angeles Times, Dec. 24, 2004

"Alou Reportedly Will Join Father In San Francisco." Los Angeles Times, Dec. 23, 2004

"Salaries See Rare Decrease." Los Angeles Times, Dec. 22, 2004

"Big Deal Isn't In, But Cora Is Out." Los Angeles Times, Dec. 21, 2004

"Paz Vega The Indisputable Heart Of 'Spanglish.'" Newsweek, Dec. 20, 2004

"Out At Third." Los Angeles Times, Dec. 17, 2004

"N.Y. Critics Look 'Sideways' Too." Los Angeles Times, Dec. 14, 2004

"Yan Is New Guy In Bullpen." Los Angeles Times, Dec. 14, 2004

"Immigrant Tale Takes Top 'European Oscar.'" Los Angeles Times, Dec. 13, 2004

"Truly A Judge Puts A Claim On A Stake." Los Angeles Times, Dec. 12, 2004

"Unholy Orders Catholic Damage In Almodovar's Bad Education." LA Weekly, Dec. 10, 2004

"Zimmer's 'Spanglish' A Melodic Mix Of Cultures." Daily Variety, Dec. 8, 2004

"Motorcycle's' Soul Fueled By Santaolalla's Melange Of Pan American Sounds." Daily Variety, Dec. 8, 2004

"Garciaparra To Stay With Cubs." Los Angeles Times, Dec. 8, 2004

"Paradise Pays Off With New Trainer." Los Angeles Times, Dec. 6, 2004

"Better Talk Now Gets Silenced In Turf Cup." Los Angeles Times, Dec. 5, 2004

"Dominguez Is Back For More." Los Angeles Times, Dec. 4, 2004

"A Low-Key Javier Bardem Runs Deep." Los Angeles Times, Dec. 3, 2004

"Nosotros Rallies Round Founder Montalban." Daily Variety, Dec. 2, 2004

"Angels, Cuban Star Morales Strike Deal." Los Angeles Times, Dec. 2, 2004

"Spirit Awards Hoist A Glass To 'Sideways.'" Daily Variety, Dec. 1, 2004

"Foreign Films Cross Kudo Category Boundaries." Daily Variety, Dec. 1, 2004

"Oscar Bids Lost In Translation." Los Angeles Times, Dec. 1, 2004

"Benitez, Giants Agree To A $21-Million Deal." Los Angeles Times, Dec. 1, 2004

"Viva La Vega." Latina Magazine, December 2004

"Alejandro Amenabar's Moving Sea." Venice Magazine, December 2004

"Javier Bardem Plumbs The Depths Of The Sea Inside." Venice Magazine, December 2004

"The Stage Is Set." Hispanic Magazine, December 2004

"Moreno Undecided On Name." Los Angeles Times, Nov. 29, 2004

"Barrera Slugs Out A Win Over Morales." Los Angeles Times, Nov. 28, 2004

"Jockey's Perfect In Track Debut." Los Angeles Times, Nov. 27, 2004

"Restoring 'Pastorela.'" Austin Chronicle, Nov. 26, 2004

"Almodovar Film Gets An NC-17." Los Angeles Times, Nov. 25, 2004

"Trainer Rasmussen Sets Record For Wins In Year." Los Angeles Times, Nov. 22, 2004

"Declan's Moon Takes Easy Stroll In The Prevue." Los Angeles Times, Nov. 21, 2004

"Santana Is Winner Of Cy Young Award." Los Angeles Times, Nov. 20, 2004

"Angeles Take A Hit With Trade." Los Angeles Times, Nov. 20, 2004

"Chivas USA Grabs Torres." Los Angeles Times, Nov. 20, 2004

"U.S. Puts Jamaica Out Of World Cup Qualifier." Los Angeles Times, Nov. 18, 2004

"U.S. Players Still Trying To Make An Impression." Los Angeles Times, Nov. 17, 2004

"Guerrero Winner Of AL MVP." Los Angeles Times, Nov. 17, 2004

"Molina Stays, Ortiz Is Out." Los Angeles Times, Nov. 16, 2004

"Bonds Wins MVP In A Walk." Los Angeles Times, Nov. 16, 2004

"Giants, Vizquel Agree To Three-Year Contract." Los Angeles Times, Nov. 15, 2004

"United Gets Its Cupful." Los Angeles Times, Nov. 15, 2004

"A Noir Departure." Los Angeles Times, Nov. 14, 2004

"A Brutal Beauty." Los Angeles Times, Nov. 14, 2004

"Wizards Believe They Can Pull Off One Final Trick." Los Angeles Times, Nov. 14, 2004

"MLS Cup History." Los Angeles Times, Nov. 14, 2004

"Byrd, Ruiz Win, But Holyfield Is Defeated." Los Angeles Times, Nov. 14, 2004

"Hoosier Park Jockeys Refuse To Ride." Los Angeles Times, Nov. 14, 2004

"MLS Award Winners." Los Angeles Times, Nov. 13, 2004

"Galaxy, Chivas Gain TV Deal." Los Angeles Times, Nov. 12, 2004

"Nickel Tour Of Latin Tunes Heats Up A Chilly Midwest." Los Angeles Times, Nov. 11, 2004

"Mexico's Depth Is Paying Dividends." Los Angeles Times, Nov. 11, 2004

"They Have The Run Of Churchill Downs." Los Angles Times, Nov. 11, 2004

"Churchill Downs Finds Its Jockeys." Los Angeles Times, Nov. 10, 2004

"MLS Goal: Broaden Ownership Base." Los Angeles Times, Nov. 10, 2004

"Anaheim Will Fight Angels' Name Change." Los Angeles Times, Nov. 9, 2004

"Jockeys' Protest Plan Sparks A Turf War." Los Angeles Times, Nov. 9, 2004

"Jockey Removed Amid Boycott Threat." Los Angeles Times, Nov. 8, 2004

"What's Up At The AFI Fest 2004." LA Weekly, Nov. 5, 2004

"Film Threat." Los Angeles CityBeat, Nov. 4, 2004

"The New It Boy." Time, Nov. 4, 2004

"Percival An Angel No More." Nov. 3, 2004

"The Longshots." Los Angeles Times, Nov. 3, 2004

"Frankel Sweeps Weekend Oak Tree Stakes." Los Angeles Times, Nov. 1, 2004

"Frankel Delivers Classic Winner." Los Angeles Times, Oct. 31, 2004

"12th San Diego Latino Film Festival." HispanicAd.com, Oct. 30, 2004

"Red Sox Finish Off Curse In Style." Los Angeles Times, Oct. 28, 2004

"Valenzuela Set To Pitch." Los Angeles Times, Oct. 28, 2004

"Bobby Avila, 78; First Mexican To Win Major League Batting Crown."

Los Angeles Times, Oct. 28, 2004
"Red Sox Only One Win Away." Los Angeles Times, Oct. 27, 2004
"Red Sox Win Despite Four Errors." Oct. 25, 2004
"St. Louis Gets To Clemens In The Sixth Inning And Eliminates Houston, 5-2." Los Angeles Times, Oct. 22, 2004
"They'll Take It To The Limit." Los Angeles Times, Oct. 21, 2004
"Red Sox Back In The World Series." Los Angeles Times, Oct. 21, 2004
"Sox Can Ace History Test." Los Angeles Times, Oct. 20, 2004
"Red Sox Find The Loop Hole." Los Angeles Times, Oct. 19, 2004
"Astros Make A B-Line For Victory To Tie Series." Los Angeles Times, Oct. 18, 2004
"Rivera Saves The Yankees." Los Angeles Times, Oct. 13, 2004
"Astros Win A Series At Last." Los Angeles Times, Oct. 12, 2004
"L.A. Can't Pull Off One More Comeback." Los Angeles Times, Oct. 11, 2004
"Hot Topic." People, Oct. 11, 2004
"New Tunes Takes A Cue From 'Q.'" Weekly Variety, Oct. 11, 2004
"New York Is Just Getting Warmed Up." Los Angeles Times, Oct. 10, 2004
"Sosa Fined For Late-Season Choices." Los Angeles Times, Oct. 8, 2004
"Scoring Successes." Weekly Variety, Oct. 4, 2004
"No Doubt About It, 'Tito' Is Back." Los Angeles Times, Oct. 3, 2004
"Guillen Agrees To Settlement With Angels." Los Angeles Times, Oct. 2, 2004
"The Bicultural Caper. Hispanic Magazine, October 2004
"Union Files Appeal On Guillen's Behalf." Los Angeles Times, Sept. 28, 2004
"Shingle To Target Latinos." Daily Variety, Sept. 27, 2004
"Angels Suspend Guillen." Los Angeles Times, Sept. 26, 2004
"Pedroza Sets Meet Record." Los Angeles Times, Sept. 26, 2004
"Pedroza Is Still King Of Fairplex." Los Angeles Times, Sept. 24, 2004
"Rongen Ready To Lead Chivas." Los Angeles Times, Sept. 24, 2004
"Rongen Will Lead MLS' Chivas USA." Los Angeles Times, Sept. 23, 2004
"Oh Cey, Can You See? Beltre Sets RBI Record." Los Angeles Times, Sept. 20, 2004
"Oscar's Bad Body Language." Los Angeles Times, Sept. 19, 2004
"Rhino Rocking With 'Beisbol.'" Daily Variety, Sept. 16, 2004
"Distrib Picks Up Latino Titles." Daily Variety, Sept. 14, 2004
"Local Pix Pique H'wood Interest." Weekly Variety, Sept. 13, 2004

"Uni's 'Gangster' Aims At Ramirez." Hollywood Reporter, Sept. 13, 2004

"A Memorable Companion." Los Angeles Times, Sept. 12, 2004

"Angels' Rodriguez Is An Animated Special." Los Angeles Times, Sept. 12, 2004

"Everything's Fair Game At This Meet." Los Angeles Times, Sept. 9, 2004

"2nd Look At Mexican Massacre." Daily Variety, Sept. 9, 2004

"Galarraga Feels Like A Rookie." Los Angeles Times, Sept. 2, 2004

"Yankees Bronx Bombed Like Never Before, 22-0." Los Angeles Times, Sept. 1, 2004

"Will 'The Cookout' Sizzle Or Fizzle? You Decide." Los Angeles Times, Aug. 30, 2004

"Ground Breaking Cultural Film Released On DVD." HispaniaNet. Com, Aug. 27, 2004

"Curtain To rise On Manhattan's Only All Latin Movie Theatre." HispanicAd.com, Aug. 21, 2004

"Tres Cubanos Selected For New York International Fringe Festival." HispanicAd.com, Aug. 21, 2004

"Fate Is Up In Smoke." Los Angeles Times, Aug. 20, 2004

"Durazo's 3 Homers Lead A's." Los Angeles Times, Aug.19, 2004

"This Thriller Really Smokes." Los Angeles Times, Aug. 16, 2004

"Last Season For Martinez." Los Angeles Times, Aug. 10, 2004

"Dance Cuba: Dreams Of Flight." Weekly Variety, Aug. 9, 2004

"Struggling Blue Jays Fire Manager." Los Angeles Times, Aug. 9, 2004

"Valenzuela Suspended For 2004." Los Angeles Times, Aug. 8, 2004

"Could That Be A Dominatrix In A Doomed-Lovers Duet?" New York Times, Aug. 6, 2004

"Team Signs 43-Year-Old Galarraga." Los Angeles Times, Aug. 5, 2004

"New Mexico Loans 'Latin' Coin." Daily Variety, Aug. 4, 2004

"Time To Shout." Los Angeles Times, Aug. 4, 2004

"L.A. Fans Eager To Cheer Chivas." Los Angeles Times, Aug. 2, 2004

"Helmers, Come Home." Weekly Variety, Aug. 1, 2004

"Garciaparra Is Traded To The Cubs." Los Angeles Times, Aug. 1, 2004

"Morales Makes Case In Unanimous Verdict." Los Angeles Times, Aug. 1, 2004

"Dodgers Get A Move On." Los Angeles Times, July 31, 2004

"MLS All-Star Game." Los Angeles Times, July 31, 2004

"Hair Is Focal Point Of Valenzuela Hearing." Los Angeles Times, July 31, 2004

"Hearing Begins On Valenzuela." Los Angeles Times, July 30, 2004

"Latino Films Roll Into Town." New York Daily News, July 25, 2004

"Latino Comedy Projects Pokes Fun At Politics." Dallas News, July 24, 2004

"Delgado Is Booed For His War Protest." July 22, 2004

"Fame: It's Hard To Swallow." USA Today, July 20, 2004

"'Punto' Primo At L.A. Latino Film Fest." Daily Variety, July 18, 2004

"Los Angeles Latino International Film Festival." LA Weekly, July 16, 2004

"Soccer Report, MLS News." Los Angeles Times, July 15, 2004

"Valenzuela Hearing Delayed Indefinitely." Los Angeles Times, July 15, 2004

"AL Is A Rocket Buster." Los Angeles Times, July 14, 2004

"Crowd Honors Homer Kings." Los Angeles Times, July 12, 2004

"Beltran Replaces Griffey For NL." Los Angeles Times, July 12, 2004

"Marvel Comic First To Star Latina Hero." Los Angeles Times, July 10, 2004

"Rapids Haven't Shown Many Defects Lately." Los Angeles Times, July 10, 2004

"Anaheim To Enforce Name Issue." Los Angeles Times, July 8, 2004

"It's 'Ladies' Night' At Latino Film Festival." Daily Variety, July 7, 2004

"Pitcher Garcia Signs Deal For $27 Million." Los Angeles Times, July 7, 2004

"What's In A Name" Plenty, To Moreno." Los Angeles Times, July 4, 2004

"Hail Mary." Hispanic Magazine, July 2004

"Big Day For Contreras, Yankees." Honolulu Advertiser, June 28, 2004

"Yankees Roar Back Into Their Comfort Zone." New York Times, June 28, 2004

"Contreras Family Watches Yankees Take 2 From Mets." Honolulu Star-Bulletin, June 28, 2004

"Contreras' Family Resolves paperwork, Prepares To Leave Miami." Honolulu Advertiser, June 24, 2004

"Contreras Is Set To Reunite With Wife And Daughters." New York Times, June 22, 2004

"Reds' Griffey Blasts No. 500." San Diego Union, June 21, 2004

"L.A. Will Get Second Pro Soccer Team." Los Angeles Times, June 5, 2004

"J.Lo Stirs Fresh Salsa." Daily Variety, June 1, 2004

"En Espanol Growing Latino Audience Fuels Demand For Spanish-Language Films." Los Angeles Times, May 25, 2004

"Del Toro's 'Tru Calling.'" Daily Variety, May 24, 2004

"From Catskills To Cuba, 'Dirty Dancing' Is Back." USA Today, May 23, 2004

"Owen, Del Toro Lured Into 'Sin City.'" Daily Variety, May 20, 2004

"'A Day Without A Mexican' Is Pure Vanilla." Los Angeles Times, May 14, 2004

"The Stories And Horrors In Brazil's Penal System." Los Angeles Times, May 14, 2004

"What If 12 Million Californians Vanished?" Wall Street Journal, May 13, 2004

"No Spanish Spoken Here." Los Angeles Times, May 13, 2004

"Partnership Gets Piece Of NBA." Miami Herald, April 30, 2004

"Perez Making Helming Debut." Hollywood Reporter, April 22, 2004

"Arenas To Light Up 'Nicotina.'" Daily Variety, April 19, 2004

"20th Anniversary Of The Chicago Latino Film Festival." Centerstage.net, April 18, 2004

"Suns' Sale A Boon For Moreno." Los Angeles Times, April 17, 2004

"Running Them Like Nobody's Business." Los Angeles Times, April 13, 2004

"Yanks' Payroll Soars As MLB Average Falls." USA Today, April 9, 2004

"Salaries Dip For first Time Since 1995." Los Angeles Times, April 8, 2004

"Changing Lineups." Hispanic Magazine, April 2004

"Bello, Leguizamo Head To 'Precinct 13.'" Daily Variety, March 9, 2004

"Once Upon A Time In Mexico." Hollywood Reporter, March 9, 2004

"Rodriguez Plans 'Mars' Trip For Paramount Pics." Hollywood Reporter, March 2, 2004

"Par, Helmer Explore 'Mars.'" Daily Variety, March 2, 2004

"Welch's Charms Have Survived Test Of Time." Los Angeles Times, March 1, 2004

"Making A Drama." Hispanic Magazine, March 2004

"Malick In 'Che' Revolution." Daily Variety, Feb. 19, 2004

"Castro Visits Redford In Havana Hotel." Los Angeles Times, Jan. 27, 2004

"Another MLS Team To Get Stadium." Los Angeles Times, Jan. 26, 2004

"Fernandez Reaches Out." Billboard, Jan. 24, 2004

"Orosco Decides To Call It A Career." Los Angeles Times, Jan. 22, 2004

"Perez Agrees, Gagne Gap Is $3 Million." Los Angeles Times, Jan. 21, 2004

"Beltre Is Signed For $5 Million." Los Angeles Times, Jan. 20, 2004

"L.A. Distribs Oxxo & Venus Team On Spanish-Lingo Pics." Daily Variety, Jan. 20, 2004

"Top-Shelf Moves." Los Angeles Times, Jan. 12, 2004

"Guerrero To Join Angels." Los Angeles Times, Jan. 11, 2004

"Gonzalez Goes To Kansas City, Alomar To Arizona." Los Angeles Times, Jan. 7, 2004

"Austin's Latino Comedy Projects Finds Success On The Road." Austin Chronicle, Aug. 22, 2003

Index
INDICE

N

O-P

T

U

V-Z